CHAPTER 7

Standard Error (p. 321)

$$\sigma_M = \frac{\sigma}{\sqrt{N}}$$

z Statistic for a Distribution of Means (p. 324)

$$z = \frac{(M - \mu_M)}{\sigma_M}$$

CHAPTER 9

Standard Deviation of a Sample (p. 385)

$$s = \sqrt{\frac{\Sigma(X - M)^2}{(N - 1)}}$$

Standard Error of a Sample (p. 387)

$$s_M = \frac{s}{\sqrt{N}}$$

t statistic for a Single Sample (p. 388)

$$t = \frac{(M - \mu_M)}{s_M}$$

Degrees of Freedom for a Single Sample t Test or a Paired Samples t Test (p. 393)

$$df = N - 1$$

Degrees of Freedom for an Independent Samples t Test (p. 410)

$$df_{Total} = df_X + df_Y$$

Independent Samples t Tests

Pooled Variance (p. 410)

$$s_{Pooled}^2 = \left(\frac{df_X}{df_{Total}}\right) s_X^2 + \left(\frac{df_Y}{df_{Total}}\right) s_Y^2$$

Variance for a Distribution of Means for the First Variable (p. 411)

$$s_{M_X}^2 = \frac{s_{Pooled}^2}{N} \qquad s_{M_Y}^2 = \frac{s_{Pooled}^2}{N}$$

Variance for a Distribution of Differences Between Means (p. 411)

$$s_{Difference}^2 = s_{M_X}^2 + s_{M_Y}^2$$

Standard Deviation of the Distribution of Differences Between Means (p. 411)

$$s_{Difference} = \sqrt{s_{Difference}^2}$$

t Statistic for an Independent Sample (p. 412)

$$t = \frac{(M_X - M_Y) - (\mu_X - \mu_Y)}{s_{Difference}}$$

Statistics for the Behavioral Sciences

Susan A. Nolan
Seton Hall University

Thomas E. Heinzen
William Paterson University

Worth Publishers

Publisher: Catherine Woods

Acquisitions Editor: Charles Linsmeier

Marketing Manager: Amy Shefferd

Development Editor: Michael Kimball

Senior Media Editor: Andrea Musick

Photo Editor: Bianca Moscatelli

Photo Researcher: Julie Tesser

Art Director, Cover Designer: Babs Reingold

Interior Designer: Kevin Kall

Layout Designer: Matrix Publishing Services and
Lee Ann Mahler

Associate Managing Editor: Tracey Kuehn

Project Editor: Francine Almash

Illustration Coordinator: Susan Timmins

Illustrations: Jade Myers, Matrix Art Services

Production Manager: Sarah Segal

Composition: Matrix Publishing Services

Printing and Binding: RR Donnelley

Cover Painting: Leslie Wayne

ISBN-13: 978-0-7167-5007-9

ISBN-10: 0-7167-5007-4

© 2008 by Worth Publishers

Printed in the United States of America

First printing 2007

Worth Publishers
41 Madison Avenue
New York, NY 1000
www.worthpublishers.com

All Systems Go, 2005
Oil on wood, 38" x 38"

Leslie Wayne was born in Germany in 1953 and grew up in California. She received her BFA from Parsons School of Design in 1984. She is the recipient of a 2006 New York Foundation for the Arts Fellowship in Painting, and has received grants from the Pollock-Krasner Foundation, the New York State Council on the Arts, Adolph and Esther Gottlieb Foundation and the Buhl Founda-tion. Her work is in the public collections of The Foundation To-Life, Inc., the Birmingham Museum of Art, Colleczion Thyssen Bornemisza, the Corcoran Gallery of Art, La Coleccion Jumex in Mexico City, Harvard University, the Museum of Contemporary Art in Miami, The Neuberger Museum, and the University of Florida in Gainesville, among others. She exhibits regularly across the country and in Europe. She is represented by Jack Shainman Gallery in New York City.

For Ivan
—Susan

For Donna
—Tom

Susan Nolan turned to psychology after suffering a career-ending accident on her second workday as a bicycle messenger. A native of Boston, she graduated from The College of the Holy Cross and earned her PhD in clinical psychology from Northwestern University. Her research involves experimental investigations of the role of gender in the interpersonal consequences of depression and studies of gender and mentoring in science and technology, funded in part by the National Science Foundation. Susan is the Associate Dean of Graduate Studies for the College of Arts and Sciences, as well as an Associate Professor of Psychology, at Seton Hall University in New Jersey. She has served as a statistical consultant to researchers at several universities, medical schools, corporations, and non-governmental organizations. Recently, she advised Bosnian high school students conducting public opinion research.

Susan's academic schedule allows her to pursue one travel adventure per year, a tradition that she relishes. In recent years she rode her bicycle across the United States (despite her earlier crash), swapped apartments to live in Montreal, and explored the Adriatic coast in an intermittently roadworthy 1985 Volkswagon Scirocco. She wrote much of this book while spending a sabbatical year in rural Bosnia-Herzegovina, where her husband, Ivan Bojanic, worked as an advisor to regional governments. Susan and Ivan fell in love with Bosnia—a beautiful country—and bought a small house in the city of Banja Luka as a base for future adventures. They currently reside in New York City, where Susan roots feverishly, if quietly, for the Red Sox.

Tom Heinzen was a 29-year-old college freshman, began graduate school when his fourth daughter was one week old, and is still amazed that he and his wife, Donna, somehow managed to stay married. A magna cum laude graduate of Rockford College, he earned his PhD in social psychology at the State University of New York at Albany in just three years. He published his first book on frustration and creativity in government two years later, was a research associate in public policy until he was fired over the shape of a graph, consulted for the Johns Hopkins Center for Talented Youth, and then began a teaching career at William Paterson State University of New Jersey. He founded the psychology club, established an undergraduate research conference, and has been awarded various teaching honors while continuing to write journal articles, books, plays, and two novels that support the teaching of general psychology and statistics. He is also the editor of *Many Things to Tell You*, a volume of poetry by elderly writers.

His wife, Donna, is a physician assistant who has also volunteered her time in relief work following Hurricane Mitch and Hurricane Katrina. Their daughters are now scattered from Bangladesh to Mississippi to New Jersey and work in public health, teaching, and medicine. He is a mediocre French horn player, an enthusiastic but mediocre tennis player, and an ardent baseball fan (Go Cubs!).

BRIEF CONTENTS

Contents

Willie's Diner is a chrome-and-mirrored New Jersey creation with a menu as thick as a dissertation, a staff with unpredictable attitudes, and as many languages as there are different types of pie in the showcase. A large booth framed by mirrors was the site of our introduction to each other as potential authors of a new statistics textbook for the behavioral sciences. We both slapped our list of things to consider down on the table about 10 seconds after we had officially and politely greeted each other.

"I have no interest in writing a statistics textbook," Tom announced, "unless we can teach the same material much more effectively and add some, let's call them, original features."

"Well, I have no interest in writing a textbook just for the sake of writing a textbook," said Susan. "And I have to warn you. I have very strong ideas about what works and what doesn't work." We stared at each other until Susan said, "Let's see what you've got."

The staff at Willie's delivered our water, but before they could take our order we were discovering some deeply shared convictions about the teaching of statistics. The perfect story would have us writing them down on a Willie's placemat, but Susan used her laptop to record and later refine our impassioned beliefs about the teaching of statistics:

1. Statistics has a success story to tell.

2. The learning of statistics has intrinsic value.

3. The language of statistics complicates understanding, but unnecessarily.

4. The concepts in statistics are already familiar to students.

5. The content and especially the technology of teaching statistics will continue to change.

6. The conceptual frame of teaching statistics needs to shift from apology to opportunity.

We eyed each other across the table. "This might work," said Susan. We outlined the order of chapters, explained the logic for our changes to each other, and convinced each other that these alterations and additions were the product of many years of intimate classroom experience and close mentoring of student projects. But there was more to the energy that created this book than these shared convictions.

"I run our internship program," said Tom, "and I do a lot of career counseling. I'm tired of convincing one student at a time how well statistics and experimental design have prepared them for great jobs. I need a bigger audience."

Here's what we want to tell our bigger audience: in addition to the customary content of a statistics course, we believe that this textbook will help students

1. To reason more clearly about their everyday lives

2. To plan their job and career searches more purposively

3. To think more deeply about the mixture of randomness and pattern on human behavior

4. To realize the many-sided benefits of everyday statistical reasoning

In short, our time at Willie's Diner allowed us to discover in each other, as co-authors, the pleasure of helping students to discover the surprising allure of learning statistics.

Teaching Approach: Narratives in Support of Familiar Material

The discipline of statistics has many success stories to tell, and this textbook weaves some of those narratives into the content of each chapter. These accounts provide students with vivid associative hooks on which to hang their memories of statistical principles while simultaneously informing them about the difficult history, colorful personalities, and diverse, exciting applications of behavioral statistics. For example, we use narratives that describe outrageous graphical lies told through statistics, tragedies resulting from the misuse of statistics, and meaningful career opportunities related to statistics. The narratives also create a way for us to support our belief that the logic of hypothesis testing should be taught early and often.

These brief, embedded narratives are the backbone of a unique approach to the teaching of statistics and create many teaching opportunities. For example, we support our assertion that statistics is best learned within the context of understanding research designs (Chapter 1) by progressively telling the story of Dr. John Snow's success at using the idea of a correlation to stem the spread of a devastating cholera epidemic in his own London neighborhood in 1854 (see page 1). We even display the famous map that demonstrates the relation between number of deaths and the distance from the well where those who perished had resided.

In a somber narrative, we demonstrate the uses and misuses of graphs (Chapter 3) and present APA guidelines for graph construction by telling the tragic story of the *Challenger* space shuttle disaster (see page 93). The decision makers at NASA had the relevant information about the relation between temperature and the resiliency of the O-rings, but the graphs displaying that information inadvertently camouflaged (with a confounding variable) the most vital information. We balance that grim account by introducing students to Florence Nightingale ("the impassioned statistician") and the life-saving coxcomb graph that pushed her onto the international stage.

Regression analysis and its power to predict (Chapter 6) are demonstrated through Charles Darwin's unlikely prediction of a tiny moth with an astonishingly long tongue. The nectar of the stunningly beautiful Madagascar star orchid is buried 8 to 12 inches deep, and Darwin used that number to predict the existence of an insect with a tongue of a corresponding length (see page 251). The giant hawk moth was discovered 40 years after Darwin's death and named *Xanthopan morganii praedicta* in honor of Darwin's ability to use a measurement of the depth of a flower to predict the length of the tongue of the hawk moth that no one had yet discovered. The discovery of this odd-looking creature demonstrates the regression formula's unique ability to make precise predictions.

Curious characters populate the story of the normal, bell-shaped curve (Chapter 7). The young, chronically underemployed, just-out-of-prison Abraham De Moivre advised gamblers about the predictability of chance events from his "office" at a London coffee house—where much later in his life he was visited daily by his friend Isaac Newton (see page 307). A different kind of frustration led astronomers to the bell shape of the normal curve: their measuring instruments jiggled. Errors in their observations of planetary movements led them to the discovery that there was a bell-shaped pattern of errors around their best estimate of reality. These several characters cohere around a stunningly simple class demonstration that allows the mysterious power of the central limit theorem to emerge from its historical context and open the way for the standardizing power of the z distribution.

The failure of facilitated communication to liberate autistic children demonstrates the benefits of using the standardized z distribution (Chapter 8) to make fair and impartial comparisons (see page 339). Putting human faces on the z distribution demonstrates both the applicability of statistical reasoning and the seductive dangers that threaten behavioral scientists when they abandon a scientific approach in favor of well-intentioned, subjective convictions. It also foreshadows the next chapter on t tests by dramatizing the theoretical clarity that can emerge out of a simple two-group design.

The logic of how ANOVA uses between-groups variability, within-groups variability, and the F distribution (Chapter 10) is demonstrated by "Shackleton's valiant voyage" (see pages 427–428). After his wooden vessel was crushed by an Antarctic ice floe, Sir Ernest Shackleton led three tiny, differently equipped lifeboats (between-boats variability) crammed with three very different groups of crew members (within-boats variability) back to civilization without a single life being lost. Twenty-eight men watched from the ice as their ship disappeared. Then 28 men crossed the planet's coldest and most dangerous ocean with ragged clothes, minimal equipment, a solitary navigation device, and an early version of a camera that documented what has been called the world's "most successful failure."

The rationale for and use of other commonly used nonparametric statistics (Chapter 14) is illustrated by the psychometric challenge of studying Alzheimer's disease (see pages 617–618). The narrative clarifies the need for alternative statistical tests when we are unable to obtain interval observations or when we are obliged to impose normality on a nonnormal situation. The variety of nonparametric statistical tests are presented as systematic alternatives to parametric tests, with guidance about when and how to use each test. The discussion also highlights the flexibility that makes statistics such useful tools of discovery about distressing, difficult disorders such as Alzheimer's disease.

Each chapter's narrative is woven into the text so that it illustrates the particular principles being taught within each subsection of each chapter. Students absorb the surprising history of statistics as they learn its detailed applications; they are inspired to value statistical reasoning not only as a meaningful career path but also for its inherent clarity. The field of statistics has a success story to tell, and these narratives tell that story while teaching its formulas, demonstrating its logic, and promoting its core concepts.

Novel Features of the Textbook

There are eight features that make this textbook distinctive among its peers. The first three are integral to every chapter:

1. **Embedded Narratives.** The narratives enhance comprehension by demonstrating the particular principles being taught within each subsection of each chapter. Narratives are empirically validated as a particularly effective teaching tool. Kaufman and Bristol's (2001) review indicates that "people understand and remember information better when it is presented in a social context." Ben-Peretz (2002) identified the "importance of

narratives" as the first theme articulated by retired teachers reflecting on effective teaching techniques. Van den Broek, Lynch, and Naslund (2003) noted how narratives improve comprehension by helping students perceive connections that in turn help them to extract main ideas.

2. **Career Opportunities.** We both deepen and broaden our students' career aspirations. Our diverse consulting experiences allow us to point students toward dozens of surprising career opportunities related to statistics. So we have permeated this textbook with allusions to career opportunities, and we describe some of them in detail. Students will learn about statistical careers in many fields highlighted throughout the book. Examples include:

   ◼ Public health (Chapter 1, pages 4, 15–21)

   ◼ Evaluation research (Chapter 2, pages 40, 54, 66)

   ◼ Communication (Chapter 3, pages 118–119, 122–125)

   ◼ Marketing (Chapter 5, pages 186–187)

   ◼ Quality control (Chapter 15, pages 678–679)

   ◼ The opportunities demonstrated by W. S. Gossett and Stella Cunliffe at the Guinness Brewing Company (Chapter 9, pages 382–383, 391–392)

3. **Everyday Applications.** We separate science from superstition by demonstrating the dangers of confusing correlation with causation (Chapter 5). At every opportunity, we clarify how confounding variables make it impossible to reach conclusions. From private reasoning to public declarations, we demonstrate how everyday statistical reasoning constrains our most unproductive hunches and energizes our most creative hypotheses. The text is filled with real-world applications from a wide variety of sources that convey the wide range of career opportunities, as well as relevance to many parts of our lives. These applied illustrations of statistical reasoning include the following:

anthropology, 660–661, 678
autism, 338–339, 351–352, 358–359, 364–365
armed services, 113–115, 120–121, 128
baseball, 30, 62, 232
clinical psychology 15–16, 55
cognitive psychology, 8
communication, 96, 118–119, 122–125
cosmetics, 186–187
dirty data, 369–370
economics, 660–662, 678–679
education/education administration, 40, 41, 43, 53–55, 66
engineering, 30, 93–95, 101, 105, 109–110
epidemiology, 4, 15–21, 124–126

gender and math ability, 81, 531
gerontology, 617–619, 623–624, 631–632
humor as medical treatment, 579–580
insurance industry, 253–254, 260, 264, 270
marketing, 186–187
neuroscience, 133
public administration and policy 171–173, 234–235
public health and policy, 4, 15–21, 266–267, 318–319
social psychology, 171–173
sociology, 171–173, 220–221, 234–235
tennis, 668
theater, 527–528, 541–543

Three chapters acknowledge existing trends in the teaching of statistics and push further and faster in those productive directions.

4. **The Link Between Research Design and Statistical Analysis.** Chapter 1 emphasizes the link between research design and statistical analysis to a far greater degree than other textbooks (an emphasis reinforced within every chapter). Because statistical observations can be interpreted only within the context of an appropriate research design, we make this connection explicit in the opening chapter and reinforce that principle at every opportunity within each chapter. For students who have already taken a research methods class, this chapter will serve as a refresher; for those who have not, this chapter will provide enough background information that they will be able to see why statistical analyses in the absence of research design are questionable. This structure leads to a background in statistics that allows students who take a follow-up research methods class to comprehend the material more easily.

5. **Graphic Literacy.** Chapter 3 energetically promotes graphic literacy by describing the purposes of graphs, how to lie with graphs, and the APA guidelines for graph construction; we also peek into the exciting future of visual displays of data. Graphing skills are so important because visual displays of data are so much more compelling than tables of numbers, and the ability to create and understand visual displays is central to so many careers. Moreover, we are persuaded by Friendly (2002) and Tufte (1990; 1997; 2006), as well as by our own teaching experience, that the time for graphic literacy is now.

6. **Choosing a Statistical Test and Reporting Statistics.** As each hypothesis test is introduced throughout the chapters in the text, we describe how the results would be reported in APA style. However, Chapter 15 takes this a step further, first collating the reporting information from each chapter and then modeling how to report statistics in context, with specific guidelines about when to use each one. The chapter also teaches students how to read Results sections that include unfamiliar statistics as well as those that include familiar ones.

We also encourage deeper learning by integrating two features within each chapter:

7. **Experience It for Yourself.** These recurring features offer unique, participatory activities that teach particularly difficult concepts by strategically inserting activities at key points within each chapter. You can think of it as the best features of a workbook strategically inserted into the text. But it is also much more than that. For example, completing the Consideration of Future Consequences (CFC) scale in Chapter 1 teaches students principles of measurement; the quincunx machines and the sampling exercise in Chapter 7 let students experience for themselves the mystery of the central limit theorem.

Transforming the Stroop Task into Numbers (p. 8)
Operationalizing Research Hypotheses (p. 19)

Listen to the Story Statistics Tell (p. 76)
Lying with Graphs (p. 96)
Reading a Graph (p. 120)

Understanding Randomness
  (p. 156)
Take the Probability Quiz (p. 175)
Becoming a Smarter Consumer
  (p. 186)
Illusory Correlations (p. 217)
Creating a Career in Health
  Psychology (p. 266)
The Bell-Shaped Normal Curve in
  Theory and in Practice (p. 304)

Creating Your Own Distributions
  (p. 315)
How Scientific Evidence Influences
  What You Believe (p. 395)
The Probability of "Four of a Kind"
  Families (p. 437)
Name That ANOVA (p. 483)
Calculating Statistical Power (p. 561)
Predicting from a Correlation
  Coefficient (p. 629)

8. **Digging Deeper into the Data.** Instructors can choose to include these optional sections that introduce more advanced statistical techniques. We created this text to provide flexibility around instructors' individual interests and opportunities for selective specialization. The end of each chapter describes an advanced statistical technique or a less known but very handy statistical tool relative to the content of each chapter. Some of the more sophisticated statistical tools in the Digging Deeper into the Data sections will be accessible to accomplished undergraduates; graduate students will be able to use the textbook to reinforce their earlier learning while increasing and applying their statistical sophistication. Because these sections are optional, the text is written so that no information from these sections is referenced at any point in the main parts of the chapters. An instructor could choose to use all, one, or none of these sections without discontinuity in the remainder of the text.

▩ Variations on Standard Research Designs, (pp. 29–31)

▩ Alternate Approaches to Descriptive Statistics, (p. 84)

▩ The Box Plot, (p. 141)

▩ The Shocking Prevalence of Type I Errors, (pp. 189–192)

▩ Partial Correlation, (pp. 235–238)

▩ Structural Equation Modeling (SEM), (pp. 281–287)

▩ The Normal Curve and Catching (Possible) Cheaters, (pp. 326–329)

▩ What to Do with Dirty Data, (pp. 368–372)

▩ More Ways to Visualize Data, (pp. 414–416)

▩ A Priori and Post-Hoc Tests to Decide Which Groups Are Different, (pp. 460–467)

▩ Variations on ANOVA, (pp. 515–518)

▩ Meta-Analysis, (pp. 563–566)

▩ A Deeper Understanding of Chi Square, (pp. 603–606)

▩ Transforming Skewed Data, the Meaning of Interval Data, and Bootstrapping, (pp. 643–648)

▩ Reporting More Sophisticated Statistical Analyses, (pp. 692–693)

Pedagogical Features

We believe that we have created a "sticky" textbook. Statistical ideas will remain in students' memories because we have provided vivid contexts, promoted comprehension, and described career opportunities that match the ambitions that brought students to the social sciences in the first place. We have reinforced strategic teaching moments by creating individual and class experiences within the flow of the text, identified as Experience It for Yourself. These experiential sections, such as the virtual quincunx machine and a way to experience the central limit theorem, are timed within the text so that they promote spaced learning. We also support the habit of timely, periodic review by providing manageable chunks of information separated by interim summaries within each chapter, each one supported by Check Your Learning exercises that smoothly reinforce the material within each subsection of the text. Check Your Learning exercises allow students to review the major concept or practice the primary technique introduced in that subsection. That same thinking led us to provide an optional outline of SPSS guidance within the text that summarizes what our SPSS supplement provides in more detail. There are also end-of-chapter exercises (answers to odd-numbered questions are in Appendix C) that imitate and expand on the particular illustrations we used in the text. In short, we offer choices that can accommodate a wide range of teaching and learning styles.

We created choices in this textbook because one of the things we learned at Willie's Diner is that we both believe that other instructors care just as much as we do about the intrinsic value of learning statistics. In fact, we believe that the best teachers can communicate everything their students need to know with a piece of chalk, a clean chalkboard, and a clear head. However, most of us need choices. Some classes will be ready for many of the Digging Deeper into the Data sections; other classes will proceed at a slower pace. But almost every class will begin experiencing "aha" moments by the time they get to Chapter 5 on correlation and Chapter 6 on regression. Some students need to do every exercise; others can do most exercises as thought experiments. But they will all remember experiencing for themselves the meaning of the central limit theorem. We view learning SPSS as an easy way to teach the concepts of statistics; others will treat it as secondary to their purposes. But we've provided everyone with choices by outlining SPSS commands at the end of each chapter and creating a separate SPSS supplement that describes SPSS procedures in more detail. Every class is a unique adventure, so we created a textbook that accommodates all those diverse teaching and learning styles while communicating that statistics does indeed have a success story worth telling.

Supplements

We understand that a book alone cannot meet the education needs and teaching expectations of the modern classroom. Therefore, we have engaged colleagues to create a comprehensive supplements package that tries to bring statistics to life for students and provide instructors with the resources necessary to effectively supplement their successful strategies in the classroom.

Instructor's Resources by Robin Freyburg, Yeshiva University, and special contributor Katherine Makarec, William Paterson University. Contents include an introduction containing general information such as Tips for Adjunct, New, or Part-Time Instructors; What to Do and What Not to Do in Class; and Sample Syllabi. Detailed Lecture Outlines for each of the chapters include suggestions for classroom discussion, ideas for student activities, handouts, research projects, and multimedia suggestions.

Test Bank by Kelly Goedert, Seton Hall University. Contents include multiple-choice questions, many of which include figures and graphs; fill-in-the-blank questions based on corresponding graphs and figures; and essay questions, many of which are multipart and similar in style to the end-of-chapter exercises. The Test Bank also includes the Web quizzes from the book's companion Web site and all the questions in and solutions to the end-of-chapter exercises.

Diploma Computerized Test Bank (available in Windows and Macintosh on one CD-ROM). The CD-ROM allows you to add an unlimited number of questions; edit questions; format a test; scramble questions; and include pictures, equations, or multimedia links. With the accompanying gradebook, you can record students' grades throughout a course, sort student records, add weight to grades, and more. This CD-ROM is the access point for Diploma Online Testing. Blackboard and WebCT-formatted versions of the Test Bank are also available in the Course Cartridge and ePack.

iClicker Radio Frequency Classroom Response System. Offered by Worth Publishers, in partnership with iClicker and available for fall 2008 classes, iClicker is Worth's new polling system, created by educators for educators. This radio frequency system is the hassle-free way to make your class time more interactive. The system allows you to pause to ask questions and instantly record responses, as well as take attendance, direct students through lectures, gauge your students' understanding of the material, and much more.

Worth Image and Lecture Gallery at www.worthpublishers.com/ilg. Using the Image and Lecture Gallery, you can browse or search and download text art, illustrations, outlines, and prebuilt PowerPoint slides for *all* Worth titles. Users can also create personal folders for easy organization of the materials.

Study Guide with SPSS by Robert Weathersby, Eastern University. Contents include a "To the Student" preface containing general information and tips for mastering statistical concepts; learning objectives; a chapter summary and review; exercises that cover key concepts from the textbook; and multiple-choice review questions. Each chapter contains a separate section on SPSS incorporating examples from the textbook, screen shots from SPSS, and review questions for each example. A short introduction to SPSS is also included in the "To the Student" preface.

Book Companion Site at http://www.worthpublishers.com/nolanheinzen. For instructors, the Web site features an online gradebook, Lecture and Illustration PowerPoints written by Katherine Makarec (William Paterson University), iClicker classroom response questions (available in Word and PowerPoint), and the Image and Lecture Gallery, featuring figures, photos, and tables from every Worth title. It also includes electronic files of the Instructor's Resources. For students, the Web site includes a bank of Web quizzes written by Kristin Ratliff, Temple University, interactive modules such as the Stroop Test and a virtual quincunx, audio downloads from Scientific American, learning objectives, chapter outlines, and flashcards.

Acknowledgments

We would like to thank the many people who have contributed directly and indirectly to the writing of this book. First, we would like to thank and are eternally grateful to Beatrix Mellauner for bringing the two of us together as co-authors. Without her encouragement, this journey might never have started. And, most important, we want to thank our students at Northwestern University, Seton Hall University, and William Paterson University for teaching us how to teach statistics in a way that makes sense.

Tom: The family members who know me on a daily basis and decide to love me anyway deserve more thanks than words can convey: Donna, Rebekah, Debbie, Amy, and Elizabeth. The close friends and colleagues who voiced encouragement and timely supports also deserve my deep appreciation: Beth, Army, Culley, and Miran Schultz; Laura Cramer-Berness; Ariana DeSimone; Sally Ellyson; Gerry Esposito; Neil Kressel; Kate Makarec; Judy Passapera; J. Allen Suddeth; and Nancy Vail.

My students, in particular, have always provided a reality check on my teaching methods with the kind of candor that only students engaged in the learning process can bring.

Susan: I am grateful to my Northwestern University professors and classmates and Vanderbilt University and Seton Hall University colleagues for demonstrating that statistics can truly be fun. Thanks especially to classmates Charan Ranganath and Zoran Martinovich for sharing their arsenal of instructional materials as I embarked on teaching my first statistics course. Thanks to Cynthia Flynn and Gregory Burton for expanding my statistical boundaries through endless debates about statistics. I also am grateful to Nicole Folchetti for illuminating the road that is textbook writing.

Much of the writing of this book took place during my sabbatical in Bosnia-Herzegovina. Thanks to Seton Hall University for the year away, and thanks to my Bosnian friends for making my sabbatical not only professionally productive but also personally rewarding. A special thank you to the members of the Nolan and Bojanic clans who have patiently weathered the barrage of studies I tend to cite in everyday conversation. And finally, I am most grateful to my husband, Ivan Bojanic, for the memorable adventures we've had (and the statistical observations that grew out of many of them); Ivan experienced the evolution of this book through countless road-trip conversations and late-night editorial sessions.

Over the course of our teaching careers, supplemental materials have continued to grow in their availability, quality, and importance. Not only do they make our lives easier (surely not an insignificant point in itself), but they make us better teachers and the possibilities for our students more achievable. Working behind the scenes and often without due reward, supplements authors have come to produce materials that, as instructors, we both rely on and yet too often take for granted. The contributions of supplements authors to the success of a textbook are innumerable, and we would like to take this moment to highlight the impressive cast of instructors who have joined our team. We are grateful to our trusted colleagues for their tireless work creating this comprehensive supplements package. Kelly Goedert, Katherine Makarec, Robert

Weathersby, and Robin Freyburg are all professionals with a deep interest in creating successful classrooms, and we appreciate the opportunity to work with people of such commitment.

Throughout the writing of this first edition, we relied on the criticism, corrections, encouragement, and thoughtful contributions from reviewers, focus group attendees, survey respondents, and class testers. We thank them for their expertise and for the time they set aside to help us develop this textbook. We would like specifically to mention the contributions of Robert Weathersby (Eastern University). Our execution owes a great deal to his comments and recommendations.

Michael Allen,
University of Mississippi

Jan Andrews,
Vassar College

Cheryl Armstrong,
Fitchburg State University

Steven Barger,
Northern Arizona University

Elizabeth Bauer,
New York University

Michael Biderman,
University of Tennessee, Chattanooga

Robert Boody,
University of Northern Iowa

Alan Bougere,
University of Southern Mississippi

Gabrielle Britton,
Lafayette College

Andrea Bubka,
Saint Peter's College

Michael Carlin,
*University of Massachusetts Medical
   School*

Marie Cassar,
Saginaw Valley State University

Sheila Chiffriller,
Pace University

Victor Cicirelli,
Purdue University

Michael Clump,
Marymount University

Dennis Cogan,
Texas Tech University

Andrew Cohen,
University of Massachusetts, Amherst

David Dodd,
Washington University, St. Louis

Betty Dorr,
Hollins College

Brian Doss,
Texas A&M University

Dennis Doverspike,
University of Akron

Beverly Dretzke,
University of Minnesota

Miguel Eckstein,
*University of California,
Santa Barbara*

Yousef Fahoum,
University of Arkansas, Little Rock

David Falcone,
La Salle University

Jinyan Fan,
Hofstra University

Whitney Fauth,
University of San Diego

David Feigley,
Rutgers University

Cary Feria,
Morehead State University

Kory Floyd,
Arizona State University

Melissa Fortner,
Transylvania University

Joel Freund,
University of Arkansas

Raymond Gamba,
City College of San Francisco

Azenett Garza,
Weber State University

Brandon Gibb,
Binghampton University, SUNY

Barry Giesbrecht,
University of California, Santa Barbara

Timothy Goldsmith,
University of New Mexico

Charles Halcomb,
Wichita State University

Jane Halpert,
DePaul University

Isaac Heacock,
Indiana University

Mike Hurley,
George Mason University

Carolyn Jagacinski,
Purdue University

David Jewett,
University of Wisconsin-Eau Claire

George Johanson,
Ohio University

Julian Keenan,
Montclair State University

Stephanie Keer,
Rutgers University, New Brunswick

Shelley Kilpatrick,
Southwest Baptist University

Meredith Kneavel,
Chestnut Hill College

David Kreiner,
University of Central Missouri

Christopher LeGrow,
Marshall University

Brad Love,
University of Texas, Austin

Jennifer Mailloux,
University of Mary Washington

Stuart Marcovitch,
University of North Carolina, Greensboro

Dawn McBride,
Illinois State University

Maureen McCarthy,
Kennesaw State University

Dawn McQuiston-Surrett,
Arizona State University, West Campus

Jackie Miller,
The Ohio State University

Joanne Miller,
Northeastern University

Simon Moon,
La Salle University

David Mostofsky,
Boston University

Morrie Mullins,
Xavier University

Michael Nielsen,
Georgia Southern University

Jonathan Page,
Minnesota State University, Mankato

Debra Pate,
Jackson State University

Peter Pfordresher,
University of Texas, San Antonio

Joshua Priddy,
University of Houston

Elaine Olaoye,
Brookdale Community College

Andrew Oswald,
North Harris Montgomery County Community College

Ron Salazar,
San Juan College

Steven Scher,
Eastern Illinois University

Eric Seeman,
University of Alabama, Huntsville

Selcuk Sirin,
Montclair State University

Glenda Smith,
North Harris Montgomery Community College

Mathew Spackman,
Brigham Young University

Jesse Spencer-Smith,
University of Illinois at Urbana-Champaign

James Spivey,
University of Texas, Austin

Megan Spokas,
Temple University

Deborah Stote,
University of Texas, Austin

Cheryl Terrance,
University of North Dakota

Alison Thomas-Cottingham,
Rider University

G. Marc Turner,
Texas State University, San Marcos

Douglas Wallen,
Minnesota State University, Mankato

Robert Weathersby,
Eastern University

Georjeanna Wilson-Doenges,
University of Wisconsin, Green Bay

Lucinda Woodward,
Ball State University

Marcel Yoder,
University of Illinois at Springfield

It has truly been a pleasure for us to work with everyone at Worth Publishers. From the moment we signed with Worth to the publication of the book you are holding, we have been impressed with the passionate commitment of everyone we encountered at Worth at every stage of the publishing process. We would like to thank Bob Worth for imposing so many positive, enduring values in textbook publishing. Publisher Catherine Woods continues to make those values real every day, instilling a legacy of quality and commitment in the culture of Worth.

Michael Kimball, our development editor, has been with us every step of the process. He is fun and easy to work with and also a brilliant writer and editor; we have learned a great deal about ourselves as writers because of him. His attention to every detail helped us achieve our vision for this book, and his impact can truly be seen on every page. Acquisitions Editor Charles Linsmeier took on the challenge of managing our first edition. His impressive ability to assess ideas and face problems from multiple angles has contributed to a successful publication. His support, timing, and humor were all welcome additions to the team.

Associate Managing Editor Tracey Kuehn managed the production of the textbook and, along with Project Editor Francine Almash, worked tirelessly to bring the book to fruition. Production Manager Sarah Segal kept us focused with her efficiency and her passionate commitment to creating a truly beautiful book. Copyeditor Karen Osborne impressed us with her ability to see the forest while walking amongst the trees; her contributions to the finished book were numerous. We appreciate Assistant Editor Justin Kruger's quiet, perceptive humor, which was displayed throughout the development and production of the book, and for wearing so many hats during the creation of this book that he could open a haberdashery. Together Tracey, Francine, Sarah, Karen, and Justin let us know precisely what needed to be done and precisely when we needed to do it. Their work is a testament to the consistent quality of Worth titles.

Babs Reingold, Art Director, is inspiring in her commitment to artistic values in textbook publishing. Kevin Kall, Designer, united beauty with clarity and content in the interior design. Photo Editor Bianca Moscatelli and Photo Researcher Julie Tesser patiently trained us in the art of photo selection. Thanks to each of you for fulfilling Worth's promise to create a book whose aesthetics so beautifully support the specific pedagogical demands of teaching statistics.

Andrea Musick, Media Editor, and Stacey Alexander, Production Manager, guided the development and creation of the supplements package, making life so much better for so many students and instructors.

Amy Shefferd, Marketing Manager, and Kirsten Watrud, Market Development Manager, quickly understood why we believe so deeply in this book, and each contributed tireless efforts as advocates of this first edition with our colleagues across the country.

Lastly, we would like to thank Laura Pople. Those early, thrilling conversations at Willie's Diner inspire happy memories and a sincere sense of gratitude. Laura believed in this book from our very first conversation, brought us to Worth, and remains one of our strongest advocates. We hope she finds as much joy holding this book in her hands as we do.

Susan A. Nolan

Thomas E. Heinzen

>

CHAPTER ONE

AN INTRODUCTION TO STATISTICS AND RESEARCH DESIGN
THE BASIC ELEMENTS OF STATISTICAL REASONING

At first, there were only worried rumors about people dying, but the rumors became fear as the death toll in little towns like New Castle and Gateshead kept climbing. Then, on August 31, 1854, cholera struck a busy London neighborhood, claiming an astonishing 127 lives in just three days. Before it was over, the epidemic would claim an estimated 19,000 lives across England (Creighton, 1894/1965). This London outbreak of cholera occurred so suddenly that Snow later described it as "the most terrible outbreak of cholera that ever occurred in this Kingdom" (Snow, 1855, p. 38). Statistics, of course, can quantify such horrors, and sometimes that is the grim task assigned to statisticians. But statistics does more than document destruction; statistics saves lives.

The first London victims all lived around Broad Street and very close to the Frith Street office of Dr. John Snow, a physician who had spent several years forming new hypotheses about how cholera was communicated from one person to the next (Vinten-Johansen, Brody, Paneth, Rachman, & Rip, 2003). Not surprisingly, the suddenness of the attack created an immediate public panic, partly because surviving families were so familiar with the disease. Even young children knew how consuming a cholera epidemic could become; only five years earlier this same disease had claimed a staggering 58,000 lives.

Nobody knew where the disease came from, and nobody knew why it left. All they knew was that death was

Life-Saving Statistics
The London cholera epidemic of 1854 was contained because John Snow used statistical reasoning to identify the source of contamination.

F U N.—August 18, 1866.

DEATH'S DISPENSARY.
OPEN TO THE POOR, GRATIS, BY PERMISSION OF THE PARISH.

Mary Evans Picture Library / The Image Works

sudden, vicious, and appeared to strike randomly. In just 10 days, the death toll in Dr. Snow's neighborhood climbed from 127 to 500, approximately 37 new deaths every day. The crisis was getting worse despite the massive exodus of those Broad Street residents who were able to leave their neighborhood. The victims vomited repeatedly; their loosened bowels produced "rice water," and the resulting dehydration contributed to a rapid death. The rumors were true. Cholera had found its way to Broad Street.

The cholera problem in 1854 was the exact same problem that had not been solved in 1849, and that in turn had been a repetition of the problem created by the cholera epidemic of 1832. Someone needed to discover the pattern, if there was one, in the apparently random distribution of deaths by cholera, both to stop this epidemic and to prevent another from occurring. The situation was desperate: The spread of cholera could be stopped only if someone could find a way to discover whether there was a reason behind the randomness, a pattern hiding within the horrifying numbers.

> TWO BRANCHES OF STATISTICS: GROWING OUR KNOWLEDGE OF HUMAN BEHAVIOR

Collecting data is exciting when we care deeply about the ideas being tested. In 1854, Dr. John Snow had to care; his own life, the lives of his neighbors, and thousands, maybe even hundreds of thousands, of lives were at risk. The payoffs for learning how to transform observations into numbers are seldom this dramatic, but they can be. Snow's research proceeded in two stages: description followed by inference. First, he described his findings with a brief visual summary that used public records and personal interviews to create a map that identified where the victims of cholera had been living. Second, he used the information from that map to make inferences about how cholera must be transmitted from person to person, not only in his neighborhood, but wherever an outbreak was taking place. The intuitive genius of Snow anticipated the two main "branches" of modern statistical thought and practice: descriptive statistics and inferential statistics.

Descriptive Statistics: Organizing, Summarizing, and Communicating Numerical Information

These two branches of statistics are exactly what their names suggest. ***Descriptive statistics*** *organize, summarize, and communicate a group of numerical observations.* Descriptive statistics reduce large amounts of data to a manageable yet meaningful size. Let's illustrate descriptive statistics by using numbers that are familiar to most of us: body weight. The Centers for Disease Control and Prevention (CDC) (2004) reported that people in the United States weigh much more now than they did four decades ago. The average weight for women increased from 140.2 pounds in 1960 to 164.3 in 2002. For men, the average weight went from 166.3 to 191.0 pounds in the same time span. These averages are descriptive statistics because they describe many weights in just one number. We can learn a great deal from these succinct summaries; a single number reporting the average is far more useful than a long list of the weights of *every* person studied by the CDC at these two points in time. In Chapter 2, we'll learn more about using descriptive statistics to summarize data with a single number.

Inferential Statistics: Using Samples to Draw Conclusions About a Population

Inferential statistics, like descriptive statistics, are exactly what their name implies. ***Inferential statistics*** *use sample data to make general estimates about the larger population.* We make informal inferences all the time. Students, for example, often use the first day of a class as a sample to make inferences about the professor so that they can predict what is likely to happen across an entire semester. Some students even decide not to take a particular course because they infer from the sample of attending one class that the content of the course will be too difficult, the room too crowded, or the professor too demanding. More formally, the CDC made inferences about weight even though they did not actually weigh *everyone* in the United States. In their research, the CDC typically studies a representative group of U.S. citizens in person or examines existing medical records of a representative group of U.S. citizens.

Distinguishing Between a Sample and a Population

*A **sample*** is a set of observations drawn from the population of interest that, it is hoped, share the same characteristics as the population of interest. A representative sample is intended to serve a similar function as the politician who is supposed to represent you and your interests to the government; in the United States, we even call them representatives and the place where they all work is called the House of Representatives. When we study how much Americans weigh, the entire group that we're interested in is everyone in the United States, called the population of interest. Although we typically study a sample, what we're really interested in is the ***population***, *which includes all possible observations about which we'd like to know something.* The average weight of the sample of women and men is

■ **Descriptive statistics** organize, summarize, and communicate a group of numerical observations.

■ **Inferential statistics** use sample data to make general estimates about the larger population.

■ A **sample** is a set of observations drawn from the population of interest that, it is hoped, share the same characteristics as the population of interest.

■ The **population** includes all possible observations about which we'd like to know something.

then used to estimate the average weight for the population of all women and men in the United States. In its report, the CDC uses the sample to infer (or make an intelligent guess about) the average weight of the population. Such a conclusion goes beyond the actual data that the CDC has. (It is important to note that the word *data* is the plural of the word *datum*. This is why we say "the data *are* interesting" and "if we examine the data, we see that *they* tell us . . . ")

Because we're using a sample, it might be even more useful to develop an interval, rather than a single numerical summary, for each data set. Given that the average weight for women is calculated using a sample, rather than the entire population of American women, an interval of possible averages might be more accurate than a single number that might be slightly off. For example, we might report that the average weight of women in 2002 was likely between 163.3 and 165.3 pounds. In Chapter 12, we'll learn more about using our data to develop such intervals.

Samples in inferential statistics are frequently used because it is rare to be able to study every person (or college student, school system, automobile, or laboratory rat) in a particular population. For one thing, it's far too expensive. In addition, it would take so much time to study everyone that whatever we were studying would probably change shape long before we finished studying it. John Snow certainly couldn't study every individual with cholera: They were dying too fast! He wanted to *help* everyone, not *study* everyone. And he would need both descriptive statistics and inferential statistics to fulfill his mission.

Snow described the data by using public records to collect information about who had died and where they had lived; after that, he interviewed members of the surviving families. He described the data even more clearly by organizing those data on a map that plotted the location of each death due to cholera and using that map to communicate his findings to the local authorities. These were grim descriptive statistics, and they told a frightening story. But Snow wasn't done yet. After carefully describing the data, he began to make inferences about the meaning of that data; he was extending the pattern he had discovered. He generalized that pattern to people and circumstances that he had not studied and never would study. Then he recommended specific action to his local board of health. The scientific process always begins with descriptions before it dares to make inferences. Making accurate inferences can be a life-saving leap, as it was for the people living near Broad Street. That's why it is so vital that we collect "clean," trustworthy data from the very beginning.

Descriptive Statistics Summarize Information
It's more useful to use a single number to summarize many people's weights than to provide a long, overwhelming list of each individual's weight.

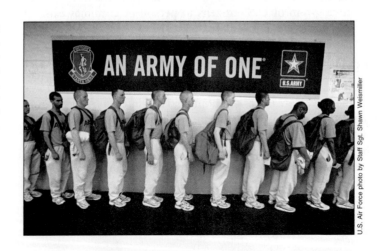

U.S. Air Force photo by Staff Sgt. Shawn Weismiller

Alex Bartel / Photo Researchers, Inc.

The Two Branches of Statistics: Descriptive and Inferential
Self-grafting branches provide mutual nourishment that strengthens the overall structure. The two metaphorical branches of statistics, descriptive statistics and inferential statistics, can also be thought of as providing mutual nourishment that strengthens the structure of our knowledge about human behavior.

Although the scientific process begins with description, the two branches—one for descriptive statistics and one for inferential statistics—are unavoidably intertwined. The branching of statistics is most accurately compared with a self-grafting tree, a tree whose branches first touch, then rub, and eventually open up to one another to provide mutual nourishment. The mutually supportive relationship between descriptive statistics and inferential statistics produces a constantly changing, well-nourished body of knowledge about human behavior that grows a little bit stronger with every published study.

In summary, statistics is divided into two branches, descriptive statistics and inferential statistics. Descriptive statistics organize, summarize, and communicate large amounts of numerical information. Inferential statistics draw conclusions about larger populations based on smaller samples of that population. Samples are intended to be representative of the larger population. Descriptive statistics are used on samples to make inferences about populations. Inferential statistics are used to make interpretations.

⊙ CHECK YOUR LEARNING

1-1 Imagine that the director of the counseling center at your university wants to examine the stress levels of students at your university. From the student directory, she randomly chooses 100 of the 12,500 students and assesses their stress levels in a diagnostic interview. She reports that the average stress level is 18 on a scale of 1–50, a score she knows to be moderately high for college students. She concludes, and reports to the school newspaper, that the students at this institution have a moderately high stress level.

a. What is the sample? _____

b. What is the population? _____

c. What is the descriptive statistic? _____

d. What is the inferential statistic? _____

> VARIABLES: TRANSFORMING OBSERVATIONS INTO NUMBERS

More than 22,000 people had died in the cholera attacks of 1831–1832, and another 54,000 died in the attack of 1848–1849. Naturally, John Snow was aware of those alarming numbers as the 1854 epidemic unfolded near his office on Frith Street. If he wanted to prevent another devastating epidemic, he needed to find some connection between those deaths and some other variable that might be causing this terrible disease. And he needed to find that variable fast.

More specifically, Snow needed to discover a variable that predicted exactly who would contract cholera. If he could pierce the apparent randomness of this disease, he might discover how chloera was being transmitted. This is part of what made Snow so powerful a researcher: He believed there must be some causal connection, a reason behind the apparent randomness of the attacks. Snow used the logic of statistics to discover that cause. So, what did he do? John Snow simply started counting.

Whether our purpose is descriptive or inferential, we begin the research process by transforming observations about behavior into numbers. Because behavior varies, it is not surprising that we refer to *observations of physical, attitudinal, and behavioral characteristics that can take on different values as* **variables**. Behavioral scientists often study abstract variables such as motivation, belief in a just world, self-esteem, and attitudes. Obviously, these ideas cannot be observed in the same way that we can observe and quantify weight or the length of a basketball player's arms or the number of people living in a particular city. In the behaviorial sciences, we call these ideas **constructs**, *hypothetical ideas that have been developed (or constructed) to describe and explain human behavior*. For example, on page 14 you have the opportunity to describe yourself using a scale that represents the construct called Consideration of Future Consequences, a variable we selected because it may be an influential variable that shapes the career choices of many students of the behaviorial sciences. Because there are many different types of constructs available for observation, we use different types of numerical observations to quantify them, choosing the type of numerical observation that best matches the characteristics of each variable of interest.

Students of the behavioral sciences will be happy to learn that the ability to transform observations into numbers is a skill that is in high demand. It is important for the same reason that computer programmers developed the guideline referred to as GIGO (garbage in, garbage out). GIGO reminds computer programmers and behavioral scientists that the quality of their work is only as good as their initial information. If we start off by using numbers that don't genuinely represent our observations, then all of our subsequent analyses will be contaminated and lead us to faulty conclusions. But if we learn how to get it right, then we have opened the door to a variety of far-reaching insights through statistical reasoning. So here's what you need to know to transform everyday observations into the kinds of numbers that genuinely represent those observations.

Discrete observations *can take on only specific values (e.g., whole numbers); no other values can exist between these numbers.* For example, if we measure the number of newspaper deliveries that are late across a particular week, the only possible values would be whole numbers. It is reasonable to assume that each household in the study could have anywhere from 1 to 7 papers delivered late in any given week, but never 1.6 or 5.92 papers delivered late. On the other

■ A **variable** is any observation of a physical, attitudinal, or behavioral characteristic that can take on different values.

■ A **construct** is a hypothetical idea that is developed (or constructed) to describe and explain human behavior.

■ **Discrete observations** can take on only specific values (e.g., whole numbers); no other values can exist between these numbers.

hand, ***continuous observations*** *can take on a full range of values (e.g. numbers out to several decimal places); there is an infinite number of potential values.* For example, in the Stroop color-naming task that you can experience for yourself on page 8, an individual who completed all the mental tasks in a total of 12.839 seconds could fall in the interval between 12.000 seconds and 12.999 seconds, whereas someone who completed them in 14.870 seconds could fall in the interval between 14.000 and 14.999 seconds. The possible values are limited only by the number of decimal places we choose to use.

Discrete and continuous variables break down into further categories. A study tip to help you remember those categories is the acronym N-O-I-R, French for "black." (If you have not studied French, perhaps you have heard the term *film noir*, used to reference dark, dramatic films, often crime stories.) You can use N-O-I-R as a mnemonic trick to remember the four increasingly specific ways of transforming observations into numbers: N (nominal), O (ordinal), I (interval), and R (ratio). The first two of these are discrete variables only, and the last two are usually continuous variables, also known as scale variables.

First, let's examine the two types of discrete observations: nominal variables and ordinal variables. As the word implies, ***nominal variables*** *are used for observations that have categories, or names, as their values.* For example, when entering data into a statistics computer program, a researcher might code male participants with the number 1 and female participants with the number 2. But those numbers serve only a naming function; they merely identify the gender category to which each participant in our study belongs. The numbers do not imply that men are better than women because they are coded as a 1, just as they do not suggest that women are twice as good as men because they happen to be coded as a 2. *Nominal* numbers only *name* category membership. Nominal variables are always discrete; when assigning numbers to categories, there would never be a need to assign anything but a whole number.

Ordinal numbers, as their name also suggests, represent a *rank-ordered* relationship. ***Ordinal variables*** *are observations that have rankings (i.e., 1st, 2nd, 3rd, . . .) as their values.* In competitive sports, you finish the season in a particular "place," or rank. Whether you go to the playoffs is determined by your rank at the end of the season. It doesn't matter if you won first place by a lucky score on the last play of the last game of the season or if you won your league championship by a wide margin. Ordinal numbers allow us to organize our observations into rankings, whereas nominal observations allow us to translate discrete observations into numbers. Like nominal observations, ordinal observations are always discrete. A participant could be first or 3rd or 12th, but could not be ranked at 1.563.

There also are two types of observations that can be continuous—interval variables and ratio variables. ***Interval variables*** *have numbers as their values; the distance (or interval) between pairs of consecutive numbers is assumed to be equal.* For example, time is an interval variable because the interval from one second to the next, or from one-tenth of a second to the next tenth of a second, is always the same. Many cognitive studies (such as the Stroop task) use reaction time to

Nominal Variables Just Categorize
If you wanted to compare the records of Republicans and Democrats, political parties would be a nominal variable. Nominal observations merely name categories; the numbers don't have any meaning beyond a name.

■ **Continuous observations** can take on a full range of values (e.g., numbers out to many decimal points); there is an infinite number of potential values.

■ A **nominal variable** is a variable used for observations that have categories, or names, as their values.

■ An **ordinal variable** is a variable used for observations that have rankings (i.e., 1st, 2nd, 3rd, . . .) as their values.

■ An **interval variable** is a variable that has numbers as its values; the distance (or interval) between pairs of consecutive numbers is assumed to be equal.

measure how quickly we process difficult information. The Stroop task assesses how long it takes to read a list of color words printed in ink of the wrong color. For example, the word *red* might be printed in blue or the word *blue* might be printed in green. If it takes you 1.264 seconds to press a computer key that accurately identifies that the word *red* printed in blue actually reads *red*, your reaction time is an interval observation.

EXPERIENCE IT FOR YOURSELF

TRANSFORMING THE STROOP TASK INTO NUMBERS

You can experience for yourself how social scientists transform observations into numbers. Observe your own cognitive processes at work by taking the short cognitive test called the Stroop task presented in the accompanying figure and at the Web site that supports this textbook at http://www.worthpublishers.com/ nolanheinzen. This version of the Stroop task gives you your response times in whole numbers—for example, 12 seconds. Reaction-time measurements of human behavior are ratio observations because time always implies a meaningful zero. That is, zero means the absence of a quality, such as no time.

Reaction Time and the Stroop Task
The Stroop task assesses how long it takes to read a list of color words printed in the wrong color, such as the word *red* printed in the color white. Try it and see how tricky (and frustrating) it can be. (from http://www.snre.umich.edu/ eplab/demos/st0/stroop_program/ stroopgraphicnonshockwave.gif)

Some interval variables are also discrete variables, such as the number of late newspapers each week. This is an interval variable because the distance between numerical observations is assumed to be equal. The difference between 1 and 2 newspapers is the same as the difference between 5 and 6 newspapers. However, this is also discrete because, as noted earlier, you cannot have anything but whole numbers. There are several social science measures (such as the CFC scale) that are treated as interval measures but also are discrete. Many scores on personality and attitude scales can only be whole numbers, but most of these scales are analyzed as interval variables.

Studies that measure time and distance are continuous, interval observations. But they are also identified as *ratio* observations because zero has meaning for time and distance—the absence of time and the absence of distance mean something, such as time running out in a basketball game or crossing the finish line in a race. ***Ratio variables are variables that meet the criteria for interval variables but also have meaningful zero points.*** Because ratio variables are typically concepts

■ A **ratio variable** is a variable that meets the criteria for interval variables but also has a meaningful zero point.

such as distance, size, and time, they are often continuous variables. Sometimes ratio variables are discrete, however, as in the frequency of an event's occurrence; for example, the number of times a rat pushes a lever to receive food would be considered a ratio variable in that it has a true zero point.

Many statistical computer programs refer to both interval numbers and ratio numbers as *scale* observations because both interval observations and ratio observations are analyzed with the same statistical tests. Computer programs such as the Statistical Program for the Social Sciences (SPSS) prompt us to identify whether the number we are entering into the computer is nominal, ordinal, or scale. Throughout this text, we use all three terms depending on what we are teaching, but we often follow their lead by referring to ratio variables and interval variables as scale variables. As a student of the behavioral sciences, you will find that knowing the different ways that observations about human behavior can be transformed into numbers (N-O-I-R) creates opportunities to indulge your curiosity, explore career opportunities, and experience some early success in your academic major.

The mnemonic makes it easy to remember the different ways to transform observations into numbers: N-O-I-R. Nominal variables name, and ordinal variables rank. Both of these can *only* be discrete variables. With interval variables, distances between observations are assumed to be equal. Ratio variables meet the criteria for interval variables but also have meaningful zero points. Both of these can be discrete or continuous variables. Software typically combines interval and ratio variables, calling both types scale variables. Table 1-1 summarizes the four types of variables.

When designing a study, our goal is to match the kind of observation we plan to make with the kind of number that most accurately represents that observation. Even though scale observations are the most specific way to transform observations into numbers, we cannot impose the assumptions of scale numbers on nominal observations. Most computer programs require us to identify what kind of numerical observation—nominal, ordinal, scale (interval)—is represented by a particular number. Simply remember the N-O-I-R distinction between numerical observations that are nominal (naming), ordinal (rank-ordered), or scale (interval or ratio).

In summary, social scientists create constructs (hypothetical ideas) as they seek to translate observations about human behavior into numbers that genuinely represent those observations. They select either nominal (naming) observations, ordinal (rank-ordered) observations, or scale (interval or ratio) observations that correspond as precisely as possible to what they are observing. Observations may also be described as either discrete or continuous. Our

TABLE 1-1. QUANTIFYING OUR OBSERVATIONS

There are four types of variables that we can use to quantify our observations. Two, nominal and ordinal, are always discrete variables. Interval variables can be discrete or nominal; ratio variables are almost always continuous.

	DISCRETE	CONTINUOUS
NOMINAL	Always	Never
ORDINAL	Always	Never
INTERVAL	Sometimes	Sometimes
RATIO	Seldom	Almost Always

ability to transform observations into numbers creates a variety of career opportunities. The Stroop task provides a way to experience how observations about mental processing are translated into numbers.

◉ CHECK YOUR LEARNING

1-2 Eleanor Stampone (1993) randomly distributed what appeared to be the same piece of paper to students in a large lecture center. Each paper contained one of three short paragraphs that described the interests and appearance of a female college student. The descriptions were identical in every way except for one adjective. The student was described as having either "short," "mid-length," or "very long" hair. At the bottom of each piece of paper, Stampone asked the participants (both female and male) to fill out a scale that indicated the probability that the student described in the scenario would be sexually harassed.

   a. What is the nominal variable used in Stampone's hair-length study? Why is this considered a nominal variable? _____

   b. What is the ordinal variable used in the study? Why is this considered an ordinal variable? _____

   c. What is the interval or ratio variable used in the study? Why is this considered an interval or ratio variable? _____

> INDEPENDENT AND DEPENDENT VARIABLES: THE MAIN INGREDIENTS OF STATISTICAL THINKING

Dr. John Snow's Broad Street neighborhood was a collection of breweries, cowsheds, workhouses (prisons), animal droppings, and slaughterhouses. Human waste, rotten food, animal waste, and other garbage were deposited near homes in "cess pits" that had not been drained for years. What a breeding ground for disease! Cholera was simply the worst of the many diseases that must have been rising out of all that swampy wastewater. Terrified parents, anxious to relieve their children's suffering must have raced from their homes to the nearest well again and again; it was the only possible comfort for a desperately dehydrated victim of cholera—and perfectly designed to ensure repeated exposure to cholera.

Fortunately, Snow had a specific hypothesis in mind, and he was determined to test it. So he started counting the cholera deaths (a descriptive statistic) and then calculated a second variable: location. Locating exactly where the cholera victims had lived allowed him to correlate two variables: the number of deaths and the location of deaths. Specifically, Snow walked around his neighborhood, interviewed the grieving families, took careful notes, and then placed dots on a map that showed the exact location of where the cholera victims had been living.

The life-saving information on this now-famous map of London jumped off the page! Almost all the deaths were near the Broad Street water well. The visual presentation of these data revealed that the closer a home was to the well, the more likely it was to have suffered a death from cholera. In 1854, this map was a virtual window into the spread of this terrible disease. The visual correlation between number of deaths and distance from the well also allowed Snow to observe that only a few deaths had occurred near a neighboring well. Furthermore, his careful interviews revealed that half of the cholera victims living near the neighboring well had actually pumped water from the Broad Street well.

Snow's hypothesis had mixed the right variables together and created new knowledge that saved thousands of lives.

At a practical level, it is helpful simply to remember that variables vary. For example, when studying a discrete, nominal variable such as *gender*, we refer to gender as the variable because it can vary as either male or female. The term *level*, along with the terms *value* and *condition*, all refer to the same idea; **levels are the discrete values or conditions that variables can take on.** For example, male is a level or value of the variable, not the variable itself; female is another level or value of the variable, not the variable itself. Gender is the variable. Similarly, when studying a continuous, scale variable, such as how fast a runner completes a marathon, we refer to time as the variable; 3 hours, 42 minutes, 27 seconds is one of an infinite number of possible times it would take to complete a marathon. Finally, when comparing the effects of an antidepressant to those of a placebo, we often describe the variable as type of treatment and its subcategories as the placebo condition versus the treatment condition. The important thing to remember is this: variables vary.

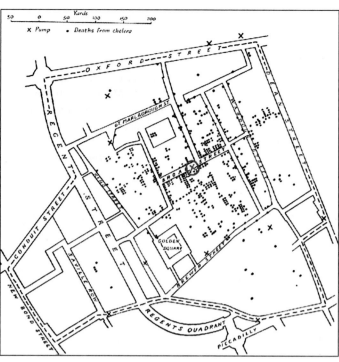

John Snow's Famous Map
John Snow mapped cholera deaths in relation to the Broad Street water well and, in doing so, solved the urgent mystery of how cholera could infect so many people so suddenly. The Xs are all neighborhood wells. The X with the red circle is the Broad Street well. Each dot indicates that a person living at this address died of cholera.

Putting Variables to Work: Independent, Dependent, and Confounding Variables

There are three types of variables. Two of these variables are necessary for research: independent variables and dependent variables. But the third type of variable, a confounding variable, is the enemy of good research. Confounding variables are so harmful to research that we cannot say enough bad things about them! They are the monkey wrench in the gears, the fly in the ointment, and the fingernails on the chalkboard! Confounding variables are so harmful to research that we expend enormous amounts of time, intellectual energy, and money to minimize or neutralize their effects.

All of the sciences use the terms *independent variable* and *dependent variable* to formulate their hypotheses. We usually conduct research to determine if one or more independent variables predicts a dependent variable. *The **independent variable** has at least two levels that we either manipulate or observe to determine its effects on the dependent variable.* For example, if we are studying the effects of caffeinated coffee on the time needed to complete the Stroop task, then the independent variable is the different numbers of cups of coffee that we, as experimenters, decide to test in our study. If we are studying whether gender predicts one's attitude about politics, then the independent variable is gender.

There is a debate about whether all variables like this, whether manipulated or observed, can be called independent variables. For example, if we hypothesize that one's gender predicts one's attitudes about politics, not all researchers would call gender an independent variable even though it functions as one. Some argue that because we're not actually manipulating gender—that is, we're not assigning people to be men or women—it's not an independent variable. To make this differentiation, some researchers use the term *independent variable* only

- ■ A **level** is a discrete value or condition that a variable can take on.
- ■ An **independent variable** is a variable that we either manipulate or observe to determine its effects on the dependent variable.

when the researcher is manipulating the variable; they use either *quasi-independent variable* or *nonmanipulated independent variable* when the variable is not manipulated. Most commonly, however, *independent variable* is used regardless of whether the variable is manipulated or merely observed. The important point is that all such variables serve as explanatory, or predictor, variables. We will refer to them simply as independent variables.

The **dependent variable** *is the outcome variable that we hypothesize to be related to, or caused by, changes in the independent variable.* For example, we hypothesize that the dependent variable (reaction time) *depends* on the independent variable (the number of cups of coffee); reaction time depends on the amount of caffeine. If you're in doubt as to which is the independent and which the dependent variable, then ask yourself which one *depends* on the other; that one is the dependent variable.

By contrast, confounding variables, often simply called *confounds*, damage the logic of our reasoning. **Confounding variables** *include anything that systematically varies with the independent variable so that we cannot logically determine which variable is at work.* For example, prior to Hurricanes Katrina and Rita during the tragic summer of 2005, many insurance companies had insured people's homes against wind damage but not against flood damage. Hurricane winds bring water in many different ways: in the rain, by causing higher tides, and by creating structural damage that allows water into the home. Consequently, both wind and water contributed to the levees' breaking around New Orleans, as well as causing billions of dollars of other damage all along the Gulf Coast. But logically, many insurance companies could argue that it was often unclear whether damage to a particular home was due to high winds or high water. Wind and water were confounded.

Another type of variable can disrupt a study in a similar way. **Extraneous variables** *are randomly distributed influences that detract from the experimenter's efforts to measure what was intended to be measured.* Imagine a room full of male and female students distributed around a lecture center. They are each reading a descriptive paragraph about a male college student. The paragraph includes details such as where he grew up, what he is studying, his hobbies, and a brief physical description. Although the paragraphs look identical, they actually vary in one respect: weight. Students in the class have been randomly assigned to read about a 5-foot, 11-inch man who weighs 125 pounds, 175 pounds, 225 pounds, or 275 pounds. At the end of the paragraph, the students are asked to rate the probable intelligence of this fictional student.

Suddenly, just outside the door to the lecture center, there is the sound of glass breaking, and the distinctive aroma of a new perfume being test-marketed by a business intern wafts into the room. Is the aroma a confound? No, because it does not systematically vary with any of the conditions. That is, the perfume will influence people in the randomly distributed conditions equivalently. However, the aroma does distract their attention and might cue other thoughts about the appearance, role, and expectations of women in society. In other words, it might raise or lower all scores. Moreover, the aroma is not something that can be quickly processed and then disregarded (like the sound of the glass breaking) because it lingers in the air. It's a disruptive, extraneous variable that entered the study by chance and contributed what experimenters refer to as noise. **Noise** *influences an experiment by making the relations between variables less clear than they really are.* The word *noise* is used by scientists in a way that is different from how we use it in everyday language. It doesn't necessarily have to be an actual sound; in fact, it's often not a sound. It could be the effect of a smell, the presence of an individual, or different times of day—anything that disturbs the clarity of the story our data are telling.

■ A **dependent variable** is the outcome variable that we hypothesize to be related to, or caused by, changes in the independent variable.

■ A **confounding variable** is any variable that systematically co-varies with the independent variable so that we cannot logically determine which variable is at work; also called a *confound*.

■ An **extraneous variable** is a randomly distributed influence that detracts from the experimenter's efforts to measure what was intended to be measured.

■ **Noise** influences an experiment by making the relations between variables less clear than they really are.

The names for these disruptive influences are well chosen. The word *confounding* implies confusion, and confusion is exactly what these variables add to a study. Similarly, the word *extraneous* suggests something external—that is, outside of or in addition to our independent variables—and that is exactly how these variables tend to confuse an otherwise well-designed study. Similarly, *noise* is the kind of static sound that makes it difficult to hear what the data are saying. Experimenters are annoyed by noise and upset about extraneous variables, but they become livid about confounding variables! Confounds introduce unrelated factors that disrupt the logic of a study.

Was the Damage from Wind or Water?
During Hurricane Katrina in 2005, high winds were confounded with high water so that often it was not possible to determine whether property damage was due to wind (insured) or to water (not insured).

Confounding variables often confuse the logic of a study simply by happening at the same time. In other words, they co-occur with the independent variable, so we cannot tell which variable is doing the "causing." For example, if cities' divorce rates appear to predict crime rates, then it could be because the confounding variable of income—which tends to decrease with divorce—is predicting crime rates. Logically, we cannot determine whether a higher divorce rate or lower income is the real predictor of higher crime rates. It could be either, neither, or both; we just can't tell because confounds confuse our understanding of the possible relations between variables.

During the Broad Street cholera outbreak, there were thousands of possible confounds, and logically any one of them might have been connected to the dependent variable of whether someone contracts cholera. For example, the local brewery in Dr. Snow's neighborhood may have started a new fermentation process; maybe cholera was being distributed in the beer, or only in particular kegs of beer. There also was a workhouse (prison) in the neighborhood; perhaps some disease was escaping from that confined world, floating on the air out into the public. Any co-occurring variable could be causing cholera: Snow's challenge was to isolate the causal variable.

Snow was faced with thousands of such potential confounds—even religion! A significant part of the public debate over cholera boiled down to sin versus sanitation. The Reverend Vaughan Thomas, for example, concluded that cholera illustrated "the reality of that universal law of Providence, whereby sin produces its own punishment . . . [for] vicious indulgences predisposed the body to take disease" (quoted in Morris, 1975). Talk about blaming the victim! Research needs to be so carefully designed that the entire range of potential explanations can be ruled out, including the idea that "catching" cholera was God's way of punishing the wicked for their own excesses.

Given the problems of confounding variables, how do we decide which is our independent variable and which might be a confounding variable we want to control? Well, it all comes down to what *you* decide to study. Scientists make these choices every time they design a new experiment. For example, if you hypothesize that a particular diet drug leads to weight loss, whether someone uses the diet drug becomes your independent variable and exercise becomes the potentially confounding variable that you would try to control. On the other hand, if you hypothesize that exercise leads to weight loss, then the level of exercise becomes your independent variable and whether people use diet drugs along with it becomes the potentially confounding variable that you have to control. In both of these cases, the dependent variable would be weight loss. But you, the researcher, have to make some decisions about which variables to treat as independent, predictor variables and which to treat as dependent variables you are hoping to predict. You, the experimenter, are in control of the experiment.

Developing and Assessing Variables: The Reliability and Validity of Tests

One recently developed variable is particularly relevant for behavioral science majors trying to sort out their careers: Consideration of Future Consequences (CFC). You will want to evaluate yourself on this scale, shown in Figure 1-1,

For each of the statements below, please indicate whether the statement is characteristic of you on a scale of 1 to 5. If the statement is extremely uncharacteristic of you write a 1 to the left of the question; if the statement is extremely characteristic of you write a 5. Use the numbers in the middle if you fall between the extremes. Please keep the scale in mind as you rate each of the statements below.

Extremely Uncharacteristic				Extremely Characteristic
1	2	3	4	5

_____ 1. I consider how things might be in the future and try to influence those things with my day-to-day behavior.

_____ 2. Often I engage in a particular behavior to achieve outcomes that may not occur for many years.

_____ 3. I act only to satisfy immediate concerns, figuring the future will take care of itself.

_____ 4. My behavior is influenced only by the immediate (i.e., a matter of days or weeks) outcomes of my actions.

_____ 5. My convenience is a big factor in the decisions I make or the actions I take.

_____ 6. I am willing to sacrifice my immediate happiness or well-being to achieve future outcomes.

_____ 7. I think it is important to take warnings about negative outcomes seriously even if the negative outcome will not occur for many years.

_____ 8. I think it is more important to perform a behavior with important distant consequences than a behavior with less important immediate consequences.

_____ 9. I generally ignore warnings about possible future problems because I think the problems will be resolved before they reach crisis level.

_____ 10. I think that sacrificing now is usually unnecessary since future outcomes can be dealt with at a later time.

_____ 11. I act only to satisfy immediate concerns, figuring that I will take care of future problems that may occur at a later date.

_____ 12. Since my day-to-day work has specific outcomes, it is more important to me than behavior that has distant outcomes.

FIGURE 1-1
Consideration of Future Consequences (CFC) Scale

Fill out the CFC scale and calculate your personal score. When calculating your score, note that items 3, 4, 5, 9, 10, 11, and 12 are reverse scored (1 = 5, 2 = 4, 3 = 3, 4 = 2, 5 = 1). For example, if you had a 4 for item number 3, that 4 would become a 2. After reverse scoring these items, simply add up the scores for the individual items to get your total score. Your score will be easier to interpret if you then divide your total score by 12 (the number of items).

for four reasons. First, you will find it interesting to compare your CFC score to the scores of others in your class. Second, we will be using your CFC score in subsequent chapters to teach you about other aspects of statistics. Third, discovering your CFC score will help you gain a sense of why reliability and validity are so critical to the social sciences. Finally, you might start to think a bit more clearly about how you are making decisions that will shape your own life and career.

This variable, the CFC scale, is an example of a variable constructed with a significant degree of reliability and validity (Eckles, Joireman, Sprott, & Spangenberg, 2003). *A **reliable** measure is one that is consistent.* If you were to weigh yourself on your bathroom scale now and again in an hour, then you would expect your weight to be almost exactly the same. If your weight remains the same when you haven't done anything to change it, then your bathroom scale is reliable.

But a reliable scale is not necessarily a valid scale. *A **valid** measure is one that measures what it was intended to measure.* Your bathroom scale could be incorrect, but be consistently incorrect. In that case, your scale would be reliable, but not valid. A more extreme example is wanting to know your weight but using a ruler to determine it. We would get a number, and that number might be reliable, but it would not be a valid measure of your weight. If the CFC scale does not have high reliability and validity, then there is no point in your filling it out because we can never know for sure what your score means.

There are many subtypes of both reliability and validity, but they are all simply specific ways of testing whether the scale is consistent (reliability) and measures what it was intended to measure (validity). For example, if your CFC score today is nearly the same as your CFC score tomorrow, then the scale appears to be somewhat reliable. Why not take the scale again tomorrow and find out? It will give you a good understanding of a particular type of reliability called test–retest reliability. ***Test–retest reliability*** *refers to whether the scale being used provides consistent information every time the test is taken.* If your CFC score also predicts a network of behaviors related to its core idea, then the scale also has high validity. The core idea of the CFC scale is that it measures individual differences in how each of us weighs the effects of our present decisions and behaviors on distant outcomes. One of the immediate applications of the CFC scale has been to public health. For example, if high CFC scores predict specific behaviors, such as whether we go to the doctor on a regular basis or buy health insurance, then the scale has a particular type of validity called predictive validity. More formally, ***predictive validity*** *refers to how well a measuring instrument (such as a personality scale) predicts actual behavior.*

Unfortunately, we now know that some very famous tests have very low reliability and validity—but it is very important that we know it! Any test with poor reliability cannot have high validity because it is not possible to measure what we intended to measure when the test itself produces varying results. The well-known Rorschach inkblot test is one example of a test whose reliability is questionable, so the validity of the information it produces is difficult to interpret (Wood, Nezworski, Lilienfeld, & Garb, 2003). For instance, two clinicians might analyze the identical set of responses to a Rorschach test and develop quite different interpretations of those responses. Although training and a specific set of guidelines for scoring the Rorschach increase its reliability, it is difficult to figure out if a particular clinical conclusion is valid. Many researchers doubt the validity of the Rorschach despite the possibility of improved

■ **Reliability** refers to the consistency of a measure.

■ **Validity** refers to the extent to which a test actually measures what it was intended to measure.

■ **Test–retest reliability** refers to whether the scale being used provides consistent information every time the test is taken.

■ **Predictive validity** refers to how well a measuring instrument (such as a personality scale) predicts actual behavior.

What Might This Be?
An example of an inkblot such as those that are used in the famous Rorschach inkblot test. A clinician would ask the test-taker, "What might this be?" Unfortunately, although there are some indications that, with proper training, the Rorschach test can be scored reliably, evidence does not support the test's validity.

reliability. Just because two clinicians using a fairly reliable system for scoring the Rorschach designate a person as psychotic, it doesn't necessarily mean that the person *is* psychotic or even that the person will occasionally behave in a psychotic manner. It might not be a valid measure of the construct of psychoticism at all. Reliability is necessary, but not sufficient, to create a valid measure.

Nevertheless, the central idea that ambiguous pictures somehow invite revealing information remains attractive to many researchers (and to laypeople, too); as a result, tests such as the Rorschach still are used frequently, even though there is much controversy about their utility (Wood et al., 2003). Projective personality tests such as the Rorschach and the Thematic Apperception Test (TAT), measures in which test-takers are asked to tell stories about ambiguous pictures, are most helpful when limited to a specific purpose and supported by a network of studies testing their reliability and validity (Birney, Burdick, & Teevan, 1969).

In summary, variables are the ingredients that social scientists mix together to create new knowledge through statistical reasoning. Independent and dependent variables express a predictor–predicted relation between variables that allows researchers to test and explore the relations between variables. Confounding variables limit our ability to understand those relations because they won't allow us to logically distinguish between alternative explanations. The CFC scale provides an opportunity for students to learn about the importance of reliability and validity, while also thinking about the role CFC plays in their own career planning. Any construct needs to be measured with reliability and validity in order to trust the information it provides.

☉ CHECK YOUR LEARNING

1-3 Let's say you wanted to study the impact of declaring a major on school-related anxiety. You recruit 50 first-year university students who have not declared a major and 50 first-year university students who have declared a major. You have all 100 complete an anxiety scale.

a. What is the independent variable in this study?

b. What are the levels of the independent variable?

c. What is the dependent variable?

d. What would it mean for the anxiety scale to be reliable?

e. What would it mean for the anxiety scale to be valid?

> AN INTRODUCTION TO HYPOTHESIS TESTING: FROM HUNCH TO HYPOTHESIS

When the cholera outbreak hit Broad Street, John Snow did not have time to consider which variable to investigate first; people were dying all around him. Fortunately, he had already spent several years testing different hypotheses about the transmission of cholera. He was reasonably certain that he knew how cholera was *not* transmitted because he had been systematically ruling out possible explanations. He had proposed and tested many hypotheses, but none of them was supported by the evidence.

The focus of John Snow's efforts was to identify something as close as possible to a cause–effect relationship. He knew he was getting close when he began to identify patterns that were more than mere coincidence. Even when interviewing families who were stricken with grief, Snow systematically, yet sensitively, asked insightful questions that produced useful, life-saving information. He elicited descriptions of exactly who was doing what, and who was standing where, when in the presence of someone with cholera; then he noted who did or did not become ill.

> [T]he above instances are quite sufficient to show that cholera can be communicated from the sick to the healthy; for it is quite impossible that even a tenth part of these cases of consecutive illness could have followed each other by mere coincidence, without being connected as cause and effect. (Snow, 1855, p. 11)

Snow was a man who knew the importance of generating hypotheses that could be tested and then rejected. He didn't mind being wrong because every unsupported hypothesis simply narrowed the field of possible causes. Eventually, the scientific process forced his brain to imagine alternative explanations that better fit the evidence for how this gruesome disease was communicated from one person to the next. Snow's statistical reasoning was racing against the urgency of grieving neighbors and the threat to his own survival. He already had some well-developed ideas about what was causing the rapid spread of this deadly disease. Now he had to put his ideas to the test.

Testing our ideas is called hypothesis testing. More formally, **hypothesis testing** is the process of drawing conclusions about whether a particular relation between variables is supported by the evidence. Typically, we examine data from a sample to draw conclusions about a population. When we formalize the process of scientific hypothesis testing, we are actually trying to shoot down our own favorite idea. Such a self-critical approach is the way science has successfully reasoned its way to innumerable medical cures, advances in psychological therapies, and technological progress. Our impulse to critically test our own long-held beliefs may be the saving grace of the human species; it certainly was the saving grace for John Snow and his neighbors.

This course in statistics is not equivalent to the kind of health crisis that John Snow faced, but it does represent a significant hurdle in your personal growth as a student of the behavioral sciences. So we can use research-based learning (Bartsch, 2006) to demonstrate how to transform a vague hunch into a scientific hypothesis. The account below is presented as a single-class experience; however, it actually represents a somewhat idealized process across many different statistics classes.

We started the very first day of a statistics class with a discussion that allowed us to sample our students about the hunches and vague questions they had coming into a statistics course. We then challenged our students to make their questions more and more specific until their questions evolved into a testable hypothesis about the value of taking a course in statistics. The following questions are representative of the responses that emerged from that initial discussion. (Sometimes we ask our students to write down these questions, but a candid discussion with careful note taking works just as well.) These initial questions in the minds of our

■ **Hypothesis testing** is the process of drawing conclusions about whether a particular relation between variables is supported by the evidence.

students on the first day of class may correspond to some of the questions you have about learning statistics. We started the discussion by simply encouraging our students: "Be honest. What are your thoughts as you begin this class in statistics?"

"Why do I have to take this class?"

"What good will this class do me?"

"Is this professor any good?"

"Why is the book so expensive?"

"Will it be hard?"

"Will I have to study a lot?

"How many tests are there?"

"What can I use statistics for, anyway?"

"Do I have to learn to use a statistics program on the computer?"

As we considered these honestly expressed questions, the class agreed that most of them revolved around the same issue:

"Will the effort I put into this class yield personal benefits?"

This is a far more specific question than those we started with, yet it remains true to the spirit of the initial set of ideas or hunches that students really have. Consequently, we have moved from a vague hunch to a specific question. However, this was not yet a question or hypothesis that we could test. So we explored more specific ways we might ask that same question and eventually we came up with:

"Have previous students at this college benefited from learning statistics?"

At this point, the class knew they were on the trail of a more specific and answerable question. If others had benefited from learning statistics, it was only a small leap for them to believe that they, too, might benefit from learning statistics. An odd but wonderful thing often happens as the research process narrows an honestly asked question into a testable hypothesis: creativity. In this case, the research process developed along this line:

"Maybe we could survey the alumni to find out if they are using statistics?"

Very soon, students were developing a scale for a survey of alumni that tested this hypothesis:

"Learning statistics will provide tangible financial benefits."

They were proposing to ask alumni such things as:

"How much money do you earn?"

"How long ago did you graduate?"

"How often do you interpret or create statistical information?"

"Rate how important statistical information is to your job."

"Rate how important a knowledge of statistics is to being promoted."

On the very first day of class, these students were doing an excellent job of working toward an operational definition of "the value of learning statistics." *An **operational definition** specifies the operations or procedures used to measure or manipulate a variable.* We could, for example, operationalize anxiety as a score on a self-report anxiety scale that an individual completed on his or her own, a

■ An **operational definition** specifies the operations or procedures used to measure or manipulate a variable.

clinician's rating of that person's anxiety following a diagnostic interview, or a physiological measure such as heart rate that might be the product of anxiety. In the statistics class described above, the students proposed to measure in a very concrete way what had started out as an inarticulate idea. Specifically, they collected the personal data described above (about income, years since graduation, and so forth, plus scaled data from a 7-point scale about the importance of statistical information to their jobs and being promoted). John Snow was doing the exact same thing: translating a hunch into a hypothesis.

OPERATIONALIZING VARIABLES

EXPERIENCE IT FOR YOURSELF

You already carry many hypotheses around in your head; you just haven't bothered to test them yet, at least not formally. For example, perhaps you believe that men use bank ATMs faster than women or that smokers simply lack will power. Maybe you are convinced that the parking problem on your campus is part of an uncaring conspiracy by administrators to make your life more difficult. Perhaps you suspect that your friends tolerate you only because you can tell a good joke. In each of these cases, as shown in the accompanying figure, we can frame our hypothesis in terms of an independent variable and a dependent variable. Once again, the best way to learn about operationalizing a variable is to experience it for yourself. So propose a way to measure each of the variables identified in the accompanying table. We've given you a start with regard to gender (an easy variable to operationalize) and how bad the parking problem is (a more difficult variable to operationalize).

The Independent Variable . . .	Predicts	The Dependent Variable
Gender		who uses ATMs the fastest
Amount of will power		level of cigarette smoking
Level of caring by administrators		parking problem
Level of joke-telling ability		number of friends

CONCEPTUAL VARIABLE	OPERATIONALIZED VARIABLE
Gender	Self-reported gender
Who uses ATMs the fastest	_____
Amount of will power	_____
Level of cigarette smoking	_____
Level of caring by administrators	_____
How bad the parking problem is	Ask students to rate the parking problem on a scale ranging from 1 (no problem) to 5 (the worst problem on campus)
Level of joke-telling ability	_____
Number of friends	_____

Learning how to operationalize variables is a skill worth developing. There are many very interesting, consequential jobs available for those creative enough to operationalize variables without spending an organization's entire budget on a single project! Moreover, the better you get at it, the sooner you can start indulging your own curiosity about human behavior by "mixing" variables together to test and explore your own hypotheses.

In summary, hypothesis testing is the process of drawing conclusions about whether a particular relation between variables is supported by the evidence. Typically, we test hypotheses by examining data from a sample and then drawing conclusions about the larger population. Transforming our vague hunches into testable hypotheses requires asking increasingly specific questions until we arrive at a question that can be answered numerically. Learning how to operationalize variables is a skill that has practical career benefits; it also provides a way to satisfy our own curiosity about human behavior.

⊙ CHECK YOUR LEARNING

1-4 For each of the following variables—both described at some point in this chapter—state (i) how the researcher operationalized the variable, and (ii) one other way in which the researcher could have operationalized the variable.

a. Cholera (in John Snow's study)

b. The water, the proposed cause of cholera (in John Snow's study)

> TYPES OF RESEARCH DESIGNS: EXPERIMENTS, NONEXPERIMENTS, AND QUASI-EXPERIMENTS

Cholera seemed to pick and choose its victims randomly, so a "miasma of the air" hypothesis had been the most appealing explanation. But it really didn't fit the evidence that John Snow had been collecting. One person developed cholera while someone else standing right next to that person did not. Surely they had breathed in the same air. But the slow progress of science was about to be jump-started, transformed by the intrinsic logic of a simple statistic: the correlation.

Even after plotting his persuasive map, Snow wanted to be sure that he accurately understood the story his map was telling. So he examined a sample of Broad Street well water under a microscope and discovered "white, flocculent particles." That is when he decided that he had seen enough evidence. As soon as a plausible reason for the correlation between deaths and location became clear to him, Snow took his findings to the Board of Guardians of St. James Parish, the governmental agency in charge of the Broad Street pump.

The Board of Guardians, however, was startled by the odd theory that cholera was communicated in the water supply. Furthermore, they were unsure how to respond to Snow's bizarre insistence that they simply remove the pump handle in order to stop the spread of

Handleless Pump Outside the John Snow Pub
John Snow's careful research convinced public health officials to remove the handle from the pump at the contaminated well. Research and statistical reasoning have enormous implications for public health and numerous other fields that affect our well-being.

Martin Jacob

the disease. How could removing a pump handle stop an epidemic? Frankly, the idea sounded ridiculous. The local government resisted, but Snow insisted. At last, the local authorities removed the pump handle and the rate of deaths from cholera declined dramatically. However, Snow soon ran into another statistical problem. The rate of deaths from cholera had started to decline even before the removal of the pump handle! Maybe his theory was nonsense; perhaps cholera wasn't really transmitted in the shared water supply. On the other hand, maybe there were statistical reasons for the decline in the death rate prior to removing the pump handle.

Why would the number of deaths in the Broad Street neighborhood decline during a full-blown cholera epidemic? The answer is both disturbing and insightful. There were fewer deaths because there were fewer people available to be infected. First of all, many people in the neighborhood had already died. Second, anyone who could get out of London had already done so. Just as Hurricane Katrina left only the poorest people in New Orleans without a way to leave the city, the wealthiest and healthiest people in the Broad Street neighborhood had found somewhere else they could go. Those who remained were too sick, too full of grief, or materially unable to leave the neighborhood.

Statistics are most meaningful within the context of a research design. For example, John Snow didn't need a statistical formula to think like a statistician. The logic of Snow's correlation research design created a map that allowed his data to "speak." In fact, the mathematical formula for the correlation would not be developed by Karl Pearson until 40 years later, near the end of the nineteenth century. But the idea of a systematic co-relation between two variables (number of deaths and proximity to the well) represented the correlational research design that was at the heart of Snow's life-saving accomplishment.

The goal of every study is to create a fair test of the hypothesis. But no single research design is suitable for every situation. For example, randomly assigning participants to either an experimental or a control group is a common and very effective way to create initial equality between the two groups. However, when we study post-traumatic stress disorder (PTSD), for example, we cannot randomly assign one participant to suffer some terrible tragedy so that we can compare his or her response to a "control" who has not been similarly traumatised. Nevertheless, it is becoming increasingly important for us to understand this particular disorder because its pattern of symptoms seems to occur following traumas such as rape, loss of a loved one, exposure to combat, or the destruction of one's home. Fortunately, we have three classes of studies that allow us to use statistics to address these questions: experiments, quasi-experiments, and nonexperiments. These different types of studies are distinguished by how their participants are selected, assigned, and treated.

The American Psychological Association (APA) (2001) offers an important insight into the everyday work of research by encouraging us to identify these research volunteers as *participants* rather than *subjects*, even though the more traditional term *subjects* lingers within the research community. Use of the word *subjects* implies an inappropriate attitude toward the people who help us, and the change in our language is long overdue. However we describe the people who help us learn about human behavior, our goal is to treat participants with respect so they can provide trustworthy information about the relations between variables.

The Ethics of Experimental Design

A disturbing pattern of psychological symptoms was called shell shock after World War I, battle fatigue and war trauma after World War II and the Korean conflict, and eventually post-traumatic stress disorder (PTSD) following the Vietnam War. Because we cannot randomly assign individuals either to participate or be exempt from a war, we must use nonexperimental designs to try to isolate the effects and develop coping strategies.

GUO LEI / Xinhua / Landov

Experiments and Causality: Controlling the Confounding Variables

In everyday conversation, we might say that we are doing an *experiment* when we try a new route to school or add a new spice to our famous chili, but this term means something very specific in science. *An **experiment** is a study in which participants are randomly assigned to a condition or level of one or more independent variables.* Neither the participants nor the researchers get to choose the condition.

Experiments are the gold standard of hypothesis testing and for a very good reason: experiments are better than any other type of research design at controlling the effects of confounding variables. This means that experiments can create a chain of cause–effect reasoning that leads to a rich, productive understanding of many different behaviors. Experiments are the most direct way to test cause–effect relations between variables, thus increasing our confidence that we understand the relations between the variables in our study. Even when researchers cannot conduct a true experiment, they include as many of the characteristics of an experiment as possible. The critical feature that makes a study worthy of the descriptor *experiment* is random assignment to groups.

Randomness is an extremely powerful way to control confounding variables. It is used in a variety of ways across science, but it always has the same underlying purpose: to provide a fair, unbiased test of the hypothesis. Experiments create an initial equality between groups by randomly assigning participants to different levels, or conditions, of the independent variable. *With **random assignment**, every participant in the study has an equal chance of being assigned to any condition.* Random assignment controls the effects of personality traits, life experiences, personal biases, or other potential confounds by distributing them across each condition of the experiment to an equivalent degree. As you might anticipate, the more participants we have in a study, the more likely it is that each randomly created group really is equivalent.

Random assignment is not the only technique that experimenters use to control the effects of potentially confounding variables. Another technique is called the ***single-blind experiment**, in which participants do not know the condition to which they have been assigned.* This reduces the possibility that participants will expect something to happen and thereby create a placebo effect. Specifically, *a **placebo effect** occurs when an expectation of an outcome either causes or appears to cause that outcome to take place.* Placebo effects are surprisingly powerful. Simply expecting that a drug will have an effect can cause the medication you take to have—or appear to have—the desired effect. To control for placebo effects, participants are not informed about the condition to which they have been randomly assigned. Moreover, sometimes even the experimenters conducting the study do not know to which condition participants have been assigned. *When neither the participants nor the experimenters know the participants' assigned conditions, the study is called a **double-blind experiment**.* A double-blind experiment reduces the possibility that the experimenter may unintentionally influence participants to respond in a certain manner.

Are you surprised that experimenters may inadvertently contaminate their own studies? Experimenters become deeply engaged in their studies and are privately—and even unconsciously—hoping that the study will turn out in a particular way, just as you will when you put your own hypotheses to the test. That is why experimenters run the risk of exhibiting ***demand characteristics** by inadvertently cueing the participants to certain responses.* For example, an experimenter might convey expectations for the participants' behavior by nodding his or her head and smiling more when administering a test to a participant in a condition that the experi-

▪ An **experiment** is a study in which participants are randomly assigned to a condition or level of one or more independent variables

▪ In **random assignment,** every participant in a study has an equal chance of being assigned to any of the groups, or experimental conditions, in the study.

▪ A **single-blind experiment** is one in which participants do not know the condition to which they have been assigned. This reduces the possibility that participants will respond as they believe they are expected to respond to a given situation.

▪ A **placebo effect** occurs when an expectation of an outcome either causes or appears to cause that outcome to take place.

▪ A **double-blind experiment** is one in which neither the experimenters conducting the study nor the participants in the study know the condition to which participants have been assigned.

▪ **Demand characteristics** refer to experimenters inadvertently cueing participants to offer certain responses.

menter hopes will turn out well. A double-blind experiment controls such confounds by hiding the experimental condition and the hypothesis being tested from both the experimenter and the participant. In other words, statistical reasoning requires us to control internal confounds that exist within ourselves, as well as to control for external confounds that exist in the environment.

As you begin to understand how difficult it is to control confounding variables, you will gain a new respect for the power of randomness to wash out so many potential confounds. For example, a school psychologist might want to study whether playing Scrabble (the independent variable) improves vocabulary (the dependent variable) as measured by a standard vocabulary test. In such a study, it would not be ideal to ask people whether they play Scrabble and then measure their vocabularies. Can you spot the confounding variable? People may choose to play Scrabble *because* they already have a large vocabulary and enjoy using it to win at Scrabble. If that is the case, then of course those who play Scrabble will have larger vocabularies—they already did before they took up the game!

It would make much more sense to set up an experiment that randomly assigns students to one of the two levels of the independent variable: play Scrabble or do not play Scrabble. Random assignment assures us that our two groups are roughly equal on all of the variables that might cause high vocabulary, such as intelligence, amount of reading, level of education, and any other variable that might be related to the size of a person's vocabulary. Random assignment washes out the effects of all such potential confounds. Specifically, random assignment to groups increases our confidence that the two groups would be similar on level of vocabulary *prior* to this experiment. (Figure 1-2 visually clarifies the difference between self-selection and random assigment.) We will explore more specifically how random assignment is implemented in Chapter 4.

In addition to using random assignment, we would want to make sure that our two groups are treated as equally as possible, except for the Scrabble playing. That would mean no encouraging, smiling experimenters in the "play

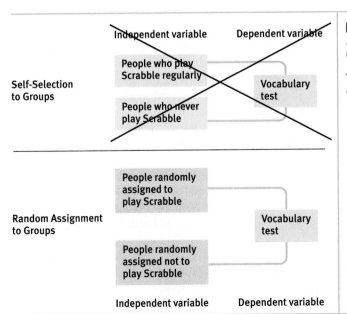

FIGURE 1-2
Self-Selected into or *Randomly Assigned* to One of Two Groups: Scrabble Players vs. Non–Scrabble Players

The design of the first study does not answer the question "Does playing Scrabble improve vocabulary?"

∎ **Nonexperiments** and **quasi-experiments** are studies in which participants are not randomly assigned to conditions.

∎ A **correlation** is an association between two or more variables.

Scrabble" group, no leaking of information to participants about what the hypothesis is, and certainly no shifting about of participants in order to help "make" the study come out in a particular way. If we can control all these confounding variables, then we can conclude whatever the results allow us to conclude. If, for example, the "play Scrabble" group is a great deal higher on vocabulary after the experimental manipulation, then we can conclude that Scrabble playing caused the higher vocabulary. But we can make this powerful assertion of causality only if the two groups are virtually equivalent in every way except for playing Scrabble.

Research Designs Other Than Experiments: Nonexperiments and Quasi-Experiments

*Nonexperiments and **quasi-experiments** are used when we cannot randomly assign participants to conditions.* There are many research designs that fall under these two headings. Quasi-experiments usually provide some kind of comparison group, but it would not be the result of random assignment. Consequently, quasi-experiments provide somewhat more trustworthy information than nonexperimental designs, but they still do not allow us to assert a cause–effect relation between variables.

One example of a nonexperiment is the one-group pretest–posttest design. To conduct the Scrabble study using a one-group pretest–posttest design (illustrated in Figure 1-3), we could measure the vocabulary levels of all participants, have them play Scrabble for a semester, and then reassess vocabulary. If vocabulary increases, it might be due to Scrabble playing, but we cannot assume causality. It might also be due to a semester's worth of learning in class or a particularly effective teacher. In nonexperiments, the design of the study does not allow us to control for any other possible causes for an increase in vocabulary.

One example of a quasi-experiment is a nonequivalent control group design with pretest and posttest. The title of this type of quasi-experiment is long, but if we examine each part of it, it's easy to understand. "Nonequivalent control group" means that there are two groups, but they are not randomly assigned, so they may be different on a number of possible confounding variables. "With pretest and posttest" means that every participant is measured on the dependent variable before and after some intervention.

A pretest–posttest design is flawed because some co-occurring variable could be responsible for any changes in the dependent variable. So a little more control is added by creating a comparison group even though it is a self-selected comparison group. For the Scrabble study (illustrated in Figure 1-4), we would administer a vocabulary pretest to both Scrabble players and non–Scrabble players and then have them continue in their current conditions (either playing Scrabble or not). After a semester, we would administer a vocabulary posttest. If Scrabble players increased their vocabularies even more than non–Scrabble players, then that would provide evidence that those who play Scrabble are more likely to learn new words than those who do not play Scrabble. But they are still nonequivalent groups because they were self-selected rather than randomly assigned. That means that any differences in vocabulary over the year could be caused by playing Scrabble or due to the fact that those who play Scrabble are those who learn new words better anyway. They're just good at it, and that's probably why they

FIGURE 1-3
Nonexperiments

Flowchart of a one-group pretest–posttest design. This is a nonexperiment because the study does not control potential confounds by randomly assigning participants to groups.

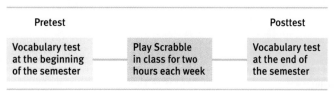

Pretest		Posttest
Vocabulary test at the beginning of the semester	Play Scrabble in class for two hours each week	Vocabulary test at the end of the semester

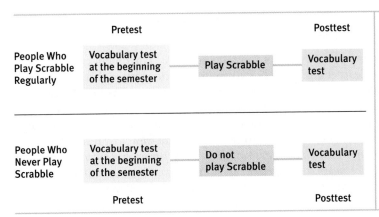

FIGURE 1-4
Quasi-Experiments

Flowchart of a nonequivalent control group design with pretest and posttest. A quasi-experiment is better than a nonexperiment because it provides a meaningful comparison group, but it is not a true experiment because it makes a comparison of groups created through self-selection rather than random assignment to groups.

like Scrabble in the first place. In a quasi-experiment, we can examine some of the other possible causes of an increased vocabulary. But because there is no random assignment, we cannot control for many other possible causes of an increased vocabulary.

John Snow's research was based on the principles of a correlational design. *A correlation is an association between two or more variables, usually interval variables.* In correlational studies, we do not manipulate either variable. We merely assess the two variables as they exist. For example, we might measure the interval variables of amount of Scrabble playing and level of vocabulary. We might find that they are related (as is shown in Figure 1-5), but we would not have evidence that playing Scrabble causes vocabulary to increase. We will discuss correlation—both its calculation and its interpretation—in much greater detail in Chapter 5.

In all of the nonexperimental studies, data can be collected in several ways. We can bring people to our laboratories to collect data in person—whether by pen and paper, videotape, observation of behavior, or even having them play computer games. We can also have people complete surveys in a variety of forms, including on the computer, using pen and paper (individually or in groups), orally over the telephone, or orally in person. Alternately, we can collect archival data by using databases that already exist, such as the medical records that the CDC uses in some of their research.

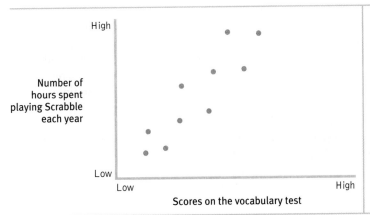

FIGURE 1-5
Correlation Between Vocabulary and Scrabble Playing

This graph depicts a relation between vocabulary and hours spent playing Scrabble for a study of 10 fictional participants. The more one plays Scrabble, the higher one's vocabulary tends to be.

One Goal, Two Strategies: Between-Groups Designs Versus Within-Groups Designs

The goal of an experiment is to answer a question. An experiment creates an opportunity for a clear, empirical answer to an intelligent question that has been expressed formally as a hypothesis. Skilled experimenters achieve this by creating meaningful comparison groups, and there are several ways in which that can be accomplished. However, most experiments are designed as either a *between-groups* research design or a *within-groups* (also called a *repeated-measures*) research design.

Between-groups research designs are those in which participants experience one, and only one, level of the independent variable. In some between-groups studies, the different levels of the independent variable serve as the only relevant distinction between two (or more) groups that otherwise have been made equal or equivalent through random assignment. An experiment that compares a control group with an experimental group is an example of a between-groups design. We also can have between-groups designs in which random assignment is not used. For example, we can compare people suffering from depression with people not suffering from depression. In this case, people are not randomly assigned to have or not have depression, but they still belong to one and only one group: either depressed or not depressed. This would however, not be an experiment.

In a within-groups research design, the different levels of the independent variable are experienced by all participants in the study. An experiment that compares the same group of people before and then after they experience an independent variable is an example of a within-groups design (also called a *repeated-measure design*). The word *"within"* emphasizes that if you experience one condition of a study, then you must experience all conditions of the study. Many applied questions in the behavioral sciences are best studied using a within-groups design, especially long-term (often called longitudinal) studies that examine how individuals and organizations change over time or studies involving a naturally occurring event cannot be duplicated in the laboratory. For example, we obviously cannot randomly assign individuals either to experience a hurricane or not experience a hurricane. However, we could use nature's predictability to anticipate hurricane season, collect some "before" data, and then collect data once again from those who did experience living through a hurricane. Such a before/after design is one version of a within-groups design.

There are particular problems, however, with the within-groups design. Specifically, a within-groups design invites a particular kind of confounding variable into a study: order effects. *Order effects*, also called *practice effects*, *refer to how a participant's behavior changes when the dependent variable is presented for a second time.* For example, if we wanted to study the effects of eating or not eating just prior to an exam (think of your midterm), we could have you take the exam, go out to eat, and then come back and take the identical exam all over again. This confound is easy to spot! You and your classmates probably would have talked about the exam during lunch; your responses the second time around would be influenced by your discussions over lunch.

The main technique used to limit the influence of order effects is counterbalancing. *Counterbalancing minimizes order effects by varying the order of presentation of different levels of the independent variable from one participant to the next.* Counterbalancing is not always effective or applicable, however, and most researchers strive to create between-groups designs. Unfortunately, sometimes we cannot conduct the kind of experiments that allow us to create strong causal links between variables, so we modify our research designs to make them as trustworthy as

- ■ In a **between-groups research design**, participants experience one, and only one, level of the independent variable.

- ■ In a **within-groups research design**, the different levels of the independent variable are experienced by all participants in the study; also called a *repeated-measures design*.

- ■ An **order effect** refers to how a participant's behavior changes when the dependent variable is presented a second time; also called **practice effect**.

- ■ **Counterbalancing** minimizes order effects by varying the order of presentation of different levels of the independent variable from one participant to the next.

circumstances allow. Social scientists are very creative researchers and frequently invent new scales, methods, and research designs to answer their questions.

In summary, the "best" approach to research matches the design to the situation. All research designs seek to articulate a cause–effect relation between an independent variable and a dependent variable. However, confounding variables often disrupt the logic of a study, especially with nonexperimental and quasi-experimental designs. Random assignment to groups is the hallmark of an experiment because it is so effective at controlling confounding variables. However, other techniques also help create studies that provide a fair test of a hypothesis. Unwanted placebo effects, order effects, and other inadvertent experimenter effects can be limited through the use of blind experiments and counterbalancing. Studies that involve many participants are either between-groups or within-groups designs; between-groups designs allow for greater control of potential confounding variables.

⊙ CHECK YOUR LEARNING

1-5 Expectations matter. Spencer, Steele, and Quinn (1999) examined how expectations based on stereotypes influence women's math performance. Some women were told that there was a gender difference on a certain math test and that, consistent with the gender stereotype, women tended to receive lower scores than men did. Other women were told that there were no gender differences on the test. Women in the first group performed more poorly than men did, whereas women in the second group did not.

a.   Briefly outline how researchers could conduct this research as a true experiment using a between-groups design.

b.   Why would researchers want to use random assignment?

c.   If researchers did not use random assignment but rather chose people who *already* were in those conditions (that is, who already believed stereotypes or not), what might be possible confounds? Name at least two.

d.   Why might researchers use a double-blind design?

e.   Briefly outline how researchers could conduct this experiment using a within-groups design (albeit one that would likely suffer from order effects).

f.   Why would order effects be a concern in a within-groups study?

g.   Why might researchers use counterbalancing?

❯ CURIOSITY, JOY, AND THE ART OF RESEARCH DESIGN

One of the most fascinating questions that arose out of the grisly story of John Snow and the cholera epidemic is the case of two mysterious deaths due to cholera in other, unaffected, parts of London. A woman in West Hampstead had died from cholera on September 2; her niece in Islington had died the following day. Statistically, we now identify such extreme data points as "outliers"— they just don't fit the pattern. It is worth noting John Snow's response to these outliers. He didn't just "throw them away" as an annoying anomaly.

Snow saddled up his horse and rode up to West Hampstead to interview the son and cousin of the two women who should not have died from cholera. Snow's interview revealed that one of the West Hampstead women who died had had a secret. She had once lived near Broad Street and had developed a taste for the wonderful-tasting water that came out of the Broad Street pump. In fact, her sons had sent her a large container of the water just three days prior to her death. The date was August 31, 1854, the very same day that the cholera outbreak began. She had shared this wonderful-tasting water with her niece. Both had died.

Snow's map now allowed him to see other clues, including what may be the only case in which lives were saved by drinking large amounts of beer. There were 70 unaffected men working at a brewery on Broad Street. They were given a free allowance of beer each day and had access to water from another well, and consequently never drank the nearby well water (Johnson, 2006). Around the corner from the Broad Street pump there was a workhouse with 535 men, but only 5 of them had contracted cholera; they had their own well inside the workhouse. However, at a nearby percussion-cap factory, there were 18 deaths due to cholera; two large tubs of Broad Street well water were always kept available for the thirsty workers. Snow even discovered the event that may have initiated the cholera outbreak in the first place: an infant's nappies (diapers) had been soaked in a bucket of water, and this now (possibly) contaminated bucket had been tossed out only a few feet from the well.

How clear it all is in retrospect! The logic of a fairly rudimentary statistic—the correlation—had saved thousands of lives. But John Snow's job still wasn't over. A few months after the epidemic had been quelled, the Board of Guardians examined Snow's data and unusual recommendation once again. They reached this conclusion: "After careful inquiry, we see no reason to adopt this belief." The idea of an invisible disease traveling in water was just too strange. And stopping an epidemic by removing a pump handle? That was much too bizarre to be believed.

Dr. John Snow's statistical problem was personal: his own life, the lives of his neighbors, and thousands more lives across the city of London were at risk. But even without a threat to our survival, we humans are a deeply introspective species. This impulse for self-knowledge and self-examination may be the product of evolutionary survival, intellectual curiosity, existential desperation, the pleasures of narcissism, or some secret recipe that includes all of those ingredients. Whatever mixture makes up the "soup" of human curiosity, behavioral scientists have invented an impressive array of methods to satisfy that curiosity.

The joy of statistics is not the elegance of its mathematical computations (Guttmannova, Shields, & Caruso, 2005); in spite of their sometimes impressive appearance, our formulas are not all that complicated. However, the very real joy of statistics is its ability to satisfy this deep human impulse called curiosity by separating chance from pattern. And statistics can only help satisfy our curiosity within the context of a sensible, appropriate research design (Christopher & Watler, 2006). Every semester, a new crop of students eagerly scans their computers to determine if their very own hypotheses have been supported by the evidence that they themselves collected. A photograph of their faces would suggest excitement, joy, and curiosity.

A close look at how John Snow went about discovering how cholera was transmitted reveals that he intuitively used several research designs. He used a correlational design when he plotted the relation between the number of deaths and the distance from the pump. But he also used a between-groups design when he compared the number of deaths near the Broad Street well with the number of deaths

The John Snow Pub
A pump without a handle and a pub in the Soho neighborhood of London commemorate the life-saving statistical achievements of John Snow, the father of epidemiology (the study of statistical patterns of diseases).

Martin Jacob

near a neighboring, uncontaminated well. And he used outlier analysis when he traveled to the far parts of London to interview the grieving families of people who were unlikely to have drunk water from the Broad Street well. Fortunately, John Snow was able to learn about the transmission of cholera quickly enough to help save lives. But he could not have accomplished this life-saving feat without the commonsense logic of a good research design.

▣ DIGGING DEEPER INTO THE DATA: VARIATIONS ON STANDARD RESEARCH DESIGNS

The creativity of research designs seems to arise spontaneously: researchers aren't trying to be creative; they're trying to test a hypothesis. But frustrating situations often provoke creativity; the two types of designs discussed here—outlier analysis and archival research—are innovative ways in which researchers use the logic of statistical reasoning to answer a specific question.

Outlier Analysis: Does the Exception Prove the Rule?

John Snow wasn't content to live with a loose end that might be a clue to something very important, such as the next cholera outbreak! Snow used outlier analysis when he sought to explain why two Londoners died in the cholera epidemic even though they lived far away from the Broad Street pump that transmitted that terrible disease. ***Outlier analysis** refers to studies that examine the outliers—those participants in a study who behave very differently or who have extremely different results from the other participants—in an effort to understand the factors that influence the dependent variable.*

Outlier analysis would prove to be crucial once again in the 1990s when researchers were desperately trying to track down effective strategies to fight the ongoing HIV/AIDS epidemic (Kolata, 2001). Unlike the woman and her niece who should not have died from cholera, in this case the outlier was someone who, according to most predictors, should not have lived. This outlier was Robert Massie, whose inspiring story is summarized by Belluck (2005). Massie was a hemophiliac who, like many others with that genetic disease, had become infected early in the HIV/AIDS epidemic through repeated exposure to the untested, contaminated blood supply. In 1994, he volunteered as a participant in a research study at the Massachusetts General Hospital, but for a very odd reason: he had yet to show any symptoms of AIDS. Massie's immune system was working exquisitely. Eventually researchers were convinced that the immune system could fight off the AIDS virus if the virus were vigorously attacked immediately after infection, allowing the helper T-cells to gain—and then maintain—the upper hand in the battle against the virus. Massie was likely among the rare 1% of infected individuals whose immune systems had gotten the upper hand right away. Identifying him as an outlier helped lead to effective, innovative treatments for HIV.

Outlier analysis is a seldom reported research design, but it is a logical extension of a well-designed experiment that helps identify outliers in the first place. Outlier analysis produced dramatic, insightful information for John Snow and HIV/AIDS researchers. Many modern researchers simply "throw out" statistical outliers, but there are several tactics they should consider. In the Digging Deeper into the Data section of Chapter 14, we discuss some of the separate literature about the different strategies a researcher can use when an extreme data point is influencing the story that the data tell.

▪ **Outlier analysis** refers to studies that examine the outliers—those participants in a study who behave very differently or who have extremely different results from the other participants—in an effort to understand the factors that influence the dependent variable.

■ **Archival studies** analyze existing records or documents rather than newly collected data.

Outlier analysis can offer distinctive insights. For example, the Army Corps of Engineers uses outlier analysis when they determine the height needed to construct canals or contain rivers; the highest (outlier) watermark represents the minimum height to which they must build so that an area will never flood, even though the outlier—the highest flood—might come along only once in a hundred years. In the social sciences, the most interesting person or group in a study may be the outlier who resists the prevailing pattern. With Stanley Milgram's famous study on obedience to authority, outlier analysis directs our attention to those interesting few who resisted the general pattern of obedience. What individual differences distinguished those who did not give in to the power of the situation? Luttke's (2004) review of Milgram's study highlights the observation that those who did not comply with that powerful situation could have been influenced by simple proximity to the victim rather than by personality or by variables that assess individual differences, such age or gender. Researchers can stumble into critical insights by paying attention to outliers.

Archival Studies: When the Data Already Exist

Archival studies analyze existing records or documents rather than newly collected data. Hospitals keep many such records, including length of stay per disease, cure rates related to particular medical procedures, and even outcome evaluations of particular surgeons. Archival data have several important benefits. They have already been compiled, so there may be much less data-collection work. The cost of research is often far lower; depending on the archive in which we are interested, the data might even be available free of charge. And often archival data allow us to study phenomena we could not study otherwise for either practical or ethical reasons.

Money Ball (Lewis, 2003), the best-selling book about former baseball player turned general manager Billy Beane, describes how Beane used archived baseball statistics about player performance to consistently help the Oakland Athletics select and draft productive baseball players and create consistently winning teams on a relatively small budget. Statisticians hired by Beane essentially observed correlations between player statistics and team outcomes to determine which player skills were most related to winning. Catcher turned first baseman Scott Hatteberg, for example, was a player who would not have been chosen by the Oakland A's without statistics based on archival data. He was not a great fielder or a noteworthy home run hitter. But he got on base consistently, a nonglamorous trait that is statistically more strongly related to wins than is the more exciting ability to hit home runs.

Archival Research to Predict Baseball Wins
The Oakland A's chose Scott Hatteberg based on a statistical analysis. He did not excel at fielding or hitting home runs, but he got on base consistently. This nonglamorous trait statistically contributes more to a team's wins than does the more dramatic ability to hit home runs.

The individual with a clear hypothesis in mind can examine archived information to test his or her ideas. Marycarmen Kunicki (Kunicki & Heinzen, 1996) won an undergraduate research award for comparing and then graphing the proportion of male versus female bylines on the front page of the *New York Times* over 50 years. Kunicki collected her data by spending hours scanning the archives in her university library, systematically sampling front pages of the *New York Times* so she could count and estimate (by name) the genders of the authors on hundreds of front pages. This also allowed her to project the year in which gender equity was likely to be realized—2017!

D.K. Simonton (1999) used archived information to study the age of peak creativity for poets, musicians, scientists, and other high achievers; in doing so, he developed a field called historiometrics that analyzes a variety of archived information. For example, Simonton (2005) recently investigated whether money produced cinematic creativity by comparing budgets with box office success and then adding the variable of critical

Lisa Blumenfeld / Getty Images

acclaim as measured by film reviews and movie guide ratings. The range and inventiveness of Simonton's archival investigations is itself an archive of a very curious mind!

Researchers can also mine archives to answer questions that may never have been considered by the people who gathered the data. Some archival data, like hospital records, might have direct social science applications, whereas other archival data, like *New York Times* bylines, seem unrelated to an issue in the behavioral sciences until a particularly creative researcher encounters them. Let your own research question guide your search through the ever-expanding mountains of already existing data. As Simonton's many investigations suggest, the data that make up the patterns already exist, just waiting for more curious brains to investigate them.

In summary, there are many variations on standard research designs that allow researchers to dig deeper into the data. Outlier analysis involves studying participants who have extremely different outcomes compared to other participants. Archival studies involve accessing and analyzing data that already exist.

⊙ CHECK YOUR LEARNING

1-6 For each of the following scenarios, identify the advanced technique that was used. Explain your answer.

a. A statistics professor used class records and a survey of alumni to test whether good grades in statistics predicted future earnings.

b. A pharmacist examined his pharmacy's call logs to determine whether different types of questions (e.g., about dosage, contraindications, side effects) were more likely to be asked by those of certain age groups.

c. A social psychologist statistically identified and then interviewed the few individuals who did not conform to intense peer pressure in an experiment.

d. An epilepsy researcher studied the few people in an epilepsy study who had surgery to reduce seizures and yet had more severe seizures following the surgery.

> Two Branches of Statistics: Growing Our Knowledge of Human Behavior

Descriptive and *inferential statistics* are the two branches of analysis, with descriptive statistics providing numerical summaries and inferential statistics allowing us to make conclusions beyond our data. With inferential statistics, we typically study a smaller group, or *sample*, to draw conclusions about the larger group, or *population*, in which we're interested.

> Variables: Transforming Observations into Numbers

We explore psychological *constructs* by examining observable variables. Statistics allow us to study two general types of variables—discrete and continuous. *Discrete variables* are those that can take on only certain numbers (e.g., whole numbers, such as 1), and *continuous variables* are those that can take on all possible numbers in a range (e.g., 1.68792). There are two types of variables that can only be discrete: nominal and ordinal. *Nominal variables* use numbers simply to give names to scores (e.g., 1 to stand for male on the nominal variable of gender). *Ordinal* variables are rank-ordered (e.g., 1st place, 2nd place). There are two types of variables that can be continuous: interval and ratio. *Interval* variables are those in which the distances between numerical values are assumed to be equal; they include physical properties such as height as well as more abstract concepts such as personality traits. Although interval variables can be continuous, they also can be discrete; the scores on many measures, such as attitude and personality scales, can only be whole numbers. Finally, *ratio variables* are those that meet the criteria for interval variables but also have a meaningful zero point. Time, for instance, is a variable for which a score of 0 has meaning.

> Independent and Dependent Variables: The Main Ingredients of Statistical Thinking

When conducting a study to test a research hypothesis, we must identify at least one *independent variable*, the variable thought to be predicting another, and at least one *dependent variable*, the variable thought to depend on the independent variable. If a variable is nominal, we refer to its categories as *levels*. *Confounding variables* are those that vary systematically with the independent variable, so that we cannot determine whether the independent variable or the confounding variable is affecting the dependent variable, and *extraneous variables* are randomly distributed external influences on the dependent variable. This kind of *noise* can make the relations among variables less clear than they are. When designing a study, researchers typically assess their independent and dependent variables' *reliability*, or consistency. With *test-retest reliability*, we assess whether results are consistent across more than one administration of the test. *Validity* is the ability to measure what they were designed to measure. With *predictive validity*, we assess how well a variable predicts another theoretically related variable.

> An Introduction to Hypothesis Testing: From Hunch to Hypothesis

Hypothesis testing is the formal process of drawing conclusions about the relation between one or more independent variables and a dependent variable. We start the process of research by developing hypotheses and then *operationalizing* our variables—creating a specific plan to measure our independent and dependent variables.

> Types of Research Designs: Experiments, Nonexperiments, and Quasi-Experiments

If we randomly assign participants to levels of the independent variable (e.g., an independent variable for the type of studying with levels of "alone," "with a tutor," or "with a study group of peers"), we are conducting an *experiment* and can draw conclusions about causality. With *random assignment*, every member of the sample has an equal chance of being assigned to every possible experimental group. An experiment in which the participant does not know to which condition he or she has been assigned is a *single-blind experiment*. One in which neither the participant nor experimenter knows to which condition the participant has been assigned is a *double-blind experiment*. If we cannot use random assignment because it is unethical, impractical, or impossible, then we must conduct a *nonexperiment*, *quasi-experiment*, or correlational study.

Two prominent research designs are between-groups and within-groups designs. In a *between-groups research design*, every participant experiences only one level of the independent variable. In a *within-groups research design*, every participant experiences all levels of the independent variable (although not at the same time). Various phenomena can affect the outcome of an experiment. *Order effects*, or *practice effects*, in which a participant's behavior under ensuing conditions of the study is affected by the earlier conditions, can affect the outcome of a within-groups study. *Counterbalancing*, in which participants are randomly assigned to different orders of conditions, can reduce this problem. *Placebo effects* occur when the mere expectancy of a certain outcome leads to that outcome. Using a control group helps us see the effects of an intervention over and above any placebo effect. *Demand characteristics* occur when an experimenter inadvertently elicits a certain response from participants. They can be reduced by standardizing the experimental protocol.

> Curiosity, Joy, and the Art of Research Design

The social sciences breed innumerable research questions in its clinicians, teachers, researchers, and students aspiring to one of those careers. Sound research design sets the stage for the implementation of the appropriate statistical analyses to answer our questions.

> Digging Deeper into the Data: Variations on Standard Research Designs

In this section, two less common research techniques were discussed. *Outlier analysis* involves studying the participant who does *not* fit the pattern. An examination of the one participant who behaved differently can either debunk our hypothesis, provide further evidence in support of our hypothesis, or lead us to explore a brand-new hypothesis. *Archival studies* examine existing data garnered from various sources—from hospital records to census databases to reports from social science graduate programs.

COMPUTING SOFTWARE FOR THE SOCIAL SCIENCES

No matter which statistical program you use, you should know that (1) the underlying mathematics are the same; (2) the companies constantly compete with each other, so they are all perpetually upgrading their capabilities; and (3) you can get answers to many questions as they come up by referring to the SPSS instructions in the study guide that complements this textbook; by accessing online tutorials by searching for "SPSS," or another software, and by using the "Help" function within the SPSS or another computer program.

> Welcome to SPSS

There are many excellent statistical software programs available to behavioral scientists. We have chosen SPSS (Statistical Package for the Social Sciences) because it is a frequently used software program across several different behavioral sciences. All statistical programs use a similar four-part structure that allow us to:

1. Identify and describe our variables
2. Enter our data in a spreadsheet format
3. Request particular kinds of statistical analyses
4. Read and manipulate the output of our data analysis

SPSS is a menu-driven statistical program, easily learned by moderately sophisticated computer users. So, we will get you started, make a few comments about the most important features, and leave the rest up to your own curiosity and your professor's wise advice.

Testing the validity of our own ideas is when statistics gets really interesting, particularly with the power of computer software to speed analyses. SPSS is also worth learning because so many employment opportunities flow out of this particular skill.

SPSS GUIDELINES FOR CHAPTER 1: NAMING AND DESCRIBING VARIABLES

SPSS is divided into two main screens. The easiest way to move back and forth between these two screens is by using the two tabs located at the lower left labeled *Variable View* and *Data View*.

In order to name the variables, go to *Variable View* and select:

Name. Write in a short version of the variable name, such as AGG (for Aggression).

Type. For nominal variables, change the type to "string" by clicking the box in the column titles "Type," or clicking the little gray box, choosing string, and clicking OK.

To tell SPSS what that name means, select:

Label. Write in the full name of the variable, such as Aggression Scale.

If there are any nominal variables, to tell SPSS what the numbers assigned to each variable actually mean, select:

Values. Click on the box in the column titles "Values" next to the appropriate variable, then click on the little gray box on the right to access the tool that allows us to identify the values (or levels) of the variables. For example, if the nominal variable Gender is part of the study, tell SPSS that for example, 1 equals male and 2 equals female. The numbers are the values and the words are the labels.

Now tell SPSS what kind of variables these are by selecting:

Measure. Highlight whether this variable is nominal, ordinal, or scale, by clicking on the box in the column titles "Measure" next to each variable, then clicking on the little blue arrow to access the tool that allows us to identify whether the variable is scale, ordinal, or nominal. Notice that this is not necessary for nominal variable if the type is already listed as "string."

After describing all the variables in the study in *Variable View*, switch over to *Data View* and notice that the entered information you entered was automatically transferred to that screen, but now the variables are displayed across the tops of the columns instead of along the left-hand side of the rows. You can now enter your data in *Data View* under the appropriate heading; each participant's data is entered across one row.

EXERCISES

1.1 Average weights of girls in the United States: The CDC reported very large weight increases for U.S. residents of both genders and of all age groups in the last four decades. Go to the Web site that reports these data: http://www.cdc.gov/ and search for the article titled *Americans Slightly Taller, Much Heavier Than 40 Years Ago.*

a. What were the average weights of 10-year-old girls in 1963 and in 2002?

b. Do you think the CDC weighed every girl in the United States to get these averages? Why would this not be feasible?

c. How does the average weight of 10-year-old girls in 2002 represent both a descriptive and an inferential statistic?

1.2 Sample vs. population: The Health Study of Nord-Trøndelag County of Norway (HUNT) surveyed more than 60,000 people in a Norwegian county and reported that "people who have gastrointestinal symptoms, such as nausea, are more likely to have anxiety disorders or depression than people who do not have such symptoms."

a. What is the sample used by these researchers?

b. What is the population to which the researchers would like to extend their findings?

1.3 The Kentucky Derby and types of variables: The Kentucky Derby is perhaps the premier event in U.S. horse racing, and it provides many opportunities for identifying types of variables. For each of the following examples, identify the type of variable: nominal, ordinal, or interval/ratio.

a. We might consider the variable of finishing position. For example, in 2005, there was a stunning upset when Giacomo, a horse with 50-1 odds, won, followed by Closing Argument, and then Afleet Alex.

b. We might be interested in the variable of finishing time. Giacomo won in 2 minutes, 2.75 seconds.

c. If we were the betting type, we might examine the variable of payoffs. Giacomo was such a long shot that a $2.00 bet on him to win paid an incredibly high $102.60.

d. We might be interested in the history of the Derby and the demographic variables of jockeys, such as gender or race. For example, in the first 28 runnings of the Kentucky Derby, 15 of the winning jockeys were African American. (http://www. kentuckyderby.com/2005/derby_history/african_americans_in_the_derby/)

e. In the luxury boxes, high fashion reigns; we might be curious about the variable of hat wearing, observing how many women wear hats and how many do not.

1.4 Discrete vs. continuous interval variables: For each of the following examples, state whether the interval variable is discrete or continuous.

a. The capacity, in terms of songs, of an iPod

b. The playing time of an individual song

c. The cost in cents to download a song legally

d. The number of posted reviews that a CD has on Amazon.com

e. The weight of an MP3 player

1.5 Reliability and validity of the Rorschach inkblot test: The article "What's Wrong with the Rorschach: Science Confronts the Controversial Inkblot Test" (Wood et al., 2003) presents an overview of scientific evidence that suggests that the Rorschach performs poorly at diagnosing psychopathology, determining personality traits, and predicting future behavior. For example, the Rorschach tends to overdiagnose, labeling many people without psychopathology as sick.

a. Do these findings relate more to reliability or validity? Explain.

b. Explain how a test such as the Rorschach could be reliable, even if it were not valid.

1.6 Assessing the merits of wine ratings: You may have been in a wine store and wondered just how useful those posted wine ratings are (usually a scale with 100 as the top score). After all, aren't ratings subjective? Corsi and Ashenfelter (2001) studied whether wine experts are consistent. Knowing that the weather is the best predictor of price, the researchers wondered how well weather predicted experts' ratings. The variables used for weather included temperature and rainfall, and the variable used for wine experts' ratings was based on the numbers they assigned to each wine.

a. Name one independent variable. What type of variable is it? Is it discrete or continuous?

b. Name the dependent variable. What type of variable is it? Is it discrete or continuous?

c. How does this study reflect the concept of reliability?

d. Let's say that you frequently drink wine that's been rated highly by Robert Parker, one of the wine experts in this study. His ratings were determined to be reliable, and you find that you usually agree with Robert Parker. How does this observation reflect the concept of validity?

1.7 Reliability and validity and personality testing: Go online and take the following personality test: http://www.outofservice.com/starwars/. This test assesses your personality in terms of the characters from the original *Star Wars* series. (You may have to scroll down to get to the questions.)

a. What does it mean for a test to be reliable? Take the test a second time. Does it seem to be reliable?

b. What does it mean for a test to be valid? Does this test seem to be valid? Explain.

1.8 Research hypotheses and the *Star Wars* personality test: The *Star Wars* personality test from Exercise 1.7 asks a number of demographic questions at the bottom. For example, it asks "in what country did you spend most of your youth?"

a. Can you think of a hypothesis that might have led the developers of this Web site to ask that question?

b. For the hypothesis in part (a), identify the independent and dependent variables.

1.9 Operationalizing dependent variables: For each of the following hypotheses, identify the likely dependent variable and a likely way of operationalizing that dependent variable. Be specific.

a. Teenagers are better at video games than are adults in their 30s.

b. Spanking children leads them to be more violent.

c. Weight Watchers leads to more weight loss if you go to meetings than if you participate online.

d. Students do better in statistics if they study with other people than if they study alone.

e. Drinking caffeinated beverages with dinner makes it harder to get to sleep at night.

1.10 Identifying independent variables: For each of the hypotheses listed in Exercise 1.9, identify the independent variable and the most likely levels of that independent variable.

a. Teenagers are better at video games than are adults in their 30s.

b. Spanking children leads them to be more violent.

c. Weight Watchers leads to more weight loss if you go to meetings than if you participate online.

d. Students do better in statistics if they study with other people than if they study alone.

e. Drinking caffeinated beverages with dinner makes it harder to get to sleep at night.

1.11 Consideration of Future Consequences and variables: Researchers at Washington State University (Eckles et al., 2003) reported that people with higher CFC scores tended to have less credit card debt and were less likely to buy on impulse.

a. Identify the independent and dependent variables in this study.

b. For the variable of impulse buying, give an example of an item that might have appeared on this scale that would likely be valid.

1.12 Consideration of Future Consequences and types of studies: Refer to the study described in the Exercise 1.11.

a. Is this study an experiment or a correlational study? Why?

b. Is it possible that there is a confounding variable that might have affected these results? If yes, suggest at least one possible confounding variable.

c. Now that you know these results, suggest a related hypothesis about the CFC that might lead to a follow-up study.

1.13 Cholera and HIV: Several studies have documented the susceptibility of people who are HIV-positive to cholera, likely because of weakened immune systems. Researchers in Mozambique (Lucas et al., 2005), a country where an estimated 20% to 30% of the population is HIV-positive, wondered whether an oral vaccine for cholera would work among people who are HIV-positive. Fourteen thousand people in Mozambique who tested positive for HIV were immunized against cholera. Soon thereafter, an epidemic of cholera spread through the region, giving the researchers an opportunity to test their hypothesis.

a. Describe a way in which the researchers could have conducted an experiment to examine the effectiveness of the cholera vaccine among people who are HIV-positive.

b. If the researchers did conduct an experiment, would this have been a between-groups or within-groups experiment? Explain.

c. Describe a way in which the researchers could have conducted a nonexperiment or a quasi-experiment to examine the effectiveness of the cholera vaccine among people who are HIV-positive.

d. The researchers did not randomly assign participants to vaccine or nonvaccine conditions; rather, they conducted a general mass immunization. Why does this limit their ability to draw causal conclusions? State at least one possible confounding variable.

1.14 Problems using random assignment: Refer to the study on cholera and HIV described in the Exercise 1.13. The researchers did not use random assignment when conducting this study.

a. List at least one practical reason that the researchers might not have used random assignment.

b. List at least one ethical reason that the researchers might not have used random assignment.

1.15 Implementing random assignment: If you had been conducting the study described in Exercise 1.13 and were unconcerned with practicality and ethics, describe how you could have used random assignment.

1.16 Within-groups vs. between-groups: Noting the marked increases in weight across the population, many researchers, nutritionists, and physicians have struggled to find ways to stem the tide of obesity in many Western countries. A number of exercise programs have been advocated by these clinicians and researchers, and there has been a flurry of research to determine their effectiveness. Pretend that you are in charge of a research program to examine the effects of an exercise program on weight loss in comparison with a no-exercise program.

a. Describe how you could study this exercise program using a between-groups research design.

b. Describe how you could study this exercise program using a within-groups design.

c. What is a potential confound of a within-groups design?

1.17 The language of statistics—*scale:* Describe two ways that statisticians might use the word *scale*.

1.18 The language of statistics—*reliable:* In your own words, define the word *reliable*—first as you would use it in everyday conversation, and then as a statistician would use it.

1.19 The language of statistics—*experiment:* In your own words, define the world *experiment*—first as you would use it in everyday conversation, and then as a researcher would use it.

1.20 The language of statistics: In statistics, it is important to pay very close attention to language. The following statements are wrong but can be corrected by substituting one word or phrase. For example, the sentence "Only correlational studies can tell us something about causality" could be corrected by changing *correlational studies* to *experiments*. Identify the incorrect word or phrase in each of the following statements, and supply the correct word.

a. In a study on exam preparation, every participant had an equal chance of being told he/she had to study alone, or being told he/she would study with a group. This was a quasi-experiment.

b. A psychologist was interested in studying the effects of the dependent variable of caffeine on hours of sleep, and he used an interval scale to measure sleep.

c. A university assessed the reliability of a commonly used scale—a mathematics placement test—to determine if it were truly measuring math ability.

d. In a within-groups experiment on calcium and osteoporosis, participants were assigned to one of two levels of the independent variable: no change in diet or calcium supplement.

e. A researcher studied a population of 20 rats to determine whether changes in exposure to light would lead to changes in the dependent variable of amount of sleep.

▪ DIGGING DEEPER INTO THE DATA: EXERCISES

1.21 Outlier analysis: Imagine that you conducted the study described in Exercise 1.16 and that one individual had *gained* many, many pounds while in the exercise program.

a. Why would this individual be considered an outlier?

b. Explain why outlier analysis might be useful in this situation.

c. What kinds of things might we be looking for in an outlier analysis?

1.22 Archival studies: Massey and Thaler (2005) wondered whether National Football League (NFL) teams overvalued the top draft picks, so they tested this idea using archival data. They used several archives, including ones on the drafts over the years as well as ensuing player performance and compensation. They found that irrational factors and biases, including overconfidence, seemed to override the information that was available to teams. Draft picks *were* overvalued. For each of the following topics, think like Massey and Thaler. What is a possible hypothesis? What are possible archival data-bases that could be used?

a. Canadian provinces and ethnic background

b. Homicide in the United Kingdom over the years

c. Shark attacks and regions of the world

d. Coffee production and political systems

e. SAT scores and the different majors at your university

f. The topic of your choice

TERMS

descriptive statistics (p. 3)

inferential statistics (p. 3)

sample (p. 3)

population (p. 3)

variable (p. 6)

construct (p. 6)

discrete observations (p. 6)

continuous observations (p. 7)

nominal variable (p. 7)

ordinal variable (p. 7)

interval variable (p. 7)

ratio variable (p. 8)

levels (p. 11)

independent variable (p. 11)

dependent variable (p. 12)

confounding variable (p. 12)

extraneous variable (p. 12)

noise (p. 12)

reliability (p. 15)

validity (p. 15)

test–retest reliability (p. 15)

predictive validity (p. 15)

hypothesis testing (p. 17)

operational definition (p. 18)

experiment (p. 22)

random assignment (p. 22)

single-blind experiment (p. 22)

placebo effect (p. 22)

double-blind experiment (p. 22)

demand characteristics (p. 22)

nonexperiments and quasi-experiments (p. 24)

correlation (p. 24)

between-groups research design (p. 26)

within-groups research design (p. 26)

order effect (p. 26)

counterbalancing (p. 26)

outlier analysis (p. 29)

archival studies (p. 30)

CHAPTER TWO

DESCRIPTIVE STATISTICS
ORGANIZING, SUMMARIZING, AND GRAPHING INDIVIDUAL VARIABLES

Two weeks after she graduated from college, Alex realized that she had no idea what to do with her degree. So she took the first job that came along, worked hard, received some raises, but hated going to work each morning. Two years after graduating, Alex had still not discovered what she wanted to do with her life, but she had discovered what she did *not* want to do with her life: retail sales. With an impulsive desperation, she quit her job and then called one of her favorite teachers from college for advice: Professor Jackson.

"So what do you want to do with your life?" asked Professor Jackson after hearing Alex's complaint.

"Maybe get a master's degree," Alex said. "You seem to be enjoying your career."

Professor Jackson heard a hesitation in her voice. "My area is called evaluation research, and I love it," she told Alex, "because I help organizations get better the same way therapists help individuals get better. But that's me, Alex. What do you want?"

Like many students drawn to the behavioral sciences, Alex had considered several different careers, from becoming some kind of a therapist to pursuing her surprising enjoyment of economics. She had also enjoyed the practical, problem-solving side of organizational psychology, and she knew that she was more interested in broader social issues than in personal problems. "I'm hoping I'll figure out what I want in graduate school," she said, "but maybe I should figure it out now, before I spend all that money."

"Just prioritize what's important to you; maybe even write down your top three choices, in order. Goals organize behavior, Alex. At least that's how I think about it."

But what Alex started thinking about came from only one word in Professor Jackson's sentence. It was almost a magical word to her because it was the very thing she had felt slipping out of her life: choices.

> ORGANIZING OUR DATA: A FIRST STEP IN IDENTIFYING PATTERNS

Comstock Images / Alamy

From Chaos to Clarity
Descriptive statistics and personal therapy take their participants on similar "journeys" by requiring them to organize, summarize, and communicate large amounts of information.

Alex was transforming her confusing life into a purposeful career. All she had to do to regain a sense of direction was reorder her life according to her *own* priorities, from most important to least important, the same way a variable can be reorganized from the highest score to the lowest score. We are usually most interested in the relations between two or more variables. For example, Alex prioritized her life goals (one variable) to gain a greater sense of purpose (a second variable). But the way to begin to understand the relations between variables is to understand the internal structure of each individual variable. That is why this chapter focuses on descriptive statistics—ways to organize, summarize, and graphically portray individual variables. As Alex was discovering, merely reorganizing the values of a variable from highest to lowest can offer surprising insights.

Statisticians and therapists are more similar than you might imagine: they both begin their work with chaotic data, reorganize those data into a sensible pattern, and then communicate that newfound clarity to others. For example, statisticians begin with numbers that might appear to be random. They then organize, summarize, and create a visual display (usually a graph) to communicate the insights buried within large amounts of numerical information. Therapists also often begin with the chaotic data from a person's life; the chaos is what drives many people to seek therapy in the first place. Therapists then organize, summarize, and decide how best to communicate the insights that slowly emerge from the therapy process. Indeed, conducting research and providing therapy are so similar that many psychology students start out wanting to be therapists but then "get hooked" on research (Weis, 2004). Whatever you eventually decide to do with your particular training in the behavioral sciences, learning how to organize, summarize, and graphically portray what a set of numbers "says" is a skill that translates into many different settings. But it is worth noting this pattern: therapists tend to learn a great deal about themselves when they commit their lives to a helping profession. As Alex discovered, the insights from statistical reasoning can challenge you just as deeply and just as unexpectedly.

So the first step in transforming chaos into clarity is to reorganize the way the data are distributed. Notice that we do not change the data, we merely reorganize the numbers so we can create something more useful—a summary or a graph that lets us see their pattern. As you grow in your statistical skills, think of yourself as a chef being trained to create something wonderful, rather than a short-order cook just slopping something together. And the first step in creating a nourishing meal is to organize your raw ingredients and find out what you've got to work with.

■ **Raw scores** are data that have not yet been transformed or analyzed.

■ A **distribution** is the pattern of a set of numbers.

■ A **frequency table** is a visual depiction of data that shows how often each value occurred; that is, how many scores were at each value. Values are listed in one column, and the numbers of individuals with scores at that value are listed in the second column.

Distributions: Four Different Ways to Describe Just One Variable

The raw ingredients of a data set are called the ***raw scores***, *data that have not yet been transformed or analyzed.* In statistics, we then organize our ingredients into *a* ***distribution*** that *displays the pattern of a set of numbers.* For example, a distribution can be the pattern of the scores from a sample of college students who performed the Stroop task, a cognitive exercise that you can experience for yourself on page 8. The numbers in the distribution may be individual scores—the raw scores—but they also may be other numbers based on samples of many individuals.

Because statisticians often need flexibility in the tools they use to understand their data, it is not surprising that there are four different ways of visually organizing the distribution of data. The first approach, the frequency table, may tell the story of a variable quite nicely, but it is also the starting point for each of the other ways. *A* ***frequency table*** *is a visual depiction of data that shows how often each value occurred; that is, how many scores were at each value.* Once organized into a frequency table, the data can be displayed as a grouped frequency table, a frequency histogram, or a frequency polygon. These four methods of visually organizing data represent the basic tools in a statistician's toolbox. If one technique doesn't give us a clear picture of the data, another one just might work better.

Organizing Data: A Frequency Table

Imagine that you ask everyone in a class of 20 first-year college students how many nights they went out to party in the previous week. In this case, we might specify that *to party* means to leave your place of residence for at least three hours after 6:00 P.M. for any purpose unrelated to academic work. This observation allows for only a very specific set of possible responses that range from not going out at all to going out every night: 0, 1, 2, 3, 4, 5, 6, or 7 nights. If we asked each of the 20 students how many nights a week they typically go out to party, we might get a data set of 20 numbers that looks like this:

1	2	7	6	1
2	6	5	4	4
0	3	2	2	3
4	3	5	4	4

At first glance, it is not very easy to find a pattern in these numbers, so imagine how much more difficult it would be if there were 100 participants or 1000, or 500,000. It would look like a blizzard of haphazard numbers. But when we reorder those numbers, a pattern begins to emerge. A frequency table is the best way to create an easy-to-understand distribution of the data. It is probably the simplest, yet single most insightful, way to bring clarity to the chaos of a data set. In this example, we simply reorder the "nights partying" data into a table with two columns, one for the range of possible responses—the values—and one for the frequencies of each of the responses—the scores. Table 2-1 portrays the frequency table for these data.

There are specific steps to follow when creating a frequency table. First, we examine our data to determine the range of scores. In this case, we see that the highest possible value is 7 nights out per week and the lowest possible value is 0 nights out per week. We then make a column of all of these numbers, with the highest (7) on top and the lowest (0) on the bottom. Next, we go through

TABLE 2-1. FREQUENCY TABLE OF NIGHTS OUT PER WEEK

A frequency table shows the counts for each value of one interval variable. In this case, the frequency table depicts the numbers of students who reported a given number of nights out per week, from 0 to 7.

NIGHTS	FREQUENCY
7	1
6	2
5	2
4	5
3	3
2	4
1	2
0	1

all of the scores in our data set and make a tally mark for each one next to its appropriate response. For example, the first score in the data set of "nights partying" is 1, so we make a mark next to 1 to indicate that so far it has occurred only once. Then, we simply count up all of the marks and place those numbers in the second column. It is important to note that we include *all* numbers in the range. If no one reported that they went out six nights a week, we still would put the value 6 in our table and just write the score 0 next to it.

A statistical description of the night habits of college students may be interesting, but it's hardly a compelling social issue. However, many seemingly harmless statistical observations lead to progressively more consequential issues. For example, this simple study of the night habits of students might lead to studies that provide guidelines related to strategies for success in college or the larger problem of reducing substance abuse on campus. The identical process of organizing data into a sensible distribution was part of the mystery addressed by the research team of Kuck, Buckner, Marzabadi, and Nolan (2007): why fewer women than men achieved high-prestige academic positions in the field of chemistry. This is a more consequential issue for research-driven economies such as that of the United States because so many women excel in science as young students. The loss of so much intellectual talent would seem to do great harm to the national economy, especially in the current context of global competitiveness. The conceptual focus of their research was on mentoring, so they created an archival research design to identify the most successful mentors: professors whose students were hired by the top 50 chemistry departments. The specific issue they investigated within the context of mentoring was whether these professors were equally successful at nurturing the talents of both male and female graduate students.

The participants in this archival study were all graduate school advisors who had had at least three former PhD students go on to jobs as professors in departments ranked in the top 50 chemistry departments. There were 54 graduate advisors who met this highly selective criterion. Many more professors had just one or two former students go on to these top jobs, and

Does Mentoring Make a Difference?
Data suggest that graduate school advisors make a difference in the field of chemistry. Some do much better than others in having their former students end up in prestigious academic positions. One professor in this distribution is an outlier and might be a role model for other mentors.

Leo Sorel / Leo Sorel Photography

even more had no students achieve this kind of success. Each score represents the number of students successfully mentored by different professors. Here are the data for the 54 top-producing graduate advisors:

3, 3, 3, 4, 5, 9, 5, 3, 3, 5, 6, 3, 4, 8, 6, 3, 3, 3, 4, 4, 4, 7, 6, 3, 5, 5, 5, 7,
13, 3, 3, 3, 3, 3, 4, 4, 4, 5, 6, 7, 6, 7, 8, 8, 3, 3, 3, 5, 3, 3, 5, 3, 5, 3, 3.

We know at a glance that the lowest score is 3, but that was expected because it was the criterion set by the research team as the minimum to be included in the study. A quick glance also reveals that the highest score is 13; one professor successfully mentored 13 high-achieving students, a most impressive number and an outlier in this data set. Simply noting that the scores range from 3 to 13 brings some clarity to the data set. But we can do even better.

After we identify the lowest and highest scores, we create the two columns that we see in Table 2-2 by counting how many graduate advisors fall at each value. This is done by going through the raw scores and determining how many fall at each value in the range. The appropriate numbers for each value are then recorded in the table. There is only one advisor with 13 students, so a 1 is marked there. There are no advisors with 12, 11, or 10 students—which further highlights the achievements of the one professor with 13—so we put a 0 next to each one, and so on.

Here is a recap of the steps to create a frequency table:

1. Determine the highest and lowest scores.

2. Create two columns: the first is labeled with the variable name, and the second is labeled "frequency."

3. List the full range of values that encompasses all the scores in the data set from highest to lowest. Include *all* values in the range, even those for which the frequency is 0.

4. Count the number of scores at each value, and write those numbers in the frequency column.

This simple reordering of the data allows us to gain even more insights from this formerly chaotic set of numbers. As demonstrated in Table 2-3, we can begin by redescribing the numbers of advisors (who had a particular number of students now in top jobs) as a percentage. To calculate a percentage, we divide the number of advisors in a category (categories based on numbers of students now in top jobs) by the total number of advisors, and then multiply by 100. As we observed earlier, one out of 54 advisors had 13 graduate students go on to top jobs. We calculate the percentage as $\frac{1}{54}$ (100) = 1.85; that is, 1 of 54 is 1.85%. Because we calculate the percentages represented by each value, we can also add them together to calculate the **cumulative percentages**, *the percentages of individuals who have scores at a given value or lower*. For example, 49 graduate advisors had a score of 7 or less (no more than 7 students who went on to top jobs); 49 of 54 is 90.74%. [This percentage was calculated as follows: $\frac{49}{54}$ (100) = 90.74.] Therefore, 90.74% of advisors had 7 or fewer graduates go on to top professorial jobs. Simply reordering the data invites meaningful comparisons within the data set, especially when we bear in mind that there are real students and professors behind each of those numbers.

Note that when we calculate statistics, we can come up with slightly different answers depending on how we round off at each step. If there are many

■ The **cumulative percentages** reflect the percentage of individuals who have scores at a given value or lower.

TABLE 2-2. FREQUENCY TABLES AND GRADUATE ADVISING

This frequency table depicts the numbers of students placed on the top 50 chemistry faculties by each top-producing graduate advisor. If you wanted a high-profile professorial job, which advisor would you want?

FORMER STUDENTS NOW IN TOP JOBS	FREQUENCY
13	1
12	0
11	0
10	0
9	1
8	3
7	4
6	5
5	9
4	8
3	23

Data from Kuck et al. (2007).

steps, we can even come up with very different answers depending on our rounding decisions. In this text, we'll round off to three decimal places, throughout our calculations, but we'll report our final answers to two decimal places, rounding up or down as appropriate. If you follow this convention, you should get the same answers that we get.

TABLE 2-3. EXPANSION OF A FREQUENCY TABLE

This frequency table is an expansion of Table 2-2, which depicts the numbers of students placed on the top 50 chemistry faculties by each top-producing graduate advisor. It now includes percentages and cumulative percentages, which are often more descriptive than the actual counts.

FORMER STUDENTS NOW IN TOP JOBS	FREQUENCY	PERCENT	CUMULATIVE PERCENT
13	1	1.85	100.00
12	0	0.00	98.15
11	0	0.00	98.15
10	0	0.00	98.15
9	1	1.85	98.15
8	3	5.56	96.30
7	4	7.41	90.74
6	5	9.26	83.33
5	9	16.67	74.07
4	8	14.81	57.41
3	23	42.59	42.59

Data from Kuck et al. (2007).

Organizing Interval Data: Grouped Frequency Tables

In the previous examples, we used data that counted the numbers of people. We refer to these data as discrete whole numbers because, well, people cannot be divided into pieces. In addition, the range was fairly limited—0 to 7 for the first example of "nights partying" and 3 to 13 for the second example of "mentoring professors." But data are often less "pretty" (easily understood) than these in three situations:

1. When data are continuous-interval variables, such as reaction time to several decimal places

2. When data cover a huge range, such as countries' populations

3. When data are both interval and very large, such as the weights of adult North Americans, which might range from under 100 pounds to several hundred pounds *and* may be reported to several decimal places

In all three of these situations, the frequency table would go on for pages and pages—and nobody, especially statisticians, wants to read all those individual data. For example, if someone weighed only 0.0003 pound more than the next weight, that person would belong to a distinctive, unique category. Not only would we be creating an enormous amount of unnecessary work for ourselves, but we also wouldn't be able to see trends in the data. Fortunately, we have a technique to deal with these situations: *a **grouped frequency table** allows us to depict our data visually by reporting the frequencies within a given interval rather than the frequencies for a specific value.* The word *Interval* is used in more than one way by statisticians. Here, it refers to a range of values (as opposed to an interval variable, the type of variable that we presume to have equal distances between values).

The following fictional data exemplify the first of these three situations in which the data aren't easily conveyed in a standard frequency table. These are the times in seconds that it took 50 individuals to complete a computer-generated Stroop task similar to that introduced in Chapter 1 (available at http://www.worthpublishers.com/nolanheinzen). If you haven't already tried this frustrating yet fascinating exercise, do so now to get a sense of how cognitive data are gathered. The online task gives responses only in whole numbers; the data reported here are from a version of the Stroop task that reported reaction times to two decimal places:

10.20	11.33	12.14	9.87	12.33
13.08	11.04	14.53	14.36	9.06
12.00	12.45	13.82	13.29	11.67
12.56	15.79	10.09	10.17	11.42
11.93	12.88	(17.15)	11.84	12.21
10.38	14.05	15.11	12.11	12.88
12.52	12.46	11.74	13.64	14.76
(8.07)	10.74	12.32	13.10	12.98
15.86	11.55	9.07	14.97	10.62
13.85	13.92	11.24	13.88	12.70

▪ A **grouped frequency table** is a visual depiction of data that reports the frequencies within a given interval rather than the frequencies for a specific value.

A quick glance at these data does not give us a very useful sense of how long it takes the typical person to complete this Stroop task. Nor would a frequency table be very helpful. The lowest score is 8.07 and the highest is 17.15. The top of a frequency table would look like Table 2-4. Such a table would be absurdly

TABLE 2-4. UNWIELDY FREQUENCY TABLES

A frequency table that lists every possible value is often not much more useful than a listing of every single score. Here we see the numbers of participants finishing the Stroop task in each possible amount of time, though it is only an excerpt of the possible times. The full table would be ridiculously long.

TIME TO COMPLETE STROOP TASK	FREQUENCY
17.15	1
17.14	0
17.13	0
17.12	0
17.11	0
17.10	0
17.09	0
17.08	0
.	.
.	.
.	.
8.07	1

long and would not convey much more interpretable information than does the list of the original raw data.

Instead of reporting every single value in the range in which these scores fall, however, we can report intervals, or ranges of values. Once again, there are a few rules aimed at generating standard tables that others can understand instantly. Here are the five steps to generate a standard grouped frequency table. We provide the steps first, rather than a description, because the steps for a grouped frequency table are a bit more complicated than are the steps for a frequency table.

1. Find the highest and lowest scores in your frequency distribution.

    In our example, these scores are 17.15 and 8.07.

2. Get the full range of data. If there are decimal places, round both scores down to the nearest whole numbers. If there already are whole numbers, use these. Subtract the lowest whole number from the highest whole number and add 1 to get the full range of the data. (Why do we add 1? Try it yourself. If we subtract 8 from 17, we get 9—but count the values from 8 through 17. There are 10 numbers, and we want to know the full range of the data.)

    In our example, 17.15 and 8.07 round down to 17 and 8, respectively. 17 − 8 = 9, and 9 + 1 = 10. Our scores fall within a range of 10.

3. Determine the number of intervals and the best interval size. There is no consensus about the ideal number of intervals, but most researchers recommend between 5 and 10, depending on the data. If we have an enormous data set with a huge range, then you might have many more intervals than 10. To find the best interval range, divide the range by the number of intervals we want, then round that answer to the nearest whole number. That whole number is ideally a "pretty" number (easily understood). With wide ranges, it's a multiple of 10 or 100 or 1000; with smaller ranges, it could be as small as 2, 3, or 5, or even 1 (or less than 1) if the numbers go to many decimal places. Try several interval sizes to get the best whole number for the interval size.

TABLE 2-5. GROUPED FREQUENCY TABLE
....

Grouped frequency tables make sense of data sets in which there are many possible values. This grouped frequency table depicts the frequencies for time to complete the Stroop task. The table provides the number of people who responded within each interval of time.

INTERVAL	FREQUENCY
16.00–17.99	1
14.00–15.99	8
12.00–13.99	22
10.00–11.99	15
8.00–9.99	4

In our example, we could choose to have 5 or 10 intervals. If we choose 5, we'll have an interval size of 2. If we choose 10, we'll have an interval size of 1. Note that with decimals, intervals of size 1 make sense. Each interval includes every value between one whole number and the next. For example, one of our intervals would range from 8.00 to 8.99. For this example, however, we'll choose 5 intervals of size 2.

4. Figure out the number that will be the bottom of the lowest interval. We want the bottom of that interval to be a multiple of our interval size. For example, if we have 8 intervals of size 5, then we want the bottom interval to start at a multiple of 5. It could start at 0, 10, 55, or 105, depending on our data. We choose which one by selecting the multiple of 5 that is below our lowest score.

    In our example, we have 5 intervals of size 2, and so the bottom of our lowest interval should be a multiple of 2. Our lowest score is 8.07, and so the bottom of our lowest interval would be 8. (If our lowest score were 7.22, we would choose 6. Note that this process might lead to one more interval than we planned for; this is perfectly fine.)

5. Finish the table by listing the intervals from highest to lowest and then counting the numbers of scores in each. This step is much like creating a frequency table (without intervals), which we discussed earlier. If you decide on intervals of size 5 and the first one begins at 10, then count the five numbers that will fall in this interval: 10, 11, 12, 13, and 14. The interval in this example runs from 10 to 14. (In reality, it runs from 10 to 14.9999, and the next one begins at 15, five digits higher than the bottom of the preceding interval.) A good rule of thumb is that the *bottoms* of the intervals should jump by the chosen interval size, 5 in the example just cited, and 2 in the example we've been working through in this list.

    In our example, the lowest interval would be 8 to 9, or 8.00 to 9.99. The next one would be 10.00 to 11.99, and so on.

The grouped frequency table in Table 2-5 gives us a much better sense of how quickly these students completed the Stroop task than either the list of raw data or a frequency table without intervals.

Graphing Our Data: Histograms

Even more than tables, graphs help us to see our data at a glance. The two most common methods for graphing interval data for one variable are the histogram and the frequency polygon. Here we will learn to construct and interpret both the more commonly used histogram and the less frequently used frequency polygon.

Histograms look like bar graphs but are typically used to depict interval data with the values of the variable on the x-axis and the frequencies on the y-axis; the bars reflect the frequencies for each value or interval. The difference between histograms and bar graphs is that bar graphs typically provide scores for nominal data (e.g., frequencies of men and women), whereas histograms typically provide frequencies for interval data (e.g., reaction times). We can construct histograms from frequency tables or from grouped frequency tables. Histograms allow for the many intervals that typically occur with interval data; the bars are stacked one against the next, and the intervals are arranged in a meaningful way—that is, lower numbers are to the left of higher numbers. With bar graphs, the categories do not need to be arranged in a particular order; the bars often have spaces between them to indicate that the arrangement from left to right has no particular numerical meaning.

Let's start by constructing a histogram from a frequency table. Table 2-2 depicted the data on chemistry graduate advisors and the numbers of students they placed in top professorial positions. We construct a histogram by drawing the x-axis (horizontal) and y-axis (vertical) of a graph. We label the x-axis with the variable of interest—in our case, "numbers of students"—and we label the y-axis "frequencies." As with most graphs, the lowest numbers start where the axes intersect and the numbers go up as we go to the right on the x-axis and as we go up on the y-axis. Ideally, the lowest number on each axis will be 0, so that the graphs will not be misleading. However, if the range of numbers on either axis is far from 0, histograms sometimes use a number other than 0 as the lowest number. Further, if there are negative numbers among the scores (such as air temperature), the x-axis could have negative numbers.

Once we've created our graph, we draw bars for each value. Each bar is *centered on* the value for which it provides the frequency. The heights of the bars represent the numbers of scores that fell at each value—the frequencies. If no one had a score at a particular value, there will be no bar. Thus, for the value of 7 on the x-axis, there will be a bar centering on 7 with a height of 4 on the y-axis, indicating that four scores had a value of 7. See Figure 2-1 for the histogram for the "chemistry advisor" data.

▪ A **histogram** looks like a bar graph but is typically used to depict interval data with the values of the variable on the x-axis and the frequencies on the y-axis.

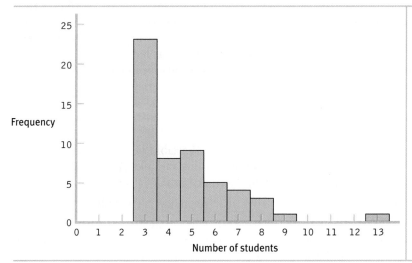

FIGURE 2-1
Histogram for the Frequency Table of Graduate Advisors

Histograms are graphic depictions of the information in frequency tables or grouped frequency tables. This histogram displays the numbers of students that each graduate advisor placed into top professorial positions.

Here is a recap of the steps to construct a histogram from a frequency table:

1. Draw the x-axis and label it with the variable of interest and the full range of values for this variable. (Include 0 unless all of the scores are so far from 0 that it's impractical.)

2. Draw the y-axis and label it "frequencies." (Include 0 unless it's impractical.)

3. Draw a bar for each value, centering the bar around that value on the x-axis and drawing the bar as high as the frequency for that value as represented on the y-axis.

Grouped frequency tables can also be depicted as histograms. Instead of listing values on the x-axis, we list the midpoints of intervals. Students commonly make mistakes in determining the midpoints of intervals. If there are three intervals that range from 0 to 9, 10 to 19, and 20 to 29, what would the midpoints be? If you said 4.5, 14.5, and 24.5, you're making a *very* common mistake. Remember, the intervals really go from 0.000000 to 9.999999, or as close as you can get to 10 without actually being 10. Given that there are 10 numbers in this range (0, 1, 2, 3, 4, 5, 6, 7, 8, and 9), the midpoint would be 5 from the bottom. So the midpoints for 0 to 9, 10 to 19, and 20 to 29 are 5, 15, and 25. A good rule: When determining a midpoint, look at the bottom of the interval that you're interested in and then the bottom of the next interval. What's the midpoint between the two interval minimums? Once you've determined your midpoints, check them; they should jump by the interval size. Here, the interval is size 10. Notice that the midpoints consistently jump by 10 (5, 15, and 25).

Let's look at the Stroop data for which we constructed a grouped frequency histogram. What are our midpoints? There are five intervals: 8.00 to 9.99, 10.00 to 11.99, 12.00 to 13.99, 14.00 to 15.99, and 16.00 to 17.99. Let's calculate the midpoint for the lowest interval. We should look at the bottom of this interval, 8, and the bottom of the next interval, 10. The midpoint of these numbers is 9; so that is the midpoint of this interval. The remaining intervals can be calculated the same way. We can then check to be sure they jump by exactly 2 each time. To calculate the midpoint of the highest interval, imagine that we had one more interval. If we did, it would start at 18.00. The midpoint of 16 and 18 is 17. Using these guidelines, we calculate our midpoints as 9, 11, 13, 15, and 17. We now can construct our histogram by placing these midpoints on the x-axis and then drawing bars that center on them and are as high as the frequency for each interval. The histogram for these data is shown in Figure 2-2.

Here is a recap of the steps to construct a histogram from a grouped frequency table:

▪ A **frequency polygon** is a line graph with the x-axis representing values (or midpoints of intervals) and the y-axis representing frequencies. A point is placed at the frequency for each value (or midpoint), and the points are connected.

1. Determine the midpoint for every interval.

2. Draw the x-axis and label it with the variable of interest and the midpoints for each interval of values on this variable. (Include 0 unless the values are so far from 0 that it's impractical.)

3. Draw the y-axis and label it "frequency." (Include 0 unless it's impractical.)

4. Draw a bar for each midpoint, centering the bar on that midpoint on the x-axis and drawing the bar as high as the frequency for that interval as represented on the y-axis.

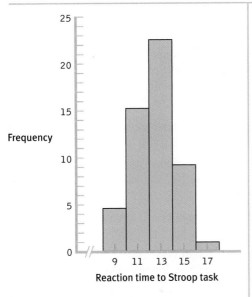

FIGURE 2-2
Histogram for the Grouped Frequency Table of Stroop Data

Histograms can also depict the data in a grouped frequency table. This histogram depicts the data seen in the grouped frequency table for Stroop task response times.

Graphing Our Data: Frequency Polygons

Frequency polygons are constructed in a very similar way to histograms. Histograms look like city skylines, but polygons look more like mountain landscapes. As the name might imply, polygons are many-sided shapes. Specifically, *frequency polygons are line graphs with the x-axes representing values (or midpoints of intervals) and the y-axes representing frequencies; a point is placed at the frequency for each value (or midpoint), and the dots are connected.* For the most part, we make frequency polygons exactly as we make histograms. Instead of constructing bars above each value or midpoint, however, we draw dots and connect them. The other difference is that we need to add an appropriate value (or midpoint) on either end of the graph so that we can draw lines down to 0, grounding our shape. Figure 2-3 shows the frequency polygon for the grouped frequency distribution of Stroop response times that we constructed previously in Figure 2-2.

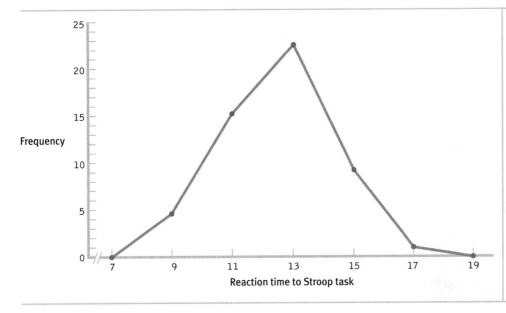

FIGURE 2-3
Frequency Polygons as Another Graphing Option for the Stroop Data

Frequency polygons are an alternative to histograms. This frequency polygon depicts the same data that were previously depicted in the histogram in Figure 2-2. In either case, the graph provides an easily interpreted "picture" of our distribution.

Here is a recap of the steps to construct a frequency polygon. When basing a frequency polygon on a frequency table, we will place specific values on the *x*-axis. When basing it on a grouped frequency table, we will place midpoints of intervals on the *x*-axis.

1. If based on a grouped frequency table, determine the midpoint for every interval. If based on a frequency table, skip this step.

2. Draw the *x*-axis and label it with the variable of interest and either the values or the midpoints. (Include 0 unless the values/midpoints are so far from 0 that it's impractical.)

3. Draw the *y*-axis and label it "frequencies." (Include 0 unless it's impractical.)

4. Mark a dot above each value or midpoint depicting the frequency, as represented on the *y*-axis, for that value or midpoint, and connect the dots.

5. Add an appropriate hypothetical value or midpoint on both ends of the *x*-axis, and mark a dot for a frequency of 0 for each value or midpoint. Connect the existing line to these dots, creating a shape rather than a "floating" line.

Applying Visual Depictions of Data: Generating Research Questions

Frequency tables provide far more information than a jumble of raw data, and they lead to more specific research questions. Think back to the study by Kuck et al. (2007) of chemistry professors and the graduate students they advised. From the frequency table, we can see that most of these professors trained just a few of these future top faculty members, whereas just a few produced many. The researchers next looked at the gender breakdown of the graduate students (all these advisors were men). They found that these advisors were placing far more male than female students in these top jobs, even when the lower numbers of women in chemistry PhD programs were taken into account. But this is only one of the important research questions stimulated by merely looking at a description of the data.

Another researcher might be interested in aspects of these data other than gender. For example, are you wondering why just a few of these advisors did extremely well in sending their students on to these prestigious jobs? This second research question suggests many other, more specific research questions. For example, you might decide to look at how many graduate students each advisor trained. Perhaps those with many students had more chances to have a student obtain one of these top jobs. Or you might look at how much grant money these professors received—grant money they could spend on laboratory equipment and other resources for their students. Perhaps those with more financial backing provided the best training for their students. Or you might examine how prestigious these advisors were themselves. It may be their prestige that's lending a "halo" to their students. From a simple description of the data, we have raised four separate but related hypotheses. We have raised research questions about (1) constraints on talented women in chemistry; (2) whether mere numbers of graduate students predicted who the most successful mentors were; (3) whether the amount of grant money affected that success; and (4) whether the perceived prestige of a professor was the best predictor of that success.

An Outlier Professor
While at the University of California at Berkeley, Dr. Yuan T. Lee advised 13 chemistry graduate students who went on to become professors in one of the top 50 U.S. chemistry departments; a frequency distribution demonstrates that this is far more than were trained by any other professor, at Berkeley or any other university, and suggests research questions about what specific qualities in an advisor lead to student success. This is a case in which the outlier may be the most interesting data point.

AP Photo / Vincent Yu

The professor who trained 13 future top faculty members? Dr. Yuan T. Lee from the University of California at Berkeley. He won a Nobel Prize. Did that have anything to do with his success in placing his students in these top jobs? Maybe. But maybe not. Many of Lee's students who went on to top professorships got their jobs *before* he won his Nobel Prize, and although there are other chemistry Nobel Prize winners in the United States who serve as graduate advisors, no one else has Lee's record in placing students. Already we're using our visual depiction of data, and any follow-up information we can find, to develop new research questions!

In summary, there are four techniques for organizing information about a single variable: frequency tables, grouped frequency tables, frequency histograms, and frequency polygons. These simple techniques reorganize data to create visual depictions that provoke more specific research questions.

⊙ CHECK YOUR LEARNING

2-1 In 2005, *U.S. News & World Report* published a list of the best psychology PhD departments in the United States. It explicitly stated that the programs are research-focused, as is typically the case with a PhD program (vs. PsyD programs, which are often more clinically focused). The top 27 departments ranged from Stanford University at number 1 through a tie among the last six universities, which include Johns Hopkins and Northwestern Universities. (Some schools appeared on the list twice if they had two separate psychology-related departments with top rankings.) Let's say you're interested in attending one of these schools, specifically one that has ethnic diversity. Data for these schools can be gathered from www. petersons.com. Seventeen of these reported the number of current students who are members of a racial or ethnic minority group. Here are those data:

17	17	8	12	3	59	41	3	32
4	10	59	20	1	9	3	27	

a. Construct a grouped frequency table of these data.

b. Construct a histogram for this grouped frequency table.

c. Construct a frequency polygon for this grouped frequency table.

d. What can we tell from the graphs and table that we cannot tell from the list of scores?

e. Why might percentages of students who are members of a minority group be more useful than these numbers? *Hint:* The numbers of full-time psychology graduate students at these schools range from 19 to 258.

f. Not all schools provided data. How might the schools that provided data on numbers of minority students be different from schools that did not provide these data?

> CENTRAL TENDENCY: DETERMINING THE TYPICAL SCORE

Alex began to realize that she could use statistical ideas to describe her emotions and that it was surprisingly helpful to do so. For example, simply recognizing that she had choices elevated her mood. Her rising spirits clarified how discouraged she had become over the past two years. Her emotions swung faster now, hitting a new low when she started worrying about how to pay for graduate school, but lifting again when she realized that more education would probably lead to more money. And they fell again with the recognition that it was going to take at least a few years to get there. Imagining a better life? Up. The possibility of failure? Down. Each point in favor of taking the big risk of going to graduate school lifted her up, and each corresponding challenge discouraged her even more. The wild swings, the variability of her emotions, were wearing on her. She was experiencing statistics in her self-observations about the variability of her moods around a central tendency, and the stress of all that variability produced one clear insight: She had to make a decision.

Professor Jackson didn't limit the options they discussed to attending graduate school in evaluation research. In fact, she emphasized that those who had the best graduate school experiences—and who were happiest with their careers after school—were those who approached the degree with a particular purpose in mind. She had even given Alex a booklet: "Five Ways to Go to Graduate School for Free (and What You Can Do About It Now)." Nevertheless, going to graduate school was such a big decision that Alex was almost trembling when she finally had to mail in her application checks. She was choosing to be poor, even if temporarily. More important, she was choosing her life, and that was exciting.

"Why didn't somebody tell me about evaluation research?" Alex asked Professor Jackson at their next meeting. "This is exactly what I want."

"Evaluation research is full of many very different opportunities," Professor Jackson replied. "There is a great deal of research that needs to be done and never enough well-trained people to do it. And deciding to study evaluation research doesn't mean you are done with your big decisions. Evaluation research is a huge field. You can do research on quasi-experimental designs for field studies, evaluations of the effectiveness of reforestation, the difference between evaluating politics and the politics of evaluation, and evaluation in the nonprofit sector."

"Wait a second," said Alex. "So evaluation research isn't like a psychology, communications, or chemistry department—it's an 'all over the place' department. So if I want to make sure that the trees that a lumber company plants after it clears a forest really grow up to be useful trees, that's all evaluation research?"

"That's evaluation research," Professor Jackson agreed. "The skills you learned in the behavioral sciences can be applied in many different ways. You could work with a consulting firm that evaluates pollution control techniques, a government agency that monitors pollution emissions, or even the company that did the polluting in the first place. You could even evaluate the effect of premature discounting on retail sales." Alex looked up just in time to notice her smiling. Professor Jackson added, "There always will be work for anyone who knows enough statistics and research design to be a good evaluator. You can help improve the world in small but very important ways."

The more she spoke with Professor Jackson, the more Alex started to feel settled and hopeful about her big decision to go to graduate school. Her average mood was higher now than it had been when all she could imagine was a dreary future in retail sales. And as she got accustomed to thinking of herself as a graduate student, her moods fluctuated less wildly. Alex still didn't recognize that she was experiencing statistics, but she was going to become a statistician, and graduate school was the way she was going to get there.

The Need for Alternative Measures of Central Tendency

Just as there is variability around the central tendency of Alex's emotional life, there is variability around a central tendency in any distribution of numbers. *Central tendency refers to the descriptive statistic that best represents the center of a data set, the particular value that all the other data seem to be gathering around.* Simply creating a visual representation of the distribution often reveals its central tendency. The central tendency is usually at (or near) the highest point in the histogram or the polygon (Figure 2-4).

There are exceptions to this easy "high point of the distribution" rule, however, and they can be very important. For example, how can you describe the central tendency of an individual with bipolar disorder? Unlike Alex, these individuals experience an abnormal emotional life characterized by desperately manic periods, severe depressive episodes, and periods of stability in between. In clinical cases of bipolar (manic-depressive) disorder, emotional highs and lows are not evenly distributed around a single central tendency. Indeed, people with bipolar disorder tend to have three central tendencies: one manic, one depressive, and one stable. If untreated, they will have approximately 10 bipolar episodes in their lifetime, with manic moods that might last from a few weeks to a few months and depressive moods that might last six months or longer. Between the episodes, their moods are relatively stable, centering around a middle mood level. Nevertheless, they still have a predictable pattern to their lives, and alternative indicators of central tendency provide a way of describing that pattern. Three different measures of central tendency—mean, median, and mode—recognize these important differences in the shapes of numerical distributions.

Mean: The Arithmetic Average

The mean is simple to calculate and is the gateway to understanding statistical formulas. The mean is such an important concept in statistics that we provide you with four distinct ways to think about it: verbally, arithmetically, visually, and symbolically (using statistical notation).

■ **Central tendency** refers to the descriptive statistic that best represents the center of a data set, the particular value that all the other data seem to be gathering around.

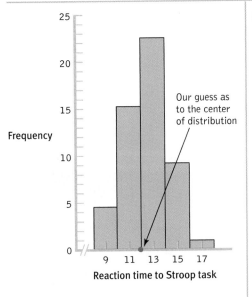

FIGURE 2-4
Estimating Central Tendency with Histograms

Histograms and frequency polygons allow us to see the likely center of our sample's distribution. The arrow points to our guess as to the center of the distribution of Stroop task response times.

▪ The **mean** is the arithmetic average of a group of scores. It is calculated by summing all the scores and dividing by the total number of scores.

▪ **Statistics** are numbers based on a sample taken from a population; they are usually symbolized by Latin letters.

The Mean, Act 1: Defining the Mean in Plain English

The most commonly reported measure of central tendency is *the mean*, *the arithmetic average of a group of scores*. The mean, often called the average, is used to represent the "typical" score in a distribution. This is different from the way we often use the word *average* in everyday conversation. We may refer to a person as average in a somewhat derogatory way, noting that someone is "just" average in athletic ability or a movie was "only" average. In statistics, however, *average* may or may not have a negative connotation. Being near the average in amount of REM sleep may have no value judgment attached to it, whereas having the average SAT score among a group of honors students might be a very good thing. The word *average* connotes so many different shades of meaning that we need to define the mean arithmetically.

The Mean, Act 2: The Mean in Plain Arithmetic

The mean is calculated by summing all the scores in a data set and then dividing this sum by the total number of scores. But you know this. You likely have calculated means many times in your life. For example, when we explore the number of "nights partying" of 20 students, the mean would be calculated by first adding

$$1 + 2 + 7 + 6 + 1 + 2 + 6 + 5 + 4 + 4 + 0 + 3 + 2 + 2 + 3 + 4 + 3 + 5 + 4 + 4 = 68$$

and then dividing by 20, the number of scores: 68/20 = 3.4.

Similarly, the 50 response times to the Stroop task summarized in Table 2-5 (page 48) represent a more complex distribution because there are more observations and they are reported to two decimal points. Consequently, we will not be able to guess the mean simply by glancing at these data, but calculating the mean will give us a precise measure of central tendency. You may want to calculate the mean for these numbers—with a calculator (but without a formula).

Did you get 12.43? Now let's consider the visual representation of these same data in Figure 2-5, but with the actual mean indicated by an arrow.

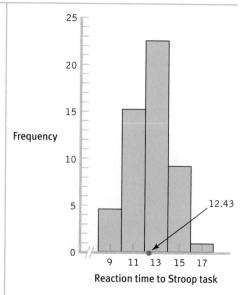

FIGURE 2-5
Calculate the Mean to Confirm Your Estimate

A histogram gives us a sense of the center of our sample's distribution, but it's much more accurate to calculate the actual mean. The arrow indicates the actual mean of 12.43.

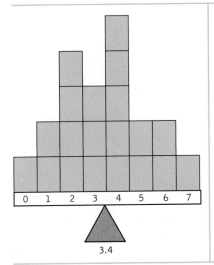

FIGURE 2-6
The Mean as the Fulcrum of Our Data

The mean, 3.4, is the balancing point for all the scores for "nights partying" for the students in our sample. Mathematically, the scores always will balance around the mean for any sample.

The Mean, Act 3: Visual Representations of the Mean

Think of the mean as the point that perfectly balances two sides of a distribution. For example, the mean of 3.4 "nights partying" is represented visually as the point that perfectly balances that distribution in Figure 2-6.

The Mean, Act 4: The Mean Expressed by Symbolic Notation

Symbolic notation may sound far more difficult to understand than it really is. After all, you just calculated a mean without symbolic notation and without a formula; however, we use only a handful of symbols to express the ideas necessary to understand statistics. We emphasize them now so that you will develop the habit of using the correct statistical terms and notations for concepts you already know.

After completing our course in statistics, one student who came back to thank us offered a unique description that reinforced our belief that the concepts in statistics are already familiar to most students. He said, "I would study the material in the book every week, not understand it, and then come to class. When I finally understood the idea, I kept finding myself saying, 'Oh, is that all it is?' You've got to tell people that statistics sounds like a more difficult subject than it really is."

We're taking that student's advice, in part simply by passing along his story. But our student's point is illustrated by the several different symbols that statisticians use to communicate information about the mean as a measure of central tendency. Although these different symbols all represent the same core idea of central tendency, they convey important nuances of meaning.

Here are the several symbols that represent the mean. For the mean of a sample, statisticians typically use M or $\bar{X}$. In this text, we'll use M; many other texts also use M, but some use $\bar{X}$ (pronounced "X bar"). For a population, statisticians use the Greek letter μ (pronounced "mew") to symbolize the mean. Although there are exceptions, Latin letters such as M tend to refer to numbers based on samples, and Greek letters such as μ tend to refer to numbers based on populations. *The numbers based on samples are called **statistics**; M is a statistic. The numbers*

Symbols: M and $\bar{X}$ ("X bar") are two different symbols for the same thing, the mean of a sample. The Greek letter μ (pronounced "mew"), is the symbol for the mean of a population.

■ **Parameters** are numbers based on the whole population; they are usually symbolized by Greek letters.

■ The **median** is the middle score of all the scores in a sample when the scores are arranged in ascending order. If there is no single middle score, the median is the mean of the two middle scores.

■ The **mode** is the most common score of all the scores in a sample.

Symbols: *N* refers to the total number of scores in a sample. Formulas: The formula for the mean is $M = \frac{\Sigma X}{N}$ in which *X* indicates each score and *N* indicates the total number of scores.

TABLE 2-6. THE MEAN IN SYMBOLS

The mean of a sample is an example of a statistic, whereas the mean of a population is an example of a parameter. The symbols we use depend on whether we refer to the mean of a sample or a population.

NUMBER	USED FOR	SYMBOL	PRONOUNCED
Statistic	Sample	M or $\bar{X}$	"M" and "X bar"
Parameter	Population	μ	"mew"

based on populations are called **parameters**; μ is a parameter. Table 2-6 presents all this information concisely. As shown in Figure 2-7, you can remember this distinction by the first letters of these words: *statistic* and *sample* both begin with *s*, and *parameter* and *population* both begin with *p*. These symbols are part of the language of statistics and help us to communicate with other statisticians. In journal articles, we typically see means reported as *M*, an indication that it is describing a sample that was taken from a larger population.

A formula to calculate the mean of a sample would use the symbol *M* on the left side of the equation. The right side would provide information on the actual calculation of the mean. A single score is typically symbolized as *X*. We know that we're summing all the scores, all the *X*s, and so the first step is to use the summation sign, Σ (pronounced "sigma"), to indicate that we're summing a list of scores. As you might guess, the full expression for summing all the scores would be ΣX. This instructs us to add up all of the *X*s in the sample. The next step is dividing by the total number of scores. The total number of scores in a sample is typically represented by *N*. (Note that the capital letter *N* is used when we refer to the number of scores in the entire data set; if we break the sample down into smaller parts, as we'll see in later chapters, we use the lowercase letter *n*.) The full equation would be: $M = \frac{\Sigma X}{N}$. It looks more complicated than it really is. After all, it's just the formula for the mean. But if you start using this formula now, you will quickly grow accustomed to symbolic notation.

Let's look at the mean for the Stroop task that we considered earlier in this section. First, we added up every score. The sum of all the scores came to 621.73. Then we divided 621.73 by the total number of scores, 50. Our result was 12.43. Here's how it would look as a formula:

$$M = \frac{\Sigma X}{N} = \frac{621.73}{50} = 12.43$$

FIGURE 2-7

Try using a mnemonic trick to remember the distinction between samples and *pa*rameters. The letter *S* means that numbers based on (*S*)amples are called (*S*)tatistics. The letter *P* means that numbers based on (*P*)opulations are called (*P*)arameters.

Statisticians tend to be as specific with their symbols as they are with their words. For example, almost all symbols are italicized, whether in the formulas to calculate statistics or in the reporting of statistics. However, the actual numerical values of the statistics are not italicized. Furthermore, whether or not a symbol is capitalized usually has meaning. Changing a symbol from uppercase to lowercase often changes what it means. When you practice calculating means, use this formula, being sure to italicize the symbols and use capital letters for *M*, *X*, and *N*. It may seem silly to use a formula for something so ingrained, but the notation will become familiar and that will make it easier to apply it to new concepts.

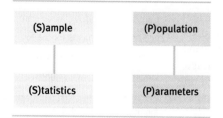

Median: The Middle Score

The second most common measure of central tendency is the median. *The **median** is the middle score of all the scores in a sample when the scores are arranged in ascending order.* We can think of the median as the 50th percentile. The median does not tend to be denoted by a symbol, although in APA style, the writing style of the American Psychological Association (APA), it can be abbreviated as *mdn*. (Note that APA style, despite the word *psychological* in its name, is used across many of the social sciences; you are likely to use it in your courses regardless of your social science major.) To determine the median, we first line up all the scores in ascending order. Second, we find the middle score. If there is an odd number of scores, there will be an actual middle score. If there is an even number of scores, there will be no actual middle score. In this case, take the mean of the two middle scores.

> Symbols: In APA style, median is sometimes abbreviated as *mdn*.

Here are specific instructions for finding the median. Keep in mind that with a distribution of only a few data points, we won't want to use the formula—just count how many numbers there are in the distribution and find the score that has the same number of scores above it and below it. Even with a distribution with many scores, the calculation is easy. All we do is divide the number of scores (N) by 2 and add $^1/_2$; that is, 0.5. That number is the ordinal position (rank) of the median, or middle score. As illustrated below, simply count that many places over from the start of your scores and report that number.

Here is an example with an odd number of scores (representing Stroop reaction times from a sample of 9 individuals):

12.52, 12.46, 11.74, 13.64, 14.76, 8.07, 10.74, 12.32, 13.10

First, we put the scores in ascending order:

8.07, 10.74, 11.74, 12.32, 12.46, 12.52, 13.10, 13.64, 14.76

Then we count them. There are 9 scores: 9/2 = 4.5. If we add 0.5 to this, we get 5. Therefore, the median is the 5th score. We now count across to the 5th score. The median is 12.46.

Here is an example with an even number of scores. We will use the same data as in the example with the odd number of scores, but we'll add one more data point: 14.97.

Arranged in ascending order, our data are now:

8.07, 10.74, 11.74, 12.32, 12.46, 12.52, 13.10, 13.64, 14.76, 14.97

Mean vs. Median
The median is that part of the roadway that divides the directions in which vehicles are permitted to drive. It can be dangerous to confuse the mean and the median, especially when you are calculating the "middle" of the roadway!

We now count 10 scores: 10/2 = 5. If we add 0.5 to this, we get 5.5; therefore, the median is the average of the 5th and 6th scores. The 5th and 6th scores are 12.46 and 12.52. The median is their mean, 12.49.

Mode: The Most Common Score

The *mode* is perhaps the easiest of the three measures of central tendency to calculate. *The **mode** is the most common score of all the scores in a sample.* It is readily picked out on a frequency table, histogram, or polygon. A memory trick to remember the mode is the letter *o* because the m*o*de is the m*o*st c*o*mmonly *o*ccuring score in a distribution.

David De Lossy / Photodisc Green / Getty Images

■ A **unimodal** distribution has one mode, or most common score.

■ A **bimodal** distribution has two modes, or most common scores.

■ A **multimodal** distribution has more than two modes, or most common scores.

Like the median, the mode does not tend to be represented by a symbol; unlike the median, it does not even have an APA abbreviation. When reporting modes, we use the word itself (e.g., the mode is . . .).

Determine the mode for the following two samples from earlier in this chapter. The mode can be found either by searching the list of numbers for the most common score or by constructing a frequency table.

1. Fictional data for 20 students; each score represents the number of "nights partying":

    1, 2, 7, 6, 1, 2, 6, 5, 4, 4, 0, 3, 2, 2, 3, 4, 3, 5, 4, 4

    Mode: _____

2. Data for 54 graduate advisors; each score represents the number of that graduate advisor's former students who went on to top jobs:

    3, 3, 3, 4, 5, 9, 5, 3, 3, 5, 6, 3, 4, 8, 6, 3, 3, 3, 4, 4, 4, 7, 6, 3, 5, 5, 7, 13, 3, 3, 3, 3, 3, 4, 4, 4, 5, 6, 7, 6, 7, 8, 8, 3, 3, 3, 5, 3, 3, 5, 3, 5, 3, 3

    Mode: _____

Did your answers match the correct answers—(1) 4 and (2) 3? If they didn't, you might have made a common mistake. The mode is the score that occurs most frequently, not the frequency of that score. So, in the second data set above, the score 3 occurs 23 times. The mode is 3, *not 23*.

The modes in these two examples were particularly easy to determine because there was one most common score in each case. Sometimes data sets have no specific mode. This is especially true when the scores are reported to several decimal places. Other data sets have more than one specific mode, where two or more different scores are the most common. When there is no specific mode, we sometimes report the most common interval as the mode. When there is more than one mode, we report both, or all, of the most common scores. *When a distribution of scores has one mode, we refer to it as* **unimodal**. *When a distribution has two modes, we call it* **bimodal**. *When a distribution has more than two modes, we call it* **multimodal**. A histogram describing bipolar disease, for example, might be multimodal, as illustrated in Figure 2-8.

FIGURE 2-8
Bipolar Disorder and the Modal Mood

Because people with bipolar disorder, especially those who are not receiving treatment, have three different mood states in their lives, it might be hard to determine a true center for their daily mood scores. The distribution might be multimodal, with one mode for depressive days, one for stable days, and one for manic days.

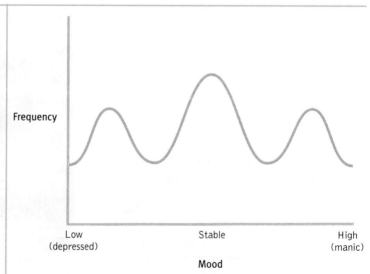

As demonstrated in the examples above, the mode can be used with interval data; however, it is most commonly used with nominal data. For example, Cancer Research UK (2003) reported that lung cancer was the most common cause of cancer death in the United Kingdom (22%). No other type of cancer came close. Colorectal cancer accounted for 10% of cancer deaths, breast cancer for 8%, and all other types for 7% or less. In this data set, the modal type of cancer death is lung cancer.

The Effect of Outliers on Measures of Central Tendency

The mean usually appears in journal articles and media reports. However, we employ the median and mode when the data are skewed (lopsided). One common reason for skewed data is a statistical outlier. To demonstrate the effect of outliers on the mean, as well as the median's resistance to the effect of outliers, let's use the statistical archives of America's national pasttime, baseball.

Some baseball players have made a career out of their ability to steal bases. But one major league player eclipsed all others in terms of the total number of stolen bases: Rickey Henderson. Presented below are the five all-time stolen base leaders according to the major league baseball Web site. As you read their stories and compare their statistics, what research questions come to mind? Outliers do more than merely change the statistical mean; they inspire your curiosity.

Hall of Fame outfielder Rickey Henderson played from 1979 to 2003, a re-markable 24-year career in which he stole 1406 bases while playing for eight different teams, most frequently the Oakland Athletics and the New York Yankees. Lou Brock, another Hall of Fame outfielder, played from 1961 to 1979 and succeeded in the face of enormous odds. He picked cotton as a child in Louisiana and still managed to represent his high school in state competitions in mathematics and chemistry. Lou Brock had 938 stolen bases. Another Hall of Fame base-stealer is Billy Hamilton, who played from 1888 to 1901. Billy Hamilton set a record by stealing 7 bases in one game and had 912 stolen bases. Centerfielder Ty Cobb was both criticized and admired for his aggressive play and stole 892 bases. He was the first inductee into the Baseball Hall of Fame after playing 22 years for the Detroit Tigers and another 2 years for the Philadelphia Athletics from 1905 to 1928. The only one of these players not in the Baseball Hall of Fame, outfielder Tim Raines, played from 1979 to 2002 and enjoyed the highest success rate at base-stealing (84.7%); he stole 808 bases.

Reported below are five top base-stealers in major league history and the number of bases stolen:

R. Henderson	1406
L. Brock	938
B. Hamilton	912
T. Cobb	892
T. Raines	808

To get a sense of the lifetime achievement of the best base-stealers, we might want to calculate a measure of central tendency for these five players, using the formula to get a little more practice with the symbols of statistics.

$$M = \frac{\Sigma X}{N} = \frac{\Sigma(1406 + 938 + 912 + 892 + 808)}{5} = \frac{4956}{5} = 991.2$$

Outshone by an Outlier
Hall of Fame baseball player Billy Hamilton once stole seven bases in a single game. Yet even his remarkable career was eclipsed by an outlier, the current and likely permanent base-stealing champion, Rickey Henderson.

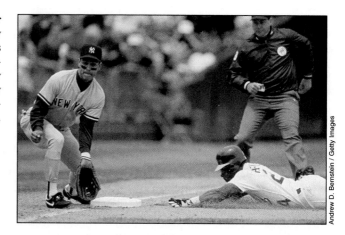

As often happens, this mean is not the same as any of the scores in the sample. The mean of 991.2 is not typical for any of these five baseball players. An important feature of the mean, however, is that it is the point at which all the other scores would balance. Figure 2-9 demonstrates this using the analogy of a balance beam with the numbers of stolen bases from 808 to 1406 marked on it. Weights are placed to represent each of the scores in our sample. The seesaw will be perfectly balanced if we put its fulcrum at the mean of 991.2.

When we look at the stolen base data, however, we notice that one score—that of Rickey Henderson—is very different from all the others. Four of the scores are between 808 and 938, not a very wide range. But Rickey Henderson stole 1406 bases. When there is an outlier, like Rickey Henderson, it is important to consider what his score will do to the mean. *An **outlier** is an extreme score that is either very high or very low in comparison with the rest of the scores in the sample.* Outliers are particularly influential when we have a small number of observations. When we eliminate Rickey Henderson's score, the data are now 808, 892, 912, and 938, and the mean is now:

$$M = \frac{\Sigma X}{N} = \frac{\Sigma(808 + 892 + 912 + 938)}{4} = \frac{3550}{4} = 887.5$$

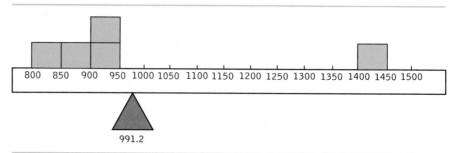

| 800 | 850 | 900 | 950 | 1000 | 1050 | 1100 | 1150 | 1200 | 1250 | 1300 | 1350 | 1400 | 1450 | 1500 |

991.2

FIGURE 2-9
Outliers and the Mean

When there is an outlier, sometimes the mean is not representative of any one actual score. With the base-stealing data, the mean of 991.2 is above the lowest four scores and well below the highest. Rickey Henderson's score pulls the mean higher, even among the very best base-stealers ever.

■ An **outlier** is an extreme score that is either very high or very low in comparison with the rest of the scores in a sample.

The mean of these scores, 887.5, is a good deal lower than the mean of the scores that included Rickey Henderson's very high number of stolen bases. We see from Figure 2-10 that this mean, like the previous mean, marks the point at which all other scores are perfectly balanced around it; however, this mean is a little more representative of the scores—887.5 does seem to be a typical score for these four players. It falls somewhere in the middle of the scores used to calculate it, whereas the mean of 991.2 is higher than all scores except Rickey Henderson's score of 1406. Even compared with the top base-stealers, Rickey Henderson brought the mean up in the same way that one truly exceptional student might be labeled "a curve buster."

An Early Lesson in Lying with Statistics: Which Measure of Central Tendency Is Best?

Different measures of central tendency can lead to very different conclusions. When there is a decision to be made about which measure to use, the choice is usually between the mean and the median. Typically, the mean is the measure of choice; however, whenever the distribution is skewed by an outlier (or when the distribution of observations itself is skewed), the median is used to convey central tendency. The mode is generally used when one particular score dominates a distribution and to indicate bimodal or multimodal distributions. The mode is also used when the data are nominal. The best way to tell the truth with statistics is to provide more details, so when you are uncertain as to which is the best indicator of central tendency, report all three. Alas, there are also so many opportunities to mislead with statistics that lying with numbers has rightfully become an issue in the popular media, particularly with regard to financial statements, advertising, and how peer-reviewed social science research is communicated to the general public.

Numerous statisticians have pointed out the problems with identifying averages, often using the humorous example of the average person (Bernstein, 1998). In *The Average American: The Extraordinary Search for the Nation's Most Ordinary Citizen*, Kevin O'Keefe (2005) used a vast array of statistics from the 2000 U.S. Census to find the American individual who was the most average in 140 different characteristics. A review of the book (Grimes, 2005) describes O'Keefe's average American as someone who

> spends 95 percent of the time indoors, thinks abortion is morally wrong but supports the right to have one, owns an electric coffeemaker, has nine friends and at least one pet, and would rather spend a week in jail than become president. He (or she) lives within a 20-minute drive of a Wal-Mart, attends church at least once a month, prefers smooth peanut butter to chunky, lives where the average annual temperature is between 45 and 65 degrees, and believes that Jews make up 18 percent of the population (the actual figure is between 2 and 3 percent).

Of course, the more criteria O'Keefe added on, the less likely it was that a single individual would be perfectly average. Most of the 94 finalists for the title of Average American failed to meet at least one criterion. As the book reviewer noted: "One by one, his prospects flunk the test. One has too many cars. Another lacks a pet. And so it goes, down to the wire." As O'Keefe's difficult search demonstrates, beware of conclusions drawn merely from means.

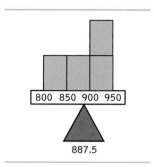

FIGURE 2-10
The Mean Without the Outlier

When the outlier—Rickey Henderson—is omitted from the base-stealing data, the mean is now more representative of the actual scores in the sample.

"Consuming" Statistics: Figures Don't lie, but Liars Figure

Central tendency communicates an enormous amount of information with a single number, so it is not surprising that measures of central tendency are among the most widely reported of descriptive statistics. We are told the mean, median, and mode not only in research articles and technical reports but also in popular media—from newspaper articles to Web sites to TV commercials. When we are conducting statistical analyses and have to report the results to nonstatisticians, measures of central tendency are easily understood. You might have read a newspaper report that the median home price for your town is $225,500; your biology professor might have told you that the average test grade for the class was 78; an online questionnaire on bioethics might have reported that the modal response to a question on one's position on stem cell research was "strongly approve." Even without a background in statistics, most people have a pretty good sense of the meaning of these reports of central tendency. But that doesn't stop many people from using them incorrectly, whether naively or intentionally.

There is one particular statistical "lie" or trick that is used on consumers more than any other: reporting the mean instead of the median. Fortunately, it requires only a little bit of critical thinking to exorcise this particular statistical demon from your thought life. When you read an article or advertisement or hear a news story or commercial, listen to reports of central tendency. First, notice whether it is reporting an average (mean) or a median. Second, if it is reporting a mean, think about whether that distribution is likely to be skewed by one extremely high number. Here are four examples in which the mean and median would lead to quite different conclusions.

Housing Prices: Misleading with the Mean

In an article on housing prices in Manhattan, the *New York Times* provided a model of responsible journalism by demonstrating that there is a story behind how central tendency is used to communicate real estate prices. "Look, up in the air! Is it a bubble? Is it froth? It's Manhattan real estate prices," wrote William Neuman (2005) in his report of record high median and average Manhattan housing prices of $750,000 and $1,276,202, respectively. The mean is inflated by a few sales in the millions, outliers that would not affect the median. The film star Gwyneth Paltrow and her husband, Chris Martin of the rock band Coldplay, sold their Manhattan apartment right around that time for about $7 million; this price certainly would have inflated the mean.

Perceived Income and Politics: Strategic Impressions Versus Statistical Precision

Statistics can be used to sway public opinion by confusing the mean and the median to overdramatize a story. In London's *Financial Times*, Vanessa Houlder (2004) pointed out that typical incomes can be perceived as quite low (£9800) or quite high (£42,000), depending on whether the typical income is presented as a mean or a median, as well as "on whether economists choose individuals or households, net or gross income" or "a subset or the whole population." Depending on one's politics and goals, one could select a statistical definition of *average* as portraying the typical UK citizen as anything from just getting by to doing pretty darned well. Holder's story demonstrates the value of critical thinking when reading reports about "average" income.

Celebrity Outliers

Reports of the cost of a typical Manhattan apartment depend on whether we report the mean or the median. Film star Gwyneth Paltrow and her husband, Coldplay lead singer Chris Martin, sold their Manhattan apartment in the spring of 2005 for around $7 million. Such a sale would be an outlier and would boost the mean; however, it would not affect the median. Of course, either way, the typical Manhattan apartment is not in the budget of the typical college graduate!

Mario Magnani / Getty Images

As the caustically humorous Sir Winston Churchill told an ambitious young supporter, "I gather, young man, that you wish to be a Member of Parliament. The first lesson that you must learn is, when I call for statistics about the rate of infant mortality, what I want is proof that fewer babies died when I was prime minister than when anyone else was prime minister. That is a political statistic."

Life Expectancy: Profiting by Planning Ahead

Be careful when you buy life insurance or plan for your retirement. Confusing the mean and the median can cost you a great deal of money. A letter to the editor (Kocich, 2005) corrected a London *Financial Times* reporter who failed to explain the flaws in the average life expectancies that he reported. The author of the letter explained that typical life expectancy at birth is calculated with a mean, not a median, and would be affected by outliers on the low end—those who die at birth or in childhood. These early deaths would dramatically decrease the life expectancy at birth. Those who survive to adulthood would have far higher life expectancies.

Don't let people lie to you with statistics! As you take in information over the course of your day—and we take in more than we realize every day—start to ask yourself: Are they using the mean when they should be using the median?

In summary, the central tendency of a distribution is the one number that best describes that distribution. If the distribution has been transformed into a histogram or frequency polygon, the high point of the distribution usually represents its central tendency. However, distributions are not always evenly balanced on either side of the center point; consequently, the mean (arithmetic average), the median (middle score), and the mode (most frequently occurring score) provide numerical indicators of central tendency. The mean is the most commonly used of the three; however, the median is preferred when the distribution is skewed (lopsided). Substituting the mean when the median should be reported is a common source of public misinformation; recognizing this one distinction will help you become a much keener consumer of statistical information.

⊙ CHECK YOUR LEARNING

2-2 Let's return to the fictional data for 20 students, but this time we'll make them seniors instead of first-year college students; again, each score represents the numbers "nights partying" in one week. The numbers used here are a bit different from the ones presented previously:

1, 0, 1, 2, 5, 3, 2, 3, 1, 3, 1, 7, 2, 3, 2, 2, 2, 0, 4, 6

a. Using the formula, calculate the mean of these scores.

b. If the researcher reported the mean of these scores to the university as an estimate for the whole university population, what symbol would be used for the mean? Why?

c. If the researcher were interested only in the scores of these 20 students, what symbol would be used for the mean? Why?

d. What is the median of these scores?

e. What is the mode of these scores?

f. Are the median and mean similar to or different from each other? What does this tell you about the distribution of scores?

> MEASURES OF VARIABILITY: EVERYONE CAN'T BE TYPICAL

After two years of graduate training in evaluation research, Alex's first consulting job developed by the chance arrival of a plastic bottle on a windy day. She had been helping Professor Jackson prepare for a presentation to the associate directors of higher education, the most powerful higher education committee in the state with representatives from every campus. Unfortunately, Professor Jackson's aging father had twisted his ankle on a plastic bottle that the wind had blown onto his front walk. Obliged to miss the meeting, Dr. Jackson had asked Alex to fill in.

"It's just a five-minute summary of the research on alumni donations that we did together," Dr. Jackson had explained to her. "Hand out the graphs, say a few words, and then answer their questions; nothing to it. Don't be nervous; they're just normal people who happen to have fancy titles."

"Sure," Alex had replied casually, hoping she could match her professor's confidence.

"There are some rules to being part of an effective committee," Professor Jackson had continued. "First of all, be prepared before you get there. You want to accomplish something by being there. Otherwise, why bother showing up? Second, listen carefully. If you know what you want to accomplish, you might be able to get it done informally, during some other agenda item. Third . . . "

"Yes?" Alex had to prompt her.

"I can't think of a third. You'll figure it out. Have fun. Oh, be on the lookout for your next consulting job. Some issue or question will come up during the meeting and you can indicate that you might be able to help them. The associate directors try to make evidence-based policy decisions, and you're the one bringing the evidence."

Statistical evidence is a language that uses words, images, and symbolic notation to communicate complicated observations about human behavior. For example, frequency tables, histograms, and frequency polygons all give us a sense of the center of our data, but they simultaneously describe variability, the spread of a distribution. Along with visual depictions and measures of central tendency, the indicators of variability we learn about next offer new ways to take snapshots that describe the distribution of our data. One way to numerically describe the variability of a distribution is by computing its range. A second way is by computing variance, an idea expressed more usefully as the standard deviation. We need alternative measures of variability partly because, well, people are so very different from one another.

Shyness, for example, can be a self-imposed prison with very little variability because the individual is consistently shy over time and across many different situations. Simply going to a new restaurant may represent a significantly new behavior for extremely shy individuals. Consequently, both the statistical range and the amount of variability may be very restricted in a shy personality. However, other individuals who also are shy most of the time may periodically break out of their shell—and with a vengeance! They might use alcohol to excuse their unusual behavior at the annual company picnic or engage in a secret life that differs dramatically from their customary behavior. Such an individual's personality would also be described as having, on average, very little variability but with a very wide range, because of their periodic outbursts. The range and the two measures of variability—variance and standard deviation—provide statisticians with a way to describe these important individual differences.

Range: From the Lowest to the Highest Score

The range is the easiest measure of variability to calculate. *The **range** is a measure of variability calculated by subtracting the lowest score (the minimum) from the highest score (the maximum).* The range is represented in formula as:

$$\text{range} = X_{highest} - X_{lowest}$$

Maximum and *minimum* are sometimes substituted in this formula to describe the highest and lowest scores, and some statistical computer programs abbreviate these as *max* and *min*.

Here are the scores for the chemistry professors we discussed earlier in the chapter. Each score represents the number of students advised by this professor who went on to obtain top professor jobs.

3, 3, 3, 4, 5, 9, 5, 3, 3, 5, 6, 3, 4, 8, 6, 3, 3, 3, 4, 4, 4, 7, 6, 3, 5, 5, 7, 13, 3, 3, 3, 3, 3, 4, 4, 4, 5, 6, 7, 6, 7, 8, 8, 3, 3, 3, 5, 3, 3, 5, 3, 5, 3, 3

We can determine the highest and lowest scores either by reading through the data or, more easily, by glancing at the frequency table for these data. The highest score is 13 and the lowest is 3. Range $= X_{highest} - X_{lowest} = 13 - 3 = 10$. The range can be a useful initial measure of the variability of our data, but the utility of the range is limited. It is affected by our highest and lowest scores only; it does not take any other data points into account. The other scores could all be very close to the highest score or all huddled near the center. They could also be spread out very evenly or have some other unexpected pattern. If we use only the range, we may miss vital information about our distribution. Whenever possible, it is far more useful to get a sense of how far the typical score differs from the mean.

Variance: The First Step in Calculating Standard Deviation

The word *variance* may be a more intuitive description of its meaning than *standard deviation*. However, both *variance* and *standard deviation* articulate the same idea. They both measure the amount of variability in a distribution. Consequently, they both provide far more information than the range. When something varies, it must vary from, or be different from, something else. That something else is the mean. So, whether we compute variance or standard deviation, the number we arrive at is a number that describes the degree to which a distribution varies with respect to the mean. In practice, the most commonly used measure of variability is the standard deviation. *The **standard deviation** is the typical amount that the scores in a sample vary, or deviate, from the mean.* The standard deviation is so basic and important to the understanding of statistics that it is customarily reported in social science papers at the same time as the mean.

We often ask our students how they might determine the typical amount that scores vary from the mean. They usually suggest that we figure out how far each score falls from the mean and take the average of those. It's a great idea and is definitely a step down the right pathway. But it doesn't work. Let's try it with an example, so we can see its fatal flaw.

Students who seek therapy at university counseling centers often do not attend many sessions. For example, in one study, the median number of therapy sessions was 3 and the mean was 4.6 (Hatchett, 2003). Let's examine the spread of fictional scores for a sample of five students: 1, 2, 4, 4, and 10 numbers of therapy sessions. Taking our students' suggestion, we'll first calculate the mean: 4.2. We'll next subtract the mean from every score. When calculating variability, and many other

Formula: range $= X_{highest} - X_{lowest}$

■ The **range** is a measure of variability calculated by subtracting the lowest score (the minimum) from the highest score (the maximum).

■ The **standard deviation** is the typical amount that the scores in a sample vary, or deviate, from the mean.

■ A **deviation from the mean** is the amount that a score in a sample differs from the mean of the sample; also called *deviation*.

■ **Variance** is the average of the squared deviations from the mean.

statistics, we usually work in columns so that we are sure to make all calculations for every score. As you might expect, we label the column that lists our scores with an X. Here, our second column will include the results we get when we subtract the mean from each score, or $X - M$. We call each of these a ***deviation from the mean*** (or just a *deviation*)—*the amount that a score in a sample differs from the mean of the sample.*

X	$X - M$
1	−3.2
2	−2.2
4	−0.2
4	−0.2
10	5.8

Finally, we'll take the mean of the deviations. Don't forget the signs—negative and positive—when calculating the mean! We get 0. In fact, every time you do this with any data set, the mean will be 0. Are you surprised? Remember, the mean is the point at which all scores are perfectly balanced. Mathematically, the scores *have* to balance out. Yet we know that there *is* variability among these scores. The variability is certainly not 0!

Now let's look at the *right* way to get the typical deviation from the mean. When we ask students for ways to eliminate the negative signs, two suggestions typically come up. (1) Take the absolute value of the deviations, thus making them all positive, or (2) square all the scores, again making them all positive. It turns out that the latter, squaring all the deviations, is how statisticians solve this problem. Once we square our deviations, we can take their average and get a measure of variability, although one that won't look like the typical deviation from the mean. In most cases, it will be much, much bigger. This number, *the average of the squared deviations from the mean, is called the* ***variance***.

Let's calculate variance for our therapy session data. We'll add a third column that will contain the squares of each of the deviations.

X	$X = M$	$(X - M)^2$
1	−3.2	10.24
2	−2.2	4.84
4	−0.2	0.04
4	−0.2	0.04
10	5.8	33.64

Now we can calculate a mean that will not be 0, unless there is no variability whatsoever. In this case, we calculate the mean of the numbers in the third column, the squared deviations. If we sum the squared deviations, we get 48.80. If we divide this sum by N, or 5, we get 9.76. The variance of this sample, therefore, is 9.76. Before we figure out the equation for variance—which, by the way, we didn't actually need here to figure out variance—we want to point out the sum of the squared deviations, 48.80, that we get along the way. *The sum of squared deviations, usually called simply the* ***sum of squares*** *(symbolized as SS), is the sum of the squared deviations from the mean for each score.* The sum of squares shows up frequently in statistics and is a useful ingredient in several types of inferential statistics. We'll see it again.

Symbols: *SS* represents the sum of squares, the sum of squared deviations from the mean.

Back to the formula for variance. Let's think about what we did to calculate it.

1. We subtracted the mean from every score to get the deviations.
2. We squared all the deviations.
3. Then we took the mean of the squared deviations by summing them and dividing by N.

Let's put this in equation form, which will make it look more complicated than it is but will continue to acclimate us to symbolic notation. We need a few new symbols at this point, because variance has several different symbols when it's calculated from a sample, including SD^2, s^2, and MS. The first two symbols come from the words *standard deviation squared*, and the third from the words *mean square* (referring to the average of the squared deviations). We'll use SD^2 at this point, but rest assured that we will alert you when we switch to other symbols for variance later. When variance is calculated from a population, it typically has just one symbol, σ^2 (pronounced "sigma squared"), and is a parameter. As with the mean, Latin letters are used for statistics, which are calculated from samples, and Greek letters are used with parameters, which are calculated from or hypothesized for populations.

We already know all the symbols needed to calculate variance: X to indicate the individual scores, M to indicate the mean, and N to indicate the sample size.

$$SD^2 = \frac{\Sigma(X - M)^2}{N}$$

Again, we don't need the formula. Variance is really just a mean—the mean of squared deviations. But it's good to get used to the ways that statisticians communicate through symbols.

Standard Deviation: Variation from the Mean

The problem with variance is that it's not very easy to understand at a glance. Remember, the numbers of therapy sessions for the five students were 1, 2, 4, 4, and 10, with a mean of 4.2. The typical score does not vary from the mean by 9.76. The variance is based on *squared* deviations, not deviations, and so it is too big. When we ask our students how to solve this problem, they invariably say "unsquare it," and that's just what we do. We take the square root of variance to come up with a much more useful number, the standard deviation. The square root of 9.76 is 3.12, and now we have a number that "makes sense" to us. We can now say that the typical number of therapy sessions for students in this sample is 4.2 and the typical amount a student varies from that is 3.12. As you read journal articles, you often will see the mean and standard deviation reported as ($M = 4.2$, $SD = 3.12$). A glance at our data tells us that these numbers make sense: 4.2 does seem to be approximately in the center, and scores do seem to vary from 4.2 roughly by 3.12. The score of 10 is a bit of an outlier, but not so much that the mean and standard deviation are not somewhat representative of the typical score and typical deviation. Good statisticians *always* ask themselves whether the statistics reported make sense. When the sample is small, we can look at the raw data to confirm that our statistics make sense, but when the sample is large, we will need a frequency table, histogram, or frequency polygon to help us make sense of our data.

Again, we didn't actually need a formula to get the standard deviation. We just took the square root of the variance. But it's useful to start using the language of statisticians. Standard deviation is symbolized with Latin letters when it pertains to a sample and Greek letters when it pertains to a population. Perhaps

■ The **sum of squares**, symbolized as *SS*, is the sum of the squared deviations from the mean for each score.

Symbols: Variance is symbolized by SD^2, s^2, or MS when calculated from a sample and by σ^2 when calculated from or estimated for a population.

Formulas: Variance is calculated using the formula

$$SD^2 = \frac{\Sigma(X - M)^2}{N},$$

where X indicates the sample scores, M indicates the sample mean, and N indicates the number of scores in the sample.

TABLE 2-7. VARIANCE AND STANDARD DEVIATION IN SYMBOLS

The variance or standard deviation of a sample is an example of a statistic, whereas the variance or standard deviation of a population is an example of a parameter. The symbols we use depend on whether we refer to the spread of a sample or a population.

NUMBER	USED FOR	STANDARD DEVIATION SYMBOL	PRONOUNCED	VARIANCE SYMBOL	PRONOUNCED
Statistic	Sample	SD or s	as written	SD^2, s^2, or MS	letters as written; if ^{2}, then followed by "squared" (e.g., "s squared")
Parameter	Population	σ	"sigma"	σ^2	"sigma squared"

Symbols: Standard deviation is represented by SD or s when calculated from a sample and by σ when calculated from a population.

Formulas: Standard deviation can be calculated directly from variance by taking the square root: $SD = \sqrt{SD^2}$, where SD^2 indicates variance. If we don't have variance, standard deviation is calculated:

$$SD = \sqrt{\frac{\Sigma(X - M)^2}{N}}$$

where X indicates the scores in the sample, M indicates the sample mean, and N indicates the sample size.

you guessed the symbols by just taking the square root of those for variance. With a sample, standard deviation is either SD or s. With a population, standard deviation is σ. Table 2-7 presents this information concisely. We can write the formula showing how standard deviation is calculated from variance:

$$SD = \sqrt{SD^2}$$

We also can write the formula showing how standard deviation is calculated from the original Xs, M, and N:

$$SD = \sqrt{\frac{\Sigma(X - M)^2}{N}}$$

In summary, there are several tools that can help us understand the distribution of an individual variable. We can look at it in table or graph form, and we can examine its center and variability. Describing the variability or spread of a distribution increases our understanding of the data. The simplest way to measure variability is the range. The range is calculated by subtracting the lowest score from the highest score. Variance and standard deviation are more precise ways to measure variability. They both measure the degree to which scores in a distribution vary from the mean; the standard deviation is simply the square root of the variance.

⊙ CHECK YOUR LEARNING

2-3 Final exam week is approaching and students are not eating as well as usual. Four students were asked how many calories of junk food they had consumed between noon and 10:00 P.M. on the day before an exam. The estimated numbers of nutritionless calories, calculated with the help of a nutritional software program, were 450, 670, 1130, and 1460.

a. Using the formula, calculate the range for these scores.

b. What information can't you glean from the range?

c. Using the formula, calculate variance for these scores.

d. Using the formula, calculate standard deviation for these scores.

e. If a researcher were interested only in these four students, what symbols would she use for variance and standard deviation, respectively?

f. If another researcher hoped to generalize from these four students to all students at the university, what symbols would he use for variance and standard deviation?

> SHAPES OF DISTRIBUTIONS: APPLYING THE TOOLS OF DESCRIPTIVE STATISTICS

To prepare Alex for her meeting with the associate directors, Professor Jackson emphasized that they were most interested in what they called "financial loyalty." They believed that loyalty to the university was expressed most sincerely with a check; one associate director even asserted that the single best way to evaluate the overall success of an institution was the proportion of alumni who gave money to the university. Before leaving to care for her father, Dr. Jackson had given Alex some additional advice: "Don't interpret the data for them unless they ask. Then keep it very simple. They don't think like researchers, Alex; they think like associate directors. On the other hand, if they say something really stupid, as they sometimes do, don't be afraid to speak up. That's really what they're paying for."

Nevertheless, Alex was nervous as she was introduced to the associate directors at the start of the meeting, as they all took places around a massive conference table. She was last on the agenda, so she quietly reviewed her notes as the meeting progressed. These were powerful people. She put her notes aside only when the committee finally arrived at the item just above hers: tuition increases for the coming year.

"We've got a huge public relations problem," one of the associate directors said. That sober observation quickened the attention of the 15 PhDs around the large conference table. Public relations mattered. "Last month we voted on tuition increases for the 13 campuses around the state. Well, it didn't look right to me, so I recomputed the numbers, and we have an average tuition increase of 13.5% over last year."

"We never would have voted for that!" said the chair of the committee. "Have the newspapers seen this piece of paper? The students would riot!"

The presenting associate director calmly distributed a single sheet of paper that listed every campus, the percentage that tuition had increased at each campus, the number of FTE (full-time-equivalent) students attending each campus, and then the simple calculation that revealed a 13.5% average increase in tuition.

AVERAGE % TUITION INCREASE PER CAMPUS	NUMBER OF FTE STUDENTS PER CAMPUS
Campus 1: 2.2%	8,037
Campus 2: 2.3%	7,241
Campus 3: 2.8%	11,760
Campus 4: 2.8%	13,789
Campus 5: 3.4%	6,452
Campus 6: 3.7%	4,239
Campus 7: 3.7%	12,365
Campus 8: 3.7%	9,452
Campus 9: 4.6%	3,563
Campus 10: 4.8%	4,223
Campus 11: 5.1%	3,335
Campus 12: 47.3%	423
Campus 13: 89.8%	217
Average % increase = 13.55%	

"All I did," said the associate director, "was add up the percentage increases and divide by the 13 colleges and universities in our system."

Alex glanced at the numbers. That's all it took: a glance. There was no problem.

These 15 PhDs weren't looking at the data correctly. Yes, it was true that the average (mean) tuition increase would be 13.55%, but the two outliers made the data lopsided, a skewed distribution. A better, more accurate, way to report the data was that most students would experience a tuition increase of only 3.7% (the mode and the median), a number that was unlikely to trigger any student protests.

"This can't possibly be right," said the chair of the meeting. "Can you help us out, Alex? What are we not understanding from these data?"

Alex took a deep breath. "You've got two outliers skewing a small distribution, you haven't weighted the means by the number of students attending each institution, and you're using an inappropriate measure of central tendency."

The 15 PhDs turned their eyes back to the paper in front of them. The presenting associate director said, "Repeat that, please, and slowly."

Alex continued, "The campuses marked as 12 and 13 are outliers, and they're skewing the distribution." At last, heads were turning to look at the actual data. "The percentage increases on those two campuses are so different that they are pulling the mean of the distribution up. But the mean doesn't represent the central tendency when the distribution is skewed. You're supposed to use the median and that is," she glanced at the paper once again, "only 3.7%. In fact, the median and the mode are both 3.7%. All you have to do is report the median increase in tuition, just like they do on the radio for housing prices."

There was a long, embarrassing silence. Finally, the presenting associate director murmured, "Anything else?"

"Well, actually," said Alex, "your FTEs on those two outlier campuses are very small, but you haven't weighted your calculations by how many students would actually be affected by those large increases in tuition." Once again, heads turned to look at the actual data.

"So, we don't really have a problem, do we?" said the committee chair. "Good. Nice job, Alex. I'm sorry we won't have time to get to your report. Next month, when you come with Professor Jackson, come early so you can stop by my office. Bring your resumé. I need someone who understands what the data are really saying working in my office."

Normal Distributions: The Silent Power Behind Statistics

Alex understood that the data about tuition increases violated what was expected; instead, the data were skewed. Many, but not all, descriptions of individual variables form a bell-shaped, or *normal*, curve. Without campuses 12 and 13, the percentage data about tuition increases would have looked much more like a normal distribution because there were more data points in the middle (around 3.7%) and a balanced difference from the average at the lower end (2.2%) and at the upper end (5.1%). Statisticians use the world *normal* to describe distributions in a very particular way. *A **normal distribution** is a specific frequency distribution in the shape of a bell-shaped, symmetric, unimodal curve.* We will need two new terms to help us describe distributions—*skewness* and *kurtosis*. ***Skewness** describes how much one of the tails of the distribution is pulled away from the center.* ***Kurtosis** describes how flat and wide versus how tall and*

▪ A **normal distribution** is a specific frequency distribution in the shape of a bell-shaped, symmetric, unimodal curve.

▪ **Skewness** describes how much one of the tails of the distribution is pulled away from the center.

▪ **Kurtosis** refers to the degree to which a curve's width and the thickness of its tails deviate from a normal curve—from very tall and skinny with thicker tails to very flat and wide with thinner tails.

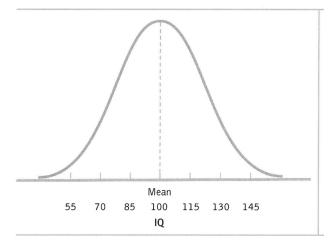

FIGURE 2-11
The Normal Distribution

The normal distribution, shown here for IQ scores, is a frequency distribution that is bell-shaped, symmetrical, and unimodal. It is central to many calculations in statistics.

skinny the distribution is. The shape of the distribution becomes even more important as we begin to use our data to make inferences that extend beyond our sample.

The normal distribution is the silent power behind both descriptive and inferential statistics because it allows us to make discriminations between observations. For example, most teachers aim for something close to a normal distribution as the basis for grading because it discriminates fairly; however, the reality is that distributions of grades are often skewed—mostly high grades, but a few low ones trailing off down toward 0. Descriptive statistics need a normal distribution to discriminate fairly between observations such as student achievement, different drug therapies, and the best baseball players. Inferential statistics also require a normal distribution because if the sample doesn't discriminate in the first place, then we can't trust the inferences based on those samples.

Statistics is a recent innovation, yet it quickly became a part of the decision-making process in public health, social policy, medical interventions, gambling, insurance, astronomy, and many other fields. This power to discriminate among observations is known by many names, including the normal distribution described above—the bell-shaped, symmetrical, unimodal curve like the one shown in Figure 2-11. Most distributions of variables found in nature—whether physical, behavioral, or even attitudinal—are normal distributions. The varied loudness of barking dogs, the varied numbers of fans attending home baseball games across an entire season, and the varied scores from an intelligence test all tend to form a bell-shaped curve. There are fewer scores at values that are farther from the center and even fewer scores at the most extreme values; most scores cluster around the middle, at the top of the bell.

Skewed Distributions: When Our Data Are Not Symmetrical

Reality is not always normally distributed. Consequently, the distributions describing those particular observations are not normally distributed. The technical descriptor for such data is skewed, but a skewed distribution also may be described as lopsided, off-center, or simply nonsymmetrical. Skewed data have an ever-thinning tail in one direction or the other. When a distribution is

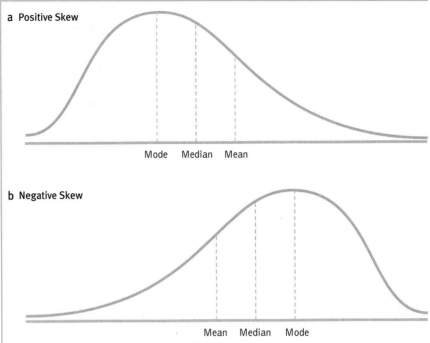

FIGURE 2-12
Two Kinds of Skew

The mnemonic "The tail tells the tale" means that the distribution with the long, thin tail to the right is positively skewed and the distribution with the long, thin tail to the left is negatively skewed.

a Positive Skew

Mode Median Mean

b Negative Skew

Mean Median Mode

positively skewed, as in Figure 2-12a, *the tail of the distribution extends to the right, in a positive direction.* Positive skew sometimes occurs when there is a *floor effect, a situation in which a constraint prevents a variable from taking values below a certain point.* For example, the "chemistry advisor" data, with scores indicating how many former students went on to top jobs, is an example of a positively skewed distribution with a floor effect. The researchers considered only professors who had had at least three former students achieve this level of success, which means that the data were constrained at the lower end of the distribution.

The distribution in Figure 2-12b shows *negatively skewed data*, data that *have a distribution with a tail that extends to the left, in a negative direction.* Not surprisingly, negative skew is sometimes a result of *a ceiling effect, a situation in which a constraint prevents a variable from taking on values above a given number.* If a professor gave an extremely easy quiz, a ceiling effect might result. A number of students would cluster around 100, the highest possible score, with a few stragglers down in the lower end. Some of the students with very high scores might have scored above 100 if the quiz had extra credit, but they were limited by the ceiling of 100.

There is a handy mnemonic you can use to remember the difference between negatively and positively skewed distributions: "the tail tells the tale." Negative scores are to the left, so when the long, thin tail of a distribution is to the left of the distribution's center, we say that it is negatively skewed. When that long, thin tail of the distribution is to the right of the distribution's center, then we say that the distribution is positively skewed. So simply keep in mind that "the tail tells the tale" when you are trying to describe a skewed distribution as either negatively or positively skewed.

■ With **positively skewed** data, the distribution's tail extends to the right, in a positive direction.

■ A **floor effect** is a situation in which a constraint prevents a variable from taking values below a certain point.

■ **Negatively skewed** data have a distribution with a tail that extends to the left, in a negative direction.

■ A **ceiling effect** is a situation in which a constraint prevents a variable from taking on values above a given number.

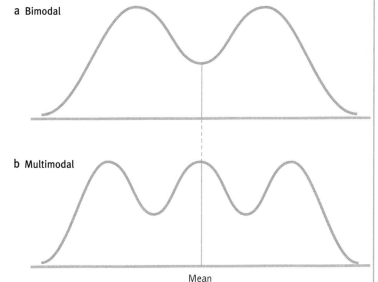

FIGURE 2-13
Distributions with More Than One Mode

A distribution with two "humps" in the data, as in the top figure, is described as being bimodal. One with more than two "humps," as in the bottom figure, is described as being multimodal.

Bimodal and Multimodal Distributions: Identifying Distinctive Populations

In addition to skewness, a distribution can deviate from normality in its number of modes. Distributions with one mode are called unimodal and resemble a single-hump camel. Distributions with two modes are bimodal and look like a double-hump camel. Distributions with more than two modes are multimodal, but nature has not, alas, provided us with an exemplary camel. Let's consider situations best described by bimodal and multimodal distributions.

Bimodal distributions, like that in Figure 2-13a, usually occur when there are two distinct types of individuals within the same data set. For example, if we were to plot men's and women's heights under one curve, the data would produce a distribution with one peak around the mean for women and another peak around the mean for men.

Multimodal distributions, such as that in Figure 2-13b, are those with more than two separate curves in the same distribution. Like bimodal distributions, the peaks don't have to be the same height. If we were recording observations of the emotional state of an individual with bipolar disorder, there likely would be one peak indicating the manic state, one for the depressive state, and one for the stable state between the poles. Multimodal distributions are rare, but it is useful to know that they occur and that statistics can describe them.

Kurtosis and Distributions: Tall and Skinny Versus Short and Wide

Statisticians describe how "skinny" or "fat" a curve is as kurtosis. There are three terms that describe the kurtosis of distributions: *mesokurtic, leptokurtic,* and *platykurtic. A normal distribution is **mesokurtic**. Meso* means "middle," and in a normal distribution, most scores occur in the middle. ***Leptokurtic*** *describes*

■ **Mesokurtic** describes a normal distribution.

■ **Leptokurtic** describes curves that are tall and thin with thicker tails.

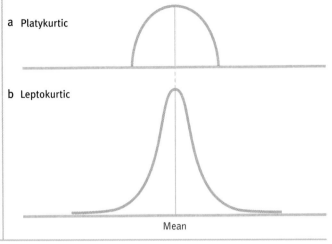

FIGURE 2-14
Kurtosis

These two curves have identical means but very different shapes. The curve on top is a platykurtic, or short and fat, curve with thinner tails, and the one below it is leptokurtic, or very tall and skinny, with thicker tails.

a Platykurtic

b Leptokurtic

Mean

■ **Platykurtic** describes curves that are short and fat with thinner tails.

curves that are tall and thin and have thicker tails. **Platykurtic** *describes curves that are short and fat and have thinner tails.* The two nonnormal distributions are depicted in Figure 2-14. Although leptokurtic and platykurtic curves are frequently described as tall and thin or short and fat, respectively, it is important to remember that the thickness of the tails is an important part of their definition (DeCarlo, 1997). As a memory device, you may want to remember that the "lept" in *leptokurtic* suggests something very tall that you could "leap" off of; the "platy" in *platykurtic* may remind you of pictures of an odd-looking animal called the duck-billed platypus that has an extremely flat, wide nose.

The statistical skills learned by students of the behavioral sciences provide them with two significant career advantages. First, so many other people fear statistics that they tend to believe you must have mysterious intellectual skills if you merely call yourself a statistician. Second, being able to create graphs and present numerical data so that they tell an accurate, meaningful story is a highly useful skill. Both of these advantages come to students in the behavioral sciences who understand the most basic ways of organizing, summarizing, and presenting descriptive statistics about individual variables.

EXPERIENCE IT FOR YOURSELF

LISTEN TO THE STORY STATISTICS TELL

In 10 to 15 years, many of today's college students will be buying homes and sending their own children off to school. The accompanying curves describe the distribution of home prices in different towns. Experience for yourself the stories that these curves tell, and consider what your responses suggest about your own values. You might consider each neighborhood's likely income, architectural diversity, ethnic diversity, values diversity, crime rates, or types of crimes being committed.

Skewness of Distribution of Housing Prices

Negatively Skewed (Town 1)   Positively Skewed (Town 2)

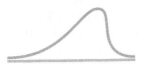   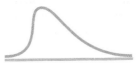

In which town would you want to raise children? Why?

Answer:

Number of Modes in Distribution of Housing Prices

Unimodal (Town 3)   Bimodal (Town 4)   Multimodal (Town 5)

   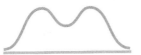   

What can you infer about the school district and the kind of people you would probably meet in each of the high schools in each of these towns?

Answer:

Kurtosis in Distribution of Housing Prices

Leptokurtic (Town 6)   Mesokurtic (Town 7)   Platykurtic (Town 8)

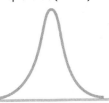   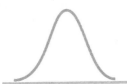   

What opportunities for friendship probably exist in each town? Which towns are towns that you would want to live in?

Answer:

The act of making choices tends to reveal a great deal about our own attitudes and values. Descriptive statistics describe exactly what those choices are.

In summary, the shapes of distributions tell a story about the data; the pervasiveness of the normal distribution is part of the power behind modern applications of statistics. A normal distribution is unimodal, symmetrical, and bell-shaped. A skewed distribution "leans" to either the left or the right; a tail to the left indicates a negative skew, and a tail to the right indicates a positive skew. The three most common causes of skewness are floor effects, ceiling effects, and outliers. Floor and ceiling effects constrain the range of the data. Outliers "pull" the mean of the data toward itself. A unimodal distribution has one mode, a bimodal distribution has two, and a multimodal distribution has three or more. Bimodal and multimodal distributions rarely occur in nature and often indicate the presence of two or more distinctive populations within a single data set. Normal distributions have a mesokurtic shape. Leptokurtic distributions are tall and skinny. Platykurtic distributions are fat and wide. Understanding the shape of a distribution can help you make important decisions such as where you might want to live, pay property taxes, and educate your children.

⊙ CHECK YOUR LEARNING

2-4 Each of the following data sets is followed by a question about its likely shape. Choose the term that is most likely to describe the distribution, and explain your answer. *Note:* Depending on your explanation, in some cases it is possible to provide a rationale for more than one answer.

a. Wait time for a table at a restaurant: normally distributed, positively skewed, or negatively skewed?

b. The time that residents spend on public transportation in a major city such as London: unimodal, bimodal, or multimodal?

c. The income of high school teachers in the Canadian province of Ontario: mesokurtic, platykurtic, or leptokurtic?

■ DIGGING DEEPER INTO THE DATA: ALTERNATE APPROACHES TO DESCRIPTIVE STATISTICS

As researchers discover the power of statistics, they develop more sophisticated techniques that can be applied to unusual circumstances. Many statistical stories are straightforward accounts that describe easily understood data. But some statistical stories require special techniques to draw out the story hiding inside the data. For instance, the interquartile range statistic describes a more precise way to provide a visual presentation of skewed data.

The Interquartile Range: An Alternative to the Range

Describing skewed distributions can be troublesome. Here's why. If you live in a leptokurtic town that has one, and only one, extremely expensive home in it, then the range statistic would tend to be misleading. That one home worth significantly more money than the others would give a misleading impression of the range of real estate prices in your town. With a normal distribution, we could quantify variability by reporting the standard deviation. But the mean is a key ingredient in the calculation of the standard deviation; hence, if the mean is not the appropriate measure of central tendency, then the standard deviation is not the appropriate measure of variability. A good way to remember the meaning of skewness is a bit crude but true: "skewness skews things up." So there are other ways to look at the data.

As we noted earlier in the chapter, the range has a major limitation: it is completely dependent on the maximum and minimum scores. The $17 million home at the high end or the shack in the middle of a wealthy, gated community at the low end of the distribution "skew up" the distribution. Whenever we have severe outliers, the range will be an exaggerated measure of the variability. Fortunately, we have an alternative to the range: the interquartile range.

*The **interquartile range** is a measure of the distance between the first and third quartiles.* As we learned earlier, the median marks the 50th percentile of a data set. Similarly, *the **first quartile** marks the 25th percentile of a data set, and the **third quartile** marks the 75th percentile of a data set.* Essentially, the first and third quartiles are the medians of the two halves of the data—the half below the median and the half above the median. These are calculated in a manner very similar to how we calculate the median. After calculating the median, look at all the scores below the median. The median of these scores, the lower half of the scores, is the first quartile, often called *Q1* for short. Next, look at all of the scores above the median. The median of these scores, the upper half of the scores, is the third quartile, often called *Q3* for short. The interquartile range, often abbreviated as *IQR*, is the difference between these: $IQR = Q3 - Q1$. Because the interquartile range is the distance between the 25th and 75th percentiles of the data, it can be thought of as the range of the middle 50% of the data.

The interquartile range has two important advantages over the range. First, because it is not based on the minimum and maximum—the most extreme scores—it is less susceptible to outliers. Second, we can use the interquartile range to identify outliers in a more formal way than just looking for them on a table or graph. Let's look at an example to see how the interquartile range helps us in both of these ways.

We start by calculating the five-number summary that we see in Figure 2-15. Here are the data from the "chemistry advisors" that we examined earlier in the chapter. You'll recall that the scores are the numbers of students advised by these professors who went on to professorial jobs at the most prestigious universities:

3, 3, 3, 4, 5, 9, 5, 3, 3, 5, 6, 3, 4, 8, 6, 3, 3, 3, 4, 4, 4, 7, 6, 3, 5, 5, 7, 13, 3, 3, 3, 3, 3, 4, 4, 4, 5, 6, 7, 6, 7, 8, 8, 3, 3, 3, 5, 3, 3, 5, 3, 5, 3, 3

To calculate the median of these scores, we must first organize the data so that they are in ascending order:

3, 3, 3, 3, 3, 3, 3, 3, 3, 3, 3, 3, 3, 3, 3, 3, 3, 3, 3, 3, 3, 3, 3, 4, 4, 4, 4, 4, 4, 4, 4, 5, 5, 5, 5, 5, 5, 5, 5, 5, 6, 6, 6, 6, 6, 7, 7, 7, 7, 8, 8, 8, 9, 13

> ▪ The **interquartile range** is the difference between the first and third quartiles of a data set.
> ▪ The **first quartile** marks the 25th percentile of a data set.
> ▪ The **third quartile** marks the 75th percentile of a data set.

Symbols: The interquartile range is abbreviated as *IQR*. The first and third quartiles are abbreviated as *Q1* and *Q3*, respectively.
Formulas: $IQR = Q3 - Q1$

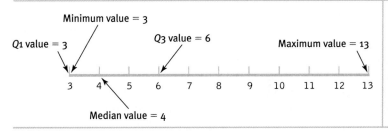

FIGURE 2-15
Five-Number Summary

Just five numbers give a good sense of our overall distribution. These five numbers represent the scores at the 0, 25th, 50th, 75th, and 100th percentiles.

We have 54 scores; if we divide 54 by 2 and add 0.5, we get 27.5. The median, then, is the average of the 27th and 28th scores. These scores are both 4, so the median is 4. We now take the first 27 scores:

3, 3, 3, 3, 3, 3, 3, 3, 3, 3, 3, 3, 3, 3, 3, 3, 3, 3, 3, 3, 3, 3, 3, 4, 4, 4, 4

The median of the 27 scores that comprise the lower half of the data set will be the first quartile, the 25th percentile of our data. There are 27 scores. If we divide 27 by 2, and add 0.5, we get 14. The median of these scores—the first quartile—is the 14th score: 3.

We'll do the same with the top half of the scores:

4, 4, 4, 4, 5, 5, 5, 5, 5, 5, 5, 5, 5, 6, 6, 6, 6, 6, 7, 7, 7, 7, 8, 8, 8, 9, 13

Again, there are 27 scores, and so the median of these scores—the third quartile—is also the 14th score. This time the 14th score is 6. The range is the maximum minus the minimum: range $= X_{highest} - X_{lowest} = 13 - 3 = 10$, whereas the interquartile range is the third quartile minus the first quartile: $IQR = Q3 - Q1 = 6 - 3 = 3$. The whole data set has a width of 10, whereas the middle 50% has a width of 3. The interquartile range is not influenced by the outlier of 13, so it is a more valid measure of variability for these data than is the range. The interquartile range, unlike the range, is resistant to outliers, even if they're far more extreme than 13. Imagine that the top chemistry advisor in this data set trained 55 students who went on to top professorships. The range would increase dramatically ($55 - 3 = 52$), but the interquartile range would be unaffected; it would still be 3.

The second important advantage of the interquartile range is its ability to help us identify potential outliers. Many researchers use the $1.5 \times IQR$ criterion to identify outliers, particularly when the median is the preferred measure of central tendency. If a score is more than $1.5 \times IQR$ below the first quartile or more than $1.5 \times IQR$ above the third quartile, it is considered an outlier. Let's examine the "chemistry advisor" data set to see if we can identify any outliers using this criterion. The IQR that we calculated for the first data set is 3.

$$1.5 \times IQR = 1.5 \times 3 = 4.5$$

The first quartile is 3, and the second quartile is 6. If we subtract 4.5 from 3, we get -1.5. No score is below -1.5 (in fact, it's impossible in this data set), so there is no outlier in the lower half of these data. If we add 4.5 to 6, we get 10.5. One score, 13, is above 10.5, and so that score is very likely to be an outlier. The $1.5 \times IQR$ criterion is useful to confirm what we suspect from tables and graphs.

$$Q1 - (1.5 \times IQR) = 3 - (1.5 \times 3) = 3 - 4.5 = -1.5$$
$$Q3 + (1.5 \times IQR) = 6 + (1.5 \times 3) = 6 + 4.5 = 10.5$$

Statistics That Don't Focus on the Mean: Letting the Distribution Guide Our Choice of Statistics

Researchers sometimes have hypotheses about descriptive statistics other than the mean, including other measures of central tendency, such as the median and mode, and measures of variability, such as variance or standard deviation. The two most common alternatives to hypotheses about the mean are hypotheses about the median and hypotheses about variability. The visual presentation of the data can suggest what features we should be paying attention to.

For example, sometimes the median or mode is a more revealing indicator of central tendency. So, paying attention to the visual presentation of the data can reveal a bimodal or even a multimodal distribution that would probably not

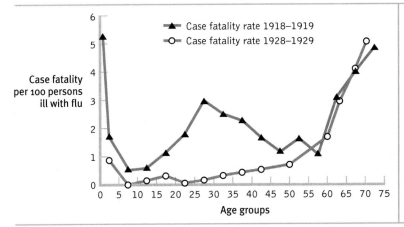

FIGURE 2-16
Skewed Distributions

Skewed distributions can be bi-modal or even multimodal. Using alternative indicators of central tendency and viewing the distribution can reveal patterns in the data that we might not perceive if we used only the mean.

be apparent if we concentrated only on the mean. For example, flu remains a worldwide threat; 50 million people died during the pandemic of 1918–1919, and recent cases of avian flu continue to worry epidemiologists. Taubenberger and Morens (2006) became interested in how we can protect ourselves from a flu pandemic and looked into archival data that described the mortality rates from two previous flu pandemics, one in 1918–1919 and another in 1928–1929. They published a graph, reproduced in Figure 2-16, that described the death rates by age during these two pandemics. They discovered that, for some still unknown reason, the death rate during the 1918–1919 flu included the deaths of many people whose age usually makes them less susceptible to dying from flu. This multimodal distribution would not be apparent if you considered only the mean number of deaths. But looking at the shape of the distribution suggests that researchers should look even more closely at the vulnerabilities of that particular population, because that particular strain of flu caused the death of a disproportionate number of people still in the prime of their life.

Differences among samples' variability might also be tested using the standard deviation or the variance. In certain cases, it might be more interesting to know that the spreads of two samples are different than to know that their central tendencies are different. For example, more boys and men than girls and women have been identified as belonging to two different groups, those with math-related learning disabilities and those identified as mathematically gifted (e.g., Feingold, 1992). In another example, some researchers have tested the effects of alcohol on tipping after restaurant meals (Lynn, 1988; Sanchez, 2002). It is possible that people who are drunk tend to leave very little or a great deal of money compared with sober, and therefore rational, people. It is also possible that the mean amount of money left as a tip might not be very different as a result of alcohol but that the variability of the amount of money is extremely different as a result of alcohol.

As a potential graduate student, there may be instances in which you want to consider the median or variability, rather than the mean, when you compare programs. The median GRE scores, for example, are likely of more interest than the mean scores. The latter are likely skewed by the occasional outlier. Alternately, you may be far more interested in comparing the variability of funding, rather than the average amount of funding, across different graduate programs. For example, your research might indicate that two schools provide the same (mean) level of funding for their PhD programs—say, a guaranteed stipend of around $12,000. However, you might discover that one school is far more variable than the other. Some students get nothing, and others get around $20,000 or more, whereas the other school gives all students the same stipend.

Gender and Math: Comparing Distributions, Not Just Means
Studies suggest that boys' math abilities are more variable than girls'. Boys are more likely to be found among both the top and the bottom scorers in tests of mathematical ability. Had you noticed? The distribution of boys' math ability scores was more platykurtic (more high and more low scores describing a distribution with more variability); the distribution of girls' math ability scores was more leptokurtic (less varied).

This statistical information may influence both your decision to apply and, if accepted, which school you choose to attend. At the very least, it will help you ask sharper questions during your interviews. And these more precise questions are likely to impress professors, who then are more likely to recommend that you receive more money. But you also need to ask yourself whether you want to spend money applying to a school where you're guaranteed a stipend or whether you prefer to take a risk and try for more money, knowing that you might get nothing. (The authors encourage you to apply to both types of schools.) Perhaps you agree with the opening thesis of this chapter: thinking like a statistician is similar to conducting many types of psychological therapy because both statisticians and therapists continually try to ask better, more precise questions.

In summary, the interquartile range represents one distinctive way to tell the story of skewed data. Alternative ways of analyzing data sets include working with extremely skewed data or multimodal data, as well as testing changes in the amount of variability rather than changes in the average. It is always helpful to conduct a visual inspection of the data, so that we can "listen with our eyes" to the story the data tell.

⊙ CHECK YOUR LEARNING

2-5

a. Calculate the interquartile range for the following set of fictional data—numbers of therapy sessions at a university counseling center. Use the IQR × 1.5 rule to determine whether there are potential outliers.

$$2 \quad 5 \quad 1 \quad 3 \quad 3 \quad 4 \quad 3 \quad 6 \quad 7 \quad 1 \quad 4$$
$$3 \quad 7 \quad 2 \quad 2 \quad 2 \quad 8 \quad 3 \quad 3 \quad 12 \quad 1$$

b. A researcher wants to compare the numbers of books in the homes of students from blue-collar families with the numbers of books in the homes of students from white-collar families.
   i. Explain why it might be useful for the researcher to compare medians instead of means.
   ii. Explain why the researcher might want to compare the variabilities of the two samples in addition to their central tendencies.

REVIEW OF CONCEPTS

In this chapter, we learned four general categories of descriptive statistics; we learned to describe and understand the *distribution* of our data through the use of visual depictions, measures of central tendency, measures of variability, and assessments of the shape of the distribution.

> Distributions: Four Ways to Describe Just One Variable

The *raw scores* of our sample can be very difficult to interpret just by glancing at them in their original form. Several techniques help us to understand our data visually. *Frequency tables* are comprised of two columns, one with all possible values and one with a count of how often each value occurs among the scores in the data set. Sometimes a third column includes *cumulative percentages. Grouped frequency tables* allow us to work with more complicated data. Instead of containing values, the first column consists of intervals. We can present larger data sets and those with scores to several decimal places in tabular form more easily when using intervals.

Graphs provide even clearer pictures of our data. *Histograms* display bars of different heights indicating the frequencies of each value that our variable can take on. Bars can be centered on values or on the midpoints of intervals. Similarly, *frequency polygons* show frequencies with dots at different heights depicting the frequencies of each value that our variable can take on. The dots can be above specific values or above the midpoints of intervals. The dots are connected to form a shape.

> Central Tendency: Determining the Typical Score

Three measures of *central tendency* are commonly used in research. The *mean* is the arithmetic average of the data. The *median* is the midpoint of the data set; 50% of scores fall on either side of the median. The *mode* is the most common score in the data set. When there's one mode, the distribution is *unimodal*; when there are two modes, it's *bimodal*; and when there are three or more modes it's *multimodal*. The mean is highly influenced by *outliers*, whereas the median and mode are resistant to outliers. It is important to consider whether outliers are present in our data set when deciding which measure of central tendency to use. Usually, however, the mean is the preferred measure. When reading reports of descriptive statistics in the media, consider whether the writer used the appropriate measure of central tendency for the data.

> Measures of Variability: Everyone Can't Be Typical

The *range* is the simplest measure of variability to calculate; it is often used when the preferred measure of central tendency is the median. It is calculated by subtracting the minimum score in our data set from the maximum score. Variance and standard deviation are much more common measures of variability; they are used when the preferred measure of central tendency is the mean. *Variance* is the average of the squared deviations. It is calculated by subtracting the mean from every score to get *deviations from the mean*, then squaring each of the deviations. *Standard deviation* is the square root of variance; it is the typical amount that a score deviates from the mean. The *sum of squares* of the deviations is used in many inferential statistics.

> Shapes of Distributions: Applying the Tools of Descriptive Statistics

There are a number of terms used to describe the distribution of our data. The easiest distribution to work with is the *normal distribution*, one that is unimodal, symmetric, and bell-shaped. Data can also display *skewness*. A distribution that is *positively skewed* has a tail in a positive direction (to the right), indicating more extreme scores above the center. Positive skew sometimes occurs because there is a *floor effect*, a constraint on the low end below which scores cannot fall. A distribution that is *negatively skewed* has a tail in a negative direction (to the left), indicating more extreme scores below the center. Negative skew sometimes occurs because there is a *ceiling effect*, a constraint on the high end above which scores cannot fall.

There are a number of additional ways to examine our distribution that have an impact on how we describe our data and on the decisions we make about the inferential statistics that we plan to use. For example, *Kurtosis* refers to the degree to which a curve's width and the thickness of its tails deviate from a normal curve. A normal distribution is *mesokurtic*. *Leptokurtic* describes curves that are tall and thin with thicker tails, whereas *platykurtic* describes curves that are short and wide with thinner tails.

▪ Digging Deeper into the Data: Alternate Approaches to Descriptive Statistics

When the median is the preferred measure of central tendency, the *interquartile range* (*IQR*) is a better measure of variability than is the range. The *IQR* is the *third quartile*, or 75th percentile, minus the *first quartile*, or 25th percentile. The *IQR* is the width of the middle 50% of the data set, and, unlike the range, is resistant to outliers. The *IQR* can also be used to determine the presence of outliers. Scores that are $1.5 \times IQR$ below the first quartile (*Q1*) or $1.5 \times IQR$ above the third quartile (*Q3*) are very likely to be outliers.

Finally, the mean is not the only descriptive statistic about which we can develop hypotheses to test with inferential statistics. We might want to estimate the population mean from a sample mean or to compare two means; we might want to estimate the population median from a sample median or to compare two medians; or we might want to estimate a population standard deviation or variance from a sample standard deviation or variance or to compare two samples' variabilities. We are not limited to means when we develop research questions.

SPSS GUIDELINES FOR CHAPTER 2: DESCRIBING INDIVIDUAL VARIABLES

The left hand column in *Data View* is prenumbered, beginning with '1.' Each column to the right of that number contains information about a particular variable; each row below that number represents a unique individual. Notice the choices at the top of the *Data View* screen. Enter some data, then start following the menu by selecting:

Analyze → Descriptive Statistics → Frequencies. Then select the variables you want SPSS to describe, by highlighting them and clicking the arrow in the middle.

To get a numerical description of each variable, select:

Analyze → Descriptive Statistics → Frequencies → Statistics → Mean, Median, Mode, Std. deviation, etc. → Continue → OK.

We will want to visualize each variable by selecting:

Analyze → Descriptive Statistics → Frequencies → Charts → Histograms with normal curve → Continue → OK.

With all of the SPSS functions, an output screen will automatically appear after we click on OK.

EXERCISES

2.1 Frequencies and the National Survey of Student Engagement (NSSE):
The National Survey of Student Engagement (NSSE) surveys freshmen and seniors about
their levels of engagement in campus and classroom activities that enhance learning. More
than 400,000 students at about 730 schools have completed surveys since 1999, the first
year that the NSSE was administered. Among the many questions on the NSSE, students
were asked how often they were assigned a paper of 20 pages or more during the academic
year. For a sample of 19 institutions classified as national universities—the 19 that made
their data publicly available through the *U.S. News & World Report* Web site—here are the
percentages of students who said they were assigned between 5 and 10 20-page papers:

0	5	3	3	1	10	2
2	3	1	2	4	2	1
1	1	4	3	5		

a. Create a frequency table for these data. Include third and fourth columns for percentages and cumulative percentages, respectively.

b. For what percentage of these schools did exactly 4% of their students report that
they wrote between 5 and 10 20-page papers that year?

c. For what percentage of schools did 4% *or fewer* students report that they wrote between 5 and 10 20-page papers that year?

d. Is this a random sample? Explain your answer.

2.2 Grouped frequency tables and alumni donations: The associate directors
for whom Alex was consulting were interested in alumni donations, as are many schools,
not only because they want the money but also because it is one of the criteria by which
U.S. News & World Report ranks U.S. institutions of higher learning. *U.S. News* includes
this criterion because higher rates of alumni giving are seen as indicative of the satisfaction of former students with their education. An increase in a school's overall ranking
by this magazine has been demonstrated to translate into an increase in applications—
and all schools want that—even though there is controversy about the validity of these
rankings. One set of rankings is for the best national universities: institutions that offer
undergraduate, master's, and doctoral degrees and have an emphasis on research.
(Harvard tops the list that was published in 2005.) Here are the alumni giving rates that
were reported in 2005; the rates are the percentages of alumni who donated to each of
the top 70 national universities in the year prior to publication of these data.

48	61	45	39	46	37	38	34	33	47
29	38	38	34	29	29	36	48	27	25
15	25	14	26	33	16	33	32	25	34
26	32	11	15	25	9	25	40	12	20
32	10	24	9	16	21	12	14	18	20
18	25	18	20	23	9	16	17	19	15
14	18	16	17	20	24	25	11	16	13

a. How was the variable of alumni giving operationalized? What is another way that
this variable could be operationalized?

b. Create a grouped frequency table for these data.

c. The data have quite a range, with the lowest scores belonging to Boston University, the University of California at Irvine, and the University of California at San Diego, and the highest belonging to Princeton University. What research hypotheses come to mind when you examine these data? State at least one research question that these data suggest to you.

2.3 Grouped histogram and frequency polygon: See the *U.S. News & World Report* data in Exercise 2.2.

a. Create a grouped histogram for these data. Be careful when determining the midpoints of your intervals!

b. Create a frequency polygon for these data.

c. Examine these graphs and give a brief description of the distribution. Are there outliers? Are the data skewed, and, if so, in what direction? What do the graphs indicate about the center of the distribution? How many modes do there appear to be?

2.4 Central tendency and baseball: Go to the Web site http://baseball-statistics.com/Greats/ and click on the "P" for pitcher on the picture of the baseball field. Scroll down to the first table—the one with Pedro Martinez's name on top. This table provides pitching stats for 11 players with the best four-year pitching performance. The third column of numbers to the right of the names is titled "Pct." and lists the percentage of games won by each pitcher.

a. List the 11 scores for this sample.

b. What is the mean of these scores?

c. What is the median of these scores?

d. Compare the mean and median. Does the difference between them suggest that the data are skewed very much?

e. This Web site determined the best pitcher in several different ways. In other words, it used several different operational definitions. The first table we examined here was based on the best four-year stretches; that is, the pitchers who had the best four years in a row at anytime in their careers. "Best pitcher" was also operationally defined in other ways. State at least one other way in which "best pitcher" was operationally defined. *Hint:* Look at the descriptions of the second and third tables.

f. According to this Web site, what is one confound that might have affected a pitcher's numbers? *Hint:* See the paragraph below the second table (the one headed by Greg Maddux).

(For you baseball fans, this is a great Web site to explore both to be entertained and to develop research hypotheses.)

2.5 Central tendency and alumni donations: Here are the *U.S. News & World Report* data again on alumni giving at the top 70 national universities.

48	61	45	39	46	37	38	34	33	47
29	38	38	34	29	29	36	48	27	25
15	25	14	26	33	16	33	32	25	34
26	32	11	15	25	9	25	40	12	20
32	10	24	9	16	21	12	14	18	20
18	25	18	20	23	9	16	17	19	15
14	18	16	17	20	24	25	11	16	13

a. Calculate the mean of these data, showing that you know how to use the symbols and formula.

b. Determine the median of these data.

2.6 What's better—median or mean?: Briefly describe a real-life situation in which the median is preferable to the mean. Give hypothetical numbers for mean and median in your explanation. Be original! (That is, don't use home prices or another example from the chapter.)

2.7 Central tendency and the business of weight loss: Find an advertisement for a weight-loss product either online or in the print media—the more unbelievable the claims, the better! It could be a drug, a book, or a program.

a. What does the ad promise that this product will do for the consumer?

b. What data does it offer for its promised benefits? Does it offer any descriptive statistics or merely testimonials? If it offers descriptive statistics, what are the limitations of what they report?

c. If you were considering this product, what measures of central tendency would you most like to see? Explain your answer, noting why not all measures of central tendency would be helpful.

d. If a friend with no statistical background were considering this product, what would you tell him or her?

2.8 The range and NSSE: The National Survey of Student Engagement (NSSE) asked students how often they asked questions in class or participated in classroom discussions. The options were "never," "sometimes," "often," and "very often." Here are the percentages, reported in 2005, of students who responded "very often" for the 31 institutions classified as liberal arts colleges that allowed their 2004 data to become public through the *U.S. News & World Report* Web site.

58	45	53	45	65	41	50	46	54
59	52	60	59	62	54	52	53	54
83	60	32	62	50	50	43	32	53
60	52	55	53					

a. What is the range of these data?

b. The top college is Marlboro College in Vermont, and the two tied for lowest are Randolph-Macon Women's College in Virginia and Texas A&M University in Galveston. What research questions do these data suggest to you? State at least one research question generated by these data.

2.9 Variance, standard deviation, and NSSE: Here again are the data from the National Survey of Student Engagement (NSSE) for a sample of 19 national universities, as reported in 2005. These are the percentages of students who said they were assigned between 5 and 10 20-page long papers.

0	5	3	3	1	10	2
2	3	1	2	4	2	1
1	1	4	3	5		

a. Calculate the mean of these data using the symbols and formula.

b. Calculate the variance of these data using the symbols and formula, but also using columns to show all calculations.

c. Calculate the standard deviation using the symbols and formula.

d. In your own words, describe what the mean and standard deviation of these data tell us about these scores.

2.10 Parameter versus statistic: For each of the following situations, state whether the mean would be a statistic or a parameter. Explain your answer.

a. According to 1991 Canadian census data, the mean income (from employment only) of French-speaking Canadians living in Ontario was $29,527, higher than the general population mean of $28,838.

b. In the 2004–2005 National Basketball Association season, the 30 teams won a mean 41.00 games.

c. The General Social Survey (GSS; see Exercise 2.14 for details) included a vocabulary test in which participants were given a series of words and were asked to choose the appropriate synonym from a multiple-choice list of five words (e.g., *beast* with the choices *afraid, words, large, animal,* and *separate*). The mean vocabulary test score was 5.98.

d. The National Survey of Student Engagement (NSSE) asked students at participating institutions how often they discussed ideas or readings with their professors outside of class. Among the 19 national universities that made their data public, the mean percentage of students who responded "very often" was 8%.

2.11 Mean, median, and the shape of distributions: Consider the many possible distributions of grades on a quiz in a statistics class; imagine that the grades could range from 0 to 100. For each of the following situations, give a hypothetical mean and median (that is, make up a mean and a median that might occur with a distribution that has this shape). Explain your answer.

a. Normal distribution

b. Positively skewed distribution

c. Negatively skewed distribution

2.12 Shape of distributions: Consider these three variables: finishing times in a marathon, number of university dining hall meals eaten in a semester on a three-meal-a-day plan, and scores on a scale of extroversion.

a. Which of these variables is mostly likely to have a normal distribution? Explain your answer.

b. Which of these variables is mostly likely to have a positively skewed distribution? Explain your answer, stating the possible contribution of a floor effect.

c. Which of these variables is mostly likely to have a negatively skewed distribution? Explain your answer, stating the possible contribution of a ceiling effect.

2.13 Number of modes: For each of the following distributions, state whether it's more likely to be unimodal or bimodal. Explain your answer.

a. Age of patients in a hospital maternity ward

b. Depression scores on a Beck Depression Inventory

c. GRE scores of applicants to sociology graduate programs

d. The cost of an AIDS drug that is sold in first world countries in Europe, as well as in third world countries in Africa.

2.14 Understanding your distribution—the General Social Survey (GSS): Since 1972, the National Opinion Research Center has interviewed approximately

2000 adults a year (almost every year). In that time, more than 38,000 people have answered more than 3000 different questions related to their opinions, attitudes, and behaviors. The GSS is meant to be analyzed by people like us—anyone with an Internet connection and an interest in social science data. Go to the GSS Web site at www.icpsr.umich.edu/GSS/. During several years of the GSS, participants were asked how many hours per day they watched television. The latest year in which this question was asked is 1998. Near the top of the GSS Web site, click "Analyze," then click the circle for "Frequencies or crosstabluation" and click "Start." Enter TVHOURS in the space next to "Row," and YEAR(1998) in the space next to "Selection Filter(s)." At the bottom of that page, under "Table Options" click the box next to "Statistics" and then click the button that says "Run the Table." (In the questions below, when asked to use a symbol, the answer would look something like this: $X = 5$. But you, of course, would use the appropriate symbol for the question!) [*Note:* you may have to select the "classic interface" if the GSS Web site does not appear as described.]

a. The frequency table, titled "Frequency Distribution," is similar to the frequency tables presented in this chapter with a couple of exceptions: the lowest value is on the top in the left-hand column, and the percentages are in bold above the frequencies in the right-hand column. What is the total number of people in this sample? Report this using the symbol for the number of people in a sample.

b. How many of the respondents reported that they watched TV four hours a day? What percentage of respondents reported that they watched TV four hours a day? Calculate the cumulative percentage for this response. That is, what percentage of respondents said they watched TV four hours or less per day?

c. Look at the box below the frequency table that is titled "Summary Statistics." Using the symbols for statistics where appropriate, report all three measures of central tendency: mean, median, and mode.

d. Do these data seem to be affected by an outlier or outliers? Would the mean or the median be a better measure of central tendency for these data? Explain your answer.

e. What is the range for these data? What does this range indicate about the responses to this question?

f. Using the symbols for samples, report the variance and standard deviation.

g. Write a one- to two-paragraph summary describing the distribution of these data. Mention center, variability, and shape. Be sure to discuss the number of modes (i.e., unimodal, bimodal, multimodal) and the presence and direction of any skew.

h. State one research question that might arise from this data set.

(If you want to "play" with this data set, you can get a full list of the variables that have been asked over the years. On the left side of the screen, click on the word "Subject" under the heading "Codebook Indexes" to find all the topics about which questions were asked.)

2.15 Understanding your distribution—wins in the NBA: Here are the numbers of wins for the 30 NBA teams for the 2004–2005 NBA season.

45	43	42	33	33	54	47	44	42	30
59	45	36	18	13	52	49	44	27	26
62	50	37	34	34	59	58	51	45	18

a. Create a grouped frequency table for these data.

b. Create a histogram based on the grouped frequency table.

c. Determine the mean, median, and mode of these data. Use symbols and the formula when showing your calculation of the mean.

d. Using software, calculate the range and standard deviation of these data.

e. Write a one- to two-paragraph summary describing the distribution of these data. Mention center, variability, and shape. Be sure to discuss the number of modes (i.e., unimodal, bimodal, multimodal), any possible outliers, and the presence and direction of any skew.

f. State one research question that might arise from this data set.

2.16 The language of statistics—*distribution*: In your own words, define the word *distribution* first as you would use it in everyday conversation and then as a statistician would use it.

2.17 The language of statistics—*interval*: Describe two ways that statisticians might use the word *interval*.

2.18 The symbols of statistics: Find the incorrectly used symbol or symbols in each of the following statements or formulas. For each statement or formula, (i) state which symbol(s) is/are used incorrectly, (ii) explain why the symbol(s) in the original statement is/are incorrect, and (iii) state what symbol(s) *should* be used.

a. The mean and standard deviation of the sample of reaction times were calculated ($m = 54.2$, $SD^2 = 9.87$).

b. The mean of the sample of high school student GPAs was $\mu = 3.08$.

c. range $= X_{highest} - X_{lowest}$

d. $\sigma = \sqrt{\dfrac{\Sigma(X - M)^2}{N}}$

2.19 Kurtosis, platykurtic, leptokurtic, and mesokurtic: Draw three graphs that describe three possible distributions (platykurtic, leptokurtic, mesokurtic) of the grade point average (GPA) for behavioral science majors at graduation. The horizontal axis will represent GPA and the vertical axis will represent the frequencies of those scores. Which distribution do you think will describe the distribution of GPA for behavioral science majors in your graduating class? Why do you anticipate such a distribution? Where do you stand in comparison with others in your graduating class?

▪ DIGGING DEEPER INTO THE DATA: EXERCISES

2.20 Interquartile range and resistance to outliers: Once again, here are the data on alumni giving rates at the top national universities.

48	61	45	39	46	37	38	34	33	47
29	38	38	34	29	29	36	48	27	25
15	25	14	26	33	16	33	32	25	34
26	32	11	15	25	9	25	40	12	20
32	10	24	9	16	21	12	14	18	20
18	25	18	20	23	9	16	17	19	15
14	18	16	17	20	24	25	11	16	13

a. What is *Q1* for these data?

b. What is *Q3* for these data?

c. Calculate the interquartile range.

d. Why is the *IQR* a better measure of variability for these data than the range? How could the range be a misleading indicator of spread for these data?

2.21 Interquartile range and determination of outliers: See the data in Exercise 2.20. According to the *IQR* × 1.5 criterion, are there any outliers? Show your calculations.

2.22 SAT/ACT scores: *U.S. News & World Report* provides the 25th through 75th percentiles of SAT/ACT scores for the institutions in its lists of best colleges and universities. A friend is interested in Spelman College in Georgia and reads that the 25th through 75th percentiles of SAT scores there is 990–1160.

a. In your own words, explain to your friend what this means.

b. Using the language of statistics and the interquartile range, explain how this was calculated.

c. Why does *U.S News & World Report* provide the interquartile range, not the range? Give a hypothetical example of a case where the range would lead to misleading information about the overall spread of SAT scores for a school.

2.23 Inferential statistics and variance: Provide an original, real-life example of a situation in which it might be preferable to compare variances as opposed to means.

TERMS

raw scores (p. 42)
distribution (p. 42)
frequency table (p. 42)
cumulative percentage (p. 44)
grouped frequency table (p. 46)
histogram (p. 49)
frequency polygon (p. 51)
central tendency (p. 55)
mean (p. 56)
statistics (p. 56)
parameters (p. 58)
median (p. 58)

mode (p. 58)
unimodal (p. 60)
bimodal (p. 60)
multimodal (p. 60)
outlier (p. 62)
range (p. 67)
standard deviation (p. 67)
deviation from the mean (p. 68)
variance (p. 68)
sum of squares (p. 69)
normal distribution (p. 72)
skewness (p. 72)
kurtosis (p. 72)

positively skewed data (p. 74)
floor effect (p. 74)
negatively skewed data (p. 74)
ceiling effect (p. 74)
mesokurtic (p. 75)
leptokurtic (p. 75)
platykurtic (p. 76)
interquartile range (p. 79)
first quartile (p. 79)
third quartile (p. 79)

SYMBOLS

X
M
$\overline{X}$
μ
N
mdn

SS
SD^2
s^2
MS
σ^2
SD

s
σ
IQR
$Q1$
$Q3$

FORMULAS

$$M = \frac{\Sigma X}{N}$$

$$SD^2 = \frac{\Sigma(X - M)^2}{N}$$

$$SD = \sqrt{\frac{\Sigma(X - M)^2}{N}}$$

$$\text{range} = X_{highest} - X_{lowest}$$

$$SD = \sqrt{SD^2}$$

$$IQR = Q3 - Q1$$

CHAPTER THREE

VISUAL DISPLAYS OF DATA
GRAPHS THAT TELL A STORY

The "I am here" message arrived from Mars at 11:29 P.M. on January 3, 2005, and it immediately touched off a joyous celebration. Thousands of tiny, statistically based decisions had come together to create this moment of sweet scientific success. The very last decision was to open the parachutes earlier than planned. The spacecraft needed more time to slow down because a Martian dust storm had heated and thinned the atmosphere. It was a complicated, statistically reasoned decision that balanced one set of risks (e.g., the speed of descent, survival of the spacecraft) against another (e.g., hitting their landing target, a parachute malfunction) while staying within the estimated margins of error for each. But chance was kind to NASA's historic mission to Mars, and a stream of data began to pour in to the computers at the Jet Propulsion Laboratory in Pasadena, California.

Unfortunately, NASA had not always been so lucky, especially with the space shuttle program. One of the first images captured by the camera onboard the Mars rover *Spirit* was a memorial to the seven *Columbia* astronauts who had died on February 1, 2003. A piece of foam had knocked loose a thermal tile during the *Columbia* launch. That small opening on *Columbia*'s left wing allowed heat to penetrate and destroy the space shuttle during its attempted reentry to Earth's atmosphere. It wasn't the first shuttle catastrophe. The *Challenger*'s seven astronauts had died on January 28, 1986. A tiny gap in the giant O-rings that separated sections of the right-side booster rocket had started leaking during launch. Cameras later revealed that puffs of black smoke were visible on the launchpad. That O-ring leak expanded to a flame that exploded the fuel-laden shuttle 73 seconds after launch as it tried to leave Earth's atmosphere. Something had gone horribly wrong, twice.

Scientists Celebrate a Successful Landing on Mars
Thousands of statistically based decisions helped make the historic Mars landing a success. The joy of discovery and profound technological achievement among scientists from NASA and the Jet Propulsion Laboratory was tempered by the sadness about lives lost as part of the space shuttle program.

AP Photo/Damian Dovarganes /Pool

Behavioral scientists addressed two distinctive needs after the *Challenger* disaster. The first publications focused on individual psychological consequences of the disaster, such as survivor guilt, reactions of schoolchildren who witnessed the event, and the ways in which memory would manage so impressive an event. Later articles, however, searched for organizational causes of the disastrous decision to launch *Challenger* on that cold Tuesday morning. Clinical psychologists put their efforts into meeting immediate needs; organizational psychologists and communications experts put their efforts into understanding the causes of the tragedy in the first place. Researchers described NASA's decision-making process as the product of groupthink, masculine management styles, and an organizational culture that ignored danger signals. In retrospect, one particular danger signal had appeared the night before the launch and seems to have been a symptom of NASA's many dysfunctional elements: a poorly drawn graph.

In this chapter, we'll explore the ways in which visual displays of data may be used both positively and negatively, to reveal but also to conceal, to clarify complicated data but also to complicate clear relations between variables out of an apparent desire to mislead. You will be a very sophisticated consumer of visual displays of data by the end of this chapter. You will know how to lie with statistics, how to recognize when others are lying to you with statistics, and what questions to ask to find out if people are snowing you with meaningless mathematical details. In the process, we will introduce the most common types of graphs, their strengths and weaknesses, when they should be used, and the guidelines that will enable you to construct a visual display of data in the most straightforward manner possible. Finally, we'll emphasize the importance of graphing literacy, both to recognize the lies that others sometimes tell with graphs, but also to be ready for the sometimes spectacular advances regarding visual displays of data.

> USES OF GRAPHS: CLARIFYING DANGER, EXPOSING LIES, AND GAINING INSIGHT

The purpose of a graph is to reveal and clarify relations between variables. But as the *Challenger* story unfolds across this chapter, you will understand that sometimes a graph can reveal more about the person(s) creating the graph than it does about the data set. At the most obvious level, the content of graphs suggests what we are most interested in, the kind of job that we have. But the graphmaker's many small choices also suggest whether he or she is more prone to truth-telling or to lying, to respecting the data or to biasing it. Sensible guidelines from the American Psychological Association (APA) inform the construction of graphs, yet the graphmaker's many small choices also tell a story that may be just as important as the story emerging from the data set. The story behind the creation of graphs leads directly to the story of the explosion of *Challenger*. So, this section first demonstrates why graphing has become a critical skill and then gleans the lessons learned from what have been called the worst and the best graphs ever created.

Graphing in the Information Age: A Critical Skill

Graphic literacy is a survival skill in our information age, even if it is only to recognize when someone is using a graph to mislead us. Graphs can reveal previously hidden information, persuade others to change their beliefs or behavior, and provoke the viewer to ask new and better questions. Cohen (1990), an active proponent of the use of graphs, even says that "we sometimes learn more from what we see than from what we compute" (p. 1305). This is why students who learn how to visually display information enjoy diverse opportunities for influence. For example, graphs now routinely appear in congressional debates to persuade both legislators and their constituents, in news articles to inform and motivate the public by exposing the depth of financial corruption in corporations, and in corporate meetings to clarify complex decision making. For each of these public presentations of data, there is a congressional staffer, an enterprising journalist, or a perceptive researcher creating the visual display of critical information. Visual displays of data are powerful, and the people who create those visual displays wield much of that power.

More immediately relevant for many of you, the Educational Testing Service (ETS) has considered revamping the Graduate Record Exam (GRE), the test required for most graduate school applications. ETS has discussed revising the quantitative reasoning section of the revised GRE so that it emphasizes geometry much less than in the past and emphasizes the interpretation of tables and graphs much more. This means that strong graphing skills may soon directly strengthen your graduate school application.

Students in the behavioral sciences are particularly well equipped to work with graphs because they learn to be skeptics; they have been trained not to overinterpret data just because they look good on a graph or sound good when expressed by a persuasive speaker. Graphic literacy is a critical thinking skill, but it is not a new skill and it certainly doesn't rely on computers. The engineers who sent their graphs to NASA the night before the *Challenger* was launched didn't need fancier graphs; they needed to think more clearly and then develop graphs to reflect that thinking. They needed to create clearer graphs to persuade others more effectively. Specifically, they needed to apply what they (hopefully) had been taught in a statistics class—to separate independent variables from extraneous, confounding variables to determine exactly what is influencing the dependent variable. A clearly conceived, hand-drawn graph on the back of an envelope could have clarified the effect of cold temperatures on O-rings more persuasively than a computer-generated, PowerPoint presentation with multicolored, bouncy graphics.

"The Most Misleading Graph Ever Published": The Cost and Quality of Higher Education

Learning how to lie with graphs empowers you to spot those lies for yourself. We are indebted to Michael Friendly of York University for collecting and managing a Web site (Friendly, 2000) that humorously demonstrates the power of graphs both to deceive and to enlighten. Figure 3-1 was awarded the title of "the worst graph ever published."

FIGURE 3-1
Graphs That Lie

Michael Friendly describes this graph as a "spectacular example of more graphical sins than I have ever seen in one image" and possibly "the most misleading graph ever published."

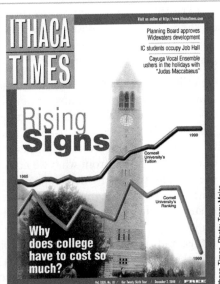

Ithaca Times, Photo: Tracy Meier

EXPERIENCE IT FOR YOURSELF

LYING WITH GRAPHS

Before reading any further, look at Figure 3-1 and then write a short sentence about what the graph seems to communicate about the relation between the two variables of (1) cost of higher education and (2) quality of higher education at Cornell University. This exercise is a setup, but go ahead and fall for it. The exercise teaches you how to lie with a graph and how to become fairly sophisticated in your lying. Anybody can lie, but communicating a complicated reality requires skill. These exercises will teach you how to do both.

At first glance, this graph appears to convey that _____
_____ .

There are at least four lies in this single graph. Some of them are fairly subtle white lies that simply leave a false impression. Try to identify some of those lies before you read about them:

Lie 1: _____

Lie 2: _____

Lie 3: _____

Lie 4: _____

This graph from the *Ithaca Times* is brilliant in its ability to deceive. At a glance, it would seem to tell a story of increasing cost and decreasing quality; the line representing tuition goes up and the line representing Cornell University's ranking goes down. It even feels vaguely scientific simply because it is a graph. But let's examine the variety of deceptions in this graph, continuing with other first impressions. Notice that the graph superimposes statistical information on a picture that is emblematic of the local Cornell University campus, so the underlying message of the graph gains credibility by being associated with this prestigious university, even though the grim message is that Cornell University students have been paying more and more money while receiving a progressively inferior education.

The graph purports to answer the headlined question: "Why does college have to cost so much?" That rising line represents rising tuition costs, as measured by the share of a student's family's median income, over 35 years. Now look for the timeline that corresponds to the plummeting lower line. Can you find it? The apparently falling line represents the ranking of Cornell University over only *11 years*—but the graph does not clearly convey that critical information. You would have no way of knowing that information, but the key is that the graph indicates nothing at all. The absence of critical information is a red flag.

Lie 1: The graph treats unequal scales as if they were equal. This lie uses identical distances (almost the width of the magazine cover) to represent very different time frames (11 years versus 35 years).

Lie 2: The graph unites incompatible scales. This lie compares an interval scale (tuition as a proportion of income) to an ordinal scale (university rank). The two scales are incompatible, yet they are treated as if they were the same. This lie also helps to set up and anticipate the next lie.

Lie 3: The graph uses misleading starting points for incompatible scales. This lie arbitrarily begins the line representing quality of education (Cornell's rank compared to other institutions) lower than the line representing tuition costs, suggesting that an institution already failing to deliver what students are paying for has, over the last either 11 or 35 years (!), become dramatically worse. There is no reason except deception to start one line higher or lower than the other. The scales are not comparable and should not even be placed in the same graph.

Lie 4: The graph *reverses* the implied meaning of up and down. This is breathtaking! It must be the best (worst) of all the lies in this graph because the impression it leaves contradicts the data. Cornell University's ranking did indeed change over this 11-year period. It *improved* from 15th place nationally to 6th place! Cornell's ranking didn't get worse; it got better! Then why does the line representing Cornell's ranking go down? Is it an outright lie? No. This astonishing graphic lie simply reversed the direction of the numbers from what makes the most sense. In the business of rankings, a low number is good, but the graphmaker made sure that the good information was portrayed by a line going down. As in Alice's Wonderland, down is good and up is down!

If this graph were true to its data, the line representing quality of education as measured by rank order compared to other universities should be rising rather impressively, from 15th place to 6th place. Yet this line for quality of education portrays Cornell's considerable stature as falling dramatically! Taken at face value, the headline and the graph tell an alarming story that would probably inspire feelings of outrage that would be likely to sell more newspapers, especially in Ithaca. As we noted at the beginning of this chapter, sometimes a graph suggests more about the person creating the graph than it reveals about the data set. Our guess is that the creator of this cover believed a dramatic, negative story would increase sales.

"The Best Statistical Graph Ever Created": Napoleon's Disastrous March to Moscow

What may be the best statistical graph ever drawn tells a horrifying story. This graph, created by the French engineer Charles Minard, and shown in Figure 3-2, stirs the imagination by telling a story of immense tragedy and human foolishness: Napoleon's ill-fated 1812 Russian campaign to Moscow—and back. The size of Napoleon's army is represented by the bandwidth as it traveled between June and December of 1812. A common estimate of Napoleon's army in June of 1812 is 600,000 men and perhaps 50,000 horses. The thin black line at the end of this journey represents the approximately 10,000 remaining men who returned in the frigid December of that same year. Napoleon's army averaged losses of approximately 3000 men *every single day* for six months! The simple inclusion of temperature data helps the viewer understand why the Russian winter all but finished off the depleted army during its return trip. This single picture tells the story of a monumental six-month disaster—and implies the human suffering through a simple but horrifying statistical graph. This graph is so effective that Michael Friendly issued a good-natured challenge for modern visualizers of data to improve upon it. The resulting collection of graphs may be found through York University (http://www.math.yorku.ca/SCS/Gallery/re-minard.html), as well as through an interactive graph supplied by James Rubarth-Lay (1997) of the University of Texas that pulls the viewer into a time-warped historical experience through links positioned on Minard's graph (http://uts.cc.utexas.edu/~jrubarth/gslis/lis385t.16/Napoleon/).

FIGURE 3-2
Graphs That Illuminate

Described as "the best statistical graph ever drawn," this graph created by French engineer Charles Minard in 1813 tells a dramatic, complicated story with horrifying clarity, using just a single picture.

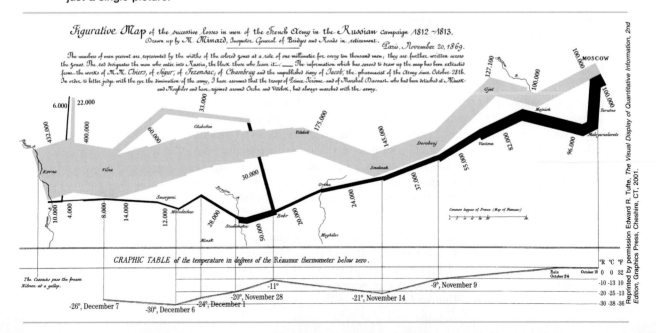

In summary, our own personalities, values, and life experiences play a role in what we choose to research, which findings we choose to report, and how we choose to portray them. In our information age, summary tools such as graphs are essential to the communication of new discoveries and ideas. Such tools can be used to deceive, both blatantly and subtly, as well as to clarify, both succinctly and insightfully.

⊙ CHECK YOUR LEARNING

3-1 Which of the accompanying two graphs is misleading? Which seems to be an accurate depiction of the data? Explain your answer.

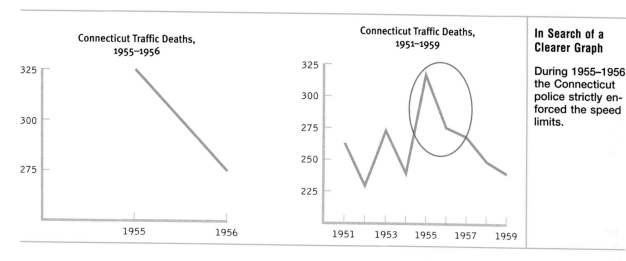

In Search of a Clearer Graph

During 1955–1956 the Connecticut police strictly enforced the speed limits.

> COMMON TYPES OF GRAPHS: A GRAPH DESIGNER'S BUILDING BLOCKS

The story told by a well-constructed graph begins with raw data. It is the responsibility of the researcher to organize that information in any way that allows the data to speak most clearly. The following is a transcript of the disastrous *Challenger* launch. (T = time, in seconds)

T + 0.000   Solid rocket ignition command is sent. Astronaut Judy Resnik, intercom: "Aaall Riight!"

T + 0.008   First of eight 25-inch-long, 7-inch-wide exploding bolts fire, four at the base of each booster, freeing *Challenger* from launch pad.

T + 0.678   Film developed later shows the first evidence of abnormal black smoke appearing slightly above the suspect O-ring joint in *Challenger*'s right-hand solid rocket booster. . . .

T + 1.000   Shuttle pilot Michael Smith, intercom: "Here we go." . . .

T + 3.375   Last positive visual indication of smoke swirling under the bottom of the external fuel tank. Launch commentator Hugh Harris, NASA-SELECT television: " . . . Liftoff of the 25th space shuttle mission, and it has cleared the tower." . . .

T + 5.674   Internal pressure in the right-side booster is recorded as 11.8 pounds per square inch higher than normal. . . .

T + 8.000   Shuttle commander Dick Scobee, air-to-ground: "Houston, *Challenger*, Roll program."

T + 10.00   Greene: "Rog, good roll."

T + 11.000   Smith, intercom: "Go, you mother." . . .

T + 19.000   Smith, intercom: "Looks like we've got a lot of wind here, today." Scobee: "Yeah." . . .

T + 21.124   The roll maneuver is completed and *Challenger* is on the proper trajectory. . . .

T + 35.379   The three main engines begin throttling down to 65% power as planned.

T + 43.000   Scobee, intercom: "OK, we're throttling down." . . .

T + 45.217   A flash is observed downstream of the shuttle's right wing.

T + 48.118   A second flash is seen trailing the right wing. . . .

T + 57.000   Scobee, intercom: "Throttling up."

           Smith: "Throttle up."

           Scobee: "Roger."

T + 58.788   Tracking cameras show the first evidence of an abnormal plume on the right-hand solid rocket booster facing away from the shuttle. . . .

T + 59.753   First visual evidence of flame on the right-side booster. 70mm tracking camera closeup: A flickering tongue of flame appears on the side of the right-side booster away from the shuttle and quickly becomes continuous.

T + 60.000   Smith, intercom: "Feel that mother go!"

           Unknown, intercom: "Wooooo Hoooooo!"

T + 60.248   First evidence of the anomalous plume "attaching" to the fitting that couples the aft end of the right-side rocket to the base of the external fuel tank. . . .

T + 63.964   The shuttle's computers order a planned change in *Challenger's* pitch to ensure the proper angle of attack during this phase of the trajectory. . . .

T + 64.705   A bright, sustained glow is photographed on the side of the external fuel tank. . . .

T + 65.524   Data show the left wing's outboard elevon move suddenly. . . .

T + 67.650   The abnormal plumes on the bottom and top of the booster appear to merge into one. This means the flame has wrapped around the joint as the leak deteriorated.

T + 70.000   Scobee, air-to-ground: "Roger, go at throttle up." . . .

T + 72.497   The nozzles of the three liquid-fuel main engines begin moving at high rates. . . .

T + 72.624   *Challenger* beams back what turns out to be its final navigation update.

T + 72.964   Main engine liquid oxygen propellant pressures begin falling sharply at turbopump inlets.

T + 73.000   (approximate) Smith, intercom: "Uh, oh . . . "

T + 73.213   An explosion occurs near the forward part of the tank where the solid rocket boosters attach. . . .

T + 73.361   End of last data frame.

T + 74.130   Last radio signal from orbiter.   (Harwood & Navias, 1986.)

Statistics matter. There had been 24 successful shuttle flights prior to the *Challenger*'s explosion, so when weather forecasters predicted an unusually cold Florida morning, it might have been easy for the engineers to assume that their "luck" would hold. It didn't. Morton Thiokol engineers and NASA officials had debated deep into the night about what the data were telling them about the effect of cold temperatures on the resiliency of the O-rings that sealed off sections of the rocket boosters. The engineers had even sent NASA officials 13 tables and graphs that documented experimental and field data about damage to the O-rings, trying to make their case to delay the launch. What had gone so wrong?

The engineers simply had not followed the conventional rules for graph construction. You must learn these standards first, so you can tell the story of your data in a way that is familiar and accessible to others. Those guidelines will then shape your unfolding graphical creativity. For example, single-variable graphs follow one set of rules while multivariable graphs emphasize different features because they are telling a more complex story. When the data tell an important, exciting story, you can hardly wait to find the best way to tell that story visually. So let's learn the rules.

In Chapter 2, we learned how to create frequency histograms and polygons, visual displays of the distribution of a single variable. Histograms and polygons are rarely presented in published research or in media accounts of research, however. This is primarily because histograms and polygons display information about only one variable and it is the relation between two or more variables that is most fascinating. We occasionally find histograms in which a researcher provides demographic information; for example, a researcher might want to present the ages or incomes of study participants. Usually, however, demographic information is presented in the text with a simple report of means, medians, and standard deviations. But don't underestimate the power of describing just one variable very thoroughly. Excellent questions evolve out of simple, clear descriptions of a single variable. For example, which type of town described in Figure 3-3 would you prefer to live in—a town with a great deal of economic diversity (as suggested by a platykurtic distribution of real estate prices) or a town in which every house is almost identical to all the others (as suggested by a leptokurtic distribution)?

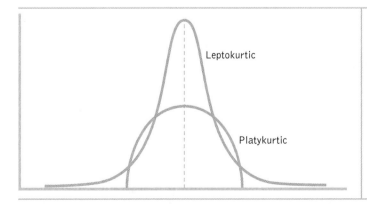

Leptokurtic

Platykurtic

FIGURE 3-3
Histograms Depict One Interval Variable

This platykurtic histogram compared to a leptokurtic histogram of real estate prices in a town provokes numerous questions, such as: Will I enjoy living in a platykurtic town with so much economic diversity? Will I be bored in a leptokurtic town with little diversity? How will the exposure to diversity in a platykurtic town affect my children? Does my preference for living in a platykurtic or leptokurtic town reveal something important about me and what I value?

A single-variable graph can provoke excellent questions, but the richer ideas that seduce students into the world of research usually involve the relations between variables. For example, after we understand the distribution of real estate prices in one town, we naturally ask ourselves, "Now I wonder how my town would compare with this one?" Suddenly, your desire to make a comparison means that you now have not one but two variables to deal with. Similarly, if you research graduate programs, you will want to make comparisons among them to figure out which ones might be right for you, such as "What do students do after graduation?" or "Does the university provide financial assistance?" This means that we need graphs that describe this multivariable story and that clarify the relation between those variables in just one image. The primary graphs that tell a multivariate story are scatterplots, line graphs, bar graphs, pictorial graphs, and pie charts.

Scatterplots: Observing Every Data Point

*A **scatterplot** is a graph that depicts the relation between two interval variables.* The values of each variable are marked along the two axes, and a mark is made to indicate the intersection of the two scores for each participant. The mark will be above the individual's score on the *x*-axis and across from the score on the *y*-axis. A scatterplot is simple to construct either by hand or by computer. Consider sketching these graphs by hand first (although it may seem retro) and then progress to the computer. Constructing a graph by hand will enhance your awareness of its components and give you the flexibility to include, eliminate, or invent various features of the graph. If you have a solid foundation in written graphs, your computer-constructed graphs will be more accurate and more elegant.

In the example in Figure 3-4, a researcher might be interested in the effect that the amount of studying had on students' grades on a statistics exam; to study this, the researcher could gather two scores for each participant—the number of hours studied and the grade on the statistics exam. We must first decide which variable we believe is the independent variable (the variable doing the predicting) and which is the dependent variable (the variable being predicted). In this example, it is more likely that hours spent studying would predict the grade on the statistics exam rather than the other way around. So, the independent variable *(x)* is hours spent studying, and the dependent variable *(y)* is the grade on the statistics exam.

As seen in Figure 3-4, these data suggest that the more one studies, the better one performs on exams. We now have a sense of our data and how the two variables are related to each other. Note that the values on both axes go down

FIGURE 3-4
Scatterplot of Hours Studied and Statistics Grades

This scatterplot depicts the relation between hours spent studying and grades on a statistics exam. Each dot represents one student's score along the independent variable on the *x*-axis and along the dependent variable on the *y*-axis.

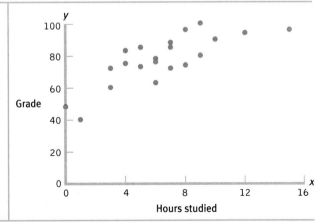

to 0, reducing the likelihood of misinterpretation. In a situation in which the scores are all very high, however, it might be too unwieldy to include all the values. In such cases, it wastes space to have the axes go all the way down to 0, and the data near the top would be compacted and more difficult to read; however, whenever practical, it's best to include 0. As we'll see later, it's very easy to mislead our audience, intentionally or not, when we cut short the scale on our graphs.

As computer technology increases the choices when creating graphs, there are calls for simplicity in graph design. One leader in this movement is Edward R. Tufte, a former Princeton and Yale professor, who has published a number of classic books on the visual presentation of data. Tufte (2001/2006) suggests several ways to redesign the traditional scatterplot in an effort to improve what he refers to as the "data–ink ratio." This refers to the goal of providing the maximum amount of data while using the minimum amount of ink. One of Tufte's suggestions involves a range-frame, rather than the traditional scatterplot. *A range-frame is a scatterplot or related graph that indicates only the range of the data on each axis; the lines extend only from the minimum to the maximum scores.* Eliminating the ends of the axes means that the lines forming the range-frame now also represent the data. More data, less ink: the data–ink ratio increases. In addition, the minimum and maximum observations themselves can be labeled with their values so that these numbers are easily discerned by the viewer. This also means that all data labels below the minimum and above the maximum can be eliminated. Figure 3-5 shows a range-frame for the scatterplot in Figure 3-5. When constructing your own graphs, consider clever ways to increase the data–ink ratio and improve your graphs' storytelling abilities.

Here is a recap of the steps to create a scatterplot:

1. Organize the data by participant; each participant will have two scores, one on each interval variable.

2. Label the horizontal *x*-axis with the name of the independent variable and its possible values, starting with 0 if practical.

3. Label the vertical *y*-axis with the name of the dependent variable and its possible values, starting with 0 if practical.

4. Make a mark on the graph above each study participant's score on the *x*-axis and next to his or her score on the *y*-axis.

5. To convert to a range-frame, simply erase the axes below the minimum scores and above the maximum scores.

▪ A **scatterplot** is a graph that depicts the relation between two interval variables. The values of each variable are marked along the two axes, and a mark is made to indicate the intersection of the two scores for each participant. The mark will be above the individual's score on the *x*-axis and across from the score on the *y*-axis.

▪ A **range-frame** is a scatterplot or related graph that indicates only the range of the data on each axis; the lines extend only from the minimum to the maximum scores.

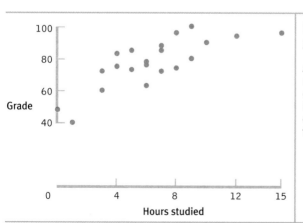

Grade

Hours studied

FIGURE 3-5
A Range-Frame Improves on a Scatterplot

A range-frame is a traditional scatterplot that indicates the minimum and maximum observed values on the axes by erasing all ink beyond these points. In this case, the *y*-axis begins at 40 instead of 0, and the *x*-axis ends at 15 instead of 16. This simple alteration increases the ratio of ink used for actual data to overall ink used in the graph.

**FIGURE 3-6
A Scatterplot and an
Outlier**

It is easy to observe
outliers on a scatterplot.
On this scatterplot, the
outlier is circled. This
individual studied for 15
hours but scored only 43
on the exam. This score
is far from the trend of
the rest of the data.

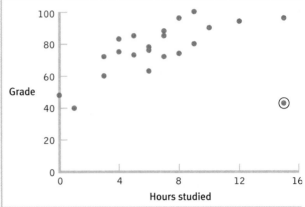

As noted in Chapter 2, outliers are extreme data points that can dramatically influence a distribution of data. As demonstrated in Figure 3-6, an important feature of a scatterplot is its ability to visually identify outliers, points that represent individuals whose scores fall away from the trend of the rest of the data. Outliers present a particular challenge for researchers and raise important questions that are both practical and theoretical. When confronted with an outlier, you need to ask questions such as these:

1. Did my finger slip from a 0 to a 9 during data entry? Perhaps I was just tired and made an honest mistake.

2. Is this outlier obscuring an otherwise distinctive trend in the data?

3. How far out does an outlier have to be before I can think about throwing it out? (There is a separate literature on this; do a computer literature search of "Mahalanobis's distance.")

4. Was one of the participants just trying to mess up our study? Perhaps someone was having a bad day or we offended somebody who tried to get revenge by giving us bad data.

5. On the other hand, is this outlier an important clue that we should be paying attention to?

Sometimes outliers provide very important information, as they did when John Snow explored why two people living far from the Broad Street well contracted cholera and found that they had nonetheless drunk water from the Broad Street well. In that case, a detail that appeared to contradict the trend in the data ended up providing distinctive support for the trend. But sometimes we don't even know that an outlier is an outlier until we look at the scatterplot.

When we are interested in the relation between two variables, we first have to understand the different ways in which the two variables *might* be related—either linearly or nonlinearly (or not at all). As the word *linear* implies, *a **linear relation** between variables means that the relation between variables is best described by a straight line.* When the linear relation is positive, the pattern of data points flows upward and to the right. When the linear relation is negative, the pattern of data points flows downward and to the right. In both cases, the relation is best described by a straight line (described more specifically in Chapter 6). For example, the data for hours studying and statistics grades shown in Figure 3-4 are

■ A **linear relation** between variables means that the relation between variables is best described by a straight line.

related in a positive, linear way; on average, as one studies more, one performs better; on average as one studies less, one performs worse. In this case, the overall flow of the data points is upward and to the right. There are no dramatic twists and turns in this data set.

*A **nonlinear relation** between variables means that the relation between variables is best described by a line that breaks or curves in some way.* Because a scatterplot depicts every observation, a visual inspection of a scatterplot is a particularly useful way to examine our data to determine if there is a linear or nonlinear relation between variables. Note that two variables are not necessarily related in a nonlinear way if they are not related in a linear way; they might not be related at all! It's important to remember that a nonlinear relation is still a relation. Because nonlinear simply means "not straight," there are several different kinds of nonlinear relations between variables, and some of them show up in behavioral science research rather frequently.

Let's consider an example. The Yerkes–Dodson law predicts the relation between level of arousal and test performance. As professors, we don't want you so relaxed that you don't even show up for the test, but we don't want you so stressed out that you can't take the test because you're having a panic attack. We want you somewhere in the happy middle because for most of us there seems to be a nonlinear relation (an upside-down U-curve) that describes the relation between arousal and test performance (Figure 3-7). Although the Yerkes–Dodson law continues to generate study and debate (e.g. Christianson, 1992; Hancock & Warm, 1989), those of you who have struggled with performance anxiety such as stage fright may recognize this principle: practice and experience can help you to perform better, even under circumstances that otherwise promote high levels of anxiety. But the best way to understand this relation between two variables is to see it in the line that summarizes the data from a scatterplot.

The performance of the *Challenger* was a group performance rather than an individual performance, so the anxiety about the launch was spread across the entire team. That means that responsibility for the performance of the space shuttle was also diffused across the entire team. But the disaster still could have been presented by a simple scatterplot describing the relation between two variables. Unfortunately, it was a scatterplot that was never properly drawn. After the disaster, a special commission was established to investigate what went wrong, clarify the lessons to be learned, and assign responsibility, if appropriate. The *Report of the Presidential Commission on the Space Shuttle* Challenger *Accident* (PCSSCA) (1986) is the source for much of the material reported here, filtered significantly through the lens of "graph guru" Edward Tufte's (1997/2005) analysis in *Visual Explanations*. Some of Tufte's conclusions have been questioned, most notably his moral judgments, which are discussed by Robison, Boisjoly, Hoeker, and Young (2002). But there is a consensus that better visual presentations of the data could have averted this tragedy.

The presidential commission recognized that a specific question had been asked the night before the launch: What is the effect of temperature on the O-ring material? Commission members examined the charts and graphs faxed to NASA officials the night before the launch. They noted that the Thiokol engineers had only had a few hours to collect this material. Conversations

■ A **nonlinear relation** between variables means that the relation between variables is best described by a line that breaks or curves in some way.

FIGURE 3-7
Nonlinear Relations

The Yerkes–Dodson law predicts that stress/anxiety improves test performance— but only to a point. Too much anxiety leads to an inability to perform at one's best. This inverted U-curve illustrates the concept, but a scatterplot would be a better clarification of the particular relation between these two variables.

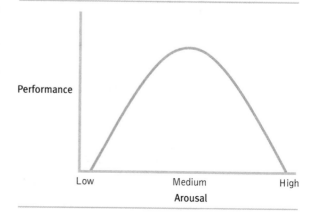

between NASA officials and Thiokol engineers about their interpretation of the data continued until midnight before the morning of the launch. Keep your eye out for the only two variables at stake in answering this specific cause–effect question: the independent variable (temperature) and the dependent variable (indicators of damage to the O-ring material). That's the only question that was being asked. Anything else is, by definition, an extraneous and dangerously distracting variable.

The accompanying chart is titled "History of O-Ring Damage on SRM Field Joints," so it would appear to be answering the question being asked on that fateful evening. (*Note*: SRM stands for solid rocket motor, the unit that experienced O-ring failure.) As several observers have noted, you don't need particular training as an engineer to understand that words like *erosion*, *damage*, and *soot blowby* suggest something bad. There had been 24 previous shuttle flights, and the shuttles had been carefully examined after each. In addition, there had been extensive lab testing of the SRMs. However, only one of the two critical variables is represented in this presentation, so it is impossible to assess the relation between the two variables. It would be like trying to understand a marriage with only one person in it—it simply can't be done.

Table Prepared for NASA Officials the Night Before the *Challenger* Disaster
This table provided detailed information about one of the key variables, damage to the O-rings. But it did not link it to information about the second, potentially causal variable: temperature.

Consider this question: If there were 24 shuttle flights and the relevant information had been collected after each, then why weren't there at least 24 data points? The extensive development and preflight testing of the rocket boosters would have provided still more data points that could have revealed whether there was a trend in the data. When you're searching for a trend, you must include all the data! In this case, knowing that there was considerably less damage to the O-rings when the shuttle was launched in warmer weather was critical

---

HISTORY OF O-RING DAMAGE ON SRM FIELD JOINTS

	SRM No.	Cross Sectional View			Top View	
		Erosion Depth (in.)	Perimeter Affected (deg)	Nominal Dia. (in.)	Length Of Max Erosion (in.)	Total Heat Affected Length (in.)
61A LH Center Field**	22A	None	None	0.280	None	None
61A LH ~~CENTER~~ FIELD**	22A	NONE	NONE	0.280	NONE	NONE
51C LH Forward Field**	15A	0.010	154.0	0.280	4.25	5.25
51C RH Center Field (prim)***	15B	0.038	130.0	0.280	12.50	58.75
51C RH Center Field (sec)***	15B	None	45.0	0.280	None	29.50
41D RH Forward Field	13B	0.028	110.0	0.280	3.00	None
41C LH Aft Field*	11A	None	None	0.280	None	None
41B LH Forward Field	10A	0.040	217.0	0.280	3.00	14.50
STS-2 RH Aft Field	2B	0.053	116.0	0.280	--	--

*Hot gas path detected in putty. Indication of heat on O-ring, but no damage.
**Soot behind primary O-ring.
***Soot behind primary O-ring, heat affected secondary O-ring.

Clocking location of leak check port - 0 deg.

OTHER SRM-15 FIELD JOINTS HAD NO BLOWHOLES IN PUTTY AND NO SOOT NEAR OR BEYOND THE PRIMARY O-RING.

SRM-22 FORWARD FIELD JOINT HAD PUTTY PATH TO PRIMARY O-RING, BUT NO O-RING EROSION AND NO SOOT BLOWBY. OTHER SRM-22 FIELD JOINTS HAD NO BLOWHOLES IN PUTTY.

Reprinted by permission Edward R. Tufte, *Visual Explanations*, Graphics Press, Cheshire, CT, 1997.

information, even though there should not have been any damage to the O-rings under any circumstances. Be very, very suspicious when people have provided only part of the data. At the worst, it's lying by omission.

Line Graphs: Searching for Trends

*A **line graph** is used to illustrate the relation between two interval variables; sometimes the line represents the predicted y scores for each x value, and sometimes the line represents change in a variable over time.* Like scatterplots, line graphs use two different interval variables. The line of fit is the line that minimizes the distances of the dots from that line. The line of best fit allows us to use the *x* value to predict the *y* value; for example, we could use "time spent studying" scores to predict "test scores." Let's say that one of our students failed the midterm and declared with some indignation that he had studied for three hours and still got a failing grade. When questioned, the student acknowledged that those three hours represented his total study time over half a term, not his weekly average (which would still be below the average college expectation of six study hours per week for each three-credit course). If we know the general relation between hours studied and the grade on the statistics exam, then we can tell other people what they might expect to score on the exam if they study a given number of hours. The line of best fit allows us to make predictions when we know only one piece of information. Specifically, we can use the line of best fit in Figure 3-8 to predict that if a person studies for two hours, she will earn a test score of about 62, whereas if she studies for 13 hours, she will earn about 100.

Here is a recap of the steps to create a scatterplot with a line of best fit:

1. Label the *x*-axis with the name of the independent variable and its possible values, starting with 0 if practical.

2. Label the *y*-axis with the name of the dependent variable and its possible values, starting with 0 if practical.

3. Make a mark above each study participant's score on the *x*-axis and next to his or her score on the *y*-axis.

4. In Chapter 6, you will learn how to use a regression equation that will draw the line of best fit through the points on the scatterplot.

5. To convert to a range-frame, erase the axes below the minimum and above the maximum.

■ A **line graph** is used to illustrate the relation between two interval variables; sometimes the line represents the predicted *y* scores for each *x* value, and sometimes the line represents change in a variable over time.

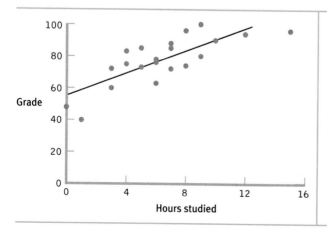

FIGURE 3-8
The Line of Best Fit

The line of best fit allows us to make predictions for an individual's values on the *y* variable from his or her values on the *x* variable.

■ A **time plot,** or **time series plot,** is a graph that plots an interval variable on the *y*-axis as it changes over an increment of time (e.g., second, day, century) labeled on the *x*-axis.

A second situation in which a line graph is more useful than just a scatterplot occurs with time-related data. *A **time plot,** or **time series plot,** is a graph that plots an interval variable on the y-axis as it changes over an increment of time (e.g., second, day, century) labeled on the x-axis.* As with a scatterplot, marks are placed above each value on the *x*-axis (e.g., at a given minute) at the value for that particular time on the *y*-axis (i.e., the score on the dependent variable).

Let's consider the hotly debated topic of gun control and its effects on homicides. Notice how clearly the time plot in Figure 3-9 seems to tell the story of the numbers of homicides in Canada from 1961 through 1994 (Gimbarzevsky, 1995). Here we see a substantial increase in gun murders between the early 1960s and the mid 1970s, and then the pattern becomes more erratic. But have we discovered the whole story about the relation between gun murders and their possible causes in Canada over this period? Absolutely not! We need to know how many guns are actually available across the population: guns per capita. This last question about gun murders *per capita* is a much more finely grained question than the one that we started with. But it is a question that comes much closer to asking the question that we really want to answer regarding the relation between the distribution of guns and gun murders. An effective graph provokes more precise questions.

Here is a recap of the steps to create a time plot:

1. Label the *x*-axis with the name of the independent variable and its possible values. The independent variable will be an increment of time (e.g., hour, month, year).

2. Label the *y*-axis with the name of the dependent variable and its possible values, starting with 0 if practical.

3. Make a mark above every study participant's score on the *x*-axis and next to her or his score on the *y*-axis.

4. Connect the dots.

5. To convert to a range-frame, erase the *y*-axis below the minimum *y* value and above the maximum *y* value.

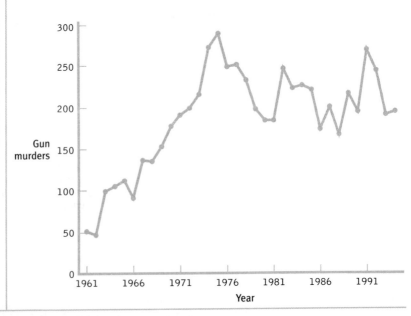

FIGURE 3-9
The Numbers of Gun Murders in Canada Between 1961 and 1994

Ask a better question. Instead of answering a question about absolute numbers of gun murders, a better graph would answer the question about the numbers of deaths *per capita* to reflect possible changes in Canada's population over time.

The Thiokol engineers seemed convinced that there was a trend in the data, but they did not present that information in a visually convincing way. They had reached the right conclusions, but they did not have a visual presentation powerful enough to impress NASA management. In their previous charts, they had included only one of the variables of interest: damage to the O-ring material. It was not clear if that damage had been caused by colder temperatures or some other cause. The only clear information was that there had been damage to some of the O-rings. That alone was a significant danger signal; in a more conservative organizational environment, that piece of information might have been sufficient to reschedule *Challenger*'s launch. However, in the two accompanying graphs (*below*), Thiokol engineers presented information that included both of the relevant variables—temperature and damage to the O-rings. Let's investigate why these graphs did not communicate effectively.

These two visual presentations demonstrate why fancy presentation software has not been good for science. Specifically, there is no good reason to use gimmicky little rockets to represent these data. They were not created between the time of the NASA request for information and the response to that request. They were created for the presidential commission investigating the disaster. Someone had the time to play with the presentation of these data. The graphmaker chose to use little rockets, even though it would seem to be a safe assumption that everyone on this project knew they were dealing with rocket boosters. So if there is nothing positive to recommend the use of this kind of gimmicky pictorial display, is there anything negative to recommend against it? Yes!

Tufte (1997/2005) identifies several problems with how these data were presented. First, these were two separate presentations. That meant that viewers had to memorize the interpretive code from the first presentation to understand the second presentation. Tufte reports that these data were actually presented on successive overheads, so viewers could not even shuffle their own pages to look at the interpretive code to double-check its meaning.

Second, the viewer's attention is not directed to the critical variables of interest: temperature and damage to the O-rings. Instead, attention is directed to all those cute little rockets and only tangentially to the indicators of damage that appear to be randomly scattered among them. As Tufte comments about this presentation, "Chartjunk indicates statistical stupidity just as weak writing often reflects weak thought" (p. 48).

Obscuring Vital Information These two graphic presentations contained the right information but obscured the vital relation between temperature and damage to the O-rings.

History of O-Ring Damage in Field Joints

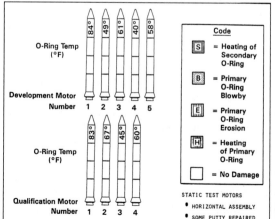

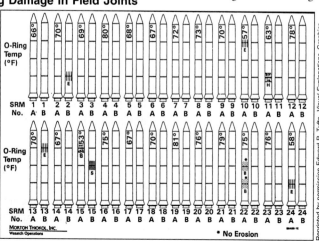

Reprinted by permission Edward R. Tufte, *Visual Explanations*, Graphics Press, Cheshire, CT, 1997.

Third, the cause–effect relation that was the answer to the only question being asked is obscured by other gimmicks made necessary by the cute little rockets. Specifically, the vital, potentially life-saving numbers revealing temperature have been turned sideways because the rockets are tall and narrow. Because the information was de-emphasized visually, a reasonable person viewing this information would be led to believe that these particular numbers were not very important.

Fourth, the second vital variable, indicating type of damage to the O-ring, was coded with arbitrary symbols: dots, diagonal bars, and vertical stripes rather than something intuitive, such as progressively darker marks indicating progressively more damage. The damage indicators cannot be seen or understood easily.

Fifth, the cause–effect relation between temperature and O-ring resiliency is obscured because the cute little rockets are not presented in the appropriate order. The data are presented in chronological order based on the dates when the O-rings were tested. That might have been an interesting relation to examine if the engineers were trying to answer a different question. But it was not the question being asked late into the night prior to the launch of *Challenger*. Nor was it the question being asked at the hearings. The critical question was about temperature, not time, so the data should have been ordered according to temperature, from coldest to warmest, rather than in chronological order.

There were consequences of this use of chartjunk instead of direct information. As the critical decision was being made about whether to launch *Challenger* the next morning, the right question was being asked. The data that provided an answer to that question were collected by the Thiokol engineers. They presented that information to the appropriate people. But a poorly constructed visual presentation and an overeager organizational culture conspired against the space shuttle and its crew. The decision makers were looking directly at the life-saving information, but all they could see were lots of cute little rockets with obscure, meaningless markings.

So what would have communicated the relation between temperature and damage to the O-ring more effectively? With the helpful wisdom of hindsight, Tufte (1997/2005) used the same information to construct a table and a graph that display the relation between temperature and damage to the O-rings. His additional piece of information was a damage index, which he describes as a "severity-weighted total number of incidents of O-ring erosion, heating, and blowby" (p. 44). Even without the damage index, the table in Figure 3-10 reveals a disturbing, clearly identifiable trend, and the corresponding graph in Figure 3-11 dramatizes the high probability of danger when launching the shuttle at a temperature well below the temperature at which the O-rings had ever been tested.

You never outgrow your need to understand the basic statistical reasoning about independent and dependent variables and the corresponding need to recognize and control the dangerous influence of extraneous or confounding variables. There was a trend in the data about damage to the O-rings, but it wasn't over time, it was over temperature. In this case, damage was the dependent variable, temperature was the independent variable, and time was nothing but a dangerously distracting, extraneous variable. Images of cute little rockets probably seemed like a clever way to present the data, but that choice cascaded into several dangerous distractions. No one at NASA or Morton Thiokol gained any information from these pictures of rockets. Instead, the rockets obscured a great deal of extremely important information. This additional confound confused the

FLIGHT	DATE	°F	EROSION INCIDENTS	BLOW-BY INCIDENTS	DAMAGE INDEX	COMMENTS
51-C	01.24.85	53°	3	2	11	Most erosion of any flight; blow-by; back-up rings heated
41-B	02.03.84	57°	1		4	Deep, extensive erosion.
61-C	01.12.86	58°	1		4	O-ring erosion on launch two weeks before Challenger.
41-C	04.06.84	63°	1		2	O-rings showed signs of heating, but no damage.
1	04.12.81	66°			0	Coolest (66°) launch without O-ring problems.
6	04.04.83	67°			0	
51-A	11.08.84	67°			0	
51-D	04.12.85	67°			0	
5	11.11.82	68°			0	
3	03.22.82	69°			0	
2	11.12.81	70°	1		4	Extent of erosion not fully known.
9	11.28.83	70°			0	
41-D	08.30.84	70°	1		4	
51-G	06.17.85	70°			0	
7	06.18.83	72°			0	
8	08.30.83	73°			0	
51-B	04.29.85	75°			0	
61-A	10.30.85	75°		2	4	No erosion. Soot found behind two primary O-rings.
51-I	08.27.85	76°			0	
61-B	11.26.85	76°			0	
41-G	10.05.84	78°			0	
51-J	10.03.85	79°			0	
4	06.27.82	80°			?	O-ring condition unknown; rocket casing lost at sea.
51-F	07.29.85	81°			0	

FIGURE 3-10
The Relation Between Temperature and Relative Damage to O-rings: Tabular Version

This Table presents a clearly indentifiable trend that the two graphic presentations on page 109 do not.

FIGURE 3-11
The Relation Between Temperature and Relative Damage to O-rings

An effective figure or table *includes* the variables of interest (temperature and amount of damage to the O-rings) and *does not include* extraneous variables such as time.

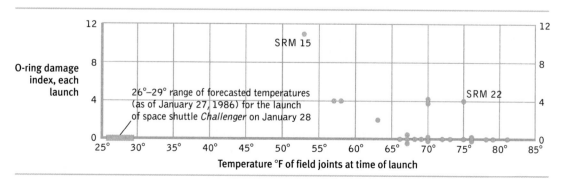

logic of a visual presentation that could have, and many say should have, saved seven lives and billions of dollars.

Perhaps you are saying to yourself that you never anticipate working on a project that, if it fails, might cost people their lives. But people seldom bother with statistics unless the variables are important to somebody. Evaluating retirement monies, calculating life insurance, understanding the efficacy of antidepressants, deciding whether to promote a struggling first-grade student, and evaluating teaching technologies are very important endeavors. Statistics matter. Avoid cutesy visual presentations!

Bar Graphs: An Efficient Communicator

Bar graphs are visual depictions of data when the independent variable is nominal and the dependent variable is interval. Each bar typically represents the mean value of the dependent variable for each category. They are one of the most commonly used types of graphs. Bar graphs and histograms both use bars and sometimes look very similar, but don't confuse them. A histogram describes only one variable, but in very great detail. A bar graph provides a summary description of the relation between two or more variables.

More specifically, the *x*-axis of a histogram includes one variable, usually an interval variable such as GPA, and the *y*-axis identifies the frequency of each value of that same variable (for example, how many scores occur between 1.5 and 1.9, between 2.0 and 2.4, etc.). In a bar graph, the *x*-axis includes a nominal variable, such as gender (with separate bars for men and women); the *y*-axis describes a second variable, an interval variable, such as Consideration of Future Consequences (CFC) scores that allow us to compare the average CFC scores of men to the average CFC scores of women.

The most straightforward way to distinguish between histograms and bar graphs is by counting the number of variables being presented. If there is only one variable, it's probably a histogram. In addition, look at the variable presented on the *x*-axis:

▪ The *x*-axis of a histogram represents values of an interval variable.

▪ The *x*-axis of a bar graph indicates discrete levels of a nominal variable.

Also look at the variable presented on the *y*-axis:

▪ The *y*-axis of a histogram represents counts or percentages.

▪ The *y*-axis of a bar graph also may represent counts or percentages. But the *y*-axis of a bar graph can indicate many other variables, such as scores on a personality scale, reaction time, preference indicators, or any other interval measure of a dependent variable.

Bar graphs are extremely flexible tools for the visual presentation of data. For example, we most often report the means of the interval variable on the vertical *y*-axis, but we could also report the medians. If there are many categories to be displayed along the horizontal *x*-axis, researchers sometimes create a *Pareto chart, a type of bar graph in which the categories along the x-axis are ordered from highest bar on the left to lowest bar on the right.* This ordering allows easier comparisons and easier identification of the most common and least common categories. The flexibility of the bar graph is the main reason it is used so often across so many different kinds of research. For example, bar graphs can be used to display the results of the General Social Survey (GSS). The National Opinion Research Center has

▪ A **bar graph** is a visual depiction of data when the independent variable is nominal and the dependent variable is interval. Each bar typically represents the mean value of the dependent variable for each category.

▪ A **Pareto chart** is a type of bar graph in which the categories along the *x*-axis are ordered from highest bar on the left to lowest bar on the right.

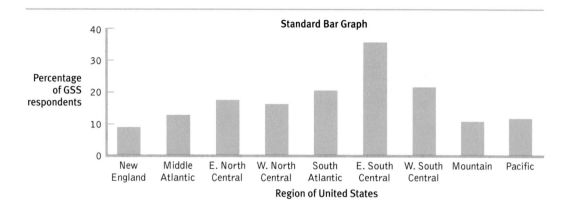

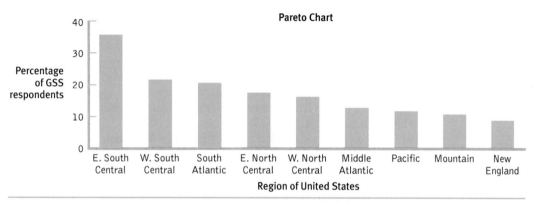

FIGURE 3-12
The Flexibility of the Bar Graph

The standard bar graph provides a comparison among nine nominal variables. The dependent variable is the percentage of respondents who said that an avowed homosexual should be "not allowed" to speak. The Pareto chart, a version of a bar graph, orders the categories from highest to lowest along the horizontal axis to allow for easier comparisons.

interviewed approximately 2000 U.S. adults a year (almost every year) since 1972. Over the years, more than 38,000 people have answered more than 3000 different questions related to people's opinions, attitudes, and behaviors. The responses provide fascinating insight into attitudes about everything from belief in heaven and hell to attitudes about laws governing seat belt use. The GSS Web site can be found at http://www.icpsr.umich.edu/GSS/, and anyone can analyze their data. It's a goldmine of archival data for social scientists. Often, it can answer questions related to current political controversies, such as the debate about gay marriage, and whether decisions made in one state should be accepted by other states. A relevant question on the GSS asked respondents to consider an "admitted homosexual [who] wanted to make a speech in your community" and asked: "Should he be allowed to speak, or not?" Figure 3-12 includes two different ways of depicting the percentages of respondents in different U.S. regions who said the individual should be "not allowed" to speak. One graph is a standard bar graph with categories ordered as the GSS orders the regions, and the other is a Pareto chart. Which one is easier to read?

Bar graphs are often used in the applied behavioral sciences. For example, Newell, Rosenfeld, and Culbertson (1995) examined the effect of sexual harassment on the intention to remain in the Navy. We can see from Figure 3-13 that female Navy officers who reported that they had not been harassed had a somewhat higher intention of staying in the Navy for at least 20 years than did those who reported that they had been harassed.

FIGURE 3-13
Bar Graphs Highlight Differences Between Means

This bar graph depicts the mean ratings of intention to stay in the Navy for two groups of female Navy officers: those who reported having been harassed and those who reported not having been harassed. A bar graph can more vividly depict differences between means than just seeing the typed numbers themselves: 3.32 and 3.64.

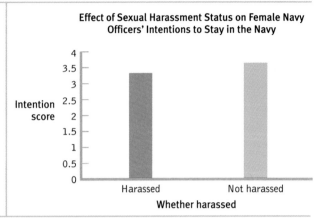

Effect of Sexual Harassment Status on Female Navy Officers' Intentions to Stay in the Navy

But how dramatic is this difference? Manipulating the range of the y-axis can change the story that these data seem to be telling. Compare Figure 3-14 to Figure 3-13, and notice what happens when the values on the y-axis do not begin at 0, and when the intervals change from 0.5 to 0.05. The exact same data, presented with a different range displayed on the y-axis, leave a very different impression. So pay close attention to the range of the y-axis.

What story does this graph tell? The difference is now exaggerated. Although there does seem to be a small difference when we look at Figure 3-13, the difference appears very large in Figure 3-14. The key word here is *appears*. Regardless of where the y-axis begins, the data are the same! It is important to remember this when creating or interpreting bar graphs. The next time you see a bar graph in a magazine or on a Web site, look at the values on the y-axis. Do they start at 0? More often than you might guess, they do not. Then ask yourself if the creator of the graph had an agenda: Did this person *want* to show an exaggerated difference?

Here is a recap of the steps to create a bar graph. The critical choice for you, the graph creator, is in step 2.

1. Label the x-axis with the name and levels (i.e., categories) of the nominal independent variable.

2. Label the y-axis with the name of the dependent variable and its possible values, starting with 0 if practical.

3. For every category, draw a bar with the height of that category's mean (or median) on the dependent variable.

FIGURE 3-14
Deceiving with the Scale

To exaggerate a difference between means, graphmakers sometimes compress the rating scale that they show on their graph. When possible, label your axis beginning with 0.

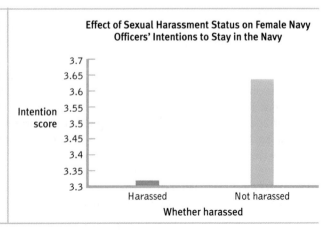

Effect of Sexual Harassment Status on Female Navy Officers' Intentions to Stay in the Navy

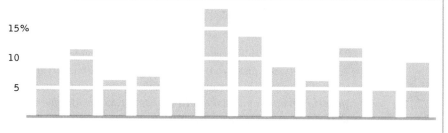

Tufte (2001/2006) would say we can go even further by redesigning bar graphs. Figure 3-15 is a redesigned bar graph in Tufte's style. Tufte has eliminated both the box around the graph and the vertical axis. He has kept the data labels on the y-axis and has replaced the tick marks that indicate the levels of the dependent variable with thin white lines through the bars. This reconfiguration leads to an improvement in the data–ink ratio. Computer software may not allow all of these changes, but we can construct graphs such as these by using software created for graphic artists or by using pencil and paper.

Bar graphs are remarkably flexible in that they allow us to depict more than one independent variable on the same graph. Figure 3-16 is a bar graph of the data on female Navy personnel's intention to stay in the Navy for two independent variables: sexual harassment status and rank. The depiction of two independent variables allows for a deeper understanding of the factors that affect this intention.

To read this graph, first notice the main difference between this bar graph and those that include only one independent variable. We now have a key on the right-hand side that tells us which one of the officer bars and which one of the enlisted bars are for those who reported having been harassed and which ones are for those who reported not having been harassed. It is best to avoid using keys because they require the reader to look back and forth between the bars and the code, but most software makes it difficult to eliminate a key and type the words right under the bars. This multivariable bar graph suggests that sexual harassment was more detrimental for female enlisted personnel than for female officers with respect to their intention to remain in the Navy. The more complex story is likely to lead us to new and more targeted research questions. We might, for example, design a study to examine why sexual harassment might have more negative consequences for female enlisted personnel than for female officers.

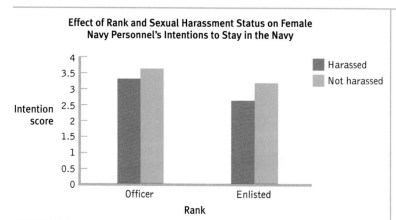

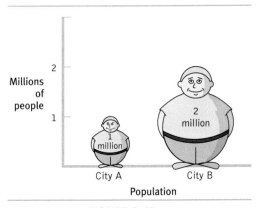

FIGURE 3-17
Distorting the Data with Pictures

With a pictorial graph, doubling the height of a picture is often coupled with doubling the width—you're multiplying by 2 twice. Instead of being twice as big, the picture is *four times* as big!

Pictorial Graphs: Choosing Clarity over Cleverness

When there are only basic differences to be depicted—the difference between just two or three categories on an interval variable, for example—a pictorial graph is sometimes used. *A **pictorial graph** is a visual depiction of data typically used for an independent variable with very few levels (categories) and an interval dependent variable. Each category uses a picture or symbol to represent its value on the interval dependent variable.* Pictorial graphs are far more common in the popular media than in research journals, primarily because the popular media often prefer eye-catching cosmetics over accuracy in their graphs. Researchers, however, better understand the difficulties and dangers of using pictorial graphs accurately and appropriately. The pictures of cute little rockets in the *Challenger* data obscured a critical relation between variables.

Pictorial graphs use pictures in place of bars. For example, the graphmaker might use stylistic drawings of people to indicate population size. If one city has double the population of another, the graphmaker might, as in Figure 3-17, make the drawing of the person twice as tall—but also twice as wide so that the taller person won't look stretched out. This has the misleading effect of making the taller drawing about four times as big in total area as the shorter one, when it is supposed to convey that the population is only twice as big. This is a very easy error to make, and for that reason many researchers avoid pictorial graphs.

Moreover, there is a body of research on flaws in human perception (e.g., Macdonald-Ross, 1977) suggesting that even if drawn correctly and in proportion, quantities depicted on pictorial graphs could still be misperceived. Indeed, because there are so many ways to depict data that are both more flexible and less misleading, we will not outline the steps for making this kind of pictorial graph here. Instead, we direct your attention to Figure 3-18, which illustrates a more subtle misuse of pictorial images to mislead. We recommend that you adopt a fairer, more scientific attitude and avoid the traditional pictorial graph in favor of a clearer, less misleading bar graph. When viewing graphs presented by others, assess whether the presenter seems to be more interested in style or substance. If the answer is style, look out.

FIGURE 3-18
Pictures in Graphs Can Distract and Mislead

Pictorial graphs can also subtly minimize real differences, as in this graph of industrial production over time. Notice what happens to the smoke rising out of each stack.

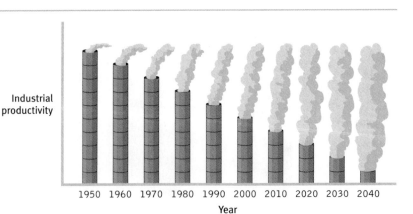

Pie Charts: Are Pie Charts Passé?

*A **pie chart** is a graph in the shape of a circle with a slice for every category. The size of each slice represents the proportion (or percentage) of each category.* A pie chart is created by drawing a circle, then creating slices for each category. The slices should *always* add up to 100% (or 1.00 if using proportions). Figure 3-19 includes a pie chart and a bar graph, both depicting the same data. As suggested by this comparison, data can almost always be presented more clearly in a table or bar graph than in a pie chart.

Tufte (2001/2006) bluntly advises: "A table is nearly always better than a dumb pie chart; the only worse design than a pie chart is several of them, for then the viewer is asked to compare quantities located in spatial disarray both within and between pies" (p. 178). It is almost always more difficult to correctly perceive the magnitude of a pie slice than of a bar and to accurately compare two or more pie slices than two or more bars. Because of the profound limitations of pie charts and the ready alternatives, we will not outline the steps for creating a pie chart here.

In summary, an understanding of the most common graphs will provide a solid foundation from which to launch more creative designs. Single-variable graphs include the frequency histograms and polygons that we encountered in Chapter 2. Multivariable graphs improve upon single-variable graphs by allowing us to observe relations among multiple variables. Scatterplots and line graphs allow us to see relations between two interval variables. Bar graphs, pictorial graphs, and pie charts depict the values of an interval variable for various levels of a nominal variable. Of these, bar graphs are preferred; pictorial graphs and pie charts can be misleading, and data are almost always more clearly represented in another fashion.

■ A **pictorial graph** is a visual depiction of data typically used for an independent variable with very few levels (categories) and an interval dependent variable. Each category uses a picture or symbol to represent its value on the interval dependent variable.

■ A **pie chart** is a graph in the shape of a circle with a slice for every category. The size of each slice represents the proportion (or percentage) of each category.

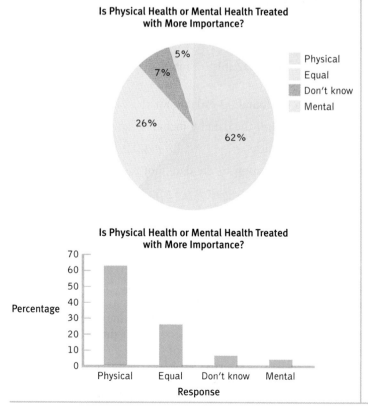

FIGURE 3-19
Pie Chart or Bar Graph?

A research firm hired by the Suicide Prevention Action Network (2004) asked participants: "Do you think that mental health and physical health are treated with equal importance in our current health care system?" We can see from the pie chart that most people (62%) believe that physical health is treated with more importance than is mental health; however, the bar graph is easier to interpret.

⊙ CHECK YOUR LEARNING

3-2 What is the best type of common graph to depict each of the following data sets and research questions? Explain your answer.

a. Depression severity and amount of stress for 150 university students. Is depression related to stress level?

b. Numbers of inpatient mental health facilities in Canada as measured every 10 years between 1890 and 2000. Has the number of facilities declined in recent years?

c. Numbers of siblings reported by 100 people. What size family is most common?

d. Mean years of education for six regions of the United States. Are education levels higher in some regions than in others?

e. Calories consumed in a day and hours slept that night for 85 people. Does the amount of food you eat predict how long a person will sleep at night?

> HOW TO BUILD A GRAPH: DOS AND DON'TS

The tragedy of *Challenger* is an opportunity to learn about the dangers and opportunities of visual displays of data. Let's review what the *Challenger* story has taught us.

1. Follow the conventional rules for the visual display of data.

2. State your hypothesis clearly.

3. Include all the data.

4. Limit your display to the variables of interest: the independent and the dependent variables.

5. Don't substitute a confounding variable for the variable of interest.

6. Make it easy to interpret the data by including an intuitive key.

7. Avoid gimmicky graphics.

8. Direct the viewer's attention to the data, not to the cleverness of the presentation.

9. Present the data in order.

10. Take responsibility for your presentation of the data by identifying yourself as the creator of the graph.

Part of the tragedy of *Challenger* is not only that it could have been prevented, but that it came so close to being prevented. As the research literature in psychology, communications, and organizational development suggests, there may have been organizational reasons that made it easy for this particular tragedy to occur. But in spite of those organizational pressures, a single, hand-drawn, clearly conceived graph created on the evening of January 27, 1986 could have changed history on the morning of January 28, 1986.

For all of us who wish to communicate the scientific excitement that comes from understanding some new piece of the puzzle we call human behavior, the first question to ask is whether to create a graph in the first place. There should be a clear and compelling reason for a graph. Specifically, a graph should provide information that our audience could not glean from the text on its own, or it should clarify an otherwise difficult-to-understand finding. We should always ask ourselves exactly what we hope to accomplish by the inclusion of a particular graph. If we conclude that a graph is appropriate to our needs, we will want to know (1) the specifics of APA style; (2) the factors to consider when choosing which graph to create; (3) the limitations of software; and (4) some general guidelines that will, like the advice gleaned from the *Challenger* disaster, keep us headed in a positive direction.

APA Style: Graphing Guidelines for Social Scientists

Most social scientists adhere to APA style when reporting the results of their research. The APA refers to graphs, and any other visual materials that are not typed text, as figures. You may have observed that, in line with this standard, we have referred to figures throughout this text. The APA (2001) has an excellent list of considerations for the decision to create a figure, while offering the general guidance that a good figure embodies "simplicity, clarity, and continuity" (p. 177). The figure, usually a graph, should be easy to read and understand; it should provide only pertinent information. The APA emphasizes the importance of planning in the creation of graphs, suggesting that we know exactly what we hope to accomplish, such as to display the trend of data over time or the particular relation between two variables. If we believe that our proposed graph will satisfy these criteria, then we can move on to the process of actually constructing our graph. At a practical level, the first decision about a graph is usually whether to use a graph or a table.

In a journal article written in APA style, the author often presents tables or figures. *A **table** is a presentation of data, typically quantitative, that is typed as text in rows and columns.* In Chapter 2, we introduced the frequency table and grouped frequency table, two examples of data presented in this manner. *A **figure** is any visual presentation of data other than a table, such as a photograph, drawing, or, most frequently, a graph.* Tables are typed as text, but figures require that an author supply artwork, which is often created using computer software.

The APA (2001) offers rough guidelines to help researchers decide whether to use a table, a figure, or neither. When we choose to report only 1, 2, or 3 numerical results, the APA suggests including them in a sentence; for example, if merely reporting a mean and standard deviation, we would write, "The mean of group 1 was 3.65 with a standard deviation of 1.12." Or we could follow a sentence in the text with the information in parentheses: "($M = 3.65$, $SD = 1.12$)." With so few results, we would not need a table or figure. However, when we choose to report more than 3, but fewer than 20, numerical results, a table is recommended. And if reporting more than 20 numbers, the APA recommends using some kind of a figure, such as a graph. These are guidelines, however, not rules; we suggest erring on the side of providing a figure and then letting the editor make the final determination.

Once we have decided between a table or a graph, the APA has specific guidelines for creating tables and figures, not only in terms of how they should look but also in terms of where they should be placed in a manuscript. When preparing a manuscript in APA style, follow these guidelines:

1. Refer to tables and figures in the text by number, and briefly describe them.

2. Place the final, camera-ready versions of the actual tables and figures at the end of the manuscript.

■ A **table** is a presentation of data, typically quantitative, that is typed as text in rows and columns (e.g., frequency table).

■ A **figure** is any visual presentation of data other than a table, such as a photograph, drawing, or graph.

3. Provide a complete and clear title, called the caption, for every figure on a separate page.

4. Write the number of the figure in pencil as close to the top right of the final copy of the figure as possible.

5. Write the manuscript's short title and the word *TOP* on the back of the final copy to indicate the top of the figure.

Choosing the Type of Graph: Understanding Our Variables

When deciding what type of graph to use, first examine the variables. Decide which are independent and which are dependent variables, and identify what type of variable—interval (scale), ordinal, or nominal—each of them is. This is important for graph construction because most of the time the independent variable will go on the horizontal x-axis and the dependent variable will go on the vertical y-axis. More important, we want to have our proposed cause–effect relation clearly in mind as we organize our data, so that we do not inadvertently propose an impossible relation between variables. For example, we recently reviewed a paper in which the author had reversed the proposed relation between the variables of where participants were raised (urban, suburban, rural) and their knowledge of sex trafficking. No amount of knowledge of sex trafficking can change where someone was raised, but where someone was raised might be a predictor of their knowledge of sex trafficking.

Once we make a thorough assessment of our variables, we can determine the appropriate graph:

1. One interval variable (with frequencies): histogram or frequency polygon

2. One interval independent variable and one interval dependent variable: scatterplot or line graph

3. One nominal independent variable and one interval dependent variable: bar graph

4. Two or more nominal independent variables and one interval dependent variable: bar graph

EXPERIENCE IT FOR YOURSELF

READING A GRAPH

Let's confirm your understanding of independent and dependent variables within the context of a graph by using the study of female Navy personnel's attitudes that we considered earlier; in particular, consider Figure 3-20a, which depicts two independent variables. Try to answer the following questions *before* looking at the answers provided after the questions.

1. What variable are the researchers trying to predict? That is, what is the *dependent variable*?

2. Is the dependent variable nominal, ordinal, or interval? _____

3. What kinds of scores can participants get on the dependent variable (e.g., if the dependent variable is gender, possible scores are male and female; if it's IQ as measured by the Wechsler Adult Intelligence Scale,

then the possible scores are the IQ scores themselves, ranging from 0 to 145)? _____

4. What variables did the researchers use to predict this dependent variable? That is, what are the *independent variables*? and

5. Are these two independent variables nominal or interval? _____

6. What kinds of scores can participants get on each of these independent variables?

Now check your answers.

1. The dependent variable is the intention of staying in the Navy for 20 years.

2. Intention to stay in the Navy is an interval variable.

3. Intention scores represent an attitude scale with a range of 1 to 5.

4. The first independent variable is rank; the second independent variable is harassment status.

5. The two independent variables, rank and sexual harassment status, are both nominal variables.

6. The possible scores for rank are officer and enlisted. The possible scores for sexual harassment status are harassed and not harassed.

Because there are two independent variables, both of which are nominal, and one interval dependent variable, we used a bar graph to depict these data.

It doesn't matter, by the way, which independent variable is listed first and which is listed second. When we graph our data, we can put one independent variable on the *x*-axis and the other independent variable in the key, but we can switch them around, too. The graph will look different, but it will tell the same story. It is useful to create both versions of the graph because it expands our own view of the data and allows us to choose the one that most clearly tells our story (Figure 3-20a and b). Which graph is easier for you to understand?

FIGURE 3-20
Same Data, Two Approaches

When we are graphing a data set that has two independent variables, we can switch the display of the independent variables back and forth between the *x*-axis and the key. The graphs will look different, but they will tell the same story. This represents another artistic choice for the creator of the graph. Notice that the dependent variable remains in its usual place along the *y*-axis in both graphs (a and b). Which graph tells the story of this data set most clearly?

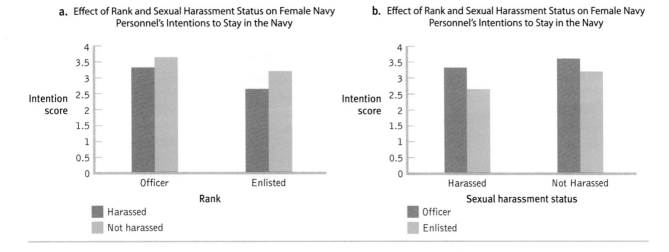

a. Effect of Rank and Sexual Harassment Status on Female Navy Personnel's Intentions to Stay in the Navy

b. Effect of Rank and Sexual Harassment Status on Female Navy Personnel's Intentions to Stay in the Navy

The Limitations of Graphic Software: Who Is Responsible for the Visual Display?

There are now many excellent computer-generated graphing programs, but be careful. The programmers had no idea how their creations would be used, so keep the context of a graph in mind: The visual communication of statistical information often represents the powerful end point of a statistical analysis. In fact, scientific graphs are so compelling and present so much information so quickly that accompanying text may be ignored in favor of a compelling picture of the data.

The creator of the graph must bear the responsibility for the impression it conveys. Many guidelines for graph construction are built into standard graphing software, but don't rely on the software to make decisions for you. That can be dangerous, because it is always the researchers, not our computer programs, who are responsible for the presentation of the data. Computer ***defaults*** *are the options that the software designer has preselected; these are the built-in decisions that the software will implement if we do not instruct it otherwise.* Often, the defaults are the options we would select anyway, but there are two problems with accepting them without consideration. First, we should always know what options we are selecting, because in letting the computer select, we *are* making a choice. Second, we will not always want the default options. Computer defaults can lead to difficult-to-interpret, misleading, or even inaccurate visual presentations of our data.

When you create graphs, do not be a passive user of software. Play with the program to figure out how to change defaults. Often you can point the cursor at a part of the graph and click to view the available options. If playing with the program doesn't yield the result you want, open the "Help" file and read the instructions. Even if you have to use white-out and a pencil, make sure that your graph celebrates accuracy over appearance and content over cosmetics.

Creating the Perfect Graph: General Guidelines

At this point, we have a good understanding of our variables, have chosen the graph that we will create, and are ready to begin creating the graph while avoiding the common pitfalls of graph construction. There are two closely related general guidelines that will always serve us well as we construct our graphs:

1. A graph should use the same terms that were used in the body of the paper.
2. A graph should tell its entire story without forcing the reader to go back to the text to understand what it says.

Both of these guidelines will be met if we label our graph appropriately and are mindful of our computer software's default features throughout the graph-creation process

A final general consideration involves the graph-corrupting fluff called *chartjunk*, a term coined by Tufte (2001/2006). According to Tufte, ***chartjunk*** *is any unnecessary information or feature in a graph that detracts from a viewer's ability to understand the data.* Chartjunk can take the form of any of three unnecessary features, all demonstrated in the rather frightening graph in Figure 3-21. (1) ***Moiré vibrations*** *refer to any of the patterns that computers provide as options to fill in bars.* Tufte recommends using shades of gray instead of patterns. In fact, he prefers gray to colors not in the white–black continuum, noting that if we

▪ **Defaults** are the options that the software designer has preselected. These are built-in decisions that the software will implement if we do not instruct it otherwise.

▪ **Chartjunk** is any unnecessary information or feature in a graph that distracts from a viewer's ability to understand the data.

▪ **Moiré vibrations** are a form of chartjunk that take the form of any of the patterns that computers provide as options to fill in bars.

▪ **Grids** are a form of chartjunk that take the form of a background pattern, almost like graph paper, on which the data representations, such as bars, are superimposed.

▪ **Ducks** are a form of chartjunk where features of the data have been dressed up to be something other than merely data.

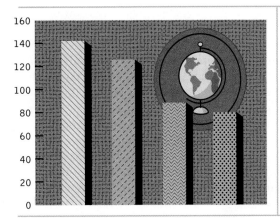

FIGURE 3-21
Chartjunk Run Amok

Moiré vibrations, such as those seen in the patterns on these bars, might be fun to use, but they detract from the viewer's ability to glean the story of the data. Moreover, the grid pattern behind the bars might appear scientific, but it serves only to distract. Ducks, like the 3-D shadow effect on the bars and the globe clip-art, add nothing to our data, and the colors are absurdly eye-straining. Don't laugh—we've had students submit carefully written research papers accompanied by graphs even more garish than this!

decide to use colors, we should be careful to choose those, such as blue, that can be distinguished from other colors even by those who are color-blind (reds and greens can be difficult for many of these people to tell apart).

We have had students who were so mesmerized by the seductive possibilities of graph-construction software that their graphs looked like sample sheets from a wallpaper store, an array of lovely designs but nary a data point to be discerned! (2) *Grids refer to a background pattern, almost like graph paper, on which the data representations, such as bars, are superimposed.* Tufte recommends the use of grids only for hand-drawn drafts of graphs. They should never be in a final version of a graph. (3) *Ducks are features of the data that have been dressed up to be something other than merely data.* Think of ducks as data in costume. Named for the Big Duck, a store in Flanders, New York, built in the form of a very large duck, graphical ducks can be three-dimensional effects, cutesy pictures, fancy fonts, or any other flawed design features. All other things being equal, simpler graphs are easier to interpret. Avoid chartjunk!

To wrap up our discussion of general guidelines, here is a short checklist of questions to ask when you've created a graph. Some we've mentioned previously, and all are wise to follow.

- Does the graph have a clear, specific title? Have you included the title in the appropriate place in your manuscript (as a figure caption at the end)?

- Are both axes labeled with the names of the variables in both upper- and lowercase letters? Do all labels read left to right—even the one on the *y*-axis? If possible, have you avoided a key that labels variables in a box separate from the graph itself?

- Are all terms on the graph the same terms that are used in the text that the graph will accompany? Have all abbreviations been eliminated?

- Are the units of measurement included in the title or data labels?

- Do the values on the axes either go down to 0 or have cut marks (double slashes) to indicate that they do not go down to 0?

- Are colors used in a simple, clear way—shades of gray instead of other colors?

- Has all chartjunk—moiré vibrations, grids, and ducks—been eliminated?

Edward Tufte's Big Duck
The graphics theorist Edward Tufte took this photograph of the Big Duck, the store in the form of a duck for which he named a type of chartjunk (graphical clutter). In graphs, ducks are any aspects of the graphed data that are "overdressed," obscuring the message of the data. Think of ducks as data in a ridiculous costume.

Franck Fotos/Alamy

When we use this simple checklist to construct our graph, we allow our data to speak as clearly and powerfully as they deserve, which is the primary reason for constructing a graph in the first place. If you feel pulled to distort your data or decorate them to make them more interesting, then ask yourself whether these data are worth reporting in the first place. As Tufte (2001/2006) says: "If the statistics are boring, then you've got the wrong numbers" (p. 80).

In summary, we have to decide how to present our data—in the text, in a table, or in a figure such as a graph. Once we've decided to use a graph, there are several guidelines to follow. Regardless of the type of graph, we must be cautious when using graphing software; we must not blindly accept the computer's default design decisions. Finally, attention to the labeling of the graph and to the avoidance of chartjunk lead to a clearer, more persuasive graph.

⊙ CHECK YOUR LEARNING

3-3 Use Figure 3-21 to represent the data testing the hypothesis that exposure to the sun can impair IQ. Imagine that the researcher has recruited groups of individuals and randomly assigned them to different levels of exposure to the sun: 0, 1, 6, and 12 hours per day (in all cases, enhanced by artificial sunlight when natural light is not available). The IQ scores are 142, 125, 88, and 80, respectively. Redesign this chartjunk graph, either by hand or using software, paying careful attention to the dos and don'ts outlined in this section.

> GRAPHING LITERACY: LEARNING TO LIE VERSUS CREATING KNOWLEDGE

The *Challenger* disaster demonstrates that a simply constructed, clearly reasoned graph could have saved many lives, as well as enormous amounts of money. Fortunately, history has provided us with a powerful example of a woman who created graphs that actually did save lives by creating new knowledge. This famous Christian feminist is not as well known for her statistical savvy as she is for her contributions to nursing, but none other than Sir Francis Galton, the famed statistician, called Florence Nightingale "the impassioned statistician."

Nightingale's adolescence was fraught with emotional conflict as she battled family expectations that she marry in order to save the family fortune. Yet she somehow used her considerable energy to transform Victorian expectations about the role of women, health care, and the responsibility of government to its people. By simply counting deaths and organizing them by month, she created descriptive statistics that allowed her to perceive genuine patterns amid the chaos of daily hospital life. She then used those data to create persuasive visual representations so that the new knowledge emerging from those data was clear, accurate, and convincing. In short, Florence Nightingale changed her world because she created powerful graphs.

The most powerful and famous of Nightingale's visual displays of data were the coxcomb graphs, so named because they resembled the profile of a rooster (Figure 3-22). She embedded three variables within this color-coded graph: the nominal variable of causes of death, the interval variable of number of deaths, and the ordinal variable of month of the year. She created two such graphs to

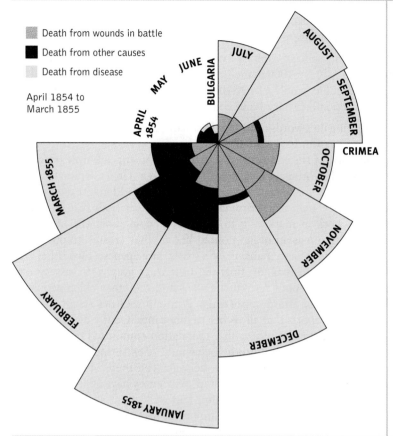

Death from wounds in battle
Death from other causes
Death from disease

April 1854 to
March 1855

FIGURE 3-22
Graphs That Persuade

Florence Nightingale's coxcomb graphs depicted "The Causes of Mortality in the Army in the East" in the years 1854–1855 (shown here). It was called a coxcomb because the data arrangement resembled the shape of a rooster's head. The 12 sections represent the ordinal variable of a year broken into 12 months. The size of the sections representing each month indicates the variable of how many people died in that particular month. The colors correspond to the different causes of death. Perhaps this graphic presentation vies with Charles Minard's graph of Napoleon's 1812 Russian campaign for the title of "the best statistical graphic ever drawn."

represent the causes of mortality in the years 1854–1855 and 1855–1856. Perhaps it was her public relations savvy that inspired her to use red to represent deaths due to wounds, blue to represent deaths due to preventable causes, and black to represent deaths due to all other causes. The visual portrayal of so much blue compared to so little red, even in wartime, forced the British government into a wide variety of health reforms. When she compared the graph representing deaths in 1854–1855 to the graph representing 1855–1856, it became clear that many more people were dying in peacetime because of preventable causes than were dying in battle!

As her fame increased, Florence Nightingale enjoyed many job opportunities that would have given her significant social power, both in government and in hospital administration. But she rejected all these job offers (just as she had rejected many offers of marriage), instead using statistics and other means of persuasion to influence public policy. She created many original descriptive statistics and graphs in support of many causes: alleviating overcrowding, implementing educational reform, and, most famously, reducing mortality in the army. But the specifically demanding question that all her statistics seemed to be asking was "Why?" People are dying unnecessarily: Why aren't we doing something about it? She united the passions of her adolescence, the wisdom of her adulthood, and the intelligence of an impassioned statistician to live a remarkably effective life with a statistically informed purpose. Her questions were not philosophical musings, but pointed barbs to people in power on the basis of undeniably persuasive information. For example, listen to how she "sucker-punched" (with sarcasm) some poor administrator resisting her reforms by asserting:

> [W]ith our present state of sanitary knowledge, it is as criminal to have a mortality of 17, 19, 20 per 1000 in the Line, Artillery, and Guards in England, when that of Civil life is only 11 per 1000, as it would be to take 1100 men per annum out upon Salisbury Plain and shoot them (Gill, 2005, p. 421).

Florence Nightingale's words reinforced brilliant, life-saving graphs that were created out of her passion to let the data speak.

As we survey some of the careers that our former students are now pursuing, we see that Florence Nightingale's legacy continues, even if in less dramatic form. For example, one of our former students often reads (but seldom creates) graphs in his work as a policy analyst in criminal justice. Another both reads and creates graphs in his work in marketing to persuade people about the life-saving importance of signing up as an organ donor. Yet another creates graphs to include in her annual reports as a manager of a foster care agency. Two other students work in different areas of finance; one uses graphs to assess and communicate projections about retirement plans and the other helps people to evaluate whether they can afford a mortgage. A friend uses her statistical skills to produce evaluation reports that allow her to more intelligently distribute millions of dollars each year as an officer in a foundation committed to improving urban education. If your attraction to the behavioral sciences includes a need to live a socially purposeful life, statistics can help get you there. The social passions that inspired Florence Nightingale's statistical legacy have continued across more than 150 years of statistics and are alive and well in our students.

It is very likely that graphs will play an important part in your life and career, whether you create them, refer to them in presentations, or read them in others' reports. Graphic literacy is a requirement for intelligent living. And remember, strong graph interpretation skills might even boost your GRE score! In this section, we will discuss the use of statistics in graphs to lie and to provide misinformation. An awareness of these 11 techniques for lying with statistics will serve you well, whether you are a consumer or a creator of graphs. We also will discuss the future of graphing, both to convince you that visual displays of data will pervade more aspects of your future career than you might predict and to stir your imagination about the possibilities of visual displays of data.

Lying With Statistics and Graphs: 11 Sophisticated Techniques

A sales manager once asserted that he never lied to his customers. "On the other hand," he acknowledged, "if they happen to believe something that is in my favor but isn't true, I won't try to change their opinion." Most of the 11 ways to lie with statistics listed here are a similar kind of white lie. A bald-faced lie is more convincing when presented in a graph, but somewhat easier to catch. A graph, with its scientific aura, is especially vulnerable to statistical white lies that subtly convey inaccurate, but credible, impressions. Most of these techniques are easily learned but sometimes less easy to recognize.

1. *The false face validity lie.* Face validity refers to whether the method used to collect our data seems (on the face of it) to represent what it says it represents. An unsophisticated lie involves labeling our graph one thing and

then supplying data for something else. A sophisticated lie involves using a plausible, but inaccurate, alternative; for example, we might label the variable "aggression" but measure how many times people shout at each other and for how long, behaviors that are probably only weakly correlated with aggression. Some fairly happy, well-adjusted families shout almost all the time, and many quiet families exchange polite comments but with lethal intent. We can catch people in this lie by reading their operational definitions. If the operational definitions don't fit the variables named in the title, be suspicious. If you can't find an operational definition, be very suspicious. Most people, however, never check, so it is an easy lie to get away with.

2. ***The biased scale lie.*** A biased scale slants information in a particular way. For example, some college course evaluation scales use categories labeled "poor," "fair," "good," "very good," and "excellent." Three out of the five categories connote very positive ratings ("good," "very good," and "excellent"), one is ambiguously weaker but potentially complimentary ("fair"), and the lonely fifth category isn't really so bad ("poor"). This scale will produce a negatively skewed distribution, and that's one way to catch this lie—a skewed distribution. To produce a bell-shaped curve, simply use more extreme end points, such as "the single worst professor I have ever had" and "the single best professor I have ever had." This forces students to identify the outliers, those rare professors who are either truly terrible or truly wonderful.

3. ***The sneaky sample lie***. A sneaky sample occurs when the people who participate in a study have been preselected so that the data will turn out in a particular way. For example, what kinds of students participate in RateMyProfessors.com? There is wide potential for bias whenever people self-select into the sample. Perhaps only students who love or hate their professors tend to participate in this Web site. Such comments can be very helpful but should be taken with a grain of salt because the information probably represents the views of a sneaky and therefore biased sample. You already know how to determine whether you are being influenced by a sneaky sample lie: the absence of random sampling.

4. ***The push-polling lie***. Push-polling is a clever variation on the sneaky sample lie that is used during political campaigns. A polling organization will call you on the phone and ask you questions designed to influence, rather than assess, your opinion. For example, a phone researcher may ask you, "How aware are you that Senator So-and-So has been accused of child abuse? Very aware, somewhat aware, or unaware?" The idea is planted in your mind, even if Senator So-and-So is completely innocent. Merely being asked the question makes you "somewhat aware" of the accusation, and that so-called research finding can then be reported in the media to a public that believes that "where there's smoke, there must be fire." Don't be a sucker! Ask for evidence.

5. ***The limited range lie***. When our scale does not allow your variable the range of expression it deserves, we are limiting the range of possible scores. For example, the *Challenger* data had a limited range because it simply excluded data about O-rings in warmer temperatures. Here are two ways to uncover the limited range lie. First, ask whoever is presenting the graph if you are being shown all of the available data, including the outliers. Second, examine the range of the data and the scale being used, and then ask yourself if there is more relevant data that could have been collected.

6. *The interpolation lie*. Interpolation occurs when we assert that some value between the data points necessarily lies on a straight line between those data points. For example, Simonton (1988) has used archival data in innovative ways to study the relation between age and creative productivity. Specifically, creative productivity tends to peak early (late 20s, early 30s) and then fall sharply in the fields of lyric poetry, pure mathematics, and theoretical physics. Creative productivity tends to appear later and rise more slowly (40s and 50s) and then decline less precipitously for novel writing, history, philosophy, and medicine. Simonton would have missed these nonlinear findings if he had measured creative productivity only at the beginning and end of a career. To spot the interpolation lie, check to be sure that a reasonable number of in-between data points have been reported.

7. *The extrapolation lie*. Extrapolation is a lie that goes beyond the available data points. *The Complete CB Handbook* (1976) makes extrapolations, hilarious in retrospect, based on the accelerating growth of citizens band (CB) radio use up until that time. These short-distance radios were first used in the 1940s but became very popular during the 1970s. Truckers used them to stay awake by chatting with other truckers, get emergency help, and check on traffic or speed traps. But when they showed up in the popular media like *The Dukes of Hazzard* TV show, the CB radio culture became a huge mainstream fad. The book predicted: "Soon every other automobile on the road will be equipped with a CB radio. . . . CB radio instruction will be a part of the elementary school curriculum in every state of the Union. . . . The CB radio industry will become a multi-billion-dollar-a-year business" (pp. xiv–xv). *The Complete CB Handbook* didn't take the invention of cell phones into account! CB radios are now rarely used except by truckers and some hobbyists. The extrapolation lie usually leads people to make grandiose, implausible assertions. Don't assume linearity.

8. *The false impression lie*. A false impression, as the phrase suggests, is an impression that contradicts the actual data. The false impression lie is accomplished in a variety of ways, but most commonly by presenting only part of the data and not labeling it clearly. The *Ithaca Times* graph discussed early in this chapter and shown in Figure 3-1 is technically accurate in one respect: Cornell's improved ranking. But the graph leaves a false impression by reversing the implied meaning of the scale, illustrating Cornell's improved ranking by a line that goes down instead of up. There are two ways to avoid being duped by a false impression lie. First, read carefully. Second, ask whether the information has gone through some form of unbiased peer review. Science articles are seldom published unless two or three other scientists have approved of the methods and conclusions proposed in an article.

9. *The change the interval lie*. The *Ithaca Times* graph (see Figure 3-1 on page 96) also lied by treating different intervals (11 years and 35 years) as if they were the same. As we also demonstrated in the description of female Navy personnel's intention to remain in the Navy for 20 years (see Figures 3-13 and 3-14 on page 114), a small change in the scale can leave a very different visual impression. If we change the interval from one graph to another, then we must clearly communicate what we did and why we did it. Simply pay attention to where the numbers actually begin or end, especially along the dependent variable (*y*-axis).

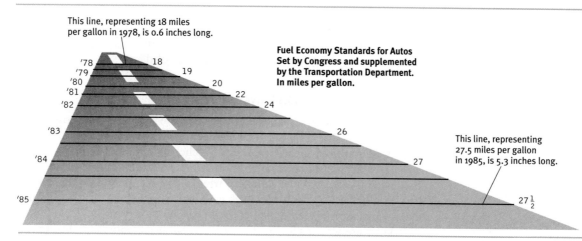

This line, representing 18 miles per gallon in 1978, is 0.6 inches long.

Fuel Economy Standards for Autos Set by Congress and supplemented by the Transportation Department. In miles per gallon.

This line, representing 27.5 miles per gallon in 1985, is 5.3 inches long.

FIGURE 3-23
The Inaccurate Values Lie

The visual lie told here is the result of a "highway" that spreads much farther apart than the data indicate. Michael Friendly (2005) asserts that "this graph, from the *New York Times*, purports to show the mandated fuel-economy standards set by the U.S. Department of Transportation. The standard required an increase in mileage from 18 to 27.5, an increase of 53%. The magnitude of increase shown in the graph is 783%, for a whopping lie factor = (783/53) = 14.8!"

10. *The inaccurate values lie*. This lie can be subtly effective. Sometimes it involves telling the truth in one part of the data but visually distorting it in another place. Notice in Figure 3-23 how wide the "highway" is when the accelerating fuel-economy savings is coming at the viewer. The proportional change in distance between the beginning and end of the highway is many times larger than the proportional change in the size of the data.

11. *The outright lie*. There is one more type of statistical lying that may use any of the techniques outlined above—plus simply making up the data! There are numerous frightening examples of outright lies with statistics and graphs. In *Freakonomics*, Levitt and Dubner (2005) reported that Mitch Snyder, an advocate for the homeless who was frequently interviewed by the media, repeatedly cited a statistic in the early 1980s that there were 3 million homeless Americans. Levitt and Dubner pointed out that that would mean more than 1 in 100 Americans are homeless; Snyder eventually admitted he had lied because he had been pushed by reporters to provide a specific number! One way to address outright lies is through strict peer review and a request to see the raw data. In 2005, for example, such a request to see the raw data resulted in Korean scientist Hwang Woo-suk's confession that he fabricated much of the data in his highly publicized cloning and stem cell research, as well as the statistics and graphs that interpreted the data for the scientific community and the media.

Lies in cancer, depression, or pension fund research mean that someone dies, suffers, or worries unnecessarily. People, unfortunately, are fooled on a regular basis. But now that you know these 11 sophisticated techniques for lying with statistical graphs, you are less likely to be among the fooled.

The Future of Graphs: Breaking the Fourth Wall

Theater actors perform in a world with three literal walls on the stage; the audience peeks in on what is happening in their lives through the fourth, invisible wall. Sometimes, however, the playwright or director instructs an actor to startle the audience by breaking the fourth wall and speaking directly to the audience. The film version of this would have actors climb out of the movie or television screen and walk into the movie theater or our living rooms—or at least look directly into the camera and speak to the audience. Graphs have that

■ **Sparklines** are datawords that are data-intense, design-simple, word-sized graphics that may be inserted into sentences.

same unnerving ability to occasionally take us into a new, unexpected dimension of understanding. Our deliberately broad scan of the literature found that graphs are already being used in many very different and unexpected ways, so we predict an exciting future for visual displays of data.

Interactive Graphing: Multilayered Information

In the creative world of visual displays, perhaps the most exciting prospect on the horizon is interactive graphing. You have probably used interactive tools already. For class, you may have used a CD-ROM, clicking a button to read more about the role of nongovernmental organizations in facilitating refugee relocation or to call up a photo of Lawrence Kohlberg while viewing a moral development timeline. Outside of school, you may have used an interactive Web site to request an online comparison of two digital cameras or clicked a swatch of color so that a store's Web site would show you what those tall black boots look like in red.

Despite the accelerating inclusion of interactive components on Web sites and CD-ROMs, few have taken advantage of their potential for creating truly inspiring graphs. One rare example, simultaneously informative and haunting, was published in the *New York Times* on September 9, 2004, to commemorate the day on which the 1000th U.S. soldier died in Iraq. Titled "The Roster of the Dead," this beautifully designed tribute is formed by photos of each of the dead servicemen and women. One can view these photographs by month of death, first letter of last name, home state, or age at death. Because the photos are the same size, the stacking of the photos serves almost as a bar graph. By clicking on two or more months successively or on two or more ages successively, one can visually compare numbers of deaths among levels of a category. Yet the graph is even more nuanced than this. In this text, we've emphasized that every score—and every person behind a score—has a story. This graph allows direct access to a part of those stories. By holding the cursor over a photo, you can learn, for example, that a photo that caught your eye is of Spencer T. Karol, regular duty in the U.S. Army, from Woodruff, Arizona, who died on October 6, 2003 at the age of 20, from hostility-inflicted wounds. A thoughtfully designed interactive graph holds even more power than a traditional flat graph to educate, evoke emotion, and even make a political statement.

The Many Layers of Interactive Graphs
Baltimore's City Paper publishes an interactive graphic called the Murder Ink Map. At the macro-level, this graph allows the viewer to see the number of people who have been murdered in the city of Baltimore in a given year, as well as where each murder took place. At the micro-level, the viewer can click on any of the numbered push-pins to read details about that particular murder—including the time, date, means, and whether the case has been solved.

Sparklines: Datawords Within Sentences

Edward Tufte (2006) proposes an innovation in the visual display of data that is more a re-capturing of the original impulse of early sci-entists: datawords. When Galileo recorded his stunning telescopic observations of the movements of planets, he embedded tiny sketches within the text that described those observations so that the reader could see the evidence at the very moment that particular evidence was being discussed. There was no need to refer to another figure on another page, take a trip to the appendix, or lift the eye from the page. At publication, Galileo arranged for the woodcuts of his drawings to be embedded within sentences such as "I saw the stars arranged in this manner. The more [sketch of stars around Jupiter] eastern star was . . . " In subsequent sentences, Galileo noted how the positions of the stars relative to Jupiter changed hour by hour.

So, Tufte (2006) suggests that we begin using *sparklines, datawords that are data-intense, design-simple, word-sized graphics that may be inserted into sentences.* For example, he suggests describing a patient's glucose levels with this sparkline **glucose** 6.6 . The dataword for this individual shows a change in glu-cose over time against the band of expected normal variation anchored by the most recent reading at the far right (6.6). An enormous amount of useful data is communicated within the prose; the reader does not even have to glance away from the text. Similarly, Tufte (2006) demonstrates the use of a sparkline to de-scribe the follow-the-herd mentality of mutual funds, plus an exception to that pattern. There are 400,000 individual data points in this word-sized sparkline (All 10 funds, overlapped, PIMCO in red) that demonstrates the distinc-tive performance of a Pimco fund compared to nine other mutual funds. Sparklines are a useful innovation in our data-intensive age and unite modern scientific expressions with the original impulses of Galileo.

Forensic Graphing: Fighting Custody Battles

Forensic psychologists sometimes use graphs in custody battles to compare prom-ised support to real support in terms of time spent with a child, money owed to a spouse, and other court-mandated requirements ("Optimal Graphs and Statistics," parentingtime.net, 2005). The simple bar chart in Figure 3-24 offers

Reprinted with permission Edward R. Tufte, Beautiful Evidence, Graphics Press, Cheshire, CT, 2006

ta imperfezzione dello ſtrumento, ò dell'occhio del riguardan-te,perche ſendo la figura di Saturno coſi ,come moſtra-no alle perfette viſte i perfetti ſtrumenti , doue manca tal perfezzione appariſce coſi non ſi diſtinguendo perfetta-mente la ſeparazione , e figura delle tre ſtelle ; ma io che mil-

Galileo: An Early User of Sparklines Galileo embed-ded his prose with drawings of his evidence. Edward Tufte describes word-sized graphics as datawords, or sparklines, word-sized graph-ics that may be inserted into sentences.

Reprinted by permission Edward R. Tufte, *The Visual Display of Quantitative Information, 2nd Edition*, Graphics Press, Cheshire, CT, 2006.

FIGURE 3-24
Graphs in the Courts

Custody battles may be fought using graphs that suc-cinctly describe the relation between the amount of time or money that a parent has promised compared to what that parent actually delivered.

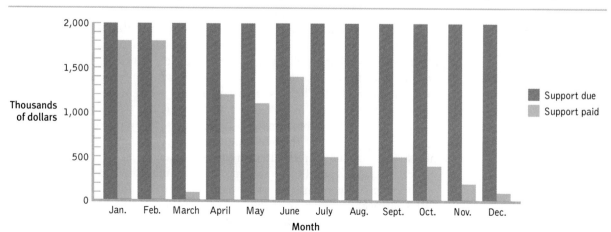

a month-by-month comparison of the extent to which a parent has fulfilled the court-mandated obligation to his or her children. Although we need to bear in mind that fake information does not magically become true just because it is in a graph, this application demonstrates the creative potential, storytelling capability, and persuasive strengths of visual displays, even of such personal data.

Computerized Mapping: A Maturing Technology

Google, Yahoo!, and others have published software that enables computer programmers to link Internet-based data to Internet-based maps (Markoff, 2005). For example, there is software that links house listings to maps so that prospective home buyers can see all the properties of interest on one map. The media predict that these mapping tools will be used mainly by businesses—from advertising companies to franchise restaurants—but the accessibility of these visual tools makes it almost certain that social scientists will find creative ways to apply them to research questions. The merging of geographical information systems (GIS) and behavioral data strikes us as having enormous potential for insight through new forms of visual data.

Sociologists use GIS more than many other social scientists, but the field of epidemiology, which includes the tracking of demographic patterns of physical and mental health problems, could likely benefit from maps that describe the prevalence of physical and psychological disorders, especially when these maps are layered with other predictive data already associated with geographic variables, many of which are publicly available through what are called TIGER Shapefiles (maps of demographic data) from the U.S. Census Bureau ("TIGER Shapefiles and 2000 U.S. Census," 2005). Organizational psychologists, public health specialists, and political scientists also could use GIS to clarify patterns related to co-morbidity, marketing, blood donations, or voting behavior relative to placement of voting machines (an issue in Ohio during the 2004 presidential election). Ironically, this advance in computerized mapping pretty much mirrors what John Snow did without a computer in 1854 when he studied the Broad Street cholera outbreak (see Chapter 1).

Clinical Applications: Graphs to Monitor Therapy

Clinical psychology researchers have developed graphing techniques, illustrated in Figure 3-25, to help therapists predict when the therapy process appears to be leading to a poor outcome (Howard, Moras, Brill, Martinovich, & Lutz, 1996). They have developed a model that is able to predict an expected rate of recovery for a specific client. The independent variables include a number of pretherapy client characteristics, such as attitude toward therapy and the severity and pattern of psychopathology; the dependent variable is rate of improvement. The predicted rate of improvement is graphed as a line, somewhat like the line of best fit we saw earlier, but typically curved—perhaps an initial quick improvement, followed by steady improvement, and then a plateau. The therapist then adds points to the graph showing a client's actual status, assessed empirically using measurement tools, at each succeeding week of therapy. This allows a therapist to determine how a client's *actual* rate of improvement compares to what would be expected for another individual with similar characteristics. If therapy progresses more slowly than expected, then both the client and the therapist may be spurred to take action by the discrepancy in the graphs.

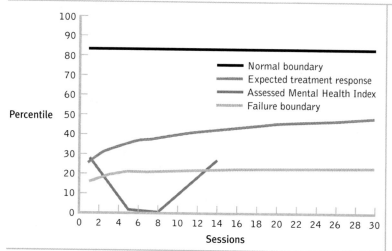

FIGURE 3-25
Graph as Therapy Tool

Some graphs allow therapists to compare the actual rate of a client's improvement with the expected rate given that client's characteristics. This client (Assessed Mental Health Index in grey) is doing worse than expected (expected treatment response in red), but has improved enough to be above the failure boundary (in yellow).

Brain Imaging: From Numbers to Pictures

Brain imaging is a visual display of data that does not appear to be based on numerical data; yet much of the final image is based on innumerable mathematical calculations using many, many numbers. The several types of brain imaging, however, represent some of the most tangible, dramatic improvements in our understanding of brain function, our treatment of traumatic brain injury, and the identification of a wide variety of illnesses. For example, positron emission tomography (PET) maps the brain's metabolic activity. Harmless radioactive molecules, injected into the bloodstream along with water, release positrons, positively charged particles that cluster where blood flow is highest. A PET camera measures the levels of radioactivity and creates an image that demarcates the areas of the brain with the highest levels of blood flow—those with the highest radiation counts.

Some researchers create two images using PET, a control image and an experimental image in which a participant is engaged in a cognitive task. By subtracting the control blood-flow pattern from the experimental blood-flow pattern, researchers can measure the change in blood flow. Then they can calculate a mean change in blood flow for a number of research participants. This is just one example of a visual display of data that has transformed both neurology and cognitive psychology. The future of visual displays of data appears to be very exciting, with promises of richer insights, more accurate information, and provocative ways of collecting and then displaying data.

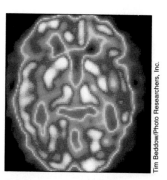

Brain Scans as Graphs
PET and other kinds of brain scans use the latest advances in graphing techniques to aid in the understanding of brain functioning.

The Uses and Misuses of Statistics: It's Not Just What You Draw, It's How You Draw It

"Lies, damn lies, and statistics." It is not clear whether these famous words first were spoken by Mark Twain or Benjamin Disraeli. But there is an alternative folk wisdom that we like much better: "Figures don't lie, but liars figure." Early in this chapter, we suggested that graphs sometimes reveal as much about the person creating the graph as about the information itself. This is because graphs are also a work of art. This means that we often need to do more than glance at a graph to decipher what it is saying, just as therapists need to listen to *how* clients speak, as well as to the content of what they are saying. So a graph should draw the viewer deeper into its meaning by seducing both the eye and the imagination with compelling information.

Almost anyone can lie with a graph, and now, thanks to what you have learned in this chapter, so can you—and with style! But why would you want to do that? There is an enormous amount of information about human behavior that still needs to be discovered. So let's become artistically mature and intellectually competent with our visual displays of data. Visual displays of data freeze some aspect of fluid human behavior, and this gives us the opportunity to enjoy a long, contemplative look at the story the data tell. We encourage you to do what Florence Nightingale did during the busiest years of her brief career: invent a new way to let a visual display of data tell a story that you believe is worth telling.

In summary, graphing literacy is becoming more and more integral to career success in our information age. Graphing savvy can help us navigate the myriad visual displays we encounter every day, many of which are riddled with statistical lies. Moreover, a deep understanding of the basic tenets of graphing is invaluable because the graphs of the future will become ever more complex. In the near future, we can expect to see an acceleration in the use of online interactive graphs, map-based graphs that use GIS, graphs based on sophisticated prediction models such as those that forecast therapy outcomes, and increasingly sophisticated brain-imaging techniques.

⊙ CHECK YOUR LEARNING

3-4 Several descriptions of graphs follow. For each, indicate the likely lie that the graphmaker is perpetrating.

a. A time series plot depicted the change in salaries, adjusted for inflation, of sociologists. It showed salaries in 1950, 1975, and 2000, with an increase at each time point. The graphmaker asserted that salaries had been increasing steadily since 1950.

b. Do smarter people attend statistics class more often? A scatterplot depicted the relation between intelligence and class attendance. Statistics grades were on the x-axis, and percentages of classes attended were on the y-axis.

c. Your professor asserts that you should not become a political scientist, showing a time plot that depicts a decrease in job openings over the last 10 years. The job prospects can only decrease, he warns.

d. Students were asked to rate the likelihood that they would attend one or more of a series of GRE preparation workshops held on campus. They could choose 1, would never go; 2, would rarely go; or 3, would always go. A bar graph depicted the mean scores for economics, criminal justice, and nursing students.

e. The bookstore manager wanted to ascertain changing student perceptions of the bookstore over four years. She added a brief questionnaire to the bookstore Web site, tallied the mean score for each of four years, and printed posters that showed a time series plot demonstrating increasingly positive perceptions over time.

f. A school initiated a zero-tolerance policy toward aggression, either physical or verbal, in the classroom. At the end of the year, the school principal showed parents a bar graph depicting girls' detention and suspension rates for the previous and the current years, stating, "Girls are becoming increasingly violent in recent years."

▪ DIGGING DEEPER INTO THE DATA: THE BOX PLOT

There are numerous advanced ways to create graphs. Many of these techniques are invented graph by graph to best portray a given data set, but others are standard forms of graphs that have not been covered in this chapter, often because they are rarely used in the behavioral sciences. One such graphing technique is the box plot, invented by John Tukey in the 1960s. Box plots help us to understand the distribution of our data, especially when the median, rather than the mean, is the measure of central tendency that communicates the most meaningful information.

Box plots are graphs that depict the overall distribution of a data set. The lower end of the box marks the first quartile, and the upper end marks the third quartile. A line through the middle indicates the median. "Whiskers" are lines that indicate the minimum and maximum scores in a sample. Box plots are powerful, descriptive graphs because they can tell a story accurately and clearly, especially when the data are skewed. And many naturally occurring phenomena are skewed. For example, a distribution of mortality data (the age at which people die) is naturally skewed by the sad reality that so many children die compared to the more gradual mortality rates among older people able to live out their natural lives. Unfortunately, mortality distributions are especially skewed in third world countries, where many children die at a very young age and a long life is a rarity. We may not enjoy hearing such stories, but box plots can tell them accurately in one powerful picture.

Box plots depict the overall distribution of the data in a sample and are based on five scores: the minimum, first quartile, median, third quartile, and maximum. In the Digging Deeper into the Data section of Chapter 2, we discussed the interquartile range (*IQR*), calculated by subtracting the first quartile from the third quartile. The first quartile (*Q1*) designates the 25th percentile, and the third quartile (*Q3*) designates the 75th percentile, so the *IQR* designates the range of the middle 50% of scores. Researchers often use the *Q1* and *Q3* as part of a "five-number summary" that includes the minimum, *Q1*, median, *Q3*, and maximum. So, box plots are information-dense visual presentations that provide distinctive information.

For example, in the wake of the September 11, 2001, terrorist attacks, regular air travelers have become familiar with having to remove shoes, go through multiple identity checks, and comply with other security-related delays associated with air travel. Many of us may grumble about both the inconvenience and the improbability that these long lines are really making us any safer. But how bad a problem is it really? Here are data presented by *USA Today* for June 1, 2004, through May 16, 2005, for the average wait in a security line (in minutes) for the 40 U.S. airports with the most traffic in terms of number of domestic passengers who flew out of that airport.

4.7	2.6	2.3	5.4	2.9	5.6	3.2	3.9	4.8	2.1
4.3	3.9	4.8	3.7	4.9	2.5	5.7	5.2	4.3	2.9
2.9	5.6	5.9	4.7	2.6	2.8	4.7	2.8	2.7	2.5
5.3	3.8	2.6	5.6	3.3	2.7	5.4	5.3	3.2	3.1

The information needed to create a box plot is provided on the next page, but if you want to do this as a mathematical exercise, you can first refer to the instructions in Chapter 2 to determine the minimum, median, and maximum. Then use

▪ A **box plot** is a graph that depicts the overall distribution of a data set. The lower end of the box marks the first quartile, and the upper end marks the third quartile. A line through the middle indicates the median. "Whiskers" indicates the minimum and maximum scores.

▪ **Whiskers** are the lines that extend from either end of the box in a box plot. The ends of the whiskers indicate the minimum and maximum scores in a sample.

the brief instructions in the Digging Deeper into the Data section of Chapter 2 on page 79 to determine *Q1* and *Q3*. These numbers form our five-number summary:

Maximum: 5.90

Q3: 5.05

Median: 3.85

Q1: 2.80

Minimum: 2.10

A box plot is created from these five numbers. The box encompasses the middle 50% of scores. That means that the horizontal bottom of the box is the 25th percentile, *Q1*, and the top is the 75th percentile, *Q3*. The box has a horizontal line through it to indicate the median. Its whiskers are the lines that extend from either end of the box. The ends of the whiskers indicate the minimum and the maximum scores in a sample. Figure 3-26 is a box plot of these data. From the box plot, we can get a sense of the distribution. For example, this tells us that the median falls pretty much in the middle. *Q3* is a little farther from the median than is *Q1*, indicating some positive skew, but this is a pretty symmetrical box plot. There is a good chance that the data are normally distributed. You may want to remember the mnemonic we suggested regarding the direction of skew: "the tail tells the tale." In other words, if the long tail is to the right (when the box plot has more space in the upper portion), then the distribution has a positive skew. If the long tail is to the left (when the box plot has more space in the lower section), then the distribution has a negative skew.

Here is a recap of the steps to create a box plot.

1. Calculate the five-number summary: minimum, *Q1*, median, *Q3*, maximum

2. Label the *y*-axis with the name of the dependent variable and its possible values, starting with 0 if practical.

3. Draw a box. The bottom of the box should fall at the value for *Q1* and the top at the value for *Q3*.

4. Draw a horizontal line across the box at the value for the median.

5. Draw vertical whiskers that extend from the bottom of the box to the minimum and from the top of the box to the maximum.

FIGURE 3-26
Box Plot of Airport Waiting Times

This box plot depicts airport waiting times (in minutes) at the 40 busiest U.S. airports. From this graph, we can see the minimum and maximum scores, as well as the scores at the 25th, 50th, and 75th percentile. As you'll recall, the 50th percentile is the median.

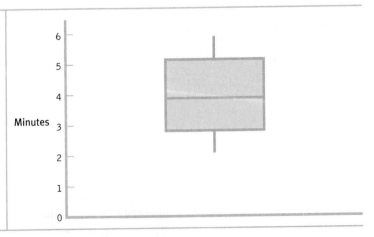

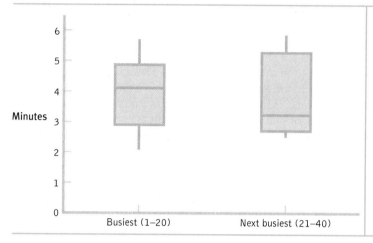

FIGURE 3-27
Side-by-Side Box Plots of Airport Waiting Times

This graph includes two box plots side by side; one depicts airport waiting times (in minutes) at the 20 busiest U.S. airports, and the other depicts times at the next 20 busiest airports. The side-by-side box plots allow for a comparison of the distributions of the two samples.

One particularly useful feature of box plots is the ability to do side-by-side box plots for different categories of the same data. So if we have a nominal independent variable and an interval dependent variable, we can do side-by-side box plots for each category. We could, for example, do side-by-side box plots for two airport categories: the 20 airports with the most traffic (ranked 1–20) and the next 20 busiest airports (ranked 21–40). Again, the dependent variable is minutes. Figure 3-27 depicts box plots for the data categorized this way.

We can read a different story from these data. First, the median for the busiest 20 airports, as we might expect, is higher than the median for the next 20 busiest airports. But there's more to the story than this. The data for the busiest 20 airports (1–20) seem to be negatively skewed, but not too severely. The median is closer to $Q3$ and the maximum than it is to $Q1$ and the minimum. On the other hand, the data for the next 20 busiest airports (21–40) seem to form a more obviously positively skewed distribution. The median is much closer to the minimum and $Q1$ than it is to the maximum and $Q3$. What about these patterns indicates skew? Well, if the median is far from the 75th and 100th percentiles, then the central tendency of the data set is not likely to be in the middle; the data stretch out in a positive direction. Similarly, if the median is far from the 0 and 25% marks, then the data are stretching out from the central tendency in a negative direction. These pictures of the data give us a very quick sense of whether there is skew. Moreover, these box plots give us *far* more information

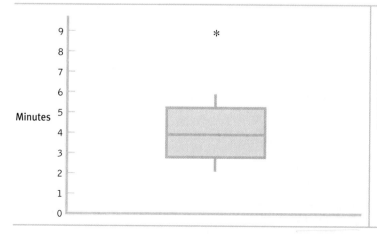

FIGURE 3-28
Box Plots and Outliers

This box plot again depicts airport waiting times (in minutes) at the 40 busiest U.S. airports, but this time the sample data include an outlier of 9 minutes. Potential outliers are identified in a box plot by a symbol, such as an asterisk.

than a bar graph depicting the two means (or medians) would give us. Why do you think that the distribution was so skewed at the less busy airports?

Another benefit of box plots is their ability to depict potential outliers in a very clear way. Figure 3-28 shows what happens if we include an outlier—nine minutes—in the data for the original box plot. Potential outliers are designated by an easy-to-see asterisk (or another symbol, such as a small circle, in some software programs). The whiskers end at the next-lowest scores below the potential outlier or outliers (or if the outliers are on the lower end of the box, the whiskers end at the next-highest score). Computer software programs that create box plots typically calculate outliers using the $1.5 \times IQR$ rule that we discussed in the Digging Deeper into the Data section of Chapter 2. The IQR is multiplied by 1.5; that number is added to $Q3$ and subtracted from $Q1$. Any scores that are beyond these points are considered potential outliers. This technique, although quite useful, is merely an estimate of which points might be outliers. It is important to examine any identified points in the context of the data to determine whether they are indeed quite far from the rest of the data.

Box plots are most useful when we suspect that our data are skewed; in such cases, the median is likely to be a better measure of central tendency than the mean, and the IQR and range are likely to be better measures of variability than the standard deviation. In general, the box plot is an excellent choice in two situations: (1) if our data are likely to be skewed and (2) if we want to make comparisons of the shape of distributions rather than comparisons of central tendency. The beauty of box plots is that they present so much interesting data in an easily understood visual depiction.

Tufte (2001/2006) suggests a redesign of the standard box plot that substantially increases the data–ink ratio. In this redesign, the box is eliminated entirely. The median is designated by a dot, and the whiskers remain. Figure 3-29 depicts a redesign of Figure 3-26. The far simpler graph imparts the same information. Because the five-number summary is conveyed within a single vertical line, it would be possible to add a number of other box plots on the same graph without sacrificing clarity.

In summary, there are many other types of standard graphs that we did not cover in this chapter, primarily because they are rarely used in the behavioral sciences. However, many of them, including the box plot, could be quite valuable by expanding the ways that we think about data. Box plots are graphs that are comprised of a five-number summary: the minimum, $Q1$, median, $Q3$, and maximum. $Q1$ and $Q3$ form the outside of a box, with the median cutting across it. Whiskers, or vertical lines, extend out to the minimum and maximum scores. The box plot is a flexible tool. It can depict two or more samples on the same plot to allow for comparison, and it can easily flag potential outliers.

FIGURE 3-29
Simplified Box Plot

Tufte's suggestions for redesigning box plots are implemented in this graph. The far simpler design conveys the same information as the more elaborate box plot. The simplicity lends itself to the inclusion of additional box plots. A simplified side-by-side box plot need not limit itself to two boxes.

⊙ CHECK YOUR LEARNING

3-5 Suppose an industrial/organizational psychologist wants to demonstrate that constructing graphs with computer software is far faster than with the old-fashioned paper-and-pencil method. He randomly assigns 15 people to construct a graph with a computer and 15 different people to construct a graph by hand. Here are the numbers of minutes for each group to complete the graph:

Computer: 12, 15, 22, 11, 15, 15, 16, 11, 12, 84, 17, 13, 13, 14, 18

By hand: 15, 16, 20, 24, 22, 17, 16, 14, 17, 19, 19, 19, 15, 15, 14

a. Compare the two sample means. Based only on the means, which graphing method appears to lead to faster graph construction?

b. Calculate the five-number summary for each sample.

	COMPUTER	BY HAND
MIN	1	14
Q1	12	15
MDN	15	17
Q3	17	19
MAX	84	24

c. Now create a side-by-side box plot for these data, either using software or by hand. What do you learn from the box plot that you do not learn from the means?

d. Use the *IQR* × 1.5 criterion for each sample to determine if there are any potential outliers.

e. Create a side-by-side box plot without the potential outlier. Now which method seems to lead to the faster graph construction? Explain.

REVIEW OF CONCEPTS

> Uses of Graphs: Clarifying Danger, Exposing Lies, and Gaining Insight

Graphs can imply information about the creator of the graph, as well as provide information about a specific data set. The volume of information available as a result of the Internet and advances in research makes graphic literacy an increasingly important skill. Consequently, the ability to create and interpret graphs is becoming an essential skill if we wish to avoid misleading and being misled by others.

> Common Types of Graphs: A Graph Designer's Building Blocks

When developing graphing skills, it is important to begin with the basics. Single-variable graphs, including frequency histograms and polygons, depict just one interval variable. Multivariable graphs depict the relations among more than one variable. There are several types of multivariable graphs commonly used by social scientists.

Scatterplots depict the relation between two interval variables. They are useful for identifying data points that are outliers and for examining the relation between the variables to determine whether it is *linear* or *nonlinear*. Some *line graphs* expand on scatterplots by including a line of best fit. Others, called *time plots*, show the change in an interval variable over time.

Bar graphs are used to compare two or more categories of a nominal independent variable with respect to an interval dependent variable. Sometimes more than one independent variable is depicted on one bar graph. A bar graph on which the categories are organized from the highest bar to the lowest bar, called a *Pareto chart*, allows for easy comparison of categories. *Pictorial graphs* are like bar graphs except that pictures are used in place of bars. *Pie charts* are used to depict proportions or percentages on one nominal variable with just a few levels. Because both pictorial graphs and pie charts are frequently constructed in a misleading way or are misperceived, bar graphs are almost always preferred to pictorial graphs and pie charts.

Recent redesigns of graphs allow us to increase the data–ink ratio and devote more of our graph to telling the story and less to distracting adornments. One example is the *range-frame*, a scatterplot or line graph that eliminates the *x*-axis and *y*-axis below the minimum score and above the maximum score.

> How to Build a Graph: Dos and Don'ts

The APA has developed guidelines to help behavioral scientists determine whether to construct a *table* (typed in text) or a *figure* (not typed in text; usually a graph). The APA also has guidelines about how to construct a figure once we've decided it is appropriate to do so. Once we have decided to create a graph, we must decide what type of graph to create by examining our independent and dependent variables.

We must then consider a number of guidelines to develop a clear, persuasive graph. We must be careful to consider our computer software's *defaults*, the design decisions that the computer programmers made and that will be implemented unless we request otherwise. It is important that all graphs be labeled thoroughly and appropriately and given a title that allows the graph to tell its story without additional text. For an unambiguous graph, it is imperative that graph creators avoid *chartjunk*, unnecessary information, such as *moiré patterns*, *grids*, and *ducks*, that clutters a graph and makes it difficult to interpret. A checklist for the creation of clear graphs is included in this section.

> Graphing Literacy: Learning to Lie Versus Creating Knowledge

With the improvement of computer technology and access to information, graphing is becoming a more central part of careers, both within and outside of the behavioral sciences. An understanding of the ways people lie with graphs and statistics can help us to identify when others are lying and avoid inadvertent lies in our own graphs. Moreover, an eye to the future of graphing—from interactive graphs to the use of GIS systems—will help us to be at the forefront of graph-making in social sciences fields. Sparklines are data words inserted within sentences that communicate large amounts of information without distracting the reader's attention away from the sentence.

▪ DIGGING DEEPER INTO THE DATA: THE BOX PLOT

There are a number of more advanced and less frequently used ways to depict our data visually. *Box plots* provide information about the shape of the distribution of our data by visually presenting the five-number summary of our data: minimum, *Q1*, median, *Q3*, and maximum. The box encompasses the range from *Q1* to *Q3*, with the median indicated by a horizontal line through the box. *Whiskers* extend from the box on either end to the minimum and maximum.

Box plots are flexible graphing tools. Side-by-side box plots enable a comparison of two or more samples. Box plots also can help to identify outliers, which are included as asterisks. These are calculated by the *IQR* × 1.5 rule—any score that is more than 1.5 times the interquartile range below the first quartile or above the third quartile is considered a potential outlier.

SPSS GUIDELINES FOR CHAPTER 3: VISUAL DISPLAYS OF DATA

We can request visual displays of data from both the *Data View* screen and the *Variable View* screen. SPSS allows us to create visual displays across several different menus; however, most graphing will be done in SPSS using the Chart Builder, a very flexible graphing tool.

Graphs → Chart Builder → Gallery

Then, under "Choose from:" select the type of graph by clicking on it. Then, drag a sample graph from the right to the large box above. Usually, we'll want the simplest graph which tends to be the upper left-hand sample graph.

Finally, drag the appropriate variable from the "Variables:" box to the appropriate places on the sample graph (e.g. "x-axis"), and click OK.

Remember: we should not rely on the default choices of the software; we are the designer of the graph. Once the graph is created, we can change the graph's appearance by double-clicking on the particular feature of the graph that we would like to modify.

EXERCISES

3.1 Cross-country cycling and scatterplots: Every summer, the touring company America-by-Bicycle conducts its Cross-Country Challenge, a seven-week bicycle journey across the United States from San Francisco to Portsmouth, New Hampshire. At some point during the trip, the exhausted cyclists usually start to complain that the organizers are purposely planning for days with lots of hill and mountain climbing to coincide with longer distances. The staff who work on the tour counter that there's no relation between climbs and mileage and that the route is organized based on practicalities such as the location of towns in which riders can stay. And the organizers who planned the route (and who also own the company) say that they actually tried to reduce the mileage on the days with the worst climbs. Here are the approximate daily mileages and climbs (in vertical feet) as estimated from one rider's bicycle computer.

MILEAGE	CLIMB	MILEAGE	CLIMB	MILEAGE	CLIMB
83	600	69	2500	102	2600
57	600	63	5100	103	1000
51	2000	66	4200	80	1000
76	8500	96	900	72	900
51	4600	124	600	68	900
91	800	104	600	107	1900
73	1000	52	1300	105	4000
55	2000	85	600	90	1600
72	2500	64	300	87	1100
108	3900	65	300	94	4000
118	300	108	4200	64	1500
65	1800	97	3500	84	1500
76	4100	91	3500	70	1500
66	1200	82	4500	80	5200
97	3200	77	1000	63	5200
		92	3900	53	2500

a. Construct a scatterplot of the cycling data, putting mileage on the *x*-axis. Be sure to label everything, and include a title.

b. We haven't learned to calculate inferential statistics on these data, so we can't really know what's going on, but do you think that amount of vertical climb is related to a day's mileage? If yes, explain the relation in your own words. If no, explain why you think there is no relation.

c. It turns out that inferential statistics do not support the existence of a relation between these variables and that the staff seem to be the most accurate in their appraisal. Why do you think the cyclists and organizers are wrong in opposite directions? What does this say about people's biases and the need for data?

3.2 Group of Eight and line of best fit: The Group of Eight, G8 for short, consists of most of the major world economic powers. It meets annually to discuss pressing world problems. In 2005, for example, the agenda included global warming, poverty in Africa, and terrorism. Decisions made by G8 nations can have an impact; in fact, the eight nations that make up the membership reportedly account for almost two-thirds of the world's economic output. Here are data for seven of the eight G8 nations for gross domestic product (GDP) in 2004 (according to the World Bank) and a measure of education. The measure of education is the percentage of the population between the ages of 25 and 64 that have at least one university degree (Sherman, Honegger, & McGivern, 2003). Russia is not included because no data point for education was available.

COUNTRY	GDP (IN TRILLIONS OF $U.S.)	% WITH UNIVERSITY DEGREE
Canada	0.98	19
France	2.00	11
Germany	2.71	13
Italy	1.67	9
Japan	4.62	18
United Kingdom	2.14	17
United States	11.67	27

a. Create a scatterplot of these data with university degree on the *x*-axis, being sure to label everything and to give it a title. Later, we'll use statistical tools to determine the equation for the line of best fit. For now, draw a line of best fit that represents your best guess as to where it would go.

b. In your own words, describe the relation between these variables that you see in the scatterplot.

c. Is there an outlier? What country is it? How do you think the outlier affects the mean of each of these variables? Calculate the mean GDP with and without this outlier. What would be a better measure of central tendency than the mean?

d. Create a scatterplot of these data without the outlier. Again include your best guess for the line of best fit. Now describe the relation between these variables. Does the relation appear to change at all? Explain.

e. We put education on the *x*-axis, indicating that education was the independent variable. Explain why it is possible that education predicts GDP. Now reverse your explanation of the direction of prediction, explaining why it is possible that GDP predicts education.

3.3 Organ donation and time series: The Canadian Institute for Health Information (CIHI) is a nonprofit organization that compiles data from a range of institutions—from governmental organizations to hospitals to universities. Among the many topics that interest public health specialists is the problem of low levels of organ donation. Medical advances have led to ever-increasing rates of transplantation, but organ donation has not kept up with medicine's ability to perform more sophisticated and more complicated surgeries. Recent data reported by CIHI (2005) provide Canadian transplantation and donation rates for 1994–2004. Here are the donor rates per million deaths.

YEAR	DONOR RATE PER MILLION DEATHS	YEAR	DONOR RATE PER MILLION DEATHS
1994	14.0	2000	15.3
1995	14.9	2001	13.5
1996	14.2	2002	12.9
1997	14.3	2003	13.5
1998	13.8	2004	13.1
1999	13.8		

a. Construct a time series plot from these data. Be sure to label and title your graph.

b. What story are these data telling?

c. Based on these data, what might you predict for 10 years from now? Explain why it might be dangerous to make that prediction. Specify which statistics lie this would represent.

d. If you worked in public health and were studying the likelihood that families would agree to donation, what research question might you ask about the possible reasons for the trend suggested by these data?

3.4 Alumni donations and bar graph: Universities are concerned with increasing the percentage of alumni who donate to the school because alumni donation rate is a factor in the *U.S. News & World Report* university rankings. What factors might play a role in alumni donation rates? Although there are numerous variables we could test, let's look at one: type of university. *U.S. News & World Report* lists the top 10 national universities (all of which are private), the top 10 public national universities, and the top 10 liberal arts colleges (also all private). National universities focus on graduate education and research, whereas liberal arts colleges focus on undergraduate education. To give you a sense of the type of institutions in each of these categories, the number-one schools for 2004 in the three categories were Harvard University, the University of California at Berkeley, and Williams College, respectively. Here are the 2004 alumni donation rates for the top 10 schools in each of these categories.

TOP TEN PRIVATE NATIONAL SCHOOLS	TOP TEN PUBLIC NATIONAL SCHOOLS	TOP TEN LIBERAL ARTS SCHOOLS
48%	15%	60%
61	14	63
45	26	52
39	16	53
46	25	66
37	26	52
38	15	55
34	9	55
33	12	53
47	32	48

a. What is the independent variable in this example? Is it nominal or interval? If nominal, what are the levels? If interval, what are the units and what are the minimum and maximum values?

b. What is the dependent variable in this example? Is it nominal or interval? If nominal, what are the levels? If interval, what are the units and what are the minimum and maximum values?

c. Construct a bar graph of these data using the default options in your computer software.

d. Construct a bar graph of these data, but change the defaults to satisfy the guidelines for graphs discussed in this chapter. Aim for simplicity and clarity.

e. What does the pattern of the data suggest?

f. Cite at least one research question that you might want to explore next if you worked for one of these universities—your research question should grow out of these data.

3.5 G8 and Pareto chart: Here are the 2004 GDPs, in trillions of U.S. dollars, of each of the G8 nations.

Canada: 0.98   Japan: 4.62
France: 2.00   Russia: 0.58
Germany: 2.71   United Kingdom: 2.14
Italy: 1.67   United States: 11.67

a. Explain how a Pareto chart is different from a bar graph.

b. Construct a bar graph of these data, arranging the countries in alphabetical order as they are here.

c. Construct a Pareto chart of these data.

d. What is the benefit of the Pareto chart over the bar graph?

3.6 Mentoring and bar graphs—two independent variables: Johnson, Koch, Fallow, and Huwe (2000) conducted a study of mentoring in two types of psychology doctoral programs: experimental and clinical. Students who graduated from the two types of programs were asked whether they had a faculty mentor while in graduate school. In response, 48.00% of clinical psychology students who graduated between 1945 and 1950 and 62.31% who graduated between 1996 and 1998 reported having had a mentor; 78.26% of experimental psychology students who graduated between 1945 and 1950 and 78.79% who graduated between 1996 and 1998 reported having had a mentor.

a. What are the two independent variables in this study, and what are their levels?

b. What is the dependent variable?

c. Create a bar graph that depicts the percentages for the two independent variables simultaneously.

d. What story is this graph telling us?

e. Why would a time series plot be inappropriate for these data? What would a time series plot suggest about the mentoring trend for clinical psychology graduate students and for experimental psychology graduate students?

f. For four time points—1945–1950, 1965, 1985, and 1996–1998—the mentoring rates for clinical psychology graduate students were 48.00, 56.63, 47.50, and 62.31, respectively. For experimental psychology graduate students, the rates were 78.26, 57.14, 57.14, and 78.79, respectively. How does the story we see here conflict with the one that we developed based on just two time points? What statistical lie was suggested by using just two time points?

g. Was this a true experiment? Explain your answer.

3.7 Pictorial graph and alumni donations: Consider the data on alumni donations presented in Exercise 3.4.

a. Explain how these data could be presented as a pictorial graph. (Note that you do not have to construct such a graph.) What kind of picture could you use? What would it look like?

b. What are the potential pitfalls of a pictorial graph? Why is a bar chart usually a better choice?

3.8 Pie chart and community-based projects: The National Survey on Student Engagement (NSSE) has surveyed more than 400,000 students—freshmen and seniors—at 730 schools since 1999. Among the many questions on the NSSE, students were asked how often they "participated in a community-based project as part of a regular course." For the students at the 19 institutions classified as national universities that made their data publicly available through the *U.S. News &World Report* Web site, here are the data. Never: 56%; sometimes: 31%; often: 9%; very often: 5%. (The percentages add up to 101% because of rounding.) Explain why a bar graph would be more suitable for these data than a pie chart.

3.9 Satisfaction with graduate advisors and defaults: The 2000 National Doctoral Program Survey asked 32,000 current and recent PhD students across all disciplines to respond to the statement: "I am satisfied with my advisor." The researchers calculated the percentage of students who responded "agree" or "strongly agree." Current students: 87%; recent graduates: 86%; former students who left without completing the PhD: 48%.

a. Use a software program that produces graphs (e.g., Excel, SPSS, Minitab) and create a bar graph for these data.

b. Play with the options available to you. List 10 aspects of the bar graph that you are able to change. Be specific.

3.10 How would you present these data?: For each of the following fictional scenarios, (i) state the independent and dependent variables, then (ii) state which graph or graphs would be appropriate to depict the data and explain why.

a. Do gender and music affect video game performance? There were 75 male and 75 female students randomly assigned to play a video game in one of the following three conditions: no music, rock music, or rap music. Their scores on the video game were recorded.

b. A social psychologist studied the effect of height on perceived overall attractiveness. Students were recruited to come to a research laboratory in pairs. They were left to sit in the waiting room for several minutes, then brought to separate rooms, where their heights were measured. They also filled out a questionnaire that asked, among other things, that they rate attractiveness of the person who had been sitting with them in the waiting room on a scale of 1–10.

c. Do people remember expletives better than other words? Students were asked to memorize a list of 20 expletives; one day later, researchers recorded how many words they remembered. Either a couple days before or after memorizing the expletives, the same students were asked to memorize a list of nonexpletives that are equally common in the English language. A day later, researchers recorded how many words they remembered.

d. A social worker tracked the depression levels of clients being treated with cognitive-behavioral therapy for depression. For each client, depression was assessed at weeks 1-20 of therapy. She calculated a mean for all her clients at week 1, week 2, and so on, all the way through week 20.

e. An epidemiologist determined adolescent suicide rates for 20 countries.

3.11 Invent a scenario: Give an example of a study—real or hypothetical—in the social sciences that might display its data using the following types of graphs. State your independent variable(s) and dependent variable, including levels for any nominal variables.

a. Frequency polygon

b. Line graph (line of best fit)

c. Bar graph (one independent variable)

d. Scatterplot

e. Time series plot

f. Pie chart

g. Bar graph (two independent variables)

3.12 What is the statistical lie in each of the following scenarios?: Identify the statistical lie (or lies) in each of the following scenarios. Explain why the scenario is an example of that lie.

a. The APA Web site (http://research.apa.org/) reported that 33.0% of new psychology doctorates in 1976 and 71.4% in 2001 were women. We could therefore infer that 52.2% of doctorates in 1988 were women.

b. Are you planning to visit New York City for a political science conference? The Web site http://www.newyork.citysearch.com/bestof/winners/2005/bagel lists the best bagels in New York City. The Web site says: "You voted for the best bagel in New York, and we tallied the results. See if your favorites are winners."

c. A researcher wanted to examine how well male versus female students interacted with each other in an academic context. She compared male and female students' responses to the question from the NSSE that asked students how often they worked with classmates on out-of-class assignments.

d. The APA Web site reported that women were 20.0% of the psychology PhDs in the workforce in 1973 and 47.9% in 2001. We could therefore predict that women will be 75.8% of psychology PhDs in the workforce in 2029.

e. *USA Today* reported that "the typical 9-year-old in the USA now reads more each day than a 17-year-old" (Toppo, 2005). The article states that 25% of children in elementary school read more than 20 pages per day, whereas 23% of high school students read at least that many pages.

f. A marketing firm hired college students wandering around a mall to rate a trailer of a romantic movie on a scale of 0–10, telling them that 0 means "I hated the trailer; it was incredibly stupid!" and 10 means "I loved the trailer; it was rather beautiful." When the average score came back 8.92, the marketing firm reported to the movie producers that "college students reported a very high level of intention to go see the movie."

g. The producer refused to pay the marketing firm, complaining that "your measurements don't support your conclusion." So it changed its measurements, telling the next sample that 1 means "The trailer is stupid"; 2 means "The trailer is OK"; and 3 means "I kind of liked the trailer." This new study produced an average score of 2.05, so the marketing firm told the producer that "this new score is only a fraction away from the highest possible score" and reasserted its conclusion that "this second sample of college students reported an even higher level of intention to go see the movie."

h. Your university's dining hall asked you whether you thought food services had improved a little, somewhat, or a lot since a new dining hall manager started three months earlier.

3.13 Rate my professor and the sneaky sample lie: Go to the Web site http://www.ratemyprofessors.com.

a. If your school is included, find one of your favorite professors. Did he or she receive any negative comments? Give one example.

b. Now find one of your least favorite professors. Did she or he receive any positive comments? Give one example.

(Note: For parts (a) and (b), if none of your professors is included, go to any university and find a professor with a good overall rating to see if he or she had any negative ratings, and then find a professor with a bad overall rating to see if he or she had any positive ratings.)

c. For most of you, there will be mixed reviews of your professors. Why is this? Explain why this is an example of the sneaky sample lie.

d. If a friend were making decisions about which courses to take based on ratemyprofessor.com, what would you tell him or her about potential problems with the ratings?

e. Give three examples of chartjunk used by the Web site developers at ratemyprofessors.com.

3.14 Advice to graph creators: What advice would you give to the creators of each of the following graphs? Consider the basic guidelines for a clear graph, chartjunk, and the 11 lies of statistics. Give three pieces of advice for each graph. Be specific—don't just say there's chartjunk; say exactly what you'd change.

a. The shrinking doctor:

THE SHRINKING FAMILY DOCTOR
In California

Percentage of Doctors Devoted Solely to Family Practice

| 1964 | 1975 | 1990 |
| 27% | 16.8% | 18.0% |

1: 4,232
5.212

1: 43,157
8.964

1: 2,247 RATIO TO POPULATION
8,023 Doctors

b. Comparison of income in Western nations:

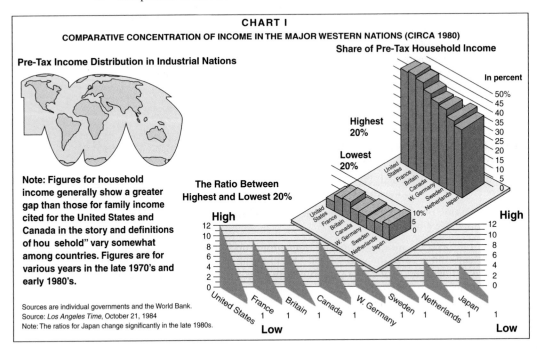

c. Workforce participation:

3.15 Pulling it all together—the popular media: Find an article in the popular media (newspaper, magazine, Web site) that includes a graph in addition to the text.

a. Briefly summarize the main point of the article and graph.

b. What are the independent and dependent variables depicted in the graph? What kind of variables are they? If nominal, what are the levels?

c. What descriptive statistics are included in the article or on the graph?

d. In one or two sentences, what story is the graph (rather than the article) trying to tell?

e. How well do the text and graph match up? Are they telling the same story? Are they using the same terms? Explain.

f. Which of the 11 lies occur in your article or graph? Explain.

g. Write a paragraph to the graph's creator with advice for improving it. Be specific, citing the guidelines from this chapter.

h. Redo the graph, either by hand or by computer, in line with your suggestions.

3.16 Pulling it all together and theory development: The Yerkes–Dodson graph demonstrates that graphs can be used to describe theoretical relations that can be tested. In a study that could be applied to the career decisions made during college, Gilovich and Medvec (1995) identified two types of regrets—regrets of action and regrets of inaction—and proposed that their intensity changes over time. You can think of these as Type I regrets, things you have done that you wish you had not done (regrets of action), and Type II regrets, things you have not done that you wish you had (regrets of inaction). They suggested a theoretical relation between the variables that might look something like the accompanying graph.

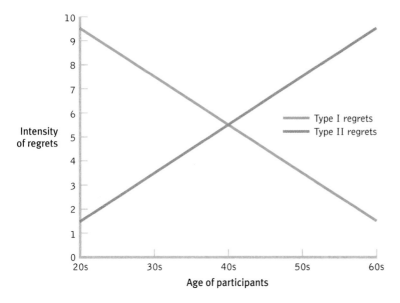

a. Briefly summarize the theoretical relations proposed by the graph.

b. What are the independent and dependent variables depicted in the graph? What kind of variables are they? If nominal, what are the levels?

c. What descriptive statistics are included in the text or on the graph?

d. In one or two sentences, what story is the graph trying to tell?

3.17 Pulling it all together and psychology degrees: The APA compiles many statistics about training and careers in the field of psychology. The accompanying graph tracks the numbers of bachelor's, master's, and doctoral degrees between the years 1970 and 2000.

a. What kind of graph is this? Why did the researchers choose this type of graph?

b. Briefly summarize the overall story being told by this graph.

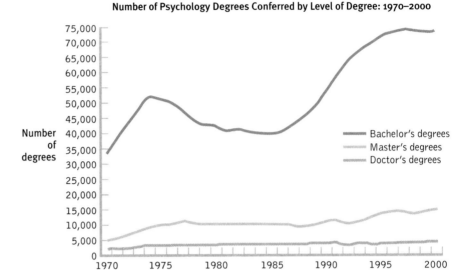

Number of Psychology Degrees Conferred by Level of Degree: 1970–2000

c. What are the independent and dependent variables depicted in the graph? What kind of variables are they? If nominal, what are the levels?

d. List at least three things that the graph creators did well (that is, in line with the guidelines for graph construction).

e. List at least one thing that the graph creators should have done differently (that is, in line with the guidelines for graph construction).

f. Why would it be dangerous to predict the numbers of degrees for 2020?

g. Name at least one variable other than number that might be used to track the prevalence of psychology bachelor's, master's, and doctoral degrees over time.

h. The increase in bachelor's degrees over the years is not matched by an increase in doctoral degrees. List at least one research question that this finding suggests to you.

3.18 The language of statistics—*bar graphs* and *histograms*: Bar graphs and histograms look very similar. In your own words, what is the difference between the two?

3.19 The language of statistics—*default*: What are two of the meanings of *default* in everyday conversation? What do we mean by *default* when we refer to computer software?

■ **DIGGING DEEPER INTO DATA**

3.20 Box plots and alumni donations: Here are the data on alumni giving rates at the top national universities.

48 61 45 39 46 37 38 34 33 47

29 38 38 34 29 29 36 48 27 25

15 25 14 26 33 16 33 32 25 34

26 32 11 15 25   9 25 40 12 20

32 10 24   9 16 21 12 14 18 20

18 25 18 20 23   9 16 17 19 15

14 18 16 17 20 24 25 11 16 13

a. Calculate the five-number summary for these data.

b. Construct a box plot for these data

c. What does the box plot indicate about the shape of the distribution?

3.21 Box plots and outliers: This question refers to the data from Exercise 3.20.

a. Calculate the interquartile range.

b. Using the *IQR* × 1.5 criterion, determine the values below which and above which scores are potential outliers.

c. According to this criterion, are there any outliers in this data set?

TERMS

scatterplot (p. 102)
range-frame (p. 103)
linear relation (p. 104)
nonlinear relation (p. 105)
line graph (p. 107)
time plot or time series plot (p. 108)

bar graph (p. 112)
Pareto chart (p. 112)
pictorial graph (p. 116)
pie chart (p. 117)
table (p. 119)
figure (p. 119)
defaults (p. 122)

chartjunk (p. 122)
Moiré vibrations (p. 122)
grids (p. 123)
ducks (p. 123)
sparklines (p. 131)
box plot (p. 135)
whiskers (p. 135)

CHAPTER FOUR

PROBABILITIES AND RESEARCH
THE RISKS AND REWARDS OF SCIENTIFIC SAMPLING

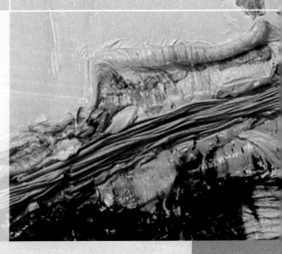

Robert was an accidental psychology major. His first love and academic major was music, especially composing in a style that blended jazz with classical music. The interaction between the two styles often produced something fascinating. He had never wanted to learn statistics; he was a musician first, foremost, and (he hoped) forever. A music major needed to understand the principles of composition, not the principles of statistics. Nevertheless, Robert's curiosity continually brought him back to psychology. Why could the simplest of melodies convey so profound a mood? How could a modification of tempo, instrument, or key produce so different a musical sensibility? He informally hypothesized that different keys communicated different moods. For example, he sensed that the key of A-flat was inherently depressive but that A major was inherently grand. But how was he ever going to test that very interesting, mysterious possibility? Psychology was the only discipline he knew that had the flexibility not only to ask so many different kinds of questions but also to answer them.

But Robert was feeling far more anxious than creative as he pulled his car into the faculty parking spot marked "Space 23: Reserved." It wasn't so much his fear of another parking ticket as it was the dread words from his mother: "The test came back positive." He was determined to make Professor Krissel understand his situation: His grandmother was in danger; the first statistics test was tomorrow; and understanding the risks and rewards of sampling statistics was the last thing he wanted to be thinking about.

Robert was not the only artist attracted to statistics. From Karl Pearson (poet, novelist) to W. Edwards Deming (composer), much of the story of statistics has been written by artistically inclined individuals because the underlying commonality between the arts and the sciences is randomness. For example, Runco (2006) has identified how randomly related activities such as playfulness promote creativity in children, and Simonton (2004) has used a wealth of archival studies to develop a more formal understanding of how chance influences scientific creativity. So the oxymoron of predictable randomness (whose curious story we learn about in Chapter 7) underlies some of the creativity in both the arts and the sciences. In this chapter, we explore randomness by learning why even the routine practice of sampling is both an art and a science, how probability theory explains coincidence, how to use probability to make predictions, the two-sided risk associated with making predictions, and the importance of statistical literacy in everyday life—as a consumer and as a patient.

> SAMPLES AND THEIR POPULATIONS: WHY STATISTICIANS ARE STINGY

To pierce the apparent randomness of who contracted cholera, John Snow interviewed the families of only 83 of the 616 (13.5%) initial victims of the Broad Street cholera outbreak. Similarly, Florence Nightingale did not record every activity in every hospital in England. Nevertheless, both were confident that their discoveries would apply to other cholera victims and to other hospitals. And they were right. The reason they could be so confident is based on principles of probability. What they learned from their respective samples turned out to be true for the larger populations they were most interested in. This is because it was unlikely that their samples would show any effect that was not genuinely present in the population. Their samples faithfully represented the larger population, in sharp contrast to the flawed presentation of incomplete data about *Challenger*'s O-rings that led to the space shuttle disaster.

The specific ways in which John Snow and Florence Nightingale gathered their original data produced samples so good that both these impassioned researchers could *generalize* their findings to similar people and situations. Their methods of collecting sampling data were imperfect according to modern guidelines, but they still made it highly probable that their samples were representative of the population. Consequently, it was highly probable that the discovery that a contaminated well or unsanitary medical conditions led to disease in their samples meant that a contaminated well or unsanitary medical conditions did the same in the population. *Generalizability refers to researchers' ability to apply findings from one sample or in one context to other samples or contexts.* This principle is also called *external validity.* Because their research designs and samples were excellent, the findings of John Snow and Florence Nightingale had high external validity, and that critical statistical detail empowered their research to save thousands of lives.

Decision Making: The Risks and Rewards of Sampling

Almost everything worth studying requires a sample, whether it is a medical test for mononucleosis, a test of memory following exposure to a chemical spill, or an organizational search for high-achieving students in a college. But there are risks and rewards when we choose to sample from a population rather than study everyone in the population.

■ **Generalizability** refers to researchers' ability to apply findings from one sample or in one context to other samples or contexts; also called *external validity.*

The risks associated with sampling are these:

1. The sample might not represent the larger population.
2. We might not know that the sample is misleading.
3. We might reach inaccurate conclusions.
4. We might make decisions based on this bad information.

The rewards of successful sampling are these:

1. The sample represents the larger population.
2. We increase our level of confidence in our own findings.
3. We reach accurate conclusions at a very low cost.
4. We remain open-minded because we know samples can mislead us.
5. We make wiser decisions based on the available evidence.

For example, a sample of a professor's teaching on the first day of a class may or may not represent what the professor will be like over an entire term. Similarly, career decisions based on a sample of psychology professors' personalities may not represent whether that academic discipline is a good fit for you. Thinking like a statistician supports intelligent, probability-based decision making, especially when circumstances are complicated by many variables.

The risks associated with sampling lead to two unpleasant possibilities. The first is that we might believe that the sample accurately represents the population when it actually does not. The second is that we might not believe the sample accurately represents the population when it actually does. We wrestle with this decision-making dilemma almost every day because we really don't want to make either kind of error. For example, when a gossip passes along some juicy information about a mutual friend, we could decide to believe the gossip and later discover that the story is not true. Or we could decide not to believe the gossip and later discover that the information really is true. Both decision-making errors can lead us to say or to do things to our friend that we might regret. So there is a two-sided risk whenever we make a judgment based on incomplete information.

We run this two-sided risk of making a wrong decision because statisticians are stingy bargain hunters. We don't want to do any more work than we absolutely have to, yet we still want the maximum amount of good information—and we want it at the lowest possible cost in terms of cash, time, and effort. Probability allows us to be so cheap. But our cheapness is not the only reason that statisticians study samples instead of entire populations. In many cases, studying every member of a population would take so long that the very thing we are studying would change by the time we had finished studying it. For example, if an industrial/organizational psychologist were studying the morale of every employee in a large organization or government agency, by the time he got to the last employee, the first participants would be ready for retirement. And sampling can work quite well; if we're making soup and it's well mixed, we don't have to sample the entire pot to know that it needs more salt. A representative sample—one spoonful of a well-mixed soup—is all we need.

There are two main types of samples: a random sample and a convenience sample. *A **random sample** is one in which every member of the population has an* *equal chance of being selected into the study. A **convenience sample** is one that uses participants who are readily available, as opposed to randomly selecting participants from the entire population of interest.* Random sampling remains the ideal, but it is usually expensive and extremely difficult to achieve. By contrast, convenience sampling is usually both inexpensive and easy, even though it introduces other problems. Which type of sampling do you imagine is used most often by stingy statisticians? Convenience sampling, of course. In fact, researchers have developed many variations on these two approaches in an effort to satisfy the goal that underlies every sampling technique: a representative sample. Most of these variations were developed as researchers tried to balance the ideal of obtaining a perfectly random sample with the real costs of collecting data in a timely manner.

Bargain Hunting for Data
Statisticians are stingy! Like bargain hunters at a flea market, they want to "buy" the best data for the lowest possible "price." And they do it all the time because the principles of probability allow them to use carefully collected sampling data to accurately generalize to larger populations.

Random Sampling: An Equal Chance of Being Selected

Theoretically, the safest way to collect a representative sample is by collecting a random sample. However, there are good reasons why collecting a random sample is far easier in theory than in practice. For example, think of the phone requests that most of us have received urging us to participate in a survey of preferences for consumer items, such as toothpaste or vacation homes, or our leanings with regard to a politician. A computerized random dialer is often used to select telephone numbers for this kind of research. The caller might even be a computer!

Using a random dialer assumes that each phone number represents, on average, the same number of people, and without bias. However, this assumption is unlikely to be correct. The young, upwardly mobile, two-income couple with no children may have six phone numbers: two landlines, two faxes, and two cell phones. At the other extreme, a large extended family may have only one phone number being used by three generations living under the same roof. So collecting a random sample is not easy; nevertheless, a random sample remains the ideal. Let's consider how to generate a random sample by using a specific example. Although most of us have an intuitive idea of what randomness means, the following exercise will demonstrate that randomness can be a surprisingly subtle concept.

If you are interested in becoming a psychological therapist, you will want to pay particular attention to this opportunity to experience randomness for yourself. The rising generation of therapists will likely be called upon to treat post-traumatic stress disorder (PTSD) connected with many different events: natural disasters, terrorism, wars, sexual assaults, or the kind of situation described below. Therapy is not glamorous work; you may never see the fruits of your labor. You may get paid late or, occasionally, not at all. Yet it remains necessary, vital work that is guided by the knowledge accumulated over many thousands of studies and shared among researchers and therapists in their professional conferences, journals, and books. And those studies can only be trusted if they are based on representative samples and random assignment to groups.

■ A **random sample** is one in which every member of the population has an equal chance of being selected into the study.

■ A **convenience sample** is one that uses participants who are readily available, as opposed to randomly selecting participants from the entire population of interest.

EXPERIENCE IT FOR YOURSELF

UNDERSTANDING RANDOMNESS

Imagine that a town has recently experienced a traumatic mass murder and that there are exactly 80 police officers in the local department. Because your training combined both clinical skills and research skills, you have been hired to determine whether peer counseling or professional counseling is the most effective way to treat officers suffering from PTSD, whether or not they were directly involved in the incident. The State Association of Chiefs of Police is financing your study because it wants to be prepared to address the needs of its officers. However, there is no line for research in its annual budget, so the sample that you can recruit must be very small, just 10 people. How do you maximize the probability that those 10 individuals will accurately represent the 80 officers?

Five officers will be randomly selected from the 80 and randomly assigned to peer counseling; another 5 will be randomly selected and randomly assigned to counseling with a therapist. Each police officer is arbitrarily assigned a two-digit number from 01 to 80. Choose 10 officers by randomly writing down any 10 numbers between 01 and 80:

_____   _____   _____   _____   _____

_____   _____   _____   _____   _____

Now arrange a list of 10 numbers, five 0's and five 1's, so that they are in random order:

__ __ __ __ __ __ __ __ __ __

Now use the accompanying random numbers table to choose a sample of 10 police officers by arbitrarily selecting a point on the table and deciding to go across, back, up, or down to read through the numbers. Decide on your starting point and direction of counting and stick to it! You can't change your method because you don't happen to like those particular numbers. For example, we could begin with the sixth number of the second row and count across. The first 10 numbers read: 97654 64501. (The spaces between sets of five numbers exist solely to make it easier to read the table.) The first pair of digits is 97, but we would ignore this number because we only have 80 people in our population. The next pair is 65. The 65th police officer in our list would be chosen for our sample. The next two pairs, 46 and 45, would also be in the sample, followed by 01. If we come across a number a second time—45, for example—we'd ignore it, just as we would ignore 00 and anything above 80.

EXCERPT FROM A RANDOM NUMBERS TABLE

This is a small section from a random numbers table used to select participants from a population to be in a sample as well as to randomly assign participants to experimental conditions.

04493	52494	75246	33824	45862	51025	61962
00549	97654	64501	88159	96119	63896	54692
35963	15307	26898	09354	33351	35462	77974
59808	08391	45427	26842	83609	49700	46058

Were you surprised that the numbers 46 and 45 occurred in a row? Did the supposedly random list that you created have any two consecutive numbers? For most of you, it will not; your numbers were generated by you, not generated randomly. *Truly random numbers often have strings of numbers that do not seem to be random.* In fact, quite often people who do not understand randomness inadvertently impose a rule that "no number can occur twice" or "consecutive numbers are not allowed." For example, in the third row of the table, you'll notice that there is a string of three 3's. A human trying to generate a list of random numbers is not likely to include such strings. We just don't think randomly, and we find the pattern-like appearance of real randomness to be confusing.

In a large study, researchers rely on random numbers generated by a computer. An especially easy one to use can be found at www.randomizer.org (Urbaniak & Plous, 2005). Once on the site, click on "randomizer," and then complete the form about the characteristics of the list you want. The Web site will even download the list into Excel. When we used the randomizer to generate a list of 10 unique numbers from the range 1–80, we were provided with the following output: 10, 23, 27, 34, 36, 67, 70, 74, 77, and 78. Of course, it will be different each time we make a request on the randomizer. You might be surprised that 4 of the 10 numbers were in the 70s. Don't be. Random numbers are truly random, and part of their subtlety is that sometimes randomness looks like a nonrandom pattern.

Variations on Random Sampling: Cluster Sampling and Stratified Sampling

The type of sample we chose in Experience It Yourself: Understanding Randomness is called a simple random sample because every police officer had an equal chance of being selected. But not all random samples are "simple random samples." A useful variation on random sampling is cluster sampling. Clusters can take many forms; they can be universities, hospitals, provinces, sides of a street, or classrooms, and so on. ***Cluster sampling*** *is a selection method in which all of the clusters in a population are identified and a certain number of these clusters are selected randomly; everyone in the selected clusters would then be recruited to participate in the study.* For example, if we're interested in studying the elementary school system in Salt Lake City, then we might treat individual classrooms as clusters. We could randomly select, for example, 30 classrooms in the school district and then include every student in the selected classrooms in our study. Cluster sampling can be easier to implement than simple random sampling; it is often easier to identify every cluster than it is to identify every individual. With cluster sampling, we only have to identify the individuals in the clusters that are selected.

Another variation on simple random sampling is ***stratified sampling***, *a sampling method in which strata, usually levels of a nominal variable, are identified, and then a random sample of the same size is taken from each stratum.* Social scientists may use many different strata in their studies, including age group, region, ethnic background, and level of education. For example, if we are interested in age differences, then our strata might include four groups of adults: those aged 20–39, 40–59, 60–79, and 80–99. We would then use simple random sampling to select the same numbers of participants from each of those strata. The entire *population* may consist of fewer people in the 80–99 range than in any of the other three age ranges,

■ **Cluster sampling** is a selection method in which all of the clusters in a population are identified and a certain number of those clusters are selected randomly. Everyone in the selected clusters would then be recruited to participate in the study.

■ **Stratified sampling** is a method in which strata, usually levels of a nominal variable, are identified, and then a random sample of the same size is taken from each stratum.

but this selection method will ensure that our *sample* consists of exactly as many people in the 80–99 year old range as there are in any of the other three age ranges.

Random samples are almost never used because we almost never have access to the whole population from which to select our sample. If we were interested in studying the mating behaviors of voles, we would never be able to list the whole population of voles so that we could select a random sample of voles. If we were interested in studying the effect of video games on the attention span of teenagers in the United States, we would not be able to identify all U.S. teenagers from which to choose a random sample. If we were interested in studying dyslexia in Canada, we could not test every Canadian for dyslexia. We just usually can't identify the entire population of interest.

The Whole Population of Voles?

If we were interested in studying the mating behaviors in voles, we would not be able to access the entire worldwide population of voles so that we could select a sample randomly. We would probably use a convenience sample from an animal supply company.

Convenience Sampling: Readily Available Participants

It is far more common to use a convenience sample. We might use voles that we bought from an animal supply company, teenagers from the local high school, and Canadians with dyslexia identified through a university counseling center. A convenience sample usually limits our generalizability—our external validity. This means that we never can be certain that results from our sample apply to the larger population of interest. Because convenience samples are so commonly used in the behavioral sciences, however, we often address the limitations through replication. A study that is well designed and is replicated with different samples can provide reliable and valid information about a concept, despite reliance on convenience samples.

We must be even more cautious when we use a ***volunteer sample***, *a special kind of convenience sample in which participants actively choose to participate in a study*. Participants volunteer, or self-select (this is also called a *self-selected sample*), when they respond to recruitment flyers or choose to complete an online survey. We should be very suspicious of such samples because a sample of volunteers may be very different from a randomly selected sample—often much more different than a convenience sample is from a randomly selected sample. For example, if money is offered for participation in a marketing study, the study may attract individuals who are unemployed or anxious about money. Geography (where the study is conducted), income, personality, and particular needs may all influence (bias) the outcomes of a study using a volunteer sample. (Note that even samples that do not meet the definition of volunteer samples—that is, those that are randomly selected—are always composed of volunteers, because participants always sign an informed consent form agreeing to participate. Ethically and legally, every participant must ultimately be a volunteer.)

Random Assignment: An Equal Chance of Being Assigned to a Condition

■ A **volunteer sample** is a special kind of convenience sample in which participants actively choose to participate in a study; also called a *self-selected sample*.

Being randomly assigned into a particular experimental condition is very different from being randomly selected into a study in the first place. If a study has two levels of the independent variable, as in the study of police officers, then we would need to assign participants to one of two groups. We could decide, arbitrarily, to number the groups 0 and 1 for the "peer-counseling" group and the "therapist-counseling" group, respectively. As before, we would select a place in the random numbers table to begin (see the table in Experience It for Yourself: Understanding Randomness) and then choose only the digits that were a 0 or 1, ignoring the others. If we began at the first number of the last row and read the numbers across, ignoring any number but 0 or 1, we would find 0010000. Hence, the first two participants would be in group 0, the third would be in group 1, and the next four would be in group 0. Again, notice the seemingly nonrandom pattern and remember that, it *is* random. Did your earlier list of 10 numbers have any strings of four 0s or four 1s in a row? How about strings of three 0s or 1s? For most of you, the answer will be no. And if your list did include strings, there might be other, less obvious ways in which it was not random. Again, humans just don't think randomly.

If we used the random numbers generator at www.randomizer.org, we would instruct the computer that we wanted one set of 10 numbers that ranged from 0–1. The numbers would *not* remain unique because we want multiple 0s and multiple 1s, and we would *not* want to sort the numbers because we would want to assign participants in the order in which the numbers are generated. When we ran the request, the 10 numbers were: 1110100000 (this is not half and half 1s and 0s, always a risk we run when we generate random numbers. We must decide in advance to use only the first five 1s and only the first five 0s). Compare the strings of 0s and 1s with any strings in the list that you generated before reading this section. It is only in the short run that randomly generated lists of numbers are this haphazard. In the long run, patterns start to emerge. As our list gets longer and longer, we'll get closer and closer to having half 0s and half 1s overall, although we will still have lots of strings of one or the other along the way. For the moment, this is a very practical consideration as we randomly assign participants to groups in a study.

As long as we don't start substituting our own notions of what is random to replace what the computer generates, we can use our common sense to resolve problems that come up; for example, what if there are many more participants assigned to one group than the other, such as nineteen 0s and one 1? It could happen, and this would lead to very unbalanced groups. Because it is best to aim for equal numbers in our groups, researchers often decide how many participants they want in each level of the independent variable and stop when one group is full. For example, if we wanted five people in each group, we'd stop when we reached five 0s (or five 1s) and assign the remaining participants to the other group. The important thing is to make our selection decisions *before* we go to the list of random numbers. This way, we don't "trick" ourselves into picking one set of numbers over another because we feel like one list is more random than another. We just can't trust ourselves to be random.

Variations on Random Assignment: Block Design and Replication

Just as there are variations on random selection, there also are variations on random assignment. Keep in mind that our goal is to create equivalent groups that will provide a fair test of our hypothesis. Random assignment just happens to be the most practical and effective way to create a state of fairness at the outset of our experiment. Another way to create equivalent groups is to match their characteristics by using a randomized block design. *A **randomized block design** creates equivalent groups by matching the participants with regard to important characteristics and then using randomization only within blocks, or groups, of participants who are similar on one or more of these characteristics.* A block could be as simple

▪ A **randomized block design** creates equivalent groups by matching the participants with regard to important characteristics and then using randomization only within blocks, or groups, of participants who are similar on one or more of these characteristics.

as two people. For example, if we were interested in the effects of alcohol on memory, we might suspect that IQ also has an impact on memory. To make sure that our conditions are the same with respect to IQ, we might take many blocks—in this case, pairs—of people with the same IQ. Within each block, one person would be randomly assigned to the "alcohol" condition and one to the control condition. So a block of two people with very high IQs of 130 would be assigned, one to each condition (one to the "alcohol" condition and one to the control condition). Another block of two people with IQs of 97 would be similarly assigned, one to each condition—and so on, for all of the blocks of two people.

A block design makes a researcher's life much easier when the experimental circumstances are more complicated. A researcher studying depression, for example, would know that psychologists have devised many different ways to treat this troubling disorder. Consequently, the researcher is interested in how previous treatments for depression might affect new efforts to treat the disorder. The new treatments could be represented by three distinct experimental conditions: therapy only, medication only, and a combination of therapy and medication. But before assigning participants to these conditions, the researcher may form two blocks: those who previously had received only outpatient treatment and those who previously had received both outpatient and inpatient treatment. In this case, the blocks include many more people than did our blocks of just two in the previous example. Those in the "outpatient-only" block would be randomly assigned to one of the three treatments; similarly, those in the "outpatient and inpatient" block would be randomly assigned to one of the three treatments (Figure 4-1). The treatments would now be balanced with respect to this "treatment history" variable, and the researcher could fairly evaluate how previous treatments for depression affect new efforts to treat this troubling disorder.

We subtitled this chapter "The Risks and Rewards of Scientific Sampling" because we always run the risk of an accidentally biased sample giving us bad

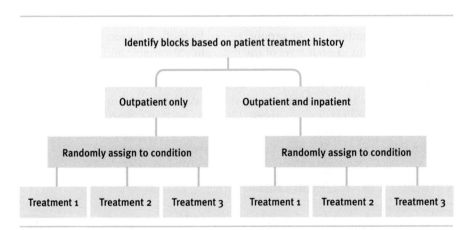

FIGURE 4-1
A Randomized Block Design

This flowchart depicts a randomized block design in which two blocks of participants are identified, people with depression who have previously only had outpatient treatment and people with depression who have previously had both outpatient and inpatient treatment. Participants are then assigned to one of the three treatments within their block. That is, those in the first block are randomly assigned to one of the three treatments, and those in the second block are randomly assigned to one of the three treatments, separately.

(unrepresentative) information. Fortunately, there is one activity that reduces the risks and increases the rewards of scientific sampling more than any other: replication. ***Replication*** *refers to the duplication of scientific results, ideally in a different context or with a sample that has different characteristics.* In other words, do the experiment again.

Some students worry that replicating a study is a form of plagiarism, but replication is actually an important characteristic of good science. One study seldom convinces any scientist, but three or four studies that produce the same finding become pretty persuasive. Twenty studies producing the same findings give us an extremely high level of confidence. Random assignment coupled with the *replication* of research goes a long way toward making up for our frequent inability to randomly select from a very large population. If we show that a manipulation makes a difference in a convenience sample, and then we replicate that finding with a different convenience sample, and then another, generalization becomes more and more appropriate.

In summary, data from a sample are used to draw conclusions about the larger population. Ideally, random sampling, in which every member of the population has an equal chance of being selected for the sample, is used. However, for practical reasons, convenience samples or variations on random sampling, such as cluster sampling and stratified random sampling, are far more common. Random assignment, in which every participant has an equal chance of being assigned to one of the experimental conditions, can go a long way toward making up for a lack of random selection. If a study that uses random assignment is replicated in several different contexts, we can start to have confidence that our findings are generalizable.

▪ **Replication** refers to the duplication of scientific results, ideally in a different context or with a sample that has different characteristics.

⊙ CHECK YOUR LEARNING

4-1 For each of the following scenarios, state whether random selection could have been used from a practical standpoint; explain your answer, including a description of the population to which the researcher likely wants to generalize. Then state whether random assignment could have been used; explain your answer.

a. A health psychologist examined whether postoperative recovery time was less among patients who received counseling prior to surgery than among those who did not.

b. The head of a school board asked a school psychologist to examine whether children in this school system would perform better in their history classes if they used an interactive textbook on CD-ROM as opposed to a traditional hard-copy textbook.

c. A social psychologist wondered whether the 2006 Olympic athletes were more likely to socialize with athletes from other countries if they were from Western countries versus Eastern countries.

d. A public health specialist studied the compliance of people diagnosed as HIV-positive to their medication regimens. He wondered whether those who received a beeper alerting them to take their medications would be more compliant than would those who did not receive a beeper.

e. A clinical psychologist studied whether people with diagnosed personality disorders were more likely to miss therapy appointments than were people without diagnosed personality disorders.

> SAMPLING IN THE BEHAVIORAL SCIENCES: WHY SAMPLING IS BOTH AN ART AND A SCIENCE

Before registering for Professor Krissel's statistics course, Robert had sampled opinions from two acquaintances who had already taken her course in statistics. He didn't exactly sample randomly; he had bumped into Alice and Ted in the food court the day he was going to register and then asked whom they had taken for statistics. He already knew he would be stuck with Professor Krissel if he wanted a class that met only one day a week, but he still tried to check her out. Robert always tried to look ahead.

"You'll survive," Ted had told him, which was not an encouraging report. "I got a C," said Alice, "so I passed, which is all I wanted. But I still don't know what I learned in the course. Look out for her first test."

Two out of two recommendations about Professor Krissel veered toward the negative, but Robert still had signed up for this course. Was he crazy, or did he just know his own priorities? Or might other students have judged Professor Krissel differently? Someone dropped a plate and silverware and Robert's mind wandered to the idea that the sounds of a cafeteria probably had a rhythm all their own, too: quiet at night, a bit louder in the morning, chaotic by lunchtime, calmer in the afternoon and into the evening, and then almost perfectly quiet again during the night. His musical memory was merging with his statistical reasoning, seeing patterns within the variability that surrounded him. He wondered, "How could I represent the 24-hour cycle of sounds within a 10-minute jazz composition?" The answer, of course, was to create a representative sample, musically.

As you develop your statistical skills, it's easy to forget that the goal of sampling is to obtain a representative sample. Any technique that nets a representative sample should be considered. But it turns out that there is nothing so reliable in creating a representative sample as the variations on random sampling you are learning about in this chapter. On the other hand, collecting a random sample is far easier in theory than it is in practice. That is why it is important to keep our focus on the goal: a representative sample that will generalize to the larger population.

Neither Random Selection nor Random Assignment: A Study of Torture

The idea of collecting a representative sample is all around us. For example, Robert was developing his own skill at musical representation because no one is interested in listening to 24 hours of music. Nevertheless, he wanted to musically convey the sounds and rhythms of an entire day. Similarly, no one is interested in reading a list of how much everyone in the United States actually weighs, yet understanding average weights alerts medical researchers to the escalating incidence of obesity and diabetes. The art of scientific sampling exists in the strategic compromises we must make when we work toward random selection and random assignment.

The distinction is important: random selection refers to a method of creating a sample from a population; random assignment refers to a method we can use once we have a sample, whether or not the sample is randomly selected. Random *selection* is almost never used, but random *assignment* is frequently used. Behavioral scientists are passionate about many different topics, from torture to children's literature. Our extreme diversity of interests has forced us to invent variations on random selection and random assignment in order to obtain a representative sample of the larger population.

For example, neither random selection nor random assignment can be used to study the PTSD that can result from torture. Nevertheless, the research team of Basoglu, Mineka, Parker, Aker, Livanou, and Gök (1997) wanted to study whether psychological preparedness protected against PTSD among torture survivors in Turkey. They compared the mental health outcomes of two groups: 55 torture survivors who had been political activists prior to their torture and 34 torture survivors who had not been political activists prior to their torture. The independent variable was activist status with two levels, political activist versus nonactivist, and the dependent variable was mental health outcome after being tortured. The research team found that political activists generally experienced more severe levels of torture than did nonactivists, but they also tended to have prepared mentally for the possibility of imprisonment and torture and had lower levels of depression, anxiety, and PTSD following the torture.

In this case, the population of interest is torture survivors in Turkey (or perhaps torture survivors worldwide, or even trauma survivors worldwide, depending on how far we're willing to generalize). The samples of torture survivors were convenience samples because the researchers could not randomly select their samples from the entire population of torture survivors. Specifically, the researchers identified torture survivors through referring sources, such as local political groups or human rights associations. Does our inability to randomly select or randomly assign participants to groups make the study invalid? Should we give up studying this important topic simply because we cannot randomly sample? Of course not.

So what should a researcher do when it is impossible to closely adhere to the rules of science, yet the topic desperately needs to be studied? Science also provides the answer: tell the truth. Science hides nothing from its reviewers. For example, there are several possible confounding variables in a study of torture, and it is important not only that we acknowledge them but also that we list them, even if we do not believe they influenced the data. For example, these particular researchers measured a number of demographic variables in both groups and reported several differences. The political activists were more likely than the nonactivists to be female (45% versus 32%) and to have higher levels of both education and income. Perhaps psychological resilience was the product of gender, education, or income rather than psychological preparedness.

Researchers need to acknowledge such confounds in their reports, as did this thorough team, because any of these variables might have provided more (or less) psychological resilience in the face of torture. This kind of interference in the logic of a study is sometimes called noise because it makes it more difficult to "hear" and understand what the data are saying. After all, we don't want to suggest a treatment for PTSD that doesn't really work, and we don't want to avoid using a treatment for PTSD that really does work. PTSD

A Sample of Torture Survivors
A study of torture survivors (Basoglu et al., 1997) found that political activists exhibited better mental health post-torture than did nonactivists. This study was worth conducting even though neither random selection nor random assignment was possible.

AP Photo / Ronald Zak

is too serious a disorder to be sloppy or untruthful about in our research. The researcher's job is to be thoroughly honest about the problems in a study so that other researchers can decide which sort of study should come next.

Students who are attracted to applied research should understand that they will need to be more (not less) sophisticated in terms of statistics and research design than their experimental counterparts. Many important topics, such as PTSD, need to be studied if we are to help its many victims, even though we cannot always apply the principles of random selection and random assignment. Hearing what the data are saying in such noisy settings requires the most powerful, discerning statistical listening devices at our disposal, accompanied by very conservative interpretations. There is an art and a science to accomplishing this scientific task with statistical (and personal) integrity.

Random Assignment but Not Random Selection: A Study of Expert Testimony

The courtroom also poses a familiar dilemma that only statistical reasoning can help to resolve: we don't want an innocent person to be found guilty, and we don't want a guilty person to be found innocent. Applied behavioral scientists (and, increasingly, lawyers) often look to the research base created by experimental behavioral scientists. The research team of Kressel and Kressel (2002) is composed of a psychologist and an attorney. In *Stack and Sway: The New Science of Jury Consulting*, they provide a particularly even-handed and well-written review of what behavioral scientists have learned about how to influence juries. They also discuss related concerns about the intersection between the social sciences and law in terms of jury selection.

Forensic psychologists, for example, draw on the knowledge base created by experimental psychologists when they provide expert testimony on the accuracy of eyewitness memory. The inherent drama of the courtroom is heightened by the finding that eyewitness memory has been shown to be both influential and inaccurate. This, of course, creates a dangerous bias against innocent defendants (Leippe, Eisenstadt, Rauch, & Seib, 2004). Consequently, researchers became interested in two additional features of eyewitness testimony: 1) when the eyewitness testimony was presented; and 2) whether the judge summarized and reminded the jury about that information.

In Leippe and colleagues' study, 385 undergraduates were randomly assigned to one of five types of expert testimony about eyewitness memory, outlined in Table 4-1. For example, one group (condition 1) heard expert testimony about the flaws of eyewitness memory before the evidence was presented and were not reminded of the testimony in the judge's final instructions. Another group (condition 4) heard the same expert testimony after the evidence was presented and were also reminded of that testimony in the judge's final instructions. Such a study can provide important information that might guide lawyers and judges in their practices. But does using undergraduates who have not been randomly selected into a study offer real guidance to judges in a courtroom? It is a question of experimental validity, and an important one, because many researchers work in universities where a very convenient pool of experimental participants is available: college students.

In this particular study, only condition 4 led to a significantly lower percentage of guilty verdicts than did other conditions. That was the condition in which the forensic psychologist's expert testimony about the flaws of eyewitness testimony was given after the evidence was presented *and* participants were reminded

TABLE 4-1. A STUDY OF EXPERT TESTIMONY: FIVE CONDITIONS

In a study of expert testimony, participants were randomly assigned to one of five conditions. The timing of the presentation of the expert testimony was varied, along with the presence or absence of a judge's summary and reminder of the expert testimony.

CONDITION	WHEN EXPERT TESTIMONY WAS PRESENTED	JUDGE SUMMARY AND REMINDER IN FINAL INSTRUCTIONS?
1	Prior to evidence	No
2	Prior to evidence	Yes
3	After evidence	No
4	After evidence	Yes
5	None presented	No

of that testimony in the judge's final instructions. Table 4-2 presents the results of this study in two different situations, one in which a stronger case with more evidence was presented and one in which a weaker case with less evidence was presented. Regardless of the level of evidence, the later timing of expert testimony and the judge's reminder combined to decrease the proportion of guilty verdicts. But the validity question persists: Can we trust these findings?

There are three ways to answer this important question: Were participants randomly selected, were participants randomly assigned to groups, and has the study been replicated? The distinction between random selection and random assignment to groups highlights the need for replication and the inherently conservative approach of science. Let's consider each of these three answers to the validity question.

The sample was based on Leippe and colleagues' intended population: all U.S. citizens who might be asked to be jurors. However, their convenience sample was composed only of those college students who signed up for the study to receive credit. Is this playing fair with science? Well, college students are among those called for jury duty, and they will continue to be called for jury duty throughout their lives. Even though college students are a convenience sample, they are part of the population of interest, so their participation would seem to

TABLE 4-2. THE INFLUENCE OF EXPERT TESTIMONY

This table depicts the proportions of guilty verdicts based on (1) the timing of expert testimony combined with the presence/absence of a judge's reminder and (2) the overall strength of the case. The proportion of guilty verdicts in both stronger and weaker cases was lower only when the expert testimony was presented after the evidence and the judge offered a reminder and summary of the expert testimony.

	TYPE OF EXPERT TESTIMONY				
	EARLY TESTIMONY		LATE TESTIMONY		NO TESTIMONY
	NO REMINDER	REMINDER	NO REMINDER	REMINDER	NO REMINDER
Stronger evidence	0.61	0.64	0.56	**0.41**	0.58
Weaker evidence	0.37	0.32	0.35	**0.21**	0.42

have some value. But we cannot call them a representative sample and are reluctant to believe this study will apply to all settings. However, because the researchers were able to use random assignment to groups, there was no biasing across experimental conditions. So perhaps we can have some cautious confidence that these findings might translate to a real jury setting.

Our confidence would be greatly increased if other researchers were able to replicate these findings using college students at other universities, as well as other convenient samples. Barbershops and hair salons might be useful places to look because most people have to get their hair cut. Churches are also natural gathering places but are more suspect because participants may share sociological attitudes relative to the justice system. The answer is always replication, even when we are able to gather a genuinely random sample in the first place. We will tend to believe a collection of studies that produce the same results from samples collected at barbershops, churches, office buildings, truck stops, and anywhere else people subject to jury duty congregate. And when they don't all produce the same results, we have the wonderful opportunity to hypothesize why the sample collected at a church differed from the sample collected at a truck stop. These are the three major ways to answer the validity question: Who was in the sample, how were they assigned to their conditions, and have the findings been replicated?

Random Selection but Not Random Assignment: A Study of Children's Literature

Populations and samples need not be people. Diekman and Murnan (2004) studied children's literature, comparing elementary-level books that had been classified by researchers and publishers as nonsexist with books that had been labeled sexist. They found that even so-called nonsexist books depicted numerous female stereotypes. Nonsexist books might depict girls and women enacting male-stereotypic roles, such as truck driver or baseball player, but they also depicted female characters in female-stereotypic roles, such as schoolteacher or mother. Moreover, male characters, even in nonsexist books, were not shown in female-stereotypic roles. The independent variable in this study is type of book with two levels, nonsexist and sexist. The dependent variable is presence of female stereotypes.

In this archival study of children's literature, the populations are all nonsexist and all sexist children's books that were classified by researchers and publishers into one of these categories. The samples were the 10 sexist and 10 nonsexist books that were randomly selected from among the larger groups for analysis. A study such as this one can use random selection because the pool of children's books that had been categorized is much smaller than the pool of, say, all U.S. citizens. From all the books that had been categorized, the researchers were able to use random selection to choose their samples. The researchers were not, however, able to use random assignment. A book could not be assigned to be nonsexist or sexist; it either was or it wasn't, a determination made by researchers and publishers according to strict criteria.

As you can see from these examples, many selection and assignment methods can be combined in doing social science. A summary of the combinations demonstrated in this section is presented in Table 4-3.

Perhaps you have noticed the conservative language we have been using throughout our discussion of variations on random selection and random assignment. We never use the word *prove*, but we have used words such as *reluctant, perhaps, cautious, might*, and *if*. This circumspection can be so frustrating

TABLE 4-3. SUMMARY OF STUDIES

Social scientists use many combinations of selection and assignment methods in their research. Three combinations, summarized here, were described in this section, but many others are possible.

TOPIC	SAMPLE	RANDOM SELECTION?	CONDITIONS	RANDOM ASSIGNMENT?
Psychological effects of torture	Torture survivors	No	Political activist or nonactivist	No
Timing of expert testimony	College students	No	One of five expert testimony presentations	Yes
Sexism in children's literature	Children's books	Yes	Labeled as sexist or nonsexist	No

that you sometimes want to throw your hands up in the air and ask, "Don't the behavioral sciences know anything?" The answer, of course, is yes. But this conservative approach to knowledge is the nature of the scientific process. In spite of our passion for statistics as a set of tools for answering interesting questions, even we have to admit that sometimes the process of science is boring (data entry), slow (peer review), and cautious (replication). We are even reluctant to believe our own findings! On the other hand, when we do succeed, science provides a sublime satisfaction that is like no other because we can firmly believe in our discovery. Random selection and random assignment are critical elements in the process of scientific discovery.

We describe samples to make intelligent inferences about populations. Basoglu and colleagues (1997) studied a sample of torture survivors to learn something about what might protect the population of torture and trauma survivors from ongoing mental health problems. Leippe and colleagues (2004) studied a sample of students to determine how the population of adults might be influenced by the timing of expert testimony about eyewitness memory. And Diekman and Murnan (2004) used a sample of children's books to learn whether the population of books labeled as nonsexist really was made up of nonsexist books. And what Robert wanted to know was whether the negative verdict about Professor Krissel elicited from his sample—his two friends in the food court—reflected the verdict he would elicit if he interviewed the entire population of everyone who had ever had Professor Krissel for statistics. This pattern will persist across everything we learn about statistics; we will describe samples to make inferences about populations. The art of scientific sampling is how behavioral scientists discover and communicate their thousands of insights into the human experience.

In summary, it is important to be able to distinguish between random sampling, a sample-selection process in which every member of the population has an equal chance of being in a study, and random assignment, a process in which every participant (regardless of how he or she was selected) has an equal chance of being in any of the experimental conditions. The concepts are easily confused but are quite different. Moreover, random assignment is far more common than is random sampling. An awareness of selection and assignment strategies as we read others' research can help us to better design and implement our own research.

⊙ CHECK YOUR LEARNING

4-2 In France in the fall of 2005, many communities of immigrants from the Middle East and North Africa saw a great deal of violence, particularly car burnings, committed by their young people. Social science research can help to diminish or avoid such violence. Answer the following questions related to hypothetical research of the French riots.

a. Of the cities that shared this demographic, Marseilles was one of the few that saw relatively little violence. A researcher wants to compare Marseilles with Lyons, a city that saw a great deal of violence, to determine what characteristics may have moderated violence, specifically among high school students. Can she use random selection? Explain. Can she use random assignment? Explain.

b. A criminal justice graduate student wants to explore whether job skills programs might reduce crime in the neighborhoods across the country that were most affected by the riots. Can he use random selection? Explain. Can he use random assignment? Explain.

> PROBABILITY THEORY: DISTINGUISHING BETWEEN MERE COINCIDENCE AND REAL CONNECTIONS

"Your grandmother?" Professor Jan Krissel's eyebrows raised slightly. Robert suspected that it was not the first time she had heard this story.

"She's been sick since the summer. They gave her some test and it came back positive."

"Oh, dear," Professor Krissel sympathized. "What was the test?" Robert realized that it was, on the surface at least, a fair question.

"I don't know. Whatever it was came back positive."

"Well, what was the diagnosis?"

"I don't know; it ended with -*itis*." Robert didn't think that she believed him. It was odd to feel as if he were lying when he knew he was telling the truth. "She's in the hospital right now, getting more tests." His explanation sounded lame, even to him. But he didn't want to bother worrying about what his professor thought. He just wanted to get home. "All I'm asking is to take the test later."

"This test is through the first chapter on hypothesis testing," Professor Krissel replied. "If you're going to drop the course, you probably should do it soon."

"I don't want to drop the course. I want to get earn a good grade, but right now I can hardly think about statistics."

"Let me think about it for a moment."

Professor Krissel closed her eyes, apparently trying to think of a solution. Robert was thinking that the longer he was in her office, the more likely he was to get a ticket. Just his luck to have a dawdling professor.

"You know, I could give you the first test from last year's class," Professor Krissel finally proposed. "What do you think of that? Have you got about an hour right now?"

A man burst into Professor Krissel's office before he could protest the idea. "Hey, there, Professor 'Space 23 Reserved.' Somebody took your parking spot. Probably some damn student. We're going to be late."

"Hello, honey. What happened?"

Of course, it just had to be Professor Krissel's parking spot that he had randomly selected. Naturally, it was on a day when her husband had dropped her off. What a coincidence!

Robert, of course, was not the first person to feel as if coincidences were somehow conspiring against him. But how do behavioral scientists explain coincidences? One student had been thinking about her best friend, and just then, the friend called. Another bought a used textbook at the bookstore, only to discover that it was previously owned by his former girlfriend. A soccer player seemed to score more goals when she wore her lucky ponytail holder. A student studying for a semester in France ran into his hometown next-door neighbor at the Eiffel Tower. A woman told her friends that she dreamed about a disaster the night before the al-Qaeda bombings in Madrid. All were amazed at the uncanny nature of these coincidences. We've all had experiences like these. The authors of this text have had many. A few years back, one of the authors signed up for a U.S. bicycle tour and was assigned a roommate. The author had Swedish ancestors in her family tree, and the roommate was from Sweden, from the same city as the author's ancestors. Moreover, the roommate's mother's maiden name was the same as the author's mother's maiden name. Long lost cousins? What's your story?

Mike Powell / Getty Images

Lucky Charms
Many athletes have a lucky article of clothing that they wear on game day because they think it helps them win. Confirmation biases lead us to notice events that match our beliefs (the occasions when the lucky object was paired with a win) and ignore those that do not (the occasions that the lucky object is paired with a loss).

Coincidence and Probability: Why Healthy Skepticism Is Healthy

Statistical reasoning can help save us from ourselves. Our tendency to read too much into bizarre but vivid occurrences results from perceptual biases that may be inherent in human cognition. Perhaps the most influential bias in intensifying our beliefs in the eerie nature of coincidence is confirmation bias. *Confirmation bias is our usually unintentional tendency to pay attention to evidence that confirms what we already believe and to ignore evidence that would disconfirm our beliefs.* For example, one father was videotaping his high school daughter playing basketball because he believed that she was being treated unfairly by the referees. He was sure that the referees were calling fouls on his daughter unfairly and complained loudly (heard on his own tape) about every injustice. But after he calmed down and reviewed the tape (two years later), he had to admit that his daughter had probably been treated fairly, maybe even committing fouls that had not been called. He was seeing only the evidence that confirmed his preexisting belief and ignoring the evidence that contradicted his belief.

Confirmation biases closely follow illusory correlations. *Illusory correlation is the phenomenon of believing one sees an association between variables when no such association exists.* This same basketball-loving father believed that one referee in particular had it in for his daughter because of her assertive play. He was sure that she fouled out of games because of unfair treatment whenever this particular referee was working a game. Once again, his more subdued examination of the recorded evidence two years later suggested he had sincerely perceived a correlation that did not exist in reality. An illusory correlation can occur when we fail to examine data in an empirical way, when we abandon the intelligent, restraining logic of statistical reasoning.

Confirmation bias and illusory correlation play roles in many aspects of human thinking, particularly those related to prejudice and discrimination. For example, a prejudiced individual who perceives Latinos as less successful than those from other ethnic groups might readily call to mind the Latino man who mows

■ **Confirmation bias** is our usually unintentional tendency to pay attention to evidence that confirms what we already believe and to ignore evidence that would disconfirm our beliefs.

■ **Illusory correlation** is the phenomenon of believing that one sees an association between variables when no such association exists.

her lawn but not the one who does her taxes. The same thing occurs with our belief in coincidence. We notice strange coincidences but do not notice the uncountable times in our life in which there are not unlikely occurrences.

The thing is, coincidences are *not* unlikely. Think about how many tiny events happen to you over the course of a week. Let's take the first example from above—the student whose friend called just as she was thinking about her. How many phone calls, e-mails, instant messages, and text messages do you receive over the course of a week? How many times do you think about your close friends over the course of a week? Is it really improbable that during one of those times, your friend would call or IM or text message you? Those are the only times you remember. Let's take the example of the dream about a disaster the night before the Madrid bombings. How many friends do you have? How many dreams do you think your group of friends has every night? Is it really improbable that one of your friends would dream about a disaster the night before one actually occurs? But it is that person's dream that will remain firmly lodged in memory because we have no reason to pay attention to all of our friends who did not have a dream about a disaster. And what about the student who encountered his hometown next-door neighbor at the Eiffel Tower? Think of the whole range of possible coincidences in one person's life. How many different coincidences could have happened to this student in his life, but didn't? We can't possibly count them. He could have found his own discarded Game Boy with his name on the back at a flea market. He could have discovered that the student across the hall in his dorm was a clown at his father's 50th birthday party. He could have met someone in class who had the same name, birthday, and piranha tattoo. You get the picture. In the course of our lives, with the uncountable number of events that happen to us, we're going to experience a good number of coincidences, just by chance.

Coincidence also plays a role in conspiracy theories. Shortly after the attacks on 9/11, several anthrax-laden letters were sent to prominent media and political figures. Soon thereafter, a number of people with links to biological weapons research died under mysterious circumstances in locations around the world, 11 in four months. One disappeared on a bridge outside of Memphis; one was hit by a car while jogging; one suffocated in an airtight laboratory in Australia; one died in a private plane crash; and seven more died under similarly peculiar circumstances in which foul play could not readily be ruled out. A conspiracy theory was born. It begins with an illusory correlation, believing there is an association where none exists, and maintains itself through the confirmation bias, paying attention to evidence that confirms what we already believe while not noticing evidence that contradicts our beliefs. Illusory correlation and confirmation bias are why developing the habit of statistical reasoning can help save us from ourselves.

Lisa Belkin (2002), reported on this and other coincidences in the *New York Times*. In her story, she carefully considered the probabilities of a number of seemingly inexplicable occurrences. She quoted Persi Diaconis, a Stanford statistician, who pointed out that because the U.S. population was 280 million, "280 times a day, a one-in-a-million shot is going to occur," and that's just in the United States. Belkin noted

Conspiracy or Coincidence?
Eleven microbiologists died of mysterious circumstances over a four-month period after anthrax-laced letters were mailed to several U.S. addresses. A careful examination of the objective data suggest this was mere coincidence, not conspiracy.

Andrew Brookes / Corbis

that most of the 11 microbiologists who died were only loosely connected to biological warfare research. Some, for example, were microbiologists who had other research focuses; they just happened to work at facilities that also did biological research. Moreover, many of the deaths were ultimately explained. One victim, who had hypertension, appeared to have had a stroke while being mugged; another with a history of seizures appeared to have tumbled over a bridge railing after a minor car accident; another was allegedly murdered by his daughter and her friends for reasons unrelated to his job.

Belkin also noted that the American Society of Microbiology has approximately 41,000 members; given that there are other organizations of microbiologists around the world, as well as numerous nonaffiliated microbiologists, 41,000 is unquestionably an underestimate of the total number of researchers in this field worldwide. It is not at all improbable that 11 microbiologists would die under mysterious circumstances during any particular four-month time frame. The reason the 11 deaths were noticed at this point in time, she concluded, was because of the political climate. In an example of an illusory correlation and then an ensuing confirmation bias, we were looking for patterns related to terrorism. Although there almost certainly were as many accountants who died strange deaths during this time—probably many more, given that there are far more accountants than microbiologists—no pattern was noticed because it would not have confirmed any preconceived ideas.

Beyond Confirmation Biases: The Dangers of Groupthink

Unfortunately, when we abandon statistical reasoning, the consequences of illusory correlations and the confirmation bias go far beyond mild misunderstandings. Even sincere government decision makers with the best educations and mountains of information are sabotaged by illusory correlations (misperceptions), confirmation biases (misreading the evidence to support a preexisting view), and their more tragic consequence: groupthink. *Groupthink refers to the overconfident, biased decision making that occurs when a group of people confirm one anothers' biases rather than relying on objective evidence.* Groupthink emerges when a group surrounds a strong leader who is uninterested in information, refuses to consider contradictory perspectives, misperceives available information, and assigns roles to individuals that establish tight informational boundaries around the group. One role, for example, is that of the gatekeeper, who determines which information is and is not allowed to be included in the decision-making process. Reasoning like a statistician is a healthy way to think, but sometimes it will make you very unpopular in a group.

Groupthink has been proposed (and debated) as a way to describe the group dynamics that led to flawed decision making during the Cuban Missile Crisis under President Kennedy, the Vietnam War decisions under President Johnson, the Watergate scandal within the Nixon administration, jury decision making, the *Columbia* space shuttle accident, and President Bush's decision to liberate Iraq by citing the threat of weapons of mass destruction that could not be found (Adema, 1986; Alter, 2002; Janis, 1972; Kramer, 1998; McKinney, 1986; Neck & Moorhead, 1992; Raven, 1998). Use of the term *groupthink* has unfortunately become a weapon in the mouths of political combatants (Alterman, 2005; Bauerlein, 2004; Nelson, 2003), but that simply means that all participants tacitly recognize its danger and that it represents a persistent psychological pattern. Mountains of information won't help us make better decisions if we are determined to misperceive all of it.

■ **Groupthink** refers to the overconfident, biased decision making that occurs when a group of people confirm one anothers' beliefs rather than relying on objective evidence.

Groupthink and Presidential Decision Making
Reasoning like a statistician undermines the dangerous processes associated with groupthink. Clockwise from upper left: the Kennedy, Johnson, Bush, and Nixon administrations have all been accused of succumbing to groupthink.

In summary, an understanding of the role of probability theory in statistics requires a healthy skepticism toward the idea of meaning in coincidence. An illusory correlation occurs when we perceive a connection where none exists. It is often followed by a confirmation bias, whereby we notice occurrences that fit with our preconceived ideas and fail to notice those that do not. Groupthink is the most dangerous result of our biases; it is the overconfident, biased decision making that occurs when several people confirm the group's preconceived ideas and no one in the group seriously examines objective evidence. Statistical reasoning helps us to overcome these very human biases.

⊙ CHECK YOUR LEARNING

4-3 Describe how illusory correlation and confirmation bias might have contributed to the following (incorrect, or at least debatable) conclusions.

a. Flying in an airplane is more dangerous than driving in a car.

b. Only women are good nurses.

c. We are more likely to be killed by a shark than a dog.

d. Depression is caused by child abuse.

e. Gay men tend to present themselves in a very sexualized manner.

> PROBABILITY THEORY: THE BASICS

Robert had to sit passively while Professor Krissel's husband complained. "I just got the car serviced and came by to pick you up so you can take me to the airport. But I had to walk just about from Siberia to get to your office. Someone parked in your spot. Now we have to walk all the way back just to get to the car. Anyway, I can't be late, so can we go soon?"

Robert could see that Professor Krissel was rapidly forgetting about him. Who could blame her? But a stupid car and a plane trip weren't more important than his dying grandmother. The whole world seemed to have the wrong priorities, and Robert could sense that Professor Krissel still didn't believe his story. But he knew why. Last term, when he had come to her office to get admitted into this statistics class, Professor Krissel had been holding a conversation with another professor. Robert had stood politely outside while the two professors continued their conversation.

"Lose any grandmothers yet?" the other professor had asked.

"Two, both in general psychology. When they say that my test is a killer, I didn't think they meant is so literally." Professor Krissel had continued, "It's a very large class. So large that I think we might lose two, maybe even three more grandmothers this week. And they're first-year students, you know."

"First-year students do seem to lose a lot of grandmothers," her colleague had agreed. "The trouble is that this is about the time of their life when their grandparents really do die."

"So maybe all these grandmothers really are dying. Some of them probably are, anyway, so how do you know what to believe?" Robert had kept on eavesdropping, partly because he had no other choice. He needed Professor Krissel's signature to get into her class. He had already shuffled his feet and made small coughing noises. What did it take to get someone's attention?

Professor Krissel and her colleague faced the dilemma of having to make judgments about the veracity of students' explanations for missing tests when they were uncertain about whether those explanations were true. Statistical reasoning is a healthy way to think because it gives us a better way to make such judgments, even under conditions of profound uncertainty. Statistics help us manage uncertainty through the use of mathematical probabilities—the probability that a particular event will occur just by chance. So in this section we can now turn our attention to two key concepts: probability and the biased ways that we humans assess probability without the sensible guidelines of statistical reasoning.

Expected Relative-Frequency Probability: The Probability of Statistics

When we discuss probability in everyday conversation, we tend to think of what statisticians would call subjective probability, also called *personal probability*. *Subjective probability refers to an individual's opinion or judgment about the likelihood that an event will occur.* We might say something like "There's a 75% chance I'll finish my paper and go out tonight." We don't mean that there is precisely a 75% chance that we'll go out; rather, this is our rating of our confidence that this will occur. It's really just our best guess, a personal estimate.

Mathematicians and statisticians, however, use the word *probability* a bit differently than we do in everyday conversation. Statisticians are concerned with a different type of probability, one that is more objective. In statistics, we are interested in the **expected relative-frequency probability**, *the expected outcome if a trial were repeated many, many times.* When flipping a coin, in the long run, the expected relative-frequency probability of heads would be 0.50. Probability refers to the likelihood that something occurs, and frequency refers to how often a given outcome (e.g., heads or tails) occurs out of a certain number of trials (e.g., coin flips). The term **trial**, in reference to probability, *refers to each occasion that a given*

■ **Subjective probability** refers to an individual's opinion or judgment about the likelihood that an event will occur; also called *personal probability*.

■ The **expected relative-frequency probability** is the expected outcome if a trial were repeated many, many times.

■ In reference to probability, a **trial** refers to each occasion that a given procedure is carried out.

Eyebyte / Alamy

Determining Probabilities
To determine the probability of heads, we would have to conduct many trials (coin flips), record the outcomes (either heads or tails), and determine the proportion of successes (in this case, heads).

■ In reference to probability, **outcome** refers to the result of a trial.

■ In reference to probability, **success** refers to the outcome for which we're trying to determine the probability.

procedure is carried out; for example, each time we flip a coin, it is a trial. ***Outcome*** *refers to the result of a trial;* for coin-flip trials, the outcome is either heads or tails. ***Success*** *refers to the outcome for which we're trying to determine the probability;* if we are testing for the probability of heads, then success is heads.

Think back to frequency tables, histograms, and frequency polygons. *Relative frequency* refers to the frequency of successes compared with the overall number of trials. How many heads do we get relative to the total number of coin flips? *Expected* means what we would expect in the long run if a very large number of trials were carried out. We cannot get at the true expected relative-frequency probability without many, many trials. The expected relative-frequency probability of getting heads on a coin flip is 0.50. If we flip that coin many, many times, we would expect that half of those flips will be heads. We calculate probability by dividing the total number of successes by the total number of trials. If we flip a coin 2000 times and get 1000 heads, then probability is 1000/2000 = 0.50.

People often confuse the terms *probability, proportion,* and *percentage.* Probability, the concept of most interest to us right now, is the proportion that we expect to see in the long run. The proportion is the number of successes divided by the number of trials. In the short run, in just a few trials, the proportion might not reflect the underlying probability. A coin flipped six times might have more or fewer than three heads, leading to a proportion of heads that does not parallel the underlying probability of heads. Both proportions and probabilities are written as decimals. A coin that comes up heads half the time in the long run would have a 0.50 probability of heads. Percentage is simply probability or proportion multiplied by 100. A flipped coin has a 0.50 probability of coming up heads and a 50% chance of coming up heads. The lowest possible probability or proportion is 0.0, and the lowest possible percentage is 0%; the highest possible probability or proportion is 1.0, and the highest possible percentage is 100%. Most people are already familiar with percentages, so simply keep in mind that probabilities focus on the long run while proportions are a strictly mathematical calculation.

One of the central characteristics of expected relative-frequency probability is that it only works in the long run. Think of the earlier discussion of random assignment in which we used a random numbers generator to create a series of 0s and 1s to assign participants to levels of the independent variable. In the short run, over just a few trials, we got strings of 0s and 1s and often did not end up with half 0s and half 1s, even though that is the underlying probability. With many trials, however, we're much more likely to get close to 0.50, or 50%, of each, although there will be many strings of 0s or 1s along the way. The pattern only becomes clear in the long run. In the short run, the results may appear haphazard. In the long run, the results are quite predictable. Without many, many trials, we cannot determine expected relative-frequency probability.

Independence and Probability: The Gambler's Fallacy

Another key factor in statistical probability is the fact that the individual trials must be independent. This is yet another use of the word *independent,* one of the favorite words of statisticians. Here we use *independent* to mean that the outcome of each trial must not depend in any way on the outcome of previous trials. If we're flipping a coin, each coin flip must be independent of every other coin flip. If we're generating a random numbers list, each number must be generated without thought to the previous numbers. In fact, that is exactly why humans can't think randomly. We automatically glance at the previous numbers we have generated in order to best make the next one random. But if our next number depends on the previous one, it is not independent and not random. A computer does not have a memory for the previous numbers, nor does a random numbers table—which, after all, is likely to have been created by a computer in the first place. Chance has no memory.

The Gambler's Fallacy
Chance has no memory. Individual trials are independent.

Just as each trial needs to be an independent event to be fair, the participants in our sample also need to be unrelated to one another. Sometimes undergraduate students suggest recruiting their family members and friends to participate in their honors research. This is problematic not only because it is unethical (it would be considered coercive to ask people you knew so well) but also because it would lead to scientifically compromised results. If you were studying attitudes about prejudice, one friend's responses might not be independent of another's—their shared prejudice might even be the basis of their friendship. Even if they disagree, it's likely that your friends and family have talked to and influenced one another. At the very least, it is likely that they share opinions and attitudes because of similar life experiences. Doing our best to obtain a representative, if not a random, sample is the best way to ensure that each participant's responses are independent of every other participant's responses. Similarly, if we plan to replicate our research, we should aim to recruit a sample that is independent of our first, preferably one from a different setting or in a different context.

TAKE THE PROBABILITY QUIZ

EXPERIENCE IT FOR YOURSELF

The concept of independence within probability can be a tricky one, so experiencing it for yourself will help you to understand the concept. The gambler's fallacy describes a common bias that can lead people to make poor decisions that may have negative consequences. Indicate whether you'd agree with each of the following statements if you were speaking to the person making that statement.

1. "That woman has been playing that slot machine without success for two hours and she just quit; let's play that one—it's got to pay off soon."

   Agree _____   Disagree _____

2. "There hadn't been a car accident on the turnpike for months, and there have been three on consecutive days this week; tomorrow is definitely going to be smooth sailing. We're due."

   Agree _____   Disagree _____

3. "My next-door neighbor has had three boys and she's pregnant again. This one's bound to be a girl."

   Agree _____   Disagree _____

■ The **gambler's fallacy** is a type of biased thinking in which an individual believes that a previous occurrence has an effect on an ensuing occurrence, when in fact the two events are unrelated.

4. "In the first game of the night, my friend Henry won $10 dollars playing High Chicago poker because he had been dealt the queen of spades as a down card, which had turned out to be the highest spade in the hole. He told us, 'I guess I should bet big tonight! The cards are falling my way!' Henry had a good strategy."

Agree _____   Disagree _____

*The **gambler's fallacy** is a type of biased thinking in which an individual believes that a previous occurrence has an effect on an ensuing occurrence, when in fact the two events are unrelated.* These perceptions "feel" as if they make sense at the time, and many students would agree with most or all of these statements. But these are all examples of the gambler's fallacy. The slot machine, the cars on the highway, the egg and sperm, and the playing cards have no memory of the ones that came before. This is a dangerous way of thinking, particularly when gambling, and has led many a risk-taker to unwittingly lose his or her life savings. On the other hand, remember that the gambler's fallacy may be influencing your competition at the poker table; because there really is no such thing as a "lucky chair" at a poker table, no matter how lucky any one individual has been, you can use your statistical reasoning to gain an edge over those who prefer to trust their superstitions. As you might guess from this, the correct answer for each of the above questions is "disagree."

Gambling and Misperceptions of Probability
The gambler's fallacy can lead to the belief that a slot machine that has not paid off in a long time is "due." A person may continue to feed coins into it in the expectation of an imminent payout. Of course, the slot machine itself, unless rigged, has no memory of its previous outcomes.

Photofusion Picture Library / Alamy

Statistician Sleuths: The Case of Chicago's Cheating Teachers

Those inclined to cheat should be wary of statisticians—and the rest of us may want to consider why a public policy seems to have encouraged cheating. In *Freakonomics*, Steven Levitt and Stephen Dubner (2005) described alleged cheating among teachers in the Chicago public school system. In the name of accountability, a public policy intended to produce higher student scores had instead pressured teachers to value the appearance of success over real success. Certain classrooms had suspiciously strong performances on standardized tests, scores that often mysteriously declined the following year when a new teacher taught the same students.

In *Freakonomics*, the authors reported that Levitt, an economist, and his research colleagues decided to look for suspicious patterns in the test—blocks of correct answers among most students for the last few questions that would indicate the likelihood that the teacher had changed responses to difficult questions for most or all students. They found blocks of answers that defied probability in 5% of the classrooms studied, likely a conservative estimate of the overall cheating rate given the many forms of more sophisticated cheating that could not be detected as easily. In one classroom, for example, 15 of 22 students gave identical answers to a string of six questions toward the end of a test where the questions were more difficult and often went unanswered. It did not take a large inferential leap to believe that these teachers were filling in the answers to artificially inflate their classes' scores.

Accusing anyone of cheating creates a familiar dilemma: We certainly do not want to accuse an innocent teacher of cheating, but neither do we want to let cheaters continue without consequences. Inferential statistics, with their foundation of probability, provide a reasonable guideline that minimizes the probability of making either kind of mistake. Statisticians are dangerous to cheaters, especially statisticians mindful of self-deceptive habits such as the confirmation bias. We enjoy a way of thinking that distinguishes between chance and reality, we embrace healthy skepticism, and we have the statistical skills to quantify the probability of particular responses relative to chance.

In summary, subjective probability refers to an individual's judgment about the likelihood that an event will occur. When statisticians refer to probability, however, they usually mean expected relative-frequency probability, the expected outcome if an experiment or trial were conducted many, many times. When calculating probabilities, it is important that each trial, or occasion that a given procedure is carried out, is independent of the others. The gambler's fallacy refers to the belief that trials depend on one another, when in fact they are independent (e.g., outcomes of each pull on a slot machine). Finally, when considering probabilities, it is important to acknowledge that short-run proportions might have many different outcomes, whereas long-run proportions are more indicative of the underlying probabilities.

⊙ CHECK YOUR LEARNING

4-4 Consider a scenario in which a student wonders whether men or women are more likely to use the ATM machine in the student center. He decides to observe those who use the ATM machine. (Assume that the university enrolls roughly equal numbers of women and men and that neither women nor men are more likely to use ATM machines.)

a. Define success as a woman using the ATM on a given trial. What proportion of successes might this student expect to observe in the short run?

b. What might this student expect to observe in the long run?

c. Let's say that the student witnessed 10 men in a row using the ATM machine. He might say, "Well, the next ATM user has got to be a woman after so many men." What bias is this an example of? What would you tell this student about his observation?

➤ STATISTICS AND PROBABILITY: THE LOGIC OF INFERENTIAL STATISTICS

"It's a funny correlation," Robert had heard Professor Krissel tell her fellow professor, "if it's a real one. All these sick grandmothers just before big tests— I'm sorry, but it makes me suspicious. How do we know for sure?"

Waltraud Grubitzsch / dpa / Corbis

Using Probability to Make Decisions

Adams (1990) wrote a humorous statistical description of the implications of so many grandmothers dying during exam weeks, providing students with an excuse not to take the test on schedule. The dilemma for professors is that a certain proportion of grandparents are likely to die among a typical college-age population. How do they decide which stories to believe?

"The trouble is, if we cut the students a break because we believe them when they tell us that their grandmothers died but grandma really didn't die, then they're getting an unfair advantage. I mean, if they take the midterm later, then they can learn what's on the test from their friends. You can be wrong by believing that a student's story is true when it's not true, or you can be wrong by believing that the story isn't true when it really is true." Robert had been surprised that two professors had thought so much about dead grandmothers—and about how much students lied.

"I wish our students wouldn't cheat," Professor Krissel had said. "I know it sounds hokey, but it's really only themselves that they're cheating. And why is it almost always grandmothers? I seldom have any grandfathers die on me."

Using Probability to Make Decisions: Dead Grandmothers

Like Professor Krissel, many professors have worried about whether students are lying when they come to them with excuses. Having a grandmother die just happens to be one of the most common ones. Ask your professors if they have observed a spike in family deaths prior to exams, but still be a little skeptical of their responses. Your professors could be suffering from a confirmation bias, remembering supportive cases while ignoring contradictory evidence. Being a professor, even a social science professor, may make you more aware of such cognitive biases, but it does not magically immunize you against their effects.

Mike Adams (1990), a professor at Eastern Connecticut State University, wrote a hilarious spoof of the "dead grandmother" phenomenon. He reported fictional data—but nonetheless data that match the observations of many professors—that suggested there was a spike in the family death rate (FDR), particularly among grandmothers, just before exams. Interestingly, this was particularly pronounced among students who were not doing well to begin with. A student with an exam coming up who was failing the course was 50 times as likely to lose a relative, Adams said, as a student getting an A who had no exam coming up. He suggested that grandmothers must be worrying themselves to death and offered three tongue-in-cheek solutions. (1) Eliminate exams entirely because they seem to be killing grandmothers. (2) Allow only orphans to enroll and, if need be, create more orphans. (3) Have students lie to their families about their enrollment at universities. He noted that even if students lie about when exams are, the family may worry all of the time; better, he suggested, that students tell families they've been abducted by aliens or joined a religious cult and then sneak off to university. He also reported an increase in the preexam FDR in recent years and made a wild extrapolation about what this increase might lead to in 100 years; at that rate (in 100 years), only the largest families would survive even the first semester of a student's college career.

Developing Hypotheses: Consideration of Future Consequences

Joking aside, an examination of data using the techniques of hypothesis testing can help us to find answers for many of our research hypotheses. In Chapter 1, you read about the Consideration of Future Consequences (CFC) scale

(Strathman, Gleicher, Boninger & Edwards, 1994). Imagine that your own university is interested in increasing its students' CFC scores, in the hope that students will pursue internships and research experiences at an earlier stage of their undergraduate careers. The university might implement a semester-long program through the career center that exposes students to the many graduate school and career options available to them. However, prior to implementing what might be a costly program, the university administrators decide to conduct a study. The first step in hypothesis testing is to collect our data, which includes identifying our population, recruiting a sample, and choosing our independent and dependent variables.

For the university administrators' study, the population in which they are interested is all second-year students. They have had enough time to get adjusted to college but still have time to explore different majors and possible careers prior to graduation. Sixty students are randomly selected from the sophomore class. These students constitute the sample. Of the 60 students, 30 are randomly assigned to the career center's program for one hour a week for one semester, and 30 are assigned to a control group—a group that meets for the equivalent amount of time but does not discuss careers or graduate programs. In general, *a control group is a level of the independent variable that is designed to match the experimental group—the group receiving the treatment or intervention of interest—in all ways but the experimental manipulation itself.* So the independent variable is program, with two levels: "career center" group and control group. At the end of the semester, all students complete the CFC scale. The dependent variable, therefore, is CFC score. The university administrators hope that the career-oriented program will increase students' CFC levels.

A next step, one that we'll see throughout this text, is the development of hypotheses. When we calculate inferential statistics, we're always comparing two hypotheses. One is *the null hypothesis—a statement that postulates that there is no mean difference between populations or that the mean difference is in a direction opposite from that anticipated by the researcher.* In most circumstances, we can think of the null hypothesis as the boring hypothesis because it proposes that nothing will happen. In the CFC study, the null hypothesis would be that the mean CFC score is the same for both the "career center" group and the control group. This hypothesis is boring because it proposes that nothing is going on, that there is no mean difference between groups, and that being part of the "career center" group makes absolutely no difference in CFC scores.

By contrast, the research hypothesis, also called the *alternate hypothesis*, is usually the exciting and interesting one. *The research hypothesis is a statement that postulates that there is a difference between populations or sometimes, more specifically, that there is a difference in a certain direction, positive or negative.* This is usually the exciting hypothesis because it proposes a distinctive difference that is worthy of even further investigation. In the CFC study, the research hypothesis would be that the CFC score is different for those in the "career center" group than for those in the control group; it also could specify a direction—that the CFC score is higher for those in the "career center" group than for those in the control group. This hypothesis is the exciting one because, if supported, the researcher has a finding that is potentially interesting, potentially publishable, potentially something the media would cover—and might encourage more financial support for career centers across many colleges and universities. Notice

Testing Hypotheses
If university administrators wanted to conduct a program through the career center to increase students' CFC scores, they might first conduct a study. Ideally, they would randomly assign students either to the group that received the career center program or to a control group.

- A **control group** is a level of the independent variable that is designed to match the experimental group in all ways but the experimental manipulation itself.

- An **experimental group** is a level of the independent variable that receives the treatment or intervention of interest in an experiment.

- The **null hypothesis** is a statement that postulates that there is no mean difference between populations or that the mean difference is in a direction opposite from that anticipated by the researcher.

- The **research hypothesis** (or *alternate hypothesis*) is a statement that postulates that there is a mean difference between populations or sometimes, more specifically, that there is a mean difference in a certain direction, positive or negative.

that for all hypotheses, we are very careful to state the comparison group. We do not say merely that the "career center" group has higher average scores; we say that it has higher average scores *than* the control group.

Making a Decision About Our Hypothesis: Consideration of Future Consequences

Here is where we introduce the logic of formal hypothesis testing. There are sensible reasons for the way that formal hypothesis testing is framed, and we will bring up the logic of hypothesis testing throughout the book. The sooner you understand this logic, the higher the probability that you'll understand and appreciate the power of inferential statistics. When we make a conclusion at the end of a study, the data leads us to conclude one of two things:

1. We decide to reject the null hypothesis.

2. We decide to fail to reject the null hypothesis.

Remember, you always begin your reasoning about the outcome of an experiment by reminding yourself that you are testing the (boring) null hypothesis.

In terms of the CFC study, the null hypothesis is that nothing happened. More specifically, the null hypothesis is that the mean CFC score for the "career center" group is the same as the mean CFC score for the control group. When trying to learn the logic of hypothesis testing, the key is to get started right. And the way to get started right is to keep repeating to yourself what the null hypothesis is proposing: there is no mean difference between groups.

After we analyze them, the data will tell us how to respond to the null hypothesis. We don't really have to make a judgment call about the null hypothesis because the data will tell us what to do. Based on the data, we will be able to do one of two things:

1. *Reject the null hypothesis.* "I reject the idea that there is no mean difference between groups." Or more specifically, "I reject the idea that the mean CFC score is the same in the 'career center' group as it is in the control group."

2. *Fail to reject the null hypothesis.* "I do not reject the idea that there is no mean difference between groups." Or more specifically, "I do not reject the idea that the mean CFC score is the same in the 'career center' group as it is in the control group."

If this language sounds confusing, that's because it is—but only at first. You will be surprised at how quickly you will get accustomed to it, because all formal hypothesis testing uses this logic. Let's take the first possible conclusion, to reject the null hypothesis. Intuitively, we would think that if the "career center" group's mean CFC score is a good deal higher than the control group's mean CFC score, then we should accept our research hypothesis that there is such a mean difference in the populations. But rather than accepting the research hypothesis, we reject the *null* hypothesis, the one that suggests there is nothing going on. We repeat: When the data suggest that there *is* a mean difference, we *reject* the idea that there is no mean difference. Rejecting sounds like a bad thing, but most of the time rejecting the null hypothesis when conducting research is a very good thing.

The second possible conclusion is failing to reject the null hypothesis. There's a very good reason for thinking about this in terms of failing to reject the null hypothesis rather than accepting the null hypothesis. Let's say there's a small mean difference, and we conclude that we cannot reject the null hypothesis (remember, rejecting the null hypothesis is what you want to do!). It could be that a real difference didn't show up in this particular sample just by chance. There are many ways in which a real mean difference in the population might not get picked up by a sample. Again, we repeat: When the data do not suggest a difference, we *fail* to reject the null hypothesis, which is the postulation that there is no mean difference. The way we decide whether to reject the null hypothesis is based directly on probability. We calculate the probability that the data would produce a difference this large and in a sample of this size *if* there were nothing else going on.

Because this logic is initially counterintuitive and perhaps unfamiliar to you, we will explain it using another perspective. Imagine that there is an omniscient behavioral scientist, Dr. X, who lives hermitlike on a mountain and who can see the actual average differences among all possible populations, no matter what we're studying. In this case, let's say Dr. X knows that there is no difference between the population mean CFC score for the "career center" group and the population mean CFC score for the control group. But samples can, just by chance, turn out to be different from the populations from which they are drawn. So it is possible that samples of the two groups would have different mean CFC scores just by chance. Even though the omniscient Dr. X. knows there is no difference between groups, the samples could show an average difference of perhaps 8 points. In other words, there could be an average difference between the samples even though there is no such difference between the populations. The omniscient Dr. X knows, but the rest of us have to depend on probability statistics.

We will be giving you many more opportunities to get comfortable with the logic of formal hypothesis testing before we start to apply numbers to it. But here are three easy rules and a table (Table 4-4) that will help keep you on track.

1. Always begin your reasoning about the idea you are testing with the null hypothesis that there is no average difference between groups.

2. Use the words *reject* and *fail to reject* only in reference to that same null hypothesis.

3. Never use the word *accept* in reference to formal hypothesis testing.

In summary, an understanding of probability is central to learning the language of statistics. When behavioral scientists conduct research, they develop two hypotheses: a null hypothesis that postulates no mean difference between levels of an independent variable and a research hypothesis that postulates a mean difference of some kind. Researchers can draw two conclusions. They can reject the null hypothesis and conclude that they have supported their exciting research hypothesis, or they can fail to reject the null hypothesis and conclude that they have not supported their exciting research hypothesis.

TABLE 4-4. HYPOTHESIS TESTING: HYPOTHESES AND DECISIONS

The null hypothesis posits no difference, on average, whereas the research hypothesis posits a difference of some kind. There are only two decisions we can make. We can fail to reject the null hypothesis if the research hypothesis *is not* supported, or we can reject the null hypothesis if the research hypothesis *is* supported.

	HYPOTHESIS	DECISION
NULL HYPOTHESIS	No mean change or difference	Fail to reject the null hypothesis (if research hypothesis is not supported)
RESEARCH HYPOTHESIS	Mean change or difference	Reject the null hypothesis (if research hypothesis is supported)

⊙ CHECK YOUR LEARNING

4-5 A university cuts the heat in wintertime to save money, and professors wonder whether students will perform more poorly, on average, under cold conditions. Several professors join forces to conduct a study in the hope of gathering data that will encourage stingy administrators to restore full heat.

a. Cite the likely null hypothesis for this study.

b. Cite the likely research hypothesis.

c. If the cold temperature appears to decrease academic performance, on average, what will the researchers conclude in terms of formal hypothesis-testing language?

d. If the researchers do not gather sufficient evidence to conclude that the cold temperatures lead to decreased academic performance, on average, what will they conclude in terms of formal hypothesis-testing language?

> TYPE I AND TYPE II ERRORS: STATISTICAL INFERENCES CAN BE WRONG

Robert blinked back to the present. Professor Krissel was saying something. "I'm sorry," Robert told her. "Please say that again. My mind wandered."

"Before my husband came in with this little car crisis, I was going to suggest that you take last year's midterm right now and then go home and take care of your family business. But as you can see, I'm in a bit of hurry, and so are you, I imagine. So let's give you a version of the test you can do in the next 10 minutes."

"Ten minutes? Right now?"

"Sure. For the multiple choice, I'll give you a random selection of questions. Let me grab a random numbers table. Here, we'll pick this row on the table." Robert looked at the table, a page with many columns and rows of numbers from 0 to 9. "There are 30 multiple-choice questions, and I'll have you answer 5. We'll go across the row looking at each pair of digits. The first two are 19, so you'll answer question 19. The next two are 03, so you'll answer question 3. The next is 89, but there is no 89, so we'll skip that." Professor Krissel pulled a test out of a drawer and began marking the questions Robert would need to answer. "It's a long test anyway, so I'm pretty sure that your answers to a random sample of these questions will let me know if you've understood the material. If you don't do well on the test, we'll discuss it later. But this way, you can just get it done now and go home without so much worry, at least for this week. And I'll have time to manage our car problem. You've got 10 minutes, 15 if you really need it. Okay?" She glanced at her husband. "Is this okay with everybody?"

Now Robert felt like he couldn't get out of it. And he really wanted to get to his car before Professor Krissel and her husband noticed it was his car in her parking spot—and certainly before the campus police issued a ticket.

Type I Errors: Sins of Commission

Robert's story is only one of the illustrations that we have been using to introduce you to an important statistical concept. For example, when we discussed the sampling difficulties of studying torture survivors, we noted that researchers are candid about those problems for two very specific reasons: A therapist doesn't want to pursue a treatment for PTSD that doesn't really work, but neither does a therapist want to avoid using a treatment that really does work. Similarly, when we discussed the importance of random assignment when studying jury decisions, we noted that there are two ways that a jury can come to a wrong decision. The jury doesn't want an innocent person to be found guilty, and the jury doesn't want a guilty person to be found innocent. If you asked a person suffering from PTSD or the judge overseeing a trial which type of error they prefer, their most honest answer would be, "Are you kidding? I don't want to make either kind of error! I want to get it right."

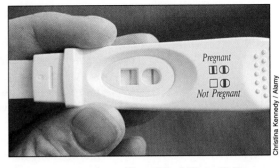

Are you starting to see why we are so impassioned about statistical reasoning? Statistical reasoning guides all of us toward minimizing the probability of making either kind of error, which of course is another way of asserting that statistical reasoning helps us maximize the probability of reaching a correct decision. Isn't it beautiful? We all make thousands of decisions every day. Most of them are minor, but a few of them will prove to be fairly consequential. Our lives are far more enjoyable and effective as we develop habits of thinking that increase the frequency of "getting it right" and decrease the frequency of making either type of error.

If we reject the null hypothesis, but it was a mistake to do so, then we have committed a Type I error. Specifically, *a **Type I error** occurs when we reject the null hypothesis, but the null hypothesis is correct.* A Type I error is like a false-positive in a medical test. If a woman believes she might be pregnant, then she might buy a home pregnancy test. In this case, the null hypothesis would be that she is not pregnant, and the research hypothesis would be that she is. If the test is positive, the woman rejects the null hypothesis—the one that postulates that she is not pregnant. Based on the test, the woman believes she is pregnant. Pregnancy tests, however, are not perfect. One urine-based test conducted only at clinics claims a false-positive rate of 0.2%, and home pregnancy tests are often far less accurate than this, particularly very early in a pregnancy and when the instructions are not followed perfectly. If the woman receives a positive test and rejects the null hypothesis, it is possible that she is wrong and it is a false-positive. Based on the test, the woman believes she is pregnant even though she is not pregnant. A false-positive is equivalent to a Type I error.

As you can easily imagine, a Type I error typically leads to action, at least until we discover that it is an error. For example, the woman with a false-positive pregnancy test might announce the news to her family and start buying baby clothes. Or a person mistakenly diagnosed with a very severe illness might begin expensive, possibly even harmful, treatments. Many researchers consider the consequences of a Type I error to be particularly detrimental because people often take action based on a mistaken finding.

Type II Errors: Sins of Omission

If we fail to reject the null hypothesis but it was a mistake to do so, this is a Type II error. Specifically, *a **Type II error** occurs when we fail to reject the null hypothesis, but the null hypothesis is false.* A Type II error is like a false-negative in medical testing. In the pregnancy example above, the woman might get a negative result on the test and fail to reject the null hypothesis, the one that says she's not pregnant. In this case, she would conclude that she's not pregnant

Type I and Type II Errors The results of a home pregnancy test are either positive (indicating pregnancy) or negative (indicating no pregnancy). If the test is positive, but the woman *is not* pregnant, this is equivalent to a Type I error in statistics. If the test is negative, but the woman *is* pregnant, this is equivalent to a Type II error in statistics. With pregnancy tests, as with hypothesis testing, people are more likely to act on a Type I error than on a Type II error.

■ A **Type I error** occurs when we reject the null hypothesis, but the null hypothesis is correct.

■ A **Type II error** occurs when we fail to reject the null hypothesis, but the null hypothesis is false.

when she really is. False-negative rates for pregnancy tests, however, tend to be higher than false-positive rates. For the urine-based test conducted in clinics, there is a 0.6% false-negative rate, and home pregnancy tests can have much higher false-negative rates. A false-negative is equivalent to a Type II error.

A Type II error typically results in a failure to take action because a research intervention is not supported or, with respect to medical testing, a given diagnosis is not received. Yet there are cases in which a Type II error can have serious consequences. For example, the pregnant woman who does not believe she is pregnant because of a Type II error may drink alcohol in a way that unintentionally harms her fetus. Similarly, a truly effective Alzheimer's drug might be kept from the market. The many thousands of people (and their families) who suffer from this terrible disease will continue to suffer. The answer is right under our noses, but we don't know it because of a Type II error.

The fact that both Type I and Type II errors do occur accentuates the importance of replication in research. From your own experience, you likely know that physicians insist on replication in the form of multiple tests when the medical stakes are high. A positive mammogram that suggests breast cancer leads to an ultrasound. A positive ultrasound leads to a biopsy. It is perhaps a bit frightening to realize that the same does not occur with a negative result (although it is understandable, given the high costs of so much testing, most of which would be unwarranted). A negative mammogram is considered good news, and typically no further testing occurs. If the woman really has undetected breast cancer, this would be a Type II error and might have serious repercussions.

Nickerson (2000) likened Type I and Type II errors to the decisions that jurors make in court. The null hypothesis, Nickerson says, is that the defendant is innocent. This hypothesis is rejected only if there is enough evidence to demonstrate that he or she is guilty beyond a reasonable doubt. In social science research, there are two possible decisions: to reject the null hypothesis or fail to reject the null hypothesis. Similarly, in court, there are two possible decisions, guilty or not guilty, which parallel the decisions researchers make after listening carefully to the numerical evidence. In court, if we listen carefully to the evidence and decide that the defendant is guilty (even though the person is really innocent), then we have committed the equivalent of a Type I error. On the other hand, if we listen carefully to the evidence and decide that the defendant is not guilty (even though the person is guilty), then we have committed the equivalent of a Type II error. Obviously, we don't want to make either error. So we strive to find the point that minimizes the probability of making either kind of error.

Notice that we use the phrase *not guilty*, which, as Nickerson points out, is not the same as *innocent*. When we fail to reject the null hypothesis, we cannot accept the null hypothesis. It is still possible that the defendant is guilty, but the evidence was not sufficient to draw this conclusion. In many countries, the justice system is set up so that it is harder to reject the null hypothesis—that is, it is more difficult to decide that someone is guilty. The U.S. system is based on the belief that it is preferable to free a guilty person than to imprison an innocent one. Whether in research, medical diagnosis, or a court of law, Type I and Type II errors can and do occur. Be sure to replicate important findings in your own research, and be sure to look for replications in the literature, especially when you read of findings that may have far-reaching consequences.

In summary, when we draw a conclusion from inferential statistics, there is always a chance we are wrong, even though we can never know for sure whether we're right or wrong. When we reject the null hypothesis, but the null hypothesis is true, we have committed a Type I error. When we fail to reject the null hypothesis, but the null hypothesis is not true, we have committed a Type II error. It is important to be perpetually aware that, regardless of our statistical decision, we may be wrong, and there may be consequences to our mistake.

⊙ CHECK YOUR LEARNING

4-6 Researchers conduct a study on perception by having participants throw a ball at a target while wearing virtual-reality glasses and while wearing glasses that allow normal viewing. The null hypothesis is that there is no difference in performance when wearing the virtual-reality glasses than when wearing the glasses that allow normal viewing.

a. The researchers reject the null hypothesis, concluding that the virtual-reality glasses lead to a worse performance than the normal glasses. What error might the researchers have made? Explain.

b. The researchers fail to reject the null hypothesis, concluding that it is possible that the virtual-reality glasses have no effect on performance. What error might the researchers have made? Explain.

❯ STATISTICS IN EVERYDAY LIFE: TYING IT ALL TOGETHER

Robert took the test in a chair outside the professor's office. He thought he would be nervous, but instead he just disappeared into the test material like it was a mental vacation. He finished the few questions and handed the test back to Professor Krissel.

"Here," Robert told Professor Krissel from her doorway. "I'm going to get going. It's a long drive." He glanced at her fidgeting husband.

"Wait a moment," she insisted as she took his test. "Let's grade it right now so you'll know what to plan for when you get back." Her pencil glided over the test, a musical pattern rising from the randomness. At last she looked up and smiled. "Go home," she said. "Be good to your family. You earned your A."

Robert moved in a daze back down the stairs toward the parking lot. His car was still there and he had no ticket! He quickly pulled out of Professor Krissel's parking space and drove away. His cell phone rang and it startled him.

"She's okay." It was his mother's voice.

"What? Wait. What about that test?"

"The doctor said that it was a false-positive. That first test came back with information that turned out not to be true. They did another test and it came back negative, too. She's okay."

"So there's nothing at all wrong with grandma?" Robert felt relieved. "How is she?"

"Oh, she's asleep. All she knows is that she's been getting a whole lot of attention, and she likes that. I hope you weren't planning on driving back or anything. Studies come first. Remember that!"

After he hung up, Robert remembered the statistics test. He had aced it! He turned the radio on, and a roaring sound came out of it. Applause. Thunderous applause.

"Bravo!!" Now there was wild cheering. A smooth voice said something about an opera and then simply let the cheering continue. It must have been an amazing performance!

"Thank you," he said modestly. "Thank you."

Like Robert, we often have to make decisions without enough information. The formal purpose of this text is to teach you how to become an intelligent consumer and creator of statistical information. But we are aiming deeper than mere skill building because we believe that statistical reasoning is a healthy, sensible way to think and make decisions about your life, even if you never read another research study. It is important to question the statistical claims that bombard you each day in magazines and newspapers, online, from friends, on TV, on billboards. Understanding the risks and rewards of statistically based decision making can make you a superior decision maker and a good consumer of research—but it also can make you a good consumer, period.

The Case of Lush: Testimonial to a Moisturizer

The spring/summer 2005 British edition of *Lush Times* is a colorful, 32-page, chatty catalog of Lush's handmade cosmetics. The newspaper-style catalog clearly aims to entertain, but its ultimate goal is to sell cosmetics. Skin's Shangri La is one of the many face moisturizers that Lush offers, and a long description of its amazing moisturizing and skin-rejuvenating powers ends with two testimonials, one of which reads in part: "I'm nearly 60, but no one believes it, which proves Skin's Shangri La works!"

EXPERIENCE IT FOR YOURSELF

BECOMING A SMARTER CONSUMER

Knowing what you've now learned about statistics and the role of samples, probability, and error, answer the following questions about the many possible flaws of this "evidence"—a brief testimonial—for the supposed effectiveness of Skin's Shangri La.

1. What is the sample size flaw? _____

2. What is the representative sample flaw? _____

3. What is the self-selection flaw? _____

4. How does probability fit in? _____

5. Do possible flaws mean that Skin's Shangri La is ineffective? _____

Testimonials as Evidence?
Does one middle-aged woman's positive experience with Skin's Shangri La—"I'm nearly 60, but no one believes it"—provide evidence that this moisturizer causes younger-looking skin? Testimonials use a volunteer sample of one person, usually a biased individual; moreover, you can bet that the testimonial that a company uses in its advertising is the most flattering one.

Susan Nolan

Let's first consider the population and sample here. The population would be all women approaching age 60. The Lush marketers would like potential customers to think that they, too, could look years younger if they used this product. The sample would be the individual who wrote to Lush to share her experience. There are two major problems with this sample. First, and most important, one person can never constitute a representative sample. It would not even make sense to conduct hypothesis testing on data from one individual. Second, this is a special kind of convenience sample, a volunteer sample. The customer who had this experience chose to write to Lush. Was she likely to write to Lush if she did not feel very strongly about this product? Moreover, was Lush likely to publish her statement if it were not positive?

A second consideration is the type of person of her age who would shop at Lush. Although Lush touts its products for people of all ages, its marketing clearly seems targeted at young people. With colorful, cartoonlike drawings and catchy product names, such as Iridescent Glitterbug, Candy Fluff, and Sonic Death Monkey, it seems likely that teens and 20-somethings are the intended consumers. What might you hypothesize about the type of 60-year-old woman who would shop at Lush in the first place? Might she have a more youthful mind-set than others her age?

Third, doing statistics comes down to decision making based on probability. How likely are we to see a certain effect just by chance? If it's very likely, we cannot reject the null hypothesis, the one that says Skin's Shangri La *does not* work. With one participant, we could never reject the null hypothesis, because we might see an effect just by chance. To reject the null hypothesis, we'd need more participants, and we'd want them to be representative of the sample, not just women who choose to shop at Lush. If we were the inventors of and investors in Skin's Shangri La, we'd want to convince consumers that our products work. But if you want to be an intelligent consumer, then you would not allow such flawed arguments to influence how you spend your money.

Which is more persuasive to you? A dubious testimonial or a well-designed study? If your honest answer is a dubious testimonial, then statistical reasoning once again leads us to ask a better question, albeit one that is more difficult to answer: What is it about you that is more responsive to unlikely fantasy than to statistical probability? Statistical thinking can challenge us in unexpected ways, inspire introspection, improve our daily decision making, and offer significant career guidance.

Understanding the Meaning of Proof: Statistical Literacy in Consumer Research

So why don't companies conduct well-designed consumer research? First, conducting a careful experiment with a large, representative sample that has been randomly assigned to conditions is not only time-consuming but also quite expensive. With hundreds of products at many companies, including Lush, it would be prohibitive to make well-designed experiments the norm. In fact, few companies do such research unless required by law; pharmaceutical companies, for example, must conduct controlled experiments that use random assignment. Second, there's no *need* to conduct well-designed experiments. P. T. Barnum's money-making observation probably says it best: "There's a sucker born every minute." The public doesn't require scientifically framed data to believe a particular product works, especially when they want it to work. For most consumers, a testimonial of the sort described above would probably yield more sales than would a report of the results of a well-designed study. Third, a vivid anecdote is likely more persuasive to most people because it is more likely to be remembered. What would a potential consumer be more likely to repeat to a friend—the results of a study or the report that one 60-year-old woman actually looks substantially younger? Statistical literacy is essential to separating claims based on solid evidence from those based on flimsy or no evidence.

It's your money, so let's think through what statistical literacy means in terms of consumer research. Just because a product is praised in a testimonial does not mean that it doesn't work; it may work wonderfully. We just can't know from a sample of one. However, keep in mind that many social science studies have demonstrated that "believing is seeing." Once we get an idea in our heads, we see the evidence that supports that idea and disregard the evidence that does not support it. So the probability is high that a 60-year-old woman who wants to believe that she looks younger would actually perceive herself as looking years younger. Even if this moisturizer were nothing more than an expensive placebo, who wants to admit that they spent their money foolishly when it feels so comforting to believe otherwise? Fortunately, statistical literacy helps us recognize that a biased sample of one does not allow us to conclude that a moisturizer works. This woman might actually look younger than her age without any assistance from an expensive moisturizer; or she might even look years older than she is without it! The evidence does not allow us to reach a conclusion either way. But one does wonder about the degree to which a nation's economy floats on a sea of placebo effects.

That leads us to a discussion about the word *proof*. Statistical literacy means that we reserve that powerful word for those rare circumstances when it deserves to be used. The word *prove* is used fairly loosely in consumer culture and in discussions of human behavior, often in ways similar to that in the Lush testimonial on the previous page. In science, however, we never prove anything; we just find evidence against alternative explanations. When we reject the null hypothesis, we are saying that the idea that nothing is happening—that a moisturizing product does not work or that the hypothalamus is not be affected by a certain procedure—does not seem likely under these circumstances. However, we have not proved that the product or procedure worked—just that it seems more and more unlikely that it did not work. In other words, science forces itself to be humble. As scientists, we're willing to believe only the last theory standing.

That said, it is irresponsible to suggest that the sciences, including the behavioral sciences, cannot draw any conclusions. Scientists confidently draw conclusions all the time, especially when based on sound research that has been replicated. For example, there is currently much debate in the United States about the theory of evolution, a theory that continues to provide valuable insights into human behavior, produce life-saving medications, and accelerate the growth of knowledge by using species such as short-lived fruit flies to test for both random and induced genetic mutations across generations. Some say that because evolution is a theory and not a proven fact, it is equivalent to a litany of other explanations about how humans came to be. This is not true. Evolution will *never* be a proven fact because that is not how science works. However, scientists have been able to reject the null hypothesis—the hypothesis that evolution does not occur—over and over again across many disciplines. As commonsense observers trying to make sense of the world around us, we're willing to believe only the last theory standing.

The irony is that for those who cite faith in their objection to evolution, this scientific perspective does not attack faith at all! Indeed, both science and religious texts clarify that faith, and faith alone, is the evidence for itself; otherwise it isn't faith. So people who look to science to buttress their faith are actually revealing their private doubts because adding any evidence to faith undermines the very definition of faith. To date, no other explanation of the origins and ancestry of humans has generated even close to the degree of evidence that evolution and natural selection have assembled. When we have rejected our null hypothesis in every way we can think of to test it, and when we have replicated our work numerous times, we can start to be confident that our alternative hypothesis is a valid one. Proof, however, we'll never have.

In summary, despite the availability of powerful statistical techniques, consumers of ideas and products in our society often accept testimonials more readily than they accept empirical evidence. Because empirical evidence is not necessary to persuade or to sell a product, few companies conduct the rigorous research necessary to support a product's efficacy. Educated consumers will consider statistical principles in their everyday decision making.

⊙ CHECK YOUR LEARNING

4-7 It is ironic that even books on statistics sometimes rely on testimonials. On the back cover of a book recounting the history of the personages who drove the field of statistics ever forward, *The Lady Tasting Tea: How Statistics Revolutionized Science in the Twentieth Century* by David Salsburg (2001), we find a testimonial from "Alvan R. Feinstein, MD, Sterling Professor of Medicine and Epidemiology, Yale University School of Medicine." Feinstein avers, "Highly readable and well-written. . . . Give it to someone you want to delight."

   a. Why does the publishing company include such a testimonial? For what outcome do they hope? Why do they note the testimonial writer's pedigree?

   b. What evidence would be better than this testimonial in convincing you that this book has merit?

   c. Both authors of this text add to Feinstein's testimonial; we, too, find this book highly entertaining, particularly for statistics geeks. Why should a potential reader of Salsburg's text not rely on our words either?

   d. This textbook also uses memorable anecdotes about statistical reasoning. What kind of evidence would convince you that story-telling is or is not an effective teaching tool?

▪ DIGGING DEEPER INTO THE DATA: THE SHOCKING PREVALENCE OF TYPE I ERRORS

Misuse of hypothesis testing—and a tendency to overlook the possibilities of error, particularly of Type I error—has led to the mass dissemination of numerous false findings. In the *British Medical Journal*, Sterne and Smith (2001) comment that the medical literature shows a strong tendency to accentuate the positive; positive outcomes are more likely to be reported than null results. This tendency arises because journals—whether reporting on medical, psychological, sociological, or any other scientific findings—tend to publish "exciting" results rather than "boring" ones.

To translate this into the terms of hypothesis testing discussed early, if a researcher rejects the boring null hypothesis, thus garnering support for the exciting research hypothesis, the editor of a journal is more likely to want to publish these results. If a researcher fails to reject the boring null hypothesis, thus not supporting the exciting research hypothesis, then the editor of a journal is far less likely to want to publish these results. The mass media compound this problem; only the *most* exciting and surprising results are likely to get picked up and disseminated to the general public. When was the last time that you read an article about a new drug that did nothing? It is a problem that a sophisticated consumer of statistical information needs to acknowledge: There is a bias against boring reality!

Estimating Type I Error in the Medical Literature: Does That Pill Really Work?

Using educated estimations, Sterne and Smith (2001) calculated some probabilities of what might occur across 1000 hypothetical studies that use hypothesis testing. First, based on the literature on coronary heart disease, they assumed that 10% of studies *should* reject the null hypothesis; that is, 10% of studies examined medical techniques that actually worked. Second, based on flaws in methodology such as small sample sizes, as well as the fact that there will be chance findings, they estimated that half of the time the null hypothesis would *not* be rejected when it should be rejected, a Type II error. That is, half of the time a new effective treatment would not receive empirical support. Finally, when a new treatment *does not* actually work, researchers will falsely reject the null hypothesis 5% of the time; just by chance, studies will lead to a false reportable difference between treatments, a Type I error. In later chapters, we'll learn more about this 5% criterion, but for now, it's only important to know that the 5% cutoff is both arbitrary yet well-established in statistical analyses. Table 4-5 summarizes Sterne and Smith's hypothetical outcomes of 1000 studies.

Let's examine their numbers. Of 1000 studies, the exciting research hypothesis is accurate in only 100; for these studies, we *should* reject the null hypothesis. In the other 900 of these studies, the null hypothesis is accurate and we *should not* reject the null hypothesis. That is, if we were always correct in our decisions, we should reject the null hypothesis only in 100 of these studies, and we should fail to reject the null hypothesis in the other 900. But remember, we are sometimes incorrect in our conclusions. Given the 5% Type I error rate that Sterne and Smith used, we will falsely reject 5%, or 45, of the 900 null hypotheses that we should not reject. Given the 50% Type II error rate that Sterne and Smith used, we will incorrectly fail to reject 50 of the 100 studies in which we should reject the null hypothesis. (Both of the numbers indicating errors are in boldface in Table 4-5.) The most important numbers in Table 4-5 are in the row labeled "reject." This is the row for which we'll have exciting results. Of the 95 total studies for which we reject the null hypothesis, we'll be wrong in 45 of these cases. We'll be wrong almost half of the time! The probabilities calculated by Sterne and Smith, using assumptions based on their knowledge of the statistical and medical literatures, suggest that almost half of published medical studies may contain Type I errors; they may be reports of findings that are simply not accurate. These rates are likely to be true for other sciences as well, including the behavioral sciences.

Several recent cases in the medical literature exemplify the premises of Sterne and Smith. In recent years, there has been a spate of claims about the health benefits of natural substances. Natural health-related products are often less

TABLE 4-5. ESTIMATES OF TYPE I ERRORS

Sterne and Smith (2001) used educated estimates to calculate the likelihood of Type I errors in published reports of medical findings. Their calculations suggest that almost half of published medical studies exhibit Type I errors!

RESULT OF STUDY	NULL HYPOTHESIS IS TRUE (TREATMENT DOESN'T WORK)	NULL HYPOTHESIS IS FALSE (TREATMENT DOES WORK)	TOTAL
Fail to reject	855	**50**	905
Reject	**45**	50	95
Total	900	100	1000

expensive than their manufactured counterparts because they do not have to be invented by big pharmaceutical companies. In addition, they are perceived to be healthy even though natural substances are not always risk-free. (Remember, cyanide and arsenic are natural products! So are rattlesnake venom and lead.) Previous research has supported the use of vitamin E to prevent various maladies, and echinacea has been championed for its alleged ability to prevent the common cold. Yet recent studies that implemented rigorous research designs have largely discredited early accounts of the effectiveness of vitamin E and echinacea in the contexts for which they were recommended.

Medical Findings and Confirmation Biases: Science Versus Self-Deception

When the general public reads first of the value of vitamin E or echinacea and then of the health care establishment's dismissal of these preventive treatments, they start to wonder what to believe and often, sadly, rely even more on their own biased common sense. It would be far better for scientists to improve their research designs from the outset, and reduce the Type I errors that so frequently make headlines. Sterne and Smith (2001) lament the general public's accelerating distrust of the medical and scientific establishments that such scientific flip-flopping leads to. Knowing what we do about the confirmation bias, however, we might add that the general public tend to be cynical mostly about findings that they do not like—those that tell them to exercise more, quit smoking, and eschew sun tanning—and are perhaps too readily accepting of those that they do like—reports of a new "cure" for a disease that ails them, particularly if the proposed cure is effort-free and inexpensive. We tend to focus on what we want in order to confirm our preexisting beliefs.

Sterne and Smith (2001), as well as the American Psychological Association, strongly recommend the use of statistical methods other than hypothesis testing to reduce the inflated publication rates of Type I errors and to begin to restore the public's trust in reported scientific findings. Among the many suggestions are the use of larger sample sizes to make it more likely that real results are detected and the reporting of the magnitude of any findings so that the public and other scientists can determine how important a finding really is.

In summary, because of the flaws inherent in much research, numerous null hypotheses are rejected falsely, resulting in Type I errors. In fact, researchers have estimated that almost half of published medical findings exhibit Type I errors. Educated consumers of research are skeptical about findings that have not been replicated across varying contexts. Moreover, educated consumers of research are aware of their own confirmation biases and how these biases might affect their tendency to believe research findings without appropriate questioning.

R E V I E W   O F   C O N C E P T S

⊙ CHECK YOUR LEARNING

4-8 Kolata (2005) reported that although echinacea is one of the most commonly used natural supplements—used by over 14 million Americans—recent research did not supports its efficacy. The journal article to which Kolata referred was published in the *New England Journal of Medicine*. Turner, Bauer, Woelkart, Hulsey, and Gangemi (2005) reported on their rigorously designed experiment of 399 volunteers who were infected with the rhinovirus that causes the common cold. This carefully designed study, however, failed to detect an effect of echinacea. The authors concluded that their findings, in conjunction with similar findings from other well-designed research, "suggest that the burden of proof should lie with those who advocate this treatment" (p. 348).

a. Explain why earlier findings may have been examples of Type I errors.

b. Given that this study is described as "rigorously" and "carefully" designed, what tactics did the researchers likely include in their design?

c. Why would a proponent of echinacea—say, a friend of yours who has taken it for years—be reluctant to believe the results of this study?

> Samples and Their Populations: Why Statisticians Are Stingy

The gold standard of sample selection is *random sampling*, a procedure in which every member of the population has an equal chance of being chosen for study participation. A random numbers table or computer-based random numbers generator is used to assure randomness. Variations on random sampling include *cluster sampling*, in which clusters (e.g., schools) are randomly selected and every member of the cluster is chosen to participate, and *stratified sampling*, in which equal numbers of participants are randomly selected from different strata (e.g., age groups).

For practical reasons, random selection is uncommon in social science research. Many behavioral scientists use a *convenience sample*, a sample that is readily available to them. One kind of convenience sample is the *volunteer sample*, in which participants themselves actively choose to participate in the study. With random assignment, every participant in a study has an equal chance of being assigned to any of the experimental conditions. One variation on random assignment is *randomized block design*, in which participants are assigned to conditions within blocks, or groups that share a characteristic thought to affect the dependent variable. *Replication*, the duplication of scientific results, in conjunction with random assignment, can go a long way toward increasing our ability to generalize our findings beyond our samples.

> Sampling in the Behavioral Sciences: Why Sampling Is Both an Art and a Science

Random sampling and random assignment are often confused, and a beginning statistics student must be careful to distinguish between these concepts. It is also important to be aware that random assignment is far more common than random sampling, mostly for practical reasons. Scrutiny of others' research designs, particularly their sampling and assignment methods, can make us better and more careful researchers.

> Probability Theory: Distinguishing Between Mere Coincidence and Real Connections

Probability forms the foundation of inferential statistics. Calculating probabilities is essential because human thinking is dangerously biased. Because of a *confirmation bias*, or tendency to see patterns that we expect to see, we tend to see meaning in mere coincidence. A confirmation bias often results from an *illusory correlation*, a relation that appears to be present but actually does not exist. *Groupthink*, overconfident and biased decision making, is a potentially dangerous outcome of a failure to rely on objective data.

> Probability Theory: The Basics

When we think of probability, many of us think of *subjective* (or *personal*) *probability*, an individual's own judgment about the likelihood that an event will occur. Statisticians, however, are referring to *expected relative-frequency probability*, or the long-run expected outcome if an experiment or trial were repeated many, many times. A *trial* refers to each occasion a procedure is carried out and an *outcome* is the result of a trial. A *success* refers to the outcome for which we're trying to determine probability. The *gambler's fallacy* is a type of biased thinking in which an individual believes that a previous occurrence has an effect on an ensuing occurrence, when in fact the two events are unrelated.

> Statistics and Probability: The Logic of Inferential Statistics

Inferential statistics, based on probability, start with the positing of a hypothesis. The *null hypothesis* is a statement that postulates no average difference between populations. The *alternative* or *research hypothesis* is a statement that postulates that there is an average difference between populations. After conducting a hypothesis test, we have only two possible conclusions. We can either reject or fail to reject the null hypothesis. When we conduct inferential statistics, we often are comparing an *experimental group*, the group subjected to an intervention, with a *control group* the group that is the same as the experimental group in every way except the intervention.

> Type I and Type II Errors: Statistical Inferences Can Be Wrong

Statisticians must always be aware that their conclusions may be wrong. If a researcher rejects the null hypothesis, but the null hypothesis is correct, the researcher is making a *Type I error*. If a researcher fails to reject the null hypothesis, but the alternative hypothesis is correct, the researcher is making a *Type II error*.

> Statistics in Everyday Life: Tying It All Together

A knowledge of statistics can help us debunk far-fetched marketing claims or judge the merits of a new medical breakthrough. Representative samples, sound research design, and replication of research are markers that can help us be more certain about reported findings. Although we can never attain proof that our research hypotheses are true, we can generate much empirical support for them.

> Digging Deeper into the Data: The Shocking Prevalence of Type I Errors

Scientific and medical journals tend to publish, and the media tend to report on, the most exciting and surprising findings. As such, Type I errors are often overrepresented among reported findings. A careful examination of a study's sample and research design can help us to judge the merits of reported findings as well as examine our own biases.

SPSS GUIDELINES FOR CHAPTER 4: ALTERNATIVE WAYS TO EXAMINE INDIVIDUAL VARIABLES

There are a variety of ways to look more closely at the individual variables.
We can request a variety of case summaries by selecting:

Analyze → Reports → Case Summaries

We then can highlight the variable of interest and click the arrow to move it under "Variables:"

If we want to break it down by a second variable, we can highlight a nominal variable and click the bottom arrow to move it under "Graphing Variable(s):"

After making our choices, we click on "OK" to see the output screen.

EXERCISES

4.1 Random selection and U.S. school psychologists: Approximately 21,000 school psychologists are members of the U.S.-based National Association of School Psychologists. Of these, about 5000 have doctoral degrees. A researcher wanted to randomly select 100 of the doctoral-level school psychologists for a survey study regarding aspects of their jobs, including types of tasks in which they engaged, settings in which they worked, and attitudes about their careers. Here is the same excerpt from a random numbers table that was presented earlier in this chapter:

04493	52494	75246	33824	45862	51025	61962
00549	97654	64051	88159	96119	63896	54692
35963	15307	26898	09354	33351	35462	77974
59808	08391	45427	26842	83609	49700	46058

a. What is the population targeted by this study? How large is it?

b. What is the sample desired by this researcher? How large is it?

c. Describe how the researcher would select his sample. Be sure to explain how the members of the population would be numbered and what sets of digits the researcher should ignore when using the random numbers table.

d. Beginning at the left-hand side of the top line and continuing with each succeeding line, list the first 10 participants that this researcher would select for his study.

4.2 U.S. school psychologists and variations on random sampling: For each of the following variations on random sampling, briefly explain the steps for selecting a sample.

a. Cluster sampling with the institutions from which the school psychologists received their doctoral degrees as the clusters

b. Cluster sampling with U.S. states as the clusters

c. Stratified sampling with men and women as the strata (if you want equal numbers of men and women)

d. Stratified sampling with U.S. regions (e.g., Northeast, Midwest) as the strata (if you want equal numbers from each region)

4.3 Random assignment and U.S. school psychologists: See Exercise 4.3 regarding school psychologists. Once the researcher had randomly selected his sample of 100 school psychologists, he decided to randomly assign 50 of them to receive, as part of their survey materials, a newspaper article about the improving job market for school psychologists; he assigned the other 50 to receive a newspaper article about the declining job market for school psychologists. Unbeknownst to the participants (until the debriefing at the end of the survey), the articles were fictional. After reading the articles, the participants would respond to questions about their attitudes toward their careers. The researcher wondered whether attitudes could be affected by external sources.

a. What is the independent variable in this experiment, and what are its levels?

b. What is the dependent variable in this experiment?

c. What features of the research design qualify this study as an experiment?

d. Describe how the researcher would randomly assign the participants to the levels of the independent variable. Be sure to explain how the levels of the independent variable would be numbered and what sets of digits the researcher should ignore when using the random numbers table.

e. Beginning at the left-hand side of the bottom line of the random numbers table excerpt in Exercise 4.1, and continuing with the left-hand side of the line above it, list the levels of the independent variable to which the first 10 participants would be assigned.

f. Why do these numbers not appear to be random? Discuss the difference between short-run and long-run proportions.

4.4 U.S. school psychologists and variations on random assignment: Consider the U.S. school psychologists scenario discussed in Exercise 4.3.

a. Briefly explain how you would assign a sample of participants to conditions using randomized block design if the blocks were pairs of participants making the same salary.

b. List three other possible blocks that could be used in this study.

4.5 Random selection and Australian school psychologists: There are approximately 2000 school psychologists in Australia. A researcher has developed a new diagnostic tool to identify conduct disorder in children and wants to study ways to train school psychologists to administer it. She wants to recruit 30 school psychologists to participate in her study.

a. What is the population and how large is it?

b. How large is the desired sample?

c. Explain how you could use the Web-based tool http://randomizer.org to randomly select 30 school psychologists for this study. State what you would enter in each of the boxes on the site: how many numbers you want to generate, how many numbers per set, number range, whether each number remains unique, and whether you wish to sort your numbers.

d. Use the randomizer to generate a list of 30 numbers. List the numbers of the 30 participants who will be chosen. (Note: Click the "Randomizer" button to begin.)

e. Repeat the process to generate a second list. State ways in which the two lists do or do not seem random to you. Are there strings of numbers? Are there several numbers close to one another in magnitude (e.g., three numbers right around 1100)?

4.6 Random assignment and Australian school psychologists: The researcher described in Exercise 4.5 has developed two training modules. One is implemented in a classroom setting and requires that school psychologists travel to a nearby city for training. The other is a Web-based training module and is far more practical and cost-effective to use. Half of the participants will be randomly assigned to classroom training and half will be randomly assigned to use the Web-based program. She will administer a test to participants after training to determine how much they learned. Her hope is that the Web-based training will work as well as the classroom training, resulting in savings of both cost and time.

a. What is the independent variable in this experiment? What are its levels?

b. What is the dependent variable in this experiment?

c. What features of the research design qualify this study as an experiment? Explain how you would use the randomizer Web site to assign the 30 participants to levels of the independent variable. State what you would enter in each of the boxes on the site: how many numbers you want to generate, how many numbers per set, number range, whether each number remains unique, and whether you wish to sort your numbers.

d. Use the randomizer to generate the assignments for the 30 participants. List the assignments.

e. Repeat the process, but this time generate assignments so that exactly 15 are in each condition. What did you do differently to achieve this goal?

f. Repeat the process one more time, but now generate assignments in blocks of 10. Be sure that half of each block of 10 is in each condition. Explain what you did.

4.7 Random numbers and the helpful roommate: Imagine that you have been hired by the Psychology Department at your school to administer a survey to psychology majors about their experiences in the department. You have been asked to randomly select 60 majors from the overall pool of 300. You are working on this project in your dorm room using a random numbers table because the server is down and you cannot use randomizer.org. Your roommate is patiently waiting for you to finish so you can go out and offers to write down a list of 60 random numbers between 001 and 300 for you so you'll be done quickly. In about three to four sentences, explain to your roommate why this would not be likely to result in a list of random numbers.

4.8 Studies and randomness: For each of the following studies, state (i) whether random selection could have been used, explaining why it would be possible or why not. Explain also to what population the researcher wanted to and could generalize and (ii) whether random assignment could have been used, explaining why it would be possible or why not.

a. A researcher recruited 1000 U.S. physicians through the American Medical Association (AMA) to participate in a study of standards of confidentiality with respect to patient information. He wanted to compare perceptions of the standard among men versus women.

b. A developmental psychologist wondered whether children born preterm (premature) had different social skills at age five than children born full-term.

c. A psychobiologist wondered whether people who were startled by an auditory stimulus responded differently on brain scans than people startled by a visual stimulus. She wondered whether different parts of the brain were affected in the two different conditions.

d. A counseling center director wanted to compare the length of therapy in weeks for students who came in for treatment for depression versus students who came in for treatment for anxiety. She wanted to report these data to the university administrators to help develop the next year's budget.

e. An industrial/organizational psychologist wondered whether a new laptop design would affect people's response time when using the computer. He wanted to compare response times when using the new laptop with response times when using two standard versions of laptops, a Mac and a PC.

4.9 Volunteer samples and U.S. college football: A volunteer sample is a kind of convenience sample in which participants select themselves to participate. On August 19, 2005, *USA Today* published an online poll on its Web site asking this question about U.S. college football: "Who is your pick to win the ACC conference this year?" Eight options—seven universities, including top vote-getters Virginia Tech and Miami, as well as "other"—were provided.

a. Describe the typical person who might volunteer to be in this sample. Why might this sample be biased, even with respect to the population of U.S. college football fans?

b. What is external validity? Why might external validity be limited in this sample?

c. What other problem can you identify with this poll?

4.10 Volunteer samples and *Cosmo* quizzes: *Cosmopolitan* magazine, *Cosmo* as it's known popularly, publishes many of its well-known quizzes on its Web site. One quiz is titled "Are You Obsessed with Appearances?" (It is at http://quiz.ivillage.com/cosmopolitan/tests/Appearances.htm if you're interested in viewing it.) As if the fact that one reads *Cosmo* isn't enough to answer the question, the quiz poses 10 situations for which participants must choose how they'd act from among three limited options. An invitation to a costume party for which one must dress as a musician offers the possibilities of Lauryn Hill in "killer cargo pants," one of the Indigo Girls in a flannel shirt, and Madonna in her "ultra-glam Marilyn Monroe phase." Consider whether you want to use the quiz data to determine how obsessed women are with their appearance.

a. Describe the typical person who might respond to this quiz. How might data from such a sample be biased, even with respect to the overall *Cosmo* readership?

b. What is the danger of relying on volunteer samples in general?

c. What other problems do you see with this quiz? Comment on the types of questions and responses.

4.11 Volunteer samples and U.S. political leanings: On the Web site http://www.theadvocates.org/quiz.html, Advocates for Self-Government offers the "World's Smallest Internet Political Quiz," focusing on the U.S. political spectrum. By means of just 10 questions, the quiz identifies an individual's political leanings. As of May 23, 2007; 9,464,924 people had taken the quiz, and the breakdown into the five possible categories is: centrist, 33.49%; conservative, 8.88%; libertarian, 32.64%; liberal, 17.09%; and statist (big government), 7.89%.

a. Do you think these numbers are representative of the U.S. population? Why or why not?

b. Describe the people most likely to volunteer for this sample. Why might this group be biased in comparison to the overall U.S. population?

c. The Web site says, "Libertarians support maximum liberty in both personal and economic matters." Libertarians are not the predominant political group in the United States. Why, then, might libertarians form the largest category of quiz respondents?

d. This is a huge sample—9,464,924. Why is it not enough to have a large sample to conduct a study with high external validity? What would we need to change about this sample to increase external validity?

4.12 Differentiating among types of selection and assignment: For each of the following hypothetical scenarios, state whether selection or assignment is being described as well as the specific selection or assignment method being used. Explain your answer.

a. For a study of stress levels in *Fortune* 500 company presidents, 25 presidents over age 60 and 25 under age 60 were chosen; every president in a given age category had an equal chance of being chosen for his or her age category sample.

b. A study of the services offered by counseling centers at Canadian universities studied 20 universities; every Canadian university had an equal chance of being in this study.

c. In a study of phobias, 30 rhesus monkeys were either exposed to fearful stimuli or not exposed to fearful stimuli. Every monkey had an equal chance of being placed in either of the exposure conditions.

d. A study of cell phone usage recruited participants by including an invitation to participate in their cell phone bills.

e. A study of visual perception recruited 120 Introduction to Psychology students to participate.

f. Fifty groups of three students matched on GPA were assigned to complete a cognitive task in one of three conditions: loud music, soft music, silence. Within each group of three, each student had an equal chance of being assigned to each condition.

g. A study of student athletes in U.S. Division I university athletic programs selected 30 of the Division I athletic programs in the United States. Every program had an equal chance of being selected. Every student athlete within each of the 30 programs was recruited for participation.

4.13 Biases and horoscopes: A friend reads his horoscope every day and is amazed at its accuracy. From your Introduction to Psychology class, you know that the accuracy of horoscopes, or of ESP for that matter, has never been verified in a well-designed experiment.

a. What is an illusory correlation, and how does your friend's perception relate to it?

b. What is a confirmation bias, and how does your friend's perception relate to it?

c. How might you design a simple experiment to demonstrate to your friend that his belief is based on biases rather than fact?

4.14 Coincidence: Pair up with another student in your statistics class whom you do not know well. Together, read through the topics in the accompanying table to see which are areas in which you have something in common, describing the commonalities when you find them. When possible, try to find at least one parallel experience; for example, for the topic of vacation destinations, list vacation spots until you hit upon a place you've both been to. Note any commonalities that you find. Skip topics for which you have nothing in common.

a. Were you surprised at how many commonalities you found? What does this tell you about the nature of coincidence? Discuss the probability of unusual occurrences when you consider the whole range of possible occurrences.

b. Read the list of commonalities to a third person, noting *only* the things you have in common. What is this person's reaction?

TOPIC	COMMONALITY
Vacation destinations	_____
Number of siblings	_____
Parents' occupations	_____
Jobs held	_____
Pets	_____
Hometown	_____
Name of high school	_____
Favorite ice cream flavor	_____
Favorite color	_____
Favorite food	_____
Toothpaste brand	_____
Favorite video game	_____
Favorite high school subject	_____
Sports played	_____
Favorite TV show	_____
Movie last watched	_____
Magazines read regularly	_____
News source (e.g., CNN)	_____
Volunteer work	_____
Career goals	_____
Favorite college course	_____
Ever had braces?	_____
Wear contacts/glasses?	_____
Favorite beverage	_____
Favorite pro sport or team	_____
Favorite musicians	_____
Instruments played	_____
Involvement in student groups	_____
Piercings	_____
Tattoos	_____

4.15 Confirmation bias, professors, and dead grandmothers: This chapter described a spoof by Adams (1990) using fictional data to postulate that more students have grandmothers die prior to examinations than at other times of the semester. Many professors, perhaps some of your own, believe that students invent dead grandmothers to avoid taking examinations. It may be true that some students do this. But it also may be merely a perception of professors due to their own confirmation biases. Write what you would say to one of your professors if she stated that she believed this (and if you worked up the nerve to call her on it!).

4.16 The components of the calculation of probability: A certain university provides every student with a laptop computer. Students complained that their computers "always" crashed when they were on the Internet and had at least three other programs open (e.g., word-processing program, music program, statistical software). One student thought this was an exaggeration and decided to calculate the probability that the campus computers would crash under these circumstances. On 100 different students' computers, he opened three programs and then went online. He recorded whether each computer crashed under these conditions.

a. Identify what the trials would be in this example.

b. Identify what would be meant by outcome in this example.

c. Identify what would be meant by a success in this example.

d. What is meant by independent trials? Would the trials be considered independent in this example? Why or why not?

e. If the student used his own computer 100 times, turning it off between each trial, would the trials be considered independent? Why or why not?

4.17 Short-run proportions versus long-run probabilities: Short-run proportions are often quite different from long-run probabilities.

a. In your own words, explain why we would expect short-run proportions to fluctuate but long-run probabilities to be more predictable.

b. What is the expected long-run probability of heads if you flip a coin many, many times? Why?

c. Flip a coin 10 times in a row. What proportion are heads? Do this 5 times (and actually do it, don't just write down numbers!).

Proportion for first 10 flips: _____

Proportion for second 10 flips: _____

Proportion for third 10 flips: _____

Proportion for fourth 10 flips: _____

Proportion for fifth 10 flips: _____

d. Do the proportions in part (c) match the expected long-run probability in part (b)? Why or why not?

e. Imagine that a friend flipped a coin ten times, got nine out of ten heads, and complained that the coin was biased. How would you explain to your friend the difference between short-term and long-term probability?

4.18 Probability, proportion, and percentage: A deck of playing cards has four suits and thirteen cards in each suit, for a total of 52 cards. From the deck you draw one card; you record what the card is and then replace it. Let's say you repeat this process 15 times, and 5 of the 15 cards are aces. Answer the following questions keeping this example in mind.

a. What does the term *probability* refer to? What is the probability of drawing an ace?

b. What does the term *proportion* refer to? What is the proportion of aces drawn?

c. What does the term *percentage* refer to? What is the percentage of aces drawn?

d. Based on these data (5 out of 15 cards were aces), do you have enough information to determine whether the deck is stacked (i.e., biased)? Why or why not? [*Note:* 4 of the 52 cards should be aces.]

4.19 Gambler's fallacy and independent trials: The gambler's fallacy describes the phenomenon by which people predict the outcome of a future trial based on the outcome of previous trials. When trials are independent, we cannot predict the outcomes of a future trial based on the outcome of previous trials. For each of the following examples, (i) state whether the trials are independent or dependent and (ii) explain why. In addition, (iii) state whether it is possible that the quote is accurate or whether it is definitely fallacious, explaining how the independence or dependence of trials influences this.

a. You are playing Monopoly and have rolled a pair of sixes in 4 out of 10 of your last rolls of the dice. You say, "Cool. I'm on a roll. I'm likely to get sixes again on my next turn."

b. You are an Ohio State University football fan and are sad because they have lost two games in a row. You say, "That is really unusual; the Buckeyes are doomed this season. That's what happens with lots of early-season injuries."

c. You have a 20-year-old car that often has trouble starting. It has started every day this week, and now it's Friday. You say, "I'm screwed. It's been reliable all week, and even though I did get a tune-up last week, today is bound to be the day it fails me."

d. It's your first week at your corporate internship and you have to wear nylon stockings to the office if you're wearing a skirt. On the first and second days, you get a run in your stockings almost immediately, an indication of a defect. The third day, you put on yet another new pair of stockings and say, "OK, this pair has to be good. There's no way I'd have three bad pairs in a row. They're even from different stores!"

4.20 Probability in the real world: In *Freakonomics*, Levitt and Dubner (2005) describe a study conducted by Levitt and Duggan (2002) that broached the question: Do sumo wrestlers cheat? Sumo wrestlers have enormous respect in Japan, where sumo wrestling is considered the national sport. The researchers examined the results of 32,000 wrestling matches over an 11-year time span. If a wrestler finishes a tournament with a losing record (7 or fewer wins out of 15 matches), his ranking goes down, along with the money and prestige that come with winning. The researchers wondered whether, going into the last match of the tournament, wrestlers with 7-7 records (needing only one more win to rise in the rankings) would have a better than expected win record against wrestlers with 8-6 records (those who are already guaranteed to rise in the rankings). Such a phenomenon might indicate cheating. One 7-7 wrestler (wrestler A), based on past matches against a given 8-6 opponent (wrestler B), was calculated to have won 48.7% of the time.

a. If there is no cheating, what is the probability that wrestler A will beat wrestler B in any situation, including the one in which A is 7-7 and B is 8-6?

b. If matches tend to be rigged so that 8-6 wrestlers frequently throw matches to help other wrestlers maintain their rankings (and to get payback from 7-7 wrestlers in future matches), what would you expect to happen to the winning percentage when these two wrestlers meet under these exact conditions—that is, the first is 7-7 in the tournament and the second is 8-6?

c. State the null hypothesis and research hypothesis for the study examining whether sumo wrestlers cheat.

d. In this particular real-life example, wrestler A was found to have beaten wrestler B 79.6% of the time when A had a 7-7 record and B had an 8-6 record. If inferential statistics determined that it was very unlikely that this would occur by chance, what would your decision be? Use the language of hypothesis testing.

4.21 Null hypothesis and research hypothesis: For each of the following studies, cite the likely null hypothesis and the likely research hypothesis.

a. A forensic cognitive psychologist wondered whether repetition of false information would increase the tendency to develop false memories, on average.

b. A clinical psychologist studied whether ongoing structured assessments of the therapy process would lead to better outcome, on average, among outpatient therapy clients with depression.

c. A corporation recruited an industrial/organizational psychologist to explore the effects of cubicles (versus enclosed offices) on employee morale.

d. A team of developmental cognitive psychologists studied whether teaching a second language to children from birth would affect children's ability to speak their native language.

4.22 Hypothesis-testing decisions: For each of the following fictional outcomes, state whether you would reject or to fail to reject the null hypothesis (contingent, of course, on inferential statistics backing up the statement). Explain the rationale for your decision.

a. When false information is repeated several times, people seem to be more likely, on average, to develop false memories.

b. Therapy clients with depression who have ongoing structured assessments of therapy seem to have lower depression levels post-therapy, on average, than do clients who do not have ongoing structured assessments.

c. Employee morale does not seem to be different, on average, whether employees work in cubicles or enclosed offices.

d. A child's native language does not seem to be different in strength, on average, based on whether the child is raised to be bilingual.

4.23 Type I and Type II errors: Examine the statements from Exercise 4.22, printed again here. If this conclusion is incorrect, what type of error have you made? Explain your answer.

a. When false information is repeated several times, people seem more likely, on average, to develop false memories.

b. Therapy clients with depression who have ongoing structured assessments of therapy seem to have lower depression levels post-therapy, on average, than do clients who do not have ongoing structured assessments.

c. Employee morale does not seem to be different, on average, whether employees work in cubicles or enclosed offices.

d. A child's native language does not seem to be different in strength, on average, based on whether the child is raised to be bilingual.

4.24 Testimonials and Harry Potter: Amazon.com and other online bookstores offer readers the opportunity to write their own book reviews, and many other potential readers scour these reviews to decide which books to buy. Harry Potter books attract a great deal of these reader reviews. One amazon.com reviewer—bel78—submitted her review of *Harry Potter and the Half-Blood Prince* from Argentina. Of the book, she said "it's simply outstandingly good" and suggested that readers of her review "run to get your copy." Do these reviews have an impact? In this case, more than 900 people had read bel78's review as of October 2005, and nearly 700 wrote in to report that the review was helpful to them.

a. Imagine that you're deciding whether to buy *Harry Potter and the Half-Blood Prince*, and you want to know what people who had already read the book thought before you invested the money and time. What is the population whose opinion you're interested in?

b. If you read only bel78's review, what is the sample from which you're gathering your data? What are some of the problems in relying on just this one review?

c. Almost 3000 readers had reviewed this book on amazon.com by October 2005. What if all reviewers agreed that this book was amazing? What is the problem with this sample?

d. Given no practical or financial limitations, what would be the best way to gather a sample of amazon.com users who had read this Harry Potter book?

e. A friend plans to order a book online to take on spring break. She is reading online reviews of several books to make her decision. Explain to her in just a few sentences why her reliance on testimonials is not likely to provide her with objective information.

4.25 Tying it all together—Treatment for alcohol problems in college students: Borsari and Carey (2005) randomly assigned 64 male students who had been ordered, after a violation of university alcohol rules, to meet with a school counselor to one of two conditions. Students were assigned to undergo either (1) a brief motivational interview (BMI), a recently developed intervention in which educational material is related to the students' own experiences, or (2) an alcohol education session (AE), a more established intervention in which educational material is simply presented with no link to students' experiences. Based on inferential statistics, the researchers concluded that those in the BMI group had fewer alcohol-related problems at follow-up than did those in the AE group.

a. What is the population of interest and what is the sample in this study?

b.   Was random selection used? Why or why not?

c.   Was random assignment used? Why or why not?

d.   What is the independent variable, and what are its levels? What is the dependent variable?

e.   What was the null hypothesis, and what was the research hypothesis?

f.   What decision did the researchers make? Use the language of inferential statistics.

g.   If the researchers were incorrect in their decision, what kind of error did they make? Explain your answer. What are the consequences of this type of error, both in general and in this situation?

4.26 The language of statistics—*replication*: In your own words, define the word *replication*, first as you might use it in everyday conversation and then as a statistician would use it.

4.27 The language of statistics—*probability*: In your own words, define the word *probability*, first as you would use it in everyday conversation and then as a statistician would use it. What is the difference between subjective (or personal) probability and expected relative-frequency probability?

4.28 The language of statistics—*independent*: The word *independent* is used in this chapter in yet another way. Explain how *independent* is used with respect to trials in probability and with respect to participants in a sample. Then, from previous chapters, explain another way that statisticians use the word *independent*.

4.29 The language of statistics—*prove*: Explain why scientists do not use the word *prove*. In your explanation, discuss how probability and inferential statistics do not allow us ever to have absolute proof that our research hypothesis is true.

■ DIGGING DEEPER INTO THE DATA

4.30 True experiments and medical research: Many medical studies are conducted as true experiments in which participants are randomly assigned to one of two or more conditions. A psychopharmacological study might, for example, assign individuals with depression to one of two or more antidepressants.

a.   What would be necessary for this study to qualify as a true experiment?

b.   What is meant by the term *placebo*? Explain how this experiment might use a placebo.

c.   What is meant by the term *double-blind*? Explain how this experiment might use double-blindness.

4.31 Medical research, the media, and Type I errors—Reducing bone fractures: The *New York Times* (Bakalar, 2005) reported that a study of 91,000 men, published in the *Archives of Internal Medicine*, found that men who took statins—drugs initially targeted at lowering cholesterol—had a significantly lower average risk for bone fractures than those who did not take statins. The newspaper article also noted, however, that previous studies that examined patient records over time did not show a similar finding.

a.   Citing information from the Digging Deeper into the Data section of the chapter, explain why it is possible that this study is an example of a Type I error.

b.   What would you want to know about this study before judging its merits? List at least four aspects of good research design that you would like to see.

c.   The study did not use random assignment; rather, it examined the outcomes for men who were and were not already using statins. Why should the lack of random assignment make you question the study's results? What are possible third variables that might explain this link?

4.32 Medical findings in the media now: Go online or open a newspaper and find a media report of a recent medical finding. Many newspapers have science and/or health sections; this is a good place to look.

a. Describe your study and its findings.

b. What were the independent variable and its levels? What was the dependent variable?

c. Was random selection used? Random assignment? Explain.

d. What would the null and research hypotheses have been?

e. If the researchers were wrong, was this a Type I or a Type II error? Explain your answer.

f. In light of the discussion of Sterne and Smith's (2001) estimates of errors in medical publications, why should you be skeptical of this finding? What should someone look for before altering their behavior based on this study?

KEY TERMS

generalizability (p. 153)

random sample (p. 155)

convenience sample (p. 155)

cluster sampling (p. 157)

stratified sampling (p. 157)

volunteer sample (p. 158)

randomized block design (p. 159)

replication (p. 161)

confirmation bias (p. 169)

illusory correlation (p. 169)

groupthink (p. 171)

subjective probability (p. 173)

expected relative-frequency probability (p. 173)

trial (p. 173)

outcome (p. 174)

success (p. 174)

gambler's fallacy (p. 176)

control group (p. 179)

experimental group (p. 179)

null hypothesis (p. 179)

research hypothesis (p. 179)

Type I error (p. 183)

Type II error (p. 183)

CHAPTER FIVE

CORRELATION
QUANTIFYING THE RELATION
BETWEEN TWO VARIABLES

"Don't do this to me," Ryan replied. "Not now, not today." It was the start of what could have been the biggest fight of their three-year marriage and it was over a horoscope.

"But listen to what it says," Kayla insisted. "Self-improvement," she read to him, "could bring amazing results. Don't overspend on luxury items. Try not to lend or borrow money today."

"You're just scared," Ryan told her. But so was he. They were about to take all their wedding money, their personal savings, and money borrowed from both their parents so they could put a down payment on their very first home.

"But what about our synastry analysis?" Kayla went to a box and pulled out a thick binder. "We were meant for each other," she said, as she opened the binder full of symbols and phrases. "The stars weren't wrong then. That's why we're so compatible. It explains it all, right here. You're a Leo and I'm a Capricorn. That's the real reason we get along so well."

"Well, we're not getting along very well right now, are we? So it must be wrong."

"But that's because you're a Leo, and you're acting just like a stubborn Leo!"

Ryan could never figure out how to argue with astrology. Kayla could always pull out something from astrology to get what she wanted. Ryan looked at Kayla, sighed deeply, and decided this was a day for telling the truth. "I have something to confess to you," he said.

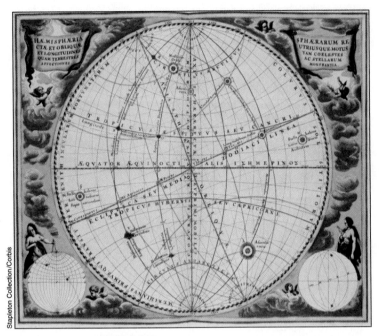

Stapleton Collection/Corbis

Superstition Versus Science
Understanding correlation is the point of separation between superstitious ways of knowing, such as astrology, and scientific ways of knowing, such as those used in the social sciences.

Perhaps you view astrology as just good fun, not harmful, and a pleasant way to start your day over a cup of coffee. Or maybe you look to astrology to help you navigate the personality differences between people you know well. Many people, however, take astrology far more seriously. A study sampling people living in Western societies found that "the incidence of astrologers and serious students of astrology is roughly 1 in 10,000 people in the general population" (Dean, Mather, & Kelly, 1996, p. 60). That's approximately 30,000 people who are *serious* about astrology in the United States, for example, with an additional 4000 living in Canada. The number of devout believers, part-time dabblers, and curiosity seekers in astrology is probably many times those estimates. As we learned in Chapter 1, *correlation* is the general term used to describe the association (or relation) between two variables, and astrology is based on the perceived correlation between planetary movements and human events. So let's *learn* about correlation by *using* correlation and commonsense statistical reasoning to test the validity of this popular belief system.

Unlike the social sciences, astrology makes really big claims. Journal articles in the social sciences typically end with comments such as "More research needs to be done" and "These conclusions are only tentative." It seems crazy, doesn't it? The researchers do all this work and then, at the very end, they give you lots of reasons why you should *not* believe their study! In sharp contrast to behavioral scientists, astrologers go way over the top in declaring what they can do for you. According to the Web site astrologycom.com, a synastry analysis of two people's astrological charts

> explains how current (or future) partners interact emotionally, mentally, sexually, and spiritually. It helps partners be more compassionate toward each other, and adopt more realistic expectations of the relationship. It describes two people's capacity to communicate, showing areas of interest. It reveals their emotional rapport and tells us about the intensity of the physical attraction between them. It can show you whether this person is right for you.

Wow! That's a lot of promises based on a presumed correlation between planetary movements and human personality. But the scientific tests of astrology go well beyond these popularized versions of astrology found in newspapers and on Web sites. Dean and Kelly's (2003) study described experiments that used astrologers with significant years of experience, allowed them to work under conditions the astrologers themselves believed were most conducive to success, and analyzed the correlations between their readings and several other variables, such as personality traits. They even evaluated how confident astrologers were in their *own* astrological readings. As you will see, even under these optimal conditions, believers in astrology are perceiving a correlation that does not seem to exist.

In this chapter, we'll learn how to use correlation to separate science from superstition. Correlation will help us avoid both self-deception and deceptions promoted by others, to discover new ways of measuring behavior, to explore careers in psychometrics, and to distinguish between the influences of overlapping variables. But first we need to learn how to calculate the most common form of correlation: r, the Pearson correlation coefficient. Then we'll use a tool called z scores to resolve the problem of exploring the relation between variables that come from two completely different scales. As we harness the power of z scores to transform different scales into standardized scales, we'll learn how to assess the direction and size of the correlation. This intimate understanding of correlation enables us to avoid the danger of faulty causal reasoning that awaits the naive consumer of statistics. Finally, we'll discover the ways in which behavioral scientists use correlation to create reliable and valid tests that are linked to a wide range of career opportunities.

> CORRELATION: ASSESSING ASSOCIATIONS BETWEEN VARIABLES

Students often enjoy the chapter on correlation because, as the saying goes, they "get it." Perhaps correlation is intuitively easier to understand because we use the idea of correlation to explain everyday events and because the word has made its way into everyday language. A correlation is exactly what its name suggests: a co-relation between two variables. Lots of things are co-related: outside temperature and the number of people going to the beach, the amount of junk food consumed and the amount of body fat, how many cars travel on a particular road and how often the road needs maintenance. We learned in Chapter 1 that correlational studies are studies that examine relations, usually between two interval variables.

The Need for Standardization: Putting Two Different Variables on the Same Scale

One of the first problems that we encounter when we attempt to quantify the relation between two variables is the fact that the two variables are indeed *different* variables. Fortunately, we can standardize these different variables by using their respective means and standard deviations to convert any raw score into a z score. *A **z score** is the number of standard deviations a particular score is from the mean.* A z score is part of its own distribution, the z distribution, just as a raw score, such as an individual's height, is part of its own distribution, a distribution of heights. (Note that as with all statistics, the z is italicized.) We will introduce the z distribution in much more detail in Chapter 7. For now, the most important thing for you to recognize is that the standardized z distribution allows us to make lots of different comparisons because any score on any measure can be converted to the same distribution: the z distribution.

Here is a memorable example of why we need standardization: comparing the weights of cockroaches. You probably know that different countries use different measures of weight; in the United Kingdom and the United States, the pound is typically used, with a number of variants that are either fractions or multiples of the pound; these include the mite, drachm, ounce, stone, and ton. In most countries in the world, the metric system is used, with the gram as the basic unit of weight. As with the pound, there are many variants that are fractions or multiples of the gram, including the milligram and kilogram.

■ A **z score** is the number of standard deviations a particular score is from the mean.

**Standardizing
Cockroach Weights**
Standardization creates
meaningful comparisons by
converting different scales to
a common, or standardized,
scale. We can compare the
weights of these cockroaches
using different measures of
weights—including drachms,
pounds, and grams.

If we were told that three imaginary species of cockroaches had mean weights of 8.0 drachms, 0.25 pound, and 98.0 grams, respectively, which one should we fear the most (assuming that a larger cockroach generates more fear)? The easiest way to answer this question is to standardize the three cockroach weights by comparing them on the same scale—for example, we could convert all these weights to grams. A drachm is 1/256 of a pound, so 8.0 drachms is 1/32 = 0.03125 of a pound. One pound equals 453.5924 grams. Based on these conversions, the weights could be standardized into grams as follows:

Cockroach 1 weighs 8.0 drachms = 0.03125 pound = 14.17 grams

Cockroach 2 weighs 0.25 pound = 113.40 grams

Cockroach 3 weights 98.0 grams

Standardizing by grams allows us to make a meaningful comparison. The second cockroach species tends to weigh the most: 113.4 grams. Fortunately, the biggest cockroach in the world weighs only about 35 grams and is about 80 millimeters (3.15 inches) long. Cockroaches 2 and 3 exist only in our imaginations. However, not all conversions are as easy as standardizing weights from different countries into grams. That's why statisticians developed the z distribution.

The z Score: Transforming Raw Scores into Standardized Scores

Our desire to make meaningful comparisons forces us to convert raw scores into standardized scores, and we can always determine any score's distance from its mean in terms of standard deviations. For example, let's say that you know that after taking the midterm examination, you are 1 standard deviation above the mean in your statistics class. Is this good news? What if you are 2 standard deviations above the mean? Are you even happier? What if you are 0.5 standard deviation below the mean? How has your mood changed based on this comparative information? Understanding a score's relation to the mean of its distribution gives us important information about that score. For a statistics test, we know that being well above the mean is a good thing; in anxiety levels, we know that being well above the mean is usually a bad thing. z scores create an opportunity to make meaningful comparisons by putting different variables on a common scale.

We were able to compare the weights of cockroaches by converting all the observations into grams. When grams became the standard distribution, the cockroaches' original weights ceased being part of the distribution of pounds or the distribution of drachmas and instead became part of the distribution of grams. Similarly, when raw scores are converted to z scores, the raw scores ceased being part of their original distribution of the original sample and instead became part of the same z distribution. This is exciting because any score that is part of a distribution with a known mean and a known standard deviation can be reexpressed on the same z distribution. So now all kinds of potentially meaningful comparisons are possible, even between very different kinds of variables.

The only information we need to convert any raw score to a z score is the mean and standard deviation of the population of interest. That is, we must know the population *parameters*, rather than sample *statistics*. (Remember our mnemonic from Chapter 2? *P* and *S*. Parameters describe *p*opulations. Statistics describe *s*amples.) Fortunately, the only population parameters we need to know

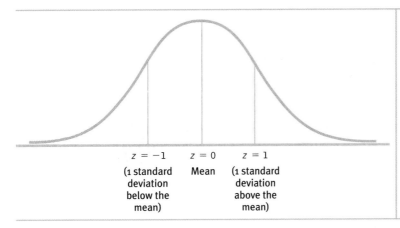

FIGURE 5-1
The z Distribution

The z distribution always has a mean of 0 and a standard deviation of 1.

to convert individual scores to z scores are the mean and standard deviation. For instance, in the midterm example above, we are probably interested only in comparing our grade with the grades of others also taking this particular statistics course. In that case, the statistics class is the entire population of interest, rather than a sample of some other larger population of students across the college or at other universities who are also studying statistics.

Let's say that your particular score on the midterm was 2 standard deviations above the mean; so your z score is 2.0. Imagine that a friend's score is 1.6 standard deviations below the mean; your friend's z score is -1.6. What would your z score be if you fell exactly at the mean in your statistics class? If you guessed 0, you're correct. You would be 0 standard deviation from the mean.

Figure 5-1 illustrates two important features of the z distribution. First, the z distribution always has a mean of 0. So, if you are exactly at the mean, then you are 0 standard deviation from the mean. Second, the z distribution always has a standard deviation of 1. If your raw score is 1 standard deviation above the mean, you will have a z score of 1.0. No matter what the mean and standard deviation of the original distribution, once we convert to the z distribution, the standard deviation will be 1.0.

Let's calculate some z scores without a calculator or formula. Let's use the distribution of scores on a statistics exam, in which the students who took the exam comprise the entire population of interest. (This example is illustrated in Figure 5-2.) If the mean on a statistics exam is 70, the standard deviation is 10, and your

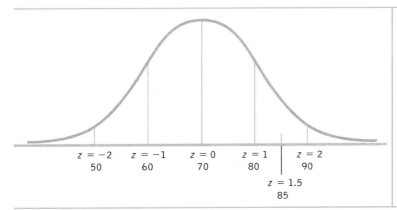

FIGURE 5-2
z Scores Intuitively

With a mean of 70 and a standard deviation of 10, we can calculate many z scores without a formula. A raw score of 50 has a z score of −2.0. A raw score of 60 has a z score of −1.0. A raw score of 70 has a z score of 0. A raw score of 80 has a z score of +1.0. A raw score of 85 has a z score of 1.5.

score is 80, what is your z score? In this case you were exactly 10 points, or 1 standard deviation, above the mean, so your z score would be 1.0. Now let's say your score is 50. Now you're 20 points, or 2 standard deviations, below the mean, so your z score would be -2.0. What if your score were 85? Now you're 15 points, or 1.5 standard deviations, above the mean, so your z score is 1.5.

As you can see, we don't need a formula to calculate a z score when we're working with easy numbers; however, it is important to learn the notation and language of statistics. So let's also convert z scores using a formula for when our numbers are not easy to work with. To calculate a particular z score, we first determine the distance of a particular person's score (X) from the population mean (μ) as part of the calculation: $X - \mu$. Then we express this distance in terms of standard deviations by dividing by the standard deviation of the population, σ. The formula, therefore, is

$$z = \frac{(X - \mu)}{\sigma}$$

Let's take an example that is not so easy to calculate in our heads. Let's say we know that the mean height for the sophomore class at your university is 64.886 with a standard deviation of 4.086. Let's pretend the entire population in which we're interested is these sophomores; if that is the case, 64.886 and 4.086 are parameters, not statistics, and can be used to calculate z scores. If you are 70 inches tall, what is your z score?

$$z = \frac{(X - \mu)}{\sigma} = \frac{(70 - 64.886)}{4.086} = 1.25$$

You would be 1.25 standard deviations above the mean.

We must be careful when we use a formula because it is easy to make a mistake when using a formula mindlessly. Always consider whether the answer makes sense. In this case, 1.25 is a positive z score, indicating that the height expressed as a z score is just over 1 standard deviation above the mean. This makes sense because the raw score of 70 is also just over 1 standard deviation above the mean of 64.886. If you do this quick check as you finish each problem on your homework or on a test, then you can correct mistakes before they cost you.

Let's take another example: What if you were 62 inches tall?

$$z = \frac{(X - \mu)}{\sigma} = \frac{(62 - 64.886)}{4.086} = -0.71$$

You would be 0.71 standard deviation *below* the mean.

Don't forget the sign of the z score. Changing a z score from negative 0.71 to positive 0.71 makes a big difference! Fortunately, even if you forgot to include the negative sign, then you could still catch your error if you considered whether the answer made sense. In this case, the height is lower than the mean, so the z score must be negative.

Now let's demonstrate that the mean of the z distribution is always 0 and the standard deviation of the z distribution is always 1. We will continue to use the mean and standard deviation of heights as given above for this demonstration, but you can try it with any distribution for which you know the mean and standard deviation, and the results will be the same every time. The mean here is 64.886. Let's calculate what the z score would be at the mean.

$$z = \frac{(X - \mu)}{\sigma} = \frac{(64.886 - 64.886)}{4.086} = 0$$

Symbols: z refers to the distance of a score from the mean of its distribution, in terms of the standard deviation of its distribution.

Formulas: The formula for the z score is $z = \frac{(X - \mu)}{\sigma}$, where X indicates the score, μ indicates the mean of the population from which the score comes, and σ indicates the standard deviation of the population from which the score comes.

Estimating z Scores
Would you guess that the person on the left has a positive or negative z score for height? What about the person on the right? A person who is very short has a below-average height and thus would have a negative z score. A person who is very tall has an above-average height and thus would have a positive z score.

Masterfile/Radius Images

The standard deviation is 4.086 inches. If someone is exactly 4.086 inches above the mean—that is, 1 standard deviation above the mean—his or her score would be $64.886 + 4.086 = 68.972$. Let's calculate what the z score would be for this person.

$$z = \frac{(X - \mu)}{\sigma} = \frac{(68.972 - 64.886)}{4.086} = 1$$

Our ability to convert raw scores from different distributions to z scores that all belong to the same distribution creates opportunities for comparing different variables. So let's start using standardized variables from different distributions to understand what the correlation statistic can, and cannot, reveal about the relation between two variables.

■ A **correlation coefficient** is a statistic that quantifies a relation between two variables.

The Characteristics of Correlation: Understanding the Coefficient at a Glance

The number that we calculate when we quantify a correlation is called a coefficient. Specifically, *a **correlation coefficient** is a statistic that quantifies a relation between two variables*. In the current chapter, we're going to learn how to quantify a relation—that is, we're going to learn to calculate a correlation coefficient—when the data are linearly related. A linear relation means that the data form an overall pattern through which it would make sense to draw a straight line. The specific correlation coefficient that we'll learn in this chapter would not be used if our data were related in some other way—for example, if the pattern of data formed a curve rather than a straight line.

Regardless of the type of relation—linear or another pattern of correlation—one of the handy things about the correlation coefficient is that it really can be understood with just a glance. There are only three main characteristics of the correlation coefficient.

1. The correlation coefficient can be either positive or negative.
2. The correlation coefficient always falls between -1.00 and 1.00.
3. It is the strength (also called the magnitude) of the coefficient, not its sign, that indicates how large it is.

The first important characteristic of the correlation coefficient is that it may be either positive or negative. When two variables are related to one another, there are two directions in which they might be related: positively or negatively. A positive correlation has a positive sign (e.g., 0.32), and a negative correlation has a negative sign (e.g., -0.32). Two variables can have a positive correlation, as depicted in Figure 5-3. *A **positive correlation** is an association between two*

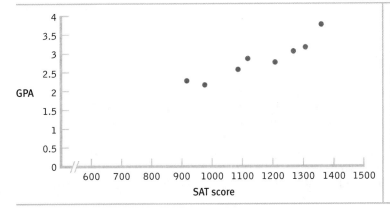

FIGURE 5-3
A Positive Correlation

These data points depict a positive correlation between SAT score and college grade point average (GPA). Those with higher SAT scores tend have better GPAs, and those with lower SAT scores tend to have lower GPAs.

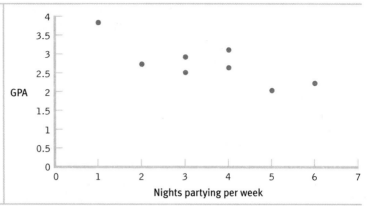

FIGURE 5-4
A Negative Correlation

These data points depict a negative correlation between nights partying per week and
GPA. Those who party more tend to have
lower GPAs, whereas those who party less
tend to have higher GPAs.

variables such that participants with high scores on one variable tend to have high scores
on the other variable as well, and those with low scores on one variable tend to have
low scores on the other variable as well. Contrary to what some people think, when
participants with low scores on one variable tend to have low scores on the
other, it is *not* a negative correlation. A positive correlation describes a situation
in which participants tend to have similar scores, with respect to the mean and
spread, on both variables—whether the scores are low, medium, or high. On a
scatterplot, we see a positive correlation as sloping upward to the right. The
scatterplot in Figure 5-3 shows a positive correlation between Scholastic
Aptitude Test (SAT) score and college grade point average (GPA). For example, the lower-left dot is for a person with a 980 on the SAT and a 2.2 GPA;
this person is lower than average on both scores. The upper-right dot is for a
person with a 1360 on the SAT and a 3.8 GPA; this person is higher than average on both scores. This makes sense, because we would expect people with
higher SAT scores to get better grades, on average.

Correlations might also take a different direction, as shown in Figure 5-4.
This is a negative correlation. *A **negative correlation** is an association between two
variables in which participants with high scores on one variable tend to have low scores
on the other variables.* On the scatterplot, we see a negative correlation as one
sloping downwards to the right. The scatterplot in Figure 5-4 shows a negative
correlation between nights partying per week and GPA. For example, the
upper-left dot is for a person who goes out one night per week and has a 3.8 GPA;
this person is lower than average on nights partying and higher than average
on GPA. The lower-right dot is for a person who goes out six nights per week
and has a 2.2 GPA; this person is higher than average on nights partying and
lower than average on GPA. This makes sense, because we would expect people who party more to get lower grades, on average.

A second important characteristic of the correlation coefficient is that it always falls between −1.00 and 1.00. Both −1.00 and 1.00 are perfect correlations. If we calculate a coefficient that is outside this range, we have made a
mistake in our calculations. 1.00 indicates a perfect positive correlation because
every point on the scatterplot falls in one line, as seen in the imaginary relation
between absences and exam grades depicted in Figure 5-5; higher scores on one
variable are associated with higher scores on the other, and lower scores on one
variable are associated with lower scores on the other. When a correlation coefficient is either −1.00 or 1.00, knowing somebody's score on one variable is

■ A **positive correlation** is an
association between two variables such that participants
with high scores on one variable tend to have high scores
on the other variable as well,
and those with low scores on
one variable tend to have low
scores on the other variable
as well.

■ A **negative correlation** is an
association between two variables in which participants
with high scores on one variable tend to have low scores
on the other variable.

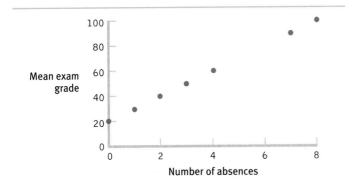

FIGURE 5-5
A Perfect Positive Correlation

When every pair of scores falls on the same line on the scatterplot, with higher scores on one variable associated with higher scores on the other (and lower scores with lower scores), there is a perfect positive correlation of 1.00, a situation that almost never occurs in real life. Also, we would not predict that the number of absences would be positively correlated with mean exam grade!

sufficient to know exactly what that person's score is on the other variable; they are perfectly related.

A correlation coefficient of −1.00 indicates a perfect negative correlation. Every point on the scatterplot falls in one line, as seen in the imaginary relation between absences and exam grades depicted in Figure 5-6, but now higher scores on one variable go with lower scores on the other. As with a perfect positive correlation, knowing one's score on one variable is sufficient to know exactly one's score on the other variable. A correlation of 0.00 falls right in the middle of the two extremes and indicates no correlation—no association between the two variables. Correlations of exactly −1.00, 0.00, and 1.00 are almost unheard of. Real-life data tend to be somewhat "messy."

The third useful characteristic of the correlation coefficient is that its sign—positive or negative—indicates only the direction of the association, not the strength or size of the association. So a correlation coefficient of −0.35 is the same size as one of 0.35. A correlation coefficient of −0.67 is larger than one of 0.55. Don't be fooled by a negative sign; the sign indicates the direction of the relation, not the strength. The strength of the correlation is determined by how close to "perfect" the data points are. The closer the data points are to the line that one could draw through them, the closer to a perfect correlation and therefore the stronger the relation between the two variables. The farther the points are from this imaginary line, the farther the correlation is from being a perfect −1.00 or 1.00, and the weaker the relation between the two variables.

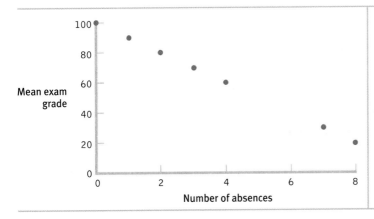

FIGURE 5-6
A Perfect Negative Correlation

When every pair of scores falls on the same line on the scatterplot and higher scores on one variable are associated with lower scores on the other variable, there is a perfect negative correlation of −1.00, a situation that almost never occurs in real life.

Ole Graf/zefa/Corbis

The Teeter-Tottering Negative Correlation
When two variables are negatively correlated, a high score on one variable indicates a likely low score on the other variable—just like children on a teeter-totter.

The scores in a positive correlation move up and down together, the same way the mercury rises in a thermometer as the temperature goes up. The scores in negative correlation move up and down in opposition to each other, like a teeter-totter. That is why knowing the direction of a correlation allows us to use one score to predict another score. Fortunately, we can be far more specific than merely identifying the direction of the correlation between variables. We can also quantify the correlation between those variables.

Correlation coefficients often surprise us because correlation coefficients that are close to -1.00 or 1.00 seldom occur in nature. These perfect correlations are unusual because almost everything that changes has some natural variability. Even trains that have a reputation for running on time, for example, aren't a perfect, positive correlation if you measure them right down to the millisecond. And a teeter-totter won't be a perfect, negative correlation if you measure some of the bounciness and spring in it. On the other hand, correlations that are close to 0 are very common because the world is full of unrelated random variability. That's one of the reasons the correlation is so powerful a statistic: correlations help us discover predictable relations amid the chaos of everyday life.

So, what magnitude of a correlation coefficient is large enough to be considered important? Cohen (1988) published standards, as seen in Table 5-1, for the size of the correlation coefficient, r. Very few findings in the social sciences have correlation coefficients of 0.50 or larger, the number that Cohen has suggested indicates a large correlation. This is usually true because any particular variable is influenced not just by one other variable but by many variables. A student's mean exam grade, for example, is influenced not only by absences from class but also by attention level in class, hours of studying, interest in the subject matter, IQ, motivation to get a high grade, and many more variables. So correlation coefficients are often surprising, usually because we expect a stronger (closer to -1.00 or 1.00) correlation than we actually observe.

You likely already have an intuitive sense of what a correlation means. You carve out time in your busy week to study for an upcoming statistics test because you know that the number of hours you devote to that task is correlated with your grade. Why? Because you recognize that there's a positive correlation between the hours you spend studying and the grade you earn on a test: the more you study, the higher your grade. You also curtail your social activities for that week because you know that the number of nights you party in the

TABLE 5-1. HOW STRONG IS AN ASSOCIATION?

Cohen (1988) published guidelines to help researchers determine the strength of a correlation from the correlation coefficient. In social science research, however, it is extremely unusual to have a correlation as high as 0.50, and many have disputed the utility of Cohen's conventions for many social science contexts.

SIZE OF THE CORRELATION	CORRELATION COEFFICIENT
Small	0.10
Medium	0.30
Large	0.50

week leading up to the statistics test is correlated with your grade. Why? Because you also recognize that there's a negative correlation between nights spent partying and the grade you earn on a test: the more nights you party, the lower your grade. In both cases, we can know something about the likely score on a second variable by knowing the score on the first variable.

When we read that two variables are correlated, we know only that they are associated with each other in some way. The first step in understanding correlation is to ascertain the direction of the association. Is it a positive correlation or a negative correlation? But that's not enough. We also need to know the size of the correlation. Is it small, medium, or large? And how big does the correlation need to be in a given context for it to have practical importance? We'll learn how to answer these questions in the next section.

In summary, a correlation coefficient is a statistic that quantifies a relation between two variables, and we need to understand z scores to calculate a correlation coefficient. A z score is the distance that a score is from the mean of its distribution in terms of standard deviations. z scores fall on the z distribution, and so when we convert two sets of raw scores (on different scales) to z scores, we can then compare them. The correlation coefficient can be understood at a glance. It always falls between −1.00 and 1.00. When two variables are related such that people with high scores on one tend to have high scores on the other and people with low scores on one tend to have low scores on the other, we describe them as positively correlated. When two such variables are related such that people with high scores on one tend to have low scores on the other, we describe them as negatively correlated. When two variables are not related, there is no correlation and they have a correlation coefficient close to 0. Finally, the strength of the correlation is independent of its sign.

⊙ CHECK YOUR LEARNING

5-1 A study of Consideration of Future Consequences (CFC) found a mean score of 3.51, with a standard deviation of 0.61, for the 664 students in the sample (Petrocelli, 2003). For the sake of this exercise, let's assume that this particular sample comprises the entire population of interest.

a. If your CFC score were 4.2, what would your z score be? Use symbolic notation and the formula. Explain why this answer makes sense.

b. If your CFC score were 3.00, what would your z score be? Use symbolic notation and the formula. Explain why this answer makes sense.

c. If your z score were 0, what would your CFC score be? Explain.

❭ THE PEARSON CORRELATION COEFFICIENT: QUANTIFYING A LINEAR ASSOCIATION

"I have something to confess to you," Ryan repeated. "It's about when we were first getting to know each other."

Kayla interrupted him. "We really got to know each other at that talk about astrology," she said. "I'd been seeing more and more of you at parties and different places, but I didn't think too much about it. Then we both had a reading and started comparing notes. I remember everything. My horoscope for that day even told me that we would meet. I've got it right here." She flipped through the binder containing her horoscope from that fateful day and the synastry analysis of relative compatibility that had brought them together. "It predicted every detail about what happened on the day we met."

"Yeah," said Ryan. "I have to explain about that." He looked at his watch. "Can't we just go? We're going to be late for our appointment at the real estate office." He went to the door again, hoping that she would just follow him.

Instead, Kayla pulled out another book of horoscopes. "I'll be fair," she said. "I'll look at another one." This time she read, "This is not a good day to make big decisions. Put them off until you can think more clearly. Someone you love will oppose you today. Find a way to assert yourself without making them resentful." Kayla looked at Ryan, pleading with him to understand. "Don't you see it? This is a confirmation," Kayla said. "Here, I'll look up a third one."

"Please don't," said Ryan.

"This is a good day to think big and to act decisively. Others may not understand your motivation. Stand your ground but also be willing to compromise. You might be surprised by getting what you really want."

"You see," said Ryan, "that one doesn't agree. It's telling you to think big and act decisively. Now let's get going."

"But it does agree," said Kayla. "I am acting decisively and I am standing my ground. I'm not going. All three astrologers are giving us the exact same guidance that we need for today. What more evidence do you need?"

"We've got two expensive lawyers already sitting at a table, a real estate agent who is waiting for a check, and a family that wants to move out of state so their kids can get started at a new school. So we can't postpone the house closing. Do you want to pay for two lawyers to sit there and do nothing?" He remained standing by the door, growing more irritated by the moment.

For the first time, Kayla thought about the financial costs of her belief in astrology. Lawyers were expensive. But astrology helped her make some sense out of things she couldn't otherwise understand: why people acted the way they did, why she could feel so differently about things from one day to the next, even why two people were attracted to each other. The more involved she got with astrology, the more convinced she became that it was a useful guide to living her life.

Ryan had had enough. "You're not letting the stars tell you what to do. You're using the stars so you get to do what you want to do anyway," Ryan accused her. "Rising moons, sun charts: it's nonsense!" Ryan only wanted to do one thing today: buy a house. Instead, they were on the verge of a major marital crisis.

"So you think our whole relationship is nonsense?" Kayla said.

Ryan knew exactly what he had to do and exactly what he had to say. He quieted himself and sat down at the kitchen table. Then he looked at Kayla and asked, "You don't want to hear what I have to confess, do you?"

Astrology claims that there is a correlation between the movements of the planets and a wide variety of human behaviors, emotions, personality traits, and events. The precise way this is actually supposed to happen is unclear, but Dean and Kelly (2003) point out that individual astrologers have profoundly different understandings of astrology, so scientific criticisms are easily dispensed with by asserting that any particular scientific study didn't examine their particular understanding of astrology. For some astrologers, the location of the planets at the precise second of your birth is far more important than the actual day of your birth. So Dean and Kelly put astrology to the test, using approaches that maximized the probability of success for astrology. One study, for example, examined personality correlates between time-twins, using hospital records to identify individuals born within a few minutes of one another. But before we summarize the scientific tests, experience for yourself how easy it is to confuse correlation with causation.

ILLUSORY CORRELATIONS

EXPERIENCE IT FOR YOURSELF

We're playing a trick on you in this section. The horoscopes below can't be your real horoscopes because they were meant for July 13, 2006. Nevertheless, try the short exercise that follows the horoscopes and pay attention to how fluent and convincing you are at post-hoc (after-the-fact) explanations. Doesn't it feel, intuitively, as if the stars somehow really know about the stuff in your personal life?

Aquarius: Jan. 21–Feb. 19   Be cautious when dealing with coworkers. You need to spend some time reflecting on past experiences and involvements. Delve a little deeper if you really want to know the score.

Pisces: Feb. 20–March 20   Romantic opportunities are evident if you get involved in large groups or organizations. You can make money if you are careful not to let it slip through your fingers. Ask a close friend for advice.

Aries: March 21–April 19   Unexpected and exciting benefits or opportunities can occur through friends, clubs, and associations. This is a time when you are inspired by new ideas and creative impulses that allow you to network with others in accomplishing your goals.

Taurus: April 20–May 20   Something you say this day may seem like your soul speaking out loud. Even if normally reserved, you may show some emotion in public now. If you're holding anger back, it might sneak out as some rash act. Something you learned early on was wrong, so now you should let that be gone.

Gemini: May 21–June 21   You do have more confidence now. If you normally get stage fright, that should disappear. Lose fat and build muscle while you sleep. Try our new diet plan. You will be delighted at your ability to assert yourself. But if you are normally rather fierce and fiery, watch out!

Cancer: June 22–July 22   You may attend conventions or seminars that stimulate your intellect as well as your imagination. Interesting and unconventional people may suddenly appear in your social life who revolutionize your way of thinking.

Leo: July 23–Aug. 22   You will be setting your goals for the future very determinedly. Cooperation will not always be easy for you, but your enthusiasm will be catching amongst companions, so they should rally round.

Virgo: Aug. 23–Sept. 22   Your co-workers or workmates enjoy having you on their team today. Group discussions find you expressive and insightful. More and more often, others realize that you are not what you appear to be.

Libra: Sept. 23–Oct. 23   Situations in your personal life are moving a little fast lately. Limitations will set in if you haven't followed the rules. Interaction with colleagues will only be upsetting.

Scorpio: Oct. 24–Nov. 22   Your independence and fearlessness are your most dominant traits. This combination leads you into all kinds of interesting places. Unfamiliar territory may be a little spooky at first, but press on with this venture.

Sagittarius: Nov. 23–Dec. 21   You will find that superiors may not see situations as you do. A passionate party for two might be just the remedy. Your interests could lead you down avenues you never realized existed.

Capricorn: Dec. 22–Jan. 20   You will have excellent ideas and you should be able to help your partner get ahead. Catch up on overdue paperwork. You will have an inaccurate assessment of your status in society. Not everything in your life is easy now.

1. Check the horoscope for your birthday and make a note of how your horoscope seems to apply to your life right now. For example, one of the authors, a Libra, wrote:

    We're trying to go on a vacation but haven't made arrangements far enough in advance, so now we're scrambling to find someplace to go. Plus, we're fussing and blaming one another for not planning ahead. So yes, we are limited because we haven't followed the rules. Not only that, when I mentioned this situation to a colleague, I got even more upset because he told me what I already knew—that we should have made arrangements months ago.

2. Now read the horoscope three months after your own (for example, a Libra will read the horoscope for Capricorn) and write a short description about how that horoscope also seems to apply to your life right now.

Were you interested in what your horoscope said, even though we announced ahead of time that it was a trick? Actually, we've played a double trick on you because these are all horoscopes for people born under the Aries sign. They were taken from 12 different astrologers based on the first 12 (free) horoscopes that came up by searching the Web under "daily horoscope." We accidentally included an advertisement in Gemini's horoscope as we were cutting and pasting from the Web, but we decided to include it anyway as a way of bringing attention to how people try to make money off your private search for meaning. If you perceived any correlation between your horoscope and your life, it probably felt like, "Wow! Somehow the stars really know what I've been going through! Amazing!" But it's all just an illusory correlation that takes advantage of (1) how richly you experience your life (even if it's a relatively boring life, you still have lots of material to work with); and (2) how fluent you are at post-hoc explanations.

So, as we summarize what science has discovered about astrology, pay attention to four points in these next two paragraphs because they reveal something both frightening and exciting about science, scientists, and the correlation coefficient. Pay attention to the following:

1. The evidence.
2. The story that the evidence tells.
3. What the scientists conclude from the evidence.
4. What the scientists do *not* conclude from the evidence.

Dean and Kelly (2003) used the technique called meta-analysis (a study of many studies). A summary of many studies is only possible because many different researchers have tested the validity of astrology. For example, the time-twin studies examined 2100 pairs of time twins, 92% of whom were born within five minutes of each other. They produced a correlation of 0.00. In other words, the time-twin studies indicated a random relation between astrological descriptions of time-twins. In another analysis, they examined 40 different studies that gathered data on 700 astrologers and 1150 astrological birth charts. This study yielded an average correlation of only 0.051. Once again, there was no evidence in support of astrology. Other similarly exhaustive studies yielded correlations of 0.002, 0.01, and 0.101. The highest correlation was when individual astrologers made repeated readings; in other words, they were tested for their levels of agreement *with themselves*. Even this produced a correlation of only 0.27; you might expect astrologers to at least remember what they had said previously. You will notice that none of these correlations (except that between an astrologer and him- or herself!) was larger than a "small" correlation, which is, according to Cohen, 0.10, and most were nonexistent.

Now notice what Dean and Kelly concluded at the end of all this effort: there is "clearly nothing here to suggest that astrologers can perform usefully better than chance, once hidden persuaders are controlled for." Now listen to the end of their article about what they were *not* willing to conclude: "The possibility that astrology might be relevant to consciousness and psi is not denied, but if psychic or spirit influences exist in astrology, they would seem to be very weak or very rare. Support for psychic ability seems unlikely." Unlikely!? Are Dean and Kelly crazy? Thousands of people were tested by many different researchers using methods designed to make it easy for astrologers to succeed. They used experienced astrologers and tested for different capabilities related to astrology. They gave astrologers every conceivable opportunity to succeed, yet every correlation produced no evidence that astrology works. And still, Dean and Kelly are unwilling to say that astrology doesn't work. Psychic ability related to astrology is only "unlikely." Are scientists crazy, or do they understand something important about what the correlation coefficient can and *cannot* do?

Everyday Correlation Reasoning: Asking Better Questions

Ryan and Kayla's efforts to manage their marriage and the everyday advances in science depend on the same process: asking better questions. Understanding what correlation can and *cannot* do compels us to ask better, more precise questions. For example, *New York Times* op-ed columnist Paul Krugman (2006) used the idea of correlation for the basis of a column when he asked, "Is being an American bad for your health?" Citing a study published in the *Journal of the American Medical Association* (Banks, Marmot, Oldfield, & Smith, 2006), Krugman explained that the United States has higher per capita spending on health care than any country in the world and yet is surpassed by many countries in life expectancy. This is a negative correlation, and it is surprising. We would normally expect a positive correlation in which more spending on health care is associated with more years of life. So why is there a negative correlation between spending on health care and longevity?

Krugman mentioned the more obvious possible causes: the lack of universal health insurance and the varied quality of health care based on class or race, both of which are problems specific to the United States. But these aren't winning

Corbis

Stress and Longevity
Are American work habits
correlated with poor health?
Higher spending on health
care and lower health outcomes represent a negative
association between these
two variables. A negative
correlation is like a teeter-
totter: When one variable
starts moving up, the other
variable starts moving down.

explanations. For example, a comparison of non-Hispanic white people from America and from England (thus taking race out of the equation) yielded a surprising finding: the wealthiest third of Americans have poorer health than do even the *least* wealthy third of the English. This is still a negative correlation, and it is probable that the wealthiest third of Americans are most likely to have health insurance. In other words, this particular negative correlation doesn't seem to be explained by differing levels of health insurance, institutionalized racial bias, or economic class. So Krugman noted the alarming tendency for Americans to be obese, the difficulty that even insured Americans have in getting preventive health care, and the long workweeks typical in the United States (a mean of 46 hours compared to a mean of 41 in the United Kingdom, France, and Germany). Whatever the cause, Krugman points out, "there's something about [the American] way of life that is seriously bad for our health." *Correlations can't tell us which explanation is right*, but they can force us to think more creatively and precisely about the possible explanations.

Let's look at a correlation that tests one of Krugman's (2006) hypotheses. Krugman hypothesized that Americans might fare worse than the British because the U.S. health insurance system generally does not cover preventive care. For example, many insurance policies cover amputations for ailing diabetics but not the regular care that might have prevented the amputation in the first place. Were we to quantify this correlation, we could gather data on two interval variables: age at death and amount of preventive health care received. Imagine that we randomly selected archival material about 100 American citizens who had died within the past year (and who were at least 50 years old at death). We could record their age at death; then we could have medical experts peruse their health records and give them a score from 1 to 10 (with 1 indicating poor preventive care and 10 indicating superior preventive care). Figure 5-7 shows an example of fictional data telling one story that might emerge in such a study. Note that we placed age at death on the *y*-axis because it is more appropriate to consider age as the dependent (outcome) variable; in fact, it wouldn't make sense that the amount of preventative care depended on one's age at death! The overall pattern of the data is roughly linear; as the score for the quality of preventive care increases, the age at death tends to increase as well. This is a positive correlation.

FIGURE 5-7
A Positive Correlation

These fictional data points depict a positive correlation between the quality of the preventive health
care that people received during their lives and
their age at death. Those with better preventive
care tended to live longer, whereas those with
worse preventive care tended to have shorter lives.

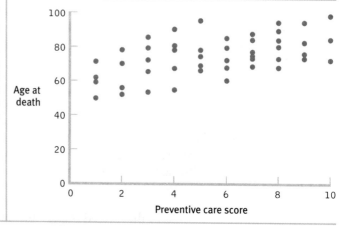

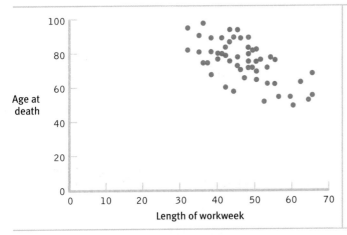

FIGURE 5-8
A Negative Correlation

These fictional data points depict a negative correlation between the mean length of an individual's workweek and his or her age at death. Those with longer workweeks tended to have died earlier, whereas those with shorter workweeks tended to have had longer lives.

Krugman also suggested that the long workweek of Americans might be related to their lower life expectancy. To explore whether there were such a relation, we could again gather data on two interval variables: age at death and length of workweek. Imagine that we randomly selected 100 Americans who had died within the past year (and who were at least 50 years old at death and had been employed full-time for at least 20 years). We could note their age at death and use employment records to calculate the mean workweek for each of them over the years during which they were employed. Figure 5-8 depicts one possible way in which the two variables might be related. The overall pattern of the data is approximately linear; those with longer workweeks tended to have shorter lives, whereas those with shorter workweeks tended to have longer lives. This is a negative correlation.

Now, what if we were to consider the relation of age at death with belief in extrasensory perception (ESP), something not posited by Krugman? Figure 5-9 depicts such a correlation. One's belief in ESP is not related to one's age at death. People at every level of belief in ESP have many different ages at death.

Understanding what correlation can and cannot do helps us to ask better, more precise questions about variables that appear to be correlated. Understanding correlation can also help us avoid wasting time trying to answer questions about variables that do not appear to be correlated. Correlation helps us to ask better questions about demographic clusters of breast cancer, the relation between depression and unemployment, or whether playing college football

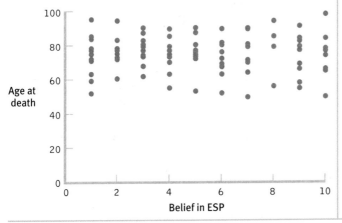

FIGURE 5-9
No Correlation

These fictional data points depict the absence of a correlation between belief in ESP and age at death. Knowing a person's level of belief in ESP tells us nothing about his or her likely age at death.

is associated with negative health outcomes later in life. Asking better questions is why it is worth the effort to understand the meaning of the correlation coefficient and how it is calculated.

Calculation of the Pearson Correlation Coefficient: Harnessing the Power of z Scores

There are several kinds of correlation coefficients, and the one that we choose to calculate depends on the specific relation between our variables. *The **Pearson correlation coefficient** is a statistic that quantifies a linear relation between two interval variables.* In other words, a single number will be used to describe the direction and strength of the relation between two variables when their overall pattern indicates a straight-line relation. The Pearson correlation coefficient, also sometimes called the Pearson product-moment correlation coefficient, is symbolized by r. The italicized symbol r is used when it is a statistic based on sample data. When we're referring to the population parameter for the correlation coefficient, such as when we're writing the hypotheses for significance testing, we use the Greek letter ρ, written as "rho" and pronounced "row," even though it looks a bit like the Latin letter p.

When we calculate the correlation coefficient, we are computing a descriptive statistic; it describes only the direction and strength of association between two variables. [However, we can also conduct a hypothesis test to determine if the correlation coefficient is significantly different from zero (no correlation).]

For many students, the Pearson correlation coefficient is the point at which their understanding of statistics starts to come together. So let's consider an example related to your everyday decision making as a student. Every couple of semesters, we have a student who avows that she does not have to attend statistics classes regularly to do well because she can learn it all from the book. What do you think? What relation would you expect between these variables? Let's look at the correlation between attendance and exam grades. Table 5-2 displays the data for 10 students in one of our recent statistics classes. The second column shows the number of absences over the semester (out of 29 classes total) for each student, and the third column shows each student's final exam grade for the semester.

Before we even start the calculations, we want to construct a scatterplot for these data, seen in Figure 5-10, to be sure that the relation is roughly linear. We can see from this scatterplot that the data, overall, have a pattern through which we could imagine drawing a straight line. So, from this graph, we can confirm that the data have an approximately linear relation, and it is safe to proceed with the calculation of a Pearson correlation coefficient. Based on the scatterplot, do you expect the correlation coefficient to be positive or negative? How large would you expect it to be (i.e., how close to -1.00 or 1.00)? It's helpful to think about what the scatterplot suggests about the correlation coefficient; if the coefficient that we calculate does not match our expectations, we can go back to find out where we went wrong.

The first step in the calculation of a correlation coefficient is figuring out a way to consider two interval variables at the same time. Almost always, a correlation coefficient is calculated based on two interval variables on different scales. In this example, we have one scale for number of absences, with a range of 0–8, and another scale for mean exam grade, with a range of 50–99. But we've already figured out how to solve that problem. We can use z scores to standardize

Symbols: r for the sample statistic

Symbols: ρ for the population parameter

■ The **Pearson correlation coefficient** is a statistic that quantifies a linear relation between two interval variables.

TABLE 5-2. IS SKIPPING CLASS RELATED TO STATISTICS EXAM GRADES?

Here are the scores for 10 students on two interval variables: (x) number of absences from class in one semester, and (y) the mean exam grade for that semester.

STUDENT	ABSENCES	MEAN EXAM GRADE
1	4	82
2	2	98
3	2	76
4	3	68
5	1	84
6	0	99
7	4	67
8	8	58
9	7	50
10	3	78

raw scores (so they are no longer on their original scales) and make them part of the z distribution. We can take both columns of raw scores and convert every raw score to a z score.

First, we have to calculate the means and standard deviations for each scale. The mean number of absences was 3.400, with a standard deviation of 2.375. The mean for a student's final exam grade was 76.000, with a standard deviation of 15.040. For every raw score for the first variable, number of absences, we'll calculate a z score using the appropriate mean and standard deviation. For the first variable, we'll call the raw scores X and will call the z scores z_X to differentiate them from those for final exam grade. For example, for the first score of 4, we'll calculate: $z_X = \dfrac{(X - M_X)}{SD_X} = \dfrac{(4 - 3.400)}{2.375} = 0.253$. Then, for every raw score for the second variable, exam grade, we'll calculate a z score using its mean and standard deviation. We'll call these raw scores Y and these z scores z_Y to differentiate them from the scores for number of absences. For the first score of 82, we'll calculate: $z_Y = \dfrac{(Y - M_Y)}{SD_Y} = \dfrac{(82 - 76.000)}{15.040} = 0.399$.

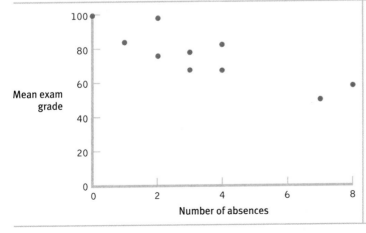

FIGURE 5-10
Always Start with a Scatterplot

Before calculating a correlation coefficient for the relation between number of absences from class and mean exam grade, we construct a scatterplot. If the relation between the variables appears to be roughly linear, we can calculate a Pearson correlation coefficient.

TABLE 5-3. CONVERTING THE RAW SCORES TO z SCORES

Transforming the raw scores into standardized z scores puts the two variables on the same scale. And that allows us to calculate the correlation coefficient in the simplest possible way.

STUDENT	ABSENCES (z_X)	MEAN EXAM GRADE (z_Y)
1	0.253	0.399
2	−0.589	1.463
3	−0.589	0.000
4	−0.168	−0.532
5	−1.011	0.532
6	−1.432	1.529
7	0.253	−0.598
8	1.937	−1.197
9	1.516	−1.729
10	−0.168	0.133

Pay very close attention to the signs of the z scores, as the signs are integral to the calculation of the correlation coefficient. Also, it's easy to forget to switch to a different mean and standard deviation when you finish the calculations for one variable and shift to the other. Be sure to use the appropriate mean and standard deviation for each variable. Table 5-3 shows the z scores for the two variables.

It takes only a few steps to calculate the Pearson correlation coefficient. We multiply each pair of z scores, being sure to keep the two scores for each student together. These are called cross-products. The average of the cross-products is r, the Pearson correlation coefficient. Table 5-4 shows the cross-products in the fourth column. To average them, we add them up and divide

TABLE 5-4. THE AVERAGE OF THE CROSS-PRODUCTS OF THE z SCORES

The Pearson correlation coefficient is calculated by taking the average of the cross-products of the z scores for the two variables. The cross-products are shown here in the fourth column.

STUDENT	ABSENCES (z_X)	MEAN EXAM GRADE (z_Y)	CROSS-PRODUCTS [$(z_X)(z_Y)$]
1	0.253	0.399	0.101
2	−0.589	1.463	−0.862
3	−0.580	0.000	0.000
4	−0.168	−0.532	0.090
5	−1.011	0.532	−0.538
6	−1.432	1.529	−2.189
7	0.253	−0.598	−0.151
8	1.937	−1.197	−2.318
9	1.516	−1.729	−2.620
10	−0.168	0.133	−0.022

by N, which here is 10. We actually don't need a formula for the Pearson correlation coefficient. We simply follow these three steps:

1. Calculate z scores for every raw score.
2. Multiply the two z scores for each participant.
3. Average these cross-products.

The average of the cross-products (try it yourself) is -0.85. So the Pearson correlation coefficient, r, is -0.85. That is a very strong negative correlation. If we examine the scatterplot in Figure 5-10 carefully, we will notice that there aren't any glaring individual exceptions to this rule; the dots are telling a consistent story. So what should our students learn from that? Go to class!

We can also calculate the Pearson correlation coefficient using a formula. To construct the formula, let's start by knowing that we have to calculate a mean cross-product. The formula for a mean is: $M = \dfrac{\Sigma X}{N}$. Except now we're not calculating a mean of scores, but rather a mean of cross-products. We can replace the X in the formula with $(z_X)(z_Y)$ to get the appropriate formula:

$$r = \frac{\Sigma[(z_X)(z_Y)]}{N} = \frac{-8.511}{10} = -0.85$$

Formulas: $r = \dfrac{\Sigma[(z_X)(z_Y)]}{N}$

Why does the formula work? Let's consider a positive correlation. High scores tend to associate with high scores, and low scores with low scores. High scores are above the mean and would convert to positive z scores. A pair of high scores, one on each variable, means a pair of positive z scores; their cross-product would be positive. Low scores are below the mean and would convert to negative z scores. A pair of low scores, one on each variable, means a pair of negative z scores; their cross-product would also be positive. The mean of mostly positive cross-products would be positive—a positive correlation coefficient.

Let's consider a negative correlation. High scores tend to associate with low scores. High scores, which are above the mean, would convert to positive z scores. Low scores, which are below the mean, would convert to negative z scores. The cross-product of a high score on one variable (positive z score) and a low score on the other (negative z score) would be negative. The mean of mostly negative cross-products would be negative—a negative correlation coefficient. Look at the cross-products for the example we considered here. Seven of the ten are negative, and so it's not surprising that their average, which is the r, is negative. Our z scores are doing the work for us!

In summary, correlation helps us to develop even better research questions because it allows us to quantify the relations that we observe. Before we calculate a correlation coefficient, we must always construct a scatterplot to be sure the two variables are linearly related. Once we have determined that any association is linear, the Pearson correlation coefficient is calculated in three basic steps. First, we convert raw scores to z scores separately for each variable. Then we multiply the two z scores for each participant, creating cross-products of the z scores. Finally, we take the average of the cross-products.

⊙ CHECK YOUR LEARNING

5-2 Is age associated with how much people study? Calculate the correlation coefficient for the accompanying data (taken from students in some of our statistics classes), and state what the correlation coefficient tells us about the direction and strength of the association. Be sure to include a scatterplot. The mean for age is 21, and the standard deviation is 1.789. The mean for hours studied is 14.2, and the standard deviation is 5.582.

STUDENT	AGE	NUMBER OF HOURS STUDIED (PER WEEK)
1	19	5
2	20	20
3	20	8
4	21	12
5	21	18
6	23	25
7	22	15
8	20	10
9	19	14
10	25	15

> MISLEADING CORRELATIONS: UNDERSTANDING THE LIMITS OF CAUSAL REASONING

Their lawyer greeted them outside the conference room. "I was getting worried about you," she said. "Kayla, I was reading the Features section of the newspaper while we were waiting, and I circled your horoscope. I knew you'd be interested about what it says for today."

Kayla accepted the newspaper and read it out loud: "Act confidently today, even if you don't feel it. Long-term decisions have a good chance of turning out well. Misunderstandings with a loved one will turn out to be no more than misunderstandings. Look for something special in the color blue."

"Your front door is blue," said their lawyer. "Let's go in."

The house closing went smoothly, and Ryan and Kayla went out for lunch before heading to the house with the blue door that was now theirs.

"I hope we did the right thing," Kayla said. Too many big things had happened in one morning: They'd had a fight, they'd purchased a home, Ryan had something to confess, and Kayla's belief in astrology had been attacked. "I'll have a grilled cheese sandwich," she told the waitress.

Ryan excused himself after he ordered, and Kayla glanced through the newspaper their lawyer had given them. Beneath the astrological readings she saw an article titled "Astrology and Its Hidden Persuaders." In their efforts to understand the appeal of astrology, Dean and Kelly had developed a list of hidden persuaders to explain why people perceive correlations that do not exist (Dean & Kelly, 2003; Hartmann, Reuter, & Nyborg, 2006; Skeptics Dictionary, 2006). Kayla already knew what real astrologers thought about scientists who didn't agree with them: they just didn't "get it." How could scientists fairly test something they didn't believe in and hadn't experienced. According to Kayla's understanding, it was the scientists who were biased, not the people who already believed. How could nonbelievers possibly create a valid test? The article identified Dean as a former astrologer.

"So he should know," Kayla thought to herself. She started reading about the hidden persuaders.

The Texas Sharpshooter Fallacy: Astrology works like a Texas sharpshooter who first shoots a hole in the side of his barn and then draws a bull's eye around the spot where the hole went in.

Pseudo-Science: Astrology offers a scientific sounding theory that can't be tested because it is consistent with every imaginable state of affairs in the empirical world. Real scientific theories are testable.

The Forer Effect: Astrology offers people vague personality descriptions that they believe are uniquely applicable to themselves without realizing that the same description could be applied to just about anyone. (This effect is named for the psychologist Butram R. Forer, who first described it.)

The Clever Hans Phenomenon: Astrologers both knowingly and unknowingly respond to cues from the person who has come to them for a reading the same way a famous horse nicknamed "Clever Hans" was credited with knowing how to solve mathematical problems by tapping his hoof. In reality, the horse was responding to subtle head movements from its owner.

Shoe-Horning: Astrologers force-fit current events into existing beliefs after they have happened and then call it evidence that supports their beliefs. In the same way, religious leaders working from very different belief systems publicly, shoe-horned the terror attacks of 9/11 as evidence that God was punishing America for its various sins.

Kayla looked up from the newspaper as Ryan returned. "So," he said, "are you ready to hear what I want to confess? I'd like to get this off my chest before we move into our new house."

The hidden persuaders alert us to the most common mistake related to correlation: assuming that correlation implies causality. If you listen to media reports of changes in the stock market on a given day, the so-called analysts usually describe some co-occurring event, such as an impending election, a report on unemployment, or rumors of a takeover of a major company. Then they confidently attribute changes in the stock market to the impending election, economic report, or rumor. Sometimes they even blame "the mood of the public." They don't know; they just sound confident. Co-occurring events are, by definition, correlated, but they are not necessarily causally related. In fact, there are millions of other co-occurring variables out there: what you ate for lunch, the weather, and (more famously) the height of hemlines in this year's fashion statement. So what are the causal possibilities when two variables are correlated?

Correlation Is Not Causation: Invisible Third Variables

Correlations provide clues to causality, but they do not demonstrate or test for causality; they only quantify the strength and direction between variables. A superstitious response to a correlation interprets strong correlations as evidence of a causal relation between variables. That is why your understanding of what correlations can and *cannot* do is what distinguishes your own reasoning as either scientific or superstitious. Let's think through the possible causal influences by using an example that we're already familiar with.

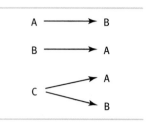

FIGURE 5-11
Three Possible Causal Explanations for a Correlation

Any correlation could be explained in one of several ways. The first variable (A) might cause the second variable (B). Or the reverse could be true—the second variable (B) could cause the first variable (A). Finally, there could be a third variable, C, that causes both A and B. In fact, there could be many third variables.

Earlier, we determined that the number of absences from statistics class was negatively correlated with students' mean grades on the exams. We concluded by encouraging you to attend class. The assumption behind this is that class attendance causes good grades. As teachers who have observed many students study statistics, we do believe that class attendance leads to better grades. But, as researchers, we also have to acknowledge that (1) the pattern isn't true for every student and (2) there might be other explanations for this association. With any association, we must consider three possible reasons for the pattern. Let's call absences from class A and mean exam grade B. We could hypothesize that lower levels of A causes higher levels of B. Yet it is possible, although somewhat less plausible, that the reverse is true. Perhaps those who get good grades get more excited about class and want to attend more often. In this case, higher levels of B lead to lower levels of A. But even more important is the possibility of one (or more) third variables. We'll refer to any third (or fourth or fifth) variable as C. The three possibilities are outlined in Figure 5-11.

What third variables might lead to a correlation between number of absences and mean exam grade? A high need for achievement might lead both to better grades and to a realization that going to class is a good thing. Having friends in class also might lead students to want to attend class and then to get better grades by having study partners. What if it's a morning class? Students who are "morning people" might be more likely to wake up alert, get to class on time, and therefore perform better on exam days. The possibilities are limitless. Never confuse correlation with causation.

A Restricted Range: When the Values of One Variable Are Limited

In many behavioral science studies, one or even both of the variables are restricted in their range. For example, a famous study by Benbow and Stanley (1980) assessed mathematical reasoning ability in a sample of boys and girls who performed in the top 2% to 3% on standardized tests. These mathematically high-achieving participants represent a much smaller range than the full population from which the researchers could have drawn their sample. We must consider the effects of a restricted range on correlation coefficients. We can always speculate and then hypothesize, but we never want to conclude or generalize

FIGURE 5-12
The Full Range of Data

This scatterplot depicts data for the full range of two variables, age and hours studied per week. The Pearson correlation coefficient for these data is 0.56.

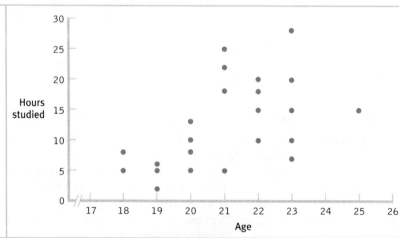

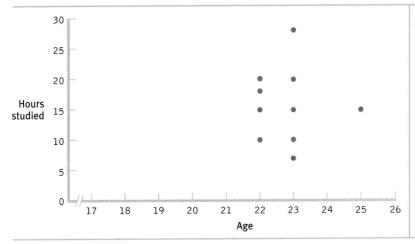

FIGURE 5-13
A Restricted Range for Age

This scatterplot depicts the same data as in Figure 5-12, but only for those between the ages of 22 and 26. The strength of the Pearson correlation coefficient for these data is now only 0.05.

about individuals who are not part of the population from which we have collected our sample.

Some of the graphs used by NASA management to decide that it was safe to launch the *Challenger* space shuttle are an alarming demonstration of what can happen when we analyze a restricted range—they neglected to include many observations at extreme ends of the temperature range and failed to project from a graph what might happen if they launched *Challenger* in extremely cold temperatures. Similarly, in Check Your Learning 5-2, we presented data on two variables, age and number of hours studied per week, for a small sample (10 students) of our statistics students. Figure 5-12 depicts a scatterplot of data on these two variables from another larger sample of our statistics students. The Pearson correlation coefficient for these data points is 0.56, a strong positive correlation.

Now let's look only at nontraditionally aged students who are 22 years old or older, illustrated in Figure 5-13. With just the restricted range of students between the ages of 22 and 25, we no longer see the pattern of a positive correlation emerging from the data. The strength of this correlation is far smaller; *r* is now just 0.05. When we calculate a correlation coefficient, we should always ask ourselves whether the ranges of the two variables are sufficient to show us their true association.

The Effect of an Outlier: The Influence of a Single Data Point

In the Digging Deeper into the Data section of Chapter 1, we introduced a form of outlier analysis when we described how Dr. John Snow traveled a long distance to interview the families of people who should not have died from cholera because they lived so far from the contaminated Broad Street pump. *Outlier analysis refers to studies that examine the extreme scores in an effort to understand the factors that influence the dependent variable.* Outliers are not always people, of course. Technically, *an outlier is a score or case that is so low or so high that it stands apart from the rest of the data* (Goodwin & Leech, 2006). Outliers can have powerful effects on the correlation coefficient.

For example, consider the correlation between monthly cell phone bills and hours studied per week, calculated from data reported by some of our statistics students. We calculated a Pearson correlation coefficient of 0.390, a medium

■ **Outlier analysis** refers to a study that examines the extreme scores in an effort to understand the factors that influence the dependent variable.

■ An **outlier** is a score or case that is so low or so high that it stands apart from the rest of the data.

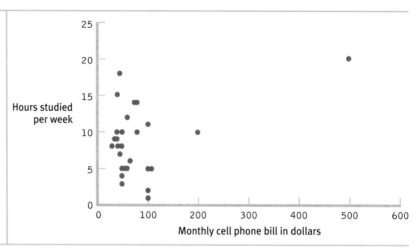

FIGURE 5-14
The Effects of an Outlier on the Correlation Coefficient

One individual who both studies and uses her cell phone more than any other individual in the sample changed the Pearson correlation coefficient from −0.135, a negative correlation, to 0.390, a much stronger and positive correlation! Always examine the scatterplot for outliers before calculating a correlation coefficient.

correlation by Cohen's standards and quite large in terms of the typical correlation in the behavioral sciences. But before you start making up a story about students spending hours studying with friends on their cell phones, let's look at the data, depicted in the scatterplot in Figure 5-14.

A single individual reported the highest number of hours studied per week and was an extreme outlier on the variable of monthly cell phone bill, reporting that she typically spends a whopping $500 a month! Did she misinterpret the question? Does she have a boyfriend in Peru? Regardless of her story, guidelines regarding outliers suggest when it might be acceptable to disregard outliers because they distort the story that the data are telling (Miyamura & Kano, 2006). For example, without this one $500 per month cell phone user, the Pearson correlation coefficient is −0.135, showing both a decrease in strength and a reversal of direction. The possibility of an outlier is yet another reason to construct a scatterplot first. A visual inspection of the scatterplot is often the most effective way to identify outliers. And once we identify an outlier, we must decide whether it makes sense to include it in the analyses; in fact, it's best to make decisions about when we will and will not exclude an outlier *before* we collect data.

In summary, correlation is not equivalent to causation. When two variables are correlated, that association might occur because the first variable (A) causes the second (B) or because the second variable (B) causes the first (A). In addition, there could be a third variable (C) that causes both of the correlated variables (A and B). In addition to problems with interpretation of correlations, there are several factors that can create problems for the calculation of correlations. A correlation can be dramatically altered by a restricted range or by an extreme outlier. These two problems can be identified by the examination of a scatterplot.

⊙ CHECK YOUR LEARNING

5-3 A writer for *Runner's World* magazine debated the merits of running while listening to music (Seymour, 2006). The writer, an avid iPod user, interviewed a clinical psychologist, whose response to the debate about whether to listen to music while running was: "I like to do what the great ones do and try to emulate that. What are the Kenyans doing? Are they running with Walkmans?" Let's say a researcher conducted a study in which he determined the correlation between the percentage of a country's marathon runners who train while using a portable music device and the average marathon finishing time for that country's runners. (Note that in this case the participants are countries, not people.) Let's say the researcher finds a strong positive correlation. That is, the more of a country's runners that train with music, the longer the average marathon finishing time. Remember, in a marathon, a longer time is bad. So this fictional finding is that training with music is associated with *slower* marathon finishing times; the United States, for example, would have a higher percentage of music use and higher (slower) finishing times than Kenya.

a.   Using the A-B-C model, provide three possible explanations for this finding.

b.   In what way might a restricted range be involved in this hypothetical study?

c.   How might an outlier affect the correlation coefficient of this study?

➤ RELIABILITY AND VALIDITY: CORRELATION IN TEST CONSTRUCTION

"To begin with," said Ryan. "I don't believe in astrology."

"Well, I've known that for a long time," said Kayla. "It's just like a Leo to lose faith."

"It's not that I lost my faith," said Ryan. "I never had it to begin with."

"Do you really think that you just happened to show up for that talk on astrology? And that I just happened to be there? That's more than a coincidence," Kayla said. "It was the stars."

"It wasn't the stars." Ryan took a deep breath. "I haven't wanted to tell you this because I didn't want to hurt you, but I never believed any of that stuff. Not even at the beginning."

"So are you trying to say that you really don't love me?"

"Of course I do. And we just bought ourselves a home, and now I feel like I can grow old with you. But it wasn't the stars that brought us together, Kayla. You know how you kept bumping into me? It was because the more I saw you, the more I liked you. That's the real correlation. I was looking for excuses to see you, and the only reason I went to that astrology thing was because I knew you would be there. It wasn't the synastry analysis that convinced me we were right for each other. I was already convinced."

"You mean you liked me before we even met at that talk?"

"Way before." Ryan took her hand.

"Let's go home," said Kayla.

Correlation, Psychometrics, and a Super-Heated Job Market: Creating the Measures Behind the Research

Social science majors don't need to wait for the stars to participate in a hot job market. And for students who recognize the value of improving their statistical skills, it looks like this hot job market will continue for some time to come. So what are statisticians actually doing? Well, they're in the field collecting data, explaining ability tests to concerned parents, creating laboratory situations that

■ **Psychometrics** is the branch of statistics used in the development of tests and measures.

■ **Psychometricians** are the statisticians and psychologists who develop tests and measures.

capture some elusive phenomenon, helping school principals gather data more intelligently, teaching bureaucrats how to interpret data, listening carefully to human resource directors concerned about morale, and using correlations to ask better questions.

The career path that specializes in the measurement of many social science variables is called **psychometrics**: *the branch of statistics used in the development of tests and measures.* Not surprisingly, *the statisticians and psychologists who develop tests and measures are called* **psychometricians.** Psychometrics involves many of the statistical procedures referred to in this text, and correlation forms the mathematical backbone of many of them. Psychometricians are needed to make sure elections are fair, to test for cultural biases in the SAT, to evaluate the effectiveness of new legislation, to identify high-achieving employees, to establish guidelines for profit sharing, and to help guide college graduates into productive, satisfying careers.

Despite the importance of psychometricians, we don't have nearly enough of them. The *New York Times* reported (Herszenhorn, 2006) a "critical shortage" of such experts in statistics, psychology, and education, leading to intense competition for the few who are available—competition that has resulted in salaries as high as $200,000 a year! The competition has become even fiercer as standardized testing becomes more widespread. The College Board's vice president for research and psychometrics said that following the implementation of the educational policy formalized in the No Child Left Behind Act and the reliance on standardized testing that it mandates, the demand for psychometricians "has just gotten ridiculous." Currently, only about 50 PhDs graduate with psychometrics degrees each year. As the *New York Times* says, "Psychometrics, one of the most obscure, esoteric, and cerebral professions in America, is also one of the hottest."

Correlation and Reliability
Correlation is used by psychometricians to help professional sports teams assess the reliability of athletic performance such as how fast a pitcher can throw a baseball. Such information is especially helpful when scouting players coming out of college or the minor leagues.

Reliability: Using Correlation to Create a Consistent Test

The demand for psychometricians exists, in part, because we need to know if a test taken by employees, students, managers, sex offenders, political candidates, or convicted criminals is trustworthy. A test demonstrates its trustworthiness by its reliability; that is, how consistently it measures what it was intended to measure. And reliability is assessed by the correlation coefficient. In Chapter 1, we defined a reliable measure as one that is consistent. For example, a baseball pitcher who consistently allows the opposition to score very few runs will get a reputation for being a reliable pitcher. Similarly, if we are measuring shyness, then a reliable measure leads to very nearly the same score every time the same person takes the shyness test.

In Chapter 1, we described one particular type of reliability: test–retest reliability. To calculate a measure's test–retest reliability, the measure is given twice to the *same sample*, typically with a delay of a week or more between tests. The participants' scores on the first test of the measure are correlated with their scores on the second test. A large correlation indicates that the measure shows good consistency over time—good test–retest reliability—and although there are several ways to assess reliability, this one is best if you want to determine a measure's reliability over

AP Photo/Michael Manning

time (Cortina, 1993). However, a problem you may also recognize from Chapter 1 is known as an order effect (also called a practice effect). An order effect occurs when taking a test the first time changes the results of taking the same test a second time. For example, if you were to take the same version of the SAT two weeks apart, your second score would likely be higher due to the order effect.

A better way to measure the reliability of a test is by measuring its internal consistency (DeVellis, 1991) to verify that all the items were measuring the same idea. Initially, researchers measured internal consistency by calculating *split-half reliability*: *a measure of the internal consistency of a test or measure that is calculated by correlating the odd-numbered items with the even-numbered items.* If the correlation of the odd-numbered items (1, 3, 5, etc.) with the even-numbered items (2, 4, 6, etc.) is large, then the test has high internal consistency, or split-half reliability. The odd–even approach is easy to understand, but computers have made possible a much more sophisticated approach to measuring internal consistency.

The computer can calculate *every possible* instance of split-half reliability. Consider a 10-item measure. The computer can calculate correlations between the odd-numbered items and even-numbered items, between the first five items and the last five items, between items 1, 2, 4, 8, 10 and items 3, 5, 6, 7, 9, and so on for every combination of two groups of five items. The computer calculates what is essentially (although not always exactly) the average of all possible split-half correlations (Cortina, 1993); the average of these is called coefficient alpha, or sometimes *Cronbach's alpha* in honor of the statistician who developed it. *Coefficient alpha*, *symbolized as* α, *is a commonly used estimate of a test's or measure's reliability and is calculated by taking the average of all possible split-half correlations.* This is a far superior method of estimating the internal consistency of a test than split-half reliability; because of this, it is commonly used across a wide range of fields, including psychology, education, sociology, political science, medicine, economics, criminology, and anthropology (Cortina, 1993).

When developing a new scale or measure, how high should our reliability be? When conducting research, a coefficient alpha of 0.80 is considered adequate; it would not be worth using a scale in our research if its coefficient alpha is less than 0.80. But, if we are using a scale to make decisions about individuals—for example, the SAT or a medical diagnostic tool—then we should aim for a coefficient alpha of 0.90 or even of 0.95 (Nunnally & Bernstein, 1994). You want high reliability when using a test that directly affects people's lives, but it also needs to be valid.

Validity: Using Correlation to Test Whether We Are Measuring What We Intend to Measure

In Chapter 1, we defined a valid measure as one that measures what it was designed or intended to measure. Nunnally and Bernstein (1994), the authors of a classic book on psychometrics, consider validity to be the most important concept in the field. It can be a great deal more work to measure validity than reliability, so that work is not always done. In fact, it is quite possible to have a reliable test, one that measures a construct consistently over time and is internally consistent, that is still not valid. Just because the items on a test all measure the same underlying construct doesn't mean that they're measuring the construct that we want them to measure or that we think they are measuring.

Symbols: α

■ **Split-half reliability** is a measure of the internal consistency of a test or measure that is calculated by correlating the odd-numbered items with the even-numbered items.

■ **Coefficient alpha**, symbolized as α, is a commonly used estimate of a test's or measure's reliability and is calculated by taking the average of all possible split-half correlations; also called *Cronbach's alpha*.

Spencer Grant/PhotoEdit

Validity and Personality Quizzes

Correlation can also be used to establish the validity of a psychological test. Establishing validity is usually much more difficult than establishing reliability. Moreover, most magazines and newspapers never examine the psychometric properties of the quizzes that they publish. Think of most of these as mere entertainment.

■ **Criterion-related validity** is a type of validity whereby the scale or measure of interest is correlated with a criterion, which is some external standard.

■ **Postdictive validity** is a type of criterion-related validity in which we correlate the scale or measure of interest with a criterion measured in the past.

■ **Concurrent validity** is a type of criterion-related validity in which we correlate the scale or measure of interest with a criterion measured at the same time.

We defined a construct in Chapter 1 as a hypothetical idea that has been developed (or constructed) to describe and explain human behavior. For instance, we can't really see shyness the same way we can see red hair. However, we can see the effects of shyness, such as withdrawing from groups, a hesitancy to speak up, and a reluctance to go out. More important, we can measure this invisible personality trait that we call shyness. So shyness is a construct, a variable that we have constructed to describe and explain behavior.

Cosmopolitan magazine has published quizzes that claim they can assess their readers' relationships with their boyfriends. If you've ever taken one of these quizzes, you might find yourself wondering what some of the quiz items have to do with the construct at hand. One such quiz, titled "Is He Devoted to You?" asks: "Be honest: Do you ever worry that he might cheat on you?" Does this item assess a man's devotion or a woman's jealousy? Another item asks: "When you introduced him to your closest friends, he said:" and then offers three options: (1) "I've heard so much about all of you! So, how'd you become friends?" (2) "'Hi,' then silence—he looked a bit bored." And 3) "'Nice to meet you' with a big smile." Does this measure his devotion or his social skills? Such a quiz might be reliable, in that you'd consistently get the same score today and again in a few days, but is it a valid measure of a man's devotion to his girlfriend? Devotion, jealousy, and social skills are different constructs; it takes a psychometrician who understands correlation to test the validity of such measures.

Correlation can be used to test validity in several different ways, which is why there are several different types of validity. But every type of validity is trying to assess the same core idea: Are we measuring what we intended to measure? *Criterion-related validity is a type of validity whereby the scale or measure of interest is correlated with a criterion, which is some external standard.* For example, the criterion for shyness might be some of the behaviors that we have already suggested: withdrawn behavior, hesitancy to speak up, and a reluctance to go out in groups. So those are the behaviors that we will measure and correlate with one another to estimate criterion-related validity. *Postdictive validity is a type of criterion-related validity in which we correlate the scale or measure of interest with a criterion measured in the past.* An archival approach could be used to measure postdictive validity by watching a home movie (the archive) of a child attending a birthday party three years earlier, counting the shy behaviors displayed by the child, and then correlating that with the child's current score on a shyness scale. *Concurrent validity is a type of criterion-related validity in which we correlate the scale or measure of interest with a criterion measured at the same time.* If we know someone's score on a shyness scale and can measure another shyness-related behavior (such as how close he will come to a woman when asking for a date), we can estimate concurrent validity. Predictive validity, first discovered in Chapter 1, refers to how well a measuring instrument (such as a personality scale) predicts future behavior. A shyness scale with predictive validity will predict how often a person will go out, how many friends he or she will have, and other shyness-related behaviors. If these tests indicate that we are not measuring what we intended to measure, then our test lacks validity. Start over.

Another way to think about what validity means is to ask ourselves whether we can actually do anything useful with the scale we have developed. In their groundbreaking treatise on affirmative action in higher education, Bowen and Bok (2000) studied more than 35,000 black and white students who graduated from one of 28 highly selective universities. They first considered the obvious outcome criteria: these students' future graduate education and career success. Their findings debunked the myth that black graduates of such institutions did not achieve the successes of their white counterparts. The researchers then went a step further and assessed a criterion very important to the social fabric of a society: graduates' levels of civic and community participation, including political involvement and community service. Bowen and Bok found that a significantly larger proportion of black than white graduates of these top institutions were actively involved in their communities. Bowen and Bok changed the nature of the debate on affirmative action by widening the pool of criteria by which we judge success. Psychometricians can change the world by asking better questions.

In summary, correlation is a central part of psychometrics, the statistics of the construction of tests and measures. Psychometricians, the statisticians who practice psychometrics, use correlation to establish the reliability and the validity of a test. Test–retest reliability can be estimated by correlating the same participants' scores on the same test at two different time points. Split-half reliability, now obsolete, is estimated by correlating participants' scores on the odd-numbered items of a test with their scores on the even-numbered items of a test. Coefficient alpha, now widely used to establish reliability, is calculated by taking the average of all possible split-half correlations (i.e., not just the odds versus the evens). The three kinds of criterion-related validity examine the correlation of participants' scores on a measure with their scores on another measure taken either in the past (postdictive validity), present (concurrent validity), or future (predictive validity). Psychometricians must carefully consider what constitute the appropriate criteria when estimating these types of validity.

⊙ CHECK YOUR LEARNING

5-4 Remember the *Cosmopolitan* devotion quiz we referred to when discussing validity? Imagine that the magazine hired a psychometrician to assess the reliability and validity of its quizzes, and she administered this 10-item quiz to 100 female readers of that magazine who had boyfriends.

a. How could the psychometrician establish the reliability of the quiz? That is, which of the methods introduced above could be used in this case? Be specific, and cite at least two ways.

b. How could the psychometrician establish the validity of the quiz? Be specific, and cite at least two ways. (*Hint:* Think about what the criteria would be—past, present, or future. Be creative in selecting the criteria!)

c. Choose one of your criteria from part (b) and explain why it might not actually measure the underlying variable of interest. That is, explain how your criterion itself might not be valid.

▪ DIGGING DEEPER INTO THE DATA: PARTIAL CORRELATION

Whatever you might believe about astrology, you probably recognize that it takes more than just two correlated variables to understand a complicated world. For example, if you were interested in why people do or do not donate blood,

▪ **Partial correlation** is a technique that quantifies the degree of association between two variables, after statistically removing the association of a third variable with both of those two variables.

then you could hypothesize that several different variables were at work: the importance of helping others, fear of needles or infection, whether someone in your family has ever needed blood, how often a bloodmobile comes near your home or workplace, or whether the blood center is located on a bus line with reliable service. Some of these variables surely have more merit than others. Even something as simple as understanding why people do or do not donate blood requires more than just two variables. The challenge of understanding a complicated world is one reason that there are so many terrific career opportunities for behavioral science majors.

Fortunately, correlation also provides a helpful way to think about the relative influence of multiple variables. ***Partial correlation** is a technique that quantifies the degree of association between two variables, after statistically removing the association of a third variable with both of those two variables.* Previously, we considered the correlation between number of absences and mean exam grade in a statistics class; in a larger sample of 26 students, we found a correlation of −0.44. Students with more absences tended to have a lower mean exam grade, whereas those with fewer absences tended to have a higher mean exam grade. We also discussed the many possible third variables that might influence this association, including the completion of homework assignments. As expected, the correlation between the percentage of completed homework assignments and mean exam grade was 0.53. Those who completed a higher percentage of homework assignments tended to earn better grades, whereas those who completed a lower percentage of homework assignments tended to earn poorer grades.

Yet we might also wonder about the correlation of number of absences with percentage of completed homework assignments. After all, how can a student turn in his homework if he isn't in class? And, in fact, the correlation between number of absences and percentage of completed homework assignments is −0.51. Those who miss class more tend to have completed a smaller percentage of homework assignments, whereas those who miss class less tend to have completed a larger percentage of homework assignments. So how can we begin to tease apart the relations among these three variables? Just when we need it, partial correlation comes to the rescue.

Partial correlation allows us to examine the association between two variables when we suspect that there is a third variable at work. We can calculate a correlation coefficient that expresses the association between two variables, over and above the association of either of these variables with a third variable. Essentially, we subtract the influence of a third variable from the correlation coefficient. Figure 5-15 is a drawing of three overlapping circles that represent the three variables: number of absences, percentage of completed homework assignments, and mean exam grade. Overlapping circles indicate correlations between pairs of variables. You'll notice that there is a portion of the diagram that represents the association among all three variables—the section where all three circles overlap (B).

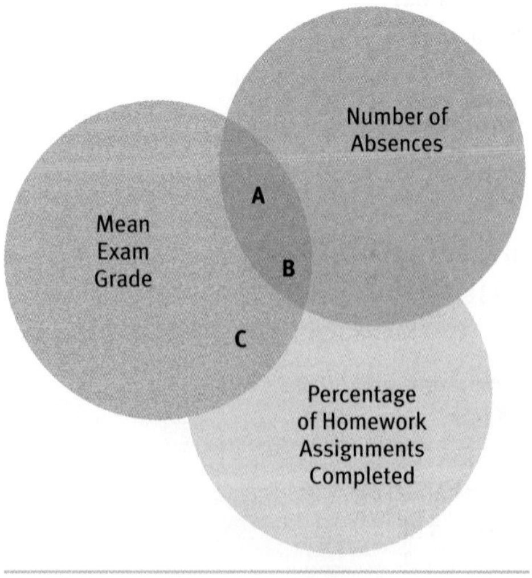

Conceptually, partial correlation quantifies the correlation between two variables by removing (or correcting for) all overlapping variability of each variable with the third. The actual calculations of partial correlations are complex, and we typically let the computer do the math for us. But the concept is that we calculate a correlation of two variables, over and above their

FIGURE 5-15
A Venn Diagram:
Partial Correlation and
Overlapping Variability

Partial correlation can help us understand the degree to which two variables are associated, independent of a third variable. We can, for example, assess the correlation between number of absences and mean exam grade, over and above the correlation of percentage of completed homework assignments with these variables.

respective correlations with a third variable. That allows us, for example, to calculate the partial correlation of number of absences and mean grade, correcting for percentage of homework assignments completed. Let's describe this same idea visually.

In terms of the Venn diagram in Figure 5-15, we calculate the association represented by A—the part left over when B, the section that accounts for the overlap among all three, is removed. The partial correlation is −0.23, smaller than the initial Pearson correlation of −0.44 but still fairly substantial. We can also calculate the partial correlation of percentage of homework assignments and mean grade, correcting for number of absences. In terms of Figure 5-15, to do this we calculate the association represented by C—the part left over when B is removed. The partial correlation is 0.40, smaller than the initial Pearson correlation coefficient of 0.53 but still substantial. The completion of homework assignments has a strong association with the mean exam grade, even after we've removed the contribution of number of absences.

It appears that the variables of number of absences and percentage of homework assignments completed both have substantial correlations, independent of each other, with the variable of mean exam grade. The partial correlation of homework and grade, controlling for absences, is stronger than the partial correlation of absences and grade, controlling for homework. What's the message for the students in this class? Coming to class is associated with good exam grades, over and above doing homework. And doing homework is even more strongly associated with good exam grades, over and above just coming to class. We can't know that these behaviors *cause* good exam grades, because correlation can never tell us about the existence or direction of causality, but these data do tell us that those students who come to class and do their homework tend to get the good exam grades. Now it doesn't seem very startling to discover that coming to class and doing your homework are associated with earning higher grades. But things always seem to make sense after the statistical analysis. Trust us, correlations can surprise you.

In summary, partial correlation enables us to quantify the association between two variables, over and above the association of a third variable with either of these variables. This technique is useful when the researcher suspects that a third variable might be associated with both variables of interest. Like correlation, partial correlation does not tell us anything about the existence or direction of causation.

⊙ CHECK YOUR LEARNING

5-5 The accompanying correlation matrix displays the Pearson correlation coefficients, as calculated by computer software, for each pair of the following variables: percentage of homework completed, number of absences, mean exam grade, and extra credit earned. The Pearson correlation coefficients for each pair of variables are at the intersection in the chart of the two variables. For example, the correlation coefficient for the association between percentage of homework completed (top row) and number of absences (second column of correlations) is −0.506.

a. What is the correlation coefficient for the association between percentage of homework completed and extra credit earned? Explain what this correlation coefficient means.

b. What is the correlation coefficient for the association between the mean exam grade and extra credit earned? Explain what this correlation coefficient means.

c. The partial correlation of extra credit earned and mean exam grade is 0.539, controlling for the percentage of homework completed. Explain what this means.

Correlations

		Percentage of Homework Completed	Number of Absences	Mean Exam Grade	Extra Credit
Percentage of Homework Completed	Pearson Correlation		-.506(**)	.532(**)	.372
	Sig. (2-tailed)		.008	.005	.062
	N		26	26	26
Number of Absences	Pearson Correlation			-.437(*)	-.399(*)
	Sig. (2-tailed)			.026	.044
	N			26	26
Mean Exam Grade	Pearson Correlation				.621(**)
	Sig. (2-tailed)				.001
	N				26
Extra Credit	Pearson Correlation				
	Sig. (2-tailed)				
	N				

** Correlation is significant at the 0.01 level (2-tailed).
* Correlation is significant at the 0.05 level (2-tailed).

REVIEW OF CONCEPTS

> Correlation: Assessing Associations Between Variables

Correlation is an association between two variables and is quantified by a correlation coefficient. To calculate a *correlation coefficient,* we have to know how to calculate *z scores,* which allow us to convert raw scores from any distribution to scores on a very specific distribution, the *z* distribution. This standardization process allows us to calculate a correlation coefficient using scores from two very different scales. A *positive correlation* indicates that a participant who has a high score on one variable is likely to have a high score on the other, and someone with a low score on one variable is likely to have a low score on the other. A *negative correlation* indicates that someone with a high score on one variable is likely to have a low score on the other. All correlation coefficients must fall between −1.00 and 1.00. The strength of the correlation is independent of its sign.

> The Pearson Correlation Coefficient: Quantifying a Linear Association

The *Pearson correlation coefficient* is used when two interval variables are linearly related, as determined from a scatterplot. To calculate the Pearson correlation coefficient, we first convert the raw scores on each variable to z scores. We multiply the pair of z scores for each person in the sample, and take the average of these cross-products.

> Misleading Correlations: Understanding the Limits of Causal Reasoning

Correlation coefficients have the ability to mislead. To accurately interpret a correlation coefficient, we must be certain not to confuse correlation with causation. We cannot know the causal direction in which two variables are related from a correlation coefficient, nor can we know if there is a hidden third variable that causes the apparent relation. Outlier analysis can be useful if we are interested in extreme scores. But, we must also be aware of the negative effects of both a restricted range or an extreme *outlier* on the correlation coefficient. All of these problems can detract from the accuracy of our correlation coefficient.

> Reliability and Validity: Correlation in Test Construction

Psychometrics, the statistics of the development of tests and measures, is a hot field right now. *Psychometricians* assess the reliability and validity of tests. Reliability is sometimes measured by a process called test–retest reliability in which participants' scores on the same measure at two different times are correlated. However, those correlations may suffer from practice, or order, effects. An antiquated technique, called *split-half reliability*, calculates reliability by correlating participants' scores on the odd-numbered items and even-numbered items of the test. *Coefficient alpha*, the most common method of estimating reliability, is an updated version of the split-half technique; the computer calculates the average of all possible split-halves. *Criterion-related validity* is one way to assess validity. There are three kinds, all of which correlate scores on a measure with a criterion that the measure is hypothesized to correlate with. *Postdictive validity* correlates scores on a measure with another measure, the criterion, from the past. *Concurrent validity* uses a present criterion. And predictive validity uses a future criterion.

> Digging Deeper into the Data: Partial Correlation

Partial correlation is used when researchers want to know the correlation between two variables, after the contribution of a third variable is removed. In other words, we quantify the degree of association between two variables that remains when the correlations of these two variables with the third variable are mathematically eliminated. Researchers use this technique when there is the possibility that a third variable is influencing the relation and the researcher is able to measure that third variable. Partial correlation is subject to the same potential pitfalls as correlation.

SPSS GUIDELINES FOR CHAPTER 5: CORRELATION

Instructing SPSS to run a correlation on our variables requires only a few choices, but those choices remind us what a correlation can and *cannot* reveal about the relation between two scale variables.

To view a scatterplot of the relations between two variables, select:

Graphs → Chart Builder → Gallery → Drag the upper-lefthand sample graph to the large box on top. Then select the variables to be included in the scatterplot by dragging the independent variable to the *x*-axis and the dependent variable to the *y*-axis. Click OK.

The default is to select for scale data and the Pearson correlation coefficient. Select:

Analyze → Correlate → Bivariate. Then, select at least two interval variables to be analyzed. If more than two variables are selected, then SPSS will build a correlation matrix of all possible pairs of variables.

After making our choices, we click on OK to see the Output screen.

EXERCISES

5.1 Sleep and the mean and standard deviation of the z distribution: A sample of 150 statistics students reported the typical number of hours that they sleep on a weeknight. The mean number of hours was 6.65, and the standard deviation was 1.24. (For this exercise, treat this sample as the entire population of interest.)

a. What is *always* the mean of the z distribution?

b. Using the sleep data, demonstrate that your answer to part (a) is the mean of the z distribution. (*Hint:* Calculate the z score for a student who is exactly at the mean.)

c. What is *always* the standard deviation of the z distribution?

d. Using the sleep data, demonstrate that your answer to part (c) is the standard deviation of the z distribution. (*Hint:* Calculate the z score for a student who is exactly 1 standard deviation above or below the mean.)

e. How many hours of sleep do you typically get on a weeknight? What would your z score be compared with this population?

5.2 The GRE and z scores without a formula: The verbal subtest of the GRE has a population mean of 500 and a population standard deviation of 100 by design (the quantitative subtest has the same mean and standard deviation).

a. Use symbolic notation to state the mean and standard deviation of the GRE verbal test.

b. Convert the following GRE scores to z scores *without* using a formula: (i) 700, (ii) 550, (iii) 400.

5.3 Breakfast and z scores: Georgiou and colleagues (1997) reported that college students had healthier eating habits, on average, than did those who were neither college students nor college graduates. The journal article reported means and standard deviations for students and nonstudents on a number of eating measures. For example, the 412 students in the study ate breakfast a mean of 4.1 times per week with a standard deviation of 2.4. For this exercise, imagine that you are one of the students in the study and that this is the entire population of interest; thus, these numbers can be treated as parameters.

a. Using symbolic notation and the formula, calculate the z score for a student who eats breakfast six times per week.

b. Again using symbolic notation and the formula, calculate the z score for a student who eats breakfast twice a week.

c. How many times a week do you typically eat breakfast? Calculate your own z score.

5.4 Correlation, the confirmation bias, and a test of astrology: The *New York Times* reported that an officer of the International Society for Astrological Research, Anne Massey, stated that a certain phase of the planet Mercury, the retrograde phase, leads to breakdowns in areas as wide-ranging as communication and travel (Newman, 2006). The *Times* reporter, Andy Newman, documented the likelihood of breakdown on a number of variables in both phases, retrograde and nonretrograde. Newman discovered that, contrary to Massey's hypothesis, New Jersey Transit commuter trains were less likely to be late, by 0.4%, during the retrograde phase. On the other hand, consistent with Massey's hypothesis, the rate of baggage complaints at LaGuardia airport increased from 5.38 during nonretrograde periods to 5.44 during retrograde periods. Newman's findings were contradictory across all examined variables—rates of theft, computer crashes, traffic disruptions, delayed plane arrivals—with some variables backing Massey and others not. Newman cited a transportation statistics expert, Bruce Schaller, who said, "If all of this is due to randomness, that's the result you'd expect." Astrologer Massey counters that the pattern she predicts would only emerge across thousands of years of data.

a. Do reporter Newman's data suggest a correlation between Mercury's phase and breakdowns?

b. Why might astrologer Massey believe there is a correlation? Discuss the confirmation bias and illusory correlations in your answer.

c. How do transportation expert Schaller's statement and Newman's contradictory results relate to what you learned about probability in Chapter 4? Discuss expected relative-frequency probability in your answer.

d. If there were indeed a small correlation that one could observe only across thousands of years of data, how useful would that knowledge be in terms of predicting events in your own life?

e. Write a brief response to Massey's contention of a correlation between Mercury's phases and breakdowns in aspects of day-to-day living.

5.5 Correlation, body fat index, and age at death: In the newspaper column discussed early in this chapter, Paul Krugman (2006) mentioned obesity (as measured by body fat index) as a possible correlate of age at death.

a. Describe the likely correlation between these variables. Is it likely to be positive or negative? Explain.

b. Draw a scatterplot that depicts the correlation that you described in part (a).

5.6 Exercise and scatterplots: Does the amount that people exercise correlate with the number of friends they have? The accompanying table contains data collected in some of our statistics classes. The first column shows hours exercised per week and the second column shows the number of close friends reported by each participant.

EXERCISE	FRIENDS
1.00	4.00
.00	3.00
1.00	2.00
6.00	6.00
1.00	3.00
6.00	5.00
2.00	4.00
3.00	5.00
5.00	6.00
8.00	4.00
2.00	4.00
10.00	4.00
5.00	7.00
4.00	5.00
2.00	6.00
7.00	5.00
1.00	5.00

a. Create a scatterplot of these data. Be sure to label both axes.

b. What does the scatterplot suggest about the relation between these two variables?

c. Would it be appropriate to calculate a Pearson correlation coefficient? Explain your answer.

5.7 Externalizing, anxiety, and scatterplots of raw scores: A study on the relation between rejection and depression in adolescents conducted by one of the authors (Nolan, Flynn, & Garber, 2003) also collected data on externalizing behaviors (e.g., acting out in negative ways, such as causing fights) and anxiety. We wondered whether externalizing behaviors were related to feelings of anxiety. Some of the data are presented in the accompanying table.

EXTERNALIZING	ANXIETY
9.00	37.00
7.00	23.00
7.00	26.00
3.00	21.00
11.00	42.00
6.00	33.00
2.00	26.00
6.00	35.00
6.00	23.00
9.00	28.00

a. Create a scatterplot of these data. Be sure to label both axes.

b. What does the scatterplot suggest about the relation between these two variables?

c. Would it be appropriate to calculate a Pearson correlation coefficient? Explain your answer.

d. Construct a second scatterplot, but this time add in the data for one more participant: (1 on externalizing, 45 on anxiety). Would you expect the correlation coefficient to be positive or negative now? Small in magnitude or large in magnitude?

c. The Pearson correlation coefficient for the first set of data is 0.61; for the second set of data it is 0.12. Explain why the correlation changed so much with the addition of just one participant.

5.8 Externalizing, anxiety, and scatterplots of z scores: Here are the means and standard deviations for the two variables in Exercise 5.7.

Externalizing ($M = 6.60$, $SD = 2.69$)

Anxiety ($M = 29.40$, $SD = 6.62$)

a. Explain why it makes sense to calculate z scores for the two variables if we want to calculate a correlation coefficient.

b. Calculate the z scores for the two variables.

c. Create a scatterplot of the z scores of the two variables.

d. Does the scatterplot differ from the one you constructed in Exercise 5.7(a)?

5.9 Expected correlations in your everyday life: For each of the following pairs of variables, would you expect a positive correlation or a negative correlation between the two variables? Explain your answer.

a.   How hard the rain is falling and your commuting time

b.   How often you say no to dessert and your body fat

c.   The amount of wine you consume with dinner and your alertness after dinner

5.10 Positive and negative correlations and cat ownership: You may be aware of the stereotype about the crazy elderly person who owns a lot of cats. Have you wondered whether the stereotype is true? As a researcher, you decide to interview 100 senior citizens in a retirement complex. You assess all senior citizens on two variables: (1) the number of cats they own and (2) their level of mental health problems (a higher score indicates more problems).

a.   Imagine that you found a positive relation between these two variables. What might you expect for someone who owns a lot of cats? Explain.

b.   Imagine that you found a positive relation between these two variables. What might you expect for someone who owns no cats or just one cat? Explain.

c.   Imagine that you found a negative relation between these two variables. What might you expect for someone who owns a lot of cats? Explain.

d.   Imagine that you found a negative relation between these two variables. What might you expect for someone who owns no cats or just one cat? Explain.

5.11 Drawing scatterplots of cat ownership and mental health: Consider the scenario in Exercise 5.10 again. The two variables under consideration were (1) number of cats owned and (2) level of mental health problems (with a higher score indicating more problems). Each possible relation between these variables would be represented by a different scatterplot. For each of the following exercises, use data for about 10 participants.

a.   Draw a scatterplot that depicts a weak positive correlation between these variables.

b.   Draw a scatterplot that depicts a strong positive correlation between these variables.

c.   Draw a scatterplot that depicts a perfect positive correlation between these variables.

d.   Draw a scatterplot that depicts a weak negative correlation between these variables.

e.   Draw a scatterplot that depicts a strong negative correlation between these variables.

f.   Draw a scatterplot that depicts a perfect negative correlation between these variables.

g.   Draw a scatterplot that depicts no (or almost no) correlation between these variables.

5.12 Describing MSG and hyperactivity data from a scatterplot: A dietician wonders whether monosodium glutamate (MSG) is related to hyperactivity in children. He assesses the amount of MSG that children consume in a meal (in grams) and their level of hyperactivity over the two hours after the meal (one a scale of 1–10).

a.   What does the accompanying fictional scatterplot suggest about the relation between MSG and hyperactivity? Be specific.

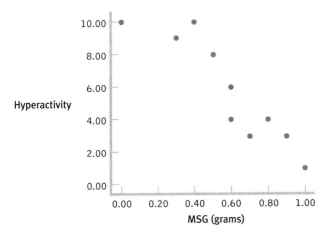

b. What does the accompanying fictional scatterplot suggest about the relation between MSG and hyperactivity? Be specific.

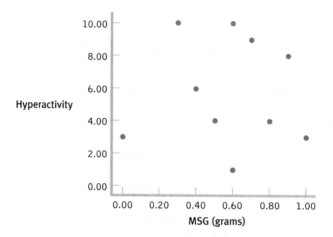

c. What does the accompanying fictional scatterplot suggest about the relation between MSG and hyperactivity? Be specific.

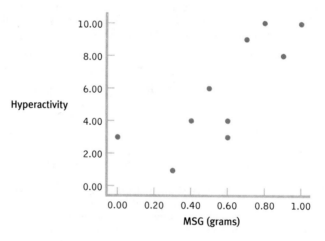

d. What does the accompanying fictional scatterplot suggest about the relation between MSG and hyperactivity? Be specific. How is this relation different from that depicted in the scatterplot in part (c)?

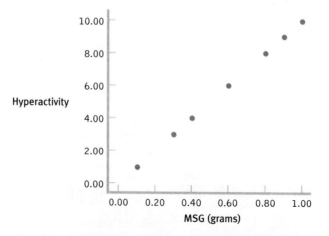

5.13 Correlation coefficients and graduate school: A researcher gathered data on psychology students' ratings of their likelihood of attending graduate school and the numbers of credits they had completed in their psychology major (Rajecki, 1998). Imagine that each of the following figures represents the Pearson correlation coefficient that quantifies the relation between these two variables. What does each coefficient suggest about the relation between the variables? Indicate whether each coefficient is roughly small, medium, or large. Specify which of these coefficients suggests the strongest relation between the two variables as well as which suggests the weakest relation between the two variables. (Any guesses as to the actual correlation in this study?)

a. 1.00

b. −0.001

c. 0.56

d. −0.27

e. −0.98

f. 0.09

[*Note:* Part (d) represents the actual correlation between these variables in this study.]

5.14 Calculating a correlation coefficient for trauma and femininity: Graduate student Angela Holiday (2007) conducted a study examining perceptions of combat veterans suffering from mental illness. Participants read a description of a person, either a man or a woman, who had recently returned from combat in Iraq and who was suffering from depression. Participants rated the situation (combat in Iraq) with respect to how traumatic they believed it was; they also rated the combat veterans on a range of variables, including scales that assessed how masculine and how feminine they perceived the person to be. Among other analyses, Holiday examined the relation between the perception of the situation as being traumatic and the perception of the veteran as being masculine or feminine. When the person was male, the perception of the situation as traumatic was strongly positively correlated with the perception of the man as feminine but was only weakly positively correlated with the perception of the man as masculine. What would you expect when the person was female? The accompanying table presents some of the data for the perception of the situation as traumatic (on a scale of 1–10 with 10 being the most traumatic) and the perception of the woman as feminine (on a scale of 1–10 with 10 being the most feminine).

TRAUMATIC	FEMININE
5	6
6	5
4	6
5	6
7	4
8	5

a. Draw a scatterplot for these data. Does the scatterplot suggest that it is appropriate to calculate a Pearson correlation coefficient? Explain.

b. Calculate the Pearson correlation coefficient.

c. State what the Pearson correlation coefficient tells us about the relation between these two variables.

d. Explain why the pattern of pairs of z scores enables us to understand the relation between the two variables. (That is, consider whether pairs of z scores tend to have the same sign or opposite signs.)

5.15 Calculating a correlation coefficient for trauma and masculinity: See the description of Holiday's experiment in Exercise 5.14. We calculated the correlation coefficient for the relation between the perception of a situation as traumatic and the perception of a woman's femininity. Now let's look at data to examine the relation between the perception of a situation as traumatic and the perception of a woman's masculinity.

TRAUMATIC	MASCULINE
5	3
6	3
4	2
5	2
7	4
8	3

a. Draw a scatterplot for these data. Does the scatterplot suggest that it is appropriate to calculate a Pearson correlation coefficient? Explain.

b. Calculate the Pearson correlation coefficient.

c. State what the Pearson correlation coefficient tells us about the relation between these two variables.

d. Explain why the pattern of pairs of z scores enables us to understand the relation between the two variables. (That is, consider whether pairs of z scores tend to share the same sign or to have opposite signs.)

e. Explain how the relations between the perception of a situation as traumatic and the perception of a woman as either masculine or feminine differ from those same relations with respect to men.

5.16 Commuting and the illusory correlation: A friend tells you that there is a correlation between how late she's running and the amount of traffic. Whenever she's going somewhere and she's behind schedule, there's a lot of traffic. And when she has plenty of time, the traffic is sparser. She tells you that this happens no matter what time of day she's traveling or where she's going. She concludes that she's cursed with respect to traffic.

a. In Chapter 4, we discussed coincidence, superstition, and the confirmation bias. Explain to your friend how these phenomena might explain her conclusion.

b. How could she quantify the relation between these two variables: the degree to which she is late and the amount of traffic? In your answer, be sure to explain how you might operationalize these variables. There are, of course, many ways that these could be operationalized.

5.17 Illusory correlations, intelligence, and an amazing Swiss waterfall: The trashy tabloid *Weekly World News* published an article—"Water from Mountain Falls Can Make You a Genius"—stating that drinking water from a special waterfall in a secret location in Switzerland "boosts IQ by 14 points—in the blink of an eye!" (exclamation point in the original). Hans and Inger Thurlemann, two hikers lost in the woods, drank some of the water, noticed an improvement in their thinking, and instantly found their way out of the woods. The more water they drank, the smarter they seemed to get. They credited "the miracle water" with enhancing their IQs. They brought some of the water home to their friends, who also claimed to notice an improvement in their thinking. Explain how a reliance on anecdotes led the Thurlemanns to perceive an illusory correlation.

5.18 Restricted range and running a race: Imagine that a sports researcher wanted to quantify the relation between miles run in training per week and running speed for a 5-kilometer race.

a. If the researcher studied a representative sample of North American adults, would you expect to find a relation between training and speed? Would it be positive or negative? Explain.

b. If the researcher studied only those who run more than 25 miles per week, would you expect to find a relation between training and speed? Would it be positive or negative? (*Hint:* There would likely be a higher percentage of people who are over-training among this sample.)

c. Explain why the researcher might find very different results in these two scenarios even when using the same two variables.

5.19 Correlation, causation, and type of schools: A *New York Times* editorial ("Public vs. Private Schools," 2006) cited a finding by the U.S. Department of Education that standardized test scores were significantly higher among students in private schools than among students in public schools.

a. What are the researchers suggesting with respect to causality?

b. How could this correlation be explained by reversing the direction of hypothesized causality? Be specific.

c. How might a third variable account for this correlation? Be specific. Note that there are many possible third variables.

(Note: In the actual study, the difference between types of school disappeared when the researchers statistically controlled for related third variables including race, gender, parents' education, and family income.)

5.20 Correlation, causation, and convertibles: How safe are convertibles? *USA Today* (Healey, 2006) examined the pros and cons of convertible automobiles. The Insurance Institute for Highway Safety, the newspaper reported, determined that, depending on the model, 52 to 99 drivers of 1 million registered convertibles died in a car crash. The average rate of deaths for all passenger cars was 87. "Counter to conventional wisdom," the reporter wrote, "convertibles generally aren't unsafe."

a. What does the reporter suggest about the safety of convertibles?

b. Can you think of another explanation for the fairly low fatality rates? (*Hint:* The same article reported that convertibles "are often second or third cars.")

c. Given your explanation in part (b), suggest data that might make for a more appropriate comparison.

5.21 Correlation, causation, and golfing as diplomacy: The *New York Times* published a satirical essay asserting that the presence of golf courses in a country is an antidote to war (Plotz, 2000). As evidence, the author observed that golfing nations, operationalized as countries with at least one golf course per 1 million people, have not fought one another in more than 50 years. Western European countries (most of which meet the definition of a golfing nation), for example, are at peace with one another, whereas Greece and Turkey have fought over Cyprus (all nongolfing nations). To end war, the author seems to suggest, we only need to build golf courses in places like Afghanistan, North Korea, and Iraq. Using the A-B-C model introduced in this chapter, explain three different ways in which these two variables might be causally related. Be specific.

5.22 Reliability and romance: Aron, Fisher, Mashek, Strong, Li, and Brown (2005) found a correlation between intense romantic love [as assessed by the Passionate Love Scale (PLS)] and activation in a specific region of the brain [as assessed by functional magnetic resonance imaging (fMRI)]. The PLS (Hatfield & Sprecher, 1986) assesses the intensity of romantic love by asking people in romantic relationships to respond to a series of questions about their partners, such as "I want _____ physically, emotionally, and mentally" and "Sometimes I can't control my thoughts; they are obsessively on _____."

a. How might we examine the reliability of this measure using test–retest reliability techniques? Be specific and explain the role of correlation.

b. Would test–retest reliability be appropriate for this measure? That is, is there likely to be an order effect? Explain.

c. How might we examine the reliability of this measure using split-half reliability? Be specific and explain the role of correlation.

d. Why is split-half reliability rarely used now?

e. How might we examine the reliability of this measure using coefficient alpha? Be specific and explain the role of correlation.

f. Coefficient alpha in this study was 0.81. Based on coefficient alpha, was the use of this scale in this study warranted? Explain.

5.23 Validity and romance: Refer to the PLS, described in Exercise 5.22.

a. What is the construct that this measure is trying to assess?

b. What would it mean for this measure to be valid? Be specific.

c. How might we assess the postdictive validity of this test? Be specific, and explain the role of correlation. Note that there are many possible criteria that could be used in this analysis.

d. How might we assess the concurrent validity of this test? Be specific, and explain the role of correlation. Note that there are many possible criteria that could be used in this analysis.

e. How might we assess the predictive validity of this test? Be specific, and explain the role of correlation. Note that there are many possible criteria that could be used in this analysis.

5.24 Reliability, validity, and holiday weight gain: The *Wall Street Journal* reported on a study of holiday weight gain (Parker-Pope, 2005). Researchers assessed weight gain by asking individuals how much weight they typically gain in the fall and winter. The average answer was 2.3 kilograms. But a study of actual weight gain over this period found that people gained, on average, 0.48 kilogram.

a. Is the method of asking individuals about their weight gain likely to be reliable? Explain.

b. Is the method of asking individuals about their weight gain likely to be valid? Explain.

5.25 Validity and Brownie the cow: New York State's fourth-grade English exam led to an outcry by parents because of a question that was perceived as an unfair measure of fourth graders' performance. Students read a story, "Why the Rooster Crows at Dawn," that described an arrogant rooster who claims to be king, and Brownie, "the kindest of all the cows," who eventually acts in a mean way toward the rooster. In the beginning the rooster does whatever he wants, but by the end, the cows, led by Brownie, have convinced him that as self-proclaimed king, he must be the first to wake up in the morning and the last to go to sleep; to the cows' delight, the arrogant rooster complies. Students were then asked to respond to several questions about the story, including one that asked: "What causes Brownie's behavior to change?" Several parents started a Web site—http://browniethecow.org—to point out problems with the test, particularly with this question. Students, they argued, were confused because it seemed that it was the rooster's behavior, not the cow's behavior, that changes. The correct answer, according to a quote on the Web site from an unnamed state official, was that the cow started out kind and ended up mean.

a. This test item was supposed to evaluate writing skill. According to the Web site, test items should lead to good student writing; be unambiguous; test for writing, not another skill; and allow for objective, reliable scoring. If students were marked down for talking about the rooster, not the cow, as alleged by the Web site, would the test item meet these criteria? Explain. Does this seem to be a valid question? Explain.

b. Psychometricians must carefully consider what constitute the appropriate criteria when estimating the three types of criterion-related validity. The item about Brownie the cow is from a test that is supposed to assess writing skills. Describe one specific criterion that could be used to estimate the postdictive validity of the test that includes this item.

c. Describe one specific criterion that could be used to estimate the concurrent validity of the test.

d. Describe one specific criterion that could be used to estimate the predictive validity of the test.

e. The Web site states that New York City schools use the tests to, among other things, evaluate teachers and principals. The logic behind this, ostensibly, is that good teachers and administrators cause higher test performance. List at least two possible third variables that might lead to better performance in some schools than in other schools, and also might lead to the presence of good teachers and administrators.

5.26 The language of statistics—*reliable:* Describe how the word *reliable* is used in everyday language. Then describe how the word is used in statistics.

5.27 The language of statistics—*valid:* Describe how the word *valid* is used in everyday language. Then describe how the word is used in statistics.

▪ DIGGING DEEPER INTO THE DATA

5.28 Partial correlation: Exercise 5.13 described a study that explored the relation between psychology students' ratings of their likelihood of attending graduate school and the number of credits they had completed in their psychology major (Rajecki, 1998). The researcher found a moderate negative correlation of −0.27.

a. What third variables might be affecting the relation between likelihood of attending graduate school and number of psychology credits completed? Describe at least two possible third variables, and explain their possible role in the relation.

b. Why would partial correlation help us to ascertain the relation between likelihood of attending graduate school and number of psychology credits completed, over and above one of the third variables you listed in part (a)?

5.29 Partial correlation: Exercise 5.7 introduced a study by Nolan, Flynn, and Garber (2003) that examined the relation between externalizing behaviors (acting out) and anxiety in adolescents. Depression has been shown to relate to both of these variables. What role might depression play in the observed positive relation between these variables? The accompanying correlation matrix displays the Pearson correlation coefficients, as calculated by computer software, for each pair of the variables of interest: depression, externalizing, and anxiety. The Pearson correlation coefficients for each pair of variables are at the intersection in the chart of the two variables. For example, the correlation coefficient for the association between depression (top row) and externalizing (second column of correlations) is 0.635, a very strong positive correlation.

Correlations

		Depression	Externalizing	Anxiety
Depression	Pearson Correlation	1	.635(**)	.368(**)
	Sig. (2-tailed)		.000	.000
	N	220	219	207
Externalizing	Pearson Correlation	.635(**)	1	.356(**)
	Sig. (2-tailed)	.000		.000
	N	219	220	207
Anxiety	Pearson Correlation	.368(**)	.356(**)	1
	Sig. (2-tailed)	.000	.000	
	N	207	207	207

** Correlation is significant at the 0.01 level (2-tailed).

a. What is the correlation coefficient for the association between depression and anxiety? Explain what this correlation coefficient tells us about the relation between these variables.

b. What is the correlation coefficient for the association between anxiety and externalizing? Explain what this correlation coefficient tells us about the relation between these variables.

c. The partial correlation of anxiety and externalizing is 0.17, controlling for the variable of depression. How is this different from the original Pearson correlation coefficient between these two variables?

d. Why is it the partial correlation coefficient different from the original Pearson correlation coefficient between these two variables? What did we learn by calculating a partial correlation?

TERMS

---

z score (p. 207)

correlation coefficient (p. 211)

positive correlation (p. 212)

negative correlation (p. 212)

Pearson correlation
 coefficient (p. 222)

outlier analysis (p. 229)

outlier (p. 229)

psychometrics (p. 232)

psychometricians (p. 232)

split-half reliability (p. 233)

coefficient alpha (p. 233)

criterion-related validity
 (p. 234)

postdictive validity (p. 234)

concurrent validity (p. 234)

partial correlation (p. 236)

SYMBOLS

---

z

r

ρ

α

FORMULAS

$$z = \frac{(X - \mu)}{\sigma}$$

$$r = \frac{\sum[(z_X)(z_Y)]}{N}$$

REGRESSION
TOOLS FOR PREDICTING BEHAVIOR

Charles had only one small piece of evidence and a theory. Nevertheless, he was convinced that there must be an unknown lover, and he was right. But the confirming evidence for their clandestine meetings would not be discovered for 41 years—20 years after Charles's death. Nevertheless, Charles's solitary observation allowed him to imagine how it all probably began. The unnamed lover would hover in the darkness until the object of its desire was correctly identified. Afterward, Charles predicted, the lover would withdraw and flit away. Charles had predicted their mutual needs, but that's all he had to go on: a single observation and a theory.

Is it the start of a romance novel or the power of prediction? Well, the statistical tool you will learn about in this chapter has the power to predict, and that is precisely what Charles was doing: predicting behavior. In this case, the impassioned lover is the Madagascar hawkmoth (*Xanthopan morgani praedicta*) and the object of its desire is the Madagascar star orchid. The last part of the moth's Latin name (*praedicta*) honors the prediction of this unusual moth's existence several decades before it was discovered. Its unusually long tongue, called the proboscis, was key to the courtship between flower and moth. And Charles is none other than Charles Darwin, who, along with his many other contributions to science, made enduring observations about the psychology of emotions indicated by facial expressions, including when we are able to mask our genuine emotions and when those emotions are likely to "leak" and tell others what we are really thinking. The theory, of course, is the theory of evolution by natural selection, and it made a stunningly precise prediction: Some late-night pollinator must exist to

Predicting the Length of a Tongue
The 11-inch depth of the nectary of the Madagascar star orchid led Darwin to predict that there must exist a moth with an 11-inch tongue.

guarantee the survival of one of nature's most beautiful orchids. Why? The Madagascar star orchid required an 11-inch tongue to reach its nectar. If it weren't attracting insects that (1) could reach that nectar and (2) in the process of drinking that nectar also rub their heads and bodies against the flower's pollen, then there was no hope of the orchid passing its genes into the next generation.

In a wonderfully clear example of co-evolution, Darwin predicted that moth and flower were using and changing one another to gain an evolutionary advantage in the contest for survival. A deepening nectary and a lengthening tongue made survival a little bit easier for each generation of blossoming flower and fluttering moth. Yet even Darwin agreed that the idea of an insect with an 11-inch tongue whose sole purpose was to gather nectar from this particular flower sounded ridiculous. "It is, however, surprising that any insect should be able to reach the nectar . . . in Madagascar there must be moths with prosboces capable of extension to a length of between ten and eleven inches!" (Darwin, 1877, p. 163; exclamation point in original).

The story of Darwin's orchid represents the use of statistics in its most productive and satisfying form: a clear theoretical context. A theoretical context becomes more important whenever we try to infer causality and predict behavior without the luxury of a controlled experiment. The experimental designs we described in Chapter 1 all hoped to achieve the same goal: to isolate causality within a relation between two or more variables. As we noted when discussing quasi-experiments, we cannot always randomly assign people (or other types of observations) to groups. We cannot, for example, study the psychological effects of surviving a category 5 hurricane by randomly assigning one group to live through such a hurricane and assigning the other group to live through a warm and pleasant summer. Nevertheless, psychologists need to predict the course of post-traumatic stress disorder in order to improve our understanding of and treatments for returning soldiers, rape victims, and individuals who have lost their homes and even their families to a natural disaster.

So what can we do to predict behavior more precisely when random assignment to groups simply isn't possible? First of all, think! We do this by using our own intuition, of course, but also by looking through the existing literature.

The Madagascar Moth
This long-tongued moth co-evolved with the Madagascar star orchid; each needed the other to survive.

Other great minds have probably asked the same research question we are try-ing to ask. Just as we hope that others will consider our ideas, we owe it to them and to plain old humility to read and consider others' ideas. So we should find out what theories and findings already predict responses to stress. We can ask whether these theoretical predictions would apply to returning soldiers as well as to victims of rape or of a natural disaster. Then we can devise a study and use statistics to test a theory that makes clear predictions. The outcome of that study will have one of three possible effects on what we believe. It will do one of the following:

1. Increase our confidence in the theory
2. Decrease our confidence in the theory
3. Lead us to modify the theory

The theory of natural selection made an astonishingly precise prediction: the existence of a moth with an 11-inch food-gathering appendage that was per-fectly designed to collect food from the Madagascar star orchid. As a social sci-ence major beginning to conduct your own research, you will save yourself a great deal of time if you can call on a sensible theory that specifies the outcomes you anticipate. A strong theory will give you something you can actually test. Like a reality television series that crowns the last surviving participant the win-ner, we start to attribute validity to any theory that is still standing after the on-slaught of scientific skepticism. As we demonstrated in the previous chapter, we can use correlation as a way to test the reliability and validity of our theories. But an even stronger way to test our ideas is by using correlation's more ma-ture sibling: regression. Regression is a statistical tool for predicting behavior.

➤ REGRESSION: BUILDING ON CORRELATION

Correlation is a marvelous tool that allows us to know the direction and strength of a relation between two variables. Yet correlation has another use. We can use a correlation coefficient to help us develop a formula, called a regression equa-tion, which allows for the prediction of an individual's score on the dependent variable from his or her score on the independent variable. The idea of using one variable to predict another variable is everywhere. Indeed, anytime we want to use data on one or more independent variables to predict scores on a de-pendent variable, we can use regression.

There are numerous real-life examples of regression. For example, just as Darwin used the depth of a flower to predict the length of a moth's tongue, many universities use regression equations to predict the success of prospective students. This regression equation includes variables such as high school grade-point aver-age (GPA) and SAT score as part of the admissions process. Similarly, insurance companies routinely use regression equations to predict the likelihood of a class of people (such as young, male drivers) to submit a claim. Do you remember what your insurance company representative asked when you applied for car insurance? Among the data he or she asked for were interval variables such as age, years of education, miles driven per year, age of the car, number of previous accidents, and number of previous traffic violations. The insurance industry is constantly looking for better predictors of who is likely to file claims, and it adjusts insur-ance premiums accordingly. But the person who answered your telephone call at

Regression and Car Insurance

When you call an insurance company for a car insurance estimate, the salesperson asks a number of questions about you (e.g., age, gender, marital status) and about your car (e.g., make, model, year, color). These characteristics are input into a type of regression equation; the output is your quote. A flashy, expensive car driven by a young, unmarried male leads to a higher quote than a basic sedan driven by a married 50-year-old woman.

the insurance company almost certainly wasn't aware of the regression equation lurking in her computer software. She entered your data, and up popped a quote for your insurance. An actuary (yet another lucrative job for statisticians!) developed the equation that resides, invisibly, on the computer.

If you like the idea of developing regression equations, you're in luck. People with statistical skills have numerous job opportunities. The magazine *Fast Company* (fastcompany.com) published a list of the top 25 jobs for 2005–2009 based on potential for growth, likely salary, necessary education, and opportunities to innovate ("The Top 25 Jobs," 2005). The list included a number of occupations that rely on statistical skills, particularly the ability to work with regression equations. *Personal financial advisors* help clients to predict how much money they will need for retirement; they focus on a range of independent variables (e.g., investment strategies, family obligations, age, health) to predict the dependent variable of the necessary retirement income. *Epidemiologists* track patterns of mental and physical health across populations; they help to make predictions from these patterns about childhood illnesses, the effects of new drugs, and flu epidemics. *Marketing managers* and *market research analysts* analyze trends to predict the future; a toy manufacturer needs that information to make the hot products for the holiday selling season. Similarly, *management analysts* use statistical tools to predict the circumstances under which a company is likely to show growth.

The FastCompany.com Web site also included *actuaries*, professionals who assess risk for institutions such as insurance companies, on its list. Although actuaries typically have a math or statistics degree, the Web site beanactuary.com encourages prospective actuaries to take courses in the social sciences "because actuaries are involved in a growing variety of social and political issues." The Web site notes that actuaries can earn as much as $100,000 a year within 10 years after starting their positions. Moreover, in keeping with our description of statisticians as storytellers, an actuary quoted on the site avows that "actuaries make a long story short through statistical analysis."

The Difference Between Regression and Correlation: Prediction Versus Relation

There is an increasing overlap between the topics studied by psychologists or sociologists and those studied by economists, particularly with respect to the influence of economic factors on behavior. For example, consider these questions that were asked recently by an economist (Ruhm, 2006). You live in the United States and the American economy is soaring: What do you predict will happen to the overall health of Americans? The American economy is tanking: Now what do you predict will happen to the overall health of Americans?

Regression—but not correlation—can provide specific quantitative information that predicts the relations between variables. More specifically, *simple linear regression is a statistical tool that enables us to predict an individual's score on the dependent variable from his or her score on one independent variable.* So we can use regression to discover how well the state of the American economy predicts health. Simple linear regression works by calculating the equation for a straight line; once we have a line, we can look at any point on the *x*-axis and find its

■ **Simple linear regression** is a statistical tool that enables us to predict an individual's score on the dependent variable from his or her score on one independent variable.

corresponding point on the *y*-axis. That corresponding point is what we'd predict for *y*. (Note that because simple linear regression helps us to determine the equation for a line, we must have data that are linearly related in order to use it—that is, the data must form an overall pattern through which it would make sense to draw a straight line. Like the Pearson correlation coefficient, simple linear regression would not be used if our data are related in some other way— for example, if the pattern of data forms a curve rather than a straight line.) We will consider an example of research that uses regression techniques, and then we'll walk through the steps to develop a regression equation.

Christopher Ruhm, an economist, often uses regression in his research. In recent research, Ruhm wanted to explore the reasons for his own previous finding (Ruhm, 2000) that the death rate *decreases* when unemployment goes up— a surprising negative relation between the death rate and an economic indicator. He took this relation a step further, into the realm of prediction: He found that an increase of 1% in unemployment predicted a decrease in the death rate of 0.5%, on average. A *poorer* economy predicted *better* health! It is a surprising finding, so Ruhm (2006) set out to explore the reasons for this negative relation between the economy and health.

Ruhm conducted regression analyses for independent variables related to health (smoking, obesity, and physical activity) and dependent variables related to the economy (income, unemployment, and the length of the work week). He analyzed data from a sample of nearly 1.5 million participants collected from telephone surveys between 1987 and 2000. Among other things, Ruhm found that a decrease in working hours predicted decreases in smoking, obesity, and physical inactivity. But all of these relations could have been identified by correlation alone. Regression can take us a step further.

Regression, like correlation, helps us ask better questions. However, regression—but not correlation—can provide specific quantitative predictions that more precisely explain relations among variables. For example, Ruhm reported that a decrease in the work week of just one hour predicted a 1% decrease in physical inactivity. So, to explain why the number of working hours predicts one's level of physical inactivity, Ruhm suggested that shorter working hours free up time for physical activity—something he might not have thought of without the more specific quantitative information provided by regression. Ruhm also noted, however, that economic decline is related to *increases* in mental health problems. So don't rush out to cut back on your hours at work, refuse a pay raise, or quit your job. Regression helps us unravel these more complicated stories. But remember, it's the stories about human behavior that are complicated, not the statistics that clarify and tell those stories. So let's develop our storytelling skills by calculating a simple linear regression using information that we're already familiar with: *z* scores.

Linear Regression: Calculating the Equation for a Line using *z* Scores Only

It is easier to predict the location of anything when it is moving along a straight line. A car driving straight across 100 miles of the flatlands of west Texas is easier to find than a car winding its way through 100 miles of the Blue Ridge Mountains of Virginia. It is also easier to predict more abstract variables when they move along a straight line. To make such straight-line (linear) predictions, we use the correlation coefficient that we just learned about in Chapter 5. The sign of the correlation coefficient is either positive (indicating a line that is moving upward and to the right) or negative (indicating a line that is moving downward and to the right). The number of the correlation coefficient (from -1 to $+1$) tells us how tightly bunched the scores are around that straight line.

For example, in Chapter 5 we calculated a Pearson correlation coefficient to quantify the relation between students' number of absences from statistics class and their mean statistics exam grade; the data for the 10 students in the sample are shown in Table 6-1. The Pearson correlation coefficient that we calculated in Chapter 5 was -0.85, an indication of a strong negative relation between the two variables. Now simple linear regression can take us a step further. We can develop an equation to predict students' mean exam grades from their numbers of absences. In other words, regression allows us to use one piece of information to make predictions about something else.

Let's say that a student (let's call him Skip) walks in on the first day of class and announces that, for a variety of complicated reasons, he intends to skip five classes. What is the most sensible way to predict Skip's average exam grade? Without knowing that Skip intends to miss five classes, the best way to predict his grade is by averaging everyone else's grade in previous classes: 76.00. But now let's imagine the same situation in relation to a regression equation. We no longer have to use the class average as our most sensible predictor of Skip's grade. Now we can refer to the size and direction of the correlation as our benchmark. If most class members miss fewer classes than Skip, we can anticipate that they will score higher than Skip, and vice versa.

So now we can unite regression with a statistic you are more familiar with: z scores. We can use a z score version of this same data set to predict what grade another student (let's call her Allie) is most likely to earn. First, we have to figure out Allie's z score. Then we multiply that z score by the correlation coefficient to get her predicted z score on mean exam grade. Finally, we transpose that z score back into a raw score representing exam scores and make our specific prediction. The formula is straightforward: $z_{\hat{Y}} = (r_{XY})(z_X)$, but it has some new features you need to learn. So let's explain the formula one letter at a time.

Formula: $z_{\hat{Y}} = (r_{XY})(z_X)$

TABLE 6-1. IS SKIPPING CLASS RELATED TO EXAM GRADES?

Here are the scores for 10 students on two interval variables, number of absences from class in one semester and the mean exam grade for that semester. The correlation between these variables is -0.85, but regression can take us a step further. We can develop a regression equation to assist with prediction.

STUDENT	ABSENCES	MEAN EXAM GRADE
1	4	82
2	2	98
3	2	76
4	3	68
5	1	84
6	0	99
7	4	67
8	8	58
9	7	50
10	3	78

The subscripts indicate that the first z score in the formula is for the dependent variable, Y, and that the second z score in the formula is for the independent variable, X. The ^ symbol over the subscript Y, called a "hat" by statisticians, refers to the fact that this variable is predicted; this is the z score for "Y hat"— the z score for the *predicted* score on the dependent variable, not the actual score. We cannot, of course, predict the actual score, and the "hat" reminds us of this. When we refer to this score, we can either say "the predicted score for Y" (with no hat, because we have specified with our words that it is predicted) or we can use the hat, $\hat{Y}$, to indicate that it is predicted. Either way of expressing that the letter Y is a predicted score is fine—the important thing is to remember that it is only that—a prediction. (We would not use both expressions because that would be redundant.)

Let's see how this formula works. If Allie's projected number of absences were identical to the mean number of absences for the entire class, then she'd have a z score of 0; if we multiply that by the correlation coefficient, then she'd have a predicted z score of 0 for mean exam grade: $z_{\hat{Y}} = (-0.85)(0) = 0$. So if she's right at the mean on the independent variable, then we'd predict that she'd be right at the mean on the dependent variable. Keep in mind that a z score is the same as a raw score except that it has been standardized around a mean of 0. So a raw score that is higher than the mean will correspond to a z score that is greater than 0. And a raw score that is lower than the mean will correspond to a z score that is less than 0. In other words, Allie's predicted z score will always fall on the same side of the mean as her raw score. The correlation coefficient helps us to determine how many standard deviations a raw score is from the line that is doing the predicting.

If Allie had a z score of 1.0 on the independent variable, then her predicted score on the dependent variable would be -0.85 because $z_{\hat{Y}} = (-0.85)(1) = -0.85$. If her z score were -2, her predicted score on the dependent variable would be 1.7: $z_{\hat{Y}} = (-0.85)(-2) = 1.7$. Notice that in both cases, the predicted z score on the dependent variable is closer to its mean than is the z score on the independent variable. Table 6-2 demonstrates this for several z scores. In other words, the score on the independent variable is actually predicting the score on the dependent variable; moreover, it is predicting the score on the dependent variable to be less extreme than is its corresponding score in the independent variable. This regressing of the dependent variable—the fact that it is closer to its

Symbols: $\hat{Y}$

TABLE 6-2. **REGRESSION TO THE MEAN**

One reason that regression equations are so named is because they predict a z score on the dependent variable that is closer to the mean than is the z score on the independent variable. This phenomenon is often called regression to the mean. The following predicted z scores for the dependent variable, Y, were calculated by multiplying the z score for the independent variable, X, by the Pearson correlation coefficient of -0.85.

z SCORE FOR THE INDEPENDENT VARIABLE, X	PREDICTED z SCORE FOR THE DEPENDENT VARIABLE, Y
-2.0	1.70
-1.0	0.85
0.0	0.00
1.0	-0.85
2.0	-1.70

▪ **Regression to the mean** is the tendency of scores that are particularly high or low to drift toward the mean over time.

mean—is called regression to the mean. *Regression to the mean is the tendency of scores that are particularly high or low to drift toward the mean over time.* In the social sciences, there are many phenomena that demonstrate regression to the mean; for example, parents who are very tall tend to have children who are shorter than they are, although probably still above average. And parents who are very short tend to have children who are taller than they are, although probably still below average. We'll explore this concept in more detail later in this chapter.

Reversing the Formula: Transforming z Scores to Raw Scores

In each example above, we predicted one z score from another z score, but we usually don't start with a z score. More typically, we want to predict one raw score from another raw score. To do this using the z score formula, we first have to convert a raw score on one variable to a z score. We then predict a z score for the second variable. Finally, we convert the z score for the second variable to a raw score. To complete this last step, we need to learn a little more about z scores.

In Chapter 5, we learned how to convert a raw score to a z score, but z scores and z distributions are incredibly versatile tools. If we already know a z score, then we can reverse our calculations to determine the raw score. The formula is the same; we just plug in all the numbers instead of the X, then solve algebraically. Let's try it. We'll use the mean and standard deviation for height that we used in Chapter 5. Remember that the mean for the population is 64.886, with a standard deviation of 4.086. So, if you had a z score of 1.79, what is your height?

$$z = \frac{(X - M)}{\sigma} \qquad 1.79 = \frac{(X - 64.886)}{4.086}$$

If we solve for X, we get 72.20. For those of you who prefer to minimize your use of algebra, we can simply do the algebra on the equation itself to derive a formula that gets the raw score directly. The following formula was derived by multiplying both sides of the equation by σ, then adding μ to both sides of the equation. That isolates the X, as follows: $X = z(\sigma) + \mu$. Let's try the same problem using this direct formula: $X = 1.79(4.086) + 64.886 = 72.20$. Regardless of whether we used the original formula or the direct formula, the height would be 72.20 inches. As always, think about whether the answer seems accurate. In this case, the answer does make sense because the height is above the mean, and the z score is positive.

What if your z score were -0.44? $X = -0.44(4.086) + 64.886 = 63.09$. Your height would be 63.09 inches. Don't forget the negative sign when doing this calculation or your answer will be way off. In this case, a consideration of whether the answer makes sense would catch this. Here, we know the height is below the mean because the z score is negative.

As long as we know the mean and standard deviation of the population, we can do two things: (1) calculate the raw score from its z score and (2) calculate the z score from its raw score.

Formulas: The formula to calculate the raw score from a z score is $X = z(\sigma) + \mu$.

Linear Regression: Calculating the Equation for a Line by Converting Raw Scores to z Scores

Using the additional information about z scores, we can now use the z score formula to predict one raw score from another raw score. Let's say that Allie plans to skip two classes. What would we predict for her mean exam grade for the semester? To use our formula, we first have to know her z score on the independent variable of number of absences. Using the mean (3.400) and the standard deviation (2.375) that we calculated in Chapter 5, we calculate: $z_X = \dfrac{(X - M_X)}{SD_X} = \dfrac{(2 - 3.400)}{2.375} = -0.589$. We can now multiply this z score by the correlation coefficient to get her predicted z score on the dependent variable, mean exam grade: $z_{\hat{Y}} = (-0.85)(-0.589) = 0.500$. Allie's number of absences was -0.589 standard deviation below the mean (that is, Allie attended class a little more often than the class average); so we predict that her mean exam grade will be 0.500, or one-half, standard deviation above the mean. The latter z score is closer to the mean; it has regressed in magnitude of standard deviations from the mean. But what would we predict for her raw score on mean exam grade? We now must convert from the z score on Y, 0.500, to a raw score for Y: $\hat{Y} = z_{\hat{Y}}$ $(SD_Y) + M_Y = 0.500(15.040) + 76.000 = 83.52$. (Note that we use the "hat" symbol, ˆ, to indicate that the raw score, Y, is predicted.) If Allie skipped two classes, that would be fewer classes than the typical students skipped, so we would expect that she would earn a higher grade. And the formula makes that very prediction—that Allie's mean exam grade would be 83.52, which is higher than the mean (76.00).

The admissions counselor and the insurance salesperson, however, are unlikely to have the time or interest to do conversions from raw scores to z scores and back. So the z score regression equation is not useful in a practical sense; however, it is useful for you to recognize that the bell-shaped curve and the standardization it makes possible are busy working their magic underneath all those raw-score, numerical observations. We need a raw-score regression equation so that we can input 2 for Allie's number of absences and get the output 83.52 for Allie's predicted mean exam grade.

Linear Regression: Calculating the Equation for a Line with Raw Scores

You may remember the equation for a line that you learned in your high school geometry class. The version you likely learned was: $y = m(x) + b$. (In this equation, b is the intercept and m is the slope.) In statistics, we use a slightly different version of this formula: $\hat{Y} = a + b(X)$. a is *the **intercept**, the predicted value for Y when X is equal to 0, which is the point at which the line crosses, or intercepts, the y-axis.* In Figure 6-1, the intercept is 5. *The **slope** is the amount that Y is predicted to increase for an increase of 1 in X.* In Figure 6-1, the slope is 2. As X increases from 3 to 4, for example we see an increase in

> ▪ The **intercept** is the predicted value for Y when X is equal to 0, which is the point at which the line crosses, or intercepts, the y-axis.
>
> ▪ The **slope** is the amount that Y is predicted to increase for an increase of 1 in X.

> Formulas: $\hat{Y} = a + b(X)$
>
> Symbols: a
>
> Symbols: b

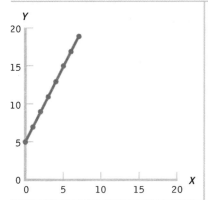

FIGURE 6-1
The Equation for a Line

The equation for a line includes the intercept, the point at which the line crosses the y-axis; here the intercept is 5. It also includes the slope, the amount that $\hat{Y}$ increases for an increase of 1 in X. Here, the slope is 2. The equation, therefore, is: $\hat{Y} = 5 + 2(X)$.

what we predict for Y of 2: from 11 to 13. The equation, therefore, is: $\hat{Y} = 5 + 2(X)$. If the score on X is 8, for example, the predicted score for Y is: $\hat{Y} = 5 + 2(8) = 5 + 16 = 21$. We can verify this on the line in Figure 6-1. Here, we were given the regression equation and regression line, but usually we have to determine these from our data. In this section, we'll learn the process of calculating a regression equation from data.

Once we have the equation for a line, it's easy to input any value for X to determine our predicted value for Y. If we had a regression equation, then we could input Allie's score of z on X and find her predicted score on Y. But first we have to develop the regression equation. And for this, we use the z score regression equation: $z_{\hat{Y}} = (r_{XY})(z_X)$. Using the z score regression equation to find the intercept and slope enables us to "see" where these numbers come from in a way that makes sense (Aron & Aron, 2002).

We start by calculating a, the intercept. We know that the intercept is the point at which the line crosses the y-axis when X is equal to 0. So we'll start by finding the z score for X.

$$z_X = \frac{(X - M_X)}{SD_X} = \frac{(0 - 3.400)}{2.375} = -1.432$$

We can then use the z score regression equation to calculate the predicted score on Y:

$$z_{\hat{Y}} = (r_{XY})(z_X) = (-0.85)(-1.432) = 1.217$$

Now we'll convert the z score for $\hat{Y}$ to its raw score:

$$\hat{Y} = z_{\hat{Y}}(SD_Y) + M_Y = 1.217(15.040) + 76.000 = 94.304$$

We have our intercept! When X is 0, $\hat{Y}$ is 94.30. That is, we would predict that someone who never misses class would earn a mean exam grade of 94.30. Let's summarize the three steps to calculate the intercept.

1. Calculate the z score for an X of 0: $z_X = \dfrac{(X - M_X)}{SD_X}$.

2. Using the z score regression equation, calculate the z score for Y that would be predicted from the z score from step 1: $z_{\hat{Y}} = (r_{XY})(z_X)$.

3. Calculate the raw score for the z score from step 2: $\hat{Y} = z_{\hat{Y}}(SD_Y) + M_Y$.

Now, we'll calculate our slope. We know that the slope is the amount that $\hat{Y}$ increases when X increases by 1. So all we need to do is calculate what we would predict for an X of 1. We can then compare our $\hat{Y}$ for an X of 0 to the $\hat{Y}$ for an X of 1. The difference between the two is the slope. So first, we'll find the z score for an X of 1:

$$z_X = \frac{(X - M_X)}{SD_X} = \frac{(1 - 3.400)}{2.375} = -1.011$$

We can then use the z score regression equation to calculate the predicted score on Y:

$$z_{\hat{Y}} = (r_{XY})(z_X) = (-0.85)(-1.011) = 0.859$$

Now we'll convert the z score for $\hat{Y}$ to its raw score:

$$\hat{Y} = z_{\hat{Y}}(SD_Y) + M_Y = 0.859(15.040) + 76.000 = 88.919$$

We would predict that a student who misses one class would achieve a mean exam grade of 88.919. As X, number of absences, increased from 0 to 1, what happened to $\hat{Y}$? First, ask yourself if it increased or decreased. An increase would mean a positive slope, and a decrease would mean a negative slope. Here, we saw a decrease in grade as number of absences increased. Next, determine how much it increased or decreased. In this case, we saw a decrease of 5.385: $94.304 - 88.919 = 5.385$. The slope here is: -5.39.

We now have our intercept and our slope and can put them into the equation: $\hat{Y} = a + b(X)$ becomes $\hat{Y} = 94.30 - 5.39(X)$. These are the four steps to determine the slope. Notice that the first three steps are identical to those for determining the intercept, except that we're now using an X of 1 instead of an X of 0.

1. Calculate the z score for an X of 1: $z_X = \dfrac{(X - M_X)}{SD_X}$.

2. Using the z score regression equation, calculate the z score for $\hat{Y}$ that would be predicted from the z score from step 1: $z_{\hat{Y}} = (r_{XY})(z_X)$.

3. Calculate the raw score for the z score from step 2: $\hat{Y} = z_{\hat{Y}}(SD_Y) + M_Y$.

4. Determine the change in $\hat{Y}$ as X increased from 0 to 1. Be sure to include the appropriate sign based on whether there was an increase or decrease in $\hat{Y}$.

We can now use our equation to predict Allie's mean exam grade based on her number of absences, two. $\hat{Y} = 94.30 - 5.39(X) = 94.30 - 5.39(2) = 83.52$. Based on the data from our statistics classes, we would predict that Allie would earn a mean exam grade of 83.52 if she skipped two classes. Notice that this is exactly what we predicted for Allie based on the z score regression equation. The difference is that now we can input any score into the raw-score regression equation, and it does all the work of converting for us. The admissions counselor, insurance salesperson, or bookie has an easy formula and doesn't have to know z scores. They only have to know how to enter the appropriate number in the computer. It takes social science majors with training in human behavior and statistics to understand that a regression equation underlies the predictions they use to maximize their profits.

In addition to plugging in a score on X to find a predicted score on Y, we also can draw our regression line to get a visual sense of what it looks like. We do that by calculating two points on the regression line, usually for one low score on X and one high score on X. We will always have $\hat{Y}$ for two scores, 0 and 1 (although in some cases these numbers won't make sense, such as for the variable of human body temperature; you'd never have a temperature that low!). These scores are low on the scale for number of absences. So we'll choose a high score as well; 8 is the highest score in our original data set, so we'll use that: $\hat{Y} = 94.30 - 5.39(X) = \hat{Y}$ $94.30 - 5.39(8) = 51.18$. For someone who skipped eight classes, we would predict a mean exam grade of 51.18. We now have three points, as shown in Table 6-3. It's useful to have three points; the third point serves as a check on the other two. If the three points do not fall in a straight line, we have made an error. (Note that 0 or 1 are not always useful as the low score, particularly if these numbers are far outside the range of values for X.)

TABLE 6-3. DRAWING A REGRESSION LINE

We calculate at least two, and preferably three, pairs of scores for X and $\hat{Y}$. Ideally, at least one is low on the scale for X and at least one is high.

X	$\hat{Y}$
0	94.30
1	88.92
8	51.18

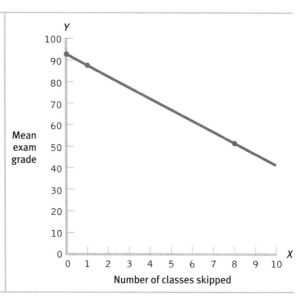

FIGURE 6-2
The Regression Line

To draw a regression line, we plot at least two, and preferably three, pairs of scores for X and $\hat{Y}$. We then draw a line through the dots.

We can now plot these three pairs of points, as seen in Figure 6-2, just as we would on a scatterplot. We then draw a line through the dots, but it's not just any line. This line is our regression line, and the regression line has another name that is wonderfully intuitive: the line of best fit. If you have ever had some clothes tailored to your particular body, perhaps for your wedding or some other really special occasion, then you know that there really is such a thing as a "best fit." There is nothing the tailor could do to make those clothes fit you any better.

The meaning of the line of best fit in regression has the same characteristic as a tailored set of clothes. We couldn't make the line a little steeper, raise it, or lower it in any way that would allow it to represent those dots any better than it already does. That is why we can look at the scatterplot around this line in Figure 6-3 and observe that the line goes precisely through the middle of the dots. This is why statisticians also call the regression line the line of best fit. Statistically, this is the line that leads to the least amount of error in prediction.

The Line of Best Fit
The line of best fit in regression has the same characteristics as tailored clothes; there is nothing we could do to that line that would make it fit those dots any better.

Notice that the negative slope means that the line we just drew starts in the upper left of the graph and ends in the lower right. Think of the word *slope*, often used when discussing, say, ski slopes. A negative slope means that the line looks like it's going downhill as we move from left to right. This makes sense because the calculations for the regression equation are based on the correlation coefficient, and the scatterplot associated with a negative correlation coefficient has dots that also go "downhill." If the slope were positive, the line would start in the lower left of the graph and end in the upper right. A positive slope means that the line looks like it's going uphill as we move from left to right. Again, this makes sense, because we base the calculations on a positive correlation coefficient, and the scatterplot associated with a positive correlation coefficient has dots that also go "uphill."

In summary, regression is a useful tool that builds on correlation; it enables us not only to quantify the relation between two variables but also to predict a score on a dependent variable from a score on an independent variable. With the z score regression equation, we simply multiply an individual's z score on an independent variable by the Pearson correlation coefficient to predict that individual's z score on a dependent variable. We can use the z score formula to convert a raw score on one variable to a z score. We then

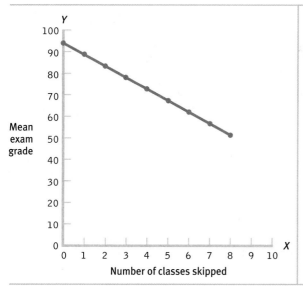

FIGURE 6-3
The Line of Best Fit

The regression line is the line that best fits the points on our scatterplot. Statistically, the regression line is the line that leads to the least amount of error in prediction.

input this z score in the z score regression equation to predict a z score on a second variable. We use the z score formula in reverse to convert the z score on the second variable to a raw score. The raw-score regression equation is easier to use in that the equation itself does the transformations from raw score to z score and back. This equation is the same one you learned back in geometry class—the equation for a line. We can use it to predict Y for any value of X. We can also graph the regression line, remembering that it is well named as the line of best fit. So now we can understand the same idea of one variable predicting another in three different ways: conceptually, symbolically, and visually.

⊙ CHECK YOUR LEARNING

6-1 Check Your Learning 5-2 asked you to calculate the Pearson correlation coefficient for the data in the accompanying table. The correlation coefficient between age and number of hours studied per week was 0.49. The mean for age was 21, and the standard deviation was 1.789. The mean for hours studied was 14.2, and the standard deviation was 5.582. Now determine the regression equation based on these data.

STUDENT	AGE	NUMBER OF HOURS STUDIED (PER WEEK)
1	19	5
2	20	20
3	20	8
4	21	12
5	21	18
6	23	25
7	22	15
8	20	10
9	19	14
10	25	15

> DRAWING CONCLUSIONS FROM A REGRESSION EQUATION: INTERPRETATION AND PREDICTION

Charles Darwin never could have made his famously precise prediction about the existence of the hawkmoth based on theory alone; he needed evidence. And the one piece of evidence he had was the existence of this peculiar star orchid that hid its nectar up to 11 inches deep within the flower. In other words, Darwin was using a particular value of one variable (the depth of the nectar buried deep within the star orchid) to predict a particular value of another variable (the length of the tongue of a moth he had never encountered). Darwin predicted an 11-inch tongue based on his observation of the depth of the star orchid's nectary. If he had observed a flower with a 13-inch nectary, he would have predicted a moth with a 13-inch tongue; if had observed a flower with a 17-inch nectary, he would have predicted a moth with a 17-inch tongue. In fact, this is one of the few real-life examples of an almost perfect correlation! Every pair of scores for depth of nectary and length of tongue would fall almost exactly on the regression line. What we teach today as statistical regression, Charles Darwin was doing spontaneously by using his scientific common sense: using a particular value of one variable to predict a particular value of another variable.

Notice how the logic of regression guided Darwin to think about evolution through natural selection. Darwin's evidence predicted the existence of a bizarre-looking moth, but Darwin also gathered evidence on other topics and from other species—from bird life, the famous Galápagos tortoises, and many other sources. Darwin used the logic of regression to predict the larger story that thousands of small pieces of evidence were telling: the theory of evolution through natural selection. So once again, we see that statistics offers us a way of reaching conclusions whose effect goes far beyond plugging information into a formula to get a quote on your car insurance.

Regression is usually a more powerful tool than correlation and is widely used across many different applications. So we'll use this next section to demonstrate first how the logic of regression is already a part of your everyday reasoning, just as it is in the process of scientific discovery. We will also address whether regression allows us to use the word and the idea of causation as we interpret our data. This will naturally lead us to a familiar caution about interpreting the meaning of regression, this time due to the naturally occurring process called regression to the mean. Finally, we'll learn how to calculate effect sizes so we can make appropriate interpretations of how good a job our regression equation is doing at predicting behavior. Chapter 5 demonstrated how cautious Dean and Kelly were when reaching conclusions about astrology, even when all the available, carefully collected evidence provided no support for its validity. Statistical reasoning requires that we remain just as cautious when interpreting the results of regression as Dean and Kelly were about correlation.

Charles Darwin, Naturalist
Charles Darwin gathered thousands of small bits of evidence before he became convinced that they were all telling the same story: the theory of evolution through natural selection.

Hulton-Deutsch Collection/Corbis

Regression: Quantifying Common Sense

Regression analysis is simply a formalized, numerical expression that can quantify scientific common sense. In fact, we all use similar reasoning whenever we use our limited knowledge to make predictions. For example, one of the authors recently had to rent storage space for some furniture. Regression helps us to predict the annual cost of storage, and we don't need a formula to do it. To begin with, the storage space company had a one-time fee of $25. This fixed cost corresponds to a in our regression formula. Now let's say that the ongoing monthly fee is about $200. This is also entered as a fixed cost and corresponds to b in our regression formula. In order to predict the annual costs from the monthly costs, it was only necessary to multiply b by 12 months of the year, a number that corresponds to X in our regression formula. So $\hat{Y}$ (the annual cost of storage) could be predicted by bX ($200 × 12 months) plus a (the annual fixed cost of $25). That is, $\hat{Y} = bX + a = (200)(12) + 25 = \$2425$.

So now, it would appear, we are equipped to estimate the annual cost from the monthly cost. Because the regression line that predicts these costs is a straight line (linear regression), we can also predict the cost of a 7-month storage, an 11-month storage, or a 29-month storage simply by substituting the appropriate number of months (7, 11, or 29) for the number 12. As a student, you also reason spontaneously using a statistical regression when you estimate the cost of textbooks and supplies for the year, when you budget for food expenses, and even when you try to predict the course of a romantic relationship. You use the information you know to make predictions about your future. But how good are we, really, at predicting the future? Well, it turns out that Darwin was better at predicting the length of an undiscovered moth's tongue than one of the authors was at predicting annual storage costs!

In reality, the prediction of annual costs for storing furniture was inaccurate. It was close, but not perfect. Why? First, someone in the family lost the keys, and that meant we needed to cut off the old lock and purchase a new one. Then the storage facility raised its prices. There are other, similar sources of error in your own estimates. Perhaps you overestimated the cost of supplies for an art class; perhaps you underestimated the cost of one of your textbooks and then lost another. Perhaps you were naively predicting that the wonderfulness of your romantic relationship would remain as fresh and invigorating over an entire year as it had been for the first month.

For many different reasons, our predictions are full of errors, and that, too, is factored into the regression analysis. Statistically speaking, such errors lead directly back to our old friend variability, who also goes by the nicknames of standard deviation and standard error. But this time, we are concerned with variability around the line of best fit rather than variability around the mean. As you might expect, data points that are closely clustered around the line of best fit are said to have very little variance. We enjoy a high level of confidence in the predictive ability of our independent variable when the data points are tightly clustered around the line of best fit, as in Figure 6-4a. And we have a low level of confidence in the predictive ability of our independent variable when the data points vary widely around the line of best fit, as in Figure 6-4b. The number that describes how far away, on average, the data points are from the line of best fit is called *the **standard error of the estimate**, a statistic indicating the typical distance between a regression line and the actual data points.* The standard error of the estimate is essentially the standard deviation of the actual data points around the regression line.

▪ The **standard error of the estimate** is a statistic indicating the typical distance between a regression line and the actual data points.

FIGURE 6-4
The Standard Error of the Estimate

Data points clustered closely around the line of best fit as in graph (a), are described by a small standard error of the estimate. Data points clustered far away from the line of best fit as in graph (b), are described by a large standard error of the estimate.

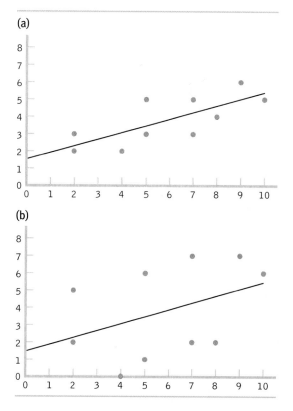

CREATING A CAREER IN HEALTH PSYCHOLOGY

Here's why Charles Darwin continues to create meaningful employment opportunities for behavioral science majors: We currently need a small army of public health specialists who can use the regression equation to test and discover interventions that lead to more compliance regarding the use of antibiotics or treatments for diabetes, increased safe behaviors regarding sexually transmitted diseases or other behavioral threats to public health. We also need people who can apply the principles of prediction, as well as the tools of persuasion from social and organizational psychology, to change the behavior of thousands of doctors and millions of patients. Are you interested in saving lives through the social sciences? You can prepare yourself through graduate programs in health psychology, applied social or organizational psychology, public health, or epidemiology. Here's an example of a very serious problem we are facing in behavioral health: the overprescription and misuse of antibiotics.

Solving this behavioral health problem requires an understanding of Darwin's theory of evolution through natural selection. We all know that antibiotics are wonderful. Strep throat used to kill people, regularly. So did pneumonia, syphilis, gonorrhea, wounds that became infected, scarlet fever, and many other infectious diseases. But then, in 1929, Alexander Fleming was cleaning up his workspace and about to discard a petri dish so old that it was growing its own mold. But before he threw it out, Fleming noticed that the bacteria surrounding the mold had died. Starting with penicillin, that simple observation opened the gate to medical interventions that have increased life expectancy for people living in the United States by 29 years! Omilusik (2007) reported that the decline in deaths by infectious diseases was so dramatic that the surgeon general of the United States declared, "It is time to close the book on infectious diseases." But the surgeon general may have spoken too soon. Fleming understood evolution through natural selection and warned us 80 years ago that inappropriate use of antibiotics would lead to resistant strains of bacteria.

Here's how evolution through natural selection is at work when you take an antibiotic. Many antibiotics require you to take the medicine "two times each day for 10 days." When you start taking your medication, it starts killing off the infectious bacteria—not all of them, but enough of them to make you feel much better. When you stop taking your antibiotic medication after only three or four days because you're feeling better, the only surviving bacteria are naturally those with the most resistance to that particular antibiotic. But the more resistant bacteria do more than survive; these stronger bugs breed within your system because you stopped taking your medicine when you felt better. So the next time you get sick because of a bacterial infection, look out! Those stronger bugs are waiting for you. In fact, we are facing an emerging public health crisis in which antibiotic-resistant bacteria are reasserting their influence and some of these once-conquered diseases are starting to make a reappearance.

This problem is behavioral, not biological. When patients with colds due to a virus plead with their doctors to give them an antibiotic, even though it will have no effect on the virus, the doctors sometimes give in, just to keep the patient happy. So, as a behavioral scientist, it is your job to describe, explain, and predict behaviors such as those described below. Experience for yourself what it means to brainstorm a possible study for each situation. We'll get you started with one possibility.

Tom, a patient with a bad cold from a virus, pleads with his doctor to give him an antibiotic: "Anything, Doc, that will make this cold go away." What three variables do you think will best predict whether this doctor inappropriately gives Tom a prescription for an antibiotic?

1. How insistent Tom is that the doctor give him a prescription.

2. _____

3. _____

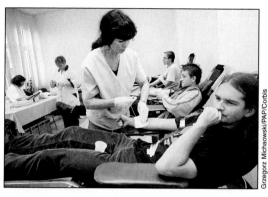

Prediction and Blood Donation
Regression can test the variables that predict the frequency with which people donate blood. Identifying the obstacles to blood donation can lead to changes in how blood donations are solicited.

Nancy is a college student with a bad case of strep throat; she is very worried about missing so many classes, and she starts feeling better after 3 days on a 10-day antibiotic. Name three variables that might predict whether Nancy will continue to take her antibiotic as directed.

1. Whether she has put the pills in a convenient place that is part of her daily routine.

2. _____

3. _____

The local Red Cross has hired you to improve the frequency of blood donations, especially of platelets. So first you decide to do a study to learn about the obstacles to donating blood. Identify the three most likely variables involved in predicting why people do or do not give blood.

1. Whether people believe giving blood is painful.

2. _____

3. _____

What Correlation Can Teach Us About Regression: Correlation Still Isn't Causation

We hope we've gotten you fairly excited about personal career opportunities related to regression. It is important, however, to understand the limitations associated with using regression. It is extremely rare that the data analyzed in a regression equation are from a true experiment (one that used randomization to assign participants to conditions). Typically, we cannot randomly assign participants to conditions when the independent variable is an interval variable (rather than a nominal variable), as is usually the case with regression. Said another way, if the independent variable is number of absences from class (with a range of 1 to more than 20), then we can't easily randomly assign participants to every possible value. When the data are not from a true experiment, the results are subject to the same limitations in interpretation that we discussed with respect to correlation.

Regression, like correlation, does not imply causality. In Experience It for Yourself: Creating a Career in Health Psychology, you may have hypothesized variables that really are correlated with the frequency of the blood donations. But that does not mean that specifically those variables:

1. Cause changes in the level of blood donation

2. Predict changes in the level of blood donation

3. Are directly related to the level of blood donations

We noted in Chapter 5 that the correlation between number of absences and exam grade could be explained if skipping class harmed one's grade, if a bad grade led one to skip more often because of frustration, or if a third variable—such as intelligence—might lead both to good grades and to an awareness that going to class is a good thing. When drawing conclusions from regression, we must consider the same set of possible confounding variables that limited our confidence in our findings following a correlation.

In fact, regression, like correlation, can be wildly inaccurate in its predictions. The predictions can be inaccurate if either of the following is true:

1. The range of one of the variables is restricted in the sample used to generate the equation.

2. There is an extreme outlier in the sample.

As with the Pearson correlation coefficient, simple linear regression should be used only if a visual inspection of the scatterplot indicates that it's sensible to proceed. A good statistician will examine the data points *before* proceeding (to check for linearity, outliers, and a restricted range) and question causality *after* the statistical analysis (to identify potential confounding variables). A good statistician will also consider whether he or she can predict beyond the data. As we noted in Chapter 3, both interpolation (predicting Y for scores on X that are in between those represented by the data set) and extrapolation (predicting Y for scores on X that are more extreme than those in our data set) are dangerous and can lead to inaccurate predictions. In other words, the scientific approach is so skeptical that researchers doubt the validity of their own work, even when they know that they have sincerely tried to do their best. But there is one more source of error that can affect fair-minded interpretations of regression analyses: regression to the mean.

Regression to the Mean: The Patterns of Extreme Scores

In the study that we considered earlier in this chapter (Ruhm, 2006), economic factors predicted several indicators of health. Ruhm also reported that "the drop in tobacco use disproportionately occurs among heavy smokers, the fall in body weight among the severely obese, and the increase in exercise among those who were completely inactive" (p. 2). What Ruhm describes captures the meaning of the word *regression*, as defined by its early proponents. Those who were most extreme on a given variable regressed (toward the mean). In other words, they became somewhat less extreme on that variable.

Francis Galton (Darwin's cousin) was the first to describe the phenomenon of regression to the mean, and he did so in a number of contexts (Bernstein, 1996). For example, Galton studied sweet peas. Galton asked nine individuals—including Darwin—to plant sweet pea seeds in the widely disparate locations in Britain where they lived. Galton found that the variability among the seeds he sent out to be planted was larger than among the seeds that were produced by these plants. The largest seeds produced seeds smaller than they were. The smallest seeds produced seeds larger than they were. Similarly, among people, Galton documented that, although tall parents tend to have taller-than-average children, their children tend to be a little shorter than their parents. And although short parents tend to have shorter-than-average children, their children tend to be a little taller than their parents. This phenomenon came to be labeled regression to the mean. Galton noted that if regression to the mean did *not* occur, with tall people and large sweet peas producing offspring even taller or larger, and short people and small

Regression to the Mean
Tall parents tend to have children who are taller than average but not as tall as they are. Similarly, short parents (like the older parents in this photograph) tend to have children who are shorter than average but not as short as they are. Francis Galton was the first to observe this phenomenon, which came to be called regression to the mean.

Jack Hollingsworth/Getty Images

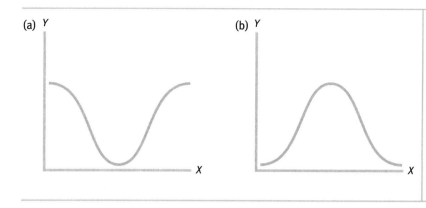

(a) Y   (b) Y

                    X   X

FIGURE 6-5
Regression to the Mean

The distribution on the left (a) demonstrates what most observations of the world would look like if regression to the mean did not occur. Trees would be either enormous or tiny. People would cry constantly or almost never. There would be no "middle ground." Instead, the distribution on the right (b) demonstrates the reality that underlies statistical reasoning: the normal, bell-shaped curve.

sweet peas producing offspring even shorter or smaller, "the world would consist of nothing but midgets and giants" (quoted in Bernstein, 1996, p. 167).

Regression to the mean is also why so much of the world is described by the bell-shaped curve, another concept often studied by Galton. If regression to the mean did not occur, the size of sweet peas, the heights of individuals, the aggressiveness of personalities, and everything else would look bimodal, like a valley (Figure 6-5a), instead of unimodal, like a hill or what we call the normal, bell-shaped curve (Figure 6-5b).

An understanding of regression to the mean can help us make better choices in our daily lives. For example, regression to the mean is a particularly important concept to remember when we begin to save for retirement and have to choose the specific allocations of our savings. Table 6-4 shows data from *Morningstar*, an investment publication; the percentages represent the increase in that investment vehicle over two five-year periods: 1984–1989 and 1989–1994 (Bernstein, 1996). As most descriptions of mutual funds remind potential investors, previous performance is not necessarily indicative of future performance. Perhaps what they really mean is that previous high performances are unlikely to continue increasing indefinitely. Consider regression to the mean in your own investment decisions. It might help you ride out a decrease in a mutual fund rather than panic and sell before the likely drift back toward the mean. And it might help you avoid buying into the fund that's been on top for several years, knowing that it stands a chance of sliding back toward the mean.

TABLE 6-4. REGRESSION TO THE MEAN: INVESTING

Bernstein (1996) presented these data from *Morningstar*, an investment publication, demonstrating regression to the mean in action. Notice that those categories that showed the highest performances during the first time period (e.g., international stocks) had declined by the second time period, whereas those with the poorest performances in the first time period (e.g. aggressive growth) had improved by the second time period.

5 YEARS TO OBJECTIVE	5 YEARS TO MARCH 1989	MARCH 1994
International stocks	20.6%	9.4%
Income	14.3%	11.2%
Growth and income	14.2%	11.9%
Growth	13.3%	13.9%
Small company	10.3%	15.9%
Aggressive growth	8.9%	16.1%
Average	13.6%	13.1%

▪ The **proportionate reduction in error** is a statistic that quantifies how much more accurate our predictions are when we use the regression line instead of the mean as a prediction tool; also called *coefficient of determination.*

The Effect Size for Regression: Proportionate Reduction in Error

Once we have calculated our regression equation, we can use it to predict individuals' scores on the dependent variable from their scores on the independent variable. Before applying the regression equation, however, it's important to determine how accurate it is—how much error there is in our predictions using the regression equation. If we don't check how well it works, then we might make predictions that have a great deal of error. We might deny candidates admission to an academic institution because a regression equation falsely predicts low performance. Or we might overcharge someone on car insurance because a regression equation falsely predicts a high number of insurance claims.

In the previous section, we developed a regression equation to predict a mean exam score from number of absences. Now we want to know: How good is this regression equation? Is it worth having our students use this equation to predict their own mean exam grades from the number of classes they plan to skip? To answer that question, we calculate *the **proportionate reduction in error**: a statistic that quantifies how much more accurate our predictions are when we use the regression line instead of the mean as a prediction tool.* (Note that the proportionate reduction in error is sometimes called the *coefficient of determination.*) More specifically, the proportionate reduction in error is a statistic that quantifies how much more accurate our predictions are when we predict scores using a specific regression equation rather than just predicting the mean for everyone.

If the mean is all we have to go by, then it's a fair predictor. In other words, using the mean is the most reasonable way to predict a baseball player's batting average if all we know is the team average. But if we know that the baseball player has been among the top five hitters for three years in a row, then we are likely to predict a batting average higher than the mean. Why? We have more

TABLE 6-5. CALCULATING ERROR WHEN WE PREDICT THE MEAN FOR EVERYONE

If we do not have a regression equation, the best we can do is predict the mean for Y for every participant. When we do that, we will, of course, have some error, because not everyone will have exactly the mean value on Y. This table presents the squared errors for each participant when we predict the mean for each of them.

STUDENT	MEAN GRADE (Y)	MEAN FOR Y	ERROR	SQUARED ERROR
1	82	76	6	36
2	98	76	22	484
3	76	76	0	0
4	68	76	−8	64
5	84	76	8	64
6	99	76	23	529
7	67	76	−9	81
8	58	76	−18	324
9	50	76	−26	676
10	78	76	2	4

information. The regression line gives us more information than the mean, and the proportionate reduction in error quantifies how much better the regression equation predicts a player's batting average than does the mean.

Earlier in this chapter, we noted that if we did not have a regression equation, the best we could do is predict the mean for everyone, regardless of number of absences. The average mean exam grade for students in this sample is 76. With no further information, we could only tell our students that our best guess for their statistics grade is a 76. There would obviously be a great deal of error if we predicted the mean for everyone. Some would fall at or near the mean, but many would fall either a good deal lower or a good deal higher than the mean. Using the mean to estimate scores is a reasonable way to proceed if that's all the information we have. But the regression line provides a more precise picture of the relation between variables, so using a regression equation reduces our error. In other words, using the regression equation means that we're not as far off in our predictions as we are when we use the mean.

Less error is the same thing as having a smaller standard error of the estimate. And a smaller standard error of the estimate means that we'd be doing much better in our predictions; visually, this means that the actual scores are closer to the regression line. And with a larger standard error of the estimate, we'd be doing much worse in our predictions; visually, the actual scores are farther away from the regression line. As the actual scores are closer to the regression line, we have less error. But we can do more than just quantify the standard deviation around the regression line. We can determine how much better the regression equation is compared to the mean; we'll calculate the proportion of error that we can eliminate by using the regression equation, rather than the mean, to predict. (In the next section, we'll teach you the long way to calculate this proportion so that you will understand exactly what this proportion represents. Then, we'll show you a shortcut.)

Using our sample, we can calculate the amount of error from using the mean as a predictive tool. We quantify that error by determining how far off an individual's score on the dependent variable (mean exam grade) is from the mean, as seen in the column titled "error" in Table 6-5. For example, for student 1, the error is $82 - 76 = 6$. We then square those errors and sum them. This is another type of sum of squares: the sum of squared errors. Here, the sum of squared errors is 2262 (the sum of the values in column 5). This is a measure of the error that results if we were to predict the mean for every person in our sample. We'll call this the sum of squares total, SS_{Total}, because it represents the worst-case scenario, the total error we would have if there were no regression equation. We can visualize this error on a graph that depicts a horizontal line for the mean, as seen in Figure 6-6. We can add the actual points, as we would in a scatterplot, and draw vertical lines from each point to the mean. These vertical lines give us a visual sense of the error that results from predicting the mean for everyone.

The regression equation can't make our predictions any worse than just predicting the mean for everyone. But it's not worth the time and effort to use a regression equation if it doesn't lead to a substantial improvement over just

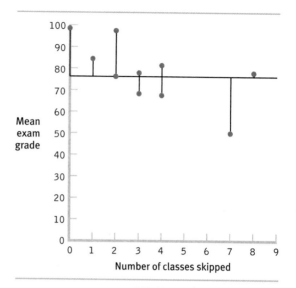

FIGURE 6-6
Visualizing Error

A graph with a horizontal line for the mean, 76, can allow us to visualize the error that would result if we predicted the mean for everyone. We draw lines for each person's point on a scatterplot to the mean. Those lines are a visual representation of error.

Symbols: SS_{Total}

predicting the mean. There will still be error with a regression equation, but there will be less error. As with the mean, we can calculate the amount of error from using the regression equation with our sample. We can then see how much better we do with the regression equation than with the mean. So let's quantify that error by determining how far each prediction is from the actual score on the dependent variable for each participant in our sample.

First, we have to calculate what we would predict for each student if we used the regression equation. We do this by plugging each X into the regression equation. Here are our calculations using the equation $\hat{Y} = 94.30 - 5.39(X)$:

$$\hat{Y} = 94.30 - 5.39(4); \ \hat{Y} = 72.74$$
$$\hat{Y} = 94.30 - 5.39(2); \ \hat{Y} = 83.52$$
$$\hat{Y} = 94.30 - 5.39(2); \ \hat{Y} = 83.52$$
$$\hat{Y} = 94.30 - 5.39(3); \ \hat{Y} = 78.13$$
$$\hat{Y} = 94.30 - 5.39(1); \ \hat{Y} = 88.91$$
$$\hat{Y} = 94.30 - 5.39(0); \ \hat{Y} = 94.30$$
$$\hat{Y} = 94.30 - 5.39(4); \ \hat{Y} = 72.74$$
$$\hat{Y} = 94.30 - 5.39(8); \ \hat{Y} = 51.18$$
$$\hat{Y} = 94.30 - 5.39(7); \ \hat{Y} = 56.57$$
$$\hat{Y} = 94.30 - 5.39(3); \ \hat{Y} = 78.13$$

The $\hat{Y}$s, or predicted scores for Y, that we just calculated are presented in Table 6-6, where the errors are calculated based on the predicted scores, rather than the mean. For example, for student 1, the error is $82 - 72.74 = 9.26$. As before, we square the errors and sum them. The sum of squared errors based on the regression equation is 705.825. We'll call this the sum of squared error, SS_{Error}, because it represents the error that we'd have if we predicted Y using our regression equation.

Symbols: SS_{Error}

TABLE 6-6. CALCULATING ERROR WHEN WE USE THE REGRESSION EQUATION TO PREDICT

When we use a regression equation for prediction, as opposed to the mean, we will have less error. We will, however, still have some error because not every participant will fall exactly on the regression line. This table presents the squared errors for each participant when we predict each one's score on Y using the regression equation.

STUDENT	ABSENCES (X)	MEAN GRADE (Y)	PREDICTED FOR Y	ERROR	SQUARED ERROR
1	4	82	72.74	9.26	85.748
2	2	98	83.52	14.48	209.670
3	2	76	83.52	−7.52	56.550
4	3	68	78.13	−10.13	102.617
5	1	84	88.91	−4.91	24.108
6	0	99	94.30	4.70	22.090
7	4	67	72.74	−5.74	32.948
8	8	58	51.18	6.82	46.512
9	7	50	56.57	−6.57	43.165
10	3	78	78.13	0.13	0.017

As before, we can visualize this error on a graph that includes the regression line, as seen in Figure 6-7. We again add the actual points, as in a scatterplot, and we draw vertical lines from each point to the regression line. These vertical lines give us a visual sense of the error that results from predicting Y for everyone using the regression equation. You'll notice that these vertical lines in Figure 6-7 tend to be shorter than those connecting each person's point with the mean in Figure 6-6.

So how much better did we do? Our error if we predict using the mean for everyone in this sample is 2262. The error if we predict using the regression equation for everyone in this sample is 623.425. Remember that this measure of how well the regression equation predicts is called the proportionate *reduction* in error. What we want to know is how much error we have gotten rid of—reduced—by using the regression equation instead of the mean. The amount of error we've reduced is $2262 - 623.425 = 1638.575$. But the word *proportionate* indicates that we want a proportion of the total error that we have reduced. We'll set up a ratio to determine this; we have reduced 1638.575 of the original 2262, or $\dfrac{1638.575}{2262} = 0.613$. We have reduced 0.613, or 61.3%, of the original error by using the regression equation versus using the mean to predict Y. This ratio can be calculated using an equation that represents what we just calculated: the proportionate reduction in error, symbolized as $r^2 = \dfrac{(SS_{Total} - SS_{Error})}{SS_{Total}} = \dfrac{(2262 - 623.425)}{2262} = 0.724$.

To recap, the worst-case scenario is predicting the mean for everyone, but if it's all the information we have, then it's much better than having no information at all. The error using the mean, the total of the sum of squares, is 2262. The regression equation that used the independent variable of number of absences to predict the dependent variable of mean exam grade still led to error, but less error. The error using the regression equation, the sum of squares, is 623.425. Knowing these two numbers enables us to determine the proportion of error that we reduced by using the regression equation to predict, rather than merely predicting the mean for everyone. We calculate the reduction in error by determining the amount of error we got rid of. We calculated this by taking a ratio, the amount of error we reduced over the total amount of error. In short, we simply have to do the following:

1. Determine the error associated with using the mean as our predictor.
2. Determine the error associated with using the regression equation as our predictor.
3. Subtract the error associated with the regression equation from the error associated with the mean.
4. Divide the difference (calculated in step 3) by the error associated with using the mean.

The proportionate reduction in error tells us how good our regression equation is. Here is another way to state it: the proportionate reduction in error is a measure of the amount of variance in the dependent variable that is explained by

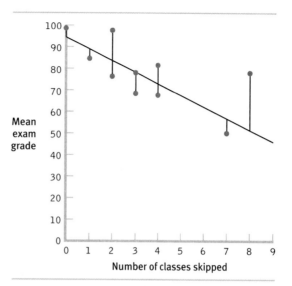

FIGURE 6-7
Visualizing Error

A graph that depicts the regression line allows us to visualize the error that would result if we predicted Y for everyone using the regression equation. We draw lines for each person's point on a scatterplot to the regression line. Those lines are a visual representation of error.

Symbols: r^2

Formulas:

$$r^2 = \frac{(SS_{Total} - SS_{Error})}{SS_{Total}}$$

the independent variable. Did you notice the symbol for the proportionate reduction in error? The symbol is r^2. Perhaps you see the connection with another number we have calculated. Yes, we could simply square the correlation coefficient! The longer calculations are necessary, however, to see the difference between the error in prediction from using the regression equation and the error in prediction from simply predicting the mean for everyone. Once you have calculated the proportionate reduction in error the long way a few times, you'll have a good sense of exactly what you're calculating.

Because the proportionate reduction in error can be calculated by squaring the correlation coefficient, we can have a sense of the amount of error that would be reduced simply by looking at the correlation coefficient. A correlation coefficient that is high in magnitude, whether negative or positive, indicates a strong relation between two variables. If two variables are highly related, it makes sense that one of them is going to be a good predictor of the other. And it makes sense that when we use one variable to predict the other, we're going to reduce error. A high correlation coefficient (whether positive or negative) indicates a high proportionate reduction in error, and both indicate a useful regression equation. So, once the long calculations have given us a sense of what r^2 means, we can simply square our correlation coefficient to assess our regression equation. Better yet, we can let the computer do it for us. But now we have some sense of where that number comes from.

In summary, because studies that analyze data using regression are not typically true experiments, findings from regression analyses are subject to the same types of limitations as correlation. For example, regression does not tell us about causation. Moreover, we must be particularly cautious when concluding that there is causality when one variable predicts another because of the well-documented phenomenon of regression to the mean; individuals with extreme scores at one point in time tend to have less extreme scores (scores closer to the mean) at a later point in time. Finally, it is important to consider the amount of variance in the dependent variable that is explained by the independent variable. We do this by calculating the proportionate reduction in error, r^2, which determines the amount of error we have eliminated by using a particular regression equation to predict an individual's score on the dependent variable versus simply predicting the mean on the dependent variable for that person.

⊙ CHECK YOUR LEARNING

6-2 Many athletes and sports fans believe that an appearance on the cover of *Sports Illustrated* (SI) is a curse. The tendency for SI cover subjects to face imminent bad sporting luck is documented in the pages of (what else?) *Sports Illustrated* and even has a name, the "SI jinx" (Wolff, 2002). Players or teams, shortly after appearing on the cover, often have a particularly poor performance, a tendency especially pronounced among individual athletes rather than teams and among those who were described on the cover with superlatives, such as *best*. In fact, of 2456 covers, SI counted 913 "victims." And their potential victims have noticed; after the New England Patriots football team won their league championship in 1996, their coach at the time, Bill Parcells, called his daughter, an SI staffer, and ordered: "No cover." Using your knowledge about the limitations of regression, what would you tell Coach Parcells?

> MULTIPLE REGRESSION: PREDICTING FROM MORE THAN ONE VARIABLE

Darwin set about measuring the length of tongue an insect would need to extract nectar by pushing a slender cylinder into the flower and using it to extract nectar from the Madagascar star orchid. The title of Darwin's book on orchids is almost as long as the tongue of a hawkmoth: *On the Various Contrivances by Which British and Foreign Orchids Are Fertilized by Insects, and on the Good Effects of Intercrossing* (Darwin, 1862). But writing an entire book about so narrow a topic signals the multiplicity of evidence Darwin used to reach his conclusions. When he described his results, Darwin (1862, p. 201) also ventured another prediction about the mysterious moth:

> The pollinia would not be withdrawn until some huge moth, with a wonderfully long proboscis, tried to drain the last drop. If such great moths were to become extinct in Madagascar, assuredly the *Angraecum* (star orchid) would become extinct.

And then some additional evidence appeared, leading Darwin to note in a second edition of this book in 1877:

> This belief of mine has been ridiculed by some entomologists, but we now know from Fritz Müller that there is a sphinx-moth in South Brazil which has a proboscis of nearly sufficient length, for when dried it was between ten and eleven inches long. When not protruded it is coiled up into a spiral of at least twenty windings.

Alfred Russel Wallace (1867, p. 488) also provided evidence when he reported measuring a moth with a proboscis "nine inches and a quarter long!" It was also from South America and safely preserved in the British Museum. Wallace asserted:

> That such a moth exists in Madagascar may be safely predicted; and naturalists who visit that island should search for it with as much confidence as astronomers searched for the planet Neptune, and I venture to predict they will be equally successful!

Now there were not two, but three separate predictors that this mysterious moth actually existed. One predictor was the existence of the star orchid itself. A second predictor was the moth from South Brazil reported by Fritz Müller. A third predictor was the moth in the British Museum. Now these last two predictors (the two moths) were very similar and made a similar point—namely, that moths with tongues of a comparable length could exist and in fact already existed, even though they were found on different continents. In regression, we describe such overlapping predictors as nonorthogonal; that is, they are *not* separate and distinct. Orthogonal variables, on the other hand, do not overlap each other. That is, *an* **orthogonal variable** *is an independent variable that makes a separate and distinct contribution in the prediction of a dependent variable, as compared to another variable.* In regression analysis, we explain more of the variability in our dependent variable if we can discover genuine predictors that are orthogonal. In other words, orthogonal predictors explain unique, additional variance the

■ An **orthogonal variable** is an independent variable that makes a separate and distinct contribution in the prediction of a dependent variable, as compared to another variable.

Confirmation of Darwin's Prediction
Three different factors predicted the discovery of the Madagascar hawkmoth. Two of the predictors (two different moths with extremely long tongues) were similar—that is, nonorthogonal, or overlapping, predictors. The third predictor was the existence of an orchid with an 11-inch nectary. Because it was a different kind of predictor, it is called an orthogonal, or nonoverlapping, predictor. Together, the three pieces of evidence predicted that a moth with an 11-inch tongue must exist on Madagascar.

Wayne P. Armstrong

same way that the existence of moths with comparable tongue lengths and the existence of a flower with an 11-inch nectary are also separate and distinct types of predictors that this strange moth with an 11-inch tongue must exist.

But three predictors and a theory still don't equal an actual moth with an 11-inch tongue! Darwin *believed* that the Madagascar moth existed, and so did Alfred Russel Wallace, but they *could not prove* that such a moth actually existed. Orthogonal variables add more confidence to your prediction, both conceptually and mathematically. But even orthogonal variables could only increase their belief in the probable existence of a Madagascar moth with an 11-inch tongue; they could not cause it to exist. Regression predicts without asserting causation.

Nevertheless, three pieces of evidence are usually better than one, whether we are trying to solve a mystery, check out a rumor, or predict what a new species of moth must look like. The behavioral sciences follow in Darwin's footsteps when it comes to using multiple pieces of evidence to reach conclusions. So the statistical technique we consider next, multiple regression, is a way of quantifying (1) whether multiple pieces of evidence really are better than one and (2) precisely how much better each additional piece of evidence actually is. Darwin (1839) was constantly collecting, measuring, and recording all kinds of objects and behaviors; orchids were only one of his many fascinations. But instead of overwhelming his intellect, Darwin's immersion in thousands of bits of evidence produced a poet's sense of beauty and awe as he observed the world around him:

> Everything was motionless, excepting the large and brilliant butterflies, which lazily fluttered about. The view seen when crossing the hills behind Praia Grande was most beautiful; the colours were intense, and the prevailing tint a dark blue; the sky and the calm waters of the bay vied with each other in splendour. . . . The scene by the dimmed light of the moon was most desolate. A few fireflies flitted by us; and the solitary snipe, as it rose, uttered its plaintive cry. The distant and sullen roar of the sea scarcely broke the stillness of the night (p. 10).

So don't confuse healthy scientific skepticism with world-weary cynicism. Evidence added to Darwin's sense of beauty, enhanced his fascination with diversity, and kept him in a state of awe. As he concluded at the end of perhaps his most famous book, *On the Origin of Species by Means of Natural Selection* (Darwin, 1859):

> There is grandeur in this view of life, with its several powers, having been originally breathed into a few forms or into one; and that, whilst this planet has gone cycling on according to the fixed law of gravity, from so simple a beginning endless forms most beautiful and most wonderful have been, and are being, evolved (p. 490).

So, as we learn how to calculate multiple pieces of evidence by using multiple regression statistics, keep in mind this small sampling of the ingredients of Darwin's life: poetry, adventure, beauty, and awe. This is the stuff of serious science. And *multiple* regression statistics are an excellent way to help us enjoy *more* of it.

Multiple Regression: Understanding the Equation

▪ **Multiple regression** is a statistical technique that includes two or more predictor variables in a prediction equation.

Just as a regression equation using one independent variable is a better predictor than the mean, a regression equation using more than one independent variable is likely to be an even better predictor. And this makes sense in the same

TABLE 6-7. PREDICTING MEAN EXAM GRADE FROM TWO VARIABLES

Multiple regression allows us to develop a regression equation that predicts a dependent variable from two or more independent variables. Here, we will use these data to develop a regression equation that predicts mean grade from number of absences *and* SAT score.

STUDENT	ABSENCES	SAT	MEAN EXAM GRADE
1	4	620	82
2	2	750	98
3	2	500	76
4	3	520	68
5	1	540	84
6	0	690	99
7	4	590	67
8	8	490	58
9	7	450	50
10	3	560	78

way that knowing a baseball player's historical batting average *plus* knowing that the player continues to suffer from a serious injury is likely to change our prediction yet again. So it is not surprising that multiple regression is far more common than simple linear regression. ***Multiple regression** is a statistical technique that includes two or more predictor variables in a prediction equation.* More specifically, multiple regression is a statistical technique that develops an equation that predicts a single dependent variable by using more than one independent variable. Multiple regression is more widely used than simple linear regression for the obvious reason that most dependent variables are best explained by more than one independent variable. Multiple regression allows us to include more than one independent variable in the equation. Let's examine an equation that might be used to predict mean exam grade from two variables, number of absences *and* score on the mathematics portion of the Scholastic Aptitude Test (SAT). Table 6-7 repeats the data from Table 6-1, with the added variable of SAT score. (Note that although the scores on number of absences and mean exam grade are real-life data from our statistics classes, the SAT scores are fictional.)

The computer gives us the printout seen in Figure 6-8. The column in which we're interested is that labeled "B" under "unstandardized coefficients." The first number, across from "(Constant)", is the intercept, so called because the intercept does not change; it is not multiplied by any value of an independent variable. The intercept here is 33.422. The second number is the slope for the independent variable, number of absences. Number of absences is negatively correlated with mean exam grade, so the slope, -3.340, is negative. The third number in this column is the slope for the independent variable of SAT score. As we might guess, SAT score and mean exam grade are positively correlated; a student with a high SAT score tends to have a higher mean exam grade. So, the slope, 0.094, is positive. We can put these numbers into a regression equation: $\hat{Y} = 33.422 - 3.34(X_1) + 0.094(X_2)$.

Once we have developed our multiple regression equation, we can input raw scores on number of absences and mathematics SAT score to determine an

Coefficients(a)

Model		Unstandardized Coefficients		Standardized Coefficients		
		B	Std. Error	Beta	t	Sig.
1	(Constant)	33.422	13.584		2.460	.043
	number of absences	-3.340	.773	-.527	-4.320	.003
	SAT	.094	.021	.558	4.569	.003

a Dependent Variable: mean exam grade

FIGURE 6-8
Software Output for Regression

Computer software provides the information necessary for the multiple regression equation. All necessary co-efficients are in column B under "unstandardized co-efficients." The constant, 33.422, is the intercept; the number next to "number of absences," −3.340, is the slope for that independent variable; and the number next to "SAT," 0.094, is the slope for that independent variable.

Symbols: R^2

individual's predicted score on Y. Imagine that our student, Allie, scored 600 on the mathematics portion of the SAT. We already know she planned to miss two classes this semester. What would we predict for her mean exam grade?

$$\hat{Y} = 33.422 - 3.34(X_1) + 0.094(X_2) = 33.422 - 3.34(2) + 0.094(600)$$
$$= 33.422 - 6.68 + 56.4 = 83.142$$

Based on these two variables, we would predict a mean exam grade of 83.142 for Allie. And how good is this multiple regression equation? From software, we calculated that the proportionate reduction in error for this equation is a whopping 0.93. We have reduced 93% of the error that would result from predicting the mean of 76 for everyone by using a multiple regression equation with the independent variables of number of absences and SAT score. Compared to using averages, the multiple regression equation represents a significant advance in our ability to predict human behavior.

When we calculate proportionate reduction in error for a multiple regression, the symbol changes slightly. The symbol is now R^2 instead of r^2. The capitalization of this statistic is an indication that the proportionate reduction in error is based on more than one independent variable.

Stepwise Multiple Regression and Hierarchical Multiple Regression: A Choice of Tactics

Researchers have a choice of several options when they conduct statistical analyses using multiple regression. One common approach is *stepwise multiple regression, a type of multiple regression in which computer software determines the order in which independent variables are included in the equation.* This method is used frequently by researchers because it is the default in many computer software programs (and probably sometimes because it doesn't involve thinking on the part of the researcher). In some circumstances, stepwise regression is a sensible way to analyze data, especially in the absence of a clear, predictive theory.

When the researcher conducts a stepwise multiple regression, the computer software implements a series of steps. In the first step, the computer identifies the independent variable responsible for the most variance in the dependent variable—that is, the independent variable that contributes the most to R^2. In other words, the computer examines each independent variable as if it were the only predictor of the dependent variable; the one with the largest R^2 "wins." Inferential statistics are then used to find out if a variable is likely to be a "true" predictor. If it is, it's referred to as statistically significant. If the winning independent variable is not a statistically significant predictor of the dependent variable, then the process stops. After all, if the independent variable that explains

■ **Stepwise multiple regression** is a type of multiple regression in which computer software determines the order in which independent variables are included in the equation.

the most variance in the dependent variable is not statistically significant, then the other independent variables won't be statistically significant either.

If, however, this first independent variable *is* a statistically significant predictor of the dependent variable, then the computer continues to the next step: choosing the second independent variable that, in conjunction with the one already chosen, is responsible for the largest amount of variance in the dependent variable. If the R^2 of both independent variables together represents a statistically significant increase over the R^2 of just the first independent variable alone, then the computer continues to the next step: choosing the independent variable responsible for the next largest amount of variance, and so on. So, at each step, the computer assesses whether the change in R^2, after adding another independent variable, is statistically significant. If the inclusion of an additional independent variable does not lead to a statistically significant increase in R^2 at any step, then the computer stops.

The strength and the weakness of using stepwise regression to analyze data revolve around the same issue: its reliance on the data, rather than theory. Having the computer select the variables that go into the regression equation is a strength when a researcher is not certain of what to expect in a study; its results can generate hypotheses that the researcher can go on to test. But that strength is also a weakness when we are working with nonorthogonal, overlapping variables. For example, imagine that both depression and anxiety are very strong predictors of the quality of one's romantic relationship; also imagine that there is a great deal of overlap in the predictive ability of depression and anxiety. That is, once depression is accounted for, anxiety doesn't add much to the equation; similarly, once anxiety is accounted for, depression doesn't add much to the equation. It is perhaps the negative affect (or mood) shared by both clusters of symptoms that predicts the quality of one's relationship. People with these psychological disorders are generally unpleasant to be with socially or to live with more intimately.

Imagine that in one sample, depression turns out to be a slightly better predictor than anxiety of relationship quality, but just barely. The computer would choose depression as the first independent variable. Because of the overlap between the two independent variables, the addition of anxiety would not make a difference. A stepwise regression would pinpoint depression, but not anxiety, as a predictor of relationship quality; that finding suggests that anxiety is not a good predictor of the quality of your romantic relationship even though it could be extremely important. Now imagine that in a second sample, anxiety is a slightly better predictor than depression of relationship quality, but just barely. This time, the computer would choose anxiety as the first independent variable. Now, the addition of depression would not make a difference. This time, a stepwise regression would pinpoint anxiety, but not depression, as a predictor of relationship quality. So the problem with using stepwise regression is that two samples with very similar data can, and sometimes do, lead to drastically different conclusions when using stepwise multiple regression.

That is why another common approach is ***hierarchical multiple regression***, *a type of multiple regression in which the researcher adds independent variables into the equation in an order determined by theory*. A researcher might want to know the degree to which depression predicts relationship quality but knows that there are other independent variables that also affect relationship quality. Based on a reading of the literature, that researcher might decide to enter other independent variables into the equation before adding depression. For example, the researcher might add age, a measure of social skills, and the number of years the relationship has lasted. After adding these independent variables, the researcher would add depression. If the addition of depression leads to a substantial

■ **Hierarchical multiple regression** is a type of multiple regression in which the researcher adds independent variables into the equation in an order determined by theory.

increase in R^2, then the researcher has evidence that depression predicts relationship quality over and above those other independent variables. As with stepwise multiple regression, we're interested in how much each additional independent variable adds to the overall variance explained. We look at the increase in R^2 with the inclusion of each new independent variable or variables and we predetermine the order (or hierarchy) in which variables are entered into a hierarchical regression equation.

The strength of hierarchical regression is that it is grounded in a theory that we can test. In addition, we're less likely to identify a predictor just by chance (a Type I error) because a well-established theory would already have identified most of our predictors. There is, however, a serious weakness associated with hierarchical regression, and it has nothing to do with the technique, its mathematics, or its concept. The problem is us. More often than we would like to admit, we researchers simply do not have a solid, predictive theory to guide us. In other words, we haven't really thought through the variables that are probably at work and why they might be there, or there's just no existing evidence to build on. A hierarchical multiple regression should not be based on a wild guess. However, in general, if we have sufficient background information to develop specific hypotheses, then we should use hierarchical multiple regression instead of stepwise multiple regression.

With the development of increasingly more powerful computers and the availability of ever larger amounts of computerized data, tools based on multiple regression have proliferated, and now the general public can access many of them online. Darlin (2006) reported on a number of Web-based search engines that now provide what are essentially regression equations that the public can use. Farecast.com predicts the price of an airline ticket for specific routes, travel dates, and, most important, purchase dates. Using the same data available to travel agents, along with additional independent variables like the weather and even which sports teams' fans might be traveling to a championship game, Farecast mimics the regression equations used by the airlines. Airlines predict how much money potential travelers are willing to pay on a given date for a given flight and use these predictions to adjust their fares accordingly and earn the most money.

Farecast.com is an attempt at an end run, using mathematical prediction tools, to help savvy airline consumers either to beat or to wait out the airlines' price hikes. Farecast claims a 70% to 75% accuracy rate for its predictions. Zillow.com does for real estate what farecast.com does for airline tickets. Using archival land record data, zillow.com predicts U.S. housing prices and claims to be accurate within 10% of the actual selling price of a given home. Another company, Inrix, predicts the dependent variable, traffic, using the independent variables of the traveling speeds of vehicles that have been outfitted with global positioning satellite (GPS) systems, the weather, and information about events such as rock concerts. It even suggests, via cell phone or "in-car navigation systems," alterative routes for gridlocked drivers. As of July 2006, Inrix was available in 15 cities. Like the future of visual displays of data, the future of the regression equation is limited only by the creativity of the rising generation of behavioral scientists and statisticians.

In summary, multiple regression is used when we want to predict a dependent variable from more than one independent variable. This procedure is more common than simple linear regression because real-world situations are more complicated than just a relation between one independent variable and one dependent variable. We can develop a multiple regression equation and input specific scores for each independent variable to determine the predicted score on the dependent variable. There are two main types of multiple regression. With stepwise multiple regression, the computer determines the contributions of the independent variable based on the sample's data. With hierarchical multiple regression, the researcher determines the order in which independent variables will be included based on a reading of the literature.

⊙ CHECK YOUR LEARNING

6-3 The accompanying computer printout shows a regression equation that predicts grade point average (GPA) from three independent variables: hours slept per night, hours studied per week, and admiration for Pamela Anderson, the B-level actress whom many view as tacky. The data are from some of our statistics classes. (*Note:* Hypothesis testing shows that all three independent variables are statistically significant predictors of GPA!)

Coefficients(a)

Model		Unstandardized Coefficients		Standardized Coefficients	t	Sig.
		B	Std. Error	Beta		
1	(Constant)	2.695	.228		11.829	.000
	Hours Slept Per Night	.069	.032	.173	2.186	.030
	Hours Studied Per Week	.015	.006	.209	2.637	.009
	Level of Admiration for Pamela Anderson	-.072	.025	-.229	-2.882	.005

a Dependent Variable: GPA

a. What is the regression equation based on these data?

b. If someone reports that they typically sleep six hours a night, study twenty hours per week, and have a Pamela Anderson admiration level of 4 (on a scale of 1–7 with 7 indicating the highest level of admiration), what would you predict for his GPA?

c. What does the negative sign in the slope for the independent variable, level of admiration for Pamela Anderson, tell you about this variable's predictive association with grade point average?

▪ DIGGING DEEPER INTO THE DATA: STRUCTURAL EQUATION MODELING (SEM)

We're going to introduce an approach to data analysis that is infinitely more flexible and visually more expressive than multiple regression. It is customarily taught only to graduate students. Yet, like most statistics, it is built on the fundamental logic of the correlation. *Structural equation modeling (SEM) quantifies how well data "fit" a theoretical model.* Here, we are discussing "fit" in much the same way you might try on some new clothes and say, "That's a good fit" or "That really doesn't fit!" If the clothes don't fit, then we can change clothes, go on a diet, or both. But if the data don't fit, we cannot then change the data

▪ **Structural equation modeling (SEM)** is a statistical technique that quantifies how well sample data "fit" a theoretical model that hypothesizes a set of relations among multiple variables.

■ A **statistical (or theoretical) model** is a hypothesized network of relations, often portrayed graphically, among multiple variables.

■ **Path** is the term that statisticians use to describe the connection between two variables in a statistical model.

■ **Path analysis** is a statistical method that examines a hypothesized model, usually by conducting a series of regression analyses that quantify the paths at each succeeding step in the model.

Understanding Networks of Variables

Structural equation modeling (SEM) displays a network of variables and how they flow from one to another to produce a specific behavior, such as cigarette smoking, the same way an aerial photograph displays a network of creeks that flow into streams that grow into a great river.

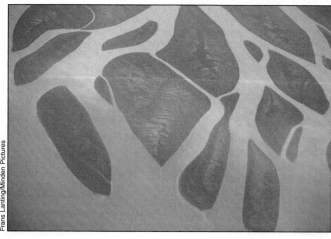

Frans Lanting/Minden Pictures

because that would be cheating science and probably deceiving ourselves. Instead, we have to change our minds. We do that by changing our statistical model, which is just our expression of how we believe several variables relate to one another.

More specifically, SEM is one of several statistical techniques that quantify how well sample data fit a theoretical model that hypothesizes a set of relations among multiple variables. SEM is one of the most sophisticated statistical approaches currently available to social scientists, and it produces graphs that portray a network of relations among several variables. Statisticians who implement SEM refer to the "model" that they are testing; in this case, *a statistical (or theoretical) model is a hypothesized network of relations, often portrayed graphically, among multiple variables.*

You have an intuitive understanding of SEM the moment you can accept that human behavior is complicated, which means that any single behavior is the product of many different influences, what we more formally call multifactorial. SEM represents the connections among the most important variables in the same way that a photograph from an airplane can help us see the connections between the many small creeks that flow into larger streams that eventually grow into rivers. Rivers don't just happen; they are "fed" by many streams. And human behavior doesn't just happen; it is the product of many smaller influences. The view from the airplane allows us to see the entire network of creeks, streams, and rivers as well as the direction in which they flow. Similarly, SEM allows us to see the network of variables and how they flow from one to another to produce a particular behavior.

Instead of thinking of variables as "independent" or "dependent" variables, SEM encourages us to think of variables as a series of connections. At various times, you have probably thought about an independent variable, such as the number of hours spent studying, and asked yourself, "But what predicts how many hours a person will study? Isn't that also a dependent variable with its own set of independent variables?" And you would be correct. Depending on what we have chosen to study, an independent variable in one study can become a dependent variable in another study. Because SEM quantifies a network of relations, some of the variables simultaneously serve as independent variables that predict other variables later in the network and as dependent variables that are predicted by other variables earlier in the network. This is why we will refer to variables without the usual adjectives of *independent* or *dependent*.

For example, many people struggle to quit smoking. But the forces (independent, predictor variables) that led up to this addiction (the dependent variable we are trying to predict) probably started out as small, fairly innocent influences. Likely candidates for these small, early (predictor) variables include (1) peer pressure, (2) the availability of cigarettes in the home, and (3) the personal importance of finding a way to relax. As a smoker grows older, these juvenile variables become less important to the behavior of smoking. Unfortunately, a new and more powerful predictor variable gradually took their place: a physiological craving for nicotine, or as one person described it, "a craving that gives you an itch that only another cigarette can scratch"—an addiction. The beauty of SEM is that it can display how all these small predictor variables merge together to create an addiction to cigarettes. Consequently, a fairly simple hypothetical model of cigarette addiction might look something like Figure 6-9.

In the historical development of SEM, the analyses based on this kind of diagram were called path analyses for the fairly obvious reason that the arrows represented "paths"—factors that lead to whatever the next variable in the model happened to be. ***Path*** *is the term that statisticians use to describe the connection between two variables in a statistical model.* ***Path analysis*** *is a statistical method that examines a hypothesized model, usually by conducting a series of regression analyses that quantify the paths at each succeeding step in the model.* Path analysis, now rendered obsolete in many cases by the more powerful technique of SEM, can quantify the relations among variables in a model. But we still find the term *path* to be a more intuitive way to describe the flow of behavior through a network of variables, and the word *path* continues to be used in structural equation models.

SEM made a significant contribution to path analysis when it quite rightly insisted on having multiple ways of measuring each of the variables in a model. Visually, that means that we now have arrows going, well, all over the place. But the arrows simply indicate the strength and direction of the relations between variables in precisely the same way that a correlation coefficient indicates strength and direction between each pair of variables.

To briefly return to our river metaphor, SEM uses a statistic much like the correlation coefficient to indicate whether the water is pretty dammed up (close to 0) or flowing freely (closer to -1.00 or 1.00). That is good to know as we try to discover the flow of variables that eventually produce a particular behavior, such as cigarette smoking, and interventions likely to dam it up, that is, decrease cigarette smoking. For example, in the path model described in Figure 6-9, it would make sense for us to try to stop late-life addiction by blocking or damming up the flow from peer pressure to youthful smoking, to avoid the development of a physiological addiction. Many such interventions, or dams, have been tried with varying degrees of success: showing high school students films of gruesome lung cancer operations and persuading them that smoking is disgusting rather than cool. But we're always on the lookout for intervening variables, such as the "rebel image" associated with cigarette smoking, that may fit somewhere in the larger SEM model that explains smoking addiction. Path analysis and SEM helps us think through our model more precisely, design interventions more intelligently, and evaluate their relative success more effectively.

A "model of smoking addiction" is fairly easy to understand, and testing such a model is precisely what a SEM model accomplishes. Do the correlations all flow in the way that we think they should flow? If they do, then we have a good fit. The visual complications enter the picture when we have at least three different ways to measure each variable, such as the variable of availability of cigarettes in the home. For example, we might measure the availability of cigarettes by using (1) ratings from parents, (2) a

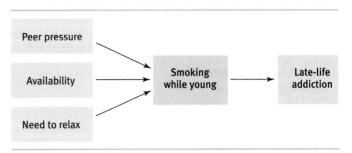

FIGURE 6-9
A Path Model of Cigarette Addiction

We can design a path model that hypothesizes the relations among the factors that might lead to cigarette addiction. Here, the hypothesized model suggests factors that lead to smoking while young, which then leads to later addiction.

Identifying the Factors that Precede Cigarette Addiction
Structural equation modeling (SEM) can help us test a model that hypothesizes a network of relations among factors, such as peer pressure or availability of cigarettes in the home, which might lead to an addiction to cigarettes.

Mika/zefa/Corbis

■ A **manifest variable** is a variable in a study that we can observe and measure.

■ A **latent variable** is the construct that we want to research but cannot directly measure.

■ A **longitudinal study** looks at ideas (constructs) by following a sample over time.

measure based on observations from a home visit, and (3) a self-report from the young smoker. And we'd also need to assess three observable variables for each of the other important variables in our model.

In SEM, these beginning measurements are called ***manifest variables,*** *the variables in a study that we can observe and that are measured.* We assess something that we can observe in an attempt to understand the underlying main idea (the construct) in which we're interested. In SEM, these main idea variables are called latent variables, ideas that we have constructed to help explain our model and that we quantify using our various scales and measures. More specifically, ***latent variables*** *are the ideas that we want to research but cannot directly measure.* Because we cannot directly observe them, we instead try to indirectly observe them using measurement tools that seem appropriate. For example, we cannot actually see the latent variable we call shyness, but we still try to measure shyness in our manifest variables using self-report scales, naturalistic observations, and reports by others about shy behavior.

We use these manifest variables and latent variables to create a model that is depicted in a visual diagram of variables. We then ask whether this model accurately describes how people tend to become addicted to cigarettes. If we can't find a path that empirically flows to our dependent variable, then we have to change our model and the variables that comprise it. In other words, a flawed model forces us to change our minds and ask better questions. But that is exactly what research does so well: test the validity of our ideas and force us to think more creatively.

Let's examine one published SEM study very closely. This particular longitudinal study helps us better understand the very unpleasant, but fairly common, experience of depression. Nolan, Flynn, and Garber (2003) were interested in the relations between depression and rejection in children and adolescents over time, so they conducted a ***longitudinal study,*** *an investigation that looks at ideas (constructs) by following a sample over time.* A good deal of research has shown that depression tends to predict rejection. But that is not terribly surprising; people just don't like to be around depressed people, so they tend to avoid them. Other research has shown that rejection leads to depression; if an individual senses that others don't like to be around him or her, it's likely to lead to negative feelings that may develop into a full-blown depressive episode.

For several decades now, researchers have posited a vicious circle whereby depression leads to rejection, which leads to more depression, and so on (e.g., Coyne, 1976). However, few researchers have tested the validity of both directions implied by this circle in a single study, especially using a longitudinal design. Remember, do not confuse a sensible-sounding model with a well-established fact. We've had to abandon lots of sensible-sounding ideas across the centuries, and we are sure to abandon still more in the future. Consequently, this theoretical model, shown in Figure 6-10, tests the proposed connections between both of these constructs—depression and rejection—through three annual assessments. One of the reasons we enjoy a fairly high level of confidence in studies using SEM is its insistence on having multiple measures of each variable in the study.

To understand the story of this model, we need to understand only three components of this graph—the six large blue circles, the three green squares attached to each large blue circle, and the arrows linking the large blue circles. For now, we can ignore everything else; we can get a basic sense of the story without understanding every component of the graph. The six large blue circles represent the underlying constructs of interest, the latent variables. These are latent variables because we cannot directly measure depression, nor can we directly "see" rejection. The large blue circles on top are labeled "T1 Rejection," "T2 Rejection,"

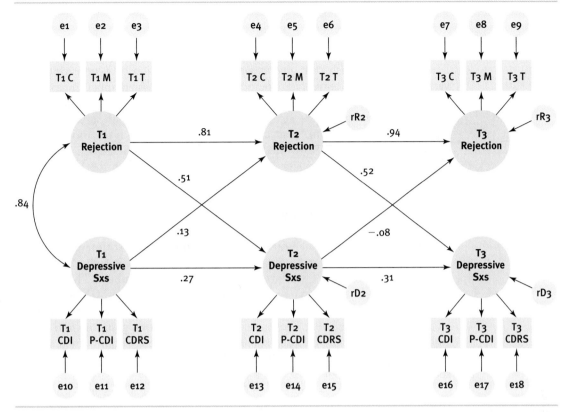

FIGURE 6-10
A SEM Diagram

This diagram depicts a structural equation model (SEM). By "reading" the numbers connecting variables, we can begin to understand the story this graph tells. For example, the path between the upper-left big circle, "T1 Rejection," and the middle-lower big circle, "T2 Depressive Sxs," has a coefficient of 0.51. This indicates a strong, positive predictive relation between a child's tendency to be rejected at the first time point of the study and her or his tendency to be depressed at the second time point of the study, one year later.

and "T3 Rejection." These refer to the constructs of rejection at each annual time point—time 1, time 2, and time 3. The large blue circles on the bottom indicate depression at each time point; for example, "T1 Depressive Sxs" refers to time 1 depressive symptoms. We cannot directly measure rejection or depressive symptoms, so we need to operationalize these variables as best we can.

The three green squares above or below each big blue circle represent the measurement tools that we used to operationalize each latent variable; these are the manifest variables, the ones that we can observe. In SEM, it is ideal to have at least three manifest variables for every latent variable, basically because it's better to look at a construct from more than one angle than to rely on only one measure that is possibly flawed. Let's look at "rejection" at time 1. There are three boxes above it: "T1 C," "T1 M," and "T1 T." These refer to three different measures of rejection, one completed by the child (T1 C), one by the child's mother (T1 M), and one by the child's teacher (T1 T). The same three rejection scales were completed at times 2 and 3, as well.

The boxes below depressive symptoms at time 1 are labeled "T1 CDI," "T1 P-CDI," and "T1 CDRS." These are three different measures of depression; the Child Depression Inventory (CDI) is completed by the child. The Parent Version of the Child Depression Inventory (P-CDI) is completed by one of the child's parents. The Child Depression Rating Scale (CDRS) is a rating scale completed by one of the experimenters during a structured interview with the child. The same three depression measures were completed at times 2 and 3, as well. The abbreviations are always defined in the Results section of the manuscript, usually at the point in the text that refers to that figure (e.g., Figure 1, Figure 2).

So far, we can see the key variable of rejection at three time points, as assessed by three measures at each time point. We also can see the equally important variable of depression at three time points as assessed by three measures at each time point. All that's left for us to understand is the arrows that represent each path. The numbers on each path give us a sense of the relation between each pair of variables. Similar to correlation coefficients, the sign of the number indicates the direction of the relation, either negative or positive, and the value of the number indicates the strength of the relation. Although this is a simplification, these basic rules will allow you to "read" the story in the diagram of the model. In the language of SEM, John Snow blocked the path of cholera to people living in the neighborhood by not allowing them to drink the water from the Broad Street well. He did this, in part, simply by removing the pump handle so that they could no longer draw water from the contaminated well.

So how does this SEM diagram address the research question: Is there a vicious circle between rejection and depression? First, look at the two paths between rejection at one time point, and depression at the next time point a year later—these are the diagonal arrows going down and to the right. The numbers are 0.51 and 0.52. These are fairly large, positive numbers. This suggests that a high level of rejection at one point generally leads to a high level of depression a year later. Now look at the two paths between depression at one point and rejection a year later. These are the diagonal arrows going up and to the right. The numbers are 0.13 and −0.08. These numbers are quite small and indicate very little relation. A high level of depression at one time point doesn't seem to say much about rejection a year later.

This is the apparent overall story: Children and young adolescents who experience rejection in interpersonal situations are likely to have increased depression a year later. However, children and young adolescents who are depressed are not likely to see a change in how frequently they are rejected a year later. Once you've read the story in the graph, read the discussion section of the journal article. The authors will discuss their conclusions in nonstatistical language. When reading a journal article, ask yourself: Does the story the authors tell in the discussion match the story you read in the graph? In the first paragraph of the discussion section of the article in which this SEM appeared, the authors stated that, "results indicated that rejection prospectively predicted depression, whereas depression did not prospectively predict rejection" (Nolan et al., 2003, p. 751).

When you encounter a model such as SEM, or one that looks similar (there are many variations out there!), follow these basic steps and you'll be on your way to a basic interpretation of very sophisticated graphs. First, figure out what variables the researcher is studying. Then look at the numbers to see what variables are related and the signs of the numbers to see the direction of the relation. Finally, check the discussion section to see if the story in the graph matches the story the authors tells.

SEM has several important strengths, including the fact that each latent variable is assessed by multiple manifest variables. In addition, we can quantify the overall fit of the data to the model; depending on the statistic used, a high or a low number indicates that the model describes the data well. SEM also has several limitations. For example, there might be another model that we did not test and that the data fit better. In addition, SEM is subject to the same limitations as correlation and regression: We cannot draw conclusions about causation from our hypothesized paths. Yet, knowing these limitations, a good researcher can tell a complex story that better describes the ways that variables interact with each other.

Predicting Depression
Do depressed children tend to get rejected in interpersonal situations? Do children who are rejected tend to become depressed? Sophisticated statistics such as structural equation modeling (SEM) can begin to answer these questions using data collected over several years. For example, Nolan, Flynn, and Garber (2003) used SEM to discover that rejection seemed to lead to depression but not the other way around.

Bill Aron/Photo Edit

In summary, more sophisticated variations of multiple regression, including structural equation modeling (SEM), have become increasingly popular in recent years. SEM allows us to examine the fit of a sample's data to a hypothesized model of the relations among multiple variables, the latent variables that we hypothesize to exist but cannot see. In SEM, each underlying latent variables is represented by at least three observable variables, the manifest variables. The relations among the latent variables, called paths, are represented by arrows, each of which is quantified. By looking at the size and sign of these numbers, we can understand the direction and strength of each relation. SEM is subject to the same drawbacks, however, as correlation: We cannot infer causation from a structural equation model.

⊙ CHECK YOUR LEARNING

6-4 University researchers were interested in the factors that might predict the success of their students and wanted to use structural equation modeling to test the model that they hypothesized.

a. List three latent variables that might predict student success. Remember, the latent variables are the more general underlying constructs—not the specific measurements that we make.

b. Choose one of these latent variables, and list three possible manifest variables for it—the observable variables that we will measure.

c. List three possible manifest variables for the latent variable of student success. (Be creative; don't limit yourself to success only while at university. Think also about the types of success that a university degree should lead to).

d. Draw a SEM diagram like that in Figure 6-10 that includes the three latent variables that might predict student success and the latent variable that you are predicting (i.e., student success). Include three manifest variables for every latent variables. You may include blank circles for the two latent variables for which you did not list manifest variables. Draw arrows that connect the boxes to the circles and the circles to each other. (You do not need to include numbers on the arrows.)

> Regression: Building on Correlation

Regression is an expansion of correlation in that it allows us not only to quantify a relation between two variables but also to quantify one variable's ability to predict another variable. We can predict a dependent variable's z score from an independent variable's z score, or we can do a bit more initial work and predict a dependent variable's raw score from an independent variable's raw score. The latter method uses the equation for a line with an *intercept* and a *slope*. We are using *simple linear regression* when we predict one dependent variable from one independent variable when the two variables are linearly related. We can graph this line using the regression equation, plugging in low and high values of X and plotting those values with their associated predicted values on Y, then connecting the dots to form the regression line. When we use regression, we must also be aware of the phenomenon called *regression to the mean*, in which

R E V I E W   O F   C O N C E P T S

extreme values tend to become less extreme over time. There is always some prediction error, which can be quantified by the *standard error of estimates*, the number that describes the typical amount that an observation falls from the regression line.

> Drawing Conclusions from a Regression Equation: Interpretation and Prediction

Regression suffers from the same drawbacks as correlation. For example, we cannot know if the predictive relation is causal; the posited direction could be the reverse (with Y causally predicting X), or there could be a third variable at work. In addition, we also must consider the degree to which an independent variable predicts a dependent variable. We also can calculate the *proportionate reduction in error*, symbolized as r^2. The proportionate reduction in error tells us how much better our prediction is with the regression equation than with the mean as the only predictive tool.

> Multiple Regression: Predicting from More Than One Variable

We use *multiple regression* when we have more than one independent variable, as is usual in most research in the behavioral sciences. Multiple regression is particularly useful when we have *orthogonal variables*, independent variables that make separate contributions to the prediction of a dependent variable. Researchers often use one of two types of multiple regression. *Stepwise multiple regression* orders the independent variables in a manner determined by the computer, using the actual data. With *Hierarchical multiple regression*, the independent variables are centered in a manner determined by the researcher, using the existing research literature.

> Digging Deeper into the Data: Structural Equation Modeling (SEM)

A number of more sophisticated statistical analyses, such as *structural equation modeling (SEM)*, have been developed in recent years. These techniques allow us to see predictive relations among a number of variables, often in *longitudinal studies* that follow participants over time. The entire network of relations forms a statistical (or theoretical) model that can be examined quantitatively. Historically, the connections between these variables, or *paths*, would have been examined using *path analysis*, a series of regression analyses that quantify each step of the model. SEM allows the model to be examined in a single analysis. SEM diagrams that depict these models look complicated but can be "read" with a basic understanding of a few concepts. *Latent variables*, represented by large circles, represent the constructs of interest that we cannot directly measure. We operationalize latent variables by measuring several *manifest variables*, represented by squares, that we believe represent each latent variable. Finally, we look at the numbers above the *paths*, represented by arrows, to determine the strength and direction of each relation between variables.

SPSS GUIDELINES FOR CHAPTER 6

The most common form of regression analysis on SPSS uses at least two scale, or interval, variables: An independent variable (predictor) and a dependent variable (the variable being predicted). Once again, begin by visualizing the data.

Request the scatterplot of the data by selecting:

Graphs → Chart Builder → Gallery → Scatter/Dot. Drag the upper-lefthand sample graph to the large box on top. Then, select the variables to be included in the scatterplot by dragging the independent variable to the *x*-axis and the dependent variable to the *y*-axis. Click OK. Then, click on the graph to make changes. To add the regression line, click Elements, then Fit Line at Total. Choose Linear, then click Apply.

To analyze the linear regression, select:

Analyze → Regression → Linear. The list of variables will appear, so select which one(s) will serve as the independent (predictor) variable(s) and which as the dependent variable being predicted.

As usual, click on OK to see the Output screen.

EXERCISES

6.1 Correlation versus simple linear regression versus multiple regression: Several studies have found a correlation between weight and blood pressure.

a. Explain what is meant by a correlation between these two variables.

b. If you were to examine these two variables with simple linear regression instead of correlation, how would you frame the question? (*Hint:* The research question for correlation would be: Is weight related to blood pressure?)

c. What is the difference between simple linear regression and multiple regression?

d. If you were to conduct a multiple regression instead of a simple linear regression, what other independent variables might you include?

6.2 Football stadiums and regression: Running a football stadium for an NFL team involves innumerable predictions. For example, when stocking up on food and beverages for sale at the game, it helps to have an idea of how much will be sold. In the football stadiums in the North, stadium managers use expected outdoor temperature to predict sales of hot chocolate.

a. What is the independent variable in this example?

b. What is the dependent variable?

c. As the value of the independent variable increases, what would we predict to happen to the value of the dependent variable?

d. What other variables might predict this dependent variable? Name at least three.

6.3 Age, studying, and predicting one z score from another z score: Check Your Learning 5-2 asked you to calculate the correlation coefficient between students' age and number of hours they study per week. The correlation between these two variables was 0.49.

a. Elif's z score for age is -0.82. What would we predict for the z score for the number of hours she studies per week?

b. John's z score for age is 1.2. What would we predict for the z score for the number of hours he studies per week?

c. Eugene's z score for age is 0. What would we predict for the z score for the number of hours he studies per week?

d. For part (c). explain why the concept of *regression* to the mean is not relevant (and why you didn't really need the formula).

6.4 The CFC scale, the z score formula, and raw scores: A study of Consideration of Future Consequences (CFC) found a mean score of 3.51, with a standard deviation of 0.61, for the 664 students in the sample (Petrocelli, 2003).

a. Imagine that your z score on the CFC score was -1.2. What would your raw score be? Use symbolic notation and the formula. Explain why this answer makes sense.

b. Imagine that your z score on the CFC score was 0.66. What would your raw score be? Use symbolic notation and the formula. Explain why this answer makes sense.

6.5 The GRE, z scores, and raw scores: The verbal subtest of the GRE has a population mean of 500 and a population standard deviation of 100 by design (the quantitative subtest has the same mean and standard deviation).

a. Convert the following z scores to raw scores *without* using a formula: (i) 1.5, (ii) -0.5, (iii) -2.0

b. Now convert the same z scores to raw scores using symbolic notation and the formula: (i) 1.5, (ii) -0.5, (iii) -2.0

6.6 Age, studying, and using the z score formula with raw scores: Check Your Learning 5-2 asked you to calculate the correlation coefficient between students' age and number of hours they study per week. The mean for age is 21, and the standard deviation is 1.789. The mean for hours studied is 14.2, and the standard deviation is 5.582. The correlation between these two variables was 0.49. Use the z score formula.

a. Joâo is 24 years old. What would we predict for the number of hours he studies per week?

b. Kimberly is 19 years old. What would we predict for the number of hours she studies per week?

c. Seung is 45 years old. Why might it not be a good idea to predict how many hours per week he studies?

d. From a mathematical perspective, why is the word *regression* used? [*Hint:* Look at parts (a) and (b), and discuss the scores on the first variable with respect to their mean versus the predicted scores on the second variable with respect to their mean.]

6.7 Studying, GPA, and predicting from a regression equation: A regression analysis of data from some of our statistics classes yielded the following regression equation for the independent variable, hours studied, and the dependent variable, grade point average (GPA): $\hat{Y} = 2.96 + 0.02(X)$.

a. If you plan to study 8 hours per week, what would you predict for your grade?

b. If you plan to study 10 hours per week, what would you predict for your grade?

c. If you plan to study 11 hours per week, what would you predict for your grade?

d. Create a graph and draw the regression line based on these three pairs of scores.

e. Do some algebra, and determine the number of hours you'd have to study to have a predicted GPA of the maximum possible, 4.0. Why is it misleading to make predictions for anyone who plans to study this many hours (or more)?

6.8 Age, studying, and regression when we already know correlation: Exercise 6.6 used the example from Check Your Learning 5-2 on whether age can predict how much people study. In Check Your Learning 6-1, you calculated the regression equation. (If you did not calculate the regression equation previously, you may do it now. The mean for age was 21, and the standard deviation was 1.789. The mean for hours studied was 14.2, and the standard deviation was 5.582. The correlation coefficient was 0.49.)

a. Use the regression equation to predict the number of hours studied for a 17-year-old student and for a 22-year-old student.

b. Using the four pairs of scores that you have (age and predicted hours studied from part (a), and the predicted scores for a score of 0 and 1 from calculating the regression equation) create a graph that includes the regression line.

c. Why is it misleading to include the ages 0 and 1 on the graph?

6.9 Regression from scratch: Researchers studied whether corporate political contributions predicted profits (Cooper, Guler, & Ovtchinnikov, 2007). From archival data, they determined how many political candidates each company supported with financial contributions, as well as each company's profit in terms of a percentage. The accompanying table shows data for five companies. (*Note:* The data points are hypothetical but are based on averages for companies falling in the 2nd, 4th, 6th, and 8th deciles in terms of candidates supported. A decile is a range of 10%, so the 2nd decile includes those with percentiles between 10 and 19.9.)

NUMBER OF CANDIDATES SUPPORTED	PROFIT (%)
6	12.37
17	12.91
39	12.59
62	13.43
98	13.42

a. Create the scatterplot for these scores.

b. Calculate the mean and standard deviation for the variable number of candidates supported.

c. Calculate the mean and standard deviation for the variable profit.

d. Calculate the correlation between number of candidates supported and profit.

e. Calculate the regression equation for the prediction of profit from number of candidates supported.

f. Create a graph and draw the regression line.

g. What do these data suggest about the political process?

h. What third variables might be at play here?

6.10 Error visually: Exercises 6.6 and 6.8 used the example from Check Your Learning 5-2 on whether age can predict how much people study. Here are the data as presented in Chapter 5.

STUDENT	AGE	NUMBER OF HOURS STUDIED (PER WEEK)
1	19	5
2	20	20
3	20	8
4	21	12
5	21	18
6	23	25
7	22	15
8	20	10
9	19	14
10	25	15

a. Construct a graph that includes both the scatterplot for these data and the regression line as determined in Exercise 6.8. Draw vertical lines that connect each dot on the scatterplot with the regression line.

b. Construct a second graph that includes both the scatterplot and a line for the mean for hours studied, 14.2. The line will be a horizontal line beginning at 14.2 on the y-axis. Draw vertical lines that connect each dot on the scatterplot with the regression line.

c. Part (a) is a depiction of the error if we use the regression equation to predict hours studied. Part (b) is a depiction of the error if we use the mean to predict hours studied (i.e., if we predict that everyone will have the mean of 14.2 on hours studied per week). Which one appears to have less error? Briefly explain why the error is less in one situation.

6.11 Error mathematically: Exercises 6.6, 6.8, and 6.10 used the example from Check Your Learning 5-2 on whether age can predict how much people study. Here are the data once again.

STUDENT	AGE	NUMBER OF HOURS STUDIED (PER WEEK)
1	19	5
2	20	20
3	20	8
4	21	12
5	21	18
6	23	25
7	22	15
8	20	10
9	19	14
10	25	15

a. Calculate the proportionate reduction in error the long way.

b. Explain what the proportionate reduction in error that you calculated in part (a) tells us. Be specific about what it tells us about predicting using the regression equation versus predicting using the mean.

c. Demonstrate how the proportionate reduction in error could be calculated using the short way. Why does this make sense? That is, why does the correlation coefficient give us a sense of how useful the regression equation will be?

6.12 Cola, osteoporosis, regression, and causation: Does one's cola consumption predict one's bone mineral density? Using regression analyses, nutrition researchers found that older women who drank more cola (but not more of other carbonated drinks) tended to have lower bone mineral density, a risk factor for osteoporosis (Tucker, Morita, Qiao, Hannan, Cupples, & Kiel, 2006). Cola intake, therefore, does seem to predict bone mineral density.

a. Explain why we cannot conclude that cola intake causes a decrease in bone mineral density.

b. The researchers included a number of possible third variables in their regression analyses. Among the included variables were physical activity score, smoking, alcohol use, and calcium intake. They included the possible third variables first, and then added the bone density measure. What type of multiple regression might the researchers have used? Explain.

c. How might physical activity play a role as a third variable? Discuss its possible relation to both bone density and cola consumption.

d. How might calcium intake play a role as a third variable? Discuss its possible relation to both bone density and cola consumption.

6.13 Rain, violence, regression, and causation: Does the level of precipitation predict violence? Dubner and Levitt (2006) reported on various studies that found links between rain and violence. They mentioned one study by Miguel, Satyanath, and Sergenti that found that decreased rain was linked with an increased likelihood of civil war across a number of African countries that they examined. Referring to the study's authors, Dubner and Levitt state, "The causal effect of a drought, they argue, was frighteningly strong."

a. What is the independent variable in this study?

b. What is the dependent variable?

c. What possible third variables might play a role in this connection? That is, is it just the lack of rain that's causing violence, or is it something else? (*Hint:* Consider the likely economic base of many African countries.)

6.14 Podcasts, scatterplots, and regression: Are podcasts a drain on students' time, or does the information they contain help students do better in school? You collect data on the number of podcasts each student downloads per month and each student's GPA. When we calculate regression equations (just as when we calculate correlation coefficients), it's important to construct a scatterplot first. Explain how each of the following might present a problem if we calculate a simple linear regression equation to predict GPA from number of podcasts downloaded, and explain how a scatterplot might help us to identify the problem.

a. One student downloads 100 per month and has a GPA of 1.2.

b. You collected data only for students in the honors program in your school.

c. It turns out that really poor students don't download podcasts very often, maybe because they don't use their computers much at all, and really good students don't download podcasts very often, maybe because they're too busy studying to have time to listen.

6.15 Tutoring and the limits of regression: A researcher conducted a study in which students with problems learning mathematics were offered the opportunity to purchase time with special tutors; the number of weeks that students met with their tutors varied from 1 to 20. He found that the number of weeks of tutoring predicted mathematics performance in these children and recommended that parents of such children send them for tutoring for as many weeks as possible—for two years if they could afford it. List three problems with that interpretation. Be sure to explain why each of these poses a problem.

6.16 Tutoring and multiple regression: Consider again the example used in Exercise 6.15. As before, the researcher is interested in predicting mathematics ability with the ultimate goal of identifying ways to improve mathematics performance.

a. If you were to develop a multiple regression equation instead of a simple linear regression equation, what additional variables might be good independent variables? List at least one variable that can be manipulated (e.g., weeks of tutoring) and at least one variable that cannot be manipulated (e.g., parents' years of education).

b. If you were to develop the multiple regression equation using stepwise multiple regression, how would you proceed? (*Note:* There is more than one specific answer. In your response, demonstrate that you understand the basic process of stepwise multiple regression.)

c. If you were to develop the multiple regression equation using hierarchical multiple regression, how you would proceed? (*Note:* There is more than one specific answer. In your response, demonstrate that you understand the basic process of hierarchical multiple regression.)

d. Describe a situation in which stepwise multiple regression might be preferred.

e. Describe a situation in which hierarchical multiple regression might be preferred.

6.17 Depression, anxiety, and the output of simple linear regression: We analyzed data from a larger data set that one of the authors used for previous research (Nolan, Flynn, & Garber, 2003). In the current analyses, we used regression to look at factors that predict anxiety over a three-year period. Here is the output for the regression analysis examining whether depression at year one predicted anxiety at year three.

Coefficients(a)

	Unstandardized Coefficients		Standardized Coefficients	t	Sig.
	B	Std. Error	Beta		
(Constant)	24.698	.566		43.665	.000
Depression Year 1	.161	.048	.235	3.333	.001

a Dependent Variable: Anxiety Year 3

a. From this software output, write the regression equation.

b. As depression at year 1 increases by 1 point, what happens to the predicted anxiety level for year 3? Be specific.

c. If someone has a depression score of 10 at year 1, what would we predict for her anxiety score at year 3?

d. If someone has a depression score of 2 at year 1, what would we predict for his anxiety score at year 3?

6.18 Depression, anxiety, and the output of multiple regression: We conducted a second regression analysis on the data from Exercise 6.17. In addition to depression at year 1, we included a second independent variable to predict anxiety at year 3. We also included anxiety at year 1. (We might expect that the best predictor of anxiety at a later point in time is one's anxiety at an earlier point in time.) Here is the output for that analysis.

Coefficients(a)

	Unstandardized Coefficients		Standardized Coefficients	t	Sig.
	B	Std. Error	Beta		
(Constant)	17.038	1.484		11.482	.000
Depression Year 1	-.013	.055	-.019	-.237	.813
Anxiety Year 1	.307	.056	.442	5.521	.000

a Dependent Variable: Anxiety Year 3

a. From this software output, write the regression equation

b. As the first independent variable, depression at year 1, increases by 1 point, what happens to the predicted score on anxiety at year 3?

c. As the second independent variable, anxiety at year 1, increases by 1 point, what happens to the predicted score on anxiety at year 3?

d. Compare the predictive utility of depression at year 1 using the regression equation in Exercise 6.17 and using this regression equation. In which regression equation is depression at year 1 a better predictor? Given that we're using the same sample, is depression at year 1 actually better at predicting anxiety at year 3 in one situation versus the other? Why do you think there's a difference?

e. The table below is the correlation matrix for the three variables. As you can see, all three are highly correlated with each other. If we look at the intersection of each pair of variables, the number next to the words "Pearson correlation" is the correlation coefficient. For example, the correlation between "Anxiety year 1" and "Depression year 1" is 0.549. Which two variables show the strongest correlation? How might this explain the fact that depression at year 1 seems to be a better predictor when it's the only independent variable than when anxiety at year 1 also is included? What does this tell us about the importance of including third variables in our regression analyses when possible?

Correlations

		Depression Year 1	Anxiety Year 1	Anxiety Year 3
Depression Year 1	Pearson Correlation	1	.549(**)	.235(**)
	Sig. (2-tailed)		.000	.001
	N	240	240	192
Anxiety Year 1	Pearson Correlation	.549(**)	1	.432(**)
	Sig. (2-tailed)	.000		.000
	N	240	240	192
Anxiety Year 3	Pearson Correlation	.235(**)	.432(**)	1
	Sig. (2-tailed)	.001	.000	
	N	192	192	192

** Correlation is significant at the 0.01 level (2-tailed).

f. Let's say you want to add a fourth independent variable. You have to choose among three possible independent variables: (1) a variable highly correlated with both independent variables and the dependent variable, (2) a variable highly correlated with the dependent variable but not correlated with either independent variable, and (3) a variable not correlated with either of the independent variables or with the dependent variable. Which of the three variables is likely to make the multiple regression equation better? That is, which is likely to increase the proportionate reduction in error? Explain.

6.19 Symbols of statistics: Which of the following equations is incorrect? For each one that's incorrect, explain why it is incorrect and then write it correctly.

$\hat{Y} = z_{\hat{Y}}(SD_Y) + M_Y$

$X = z(\sigma) + M$

$\hat{Y} = 83 + 5(X)$

$z_Y = (r_{XY})(z_X)$

$\hat{Y} = 2.2 - 1.6(X_1) + 8.1(X_2)$

6.20 Language of statistics—*regression*: How is the word *regression* used in everyday language? How do statisticians use the word *regression*? (*Hint:* When you're describing the use of *regression* in everyday language, think of how we use the shorter version of the word, *regress*.)

▪ DIGGING DEEPER INTO THE DATA

6.21 The language of statistics—*latent variables* and *manifest variables*: In your own words, what is the difference between a latent variable and a manifest variable. Give examples of a construct and measure from a social science field that would represent a latent and manifest variable, respectively.

6.22 The language of statistics—*path*: How would you use the word *path* in everyday conversation? How would a statistician use the word *path*?

6.23 Structural equation modeling (SEM) and neighborhood social disorder: The accompanying figure is from a journal article entitled "Neighborhood Social Disorder as a Determinant of Drug Injection Behaviors: A Structural Equation Modeling Approach" (Latkin, Williams, Wang, & Curry, 2005).

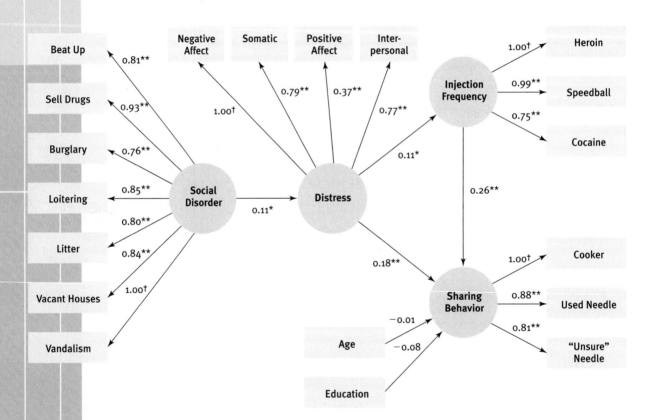

a. What are the four latent variables examined in this study?

b. What manifest variables were used to operationalize social disorder? Based on these manifest variables, in your own words, what do you think the authors mean by "social disorder"?

c. Looking only at the latent variables, which two variables seem to be most strongly related to each other? What is the number on that path? Is it positive or negative, and what does the sign of the number indicate about the relation between these variables?

d. Looking only at the latent variables, what overall story is this model telling? (Note that asterisks indicate relations that inferential statistics suggest are likely "real," even if they are fairly small.)

TERMS

simple linear regression
(p. 254)

regression to the mean
(p. 258)

intercept (p. 259)

slope (p. 259)

standard error of the
estimate (p. 265)

proportionate reduction in
error (p. 270)

orthogonal variable (p. 275)

multiple regression (p. 276)

stepwise multiple regression
(p. 278)

hierarchical multiple
regression (p. 279)

structural equation modeling
(SEM) (p. 281)

statistical (or theoretical)
model (p. 282)

path (p. 282)

path analysis (p. 282)

manifest variable (p. 284)

latent variable (p. 284)

longitudinal study (p. 284)

SYMBOLS

$\hat{Y}$

a

b

SS_{Total}

SS_{Error}

r^2

R^2

FORMULAS

$z_{\hat{Y}} = (r_{XY})(z_X)$

$X = z(\sigma) + \mu$

$\hat{Y} = a + b(X)$

$$r^2 = \frac{(SS_{Total} - SS_{Error})}{SS_{Total}}$$

INFERENTIAL STATISTICS
THE SURPRISING STORY OF
THE NORMAL CURVE

This is the story of an idea, but it begins when a shy, misunderstood teenager named A.D. was put in prison. It wasn't A.D.'s fault that he was in prison, unless you count being born into a particular religious tradition a crime. Nevertheless, a government-sanctioned religious persecution had plucked the quiet young man from a placid family life and redeposited him as an unwilling inmate inside a falling-down former monastery. So, without ever meaning to, the studious 18-year-old suddenly had lots of time to ruminate about the randomness of life-changing events.

When he was released from prison two years later, A.D. immediately fled the country of his birth and somehow arrived at a table at a coffeehouse in London. Descriptions of the young man suggest that he was still very shy, deeply religious, and probably still recovering from the random disruption of his quiet life. By contrast, Old Slaughter's Coffee House was a noisy, caffeinated explosion of intellectual freedom, impassioned political squabbles, and artists hustling for work. Desperate for money, the precocious scholar soon found other students who needed tutoring. But A.D. was so desperate to continue his own education that he tore out pages from his favorite book (Newton's *Principia*) so he could read them as he walked from one tutoring session to the next.

A.D. had experienced for himself how random events could transform a life, so it is not surprising that he turned his intellect to figuring out how chance influenced events. From his table at Old Slaughter's Coffee House, the young man worked on a mathematical equation that he believed could predict random events; he soon discovered that he was not the only one at Old Slaughter's interested in predicting random events. The local gamblers and insurance brokers sensed that something of great value was buried inside A.D.'s mathematical equations. After all, if you could predict the frequency of success and failure over the long run, then you could transform the many risks of day-to-day life into significant money-making opportunities. They were betting men, interested in gaining a financial edge; A.D. was interested in something deeper and longer lasting.

Even as he scribbled away at his table, A.D. knew that *predicting* and *randomness* were two words that contradicted each other: an oxymoron. But A.D. persevered until he had worked out a description of predictable randomness through a mathematical formula. He had the concept right; he even had the mathematical formula right. But he didn't have the picture. Perhaps he had not even tried to visualize the image his formula produced, the image that we now so easily accept as the idea that transformed the sciences by forming the foundation for inferential statistics: the normal curve (Figure 7-1). But that was a lot to expect from someone so young, especially because Abraham De Moivre was working alone, struggling for his daily bread in an unfriendly country, and still recovering from the religious persecution of French Huguenots in 1685.

Caffeinated Creativity?
Abraham De Moivre advised gamblers and insurance brokers from a table at Old Slaughter's Coffee House in London. The first formula predicting the probability of random events may have been created in that famously noisy place, an equivalent of today's coffee shop.

> THE NORMAL CURVE: IT'S EVERYWHERE!

Abraham De Moivre's discovery is what we now call the **normal curve,** *a specific bell-shaped curve that is unimodal, symmetric, and defined mathematically.* Less formally, this visual pattern looks like a camel with one hump (unimodal) that forms precisely the same slope toward the front as it does toward the back—a mirror image (symmetric). The normal curve seems to be everywhere—you just haven't noticed it before. There are many things that we don't notice until someone points them out to us: a speaker who habitually says "um" or "uh," the sound of a ticking clock, the number of people who wear their hair in a particular style, or even how much litter there is on your campus. But once you notice the normal curve, you start to see it almost everywhere. Formally, *the ubiquity of the normal curve indicates that the bell-shaped curve describes the approximate shape of the distributions of a surprising number of characteristics that vary.* Less formally, this simply means that the normal curve (or, more accurately,

■ A **normal curve** is a specific bell-shaped curve that is unimodal, symmetric, and defined mathematically.

■ The **ubiquity of the normal curve** indicates that the bell-shaped curve describes the approximate shape of the distributions of a surprising number of characteristics that vary.

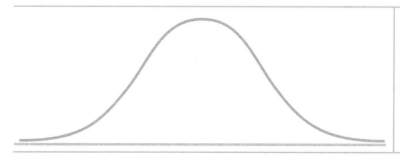

FIGURE 7-1
The Bell-Shaped Curve

Abraham De Moivre developed the first mathematical formula for the bell-shaped curve.

very good approximations of the normal curve) seems to be everywhere (ubiquity means "everywhere at the same time").

An approximation of the normal curve first appeared in this text in Chapter 2 when we rearranged the random collection of scores on the Consideration of Future Consequences (CFC) scale to the more orderly pattern of the lowest score to the highest score. There were only a few very low scores and only a few very high scores; most scores, probably including yours, could be found somewhere in the middle of the distribution. Similarly, imagine that a thief stopped the movie at your local movie theater on a busy Saturday night and ordered everyone to empty their pockets and purses. The resulting distribution of money from each person would reveal only a few people with almost no money at all, a few other people with a great deal of money, and a large number of people somewhere in the middle. When the gamblers seeking advice from Abraham De Moivre threw their dice, they would occasionally roll a 1 + 1 to make a total of 2, and they would occasionally roll a 6 + 6 to make a total of 12. But the numbers totaling 5, 6, and 7 would turn up quite frequently because they could be formed in multiple, predictable ways. For example, a 5 could be achieved by rolling 1 + 4, 2 + 3, 3 + 2, and 4 + 1. The dice are both random in the short term and predictable in the long term. The frequency with which each number turns up after many rolls of the dice conforms, roughly, to the bell-shaped curve.

De Moivre never drew the bell-shaped curve, but he did devise the mathematical formula that described it and, in so doing, opened the door to inferential statistics. His discovery transformed the sciences, provided an empirical foundation for risk management, and gave rise to the insurance industry. Not bad for a formula probably devised on a dirty table in a crowded coffeehouse. Inferential statistics will never, of course, conquer all uncertainty or eliminate all risk. Inferential statistics do, however, make uncertainty and risk more manageable by clarifying the probabilities of particular events.

Curiously, the existence of the normal curve seems to bother many people. For example, some people are reluctant to embrace the use of statistics in the behavioral sciences (especially in psychology) because they believe it represents an effort to use an objective approach to understanding subjective experience. There is likely some validity to that viewpoint; the social sciences don't pretend to be able to answer many of the most interesting questions. But with a little creativity, the debate between objective ways of knowing and subjective ways of knowing can be turned into an empirical question: How does the subjective approach compare to the objective approach?

Fortunately, this very question has been asked, and answered, by so many different people that one team of researchers (Grove, Zald, Lebow, Snitz, & Nelson, 1996) was able to conduct a study of all the studies testing this very idea. This kind of study is called a *meta-analysis*, *a type of statistical analysis that simultaneously examines as many studies as possible for a given research topic*. A meta-analysis lets us see the overall pattern of results about a particular topic rather just the results of a single study. Grove and colleagues examined 136 studies that compared objective prediction methods with the subjective judgments of professionals in their relevant fields.

In these studies, objective prediction methods were those that used only data such as test scores or specific diagnostic criteria; by contrast, subjective prediction methods utilized *both* the brainpower and intuition of professionals *plus* access to the same data. For example, an objective prediction method might use an equation that includes *only* one's college grade point average (GPA) and

■ A **meta-analysis** is a type of statistical analysis that simultaneously examines as many studies as possible for a given research topic.

Graduate Record Exam (GRE) score to predict graduate school performance; a subjective prediction method might involve the educated (subjective) guesses of a team of professors who base their prediction on information about students' GPAs and GRE scores, *plus* information from recommendations, and personal essays. Because we are confronted with both objective and subjective decision-making opportunities every day, it is not surprising that researchers have compared the effectiveness of these two approaches in a variety of ways.

Among the *many* types of outcomes that were included in this meta-analysis were objective and subjective predictions of military training success, outcome of psychotherapy, medical diagnosis, graduate school success, job performance, magazine advertising sales, choice of occupation, criminal behavior, and suicide. As you might expect from so many researchers with so many different interests, this was an extremely broad-based comparison of objective and subjective approaches. Use your own subjective intuition about the results of this meta-analysis: What do you predict about the results of this broadly based summary testing the superiority of objective or subjective prediction methods?

When these 136 studies were combined in the meta-analysis, the objective methods of prediction were approximately 10% more accurate, on average, than were the subjective methods. Of the 136 studies, the objective method was superior in 64 cases. Sixty-four other studies showed that objective and subjective methods were equally accurate. In only eight studies did the subjective judgments of professionals make better predictions than objective criteria. Moreover, in many cases, those making the subjective judgments had *more* information than was used by the objective prediction method, yet most of the time they still didn't do as well. This meta-analysis indicates that objectively based prediction tends to outperform subjectively formed professional judgment. And it is De Moivre's formula that opened the door to this kind of inferential, statistically based decision making. The shy young man writing at a table in a London coffeehouse was changing the world in ways that he could not have imagined, simply by following his curiosity to a calculation of chance events.

Happily, there are only three things that we need to know to understand the basis of inferential statistics. These three surprisingly easy-to-understand ideas took about 300 years to articulate, but today we can understand them much more quickly than that. Here they are:

1. The approximate shape of the normal curve is everywhere (ubiquity).

2. The bell shape of the normal curve may be translated into percentages (standardization).

3. A distribution of means produces a bell-shaped curve even if the original distribution of individual scores is not bell-shaped, as long as the means are from sufficiently large samples (the central limit theorem).

But the remarkable story of the normal curve is far more than a mathematical struggle toward enlightenment. It is a tale of religious persecution and personal perseverance, poverty and greed, ego and discovery. The seductive normal curve captured the fancy of atheists and theologians, astronomers and brewers, psychologists and physicians. And the story travels across time from Old Slaughter's Coffee House in the 1600s, through the Guinness brewery in Ireland in the early 1900s, and into the recent successes in space exploration by the Mars rovers at the beginning of the twenty-first century. So, before we follow this trail of dramatic successes, let's strengthen our current understanding by reviewing some of the useful things that we have already learned about distributions and the normal curve. In previous chapters, we have done the following:

1. Reorganized distributions of scores by rearranging them in order of magnitude, that is, from highest to lowest or from lowest to highest (Chapter 2, frequency tables)

2. Observed the predictable, often bell-shaped pattern into which distributions of scores fall (Chapter 2, histograms and frequency polygons)

3. Learned how to describe distributions of scores using measures of central tendency, variability, skewness, and kurtosis (Chapter 2)

4. Created visual representations of distributions of scores using histograms and frequency polygons (Chapter 2)

5. Learned that we can have distributions of scores based on samples, as well as distributions of scores based on entire populations (Chapter 4, sampling from a population)

So let's combine our previous learning with our growing understanding of the importance of the normal curve. For example, let's consider the heights, in inches, of a sample of 5 students taken from a larger sample that included several of the authors' statistics classes:

52   77   63   64   64

Figure 7-2 shows a histogram of those heights, with a bell-shaped curve superimposed upon the histogram. With so few scores, we can only begin to guess at the emerging shape of a normal distribution. Notice that three of the observations (63 inches, 64 inches, and 64 inches) are represented by the middle bar; that is why it is three times higher than the bars representing a single observation

FIGURE 7-2
Sample of 5

Here is a histogram of the heights in inches of 5 students. With so few students, the data are unlikely to closely resemble the normal curve that we would see for an entire population of heights.

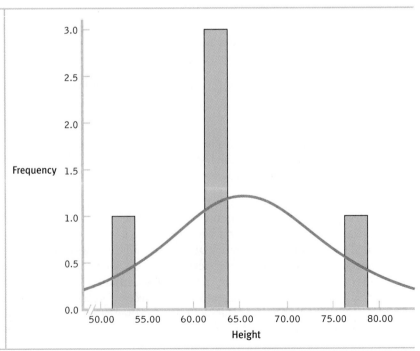

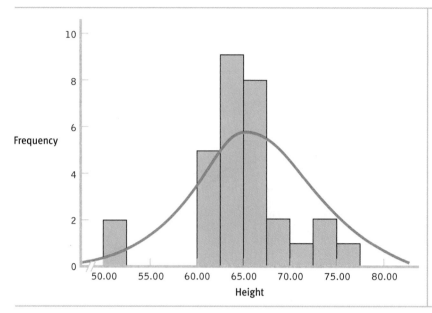

FIGURE 7-3
Sample of 30

Here is a histogram of the heights in inches of 30 students. With a larger sample, the data begin to resemble the normal curve of an entire population of heights.

of 52 inches and another observation of 77 inches. Now, here are the heights in inches from a random sample of 30 students:

52	77	63	64	64	62	63	64	67	52
67	66	66	63	63	64	62	62	64	65
67	68	74	74	69	71	61	61	66	66

Figure 7-3 shows the histogram for these data. You'll notice that the heights of 30 students resemble a bell curve more so than do the heights of just 5 students, although certainly not perfectly. Now, Table 7-1 gives the heights

TABLE 7-1. A SAMPLE OF HEIGHTS

These are the heights, in inches, of 140 students.

52	77	63	64	64	62	63	64	67	52
67	66	66	63	63	64	62	62	64	65
67	68	74	74	69	71	61	61	66	66
68	63	63	62	62	63	65	67	73	62
63	63	64	60	69	67	67	63	66	61
65	70	67	57	61	62	63	63	63	64
64	68	63	70	64	60	63	64	66	67
68	68	68	72	73	65	61	72	71	65
60	64	64	66	56	62	65	66	72	69
60	66	73	59	60	60	61	63	63	65
66	69	72	65	62	62	62	66	64	63
65	67	58	60	60	67	68	68	69	63
63	73	60	67	64	67	64	66	64	72
65	67	60	70	60	67	65	67	62	66

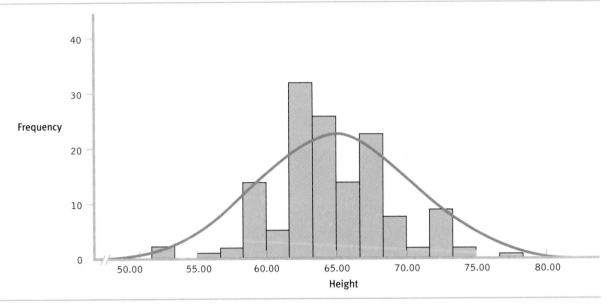

FIGURE 7-4
Sample of 140

Here is a histogram of the heights in inches of 140 students. As the sample increases, the shape of the distribution becomes more and more like the normal curve we would see for an entire population. Imagine the distribution of the data for a sample of 1000 students or of 1 million.

in inches from a random sample of 140 students. Figure 7-4 shows the histogram for these data.

We first introduced the idea of sample size in Chapter 2. As we learned, sample size refers to frequency, that is, the number of individuals who comprise the sample from which we generated data. Now we will learn why sample size is so important for gaining a representative sample that is also more likely to be bell-shaped. We can see that as the sample size increases from 5 to 30 to 140, the distribution more and more closely resembles a normal curve, as long as the underlying population distribution is normal. Imagine even larger samples—a sample of 1000 or of 1 million. Eventually, the size of the sample itself would approach that of the population of interest; as it does so, the shape of the distribution of the sample scores would approach the smoother, more symmetric shape of the distribution of the entire population.

Statistics becomes most exciting when we recognize that it is simply a remarkably handy tool that allows us to test our own ideas (as long as we are willing to let the evidence change our minds). As we will discover, the data in your sample and in the population from which the data are taken will tend to be normally distributed, and this pattern will become more evident as our sample size increases. We anticipate a fairly normal distribution whether we want to study a sample of jealousy scores, distances that people sit from each other in the student center, levels of credit card debt among college students, reaction times to the Stroop task, or the scores from our current example: heights. They all support the idea that the normal curve describes many things that vary.

EXPERIENCE IT FOR YOURSELF

THE BELL-SHAPED NORMAL CURVE IN THEORY AND IN PRACTICE

For a theoretical understanding of how chance is related to the bell-shaped curve, start playing with the virtual quincunx (pronounced "quinn-cux") machine, which was first developed by Francis Galton to demonstrate how chance invariably evolves into a bell-shaped curve. Give yourself time to play—watching what seems like chaos become coherent over the long run can be oddly addictive. You can experience the central limit theorem for yourself by using the Web site for this text or searching the Web under the terms "quincunx," "quincunx board," or "Galton board."

As you start fooling around with chance, notice the following:

1. More observations (balls dropped into the machine) continually refine the smoothness of the curve.

2. Modifying the probability parameters produces an increasingly skewed distribution.

Approximations to the normal curve are so common that certain deviations from the normal curve are used to detect fraud. In Chapter 4, for example, we discussed the method by which Chicago schoolteachers, under administrative pressure to produce results (which would get them merit pay raises), were caught cheating by changing student answers on standardized tests (Levitt & Dubner, 2005). Too many students were performing at too high a level, and the fraud was revealed by a negatively skewed distribution of test scores for the students in a given class: too many students were bunched up on the right-hand side of the curve (high test scores).

Bernstein (1996) reported another example of the normal curve as a sleuthing tool—this one from the nineteenth century—when the statistician Adolphe Quetelet used deviations from the normal curve to identify widespread cheating in the military. Being too short qualified as an excuse for soldiers to avoid combat duty. When Quetelet examined the distribution of the heights of 100,000 French soldiers, too many of them were identified as being very short. The fraud was revealed by a positively skewed distribution of heights: too many soldiers were bunched up on the left-hand side of the curve (short in height). The ubiquity of the normal curve means that we have a right to raise serious questions whenever we are confronted with a non-normal distribution. Identifying fraud is just one more of the many success stories made possible by statistics.

We should note that there are exceptions to the ubiquity of the normal curve within the behavioral sciences. Micceri (1989) pointed out that many commonly used measures, such as academic achievement tests used by school systems, do not invariably lead to distributions that are approximately normal. Despite the fact that approximately normal distributions occur frequently, it is important that researchers examine their own data graphically before conducting statistical analyses.

In summary, understanding probability is a powerful way to manage the risks of everyday living. Using the power of the normal curve to make such inferences depends on the ubiquity of the normal curve, our ability to use the normal curve for standardization, and the central limit theorem. *Ubiquity* means that the normal curve describes the distributions of almost everything that varies. *Standardization* means that we can use the normal curve to determine percentages, which allows us to compare individual scores to the whole collection of scores that forms the distribution. According to the *central limit theorem*, a distribution of means calculated from sufficiently large samples of observations will approximate a normal curve more than will samples of individual scores, even when the population of scores from which the samples were selected is not bell-shaped.

⊙ CHECK YOUR LEARNING

7-1 A sample of 225 students completed the CFC scale in 2005. The scores are means of responses to the 12 items, with some responses reversed so that a high score indicates higher consideration of future consequences. Overall CFC scores, the mean of the item ratings for each participant, range from 1 to 5.

a. Here are CFC scores for 5 of those students, rounded to the nearest whole or half number to facilitate creation of a histogram: 3.50, 3.50, 3.0, 4.0, and 2.0. Create a histogram for these data, either by hand or using software.

b. Now create a histogram for the scores of 30 students. As before, the scores have been rounded to the nearest whole or half number.

3.5	3.5	3.0	4.0	2.0	4.0	2.0	4.0	3.5	4.5
4.5	4.0	3.5	2.5	3.5	3.5	4.0	3.0	3.0	2.5
3.0	3.5	4.0	3.5	3.5	2.0	3.5	3.0	3.0	2.5

c. The accompanying histogram for 225 students uses the actual (not rounded) CFC scores. What do you notice about the shape of this distribution of scores as the size of the sample increases from 5 to 30 to 225?

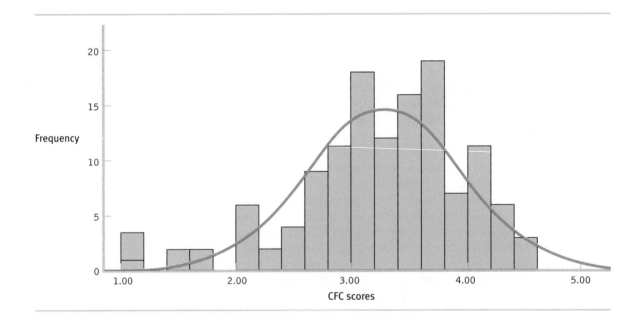

> STANDARDIZATION, *z* SCORES, AND THE NORMAL CURVE: DISCOVERING REASON BEHIND THE RANDOMNESS

Perhaps the French would not have rejected Abraham De Moivre if they had been able to look into the future of his mathematical idea. Fortunately, De Moivre's new English colleagues quickly recognized his genius; in fact, they elected him to the Royal Society of Statisticians while he was still in his early 30s. Unfortunately, they never offered him regular employment simply because he was French. Consequently, De Moivre decided never to marry because he did not believe he would be able to support a family. De Moivre was described as

> one of Newton's closest friends . . . sitting daily in Slaughter's Coffee House in Long Acre . . . at the beck and call of gamblers. . . . Every evening Newton would come and fetch De Moivre from the Coffee House. . . . I picture De Moivre working at a dirty table with a broken-down gambler beside him and Isaac Newton walking through the crowd to his corner to fetch out his friend. When asked difficult mathematical questions, Isaac Newton frequently told people, "Go to Mr. De Moivre. He knows these things better than I do" (Pearson, 1978, p. 143).

Curiously, De Moivre lived and died in a manner oddly consistent with the diminishing tails of the bell-shaped curve he helped discover. He remained mentally alert as he aged, so he self-observed his pattern of progressively greater sleepiness each day, an observation he used to predict the day on which he would sleep for 24 hours and finish his life.

One of the many benefits of De Moivre's discovery of the bell-shaped curve is that it creates opportunities for meaningful comparisons. As you may have observed, we humans spend a great deal of time comparing ourselves with one another (e.g., Suls, Martin, & Wheeler, 2002). However, without the clarity of statistics, we often make comparisons in a self-serving and biased manner by comparing ourselves in a way that fulfills particular psychological needs. For example, we will compare our academic ability to that of others if academics is our strength but choose an athletic comparison if that is where we excel. We may choose the trendiness of our wardrobe, the tidiness of our lawn, the newness of our car, or the appearance of wealth—usually anything that will bolster our self-esteem. Fortunately, the ubiquity of the normal curve helps us overcome our own self-serving biases because it allows us to make fairer, and therefore more meaningful, comparisons.

The normal curve allows us to standardize and then make such comparisons. Specifically, when the data are normally distributed, we can compare our own score on a particular variable, such as our score on a statistics test, to the entire distribution of scores, such as the distribution of all students' scores on that statistics test. We do this by converting our raw score—our grade—to a standardized score for which percentiles are already known. *The process of standardization converts individual scores to standard scores for which we know the percentiles (if the data are normally distributed).* Standardization does this by converting individual scores from different normal distributions to a shared normal distribution with a known mean, standard deviation, and percentiles.

Another way to express standardization is to play on the familiar complaint that "you can't compare apples and oranges." Well, yes we can, and in a most interesting way. We can take any apple from a normal distribution of apples, find its particular z score using the mean and standard deviation for the distribution of apples, convert the z score to a percentile, and discover that a particular apple is, say, larger than 85% of all the other apples. Similarly, we can take any orange from a normal distribution of oranges, find its particular z score using the mean and standard deviation for the distribution of

■ The process of **standardization** converts individual scores from different normal distributions to a shared normal distribution with a known mean, standard deviation, and percentiles.

Apples and Oranges
Standardization allows us to compare apples with oranges. If we can standardize the raw scores on two different scales, converting both scores to z scores, we can then compare the scores directly.

■ The **z distribution** is a normal distribution of standardized scores.

■ The **standard normal distribution** is a normal distribution of z scores.

oranges, convert the z score to a percentile, and discover that this particular orange is, say, larger than 97% of all the other oranges. The orange (with respect to other oranges) is bigger than the apple (with respect to other apples), and yes, that is an honest comparison of apples and oranges. We simply compare their standardized scores, each relative to its own group. Now substitute tennis for apples and golf for oranges and you can determine if Roger Federer is better at tennis than Tiger Woods is at golf. As you can imagine, standardization is an extremely powerful tool.

The ubiquity of the normal curve allows us to convert scores to percentiles because, theoretically, 100% of the population is represented under the bell-shaped curve. This means that the midpoint (which is the mean, the median, and the mode in a normal curve) is the 50th percentile. If your individual score on some test happens to be located to the right of the mean, you know that your score lies somewhere above the 50th percentile; a score to the left of the mean indicates that your score is somewhere below the 50th percentile. To make more specific comparisons, we convert raw scores to their percentiles by first converting them to z scores. As we learned in Chapter 5, a z score is the number of standard deviations a particular score is from the mean. The z score is part of a very specific distribution; the **z distribution** is a distribution of standardized scores—a distribution of z scores. And the **standard normal distribution** is a distribution of z scores.

But most people are not content merely with knowing whether their own score is above or below the average score. When we discover that we're different from others, we want to know by how much, and the z distribution allows us to make that comparison, as shown in Figure 7-5. After all, there is likely a big difference between scoring at the 51st and the 99th percentile in height. Both are above average, but the person whose height is at the 99th percentile is likely to be much, much taller than the person whose height is at the 51st percentile. The standardized z distribution allows us to do the following:

1. Transform raw scores into standardized scores called z scores (Chapter 5)

2. Transform z scores back into raw scores (Chapter 6)

3. Compare z scores to each other—even when the z scores represent raw scores on different scales (as we'll learn to do in this chapter)

4. Transform z scores into percentiles that are more easily understood (as we'll also learn to do in this chapter)

Standardization is a powerful tool because it creates many opportunities for precise, unbiased comparisons. Because social comparisons are critical to our

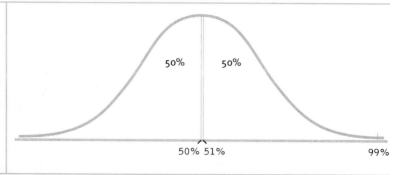

FIGURE 7-5
The All-Encompassing z Distribution

The z distribution theoretically includes all possible scores, so, when it's based on a normal distribution, we know that 50% of the scores are above the mean and 50% are below the mean. But the 51st percentile and the 99th percentile are still far from each other, so two people making a comparison usually want more precise information than whether or not they are above average.

identity development, standardization makes it possible for us to acquire a far more realistic sense of our own abilities, strengths, and weaknesses. So let's begin with an illustration that demonstrates how standardization makes meaningful comparisons possible, even when those comparisons belong to different distributions.

Standardization: Comparing *z* Scores

Imagine that a friend is taking a course in statistics at the same time that you are, but with a different professor. Each professor has a different grading scheme, so each professor's class produces a different distribution of test scores that has meaning only within the context of that particular class. But now, thanks to standardization, we can convert each raw score to a *z* score and compare raw scores from *different* distributions. For example, let's say that you both took a quiz this week. You got a 92 out of a possible 100; the distribution of your class had a mean of 78.1 and a standard deviation of 12.2. Your friend got an 8.1 out of a possible 10; the distribution of his class had a mean of 6.8 with a standard deviation of 0.74. Again, we're only interested in the classes that took the test, so these are populations rather than samples. Who did better?

If we standardize the two scores in terms of their respective distributions, then we can make a direct comparison of the two *z* scores:

Making Comparisons
z scores create a way to compare students taking different exams from different courses. If each exam score can be converted to a *z* score with respect to the mean and standard deviation for its particular exam, the two scores can then be compared directly.

$$\text{Your score: } z = \frac{(X - \mu)}{\sigma} = \frac{(92 - 78.1)}{12.2} = 1.14$$

$$\text{Your friend's score: } z = \frac{(X - \mu)}{\sigma} = \frac{(8.1 - 6.8)}{0.74} = 1.76$$

First, let's check our work. Do these answers make sense? Yes—both you and your friend scored above the mean, so you both have positive *z* scores. Second, we'll compare the *z* scores, the standardized versions of the two raw scores. Although you both scored well above the mean in terms of standard deviations, your friend did better with respect to his class than you did with respect to your class.

The standardized *z* distribution brings an enormous advantage to the world of research: it allows us to compare observations from different distributions. It's an idea we have been preparing you for throughout this text. For example, most of the examples we used just in Chapter 5 involved making comparisons from extremely different kinds of distributions, such as these:

1. Astrology and personality

2. The weight of cockroaches measured in drachmas, pounds, and grams

3. Outside temperature and the number of people going to the beach

4. The amount of junk food consumed and the amount of body fat

5. How many cars travel on a particular road and how often the road needs maintenance

6. Nights partying and GPA

7. Spending on health care and life expectancy

8. Cell phone bills and number of hours spent studying

The z distribution allows us to make meaningful comparisons between very different kinds of observations, which means that we can conduct research on all sorts of different topics.

Putting *z* Scores to Work: Transforming *z* Scores to Percentiles

So z scores are useful in and of themselves because they do both of the following:

1. They give us a sense of where a score falls in relation to the mean of its population (in terms of the standard deviation of its population).
2. They allow us to compare scores from different distributions.

Yet we can be even more specific about where a score falls. So, an additional and particularly helpful use of z scores is that they also have this property:

3. They can be transformed into percentiles.

Because the shape of a normal curve is standard (unimodal and symmetric), we automatically know something about the percentage of any particular area under the curve. Think of the normal curve and the horizontal line below it as forming a shape. (In fact, it *is* a shape; it's actually a frequency polygon that shows the frequencies for each score in the distribution. Because it includes every score in the population, the frequency polygon is smoothed out and curved, unlike the city skyline frequency polygons that we created in Chapter 2.) Like any shape, the area below the normal curve can be measured. Rather than quantifying the space in terms of some kind of measurement such as square centimeters, however, we quantify the space below a normal curve in terms of percentages. We can determine what percentage of the curve falls below or above any vertical line drawn from the line below the curve to the top of the curve.

The normal curve is such a useful tool because statisticians have determined the specific percentages that fall within each particular area. To start, the normal curve is, by definition, symmetric, so we know that exactly 50% of scores fall below the mean and 50% fall above the mean; that is, one side is a mirror image of the other. Yet, as we see in Figure 7-6, we can be more specific than this. For example, we know that approximately 34% of scores fall between the mean and a z score of 1.0; and because of symmetry, 34% of scores also fall between the mean and a z score of -1.0. We also know that approximately 14% of scores fall between the z scores of 1.0 and 2.0, and, by symmetry, 14% of scores fall between the z scores of -1.0 and -2.0. Finally, we know that

FIGURE 7-6
The Normal Curve and Percentages

The standard shape of the normal curve allows us to know the approximate percentages under different parts of the curve. For example, about 34% of scores will fall between the mean and a *z* score of 1.0.

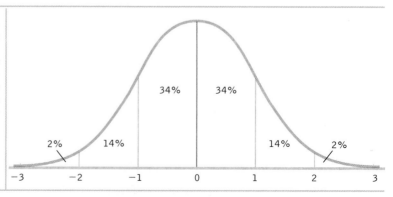

approximately 2% of scores fall between the z scores of 2.0 and 3.0 and 2% of scores fall between the z scores of -2.0 and -3.0.

By simple addition, we can determine that approximately 68% (34 + 34 = 68) of scores fall within 1 standard deviation—or one z score—of the mean; that approximately 96% (14 + 34 + 34 + 14 = 96) of scores fall within 2 standard deviations of the mean; and that all or nearly all (2 + 14 + 34 + 34 + 14 + 2 = 100) scores fall within 3 standard deviations of the mean. These percentages are useful guidelines for determining the percentage associated with a given z score. For example, if you know you are about 1 standard deviation above the mean on your statistics quiz, then you can add the 50% below the mean to the 34% between the mean and the z score of 1.0 that you earned on your quiz, and know that your score corresponds to approximately the 84th percentile.

If you know that you are about 1 standard deviation below the mean, you know that you are in the lower 50% of scores and that 34% of scores fall between your score and the mean. By subtracting, you can calculate that 50 − 34 = 16% of scores fall below you. Your score corresponds to approximately the 16th percentile. You may remember that scores indicating performance on standardized tests, such as the SAT, are frequently expressed as percentiles.

In the next chapter, we'll learn how to use a z table to calculate even more specific percentages for particular z scores. For now, it's important to understand that the z distribution forms a normal curve with a unimodal, symmetric shape; because the shape is known and 100% of the population falls beneath the bell-shaped curve, we can determine the percentage of any area under the curve. So now, in addition to the observation that the normal curve is almost everywhere (ubiquity), we have a name for this second important characteristic of the bell-shaped curve: standardization. Through standardization we can use the predictable bell shape of the normal curve to convert raw scores to z scores and z scores to percentiles.

In summary, standardization is a way to create meaningful comparisons between observations from different distributions. It is accomplished by first transforming raw scores from different distributions into z scores, also known as standardized scores. An individual's standardized z score may then be compared to the standardized distribution in order to understand an individual's performance relative to all others in the distribution. In addition, z scores may be transformed back into raw scores simply by reversing the formula. z scores correspond to percentiles that more clearly communicate how an individual compares with the larger distribution.

⊙ CHECK YOUR LEARNING

7-2 A study of CFC that we've used as an example in previous chapters found a mean CFC score of 3.51, with a standard deviation of 0.61, for the 664 students in the sample (Petrocelli, 2003).

a. If a student had a CFC score of 2.3, what would her z score be? Roughly, to what percentile does that z score correspond?

b. If a student had a CFC score of 4.7, what would his z score be? Roughly, to what percentile does that z score correspond?

c. If a student had a CFC score at the 84th percentile, what would her z score be?

d. What is the raw score of the student at the 84th percentile? Use symbolic notation and the formula. Explain why this answer makes sense.

> THE CENTRAL LIMIT THEOREM: HOW SAMPLING CREATES A LESS VARIABLE DISTRIBUTION

De Moivre's powerful mathematical idea needed to be expressed as a picture. Yet, surprisingly, simply drawing a sketch of the normal curve took about 200 years. Even after we knew that the normal curve looked like a bell, it took us another 100 years to understand its power and importance. Perhaps De Moivre sketched the normal curve on some coffee-stained piece of paper at Old Slaughter's Coffee House. We'll never know.

We do know that in 1769, Daniel Bernoulli created the visual approximation of the normal curve. Then, 80 years later, in 1849, Augustus De Morgan made an informal sketch of the normal curve and sent it by mail to the astronomer George Airy. (Both curves are shown in Figure 7-7.) The two men were stumbling toward the normal curve from a somewhat different direction than the approach that De Moivre had used; they were worried about measurement errors. Like other astronomers, De Morgan and Airy were trying to precisely record the time at which, for example, particular planets touched the horizon. Airy had adopted the plan of averaging those errors in order to obtain a best estimate. When he combined all those observations into a distribution, that distribution began to take on the shape that is so familiar to us today. Airy replied to De Morgan by mail the very next day, urging him to draw a picture of the curve. "I recommend you to do what I never did myself . . . to graphicize" (quoted in Stigler, 1999, p. 408–409).

Two critical features of the normal curve were apparent to these early scientists. First, the normal curve was symmetric: the left side was a mirror image of the right. Second, the middle of the normal curve represented their best estimate of reality because it averaged unavoidable (in effect, random) errors. This evenly balanced variability around the middle of the normal curve could be the result of many things in addition to measurement error, such as individual differences or noisy data. But the average still represented the best estimate of whatever was being measured, and the surrounding pattern of errors looked like a bell: Only a few errors were way off by being extremely high or extremely low; most errors clustered tightly around the middle.

But after 300 years of work on the normal curve, the ability to visualize it was about to establish statistics as a wonderfully practical tool. Making statistical inferences from samples was a tool that could be used by botanists, geographers, biologists, astronomers, political scientists, and soon by the researchers

FIGURE 7-7
The Bell Curve is Born

Daniel Bernoulli (a) created an approximation of the bell-shaped curve in this 1769 sketch "describing the frequency of errors." Augustus De Morgan (b) included this second sketch in a letter to astronomer George Airy in 1849.

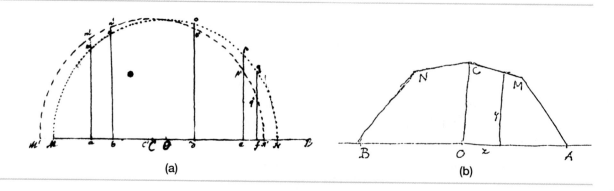

(a)   (b)

in the emerging sciences of psychology and sociology. But first, the idea of the normal curve had to pass through a brewery, where its power became a prized industrial secret. In the early 1900s, W. S. Gossett started to apply this oddly shaped sketch of the normal curve to his job: quality control in the Guinness ale factory. Gossett's work represented the intersection of theoretical and applied statistics.

One of the practical problems that Gossett faced at the Guinness factory was related to sampling yeast cultures in order to produce a more reliable ale. Too little yeast led to an incomplete fermentation, whereas too much led to bitter-tasting beer. To sample both accurately and economically, Gossett tested the idea of using the average of samples from four observations. He did this to determine how quickly the average of samples from four would come to represent a population of 3000 (Gossett, 1908, 1942; Stigler, 1999). This small adjustment (taking the *average* of a sample from four rather than a sample from one) is possible because of the central limit theorem.

The central limit theorem is the culmination of the work of many different scholars (Stigler, 1986, 1999). It first evolved from the work of theoretical mathematicians like Abraham De Moivre. Later, the central limit theorem developed because of the work of applied researchers like Frederick Bessel, who was annoyed because the instrument he used to measure the planets' movements kept producing errors (it jiggled accidentally or the observers' judgment was affected by small, random bursts of light). Bessel graphed those observations, noticed that the errors surrounded what could be considered his best-guess estimate, and further noticed that the shape of those errors was a predictable curve *and* that more observations produced a smoother-looking curve. You experienced the central limit theorem for yourself by playing with the virtual quincunx machine. So you understand why the ***central limit theorem*** *asserts that a distribution of sample means approaches a normal curve as sample size increases*. In other words, the central limit theorem demonstrates two important principles:

1. Repeated sampling will approximate a normal curve, *even when the original population is not normally distributed*.

2. A distribution of means is less variable than a distribution of individual scores.

Instead of randomly sampling a single data point, Gossett randomly sampled four data points from the population of 3000, computed the average of those four scores, and compared it to a distribution of means. *A **distribution of means** is a distribution composed of many means that are calculated from all possible samples of a given size, all taken from the same population*. It is often more formally called the sampling distribution of the mean. Put another way, the numbers that make up the distribution of means are not individual scores; they are *means* of samples of individual scores. The resulting distribution of means more consistently produces a normal distribution (although with less variance) *even when the population distribution is not normal*. The fact that Gossett used samples of four rather than three, five, or some other size is not important. The important point is that he created his data points from averages of multiple observations rather than from individual observations. The average of a sample is a more precise estimate of the population mean than an individual score; it also limits the effects of a single outlier because that outlier also would become part of an average.

■ The **central limit theorem** refers to how a distribution of sample means is a more normal distribution than a distribution of scores even when the population distribution is not normal.

■ A **distribution of means** is a distribution composed of many means that are calculated from all possible samples of a given size, all taken from the same population.

This second principle of the central limit theorem is the most counterintuitive, at least until you see it actually take place before your eyes: repeated sampling of means will produce a normal distribution even when the original distribution of scores is not normal. Perhaps you will initially react to this feature of the central limit theorem in the same way that the authors reacted when it first was presented to them. We reasoned, "If the original distribution of scores is not normal, why in the world should sampling means from this distribution create something closer to a normal distribution?" On the other hand, if this central limit theorem is true, then we could use sampling strategies to calculate the probabilities of almost anything we can imagine. Well, not only could we, we can!

Creating a Distribution of Means: Understanding Why It Works

The central limit theorem is important for many reasons, but one of its most pragmatic benefits is how richly it helps the research process. Our understanding of the central limit theorem allows us to conduct research across a vast array of topics because calculating a probability allows us to learn how *un*usual a given occurrence is, how extreme a difference might be. Because of this, it is the central limit theorem that underlies so many statistical processes. Let's first review some of the information we already know about distributions before we move on to the almost magical power of the central limit theorem. We have learned the following:

1. There are many different possible shapes of distributions, such as leptokurtic, mesokurtic, and platykurtic; skewed; unimodal, bimodal, and multimodal; and bell-shaped (Chapter 2).

2. Our sample has a distribution that tends to become increasingly normal (i.e., bell-shaped) as the sample size increases, as long as the underlying population from which our sample is drawn is normally distributed (this chapter).

3. The population from which our sample comes is not necessarily normally distributed (Chapter 2).

4. We use standardization to express raw scores as percentiles, via the z distribution (this chapter).

We can now add to these pieces of understanding the principle we have noted from the central limit theorem:

5. Repeated sampling of means rather than scores will approximate a normal curve, *even when the original population is not normally distributed.*

At a personal level, we all like to know how our individual score compares with all other scores, whether we're comparing height, income, GPA, number of publications, or a particular personality trait. But at a research level, we want to compare the sample *means* calculated on many individuals to other means, not individual scores to other individual scores. For example, if we calculate a mean height for a group of students who have been given a special growth drug, we want to know how different the mean height of that group of students is from the mean height of the population of students who have not taken the growth drug. We would never study only one student because we couldn't be sure that any difference in growth was due to the drug or to the normal development of that particular individual. Instead, we would study a sample of many students as a way to replicate our findings within the very same study. If the mean score is extreme, then we might be able to reject a null hypothesis that says that the drug does not work.

But this scenario presents us with a distribution of means, not the distribution of scores with which we're familiar, and this is precisely the point at which the central limit theorem becomes so important. The distribution of means is not exactly like the distribution of scores—most important, the distribution of means is more tightly clustered (has a smaller standard deviation) than a distribution of scores. Like most learning in statistics, understanding this feature of the central limit theorem is much easier if you experience it for yourself. This is most fascinating as a class exercise because you can observe your classmates and so compare your own reaction to their reactions as the distribution unfolds—there is reliably a great moment when various members of the class "get it" and experience the central limit theorem for themselves. But the illustration is also effective if you use it only as a thought experiment; you can still experience the central limit through the power of your imagination.

CREATING YOUR OWN DISTRIBUTIONS

EXPERIENCE IT FOR YOURSELF

Write the numbers in Table 7-1 on 140 individual index cards or equally sized pieces of paper that can be mixed together in a hat or bowl. The numbers represent the observations in Table 7-1 (p. 303)—the heights, in inches, of 140 college students from some of the authors' classes. As before, we will assume that we are interested in only these 140 students—that they comprise our entire population.

1. Either individually, with a group of classmates, or with your entire class, randomly pull one card at a time and record its score by marking it on a histogram chart above the appropriate value. (It works well to draw a square for each score, because a stack of squares resembles a bar.) After recording each score, return the card to the container and mix all the cards well before pulling the next card. (Not surprisingly, this is known as sampling with replacement.) Continue until you have plotted at least 30 scores, drawing a square for each one above the appropriate value on the x-axis, so that bars emerge above each value. This will create the beginning of a *distribution of scores* like the one in Figure 7-8 (see page 316).

2. Now, randomly pull three numbers at a time, compute the mean of those three scores (rounding to the nearest whole number), and record that number on a different histogram chart. (Ideally, you'd use sampling with replacement, returning each number to the population before pulling the next.) As before, draw a square for each mean above the appropriate value; a stack of squares will resemble a bar. Again, return each set of three cards to the container and mix well before pulling the next set of three. Continue until you have plotted at least 30 values. This will be the beginning of a *distribution of means* like the one in Figure 7-9 (see page 316). (If working alone, you will create your own hand-drawn histogram. If working in a group, you may designate one person to do it on a large computer display, white board, or poster while others watch.)

3. Compare the two histograms. When we did this exercise, we created the distribution of scores seen in Figure 7-8 and the distribution of means seen in Figure 7-9.

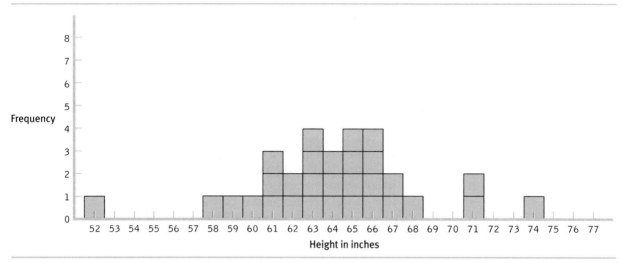

FIGURE 7-8
Creating a Distribution of Scores

This distribution is one of many that could be created by pulling 30 numbers, one at a time and replacing the numbers between pulls, from our population of 140 heights.

FIGURE 7-9
Creating a Distribution of Means

This distribution is one of many that could be created by pulling 30 means, the average of three at a time and replacing the numbers between pulls, from our population of 140 heights.

The two distributions that you created likely resemble ours, particularly if you mixed the scores thoroughly before pulling each number. In the distribution of scores, there are probably a few scores at the far tails of the distribution, with many more in the middle. Ours range from 52 to 74, with a peak in the middle. As you might imagine, if we had a larger population, and if we pulled many more numbers, our distribution would become more and more normal. Notice that the distribution is centered roughly around the actual population mean, 64.89. Also notice that all or nearly all scores fall within 3 standard deviations of the mean. The population standard deviation of these scores is 4.09. So scores should fall between $64.89 - 3(4.09) = 52.62$ and $64.89 + 3(4.09) = 77.16$. In fact, the range of scores in this population of 140 heights is very close to this, 52 through 77 (even though the highest score we pulled was 74).

Is there anything different about the distribution of means? Yes, but it may not be immediately apparent. Notice that there (probably) are not as many means at the far tails of the distribution as we see in the distribution of scores. In our distribution of means, we have a smaller range; we no longer have any

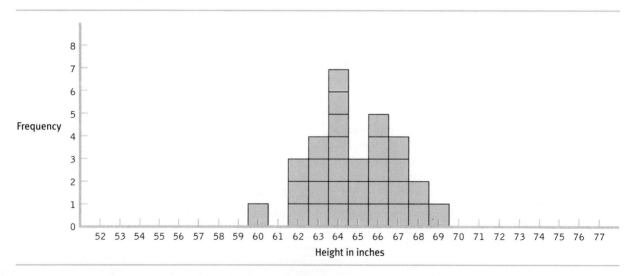

values in the 50s or 70s. There are not, however, any changes in the center of the distribution as a result of shifting from scores to means. There might be minor shifts due to random variation in the numbers and the means we pulled, but there will be no change in the mean if we include enough means in the distribution. The distribution of means should still be centered around the actual mean of 64.89. This makes sense; the means of three scores each come from the same set of scores, so the mean of the individual sample means should be exactly the same as the mean of the whole population of scores.

Notice, however, that the spread in the distribution of means is much less. This is a key point in understanding distributions of means and the central limit theorem. *Why does the spread decrease when we create a distribution of means rather than a distribution of scores?* You will have noticed when you conducted this exercise that you occasionally pulled an extreme score. *When you were plotting* **scores**, *that extreme score was plotted on the distribution. But when you were plotting* **means**, *you averaged that extreme score with two other scores. It is unlikely that all three scores were that extreme in the same direction.* So, each time you pulled a score in the 70s, you likely pulled two lower scores as well, and the mean would have been lower than the 70s. When you pulled a score in the 50s, you likely pulled two higher scores as well, and the mean would have been higher than the 50s.

What do you think would happen if we created a distribution of means of 10 scores rather than 3? As you might guess, the distribution would be even narrower, because there would be more scores to balance the occasional extreme score. Pull just two or three groups of 10 scores from the container; you'll find that the means of 10 scores are likely even closer to the actual mean of 64.89. What if we created a distribution of means of 100 scores or 10,000 scores? The larger the sample size, the smaller the spread of the distribution of means.

Larger sample sizes will shift a severely skewed distribution of a population's scores toward a normal distribution of means from that population, but that's all that the central limit theorem requires to work its magic: a distribution comprised of many sample means. In fact, distributions of means computed from samples of at least 30 are usually approximately normal, even for a skewed distribution of individual scores in the population. Although a sample size of 30 is usually sufficient for many studies in the behavioral sciences, for very skewed distributions, some suggest that a sample size of 100 is necessary to achieve a normal distribution of means (e.g., Freedman, Pisani, & Purves, 1998). So even when the population distribution is extremely skewed, repeated sampling of means from that distribution will produce a normal curve. It's not really magic; it's the central limit theorem.

Characteristics of the Distribution of Means: Understanding Why It's So Powerful

In the social sciences, as in everyday decision making, we make progress by asking better questions and asking them in a way that produces an answer. The characteristics of the distribution of means allow researchers to achieve that goal. In particular, researchers need to know when it is appropriate to reject the null hypothesis. As you may recall from Chapter 4, the *null hypothesis* is a statement about the relation between populations that are being compared. Specifically, the null hypothesis suggests that there is no difference between populations or that the difference is in a direction opposite from that proposed by the researcher. You can think of the null hypothesis as the boring hypothesis that there is nothing going on in your study. By contrast, the *research hypothesis* is the exciting and interesting one. The research hypothesis (also called the alternate hypothesis) is a statement about populations that suggests that there is a difference between populations or, sometimes more specifically, that there is a difference in a certain direction, positive or negative. This is usually the exciting hypothesis because it proposes a distinctive difference between groups that is worthy of further investigation.

For example, one of our friends works in public health trying to reduce the number of children who drown in Bangladesh. Although Bangladesh has lots of water, the water is mostly used for household needs and very few people know how to swim. Typically, a drowning seems to occur during the hour prior to the evening meal, when the mother is preoccupied with cooking. So there are several possible interventions, including something as straightforward as providing swimming lessons. The null hypothesis is that that swimming lessons will not reduce the number of children who drown. The research (alternate) hypothesis is that swimming lessons will reduce the number of children who drown. Many different agencies are eager to spend money on public health interventions that save children's lives, but they don't want to spend their money foolishly or irresponsibly. So the results of this study might direct the flow of millions of dollars toward the most effective interventions. If the data indicate that the null hypothesis can be rejected, then we have evidence that supports the idea that providing swimming lessons reduces the incidence of children who drown.

If the social sciences are going to make such discoveries, then we need to discover the relative effectiveness of such interventions so that we can draw conclusions about the null hypothesis. In this case, we would hope to reject the null hypothesis that swimming lessons will not reduce the incidence of children who drown. But it is possible that there will not be enough evidence to reject the null hypothesis. Not rejecting the null hypothesis is also important because we don't want to spend money on an intervention that only makes us feel good; we want to spend money on an intervention that actually saves children's lives. So the statistical question becomes much clearer: When are we justified in rejecting the null hypothesis?

First of all, remember that for nearly all distributions, the scores fall within 3 standard deviations of the mean. In the illustration from Experience It for Yourself: Creating Your Own Distributions, the size of 1 standard deviation of the sample *scores* is 4.09 whereas the size of 3 standard deviations of the sample *scores* is 12.27; based on this, the range of scores is expected to be roughly 52.62 to 77.16, which matched quite well with the actual population scores of 52 to 77. However, after sampling and using the average of those samples, this standard deviation based on scores is no longer useful to us because now we are working with a distribution of *means*. The range of means that we've calculated so far is only 60 to 69. Based on a standard deviation of 4.09 (which means that 3 standard deviations is $3 \times 4.09 = 12.27$), none of these means is very extreme. In other words, the z table would almost *never* indicate that any of these means was extreme. For example, a sample mean of 68 would be extreme given the range of means we calculated. But in a z distribution, those scores would be just 1 standard deviation above the population mean. Unfortunately, we can't use the standard deviation for the population to describe a sample of that population. It's like trying to use a Phillips head screwdriver on a slotted screw head—you've got the right idea, but not the right tool. So we need to make an adjustment to the standard deviation that recognizes that we are now working with sample means from the population rather than individual scores from the population.

Let's remember why we need to make this adjustment in the first place: We're sampling, and we're sampling because it is too expensive and practically impossible to study the entire population of children in Bangladesh. Fortunately, our ability to study a representative sample liberates us from the impossibility of conducting research on the whole population. But we have to use the kind of standard deviation that is meant to be used with a sample because using the population standard deviation means that we would never be able to discover which intervention, if any, really worked. If we don't use the appropriate measure of variability for a sample, then we can almost never identify a score as extreme. And if we can almost never identify a score as extreme, then we would almost never be able to reject the null hypothesis. If we can almost never reject the null hypothesis, then we won't be able to discover whether providing swimming lessons, building lots of fences, educating parents, or some other intervention is most effective at saving lives. So using the appropriate form of the standard deviation is a small statistical adjustment, but it has very big consequences.

Fortunately, there is a solution and it is very simple: The distribution of means needs its own standard deviation—a smaller standard deviation than the one we used for the distribution of individual scores. We need to use the standard deviation that is tailored to the distribution of means so we can calculate an appropriate z score for the distribution of means. As you will recall from Experience It for Yourself: Creating Your Own Distributions, the distribution of means is more tightly clustered around the mean, so we would expect that the standard deviation would also be smaller. And it is. But let's confirm our verbal explanation of this smaller standard deviation by looking at it visually.

We can use the data presented in Figure 7-10 to visually verify that the distribution of means needs its own (smaller) standard deviation (rather than the standard deviation that describes the population). Using the population mean of 64.886 and the population standard deviation of 4.086, the z scores for 60 and 69 are -1.20 and 1.01, respectively—not even close to 3 standard deviations. These z scores are wrong for this distribution. We need to use a standard deviation of the sample *means* rather than a standard deviation of the individual *scores*. And this is a very good thing because now science can distinguish between the dull null hypothesis and the exciting research (altenative) hypothesis.

FIGURE 7-10
Using the Appropriate Measure of Spread

Because the distribution of means is narrower than the distribution of scores, it has a smaller standard deviation. This standard deviation has its own name: standard error.

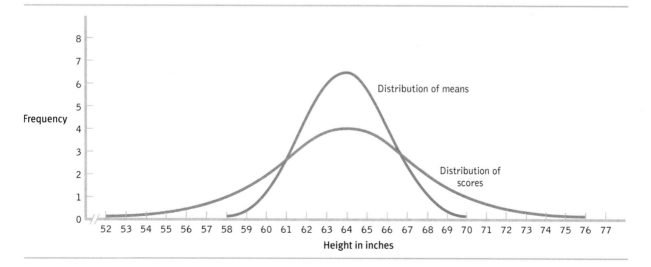

■ **Standard error** is the name for the standard deviation of a distribution of means.

Understanding distributions of means opens the door to inferential statistics—and making reasonable inferences from samples is very powerful, whether we are conducting market research about the color of packaging, theoretical research about the relation between frustration and creativity, or applied research about how to reduce the number of children who drown.

At this point, it probably won't surprise you that we will be using slightly modified language and symbols to distinguish this new standard deviation of the sampling distribution of means from the standard deviation of the population distribution of scores. As we noted previously, the mean of the distribution of means is the same as the mean of the population of scores. However, even though the value is the same, it has a different symbol. To indicate that this is the mean of a distribution of means, the symbol is μ_M (pronounced "mew sub m"). The μ indicates that it is the mean of a *population* and the subscript M indicates that the population is composed of *sample means*—the means of all possible samples of a given size from a particular population of individual scores.

Symbols: μ_M refers to the mean of a distribution of means.

We also need a new symbol and a new name for the standard deviation of the distribution of means—the typical amount that a sample mean varies from the population mean. Because of sampling error, we wouldn't expect every sample mean to fall exactly at the population mean; the standard deviation of the distribution of means helps us quantify this. But first, notice the visual verification in Figures 7-8 and 7-9 that the spread of numbers in the distribution of means is more tightly gathered around the mean than was the case in the distribution of scores. That visually confirms that the standard deviation of the distribution of means is smaller than the standard deviation of the scores. This is why we must calculate the standard deviation of the distribution of means, which also has its own symbol, σ_M (pronounced "sigma sub m"). The subscript M again stands for mean; this is the standard deviation of the population of means calculated for *all possible samples* of a given size. The symbol also has its own name to differentiate it from the standard deviation of a set of individual scores; ***standard error** is the name for the standard deviation of a distribution of means.* Table 7-2 summarizes the alternative names that describe these related ideas.

Symbols: σ_M refers to standard error, which is the standard deviation of a distribution of means.

Fortunately, there is a simple calculation that lets us know exactly how much smaller the standard error, σ_M, is than the standard deviation, σ. As we've noted, the larger the sample size, the narrower the distribution of means. This also means that the larger the sample size, the smaller the standard deviation of the distribution of means—the standard error. We calculate the standard error by using the size of the sample that was used to calculate the many means that make up the distribution. The standard error is the standard deviation of the population divided by the square root of the sample size, N. When we divide a given standard deviation by a positive number greater than 1, the outcome is a

TABLE 7-2. PARAMETERS FOR DISTRIBUTIONS OF SCORES VERSUS MEANS

When we determine the parameters of a distribution, we must consider whether the distribution is composed of means or scores.

DISTRIBUTION	MEAN	SYMBOL FOR SPREAD	NAME FOR SPREAD
Scores	μ	σ	Standard deviation
Means	μ_M	σ_M	Standard error

smaller number. As the denominator gets larger, the outcome of the calculation gets smaller, indicating less and less spread. The formula is:

$$\sigma_M = \frac{\sigma}{\sqrt{N}}$$

Imagine that the standard deviation of the distribution of individual scores is 5 and we have a sample of just 10 people. The standard error would be: $\sigma_M = \frac{\sigma}{\sqrt{N}} = \frac{5}{\sqrt{10}} = 1.58$. The spread is smaller because when we calculate a mean for 10 individuals, any extreme scores are balanced by less extreme scores. With a larger sample size of 200, the spread would be even smaller. There would be many more scores close to the mean to balance off any extreme scores. It would be rare to get a sample mean very far from the actual mean. The standard error would now be: $\sigma_M = \frac{\sigma}{\sqrt{N}} = \frac{5}{\sqrt{200}} = 0.35$. As sample size increases, the means that make up the distribution of means tend to be closer to the actual population mean, and so the spread decreases.

The most dramatic and statistically powerful feature of a distribution of means is how faithfully it obeys the central limit theorem. Even if the population of individual scores is *not* normally distributed, the distribution of means usually will be approximately normal if the samples are composed of at least 30 scores. This means that even if the population is skewed (pushed to one side or the other) or kurtotic (either very tall and skinny or very flat and wide), we can still determine how extreme that sample mean is by using the z table, *if* we take a sample of at least 30 scores. Even more important, as long as our sample includes at least 30 scores, the distribution of means will usually be approximately normal even though the population of individual scores is not normally distributed. The three graphs in Figure 7-11 depict: (a) a distribution of individual scores that

Formulas: The formula for standard error is $\sigma_M = \frac{\sigma}{\sqrt{N}}$, where σ indicates the standard deviation of the population and *N* indicates the sample size.

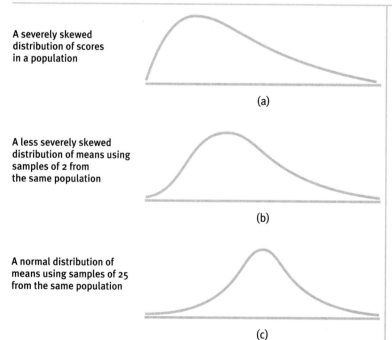

A severely skewed distribution of scores in a population

(a)

A less severely skewed distribution of means using samples of 2 from the same population

(b)

A normal distribution of means using samples of 25 from the same population

(c)

FIGURE 7-11
The Mathematical Magic of Large Samples

Even with a population of individual scores that are not normally distributed, the distribution of means will approximate a normal curve as the sample gets larger.

is extremely skewed in the positive direction (remember the mnemonic: "the tail tells the tale"), (b) the less skewed distribution that results when we create a distribution of means using samples of 2, and (c) the approximately normal curve that results when we create a distribution of means using samples of 25. In other words, the central limit theorem really works. The originally skewed distribution almost magically becomes bell-shaped. But it's not magic—it's math.

We have learned three important characteristics of the distribution of means:

1. As sample size increases, the mean of a distribution of means approaches the mean of the population of individual scores.

2. The standard deviation of a distribution of means (called the standard error) is smaller than the standard deviation of a distribution of scores. The standard error can be calculated by dividing the standard deviation of the population of individual scores by the square root of the sample size. As sample size increases, the standard error becomes ever smaller.

3. The shape of the distribution of means will have an approximately normal shape if the distribution of the population of individual scores has a normal shape or if the size of each sample that comprises the distribution is sufficiently large, usually at least 30 (central limit theorem).

In summary, the central limit theorem may be understood by learning the distinction between a distribution of scores and a distribution of means. A demonstration of the central limit theorem illustrates how a distribution of scores can have the same mean as a distribution of means. However, a distribution of scores contains more extreme scores, a bigger range, and a bigger standard deviation than a distribution of means. When used to describe a distribution of means, both the symbolic and the written languages of statistics are slightly different, even though the concepts to which they refer are familiar. The central limit theorem is especially powerful because, given a sufficiently large sample size (usually at least 30 scores in each sample), it will transform a non-normal distribution of scores into a bell-shaped curve of means. The central limit theorem enlarges the range of topics that behavioral scientists can study.

⊙ CHECK YOUR LEARNING

7-3 Let's return to the selection of 30 CFC scores that we considered in Check Your Understanding 7-1(b):

3.5	3.5	3.0	4.0	2.0	4.0	2.0	4.0	3.5	4.5
4.5	4.0	3.5	2.5	3.5	3.5	4.0	3.0	3.0	2.5
3.0	3.5	4.0	3.5	3.5	2.0	3.5	3.0	3.0	2.5

a. What is the range of these scores?

b. Take three means of 10 scores each from this sample of scores, one for each row. What is the range of these means?

c. Why is the range smaller for the *means* of samples of 10 scores than for the *individual* scores themselves?

d. The mean of these 30 scores is 3.32. The standard deviation is 0.69. Using symbolic notation and formulas (where appropriate), determine the mean and standard error of the distribution of means computed from samples of 10.

> HOW TO TAKE ADVANTAGE OF THE CENTRAL LIMIT THEOREM: BEGINNING WITH z SCORES

The idea of the bell-shaped curve matured from a theoretically interesting idea to an applicable principle under W. S. Gossett's patient attention. Gossett had been hired by Lord Guinness to work for the Guinness Brewing Company in Dublin, Ireland, shortly after Gossett received his degree in chemistry from the University of Oxford. Lord Guinness hoped to improve the beer—and the company's bottom line—by incorporating scientific techniques into the manufacturing process. Although Gossett was both a chemist and a mathematician by training, he was a statistician by inclination. But Gossett also played a subtle and more powerful role in the development of statistics.

In fact, Gossett's life can be a role model for students of the behavioral sciences for a couple of reasons. First, Gossett loved his work and his rise within the Guinness company demonstrated that a career in statistics can be financially rewarding. Second, and more important, Gossett's work demonstrated the practical, problem-solving side of statistics (which anticipated the fields of industrial and organizational psychology) and highlights the fact that a knowledge of statistics is a very marketable skill for graduates in the behavioral sciences. Organizations are eager to employ people who help them solve their problems.

Gossett's career was built by using statistics to solve many small, day-to-day problems at the Guinness brewery. His practical problem in the brewery was how to use small samples to answer questions about big numbers, and his solution still shapes the practice of modern-day research. Studies of beer making, voter preferences, and cancer research all use small samples relative to the overall population, and then use those samples to confidently reach conclusions about many thousands of people. How can they dare be so confident? To answer that question, we are going to apply the three things we have learned about the normal curve. Let's review them once again:

Quality Control at Breweries
Industrial and organizational psychologists are among those who work in industry to maintain high levels of quality control when producing everything from beer to chocolate to computer chips.

1. The approximate shape of the normal curve exists almost everywhere (ubiquity).

2. The predictable bell shape of the normal curve may be translated into percentages (standardization).

3. A distribution of means produces a less variable and more normal bell-shaped curve better than a distribution of individual scores, even when the original distribution is not normal (the central limit theorem).

Cancan Chu/Getty Images

These three characteristics of the normal curve allow statisticians to make inferences from small samples by using three closely related types of theoretical distributions: the z distribution, which we are about to learn more about, plus the t distributions explained in Chapter 9 and the F distributions explained in Chapter 10.

Creating Comparisons: Applying z Scores to a Distribution of Means

Remember z scores? They are a standardized version of raw scores based on the population of people we are studying. But in Gossett's everyday reality, he (and we) seldom have the entire population to work with. So we calculate a z score based on a distribution of means. When we calculate our z score, we simply use a distribution of means instead of a distribution of scores. The z formula changes only in the symbols it uses: $z = \dfrac{(M - \mu_M)}{\sigma_M}$. Note that we now use M instead of X because we are calculating a z score for a sample mean rather than for an individual score. Because the z score now represents a mean, not an actual score, it is often referred to as a z *statistic*. Specifically, the z statistic tells us how many standard errors a sample mean is from the population mean.

> **Formulas:** The formula for the z statistic for a distribution of means is $z = \dfrac{(M - \mu_M)}{\sigma_M}$, where M indicates the sample mean, μ_M indicates the mean of the distribution of means, and σ_M indicates the standard error of the distribution of means.

Let's consider a distribution for which we know the population mean and the population standard deviation. As you may have learned in another social science course, scores on IQ measures are calibrated to have a population mean of 100 and a standard deviation of 15. Imagine that, as part of your senior honors project, you devise a set of brain exercises that you believe will increase IQ. You take a sample of 90 representative adults in your country and enroll them in your brain boot camp. After they've performed three months of mental aerobics, you measure their IQ scores and find that the mean IQ score is 102. Is this an extreme sample mean given the population?

To find out, let's imagine the distribution of IQ scores collected after participants have performed their three months of mental aerobics. The distribution of means for samples of 90 IQ scores would be collected the same way we collected the means of three heights in Experience It for Yourself: Creating Your Own Distributions—just with far, far more means. The population of IQ scores is normally distributed, but even if it were not, the sample is made up of at least 30 scores, so the distribution of means will be normally distributed. It will have the same mean as the population, but the spread will be smaller and will have to be calculated. Any extreme IQ scores are likely to be balanced by less extreme scores when each mean is calculated, so the distribution will be less variable. Before we calculate the z statistic, let's use proper symbolic notation to indicate the mean and the standard error of the sample of individuals fortunate enough to have been selected into our brain boot camp:

$$\mu_M = \mu = 100$$

$$\mu_M = \frac{\sigma}{\sqrt{N}} = \frac{15}{\sqrt{90}} = 1.581$$

At this point, we have all the information we need to calculate the z statistic:

$$z = \frac{(M - \mu_M)}{\sigma_M} = \frac{(102 - 100)}{1.581} = 1.27$$

From this z statistic, we could use a z table to determine how extreme the mean IQ is in terms of a percentage. Then we could draw a conclusion about whether we would be likely to find a mean IQ of 102 in a sample of 90 people if the brain aerobics did *not* work. For now, simply recognize that we are connecting back to the population that we actually care about by drawing a conclusion that—we hope—applies to that population.

Estimating Population Parameters From Sample Statistics: Connecting Back

Keep in mind that researchers usually aren't very interested in the sample itself. It's likely that they don't even know the people who participate in a research study. But researchers are extremely interested in the population that the sample represents. For example, a school psychologist working with adolescents who have substance-abuse problems might read about a research study on ways to persuade adolescent drug abusers to accept help. The school psychologist isn't really interested in the sample the researchers studied because she doesn't know them as individuals. But she is keenly interested in whether the researchers discovered anything that will work for the teenagers she is trying to help. Well, her teenagers are probably part of the larger population that the researchers themselves were also interested in helping. So let's start putting what we know about the normal curve to work. In coming chapters, we will learn how to connect what we learn from the sample back to the population.

Clinical Uses for Statistics Applied psychologists study statistics in order to evaluate whether what they are reading in their professional journals is likely to be effective with the people they are trying to help. For example, school psychologists apply their knowledge to the students with whom they work.

Statisticians refer to this idea of connecting back from the sample to the population as "estimating population parameters from sample statistics." This means that researchers use the findings from the sample to learn something about the real-world population they are most interested in. To do this, in the next chapter, we will apply z statistics to our new situation: working with a distribution of means from samples instead of working with the entire population.

In summary, z scores may be calculated from a distribution of scores or from a distribution of means. The logic of the two calculations is identical, but they use slightly different symbols. Also, for the measure of spread, the two calculations use different terms: *standard deviation* for a distribution of scores and *standard error* for a distribution of means. However, the z statistic may only be used when we know the population parameters. Because we usually do not know the population parameters, we are obliged to estimate them.

⊙ CHECK YOUR LEARNING

7-4 Check Your Learning 7-2 presented summary parameters for CFC scores for the population of participants in a study by Petrocelli (2003). The mean CFC score was 3.51, with a standard deviation of 0.61. (Remember that even though this was a sample, we treated the sample of 664 participants as the entire population.) Imagine that you randomly selected 40 individuals from this population and had them watch a series of videos on financial planning after graduation. The mean CFC score after watching the video was 3.62. We want to know whether watching these videos might change CFC scores in the population. But we'll start by standardizing this mean so that we can make comparisons.

a.   Why would it not make sense to compare this sample with the distribution of scores? Be sure to discuss the spread of distributions in your answer.

b. In your own words, what would the null hypothesis predict? What would the research hypothesis predict?

c. Using symbolic notation and formulas, what are the appropriate measures of central tendency and variability for the distribution from which this sample comes?

d. Using symbolic notation and the formula, what is the z statistic for this sample mean?

e. Roughly, to what percentile does that z statistic correspond?

▪ DIGGING DEEPER INTO THE DATA: THE NORMAL CURVE AND CATCHING (POSSIBLE) CHEATERS

The normal curve is a simple drawing of everyday reality that, over its long history, grew more provocative as we learned more about it. For example, in the 1600s, Abraham De Moivre believed that his mathematical discovery of a predictable pattern behind random events was evidence for the existence of God, what he called a "natural theology." In the 1800s, Sir Francis Galton was equally impressed with the normal curve's "wonderful form of cosmic order," but he reached a very different theological conclusion (Galton, 1889; see also Peters, 1986; Yule & Kendall, 1950). In the twentieth century, Youden (1994) became so enamored with the enriching contributions of the bell-shaped curve that he imprinted a text visualization of the normal curve (Figure 7-12) on his business cards. So the normal curve has been tantalizing the imagination of scholars for 400 years!

Modern applications of the normal curve challenge the commonly expressed cynical attitude that "people can prove anything they want with statistics." That is true only when communicating to an audience that doesn't know how to ask better questions, usually about whether there is a bias in how the data were originally collected. By contrast, we've celebrated several ways in which statisticians have used statistical reasoning and the bell-shaped curve to save lives (the cholera epidemic), manage risk (the insurance industry), and catch cheaters (teachers faking student scores). But in the long run, science may be damaged more by subtle forms of bias than by blatant cheating. Fortunately, the normal curve can also indicate when the scientific culture itself has been peppered with tiny shots of corruption.

For example, Alan Gerber and Neil Malhotra (2006) looked at all studies published between 1995 and 2004 in two political science journals, the *American Political Science Review* and *American Journal of Political Science*, and recorded the z statistics reported in these studies. (When Gerber and Malhotra reported their

---

FIGURE 7-12
Youden's (1994) Text Version of the Normal Bell-Shaped Curve

THE
NORMAL
LAW OF ERROR
STANDS OUT IN THE
EXPERIENCE OF MANKIND
AS ONE OF THE BROADEST
GENERALIZATIONS OF NATURAL
PHILOSOPHY ◆ IT SERVES AS THE
GUIDING INSTRUMENT IN RESEARCHES
IN THE PHYSICAL AND SOCIAL SCIENCES AND
IN MEDICINE AGRICULTURE AND ENGINEERING ◆
IT IS AN INDISPENSABLE TOOL FOR THE ANALYSIS AND THE
INTERPRETATION OF THE BASIC DATA OBTAINED BY OBSERVATION AND EXPERIMENT

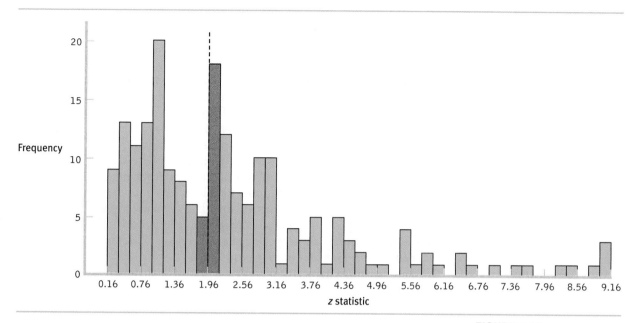

FIGURE 7-13
Identifying Cheaters

An understanding of distributions can help us identify cheaters. This histogram of *z* statistics for one of the journals studied by Gerber and Malhotra (2006) shows an unexpectedly short bar for findings with *z* statistics slightly smaller than 1.96 and an unexpectedly tall bar for findings with *z* statistics slightly larger than 1.96. This pattern is an indication that researchers might be manipulating their analyses to push their *z* statistics beyond the cutoffs and into the tails so that they can reject the null hypothesis.

own results, they combined positive and negative z statistics, so any z statistic above 1.96 indicates that it fell in the 5% of values to be found in the two tails. Note that the behavioral sciences tend to disseminate findings in which a sample mean falls in the 5% most extreme of its sampling distribution. This includes any z statistic greater than 1.96 or less than -1.96. Then they constructed a histogram (Figure 7-13) that depicted the frequencies of the z statistics in these articles, documenting an apparent publication bias among researchers! What might be the source of this possible bias? There is nothing magical about the 5% demarcation used in the behavioral sciences; it is simply a reasonable standard that minimizes the probability of committing either a Type I or a Type II error. But it is the standard used by journal editors. However, the data don't know about the 5% standard, so we would not expect any clustering of reported findings that, for example, just *barely* achieves that standard. Let's look at the data.

If you think of this histogram as one half of a normal curve, then you'll notice far fewer z statistics in the middle than you'd see in a normal curve. Once again, the absence of a normal curve is a red flag that commands our attention but this is not that surprising because z statistics in the middle, close to the mean, would be less likely to be published. However, Gerber and Malhotra also found another interesting deviation from the normal curve. There was a much lower frequency that would be expected for z statistics just below 1.96 (the 5% standard), as seen in the red bar just to the left of the dashed vertical line. And there was a much higher frequency than would be expected for z statistics just above 1.96, as seen in the red bar just to the right of the dashed vertical line. Gerber and Malhotra described these features of the graph as resembling "a very steep cliff that drops into a river valley, suggesting that a portion of the density below the critical values have been cut out and deposited above the critical value" (p. 17). What might account for this?

The authors suggest that the strict 5% cutoff is encouraging researchers to "play" with their data until it beats the cutoff. Some researchers may cheat in this way unwittingly, not realizing that they are biased. There are so many slightly different ways to conduct an analysis, it is often possible to reject the null hypothesis by using some variations of analyses but not others; so some researchers might unwittingly pay more attention to the findings that might help them to publish. However, other researchers might cheat consciously, massaging the data with various analyses until it performs as they hope.

Unfortunately, researchers are often rewarded for these kinds of cheating, which increase publication rates and the frequency of being referenced by others (Sterling, Rosenbaum, & Weikam, 1995), essential elements to career success for social science researchers. Regardless of the ways in which data were manipulated, this pattern is unlikely to have occurred by chance. Gerber and Malhotra cite a "1 in 100 million" probability that the patterns they observed occurred just by chance (p. 3). But the ubiquity of the normal curve urges us to somehow explain this violation of its shape. It is certainly possible that the academic culture of publish or perish corrupts some university professors and researchers. How can we know if this pattern is real or if such an interpretation is justified? Replication and more research.

The normal curve helped to identify a pattern of apparent cheating in social science publishing. Identifying this problem is the first step to eliminating it. Gerber and Malhotra offer some possible remedies for reducing the effects of researcher manipulations. They suggest audits of randomly selected studies, which might be conducted after studies are accepted by research journals but before actual publication. In these audits, a disinterested researcher would reanalyze the data, which might uncover problems. But even more important, the knowledge that an audit may be conducted might lead researchers to be more ethical in their own data analyses.

Gerber and Malhotra also suggest the establishment of registries. They report that in the field of medicine, some top journals will only publish results of studies that were registered before the data were collected. Registration involves a description of the research design and statistical analyses to be implemented. Researchers cannot then conduct numerous variations of analyses until one produces results that seem publishable. The normal curve makes reform like this possible in a range of scientific fields.

Paying attention to the shape of distributions is not a sophisticated form of analysis. Yet it could have flagged the enormous level of corruption at companies such as Enron, Global Crossing, and WorldCom—and prevented thousands of workers from losing their retirement monies. Given the monstrous level of corruption in these large corporations, the outsized financial rewards for cheating, and the historical documentation of cheating at the highest levels of government, should we be surprised that cheating is increasingly accepted by students? Kevin Bushweller (1999) describes the pervasiveness and creativity of cheating in high schools and notes that the "high achievers—the nation's future business and political leaders—could be the worst offenders." McCabe, Trevino, and Butterfield (2001) describe a similar pervasiveness of cheating in higher education, the rationales used by students, and the contextual and individual predictors that explain the high rates of cheating. All these issues are clarified if we begin our analysis with an understanding of the normal, bell-shaped curve. There is no other way to identify performance that is dramatically different from what we can expect by chance. The implications of the normal, bell-shaped curve reach far beyond its mathematical beginnings.

In summary, the bell-shaped curve can be used in many ways, including identifying observations caused by cheating that violate what we would expect by chance. In addition to blatant cheating, the pattern may be part of an academic culture that encourages researchers to "play" with their data until they produce results more likely to lead to a publication.

⊙ CHECK YOUR LEARNING

7-5 The following percentages represent the final grades of a class of 15 students in the notoriously difficult course of organic chemistry:

37, 42, 48, 52, 59, 63, 65, 67, 67, 67, 67, 68, 69, 72, 99

a. What is the median score?

b. Is this distribution approximately bell-shaped?

c. Which, if any, of these students would you suspect of cheating?

d. Do you have enough information to accuse the student of cheating?

e. What are three alternative explanations for the one student's extremely high score?

f. Do you believe the professor should grade on the curve so that more students pass the course?

REVIEW OF CONCEPTS

> The Normal Curve: It's Everywhere!

Inferential statistics are important because objective prediction based on statistics tends to outperform subjective prediction. This premise was demonstrated in a *meta-analysis*, a study of many studies. There are three ideas that will help you to understand inferential statistics. First, the *normal curve* describes the variability of many physical, psychological, and behavioral characteristics; it can be said to be *ubiquitous*. Second, the normal curve may be translated into percentages, standardization. Third, a distribution of means, rather than scores, produces a more normal curve. The last idea is based on the central limit theorem, by which we know that a distribution of means will be normally distributed as long as the samples from which the means are computed are of a sufficiently large size, usually at least 30. These characteristics allow us to apply three closely related types of distributions to make inferences from small samples: the z distribution, the t distributions, and the F distributions.

> Standardization, z Scores, and the Normal Curve: Discovering Reason Behind the Randomness

The process of *standardization* converts raw scores into z scores. Raw scores from any normal distribution—from heights to psychosis scores—can be converted to the z *distribution*. z scores tell us how far a given raw score falls from its mean in terms of standard deviation. Standardization using z scores has two important applications. First, standardized scores—that is, z scores—can be looked up on a z table to determine the percentile rank of given raw scores.

Second, we can directly compare z scores from different raw-score distributions. z scores work the other way around, as well; if we know an individual's percentile, we can look up her or his z score and then convert it to a raw score.

> The Central Limit Theorem: How Sampling Creates a Less Variable Distribution

The z distribution can be used with a *distribution of means* in addition to a distribution of scores. Distributions of means have three characteristics. First, they have the same mean as the population of individual scores from which they are calculated. Second, they have a smaller spread, which means we must adjust for sample size. The standard deviation of a distribution of means is called the *standard error*. The decreased variability is due to the fact that extreme scores will be balanced by less extreme scores when means are calculated. Third, distributions of means are normally distributed in two situations: (1) the underlying population of scores is normal or (2) the means are computed from sufficiently large samples, usually at least 30 individual scores. This second situation is described by the *central limit theorem*, the principle that a distribution of sample means will be normally distributed even if the underlying distribution of scores is not normally distributed, as long as there are enough scores, usually at least 30, comprising each sample.

> How to Take Advantage of the Central Limit Theorem: Beginning with z Scores

The characteristics of the normal curve allow us to make inferences from small samples using standardized distributions, such as the z distribution. The z distribution can be used for means, as well as individual scores, if we determine the appropriate mean and standard deviation.

> Digging Deeper Into the Data: The Normal Curve and Catching (Possible) Cheaters

The bell-shaped curve can be used in many ways, including identifying observations caused by cheating that violate what we would expect by chance. In addition to blatant cheating, a corrupting pattern may be part of an academic culture that encourages researchers to "play" with their data until they produce results more likely to lead to a publication.

SPSS GUIDELINES FOR CHAPTER 7

SPSS lets us understand each variable and identify its skewness, kurtosis, and how well it fits with a normal distribution.

We can identify outliers that might skew the normal curve by selecting:

Analyze → Descriptive Statistics → Explore → Statistics → Outliers. Be sure to choose the variable of interest.

We can numerically gain information about the mean, median, mode, skewness, kurtosis, range, variance, and standard deviation of each variable by selecting:

Analyze → Descriptive Statistics → Frequencies → Statistics. Then select the characteristic of interest, as well as the variable of interest.

We encourage you to play with the data so you can explore the many features within SPSS. It is always helpful when we work with our own data. SPSS is probably easiest to learn when we know the source of every number and why we decided to include it in our study in the first place. It's also much more interesting to test our own ideas!

EXERCISES

7.1 The normal curve in real life: For each of the following variables, state whether the distribution of scores would likely approximate a normal curve. Explain your answer.

a. Number of movies that a college student rents in a year

b. Number of full-page advertisements in a magazine

c. Human birth weight in Canada

7.2 Statistical versus clinical prediction: Darius, the editor-in-chief of the school newspaper, is graduating next year. It is his task to choose next year's editors for the various newspaper departments. He has an equation, based on objective criteria (e.g., grades in writing classes, scores on a leadership scale, ratings by faculty advisors), that has predicted editorial prowess well in the past. However, he tells you that he knows these individuals and can use this extra information to make better choices than he can with these objective criteria. Citing Grove and colleagues (1996) and providing specific examples, explain to Darius why he should rethink his decision.

7.3 Getting ready for a date and the normal curve: We asked 150 students (in our statistics classes) how long, in minutes, they typically spent getting ready for a date. The scores range from 1 minute to 120 minutes, and the mean is 51.52 minutes. Here are the data for 40 of those students:

30	90	60	60	5	90	30	40	45	60
60	30	90	60	25	10	90	20	15	60
60	75	45	60	30	75	15	30	45	1
20	25	45	60	90	10	105	90	30	60

a. Construct a histogram for the 10 scores in the first row of these data.

b. Construct a histogram for all 40 of these scores.

c. What happened to the shape of the distribution as you increased the number of scores from 10 to 40? What do you think would happen if the data for all 150 students were included? What if we included 10,000 scores? Explain this phenomenon.

d. Are these distributions of scores or distributions of means? Explain.

e. The data here are self-reported. That is, our students wrote down how many minutes they believe that they typically take to get ready for a date. This accounts for the fact that the data include many "pretty" numbers, such as 30, 60, or 90 minutes. What might have been a better way to operationalize this variable?

f. Do these data suggest any hypotheses that you might like to study? List at least one.

7.4 Hillary Rodham Clinton and the z distribution: A sample of 148 of our statistics students rated their level of admiration for Hillary Rodham Clinton on a scale of 1 to 7. The mean rating was 4.06, and the standard deviation was 1.70. (For this exercise, treat this sample as the entire population of interest.)

a. Use these data to demonstrate that the mean of the z distribution is always 0.

b. Use these data to demonstrate that the standard deviation of the z distribution is always 1.

c. Calculate the z score for a student who rated his admiration of Hillary Rodham Clinton as 6.1.

d. A student had a z score of -0.55. What rating did she give for her admiration of Hillary Rodham Clinton?

7.5 Breakfast, z scores, and percentiles: Exercise 5.3 referenced a study by Georgiou and colleagues (1997), who reported that college students had healthier eating habits, on average, than did those who were neither college students nor college graduates. The 412 students in the study ate breakfast a mean of 4.1 times per week with a standard deviation of 2.4. For this exercise, imagine that this is the entire population of interest; thus, these numbers can be treated as parameters.

a. Roughly, what is the percentile for a student who eats breakfast four times per week?

b. Roughly, what is the percentile for a student who eats breakfast six times per week?

c. Roughly, what is the percentile for a student who eats breakfast twice a week?

7.6 Cross-sports comparisons and z scores: A common quandary faces sports fans who live in the same city but avidly follow different sports. How does one determine whose team did better with respect to its league division? In 2004, the Boston Red Sox won the World Series; just months later, their local football counterparts, the New England Patriots, won the Super Bowl. In 2005, both teams made the playoffs but lost early on. Which team was better in 2005? The question, then, is: Were the Red Sox better, as compared to other teams in the American League (AL) of major league baseball, than the Patriots, as compared to the other teams in the American Football Conference (AFC) of the National Football League? Some of us could debate it for hours, but it's better to examine some statistics. Let's operationalize performance over the season as the number of wins during regular season play.

a. In 2005, the mean number of wins for baseball teams in the American League was 81.71, with a standard deviation of 13.07. Because all teams were included, these are population parameters. The Red Sox won 95 games. What is their z score?

b. In 2005, the mean number of wins for football teams in the AFC was 8.13, with a standard deviation of 3.70. The Patriots won 10 games. What is their z score?

c. Which team did better, according to these data?

d. How many games would the team with the lower z score have had to win to beat the team with the higher z score?

e. List at least one other way we could have operationalized the outcome variable (i.e., team performance).

7.7 Standardizing Maria Sharapova and Tiger Woods: Who is doing better financially—Maria Sharapova, with respect to the 10 tennis players with the highest incomes, or Tiger Woods, with respect to the 10 golfers with the highest incomes? In 2005, Forbes.com listed the 10 most powerful tennis players in terms of earnings and media exposure, regardless of gender. Sharapova, the first Russian (man or woman) to be ranked number one internationally in tennis, ranked second in earnings, with an income of $18.2 million, much of it from endorsements for companies such as Canon and Motorola. In 2005, Golfdigest.com listed the top 50 earners in golf, regardless of gender. Woods placed first, with $89.4 million (over one-fourth of it just from Nike endorsements!). But top golfers tend to make more than top tennis players. In comparison to his top-10 peers, did Woods really do better financially than Sharapova did in comparison to her top-10 peers?

a. For tennis, the mean for the top 10 was $11.58 million, with a standard deviation of $6.58 million. What was Maria Sharapova's z score?

b. Roughly, what was Maria Sharapova's percentile rank?

c. For golf, the mean for the top 10 was $30.01 million, with a standard deviation of $28.86 million. What was Tiger Woods's z score?

d. Roughly, what was Tiger Woods's percentile rank?

e. Who did better in comparison to the top-10 earners in their respective sports, Sharapova or Woods?

f. The 10 golfers with the highest incomes earn the following amounts (in millions of dollars): 10.3, 10.4, 11.7, 12.3, 18.6, 20.2, 23.7, 25.9, 77.6, and 89.4. Describe the shape of this distribution. What does the shape suggest about whether we should assume the z distribution is normal (i.e., the standard normal distribution)?

7.8 Comparisons and admiration of celebrities: Our statistics students, as noted in Exercise 7.4, were asked to rate their admiration of Hillary Rodham Clinton on a scale of 1 to 7. They also were asked to rate their admiration of Jennifer Lopez and Venus Williams on a scale of 1 to 7. As noted earlier, the mean rating of Clinton was 4.06 with a standard deviation of 1.70. The mean rating of Lopez was 3.72 with a standard deviation of 1.90. The mean rating of Williams was 4.58 with a standard deviation of 1.46. One of our students rated her admiration of Clinton and Williams at 5 and her admiration of J. Lo at 4.

a. What is her z score for her admiration rating of Clinton?

b. What is her z score for her admiration rating of Williams?

c. What is her z score for her admiration rating of J. Lo?

d. Compared to the other statistics students in our sample, which celebrity does this student most admire? (We can tell by her raw scores that she prefers Clinton and Williams to Lopez, but when we take into account the general perception of these celebrities, how does this student feel about them?)

e. How do z scores allow us to make comparisons that we cannot make with raw scores? That is, describe the benefits of standardization.

7.9 Sports teams and raw scores: Let's look at baseball and football again, but this time we'll look at data for all of the teams in major league baseball (MLB) and the National Football League (NFL), respectively.

a. In 2005, the mean number of wins for MLB teams was 81.00, with a standard deviation of 10.83. The perennial underdogs, the Chicago Cubs, had a z score of −0.18. How many games did they win?

b. In 2005, the mean number of wins for all NFL teams was 8.00, with a standard deviation of 3.39. The New Orleans Saints had a z score of −1.475. How many games did they win?

c. The Pittsburgh Steelers were just below the 84th percentile in terms of NFL wins. How many games did they win? Explain how you obtained your answer.

d. Explain how you can examine your answers in parts (a), (b), and (c) to determine if the numbers make sense.

7.10 HIV and a distribution of scores versus a distribution of means: Researchers have reported that the projected life expectancy for people diagnosed with human immunodeficiency virus (HIV) and receiving antiretroviral therapy (ART) is 24.2 years (Schackman et al., 2006). Imagine that the researchers determined this by following 250 people with HIV who were receiving ART and calculating the mean. (The 24.2 is actually a projected number rather than a mean for a sample.)

a. What is the variable of interest?

b. What is the population?

c. What is the sample?

d. For the population, describe what the distribution of *scores* would be.

e. For the population, describe what the distribution of *means* would be.

f. If the distribution of the population were skewed, would the distribution of scores likely be skewed or approximately normal? Explain your answer.

g. Would the distribution of means be skewed or approximately normal? Explain your answer.

7.11 Different types of distributions and language acquisition: Imagine that a language development specialist assessed the vocabulary abilities of a sample of 50 eight-year-old Canadian children using a vocabulary test with established norms.

a. What is the sample in this study, and what is the population from which the sample is taken?

b. Describe how one could (hypothetically) create a distribution of scores based on the population of interest.

c. Describe how one could (hypothetically) create a distribution of means based on this population and with this sample size.

d. How would the mean of the distribution of scores change (if at all) when the distribution of means is created?

e. How would the standard deviation of the distribution of scores change (if at all) when the distribution of means is created?

f. Which distribution would the specialist want to use if he wanted to compare the mean score of his sample with the established norms? Explain your answer.

g. If the distribution of the population is skewed, can we still use a distribution based on the normal curve (such as the z distribution)? Explain your answer.

7.12 The MMPI and a distribution of means: The revised version of the Minnesota Multiphasic Personality Inventory (MMPI-2) is the most frequently administered self-report personality measure. Test-takers respond to more than 500 true/false statements; their responses are scored, typically by a computer, on a number of scales (e.g., hypochondriasis, depression, psychopathic deviation). Respondents receive a T score on each scale that can be compared to norms. (It is important to note that T scores are different from the t statistic we will learn about in Chapter 9; you're likely to encounter T scores if you take psychology classes, and it's good to be aware that they're different from the t statistic.) T scores are another way to standardize scores so that percentiles and cutoffs can be determined. The mean T score is always 50, and the standard deviation is always 10. Imagine that you administer the MMPI-2 to 95 respondents who have recently lost a parent; you wonder whether their scores on the depression scale will be, on average, higher than the norms. You find a mean score on the depression scale of 55 in your sample.

a. Using symbolic notation, report the mean and standard deviation of the population.

b. Using symbolic notation and formulas (where appropriate), report the mean and standard error for the distribution of means to which your sample will be compared.

c. In your own words, explain why it makes sense that the standard error is smaller than the standard deviation.

7.13 The z statistic, distributions of means, and apartment rentals: Many of you will have to find an apartment to rent upon graduation. The Internet is a valuable source of data to aid you in your search. From neighborhood safety to available transportation to housing costs, recent data can steer you in the right direction. On a Web site, San Mateo County in California published extensive descriptive statistics from its 1998 Quality of Life Survey. The county reported that the mean house payment (mortgage or rent) was $1225.15, with a standard deviation of $777.50. It also reported that the mean cost of an apartment rental, rather than a house rental or a mortgage, was $868.86. For this exercise, treat the overall mean housing payment as a parameter, and treat the mean apartment rental cost as a statistic based on a sample of 100.

a. Using symbolic notation and formulas (where appropriate), determine the mean and the standard error for the distribution of means for the overall housing payment data.

b. Using symbolic notation and the formula, calculate the z statistic for the cost of an apartment rental.

c. Why is it likely that the z statistic is so large? (*Hint:* Is this distribution likely to be normal? Explain.)

d. Why is it permissible to use the normal curve percentages associated with the z distribution even though the data are not likely normally distributed?

7.14 The General Social Survey (GSS) and distributions of means: Exercise 2.14 describes the GSS, a survey of approximately 2000 adults a year since 1972, for a total of more than 38,000 people. Go to the GSS Web site at http://www.icpsr.umich.edu/GSS/. During several years of the GSS, participants were asked how many close friends they have. Near the top of the GSS Web site, click "Analyze," then type FRINUM (short for number of friends) in the space next to "Row," and then enter YEAR (1972–2004) in the space next to "Selection Filter(s)." Under "TABLE OPTIONS," click the box next to "Statistics" and then click the button that says "Run the Table." Scroll down to the Summary Statistics.

a. For the data for number of friends, list the mean, standard deviation, median, and mode. Are these data for a distribution of scores or a distribution of means? Explain.

b. What do the mean and standard deviation suggest about the shape of the distribution? (*Hint:* Compare the sizes of the mean and the standard deviation.)

c. What do the three measures of central tendency suggest about the shape of the distribution?

d. Let's say that these data represent the entire population. Pretend that you randomly selected an individual from this population and asked how many close friends she or he had. Would you compare this person to a distribution of scores or a distribution of means? Explain your answer.

e. Now pretend that you randomly selected a sample of 80 people from this population. Would you compare this sample to a distribution of scores or a distribution of means? Explain your answer.

f. Using symbolic notation, calculate the mean and standard error of the distribution of means.

g. What is the likely shape of the distribution of means? Explain your answer.

7.15 The GSS and z scores: Refer to Exercise 7.14. Again, pretend that the GSS sample is the entire population of interest.

a. Imagine that you randomly selected one individual from this population who reported that he had 18 close friends. Would you compare his score to a distribution of scores or a distribution of means? Explain your answer.

b. What is his z score? Based on this z score, what is his approximate percentile?

c. Does it make sense to calculate a percentile for this person? Explain your answer. (*Hint:* Consider the shape of the distribution.)

d. Imagine that you randomly selected 80 individuals from this population who had a mean of 8.7. Would you compare this sample mean to a distribution of scores or a distribution of means? Explain your answer.

e. What is the z statistic for this mean? Based on this z statistic, what is the approximate percentile for this sample?

f. Does it make sense to calculate a percentile for this sample? Explain your answer. (*Hint:* Consider the shape of the distribution.)

7.16 GSS and z scores—pulling it all together: Refer to the example used in Exercises 7.14 and 7.15. Let's say that you decide to use the GSS data to test whether people who live in rural areas have a different mean number of friends than does the overall GSS sample. Again, treat the overall GSS sample as the entire population of interest. Let's say that you select 40 people living in rural areas and find that they have an average of 3.9 friends.

a. What is the independent variable in this study? Is this variable nominal, ordinal, or interval?

b. What is the dependent variable in this study? Is this variable nominal, ordinal, or interval?

c. What is the null hypothesis for this study?

d. What is the research hypothesis for this study?

e. Would we compare our data to a distribution of scores or a distribution of means? Explain your answer.

f. Using symbolic notation and formulas, calculate the mean and standard error for the distribution of means.

g. Using symbolic notation and the formula, calculate the z statistic for this sample.

h. What is the approximate percentile for this sample?

7.17 The language of statistics—*standardize*: Explain how the word *standardize* is used in everyday conversation; then explain how statisticians use it.

7.18 The language of statistics—*normal*: Explain how the word *normal* is used in everyday conversation; then explain how statisticians use it.

7.19 The symbols of statistics: For each of the following, (i) identify the incorrect symbol, (ii) state what the correct symbol should be, and (iii) explain why the initial symbol was incorrect.

a. $\sigma_M = \dfrac{\mu}{\sqrt{N}}$

b. $z = \dfrac{(\mu - \mu_M)}{\sigma_M}$

c. $z = \dfrac{(M - \mu_M)}{\sigma}$

d. $z = \dfrac{(X - \mu)}{\sigma_M}$

▪ DIGGING DEEPER INTO THE DATA

7.20 Treatment for heart disease, probability, and fraud: The three most common treatments for blocked coronary arteries are medication, bypass surgery, or angioplasty, a medical procedure that leads to higher profits for doctors than do the other two procedures. The highest rate of angioplasty in the United States is in Elyria, a small city in Ohio. A *New York Times* article stated that "the statistics are so far off the charts—Medicare patients in Elyria receive angioplasties at a rate nearly four times the national average—that Medicare and at least one commercial insurer are starting to ask questions" (Abelson, 2006). The rate, in fact, is three times as high as that of Cleveland, Ohio, which is located just 30 miles from Elyria.

a. How did probability play a role in the decision of Medicare and the commercial insurer to begin investigations?

b. How might the normal distribution help the investigators to detect fraud in this case?

c. Does Elyria's extremely high percentile mean that the doctors in town are committing fraud? Cite two other possible reasons for Elyria's status as an outlier.

7.21 Detection of credit card theft and the normal distribution: Credit card companies will often call credit card holders if the pattern of use indicates that the card might have been stolen. Let's say that you spend an average of $280 a month on your credit card, with a standard deviation of $75, and your monthly credit card purchases are approximately normally distributed. The credit card company will call you anytime your purchases for the month exceed the 98th percentile. What is the dollar amount beyond which you'll get a call from your credit card company? Show all of the steps of your calculations.

TERMS

---

normal curve (p. 299)

ubiquity of the normal curve
  (p. 299)

meta-analysis (p. 300)

standardization (p. 307)

z distribution (p. 308)

standard normal distribution
  (p. 308)

central limit theorem
  (p. 313)

distribution of means (p. 313)

standard error (p. 320)

SYMBOLS

μ_M

σ_M

FORMULAS

$$\sigma_M = \frac{\sigma}{\sqrt{N}}$$

$$z = \frac{(M - \mu_M)}{\sigma_M}$$

CHAPTER EIGHT

HYPOTHESIS TESTING WITH z TESTS
MAKING MEANINGFUL COMPARISONS

Just one fair-minded, standardized test could have saved Henry and his wife enormous heartache and a great deal of money. Fortunately, Henry's love for his son was deep. It gave him strength when the police arrived at his doorstep and insisted that he come with them, saying, "Your son, Gordon, has charged you with sexual abuse."

"But that's not even possible," Henry told them. "He's at his school; I'll be picking him up in just half an hour."

"No. He's in protective custody," replied the taller officer. He looked around the peaceful rural scene and then added, "Pretty isolated out here, isn't it?"

Henry didn't know it yet, but the label of "family sex offender" had been slapped on him. As they got into the police car, one of the policemen told Henry that he might not want to say too much until he had met with an attorney. Henry's comment—"You mean this really isn't some kind of joke?"—produced only silence.

Henry knew his son. Gordon was 15 years old and still lacked the motor skills to ride a bicycle, although he certainly loved trying. He'd been trying for almost 10 years. No, Henry thought, Gordon couldn't have told such a story. And then, suddenly, he knew exactly what had happened. "It's those therapists!" he muttered in the back seat. After Henry noticed that the officer in the passenger seat had taken out a notepad, he decided he had said enough, maybe too much. But what Henry should have said was, "Why in the world didn't someone test the hypothesis that facilitated communication really works before accepting it as evidence of an actual crime?"

One fair-minded statistical test could have spared many families from similar traumas. Instead, this chapter tells the story of a modern, many-sided tragedy

in which well-meaning people became trapped by their own good intentions into doing harmful things. It happened because passionate researchers, sincere social workers, and the people who uncritically accepted their research ignored the principles of statistical reasoning that were supposed to guide them.

Facilitated communication (FC) is a technique intended to tap the latent intelligence of people with autism. It appeared to be the product of plain old common sense, but it turned out to be uncommonly dangerous. By contrast, statistical reasoning clarifies the rules of what can be called "scientific common sense," which begins with hypothesis testing. Hypothesis testing is a way of thinking that provides evidence either supporting our commonsense observations or debunking them. Hypothesis testing in the behavioral sciences tries to ask yes-or-no questions so that we can test our so-called common sense empirically. To apply hypothesis testing to problems such as facilitated communication, we will focus our discussion on how the z distribution and the z test make fair comparisons possible through standardization. Specifically, we will learn the following:

1. How to use a z table
2. How to implement the basic steps of hypothesis testing
3. How to conduct a single sample z test to compare a single sample to a known population.

> THE VERSATILE z TABLE: RAW SCORES, z SCORES, AND PERCENTAGES

This chapter focuses on the z test, the simplest of the hypothesis tests. Understanding its logic and when it can be used provides a foundation for the more commonly used hypothesis tests that you will learn about in later chapters. With the z test, as with all the other hypothesis tests, there are three different ways to say the same thing: raw scores, z scores, and percentile rankings. More specifically, these are three useful, but slightly different, ways to identify the exact same point beneath the bell-shaped curve. This is not unusual. The same individual may be called by her formal name by teachers, a nickname by her family, and yet another name by her friends. But it's still the same person, operating in a slightly different setting. Similarly, how your performance compares relative to others in the same distribution of scores may be identified by your raw score, your z score, and your percentile rank. But it's still the same information, operating in a slightly different setting.

From z Scores to Percentages: The Benefits of Standardization

Standardization (Chapter 7) allows us to make fair comparisons because it allows us to translate the standardized z distribution into percentages, and individual z scores into percentile ranks. This builds on what we have already learned about normal distributions. Specifically, we learned that (1) about 68% of scores fall within one z score of the mean, (2) about 96% of scores fall within two z scores of the mean, and (3) nearly all scores fall within three z scores of the mean. These guidelines are useful, but fortunately we can be even more specific simply by using a table of z scores and percentages. The z table is printed

TABLE 8-1. EXCERPT FROM THE z TABLE

The z table provides the percentage of scores between the mean and a given z value. The full table includes positive z statistics from 0.00 to 4.50. The negative z statistics are not included because all we have to do is change the sign from positive to negative. The percentage between the mean and a positive z statistic is identical to the percentage between the mean and the negative version of that z statistic. Remember, the normal curve is symmetric: one side always mirrors the other.

z	% BETWEEN MEAN AND z
.	.
.	.
.	.
0.97	33.40
0.98	33.65
0.99	33.89
1.00	34.13
1.01	34.38
1.02	34.61
.	.
.	.
.	.

in its entirety in Appendix B, but an excerpt from it is reproduced here for your convenience (in Table 8-1).

After converting a raw score into a z score, we can use the z table to look up a given z score and find the percentage of scores *between the mean and that z score*. First, we have to calculate the z score from the raw score. Note that the z scores in a z table are all positive. Because the normal curve is symmetric, calculating the percentage between the mean and a given positive z score is identical to calculating the percentage between the mean and the negative version of that z score. So inclusion of the negative z scores would be redundant. Like many statistical principles, this is most easily understood with a picture, as shown in Figure 8-1.

Let's learn how to use the z table. To do so, we'll consider a study about a controversial subject: the effect of height on peer relations and social adjustment among adolescents in grades 6 through 12 (Sandberg, Bukowski, Fung, & Noll, 2004). Researchers conducted the study to see whether very short children and adolescents tended to have poorer psychological adjustment than taller children and, therefore, should be treated with growth hormone. To begin, researchers categorized children

FIGURE 8-1
The Standardized z Distribution

We can use a z table to determine the percentages below and above a particular z score. For example, 34% of scores fall between the mean and a z score of 1.

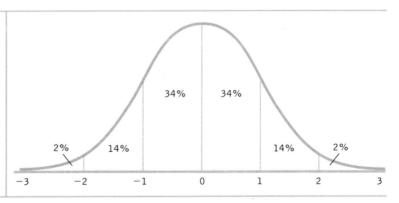

into one of three groups—short, average, or tall stature—using published norms, such as those on the Centers for Disease Control (CDC) growth charts (National Center for Health Statistics, 2000). The term *normed data* is another way of expressing the idea of standardized data that can be transformed into percentages. It is the presence of these normed data that allowed these researchers to create a fair test of the connection between height and psychological adjustment.

Now that they had a representative sample from the schools and a standardized comparison group from the normed data, Sandberg and colleagues (2004) could begin making meaningful comparisons. They decided to classify children as short in stature if they were in the bottom 5% of heights, according to published norms for a given age and gender. They were classified as tall in stature if they were in the top 5%, also according to published norms for a given age and gender. They were classified as average height if they were in the middle 90%. The CDC growth charts indicated that for 15-year-old boys the mean height was approximately 67.00 inches with a standard deviation of 3.19. For 15-year-old girls, the mean height was approximately 63.80 inches with a standard deviation of 2.66. However, even if we did not have access to the CDC norms, we could make meaningful comparisons among the children in the study by calculating *z* scores and then looking up percentages in the *z* table.

Let's consider two fictional examples related to the CDC height data, one for a score above the mean and then one for a score below the mean. Notice how uncomplicated it is to convert someone's individual raw score to a *z* score and from there to a percentile ranking. (*Note:* We'll consider the norms to represent population parameters.)

Jessica, a 15-year-old girl in one of the recruited classes, is 66.41 inches tall (just over 5 feet, 6 inches). First, we'll convert her raw score to a *z* score, as we learned how to do in Chapter 7; we'll use the mean ($\mu = 63.80$) and standard deviation ($\sigma = 2.66$) for the heights of girls: $z = \dfrac{(X - \mu)}{\sigma} = \dfrac{(66.41 - 63.80)}{2.66} = 0.98$. If we look up 0.98, we find that the associated percentage between the mean and Jessica's *z* score is 33.65%. Knowing this, we can determine a number of percentages related to her *z* score. Here are three.

1. *Jessica's percentile score, the percentage of scores below her score:* We add the percentage between the mean and the positive *z* score to 50%, which is the percentage of scores below the mean (50% of scores are on each side of the mean). Jessica's percentile is 50% + 33.65% = 83.65%. Figure 8-2 shows this visually. As with the calculation of *z* scores, we can run a quick mental

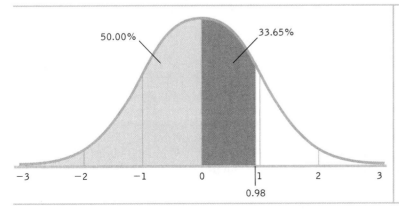

FIGURE 8-2
Calculating the Percentile for a Positive *z* Score

Drawing curves helps us to determine the appropriate percentage. For a positive *z* score, we add 50% to the percentage between the mean and that *z* score to get the total percentage below that *z* score, the percentile. Here, we add the 50% below the mean to the 33.65% between the mean and a *z* score of 0.98 to calculate the percentile, 83.65%.

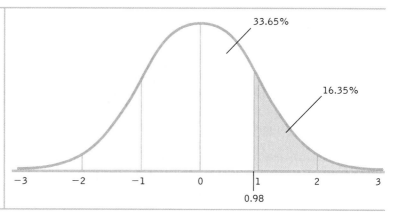

FIGURE 8-3
Calculating the Percentage Above a Positive *z* Score

For a positive *z* score, we subtract the percentage between the mean and that *z* score from 50% (the total percentage above the mean) to get the percentage above that *z* score. Here, we subtract the 33.65% between the mean and the *z* score of 0.98 from 50%, which yields 16.35%.

check of the likely accuracy of our answer. We're interested in calculating the percentile of a *positive z* score. Because it is above the mean, we know that the answer must be higher than 50%. And it is. If it were not, we would know to work through our calculations again to catch our error.

2. *The percentage of scores above Jessica's score:* We subtract the percentage between the mean and the positive *z* score from 50%, which is the full percentage of scores above the mean: $50\% - 33.65\% = 16.35\%$. So 16.35% of 15-year old girls' heights fall above Jessica's height. Figure 8-3 shows this visually. Here, it makes sense that the percentage would be smaller than 50%; because the *z* score is positive, we could not have more than 50% above it. An alternative approach may strike you as a simpler way to compute the percentage of scores above Jessica's score: subtract Jessica's percentile rank of 83.35% from 100%. This gives you the same 16.35%. (*Note:* Alternately, you could look under the column in the *z* table labeled "in the tail.")

3. *The scores at least as extreme as Jessica's z score, in both directions:* When we begin hypothesis testing, it will be useful to know the percentage of scores that are at least as extreme as a given *z* score. In this case, 16.35% of heights are extreme enough to have *z* scores above Jessica's *z* score of 0.98. But remember that the curve is symmetric. This means that another 16.35% of the heights are extreme enough to be below a *z* score of −0.98. So we can double 16.35% to find the total percentage of heights that are as far as or farther from the mean than 0.98: $16.35\% + 16.35\% = 32.70\%$. So 32.7% of heights are at least as extreme as Jessica's height in either direction. Figure 8-4 shows this visually.

What group would Jessica fall in? 16.35% of 15-year-old girls are taller than Jessica. She is not in the top 5%; so, she would be classified as average height according to the definition of *average* created *before* the researchers started examining the data.

Now let's repeat this process for a score below the mean. Manuel, a 15-year-old boy in one of the recruited classes, is 61.20 inches tall (about 5 feet, 1 inch). Keeping in mind that the height norms for boys are different from the height norms for girls, we want to know if Manuel is short enough to be classified as being of short stature (again using the 5%, 90%, 5% criteria chosen by the researchers). Remember, for boys the mean height is 67.00 inches,

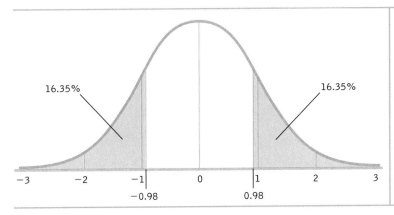

FIGURE 8-4
Calculating the Percentage at Least as Extreme as Our z Score

For a positive z score, we double the percentage above that z score to get the percentage of scores that are at least as extreme—that is, at least as far from the mean—as our z score is. Here, we double 16.35% to calculate the percentage at least this extreme: 32.70%.

and the standard deviation for height is 3.19 inches. First, we'll convert his raw score to a z score:

$$z = \frac{(X - \mu)}{\sigma} = \frac{(61.20 - 67.00)}{3.19} = -1.82$$

We'll use the full table in Appendix B this time. The z table includes only positive z scores; so we look up 1.82 and find 46.56%. Of course, percentages are always positive, so don't add a negative sign here! Let's calculate the percentile, the percentage above, and the percentage at least as extreme for the negative z score for Manuel's height. Throughout, consider whether the answers make sense. Make this assessment a habit throughout this course. When in doubt, simply sketch a normal curve and relabel it at the mean, as shown below in Figure 8-5. In other words, these are simply different ways of saying the same thing:

z = 0 = 50th percentile = the mean = the midpoint of the distribution

1. *Manuel's percentile score, the percentage of scores below his score:* For a negative z score, we subtract the percentage between the mean and the z score from 50%, the total percentage below the mean: 50 − 46.56 = 3.44. Manuel's percentile is 3.44% (Figure 8-5).

2. *The percentage of scores above Manuel's score:* We add the percentage between the mean and the negative z score to 50%, the percentage above the mean:

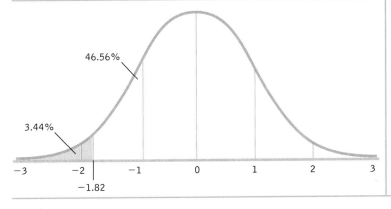

FIGURE 8-5
Calculating the Percentile for a Negative z Score

As with positive z scores, drawing curves helps us to determine the appropriate percentage for negative z scores. For a negative z score, we subtract the percentage between the mean and that z score from 50% (the percentage below the mean) to get the percentage below that negative z score, the percentile. Here we subtract the 46.56% between the mean and the z score of −1.82 from 50%, which yields 3.44%.

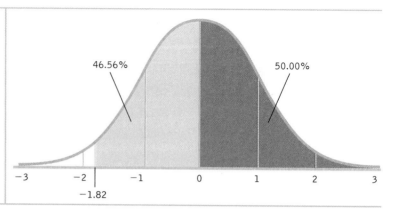

FIGURE 8-6
Calculating the Percentage Above a Negative *z* Score

For a negative *z* score, we add the percentage between the mean and that *z* score to 50% (the percentage above the mean) to get the percentage above that *z* score. Here we add the 46.56% between the mean and the *z* score of −1.82 to the 50% above the mean, which yields 96.56%.

50 + 46.56 = 96.56. So 96.56% of 15-year-old boys' heights fall above Manuel's height (Figure 8-6). (*Note:* Alternately, you could look under the column in the *z* table labeled "in the tail.")

3. *The scores at least as extreme as Manuel's z score, in both directions:* In this case, 3.44% of 15-year-old boys have heights that are extreme enough to have *z* scores below −1.82. And because the curve is symmetric, another 3.44% of heights are extreme enough to be above a *z* of score of 1.82. So we can double 3.44% to find the total percentage of heights that are as far as or farther from the mean than is Manuel's height: 3.44 + 3.44 = 6.88. So 6.88% of heights are at least as extreme as Manuel's in either direction (Figure 8-7).

In what group would the researchers classify Manuel? Manuel has a percentile rank of 3.44%. He is in the lowest 5% for heights for boys of his age, so he would be classified as having short stature. Now we can get to the question that drives this research. Does Manuel's short stature doom him to a life of few friends and poor social adjustment? When Sandberg and colleagues (2004) compared the means of the three groups—short, average, and tall—on several measures of peer relations and social adjustment, they did not find evidence of psychological differences among these three groups.

Sandberg and colleagues' study represents the kind of question that we hope psychotherapists and other clinicians ask: Do we really have a problem

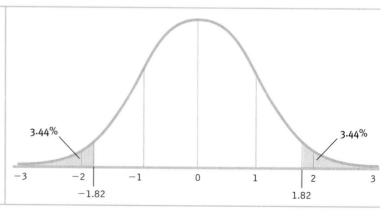

FIGURE 8-7
Calculating the Percentage at Least as Extreme as Our *z* Score

With a negative *z* score, we double the percentage below that *z* score to get the percentage of scores that are at least as extreme—that is, at least as far from the mean—as our *z* score is. Here, we double 3.44% to calculate the percentage at least this extreme: 6.88%.

here? For now, why not compare yourself with the national norms? If you're 20 years old or younger, you can look at the CDC height norms listed at www.cdc.gov/nchs/about/major/nhanes/growthcharts/charts.htm to determine your percentile score. People usually do not grow much beyond age 20, so even if you are older, you can get a sense of your percentile score by examining these charts.

Now, here is what may sound like an odd request from teachers of statistics, but it is one that we feel very strongly about: *Please do not memorize.* Please do not memorize the directions outlined below. Instead, use them only for practice until you get comfortable with the concepts underlying them. If you attempt to memorize these directions, you invite innumerable opportunities to make mistakes when you attempt to calculate the appropriate percentages on your own. There are many permutations, and it is difficult to have rote rules for every possible situation. However, here is a simple procedure that you should remember instead (one we also used in our calculations of height):

1. Draw the normal curve, shown in Figure 8-8.

2. Play around with the drawing.

Even professors make mistakes with calculations of percentages if they do not routinely use drawings. Moreover, in preliminary studies in some of our statistics classes, we found that students who drew their curves on quizzes and tests tended to be correct more often than students who did not draw and label normal curves as a guide to their thinking. *Always* use this procedure when you do your homework or take a test, and you'll have no need to memorize rules. Here's why drawing and labeling the bell-shaped curve is so effective:

1. A drawing is more likely to stay clearly implanted in your memory, especially as you keep using it.

2. A drawing at the top of your exam or quiz remains there as a handy reminder and a practical reference for future test questions.

3. A drawing condenses information, which makes it an efficient way to store and to retrieve large amounts of information.

So draw a picture instead and start playing with it. You will find yourself doing everything you need to do to obtain a correct answer. More important, you will

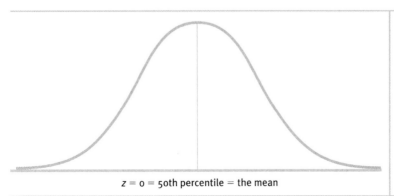

z = 0 = 50th percentile = the mean

FIGURE 8-8
z = 0 = 50th Percentile = the Mean

A *z* score of 0 represents the mean as well as the median, the 50th percentile.

understand why the answer is correct. Here is a list of things you can do while playing with your drawing.

1. *Draw* a bell-shaped curve.

2. *Label* the midpoint beneath the curve that represents a *z* score of 0 (with the mean raw score below the *z* score; remember that the mean of a *z* distribution is always 0), and *draw* a vertical line from the mean to the top of the curve.

3. *Convert* the raw score of interest to a *z* score (use the *z* formula).

4. *Add* this *z* score (with the original raw score below the *z* score) to the bell curve, and *draw* a vertical line connecting this score to the top of the curve.

5. *Shade* the portion of the curve for which you are trying to calculate the percentage.

6. *Look up the* z *score* on the table, and write the percentages that you now know under the appropriate parts of the curve. (Remember that the curve tells you the percentage between the mean and your *z* score. Also remember that each half of the curve is 50%.)

7. Use addition or subtraction as necessary to *calculate the percentage* of the shaded portion.

8. Finally, simply *ask yourself*: Does this answer make sense?

From Percentages to *z* Scores: The Benefits of Sketching the Normal Curve

One of the advantages of playing with your drawing of a bell curve is that doing so makes it is very easy to see that raw scores, *z* scores, and percentile rankings are three ways to describe the same location of a particular score within the bell-shaped curve. This means that the *z* table can be used in reverse. If we know a percentage, then we can calculate the appropriate *z* score. Once we have a *z* score, we can convert it back to a raw score. Here are the simple procedures:

1. *Draw* a picture of the curve that includes the percentage with which you are starting.

2. *Draw* vertical lines at that percentage and at the mean.

3. *Shade* only the area of the curve between the mean and the *z* score of interest.

4. From the drawing, and using addition or subtraction as needed, *calculate the percentage* between the mean and the *z* score of interest—the shaded portion.

5. *Look up the percentage* you noted in step 2 on the *z* table. (Be sure to add a negative sign if it is below the mean.)

6. *Convert* the *z* score to a raw score.

7. *Ask yourself*: Does this answer make sense?

Here are two examples demonstrating that raw scores, *z* scores, and percentile rankings are three different ways to say the same thing. Many high school students in North America take the Scholastic Aptitude Test (SAT), a common university admissions requirement. The mean SAT score is 500 and

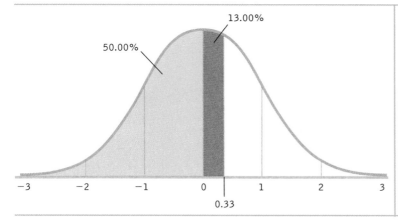

FIGURE 8-9
Calculating a Score from a Percentile

We can convert a percentile to a raw score by calculating the percentage between the mean and the z score, and looking up that percentage on the z table to find the associated z score. We would then convert the z score to a raw score using the formula. Here, we look up 13.00% on our z table (12.93% is the closest percentage) and find a z score of 0.33, which we can then convert to a raw score.

the standard deviation is 100. Because the SAT is actually calibrated to have this mean and standard deviation, we know that these are meant to be the population parameters. So let's imagine that Jo took the SAT and scored at the 63rd percentile. What was her raw score? First, we'll draw a curve, as in Figure 8-9. We will make a line at the point below which approximately 63% of scores fall. This score will be above the mean because we know that 50% of scores fall below the mean, and 63% is larger than 50%.

Using the drawing as a guideline, we see that we have to calculate the percentage between the mean and the z score of interest. We calculate this by subtracting the 50% below the mean from Jo's score, 63%: $63 - 50 = 13$. We look up the closest percentage to 13% in the z table (which is 12.93%) and find an associated z score of 0.33. This is above the mean, so we do not need to label it with a negative sign. We can then convert the z score to a raw score using the formula that we learned in Chapter 7: $X = z(\sigma) + \mu = 0.33(100) + 500 = 533$. Jo, whose SAT score was at the 63rd percentile, had a raw score of 533.

Let's do our quick mental check of the answer: this score is above the mean, just as we would expect given a percentage above 50.

Explaining test scores, such as those from the SAT, to students (and their parents) is one of the many tasks often assigned to school psychologists. Social science students contemplating a career as a school psychologist should know that interpreting test scores to nervous students and parents requires a sophisticated knowledge of statistics, as well as excellent human relations skills. But school psychologists also know how to collect and present new data. Creating new local knowledge about students in a particular district can help the board of education and the superintendent direct monies more appropriately, hire staff more intelligently, and achieve a superior education with fewer resources. Your knowledge of statistics creates opportunities to accomplish many such worthwhile goals.

For example, a school psychologist might be interested in the educational backgrounds of the best and worst performers on the SAT in her or his particular school district. To identify these students, let's say that the school psychologist needs to identify the cutoff SAT scores of the best 10% and the worst 10%— that is, the 20% who are the most extreme at both ends of the distribution.

FIGURE 8-10
Calculating Cutoffs

If we want to determine values that serve as the cutoffs for the most extreme areas of a distribution, then we calculate the percentage between the mean and one of the cutoffs, and look up that percentage on the *z* table to find its associated *z* statistic. The negative and positive *z* statistics will have the same value because the distribution is symmetric. In this case, we want to demarcate the most extreme 10% in the negative tail and the most extreme 10% in the positive tail. We look up 50 − 10 = 40% on the *z* table and find a *z* score of 1.28. So −1.28 and 1.28 are our cutoff.

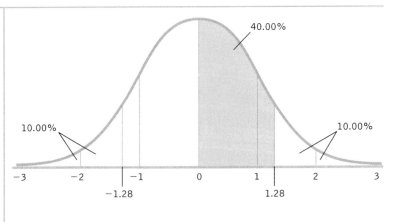

To do this, we'll first draw a curve, as in Figure 8-10. Then we'll draw vertical lines at approximately 10% from the end of the negative tail and 10% from the end of the positive tail. Next, we'll shade the area between the mean and the positive *z* score. Because the curve is symmetric, we need to calculate only one of these *z* scores. If we calculate the positive *z* score, the negative *z* score will be identical, but with a negative sign. Here, we shade the area between the mean and the positive *z* score. Because 10% of scores fall above this point and 50% fall above the mean, we subtract to find the difference: 50 − 10 = 40. So 40% of scores fall between the mean and the *z* score in which we're interested. When we look up the closest percentage to 40% on the *z* table (which is 39.97%), we find a *z* score of 1.28. Next, we convert the positive and negative versions of this *z* score to raw scores to get the school psychologist's cutoffs. Again, we use the mean of 500 and the standard deviation of 100.

$$X = z(\sigma) + \mu = 1.28(100) + 500 = 628$$

$$X = z(\sigma) + \mu = -1.28(100) + 500 = 372$$

Psychological Tests
School psychologists interpret tests to the parents of students. Your knowledge of statistics will help you to precisely communicate helpful information.

The school psychologist will study students who scored 628 or higher on the SAT as well as those who scored 372 or lower. Together, these students constitute the 20% most extreme scores. However, as a school psychologist, you will need to convey this kind of information about a particular student's score to worried parents who aren't really listening to you—and in about 10 seconds. Trust us, a drawing will help you then just as much as it does right now.

The *z* Table and Distributions of Means: The Benefits of Unbiased Comparisons

We all tend to be most interested in our own scores, especially on tests that compare our scores to other people's scores. Such comparisons are a way to learn a great deal about ourselves, but researchers are seldom interested in studying only one individual. It is difficult to have much confidence that one individual, even if randomly selected, is representative of a larger population. Fortunately, the *z* table can also be used to determine percentages and *z* statistics for distributions of means calculated from many people. The process is identical to that described for distributions of scores, but with the additional step that we first need to calculate the mean and the standard error for the distribution of means. Then we take that information to the *z* table.

Many graduate programs select students based, in part, on their Graduate Record Exam (GRE) scores, both on the general GRE and on the subject test specific to that graduate degree. For example, about half of the doctoral programs and one third of the master's programs in psychology in the United States require that students take the GRE psychology test (Matlin & Kalat, 2001). Most of these subject tests have been used for many years, so we know the population mean and the population standard deviation. In fact, Psi Chi, the national honor society in psychology, published a useful online article that provides valuable information, as well as some descriptive statistics, about the GRE psychology test for prospective graduate students (Matlin & Kalat, 2001; go to http://www.psichi.org/pubs/ and click on "articles and issues" under Eye on Psi Chi, then click on "Volume 5, Issue 2"). The authors also report data from the Educational Testing Service (ETS) based on all GRE psychology test scores between October 1, 1995, and September 30, 1998; in particular, they report that the mean score for these years was 554 and the standard deviation was 99.

Now, imagine that you were asked to figure out statistically how well psychology students at your institution perform on the GRE psychology test compared to all psychology students who have taken this test (assume that the mean and standard deviation have not changed greatly since 1998). You record the psychology test scores of a representative sample, 90 graduating seniors in your psychology department, and find that the mean score is 568. You want to know how much better (or worse) students in your department are doing by comparison to the mean score of the population. *z* statistics make that comparison possible.

First, let's imagine what that distribution of means for GRE psychology test scores probably looks like. You can actually imagine this distribution fairly accurately because of one of the three concepts related to the normal curve that we learned about in Chapter 7: the central limit theorem. For example, we are comparing the mean from our sample of 90 to a distribution of means that is created by plotting the means of every possible sample of 90. Think back to the exercise we did in Chapter 7 with means of samples of three heights. The distribution of means for samples of 90 GRE scores would be created in a similar way—just with far, far more means. The population of GRE scores is likely normally distributed, but even if it were not, the sample is at least 30, so the distribution of means will be approximately normal.

As we discovered from the central limit theorem, the distribution of means will have the same mean as the distribution of scores for the population, but the spread will be smaller and will have to be calculated. Any extreme GRE score in a given sample is likely to be balanced by less extreme scores when the mean is calculated, and so the distribution of means will be less variable than the distribution of scores. If you imagined a symmetric distribution with very little variability around the mean, then you are probably well on the way to understanding the mystery of the central limit theorem. Before we calculate the *z* statistic, let's use proper symbolic notation to indicate the mean and the standard error of this distribution of means:

$$\mu_M = \mu = 554$$

$$\sigma_M = \frac{\sigma}{\sqrt{N}} = \frac{99}{\sqrt{90}} = 10.436$$

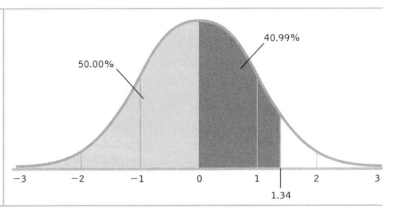

FIGURE 8-11
Percentile for the Mean of a Sample

We can use the *z* table with sample means, just as we can use it with sample scores. The only difference is that we must use the mean and the standard error of the distribution of means rather than of the distribution of the population of scores. Here, our *z* score for 1.34 is associated with a percentage of 40.99 between the mean and the *z* score. Added to the 50% below the mean, the percentile is 50 + 40.99 = 90.99.

At this point, we have all the information we need to calculate the percentile using the procedure we learned when working with distributions of individual scores. First, we convert to a *z* statistic using the mean and standard error that we just calculated.

$$z = \frac{(M = \mu_M)}{\sigma_M} = \frac{(568 - 554)}{10.436} = 1.34$$

Then we draw a curve that includes the mean of the *z* distribution, 0, and this *z* statistic, 1.34 (Figure 8-11). We will shade the area in which we are interested, everything below 1.34. Then we will look up the percentage between the mean and the *z* statistic of 1.34. The *z* table indicates that this percentage is 40.99, which we will write in the section of the curve between the mean and 1.34. We will write 50% in the half of the curve below the mean. We will add 40.99% to the 50% below the mean to get the percentile rank, 90.99%. (Subtracting from 100%, only 9.01% of mean scores would be higher than our mean if they come from this population.) Based on this percentage, the mean GRE psychology test score of our sample is quite high. There may be several reasons for such a high mean score, but for now, it suggests some very good news. You appear to be part of a psychology department whose students compare very well, on average, with other psychology departments across the country.

In the next section, we will learn how to conduct a hypothesis test using the tools of distributions. We'll learn the steps to reject, or fail to reject, the null hypothesis that the students in this department do *not* receive different scores on average than do students in the entire population. Only then can we draw a conclusion about what the data are saying.

In summary, raw scores, *z* scores, and percentile rankings are three ways to describe the same thing: the location of a particular score within a normal distribution. If we know the mean and the standard deviation of a population, we can convert a raw score to a *z* score and then use the *z* table to determine percentages below, above, or at least as extreme as this *z* score. We can use the *z* table in reverse as well, taking a percentage and converting it into a *z* score and then a raw score. These same transformations can be conducted on a sample mean instead of a score. The procedures are identical, but we must use the mean and the standard error of the distribution of means, instead of the mean and the standard deviation of the distribution of scores. The mean is identical, but the standard deviation, called standard error, is smaller; we must divide the standard deviation by the square root of the sample size.

⊙ CHECK YOUR LEARNING

8-1 Every year, the ETS administers the Major Field Test in Psychology (MFTP) to graduating psychology majors. In 2003, Baylor University wondered how its students compared to the national average. On its Web site, Baylor reported that the mean and the standard deviation of the 18,073 U.S. students who took this exam were 156.8 and 14.6, respectively. Thirty-six students in the Psychology and Neuroscience Department at Baylor took the exam; these students had a mean score of 164.6.

a.   What is the percentile rank for the sample of students at Baylor? Use symbolic notation and write out your calculations.

b.   What percentage of samples of this size scored higher than the students at Baylor?

c.   The Web site suggests that these data are evidence of the superior psychology training offered by Baylor. What more would you want to know about this sample of 36 students before drawing such a conclusion?

❯ HYPOTHESIS TESTS: AN INTRODUCTION

One of Henry's clients saw him and started to wave hello just as he was being escorted into the police station. What would happen to his accounting business? His marriage? His life? When he finally sat down with a detective, Henry decided to tell him about the therapists. "It's those facilitated communication people," he said. The detective remained quiet. "Gordon, my son, has autism, but these FC people insisted that they had discovered a way that allowed Gordon to communicate."

"Wait a second," said the detective. "I've heard of autism. It's where kids go into their own world, can't relate to others, that sort of thing, right?"

"Yes," Henry told the detective. "The facilitator holds Gordon's sleeve or part of his arm as his hand hovers over an alphabet board. Supposedly, the facilitator can sense which letters Gordon wants to press and then help him spell out words, sentences, and even entire messages."

"Hold his sleeve?" the detective asked, and reached across with his right arm to hold the shirtsleeve of his left. "Like this?"

"That's the idea," said Henry. "I couldn't do it. The facilitator told me Gordon could only do FC with people he could trust. I should have been more insulted, but at the time I was just happy that Gordon was getting some attention. At first, the facilitator reported that Gordon was telling him wonderful things, like 'Thank you, Mom and Dad, for all you've done for me.' Can you imagine, detective, how desperately a parent wants to hear that their autistic child loves them?"

"I suppose so," said the detective in a neutral tone of voice. He didn't want to make the mistake of believing that Henry had sexually abused Gordon when he really hadn't, but neither did he want to make the mistake of believing that Henry had not sexually abused Gordon when he really had. He could make either a Type I error or a Type II error—and he didn't want to make either kind. The detective had taken a college course in statistics as part of his

Facilitated Communication Quantitative and qualitative research approaches reached different and incompatible conclusions about facilitated communication. Here, a facilitator holds the sleeve of the child with autism to help him spell out words, sentences, even entire messages.

▪ **Assumptions** are the requirement that the population from which we are sampling has specific characteristics that will allow us to make accurate inferences.

criminal justice major but had never realized how its logic could help him navigate the uncertain world of detection. "Does FC really work?"

"I wanted FC to work," Henry told him. "I assumed that even if FC didn't work, Gordon wouldn't be harmed by it. And I assumed that his facilitator was sincere. In fact, I still believe that. I also assumed that good intentions somehow canceled out the possibility of a harmful outcome."

"That famous road to hell," agreed the detective. "You have to be careful when you make assumptions."

The most dangerous assumptions are the ones we don't know we are making. Fortunately, the formal process of hypothesis testing articulates its assumptions. We have also discovered when it is relatively safe to violate those assumptions. Knowing that our reasoning is based on assumptions about the data means that major, and even minor, violations of those assumptions lead us to be much more careful. So this next section focuses first on the assumptions connected with hypothesis testing. Then we introduce the six steps of formal hypothesis testing.

Assumptions: The Requirements to Conduct Analyses

We all make assumptions, whether it is assuming that the accused are guilty, that most cars will stop at red lights, or that a friend will pay back money we have lent. A detective might assume that a witness is lying but be mistaken. But even a mistaken assumption does not mean that a detective can't get to the bottom of a case—it just makes it slower and much more difficult. Circumstances and evidence first have to force the detective into recognizing the error. Then the detective has to be willing to admit to the error, separate assumptions from evidence, and follow the trail of evidence with a more open mind. Statisticians also make assumptions and run the corresponding risks of being wrong—while hoping that if we are wrong, it still won't make a difference in the outcome.

In statistics, *assumptions are the requirements that the population from which we are sampling has specific characteristics that will allow us to make accurate inferences.* Our goal is to discover something real about our population. So we want to analyze our data using the appropriate statistical test, and we would like to make as few assumptions as possible. The following assumptions hold for the hypothesis test that we'll learn in this chapter, the *z* test But they also hold for several more sophisticated hypothesis tests that we'll learn about in the next few chapters.

First, we assume that the dependent variable is measured on an interval scale. This simply means that the numbers represent equal distances from one another. For example, the difference between 30 and 31 seconds is the same as the difference between 109 and 110 seconds; time is a scale variable. However, for other measures, the assumption of equal intervals is more difficult to defend. On a depression measure with a scale of 1–10, is the difference between 1 and 2 the same as between 9 and 10? What if we knew that a score went from 1 to 2 because someone admitted to problems sleeping, whereas another score went from 9 to 10 because someone admitted to suicidal thoughts? They are both symptoms of depression, but they may not be equivalent symptoms of depression. Nevertheless, many psychological tests assume that the dependent variable is an interval variable.

Second, we assume that the participants are randomly selected. For hypothesis tests to provide accurate results, the participants in the sample must have been selected

Career Planning
Your ability to measure and test hypotheses about behavior is the most marketable skill you learn as a social science major.

Peter Turnley/Corbis

randomly. Every member of the population of interest must have had an equal chance of being chosen for participation in the study, something that rarely occurs in social science research. It is more likely that research is guided by a convenience sample (availability) than by pure random selection.

Third, the distribution of the population of interest must be approximately normal. Although many distributions are approximately normal, it is important to remember that there are important exceptions to this guideline (Micceri, 1989). Unless the sample is very small, we can usually get a sense of whether the distribution is normal by examining the sample itself. If the sample data are normally distributed, it is likely that the underlying population distribution is well approximated by a normal curve. Moreover, the application of the central limit theorem tells us that, in most cases, as long as there are at least 30 participants in our sample, the distribution of *means* will be approximately normal, regardless of the distribution of individual scores. Because hypothesis tests deal with sample means rather than individual scores, as long as the sample size is at least 30, it is likely that this assumption is met.

As you may have anticipated, inferential statistics are based on assumptions that aren't always met. However, it is permissible to conduct many hypothesis tests even if the assumptions are not met (Table 8-2). Often, the inferential statistics that we want to use are robust against violations of these assumptions. *Robust hypothesis tests are those that produce fairly accurate results even when the data suggest that the population might not meet some of the assumptions.* With respect to the first assumption, researchers often conduct successful hypothesis tests when it is not clear whether the dependent variable is measured on an interval scale. Researchers also often conduct hypothesis tests in the absence of meeting the second assumption, the one that assumes random selection; this is done legitimately *if* we add a disclaimer to reports of our research. We must limit the extent to which we generalize our findings if we cannot be certain that our sample is representative of the population. Finally, hypothesis tests are most robust in the face of a violation of the third assumption, the one that assumes a normal distribution; numerous statisticians have demonstrated the accuracy of results from distributions that are not approximately normal. For example, Sawiloswky and Blair (1992) demonstrated the robustness of hypothesis tests under certain conditions, such as when the sample size is sufficiently large.

▪ **Robust** hypothesis tests are those that produce fairly accurate results even when the data suggest that the population might not meet some of the assumptions.

TABLE 8-2. THE THREE ASSUMPTIONS FOR HYPOTHESIS TESTING

We must be aware of the assumptions for the hypothesis test that we choose, and we must be cautious in choosing to proceed with a hypothesis test even though our data may not meet all of the assumptions. Note that in addition to these three assumptions, for many hypothesis tests, including the *z* test, the independent variable must be nominal.

THE THREE ASSUMPTIONS	BREAKING THE ASSUMPTIONS
1. Dependent variable is measured on an interval scale.	Usually OK if the data are not clearly nominal or ordinal.
2. Participants are randomly selected.	OK if we are cautious about generalizing.
3. Population distribution is approximately normal.	OK if the sample includes at least 30 scores.

▪ **Parametric tests** are inferential statistical analyses that are based on a set of assumptions about the population.

▪ **Nonparametric tests** are inferential statistical analyses that are not based on a set of assumptions about the population.

With many scales, we are making an assumption that the dependent variable qualifies as an interval variable. However, when we know that the dependent variable is not interval, we don't play pretend. If I am betting on a horse race and don't have a stopwatch to calculate the actual times of each horse in the race, then I can't pretend to have interval data. As a bettor, I don't actually care whether my horse won by a nose or by 15 lengths. The relevant dependent variable in that circumstance is order of finish, an ordinal variable, and we would analyze that horse race accordingly. *Parametric tests are statistical analyses based on a set of assumptions about the population.* By contrast, *nonparametric tests are statistical analyses that are not based on a set of assumptions about the population.* Our goal is to match the appropriate statistical test with the characteristics of our data so that we can trust whatever we might discover through our statistical analysis.

Inferential statistics are based on assumptions about the population that may not be true, but most statistics are robust against violations of the assumptions. So a reasonable question is: Why bother? Why bother learning about all the assumptions when we know that it is often allowable to violate them? It really is an excellent question and that is why it leads to an excellent answer: These three statistical assumptions represent the ideal conditions of most parametric research and so the researcher who is able to meet them tends to produce more trustworthy (valid) research. *Meeting the assumptions improves the quality of our research, but not meeting the assumptions doesn't necessarily invalidate our research.* Like a detective trying to solve a case, making inappropriate statistical assumptions doesn't mean that we can't make new discoveries. It just makes it more difficult to get to the bottom of what actually happened.

The Six Steps of Hypothesis Testing: A Reliable Framework for Hypothesis Testing

If a hypothesis is supported by the findings of a hypothesis test, then it becomes part of our house of scientific knowledge, but this knowledge is more like a renter than an owner. But even as a renter, knowledge becomes very difficult to evict from our house of knowledge even if it doesn't conform to later discoveries. That is why good scientists are chronically skeptical and use the same six steps for every hypothesis test. There are variations within the six steps based on each specific distribution and its appropriate hypothesis test, but the framework is always the same for all hypothesis tests.

Step 1. *Identify the populations, distribution, and assumptions.*

The first step of hypothesis testing is to identify the populations to be compared, the comparison distribution, the appropriate test, and its assumptions. The purpose of step 1 is to be convinced that it is OK to proceed with a particular statistical analysis. When we first approach hypothesis testing, we consider the characteristics of our data to determine the distribution to which we will compare our sample. First, we state the populations represented by each of our samples. Then we list the comparison distribution (e.g., distribution of means). Finally, we list the hypothesis test that we would use for that distribution and check the assumptions for that hypothesis test.

Step 2. *State the null and research hypotheses.*

The second step is to state the null and research hypotheses. Once we state our hypothesis, we can't restate it just because we notice that the data don't seem to be supportive. In Chapter 4, we presented the null and research hypotheses on which hypothesis testing is based. The null hypothesis is usually the "boring" one, positing no change or no difference. In fact, the word *null* comes from the Latin *nullus*, which means "not any," as in "not any change or difference." The research hypothesis is the "exciting" one, the one positing that, for example, a given intervention will lead to a change or a difference. While you are still learning hypothesis testing, it is best to state the null and research hypotheses in both words and symbolic notation. A useful way to remember the meaning of the null hypothesis is by focusing on the letter *n*: the *n*ull hypothesis proposes that there is *no* difference between groups and *no* effect of the independent variable on the dependent variable—in fact, the null hypothesis proposes that *n*othing at all is going on in this study. It's a handy little mnemonic that will help you think through the logic of hypothesis testing:

*n*ull hypothesis = *n*o difference = *n*o effect = *n*othing going on.

When we start with a proper understanding of the null hypothesis, we develop the habit of thinking clearly about the comparison we are making. If we are hypothesizing that college graduates, for example, have higher lifetime earnings, we don't leave it at that; we always state the other half of the comparison: College graduates have higher lifetime earnings *than whom*? For example, we might hypothesize that college graduates have higher lifetime earnings than high school graduates. Too frequently, the second part of the comparison is omitted. So the research hypothesis is that college graduates have higher lifetime earnings than high school graduates, and the null hypothesis is that there is no difference between these two groups.

Step 3. Determine the characteristics of the comparison distribution.
The third step is to explicitly state the relevant characteristics of the comparison distribution, the distribution based on the null hypothesis. Hypothesis testing requires clarity so that after the study we don't find ourselves saying, "Well, maybe it's true and maybe it isn't. I can't tell for sure because our comparison group wasn't quite right." There is no point in doing a study if we can't come to a sensible decision after the study. In all cases, we compare the data from our sample (or samples) to a comparison distribution based on the null hypothesis to determine how extreme our sample data are. At this step, we determine the appropriate numbers to describe the distribution to which we hope to compare our sample. For *z* tests, we will determine a mean and some measure of the spread of the comparison distribution. These numbers describe the distribution represented by the null hypothesis. The numbers that we determine in this step will be used in the actual calculations of our test statistic.

Step 4. Determine critical values, or cutoffs.
The fourth step is to determine critical values, or cutoffs, indicating how extreme our data must be to reject the null hypothesis. In hypothesis testing, we determine a specific cutoff number or numbers in terms of the test statistic (e.g., *z*). Often called simply *cutoffs*, these numbers are also called critical values; **critical values** *are the test statistic values beyond which we will reject the null hypothesis*. We do this so we can easily compare the test statistic, such as the *z* statistic, that we calculate for our sample. In most cases, we determine two cutoffs, one for extreme samples below the mean and one for extreme samples above the mean. Typically, the critical values, or cutoffs, are based on a standard that statisticians have somewhat arbitrarily adopted—the most extreme 5% of the distribution curve: 2.5%

■ **Critical values** are the test statistic values beyond which we will reject the null hypothesis; often called *cutoffs*.

■ The **critical region** refers to the area in the tails of the distribution in which we will reject the null hypothesis if our test statistic falls there.

■ The probabilities used to determine the critical values, or cutoffs, in hypothesis testing are called **p levels**.

■ A **statistically significant** finding instructs us to reject the null hypothesis because the pattern in the data differs from what we would expect by chance.

on either end. At times, cutoffs are based on a less conservative percentage, such as 10%, or a more conservative percentage, such as 1%. Regardless of the chosen cutoff, the area beyond the cutoff, or critical value, is often referred to as the critical region. Specifically, *the **critical region** refers to the area in the tails of the distribution in which we will reject the null hypothesis if our test statistic falls there.*

These percentages are typically written as probabilities; that is, 5% would be written as 0.05. *The probabilities used to determine the critical values, or cutoffs, in hypothesis testing are called* **p levels**. (*p* levels are sometimes called alphas, but because alpha has other meanings in statistics, we will call them *p* levels in this text.) We call the cutoff probabilities *p* levels, rather than *p* values, to distinguish them from the cases in which we do refer to a *p* value. Specifically, using software, we can calculate the exact *p* value of a given test statistic. For example, a certain *z* statistic might be beyond a *p* level of 0.05 but might have an actual *p* value of 0.022. This would mean that we would expect a test statistic this extreme only 2.2% of the time if the null hypothesis were true.

Step 5. Calculate the test statistic.

In the fifth step, we calculate our test statistic. Hypothesis testing requires the calculation of a statistic to determine whether the numbers really add up to a trustworthy scientific finding. At this point, we use the information from step 3 to calculate our test statistic, such as a *z* statistic. Because the critical values, or cutoff values, are determined in terms of the test statistic, we can directly compare our test statistic to them to determine if our sample is extreme enough to warrant a rejection of the null hypothesis.

Step 6. Make a decision.

In the final step, we decide whether to reject or fail to reject the null hypothesis. Researchers never know for sure whether what they discover in their samples genuinely represents the population. However, we use statistical analyses to "load the dice" toward validity. This means that if the test statistic falls in the critical region, then we know that it is in the most extreme 5% of possible test statistics, but only *if* the null hypothesis is true. Just by chance, the data could have guided us toward an inaccurate conclusion, and we openly acknowledge that possibility. If we rejected the null hypothesis but should not have, we have committed a Type I error; if we failed to reject the null hypothesis but should have, we have committed a Type II error. Nevertheless, we still have to make a decision, and we do so based on the available evidence. Either we reject the null hypothesis or we fail to reject the null hypothesis. If the results of our study force us to change our minds, so be it. We can always run another study—but what we can't do is look at the data and say, "Oh, that is what I meant to hypothesize in the first place."

As with the writing of hypotheses, the writing of conclusions should always include both parts of the comparison. If we can reject the null hypothesis, we should not conclude that, for example, college graduates have higher lifetime earnings. Rather, we should state: College graduates have higher lifetime earnings *than high school graduates*. Always include the comparison so that your conclusion will be clear to your reader.

These six steps of hypothesis testing are summarized in Table 8-3.

When we are able to reject the null hypothesis, we often refer to our results as "statistically significant." *A **statistically significant** finding instructs us to reject the null hypothesis because the pattern in the data differs from what we would expect by chance.* The word *significant* is another one of those statistical terms with a very particular meaning. The phrase statistically *significant* does not necessarily

---

TABLE 8-3. THE SIX STEPS OF HYPOTHESIS TESTING

We use the same six basic steps with each type of hypothesis test.

1. Identify the populations, distribution, and assumptions and then choose the appropriate hypothesis test.
2. State the null and research hypotheses in both words and symbolic notation.
3. Determine the characteristics of the comparison distribution.
4. Determine the critical values, or cutoffs, that indicate the points beyond which we will reject the null hypothesis.
5. Calculate the test statistic.
6. Decide whether to reject or fail to reject the null hypothesis.

---

mean that the finding is important or meaningful; it means that we are justified in believing that the pattern in the data is genuine. In fact, some have called for the replacement of the term *significant* because it is so confusing. Scarr (1997), for example, said: "Let us replace the term significance with the more accurate term reliability immediately!" (p. 17, exclamation point in original). The important distinction between statistical significance and practical significance is addressed more thoroughly in Chapter 12 when we discuss effect sizes. We can calculate a statistic called an effect size that provides an estimate of the practical importance of a difference; researchers should always provide a measure of effect size in addition to the results of hypothesis testing.

In summary, hypothesis testing proceeds in discrete stages to ensure the validity of a finding. When we conduct hypothesis testing, we have to consider the assumptions for that particular test. Tests that require assumptions that the population distribution is normal are parametric tests, whereas tests that do not are nonparametric tests. There are six standard steps for hypothesis testing. First, we identify our population, comparison distribution, hypothesis test, and assumptions. Second, we explicitly state our null and research hypotheses. Third, we determine the characteristics of the comparison distribution. Fourth, we determine the critical values, or cutoffs, on the comparison distribution. Fifth, we calculate our test statistic. Sixth, we decide whether to reject or fail to reject the null hypothesis.

⊙ CHECK YOUR LEARNING

8-2 For each of the following scenarios, state whether each of the three basic assumptions for parametric hypothesis tests is met. Explain your answers and label the three assumptions (1) through (3).

a. Researchers compared the ability of experienced clinical psychologists versus clinical psychology graduate students to diagnose a patient based on a one-hour interview. For two months, either a psychologist or a graduate student interviewed every outpatient at the local community mental health center who had already received diagnoses based on a number of criteria. The psychologists and graduate students were given a score of correct or incorrect for each diagnosis.

b. Behavioral scientists wondered whether animals raised in captivity would be healthier with diminished human contact. Twenty large cats (e.g., lions, tigers) were randomly selected from all the wild cats living in zoos in North America. Half were assigned to the control group—no change in human interaction. Half were assigned to the experimental group—no humans entered their cages except when the animals were not in them, one-way mirrors were used so that animals could not see zoo visitors, and so on. Animals received a score for health over one year; points were given for various illnesses; a very few sickly animals had extremely high scores.

> HYPOTHESIS TESTS: SINGLE-SAMPLE TESTS

"This is an informal hearing," said the judge. "Our purpose is to determine the suitability of Gordon's father returning to his home, pending resolution of a charge of sexual abuse."

There were four people seated in the judge's small office in the county courthouse: Henry, Henry's lawyer, the judge herself, and a representative of the social service agency reporting the alleged sexual abuse. She looked first to Henry's lawyer. "What's the story?"

"At this stage," said Henry's lawyer, "we're simply trying to get permission for Henry to return to his home, your honor. He poses no threat to his son, he has no previous record of abuse, and he categorically denies these allegations. My client has been an exceptional, conscientious citizen. He doesn't even have a driving violation."

The judge faced the same problem as the detective. She didn't want Henry in the home if he really was abusing Gordon, and she didn't want him kept away from Gordon if he hadn't been abusing him. She turned to the social service representative. "Start talking."

"Gordon reported to his social worker that he loves his father very much, but he doesn't like it when his father does certain things to him. See page 7, your honor."

"Child sexual abuse is a very serious crime," said the judge, who was starting to read page 7.

Henry's lawyer spoke up. "We completely agree with you, your honor. But there is no evidence that Gordon even accused his father of sexual abuse. I can't explain why Gordon's social worker reported that Gordon said all those things, your honor. Gordon seldom says anything at all."

The judge lifted the notebook. "Seldom?" she asked. "He certainly seemed to have a lot to say on page 7. I assume that you do acknowledge that Gordon speaks for himself."

"No, we do not, your honor. Gordon was diagnosed with severe autism when he was an infant. What Gordon actually says is described as echolalia, simply repeating sounds that he hears. Even among the population of people diagnosed with autism, Gordon's standardized scores are consistently in the lowest 5% of the bell curve." Henry's lawyer started presenting statistical evidence from the standardized tests Gordon had taken over the last 14 years. "Even Gordon's so-called facilitator is only asserting that Gordon spelled out his communications, one finger at a time, on an alphabet board suspended in the air. They're using something called FC, facilitated communication."

"Is there a direct test of facilitated communication in all those pieces of paper?" asked the judge.

Henry's lawyer only shook his head. "I don't know yet, your honor."

"Well, if Gordon didn't communicate all this information, then who did? And why would anyone make up such accusations?" They waited for her ruling. "I need more information," she finally said. She turned first to Henry's lawyer and then to the social service representative. "Both of you need to get me more information about facilitated communication."

"What about my client?" asked Henry's lawyer.

She turned to face Henry. "Until I find out more about facilitated communication, my first responsibility is to protect Gordon. Your request to return home is denied."

Henry's lawyer started to object, but Henry stopped him. "Your honor," he said to the judge. "What will it take to convince you that Gordon never communicated any of those messages?"

"I need a fair test of whether facilitated communication really works."

Henry was trained as an accountant, but he knew that someone must have conducted research on facilitated communication. He was soon to find out that in the case of facilitated communication, poorly conducted research had punished innocent people until properly conducted research eventually vindicated them. A fair test of a hypothesis about the relation between variables depends on being able to make a fair comparison. And a fair comparison depends on the existence of a predictable, standardized distribution. So this next section first clarifies what the standardized *z* distribution can do and then applies those characteristics to hypothesis testing.

Forensic Psychology
Forensic psychologists interact with the legal system in many ways, often using statistics to clarify complex circumstances.

The *z* Test: When We Know the Population Mean and Standard Deviation

When thinking about the judge's dilemma, consider hypothesis testing that uses a *z* test for a sample mean. It is the simplest hypothesis test that might actually be published in a peer-reviewed journal and presented as evidence in a court of law. But there are other applications of the *z* test that students nearing graduation should be aware of. For example, it would be useful for you to know how your learning stacks up against your competition: students graduating from other colleges and universities. You learned how to do that earlier in Check Your Learning 8-1. That exercise considered the Major Field Test in Psychology (MFTP), administered by the Educational Testing Service (ETS) to graduating psychology majors. This test allows individual students, as well as entire departments, to compare their scores to national norms—exactly the information students might want to know as they start applying for internships, graduate programs, and various careers.

Baylor University published the data on its 36 students but did not conduct hypothesis testing to determine whether its students' mean score was significantly different from the population mean score. Frazier and Edmonds (2002), however, did use hypothesis testing to compare the MFTP scores of graduating psychology majors at Ursuline College in Ohio to those of the entire population. The authors reported that they used the national mean of 156.5, a bit different from that used by Baylor, though probably because it was from an earlier year. They did not indicate the national standard deviation, but let's assume that it was the same as that used by Baylor, 14.6. The 97 students in the Ursuline College sample, who took the MFTP between 1996 and 1999, had a mean score of 156.11. Here's how to apply hypothesis testing when comparing a sample of psychology majors in one department to psychology majors nationwide.

The *z* Test: The Six Steps of Hypothesis Testing

We will use the six steps of hypothesis testing to analyze the MFTP data from the Ursuline College psychology department, just as we will use this six-step approach for many other statistical tests. In fact, we will use the six-step approach so often in this text that it won't be long before it becomes an automatic way of thinking for you. Below, each step is followed by a summary that models how we should report hypothesis tests on practice exercises, test problems, and research projects.

Step 1. *Populations, distribution, and assumptions.*

First, we identify our populations, comparison distribution, hypothesis test, and assumptions. The *populations* are (1) all students at Ursuline College who took the MFTP between 1996 and 1999 (whether or not they are in our sample) and (2) all students nationwide who took the MFTP between 1996 and 1999. Because we have a sample of many individuals, the *comparison distribution* will be a distribution of means. We will compare our sample mean based on 97 students to a distribution of all possible means of samples of 97 students selected from the population of psychology majors who took this test. The *hypothesis test* will be a *z* test because we have only one sample and we know the mean and the standard deviation of the population from the published norms.

Let's examine the assumptions for a *z* test. (1) The data seem to be interval; study participants received scores from 120 to 200. (2) Frazier and Edmonds (2002) do not report whether sample participants were selected randomly from among all Ursuline psychology majors. If they were not, this limits our ability to generalize beyond this sample to other Ursuline students. (3) The comparison distribution must be normal. In this case, we have a sample size of 97, which is greater than 30, so based on the central limit theorem, we know that our comparison distribution will be approximately normal.

Summary: Population 1 is all students at Ursuline College who took the MFTP between 1996 and 1999. Population 2 is all students nationwide who took the MFTP between 1996 and 1999.

The comparison distribution will be a distribution of means. The hypothesis test will be a *z* test because we have only one sample and we know the population mean and standard deviation. This study meets two of the three assumptions and may meet the third. The dependent variable is interval. In addition, there are more than 30 participants in the sample, indicating that the comparison distribution will be normal. We do not know whether the data were randomly selected, however, so we must be cautious when generalizing.

Step 2. *State the null and research hypotheses.*

Next we state the null and research hypotheses both in words and in symbols. Remember, the hypotheses are always about populations, not samples. In this case, there are two possible sets of hypotheses: directional (predicting either an increase or decrease, but not both) or nondirectional (predicting a difference in either direction). The first possible set of hypotheses is directional. The null hypothesis is that those at Ursuline College who took the MFTP do *not* do better on average than those in the nationwide population who took the test; in other words, they could have the same or lower mean levels, but not higher. The research hypothesis is that students at Ursuline College who took the MFTP do better on average than those in the nationwide population who take the test. (Note that the direction could be reversed; the research hypothesis could posit that Ursuline College students do worse on average than the nationwide population.) When we wrote these hypotheses, notice that we included both halves of the comparison; we stated that we thought the Ursuline College students would do better *than the nationwide population*, not just that they would do better.

The symbol for the null hypothesis is H_0. The symbol for the research hypothesis is H_1. Throughout this text, we will use μ for the mean because hypotheses are about populations and their parameters, not about samples and their statistics. So, in symbolic notation, the hypotheses are:

$$H_0: \mu_1 \leq \mu_2$$

$$H_1: \mu_1 > \mu_2$$

These express in symbols what was previously expressed in words. For the null hypothesis, the symbolic notation says that the mean MFPT score for those in population 1, the Ursuline College students, is not greater than the mean MFPT score of the nationwide students in population 2. For the research hypothesis, the symbolic notation says that the mean MFPT score in population 1 is greater than the mean MFPT score in population 2.

This hypothesis test is considered a one-tailed test. *A **one-tailed test** is a hypothesis test in which the research hypothesis is directional, positing either a mean decrease or a mean increase in the dependent variable, but not both, as a result of the independent variable.* One-tailed tests are rarely seen in the research literature; they are used only when the researcher is absolutely certain that the effect cannot go in the other direction or would not be interested in the result if it did.

The second set of hypotheses is nondirectional. The null hypothesis states that the Ursuline College students who took the MFTP (whether or not in our sample) have the same average score as do those in the nationwide population of students. The research hypothesis is that the Ursuline College students who took the MFTP have a different average score from those in the nationwide population. The means of the two populations are posited to be different, but neither mean is predicted to be lower or higher.

The hypotheses in symbols would be:

$$H_0: \mu_1 = \mu_2$$

$$H_1: \mu_1 \neq \mu_2$$

Again, these express in symbols what was previously expressed in words. For the null hypothesis, the symbolic notation says that those in population 1, the Ursuline College students, perform the same, on average, as the students comprising population 2, the nationwide students. For the research hypothesis, the symbolic notation says that the mean MFPT score for the students in population 1 is not the same as the mean MFPT score for the students in population 2.

This hypothesis test is considered a two-tailed test. *A **two-tailed test** is a hypothesis test in which the research hypothesis does not indicate a direction of mean difference or change in the dependent variable, but merely indicates that there will be a mean difference.* Two-tailed tests are much more common than are one-tailed tests. If a researcher expects a difference in a certain direction, he or she might have a one-tailed hypothesis; however, if the results come out in the opposite direction, the researcher cannot then switch the direction of the hypothesis. It is more conservative to use a two-tailed test to begin with.

Symbol: H_0 is the symbol for the null hypothesis.

Symbol: H_1 is the symbol for the research hypothesis.

■ A **one-tailed test** is a hypothesis test in which the research hypothesis is directional, positing either a mean decrease or a mean increase, but not both, as a result of the independent variable.

■ A **two-tailed test** is a hypothesis test in which the research hypothesis does not indicate a direction of mean difference or change in the dependent variable but merely indicates that there will be a mean difference.

Summary: Null hypothesis: Ursuline College students who took the MFTP have the same scores on average as do those in the nationwide population of students—H_0: $\mu_1 = \mu_2$.

Research hypothesis: Ursuline College students who took the MFTP have different scores on average from those in the nationwide population—H_1: $\mu_1 \neq \mu_2$.

Step 3. Determine the characteristics of the comparison distribution.

Now we determine the appropriate numbers to describe the distribution with which we hope to compare our sample. For *z* tests, the population mean and standard deviation must be given, and the standard error for samples of this size is calculated from the population standard deviation. We must know the mean and the standard deviation of the population of scores to conduct a *z* test. Here, we have been informed that the population mean for the students who took the MFTP nationwide is 156.5 and the standard deviation for this population is 14.6. Because we are using a sample mean, rather than a single score, we must use the standard error of the mean instead of the population standard deviation (of the scores). These are determined as follows:

$$\mu_M = \mu = 156.5$$

$$\sigma_M = \frac{\sigma}{\sqrt{N}} = \frac{14.6}{\sqrt{97}} = 1.482$$

Summary: $\mu_M = 156.5$; $\sigma_M = \dfrac{14.6}{\sqrt{97}} = 1.482$.

Step 4. Determine critical values, or cutoffs.

It is time to be specific. We must determine numerical critical values, or cutoffs, to which we can compare our test statistic. As stated previously, the convention in behavioral science research is to set the cutoffs to a *p* level of 0.05. This indicates the most extreme 5%—that is, the 2.5% at the bottom of the comparison distribution and the 2.5% at the top. Because we will be calculating a test statistic—specifically, a *z* statistic for our sample—we will report cutoffs in terms of *z* statistics. We will use the *z* table to determine the scores for the top and bottom 2.5%.

First let's draw a curve (as in Figure 8-12). We will draw vertical lines to indicate roughly where the lowest and highest 2.5%, as well as the mean, will fall. The *z* table provides the percentage between the mean and a given *z* value. Because the curve is symmetric, we will determine one critical value—the positive *z* value—and simply make it negative to determine the other critical value. We need, therefore, to know the percentage between the mean and the positive

Graduation
Psychology majors from different universities compete with one another for places in graduate programs, internships, and jobs. The MFTP provides an indication of how well a given university has prepared its students.

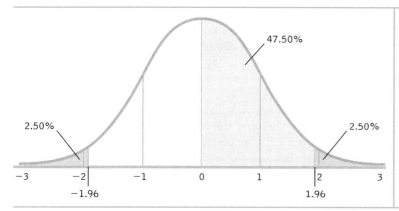

FIGURE 8-12
Determining Critical Values for a *z* Distribution

We typically determine critical values in terms of *z* statistics so that we can easily compare a test statistic to determine whether it is beyond the critical values. Here the *z* scores of −1.96 and 1.96 indicate the most extreme 5% of the distribution, 2.5% in each tail.

z statistic that we want to determine. We know that 50% of the curve falls above the mean, and we know 2.5% falls above the relevant *z* statistic. By subtracting (50 − 2.5 = 47.5), we determine that 47.5% of the curve falls between the mean and the relevant *z* statistic. When we look up this percentage on the *z* table, we find a *z* statistic of 1.96. So the critical values are −1.96 and 1.96.

Summary: Our cutoff *z* statistics are −1.96 and 1.96. (*Note:* It is helpful to include the drawn curve, indicating the cutoff *z* statistics on the curve.)

Step 5. Calculate the test statistic.

In step 5, we calculate our test statistic, in this case a *z* statistic, to find out what the data really say. We use the mean and standard error calculated in step 3:

$$z = \frac{(M - \mu_M)}{\sigma_M} = \frac{(156.11 - 156.5)}{1.482} = -0.26.$$

Summary: $z = \dfrac{(156.11 - 156.5)}{1.482} = -0.26$

Step 6. Make a decision.

Finally, we compare our test statistic to our critical values so that we can make a decision about this finding. We first add the test statistic to the drawing of the curve that includes the critical *z* statistics (Figure 8-13). If the test statistic is beyond the cutoffs—that is, if it is in the critical region—we can reject the null hypothesis. Because we now have data, we also know the direction of the effect and so would be expected to report it; in this example, if the test

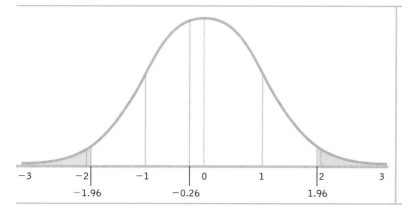

FIGURE 8-13
Making a Decision

To decide whether to reject the null hypothesis, we compare our test statistic to our critical values. In this instance, our *z* score of −0.26 is not beyond the critical value of −1.96, so we cannot reject the null hypothesis.

statistic were in the critical region, we would report whether the Ursuline College students are higher or lower on average than the nationwide population (again being sure to include this comparison group, the nationwide population, in the conclusion). If the test statistic is not beyond the cutoffs, we fail to reject the null hypothesis. This means that we can only conclude that there is no evidence from this study to support the research hypothesis. We will explore the reasons we cannot conclude that we have support for the null hypothesis in later chapters; for now, the major point is that there might be a mean difference that is not extreme enough to be picked up by the hypothesis test. It is possible that the means of our populations are different, but not different enough for us to detect in this manner. We just can't know. So our conclusions will always be expressed with respect to the research hypothesis—whether it was supported or not supported by a given study. In the current example, the test statistic of -0.26 is not even near either critical value. So we must fail to reject the null hypothesis. We conclude that there is no evidence from this study to support the research hypothesis.

Summary: Fail to reject the null hypothesis; we conclude that there is no evidence from this study to support the research hypothesis.

⊙ CHECK YOUR LEARNING

8-3 Conduct all six steps for a *z* test for the following scenario, using a *p* level of 0.05 and a two-tailed test. Check Your Learning 5-1 reported Consideration of Future Consequences (CFC) summary data from Petrocelli (2003). Petrocelli found a mean CFC score of 3.51 with a standard deviation of 0.61 for a large sample. For the sake of this exercise, let's assume that Petrocelli's sample comprises the entire population of interest. You wonder whether students who joined a career discussion group might have improved CFC scores compared with the population. Forty-five students in your Psychology Department regularly attend these discussion groups and then take the CFC scale. The mean for this group is 3.7.

Knowledge in the Behavioral Sciences
What behavioral scientists have learned is stored in academic journals. Most journals may now be accessed electronically.

> THE EFFECT OF SAMPLE SIZE: A MEANS TO INCREASE THE TEST STATISTIC

Henry left the court and headed for the most powerful institution in the United States: the public library. The librarian directed him into the psychology research database PsycINFO, and the educational research database Educational Resources Information Center (ERIC). He entered the words "facilitated communication." Henry discovered scientific journals devoted to autism, others devoted to communication, and still others devoted to communication by people with varied disabilities. He read specific articles, summaries of several articles, and reviews of collected articles. The people in favor of FC were passionate about it, no doubt about that. Henry copied every thing he could before the library closed and then started making phone calls on the sidewalk outside the library. To his surprise, the judge agreed to meet the very next day. "Only one more night away from my son," Henry thought.

The next day they all gathered once again in the judge's office, but this time there was one more person present: the social worker who had been Gordon's facilitator. Henry did not even allow the judge to welcome them before he said, "Much of the qualitative research on FC is positive, but all of the quantitative research on FC is negative." Henry laid the thick pile of articles on the judge's desk. "Look at these articles," he said. "Here's one on children with autism. If both the child with autism and the facilitator see a picture of a boat, then the person with autism spells out B-O-A-T on the letter board. But if the child sees a boat and the facilitator sees a picture of a cat, then the autistic child spells out C-A-T, what the facilitator saw. FC is hopelessly confounded when both the facilitator and the person being facilitated see the same thing regardless of what's in front of them."

Henry grabbed the article from the *American Psychologist* that reviewed FC. "In this study, Klewe tested 13 participants and found zero confirmations of FC. Zero. If you don't believe a study with 13 people, here's another one by some people named Regal, Rooney, and Wandas from 1994. They tested 19 children and found zero confirmations of FC. Zero. If you don't believe a study with 19 people, Szempruch and Jacobson in 1993 tested 23 participants and guess what?"

"Zero?" said the judge.

"Zero! The only possible confirmations, and they are rare, have obvious alternative explanations because of poor methodology."

The judge turned her gaze to the social service representative. "Do you have any problem with this?"

"We looked it up, too," he said. "I guess I can't argue with science. Especially when there is so much of it."

"What about you?" the judge asked the social worker. "You seem to be at the heart of this thing."

The young man was silent for a long time, struggling to answer. "I believed in FC," he said at last. "I went to a conference, and the FC people told me that science was too cold and that scientists couldn't understand concepts like trust. They told me that the words coming through the facilitators were all the evidence they needed—and, well, I wanted to believe them. I wanted to believe that Gordon was one of those children with special abilities."

The judge had been doing her homework, too. "FC is not new to the court system," she told Henry. "One study with only a few participants could be explained away," she said, gesturing to Henry's pile and a similar collection on her desk. "But lots of studies with lots of participants that all tell the same story are difficult to argue against. Barring any objection," she looked to the social service representative, "this case is over. Next time, do your homework."

Henry had been prepared to do battle with everyone in the room, even his own lawyer. But now he only felt disoriented. The obstacles between him and his son were gone, except for the one giant obstacle that had always been there: autism. Instead of rushing out the door, Henry sank back into a chair. "How did this happen?" he said to all of them. But a better question would have been, "Why in the world didn't somebody just read what the scientific literature had already discovered about FC before they started using it on my son?"

Testing Facilitated Communication
Facilitated communication was discredited when researchers were unable to document its effects. When the facilitator and the child with autism saw different stimuli, the facilitator always guided the child's hand to describe what the facilitator saw.

This has been a fictionalized account of people affected by the unfortunate scandal of facilitated communication. Sadly, the stories of self-deceived facilitators, accused parents, and legal charges are true. The American Psychological Association (1994) reviewed all the available literature on facilitated communication and eventually produced a statement of nonsupport expressed by the following resolution:

> **THEREFORE, BE IT RESOLVED** that APA adopts the position that facilitated communication is a controversial and unproved communicative procedure with no scientifically demonstrated support for its efficacy.

Statistics matter because the logic of hypothesis testing is a healthy way to think, not because there are lots of impressive-looking numbers and intimidating formulas. As too many people learned through the tragedy of facilitated communication, lots of qualitative observations do not guarantee validity. Many observations, if they all are contaminated in the same way, simply become more convincing and only produce a bigger, more persuasive lie. An illusory correlation is born, and it is maintained by the confirmation biases of all who believe in that illusory correlation. But just because large numbers of people can be deceived, do not conclude that a large sample size is unimportant to statistics. It's just that the experimental design is even more important than sample size.

Sample size has a powerful effect on our ability to reject the null hypothesis, but only when those large numbers of participants are safely embedded in an appropriate experimental design. In particular, a larger sample size makes it easier to have a test statistic that is beyond one of our cutoffs and, therefore, to reject the null hypothesis. But in an experiment that is poorly designed or confounded, the large sample size might just better enable us to *falsely* reject a null hypothesis. We will demonstrate this effect and then discuss why this occurs—and what we, as students of the behavioral sciences, can do about it.

Increasing Our Test Statistic Through Sample Size: A Demonstration

Increasing our sample size increases our test statistic for every hypothesis test, including the *z* test. Earlier in this chapter, we considered data from the GRE psychology test. Matlin and Kalat (2001) reported data for GRE psychology test scores over several years in the 1990s: $\mu = 554$, $\sigma = 99$. In our fictional example, we reported that 90 graduating seniors had a mean of 568. Based on the sample size of 90, we reported the mean and standard error for the distribution of means as: $\mu_M = 554$; $\sigma_M = \dfrac{\sigma}{\sqrt{N}} = \dfrac{99}{\sqrt{90}} = 10.436$. The test statistic calculated from these numbers was $z = \dfrac{(M - \mu_M)}{\sigma_M} = \dfrac{(568 - 554)}{10.436} = 1.34$.

What would happen if we increased our sample size to 200?

$$\mu_M = 554; \ \sigma_M = \dfrac{\sigma}{\sqrt{N}} = \dfrac{99}{\sqrt{200}} = 7.000$$

$$z = \dfrac{(M = \mu_M)}{\sigma_M} = \dfrac{(568 - 554)}{7.000} = 2.00$$

What if we increased it to 1000?

$$\mu_M = 554; \ \sigma_M = \frac{\sigma}{\sqrt{N}} = \frac{99}{\sqrt{1000}} = 3.131$$

$$z = \frac{(M - \mu_M)}{\sigma_M} = \frac{(568 - 554)}{3.131} = 4.47$$

What if we increase it to 100,000?

$$\mu_M = 554; \ \sigma_M = \frac{\sigma}{\sqrt{N}} = \frac{99}{\sqrt{100,000}} = 0.313$$

$$z = \frac{(M - \mu_M)}{\sigma_M} = \frac{(568 - 554)}{0.313} = 44.73$$

Notice that each time we increased our sample size, our standard error decreased and our test statistic increased. The original test statistic, 1.34, was not beyond the critical values of 1.96 and −1.96. However, the remaining test statistics (2.00, 4.47, and 44.73) were all more extreme than the positive critical value, 1.96, with each succeeding test statistic beating the critical value by larger and larger amounts. When used properly, a large sample size makes a statistic more powerful.

The Effect of Increasing Sample Size: What's Going On

Increasing sample size—to a point—is important to the quality of good science. An increase in sample size leads to an increase in the ability of the test statistic to detect genuine patterns among an array of numbers. Let's explore the logic of sample size with a closer look at the simple mathematical relation embedded in statistical formulas. Sample size, or the number of people actually in a study, enters into the equation as part of the denominator indicating the standard error. That is why an increase in sample size means that the denominator for standard error is larger. Anytime the numerator remains the same but the denominator gets larger, the outcome gets smaller.

Let's demonstrate this with a simple example. If we divide 100 by 5, we get 20. If we divide 100 by 25, we get 4. As long as the numerator stays the same, the bigger the denominator, the smaller the outcome. Here, the outcome is the test statistic and the standard error is the denominator. Conversely, if the denominator is smaller, the outcome is bigger. Look at our example with 100 divided by 5 versus by 25. The smaller denominator leads to a larger outcome. That is why when our sample size increases, the standard error decreases, and the test statistic becomes larger.

Let's now consider why this logically makes sense. If we have a larger sample size, there is much less spread to the distribution of means. If the null hypothesis were true, any sample mean would be very close to the population mean because the occasional extreme score would be balanced by all the less extreme scores. Any difference between the sample mean and the population mean would be likely to be a real difference, not just one that occurred by chance if there is a larger sample size. If we randomly selected 5 people among all those who had taken the GRE and they had GRE scores well above the national average, we might say, "Well, it's possible that we just happened to choose 5 people with high scores." But if we selected 1000 people with GRE scores well above the national average, it seems very unlikely that this would have occurred by chance—that we just happened to choose 1000 people with high scores. That is why we can be more confident that a difference that occurs with a large sample is a real difference.

Yet the difference that we found with 5 people might be exactly the same as the difference we found with 1000 people. As we demonstrated with multiple *z* tests and different sample sizes, we might fail to reject the null hypothesis with a small sample but then reject the null hypothesis for the same-size difference between two means with a large sample. Our conclusions can be different simply because of a difference in the size of our sample! In coming chapters, we will consider why this characteristic of sample size inspired new ways to tell the story of a set of data that go beyond hypothesis testing. Just as with our discussion of assumptions and violations of the assumptions, we also will consider a range of solutions aimed at improving the conclusions that we draw from our data. Our goal, as so many families had to learn through the tragedy of facilitated communication, is to listen and understand more clearly what the data are really saying instead of imposing on the data the kind of story we are hoping to hear.

In summary, the size of the sample has a direct effect on our ability to reject the null hypothesis. Larger samples lead to smaller standard errors, which in turn lead to larger test statistics. The end result is that the same-size difference might lead us to fail to reject the null hypothesis with a small sample and then reject the null hypothesis with a large sample. This is a potential flaw of hypothesis testing that led to new ways of analyzing and understanding data.

⊙ CHECK YOUR LEARNING

8-4 Check Your Learning 8-3 asked you to conduct a *z* test using summary data from Petrocelli (2003): the population mean ($\mu = 3.51$) and the population standard deviation ($\sigma = 0.61$) for CFC scores. For this exercise, you were told that a sample of 45 students had a mean of 3.7.

a. Calculate the test statistic for a sample of 5 students.

b. Calculate the test statistic for a sample of 1000 students.

c. Calculate the test statistic for a sample of 1,000,000 students.

d. Explain why the test statistic varies so much even though the population mean, population standard deviation, and sample mean do not change.

e. Why might sample size pose a problem for hypothesis testing and the conclusions we are able to draw?

▪ DIGGING DEEPER INTO THE DATA: WHAT TO DO WITH DIRTY DATA

Facilitated communication became popular, in part, because qualitative studies took precedence over quantitative studies. It is the kind of mistake that could easily happen to any of us, perhaps especially to those who care deeply about the welfare of others. Good research can be very difficult, especially in the behavioral sciences. So when we run into problems while conducting a study, we don't pretend that the problem isn't there. To the contrary, we carefully bring the problem to the attention of reviewers and readers. This is important because, as the Nobel Prize–winning physicist Richard Feynman (1986) expressed it after reviewing the causes of the *Challenger* space shuttle disaster, "For a successful technology, reality must take precedence over public relations, for Nature cannot be fooled" (p. 26).

But what kind of problems do studies in the behavioral sciences actually run into? Lots of them! For the moment we'll consider three sources of what are sometimes called "dirty data" and what we can do about each problem. Even though they are called dirty, we often don't know why they are dirty; we just know that we can't trust them. Fortunately, *z* scores and standardization often play a role in "scrubbing" the data. But don't get your priorities confused. The best approach is to collect clean data in the first place. We sincerely hope you never have to use what we are about to teach you, but we also know that you will probably need to take advantage of the tips we offer in this section. Three common sources of dirty data are missing data, misleading data, and outliers.

Missing data show up—or, more accurately, don't show up!—in a study for several different reasons. Someone filling out a scale designed to measure depression may get so discouraged by the items she is reading that she can't even finish filling out the scale. But most of the time, the problems we confront are from less dramatic causes: We can't read someone's handwriting, two pages stick together without anyone noticing the problem until it comes time to enter the data, the copy machine fails to copy a page, or someone becomes distracted by something else in the room. In a computerized study, a participant may hit "enter" before he selected a response. Missing data are a particular problem in longitudinal and clinical studies (Wisniewski, Leon, Otto, & Trevedi, 2006). Sometimes participants in longitudinal studies move away, become severely ill, are unable to obtain transportation, just forget to come to a scheduled meeting, and so on.

A second source of dirty data is misleading data. Occasionally participants are just having a bad day or feel they have been manipulated into participating in a study against their better judgment. Angry participants might deliberately provide misleading data just to get back at us. Or perhaps we have used a word in the directions and mistakenly assumed that all the participants knew its meaning. There are many possible sources of misleading data. You get the picture. Stuff happens, even in the most carefully controlled experiments.

Even the cosmetic design of items on the page is important. With the famous Florida "butterfly ballot" in 2000, a cosmetic flaw probably changed the outcome of a presidential election. This ballot was actually arranged as a book (note the instructions at the bottom to "TURN PAGE TO CONTINUE VOTING"). So voters were encouraged to perceive the page of candidates as part of a book, both by the instructions and by the physical layout of items on the page. The customary style for reading a book in English is to read the entire left hand page, reading from left to right, top to bottom, followed by reading the entire right-hand page, reading from left to right, top to bottom. In the butterfly ballot, the voter was asked

Misleading Data
The famous butterfly ballot used in Florida during the 2000 presidential election demonstrated the importance of the cosmetic arrangement of items on a page. Missing and misleading data are common problems in research that need to be faced candidly and resolved fairly.

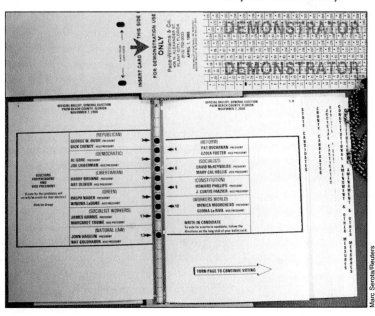

Marc Serota/Reuters

to read the top of the left-hand page first, then to read the slightly lower right-hand page next, then to match that content with the next-lower voting opportunity located in the middle of the page. People who didn't scrutinize the cosmetic arrangement of the ballot, but instead assumed that conventional reading styles were being used, could have registered an unintended vote, or have been disqualified for registering two votes.

A third source of dirty data is the presence of outliers. Outliers present an interesting problem to researchers because we don't always know how to explain them. In Chapter 1, we asserted that outliers may provide us with a unique opportunity to discover useful information. However, the bulk of the statistical literature discusses how to evaluate the influence of outliers and then describes the conditions and methods for identifying, removing, or ignoring them. And that is a justifiable concern. A single outlier can do significant damage to an otherwise cleanly collected and extremely useful data set. It can also lead us to believe that a measure is reliable when it really isn't.

Outliers can happen for any number of reasons. For example, participants may provide less-than-truthful answers on self-report measures, particularly when sensitive questions, such as those about sex or substance use, are asked. There can also be quite innocent explanations for outliers. Imagine that while making thousands of data entries, your finger occasionally slipped so that the number 0 you intended to record shows up in the data field as the number 9. A few mistakes like that and you'll think you're ready for the Nobel Prize until you discover that your dirty data have deceived you.

So what can we do? The most important thing to recognize is that our goal is to play fair with science. Remember, Richard Feynman emphasized that reality must take precedence over public relations, wishful thinking, and our private certainty that the data will come out in a certain way. If the data tell a story that contradicts our strong belief, then we either have to change our belief or figure out what went wrong with our study. The data are what the data are. So when we run into dirty data, our goal is to scrub the data, not massage them into supporting our hypothesis. So let's consider some ways we can clean up dirty data.

Let's say it again: Remember that our goal is to play fair with science. So our first question is, "Why is this data point missing?" Perhaps we asked too many questions and participants got bored or resentful and simply stopped filling out our scale. Or perhaps we offended an entire group of people by the way we asked our questions. We may be wiser to throw the data out in any of the following circumstances:

1. The data loss is widespread.

2. The data loss is systematic (because it applies across an entire group of people).

3. The data loss affects most of the participants in a particular experimental condition.

4. The data loss affects only a few individuals but almost all of their data.

But we still don't ignore the problem; we report it in the Methods section. If the problem is truly widespread, then we may have to scrap our entire study, learn our lessons, and start over again. Painful? Yes. Expensive? Yes, again. But it happens. Be willing to throw the data out if they are just too dirty to salvage. The quality of our studies is only as good as that moment when an observation gets transformed into a number, no matter how many fancy statistics we may use later on in the process.

On the other hand, if we only have occasional, nonsystematic loss of data, then we might be able to save the situation. The question to ask ourselves now is, "How can I best predict what number this participant would have indicated if he or she had answered the question?" We could assign that participant one of these numbers:

1. The modal or median score for that variable
2. The modal or median score from her or his own responses if there are similar items in our database
3. A random number, but naturally one within the range of possible numbers (not 8, say, if you are using a 1–7 scale).

Essentially, these approaches address the problem of missing data by doing what we suggested above: estimate the values that probably would have been there. The most important consideration here is that we don't get to pick the numbers based on our intuition. We decide ahead of time what technique for data replacement we are going to use. Then we report precisely what we did in our Methods section, with a comment such as, "Four participants neglected to fill in a response to one of the 12 items on the CFC scale, so we assigned them the modal score for that item based on the entire sample." A good rule of thumb is to err on the side of being more specific. When in doubt, report it.

Misleading data present a slightly different problem from missing data, but with similar solutions. For example, if we believe that a participant didn't take our study seriously because he or she left much earlier than anyone else and drew a large circle around all the numbers 7, then we should probably just ignore those data and report why we ignored it in our Methods section. We report such problems because if a scale takes such a long time to fill out that participants are dropping out of the study, then that is useful information for the next experimenter who will try to replicate and improve on our study. But if the possibly misleading data are only occasional and appear to be inadvertent, then we have to make a judgment call. We can ignore that section of data or assign it the modal value of the entire sample. Whatever we do, we report it.

Outliers present a similar problem because they also may be misleading data. Outliers can influence data a great deal when we have only a few data points; this is another good reason for recruiting as many participants into our study as we reasonably can. Some problems with outliers are easy to resolve. For example, if the 120 other participants in the sample completed a series of responses to the Stroop task within the range of 93 to 152 seconds and one participant completed her responses in 12 seconds, then we have a right to be suspicious. But be careful; we also might have a visual-processing genius on our hands. One way to identify an outlier is the 1.5 X IQR criterion introduced in the Digging into the Data section of Chapter 2. *z* scores provide another way to identify an outlier because it is not always easy to declare precisely when an outlier becomes an outlier. After all, how different does a data point have to be before we call it an outlier? Because *z* scores correspond to percentiles, they can specify precisely how different a particular data point actually is compared to all the other data points in our study.

The problem of dirty data gets a lot of attention from researchers because we all run into a variety of such problems. All of the possible solutions to the identification of outliers depend on our ability to use a standardized distribution because we can only answer the question "How different must a score be to be considered an outlier?" if we first answer the question "How different from what?"

At this stage, it is most useful for you simply to know that different approaches to identifying outliers seem appropriate to different circumstances. But the core idea of having a standardized distribution in the first place provides the starting point for making meaningful comparisons and practical decisions about outliers.

Perhaps the most interesting feature of these three sources of dirty data is how we, the experimenters, react to the problem. Judgment calls need to be made, of course, and the best guidance we can give is to report everything so that the reviewers and eventual readers can assess for themselves if we made sensible trade-offs. However, the best answer to the problem of dirty data is replication. If we replicate our finding several times, then we just might be on to some new understanding of human behavior that is extremely interesting—and trustworthy.

⊙ CHECK YOUR LEARNING

8-5 You have just conducted a study testing how well daily sugar intake and daily physical activity predicted blood sugar levels. There were only 17 participants to start with, and 3 of them dropped out prior to having their blood sugar levels assessed. In addition, 2 participants left one item blank on the physical activity scale, and 4 other participants left most of the data on their eating habits blank. At their debriefing interview, they said they just couldn't estimate food intake with any accuracy.

    a.   What will you do with the 3 participants who dropped out just prior to having their blood sugar levels assessed?

    b.   What are your choices with regard to the 2 participants who left one item blank?

    c.   What are your choices with regard to the 4 participants who left out all information about eating habits?

    d.   Do you recommend using these data at all? If so, how?

REVIEW OF CONCEPTS

> The Versatile *z* Table: Raw Scores, *z* Scores, and Percentages

The *z* table has several uses when we have normally distributed data. If we know an individual raw score, we can convert it to a *z* score to determine percentages above, below, or at least as extreme as this score. Alternately, if we know a percentage, we can look up a *z* score on the table and then convert it to a raw score. The table can be used in the same way with means instead of scores.

> Hypothesis Tests: An Introduction

Assumptions are the criteria that are met, ideally, before conducting a hypothesis test. *Parametric tests* are those that require assumptions, whereas *nonparametric tests* are those that do not. There are three basic assumptions that apply to many tests. First, the dependent variable should be interval or scale. Second, the data should be from a randomly selected sample. Third, the population distribution should be normal (or there should be at least 30 scores in the sample). A *robust* hypothesis test is one that produces valid results even when all assumptions are not met. There are six steps that apply to every hypothesis test. First, we determine the population, comparison distribution, appropriate hypothesis test, and assumptions. Second, we state our null and research hypotheses. Third, we determine the characteristics of the comparison distribution that we will use to calculate the test statistic. Fourth, we determine our *critical values*, or *cutoffs*, usually based on a *p level* of 0.05, demarcating the 5% most extreme part of the comparison distribution. The area in the most extreme 5% of the tails is called the *critical region*. Fifth, we calculate our test statistic. Sixth, we use that test statistic to decide to reject or fail to reject the null hypothesis. A finding is deemed *statistically significant* when we have rejected the null hypothesis.

> Hypothesis Tests: Single-Sample Tests

z tests are conducted in the rare cases in which we have one sample and we know both the mean and the standard deviation of the population. We must decide whether to use a *one-tailed test*, in which the hypothesis is directional, or a *two-tailed test*, in which the hypothesis is nondirectional.

> The Effect of Sample Size: A Means to Increase the Test Statistic

Sample size directly affects our ability to reject the null hypothesis. It becomes easier to reject the null hypothesis as sample size increases. Larger sample sizes lead to the calculation of smaller standard errors, which in turn lead to the calculation of larger test statistics. A difference that does not allow us to reject the null hypothesis with a small sample might allow us to reject the null hypothesis with a big sample. This flaw of hypothesis testing will be explored further in coming chapters.

> Digging Deeper into the Data: What To Do with Dirty Data

The problem of dirty data often shows up in three ways: missing data, misleading data, and outliers. Clinical and longitudinal studies are particularly susceptible to the problem of missing data. Fortunately, a variety of techniques can be used to address these problems. The techniques are all framed within the goal of playing fair with science. These approaches are guided by estimating how a participant probably would have responded. One way is to replace the missing data with the modal response to that particular variable, because it is reasonable to believe that the best predictor of how someone would have responded is how most other people responded. A similar logic guides the problem of misleading data. The problem of outliers focuses on first identifying outliers. The presence of a standardized distribution makes it possible to identify an outlier because it provides a standard of comparison.

SPSS GUIDELINES FOR CHAPTER 8

SPSS can transform raw data from different scales into standardized data on one scale that is based on the *z* distribution. SPSS gives us many opportunities to look at standardized scores instead of raw scores.

We can standardize our variable by selecting:

Analyze → Descriptive Statistics → Descriptive and then checking the box identified as "Save standardized values as variable." Click OK.

As we noted, we can also identify outliers that might skew the normal curve by selecting:

Analyze → Descriptive Statistics → Explore → Statistics → Outliers, then choosing the variable of interest.

Because raw scale data can be re-expressed as standardized data, SPSS gives us a variety of opportunities within different menus to listen to the story of our data in the language of *z* scores.

EXERCISES

8.1 The *z* table—weather patterns: Hurricane Katrina hit New Orleans on August 29, 2005. The National Weather Service Forecast Office maintains online archives of climate data for all U.S. cities and areas. These archives allow us to find out, for example, how the rainfall in New Orleans that August compared to the other months of 2005. The accompanying table shows the National Weather Service data (rainfall in inches) for New Orleans in 2005.

January	4.41		July	10.65
February	8.24		August	3.77
March	4.69		September	4.07
April	3.31		October	0.04
May	4.07		November	0.75
June	2.52		December	3.32

a. Calculate the *z* score for August. (*Note:* These are raw data for the population, rather than summaries, so you will have to calculate the mean and the standard deviation first.)

b. What is the percentile for the rainfall in August? Does this surprise you? Explain.

c. When our results surprise us, it is worthwhile to examine the individual data more closely, or even to go beyond the data we have. If we look at the daily data for August 2005 (go to http://www.srh.noaa.gov/lix/html/msy/climate.htm, then click "August, 2005"), we find the code M next to August 29, 30, and 31 for all climate statistics. At the bottom is printed: "[REMARKS] ALL DATA MISSING AUGUST 29, 30, AND 31 DUE TO HURRICANE KATRINA." Pretend it was your consulting job to determine the percentile for that August. Write a brief paragraph for your report, explaining why the data you generated are likely to be inaccurate.

d. What raw scores would mark the cutoff for the top and bottom 10% for these data? Based on these scores, what months had extreme data for 2005? Why should we not trust these data?

8.2 The *z* table—IQ: IQ scores are designed to have a mean of 100 and a standard deviation of 15. IQ testing is one way in which individuals are categorized as having different levels of mental disabilities; there are four levels of mental retardation between the IQ scores of 0 and 70.

a. People with IQ scores of 20–35 are said to have severe mental retardation and can learn only basic skills (e.g., how to talk, basic self-care). What percentage of people fall in this range?

b. People with IQ scores of 50–70 are in the topmost category of IQ scores that qualify as impairment. They are said to have mild mental retardation. They can attain as high as a sixth-grade education and are often self-sufficient. What percentage of people fall in this range?

c. An individual has an IQ score of 66. What is her percentile?

d. An individual falls at the 3rd percentile. What is his IQ score? Would he be classified as having a mental disability?

8.3 Which sibling is taller? Imagine two siblings, Kari (age 14) and Jacob (age 13), who have an ongoing rivalry. Among the many characteristics on which they compete is height. Kari is 60 inches tall, and Jacob is 59 inches tall. Kari points out that she is 1 inch taller, and Jacob says that if we take the fact that he is one year younger into account, he is actually ahead on height. From the CDC growth charts, we can find the approximate means and standard deviations for boys and girls of specific ages. The mean for 14-year-old girls is 63 inches with a standard deviation of 2.7, and the mean for 13-year-old boys is 61.8 inches with a standard deviation of 3.2.

a. Explain to Kari and Jacob how their debate can be resolved using statistics. Remember, they're young teenagers, so be sure to use simple language.

b. Conduct the necessary calculations to determine who wins the argument.

c. Determine Kari's and Jacob's percentiles so that they can see for themselves who is taller.

8.4 Comparing physician assistant incomes using *z* scores and percentiles: Physician assistants (PAs) are increasingly central to the health care system in North America. Students who graduated from PA programs in 2004 reported their income (American Academy of Physician Assistants, 2005). Those who chose to work in emergency medicine had a mean income of $76,553 with a standard deviation of $14,001. Their median *z* score was $74,044. Those who chose to work in family/general medicine had a mean income of $63,521, with a standard deviation of $11,554. Their median *z* score was $62,935.

a. The *z* distribution should only be used with individual scores if the distribution is approximately normal. What can we know about these two distributions from their means, standard deviations, and medians? Be specific. Is it appropriate to use the distribution to determine percentiles?

b. Gabrielle chose to work in emergency medicine and earned $75,500 in her first year out of her PA program. What is her *z* score? What is her percentile on income—that is, what percentage of PAs working in emergency medicine make less than she does?

c. Colin chose to work in family/general medicine and earned $64,300 in his first year out of his PA program. What is his *z* score? What is his percentile on income?

d. In comparison to those in their chosen fields, which PA is doing better financially, Gabrielle or Colin? Explain your answer using *z* scores and then explain your answer again using percentiles.

8.5 Step 1—testing of psychiatric inpatients: Boone (1992) examined scores on the Wechsler Adult Intelligence Scale—Revised (WAIS-R) for 150 adult psychiatric inpatients. He determined the "intrasubtest scatter" for each of these inpatients; each participant receives a score for his or her intrasubtest scatter. Intrasubtest scatter refers to patterns of responses in which respondents are almost as likely to get easy questions wrong as hard ones. High levels of intrasubtest scatter indicate unusual patterns of responses; because the questions start at low levels of difficulty and get increasingly more difficult, we would expect more wrong answers near the end. Boone wondered if psychiatric patients would have different response patterns than nonpatients. He compared the intrasubtest scatter for his sample of 150 patients to population data from the WAIS-R standardization group. Assume that he had access to both means and standard deviations for this population. Boone reported that "the standardization group's intrasubtest scatter was significantly greater than those reported for the psychiatric inpatients" and concluded that such scatter is normal.

a. What are the two populations?

b. What would the comparison distribution be? Explain.

c. What hypothesis test would you use? Explain.

d. Check the assumptions for this hypothesis test and label your answer (1) through (3).

e. What does Boone mean when he says *significantly*?

8.6 Step 2—psychiatric inpatients: Refer to the scenario described in Exercise 8.5.

a. State the null and research hypotheses for a two-tailed test in both words and symbols.

b. Imagine that, based on these findings, you wanted to replicate this study. Based on the findings described in Exercise 8.5, state the null and research hypotheses for a one-tailed test in both words and symbols.

8.7 Division I college football and the assumptions for hypothesis testing: Do college football teams tend to be more likely or less likely to be mismatched in the upper National Collegiate Athletic Association (NCAA) divisions. The highest division, Division I (technically, Division I-A), includes such vaunted teams as the Ohio State University Buckeyes and the University of Michigan Wolverines. During week 11 of the fall 2006 college football season, Ohio State beat Illinois by 7 points and Michigan beat Ball State by 8. Overall, however, the 53 Division I games had a mean spread (winning score minus losing score) of 16.189 that week, with a standard deviation of 12.128. We took a sample of four games that were played that week in the next-highest league, Division I-AA, to see if the spread was different; one of the many leagues within Division I-AA, the Patriot League, played four games that weekend.

a. List the independent variable and dependent variable in this example.

b. Did we use random selection? Explain.

c. Identify the populations of interest in this example.

d. State the comparison distribution. Explain your answer.

e. Check the assumptions for this test.

8.8 Division I college football and hypotheses: Refer to Exercise 8.7.

a. State the null hypothesis and the research hypotheses for a two-tailed test in both words and symbols.

b. One of our students hypothesized that the spread would be bigger among the Division I-AA teams because "some of them are really bad and would get trounced." State the one-tailed null hypothesis and research hypothesis based on our student's prediction in both words and symbols.

8.9 Division I college football and a z test: Refer to Exercise 8.7. The results for the four Patriot League games are as follows:

Holy Cross, 27/Bucknell, 10

Lehigh, 23/Colgate, 15

Lafayette, 31/Fordham, 24

Georgetown, 24/Marist, 21

a. Conduct steps 3 through 6 of hypothesis testing. (You already conducted steps 1 and 2 in Exercises 8.7(e) and 8.8(a), respectively.)

b. Would you be willing to generalize these findings beyond our sample? Explain.

8.10 College football and a z test with a different sample: Refer to Exercises 8.7–8.9. Again, use the Division I-A teams as the population.

a. Which steps of hypothesis testing would be different if we were to conduct the same hypothesis test with a different sample, the three games in the Division III league, the Empire 8, for that same weekend? Explain why those steps would be different.

b. Redo those steps for the sample that includes the three Empire 8 games. Here are the results:

Alfred, 28/Ithaca, 17

Springfield, 20/Hartwick, 44

Norwich, 7/Utica, 20

8.11 z test—the Graded Naming Test and cross-cultural differences: z tests are often used when a researcher wants to compare her or his sample to known population norms. The Graded Naming Test (GNT) asks respondents to name objects in a set of 30 black-and-white drawings. The test, often used to detect brain damage, starts with easy words like *kangaroo* and gets progressively more difficult, ending with words like *sextant*. The GNT population norm for adults in England is 20.4. Roberts (2003) wondered whether a sample of Canadian adults had different scores from adults in England. If they were different, the English norms would not be valid for use in Canada. The mean for 30 Canadian adults was 17.5. For the purposes of this exercise, assume that the standard deviation of the adults in England is 3.2.

a. Conduct all six steps of a z test. Be sure to label all six steps.

b. Some words on the GNT are more commonly used in England. For example, a *mitre*, the headpiece worn by bishops, is worn by the Archbishop of Canterbury in public ceremonies in England. No Canadian participant correctly responded to this item, whereas 55% of English adults correctly responded. Explain why we should be cautious about applying norms to people different from those on whom the test was normed.

8.12 One-tailed versus two-tailed tests—the Graded Naming Test: When we conduct a one-tailed test instead of a two-tailed test, there are small changes in steps 2 and 4 of hypothesis testing. Let's consider Exercise 8.11 on the Graded Naming Test. (*Note:* For this example, assume that those from populations, other than the one in which it was named, will score lower, on average. That is, hypothesize that the Canadians will have a lower score.)

a. Conduct step 2 of hypothesis testing for a one-tailed test—stating the null and research hypotheses in words and in symbols.

b. Conduct step 4 of hypothesis testing for a one-tailed test—determining the cutoff and drawing the curve.

c. Conduct step 6 of hypothesis testing for a one-tailed test—making a decision.

d. Under which circumstance—a one-tailed or a two-tailed test—is it easier to reject the null hypothesis? Explain.

e. If it becomes easier to reject the null hypothesis under one type of test (one-tailed versus two-tailed), does this mean that there is now a bigger difference between the samples? Explain.

8.13 p levels—the Graded Naming Test: When we change the p level that we use as a cutoff, there is a small change in step 4 of hypothesis testing. Although 0.05 is the most commonly used p level, other values, such as 0.01, are often used. Let's consider Exercise 8.11 on the Graded Naming Test.

a. Conduct step 4 of hypothesis testing for a p level of 0.01—determining the cutoff and drawing the curve.

b. Conduct step 6 of hypothesis testing for a p level of 0.01—making a decision.

c. With which p level—0.05 or 0.01—is it easiest to reject the null hypothesis? Explain.

d. If it is easier to reject the null hypothesis with certain p levels, does this mean that there is now a bigger difference between the samples? Explain.

8.14 Effect of sample size—the Graded Naming Test: Exercise 8.11 asked you to conduct a z test to ascertain whether the GNT scores for 30 Canadian participants differed from the GNT norms based on adults in England.

a. Calculate the test statistic for 3 participants. How does the test statistic change? Conduct step 6 of hypothesis testing. Does your conclusion change? If so, does this mean that the actual difference between groups changed? Explain.

b. Calculate the test statistic for 100 participants. How does the test statistic change?

c. Calculate the test statistic for 20,000 participants. How does the test statistic change?

d. What is the effect of sample size on the test statistic?

e. As the test statistic changes, has the underlying difference between groups changed? Why might this present a problem for hypothesis testing?

8.15 Cheating with hypothesis testing: Unsavory researchers know that one can cheat with hypothesis testing. That is, they know that a researcher can stack the deck in her or his favor, making it easier to reject the null hypothesis. (The best researchers always stack the deck against themselves, knowing that their results are more reputable if they reject the null hypothesis even under conservative conditions.)

a. If you wanted to make it easier to reject the null hypothesis, what are three specific things you could do?

b. Would it change the actual difference between your samples? Why is this a potential problem with hypothesis testing?

8.16 Tying it all together—orthodontics and the z test: Among those who specialize in pubic health, patient compliance is an important research topic. If patients don't adhere to a treatment, it may not work as well—or at all. A recent research report (Behenam & Pooya, 2006) began, "There is probably no other area of health care that requires a cooperation to the extent that orthodontics does," and explored factors that affected the number of hours per day that patients wore their orthodontic appliances. The patients in the study reported that they used their appliances, on average, 14.78 hours per day, with a standard deviation of 5.31. We'll treat this group as the population for the purposes of this example. Let's say a researcher wanted to study whether a DVD with information about orthodontics led to an increase in the amount of time patients wear their appliances but decided to use a two-tailed test to be conservative. Let's say he studied the next 15 patients at his clinic, asked them to watch the DVD, and then found that they wore their appliances, on average, 17 hours per day.

a. What is the independent variable? What is the dependent variable?

b. Did the researcher use random selection to choose his sample? Explain your answer.

c. Conduct all six steps of hypothesis testing. Be sure to label all six steps.

d. If the researcher's decision in step 6 was wrong, what type of error would he have made? Explain your answer.

8.17 Tying it all together—facilitated communication: Use an online database such as PsycINFO or Educational Resources Information Center (ERIC) to locate the abstract for the study of facilitated communication conducted by Klewe (1993) and titled "An Empirical Evaluation of Spelling Boards as a Means of Communication for the Multihandicapped."

a. What was the independent variable and what were its levels? Based on this, what two populations were being compared?

b. What was the dependent variable?

c. Comparing just series A and B, state the research and null hypotheses in words and symbols for a two-tailed test.

d. Comparing just series A and B, state the research and null hypotheses in words and symbols for a one-tailed test.

e. Based on the outcome described in the abstract, conduct step 6 of hypothesis testing.

f. If the researchers' decision in step 6 was wrong, what type of error would they have made? Explain your answer.

8.18 The language of statistics—*assumption*: In your own words, define the word *assumption* first as you would use it in everyday conversation and then as a statistician would use it.

8.19 The language of statistics—*critical regions* and *cutoffs*: Researchers often use the words *critical region* and *cutoff* interchangeably to describe the way in which they make a decision whether to reject the null hypothesis.

a. Using everyday language, rather than statistical language, explain why the words *critical region* might have been chosen to define the area in which we'll reject the null hypothesis.

b. Using everyday language, rather than statistical language, explain why the word *cutoff* might have been chosen to define the point beyond which we'll reject the null hypothesis.

8.20 The language of statistics—*significant*: In your own words, define the word *significant* first as you would use it in everyday conversation and then as a statistician would use it.

8.21 The language and symbols of statistics: Find the incorrectly used symbol(s) or word(s) in each of the following statements or formulas. For each statement or formula, (i) state which symbol(s) and/or word(s) is/are used incorrectly, (ii) explain why each of these is incorrect, and (iii) state what symbol(s)/word(s) *should* be used.

a. The research hypothesis is usually stated in symbols as $\mu_1 = \mu_2$.

b. A researcher determined the critical value, or cutoff, for his nondirectional hypothesis as a *p* level of 1.64.

c. A scientist calculated the mean and the standard error for the scores of his sample of pigeons to conduct a *z* test to compare their performance with the known population mean for pigeons.

d. For a study of a sample of third graders' reading ability versus the national norms, the researcher calculated: $z = \dfrac{X - \mu_M}{\sigma_M}$.

▪ DIGGING DEEPER INTO THE DATA

8.22 Dirty data and attitude research: You have conducted a study with 120 participants (60 men and 60 women) about the relation between attitudes toward cohabitation prior to marriage and self-reported sexual behaviors. Most respondents filled out both 20-item scales completely. Everyone completed the scale assessing attitudes toward cohabitation, but 1 participant indicated the highest possible scores on every item on both scales and finished very quickly. In addition, 13 women and 4 men failed to complete the 20 questions about sexual behavior; 9 women and 2 men did not respond at all; 3 women and 1 man answered just 10 questions; and 2 women and 1 man failed to answer just 1 item.

a. What are the possible causes of incomplete data?

b. What choices do you have regarding the missing data?

c. What data should be ignored, if any?

d. What do you recommend for the participant who reported the highest possible score on each item?

e. Explain why you would or would not report your decisions in your write-up of this experiment.

8.23 Movie earnings and using the *z* distribution to identify outliers: In the Digging Deeper into the Data section of this chapter, we noted that the standardized *z* distribution is sometimes used to identify potential outliers in a data set. The Web site http://www.boxofficemojo.com provides data on U.S. box office receipts for major films. The accompanying table shows domestic box office grosses (in millions of dollars) for a randomly selected sample of 15 of the 100 top-grossing films of 2005. Note that we have rounded figures to the nearest million. (For the sake of this exercise, assume that these scores represent the entire population.)

MOVIE	MILLIONS OF DOLLARS
Walk the Line	120
The Exorcism of Emily Rose	75
Serenity	26
Star Wars: Episode III—Revenge of the Sith	380
Fever Pitch	42
The Constant Gardener	34
The Fog	30
Sky High	64
Tim Burton's Corpse Bride	53
Wedding Crashers	209
Yours, Mine and Ours	53
Just Like Heaven	48
Capote	29
Kingdom of Heaven	47
Brokeback Mountain	83

a. Eyeball the data. What score or scores seem like they might be outliers?

b. Sometimes potential outliers are defined as scores that are beyond 2 standard deviations from the mean—that is, scores with *z* scores less than -2.00 or greater than

2.00. Based on that criterion, are any of these scores potential outliers? (*Hint:* You will have to calculate the mean and standard deviation first.)

c. Sometimes potential outliers are defined as scores that are beyond 3 standard deviations from the mean—that is, scores with *z* scores less than -3.00 or greater than 3.00. Based on that criterion, are any of these scores potential outliers?

d. Why might it make sense to eliminate potential outliers from any data analyses?

e. Explain why the decision of how to identify potential outliers should be made *before* collecting data.

TERMS

assumptions (p. 352)

robust (p. 353)

parametric tests (p. 354)

nonparametric tests (p. 354)

critical values (p. 355)

critical region (p. 356)

p levels (p. 356)

statistically significant (p. 356)

one-tailed test (p. 361)

two-tailed test (p. 361)

SYMBOLS

H_0

H_1

CHAPTER NINE

HYPOTHESIS TESTING WITH *t* TESTS
COMPARING TWO GROUPS

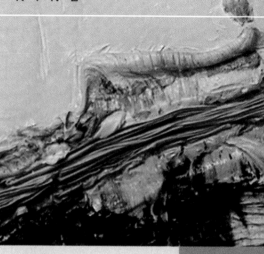

Imagine that you are a taste-tester at the Guinness ale factory. To a beer lover, this probably sounds like the perfect job. But to the master brewers at Guinness, taste-testing was part of a far-reaching economic problem: If the beer in one barrel tastes very different from the beer in another barrel, then you have high variability between the kegs of beer, an indication of poor quality control. And it's very bad for business when your thirsty customers take their first sip and announce to everyone else in the bar, "Hey! This beer doesn't taste right." Furthermore, quality control has always been important across the many centuries of beer brewing, both for maintaining consistency in the flavor and for its antiseptic effects during times when the water supply was infected (as it was during the cholera crisis of 1854).

So now you have the job of professional taste-tester at the Guinness factory. Congratulations. Early Monday morning you go to work and walk downstairs to the factory's cool storage facility in Dublin, Ireland. There you see two kegs of ale, marked keg A and keg B. You swallow a sample from keg A, record your impression with a few numerical ratings, and then move on to keg B. The whole process takes about 15 minutes. What's wrong with that as a way to taste-test your product? The first problem is that the taste from keg A lingers in your mouth and probably influences your impressions of the taste from keg B. It doesn't matter whether you are assessing the taste of ice cream, the aroma of perfume, or the qualifications of job candidates. The order of exposure influences your later assessments, so you need to find a way around this problem, which we first identified in Chapter 1 as "order effects."

As the official taste-tester at Guinness, you have another problem: How many samples of beer could you swallow before your taste-testing was impaired, not only by the taste in your mouth but also by the disorientation caused by drinking all that beer? Keep in mind that this is not a one-day, 15-minute visit to the brewery; this is the job you do all day, every day. An alcoholic makes a very poor quality control officer, especially in a brewery! After you get past keg A and keg B, you still have hundreds, perhaps thousands, of more sips of beer to taste. This is the sort of practical problem that W. S. Gossett faced at many different levels of the manufacturing process and drove him to develop the *t* test, which bestows the ability to make accurate inferences from small samples.

One of the specific problems Gossett faced at the Guinness factory was related to sampling yeast cultures in order to produce a more reliable ale. Too little yeast led to incomplete fermentation, whereas too much yeast led to bitter-tasting beer. To sample both accurately and economically, Gossett first *increased* the number of individual samples. That is, he took four samples instead of just one, but he counted only the average (mean) of those four samples in his distribution; in other words, Gossett created a distribution of means rather than a distribution of scores. Gossett also contributed to another statistical innovation by *simulating* the situation he faced in the brewery; to do this, he used a known population distribution of 3000 cards (each printed with a numerical observation), then sampled 4 cards at a time and averaged them. His goal was to determine how quickly the average of samples of 4 would come to represent the average for a population (Gossett, 1908, 1942; Stigler, 1999).

As we noted in Chapter 7, Gossett's small adjustment (taking the *average* of a sample of 4 observations rather than a sample of only 1) represented a practical application of the central limit theorem—and a solution for many problems in applied statistics. Nevertheless, his most profound contribution to statistics may have been his demonstration that good statistical hypotheses could provide practical solutions to everyday problems in industry and elsewhere. Fortunately, Gossett wasn't the only Guinness employee to demonstrate how statistical reasoning could improve the quality of a product. About 10 years after Gossett's death, the Guinness Brewing Company hired another statistician—Stella Cunliffe. Gossett's genius was to find ways to reach big conclusions from small samples. Cunliffe's genius was to wander about the Guinness fields and laboratories watching people and industrial operations at the precise moment when their behavior was being turned into a data point.

United in their passion to use statistics to improve the quality of Guinness ale, these two remarkable personalities helped the story of the normal, bell-shaped curve mature from a theoretical toy to an industrial tool. Gossett did this with the development of the *t* test; Cunliffe, by recognizing that statistics such as the *t* test had meaning only within the context of an appropriate experimental design. This chapter uses their contributions at the Guinness Brewing Company to explore three different ways that the *t* test may be used to calculate comparisons between two groups: comparing a sample to a known population, comparing two samples of the same individuals under two different conditions and comparing samples from two distinct populations.

> THE *t* DISTRIBUTIONS: DISTRIBUTIONS OF MEANS WHEN THE PARAMETERS ARE NOT KNOWN

Gossett's *t* test is much more versatile than a *z* test, even though it is limited to analyzing comparisons of two groups. In fact, we can use a mnemonic to remember when to use the *t* statistic by simply remembering that the letter *t* is only used for *t*wo-group comparisons. This chapter introduces the *t* test and Gossett's remarkable discovery: how to make inferences about the population using relatively small samples. Specifically, this chapter demonstrates:

1. How the *t* distributions relate to the *z* distribution
2. How to use the table associated with the *t* distributions
3. How to conduct a single-sample *t* test
4. How to conduct hypothesis tests to compare two samples
   a. paired-samples *t* test (a within-groups design)
   b. independent-samples *t* test (a between-groups design)

Using the *t* Distributions: Estimating the Population Standard Deviation from the Sample

One of the odd pleasures of spending time with well-trained scientists is how comfortable they are with the words "I don't know." Behavioral scientists seldom know even the most basic information about the people we are studying, such as the amount of variability in the behavior we are measuring. To conduct a *t* test, we use our sample data to estimate the variability—the standard deviation—of the entire population. Even when we begin with a representative sample, the estimated standard deviation from the sample is not likely to be exactly equal to the population standard deviation. So our estimate of the standard deviation is likely to be wrong to some degree, sometimes by quite a bit. In other words, we know that our estimates are wrong but we don't know how wrong.

The honesty inherent in statistical reasoning requires that we acknowledge our errors in estimation and make adjustments to those estimates. We first made reference to this idea of error in Chapter 6, while discussing regression, but it is worth reminding ourselves that statisticians often use the term *error* to refer to how inaccurate we are when making estimates. As you would expect, we are less confident about the accuracy of estimates that have a great deal of error, just as we are more confident about the accuracy of estimates that have a small amount of error.

Fortunately, the mathematical calculation that corrects for this error is incredibly easy: subtraction. That's it. But understanding why we need to make the correction gives us insight into how a sample can best represent the larger population. For example, imagine a sample of only 3 people. This sample is unlikely to include the most extreme scores that we find in the population, so the spread tends to be much less. A sample of 10 people would have more spread, but not by much. A sample of 1000 people, however, might have a spread much closer to that in the population from which the sample is taken. In other words, we anticipate that a small sample has a less precise spread (contains more error) than a large sample. So the smaller the sample, the more we have to adjust it to acknowledge the existence of this probable error. We make this adjustment by bumping up our estimate of the standard deviation for smaller samples.

The standard deviation formula that we used with samples is $SD = \sqrt{\dfrac{\Sigma(X - M)^2}{N}}$. We took the deviation from the mean of each score, squared each deviation, and took the mean of all the squared deviations to get variance. We then took the square root of the variance to get the standard deviation. One tiny alteration of this formula leads to a slightly larger standard deviation. Instead of dividing by N, we will divide by $(N - 1)$ to get the mean of the squared deviations. Subtraction is the key. Dividing by a slightly smaller number, $(N - 1)$, instead of by N increases the value of the standard deviation. For example, if the numerator were 90 and the denominator, N, were 10, the answer would be 9; if we divide by $(N - 1) = (10 - 1) = 9$, the answer would be 10, a slightly larger value. So the formula for estimating the standard deviation of the population from the standard deviation of the sample is $s = \sqrt{\dfrac{\Sigma(X - M)^2}{(N - 1)}}$. Notice that we call this standard deviation s instead of SD. It still uses Latin rather than Greek letters because it is a statistic (from a sample) rather than a parameter (from a population); however, we have changed from SD to s to indicate that this is a slightly different standard deviation, one that is corrected to eliminate error. From now on, we will be calculating the standard deviation in this way (because we will be using the sample standard deviation to estimate the population standard deviation), and we will be calling our standard deviation s.

Let's apply t tests to an everyday situation that many of us can relate to: multitasking. Many people equate multitasking with greater personal productivity, but it is not necessarily a good thing. For example, Strayer, Drews, and Johnston (2003) found support for the idea that multitasking on a cell phone while driving reduces visual attention by using a t test. A t test could also be used to test whether multitasking at work reduces productivity by distracting employees from other tasks. Mark, Gonzalez, and Harris (2005) conducted a study in which employees were observed at one of two high-tech companies for over 1000 hours. The employees spent just 11 minutes, on average, on one project before an interruption; moreover, after each interruption, they needed an average of 25 minutes to get back to the original project! So even though a person who is busy multitasking appears to be productive, maybe the underlying reality is that multitasking actually *reduces* overall productivity. How can we use a t test to determine the effects of multitasking on productivity?

Suppose you were a manager at one of these firms. You naturally would want to increase the time spent on a project before an interruption. So you decided to reserve a period from 1:00 to 3:00 each day during which employees could not interrupt one another. An interesting idea, right? To test your intervention, you observe 5 employees during those periods and develop a score for each—the time she or he spent on a selected task before being interrupted. Here are your fictional data: 8, 12, 16, 12, and 14 minutes. Remember, to use the z distribution, we need to know the population mean and population standard deviation. We also need to know the population mean when we use

Formulas: The formula for standard deviation as estimated from a sample is $s = \sqrt{\dfrac{\Sigma(X - M)^2}{(N - 1)}}$, where s is the estimated standard deviation, X is each score in the sample, M is the mean of the sample, and N is the sample size.

Multitasking
If multitasking reduces productivity in a sample, we can statistically determine the probability that multitasking reduces productivity among a much larger population.

Corbis

the *t* distributions. In this case, we are treating 11 minutes as the population mean. However, we need to estimate the standard deviation of the population from the sample.

To calculate our estimated standard deviation for the population, first we'll calculate our sample mean. Even though we are given a population mean (i.e., 11), we will use the *sample* mean to calculate the corrected standard deviation for the *sample*. The mean for these 5 sample scores is $M = \dfrac{(8 + 12 + 16 + 12 + 14)}{5} = 12.4$.

The formula for the corrected standard deviation is $s = \sqrt{\dfrac{\Sigma(X - M)^2}{(N - 1)}}$. Remember, the easiest way to calculate the numerator under the square root sign is by first organizing our data using columns, as shown here:

X	X − M	(X − M)²
8	−4.4	19.36
12	−0.4	0.16
16	3.6	12.96
12	−0.4	0.16
14	1.6	2.56

Thus, the numerator is: $\Sigma(X - M)^2 = \Sigma(19.36 + 0.16 + 12.96 + 0.16 + 2.56) = 35.2$. And given a sample size of 5, the corrected standard deviation is

$$s = \sqrt{\dfrac{\Sigma(X - M)^2}{(N - 1)}} = \sqrt{\dfrac{35.2}{(5 - 1)}} = \sqrt{8.8} = 2.97$$

It is interesting to observe that the correction makes a much bigger difference for small samples. For a sample of 5 like the one we just used, subtracting 1 removes one-fifth (20%) of the total. For a sample of 100, 1 is only 1% of the total. This sample correction, therefore, automatically corrects to a greater degree for the small samples, which are less likely to be accurate, than for the large samples, which are more likely to be accurate.

After we make the correction, we have an estimate of the standard deviation of the distribution of scores but not an estimate of the spread of a distribution of means, the standard error. As we did with the *z* distribution, we need to make

A Simple Correction:
$N - 1$
When estimating variability, subtracting 1 person from a sample of 4 makes a big difference. Subtracting 1 person from a sample of thousands makes only a small difference.

our spread smaller to reflect the fact that a distribution of means is less variable than a distribution of scores. We do this in exactly the same way that we adjusted for the *z* distribution. We divide *s* by $\sqrt{N}$. The formula for the standard error as estimated from a sample, therefore, is $s_M = \dfrac{s}{\sqrt{N}}$. Notice that we have replaced σ with *s* because we are using the corrected standard deviation from the sample rather than the actual standard deviation from the population.

Here's how we would convert our corrected standard deviation of 2.97 (from the data above on minutes before an interruption) to a standard error. Our sample size was 5, so we divide by the square root of 5: $s_M = \dfrac{s}{\sqrt{N}} = \dfrac{2.97}{\sqrt{5}} = 1.33$.

So the appropriate standard deviation for the distribution of means—that is, its standard error—is 1.33. Just as the central limit theorem predicts, the standard error for the distribution of sample means is smaller than the standard deviation of sample scores (1.33 < 2.97).

This step leads to one of the most common errors that we see among our students. Because we have implemented a correction when calculating *s*, students want to implement an extra correction here by dividing by $\sqrt{(N-1)}$. Do not do this! We still divide by $\sqrt{N}$ in this step. We are making our standard deviation smaller to reflect the size of the sample; there is no need for a correction.

> **Symbols:** s_M refers to the standard error of a distribution of means as estimated from a sample.
>
> **Formulas:** The formula for the standard error as estimated from a sample is $s_M = \dfrac{s}{\sqrt{N}}$, where *s* is the standard deviation as estimated from a sample and *N* is sample size.

Calculating a *t* Statistic for the Mean of a Sample: Using the Standard Error

We cannot use the *z* distribution to make estimates because the *z* distribution applies only to situations in which we know the exact mean and standard deviation for the whole population in which we're interested. When we actually know the standard deviation for the population, we don't have to estimate it. But when we are uncertain about aspects of the population, we can use our sample to help us estimate. As you can see from Figure 9-1, this uncertainty about what the population really looks like leads us to use the *t* distribution, which is wider than the *z* distribution. In fact, there are many *t* distributions—one for each possible sample size; as the sample size gets smaller and we are less and less certain that we are accurate, the *t* distributions get wider. The *t* distributions are wider than the *z* distribution because whenever we estimate the standard deviation for a population (instead of using the actual standard deviation of a population), we are less certain of our findings. The wider distributions accommodate that uncertainty. However,

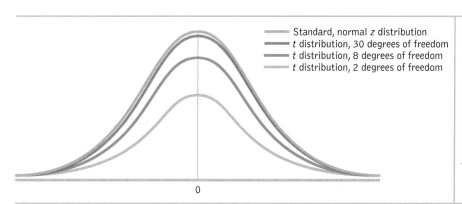

Standard, normal *z* distribution
t distribution, 30 degrees of freedom
t distribution, 8 degrees of freedom
t distribution, 2 degrees of freedom

0

FIGURE 9-1
The Wider and Flatter *t* Distributions

For smaller samples, the *t* distributions are wider and flatter than the *z* distribution. As the sample size increases, however, the *t* distributions approach the shape of the *z* distribution.

■ The *t* **statistic** indicates the distance of a sample mean from a population mean in terms of standard error.

Symbols: *t* refers to the distance of a mean (or a difference between means) from the mean of its distribution in terms of the standard error of its distribution. Formulas: The formula for a *t* statistic is $t = \dfrac{(M - \mu_M)}{s_M}$, where *t* is the *t* statistic, *M* is the sample mean, μ_M is the mean of the distribution of means, and s_M is the standard error as estimated from a sample.

as Figure 9-1 also demonstrates, the *t* distributions begin to merge with the *z* distribution as we gain confidence by adding more and more participants to our study.

The formula to calculate the *t* statistic is identical to that for the *z* statistic, except that it uses the *estimated* standard error rather than the *actual* standard error of the population of means. So, *the **t** statistic indicates the distance of a sample mean from a population mean in terms of the standard error.* That distance is expressed numerically as the estimated number of standard errors between the two means. Here is the formula for the *t* statistic for a distribution of means:

$$t = \frac{(M - \mu_M)}{s_M}$$

Note that the denominator is the only difference between this formula for the *t* statistic and the formula used to compute the *z* statistic for a sample mean. The corrected denominator makes the *t* statistic smaller and thereby reduces the probability of observing an extreme *t* statistic. That is, a *t* statistic is not as extreme as a *z* statistic; in scientific terms, it's more conservative.

The *t* statistic for our sample of five scores representing minutes until interruptions would be $t = \dfrac{(M - \mu_M)}{s_M} = \dfrac{(12.4 - 11)}{1.33} = 1.05$. With this *t* statistic, we are well on our way to making an inference about whether the communication ban from 1:00 to 3:00 affected the average number of minutes until an interruption.

As we demonstrated in Figure 9-1, *t* distributions are wider and flatter than the *z* distribution. That is why the same sample mean appears to be less extreme when plotted along a *t* distribution than when plotted along a *z* distribution. The correction of $N - 1$ flattens the distribution just a little bit, so a sample mean must be farther from the mean of the distribution of means before it can be considered to be extreme. This is particularly true for small sample sizes, for which the correction makes a much larger difference in the calculations. So, for example, when we make the correction by subtracting 1 from the sample size in the denominator, we remove 1/4, or 25%, of a sample size of 4, but only 1/100, or 1%, of a sample size of 100.

Because the correction has varying effects on the *t* distribution (depending on sample size), there is a different *t* distribution for every possible sample size. As with the *z* distribution, statisticians have developed *t* tables that include probabilities under any area of the *t* curve. There are many, many *t* tables—one for every possible sample size. Rather than include an extra book filled with every possible *t* table, we provide you with Appendix B, one *t* table for many different sample sizes. The *t* table includes only the percentages of most interest to researchers—those indicating the extreme scores that suggest large differences between groups. The *t* table allows us to determine what the most extreme *t* statistics would be for a number of different sample sizes.

When *t* and *z* Are Equal: Very Large Sample Sizes

When the sample size is large enough, the standard deviation of a sample is more likely to be equal to the standard deviation of the population. Accordingly, the correction has less of an effect on the estimate. At large enough sample sizes, in fact, the *t* distribution is identical to the *z* distribution. Most *t* tables include a sample size of ∞, infinity, to indicate a very large sample size (a sample size of infinity itself is, of course, impossible); a very large sample size would provide statistics exceedingly close to the parameters of the population. The *t* statistics at extreme percentages for very large sample sizes are identical to the *z* statistics at the very same percentages. Check it out for yourself by comparing the *z* table in Appendix B and the *t* table in Appendix B. For example, the *z* statistic for the 95th percentile is between 1.64 and 1.65; at a sample size of infinity, the *t* statistic for the 95th percentile is 1.645.

Let's remind ourselves why the *t* statistic merges with the *z* statistic as sample size increases. The underlying principle is easy to understand: more observations lead to greater confidence. For example, imagine that one of your friends reports, "Jan just received a job offer as a statistical consultant with a starting salary of $80,000 dollars a year with a $10,000 signing bonus." Naturally, you are excited for her, though maybe a little dubious about the details. But when a second friend says that he, too, has just spoken with Jan and heard the same information, you are more confident that the information is accurate. When you bump into Jan's parents and they tell the same story, your confidence increases even more. Remember, it's still all just rumor and inference, but your confidence increases with every observation. Theoretically, of course, it could all be an elaborate conspiracy. But at some point, inference naturally merges with an extremely high level of confidence.

In the same way, more participants in a study—if they are a representative sample—correspond to increased confidence that we are making an accurate observation. This is why the *t* distributions expand until they become identical with the *z* distribution; specifically, the *z* distribution matches the *t* distribution for one situation (that of a very large sample), but there are other *t* distributions for smaller samples. The *t* distributions, therefore, account for a wider range of situations. As the sample size gets smaller and the standard deviation estimated from it gets less and less likely to be accurate, the *t* distributions get progressively wider and wider, as seen in Figure 9-1. So don't think of the *t* distributions as completely separate from the *z* distribution; rather, think of them as more versatile because they allow us to make fair-minded estimates even when we have fewer observations. Similarly, we have no need of the *z* table if we have the *t* table. We can always look up a *z* statistic in the *t* table by using a sample size of infinity. Think of the *z* statistic as a single-blade Swiss Army knife and the *t* statistic as a two-blade Swiss Army knife that includes the single blade that is the *z* statistic.

The *t* Distributions: Distributions of Differences Between Means

Radio humorist Garrison Keillor describes the small fictional Minnesota hometown in his stories as a place where ". . . all the children are above average." That statistical impossibility reminds us that when we are making comparisons, we need to ask, "Compared to what?" The *t* distributions allow us to compare two samples. There are two familiar ways to create this comparison. We can use a within-groups design (as when the same people taste-test beer from both keg A *and* keg B) or between-groups design (as when different people have been randomly assigned to taste-test either keg A *or* keg B). We'll discuss the particulars of each of these distributions when we learn the hypothesis tests that accompany each. Whether we use a within-groups design or a between-groups design to collect the data, we use a *t* test to compare the distribution of responses to keg A to the distribution of responses to keg B. In both situations, the null hypothesis is that the differences in the two population distributions will have a mean of 0. The mnemonic we suggested in Chapter 8—focusing on the letter *n*—will help you to keep the meaning of the null hypothesis clearly in mind:

*n*ull = *n*o differences = *n*o effect = *n*othing going on

Think back to Experience It for Yourself 7-2, in which you first pulled 30 different scores and plotted them, and then pulled 30 different sets of three scores and plotted their means. The former was a distribution of scores, the latter a distribution of means. Now we need to develop a distribution of *differences* between means so that we can establish a distribution that specifies the null hypothesis. Let's use our data about heights to demonstrate how to create a distribution of differences between means, the distribution that accompanies a between-groups design. First, you would randomly choose 3 cards and calculate the mean of the heights listed on them. That's the first group. Then you would randomly choose 3 other cards and calculate their mean. That is the second group. Then subtract the second mean from the first. That's really all there is to it except that we do that procedure many more times (although we are simplifying a bit here; we would actually replace every card before selecting the next). So there are two samples and two sample means, but we're building just *one* curve of differences.

Let's say the first mean was 66 and the second was 64; the difference between means would be 66 − 64 = 2. Next, we put all the cards back and repeat the process. Let's say that this time we calculate means of 65 and 68 for our two samples of 3; now the difference between means would be 65 − 68 = −3. Eventually, we would have 30 differences between means—some positive, some negative, and some right at 0—and could plot them on a curve, but this would only be the beginning of what this distribution would look like. If we were to calculate the whole distribution, then we would do this an uncountable number of times, not just 30. When the authors calculated 30 differences between means from the height example, we got the distribution in Figure 9-2.

In summary, the *t* distributions are used when we do not know the population parameters and are comparing only two groups. The two groups may, as with the *z* distribution, be a sample and a population. In addition, the two groups may be two samples as part of a within-groups design or a between-groups design. Because we do not know the population standard deviation, we must estimate it, and estimating invites the possibility of more error. Consequently, the *t* distributions are a little flatter than the *z* distribution. However, the *t* distribution

FIGURE 9-2
Distribution of Differences Between Means

This curve represents the beginning of the development of a distribution of differences between means. It includes only 30 differences, whereas the actual distribution would include all possible differences.

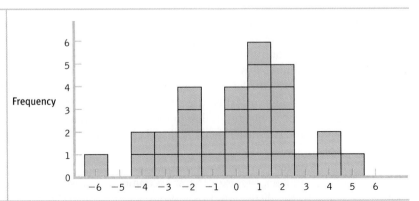

becomes comparable to the *z* distribution whenever we are able to use very large samples. A useful mnemonic for when to use the *t* statistic is simply to remember that the letter *t* is only used for *t*wo-group comparisons.

⊙ CHECK YOUR LEARNING

9-1 Earlier, we discussed a study on multitasking; the authors (Mark et al., 2005) reported that when an employee was interrupted from a task, it took an average of 25 minutes to return to that task. We imagined a follow-up study in which 5 employees were observed following a companywide intervention, a communication ban from 1:00 to 3:00. For each of the 5 employees, one task was selected. Earlier we examined the time each employee spent on a task before being interrupted; here we'll examine the time until work on that task was resumed. The fictional data for the 5 employees were 20, 19, 27, 24, and 18 minutes until work on the given task was resumed.

a. What distribution will be used in this situation? Explain your answer.

b. Determine the appropriate mean and standard deviation (or standard error) for this distribution. Show all your work; use symbolic notation and formulas where appropriate.

c. Calculate the *t* statistic.

➤ HYPOTHESIS TESTS: THE SINGLE-SAMPLE *t* TEST

The Guinness Brewing Company was a proud organization, but also a strict one. For many years, it even refused to advertise its product because it believed that because "Guinness is the best beer available, it does not need advertising as its quality will sell it, and those who do not drink it are to be sympathized with rather than advertised to" (Cunliffe, 1976; see also Salsburg, 2001). Those strict rules also explain why there is no statistic named after W. S. Gossett even though many statistics are named after the people credited with developing them (such as Pearson's correlation coefficient). Because previous employees of the Guinness Brewing Company had leaked industrial secrets to its competitors, the company had barred employees from publishing research conducted at Guinness. So Gossett published a number of groundbreaking papers without the knowledge of the company, using the pseudonym "Student."

Neither Guinness nor its competitors knew what was going on, and the secrecy of "Student's" identity was such that when an American statistician wanted to meet with Gossett in the 1930s, "arrangements were made to meet him secretly, with all the aspects of a spy mystery" (Salsburg, 2001, p. 28). It remains unclear whether Gossett's employers ever discovered his secret identity, but they were startled when someone wanted to publish his collected papers after his death. "Student's *t*," not "Gossett's *t*," continues to be a part of the teaching of statistics. But why was the *t* test so valuable an industrial secret?

Gossett discovered what you can see for yourself in Figure 9-1: that the *t* distribution gradually looks more and more like the *z* distribution when we have many observations (often called a big *N*, indicating a big number of observations; that is, a big sample size). Notice that when we have a *t* distribution for a smaller *N*, the shape of the bell is a little bit different; specifically, it is spread out more, so it is a little bit flatter and wider. A flatter, wider *t* distribution is more spread out (or varied) when it has only a few observations; with only a few observations, we have to allow for unknown observations that might be quite extreme. That makes sense, though; we will have more confidence after recording many observations than after recording only a few observations.

So Gossett had discovered the relation between the number of observations and the confidence that those observations corresponded to what we would discover in the larger population. He was creating an inferential statistic. For example, if we have the results from 10,000 sips (samples) of beer, then we are going to be far more confident in our findings than if we have results from only 1 or 2 sips (samples) of beer. That is why the theoretical *t* distributions gradually become synonymous with the *z* distribution when we have many, many observations: If we keep on increasing the number of observations, then we eventually have an observation from every possible member of the population (or at least close enough that the means are almost identical); that is, the *z* distribution. But the *t* table also demonstrates how much more our confidence increases with each additional sample. After all, there's a great deal of room between 1 or 2 sips of beer and 10,000. Gossett helped us find that middle ground that is most effective for solving real-world problems related to sampling.

Let's think in economic terms about why quantifying the relation between number of observations and confidence in those observations provides such powerful information. Gossett's *t* distributions meant that the Guinness Brewing Company could combine random sampling with a *t* test to produce high-quality, consistent-tasting ale. As a result, Guinness could draw conclusions from smaller samples and therefore had more leeway to innovate; it could test changes in the manufacturing process without risking that an expensive modification (such as using a different strain of barley or a different wood for its barrels) might end up harming the quality of thousands of barrels of overall product. Random sampling and the *t* test liberated Guinness's ability to take risks by making risk-taking more manageable.

Not surprisingly, Gossett's discovery also helped liberate the sciences from having to make thousands of unnecessary, costly observations. At a practical level, for example, physicians are highly confident in the accuracy of tests for strep throat, mononucleosis, pneumonia, and most of the common infectious diseases. They may run only one, occasionally two, and rarely three tests "just to be sure." But they don't run 200 tests because the processes involved have been quantified and improved through the power of inferential statistics made possible by Gossett's innovations.

So the idea of the normal curve turns out to be an extremely powerful idea, especially because Gossett helped us understand that the *t* distributions start looking like the *z* distribution with repeated observations. In Chapter 7 and Chapter 8, we introduced the *z* distribution and showed how it can help us conduct a hypothesis test, the *z* test. Now we'll extend that learning by demonstrating three ways to use the *t* test that correspond with three different experimental designs: (1) a single-sample *t* test that uses a distribution of means, (2) a paired-samples *t* test that uses a distribution of mean differences (used with a within-groups research design), and (3) an independent-samples *t* test that uses a distribution of differences between means (used with a between-groups research design).

The Single-Sample *t* Test: When We Know the Population Mean but Not the Standard Deviation

A ***single-sample* t *test*** *is a hypothesis test in which we compare data from one sample to a population for which we know the mean but not the standard deviation.* We need to know only the population mean to use a single-sample *t* test, so it has more uses than the *z* test. However, because we need some information about the population parameters (i.e., the mean), its use is still fairly limited. But we'll begin with the single-sample *t* test because understanding it will help us use the more sophisticated *t* tests that let us compare two samples.

As expected, when we use the *t* distributions, we use the *t* table instead of the *z* table. As we've already noted, there are different *t* distributions for every sample size, so we must take sample size into account when using the *t* table. However, we do not look up our actual sample size on the table; rather, we look up something called degrees of freedom. ***Degrees of freedom*** *is the number of scores that are free to vary when estimating a population parameter from a sample.* The phrase *free to vary* refers to the number of scores that can take on different values if we know a given parameter. For example, the manager of a baseball team needs to assign nine players to particular spots in the batting order but only has to make eight decisions ($N - 1$). Why? Because there will be only one option remaining after making the first eight decisions. So before the manager makes any decisions, there are $N - 1$, or $9 - 1 = 8$, degrees of freedom. After the second decision, there are $N - 1$, or $8 - 1 = 7$, degrees of freedom, and so on.

Consider this in the context of the *t* distribution. Because we are sampling, we have to calculate the standard deviation from our sample when we do a *t* test, and for this we need the mean. If we know the actual mean and all but one of the scores in the sample, then we can calculate the missing score with a little algebra; this number is *not* free to vary. So if the mean of four scores is 6 and we know that three of the scores are 2, 4, and 8, then the last score must be 10. If we know the mean and all the scores but two, however, then we cannot calculate these two other scores; both are free to vary. So in this second situation, if we only know the scores 2 and 4, then the other two scores could be 8 and 10, or 7 and 11, or a number of other combinations that add up to 18. This means that the degrees of freedom is the number of scores in the sample minus 1; there is always one score that cannot vary. Degrees of freedom is written in symbolic notation as *df*, which is always italicized. The formula for degrees of freedom for a single sample *t* test, therefore, is $df = N - 1$.

Even though there are *t* tables for every possible sample size as represented by degrees of freedom, we do not need to know the *t* values for every possible percentage; this is because statisticians tend to use very specific percentages as critical values, or cutoffs. We first noted in Chapter 7 then more specifically in Chapter 8 that the most common cutoff percentage is 5%, typically written as a proportion, 0.05, and called the *p* level. Two other common cutoff percentages are 10%, written as a *p* level of 0.10, and 1%, written as a *p* level of 0.01. The typical *t* table will give us *t* critical values, or cutoffs, for these three *p* levels for both one-tailed and two-tailed tests. So we will have six *t* values in a row for every degrees of freedom.

Why do we need to separate critical *t* values for one-tailed and two-tailed tests? When we use a one-tailed test, our research hypothesis is that the effect is in a specific direction, either an increase or a decrease but not both. In this case, we will have just one critical value in the positive tail of the distribution; if we use a

■ A **single-sample *t* test** is a hypothesis test in which we compare data from one sample to a population for which we know the mean but not the standard deviation.

■ **Degrees of freedom** is the number of scores that are free to vary when estimating a population parameter from a sample.

Symbols: *df* is the symbol for degrees of freedom.
Formulas: The formula for degrees of freedom for a single sample *t* test is $df = N - 1$, where *N* is the number of scores in the sample.

FIGURE 9-3
One-Tailed Versus Two-Tailed Tests

For a one-tailed test, the entire 5% of the critical region is in just one tail. For a two-tailed test, the 5% is divided between the two tails, with 2.5% in each.

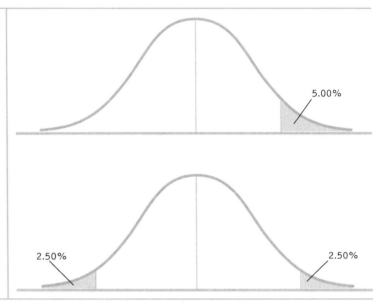

p level of 0.05, the whole 5% goes in the positive tail. With a two-tailed test, the research hypothesis is that the effect could go in either direction. Here we will have two critical values; if the *p* level is 0.05, then the 5% will be split, with 2.5% in each tail. (Both one-tailed and two-tailed tests are illustrated in Figure 9-3.) Notice that the one-tailed test makes it easier for our *t* statistic to be beyond the critical value. Putting the whole 5% in one tail brings the critical value closer to the mean. This is why the two-tailed test is considered more conservative. It leads to a more extreme cutoff; if our test statistic is beyond a more extreme cutoff, this is better evidence that we should have rejected the null hypothesis.

The *t* Table: Understanding Degrees of Freedom

Degrees of freedom can seem like a difficult concept. Fortunately, there is one key piece of information to keep in mind as you begin working with the *t* table. In the behavioral sciences, the degrees of freedom usually correspond to how many people there are in our study; more precisely, the degrees of freedom usually correspond to how many observations we are making.

It is not surprising that more degrees of freedom correspond to a higher level of confidence in whatever it is we are observing. After all, if seven different people independently report that they have seen a bear walking across the local baseball field, then our confidence that there really is a bear walking across the local baseball field naturally increases. It is also very important to understand that they could all be mistaken. Perhaps what people actually saw was just a large dog that looked even larger in the evening light. That is, there is always the possibility of a false-positive that leaves us believing something to be true when it really isn't—a Type I error. Nevertheless, more degrees of freedom increase our confidence in the validity of our observations.

Table 9-1 is an excerpt from a *t* table, but an expanded table is included in Appendix B. Consider the relation between degrees of freedom and the cutoff point needed to declare statistical significance in Table 9-1. In the column corresponding to a one-tailed test at a *p* level of 0.05 with only 1 degree of

TABLE 9-1. EXCERPT FROM THE *t* TABLE

When conducting hypothesis testing, we use the *t* table to determine critical values for a given *p* level, based on the degrees of freedom and whether the test is one- or two-tailed.

DF	ONE-TAILED TESTS 0.10	0.05	0.01	TWO-TAILED TESTS 0.10	0.05	0.01
1	3.078	6.314	31.821	6.314	12.706	63.657
2	1.886	2.920	6.965	2.920	4.303	9.925
3	1.638	2.353	4.541	2.353	3.182	5.841
4	1.533	2.132	3.747	2.132	2.776	4.604
5	1.476	2.015	3.365	2.015	2.571	4.032

freedom, the critical *t* value is 6.314. With only 1 degree of freedom, the two means have to be extremely far apart and the standard deviation has to be very small in order to declare that there is a statistically significant difference. But with 2 degrees of freedom (two observations), the critical *t* value drops to 2.920. With 2 degrees of freedom, the two means don't have to be quite so far apart or the standard deviation so small. That is, it is easier to reach the critical level of 2.920 needed to declare that there is a statistically significant difference. This makes sense because we're more confident with two observations than with just one.

Now notice what happens when we *increase* the number of observations once again from two observations to three observations. The critical *t* value needed to declare statistical significance once again *decreases*, from 2.920 to 2.353. Our level of confidence in our observation increases with each additional observation, but the increase in confidence from two observations to three observations is not as large as the increase from one observation to two observations. The degrees of freedom correspond to how many observations we are making. The number needed to declare statistical significance decreases as the degrees of freedom increase.

HOW SCIENTIFIC EVIDENCE INFLUENCES WHAT YOU BELIEVE

EXPERIENCE IT FOR YOURSELF

You'll notice that we've used the word *conservative* at several points in the text. It's use in science and statistics is different from its use in politics. Generally, when scientists say they are being conservative, they mean that they're reluctant to overturn the scientific status quo without strong evidence. Researchers must demonstrate why the null hypothesis should be rejected, so they stack the deck against rejecting it. If the null hypothesis is then rejected, it is even stronger evidence that the research hypothesis has been supported and that existing scientific knowledge should be revised. So being conservative in science means that we want to revise what we believe only when the evidence clearly gives us permission to do so.

We don't want to be *too* conservative, though. We don't want to continue to believe something that is not true in the face of convincing evidence. That is why a conservative scientific attitude simultaneously embraces a willingness to change our minds. More practically, this cautious openness to change is systematically reflected in the *t* table as we consider the relation between degrees of freedom and the number needed to declare statistical significance. You can experience this cautious openness to change in the relation between degrees of freedom and changes in the cutoff point needed to declare statistical significance. Identify the critical *t* value from Table 9-1 in each of the following circumstances:

A one-tailed test with 5 degrees of freedom at a *p* level of 0.05: _____

A one-tailed test with 4 degrees of freedom at a *p* level of 0.05: _____

A one-tailed test with 3 degrees of freedom at a *p* level of 0.05: _____

A one-tailed test with 2 degrees of freedom at a *p* level of 0.05: _____

A one-tailed test with 1 degree of freedom at a *p* level of 0.05: _____

A two-tailed test with 5 degrees of freedom at a *p* level of 0.01: _____

A two-tailed test with 3 degrees of freedom at a *p* level of 0.01: _____

A two-tailed test with 1 degree of freedom at a *p* level of 0.01: _____

A one-tailed test with 5 degrees of freedom at a *p* level of 0.10: _____

Based on this exercise, you can see for yourself that different statistical tests vary in terms of how conservative they are. Researchers select different significance levels for different circumstances. For example, imagine that you are testing a new drug to treat Alzheimer's disease (AD). Based on previous research, (1) you believe that the drug will definitely do *something* dramatic to the victim of AD, but (2) you are not sure if the drug will help or harm the patient. In this circumstance, you might want to use a two-tailed test at the 0.05 level of significance. A second approach might be appropriate if previous research has indicated that (1) the drug only helps people with AD, (2) patients might benefit enormously, and (3) there are no serious side effects to the treatment. In this circumstance, you might want to use a fairly liberal one-tailed test at the 0.10 level of significance. A third, more dangerous, possibility exists when previous research indicates that the drug (1) might help only a little bit or (2) has potentially devastating side effects. In this circumstance, you will want to make it very difficult to declare statistical significance. You will want to be extremely conservative and may use a one-tailed test at a *p* level of 0.001 before you are willing to declare statistical significance. The important thing is to know the literature and think through your hypothesis ahead of time. Then make your decision about what level of significance to use *before* you analyze your data.

Let's consider two situations that are representative of the kinds of situations researchers often face and determine the cutoff *t* value(s) for each. For the first situation, you may use the excerpt in Table 9-1. The second situation will require the full table in Appendix B.

1. *The situation:* A researcher collects Stroop reaction times for 5 participants who have had reduced sleep for three nights. She wants to compare this sample to the known population mean. Her research hypothesis is that the lack of sleep will slow participants down, leading to an increased reaction time. She will use a *p* level of 0.05 to determine her critical value.

The cutoff(s): This is a one-tailed test because the research hypothesis posits a change in only one direction—an increase in reaction time. There will be only a positive critical *t* value. There are 5 participants, so the degrees of freedom is: $df = N - 1 = 5 - 1 = 4$. Her stated *p* level is 0.05. When we look in the *t* table under one-tailed tests, in the column labeled 0.05 and in the row for a *df* of 4, we see a critical value of 2.132. For one-tailed tests, be sure to consider the sign of the critical value; in this case, we leave it as positive because we are hypothesizing an increase. (Note that for a two-tailed test, the cutoffs would be −2.776 and 2.776, more extreme values that are more difficult for a test statistic to "beat.")

2. *The situation:* A researcher knows the mean number of calories a rat will consume in half an hour if unlimited food is available. He wonders whether a new food will lead rats to consume a different number of calories—either more or fewer. He studies 38 rats and uses a conservative critical value based on a *p* level of 0.01.

The cutoff(s): This is a two-tailed test because the research hypothesis allows for change in either direction. There will be both negative and positive critical *t* values. There are 38 rats, so the degrees of freedom is: $df = N - 1 = 38 - 1 = 37$. His stated *p* level is 0.01. We want to look under two-tailed tests, under the column for 0.01, and next to a *df* of 37; however, there is no *df* of 37. In this case, we err on the side of being more conservative and we choose the more extreme (i.e., larger) of the two possible critical *t* values, which is always the smaller *df*. Here, we will look next to 35, where we see a value of 2.724. Because this is a two-tailed test, we will have critical values of −2.724 and 2.724. Be sure to list both values. (Note that for the less conservative *p* level of 0.05, the cutoffs would be −2.030 and 2.030, less extreme values that are easier for a test statistic to "beat.")

The *t* Test: The Six Steps of Hypothesis Testing

Now we have all the tools necessary to conduct a single sample *t* test. So let's consider a hypothetical study and conduct all six steps of hypothesis testing. Even though this study is hypothetical, it touches on an important issue for some psychology majors: participation rates in therapy. Unfortunately, some people still believe anyone using a psychotherapist is admitting that they are insane, weak, lacking character, or somehow not as strong as they ought to be. This is why many people who could benefit from therapy either don't start or drop out prematurely; some subsequently damage their own lives and others' lives unnecessarily. Missed appointments also mean that the therapist has rented space for a session that never took place and for which he or she cannot bill. So participation rates are an important practical concern for everyone involved in the process.

Chapter 2 presented data that included the mean number of sessions attended by clients at a university counseling center. We noted that one study reported a mean of 4.6 sessions (Hatchett, 2003). Let's imagine that the counseling center hoped to increase participation rates by having students sign a contract to attend at least 10 sessions. Five students sign the contract, and these students attend 6, 6, 12, 7, and 8 sessions, respectively. The researchers are interested only in their university, so we'll assume that the mean of 4.6 sessions is a population mean.

Nonparticipation in Therapy
Clients missing appointments can be a problem for their therapists. A *t* test can compare the consequences between those who do and those who do not commit themselves to participating in therapy for a set period.

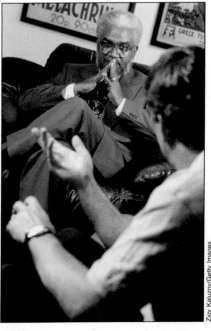

Zigy Kaluzny/Getty Images

Step 1: *Identify the populations, distribution, and assumptions.*

Population 1 is all clients at this counseling center who sign a contract to attend at least 10 sessions. Population 2 is all clients at this counseling center who do not sign a contract to attend at least 10 sessions.

The comparison distribution will be a distribution of means. The hypothesis test will be a single-sample *t* test because we have only one sample and we know the population mean but not the population standard deviation. This study meets one of the three assumptions and may meet the other two. The dependent variable is interval or scale. We do not know whether the population is normally distributed, and there are not at least 30 participants. However, the data from our sample do not suggest a skewed distribution. We do not know whether the data were randomly selected, however, so we must be cautious with respect to generalizing to other clients at this university who might sign the contract.

Step 2: *State the null and research hypotheses.*

Null hypothesis: Clients at this university who sign a contract to attend at least 10 sessions attend the same number of sessions, on average, as clients who do not sign such a contract—H_0: $\mu_1 = \mu_2$.

Research hypothesis: Clients at this university who sign a contract to attend at least 10 sessions attend a different number of sessions, on average, from clients who do not sign such a contract—H_1: $\mu_1 \neq \mu_2$.

Step 3: *Determine the characteristics of the comparison distribution.*

$\mu_M = 4.6$; $s_M = 1.114$

Calculations:

$\mu_M = \mu = 4.6$

$$M = \frac{\Sigma X}{N} = \frac{(6 + 6 + 12 + 7 + 8)}{5} = 7.8$$

X	X − M	(X − M)²
6	−1.8	3.24
6	−1.8	3.24
12	4.2	17.64
7	−0.8	0.64
8	0.2	0.04

Numerator: $\Sigma(X - M)^2 = \Sigma\ (3.24 + 3.24 + 17.64 + 0.64 + 0.04) = 24.8$

$$s = \sqrt{\frac{\Sigma(X - M)^2}{(N - 1)}} = \sqrt{\frac{24.8}{(5 - 1)}} = \sqrt{6.2} = 2.490$$

$$s_M = \frac{s}{\sqrt{N}} = \frac{2.490}{\sqrt{5}} = 1.114$$

Step 4: *Determine critical values, or cutoffs.*

$df = N - 1 = 5 - 1 = 4$; for a two-tailed test with a *p* level of 0.05 and 4 *df*, the critical values are -2.776 and 2.776 (as seen in the curve in Figure 9-4). (*Note:* It is helpful to draw a curve when conducting a hypothesis test; indicate the cutoffs and, later, the *t* statistic on the curve.)

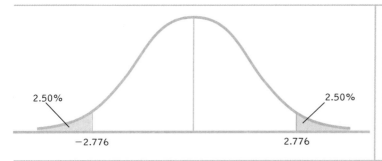

FIGURE 9-4
Determining Cutoffs for a *t* Distribution

As with the *z* distribution, we typically determine critical values in terms of *t* statistics rather than means of raw scores so that we can easily compare a test statistic to them to determine whether the test statistic is beyond the cutoffs. Here, the cutoffs are −2.776 and 2.776, and they mark off the most extreme 5%, with 2.5% in each tail.

Step 5: *Calculate the test statistic.*

$$t = \frac{(M - \mu_M)}{s_M} = \frac{(7.8 - 4.6)}{1.114} = 2.873$$

Step 6: *Make a decision.*

Reject the null hypothesis; it appears that counseling center clients who sign a contract to attend at least 10 sessions attend more sessions, on average, than do clients who do not sign such a contract. (*Note:* Include a drawing like the one in Figure 9-5, or add the test statistic to the drawing you created for the critical values. Also, note that because we rejected the null hypothesis, we stated a specific, directional conclusion. We use words and expressions such as *appears that* or *seems that* to indicate the possibility that we have made a Type I error.)

After completing our hypothesis test, we want to present the primary statistical information in a report. There is a standard American Psychological Association (APA) format for the presentation of statistics across the behavioral sciences so that the results are easily understood by the reader. You'll notice this format in almost every journal article that reports results of a social science study.

1. Write the symbol for the test statistic (e.g., *z* or *t*).

2. Write the degrees of freedom, in parentheses.

3. Write an equal sign and then the value of the test statistic, typically to two decimal places.

4. Write a comma and then whether the *p* value associated with the test statistic was less than or greater than the cutoff *p* level of 0.05.

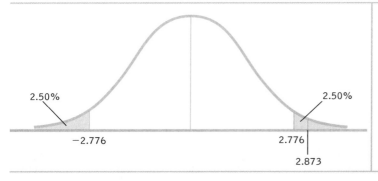

FIGURE 9-5
Making a Decision

To decide whether to reject the null hypothesis, we compare our test statistic to our critical *t* values. In this figure, the test statistic, 2.873, is beyond the cutoff of 2.776, and so we can reject the null hypothesis.

For example, if the *p* value were less than 0.05, as it was in our example, then we reject the null hypothesis and the statistics would read: $t(4) = 2.87, p < 0.05$. The statistic typically follows a statement about the finding (e.g., "it appears that counseling center clients who sign a contract to attend at least 10 sessions, on average, attend more sessions than do clients who do not sign such a contract."), after a comma or in parentheses. The report would also include the sample mean and the standard deviation (not the standard error) to two decimal points. The descriptive statistics, typically in parentheses, would read, for our example: ($M = 7.80, SD = 2.49$). Notice that, due to convention, we use *SD* instead of *s* to symbolize the standard deviation.

In summary, *z* tests and single-sample *t* tests are rare but, if conducted, are used with means, not individual scores. As with any hypothesis test, we identify the populations and comparison distribution and check the assumptions. We then state the null and research hypotheses. We next determine the characteristics of the comparison distribution, a distribution of means based on the null hypothesis. For both of these single-sample tests, the mean of the distribution of means is the same as the null-hypothesized value of the population mean. For the *z* test, the standard error has to be calculated by dividing the population standard deviation by the square root of the sample size. For the single-sample *t* test, we must first estimate the standard deviation from our sample; then we must calculate the standard error. We then determine critical values, usually for a *p* level of 0.05. The test statistic is then calculated and compared to these critical values, or cutoffs, to determine whether to reject or fail to reject the null hypothesis. The null hypothesis is only rejected if the test statistic falls in the tails beyond the cutoffs. When the null hypothesis is rejected, we state a specific, directional conclusion, even for two-tailed tests.

⊙ CHECK YOUR LEARNING

9-2 Check Your Learning 8-3 asked you to conduct a *z* test for data from the Consideration of Future Consequences (CFC) scale (Petrocelli, 2003). We now ask you to conduct all six steps for a single sample *t* test for the same data, using a *p* level of 0.05 and a two-tailed test. Then present the statistics as you would in a journal article. For this exercise, use a population mean CFC score of 3.51, but pretend that you no longer know the population standard deviation. As before, you wonder whether students who joined a career discussion group might have improved CFC scores, on average, compared with the population. Forty-five students in the social sciences regularly attend these discussion groups and then take the CFC scale. The mean for this group is 3.7. The standard deviation for this sample is 0.52.

> HYPOTHESIS TESTS: TESTS FOR TWO SAMPLES

Stella Cunliffe faced an uphill battle to being accepted by her colleagues at the Guinness Brewing Company. First of all, W. S. Gossett was revered by almost everyone. Second, Cunliffe was a woman breaking through the firmly established traditional male culture of the Guinness company. Fortunately, she was clever and perceptive. In the days before women were encouraged to exercise their intellects in public, Cunliffe tempered her enormous talents with humor and perspective.

In her presidential address to the Royal Statistical Society in 1975, Cunliffe (1976, p. 2) described how, in contrast to the free and independent life she had been living as a consultant, the supervisor of the Ladies Staff informed her

> what a privilege it was to have been chosen to work for Guinness, and reminded me that I was expected to wear stockings and a hat and, if I was lucky enough to meet one of the chosen race known as "brewers" in the corridor, on no account was I to recognize him, but should lower my eyes until he had passed.

Like Gossett, Cunliffe left an important legacy to modern students of statistics. It was Gossett who demonstrated that a good theory produced practical benefits, but it was Cunliffe who demonstrated two equally important principles of applied statistics. First, get close to the original observations. Second, recognize that statistics have meaning only in the context of an appropriate experimental design. Stella Cunliffe put Gossett's *t* test, and the underlying statistical reasoning, to work in many new ways.

Think about handmade beer casks, for example. Cunliffe observed the approximately 200 different craftsmen (called coopers) at their Dublin factory who actually made the wooden casks. Much of this work was done by eye, and then the volume of beer that each cask could hold was tested by filling it with water. Guinness didn't want to put too much beer in a cask, because that would reduce their profits. But neither did it want to put in too little beer, because that would annoy their customers. So Cunliffe expected that a certain number of casks would be rejected for being the wrong size. When she looked at the actual numbers, however, she was surprised to learn that very few casks were being rejected.

To find out why, Cunliffe spent time at the workstation of the person who weighed the casks. By observing the moment when an observation was being turned into a datum, Cunliffe realized that the woman weighing the casks was required to roll the rejections uphill; on the other hand, casks that were within the acceptable volume limits only had to be kicked downhill. Who could blame the woman for possibly fudging the numbers just a little bit so she wouldn't have to push so many heavy casks uphill, hour after hour? Cunliffe solved the problem by creating more equivalent conditions for the woman testing the casks. Specifically, she rearranged the woman's workstation so it became equally convenient for her to reject or accept each cask—both accepted and rejected casks were kicked downhill. Cunliffe understood the importance of creating equivalent conditions to conduct a fair test.

It is not surprising, then, that Cunliffe's second legacy to statistics is the importance of creating equivalent conditions by using the appropriate experimental design. Like most of us, she learned some lessons the hard way. She described one expensive disaster while trying to discover the best temperature at which to serve beer. The staff controlled for all kinds of potential confounds by monitoring the temperature with thermometers and rushing varying buckets of beer to various rooms while they waited for the verdict from a drinking panel of taste-testers. But the only thing the drinking panel indicated was that people did not like beer that had been labeled and identified with a yellow seal. In spite of all their efforts, a confound had still entered the experiment: the color of the label. But Cunliffe was alert enough to realize "how impossible it is to find human beings without biases, without prejudices, and without the delightful idiosyncrasies which

Stella Cunliffe
Stella Cunliffe created a remarkable career through her statistical reasoning and became the first female president of the Royal Statistical Society.

Royal Statistical Society

make them so fascinating (p. 5)." A statistical *t* test cannot control for a confounding variable; only the appropriate experimental design can do that.

But even the yellow label bias is the kind of prejudice that would not have been revealed without the fine-grained observations and comparisons made possible through statistical reasoning. All the other obvious variables were controlled for, but they hadn't controlled for the color of the labels. Such observations provided the kinds of information marketing professionals love because it helps them sell more product. The quirky unpredictability of humans is why students of the behavioral sciences have to become *more* sophisticated in statistics and research design than many of their peers in the other sciences: understanding human behavior requires more sophisticated statistical tools to distinguish between behaviors that are due merely to chance and those that represent some more reliable pattern.

For example, there are two general strategies for running a taste-test of casks of beer, and there are two versions of the modern-day *t* test that accommodate these two strategies. We know that order effects are the general name for the problem of how getting tipsy interferes with later judgments. An order effect can only occur when we use a within-groups design, such as the before/after design in which the same people experience both levels (before and after) of the independent variable. It is a popular design, but it is often not a very good one because it invites confounding variables into a study: Any co-occurring event may be the cause of any observed change, not just the one that we chose to focus on.

In spite of its problems, there are (usually applied) situations in which the before/after design might be the best—or even the only—design we can use. For example, how else might we measure the psychological effects of going through a natural disaster? But it is better to conduct a taste-test for beer by using random assignment to groups, a between-groups design. This between-groups design is usually a control group–experimental group design that randomly assigns different groups of people to different levels of the independent variable (such as to different casks of beer). Because both situations allow us to make comparisons between two groups, there are two different formulas used to calculate the *t* test when we have two groups. Let's work the formula for the within-groups design first.

We remind you that the peculiar history of statistics has created multiple terms with similar meanings. So, a within-groups design is also called a repeated-measures design. When discussing how to analyze a within-groups design with a *t* test, the test is also referred to both as a dependent-samples *t* test and a paired-samples *t* test. Depending on the situation you are studying and how you hope to analyze it, you may find yourself using each of these terms as you describe each circumstance.

The Paired-Samples *t* Test: Two Sample Means and a Within-Groups Design

■ The **paired-samples *t* test** is used to compare two means for a within-groups design, a situation in which every participant is in both samples; also called a *dependent-samples* t *test.*

Also called a *dependent-samples* t test, the **paired-samples** t *test* *is used to compare two means for a within-groups design, a situation in which every participant is in both samples.* Although both terms—*paired* and *dependent*—are used frequently, we will use the term *paired* in this text because it matches the language of some of the most-used statistical software packages. If an individual in the study participates in both conditions (such as a memory task after ingesting a caffeinated beverage and again after ingesting a noncaffeinated beverage), then her score in one depends on her score in the other; that's when we use the *dependent*-samples, or *paired*-samples, *t* test. But another type of test is the independent-samples *t* test. If an individual in the study participates in one and only one condition of the two-group study (such as being assigned either to the experimental group or to the control group), then his score is independent of what someone else might do in the different condition. Once you understand the single-sample *t* test, the paired-samples *t* test is simple. The major difference for the paired-samples *t* test is that we must create difference scores for every individual.

Initially, each participant will have two scores—one in each condition. When we conduct a paired-samples *t* test, we write the pairs of scores in two columns, being sure that the scores that are placed side by side belong to the same individual. We then subtract each score in one column from its matching score in the other column to create difference scores. Ideally, a positive difference score indicates an increase, and a negative difference score indicates a decrease. Often we subtract the first score from the second so that our difference scores match this logic. Now we implement the steps of the single-sample *t* test with only minor changes, as discussed in the steps below.

Let's try an example from the social sciences. Specialists in organizational dynamics are essential to many kinds of institutions—from medical to nonprofit to corporate—to streamline the institution, maximize human resources, and increase productivity. Earlier in this chapter, we discussed data collected by Mark and colleagues (2005) on the *reduced* productivity caused by multitasking, an activity that many students understand very well. If we simultaneously attempt to study, listen to music, eat a sandwich, talk on the phone, send and receive instant messages, download files, play computer games, and search for information on the Internet, then we are definitely multitasking. But behavioral scientists are interested in how the computer actually facilitates our productivity in an age of electronic multitasking.

The companies that manufacture computers and software, from IBM to Apple to Microsoft, all employ social scientists to research ways in which their products can better benefit users. A better product, they hope, will sell better. Among the employees in Microsoft's research division is a cognitive psychologist, Mary Czerwinski, who, along with several colleagues, studied how 15 volunteers performed on a set of tasks. All volunteers performed two sets of tasks. The researchers compared the volunteers' performance while using a standard size 15-inch computer monitor to their performance while using a very large 42-inch monitor (Czerwinski, Smith, Regan, Meyers, Robertson, & Starkweather, 2003). The 42-inch monitor, pictured at right and far larger than most of us have ever used, allows the user to have multiple programs in view at the same time. The participants were recruited from the community and screened to be sure they were well versed in the workings of Microsoft Windows and Office. They were asked to complete various tasks using first one monitor and then the other. The researchers used counterbalancing so that participants did not all start with the same monitor.

Here are 5 participants' fictional data, which reflect the actual means reported by Czerwinski and colleagues. Note that a smaller number is good—it indicates a faster time. The first person completed the tasks on the small monitor in 122 seconds and on the large monitor in 111 seconds. The second person: 131 and 116. The third: 127 and 113. The fourth: 123 and 119. The fifth: 132 and 121.

Large Monitors and Productivity
Microsoft researchers and cognitive psychologists (Czerwinski et al., 2003) reported a 9% increase in productivity when research volunteers used an extremely large 42-inch display versus a more typical 15-inch display. Every participant used both displays and thus was in both samples. A paired-samples *t* test is the appropriate hypothesis test for this two-group design.

Courtesy of Microsoft Research

Step 1: Identify the populations, distribution, and assumptions.

The paired-samples *t* test is like the single-sample *t* test in that we analyze a single sample of scores—individual scores for the single-sample *t* test and difference scores for the paired-samples *t* test. There will be one population reflected by each condition, but the comparison distribution will be a distribution of mean difference scores, rather than a distribution of means. The comparison distribution, as with the single-sample *t* test, is based on the null hypothesis. The null hypothesis posits no difference. So the mean of the comparison distribution is 0; this indicates a mean difference score of 0. The assumptions are the same as for the single-sample *t* test.

Summary: Population 1 is people performing tasks using a 15-inch monitor. Population 2 is people performing tasks using a 42-inch monitor.

The comparison distribution will be a distribution of mean difference scores based on the null hypothesis. The hypothesis test will be a paired-samples *t* test because we have two samples of scores, and every individual contributes a score to each sample. This study meets one of the three assumptions and may meet the other two. The dependent variable is time, which is interval or scale. We do not know whether the population is normally distributed, and there are not at least 30 participants. However, the data from our sample do not suggest a skewed distribution. The participants were not randomly selected, however, so we must be cautious with respect to generalizing our findings.

Step 2: State the null and research hypotheses.

This step is identical to that for the single-sample *t* test. Remember, hypotheses are always about populations, not about our specific samples.

Summary: Null hypothesis: People who use a 15-inch screen will complete a set of tasks in the same amount of time, on average, as people who use a 42-inch screen—H_0: $\mu_1 = \mu_2$.

Research hypothesis: People who use a 15-inch screen will complete a set of tasks in a different amount of time, on average, from people who use a 42-inch screen—H_1: $\mu_1 \neq \mu_2$

Step 3: Determine the characteristics of the comparison distribution.

This step is similar to that for the single-sample *t* test in that we determine the appropriate mean and the standard error of the comparison distribution—the distribution based on the null hypothesis. In the single-sample *t* test, there was a comparison mean, and the null hypothesis posited that the sample mean would be the same as that of the comparison distribution. With the paired-samples *t* test, we have a sample of difference scores. According to the null hypothesis, there is no difference; that is, the mean difference score is 0. So the mean of the comparison distribution is always 0, as long as the null hypothesis posits no difference.

The standard error is calculated exactly as it is calculated for the single-sample *t* test, only we use the difference scores rather than the scores in each condition. Note that to get the difference scores, we think about what makes the most sense. In the current example, we want to know what happens when we go from the control condition (small screen) to the experimental condition (large screen), so we actually subtract the first score from the second. Therefore, a negative difference indicates a decrease in time and a positive difference indicates an increase in time when the screen goes from small to large. The test statistic will be the same if we reverse the order in which we subtract, but the sign will change. In some cases, you can think about it as subtracting the "before" score from the "after" score.

Another helpful strategy is to cross out the original scores once we've created the difference scores so that we'll remember to use only the difference scores from that point on. If we don't cross out the original scores, it is very easy to use them in our calculations and end up with an incorrect standard error.

Summary: $\mu_M = 0$; $s_M = 1.923$

Calculations: (Notice that we crossed out the original scores once we created our column of difference scores. We did this to remind ourselves that all remaining calculations involve the differences scores, not the original scores.)

X	Y	DIFFERENCE	DIFFERENCE − MEAN DIFFERENCE	SQUARED DEVIATION
122	111	−11	0	0
131	116	−15	−4	16
127	113	−14	−3	9
123	119	−4	7	49
132	121	−11	0	0

The mean of the difference scores: $M_{Difference} = -11$

Numerator is the sum of squares: $0 + 16 + 9 + 49 + 16 = 74$

$$s = \sqrt{\frac{74}{(5-1)}} = \sqrt{18.5} = 4.301$$

$$s_M = \frac{4.301}{\sqrt{5}} = 1.923$$

Step 4: *Determine cutoffs.*

This step is the same as that for the single-sample *t* test. The degrees of freedom is the number of *participants* (not the number of scores) minus 1.

Summary: $df = N - 1 = 5 - 1 = 4$; our critical values, based on a two-tailed test and a *p* level of 0.05, are −2.776 and 2.776, as seen in the curve in Figure 9-6. (*Note*: It is helpful to draw a curve when conducting a hypothesis test; indicate the cutoff *t* statistics and, later, the *t* statistic on the curve.)

Step 5: *Calculate the test statistic.*

This step is identical to that for the single-sample *t* test.

Summary: $t = \dfrac{(-11 - 0)}{1.923} = -5.72$

Formula: The formula for degrees of freedom for a paired samples *t* test is $df = N - 1$, where N is the number of participants (or difference scores) in the sample. This is the same as the formula for the degrees of freedom for a single-sample *t* test except that N now refers to the number participants (or of difference scores) rather than the number of individual scores.

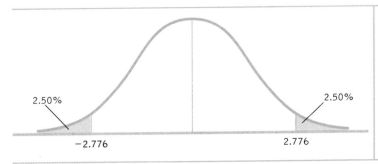

FIGURE 9-6
Determining Cutoffs for a Paired Samples *t* Test

We typically determine critical values in terms of *t* statistics rather than means of raw scores so that we can easily compare a test statistic to them to determine whether the test statistic is beyond the cutoffs. With a paired-samples *t* test, the degrees of freedom are calculated by subtracting 1 from the number of participants rather than the number of scores.

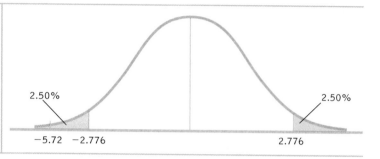

FIGURE 9-7
Making a Decision

To decide whether to reject the null hypothesis, we compare our test statistic to our critical values. In this figure, the test statistic, −5.72, is beyond the cutoff of −2.776, so we can reject the null hypothesis.

2.50%   2.50%

−5.72 −2.776   2.776

Step 6: Make a decision.

This step is identical to that for the single-sample *t* test. If we reject the null hypothesis, we will examine the means of the two conditions (in this case, $M_X = 127$; $M_Y = 116$) so that we know the direction of the effect. Remember, even though the hypotheses are two-tailed, we report the direction of the effect.

Summary: Reject the null hypothesis. It appears that, on average, people perform faster when using a 42-inch monitor than when using a 15-inch monitor (as shown by the curve in Figure 9-7).

The statistics, as reported in a journal article, follow the same APA format as for a single-sample *t* test. We report the degrees of freedom, the value of the test statistic, and whether the *p* value associated with the test statistic was less than or greater than the cutoff *p* level of 0.05. In the current example, the statistics would read: $t(4) = -5.72, p < 0.05$. We would also include the means and the standard deviations for the two samples. We calculated the means in step 6 of hypothesis testing, but we would also have to calculate the standard deviations for the two samples to report them.

Czerwinski and colleagues (2003) note that the faster time with the large display might not *seem* much faster but that, in their research, they have had great difficulty identifying any factors that might lead to faster times. Based on their previous research, therefore, this is an impressive difference. Of course, replication with other samples and with other tasks is warranted before companies spend money to buy enormous monitors for employees. What other aspects of technology might have been driven by behavioral research? The wheel to select songs on your iPod? The keypad to text message on your cell phone? Cognitive psychologists and organizational specialists across the behavioral sciences are among those on the front lines of research into technologies to improve our lives—and sell products.

The Independent-Samples *t* Test: Two Sample Means and a Between-Groups Design

Often we do not—or cannot—have the same participants in both samples, so we must use an independent-samples *t* test. The ***independent-samples t test*** *is used to compare two means for a between-groups design, a situation in which each participant is assigned to only one condition.* This test uses a distribution of differences between means. This affects our *t* test in a few minor ways, described below. As we will see, the biggest difference is that it takes more work to estimate the appropriate standard error. It's not difficult, just a bit time-consuming. Let's look at an interesting example from the area of gender differences and similarities; we will introduce the specifics of the independent-samples *t* test in each step below.

▪ The **independent-samples *t* test** is used to compare two means for a between-groups design, a situation in which each participant is assigned to only one condition.

Who do you think has a better sense of humor—women or men? Researchers at Stanford University examined brain activity in women and men during exposure to humorous cartoons (Azim, Mobbs, Jo, Menon, & Reiss, 2005). Using a brain-scanning technique called functional magnetic resonance imaging (fMRI), researchers observed many similarities between the genders in their responses to humor. However, these brain scans indicated that women tended to use more language and more executive functioning (such as verbal abstraction and screening for irrelevant features) when processing humor than did men. There was also more activity in the reward centers of women's brains than men's, the same reward centers that respond when receiving money, feeling happy, or ingesting cocaine. The researchers suggested that this might be because women have lower expectations of humor than do men and so find it more rewarding when something is actually funny.

However, the researchers were aware of other possible explanations for these findings. For example, they considered whether one gender were more likely to find humorous stimuli funny to begin with. They asked the 10 men and 10 women in their study to categorize 30 ostensibly funny cartoons as either "funny" or "unfunny." Each participant received a score that represented her or his percentage of cartoons found to be "funny." The researchers conducted an independent-samples *t* test. Below are fictional data for 9 individuals, 4 women and 5 men; these fictional data have approximately the same means as were reported in the original study. Notice that we do not have to have exactly the same number of participants in each sample, although it is best if the sample sizes are fairly close.

Percentage of cartoons labeled as "funny":

Women: 84, 97, 58, 90

Men: 88, 90, 52, 97, 86

Step 1: *Identify the populations, distribution, and assumptions.*

This step is similar to that for the paired-samples *t* test for the populations. There will be two populations, men and women. The comparison distribution, however, will be a distribution of differences between means rather than a distribution of mean difference scores. The difference is that with a paired-samples *t* test, we take the difference score of each participant and then take the mean of all the difference scores (a mean difference score), whereas with an independent-samples *t* test, we take the mean of each sample and then

What Is Humor?
Who has a better sense of humor: men or women? An independent-samples *t* test is the appropriate hypothesis test for this two-group design.

TABLE 9-2. HYPOTHESIS TESTS AND THEIR DISTRIBUTIONS

We must consider the appropriate comparison distribution when we choose which hypothesis test we will use.

HYPOTHESIS TEST	NUMBER OF SAMPLES	COMPARISON DISTRIBUTION
z test	one	Distribution of means
Single-sample *t* test	one	Distribution of means
Paired-samples *t* test	two (same participants)	Distribution of mean difference scores
Independent-samples *t* test	two (different participants)	Distribution of differences between means

calculate the difference between the means (a difference between two means). Table 9-2 summarizes the distributions we have encountered with the hypothesis tests in this chapter. As usual, the comparison distribution is based on the null hypothesis. As with the paired-samples *t* test, the null hypothesis for the independent-samples *t* test posits no mean difference. So the mean of the comparison distribution would be 0; this reflects a mean difference between means of 0. We compare the difference between our sample means to a difference of 0, which is what would occur if there were no difference between groups. The assumptions are the same as for the single-sample *t* test and the paired-samples *t* test.

Summary: Population 1 is women exposed to humorous cartoons. Population 2 is men exposed to humorous cartoons

The comparison distribution will be a distribution of differences between means based on the null hypothesis. The hypothesis test will be an independent-samples *t* test because we have two samples composed of different groups of participants. This study meets one of the three assumptions; the dependent variable is a percentage of cartoons categorized as "funny," which is an interval variable. We do not know whether the population is normally distributed, and there are not at least 30 participants. Moreover, the data suggest some negative skew; although this test is robust with respect to this assumption, we must be cautious. Finally, it is clear that the men and women in this study were not randomly selected from among all men and women, so we must be cautious with respect to generalizing our findings.

Step 2: State the null and research hypotheses.

This step is identical to that for the previous *t* tests.

Summary: Null hypothesis: On average, women will categorize the same percentage of cartoons as "funny" as will men—H_0: $\mu_1 = \mu_2$.

Research hypothesis: On average, women will categorize a different percentage of cartoons as "funny" as compared with men—H_1: $\mu_1 \neq \mu_2$

Step 3: Determine the characteristics of the comparison distribution.

This step is similar to that for previous *t* tests in that we determine the appropriate mean and the appropriate standard error of the comparison distribution—the distribution based on the null hypothesis. According to the null hypothesis, there is no mean difference between the populations; that is, the difference between means would be 0. So the mean of the comparison distribution is always 0, as long as the null hypothesis posits no mean difference. Because we have two samples, however, it is more complicated to calculate the appropriate measure of spread. There are five stages to this process. First, let's consider them in words; then we'll learn the calculations. These verbal instructions are basic; you'll understand them better when you do the calculations. But they'll help you to keep the overall framework in mind. (These verbal descriptions are keyed by letter to the calculation stages below.)

(a) Calculate the variance for each sample. (Notice that we're working with variance, not standard deviation.)

(b) Pool the variances; pooling involves taking an average of the two sample variances, accounting for any differences in the sizes of the two samples. Pooled variance is an estimate of the common population variance.

(c) Take the pooled variance and convert from squared standard deviation (i.e., variance) to squared standard error (another version of variance) by dividing the pooled variance by the sample size, first for one sample and then again for the second sample. These are the estimated variances for each sample's distribution of means.

(d) Add the two variances (*squared* standard errors), one for each distribution of sample means, to calculate the estimated variance of the distribution of the mean differences.

(e) Take the square root of this form of variance (*squared* standard error) to get the estimated standard error of the distribution of mean differences.

Notice that stages (a) and (b) are an expanded version of the usual first calculation for a *t* test. Instead of calculating one corrected estimate of standard deviation, we're calculating two—one for each sample; and we're using variances instead of standard deviations. Because there are two calculations of variance, we have to combine them (i.e., the pooled variance). Stages (c) and (d) are an expanded version of the usual second calculation for a *t* test. Once again, we are converting to the standard error (only this time it is squared because we are working with variances). Once again, we will combine the variances from each sample. And in stage (e) we will use the square root so that we have the standard error. Let's examine the calculations.

(a) We take the corrected variance for each sample; the corrected variance is the one that uses $N - 1$ in the denominator. First, we'll do it for X, the women. Be sure to use the mean for the women's scores only, which is 82.25. Notice that the symbol for this variance now uses just the s^2, instead of the SD^2, just as the standard deviation uses s instead of SD in the previous *t* tests. Also, we have included the subscript X to indicate that this is the variance for the first sample, whose scores are arbitrarily called X. (Remember, don't take the square root. We want variance, not standard deviation.)

X	X − M	(X − M)²
84	1.75	3.063
97	14.75	217.563
58	−24.25	588.063
90	7.75	60.063

$$s_X^2 = \frac{\Sigma(X - M)^2}{N - 1} = \frac{(3.063 + 217.563 + 588.063 + 60.063)}{4 - 1} = 289.584$$

▪ **Pooled variance** is a weighted average of the two estimates of variance—one from each sample—that are calculated when conducting an independent-samples *t* test.

Now we'll do the same for Y, the men. Remember to use the mean for Y; it's easy to forget and use the mean we calculated earlier for X. The mean for Y is 82.6. The subscript Y indicates that this is the variance is for the second sample, whose scores are arbitrarily called Y. (We could call these scores by any letter, but statisticians tend to call the scores in the first two samples X and Y.)

Y	$Y - M$	$(Y - M)^2$
88	5.4	29.16
94	11.4	129.96
52	−30.6	936.36
97	14.4	207.36
86	3.4	11.56

$$s_Y^2 = \frac{\Sigma(Y - M)^2}{N - 1} = \frac{(29.16 + 129.96 + 936.36 + 207.36 + 11.56)}{5 - 1} = 328.6$$

(b) We must pool the two estimates of variance. Because there are often different numbers of people in each sample, we cannot simply take their mean. We mentioned earlier in this text that estimates of spread taken from smaller samples tended to be less accurate. This is why we will weight the estimate from the smaller sample a bit less and weight the estimate from the larger sample a bit more. We do this by calculating the proportion of degrees of freedom represented by each sample. Each sample has degrees of freedom of $N - 1$. We also will calculate a total degrees of freedom that sums the degrees of freedom for the two samples. Here are the calculations for degrees of freedom for this independent-samples *t* test.

$$df_X = N - 1 = 4 - 1 = 3$$
$$df_Y = N - 1 = 5 - 1 = 4$$
$$df_{Total} = df_X + df_Y = 3 + 4 = 7$$

Formula: The formula for degrees of freedom for an independent-samples *t* test is $df_{Total} = df_X + df_Y$, where df_X is the number of participants in the first sample minus 1 ($df_X = N - 1$) and df_Y is the number of participants in the second sample minus 1 ($df_Y = N - 1$).

Symbol: s_{Pooled}^2 is the pooled estimate of the population variance.

Formulas:

$$s_{Pooled}^2 =$$

$$\left(\frac{df_X}{df_{Total}}\right) s_X^2 + \left(\frac{df_Y}{df_{Total}}\right) s_Y^2$$

Using these degrees of freedom, we can calculate a sort of average variance called a pooled variance. **Pooled variance** *is a weighted average of the two estimates of variance—one from each sample—that are calculated when conducting an independent-samples* t *test.* The estimate of variance from the larger sample counts for more in the pooled variance than does the estimate from the smaller sample because larger samples tend to lead to somewhat more accurate estimates than do smaller samples. Here's the formula for pooled variance, and the calculations for this particular example:

$$s_{Pooled}^2 = \left(\frac{df_X}{df_{Total}}\right) s_X^2 + \left(\frac{df_Y}{df_{Total}}\right) s_Y^2 = \left(\frac{3}{7}\right) 289.584 + \left(\frac{4}{7}\right) 328.6$$

$$= 124.107 + 187.771 = 311.878$$

Note that if we had exactly the same number of participants in each sample, this would be an unweighted average—that is, we could compute the average in the usual way by summing the two sample variances and dividing by 2. Let's say we had 5 participants in each sample, and so each sample had 4 degrees of freedom. There would be 8 total degrees of freedom.

So each sample's estimate of variance would account for 4/8—which reduces to 1/2—of the pooled variance. Taking half of each is the same as adding them together and dividing them by 2.

(c) Now that we have pooled the two variances, we have an estimate of spread; this is similar to the estimate of the standard deviation in the previous t tests, but now it's based on two samples (and it's an estimate of the variance rather than the standard deviation). The next calculation in the previous t tests was dividing by $\sqrt{N}$ to get the standard error. (Remember, our spread will be smaller because we are dealing with means rather than individual scores.) Think back to Experience It for Yourself 7-2 in which we created distributions of scores and distributions of means by hand; the distributions of means were less spread out than the distributions of scores. In this case, we divide by N instead of $\sqrt{N}$. Why? Because we are dealing with variances, not standard deviations. Variance is the square of standard deviation, so we divide by the square of $\sqrt{N}$, which is simply N. We will do this once for each sample, using the pooled variance as the estimate of spread. We use the pooled variance because an estimate based on two samples is likely better than an estimate based on one. The key here is to divide by the appropriate N; that is, when we do the calculations for the first sample, we divide by its N, 4. And when we do the calculations for the second sample, we divide by its N, 5.

$$s^2_{M_X} = \frac{s^2_{Pooled}}{N} = \frac{311.878}{4} = 77.970$$

$$s^2_{M_Y} = \frac{s^2_{Pooled}}{N} = \frac{311.878}{5} = 62.376$$

> Formula: $s^2_{M_X} = \frac{s^2_{Pooled}}{N}$ is the formula for the version of variance for a distribution of means for the first variable. The formula is the same for the second variable, but with a subscript of Y instead of X to represent the second variable.

(d) In stage (c), we calculated the variance versions of standard error for each sample, but we want only one such measure of spread when we calculate the test statistic. We must combine the two variances, similar to the way in which we combined the two estimates of variance in stage (b). This stage is even simpler, however. We merely add the two variances together. When we sum them, we get the variance of the distribution of differences between means, symbolized as $s^2_{Difference}$. Here are the formula and the calculations for this example.

> Symbol: $s^2_{Difference}$ is the symbol for the variance of the distribution of differences between means.

$$s^2_{Difference} = s^2_{M_X} + s^2_{M_Y} = 77.970 + 62.376 = 140.346$$

> Formula: $s^2_{Difference} = s^2_{M_X} + s^2_{M_Y}$ is the formula for the variance based on a distribution of means, but one that includes estimates from each of the two samples. This is the variance of the distribution of differences between means.

(e) Now we have paralleled the two calculations of the previous t tests by doing two things: (1) we calculated an estimate of spread (we made two calculations, one for each sample, then combined them) and (2) we then adjusted our estimate for the sample size (again, we made two calculations, one for each sample, then combined them). The main difference is that we have kept all calculations as variances rather than standard deviations. At this final stage, we must convert from variance form to standard deviation form. Because standard deviation is the square root of variance, we do this by simply taking the square root:

> Symbol: $s_{Difference}$ is the standard deviation of the distribution of differences between means.

$$s_{Difference} = \sqrt{s^2_{Difference}} = \sqrt{140.346} = 11.847$$

> Formula: $s_{Difference} = \sqrt{s^2_{Difference}}$ is the formula for the standard deviation of the distribution of differences between means.

Summary: The mean of the distribution of differences between means: $\mu_X - \mu_Y = 0$. The standard deviation of the distribution of differences between means: $s_{Difference} = 11.847$. [*Note:* It is helpful to include all calculations in the summary, and label them as stages (a)–(e).]

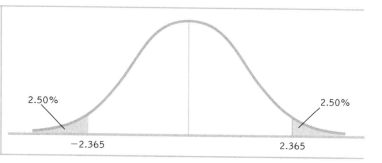

FIGURE 9-8
Determining Cutoffs for an Independent Samples *t* Test

To determine the critical values for an independent-samples *t* test, we use the total degrees of freedom, df_{Total}. This is the sum of the degrees of freedom for each sample, which is $N - 1$ for each sample.

2.50%   2.50%

−2.365   2.365

Step 4: *Determine critical values, or cutoffs.*

This step is similar to those for previous *t* tests, but we use the total degrees of freedom, df_{Total}.

Summary: Our critical values, based on a two-tailed test, a *p* level of 0.05, and df_{Total} of 7, are −2.365 and 2.365 (as seen in the curve in Figure 9-8). (*Note:* It is helpful to draw a curve when conducting a hypothesis test; indicate the cutoff *t* statistics and, later, the *t* statistic on the curve.)

Step 5: *Calculate the test statistic.*

This step is very similar to those for the previous *t* tests. Here we subtract the population difference between means based on the null hypothesis from the difference between means for our samples. The formula is

$$t = \frac{(M_X - M_Y) - (\mu_X - \mu_Y)}{S_{Difference}}$$

Formula:

$$t = \frac{(M_X - M_Y) - (\mu_X - \mu_Y)}{S_{Difference}}$$

is the formula for the test statistic for an independent-samples *t* test.

As in previous *t* tests, the test statistic is calculated by subtracting a number based on the populations from a number based on the samples, and then dividing by a version of standard error. Because the population difference between means (as per the null hypothesis) is always 0, many statisticians choose to eliminate the latter part of the formula. So the formula for the test statistic for an independent samples *t* test is often abbreviated as: $t = \dfrac{(M_X - M_Y)}{S_{Difference}}$. You might find it easier to use the first formula, however, as it reminds us that we are subtracting the population difference between means as per the null hypothesis (0) from the actual difference between the sample means. This format more closely parallels the formulas of the test statistics we calculated previously in this chapter.

Summary: $t = \dfrac{(82.25 - 82.6) - (0)}{11.847} = -0.03$

Step 6: *Make a decision.*

This step is identical to that for the previous *t* tests. If we reject the null hypothesis, we need to examine the means of the two conditions so that we know the direction of the effect.

Summary: Fail to reject the null hypothesis. We conclude that there is no evidence from this study to support the research hypothesis that either men or women are more likely than the opposite gender, on average, to find cartoons funny (as shown by the curve in Figure 9-9).

The statistics, as reported in a journal article, follow the standard APA format, including the degrees of freedom, the value of the test statistic, and whether the *p* value associated with the test statistic was less than or greater than the critical

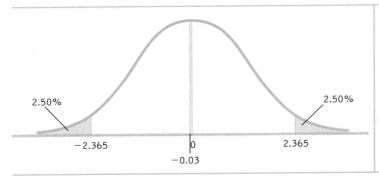

FIGURE 9-9
Making a Decision

As in previous *t* tests, to decide whether or not to reject the null hypothesis, we compare our test statistic to our critical values. In this figure, the test statistic, −0.03, is not beyond either −2.365 or 2.365. We fail to reject the null hypothesis and can only conclude that there is no evidence from this study to support the research hypothesis.

p level of 0.05. In the current example, the statistics would read: $t(7) = -0.03$, $p > 0.05$. The *p* value is listed as greater than the cutoff of 0.05 because we failed to reject the null hypothesis. The difference between men and women was *not* large enough that we could conclude that it was unlikely to have happened by chance. (The APA strongly encourages the inclusion of the statistics in cases in which we fail to reject the null hypothesis in addition to cases in which we reject the null hypothesis.) We would also include the means and standard deviations for the two samples. We calculated the means in step 3 of hypothesis testing, and we also calculated the variances (289.584 for women and 328.6 for men). We can calculate the standard deviations by taking the square roots of the variances. The descriptive statistics can be reported in parentheses as: (Women: $M = 82.25$, $SD = 17.02$; Men: $M = 82.60$, $SD = 18.13$). Always include the means and the standard deviations, as these are often the first statistics to which the reader will turn after noting the result of the hypothesis test.

In summary, the paired-samples *t* test and the independent-samples *t* test are versatile tools that are widely used in social science research. With both *t* tests, we compare two sample means, but in different ways. In the paired-samples *t* test, we calculate a difference score for every individual. We then take the mean of these difference scores and essentially conduct a single-sample *t* test with difference scores. In the independent-samples *t* test, we cannot calculate individual difference scores. That is why we compare the mean of one sample with the mean of the other sample. Because we maintain two separate samples, it is more time-consuming to calculate a measure of spread. We must calculate variance for each sample, then combine the two variances (squared standard deviations). We must then adjust for sample size for each sample, then combine the two squared standard errors. Finally, we must take the square root to go from variance to standard deviation. For both *t* tests, we use the same six steps of hypothesis testing that we used with the *z* test and with the single-sample *t* test.

⊙ CHECK YOUR LEARNING

9-3 Conduct all six steps for an independent-samples *t* test for the following scenario. Then report the statistics as you would in a journal article. Conduct a two-tailed test with critical values based on a *p* level of 0.05. Scenario: There are many different cell phone plans available, including monthly plans and prepaid plans. In a given month, do people use more cell phone minutes if they have a monthly plan in which they have paid in advance for a certain number of minutes or if they have a prepaid plan in which they pay per minute used?

From a directory of cell phone numbers, four people with a monthly plan and three with a prepaid plan were randomly selected. The minutes used over the previous month were recorded. Here are the data:

Monthly plan: 955, 1067, 1121, and 1258
Prepaid plan: 856, 1000, and 732

■ DIGGING DEEPER INTO THE DATA: MORE WAYS TO VISUALIZE DATA

When we conduct hypothesis tests that compare two (or more) samples, we must be concerned with the shapes of the distributions of the underlying populations. We often use the shapes of our samples to assess the shapes of the populations from which they are drawn. In earlier chapters, we learned to construct frequency histograms and frequency polygons to examine the shape of the data in our sample, but these graphs do not easily allow for the examination of more than one sample simultaneously. In an earlier Digging Deeper into the Data (Chapter 3), we explored box plots that allow for side-by-side comparisons of multiple distributions but do not allow us to see every data point. Two graphs that are frequently used in a range of fields, but less so in the behavioral sciences, permit us to view the shapes of two samples simultaneously, including all individual data points: the stem-and-leaf plot and the dot plot. These graphs are particularly useful when we plan to use an independent-samples *t* test.

The Stem-and-Leaf Plot: Searching for Outliers and Comparing Distributions

*The **stem-and-leaf plot** is a graph that displays all the data points of a single variable both numerically and visually.* There are two important advantages to describing a variable with a stem-and-leaf plot. First, it helps identify outliers very quickly. Second, it allows for quick visual comparisons with a second variable. A stem-and-leaf plot provides the same information as a histogram, but with more detail.

One of our in-class examples used students' reports of the numbers of minutes they typically spend in the shower. Here are the data for 30 women, already arranged in order from lowest to highest:

5, 8, 10, 10, 10, 10, 12, 15, 15, 15,

15, 15, 15, 18, 20, 20, 20, 20, 20, 23,

25, 30, 30, 30, 30, 30, 35, 40, 45, 60

In this example, the stem will consist of the first digit for each of these numbers, as follows:

6

5

4

3

2

1

0

■ The **stem-and-leaf plot** is a graph that displays all the data points of a single variable both numerically and visually.

Note three features of this particular stem:

1. We group the digits by 10s (0–9, 10–19, 20–29, 30–39, 40–49, 50–59, 60–69).

2. The first digit for numbers below 10 will be a 0.

3. The category is represented even if there is no digit represented for that category (e.g., no digit in the category 50–59).

Now we will add the leaves, the last digit for each score, shown in Table 9-3.

The only scores between 0 and 9 are 5 and 8, so these two leaves will be added next to 0. There are 10 scores between 10 and 19. Some, like 10 and 15, are repeated. In these cases, a 5, to represent 15, is added as a leaf for every instance of 15. There are six 15s, so there will be six 5s next to the stem of 1. There are no scores between 50 and 59, so the part of the stem that begins with 5 will have no leaves; once again, note that we include every part of the stem in the range of scores, even if it has no leaves. For each part of the stem that does have leaves, the leaves are arranged in ascending order.

The stem-and-leaf plot displays the same information as a histogram, but in a slightly different way and with a little more detail. In fact, the stem-and-leaf plot looks like a histogram if turned on its side. Note the similarity between the stem-and-leaf plot and the histogram of the same data in Figure 9-10.

The stem-and-leaf plot is particularly useful to visualize the scores of two samples side by side. For our shower example, we can include a sample of men on the other side of the same stem. Here are the scores for 30 men who also reported how many minutes they typically spend in the shower:

$$5, \ 7, \ 8, \ 8, \ 9, \ 10, \ 10, \ 10, \ 10, \ 10,$$

$$10, \ 10, \ 10, \ 10, \ 12, \ 15, \ 15, \ 15, \ 15, \ 15$$

$$15, \ 15, \ 15, \ 15, \ 20, \ 20, \ 20, \ 20, \ 20, \ 25$$

TABLE 9-3.	**A STEM-AND-LEAF PLOT**

For numbers with two digits, a stem-and-leaf plot includes the first digits as the stem and the second digits as the leaves. This graph allows us to see the shape of the data, along with the individual scores.

MINUTES TYPICALLY SPENT IN THE SHOWER—WOMEN:

6	0
5	
4	05
3	000005
2	0000035
1	000025555558
0	58

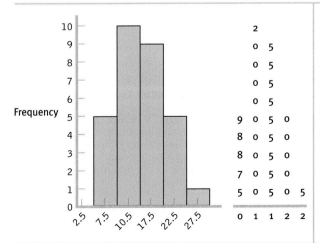

FIGURE 9-10
A Histogram and a Stem-And-Leaf Plot

The stem-and-leaf plot displays the same information as a histogram but in a slightly different way and with a little more detail.

TABLE 9-4. A SIDE-BY-SIDE STEM-AND-LEAF PLOT

Stem-and-leaf plots can be expanded to include scores for two samples on the same measure, a helpful technique for examining shapes of distributions in research designs that involve two groups.

MINUTES TYPICALLY SPENT IN THE SHOWER:		
MEN		WOMEN
	6	0
	5	
	4	05
	3	000005
500000	2	0000035
5555555552000000000	1	000025555558
98875	0	58

We now will add those scores to the stem that already exists for the women, but to the left of the stem instead of the right, shown in Table 9-4. In this case, we do not have to extend our stem, but if there were scores of 70 or above (or if there were negative scores), then we would extend our stem to include them.

The stem-and-leaf plot allows us to easily compare the two samples. We can see, without having to calculate summaries, that the central tendency of the distribution of women's scores is slightly higher than that of the distribution of men's scores, and that the distribution of women's scores has a larger spread than the distribution of men's scores. The distribution of women's scores might be somewhat skewed to the right, and the outlier (60 minutes in the shower!) is evident. Computers can quickly generate stem-and-leaf plots such as this, as well as more complicated ones that group our data into intervals. Graphs such as this are particularly useful with two-group research designs. A glance at our actual data can help us to determine how we should proceed with our analyses. The best researchers and statisticians know the overall array of their data, and not just the summary statistics and decisions of hypothesis testing.

The Dot Plot: Making It Easy on Your Eyes

*The **dot plot** is a graph that displays all the data points in a sample, with the range of scores along the x-axis and a dot for each data point above the appropriate value.* Dot plots serve a similar function to stem-and-leaf plots in that they allow us both to view the overall shape of a sample and to retain all the individual data points. Moreover, a dot plot makes it easy on the eyes by placing the dots for one group directly above the dots for the other, allowing us to view two groups simultaneously. Like the stem-and-leaf plot, the dot plot is a great first step when approaching data from a two-group research design because we can compare two distributions of data with only a glance.

To create a dot plot, we determine the range of the scores, label the x-axis and include the values from the lowest through highest scores, then place a dot above the appropriate value for every score. Figure 9-11 displays a dot plot for the samples of male and female students' minutes spent in the shower. As with the stem-and-leaf plot, we can easily observe the slightly higher central

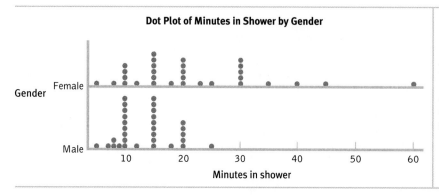

Dot Plot of Minutes in Shower by Gender

FIGURE 9-11
Dot Plot for Two Groups

A dot plot allows us to view all of the data points in our sample. Moreover, as in this dot plot, we can simultaneously view all the data points in more than one sample.

tendency and larger spread for the women than the men, as well as the potential outlier in the sample of women.

We have already described three instances when describing the data made a profound difference in the lives of many people. John Snow constructed his map of data points and helped stop an epidemic. Florence Nightingale saved thousands of lives by creating her coxcomb graph of the causes of mortality in the British army. And the astronauts aboard the space shuttle *Challenger* quite possibly would have been spared their gruesome fate if those who decided whether the launch would occur had had access to visual displays that valued clarity over cleverness. As we explore more sophisticated applications of hypothesis testing, as well as other methods to draw conclusions from our data, it is important to remember that some of the most basic lessons of statistics are not merely building blocks to the more complicated lessons. Many of these basic methods are ends in and of themselves. The visual display of our data through simple graphs and an examination of summary statistics remain central to the understanding of our data, no matter how sophisticated the techniques we use for our analyses. Had the proponents of facilitated communication examined quantitative data in even these rudimentary ways, much of the expense, time, and trauma to affected families probably would have been avoided.

In summary, stem-and-leaf plots and dot plots are two ways in which we can view the shape of our sample's distribution; both display every single data point in our sample. Moreover, both types of plots easily depict the scores of two samples side by side to allow for comparisons of distributions.

■ The **dot plot** is a graph that displays all the data points in a sample, with the range of scores along the *x*-axis and a dot for each data point above the appropriate value.

⊙ CHECK YOUR LEARNING

9-4 The following data are Consideration of Future Consequences (CFC) scores for 20 students, already arranged in order from lowest to highest:

2.0, 2.0, 2.5, 2.5, 3.0, 3.0, 3.0, 3.0, 3.5, 3.5,

3.5, 3.5, 3.5, 3.5, 3.5, 4.0, 4.0, 4.0, 4.5, 4.5

a. Construct a single stem-and-leaf plot for these data.

b. Construct a dot plot for these data.

c. What can you learn about the shape of this sampling distribution from these plots?

REVIEW OF CONCEPTS

> The *t* Distributions: Distributions of Means When the Parameters Are Not Known

The *t* distributions are similar to the *z* distribution, except that we must estimate the standard deviation from the sample. When estimating the standard deviation, we must make a mathematical correction to adjust for the increased likelihood of error. After estimating the standard deviation, the *t statistic* is calculated exactly like the *z* statistic for distributions of means. The *t* distributions can also be used to compare means of two samples using a distribution of differences between means.

> Hypothesis Tests: The Single-Sample *t* Test

Like *z* tests, single-sample *t* tests are conducted in the rare cases in which we have one sample that we're comparing to a known population. The difference is that we must know the mean and the standard deviation of the population to conduct a *z* test, whereas we only have to know the mean of the population to conduct a single-sample *t* test. There are many *t* distributions, one for every possible sample size. We look up the appropriate critical values on the *t* table based on *degrees of freedom*, a number calculated from a sample size.

> Hypothesis Tests: Tests for Two Samples

A *paired-samples* t *test* or an *independent-samples* t *test* is used when we have two samples. These two tests are much more common than single-sample tests. We use paired-samples *t* tests when the same participants are in both samples; to conduct the test, we calculate a difference score for every individual. The comparison distribution is a distribution of mean difference scores. We use independent-samples *t* tests when different participants are in each sample. We cannot calculate difference scores because the samples are comprised of different people. The comparison distribution is a distribution of differences between means. Because we are working with two separate samples of scores (rather than one set of difference scores), when we conduct an independent samples *t* test, we have additional steps to calculate an estimate of spread. We calculate two variances, then take a weighted average to calculate *pooled variance*. We convert the pooled variance to a version of variance for a distribution of means, one for each sample, then add them to combine them. Finally, we take the square root.

▪ DIGGING DEEPER INTO THE DATA: MORE WAYS TO VISUALIZE DATA

We previously learned to use frequency histograms and polygons to view the shape of our sample's distribution, but when comparing two distributions, it can be difficult to visually compare two of these graphs side by side. A *stem-and-leaf plot* and a *dot plot* are two methods that allow us to view the shape of our distribution, displaying every single score in a sample. Moreover, we can create side-by-side versions of these plots to easily compare the distributions of two samples.

SPSS GUIDELINES FOR CHAPTER 9: *t* TESTS

The *t* test is used to compare only two groups, and there are slightly different formulas depending upon whether it is a between-groups design or a within-groups design.

We can access these different ways to conduct a *t* test by selecting for a single-sample *t* test:

> **Analyze** → Compare Means → One-Sample T Test.
>> Then highlight the dependent variable and click the arrow in the center to choose it. Type the population mean to which we're comparing our sample next to "Test Value" and click "OK."

for a paired-samples *t* test:

> **Analyze** → Compare Means → Paired-Samples T Test

Choose the dependent variable under the first condition by clicking it. Choose the dependent variable under the second condition by clicking it. Then, click the arrow in the center and click "OK."

for an independent samples *t* test:

Analyze → Compare Means → Independent-Samples T Test

Choose the dependent variable by clicking it, then clicking the arrow in the upper center. Choose the independent variable by clicking it, then clicking the arrow in the lower center. Click the "Define Groups" button, then provide the values for each level of the independent variable, after "1" for Group 1 and "2" for Group 2. Then click "OK."

EXERCISES

9.1 The *t* statistic and the *Princeton Review*: On its Web site, the *Princeton Review* claims that students who have taken its course improve their GRE scores, on average, by 210 points. (No other information is provided about this statistic.) Treating this average gain as a population mean, a researcher wonders whether the far cheaper technique of practicing for the GRE on one's own using books and CD-ROMS will lead to a different average gain. She randomly selects five students from the pool of students at her university who plan to take the GRE. The students take a practice test before and after two months of self-study. They reported (fictional) gains of 160, 240, 340, 70, and 250 points. (Note that many experts suggest that the results from self-study are similar to those from a structured course if you have the self-discipline to go solo. Regardless of the format, preparation has been convincingly demonstrated to lead to increased scores.)

a. Using symbolic notation and formulas (where appropriate), determine the appropriate mean and standard error for the distribution to which we will compare this sample. Show all steps of your calculations.

b. Using symbolic notation and the formula, calculate the *t* statistic for this sample.

c. As an interested consumer, what critical questions would you want to ask about the statistic reported by the *Princeton Review*? List at least three questions.

9.2 The *t* statistic and death row: The Florida Department of Corrections publishes an online death row fact sheet (http://www.dc.state.fl.us/oth/deathrow/index.html). The site reports the average time on death row prior to execution as 11.72 years but provides no standard deviation. This mean is a parameter, as it is calculated from the entire population of executed prisoners in Florida. Has the time spent on death row changed in recent years? According to the execution list linked to this Web site, the six prisoners executed in Florida during the years 2003, 2004, and 2005 spent 25.62, 13.09, 8.74, 17.63, 2.80, and 4.42 years on Death Row, respectively. (All were men, although Aileen Wuornos, the serial killer portrayed by Charlize Theron in the 2003 film *Monster*, was among the three prisoners executed by the state of Florida in 2002; Wuornos spent 10.69 years on death row.)

a. Using symbolic notation and formulas (where appropriate), determine the appropriate mean and standard error for the distribution of means. Show all steps of your calculations.

b. Using symbolic notation and the formula, calculate the *t* statistic for time spent on death row for the sample of recently executed prisoners.

c. The execution list provides data on all prisoners executed since the death penalty was reinstated in Florida in 1976. Included for each prisoner are the name, race, gender, date of birth, date of offense, date sentenced, date arrived on death row, data of execution, number of warrants, and years on death row. State at least one hypothesis, other than year of execution, that could be examined using a *t* distribution and the comparison mean of 11.72 years on death row. Be specific about your hypothesis (and if you are truly interested, the data are available online).

d. What additional information would you need to calculate a *z* score for the length of time Aileen Wuornos spent on death row?

9.3 A distribution of differences between means and depression in China: Researchers examined depression in Chinese children (Chen, Rubin, & Li, 1995). They reported a mean score on the Children's Depression Inventory (CDI) of 11.67 for the 134 boys in the study and of 9.78 for the 127 girls. They wanted to make a comparison to determine whether Chinese boys and girls had different CDI scores, on average.

a. What are the populations of interest in this study, and what are the samples?

b. Explain the process by which you would develop a distribution of differences between means for this study.

c. What would be the mean of this distribution of differences between means—the distribution to which we would compare the difference between means from our samples? Explain why this is typically the case.

9.4 Which distribution? For each of the following situations, state whether the distribution of interest is a distribution of scores, distribution of means, distribution of mean differences, or distribution of differences between means. Explain your answer.

a. A Gallup poll conducted in November, 2005, asked 1011 American adults: "Just your best guess: What is the current minimum wage rate per hour worked?" The mean response was $6.09, almost a dollar over the actual minimum wage of $5.15. Let's say that a researcher wanted to compare the data from this sample to the actual minimum wage to see if there is a difference.

b. A professor wondered whether his students learned more when studying in silence or with music. Fifty students were randomly assigned to study for an upcoming test in silence, and 50 were randomly assigned to study for the same test while listening to music of their choice.

c. The National Doctoral Program Survey (http://survey.nagps.org) publishes data comparing individual programs, such as Loyola University of Chicago's developmental psychology program, to other programs in the same discipline on a number of measures. For example, for the category Career Guidance and Placement Services, the mean score for the 11 Loyola students who responded was 72; Loyola might wonder how this compares to other programs. The mean for this category for 75 U.S. psychology programs is 51. Assume that Loyola has access to the 11 students' scores and that the mean for all psychology students is a population parameter. (*Note:* This is a great Web site for learning more about schools, but remember that these are volunteer samples and thus are subject to bias.)

d. Your little sister got a 660 on the quantitative subtest of the SAT. Knowing that the mean is 500, with a standard deviation of 100, you help her determine her percentile.

e. Thirty students take a test assessing their knowledge of world politics. They are then assigned to listen to a daily news program on National Public Radio for one week. Their knowledge of world politics is assessed again.

9.5 Step 1—should we separate twins in the classroom? Over the years, parents and educators have debated the wisdom of keeping twins together in the classroom versus placing them in different classrooms (Bellafante, 2006). Some argue that twins support each other throughout the school years and would be distressed at being separated. Others argue that twins suffer from direct comparisons between them when in the same classroom and that they do not develop independence as readily. Imagine that you designed a study in which 200 children who had a twin were randomly selected from all North American twins who are about to start school. Note that *only one* member of each pair of twins participated in this study. The children were randomly assigned to be separated from or kept together with their twin throughout their school years. One dependent variable was a measure of academic performance.

a. Let's go through step 1 of hypothesis testing. What are the two populations?

b. What would the comparison distribution be? Explain.

c. What hypothesis test would you use? Explain.

d. Check the assumptions for this hypothesis test.

9.6 Step 1—big box stores: Many communities worldwide are lamenting the effects of so-called big box retailers (e.g., Wal-Mart) on their local economies, particularly on small, independently owned shops. Do these large stores affect the bottom lines of locally owned retailers? Imagine that you decide to test this premise. You assess earnings at 20 local stores for the month of October, a few months before a big box store opens. You then assess earnings the following October, correcting for inflation.

a. What are the two populations?

b. What would the comparison distribution be? Explain.

c. What hypothesis test would you use? Explain.

d. Check the assumptions for this hypothesis test.

e. What is one flaw in drawing conclusions from this comparison over time?

9.7 Step 2—twins and big box scores: For each of the scenarios described in Exercises 9.5 and 9.6, state the null and research hypotheses in both words and symbols.

a. Twins—to separate or not to separate

b. Big box scores—their effect on local retailers

9.8 Single-sample *t* test—high-altitude military training: Bardwell, Ensign, and Mills (2005) assessed the moods of 60 male U.S. Marines following a month-long training exercise conducted at cold temperatures and high altitudes. Negative moods, including fatigue and anger, increased substantially during the training and lasted up to three months after the training ended. Mean mood scores were compared to population norms for three groups: college men, adult men, and male psychiatric outpatients. Let's examine anger scores for six men at the end of training; these scores are fictional, but their mean and standard deviation are very close to the actual descriptive statistics for the sample: 14, 12, 13, 12, 14, 15.

a. The population mean anger score for college men is 8.90. Conduct all six steps of a single-sample *t* test. Be sure to label all six steps. Report the statistics as you would in a journal article.

b. Now calculate the test statistic to compare this sample mean to the population mean anger score for adult men ($M = 9.20$). You do not have to repeat all the steps from part (a), but conduct step 6 of hypothesis testing and report the statistics as you would in a journal article.

c. Now calculate the test statistic to compare this sample mean to the population mean anger score for male psychiatric outpatients ($M = 13.5$). Do not repeat all the steps from part (a), but conduct step 6 of hypothesis testing and report the statistics as you would in a journal article.

d. What can we conclude overall about Marines' moods following high-altitude, cold-weather training. Remember, if we fail to reject the null hypothesis, we can only conclude that there is no evidence from this study to support the research hypothesis. We cannot conclude that we have supported the null hypothesis.

9.9 Paired-samples *t* test—minimum GPAs: Is it harder to get into graduate programs in psychology or history? We randomly selected five institutions from among all U.S. institutions with graduate programs. The first number for each is the minimum GPA for applicants to the psychology doctoral program, and the second is for applicants to the history doctoral program. Both GPAs are posted on www.petersons.com for each school.

Wayne State University: 3.0, 2.75

University of Iowa: 3.0, 3.0

University of Nevada–Reno: 3.0, 2.75

George Washington University: 3.0, 3.0

University of Wyoming: 3.0, 3.0

a. The participants are not people; explain why it is appropriate to use a paired-samples *t* test for this situation.

b. Conduct all six steps of a paired-samples *t* test. Be sure to label all six steps.

c. Report the statistics as you would in a journal article.

9.10 Paired-samples *t* test—hypnosis and the Stroop effect: Earlier in the text, you were given an opportunity to take the Stroop task in which color words are printed in the wrong color; for example, the word *red* might be printed in the color blue. The conflict that arises when we try to read the words, but are distracted by the colors, increases our reaction time and decreases our accuracy. Several researchers have suggested that the Stroop effect can be decreased by hypnosis. Raz (2005) used brain-imaging techniques [i.e., functional magnetic resonance imaging (fMRI)] to demonstrate that posthypnotic suggestion led highly hypnotizable individuals to see Stroop words as nonsense words. Imagine that you are working with Raz and your assignment is to determine if reaction times decrease (remember, a decrease is a good thing; it indicates that participants are faster) when highly hypnotizable individuals receive a posthypnotic suggestion to view the words as nonsensical. You conduct the experiment on six individuals, once in each condition, and receive the following data; the first number is reaction time in seconds without the posthypnotic suggestion, and the second number is reaction time with the posthypnotic suggestion:

Participant 1: (12.6, 8.5)   Participant 4: (12.2, 9.2)

Participant 2: (13.8, 9.6)   Participant 5: (12.1, 8.9)

Participant 3: (11.6, 10.0)   Participant 6: (13.0, 10.8)

a. What is the independent variable and what are its levels? What is the dependent variable?

b. Conduct all six steps of a paired-samples *t* test. Be sure to label all six steps.

c. Report the statistics as you would in a journal article.

9.11 Independent-samples *t* test—hypnosis and the Stroop effect: Using the data from Exercise 9-10 on the effects of posthypnotic suggestion on the Stroop effect, conduct an independent-samples *t* test. Pretend two sets of people participated in the study. The first score for each participant in Exercise 9-10 will be in the first sample—those not receiving a posthypnotic suggestion. The second score for each participant in Exercise 9-10 will be in the second sample—those receiving a posthypnotic suggestion.

a. Conduct all six steps of an independent-samples *t* test. Be sure to label all six steps.

b. Report the statistics as you would in a journal article.

c. What happens to the test statistic when you switch from having all participants in both samples to having two separate samples? Given the same numbers, is it easier to reject the null hypothesis with a within-groups or between-groups design?

d. In your own words, why do you think it is easier to reject the null hypothesis in one of these situations than in the other?

9.12 Independent-samples *t* test—getting ready for a date: In an example we sometimes use in our statistics classes, several semesters worth of male and female students were asked how long, in minutes, they spend getting ready for a date. The data reported below reflect the actual means and the approximate standard deviations for the actual data from 142 students.

Men: 28, 35, 52, 14

Women: 30, 82, 53, 61

a. Conduct all six steps of an independent-samples *t* test. Be sure to label all six steps.

b. Report the statistics as you would in a journal article.

9.13 One-tailed versus two-tailed tests—Stroop and hypnosis: When we conduct a one-tailed test instead of a two-tailed test, there are small changes in steps 2 and 4 of hypothesis testing. Let's consider Exercise 9-10 on the Stroop task and posthypnotic suggestion.

a. Conduct step 2 of hypothesis testing—stating the null and research hypotheses in words and in symbols—for a one-tailed test.

b. Conduct step 4 of hypothesis testing—determining the critical value and drawing the curve—for a one-tailed test.

c. Conduct step 6 of hypothesis testing—making a decision—for a one-tailed test.

d. Under which circumstance—a one-tailed or a two-tailed test—is it easier to reject the null hypothesis? Explain.

e. If it becomes easier to reject the null hypothesis under one type of test (one-tailed versus two-tailed), does this mean that there is a bigger mean difference between the samples? Explain.

9.14 *p* values—Stroop and hypnosis: When we change the *p* level that we use as a cutoff, there is a small change to step 4 of hypothesis testing. Although 0.05 is the most commonly used *p* level, other levels, such as 0.01, are also often used. Let's consider Exercise 9-10 on the Stroop task and posthypnotic suggestion.

a. Conduct step 4 of hypothesis testing—determining the critical value and drawing the curve—for a *p* level of 0.01.

b. Conduct step 6 of hypothesis testing—making a decision—for a *p* level of 0.01.

c. With which *p* level—0.05 or 0.01—is it easiest to reject the null hypothesis? Explain.

d. If it is easier to reject the null hypothesis with certain *p* levels, does this mean that there is a bigger mean difference between the samples? Explain.

9.15 Effect of sample size—Stroop and hypnosis: Changing the sample size can have an effect on the outcome of a hypothesis test. Consider Exercise 9-10 on the Stroop task and posthypnotic suggestion.

a. Calculate the test statistic using only participants 1–3.

b. Is this test statistic closer to or farther from the cutoff? Does reducing the sample size make it easier or more difficult to reject the null hypothesis? Explain.

9.16 Choose the correct test, Part I: For each of the following three scenarios, state which hypothesis test you would use from among the four introduced so far: the *z* test, the single-sample *t* test, the paired-samples *t* test, and the independent-samples *t* test. (*Note:* In the actual studies described, the researchers did not always use one of these tests, often because the actual experiment had additional variables.) Explain your answer.

a. A study of children who had survived a brain tumor revealed that they were more likely to have behavioral and emotional difficulties than were children who had not experienced such a trauma (Upton & Eiser, 2006). Forty families participated in the study. Parents rated children's difficulties, and the ratings data were compared with known means from published population norms.

b. Talarico and Rubin (2003) recorded the memories of 54 students just after 9/11/01—some memories related to the terrorist attacks on that day (called flashbulb memories for their vividness and emotional content) and some everyday memories. They found that flashbulb memories were no more consistent over time than everyday memories, even though they were perceived to be more accurate.

c. The HOPE VI Panel Study (Popkin & Woodley, 2002) was initiated to test a U.S. program aimed at improving troubled public housing developments. Residents of five HOPE VI developments were studied at the beginning of the study so researchers could later ascertain whether their quality of life had improved. Means at the beginning of the study were compared to known national data sources (e.g., the U.S. Census, the American Housing Survey) that had summary statistics, including means and standard deviations.

9.17 Choose the correct test, Part II: For each of the following three scenarios, state which hypothesis test you would use from among the four introduced so far: the *z* test, the single-sample *t* test, the paired-samples *t* test, and the independent-samples *t* test. (*Note:* In the actual studies described, the researchers did not always use one of these tests, often because the actual experiment had additional variables.) Explain your answer.

a. Taylor and Ste-Marie (2001) studied eating disorders in 41 Canadian female figure skaters. They compared the figure skaters' data on the Eating Disorder Inventory to the means of known populations, including women with eating disorders. On average, the figure skaters were more similar to the population of women with eating disorders than to those without eating disorders.

b. In article titled "A Fair and Balanced Look at the News: What Affects Memory for Controversial Arguments," Wiley (2005) found that people with a high level of previous knowledge about a given controversial topic (e.g., abortion, military intervention) had better average recall for arguments on both sides of that issue than did those with lower levels of knowledge.

c. Engle-Friedman and colleagues (2003) studied the effects of sleep deprivation. Fifty students were assigned to one night of sleep loss (students were required to call the laboratory every half-hour all night) and then one night of no sleep loss (normal sleep). The next day, students were offered a choice of math problems with differing levels of difficulty. Following sleep loss, students tended to choose less challenging problems.

9.18 Tying it all together—school lunches: Alice Waters, the owner of the Berkeley, California restaurant Chez Panisse, has long been an advocate of the use of simple, fresh, organic ingredients in both home and restaurant cooking. More recently, she has turned her considerable expertise to school cafeterias and their fare. Waters (2006) praises recent changes in school lunch menus that have expanded nutritious offerings, but she hypothesizes that students are likely to circumvent healthy lunches by avoiding vegetables and smuggling in banned junk food unless they receive accompanying nutrition education and hands-on involvement in their meals. She has spearheaded an Edible Schoolyard program in Berkeley, which involves public school students in the cultivation and preparation of fresh foods, and states that such interactive education is necessary to combat growing levels of childhood obesity. "Nothing less," Waters writes, "will change their behavior."

a. In your own words, what is Waters predicting? Citing the confirmation bias, explain why Waters's program, although intuitively appealing, should not be instituted nationwide without further study.

b. Describe a simple between-groups experiment with a nominal independent variable with two levels and an interval dependent variable to test Waters's hypothesis. Specifically identify the independent variable, its levels, and the dependent variable. State how you will operationalize the dependent variable.

c. Explain how you could use a form of random sampling and a form of random assignment to conduct this experiment.

d. Which hypothesis test would be used to analyze this experiment? Explain your answer.

e. Conduct step 1 of hypothesis testing.

f. Conduct step 2 of hypothesis testing.

g. State at least one other way you could operationalize the dependent variable.

h. Let's say, hypothetically, that Waters discounted the need for the research you propose by citing her own data that the Berkeley school in which she instituted the program has lower rates of obesity than other California schools. Describe the flaw in this argument by discussing the importance of random selection and random assignment.

9.19 Many different hypothesis tests, one research question: Consider the study that you designed in Exercise 9.18 to test whether the Edible Schoolyard program reduces obesity.

a. How could you conduct this study so that you would use a *z* test? What information would you need to calculate the test statistic? Be specific. What is one flaw with this type of research design for this question?

b. How could you conduct this study so that you would use a single-sample *t* test? What information would you need to calculate the test statistic? Be specific.

c. How could you conduct this study so that you would use a paired-samples *t* test?

d. From a mathematical standpoint, explain why all these tests are essentially getting at the same thing. (*Hint:* Discuss the denominators and numerators of the various tests.)

9.20 Tying it all together—the shape of a glass and how much we drink: Researchers at the Cornell University Food and Brand Lab conducted an experiment at a fitness camp for adolescents (Wansink & van Ittersum, 2003). Campers were given either a 22-oz. glass that was tall and thin or a 22-oz. glass that was short and wide. Campers with the short glasses tended to pour more soda, milk, or juice than campers with the tall glasses.

a. Is it likely that the researchers used random selection? Explain.

b. Is it likely that the researchers used random assignment? Explain.

c. What is the independent variable, and what are its levels?

d. What is the dependent variable?

e. What hypothesis test would the researchers use? Explain.

f. Conduct step 1 of hypothesis testing.

g. Conduct step 2 of hypothesis testing.

h. How could the researchers redesign this study so that they would use a paired-samples *t* test?

9.21 The language of statistics—*conservative:* In your own words, define the word *conservative* as you would use it in everyday conversation. Provide at least two meanings that might be used, including the political meaning. Then define the word *conservative* as scientists use it.

9.22 The symbols of statistics: Find the error in symbolic notation in each of the following formulas. Explain why it is incorrect and provide the correct symbolic notation.

a. $z = \dfrac{(X - M)}{\sigma}$

b. $X = z(\sigma) - \mu_M$

c. $\sigma_M = \dfrac{\sigma}{\sqrt{N - 1}}$

d. $t = \dfrac{(M - \mu_M)}{\sigma_M}$

■ **DIGGING DEEPER INTO THE DATA**

9.23 Graphing and Stroop reaction times: Here is the Stroop reaction time data set from Chapter 2, but now rounded to one decimal place instead of two.

10.2	11.3	12.1	9.9	12.3
13.1	11.0	14.5	14.4	9.1
12.0	12.5	13.8	13.3	11.7
12.5	15.8	10.1	10.2	11.4
11.9	12.9	17.2	11.8	12.2
10.4	14.1	15.1	12.1	12.9
12.5	12.5	11.7	13.6	14.8
8.1	10.7	12.3	13.1	13.0
15.9	11.6	9.1	15.0	10.6
13.9	13.9	11.2	13.9	12.7

a. Construct a stem-and-leaf plot for these data.

b. Construct a dot plot for these data.

c. What can we learn about this sampling distribution from these graphs?

9.24 Graphing comparisons of means and credit card debt: Below are the amounts of credit card debt reported by 27 men and 23 women.

Men:	0	0	0	0	0	0	0	0	0	0
	0	0	0	0	0	0	0	0	0	0
	0	0	700	2000	3000	3000	3000			

Women:	0	0	0	0	0	0	0	0	0	0
	0	0	0	0	200	600	900	1700	2000	3000
	4000	4500	10,000							

a. Construct side-by-side stem-and-leaf plots for these data. (*Hint:* Here and in part (b), report in hundreds, e.g., 700 will be reported as 7, and 2000 as 20.)

b. Construct side-by-side dot plots for these data.

c. What can we learn about these two distributions from these graphs?

TERMS

t statistic (p. 388)

single-sample *t* test (p. 393)

degrees of freedom (p. 393)

paired-samples *t* test (p. 402)

independent-samples *t* test (p. 406)

pooled variance (p. 410)

stem-and-leaf plot (p. 414)

dot plot (p. 417)

SYMBOLS

s_M

t

df

s^2_{Pooled}

$s^2_{Difference}$

$s_{Difference}$

FORMULAS

$$s = \sqrt{\frac{\Sigma(X - M)^2}{(N - 1)}}$$

$$s_M = \frac{s}{\sqrt{N}}$$

$$t = \frac{(M - \mu_M)}{s_M}$$

$$df = N - 1$$

$$df_{Total} = df_X + df_Y$$

$$s^2_{Pooled} = \left(\frac{df_X}{df_{Total}}\right) s^2_X + \left(\frac{df_Y}{df_{Total}}\right) s^2_Y$$

$$s^2_{M_Y} = \frac{s^2_{Pooled}}{N}$$

$$s^2_{Difference} = s^2_{M_X} + s^2_{M_Y}$$

$$s_{Difference} = \sqrt{s^2_{Difference}}$$

$$t = \frac{(M_X - M_Y) - (\mu_X - \mu_Y)}{s_{Difference}}$$

CHAPTER TEN

HYPOTHESIS TESTING WITH ONE-WAY ANOVA
COMPARING THREE OR MORE GROUPS

> WHEN TO USE AN *F* DISTRIBUTION: WORKING WITH MORE THAN TWO SAMPLES

More than 5000 men applied for the voyage to Antarctica, but only 28 would make the final trip. The leader of the expedition was Ernest Shackleton, and their scientific mission was to sail to Antarctica, establish supply camps, collect geological specimens, study fauna, and make meteorological observations. They would begin at the Weddell Sea, using dog sleds first to get to the South Pole and then to continue across the continent. The British public was so inspired by this grand adventure that schoolchildren raised money to purchase dogs, which were named after the sponsoring schools.

Tragically, World War I broke out on July 28, 1914. Shackleton offered both ship and crew to the British Admiralty for war service. But England anticipated only a brief, glorious war, and Winston Churchill insisted that they proceed with the expedition. Eleven days later, what may be the most successful failure in the history of exploration began its long journey from England. Their ship was rightly named the *Endurance*. Every leg of their journey required an extraordinary measure of psychological toughness and physical stamina, traits that were exemplified by their leader. In the events that unfolded, Shackleton and his crew demonstrated what positive psychology (Eid & Morgan, 2006; Maddi, 2006) now recognizes as the trait that encourages the very best in human endurance: resiliency.

The *Endurance*
Resiliency was the personality trait that helped Ernest Shackleton and his crew survive their ill-fated journey on the ship *Endurance*.

Almost 100 years after Shackleton's valiant voyage, clinical and health psychologists recognize that resiliency (also known in the psychological literature as hardiness) is a potentially life-saving psychological variable that we would like to define, measure, and validate. Why? Resiliency serves as both a buffer against stress and a health-promoting personality trait in a world of increasing threat. Many people will benefit as researchers learn how to articulate and measure resiliency. Therapists can better treat post-traumatic stress disorder (PTSD), depression, and anxiety. Families can better nurture children, who then will be better equipped to cope with everyday living. Sir Ernest Henry Shackleton may be our human model of resiliency, but it takes a statistical model of resiliency to articulate and distribute its many benefits.

Understanding the benefits of a resilient personality would take far longer than necessary if we could only compare two levels of a variable at a time. For example, we might want to make a three-group comparison testing whether authoritarian, authoritative, or permissive parenting styles best nurture resiliency. A single three-group comparison would be a much better use of our time and resources than conducting three separate, two-group studies. Furthermore, it could be useful to compare resiliency among four or more very different cultures. Multiple comparisons could also help us understand the consequences of overwhelming stress and its effects on PTSD.

So, as we expand our ability to analyze two groups with a *t* test, it is helpful to understand that the tests based on the *z* distribution, the *t* distributions, and the *F* distributions (which you learn about in this chapter) are all variations on a familiar theme: the reliable characteristics of the normal, bell-shaped curve. These three distributions are like progressively more complex versions of the Swiss Army knife. We noted in Chapter 9 that the *z* test is akin to a Swiss Army knife with only a single blade, whereas the *t* tests are like a Swiss Army knife with more than one blade, one of which is the single blade that is the *z* test.

Building on that analogy, the *F* distributions are the most complex of these distributions and allow you to do the most varied types of statistical analyses, just as the most expensive Swiss Army knife allows you to do the most different things with it. Think of the *F* distributions as an elaborate Swiss Army knife that includes the single-blade knife that represents the *z* distribution, the multi-bladed knife that represents the *t* distributions, and then even more tools that make it much more versatile. And just as the *z* distribution is still part of the *t* distributions, the *t* distributions are also part of the *F* distributions; they are all based on the characteristics of the normal bell-shaped curve.

These three tests are all known as parametric tests because they test hypotheses about populations by using interval data. Nonparametric tests also test hypotheses about populations by using nominal or rank-ordered data. The distinction is important because using a parametric test on nonparametric observations (or vice versa) can lead us to a false conclusion—and why bother doing research if we end up believing something to be true when it really isn't? So select the right statistical test for each research situation.

For example, we can use the *z* test only when we know the mean and standard deviation of an entire population. The *t* test is more flexible and, among other things, allows us to analyze variables in a two-group design. And the hypothesis test that uses the F distributions, the analysis of variance (ANOVA), is often appropriate when we have anything more elaborate than a two-group design. Not surprisingly, much advanced research involves the F distributions, so, in preparation for learning about the F distributions, let's recall some of the things we have accomplished prior to this chapter. They are quite impressive, and there is a pattern emerging that we can apply to the F distributions.

1. We have learned that standardized z distributions of scores and of means can be represented as percentile rankings.

2. We have demonstrated that the t distributions of means can also be standardized, as can t distributions of mean differences and t distributions of differences between means; this enables us to analyze the differences between two means.

3. We have discovered that both statistics—the z and the t—may be calculated by dividing a numerator by a denominator.

4. We have observed that the numerator describes some kind of difference (between scores, between means, between mean differences, or between differences between means).

5. We have noted that the denominator represents some measure of variability; that is, some variation on a standard deviation.

Notice the pattern in items 3, 4, and 5. The statistic is calculated simply by dividing a numerator that represents the difference between groups by a denominator that represents the variability within the groups. Think about how simple and intuitive that is: between-groups variability/within-groups variability. For example, men are, on average, a little taller than women are, on average. Well, that's between-groups variability. Yet not all men are the same height and not all women are the same height. That's within-groups variability. As you have noticed, there is considerable overlap between the two distributions. Even though men are, on average, taller than women are, on average, there are many women who are taller than many men.

The bottom line is that there are both differences *between* groups of people and differences *within* groups of people. Uniting these two types of differences within a single equation is especially appealing because the F distributions allow us to analyze far more complex situations by including more than just two levels of a variable. The F distributions allow us to compare three, four, five, six, and many more levels of a variable within a single study. If you enjoy unraveling the mysteries of human behavior, then the versatile F statistic is just the tool for you.

z, t, and F Distributions
The z, t, and F distributions are three increasingly complex variations on one great idea: the normal curve.

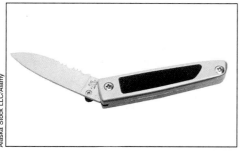

■ **ANOVA** is a hypothesis test typically used with one or more nominal independent variables (with at least three groups overall) and an interval dependent variable.

■ The **F statistic** is a ratio of two measures of variance: (1) between-groups variance, which indicates differences among sample means, and (2) within-groups variance, which is essentially an average of the sample variances.

■ **Between-groups variance** is an estimate of the population variance based on the differences among the means.

Symbol: **F** refers to a statistic that allows for a comparison of more than two means. It is calculated as a ratio of between-groups to within-groups variance.

A Mnemonic for When to Use a *t* Distribution or an *F* Distribution: *t* for Two

In Chapter 9, we suggested an easy way to remember when to use the *t* distributions: The letter *t*. The *t* test is used only for *two*-group comparisons. For example, if we want to compare the amount of yeast in two different samples of ale, we use a *t* test. If we want to compare the winning percentages of the Yankees and the Red Sox across the many years of their baseball rivalry, we use a *t* test. However, if we want to compare the amount of yeast in *three or more* different samples of ale, we use an *F* distribution and conduct an analysis of variance (ANOVA). *ANOVA* (pronounced "ah-**noe**-vah," with the emphasis on the second syllable) *is a hypothesis test typically used with one or more nominal independent variables (with at least three groups overall) and an interval dependent variable.* So, if we want to compare the Yankees and Red Sox, plus the Chicago Cubs (sigh), we use ANOVA. The *t* distributions are only used for two-group comparisons—anything more complicated than that requires the use of the *F* distributions.

The *F* Distributions: Analyzing Variability to Compare Means

Calculating the between-groups variability of the *t* test is relatively easy because all you're really doing is subtracting to obtain a number that represents how far apart the two distributions are. But when we have more than two groups, we can't just subtract one mean from another to find the numerator. Instead, we must turn to an *F* distribution to obtain a number that will estimate the variability among the numbers. The *F* statistic achieves the same outcome as the *z* statistic and the *t* statistic: an estimate of between-groups variability. But it calculates between-groups variability in a slightly different way. Rather than a difference calculated by simple subtraction and then division by a measure of variability, *F* is a ratio of two measures of variability. Specifically, *the F statistic is a ratio of two measures of variance: (1) between-groups variance, which indicates differences among sample means, and (2) within-groups variance, which is essentially an average of the sample variances.*

$$F = \frac{\text{between-groups variance}}{\text{within-groups variance}}$$

So let's think through the basic logic of the calculation of an *F* statistic. For now, the description of the calculations will be simplified to emphasize the logic of the *F* distributions.

First, let's consider how we calculate the numerator in the *F* ratio, the part of the formula that specifies differences between groups. We cannot subtract one mean from another when we have several means, yet we still want to know how different the means are from one another. The clever solution that past statisticians have devised is to determine the variability (the spread) among the three (or more) means. If there is a great deal of spread among several means, that suggests there is a difference among them. If there is not much, or no, spread among the means, that suggests there is no reliable difference among them. So, to determine the numerator, we calculate the variance among the means of the samples of interest. We call this variance *the **between-groups variance** because it is an estimate of the population variance based on the differences among the means.*

For example, if we wanted to compare how fast people talk in Philadelphia, Memphis, Chicago, and San Diego, then the between-groups (in this case, the between-cities) variance is an estimate of the variability among the average number of words per minute spoken by the people representing each of those four cities. We use the arithmetic average in these calculations; that is, the mean. The more different the average talking speeds of these four samples, the larger the between-cities variance. The difference, or variance, will be represented in the numerator.

The denominator of the F statistic is similar to the denominators of the z and t statistics. Instead of calculating a version of standard deviation, however, we calculate a version of variance. This variance is called *the **within-groups variance*** because it *is an estimate of the population variance based on the differences within each of the three (or more) sample distributions.* For example, not everyone living in Philadelphia speaks at the same pace. Neither does everyone living in Memphis, Chicago, or San Diego. There are within-city differences in talking speeds, so within-groups variance refers to the average of the amounts of variability within each city. Within-groups variance is essentially an average of the four variances, one for each city. The between-groups differences among the means of the four cities are not taken into account in this within-groups estimate of the variability of talking speeds in each city.

To calculate the F statistic, we simply divide the between-groups variance by the within-groups variance. If the between-groups variance is much larger than the within-groups variance, then we can infer that the sample means are different from one another. (Remember, between-groups variance is based on the differences among the means; within-groups variance is unaffected by differences among the means.) On the other hand, if the between-groups variance is similar to the within-groups variance, then we cannot infer that the sample means are different from one another. We use the F table to determine whether the difference among our means, as compared to the difference within the means, is extreme enough to reject the null hypothesis and conclude that there is a difference. The variability used to calculate F is simply a way of measuring how more than two groups vary from one another. The z, t, and F statistics represent the same idea: between-groups variability divided by within-groups variability.

To summarize these concepts, we can think of within-groups variance as reflecting the difference between means that we'd expect just by chance. There is variability within any population, and so we would expect some difference among means just by chance. Between-groups variance reflects the difference between means that we found in our data. If this is much larger than the within-groups variance, what we'd expect by chance, then we can reject the null hypothesis and conclude that there is some difference between means.

> ▪ **Within-groups variance** is an estimate of the population variance based on the differences within each of the three (or more) sample distributions.

Relation of *F* to *t* (and *z*): *F* as a Squared *t* for Two Groups (and Large Samples)

The relation among these three distributions is both mathematical and conceptual. When we divide the between-groups variance by the within-groups variance, we parallel the structure of the z and t statistics: difference between means divided by a measure of variability. As we saw, the F is a measure of the variability among samples as compared to the variability within samples. The z statistic and the t statistic simply calculate this identical conceptual relation with slightly different formulas.

Because of the similar structure of the test statistic calculations, the F table is essentially an expansion of the t table. In the previous chapter, we explained that there are many t distributions—one for each possible sample size. Similarly, there are many F distributions represented in the F table. Like the t table, the F table includes several extreme probabilities and the range of sample sizes, represented by degrees of freedom. But it also includes a third factor, the number of samples. The number of samples is unnecessary for the t table because there cannot be more than two samples if a t statistic has been used. There is an F distribution for every possible combination of sample size, represented by one type of degrees of freedom, and number of samples, represented by another type of degrees of freedom.

If we look in the F table under two samples (Between-Groups Degrees of Freedom of 1), we'll find the same numbers that we see in the t table—except that they're squared. F is based on variance and t, on standard deviation; this means that if we take the square root of the F for a two-group comparison, it will match the t exactly (just as if we take the square root of variance, it will match the standard deviation exactly). Moreover, if we look in the F table under two samples for a sample size of infinity, we'll find the square of the same number that we see in the z table!

For example, if we look under two samples for a sample size of infinity for the equivalent of the 95th percentile, we see 2.71. If we take the square root of this, we get 1.646. We can find 1.645 on the z table for the 95th percentile and on the t table for the 95th percentile with a sample size of infinity. (The slight differences are due only to rounding decisions.) Like Swiss Army knives, the small z distribution is part of the larger—but still small—tool that is the family of t distributions, which in turn is part of the larger tool that is the family of F distributions. These connections are summarized in Table 10-1.

When we learn how to use the F table later in this chapter, you will be able to use all three tables—z, t, and F—to verify the connections among the distributions for yourself. In the meantime, you may wonder why there are three types of distributions when we really need only one. Well, this, too, is tied to the peculiar history of statistics. Perhaps someday we will no longer have z and t distributions, but there are two reasons that they continue to be widely used. The first reason is that it is easier to learn hypothesis testing when we build from the simple z test to the more sophisticated ANOVA. We learn to consider exactly what kinds of distributions our samples form, and we learn to visualize the distributions to which our samples will be compared.

TABLE 10-1. CONNECTIONS AMONG DISTRIBUTIONS

The z distribution is subsumed under the t distributions in certain specific circumstances, and both the z and t distributions are subsumed under the F distributions in certain specific circumstances.

	WHEN USED	LINKS AMONG THE DISTRIBUTIONS
z	One sample; μ and σ are known	Subsumed under the t and F distributions
t	(1) One sample: only μ is known (2) Two samples	Same as z distribution if there is a sample size of ∞ (or just very large).
F	Three or more samples	Square of z distribution if there are only two samples and a sample size of ∞ (or just very large); square of t distribution if there are only two samples

The second reason, however, is the primary reason we continue to use all three distributions. Before computers made calculations instantaneous and effortless, researchers in the various behavioral sciences spent countless hours analyzing their data by hand or using basic calculators. In such cases, it made sense to use the simplest tool available. If those researchers only needed a z statistic, then they would have been foolish to calculate the more time-consuming F statistic. The legacy of the early researchers is that current researchers use the simplest test available, even though computers have since made it just as easy for us to use the sophisticated F statistic for all comparisons of means.

In summary, the three main properties of the normal curve can be applied to several related distributions. The F statistic is essentially an expansion of the z statistic and the t statistic that can be used to compare more than two samples. Similar to the z statistic and the t statistic, the F statistic is a ratio of a difference between means (in this case, using a measure of variability) to a measure of variability within samples. The z, t, and F are closely related distributions. The t is a z when the sample size is extremely large. The F is a squared t when there are only two samples, and the F is a squared z when there are two samples and the sample size is extremely large. Although we could use the F statistic in lieu of the t or z, we continue to learn to use all three both because it facilitates learning to move from a simpler to a more complicated test, and because in the early years of statistics, when calculations were done by hand, it made more sense to calculate the simplest statistic.

⊙ CHECK YOUR LEARNING

10-1 Again consider the research on multitasking that we explored in Chapter 9 (Mark, Gonzalez, & Harris, 2005). Let's say we compared three conditions to see which one would lead to the quickest return to working on a task following an interruption. In one condition, the control group, no changes are made to their working environment. In the second condition, a communication ban is instituted from 1:00 to 3:00. In the third condition, a communication ban is instituted from 11:00 to 3:00. We recorded the time, in minutes, until work on an interrupted task was resumed.

   a. What type of distribution will be used in this situation? Explain your answer.

   b. In your own words, explain how we would calculate between-groups variance. Focus on the logic rather than the calculations.

   c. In your own words, explain how we would calculate within-groups variance. Focus on the logic rather than the calculations.

   d. If between-groups variance were 8.6 and within-groups variance were 3.7, what would the test statistic be?

> ANALYSIS OF VARIANCE: BEYOND t TESTS

Ernest Shackleton and his crew began to look for a way into the Weddell Sea so they could begin their glorious trans-Antarctic mission. But the ice was unusually thick that year. They fought through the ice floes, but occasionally the *Endurance* became hemmed in by the ice and they would have to wait until the ice pack shifted. Shackleton let the men hunt for seals and play football on the

Corbis

**How Resilient Would
You Be?**
Ernest Shackleton and his
crew had to overcome nu-
merous difficulties, including
sea leopards who confused
them with seals, tracked their
shadows, and exploded up-
ward through the ice to hunt
them. Without high levels
of resiliency among most
members, the crew might
not have survived.

ice, at least until Frank Worsley was barely rescued after falling through softening ice and the
crew discovered that sea leopards were stalk-
ing them as food from beneath the thin ice so
that they could explode upward and attack
them. Winter was approaching. Their ship was
frozen fast, and the excitement of the great adventure was quickly giving way to greater anxiety. The crew of the *Endurance* began taking
the measure of their own endurance, as well as
that of their ship and their leader.

The crew chipped ice, fought to keep the
ship's rudder free, and desperately hoped for a
break in the weather. According to their diaries, a small break suddenly appeared
in the ice on January 24, 1915. Shackleton immediately set sail, put the steam
engine at full speed—and made no real progress. When their coal supply began to run low, Shackleton accepted their temporary fate. He ordered the steam
engine shut down to preserve their remaining fuel, and the crew settled in for
the long winter firmly in the grip of Antarctic ice.

Shackleton anticipated the fearful decisions he might have to make, applying statistical reasoning to a nonstatistical situation. If they lost their ship, the
strategic composition of each lifeboat needed to include men who could get
along with each other well enough to rotate rowing duties, stay awake during
their watch, share diminishing fresh water and food, navigate their boat independently if needed, confront rogue waves, negotiate dangerous reefs, and wait
through freezing nights for winds to abate. Shackleton was using statistical reasoning as he considered how to man three separate boats of different sizes and
seaworthiness (between-boats variance) that would carry crews composed of men
with different personalities and different needs (within-boats variance). Their
shared dependent variable was plain and simple: survival.

Shackleton could not predict if, or when, the ice might heave and suddenly
crush the *Endurance*. On October 27, 1915, he ordered the men to abandon
ship, and they began shifting their gear and their three small lifeboats onto the
ice. The first, the *Stancomb Wills*, could carry 8 men. The second, the *Dudley
Docker*, could carry 9 men. The third, the *James Caird*, could carry the remaining 11 men. For now, they were safe on the ice, but Shackleton had to decide
whether they should wait for the ice to break up in the warmer weather or try
to find a way to open water so they could begin their long journey home.
Meanwhile, the thick planking of the *Endurance* began to bend and split.

They waited. The crew and their damaged ship drifted north as the weather
warmed. The ice was softening and slowly becoming "rotten"—just one more
random threat to their survival. They fashioned a canvas chute from the ship
down to the ice to off-load the remaining supplies. The original plan was to
drag two of their three boats 350 miles over the ice until it broke up, and then
sail them through open water to tiny Paulet Island. It would be like walking
across icy randomness. The ice pack was a massive, shifting jigsaw puzzle that
could separate or swallow them without warning. Yet critical decisions still had
to be made because their floating home of ice was beginning to melt. They began their journey but soon discovered that their plan could not succeed, so they
re-established camp near the *Endurance* and waited for their ship to die.

Eventually, the ice heaved yet again and wrecked the *Endurance* beyond hope
of ever sailing again. Lansing (1960) wrote that as "the killing pressure mounted

... her timbers could no longer stand the strain, they broke with a report like artillery fire" (p. 2). On November 21, 1915, James Hurley was watching the ship when the smokestack suddenly shifted downward. "She's going down!" he shouted, and 28 men watched their crippled home disappear beneath the ice. Forward-looking decisions had to be made in a new and profoundly uncertain world. But that night Shackleton recorded only one short sentence in his diary: "I cannot write about it."

No single variable can explain why an individual is more or less resilient. Examining a complex personality trait such as resiliency may require more sophisticated statistical methods than a *t* test because a *t* test can explore only two levels of one independent variable. We could use a *t* test, for example, to compare levels of resiliency under two conditions of stress: low stress versus high stress. But we couldn't use a *t* test to compare levels of resiliency under three conditions, such as low stress, moderate stress, and high stress. For any research design that includes more than two levels of an independent variable, we must use a more versatile statistical analysis: analysis of variance (ANOVA).

The Randomness of an Antarctic Ice Floe
Researchers use hypothesis testing to help them make sense out of seemingly random data.

The Problem of Too Many *t* Tests: Fishing for a Finding

When a research design has more than two groups, it is tempting to evaluate the differences between those groups by simply conducting a *t* test on each of the possible comparisons. But it can be unwise to conduct numerous *t* tests to compare more than two samples. The probability of a Type I error (rejecting the null hypothesis when the null hypothesis is true) greatly increases along with the number of comparisons. ANOVA provides a way to test differences among more than two groups in just one test, increasing confidence in our findings. Let's use an example related to career counseling and the Consideration of Future Consequences (CFC) scale to learn how multiple comparisons, such as many *t* tests, inflate the possibility of making Type I error.

Imagine that a university career center director, Dr. Khoury, has asked a randomly selected sample of the undergraduates at his institution to complete the CFC scale. He used stratified random sampling, selecting the same number in the freshman, sophomore, junior, and senior classes. He has hypothesized that CFC scores would change over the four years of a university education and wants to compare the four levels of the independent variable, year in school, with one another. How many comparisons would he have to make?

freshman—sophomore

freshman—junior

freshman—senior

sophomore—junior

sophomore—senior

junior—senior

That's 6 comparisons. If Dr. Khoury had five groups (by adding on high school seniors), that would mean 10 comparisons. With six groups (say, by adding first-year graduate students), that would mean 15 comparisons, and so on. With the original four groups, the null hypothesis is that average CFC scores are the same

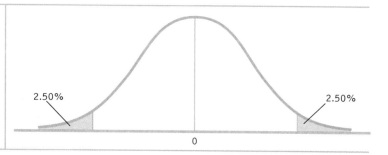

FIGURE 10-1
Extreme Means Sometimes Occur by Chance

If the null hypothesis is true, some sample means will be extreme just by chance: 5% will fall beyond the cutoffs *if* the null hypothesis is true. If we conduct enough hypothesis tests, eventually we'll be able to reject the null hypothesis—just by chance—even if the null hypothesis is true.

2.50%   2.50%

0

for all four undergraduate classes. The research hypothesis is that, on average, at least one group is different from the others. Were Dr. Khoury to use independent-samples *t* tests to tackle this problem within four groups, he'd have to conduct six *t* tests, one for each pair. If the null hypothesis is true and there really are no differences among the groups, then all four samples come from a population with the same mean; if the samples had the same mean as the population, then each mean difference would be 0. That sampling distribution of differences between means is shown in Figure 10-1. As we can see, extreme differences (those far from 0) are rare but certainly possible. In fact, sometimes they even occur by chance. When we decide to use a *p* level of 0.05, then 5% of the time we'll get a difference between means extreme enough to reject the null hypothesis just by chance when we actually should *not* reject the null hypothesis. When this happens, we make a Type I error, rejecting the null hypothesis when there is no actual difference.

Now let's apply this same reasoning to the probability of Type I errors, keeping in mind that we would prefer, if somehow possible, not to make any decision errors. As we mentioned, with a *p* level of 0.05, there is a 0.05 chance of a Type I error in any given analysis if the null hypothesis is true and therefore a 0.95 chance of *not* having a Type I error when the null hypothesis is true. These are pretty good odds, and we would tend to believe the conclusions in that study. What if we conduct more analyses, however? What are the chances of not having a Type I error on the first *and* not having a Type I error on the second? In the world of probability calculations, the word *and* indicates multiplication.

TABLE 10-2. THE PROBABILITY OF A TYPE I ERROR INCREASES AS THE NUMBER OF STATISTICAL COMPARISONS INCREASES

As the number of samples increases, the number of *t* tests necessary to compare every possible pair of means increases at an even greater rate. And with that, the probability of a Type I error quickly becomes far larger than 0.05.

NUMBER OF MEANS	NUMBER OF COMPARISONS	PROBABILITY OF A TYPE I ERROR
2	1	0.05
3	3	0.143
4	6	0.265
5	10	0.401
6	15	0.537
7	21	0.659

When we want to know what the chances are that two things will occur, we multiply the chances that each will occur. For example, if the null hypothesis is true, the chance of not having a Type I error on the first analysis *and* the second analysis is the product of the chance of each occurrence: $(0.95)(0.95) = (0.95)^2 = 0.903$. Those are almost 5% lower odds. Expressed another way, there is a $(1 - 0.903) = 0.097$ chance (almost 10%) of having at least one Type I error if we run two analyses.

And if we run six analyses? The chance of escaping six analyses without a Type I error, if the null hypothesis is true, is the chance of no Type I error on the first *and* no Type I error on the second *and* no Type I error on the third and so on. For six times, the calculation is $(0.95)(0.95)(0.95)(0.95)(0.95)(0.95) = (0.95)^6 = 0.735$. Therefore, the chance of having at least one Type I error is $(1 - 0.735) = 0.265$, or 26.5%. As you can see, the chance of a Type I error becomes increasingly higher than 0.05 as we add additional comparisons. Table 10-2 shows the chances of at least one Type I error, if the null hypothesis is true, for the numbers of t tests that would be required as the number of samples increases. As you can see, the probability of a Type I error increases quite a bit as the number of samples increases.

Researchers refer to the scattershot hypothesis testing involved in running multiple t tests as fishing, and statisticians today certainly view the findings from such an expedition as fishy. As Bernstein (1996) puts it in his book tracing the history of the calculation of risk, "If you torture the data long enough, the numbers will prove anything you want" (p. 161). So if we conduct many hypothesis tests, eventually we are likely to reject the null hypothesis—just by chance—even if there are no real differences. But science is not interested in torturing the data. Instead, statisticians developed ANOVA to help us minimize the probability of making such Type I errors.

Phil Schermeister/Corbis

A Fisher of Data
When a researcher is arbitrarily analyzing a mountain of data without regard to specific hypotheses, it's often referred to pejoratively as fishing and the results might be derided as fishy. The lazy researcher fishes; the careful researcher targets his or her analyses.

THE PROBABILITY OF 'FOUR OF A KIND' FAMILIES

EXPERIENCE IT FOR YOURSELF

You can experience for yourself how multiple trials affect the probability of a particular event. Imagine a couple who hope to have a family with at least one girl. Assume that the probability of having either a girl or a boy is 0.5 (50/50).

On the first "trial" (she's pregnant!), you ask:

What is the probability that they will *not* have a girl? _____

On the second "trial" (she's pregnant again!), you ask:

What is the probability that they will *not* have a girl? _____

The probability for each of these separate events is 0.5. In other words, there is a 50% chance of not having a girl at each pregnancy. As we mentioned previously, the word *and* indicates multiplication. So when we want to know what the chances are that this couple will not have a girl on the first trial *and* on the second trial, we multiply the two probabilities.

Based on two pregnancies, you ask:

What is the probability that they will not have a girl after two pregnancies?

_____

We simply multiply 0.50 by 0.50: $(0.50)(0.50) = (0.50)^2 = 0.25$. And this makes sense. There is a 25% (or one-in-four) chance that they will not have a girl, which means that if they have two children, there is a $(1 - 0.25) = 0.75$ chance that they will have at least one girl.

Many young couples naturally think about such probabilities as they plan their lives. If they intend to have a small family, they don't even need mathematics to calculate the odds of having at least one girl. They can use letter symbols to sketch out the probabilities. For two children, there are four combinations of boy (B) and girl (G) babies that they can have: BB, GG, BG, and GB. Only one of these four combinations (25%) includes no girl (BB). Or, if you prefer, three out of four (75%) include at least one girl.

> Now calculate the chances that they will not have a girl after four pregnancies.

> There are too many possible combinations of Bs and Gs to conveniently visualize the possibilities, so use a mathematical approach: _____

We now multiply 0.50 by 0.50 by 0.50 by 0.50: $(0.50)(0.50)(0.50)(0.50) = (0.50)^4 = 0.0625$. There's a 6.25% chance that they will not have a girl, and a $(1 - 0.0625) = 0.9375$ chance that they will have at least one girl. The probability of having at least one girl increases with additional trials (in this case, pregnancies).

Here's an interesting pair of questions. One of the authors has four daughters but no sons.

> What is the probability of a family of four daughters? _____

> Do you consider this to be an unusual event? Why or why not? _____

Your sense of how unusual it is for a family to have four children of the same gender needs to be understood in context. It may seem like a relatively rare event, but given the sheer number of families, it is likely to happen to somebody! You might ask your classmates how many of them know of a family with "four of a kind," all boys or all girls. Mathematically, we would expect a family with four children to have no boys $(0.50)(0.50)(0.50)(0.50) = 0.0625$, or 6.25%, of the time. That's 6.25% of the time that a family of four will have *all* girls. This is the same as the probability of having no girls that we calculated earlier; that is, 6.25% of the time, a family of four will have *all* boys.

So what is the probability that a family of four will have all boys or all girls? With probability theory, when we use the word *or*—as in the previous sentence—we add probabilities, just as we multiply when we use the word *and*. The probability that a family will have all boys *or* all girls, then, is $0.0625 + 0.0625 = 0.125$; 12.5% of the time, a family of four will include all boys or all girls. If you were to survey 10 classmates who come from families of four children, chances are at least one will have "four of a kind," composed of either four boys or four girls.

The probability of any random event occurring is affected by the number of trials (often called events; in this case, pregnancies). This principle of probability applies whether it is the probability of having at least one girl among a family of four children or the probability of a Type I error in a statistical analysis. Understanding how to calculate probabilities can help you understand why multiple comparisons, like multiple pregnancies, increase the odds of a having a statistically significant finding simply by chance.

The Assumptions for ANOVA: The Ideal Conditions for the Perfect Study

In this chapter, we'll focus on a particular kind of ANOVA, but we can help you by getting you comfortable with the language that statisticians use (Landrum, 2005) to describe ANOVAs in general. When naming a particular type of ANOVA, statisticians describe the research design that guides the statistical analysis. So, the word *ANOVA* is almost always preceded by two adjectives, one indicating the number of independent variables and one indicating whether the participants are in one condition (between-groups) or all conditions (within-groups). In this chapter, we'll learn how to conduct an ANOVA with just one independent variable. For example, we might conduct a study with a year in school as the independent variable and CFC scores as the dependent variable. There is just one independent variable, year in school, but it has more than two levels, so we cannot use an independent-samples *t* test; rather, we must use an ANOVA. An ANOVA that analyzes a study with just one independent variable is called a one-way ANOVA. *A **one-way ANOVA** is a hypothesis test that includes one nominal independent variable with more than two levels, and an interval dependent variable.*

A one-way ANOVA can have one of two research designs, one in which all participants are in all levels of the independent variable and one in which participants are in only one level of the independent variable. When participants are in all levels, we are using a within-groups design: *A **within-groups ANOVA** is a hypothesis test in which there are more than two samples, and each sample is composed of the same participants.* This test is also called a *repeated-measures ANOVA.* The descriptor *within-groups* refers to a research design in which all participants are in all groups, and *repeated-measures* refers to the fact that participants complete the same dependent measure in more than one condition. These terms are used interchangeably. We'll learn more about this type of ANOVA in Chapter 11.

When participants are in only one level of the independent variable, we are using a between-groups design. *A **between-groups ANOVA** is a hypothesis test in which there are more than two samples, and each sample is composed of different participants.* For a comparison of CFC scores across years in school, participants can be in only one level of the independent variable. In this chapter, we'll focus on the between-groups ANOVA. As we said earlier, though, ANOVAs are always described by two adjectives. The ANOVA used to analyze the study that compares CFC scores across years in school would have two adjectives: *one-way* and *between-groups.* It would be a one-way between-groups ANOVA. Regardless of the type of ANOVA, they all share the same assumptions. We'll start the process of learning how to conduct a one-way between-groups ANOVA by learning the assumptions for ANOVA in general.

The assumptions for ANOVA represent the optimal conditions for a valid analysis of the results. Every study has its flaws, but the difficulty of creating the perfect study doesn't mean that we shouldn't continue to try. With all parametric hypothesis testing, for example, the first assumption is that the sample should be randomly selected from all members of the population. Second, the population distributions for the samples should be normal. Third, the populations from which the samples are drawn should have the same spread, usually as measured by variance. Researchers frequently violate these assumptions because the ANOVA, like *z* and *t* tests, is robust against violations of these assumptions. However, this does not mean that we pretend that those violations did not occur.

■ A **one-way ANOVA** is a hypothesis test that includes one nominal independent variable with more than two levels, and an interval dependent variable.

■ A **within-groups ANOVA** is a hypothesis test in which there are more than two samples, and each sample is composed of the same participants; also called a *repeated-measures ANOVA.*

■ A **between-groups ANOVA** is a hypothesis test in which there are more than two samples, and each sample is composed of different participants.

We sometimes tell our students that describing the results of statistical analyses in the Results section of a research report could be the most honest thing they have ever done. We don't mean to imply that our students are chronically dishonest, but rather that the rules of science are scrupulously honest. If the conclusions of a study might be jeopardized by a huge deviation from the assumptions, then researchers either report and justify their decision to violate those assumptions in the write-up of their results or choose to conduct a more conservative nonparametric test, such as those we will introduce in Chapter 14. In other words, when researchers have to make a tough judgment call, they don't hide that fact—they report it! Let's consider each of the three assumptions and the impact of violating them.

The first assumption, that our samples are selected randomly, is necessary if we want to generalize beyond our sample. As with all hypothesis tests, if the study participants are not selected randomly, then our external validity—our ability to generalize beyond our sample—is limited. Because it is often impossible from a practical standpoint to use random selection, most researchers use ANOVA even when this assumption is violated. Conscientious researchers explicitly describe the limitations of external validity, usually in the Discussion section of their paper, although they may also refer to the limitations of their sampling technique in the Methods section. They don't hide the problem; they report it.

The second assumption is that the population distribution is normal. As with the hypothesis tests we learned previously, we can examine the distributions of our samples to get a sense of what the underlying population distribution might look like. Moreover, adherence to a normal curve becomes less important as the sizes of our samples increase. It is helpful to look at a graph of the data before proceeding, although such a graph is useful only if the sample is truly representative of the population. Remember, as we discussed in Chapter 2, that if the data are highly skewed, then the mean may not be a good indication of the center of the data. Once again, scientific papers describe their samples well so that reviewers can make the judgment about whether the study is worthy of publication. In other words, if the data are skewed, then researchers don't hide that fact; they report it.

The third assumption is that the samples all come from populations with the same variances, an assumption called homoscedasticity. *Homoscedastic populations are those that have the same variance.* *Heteroscedastic populations are those that have different variances.* (Note that homoscedasticity is also often called *homogeneity of variance*.) We hope that the sample variances are quite similar (homoscedastic), but in real-life research we often find that the variances are quite different (heteroscedastic), particularly with smaller samples. And you know what to do if your data are heteroscedastic: report it.

A good test of whether it is wise to proceed with ANOVA in light of the assumption of equal variances is to examine the smallest and largest sample variances. If the sample sizes are equal, and the largest variance is no more than five times the smallest, then it is usually safe to proceed. If the sample sizes are not equal, then the test is usually accurate as long as the largest variance is no more than twice the smallest variance. Table 10-3 outlines the assumptions for ANOVA and provides information about when it is permissible to violate the assumptions.

When you consider all these assumptions, the degree to which they are violated, and the several other cautions about not overinterpreting results, you may wonder how the knowledge base in the behavioral sciences manages to increase year after year. And the best answer to that question is "slowly." Our knowledge

■ **Homoscedastic** populations are those that have the same variance; homoscedasticity is also called *homogeneity of variance*.

■ **Heteroscedastic** populations are those that have different variances.

TABLE 10-3. THE ASSUMPTIONS FOR ANOVA: LEARNING AND BENDING THE RULES

We must be aware of the assumptions for ANOVA, and we must be cautious in proceeding with a hypothesis test when our data may not meet all of the assumptions.

LEARNING THE RULES: ASSUMPTIONS	BREAKING THE RULES: WHEN IT IS OK
Data are selected randomly.	OK if cautious about generalizing.
Population is normally distributed.	Usually OK, especially with large sample sizes.
Variances are equal (homoscedasticity, or homogeneity of variance).	*Same-size samples:* OK if largest variance is less than 5 times the smallest.
	Different-size samples: OK if largest variance is less than twice the smallest.

base about human behavior increases by many small increments, with occasional bursts of insight and activity. One study gives us a little more confidence in one area, while another study reduces our confidence that we know what's going on in another area. Because we are chronic skeptics and critical thinkers, we are reluctant to believe even our own studies. Nevertheless, we keep trying to conduct the perfect study, partly for the thrill of trying but also because the costs of ignorance and the persistence of our curiosity continually propel us forward.

In summary, it can be dangerous to conduct numerous t tests to compare more than two samples because the probability of a Type I error greatly increases with the number of samples. Analysis of variance (ANOVA) provides a way to test differences among more than two groups in just one test, increasing confidence in our findings. There are many different types of ANOVA, but in this chapter, we're going to focus on the one-way between-groups ANOVA, an analysis in which there is one independent variable with at least three levels and in which different participants are in each level of the independent variable. The assumptions for ANOVA are that participants are randomly selected, the populations from which the samples are drawn are normally distributed, and the populations of the groups have the same variance (an assumption known as homoscedasticity).

⊙ CHECK YOUR LEARNING

10-2 Near the beginning of this chapter, we described Dr. Khoury's fictional study comparing CFC scores across the four years in college: freshman, sophomore, junior, and senior.

a. In your own words, explain why this is a one-way ANOVA.

b. In your own words, explain why this is a between-groups ANOVA.

c. How could Dr. Khoury redesign this study so that it would be a one-way within-groups ANOVA?

> THE ONE-WAY BETWEEN-GROUPS ANOVA: APPLYING THE SIX STEPS OF HYPOTHESIS TESTING

Shackleton's initial decision to drag two lifeboats 350 miles across heaving ice had been a bad one—but he learned from it and he learned quickly. Needing to find a way off the rotting ice, Shackleton had chosen speed over endurance in an effort to reach open water. When explaining the plan to the crew, he emphasized the importance of traveling light and threw his remaining personal items onto the ice—including his gold coins. Then he ripped a solitary page from his Bible, put it in his pocket, laid the book on the ice, and walked away. As the strange-looking pile grew higher, the only nonessential items the men insisted on taking were photographic equipment, their diaries and a 12-pound banjo. Dragging the lifeboats, they had averaged one mile per day. It had been a dramatic, emotional decision to sacrifice endurance for speed, yet Shackleton abandoned his plan almost immediately when he saw that it wasn't working. Instead, they would have to wait until the melting ice broke up literally beneath their feet. Then, the *Stancomb Wills*, the *Dudley Docker*, and the *James Caird* would have to take 28 men from the edge of the Antarctic back to civilization without any help from a world now consumed by war.

Shackleton's calculations mimicked the logic of ANOVA: between-groups variability divided by within-groups variability. For example, the slightly longer, faster *James Caird* was a whale boat with two masts plus a jib. The *Dudley Docker* carried only a small lug sail, so it was much slower. The *Stancomb Wills* could put up a small mainsail and a jib, so it could outsail the *Dudley Docker*, but not by much. There were wide between-boats differences, especially when comparing the *James Caird* with the other two. The ANOVA is a just a formal way of assigning numbers that describe the kind of situation that Shackleton and his crew faced. The research hypothesis usually proposes that there will be a statistically significant difference between groups, that the between-groups differences will outweigh the within-groups differences. But Shackleton and the crew were trying to minimize those differences. They had a different goal: the survival of each boat and every crew member. Like a good scientist, Shackleton had formed a hypothesis, tested it, and then quickly abandoned it when he learned that dragging the boats was a bad idea.

Shackleton had also decided that their immediate goal would be Paulet Island, but now they watched in misery as their ice floe drifted far past Paulet Island and into warmer waters. When the ice finally broke up, Shackleton reset their goal for Elephant Island, another uninhabited speck on their water-logged map. The men struggled against frostbite, saltwater boils, frozen oars, and slippery decks, but the three tiny boats had at last made it into water. Each boat fought to keep in sight of the others, and several days after leaving their ice floe, one of the men sighted their destination from the peak of an ocean swell. It was an astonishing navigational feat; all 28 men reached shore safely. But they were all malnourished, many appeared to be suffering from stress-related mental illnesses, and some required amputations that were executed with as much care as their conditions allowed. Now Shackleton faced another grim decision: How to reach civilization?

After stocking up on seal and gull meat, Shackleton and five crew members set off in the *James Caird* for South Georgia island, 800 miles across the ocean. The seas washed over them, their sleep was disrupted, and they navigated by the stars from a tiny, rocking boat tossed about on giant ocean swells. Yet 14 days after setting out, they spotted kelp, bird life, and, finally, the black cliffs of South Georgia Island. The exhausted men crash-landed their tiny craft. Unfortunately, it was at the wrong end of an unexplored, mountainous island, still another 17 icy miles from the Stromness whaling station. With two of the six men too ill to travel, Shackleton left with Thomas Crean and Frank Worsley. They picked their way down dangerous, frozen streams and slid blindly into unknown valleys, lost one another and then found each other once again.

But at 6:30 in the morning, 17 months after beginning their grand expedition, the three men heard a steam whistle calling the men at the whaling station to work. As they approached the whaling station from the unexplored interior of the island, two young boys spotted them and ran away. This part of the story ends in a conversation, faithfully recorded in diaries, between the astonished manager of the whaling station and "three funny-looking men." The other three crew members at the opposite end of South Georgia Island were rescued the very next day. But it was to be 105 days of international intrigue, broken engines, stubborn ice floes, and foul weather until the remaining 22 men were rescued from Elephant Island, more than four months after they had waved good-bye to the men aboard the *James Caird*. Twenty-eight men set sail from England for a grand Antarctic adventure; 28 men lost their ship; 28 men returned.

How did they survive against such enormous odds? Among Shackleton's many strengths were his abilities to form a hypothesis, test his hypothesis with action, and then change his mind quickly based on the results. The idea of sliding the boats across the heaving ice had seemed like the best decision at the time, but it almost killed them. Aiming for Paulet Island had also seemed like a sensible plan—until they drifted past it and into more dangerous waters. Shackleton changed his mind easily and often whenever he perceived that his plan wasn't working, the same way that scientists form new hypotheses as a result of statistical feedback. Statistical reasoning coerces creativity; not being able to reject the null hypothesis forces us to hypothesize something new.

Everything About ANOVA but the Calculations: The Six Steps of Hypothesis Testing

Let's apply the principles of ANOVA to hypothesis testing of other ideas that influence our lives. We'll use an ongoing study about how foreign graduate students decide which U.S. institutions to attend to introduce the steps of hypothesis testing for a one-way between-groups ANOVA. We've selected this study for two reasons. First, it anticipates decisions about the future that we know students are facing even as they take this course. Second, it is a relatively easy-to-conduct study that represents ideas that may have profound educational, policy, and economic consequences. It is yet another demonstration that statistics matter.

Catherine Ruby (2006), a doctoral student in the education program at New York University, wondered what factors influenced foreign students' decisions to study at a particular U.S. university. Her interest in this topic sharpened after reading reports that applications from graduate students had decreased in the first few years after the terrorist attacks of September 11, 2001. She was asking a very important question with profound economic consequences: How could U.S. universities compete for the top foreign students?

Cindy Charles/Photo Edit

Criteria in Graduate School Selection and ANOVA

What criteria do foreign students consider when choosing a graduate program in the United States? A doctoral student examined this topic in her dissertation, exploring the effects of a number of factors, including characteristics both of the students and the programs, on the decision-making process. With more than two samples in most analyses, ANOVA was the hypothesis test of choice.

Just as sports franchises compete for the top athletes each year, universities also solicit the highest-achieving students (but with considerably less money). Ruby developed a survey asking current U.S. graduate students who were originally from foreign countries to rate many factors that influenced their decision to attend their current graduate program. As one aspect of her study, Ruby asked them to use a 1–5 rating of the importance of various financial aspects (e.g., availability of scholarships, amount of financial aid) in their decision to attend their university. If you are seriously considering graduate school, how important are these financial aspects in your decision? Would they be more or less important if you chose to attend a university in a different country? Ruby then separated their responses according to the four types of academic programs students were pursuing, programs in Arts and Sciences, Education, Law, and Business.

We can see the outlines of a one-way between-groups ANOVA that uses the importance of financial aspects as the dependent variable. There is one independent variable (type of academic program) and it has four levels (arts and sciences, education, law, and business). It is a between-groups design because each student was earning a degree from one and only one of those programs. And it is an ANOVA because that is precisely what Ruby proposed to do: analyze variance by estimating the variability between the types of programs and dividing it by the variability within the types of programs. The importance scores below are from 17 fictional foreign graduate students. Although the data points are fictional, they have almost the same mean importance ratings of financial aspects as Ruby observed in her actual (much larger) data set.

Arts and sciences: 4, 5, 4, 3, 4

Education   4, 3, 4, 4

Law   3, 3, 2, 3

Business   4, 4, 4, 3

Let's consider the six steps of hypothesis testing in the context of this particular one-way between-groups ANOVA. At this point, we will not calculate the test statistic. We will go through the framework of the test and then learn the calculations in the next section.

Step 1: Identify the populations, distribution, and assumptions.

The first step of hypothesis testing is the identification of the populations to be compared, the comparison distribution, the appropriate test, and its assumptions. Let's summarize Ruby's study with respect to this first step of hypothesis testing.

Summary:

Identification of populations to be compared: Population 1 is all foreign graduate students enrolled in arts and sciences programs in the United States. Population 2 is all foreign graduate students enrolled in education programs in the United States. Population 3 is all foreign graduate students enrolled in law schools in the United States. Population 4 is all foreign graduate students enrolled in business schools in the United States.

The comparison distribution and hypothesis test: The comparison distribution will be an F distribution. The hypothesis test will be a one-way between-groups ANOVA.

Assumptions: The data are not selected randomly, so we must generalize only with caution. We do not know if the underlying population distributions are normal, but the sample data do not indicate severe skew. To see if we meet the homoscedasticity assumption, we will check to see if the variances are equal when we calculate the test statistic (*Note:* When conducting an ANOVA, be sure to return to this step to indicate whether we meet the assumption of equal variances).

Step 2: State the null and research hypotheses.

The second step is to state the null and research hypotheses. As usual, the hypotheses are about population means. The null hypothesis, as in previous hypothesis tests, posits no difference among the population means. The symbols are the same as before, but with more populations. The research hypothesis, however, is a bit different. We can reject the null hypothesis in ANOVA even if only one group is different, on average, from the others. A statistically significant ANOVA can indicate that one group has a different mean from all other groups, that two groups have different means from two others, or that all groups have different means from each other. Any combination of differences between means is possible when we reject the null hypothesis, so the research hypothesis is that at least one population mean is different from at least one other population mean. Because there are several populations, we do not use symbols to express the research hypothesis. Only one group needs to be different, so $\mu_1 \neq \mu_2 \neq \mu_3 \neq \mu_4$ does not include all possible outcomes, just that in which all four population means are not equal to one another.

Summary: Null hypothesis: Foreign graduate students in arts and sciences, education, law, and business programs all rate financial factors the same, on average— H_0: $\mu_1 = \mu_2 = \mu_3 = \mu_4$.

Research hypothesis: Foreign graduate students in arts and sciences, education, law, and business programs do not all rate financial factors the same, on average.

Step 3: Determine the characteristics of the comparison distribution.

The third step is to explicitly state the relevant characteristics of the comparison distribution. This step is an easy one in ANOVA because most calculations for ANOVA are in step 5. Here we merely state that the comparison distribution is an F distribution and provide the appropriate degrees of freedom. As we discussed, the F statistic is a ratio of two independent estimates of the population variance, between-groups variance and within-groups variance (both of which we calculate in step 5). Each variance estimate has its own degrees of freedom. The sample between-groups variance estimates the population variance through the difference among the means of the samples, four in this case. The degrees of freedom for the between-groups variance estimate is the number of samples minus 1: $df_{Between} = N_{Groups} - 1 = 4 - 1 = 3$. The between-groups degrees of freedom for this example is 3.

> **Symbol:** $df_{Between}$ refers to the between-groups degrees of freedom in ANOVA.
>
> **Formula:** $df_{Between} = N_{groups} - 1$

The sample within-groups variance estimates the variance of the population by averaging the variances of the samples, without regard to differences among the sample means. We first must calculate a degrees of freedom for each sample. For the first sample, we would calculate: $df_1 = n_1 - 1 = 5 - 1 = 4$; n represents the number of participants in the particular sample. We would then do this for the remaining samples. For this example, there are four samples, so the formula would be: $df_{Within} = df_1 + df_2 + df_3 + df_4$. For this example, the calculations would be:

> **Symbol:** df_{Within} refers to the within-groups degrees of freedom in ANOVA.
>
> **Formula:** $df_{Within} = df_1 + df_2 + \ldots + df_{Last}$

$$df_1 = 5 - 1 = 4$$

$$df_2 = 4 - 1 = 3$$

$$df_3 = 4 - 1 = 3$$

$$df_4 = 4 - 1 = 3$$

$$df_{Within} = 4 + 3 + 3 + 3 = 13$$

Summary: We would use the F distribution with 3 and 13 degrees of freedom. (*Note:* Convince yourself that you understand this section by including your *df* calculations in this step.)

Step 4: Determine critical values, or cutoffs

The fourth step is to determine a critical value, or cutoff, indicating how extreme our data must be to reject the null hypothesis. For ANOVA, we use an F distribution, which means that our critical value must be on an F distribution. For an F distribution, there is just one critical value. Moreover, because the F is based on estimates of variance instead of standard deviation or standard error in both the numerator and denominator, and because variances are always positive, the F statistic is always positive. There is no negative F cutoff.

To determine the critical value, we examine the F table in Appendix B, a portion of which we have excerpted in Table 10-4. The between-groups degrees of freedom are found in a row across the top of the table. You'll notice that it only goes up to 6, as it is quite rare to have more than seven conditions or groups in a study. The within-groups degrees of freedom are in a column along the left-hand side of the table. Because the number of people in a study can range from few to many, the column continues for several pages with the same range of values of between-groups degrees of freedom on the top of each page.

When using the F table, first find the appropriate within-groups degrees of freedom along the left-hand side of the page, in this case 13. Then find the appropriate between-groups degrees of freedom along the top, in this case 3. The place in the table where this row and this column intersect contains three numbers. Again, if you look to the left-hand side of the page, you'll see three possible p levels next

TABLE 10-4. EXCERPT FROM THE *F* TABLE

We use the *F* table to determine critical values for a given *p* level, based on the degrees of freedom in the numerator (between-groups degrees of freedom) and the degrees of freedom in the denominator (within-groups degrees of freedom). Note that critical values are in italics for 0.10, regular type for 0.05, and boldface for 0.01.

DEGREES OF FREEDOM: DENOMINATOR	*p* LEVEL	DEGREES OF FREEDOM: NUMERATOR 1	2	3	4. . .
. . .					
12	**0.01**	**9.33**	**6.93**	**5.95**	**5.41**
	0.05	4.75	3.88	3.49	3.26
	0.10	*3.18*	*2.81*	*2.61*	*2.48*
13	**0.01**	**9.07**	**6.70**	**5.74**	**5.20**
	0.05	4.67	3.80	3.41	3.18
	0.10	*3.14*	*2.76*	*2.56*	*2.43*
14	**0.01**	**8.86**	**6.51**	**5.56**	**5.03**
	0.05	4.60	3.74	3.34	3.11
	0.10	*3.10*	*2.73*	*2.52*	*2.39*
. . .					

to every value of within-groups degrees of freedom. From top to bottom, the table provides cutoffs for p levels of 0.10, 0.05, and 0.01. Researchers usually use the middle one, 0.05. For our test, we will choose the critical value, or cutoff, for a p level of 0.05: 3.41. We will reject the null hypothesis if the test statistic is greater than or equal to 3.41, as shown in the curve in Figure 10-2.

Summary: Our cutoff, or critical value, for the F statistic for a p level of 0.05 is 3.41, as displayed in the curve in Figure 10-2. (*Note:* It is helpful to include the drawn curve in your solutions to exercises; indicate the cutoff F statistic on the curve.)

Step 5: Calculate the test statistic.

In the fifth step, we calculate our test statistic. At this point, we calculate two estimates of the population variance. One, between-groups variance, is based on the differences among the sample means. The other, within-groups variance, is based on the variances of the samples without regard to how spread out the sample means are. We use the two estimates to calculate the F statistic. We directly compare this statistic to our cutoff to determine whether to reject the null hypothesis. We will learn to do these calculations in the next section.

Summary: To be calculated in the next section.

Step 6: Make a decision.

In the final step, we decide whether to reject or fail to reject the null hypothesis. If the F statistic is beyond the critical value, then we know that it is in the most extreme 5% of possible test statistics *if* the null hypothesis is true. We can then reject the null hypothesis. If we are able to reject the null hypothesis, then we can draw a specific conclusion, such as "It seems that foreign graduate students studying in the United States rate financial factors differently depending on the type of program in which they are enrolled." Notice that we do not say *which* programs are different. ANOVA does not tell us where differences lie; ANOVA only tells us that at least one mean is significantly different from another.

If the test statistic is not beyond the critical value, then we must fail to reject the null hypothesis. The test statistic would not be very rare if the null hypothesis were true. In this circumstance, we report only that there is no evidence from the present study to support the research hypothesis.

Summary: We will be making an evidence-based decision, so we cannot make that decision until we complete step 5, in which we calculate the probabilities associated with that evidence. We will defer this decision until the Bringing It All Together section.

The F Statistic: Logic and Calculations

We now know all the steps of hypothesis testing except how to calculate the F statistic. In this section, we will learn the logic of ANOVA, the logic of calculating the between-groups variance and the within-groups variance, and the actual calculations necessary to compute the F statistic. Then we will return to the steps of hypothesis testing to learn how to use data to make a decision for the specific example we have been considering. Fortunately, both the concept and the calculation of the F statistic express ideas that you are already familiar with.

Let's demonstrate how to use the statistical reasoning associated with the F statistic. You already have observed that grown men on average are slightly taller than grown women, on average. The language of statistics calls that kind of

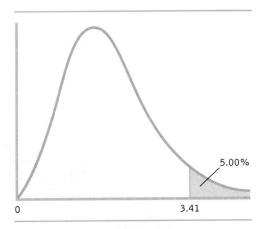

FIGURE 10-2
Determining Cutoffs for an F Distribution

We determine a single critical value on an F distribution. Because F is a squared version of a z or t in some circumstances, we have only one cutoff for a two-tailed test.

Bianca Moscatelli

Gender Differences in Height

Men, on average, are slightly taller than women (between-groups variance). However, neither men nor women are all the same height within their groups (within-groups variance). F = between-groups variability/within-groups variability.

variability "between-groups variability." Our mathematical formulas provide a way to assign a number that represents how different the groups are from one another. You also know that not all women are the same height and not all men are the same height. The language of statistics calls that kind of variability within-groups variability. Our mathematical formulas provide a way to assign a number that represents, on average, how much variability there is within each group. The F statistic is simply an estimate of between-groups variability divided by an estimate of within-groups variability. $F = \dfrac{\text{between-groups variability}}{\text{within-groups variability}}$. Behind all the fancy calculations, that's all the F statistic amounts to: simple division. But, you might ask, what about the overlap, the fact that there are many women who are taller than many men? Well, ANOVA carefully factors those individual differences directly into the equation.

The Logic of ANOVA: Quantifying Overlap

The F statistic is a ratio of two estimates of the population variance: between-groups variance and within-groups variance. The estimate of the between-groups variability appears in the numerator. Large differences among the sample means will be expressed as greater between-groups variability, making the numerator larger relative to the denominator. The estimate of the within-groups variability appears in the denominator. The less spread there is within each of the sample distributions, the less variability there is within each group, and the smaller the number will be in the denominator.

In contrast, large differences among the scores within each group will be expressed as greater within-groups variability, making the denominator larger relative to the numerator. Because the F statistic is a ratio of between-groups variability to within-groups variability, its value will be large whenever the numerator is large and the denominator is small; its value will be small whenever the numerator is small and the denominator is large. In other words, when the means of the groups are far apart from each other and the scores within each group are not very spread out, there won't be very much overlap among the groups and the F statistic will be large.

Let's consider this same idea in a graphical way. In Figure 10-3, there are three sets of three distributions of scores, one set for each study. Each distribution of scores represents one level of the independent variable, and each set of three curves represents a different study. The top set of three curves (a), for example, represents one study that will be analyzed by a between-groups ANOVA; there is one independent variable with three levels, and the scores for each level are represented by one distribution. In the top set of three curves, there is a great deal of overlap among the sample distributions. This occurs both because the means are fairly close together and because there is much variability within each of the samples. Would you be surprised if these three samples of scores came from the same population? Three overlapping distributions like these could easily result from the same population just by chance.

The second set of distributions, the middle set of three curves (b), illustrates a scenario in which the three sample means are more widely separated but the variability among the scores in each group remains the same. There is much less overlap, but the decrease in overlap is due only to the increase in the difference

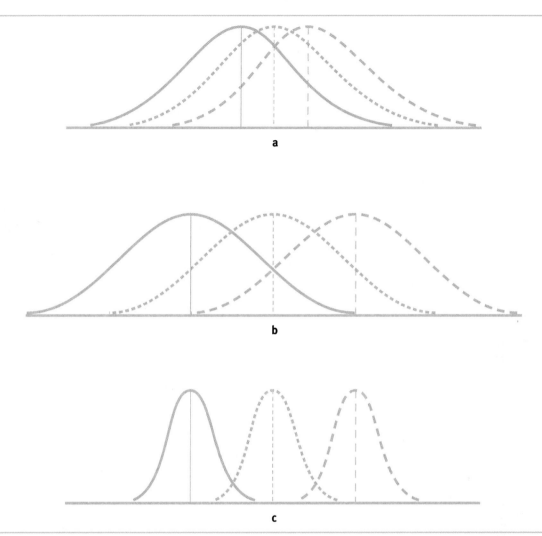

FIGURE 10-3
The Logic of ANOVA

between means. This is because the increased difference between means increases the between-groups variance, but the within-groups variance is unchanged. Said another way, the F statistic is larger, but only because the numerator is larger; the denominator has not changed. Overall, there is less overlap than in the top set of three curves; by looking at these distributions, we can see that it would be somewhat surprising to draw these three samples from the same population just by chance.

The third set of distributions, the bottom set of three curves (c), represents what would occur if we kept the increased variability between the three means but decreased the variability within each of the samples. Compared to the top set of three curves (a), we have increased our between-groups variance (the numerator) *and* decreased our within-groups variance (the denominator). Both changes lead to a larger F statistic. Compared to the middle set of three curves (b), the only change is the decrease in the within-groups variance. But even this change leads to less overlap. Just from this graph (before calculating any numbers), it would be difficult to convince someone that these three samples were drawn by chance from the very same population. These three sets of curves

Compare the top (a) and middle (b) sets of sample distributions. As the variability between means increases, the F statistic is larger. Compare the middle (b) and bottom (c) sets of sample distributions. As the variability within the samples themselves decreases, the F statistic is larger. The F statistic is larger as the curves overlap less. Both the increased spread among the sample means and the decreased spread within each sample contribute to this increase in the F statistic.

demonstrate how the F statistic captures the amount of overlap among samples by including two measures: (1) between-groups variance, a measure of how variable the means are with respect to one another, and (2) within-groups variance, a measure of how variable the scores are within each sample.

Two Ways to Estimate Population Variance: Between-Groups Variability and Within-Groups Variability

The only reason to sample, design, and analyze data is to understand the underlying population—or populations. Between-groups variability and within-groups variability are both estimates of population variance. To recap what we learned in the previous section, if there is a great deal of overlap among our three (or more) samples, then we cannot reject the null hypothesis; it is plausible that all three come from the same population. On the other hand if there is not much overlap among our samples, then we can reject the null hypothesis; it becomes less plausible that all three samples come from the same population. We assess the overlap by examining two forms of variance, one of which—between-groups variance—depends solely on the difference among the sample means. If the between-groups variance is the same as the other estimate, the one in the denominator, then it is likely that the means are the same. If the between-groups variance is greater than the other estimate, then it is possible that the means are quite different.

Mathematically, if we calculate two estimates of variance and both are identical, then the F statistic, which is a ratio of the two estimates, will be 1.0. For example, if the estimate of the between-groups variance is 32 and the estimate of the within-groups variance is also 32, then the F statistic will be $32/32 = 1.0$. Notice that this is a bit different from the z and t tests in which a z or t of 0 would mean no difference at all; here, an F of 1 means no difference at all. As the sample means get farther apart, the between-groups variance (the numerator) increases, which means that the F statistic also increases.

Let's first consider the within-groups variance, the variance that goes in the denominator when calculating the F statistic, because it's the easier of the two to understand. We simply calculate a weighted variance, much like the pooled standard deviation of the independent-samples t test. Because the within-groups variance is essentially an average of the individual variances of the samples, it is already a variance for a distribution of scores, so there is no need to perform any further calculations. Remember, we're trying to estimate the population variance, so we want the variance for a distribution of *scores*.

The numerator variance—the between-groups variance—starts out as a measure of variability among means (the means of the samples), so we have an added step. We have to convert it from a variance of a distribution of means to a variance of a distribution of scores so that it will match the form of our within-groups variance. This is the opposite of what we had to do with z and t tests. Let's review what we did with z and t tests to go from a measure of spread for a distribution of scores (usually standard deviation) to a measure of spread for a distribution of means (usually standard error) so that we can consider how to do the opposite of this.

Remember that with z and t tests we used distributions of means. Because of this, with z and t tests, we had to divide by the size of the sample in our study (N) to go from the variance version of the *larger* standard deviation to the variance version of the *smaller* standard error. (If we were working with standard deviations rather than variances, we divided by the square root of the sample size, $\sqrt{N}$.) To do the reverse for the between-groups variance, you might guess we'd multiply by the size of each sample in our study (N) to go from the *smaller* variance of a distribution of means to the *larger* variance of a distribution of scores. And you'd be right—to a degree.

The variation that often occurs in ANOVA is that we typically have samples of different sizes. For example, in our smaller version of Ruby's study of foreign graduate students, we have one sample of 5 and three samples of 4. So we'll have to include a method to weight the samples in our calculations. We cannot merely multiply the variance for the three means by a given sample size (unless the sample sizes are identical, which is a rare situation in the messiness of real-life research). We'll learn exactly how this works later, but the bottom line is that, essentially, we multiply the variance between our sample means by sample size to go from a measure of spread for a distribution of means to the measure of spread for a distribution of scores necessary for ANOVA.

Calculating the *F* Statistic: The Source Table

Our goal in performing the calculations of ANOVA (or, more likely, instructing the computer to perform them for us) is to understand the *sources* of all the variability in a study. The word *source* is carefully chosen because we may be tempted to think of the various "causes" of variability rather than "sources" of variability. But causality can be a dangerous and misleading inference, so statisticians use the term *sources* rather than *causes*.

Here is how we get to the source table. You may remember that we alerted you in Chapter 2 that the sum of the squared deviations (the number just before we divide by $N - 1$) is also known as the *sum of squares* and that it would return later in the text. Well, later is now. The measurement of variance is built on the idea of squared deviations from the mean, and that is how we calculate most of the numbers that we use to calculate variance in ANOVA: squared deviations. We will be working with variances (the squares of standard deviations), so here's a reminder of the formula we use:

$$\text{variance} = \frac{\Sigma(X - M)^2}{N - 1}$$

To conduct an ANOVA, we calculate many squared deviations, and three sums of squares. We use a source table to help us to keep track of all the sources of variability that we discover in our study. *A **source table** presents the important calculations and final results of an ANOVA in a consistent and easy-to-read format.* A source table is shown in Table 10-4; the symbols in the chart will be replaced by numbers in an actual source table.

Learning how the source table is organized now will pay dividends later when you learn to use the computer to conduct statistical analyses. Almost all statistical software presents ANOVA results in the form of a source table. So if you can understand a table that reports the sources of all the variability in the study, then you will know how to read even very complex ANOVAs in computer printouts of your own analyses, as well as reports of ANOVAs from the most sophisticated journals in psychology, medicine, biology, sociology, communications, or any discipline that uses the tools of statistics to create new knowledge. It is surprisingly easy to understand the source table if you simply keep its purpose clearly in mind: to describe the sources of numerical variability in a study.

■ A **source table** presents the important calculations and final results of an ANOVA in a consistent and easy-to-read format.

■ The **grand mean** is the mean of every score in a study, regardless of which sample the score came from.

TABLE 10-5. THE SOURCE TABLE ORGANIZES OUR ANOVA CALCULATIONS

A source table helps researchers organize the most important calculations necessary to conduct an ANOVA as well as the final results. The numbers 1–5 in the first row are used in this particular table only to help you understand the format of source tables; they would not be included in an actual source table.

1 SOURCE	2 SS	3 df	4 MS	5 F
Between	$SS_{Between}$	$df_{Between}$	$MS_{Between}$	F
Within	SS_{Within}	df_{Within}	MS_{Within}	
Total	SS_{Total}	df_{Total}		

We're going to explain the source table by discussing the meaning of each of the five columns in the source table shown in Table 10-5. For teaching purposes, we're going to explain column 1 first and then work backwards from column 5 to column 4 to column 3 and finally to column 2.

Column 1: The first column, labeled "source," lists the sources, or origins, of the two estimates of population variance. One source of variability comes from the spread *between* means and another source of variability comes from the spread among the scores *within* each sample. As far as we're concerned in this chapter, the main function of the row labeled "total" is to check our sum of squares (SS) and degrees of freedom (df) calculations. So now let's work backwards through the source table to learn how it describes the different sources of variability.

Column 5: The fifth column is labeled "*F*." As you may remember, we need only simple division to calculate the *F* statistic: We divide the estimate of the between-groups variance by the estimate of the within-groups variance.

Column 4: The fourth column, labeled "*MS*," describes how we arrived at that numerical estimate. But here's a handy observation: You already know what *MS* is. Back when we first learned variance, you learned several different symbols for variance, including SD^2, s^2, and even the symbol for variance we will use now: *MS*. *MS* is the conventional symbol for variance in ANOVA. It stands for "mean square" because variance is the arithmetic mean of the squared deviations. $MS_{Between}$ and MS_{Within}, therefore, refer to between-groups variance and within-groups variance, respectively. As we already noted, we divide $MS_{Between}$ by MS_{Within} to get *F*.

Symbol: $MS_{Between}$ refers to the between-groups variance in ANOVA.

Symbol: MS_{Within} refers to the within-groups variance in ANOVA.

Symbol: df_{Total} refers to the total degrees of freedom in ANOVA.

Formulas: $df_{Total} = df_{Between} + df_{Within}$ or $df_{Total} = N_{Total} - 1$

Column 3: The third column is labeled "*df*." This column shows the degrees of freedom, and we already have learned to calculate the $df_{Between}$ and df_{Within}. It's so easy to calculate the df_{Total} that we won't bother holding you in suspense until we get to the rest of the calculations. Any guesses on the calculation of the df_{Total}? Most of you probably said: add up the other two. And you're right: $df_{Total} = df_{Between} + df_{Within}$. In our version of Ruby's study, $df_{Total} = 3 + 13 = 16$. There is a second way to calculate it; when you are creating a source table by hand instead of through a computer program, we recommend that you check your work by calculating df both ways. This second way is $df_{Total} = N_{Total} - 1$. N_{Total} refers to the total number of people in the entire study. In our abbreviated version of Ruby's study, there were four groups with 5, 4, 4, and 4 participants in the groups, and $5 + 4 + 4 + 4 = 17$. We calculate total degrees of freedom for this study as $df_{Total} = 17 - 1 = 16$. If we always calculate degrees of freedom both ways, we know when they don't match up, indicating that we have to go back and check all our calculations.

Column 2: The all-important second column is labeled "*SS.*" This column includes the sums of squares, *SS*. We calculate three sums of squares, one for between-groups variability ($SS_{Between}$), one for within-groups variability (SS_{Within}), and one for total variability (SS_{Total}). As with degrees of freedom, the first two sums of squares add up to the third. We should always calculate all three, however, to be sure they match; this check ensures that our calculations are correct.

The source table simply collects many of the things that we have already learned to do into one, more meaningful, table. More specifically, it describes everything that we have learned about the sources of numerical variability in a particular study. In Chapter 2, for example, we learned to estimate variance by dividing the sum of squares by $(N - 1)$. You may have noticed that most degrees of freedom are based on some variation of $(N - 1)$. The $(N - 1)$ of the variance equation is essentially a version of a degrees of freedom. And that's the secret to the entire source table. Once we calculate our sums of squares for between-groups variance and within-groups variance, we simply divide each sum of squares by the appropriate degrees of freedom—the appropriate version of $(N - 1)$. We divide the $SS_{Between}$ by the $df_{Between}$, and the SS_{Within} by the df_{Within}. We then have the two variance estimates ($MS_{Between}$ and MS_{Within}), and we calculate their ratio to get our *F*. This means that once we have our sums of squared deviations, the rest of the calculation is simple division.

Symbol: $SS_{Between}$

Symbol: SS_{Within}

Symbol: SS_{Total}

Sums of Squared Deviations: The Backbone of the Source Table

Just as clinical psychology sometimes defines deviance as variations from particular social norms, statistics defines deviance as variations from particular statistical norms. For ANOVA, there are three different types of statistical deviations because we are measuring deviations from three different means used to calculate (1) deviations between groups, (2) deviations within groups, and (3) total deviations. Calculating the amount of deviance is the first step needed to calculate each sum of squares: between, within, and total.

Let's start with the total sum of squares, SS_{Total}, because it is most similar to what we calculated in Chapter 2. The best way to start is to organize all the scores, placing them in a single column with a horizontal line dividing each sample from the next. You can use the data (from our version of Ruby's study) in the column labeled "*X*" of Table 10-6 as your model, especially when calculating practice problems that have only a few data points in each group. The symbol *X* stands for individual scores, which is why there are 17 individual scores listed under that symbol in the table. Each set of scores is next to its sample, and the means of each sample are included underneath the names of each sample. [We have included subscripts on each mean in the first column (e.g., *A&S* for arts and sciences) to indicate its sample.]

Previously, we calculated the sum of squares by calculating how much each score deviated from the mean, squaring the deviations, and then summing all those squared deviations. In this case, we want to know the total sum of squares, so we will subtract the overall mean from each score, including everyone in the study, regardless of sample. The mean of all the scores is called the grand mean, and its symbol is *GM*. The ***grand mean*** *is the mean of every score in a study, regardless of which sample the score came from:* $GM = \dfrac{\Sigma(X)}{N_{Total}}$. The grand mean of

Symbol: *GM* refers to the grand mean, the mean of all scores in a study, regardless of their sample.

Formula: $GM = \dfrac{\Sigma(X)}{N_{Total}}$, where *X* is every score in the study, regardless of their sample.

these scores is 3.588. (Don't make the mistake of attempting a shortcut by taking the mean of the four sample means; because there are usually different numbers of people in each sample, you will not get the correct overall mean.) As we have been doing so far, we will write each number to three decimal places until we get to the final answer, F. As we have done throughout this book, we will report the final answer to two decimal places.

The third column in Table 10-6 shows the deviation of each score from the grand mean, and the fourth column shows the squares of these deviations. For example, for the first score, 4, we subtract the grand mean: $4 - 3.588 = 0.412$, and then square the deviation: $(0.412)^2 = 0.170$. Below the fourth column, we have summed the squared deviations: 8.122. This is the total sum of squares, SS_{Total}. The formula for total sum of squares is $SS_{Total} = \Sigma(X - GM)^2$. To calculate the total sum of squares, notice that we used the grand mean (GM) as the standard against which we measured all our deviations. That will change in the next step, when we calculate within-groups variance.

Formula: $SS_{Total} = \Sigma(X - GM)^2$

The within-groups sum of squares is the next most similar to what we've already learned, and your model for this calculation is shown in Table 10-7. Keep in mind that in the real world of research, we seldom have precisely the same number of participants in each sample. That is one of the reasons that, instead of calculating four variances and pooling them, we do the pooling at the sums-of-squares level. We create deviations for each set of sample scores, but this

TABLE 10-6. CALCULATING THE TOTAL SUM OF SQUARES

The total sum of squares is calculated by subtracting the overall mean, called the grand mean, from every score to create deviations, then squaring the deviations and summing the squared deviations.

SAMPLE	X	$(X - GM)$	$(X - GM)^2$
Arts and sciences	4	0.412	0.170
	5	1.412	1.994
$M_{A\&S} = 4.0$	4	0.412	0.170
	3	−0.588	0.346
	4	0.412	0.170
Education	4	0.412	0.170
	3	−0.588	0.346
$M_{Ed} = 3.75$	4	0.412	0.170
	4	0.412	0.170
Law	3	−0.588	0.346
	3	−0.588	0.346
$M_{Law} = 2.75$	2	−1.588	2.522
	3	−0.588	0.346
Business	4	0.412	0.170
	4	0.412	0.170
$M_{Bus} = 3.75$	4	0.412	0.170
	3	−0.588	0.346
	$GM = 3.588$		$SS_{Total} = \mathbf{8.122}$

TABLE 10-7. CALCULATING THE WITHIN-GROUPS SUM OF SQUARES

The within-groups sum of squares is calculated by taking each score and subtracting the mean of the sample from which it comes—not the grand mean—to create deviations, then squaring the deviations and summing the squared deviations.

SAMPLE	X	$(X - M)$	$(X - M)^2$
Arts and sciences	4	0	0
	5	1	1
$M_{A\&S} = 4.0$	4	0	0
	3	−1	1
	4	0	0
Education	4	0.25	0.063
	3	−0.75	0.563
$M_{Ed} = 3.75$	4	0.25	0.063
	4	0.25	0.063
Law	3	0.25	0.063
	3	0.25	0.063
$M_{Law} = 2.75$	2	−0.75	0.563
	3	0.25	0.063
Business	4	0.25	0.063
	4	0.25	0.063
$M_{Bus} = 3.75$	4	0.25	0.063
	3	−0.75	0.563
	GM = 3.588		$SS_{Within} = $ **4.256**

time the deviations are around the mean of that particular group. For the five scores in the first sample, we subtract their sample mean, 4.0. For the example, the calculations for the first score are: $(4 - 4)^2 = 0$. For the four in the second sample, we subtract their sample mean, 3.75. And so on for all four samples. (*Note:* As a practical matter, the horizontal line in between each sample serves as a reminder to start using a new mean when calculating these within-groups deviations. Don't forget to switch means when you get to each new sample!) Once we have all our deviations, we square them and sum them to calculate our within-groups sum of squares, 4.256, the number below the fourth column. (*Note:* Some texts instruct students to calculate a separate sum of squares for each group and then sum them. The method introduced here, which uses a single column, saves a step. The single sum of squares includes the squared deviations for all groups.) The formula is $SS_{Within} = \Sigma(X - M)^2$ because we subtract the sample mean, rather than the grand mean, from each score. Notice that the weighting for sample size is built into the calculation. The first sample has five scores and contributes five squared deviations to the total, whereas the other samples have only four scores and so only contribute four squared deviations.

Finally, we'll calculate the between-groups sum of squares. This step is easy to understand if you keep in mind that our goal for this step is to estimate how much each *group*, not each *individual*, deviates from the overall grand mean. This step uses the same format as the other two sums of squares and almost the same calculations. For each of the 17 individuals in this study, we subtract the grand mean from the mean of the group to which that individual belongs.

Formula: $SS_{Within} = \Sigma(X - M)^2$

For example, the first person has a score of 4 and belongs to the group labeled "Arts and Sciences," which has a mean that also happens to be 4. However, the grand mean is 3.588. We ignore this individual's personal score and subtract 3.588 (the grand mean) from 4 (the group mean) to get the deviation score 0.412. The next person, also in the group labeled "Arts and Sciences," has a score of 5. The group mean of that sample is 4, and the grand mean is 3.588. Once again, we ignore that individual's personal score and subtract 3.588 (the grand mean) from 4 (the group mean) to get the deviation score, also 0.412. In fact, we will subtract 3.588 from 4 for all five scores. We conduct the same calculation for every score in that group, as you can see in Table 10-8. When we get to the line between samples, we look for our next sample mean. For all four scores in the next sample, we subtract the grand mean, 3.588, from the sample mean, 3.75, and so on.

To summarize the calculation of the between-groups sum of squares, each deviation score within each group is computed by subtracting the grand mean from the mean of that group. To expedite the calculations, this subtraction can be performed just once for each group, and the squared deviation score will be multiplied by the number of participants in the group. Notice that the individual scores are *never* involved in our calculations, just their sample means and the grand mean! Also notice that the first group (arts and sciences) will have a little bit more weight in the calculation because it has 5 participants while the

---

TABLE 10-8. CALCULATING THE BETWEEN-GROUPS SUM OF SQUARES

The between-groups sum of squares is calculated by subtracting the grand mean from the sample mean for every score to create deviations, then squaring the deviations and summing the squared deviations. The individual scores themselves are not involved in any calculations.

SAMPLE	X	$(M - GM)$	$(M - GM)^2$
Arts and sciences	4	0.412	0.170
	5	0.412	0.170
$M_{A\&S} = 4.0$	4	0.412	0.170
	3	0.412	0.170
	4	0.412	0.170
Education	4	0.162	0.026
	3	0.162	0.026
$M_{Ed} = 3.75$	4	0.162	0.026
	4	0.162	0.026
Law	3	−0.838	0.702
	3	−0.838	0.702
$M_{Law} = 2.75$	2	−0.838	0.702
	3	−0.838	0.702
Business	4	0.162	0.026
	4	0.162	0.026
$M_{Bus} = 3.75$	4	0.162	0.026
	3	0.162	0.026
	$GM = 3.588$		$SS_{Between} = \mathbf{3.866}$

TABLE 10-9. THE THREE SUMS OF SQUARES OF ANOVA

The calculations in ANOVA are built on the foundation we learned in Chapter 2, sums of squared deviations. We calculate three types of sums of squares, one for between-groups variance, one for within-groups variance, and one for total variance. Once we have our three sums of squares, most of the remaining calculations involve simple division.

SUM OF SQUARES	TO CALCULATE THE DEVIATIONS, SUBTRACT THE . . .	FORMULA
Between-groups	grand mean from the sample mean (for each score)	$SS_{Between} = \Sigma(M - GM)^2$
Within-groups	sample mean from each score	$SS_{Within} = \Sigma(X - M)^2$
Total	grand mean from each score	$SS_{Total} = \Sigma(X - GM)^2$

other three groups have only 4. The third column of Table 10-8 includes the deviations and the fourth includes the squared deviations. The between-groups sum of squares, in bold under the fourth column is: 3.866. The formula for between-groups sum of squares is: $SS_{Between} = \Sigma(M - GM)^2$.

Now is the moment of arthmetic truth. Were our calculations correct? To find out, we will add our within-groups sum of squares (4.256) to our between-groups sum of squares (3.866) to see if they equal the total sum of squares (8.122). Here's the formula: $SS_{Total} = SS_{Within} + SS_{Between} = 8.122 = 4.256 + 3.866$. Indeed, the total sum of squares, 8.122, does equal the sum of the other two sums of squares, 4.256 and 3.866. Our calculations were correct. The calculations are time-consuming but not terribly difficult. Still, it is important to walk through these calculations at least once, doing them by hand, and then learn as soon as possible how to instruct the computer to do those calculations for you.

To recap (see Table 10-9), for the total sums of squares, we subtract the *grand mean* from each individual *score* to get the deviations. For the within-groups sum of squares, we subtract the appropriate *sample mean* from every *score* to get the deviations. And then, for the between-groups sum of squares, for every score, we subtract the *grand mean* from the appropriate *sample mean*, once for each score, to get the deviations; for the between-groups sum of squares, the actual scores are never involved in any calculations.

Now we insert these numbers into our source table to calculate our F statistic. See Table 10-10 for the source table that lists all the formulas and

Formula: $SS_{Between} = \Sigma(M - GM)^2$

Formula: $SS_{Total} = SS_{Within} + SS_{Between}$

TABLE 10-10. A SOURCE TABLE WITH FORMULAS

This table summarizes the formulas for calculating an F statistic.

SOURCE	SS	df	MS	F
Between	$\Sigma(M - GM)^2$	$N_{Groups} - 1$	$\dfrac{SS_{Between}}{df_{Between}}$	$\dfrac{MS_{Between}}{MS_{Within}}$
Within	$\Sigma(X - M)^2$	$df_1 + df_2 + \ldots + df_{Last}$	$\dfrac{SS_{Within}}{df_{Within}}$	
Total	$\Sigma(X - GM)^2$	$N_{Total} - 1$		

[Expanded formula: $df_{Within} = (N_1 - 1) + (N_2 - 1) + \ldots + (N_{Last} - 1)$]

TABLE 10-11. A COMPLETED SOURCE TABLE

Once we've calculated the sums of squares and the degrees of freedom, the rest is just simple division. We use the first two columns of numbers to calculate the variances and the F statistic. We divide the between-groups sum of squares and within-groups sum of squares by their associated degrees of freedom to get the between-groups variance and within-groups variance. Then we divide between-groups variance by within-groups variance to get the F statistic, 3.94.

SOURCE	SS	df	MS	F
Between	3.866	3	1.289	**3.94**
Within	4.256	13	0.327	
Total	8.122	16		

Formula: $MS_{Between} = \dfrac{SS_{Between}}{df_{Between}}$

Formula: $MS_{Within} = \dfrac{SS_{Within}}{df_{Within}}$

Formula: $F = \dfrac{MS_{Between}}{MS_{Within}}$

Table 10-11 for the completed source table. We divide the between-groups sum of squares and the within-groups sum of squares by their associated degrees of freedom to get the between-groups variance and the within-groups variance. The formulas are $MS_{Between} = \dfrac{SS_{Between}}{df_{Between}} = \dfrac{3.866}{3} = 1.289$ and $MS_{Within} = \dfrac{SS_{Within}}{df_{Within}} = \dfrac{4.256}{13} = 0.327$. We then divide the between-groups variance by the within-groups variance to get the F statistic. The formula is $F = \dfrac{MS_{Between}}{MS_{Within}} = \dfrac{1.289}{0.327} = 3.94$, in bold in Table 10-10.

Bringing It All Together: What's Our Decision?

Lest we forget, the point of learning all these concepts is so that we can make better decisions, especially about consequential issues. So now we have to come back to the six steps of hypothesis testing for ANOVA to fill in the gaps in steps 1 and 6. We finished step 5 in The F Statistic section.

Step 1

We have to be sure that our variances were roughly equal in our four groups; researchers use statistical software such as SPSS to test whether the groups were selected from populations with equal variances. For now, we can use our within-groups variance column to determine this. Variance is computed by dividing the sum of squares by the sample size minus 1. We can add the squared deviations for each sample, then divide by the sample size minus 1. Table 10-12 shows the calculations for variance within each of the four samples. Because the largest variance, 0.500, is not more than twice the smallest variance, 0.251, we have met the assumption of equal variances for ANOVA.

Step 6

Now that we have our test statistic, we can compare it with our critical value. Previously, in step 4, we determined that the cutoff F statistic for the foreign graduate student example, per the table in Appendix B, was 3.41. The F statistic we calculated for these data was 3.94. As seen in Figure 10-4, the F statistic for this study is beyond the cutoff; therefore, we can reject the null hypothesis. It appears that foreign graduate students applying to some types of programs rate financial factors as more important than do foreign graduate students applying to other types of programs. The ANOVA, however, does not allow us to

TABLE 10-12. CALCULATING SAMPLE VARIANCES

We calculate the variances of the samples by dividing each sum of squares by the sample size minus 1 to check one of the assumptions of ANOVA. For unequal sample sizes, as we have here, we want our largest variance (0.500 in this case) to be no more than twice our smallest (0.251 in this case). Two times 0.251 is 0.502, and so we meet this assumption.

SAMPLE	ARTS AND SCIENCES	EDUCATION	LAW	BUSINESS
	0	0.063	0.063	0.063
Squared	1	0.563	0.063	0.063
deviations:	0	0.063	0.563	0.063
	1	0.063	0.063	0.563
	0			
Sum of squares:	2	0.752	0.752	0.752
$N - 1$	4	3	3	3
Variance	**0.500**	**0.251**	**0.251**	**0.251**

■ A **post-hoc test** is a statistical procedure frequently carried out after we reject the null hypothesis in an analysis of variance; it allows us to make multiple comparisons among several means.

say more than this. We only know that there is at least one mean that is different from at least one other mean. We do not know exactly where the difference or differences lie. We must conduct a follow-up analysis, called a post-hoc test, to ascertain what the differences might be.

Summary: We can reject the null hypothesis. It appears that the importance placed on financial factors differs based on type of program to which foreign graduate students are applying, as seen in the curve in Figure 10-4. (*Note:* It is helpful to include the drawn curve in your solutions to exercises; indicate the cutoff F and the test statistic on the curve.)

Why the ANOVA Is Not Sufficient: Post-Hoc Tests

The output of a statistically significant ANOVA is like a child taunting a playmate: "I know something you don't know, nah nah na-nah nah, but I'm not going to tell you." That is, a statistically significant ANOVA asserts that something important is going on somewhere in the study, but it does not specify which specific pairs of means are responsible for a statistically significant difference between groups. That's the moment when it becomes appropriate to look backwards: after a statistically significant finding.

To determine where statistically significant differences probably are, we can start by looking at a graph of the data to figure out which means are farthest apart (because the ANOVA itself doesn't let us know). We can't know for sure, however, until we conduct an additional test, a post-hoc test. *A **post-hoc test** is a statistical procedure frequently carried out after we reject the null hypothesis in an analysis of variance; it allows us to make multiple comparisons among several means.* The name of the test, post-hoc, means "after this" in Latin, and these tests are often referred to as follow-up tests. Post-hoc tests are not conducted if we fail to reject the null hypothesis; in this case, there are no statistically significant differences among means, so it would not make sense to ask where differences are.

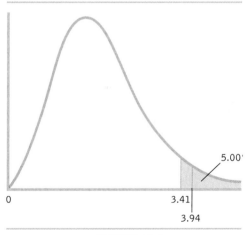

FIGURE 10-4
An *F* Distribution: Making a Decision

We compare the *F* statistic that we calculated for our samples to a single cutoff, or critical value, on the appropriate *F* distribution. We can reject the null hypothesis if the test statistic is beyond—more to the right than—the cutoff. Here, our *F* statistic of 3.94 is beyond the cutoff of 3.41, so we can reject the null hypothesis.

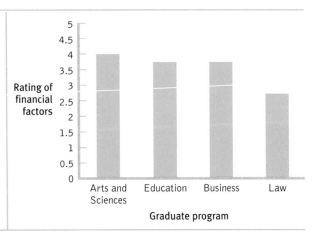

FIGURE 10-5
Which Graduate Programs Are Different?

This figure depicts the mean ratings of the influence of financial factors in decisions to attend graduate school among foreign graduate students in four different types of programs in the United States. When we conduct an ANOVA and reject the null hypothesis, we only know that there is a difference somewhere; we do not know where the difference lies. We can see several possible combinations of differences by examining the means on this graph. Further testing will let us know which specific pairs of means are different from one another.

For example, Ruby's study of foreign graduate students produced a statistically significant ANOVA. The mean of financial factor ratings of students in the different types of graduate programs (as seen in our example) are depicted in Figure 10-5. The means (which are almost identical to those in Ruby's study) were: arts and sciences, 4.00; education, 3.75; law, 2.75; and business, 3.75. Notice that the graph is a Pareto chart because it organizes the bars from highest to lowest means. We conducted an ANOVA and were able to reject the null hypothesis. So we can say that there is an overall difference between the means. But where?

First, look at the graph and then consider the possibilities. Arts and sciences graduate students might rate financial factors higher than only the law students, with no other significant differences among means. Or arts and sciences graduate students might rate financial factors higher than graduate students in all three other programs. Or law students might rate financial factors as less important than graduate students in the other three programs. There are several possibilities, and we cannot state our conclusion until we examine each of them statistically using a post-hoc test.

There are a number of post-hoc tests, and most are named for their founders, almost exclusively people with fabulous names—Bonferroni, Scheffé (pronounced "sheff-ay"), Tukey (pronounced "too-kee"). All these tests allow us to determine which means are statistically significantly different from one another once we determine that there is a difference somewhere. More important, these post-hoc tests avoid the increase in Type I errors that comes with conducting multiple *t* tests. To learn more about specific post-hoc tests, continue on to the Digging Deeper into the Data section of this chapter.

In summary, ANOVA uses the same six steps of hypothesis testing that we learned in Chapter 8, but with a few minor changes in step 3 and step 5. In step 3, we merely state the comparison distribution and provide the degrees of freedom, but we do no other calculations. In step 5, we complete the calculations, using a source table to organize the results. First, we estimate population variance by considering the differences among means (between-groups variance). Second, we estimate population variance by calculating a weighted average of the variances within each sample (within-groups variance). We divide between-groups variance by within-groups variance to calculate our *F* statistic. A higher *F* statistic indicates less overlap among the sample distributions, evidence that the samples come from different populations. If we are able to reject the null hypothesis, however, we're not finished. We must conduct a post-hoc test to determine exactly which pairs of means are significantly different from one another.

⊙ CHECK YOUR LEARNING

10-3 Irwin and colleagues (2004) are among a growing body of behavioral health researchers who are interested in adherence to medical regimens. Even people who are high-functioning in many other areas of their life may not take medications as prescribed, schedule regular doctors' appointments to monitor potentially life-threatening conditions, or undertake physician-recommended behavioral changes (e.g., to exercise more). Irwin and colleagues studied adherence to an exercise regimen over one year in postmenopausal women, a time when women are increasingly at risk for medical problems that may be reduced by exercise. Among the many factors that the research team examined was attendance at a monthly group education program that taught tactics to change exercise behavior; the researchers kept attendance and divided participants into three categories based on the number of sessions they attended. (*Note:* The researchers could have kept the data as numbers of sessions, an interval variable, rather than dividing them into categories, a nominal variable.) Here is an abbreviated version of this study with fictional data points; the means of these data points, however, are the actual means of the study. The dependent variable was number of minutes of exercise per week.

<5 sessions: 155, 120, 130

5–8 sessions: 199, 160, 184

9–12 sessions: 230, 214, 195, 209

a. State the independent variable and its levels. Explain why it is a nominal variable. State the dependent variable. Explain why it is an interval or scale variable.

b. Conduct all six steps of hypothesis testing. Show your work, as described in the summaries of steps in this section.

c. Do we know where specific differences lie based solely on the results of the ANOVA? Explain. What would we need to do to determine where specific differences lie?

d. From the description of the study, did the researchers use random assignment? Can you think of a confounding variable? What might have led to differences in minutes per week exercised other than what was learned in the group education?

■ **DIGGING DEEPER INTO THE DATA: A PRIORI AND POST-HOC TESTS TO DECIDE WHICH GROUPS ARE DIFFERENT**

Bad decisions often seem so obviously bad that we marvel that anyone dared to make them. But we only possess this magical insight after we know how events have turned out. For example, in retrospect, it is clear that Shackleton never should have attempted to use exhausted men to drag two lifeboats across heaving ice. Nevertheless, he had to learn from his mistakes—and quickly.

Fortunately, statisticians usually don't die if they make a Type I or Type II error. But it's still best for statisticians to be cautious, and there are several ways of analyzing mean differences among several groups. These ways can be divided into two main categories: planned comparisons and post-hoc tests. In this section, we'll first demonstrate how clear thinking on your part allows you to test planned comparisons. Then we'll provide a detailed look at two commonly used post-hoc tests, the Tukey *HSD* test and the Bonferroni test. A statistician should carefully consider her or his data and then use the wisest approach to comparing means.

Planned and A Priori Comparisons: When Comparisons Between Pairs Are Guided by Theory

As we noted earlier in the chapter, post-hoc tests are commonly used to compare multiple means, but they are not our only option when faced with multiple comparisons. Before we collect our data, we might decide, based on our reading of the research literature, to make only certain specific comparisons. If so, we don't need to be as stringent in our decision of whether to reject the null hypothesis in comparisons between means. We can use what's called *a **planned comparison**, a test that is conducted when there are multiple groups of scores, but specific comparisons have been specified prior to data collection*. This test is also called an *a priori comparison.*

Specific a priori comparisons are usually guided by an existing theory or a previous finding. Ruby (2006), for example, might have predicted, based on previous research, that graduate students in arts and sciences programs would have a different mean from the other three groups but that there would be no differences among the other three groups. In this case, she would have specified just three comparisons: arts and sciences versus education, arts and sciences versus business, and arts and sciences versus law. She would not typically test any other comparisons (e.g., education versus business).

In such a case, the researcher has several choices but always states the exact comparisons that he or she will make before collecting any data. These choices usually involve:

1. Conducting one or more independent-samples *t* tests with a *p* level of 0.05

2. Conducting one or more independent-samples *t* tests using a more conservative *p* level, such as that determined by the Bonferroni test, described below

Because the comparisons are planned (we are not exploring every possible comparison), we do not have to use a more stringent post-hoc test.

Statisticians use statistics to make judgment calls. The important thing is to be honest with yourself so that statistics become a guide to scientific reasoning rather than finding ways to make the data come out the way you want. For example, in some cases, the planned comparisons are conducted instead of, rather than in addition to, an overall ANOVA. This is not wrong if you genuinely planned this comparison before you collected the data. Similarly, a planned comparison may be conducted even if the ANOVA does not produce a statistically significant result. Ideally, the planned comparisons are done in addition to a statistically significant ANOVA because the significant ANOVA protects against inflated Type I error rates incurred by multiple *t* tests (even if planned). The

■ A **planned comparison** is a test that is conducted when there are multiple groups of scores but specific comparisons have been specified prior to data collection; also called an *a priori comparison.*

■ The **Tukey *HSD* test** is a widely used post-hoc test that determines the differences between means in terms of standard error; the *HSD* is compared to a critical value; sometimes called the *q test.*

success stories in statistics are built not on getting the data to come out a certain way but on the quality of your scientific reasoning, your willingness to play fair with science, and your open-mindedness in letting the data speak.

Tukey *HSD*: An Honest Approach

One of the most commonly used post-hoc tests is the Tukey *HSD* test (sometimes called the *q test* because of the statistic on which it is based). *HSD* stands for "honestly significant difference" and indicates that we adjusted for the fact that we are making multiple comparisons. We only want to find differences that are "honestly" there. *The **Tukey HSD test** is a widely used post-hoc test that determines the differences between means in terms of standard error; the HSD is compared to a critical value.* The Tukey *HSD* test involves (1) the calculation of differences between each pair of means and (2) the division of each difference by the standard error. As with the *z* and *t* tests, we compare the *HSD* for each pair of means to a critical value (a *q* value found in the table for the *q* statistic in Appendix B) to determine if the means are different enough to reject the null hypothesis. The Tukey *HSD* test, therefore, is basically a variant of the *z* and *t* tests; the parallel is easily seen in its formula: $HSD = \dfrac{(M_1 - M_2)}{s_M}$, for any two sample means. The formula for the standard error is: $s_M = \sqrt{\dfrac{MS_{Within}}{N}}$. *N* in this case is the sample size within each group, with the assumption that all samples have the same number of participants. (*Note:* Alternately, some researchers implement a Tukey *HSD* test by calculating a single critical difference. They then compare each mean difference to the critical difference, the critical *HSD*. If a mean difference is larger than the critical difference, they reject the null hypothesis for that pair of means. Regardless of the method used, the findings will be the same.)

The above calculations are easily done if all samples are the same size. However, when there are different-size samples, as in our example of foreign graduate students, we have to add one additional step. We have to calculate a weighted sample size, also known as a harmonic mean. N' (pronounced "N prime") is weighted sample size, the harmonic mean. Its formula is $N' = \dfrac{N_{Groups}}{\Sigma(1/N)}$. We calculate N' by dividing the number of groups (the numerator) by the sum of 1 divided by the sample size for every group (the denominator). For the example in which there were five students in arts and sciences programs and four in each of the other three programs, $N' = \dfrac{4}{\left(\dfrac{1}{5} + \dfrac{1}{4} + \dfrac{1}{4} + \dfrac{1}{4}\right)} = \dfrac{4}{(0.20 + 0.25 + 0.25 + 0.25)}$

$= \dfrac{4}{0.95} = 4.211$. When sample sizes are not equal, we use a formula for s_M based on N' instead of N:

$$s_M = \sqrt{\dfrac{MS_{Within}}{N'}} = \sqrt{\dfrac{0.327}{4.211}} = 0.279$$

Now we will calculate *HSD* for each pair of means. It does not matter in which order we decide to subtract our means. For example, we could subtract the mean for business from the mean for law, or the mean for law from

Symbol: *HSD*

Formula: $HSD = \dfrac{(M_1 - M_2)}{s_M}$, for any two sample means

Formula: $s_M = \sqrt{\dfrac{MS_{Within}}{N}}$, if equal sample sizes

Symbols: N' is the weighted sample size used in ANOVA

Formula: $N' = \dfrac{N_{Groups}}{\Sigma(1/N)}$

Formula: $s_M = \sqrt{\dfrac{MS_{Within}}{N'}}$, if unequal sample sizes the mean for business. Because of this, we will ignore the sign of the answer; it is contingent on the arbitrary decision of which mean to subtract from the other.

Arts and sciences (4.00) versus education (3.75):
$$HSD = \frac{(4.00 - 3.75)}{0.279} = 0.896$$

Arts and sciences (4.00) versus business (3.75):
$$HSD = \frac{(4.00 - 3.75)}{0.279} = 0.896$$

Arts and sciences (4.00) versus law (2.75):
$$HSD = \frac{(4.00 - 2.75)}{0.279} = 4.480$$

Education (3.75) versus business (3.75):
$$HSD = \frac{(3.75 - 3.75)}{0.279} = 0$$

Education (3.75) versus law (2.75):
$$HSD = \frac{(3.75 - 2.75)}{0.279} = 3.584$$

Business (3.75) versus law (2.75):
$$HSD = \frac{(3.75 - 2.75)}{0.279} = 3.584$$

Now all we need is a critical value to which we can compare our *HSD*s. Then we can determine which pairs of means are significantly different from one another. Appendix B lists the cutoffs for the *HSD* in a *q* table because the *HSD*

TABLE 10-13. EXCERPT FROM THE q TABLE

Like the *F* table, we use the *q* table to determine critical values for a given *p* level, based on the number of means being compared and the within groups degrees of freedom. Note that critical values are in regular type for 0.05 and **boldface for 0.01**.

WITHIN-GROUPS DEGREES OF FREEDOM	··· 3	k = NUMBER OF TREATMENTS (LEVELS) 4	5 ···
. . ..			
12	3.77	4.20	4.51
	5.05	**5.50**	**5.84**
13	3.73	4.15	4.45
	4.96	**5.40**	**5.73**
14	3.70	4.11	4.41
	4.89	**5.32**	**5.63**
. . .			

Who Considers the Costs of Graduate School?
A study of foreign graduate students, analyzed with an ANOVA and a post-hoc Tukey *HSD* test, found that students in arts and sciences programs considered the costs of the program more than students in law programs did. Future research might explore why such a difference occurs. The availability of assistantships to arts and sciences graduate students? The expectations of high earnings among law students?

cutoffs are values of the q statistic; we have excerpted a portion of the q table in Table 10-13. The numbers of means being compared (levels of the independent variable) are in a row along the top of the q table, and the within-groups degrees of freedom are in a column along the left-hand side. We first look up the within-groups degrees of freedom for our test, 13, along the left column. We then go across from 13 to the numbers below the number of means being compared, 4. For a p level of 0.05, the cutoff q is 4.15. Again, the sign of our *HSD* does not matter because the order in which we subtract means is arbitrary. This is a two-tailed test, and any *HSD* above 4.15 or below −4.15 would be considered statistically significant.

By comparing the *HSD*s that we calculated above to the critical value of 4.15, we can see that there is only one statistically significant difference between means in this ANOVA. It appears that foreign graduate students in arts and sciences programs in the United States rate the importance of financial factors higher, on average, than do foreign graduate students in law programs in the United States. Because we have not rejected the null hypothesis for any other pairs, we can only conclude that there is not enough evidence to determine that these pairs of means are different. So, as with any hypothesis test, we cannot accept the null hypothesis—we only reject or fail to reject the null hypothesis.

It is important to note that sometimes, when we conduct an ANOVA, we have a statistically significant result, but we do not show statistically significant differences between means when we conduct post-hoc tests. In particular, this can occur when the sizes of the individual samples are small. If the post-hoc test yields no significant differences, even though there is a statistically significant ANOVA, we cannot conclude that any particular pairs of means are different from one another.

What are some of the possible explanations for the graduate school findings? Perhaps law students expect to make a great deal of money upon graduation, so they don't mind racking up large loans. Or, perhaps Ruby happened to recruit a group of law students, just by chance, who did not concern themselves with the cost of graduate school. Either way, the next step is replication.

The Bonferroni Test: A More Stringent Post-Hoc Test

Post-hoc tests are used when we have not planned specific comparisons based on theory. For many researchers, the Tukey *HSD* test is the default post-hoc test, and in many cases, it really is the best choice. But the wise researcher thinks

■ The **Bonferroni test** is a post-hoc test that provides a more stringent critical value for every comparison of means; sometimes called the *Dunn Multiple Comparison test.*

about which test to choose before automatically conducting a Tukey *HSD* test and can justify her or his choice when writing a research report. One other post-hoc test that is often used is the Bonferroni test. It is more conservative than the Tukey *HSD* test; that is, the test makes it more difficult to reject the null hypothesis. It also is easy to implement. When we really are fishing, we just admit it, and use a more conservative test such as the Bonferroni test rather than the Tukey *HSD*.

Sometimes called the *Dunn Multiple Comparison test, the* **Bonferroni test** *is a post-hoc test that provides a more stringent critical value for every comparison of means.* Normally, as we've learned, social scientists use a cutoff level of 0.05; with a Bonferroni test, we use a smaller cutoff level to make it more difficult to reject the null hypothesis. To use a Bonferroni test, we determine the number of comparisons we plan to make. Table 10-14 states the number of comparisons for three through seven means.

The Bonferroni test is straightforward. We merely divide the p level by the number of comparisons. For a p level of 0.05 and four means, we would make six comparisons using the $(0.05/6) = 0.008$ p level for each comparison. We then conduct a series of independent-samples t tests using the more extreme p level to determine the critical values. That is, the differences between means would have to be in the extremely narrow tails of a t distribution, at 0.008 (0.8%), before we would be willing to reject the null hypothesis. For seven means, we would make 21 comparisons using the $(0.05/21) = 0.002$ p level for each comparison. The differences would have to be in the most extreme 0.2% of a t distribution before we would reject the null hypothesis!

In each case, the p levels for every comparison add up to 0.05, so we are still using a 0.05 p level overall. For example, when we make six comparisons at the 0.008 level, we have a $(0.008 + 0.008 + 0.008 + 0.008 + 0.008 + 0.008) = 6(0.008) = 0.05$ p level overall. Even though the overall p level remains at 0.05, the p levels for the individual comparisons rapidly become very extreme (see Table 10-14). The difference between two means must be quite

TABLE 10-14. THE BONFERRONI TEST: FEW GROUPS, MANY COMPARISONS

Even with a few means, we must make many comparisons to account for every possible difference. Because we run the risk of incorrectly rejecting the null hypothesis just by chance if we run so many tests, it is a wise idea to use a more conservative procedure, such as the Bonferroni test, when comparing means. The Bonferroni test requires that we divide an overall p level, such as 0.05, by the number of comparisons we will make.

NUMBER OF MEANS	NUMBER OF COMPARISONS	BONFERRONI p LEVEL (OVERALL $p = 0.05$)
2	1	0.05
3	3	0.017
4	6	0.008
5	10	0.005
6	15	0.003
7	21	0.002

extreme before we can reject the null hypothesis, and we may fail to detect real differences that are not quite extreme enough. If we fail to detect a difference that really is there, we have committed a Type II error. The Bonferroni test greatly reduces the incidence of Type I errors but can lead to Type II errors instead. When conducting hypothesis tests, we are always striking a balance between reducing Type I errors and reducing Type II errors. As we decrease the chances of one type of error, we are, by necessity, increasing the chances of the other.

In the example with the foreign students' ratings of factors used to choose a graduate school, there were six comparisons among the four means. With a Bonferroni test, we'd divide 0.05 by 6; the new p level would be $(0.05/6) = 0.008$. The critical value would be based on this more extreme p level. We would conduct independent-samples t tests but use a critical value based on 0.008. (In our t table, we could only look up the closest p level to 0.008, 0.01, but software can help us be more specific.) Using software, we conducted an independent-sample t test to compare the means for students in arts and sciences versus law programs and calculated a t statistic of 2.973. For a test of two groups with 5 and 4 participants, respectively, the total degrees of freedom, 7, would be the sum of the degrees of freedom for each group: 4 and 3 (sample size minus 1 for each group). The critical t value for a two-tailed independent-samples t test with 7 degrees of freedom at a p level of 0.01 (the closest to 0.008) would be 3.50. This comparison is not statistically significant. Unlike the Tukey *HSD*, the Bonferroni test does not allow us to conclude that arts and sciences students place more importance on financial factors, on average, than do law students in their decision where to attend graduate school. The test statistic is no longer beyond the critical value, because the critical value based on a Bonferroni test is more extreme than the critical value based on a Tukey *HSD* test.

Even if you never use anything but a Tukey *HSD* post-hoc test yourself, you are likely to encounter other tests as you read journal articles, and you will want to judge researchers' post-hoc test decisions. Do they seem to have used the Tukey *HSD* test by default? If they choose a more liberal post-hoc test, or a planned comparison, do they justify their decision? The more you know about statistics, the better you will be able to sift through good and bad data and decide for yourself which results to rely on.

In summary, a statistically significant ANOVA does not tell us where differences between means lie. Planned tests are those comparisons that we decide to conduct in advance of data collection, usually based on a particular theoretical model or previous finding. Post-hoc tests—like the Tukey *HSD* test and its more conservative counterpart, the Bonferroni test—are used when we have less-targeted hypotheses with respect to comparisons.

⊙ CHECK YOUR LEARNING

10-4 Check Your Learning 10-3 asked you to conduct an ANOVA on an abbreviated data set from research by Irwin and colleagues (2004) on adherence to an exercise regimen. Participants were asked to attend a monthly group education program to help them change their exercise behavior. Attendance was taken, and participants were divided into three categories:

those who attended fewer than 5 sessions, those who attended between 5 and 8 sessions, and those who attended between 9 and 12 sessions. The dependent variable was number of minutes of exercise per week. Here are the data once again:

> <5 sessions: 155, 120, 130
>
> 5–8 sessions: 199, 160, 184
>
> 9–12 sessions: 230, 214, 195, 209

a. What conclusion did you draw in step 6 of the ANOVA? Why could you not be more specific in your conclusion? That is, why is an additional test necessary when our ANOVA is statistically significant?

b. Conduct a Tukey *HSD* test for this example. State your conclusions based on this test. Show all calculations.

c. If we did not reject the null hypothesis for every possible pair of means, then why can't we conclude that the two means are the same?

> When to Use an *F* Distribution: Working with More Than Two Samples

The *F statistic* is used when we want to compare more than two means. As with the z and t statistics, the F statistic is calculated by dividing a measure of the differences among sample means (between–groups variance) by a measure of variability within the samples (within–groups variance). The z, t, and F distributions are closely related. The t statistic is a z statistic when the sample size is extremely high. The F statistic is a squared t statistic when there are only two samples and is a squared z statistic when there are two samples *and* the sample size is extremely high. The hypothesis test based on the F statistic is called *analysis of variance (ANOVA)*.

> Analysis of Variance: Beyond *t* Tests

Analysis of variance (ANOVA) offers a solution to the problem of running multiple *t* tests. As we run more and more comparisons of pairs, we markedly increase our risk of a Type I error. ANOVAs allow for multiple comparisons in just one statistical analysis. There are several different types of ANOVA, and each has two descriptors. One indicates the number of independent variables, such as *one-way ANOVA* for one independent variable. The other indicates whether participants are in only one condition (*between-groups ANOVA*) or in every condition (*within-groups ANOVA*). The major assumptions for ANOVA are random selection of participants, normally distributed underlying populations, and *homoscedasticity*, which means that all populations have the same variance. As with previous statistical tests, most real-life analyses do not meet all of these assumptions.

> The One-Way Between-Groups ANOVA: Applying the Six Steps of Hypothesis Testing

ANOVA uses the six steps of hypothesis testing that you have already learned, but with some modifications, particularly to step 3 and step 5. Step 3 is simpler than with t tests; we only have to state that the comparison distribution is an F distribution and provide the degrees of freedom. In step 5, we calculate the F statistic; a *source table* helps us to keep track of our calculations. The F statistic is a ratio of two different estimates of population variance, both of distributions of scores rather than distributions of means. The denominator, within-groups variance, is similar to the pooled variance of the independent-samples t test; it's basically a weighted average of the variance within each sample. The numerator, between-groups variance, is an estimate based on the difference between the sample means, but it is then inflated to represent a distribution of scores rather than a distribution of means. A large between-groups variance and a small within-groups variance indicate a small degree of overlap among samples and likely a small degree of overlap among populations. A large between-groups variance divided by a small within-groups variance produces a large F statistic. If the F statistic is beyond a proscribed cutoff, or critical value, then we can reject our null hypothesis.

The F statistic developed out of the need to ask more complicated questions that involve more than two groups. But when there are more than two groups, we need techniques to compare multiple means. When we reject the null hypothesis in ANOVA, we only know that at least one of the means is different from at least one other mean. But we do not know exactly where the differences lie. We must conduct follow-up analyses called *post-hoc tests*, to determine where differences lie.

> Digging Deeper into the Data: Post-Hoc Tests to Decide Which Groups Are Different

When we have specific hypotheses based on the existing research literature, we can conduct *planned* (or *a priori*) *comparisons*. In the absence of theoretical predictions, we conduct post-hoc tests, follow-up analyses that allow us to identify the specific statistically significant differences among means, given a statistically significant ANOVA. The *Tukey HSD* test is one of the most frequently used post-hoc tests. The calculation of the *HSD* statistic involves dividing a difference between two means by a standard error, then comparing the *HSD* to a critical value from a q table; this procedure is quite similar to that used to calculate z and t statistics. Another common post-hoc test, the *Bonferroni test*, is more conservative than the Tukey *HSD* test; that is, it is more difficult to reject the null hypothesis when we use it. Good researchers consider their options and do not automatically use a default test, such as the Tukey *HSD* test.

SPSS GUIDELINES FOR CHAPTER 10

The one-way ANOVA is used when we wish to make a comparison between three or more groups that all represent different levels of one nominal independent variable. For example, we might want to compare three different breeds of dogs (the nominal independent variable) in how easy they are to train (the interval dependent variable).

Then we can instruct SPSS to analyze our ANOVA by selecting:

Analyze → Compare Means → One-Way ANOVA. Now select the variables. The independent variable goes in the box marked "Factor" and the dependent variable goes in the box labeled "Dependent." To request various descriptive statistics, select "Options."

We may conduct planned comparisons or post-hoc comparisons of means by selecting:

Analyze → Compare Means → One Way ANOVA and then choosing "Post Hoc." Choose the post-hoc test you'd like to conduct along with an ANOVA.

EXERCISES

10.1 *The Daily Show* as real news and *t* tests versus ANOVAs: Focusing on coverage of the 2004 U.S. presidential election, Julia R. Fox, a telecommunications professor at Indiana University, coded a number of half-hour episodes of *The Daily Show* as well as a number half-hour episodes of the network news (Indiana University Media Relations, 2006). Fox reported that the average amounts of "video and audio substance" were not statistically significantly different between the two types of shows. Her analyses are described as "second-by-second," so for this exercise, assume that all outcome variables are measures of time.

a. As the study is described, what are the independent and dependent variables? For nominal variables, state the levels.

b. As the study is described, what type of hypothesis test would Fox use?

c. Now imagine that Fox added a third category, a cable news channel such as CNN. Based on this, state the independent variable or variables and the levels of any nominal independent variables. What hypothesis test would she use?

10.2 Which distribution? Part I. For each of the following situations, state whether the distribution of interest is a *z* distribution, a *t* distribution, or an *F* distribution. Explain your answer.

a. A city employee locates a U.S. Census report that includes the mean and standard deviation for income in the state of Wyoming and then takes a random sample of 100 residents of the city of Cheyenne. He wonders whether residents of Cheyenne earn more, on average, than Wyoming residents as a whole.

b. A researcher studies the effect of different contexts on work interruptions. Using discreet video cameras, she observes employees working in enclosed offices in the workplace, in open cubicles in the workplace, and in home offices.

c. An honors student wondered whether an education in statistics reduced the tendency to believe advertising that cited data. He compared social sciences majors who had taken statistics and social science majors who had not taken statistics with respect to their responses to an interactive advertising assessment.

10.3 Which distribution? Part II. For each of the following situations, state whether the distribution of interest is a *z* distribution, a *t* distribution, or an *F* distribution. Explain your answer.

a. A student reads in her *Introduction to Psychology* textbook that the mean IQ is 100. She asks 10 friends what their IQ scores are (they attend a university that assesses everyone's IQ score) to determine whether her friends are smarter than average.

b. Is the presence of books in the home a marker of a stable family? A social worker counted the number of books on view in the living rooms of all the families he visited over the course of one year. He categorized families into four groups: no books visible, only children's books visible, only adult books visible, and both children's and adult books visible. The department for which he worked had stability ratings for each family based on a number of measures.

c. Which television show leads to more learning? A researcher assessed the vocabularies of a sample of children randomly assigned to watch *Sesame Street* as much as they wanted for a year but to not watch *The Wiggles*. She also assessed the vocabularies of a sample of children randomly assigned to watch *The Wiggles* as much as they wanted for a year but not to watch *Sesame Street*. She compared the average vocabulary scores for the two groups.

10.4 Relations among the distributions: The z, t, and F distributions are closely linked. In fact, it is possible to use an F distribution in all cases in which a t or a z could be used.

a. If you calculated an F statistic of 4.22 but you could have used a t statistic (i.e., the situation met all criteria for using a t statistic), what would the t statistic have been? Explain your answer.

b. If you calculated an F statistic of 4.22 but you could have used a z statistic, what would the z statistic have been? Explain your answer.

c. If you calculated a t statistic of 0.67 but you could have used a z statistic, what would the z statistic have been? Explain your answer.

d. Cite two reasons that all three types of distributions (i.e., z, t, and F) are still in use when we really only need an F distribution.

10.5 Escalating Type I error—too many *t* tests: As we conduct numerous comparisons using t tests, the chances of a Type I error increase dramatically. In this chapter, we considered the escalation of the probability of a Type I error when the p level was set at 0.05 for each comparison. Now let's consider what happens to the chances of a Type I error when we set the p level to 0.01, a more conservative cutoff.

a. Using the format introduced in this chapter, calculate the probability of a Type I error if you conduct all possible comparisons of three groups. (*Hint:* First, determine how many comparisons would be necessary with three groups.)

b. Now calculate the probability of a Type I error if you conduct all possible comparisons with six groups.

c. Does the more conservative p value of 0.01 help much once we have many comparisons? Explain.

10.6 Choosing a graduate school: name that ANOVA: Catherine Ruby (2006), a doctoral student at New York University, conducted an online survey to ascertain the reasons that foreign students chose to attend graduate school in the United States. One of several dependent variables that she considered was reputation; students were asked to rate the importance in their decision of factors such as the reputation of the institution, the institution and program's academic accreditations, and the reputation of the faculty. Students rated factors on a 1–5 scale, and then all reputation ratings were averaged to form a summary score for each respondent. For each of the following scenarios, state the independent variable with its levels (the dependent variable is reputation in all cases). Then state what kind of an ANOVA she would use.

a. Ruby compared the importance of reputation among graduate students in different types of programs: arts and sciences, education, law, and business.

b. Imagine that Ruby followed these graduate students for three years, assessing their rating of reputation once a year.

c. Ruby compared foreign students working toward a master's, a doctorate, or a professional degree (e.g., MBA) on reputation.

d. Imagine that Ruby followed foreign students from their master's program to their doctoral program to their postdoctoral fellowship, assessing their ratings of reputation once at each level of their training.

10.7 The varieties of ANOVA—memory for names: Do people remember names better under different circumstances? In a fictional study, a cognitive psychologist studied memory for names after a group activity that lasted 20 minutes. Participants were not told that this was a study of memory. After the group activity, participants were asked to name the other group members. The researcher randomly assigned 120 participants to one of three conditions: (1) group members introduced themselves once (one introduction only), (2) group members were introduced by the experimenter and by themselves (two introductions), and (3) group members were introduced by the experimenter and themselves and also wore nametags throughout the group activity (two introductions and nametags).

a. Identify the type of ANOVA that should be used to analyze the data from this study.

b. State what the researcher could do to redesign this study so it would be analyzed with a one-way within-groups ANOVA. Be specific.

10.8 Study design and personal ads: A researcher wondered about the degree to which age was a factor for those posting personal ads on match.com. He randomly selected 200 ads and examined data about the poster (the person who posted the ad). Specifically, for each ad, he calculated the difference between the poster's age and the oldest age he or she would be open to in a romantic prospect. So, if someone were 23 years old and would date someone as old as 30, his or her score would be 7, and if someone were 25 and would date someone as old as 23, his or her score would be −2. He calculated these scores for all 200 posters and categorized them into three groups based on where they lived: exurban, suburban, or urban.

a. List the independent variable, along with its levels.

b. What is the dependent variable?

c. What kind of ANOVA is this?

10.9 Study design and football players' black grease: Does the black grease beneath football players' eyes really reduce glare or just make them look mean? In a variation of a study actually conducted at Yale University, 46 participants placed one of three substances below their eyes: black grease, black antiglare stickers, or petroleum jelly. The researchers assessed eye glare using a contrast chart that gives a value for each participant on an interval scale. Every participant was assessed with each of the three substances, one at a time. Black grease led to a reduction in glare compared with the two other conditions, antiglare stickers or petroleum jelly (DeBroff & Pahk, 2003).

a. List the independent variable, along with its levels.

b. What is the dependent variable?

c. What kind of ANOVA is this?

10.10 ANOVA and assumptions—football players' black grease: Refer to the study described in Exercise 10.9.

a. What is the first assumption for ANOVA? Is it likely that the researchers met this assumption? Explain your answer.

b. What is the second assumption for ANOVA? How could the researchers check to see if they had met this assumption. Be specific.

c. What is the third assumption for ANOVA? How could the researchers check to see if they had met this assumption. Be specific.

10.11 Between and within algebra classrooms: Imagine that your cousin, a high school student, has been assigned to an algebra class based on previous performance. Like many high schools, his high school has three levels of algebra classes: (1) one that includes the standard curriculum plus remedial lessons, (2) one that includes the standard curriculum, and (3) one that includes the standard curriculum plus an advanced component. At the end of the semester, students' performance will be assessed on a statewide standardized mathematics exam.

a. Using this example, explain the concept of between variance.

b. Using this example, explain the concept of within variance.

c. How would you draw a curve for each distribution (1, 2, and 3) that demonstrates the concepts of between variance and within variance, while also showing what you'd expect these three distributions to look like in comparison with one another.

10.12 The *F* distribution, politics, and religion: Researchers asked 180 U.S. students to identify their political viewpoint as most similar to that of the Republicans, most similar to that of the Democrats, or neither. All three groups then completed a religiosity scale. The researchers wondered whether political orientation affected levels of religiosity, a measure that assesses how religious one is, regardless of the specific religion with which one identifies.

a. What is the independent variable, and what are its levels?

b. What is the dependent variable?

c. What are the populations and what are the samples?

d. Using this example, explain how you would calculate the *F* statistic.

10.13 One-way ANOVA and eBay: Do some genres of music tend to sell for more money than other genres on eBay? We randomly selected several CDs from the eBay lists for four genres: classical, rap/hip-hop, pop, and jazz. We include prices only for CDs with no bids yet, and we list the CDs as the sellers did on the eBay Web site. These prices indicate the lowest bid that the seller will accept.

Classical:

Weber: Piano concertos by Nikolai Demidenko: $2.99

Mozart: Concertos for two and three pianos: $1.91

Mahler: Symphony No. 4 and *Der Abschied*: $1.45

Rap/Hip-Hop:

Rapmania: Roots of Rap—Various Artists: $0.99

No More Drama—Mary J. Blige: $0.01

St. Lunatics—Free City: $0.99

Nelly Furtado—Man Eater: $0.77

Pop:

Sugar Ray 14:59: $0.99

Christmas Through Your Eyes—Gloria Estefan: $1.00

R.E.M.—Monster: $0.01

Jazz:

Sketches of Spain—Miles Davis: $5.79

Buddy Clark Collection 1942–1949: $14.99

Joe Gordon/Scott LaFaro—West Coast Days: $8.99

Chet Baker—Compact Jazz: $0.99

a. What is the independent variable? What are its levels?

b. What is the dependent variable?

c. Conduct all six steps of hypothesis testing.

d. Report the statistics as you would in a journal article.

10.14 ANOVA and orthodontics: Iranian researchers studied factors affecting patients' likelihood of wearing orthodontic appliances, noting that orthodontics is perhaps the area of health care with the highest need for patient cooperation (Beheram & Pooya, 2006). Among their analyses, they compared students in primary school, junior high school, and high school. The data that follow have almost exactly the same means as they found in their study, but with far smaller samples. The score for each student is his or her daily hours of wearing the orthodontic appliance.

> Primary school: 16, 13, 18
>
> Junior high school: 8, 13, 14, 12
>
> High school: 20, 15, 16, 18

a. What is the independent variable? What are its levels?

b. What is the dependent variable?

c. Conduct all six steps of hypothesis testing.

d. Report the statistics as you would in a journal article.

10.15 The language of statistics—*source*: In your own words, define the word *source* as you would use it in everyday conversation. Provide at least two different meanings that might be used. Then define the word as a statistician would use it.

10.16 The language of statistics: Find the error in language in each of the following statements about z, t, or F distributions or their related tests. Explain why it is incorrect and provide the correct word.

a. The professor reported the mean and standard error for the final exam in the statistics class.

b. Before we can calculate a t statistic, we must know the population mean and the population standard deviation.

c. The researcher calculated the parameters for her three samples so that she could calculate an F statistic and conduct an ANOVA.

d. For her honors project, Evelyn calculated a z statistic so that she could compare a sample of students who had ingested caffeine and a sample of students who had not ingested caffeine on their video game performance mean scores.

10.17 The symbols of statistics: Find the incorrectly used symbol or symbols in each of the following statements or formulas. For each statement or formula, (i) state which symbol(s) is/are used incorrectly, (ii) explain why the symbol(s) in the original statement is/are incorrect, and (iii) state what symbol(s) *should* be used.

a. When calculating an F statistic, the numerator includes the estimate for the between variance, s^2.

b. $SS_{Between} = (X - GM)^2$

c. $SS_{Within} = (X - M)$

d. $F = \sqrt{t}$

10.18 CFC scores and major—statistical software output and the relation between t and F distributions: Two samples of students, one comprised of social science majors and one comprised of students with other majors, completed the CFC. The accompanying tables include the output from software for a t test and an ANOVA on these data.

Independent Samples Test

	t	Df	Sig. (2-tailed)	Mean Difference	Standard Error Difference	95% Confidence Interval of the Difference	
						Lower	Upper
CFC Scores	-.650	28	.521	-.17500	.26930	-.72664	.37664

ANOVA

CFC Scores

	Sum of Squares	df	Mean Square	F	Sig.
Between Groups	.204	1	.204	.422	.521
Within Groups	13.538	28	.483		
Total	13.742	29			

Group Statistics

Major		N	Mean	Standard Deviation	Standard Error Mean
CFC Scores	Other	10	3.2000	.88819	.28087
	Social Science	20	3.3750	.58208	.13016

a. Demonstrate that the results of the *t* test and the ANOVA are the same. (*Hint:* Find the *t* statistic for the independent-samples *t* test and the *F* statistic for the ANOVA.)

b. In statistical software output, "Sig" refers to the actual *p* level of the statistic. We can compare the actual *p* level to a cutoff *p* level such as 0.05 to decide whether or not to reject the null hypothesis. What are the "Sig." levels for the two tests here— the independent-samples *t* test and the ANOVA? Are they the same or different? Explain why this is the case.

c. In the ANOVA, the column titled "Mean Square" includes the estimates of variance. Show how the *F* statistic was calculated from two types of variance. (*Hint:* Look at the far left column to determine which estimate of variance is which.)

d. Looking at the table titled "Group Statistics," how many participants were in each sample?

e. Looking at the table titled "Group Statistics," what is the mean CFC score for the social science majors?

10.19 A comparison of GPAs—statistical software output and the relation between *t* and *F* distributions: Based on your knowledge of the relation of the *t* and *F* distributions, complete the accompanying software output tables. The table for the independent-samples *t* test and the table for the ANOVA were calculated using the identical fictional data.

a. What is the *F* statistic? Show your calculations. (*Hint:* The "Mean Square" column includes the two estimates of variance used to calculate the *F* statistic.)

b. What is the *t* statistic? Show your calculations. (*Hint:* Use the *F* statistic that you calculated in part (a).)

c. In statistical software output, "Sig" refers to the actual *p* level of the statistic. We can compare the actual *p* level to a cutoff *p* level such as 0.05 to decide whether to reject the null hypothesis. For the t test, what is the "Sig."? Explain how you determined this. (*Hint:* Would we expect that the "Sig." for the independent-samples t test be the same as or different from that for the ANOVA?)

Independent Samples Test

			t-test for Equality of Means				
	T	Df	Sig. (2-tailed)	Mean Difference	Standard Error Difference	95% Confidence Interval of the Difference	
						Lower	Upper
GPA		82		-.28251	.12194	-.52508	-.03993

ANOVA

GPA	Sum of Squares	Df	Mean Square	F	Sig.
Between Groups	4.623	1	4.623		.005
Within Groups	42.804	82	.522		
Total	47.427	83			

■ DIGGING DEEPER INTO THE DATA

10.20 eBay and a Tukey test: In Exercise 10.13, you conducted an ANOVA on the prices of used records on eBay.

a. When we conduct an ANOVA and reject the null hypothesis, why are we not able to say what means are different from each other?

b. Conduct a Tukey *HSD* test. Which of these types of music have statistically significantly different average prices?

10.21 Post-hoc tests and changing critical values: Consider the abbreviated study by Irwin and colleagues (2004) that we analyzed in Check Your Learning 10-3 and 10-4.

a. With a desired p level of 0.05 overall, what would the critical p value be for each comparison using a Bonferroni test?

b. With a desired p level of 0.01 overall, what would the critical p value be for each comparison using a Bonferroni test?

10.22 A priori versus post-hoc tests: Researchers who conducted a study of brain activation and romantic love divided their analyses into two groups (Aron, Fisher, Mashek, Strong, Li, & Brown, 2005). Some analyses—those for which they had developed specific hypotheses prior to data collection—used a p level of 0.05. The rest of the analyses used a p level of 0.001.

a. Explain why the researchers' plan to have different p levels for the two groups was a wise one.

b. Suggest one method by which the researchers might have come up with a p level of 0.001 as their cutoff.

TERMS

ANOVA (p. 430)

F statistic (p. 430)

between-groups variance (p. 430)

within-groups variance (p. 431)

one-way ANOVA (p. 439)

within-groups ANOVA (p. 439)

between-groups ANOVA (p. 439)

homoscedastic (p. 440)

heteroscedastic (p. 440)

source table (p. 451)

grand mean (p. 452)

post-hoc test (p. 459)

planned comparison (p. 462)

Tukey HSD test (p. 462)

Bonferroni test (p. 466)

SYMBOLS

F

$df_{Between}$

df_{Within}

$MS_{Between}$

MS_{Within}

df_{Total}

$SS_{Between}$

SS_{Within}

SS_{Total}

GM

HSD

N'

FORMULAS

$df_{between} = N_{Groups} - 1$

$df_{Within} = df_1 + df_2 + \ldots + df_{Last}$ (in which df_1 etc. are the degrees of freedom, $N - 1$, for each sample)

$df_{Total} = df_{Between} + df_{Within}$ or $df_{Total} = N_{Total} - 1$

$GM = \dfrac{\Sigma(X)}{N_{Total}}$

$SS_{Total} = \Sigma(X - GM)^2$

$SS_{Within} = \Sigma(X - M)^2$

$SS_{Between} = \Sigma(M - GM)^2$

$SS_{Total} = SS_{Within} + SS_{Between}$

$MS_{Between} = \dfrac{SS_{Between}}{df_{Between}}$

$MS_{Within} = \dfrac{SS_{Within}}{df_{Within}}$

$F = \dfrac{MS_{Between}}{MS_{Within}}$

$HSD = \dfrac{(M_1 - M_2)}{s_M}$, for any two sample means

$s_M = \sqrt{\dfrac{MS_{Within}}{N}}$, if equal sample sizes

$N' = \dfrac{N_{Groups}}{\Sigma(1/N)}$

$s_M = \sqrt{\dfrac{MS_{Within}}{N'}}$, if unequal sample sizes

TWO-WAY ANOVA
UNDERSTANDING INTERACTIONS

"It depends," Julie said to herself. She was trying to figure out what had caused the sudden "ka-boom" in the deep pool of water about 200 feet downstream from where she was fishing. If it was a trout, then it was the biggest trout in the world. If it wasn't a trout, then it was worth figuring out what it was. Her grandpa had said that the pool held very large fish, so that was one of the hypotheses that swam through her 12-year-old imagination: a very big fish. But there were other possible explanations. The sound was more like something plunging into the water than like the pancake splash of a very big fish—and it was much louder.

Her grandpa had told her never to fish the pool unless he was with her. But he had also told her that it was never wrong to avoid noisy, inexperienced fishermen. Two annoying up-from-the-city fishermen sporting expensive waders and fly rods splashed noisily into the water upstream near the bridge. So Julie's decision to fish closer to the pool depended on these conditions.

She heard a more modest splash as a trout surfaced for a fly. Then she heard more splashes as the trout suddenly began feeding on something in the water. "Since they're jumping," Julie thought to herself, "this might be the time to tie on Grandpa's birthday fly." He had given it to her on her birthday and told her, "Keep this one for a really big fish, Julie." She was about to tie it on when another thunderous "ka-boom" startled it right out of her fingers and into the water. She could only watch as it slipped away from her, downstream, riding high on the water just the way Grandpa had meant it to. Tears started, but then she asked herself, "What would Grandpa want me to do?" She tied on a new fly and cast toward the splashing trout. It bothered her, losing something that her grandpa had spent so many hours creating just for her. But the trout were rising, so she didn't have time for sadness. The effect of a losing a treasured birthday gift? It depends on whether the trout are feeding.

The idea of "it depends" infected Julie's thoughts in many other ways. She preferred to fish the Willowemoc because it was smaller and more varied than the Beaverkill. They were both famous trout streams and, on average, the Beaverkill produced bigger fish. But it was easier to find privacy on the Willowemoc, and she knew her grandpa thought it was a little safer. Unfortunately, the best place to fish was also the worst place to fish: Junction Pool. Junction Pool was the spot where the Willowemoc joined with the Beaverkill and produced a deep pool of cold, oxygenated water that was filled with all the kinds of food that trout loved: mayflies, caddis flies, and stone flies.

Unfortunately, it seemed like everyone who had ever been slightly interested in trout fishing had also heard about Junction Pool. It was too famous a fishing spot. Presidents with all their reporters and security personnel could meet up with local fishing clubs at Junction Pool. Strange, unpredictable things happened there. To Julie, the interaction of the two streams at Junction Pool meant that the enjoyment of fishing there depended on whether it was crowded with noisy fishermen. "It depends" was a regular a feature in Julie's decisions about school, friends, and trout fishing.

Fly-fishing for trout is more complicated than dropping a hook with a large worm into a pool of hungry fish. Success in fly-fishing requires a working knowledge of entomology (the study of insects), the ecology of streams, the seasonal preferences of trout, working equipment, and good luck (random influences). There are too many variables at work, so real-world outcomes (dependent variables) are never predicted by just one or even two predictor variables (independent variables). In the social sciences, there are also always more predictor variables that we don't know about. We sometimes call them "stuff-we-can't-explain variance"—those predictor variables that we just haven't thought of or haven't figured out how to measure. But the inclusion of potentially interacting variables goes a long way toward explaining many otherwise mysterious human behaviors. Humans are even more complicated than trout, so we need research designs and statistical tests that can explore the multivariable complexity of our daily lives. Statistical interactions are what happen when multiple variables meet up in places like Junction Pool.

In this chapter, we will examine the hypothesis test used for research designs that can test for the presence of interactions. Specifically, we will learn about research designs that have two nominal independent variables and one interval dependent variable. We will focus on between-groups designs for most of the chapter, but, in the Digging Deeper into the Data section, we will discuss how the concepts of two-way ANOVA can be applied to other research designs.

Fishing and Interactions Between Multiple Variables
The probability of success in fishing, on the Willowemec, shown here, or anywhere else, depends on multiple variables that interact with one another. To use one obvious example, the effectiveness of the fishing line depends on the presence or absence of a hook, just as how much a person enjoys fishing might depend on the interactions among privacy, success, and safety.

Michael Gadomski

■ A **two-way ANOVA** is a hypothesis test that includes two nominal independent variables, regardless of their numbers of levels, and an interval dependent variable.

■ A **factorial analysis of variance** is a statistical analysis used with one interval dependent variable and at least two nominal independent variables (also called *factors*); also called a *multifactorial analysis of variance*.

■ **Factor** is a term used to describe an independent variable in a study with more than one independent variable.

> TWO-WAY ANOVA: WHEN THE OUTCOME DEPENDS ON MORE THAN ONE VARIABLE

In Chapter 10, we learned that there are several kinds of ANOVA and that ANOVAs are described by two adjectives, one indicating the number of independent variables and one indicating the research design (between-groups or within-groups). We also learned that the first category of adjectives includes the term *one-way*; we learned only this one term in Chapter 10 because, until now, we have considered just one independent variable. A one-way ANOVA allows us to compare several levels of one independent variable, each level represented by a sample. But we can also use more than one independent variable. For example, *a **two-way ANOVA** is a hypothesis test that includes two nominal independent variables, regardless of their numbers of levels, and an interval dependent variable.* As the number increases—three-way, four-way, five-way—the number of independent variables increases. Table 11-1 shows a range of possibilities for naming ANOVAs. In this chapter, we'll focus on the ANOVA that uses the second adjective from column 1 and the first adjective from column 2: the two-way between-groups ANOVA.

It is sometimes difficult to determine the number of independent variables because it is easy to fall into the trap of confusing the number of variables with the number of levels of the variables. If there is a study comparing freshmen, sophomores, juniors, and seniors, it is easy, but incorrect, to think that there are four independent variables (freshmen, sophomores, juniors, and seniors) rather than one independent variable (year in school) with four levels (freshmen, sophomores, juniors, and seniors). To be sure that you're not making this mistake, always identify the independent variables *and* their levels at the same time.

There is a catch-all phrase for two-way, three-way, and higher order ANOVAs; any ANOVA with at least two independent variables can be called a factorial (or sometimes a multi-factorial ANOVA). *A **factorial analysis of variance** is a statistical analysis used with one interval dependent variable and at least two nominal independent variables (also called factors).* This is also called a *multifactorial analysis of variance.* **Factor** *is another word used to describe an independent variable in a study with more than one independent variable.* When discussing factorial ANOVAs,

---

TABLE 11-1. HOW TO NAME AN ANOVA

ANOVAs are typically described by two adjectives, one from the first column and one from the second. We will always have one descriptor from each column. So, we could have a one-way between-groups ANOVA or a one-way within-groups ANOVA, a two-way between-groups ANOVA or a two-way within-groups ANOVA, and so on.

NUMBER OF INDEPENDENT VARIABLES: PICK ONE	PARTICIPANTS IN ONE OR ALL SAMPLES: PICK ONE	ALWAYS FOLLOWS DESCRIPTORS
One-way	Between-groups	ANOVA
Two-way	Within-groups	
Three-way		

several different words are used interchangeably. For example, *independent variable*, *factor*, and even the word *way* (as in two-way ANOVA) all mean the same thing. New terms don't always refer to new ideas, so we will continue to alert you whenever a new term is used to express a familiar idea.

Why Use a Two-Way ANOVA: A Three-for-One Design

Grapefruit juice. What came to mind when you read those words? A nutrition-packed breakfast beverage? A wise choice for dieters? Something your mother would make you drink? Over the last 15 years, numerous studies (e.g., Bailey & Dresser, 2004; Mitchell, 1999) have documented the potential for grapefruit juice to increase the blood levels of certain medications, sometimes to toxic levels, by boosting the absorption of one or more of the active ingredients. Even scarier, this potentially life-threatening increase cannot be predicted for a given individual; it is found only by trial and error. For that reason, many physicians suggest that patients who take a wide range of medications, from some blood pressure drugs to many antidepressants, avoid grapefruit juice entirely. One commonly used anticholesterol drug whose effect is moderately boosted, sometimes dangerously, by the consumption of grapefruit juice is Lipitor (e.g., Bellosta, Paoletti, & Corsini, 2004). Let's use this particular interaction to understand the unique insights made possible by a two-way ANOVA.

Let's say that an investigator, Dr. Goldstein, wanted to know how to treat cholesterol, but only knew how to analyze hypothesis tests that used one independent variable, the one-way ANOVA that we learned about in Chapter 10. She would have to conduct one study to compare the effect of Lipitor on cholesterol levels with the effect of another another drug or a placebo. Then she would have to conduct a second study to compare the effect of grapefruit juice on cholesterol levels with that of another beverage or with no beverage, a study that might not even make much sense; after all, no one is predicting grapefruit juice on its own to be a treatment for high cholesterol. So how could she discover whether Lipitor works differently when combined with grapefruit juice?

In Chapter 4, we described researchers as bargain hunters, and a two-way ANOVA appears to be similar to a two-for-one sale by providing us with two independent variables, or factors, in one study. For example, a single study simultaneously examining medications like Lipitor *and* beverages like grapefruit juice is more efficient than two studies examining each independent variable individually. Two-way ANOVAs allow researchers to examine both hypotheses with the resources, time, and energy of a single study. But when Lipitor and grapefruit juice are used together, they interact and potentially create something entirely new, just like the Willowemoc and the Beaverkill Rivers join together and interact at Junction Pool. So a two-way ANOVA is even better than a two-for-one sale; it's a three-for-one sale.

Specifically, a two-way ANOVA allows researchers to explore exactly what Dr. Goldstein wanted to explore above: interactions. Does the effect of some medications, but not others, depend on the particular levels of another independent variable, the beverages that accompany them? A two-way ANOVA can examine (1) the effect of Lipitor versus other medications, (2) the effect of grapefruit juice versus other beverages, *and* (3) the ways in which a drug and a juice might combine to create some entirely new, and often unexpected, effect.

The Perils of Grapefruit Juice
Studies have demonstrated that grapefruit juice (a level of one independent variable) can interact with many common medications (levels of a second independent variable) and cause higher levels of active ingredients (the dependent variable) to be absorbed into the bloodstream. The medical journals that physicians read report the results of such two-way ANOVAs because interactions have the potential to be toxic. That is why some physicians recommend that patients who take certain medications avoid grapefruit juice entirely.

Lew Robertson/Corbis

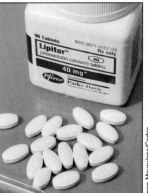
Tannen Maury/epa/Corbis

▪ A **cell** is a box that depicts one unique combination of levels of the independent variables in a factorial design.

The More Specific Vocabulary of Two-Way ANOVAs: Describing the Research Design

Every ANOVA, we learned, has two descriptors, one indicating the number of independent variables and one indicating the research design. Many researchers expand the first descriptor to provide even more information about the independent variables. Let's consider these expanded descriptors in the context of Dr. Goldstein's research. Were she to conduct just one study that examined both medication and beverage, she'd assign each participant to one level of medication (perhaps Lipitor, another cholesterol medication like Zocor, or a placebo) *and* to one level of beverage (perhaps grapefruit juice or water). This research design is shown in Table 11-2.

When we draw the design of a study, such as in Table 11-2, we call each box of the design a *cell*, *a box that depicts one unique combination of levels of the independent variables in a factorial design.* When cells contain numbers, they are usually means of the scores of all participants who were assigned to that combination of levels. In Dr. Goldstein's study, there are six cells to which participants might be assigned. Each participant is randomly assigned to one of the three levels of the variable medication: Lipitor, Zocor, or placebo. Each level of medication is in one column of the table of cells. Each participant is *also* assigned to one of the two levels of the variable beverage: grapefruit juice or water. Each level of beverage is in one row of the table of cells. A participant might be assigned to take Lipitor and grapefruit juice (upper-left cell), placebo and water (lower-right cell), or any of the other four combinations. In this case, there are two independent variables, or factors: medication and beverage. Medication, in the columns of the table, has three levels, and beverage, in the rows of the table, has two levels.

This leads us to the new ANOVA vocabulary. Instead of the descriptor *two-way*, many researchers refer to an ANOVA with this arrangement of cells as a 3 × 2 ANOVA (pronounced "three by two," not "three times two"). As with the *two-way* descriptor, the ANOVA is described with a second adjective—usually *between-groups* or *within-groups*. Because participants would receive only one medication and only one beverage, the hypothesis test for this design could be called either a *two-way between-groups ANOVA* or a *3 × 2 between-groups ANOVA*. An added benefit to the method of naming ANOVAs by the numbers of levels in each independent variable is the ease of calculating the total number of cells. Simply multiply the levels of the independent variables—the number of rows by the number of columns. In this case, the 3 × 2 ANOVA would have (3 × 2) = 6 cells. Sometimes researchers are even more specific, naming each independent variable by its number of levels, followed by the actual levels in parentheses: a 3 (Lipitor, Zocor, placebo) × 2 (grapefruit juice, water) between-groups ANOVA.

TABLE 11-2. INTERACTIONS WITH GRAPEFRUIT JUICE

A two-way ANOVA allows researchers to examine two independent variables, as well the ways in which they might interact, simultaneously.

	LIPITOR (L)	ZOCOR (Z)	PLACEBO (P)
GRAPEFRUIT JUICE (G)	L & G	Z & G	P & G
WATER (W)	L & W	Z & W	P & W

NAME THAT ANOVA

Experience for yourself some additional two-way ANOVAs. What if Dr. Goldstein added a fourth anticholesterol medication, Mevacor?

Using the new ANOVA vocabulary, what would she call the ANOVA?

_____

How many cells would there be? _____

The fourth medication would mean there were four levels of the independent variable, medication. There would still be two levels of the second independent variable, beverage. So this would be a 4×2 between-groups ANOVA. If we multiply the levels of the independent variable, we can calculate that there would be $(4 \times 2) = 8$ cells.

What if Dr. Goldstein used just two medication levels, Lipitor and placebo, along with the two levels of beverage?

Using the new ANOVA vocabulary, what would she call the ANOVA?

_____

How many cells would there be? _____

Now she has two levels of each variable, so this would be a 2×2 between-groups ANOVA, with $(2 \times 2) = 4$ cells.

This procedure can be used for expanded designs. If a third variable, such as dosage of medication (with two levels: low dose and high dose) were added to Dr. Goldstein's original study, she'd have a 3 (Lipitor, Zocor, placebo) $\times$ 2 (grapefruit juice, water) $\times$ 2 (low dose, high dose) between-groups ANOVA with $(3 \times 2 \times 2) = 12$ cells.

Two Main Effects and an Interaction: Three *F* Statistics and Their Stories

Good storytelling, whether in a TV sit-com or a lengthy novel, often keeps your interest by interweaving multiple plotlines. Two-way ANOVAs tell three stories simultaneously and produce *three F* statistics: one for the first independent variable, one for the second independent variable, and one for the interaction between the two independent variables. The *F* statistics for each of the two independent variables are referred to as main effects. *A **main effect** occurs in a factorial design when one of the independent variables has an influence on the dependent variable.* We evaluate whether there is a main effect by disregarding the influence of any other independent variables in the study—we temporarily pretend that the other variable doesn't exist.

So, with two independent variables, Dr. Goldstein would have two possibilities for a main effect. For example, after testing her participants in a two-way ANOVA, she might find a main effect of type of medication, and she would test for that main effect by temporarily pretending that the variable beverage hasn't even been included in the study. For example, Lipitor and Zocor might both work better than placebo at lowering cholesterol. That's the first story, and it completely disregards the variable beverage. She also might find a main effect of "beverage," and she would test for that main effect by temporarily pretending that the variable type of medication hasn't even been included in the study. For example, drinking grapefruit juice may reduce cholesterol, at least as

■ A **main effect** occurs in a factorial design when one of the independent variables has an influence on the dependent variable.

■ A statistical **interaction** occurs in a factorial design when the two independent variables have an effect in combination that we do not see when we examine each independent variable on its own.

compared to water. That's the second story, and it completely disregards the variable medication. But what is the third story?

Just as characters in a movie are more interesting when they have to overcome complicated circumstances, the third story in a two-way ANOVA is usually the most interesting because it is complicated by multiple, interacting variables. *A statistical **interaction** occurs in a factorial design when the two independent variables have an effect in combination that we do not see when we examine each independent variable on its own.* In other words, an interaction occurs when the effect of one independent variable on the dependent variable depends on the particular level of the other independent variable. For example, Dr. Goldstein might find that both Lipitor and Zocor (but not placebo) have more extreme effects on cholesterol when taken in combination with grapefruit juice versus water. In other words, the presence of the grapefruit juice changes the effect of Lipitor and Zocor, but not placebo. We also analyze the variability in terms of interactions because reality is usually more complicated than main effects. Fortunately, the way we analyze the variability of complicated circumstances involves only a minor variation on the skills you already have developed in previous chapters.

Each of the three F statistics has its own between-groups sum of squares (SS), degrees of freedom (df), mean square (MS), and critical value, but they all share a mean square within (MS_{Within}). Understanding the three stories of a two-way ANOVA provides far deeper insight into the factors that predict an outcome than does a series of several studies using only one independent variable at a time. The source table we used in Chapter 10 told only one story. The source table shown in Table 11-3 tells three stories, so naturally it is a little bigger. The symbols in the body of the table are be replaced by the actual calculations in an actual source table.

In summary, factorial ANOVAs are used because they allow us to examine several hypotheses in a single study, thus saving money, time, and other resources. Factorial ANOVAs also allow us to explore interactions. Factorial ANOVAs are often referred to by the levels of their independent variables (e.g., 2×2) rather than the number of independent variables (e.g., two-way), and sometimes the independent variables are called *factors*. A two-way ANOVA can tell three stories within a single study: two main effects (one about each independent variable) and one interaction (the combined influence of both variables). Each story has its own set of statistics, including its own F statistic, displayed in an expanded source table.

TABLE 11-3. AN EXPANDED SOURCE TABLE

This source table is the framework into which we would place the calculations for the two-way between-groups ANOVA with independent variables of medication and beverage. It tells three stories: The two main effects are listed first, then the interaction.

SOURCE	SS	df	MS	F
Medication	$SS_{Medication}$	$df_{Medication}$	$MS_{Medication}$	$F_{Medication}$
Beverage	$SS_{Beverage}$	$df_{Beverage}$	$MS_{Beverage}$	$F_{Beverage}$
Medication × Beverage	$SS_{Medication \times Beverage}$	$df_{Medication \times Beverage}$	$MS_{Medication \times Beverage}$	$F_{Medication \times Beverage}$
Within	SS_{Within}	df_{Within}	MS_{Within}	
Total	SS_{Total}	df_{Total}		

⊙ CHECK YOUR LEARNING

11-1 Adam Alter, a graduate student at Princeton University, and his advisor, Daniel Oppenheimer, studied whether names of stocks affected selling prices (Alter & Oppenheimer, 2006). They found that stocks with pronounceable ticker-code names, like "BAL," tended to sell at higher prices than did stocks with unpronounceable names, like "BDL." They examined this effect one day, one week, six months, and one year after the stock was offered for sale. (*Note:* For the purposes of this study, assume that the different stocks were assessed at each time period.) The effect was strongest one day after the stock was initially offered.

a. What are the "participants" in this study?

b. What are the independent variables and what are their levels?

c. What is the dependent variable?

d. Using the new descriptors from the *previous* chapter, what would you call the hypothesis test that would be used for this study?

e. Using the new descriptors from *this* chapter, what would you call the hypothesis test (i.e., statistical analysis) that would be used for this study?

f. How many cells are there? Explain how you calculated this answer.

➤ THE LAYERS OF ANOVA: UNDERSTANDING INTERACTIONS

The two noisy fishermen had watched Julie catch four trout in 30 minutes, so they splashed to the bank to ask her what they should tie on to the end of their leaders. Julie told them, "It depends."

"Depends on what?" they demanded.

"It depends on where you're fishing, how deep the water is, how cold the water is, what bugs are hatching, whether you're any good with a dry fly, whether you can see into the water, whether the terrestrials are out, whether you're trying to fish close to an overhanging tree, whether you have enough leader, and lots of other things." Julie wished she still had her grandpa's birthday present now that the trout were feeding.

"Oh."

Julie was too polite to tell them that the main effect of all their noisy splashing in the water overwhelmed all the other interacting details. Anyway, it was always possible they would just get lucky. Julie knew that chance always played a part in trout fishing; but it was always difficult to say exactly how much of successful trout fishing was due to chance and how much was due to skill. She hoped the noisy men would go away because she had a good spot. They had just ruined it with their splashing, but the trout would probably come back if she waited about 20 minutes.

The two men sat down on the bank and began to eat some sandwiches, so Julie pulled in her line and started staring into the water. She was interested in a large boulder about 10 to 15 feet away from her. The stream bumped up against the boulder and then rushed around its edges. But immediately below the boulder, the water swirled more quietly, creating what Julie's grandpa called "a soft spot" in the

Zig Leszczynski/Earth Scenes

Interactions
The ANOVA analyzes both the individual effectiveness of each variable and the inter-action effects of combined variables. Understanding success or failure in fishing also requires taking apart the various individual components so that they can be an-alyzed both separately and for how well they interact with each other.

water. The effect of how well a boulder in the stream created a friendly place for trout to hide depended on how deep the water was in this soft spot and how much food came flowing around the edges of the boulder. Julie understood interactions.

Julie was especially interested in this particular boulder be-cause there was a large overhanging tree about 20 feet up-stream. The leaves drooped into the water, and the current was vibrating the branches. To Julie, this meant that ants and bugs and other things that trout love to eat were probably falling off the branches and into the stream directly above the boulder. So the effect of a tree providing food for the trout depended on how well the current vibrated bugs off the tree and into the water. It was the interaction that produced the food. But the two men eating sandwiches on the bank saw only a 12-year-old girl staring into the water, apparently try-ing to mesmerize a trout into the net that hung from her waist.

After about five minutes of quietly watching the water, Julie tied an artificial ant to the end of her slender, almost invisible line. Rather than beat the water with repeated casts, she used the rod to cast the artificial ant just above the boul-der and worked the line so that there was very little slack by the time it came close to the boulder. As the artificial ant drifted past the soft spot in the water below the boulder, a trout darted out from the soft water, grabbed the artificial ant, and bent Julie's fly rod into a sharp **C** shape. The fish dove deep into the stream and Julie played it. Then it jumped once in the air, trying to get free of the hook. But it soon tired, and Julie netted it directly in front of the two astonished men. It was speckled with a red underbelly and was about 14 inches long. She admired it for a few moments, removed the hook, and then held it nose forward in the stream. The trout's gills pulsed beneath the water until, with a sudden burst, it wriggled out of her hand and back into the dark waters of the Willowemoc.

"Wow," said one of the men. "How did you do that?"

"And how did you know what to tie on?" asked the other.

Julie just shrugged. There was so much she could teach them, but it required only two words to summarize the main idea. "It depends," she told them.

The art and science of trout fishing illustrates that the statistical idea of in-teracting variables is all around us. Understanding interactions can guide us to-ward catching more trout and toward better decision making in other parts of our lives. The core idea of an interaction is expressed by the phrase "it depends." More specifically, an interaction occurs when the effect of one variable depends on the specific level of another variable.

Interactions and Public Policy: Using Two-Factor ANOVA to Improve Planning

Many of our students voice an idealistic ambition to do something meaningful with their lives, to use their skills as social scientists to improve the quality of life for themselves and others. They are drawn to psychology or social work, to behavioral economics or nonprofit political organizations. So let's apply the con-cept of interactions to an event that affected many lives: Hurricane Katrina demonstrates the importance of understanding interactions. First, the hurricane itself was an interaction among several weather variables. The devastating effects of the hurricane depended on particular levels of other variables, such as where it made landfall and the speed of its movement across the Gulf of Mexico. We can't understand Hurricane Katrina at a meteorological level without understanding the concept of interactions.

As behavioral scientists, our job is not to predict the weather but to describe, predict, and explain human behavior. It doesn't matter whether we are public health specialists coordinating resources, epidemiologists monitoring disease outbreaks, or volunteers providing immediate help to victims. The world is a complicated, multivariable place, which is why we need a fluent understanding of statistical interactions. Fortunately, clarifying complicated circumstances is the strength of factorial ANOVA. To put it more plainly, if you're serious about a career in the social sciences, you need to understand the thinking that underlies interactions, both conceptually and mathematically.

Interactions often surprise us. For example, we would think that Hurricane Katrina would have been universally bad for the health of all those displaced people—a main effect of a hurricane on health care. However, three researchers from the Tulane University School of Public Health and Tropical Diseases in New Orleans proposed a startling interaction regarding the effects of the hurricane on health care for pregnant women (Buekens, Xiong, & Harville, 2006):

> Women gave birth in the squalor of the Superdome or in alleys while waiting for rescuers. When it comes to pregnant women, the first priority of disaster relief agencies is to provide obstetrical and neonatal care. Massive relief efforts sometimes mean that access to care for pregnant women is actually improved in the aftermath of a disaster. (p. 91)

Of course, the quality of health care certainly didn't improve for everybody, which means that an interaction was involved. So we could create a hypothesis for why the quality of health care might improve for pregnant women in the aftermath of a disaster, while it becomes worse for almost everyone else. In the language of two-factor ANOVA, we could hypothesize that the effect of a disaster (one independent variable with two levels: disaster versus no disaster) on the quality of health care (the dependent variable) depends on the type of health care needed (the second independent variable, also with two levels: obstetrics/neonatal versus all other types of health care).

Why might health care improve for pregnant women but not for others? Pregnant women are among the most vulnerable people during a natural catastrophe, so perhaps they were given more attention by the rescue workers. Or perhaps the pregnant women were more assertive in seeking help. Perhaps both variables were interacting with each other. At this point, we don't know how to explain the researchers' findings, so we can only hypothesize. But in our complicated world, the influence of one variable usually depends on a specific level of another variable. Because we need to understand the logic of interactions to understand complicated circumstances, we'll next learn how to interpret interactions.

Interpreting Interactions: Understanding Complexity

As you may recall, the very name ANOVA (analysis of variance) expresses the goal of separating the numerical variability in a study into its component parts. At its most basic level, the variability in ANOVA is composed of three categories: between-groups variance, within-groups variance, and the unaccounted-for variance that we called stuff-we-can't-explain variance. Fortunately, the two-way between-groups ANOVA allows us to separate the between-groups variance into

■ A **quantitative interaction** is an interaction in which one independent variable exhibits a strengthening or weakening of its effect at one or more levels of the other independent variable, but the direction of the initial effect does not change.

■ A **qualitative interaction** is a particular type of quantitative interaction of two (or more) independent variables in which one independent variable reverses its effect depending on the level of the other independent variable.

■ **Marginal means** are the means of the rows and the columns in a table that shows the cells of a study with a two-way ANOVA design.

three finer categories: the two main effects, one for each independent variable, and an interaction effect. The interaction is a third effect; however, it is not a separate individual variable. The interaction effect is a blended effect resulting from the interaction between the two independent variables. The interaction effect is like mixing chocolate syrup into a glass of milk; the two foods blend into something familiar yet new.

Quantitative Interactions: Words, Tables, and Graphs

There are two terms that are often used to describe interactions: *quantitative* and *qualitative* (e.g., Newton & Rudestam, 1999). *A **quantitative interaction** is an interaction in which one independent variable exhibits a strengthening or weakening of its effect at one or more levels of the other independent variable, but the direction of the initial effect does not change.* More specifically, the effect of one independent variable is modified in the presence of another independent variable. *A **qualitative interaction** is a particular type of quantitative interaction of two (or more) independent variables in which one independent variable reverses its effect depending on the level of the other independent variable.* In a qualitative interaction, the effect of one variable doesn't just become stronger or weaker; it actually reverses direction in the presence of another variable. Let's first examine the quantitative interaction.

Our grapefruit juice example is a helpful illustration of a quantitative interaction. Lipitor and Zocor lead to elevations of some liver enzymes in combination with water, but the absorption levels are even higher with grapefruit juice. This effect is not seen with placebo, which has an equal effect regardless of beverage. The effects of Lipitor and Zocor, therefore, depend on what type of beverage they are paired with, and the effect of placebo does not. Let's invent some numbers to demonstrate this. The numbers in the cells in Table 11-4 don't represent actual absorption levels; rather, they are numbers that are easy for us to work with in our understanding of interactions. For this exercise, we will consider every difference between numbers to be statistically significant. (Of course, if we really conducted this study, we would conduct the two-way ANOVA to determine exactly which effects were statistically significant.)

First, we'll consider main effects; then we'll consider the overall pattern that constitutes the interaction. If there is a significant interaction, we then ignore any significant main effects; the significant interaction supersedes any significant main effects. Table 11-4 includes mean absorption levels for the six cells of the study. It also includes numbers in the margins of the table, to the right of and below the cells. The numbers in the margins are also means, but for every participant in a given row or in a given column. (We are assuming that there were equal numbers of participants in each cell; if this were not the case, the means in the margins would be weighted means.) As you might expect, these are called **marginal means,** *the means of the rows and the columns in a table that shows the cells of a study with a*

TABLE 11-4. A TABLE OF MEANS

We use a table to display the cell and marginal means so that we can interpret any main effects.

	LIPITOR (L)	ZOCOR (Z)	PLACEBO (P)	
GRAPEFRUIT JUICE (G)	60	60	3	41
WATER (W)	30	30	3	21
	45	45	3	

TABLE 11-5. THE MAIN EFFECT OF BEVERAGE

This table shows only the marginal means that demonstrate the main effect of beverage. Because we have isolated these marginal means, we cannot get distracted or confused by the other means in the table.

GRAPEFRUIT JUICE	41
WATER	21

TABLE 11-6. THE MAIN EFFECT OF MEDICATION

This table shows only the marginal means that demonstrate the main effect of medication. Because we have isolated these marginal means, we cannot get distracted or confused by the other means in the table.

LIPITOR (L)	ZOCOR (Z)	PLACEBO (P)
45	45	3

two-way ANOVA design. In Table 11-4, for example, the mean across from the row for grapefruit juice, 41, is the mean absorption level of every participant who was assigned to drink grapefruit juice, regardless of the medication level to which he or she was assigned. The mean below the column for placebo, 3, is the mean absorption level of every participant who took placebo, regardless of the beverage level to which he or she was assigned. (Although we wouldn't expect any absorption with placebo, we gave it a small value, 3, to facilitate our explanation of interactions.)

The easiest way to understand the main effects is to make a smaller table for each, with only the appropriate marginal means. Separate tables let us focus on one main effect at a time without being distracted by the means in the cells. For the main effect of beverage, we will construct a table with two cells, as shown in Table 11-5. Notice that we have only the means for beverage, as if medication were never even included in the study. The table makes it easy to see that the absorption level was higher, on average, for grapefruit juice than for water. Still, we would have to conduct a two-way ANOVA and reject the null hypothesis before drawing this conclusion.

We will now consider the second main effect, that for medication. As before, we will construct a table (see Table 11-6) that shows only the means for medication, as if beverage were never even included in the study. We kept the means for beverage in rows and for medication in columns, just as they were in the original table. You may, however, arrange them either way, whichever makes sense to you. Table 11-6 demonstrates that the absorption levels for Lipitor and Zocor were higher, on average, than for placebo, which led to almost no absorption. This would still need to be verified with a hypothesis test, but we seem to have two main effects: (1) a main effect of beverage (grapefruit juice leads to higher absorption, on average, than water does), and (2) a main effect of medication (Lipitor and Zocor lead to higher absorption, on average, than placebo does).

But that's not the whole story. Grapefruit juice, for example, does not lead to higher absorption, on average, among placebo users. Here's where the interaction comes in. Now we'll ignore the marginal means and get back to the means in the cells themselves, seen again in Table 11-7. Here we can see the overall pattern by framing it in two different ways. We can start by considering beverage. Does grapefruit juice boost mean absorption levels as compared to water? It depends. It

TABLE 11-7. EXAMINING THE OVERALL PATTERN OF MEANS

A first step in understanding an interaction is examining the overall pattern of means in the cells.

	LIPITOR (L)	ZOCOR (Z)	PLACEBO (P)
GRAPEFRUIT JUICE (G)	60	60	3
WATER (W)	30	30	3

depends on the level of the other independent variable, medication; specifically, it depends on whether the patient is taking one of the two medications or a placebo. We can also frame the question by starting with medication. Do Lipitor and Zocor boost mean absorption levels as compared to placebo? It depends. They do anyway, even when just drinking water, but they do so to a far greater degree when drinking grapefruit juice. This is a quantitative interaction because the strength of the effect varies under certain conditions, but not the direction.

Yet people sometimes perceive interactions where there are none. If Lipitor, Zocor, and placebo all had higher mean absorption rates when drinking grapefruit juice (versus water), there would be no interaction. Lipitor and Zocor would *always* lead to a particular increase in average absorption levels versus placebo—this would occur in the presence of any beverage. And grapefruit juice would *always* lead to a particular increase in average absorption levels versus water—this would occur in the presence of any medication. On the other hand, there is an interaction in the example we have been considering because grapefruit juice has a special effect with the two medications that it does not have with placebo. The tendency to see interactions when there are none can be diminished by constructing a bar graph, as in Figure 11-1. (*Note:* Many researchers use just lines, not bars, to depict interactions because it seems easier to "see" the interaction. Others argue that lines are misleading because they suggest points between categories that do not exist in the study. We have chosen to use bars because they more accurately reflect that each category has a mean and that we should not interpolate between means.)

The bar graph helps us to see the overall pattern, but one further step is necessary. Once we have created our bar graph, we connect each set of bars with a line. We have two choices that match the two ways we framed the interaction in words above. (1) As in Figure 11-2, we could connect the bars for the first independent variable, medication. We would connect the three medications for the grapefruit condition, and then we would connect the three medications for the water condition. 2) Alternately, as in Figure 11-3, we could connect the bars for the two beverages. We would connect the two beverages for Lipitor, then for Zocor, then for placebo. In Figure 11-3, notice that the lines do not intersect, but they're not all parallel either. If the lines were long enough, eventually they would intersect. Perfectly parallel lines indicate the likely absence of an interaction, but we almost never see perfectly parallel lines emerging from real-life data sets; real-life data are usually messy. Nonparallel lines may indicate an interaction, but we'll have to conduct an ANOVA and compare the *F* statistic with

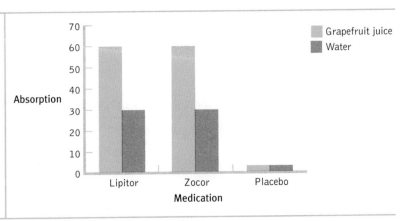

FIGURE 11-1
Bar Graphs and Interactions

Bar graphs help us determine if there really is an interaction. We can look at the pattern of the bars to determine whether there is an interaction. The bars help us to see that, among those taking placebo, absorption is the same whether the placebo is accompanied by grapefruit juice or water, whereas, among those taking Lipitor or Zocor, absorption is higher when accompanied by grapefruit juice than when accompanied by water.

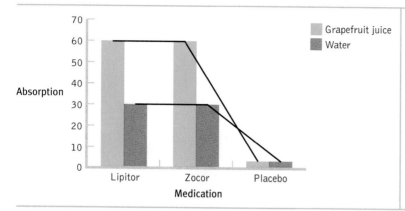

FIGURE 11-2
Are the Lines Parallel? Part I

We add lines to bar graphs to help us to determine whether there really is an interaction. We draw a line connecting the three medications under the grapefruit juice condition. We then draw a line connecting the three medications under the water condition. These two lines intersect, an indication of an interaction that can be confirmed by conducting a hypothesis test.

its cutoff to be sure. Only if the lines are significantly different from parallel can we reject the null hypothesis that there is no interaction; and we only want to interpret an interaction if we reject the null hypothesis.

Remember that the core idea of an interaction is summed up by the phrase "it depends." Main effects and interactions are best represented graphically. For example, when the lines connecting the bars are flat and all lying virtually on top of one another, then there are no main effects and no interactions. None of the independent variables influences the dependent variable in any distinctive way, so nothing is going on. However, when the lines connecting the bars are separated from one another but still parallel, then there is a main effect for at least one of the independent variables. Finally, when the lines connecting the bars are significantly different from parallel, the dependent variable is responding to different levels of one independent variable in different ways, depending on the level of the other independent variable.

Some social scientists refer to an interaction as a significant difference in differences. In the context of the grapefruit juice study, the mean difference between grapefruit juice and water is larger when participants are taking one of the medications than when they are taking placebo. In fact, for those taking placebo, there is no mean difference between grapefruit juice and water. This is an example of a significant difference between differences. Whenever the effect of one independent variable on the dependent variable depends on a particular level of the other independent variable, there is an interaction. That interaction is represented graphically whenever the lines connecting the bars are significantly different from parallel.

On the other hand, if grapefruit juice also led to an increase in mean absorption levels among those taking placebo, the graph would look like that in

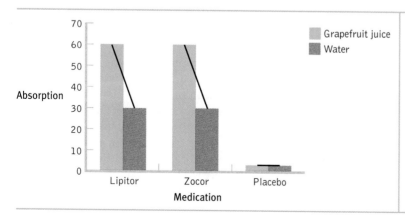

FIGURE 11-3
Are the Lines Parallel? Part II

There are always two ways to examine the pattern of our bar graphs. Here, we have drawn three lines, one connecting the two beverages under each of the three medication conditions. Were the three lines to continue, the two medication lines would eventually intersect with the horizontal placebo line, an indication of an interaction that can be confirmed by conducting a hypothesis test.

FIGURE 11-4
Parallel Lines

The three lines are exactly parallel. Were they to continue indefinitely, they would never intersect. Were this true among the population (not just this sample), there would be no interaction.

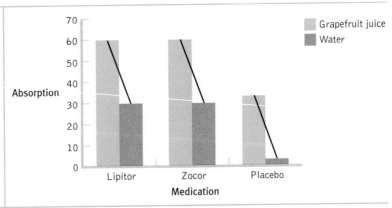

Figure 11-4. In this case, the mean absorption levels of Lipitor and Zocor do increase with grapefruit juice, but so does the mean absorption level of placebo. There is likely no interaction. Grapefruit juice has the same effect, regardless of the level of the other independent variable of medication. When in doubt about whether there is an interaction or just two main effects that add up to a greater effect, draw a graph and connect the bars with a line.

Qualitative Interactions: Words, Tables, and Graphs

Let's recall the definition of a qualitative interaction: a particular type of quantitative interaction of two (or more) independent variables in which the effect of one independent variable reverses its effect, depending on the level of the other independent variable. Here's an example that may be particularly interesting for students interested in how people integrate information and make decisions.

Do you think that, on average, people make better decisions when they consciously focus on the decision? Or do they make better decisions when the decision-making process is unconscious (that is, although they learn the facts about their choices, they make their decision after being distracted by other tasks, rather than focusing on the facts)? Which decision-making method do you think is superior, and why?

Research by Dijksterhuis, Bos, Nordgren, and van Baaren (2006) offers intriguing evidence about decision-making styles that forced many people to readjust their thinking about how to approach major and minor life choices. The authors conducted a series of studies that were analyzed with two-way ANOVAs. Participants were asked to decide between two options following either conscious or unconscious thinking about the choice.

In one study, participants were asked to choose one of four cars; one car was objectively the best of the four, and one was objectively the worst. Some participants made a less complex decision; they were told 4 characteristics of each car. Some participants made a more complex decision; they were told 12 characteristics of each car. After learning about the characteristics of the cars, half the participants in each group were randomly assigned to think consciously about the cars for four minutes before making a decision. Half were randomly assigned to distract themselves for four minutes by solving anagrams before making a decision.

Choosing the Best Car
When making decisions, such as which car to buy, do we make better choices after conscious or unconscious deliberation? Research by Dijksterhuis and colleagues (2006) suggests that less complex decisions are typically better when made after conscious deliberation, whereas more complex decisions are typically better when made after unconscious deliberation.

Franco Vogt/Corbis

TABLE 11-8. A TWO-WAY BETWEEN-GROUPS ANOVA

Dutch researchers designed a study to examine what style of decision making led to the best choices in less complex and more complex situations. Would you predict an interaction? In other words, would the lines connecting bars on a graph be different from parallel? And if they are different from parallel, how are they different? If they are different just in strength, you are predicting a quantitative interaction. If the direction of effect actually reverses, you are predicting a qualitative interaction.

	CONSCIOUS THOUGHT	UNCONSCIOUS THOUGHT (DISTRACTION)
LESS COMPLEX (4 ATTRIBUTES OF EACH CAR)	less complex; conscious	less complex; unconscious
MORE COMPLEX (12 ATTRIBUTES OF EACH CAR)	more complex; conscious	more complex; unconscious

The research design, with two independent variables, is shown in Table 11-8. The first independent variable is complexity, with two levels: less complex (4 attributes) and more complex (12 attributes). The second is type of decision making, with two levels: conscious thought and unconscious thought (distraction).

The researchers then evaluated how well people made their decisions; specifically, they calculated a score for each participant that reflected his or her ability to differentiate between the objectively best and objectively worst cars in the group. This score represents the dependent variable, and higher numbers indicate a better ability to differentiate between the best and worst cars. Let's look at Table 11-9, which presents cell means and marginal means for this experiment. Note that the means are approximate and that the marginal means are created by assuming the same number of participants in each cell. As we consider these findings, we will assume that all differences are statistically significant. (In a real research situation, we would conduct an ANOVA to determine whether the main effects and interaction were statistically significant.)

Because there was an overall pattern—an interaction—the researchers did not pay attention to the main effects in this study; an interaction trumps any main effects. However, we will examine the main effects—to get some practice—first for the independent variable of complexity and then for the independent variable of type of decision making. We will create tables for each of the two main effects so that we can examine them independently

TABLE 11-9. DECISION-MAKING TACTICS

To understand the main effects and overall pattern of a two-way ANOVA, we start by examining the cell means and marginal means.

	CONSCIOUS THOUGHT	UNCONSCIOUS THOUGHT (DISTRACTION)	
LESS COMPLEX	5.5	2.3	3.9
MORE COMPLEX	0.6	5.0	2.8
	3.05	3.65	

TABLE 11-10. MAIN EFFECT OF COMPLEXITY OF DECISION	
These marginal means suggest that, overall, participants are better at making less complex decisions.	
LESS COMPLEX	3.9
MORE COMPLEX	2.8

TABLE 11-11. MAIN EFFECT OF TYPE OF DECISION MAKING	
These marginal means suggest that, overall, participants are better at making decisions when the decision making is unconscious—that is, when they are distracted.	
CONSCIOUS	UNCONSCIOUS
3.05	3.65

(Tables 11-10 and 11-11). The marginal means indicate that when type of decision making is ignored entirely, people make better decisions, on average, in less complex situations than in more complex situations. Further, the marginal means also suggest that, when complexity of decision is ignored, people make better decisions, on average, when the decision-making process is unconscious than when it is conscious.

However, if there is also a significant interaction, these main effects are limited in their contribution to our understanding of how to best approach decisions. Without an interaction, we'd only know that we tend to make better decisions in less complex situations than in more complex situations and that we tend to make better decisions when our thought processes are unconscious than when they are conscious. But this is not the whole story. The overall pattern of cell means renders this knowledge misleading, even inaccurate, under certain conditions. The interaction offers far more nuanced information on the best method for making decisions. It demonstrates that the effect of the decision-making method *depends* on the complexity of the decision. Conscious decision making tends to be better than unconscious decision making in less complex situations, but unconscious decision making tends to be better than conscious decision making in more complex situations. This reversal of direction is what makes this a qualitative interaction. It's not just the strength of the effect that changes, but the actual direction!

A bar graph, shown in Figure 11-5, makes the pattern of the data far clearer. We can actually see the qualitative interaction. The direction of the effect of type of decision making in less complex situations is opposite that in more complex situations.

As with a quantitative interaction, we would add lines to determine whether they are parallel (no matter how long the lines were drawn) or intersect (or would do so if extended far enough), as in Figure 11-6. Here we see that the lines intersect without even having to extend them beyond the graph. This is likely an interaction. Further, the fact that the direction reverses indicates that this is a qualitative, not a quantitative, interaction. Again, we see the importance of the words "it

FIGURE 11-5
Graphing Decision-Making Methods

This bar graph displays the traditional form of the interaction far better than does a table or words. We can see that it is a qualitative interaction; there is an actual reversal of direction of the effect of decision-making method in less complex versus more complex situations.

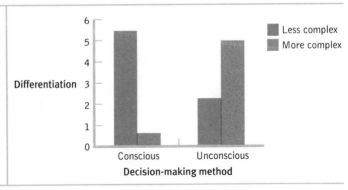

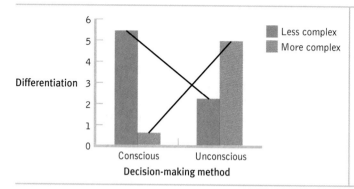

FIGURE 11-6
The Intersecting Lines of a Qualitative Interaction

When we draw two lines, one for the two bars that represent less complex situations and one for the two bars that represent more complex situations, we can easily see that they intersect. Lines that intersect, or would intersect if we extended them, indicate an interaction.

depends." Does type of decision making have an effect on the quality of the decision? Yes, but it depends on the complexity of the decision. Those making a less complex decision tend to make better choices if they use conscious thought. Those making a more complex decision tend to make better choices if they use unconscious thought. We would, as usual, verify this finding by conducting a hypothesis test before rejecting the null hypothesis that there is no interaction.

What if we conducted this study and found no statistically significant interaction; that is, what if we were not able to reject the null hypothesis for the interaction? Now, we would focus on any statistically significant main effects. The main effects would not be qualified—that is, modified—by an interaction. What if we were not able to reject the null hypothesis for either main effect? Then we could not reject the null hypothesis for any of the three possible findings—two main effects and an interaction—of a two-way ANOVA; we could only conclude that there is no evidence from this study to support any of the research hypotheses.

The qualitative interaction of decision-making method and complexity of situation was not likely to have been predicted by common sense. When this occurs, we should be cautious before generalizing the findings, particularly to our own lives. In this case, the research was carefully conducted and the researchers replicated their findings across several situations. For example, the researchers found similar effects in a real-life context when the less complex situation was shopping at a department store that sells clothing and kitchen products, and the more complex situation was purchasing furniture at IKEA. In addition to being based on good research, the results were surprising, and perhaps because of this, they were published in a top journal (*Science*) and reported by the media (e.g., Carey, 2006). Such an intriguing finding would not have been possible without the inclusion of two independent variables in one study, which required that researchers use a two-way ANOVA capable of testing for two main effects *and* interactions.

So what do these findings mean for us as we approach the decisions we face every day. Which sunblock should we buy to best protect against UV rays? Should we go to graduate school or get a job following graduation? Should we consciously consider characteristics of sunblocks but "sleep on" graduate school–related factors? Dijksterhuis and colleagues' (2006) findings would suggest yes. Yet, if the history of social science research is any indication, there are other factors that were not included in these studies but likely affect the quality of our decisions. And so the research process continues. In your social science classes, you'll probably notice that some of the most fascinating findings are qualitative interactions. You'll also notice that the story told by an interaction is far clearer in the form of a graph.

Visual Representations of Main Effects and Interactions: Bar Graphs

Graphs are almost always the best way to understand the overall pattern of main effects and interactions. To demonstrate this, let's return to a familiar example from Check Your Learning 1-2: the effect of hair length and gender of rater on the probability of a woman being sexually harassed. As you may recall, this study provided both male and female college students with a brief written description

FIGURE 11-7
A Main Effect of Gender

On average, women perceived a higher probability of the woman being sexually harassed than did men. Hair length had no effect. There is no interaction. (*Note:* On all of these graphs, feel free to add lines so that you can see whether there are likely to be interactions.)

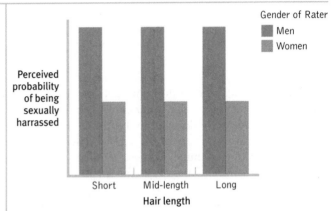

FIGURE 11-8
A Main Effect of Hair Length

On average, those with long hair were deemed most likely to be harassed, followed by those with mid-length hair, then by those with short hair. Gender of the participant had no effect. There is no interaction.

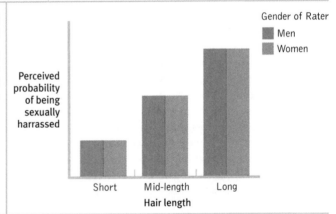

FIGURE 11-9
A Main Effect of Gender, and a Main Effect of Hair Length

On average, the longer the woman's hair, the higher the perceived probability that she would be sexually harassed. In addition, on average, women were more likely to perceive that the women would be harassed, regardless of her hair length. There is no interaction.

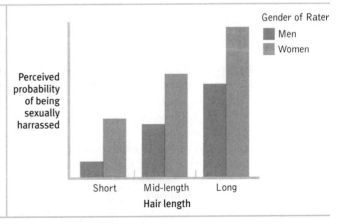

of a woman. Each description was identical except for her hair length. Some descriptions said she had "short" hair, others that she had "mid-length" hair, and a third that she had "long" hair. Participants were then asked to fill out a scale indicating their perceived probability of this woman being sexually harassed. So we have two independent variables, gender of the student rater (male, female) and hair length (short, mid-length, long), and one dependent variable (perceived probability of being sexually harassed). Figures 11-7 through 11-12 examine some possible outcomes and indicate whether they are main effects or interactions or both.

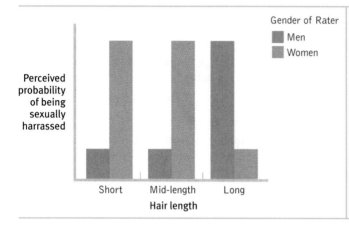

FIGURE 11-10

A Main Effect of Gender, and an Interaction Between Hair Length and Gender

There is a main effect of gender such that women, on average, were more likely to perceive that the woman would be sexually harassed. There is no main effect of hair length. In addition, there was an interaction such that women had higher average ratings than men of the probability of harassment when the woman had short or mid-length hair, whereas the men had higher average ratings than women when she had long hair.

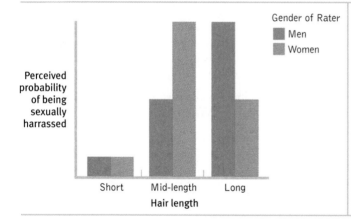

FIGURE 11-11

An Interaction Between Hair Length and Gender, and a Main Effect of Hair Length

There is no main effect of gender. There is a main effect of hair length such that women with short hair, on average, are seen as less likely to be harassed than those with mid-length or long hair. There is an interaction. Specifically, on average, men predict higher probabilities of being sexually harassed as hair length increases whereas women, on average, rate women with mid-length hair as having the highest probability, followed by those with long hair, then by those with short hair.

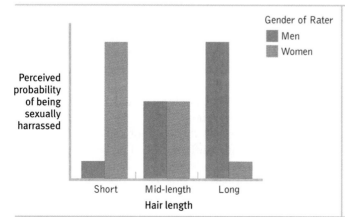

FIGURE 11-12

An Interaction Between Hair Length and Gender, and No Main Effects

The effect of hair length on the perceived probability of a woman being sexually harassed depends on the particular levels of gender. Specifically, women rate the probability of being sexually harassed as declining as hair length increases; men rate the probability of being sexually harassed as increasing as hair length increases. There are no main effects.

In summary, when there is a statistically significant interaction, the main effects are considered to be qualified (modified) by an interaction. We focus only on the overall pattern of cell means. There are two categories that describe the overall pattern. The most common interaction is a quantitative interaction in which the effect of the first independent variable depends on the levels of the second independent variable, but only in the strength of the effect. Qualitative interactions are those in which the effect of the first independent variable depends on the levels of the second independent variable, but the direction of the effect actually reverses from one level to another level of the second independent variable. There are three ways to identify a statistically significant interaction: (1) Visually, whenever the lines connecting the means of each group are significantly different from parallel; (2) conceptually, when you need to use the word-idea of "it depends" to tell the data's story; and (3) statistically, as with other hypothesis tests when the probability associated with an interaction in a source table is < 0.05.

⊙ CHECK YOUR LEARNING

11-2 For each of the following situations involving a real-life interaction, (i) state the independent variables, (ii) state the likely dependent variable, (iii) construct a table showing the cells, and (iv) explain whether it describes a qualitative or quantitative interaction.

a. Caroline and Mira are both really smart and do equally well in their psychology class, but something happens to Caroline when she goes to their philosophy class. She just can't keep up, whereas Mira does even better.

b. Our college baseball team has had a great few years. The team plays especially well at home versus away if playing teams in its own conference. However, they play especially well at away games (versus home games) if playing teams from another conference.

c. Caffeinated drinks get me wired and make it somewhat difficult to sleep. So does working out in the evenings. When I do both, I'm so wired that I might as well stay up all night.

> THE EXPANDED SOURCE TABLE: CONDUCTING A TWO-WAY BETWEEN-GROUPS ANOVA

"It depends," repeated one of the men, still staring at Julie. "But how did you know exactly what it depends on?"

"I guess I've been fly-fishing my entire life," she explained, and then added, "Why don't you fish my spot?" She knew that was what they really wanted. New fishermen could only think in terms of one thing, usually the right place to fish or the right fly to tie on. Only repeated failure, trial and error, and hours of futility could get them to the point of recognizing that the right fly depended on what kind of place you were trying to fish. Twelve-year-old Julie didn't know how to explain it to them. It was an interaction.

She moved farther downstream, closer to the big pool and just out of sight of the two noisy fishermen. She tied on a different fly. The water was deeper closer to the pool; the right fly to use depended on the speed and depth of the water. Grandpa's gift would have been perfect.

She stood in the middle of the stream, her legs protected inside her brown waders, and watched the water. She could see through to the bottom of the stream and looked for the little creatures caught in the current, struggling to break through the water's surface tension. Julie was concentrating so intently that when the second "ka-boom" sounded she almost fell into the stream just above the pool. She jerked her head up and saw only powerful ripples that located the spot. If it was fish, it was a monster. But it didn't sound like a fish.

She heard the voices of the two fishermen, coming to investigate the sound. Julie tied on a wooly bugger, knowing she could drift it down deep into the pool and give herself a chance at catching whatever might be there. But she had to do it quickly before the two fishermen got tired of lathering up the water and moved farther downstream to see if Julie was catching anything. She inched closer to the pool. She had to play out a great deal of line to get the wooly bugger into the deep water. At that moment, the effectiveness of Julie's fishing depended on many things interacting perfectly together: the amount of line she had out, whether the wooly bugger was really what the trout wanted, and whether she could get the fly to the trout before the two fishermen ruined the water.

The point of this fish story isn't subtle: Interactions are part of everyday life. Behavioral scientists explore these interactions by using two-factor ANOVAs. Fortunately, hypothesis testing for two-factor ANOVA uses the same logic as hypothesis testing for one-factor ANOVA. For example, the null hypothesis is exactly the same: There is no difference between groups. Type I and Type II errors still pose the same threats to our decision making: rejecting the null hypothesis when we shouldn't reject it or not rejecting the null hypothesis when we should reject it. The only way that a two-factor ANOVA differs from the one-factor ANOVA is that there are three ideas being tested and each idea is a separate source of variability.

The three ideas being tested in a two-factor ANOVA are the main effect of the first independent variable, the main effect of the second independent variable, and the interaction effect of the two independent variables. A fourth source of variability in two-factor ANOVA is our old friend stuff-we-can't-explain variance, which we more formally refer to as "error." Let's learn how to separate and measure these four sources of variance by evaluating a commonly used educational method to improve public health: myth-busting.

Two-Way ANOVA: The Six Steps of Hypothesis Testing

Does myth-busting really improve public health? Here are some myths and facts. Would this tactic increase your knowledge?

From the Web site of the Headquarters Counseling Center (2005) in Lawrence, Kansas:

Myth: "Suicide happens without warning."

Fact: "Most suicidal persons talk about and/or give behavioral clues about their suicidal feelings, thoughts, and intentions."

From the Web site for the World Health Organization (2007):

Myth: "Disasters bring out the worst in human behavior."

Fact: "Although isolated cases of antisocial behavior exist, the majority of people respond spontaneously and generously."

A group of Canadian researchers examined the effectiveness of myth-busting (Skurnik, Yoon, Park, & Schwartz, 2005). They wondered if the effectiveness of debunking false medical claims depends on the age of the person targeted by the message. In one study, they compared two groups of adults: one group of 32 younger adults, ages 18–25, and a second group of 32 older adults, ages 71–86, for a total

Do We Remember the Medical Myth or the Fact? Skurnik and colleagues (2005) studied the factors that influenced the misremembering of false medical claims as fact. They asked: When a physician tells a patient a false claim, then debunks it with the facts, does the patient remember the false claim or the facts? A source table will examine each factor in our study and tell us how much of the variability in the dependent variable is explained by that factor.

of 64 participants. Participants were presented with a series of claims and were told that each claim was either true or false. (In reality, all claims were true, partly because researchers did not want to run the risk that participants would misremember false claims as being true.) In some cases, the claim was presented once, and in other cases, it was repeated three times. (Note that we have altered the study's design somewhat in our description to make the study simpler for our purposes, but the results are the same.)

There were two independent variables in this study: age, with two levels (younger and older), and number of repetitions, with two levels (once and three times). The dependent variable, proportion of responses that were wrong after a three-day delay, was calculated for each participant. This was a two-way between-groups ANOVA. Alternately, we could label it a 2 × 2 between-groups ANOVA. From this, we know that there are four cells: (2 × 2) = 4. There were 64 total participants—16 in each cell. But for our purposes here, we'll use an example with 12 participants—3 in each cell. Here are the data that we'll use. These data have similar means to those in the actual study, and the F statistics are similar to those in the actual study.

Experimental Conditions	Proportion of Responses That Were Wrong
Younger, one repetition: 0.25, 0.21, 0.14	Mean: 0.20
Younger, three repetitions: 0.07, 0.13, 0.16	Mean: 0.12
Older, one repetition: 0.27, 0.22, 0.17	Mean: 0.22
Older, three repetitions: 0.33, 0.31, 0.26	Mean: 0.30

Let's consider the steps of hypothesis testing for a two-way between-groups ANOVA in the context of this example.

Step 1. Identify the populations, distribution, and assumptions.

The first step of hypothesis testing for a two-way between-groups ANOVA is very similar to that for a one-way between-groups ANOVA. First, we state the populations, but we specify that they are broken down into more than one category. In the current example, there are four populations, so there will be four cells. Table 11-12 shows the cells. With 12 participants, there would be 3 in each cell. As we do the calculations, we'll think of the first independent variable, age, as being in the rows of the table, and we'll think of the second independent variable, number of repetitions, as being in the columns of the tables.

There are four populations, each with labels representing the levels of the two independent variables to which they belong. Population 1 (Y; 1): is younger adults who hear one repetition of a false claim. Population 2 (Y; 3) is younger adults who hear three repetitions of a false claim. Population 3 (O; 1) is older adults

TABLE 11-12. STUDYING THE MEMORY OF FALSE CLAIMS USING A TWO-WAY ANOVA

The study of memory for false claims has two independent variables, age (younger, older) and number of repetitions (one, three).

	ONE REPETITION (1)	THREE REPETITIONS (3)
YOUNGER (Y)	Y; 1	Y; 3
OLDER (O)	O; 1	O; 3

who hear one repetition of a false claim. Population 4 (O; 3) is older adults who hear three repetitions of a false claim.

We next consider the characteristics of our data to determine the distribution to which we will compare our sample. We have more than two groups, so we need to consider variances to analyze differences among means. Therefore, we will use the F distribution. Finally, we list the hypothesis test that we would use for that distribution and check the assumptions for that hypothesis test. For an F distribution, we will use ANOVA, and as we already determined, we will use a two-way between-groups ANOVA.

The assumptions are the same for a two-way between-groups ANOVA as for a one-way between-groups ANOVA. First, the sample should be selected randomly. Second, the populations should be distributed normally. Third, the population variances should be equal. These data were not randomly selected. Younger adults were recruited from a university setting, and older adults were recruited from the local community. Because random sampling was not used, we must be cautious when generalizing from these samples. The researchers did not report whether they investigated the shapes of the distributions of their samples to assess the shapes of the underlying populations, nor did they provide standard deviations of the samples as an indication of whether the population spreads might be approximately equal, a condition known as homoscedasticity (*Note:* Homoscedasticity is also called homogeneity of variance). If we were analyzing our own data, we would explore these assumptions using our sample data.

Summary: Population 1 (Y; 1) is younger adults who hear one repetition of a false claim. Population 2 (Y; 3) is younger adults who hear three repetitions of a false claim. Population 3 (O; 1) is older adults who hear one repetition of a false claim. Population 4 (O; 3) is older adults who hear three repetitions of a false claim.

The comparison distribution will be an F distribution. The hypothesis test will be a two-way between-groups ANOVA. Assumptions: The data are not from random samples, so we must generalize only with caution. From the published research report, we do not know if the underlying population distributions are normal or if the population variances are approximately equal (homoscedasticity).

Step 2. State the null and research hypotheses.

The second step, to state the null and research hypotheses, is similar to that for a one-way between-groups ANOVA, except that we now have three sets of hypotheses, one for each main effect and one for the interaction. Those for the two main effects are the same as those for the one effect of a one-way between-groups ANOVA (see summary section below). If an independent variable has more than two levels, the research hypothesis would be that any two levels of the independent variable are not equal to one another. If there are only two levels, then we can simply say that the two levels are not equal; if there are only two levels and there is a statistically significant difference, then it must be between those two levels. Note that because there are two independent variables, we clarify which variable we are referring to by using initial letters or abbreviations for the levels of each (e.g., Y for younger and O for older).

The hypotheses for the interaction are stated in words but not in symbols. The null hypothesis is that the effect of one independent variable is not dependent on the levels of the other independent variable. The research hypothesis is that the effect of one independent variable depends on the levels of the other independent variable. It does not matter which independent variable we list first (i.e., "the effect of age is not dependent . . . " or "the effect of number of repetitions is not dependent . . . "). Write the hypotheses in the way that makes the most sense to you.

Summary: The main effect of the first independent variable, age, is as follows. Null hypothesis: On average, younger adults have the same proportion of responses that are wrong when remembering which claims are myths compared with older adults—H_0: $\mu_Y = \mu_o$.

Research hypothesis: On average, younger adults have a different proportion of responses that are wrong when remembering which claims are myths compared with older adults—H_1: $\mu_Y \neq \mu_o$

The main effect of the second independent variable, number of repetitions, is as follows.

Null hypothesis: On average, those who see one repetition have the same proportion of responses that are wrong when remembering which claims are myths compared with those who see three repetitions—H_0: $\mu_1 = \mu_3$.

Research hypothesis: On average, those who see one repetition have a different proportion of responses that are wrong when remembering which claims are myths compared with those who see three repetitions—H_1: $\mu_1 \neq \mu_3$.

The interaction, age × number of repetitions, is as follows.

Null hypothesis: The effect of number of repetitions is not dependent on the levels of age.

Research hypothesis: The effect of number of repetitions depends on the levels of age.

Step 3. Determine the characteristics of the comparison distribution.

The third step is similar to that of a one-way between-groups ANOVA, except that there are three comparison distributions, all of them F distributions. We need to provide the appropriate degrees of freedom for each of these: two main effects and one interaction. As before, the F statistic is a ratio of two types of variance, between-groups variance and within-groups variance. Because there are three effects for a two-way ANOVA, there will be three between-groups variance estimates, each with its own degrees of freedom. There is only one within-groups variance estimate for all three, so the within-groups variance (and its degrees of freedom) will be the same for all three possible effects.

For each main effect, the between-groups degrees of freedom is calculated as for a one-way ANOVA: the number of groups minus 1. The first independent variable, age, is in the rows of the table of cells, so the between-groups degrees of freedom is $df_{Rows(age)} = N_{Rows} - 1 = 2 - 1 = 1$. The second independent variable, number of repetitions, is in the columns of the table of cells, so the between-groups degrees of freedom is also: $df_{Columns(reps)} = N_{Columns} - 1 = 2 - 1 = 1$. We now need a between-groups degrees of freedom for the interaction. This is calculated by multiplying the degrees of freedom for the two main effects: $df_{Interaction} = (df_{Rows(age)})(df_{Columns(reps)}) = (1)(1) = 1$.

Formula: $df_{Rows} = N_{Rows} - 1$

Formula: $df_{Columns} = N_{Columns} - 1$

Formula: $df_{Interaction} = (df_{Rows})(df_{Columns})$

The within-groups degrees of freedom is calculated like that for a one-way between-groups ANOVA, the sum of the degrees of freedom in each of the cells. In the current example, there are 3 participants in each cell, so the within-groups degrees of freedom is calculated as follows, with N representing the number in each cell:

$$df_{Y,1} = N - 1 = 3 - 1 = 2$$
$$df_{Y,3} = N - 1 = 3 - 1 = 2$$
$$df_{O,1} = N - 1 = 3 - 1 = 2$$
$$df_{O,3} = N - 1 = 3 - 1 = 2$$
$$df_{Within} = df_{Y,1} + df_{Y,3} + df_{O,1} + df_{O,3} = 2 + 2 + 2 + 2 = 8$$

For a check on our work, we can calculate the total degrees of freedom just as we did for the one-way between-groups ANOVA. We subtract 1 from the total number of participants: $df_{Total} = N_{Total} - 1 = 12 - 1 = 11$. We can now add up the three between-groups degrees of freedom and the within-groups degrees of freedom to see if they equal 11. If they do not, we can check our calculations to find our error. In this case, they match: $11 = 1 + 1 + 1 + 8$.

Finally, for this step, we list the distributions with their degrees of freedom for each of the three effects. Note that, although the between-groups degrees of freedom for each effect are the same in this case, they are often different. For example, if one independent variable had three levels and the other had four, the between-groups degrees of freedom for the main effects would be 2 and 3, respectively, and the between-groups degrees of freedom for the interaction would be 6.
Summary: Main effect of age: F distribution with 1 and 8 degrees of freedom. Main effect of number of repetitions: F distribution with 1 and 8 degrees of freedom. Interaction of age and number of repetitions: F distribution with 1 and 8 degrees of freedom. (*Note:* It is helpful to include all df calculations in this step.)

Step 4. Determine critical values, or cutoffs.

Again, this step for the two-way between-groups ANOVA is just an expansion of that for the one-way version. We now need three cutoffs, or critical values, but they're determined just as we determined them before. We use the F table in Appendix B. For each main effect and for the interaction, we'll look up the within-groups degrees of freedom, which is always the same for each effect, along the left-hand side and the appropriate between-groups degrees of freedom across the top of the table. The place on the grid where this row and this column intersect contains three numbers. From top to bottom, the table provides cutoffs for p levels of 0.01, 0.05, and 0.10. As usual, we typically will use 0.05. In this instance, it happens that the critical value will be the same for both main effects and for the interaction because the between-groups degrees of freedom is the same for all three. But when the between-groups degrees of freedom are different, as often happens, there will be different critical values. Here, we look up the between-groups degrees of freedom of 1, the within-groups degrees of freedom of 8, and a p level of 0.05. The cutoff for all three is 5.32, as seen in Figure 11-13.
Summary: There are three critical values, as seen in the curve in Figure 11-13. (*Note:* It is very helpful to include the drawn curve in your answers to exercises—three curves if the cutoffs are different. Indicate the critical F statistics on the curves.) The cutoff F for the main effect of age is 5.32. The cutoff F for the main effect of number of repetitions is 5.32. The cutoff F for the interaction of age and number of repetitions is 5.32.

Step 5. Calculate the test statistic.

As with the one-way between-groups ANOVA, the fifth step for the two-way between-groups ANOVA is the most time-consuming. As you might guess, it's similar to what we already learned, but we have to calculate three F statistics instead of one. In the next section, we'll learn the logic and the specific calculations for this step.

Step 6. Make a decision.

This step is the same as for a one-way between-groups ANOVA, except that we compare each of the three F statistics to its appropriate cutoff F statistic. If the

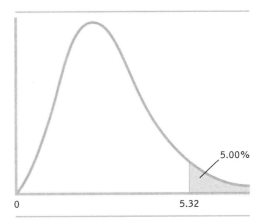

FIGURE 11-13
Determining Cutoffs for an F Distribution

We determine the cutoffs, or critical values, for an F distribution for a two-way between-groups ANOVA just as we did for a one-way between-groups ANOVA, except that we must calculate three cutoffs, one for each main effect and one for the interaction. In this case, the between-groups degrees of freedom are the same for all three, and so the cutoffs are the same.

F statistic is beyond the critical value, then we know that it is in the most extreme 5% of possible test statistics *if* the null hypothesis is true. After making a decision for each *F* statistic, we present our results in one of three ways.

First, if we are able to reject the null hypothesis for the interaction, then we can draw a specific conclusion with the help of a table and graph. Because we have more than two groups, we will use a version of one of the post-hoc tests we learned in Chapter 10. Because there are three effects, post-hoc tests are typically implemented separately for each main effect and for the interaction (Hays, 1994). If the interaction is statistically significant, then it might not matter whether the main effects also are significant; if they are also significant, then those findings are usually qualified by the interaction, and they are not described separately. The overall pattern of cell means can tell the whole story.

Second, if we are not able to reject the null hypothesis for the interaction, then we focus on any significant main effects, drawing a specific directional conclusion for each. In this study, each independent variable has only two levels, so there is no need for a post-hoc test. If there were three or more levels, however, then each significant main effect would require a post-hoc test to determine exactly where differences lie. Third, if we do not reject the null hypothesis for either main effect or the interaction, then we can only conclude that there is insufficient evidence from this study to support our research hypotheses. We will complete step 6 of hypothesis testing for this study in the next section, after we consider the calculations of the source table for a two-way between-groups ANOVA.

Two-Way ANOVA: Identifying Four Sources of Variability

In this section, we will complete Step 5 for a two-way ANOVA. The calculations for a two-way ANOVA are similar to those for a one-way ANOVA, except that we calculate three *F* statistics. We will use a source table. The elements are like those in Table 11-3, shown earlier in the chapter.

TABLE 11-13. CALCULATING THE TOTAL SUM OF SQUARES

The total sum of squares is calculated by subtracting the overall mean, called the grand mean, from every score to create deviations, then squaring the deviations and summing them: $\Sigma(X - GM)^2 = 0.0672$.

	X	(X − GM)	(X − GM)^2
Y, 1	0.25	(0.25 − 0.21) = 0.04	0.0016
	0.21	(0.21 − 0.21) = 0.00	0.0000
	0.14	(0.14 − 0.21) = −0.07	0.0049
Y, 3	0.07	(0.07 − 0.21) = −0.14	0.0196
	0.13	(0.13 − 0.21) = −0.08	0.0064
	0.16	(0.16 − 0.21) = −0.05	0.0025
O, 1	0.27	(0.27 − 0.21) = 0.06	0.0036
	0.22	(0.22 − 0.21) = 0.01	0.0001
	0.17	(0.17 − 0.21) = −0.04	0.0016
O, 3	0.33	(0.33 − 0.21) = 0.12	0.0144
	0.31	(0.31 − 0.21) = 0.10	0.0100
	0.26	(0.26 − 0.21) = 0.05	0.0025

TABLE 11-14. MEANS FOR FALSE MEDICAL CLAIMS STUDY

The study of the misremembering of false medical claims as true had two independent variables, age and number of repetitions. The cell means and marginal means for error rates are shown in the table. The grand mean is 0.21.

	ONE REPETITION (1)	THREE REPETITIONS (3)	
YOUNGER (Y)	0.20	0.12	0.16
OLDER (O)	0.22	0.30	0.26
	0.21	0.21	0.21

First, we'll calculate the total sum of squares. We calculate this in exactly the same way as for a one-way ANOVA. We subtract the grand mean from every score to create deviations, then square the deviations, and finally sum the squared deviations: $\Sigma(X - GM)^2 = 0.0672$ (Table 11-13).

We'll now calculate the between-groups sums of squares for the two main effects—the one in the rows and then the one in the columns of the table. Both are calculated similarly to the one between-groups sum of squares for a one-way between-groups ANOVA. The table with the cell means and marginal means is shown in Table 11-14. The between-groups sum of squares for the main effect of the independent variable age would be the sum, of the squares of the differences, for every score, between the marginal mean and the grand mean. We list all 12 scores (Table 11-15), marking the divisions among the cells. For each of the 6 younger participants, those in the top 6 rows of Table 11-15, we subtract the grand mean, 0.21, from the marginal mean, 0.16. For the 6 older participants, those in the bottom 6 rows of Table 11-15, we subtract 0.21 from the marginal mean, 0.26. We square all of these deviations and then add them to calculate the sum of squares for the rows, the independent variable of age: $\Sigma(M_{Row(age)} - GM)^2 = 0.03$.

We would repeat this process for the second possible main effect, that of the independent variable in the columns of the tables, number of repetitions

Formula: $SS_{total} = \Sigma(X - GM)^2$

Formula: $SS_{Between/row} = \Sigma(M_{Row} - GM)^2$

TABLE 11-15. CALCULATING THE SUM OF SQUARES FOR THE FIRST INDEPENDENT VARIABLE

The sum of squares for the first independent variable is calculated by subtracting the overall mean, called the grand mean, from the mean for each level of that variable—in this case, age—to create deviations, then squaring the deviations and summing them: $\Sigma(M_{row(age)} - GM)^2 = 0.03$.

	X	$(M_{Row(age)} - GM)$	$(M_{Row(age)} - GM)^2$
Y, 1	0.25	$(0.16 - 0.21) = -0.05$	0.0025
	0.21	$(0.16 - 0.21) = -0.05$	0.0025
	0.14	$(0.16 - 0.21) = -0.05$	0.0025
Y, 3	0.07	$(0.16 - 0.21) = -0.05$	0.0025
	0.13	$(0.16 - 0.21) = -0.05$	0.0025
	0.16	$(0.16 - 0.21) = -0.05$	0.0025
O, 1	0.27	$(0.26 - 0.21) = 0.05$	0.0025
	0.22	$(0.26 - 0.21) = 0.05$	0.0025
	0.17	$(0.26 - 0.21) = 0.05$	0.0025
O, 3	0.33	$(0.26 - 0.21) = 0.05$	0.0025
	0.31	$(0.26 - 0.21) = 0.05$	0.0025
	0.26	$(0.26 - 0.21) = 0.05$	0.0025

TABLE 11-16. CALCULATING THE SUM OF SQUARES FOR THE SECOND INDEPENDENT VARIABLE

The sum of squares for the second independent variable is calculated by subtracting the overall mean, called the grand mean, from the mean for each level of that variable—in this case, number of repetitions—to create deviations, then squaring the deviations and summing them: $\Sigma(M_{Column(reps)} - GM)^2 = 0$.

	X	$(M_{Column(reps)} - GM)$	$(M_{Column(reps)} - GM)^2$
Y, 1	0.25	$(0.21 - 0.21) = 0$	0
	0.21	$(0.21 - 0.21) = 0$	0
	0.14	$(0.21 - 0.21) = 0$	0
Y, 3	0.07	$(0.21 - 0.21) = 0$	0
	0.13	$(0.21 - 0.21) = 0$	0
	0.16	$(0.21 - 0.21) = 0$	0
O, 1	0.27	$(0.21 - 0.21) = 0$	0
	0.22	$(0.21 - 0.21) = 0$	0
	0.17	$(0.21 - 0.21) = 0$	0
O, 3	0.33	$(0.21 - 0.21) = 0$	0
	0.31	$(0.21 - 0.21) = 0$	0
	0.26	$(0.21 - 0.21) = 0$	0

(Table 11-16). So the between-groups sum of squares for number of repetitions, then, would be the sum, for every score, of the marginal mean minus the grand mean, squared. We would again list all 12 scores, marking the divisions among the cells. For each of the 6 participants who had one repetition, those in the left-hand column of Table 11-14 and in rows 1–3 and 7–9 of Table 11-16, we'd subtract the grand mean, 0.21, from the marginal mean, 0.21. For each of the 6 participants who had three repetitions, those in the right-hand column of Table 11-14 and in

TABLE 11-17. CALCULATING THE WITHIN-GROUPS SUM OF SQUARES

The within-groups sum of squares is calculated the same way for a two-way ANOVA as for a one-way ANOVA. We take each score and subtract the mean of the cell from which it comes—not the grand mean—to create deviations; then we square the deviations and sum them: $\Sigma(X - M_{Cell})^2 = 0.018$.

	X	$\Sigma(X - M_{Cell})^2$	$\Sigma(X - M_{Cell})^2$
Y, 1	0.25	$(0.25 - 0.20) = 0.05$	0.0025
	0.21	$(0.21 - 0.20) = 0.01$	0.0001
	0.14	$(0.14 - 0.20) = -0.06$	0.0036
Y, 3	0.07	$(0.07 - 0.12) = -0.05$	0.0025
	0.13	$(0.13 - 0.12) = 0.01$	0.0001
	0.16	$(0.16 - 0.12) = 0.04$	0.0016
O, 1	0.27	$(0.27 - 0.22) = 0.05$	0.0025
	0.22	$(0.22 - 0.22) = 0.00$	0.0000
	0.17	$(0.17 - 0.22) = -0.05$	0.0025
O, 3	0.33	$(0.33 - 0.30) = 0.03$	0.0009
	0.31	$(0.31 - 0.30) = 0.01$	0.0001
	0.26	$(0.26 - 0.30) = -0.04$	0.0016

TABLE 11-18. THE EXPANDED SOURCE TABLE AND THE FORMULAS

This source table includes all of the formulas for the calculations necessary to conduct a two-way between-groups ANOVA.

SOURCE	SS	df	MS	F
Age (A)	$\Sigma(M_{Row(age)} - GM)^2$	$N_{Rows} - 1$	$\dfrac{SS_{Age}}{df_{Age}}$	$\dfrac{MS_{Row(age)}}{MS_{Within}}$
Repetitions (R)	$\Sigma(M_{Column(reps)} - GM)^2$	$N_{Columns} - 1$	$\dfrac{SS_{Reps}}{df_{Reps}}$	$\dfrac{MS_{Column(reps)}}{MS_{Within}}$
A × R	$SS_{Total} - (SS_A + SS_R + SS_W)$	$(df_{Rows})(df_{Columns})$	$\dfrac{SS_{A \times R}}{df_{A \times R}}$	$\dfrac{MS_{Interaction(A \times R)}}{MS_{Within}}$
Within	$\Sigma(X - M_{Cell})^2$	$df_{Y,1} + df_{Y,3} + df_{O,1} + df_{O,3}$	$\dfrac{SS_{Within}}{df_{Within}}$	
Total	$\Sigma(X - GM)^2$	$df_{Total} = N_{Total} - 1$		

the rows 4–6 and 10–12 of Table 11-16, we'd subtract 0.21 from the marginal mean, 0.21. (*Note:* It is a coincidence that in this case the marginal means are exactly the same.) We'd square all of these deviations and add them to calculate the between-groups sum of squares for the columns, the independent variable of number of repetitions. Again, the calculations for the between-groups sum of squares for each main effect are just like the calculations for the between-groups sum of squares in a one-way between-groups ANOVA: $\Sigma(M_{Column(reps)} - GM)^2 = 0$

The within-groups sum of squares is calculated in exactly the same way as for the one-way between-groups ANOVA (Table 11-17). For each of the 12 scores, the cell mean is subtracted from the score. The deviations are squared and summed:

$$\Sigma(X - M_{Cell})^2 = 0.018$$

All we need now is the between-groups sum of squares for the interaction. We can calculate this by subtracting the other between-groups sums of squares (those for the two main effects) and the within-groups sum of squares from the total sum of squares. The between-groups sum of squares for the interaction is essentially what is left over when the main effects are accounted for. Mathematically, any variability that is predicted by these variables, but is not directly predicted by either independent variable on its own, is attributed to the interaction of the two independent variables. The formula is $SS_{A \times R} = SS_{Total} - (SS_A + SS_R + SS_{Within})$, and the calculations are $SS_{A \times R} = 0.0672 - (0.03 + 0 + 0.018) = 0.0192$

Formula: $SS_{Between/column} = \Sigma(M_{Column} - GM)^2$

Formula: $SS_{within} = \Sigma(X - M_{Cell})^2$

Formula: $SS_{Rows \times Columns}$ (or $SS_{Interaction}$) $= SS_{Total} - (SS_{Rows} + SS_{Columns} + SS_{Within})$

TABLE 11-19. THE EXPANDED SOURCE TABLE AND FALSE MEDICAL CLAIMS

This expanded source table shows the actual sums of squares, degrees of freedom, mean squares, and F statistics for the study on false medical claims.

SOURCE	SS	df	MS	F
Age (A)	0.0300	1	0.0300	13.04
Repetitions (R)	0.0000	1	0.0000	0.00
A × R	0.0192	1	0.0190	8.26
Within	0.0180	8	0.0023	
Total	0.0672	11		

FIGURE 11-14
Interpreting the Interaction

The nonparallel lines demonstrate the interaction. The bars tell us that repetition increases accuracy for younger people but decreases it for older people. Because the direction reverses, this is a qualitative interaction.

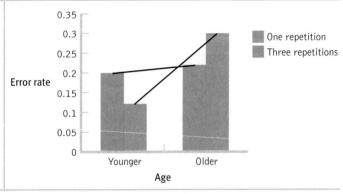

Now we can complete step 6 of hypothesis testing by calculating the F statistics using the formulas in Table 11-18 (page 507). The results are in the source table, Table 11-19 (page 507). There is a significant main effect of age because the F statistic, 13.04, is larger than the cutoff of 5.32. The means tell us that older participants tend to make more mistakes, remembering medical myths as true, than do younger participants. There is no statistically significant main effect of number of repetitions, however. The F statistic of 0.00 is not larger than the cutoff of 5.32. It is unusual to have an F statistic of 0.00. Even when there is no statistically significant effect, there is usually some difference among means due to random sampling. There also is a significant interaction. The F statistic of 8.26 is larger than the cutoff of 5.32. We will construct a bar graph of the cell means, as seen in Figure 11-14, to interpret the interaction.

The lines are not parallel; in fact, they intersect without even having to extend them beyond the graph. We can see that among younger participants, the proportion of responses that were incorrect was *lower*, on average, with three repetitions than with one repetition. Among older participants, the proportion of responses that were incorrect was *higher*, on average, with three repetitions than with one repetition. Does repetition help? It depends. It helps for younger people but is detrimental for older people. Specifically, repetition tends to help younger people distinguish between myth and fact. But the mere repetition of a medical myth tends to lead older people to be more likely to view it as fact. The researchers speculate that older people remember that they are familiar with a statement but forget the context in which they heard it; they forget that it's a false claim. Because the direction of the effect of repetition reverses from one age group to another, this is a qualitative interaction.

In summary, the six steps of hypothesis testing for a two-way between-groups ANOVA are similar to those for a one-way between-groups ANOVA. Because we have the possibility of two main effects and an interaction, each step is broken down into three parts; we will have three sets of hypotheses, three comparison distributions, three critical F statistics, three F statistics, and three conclusions. An expanded source table helps us to keep track of the calculations.

⊙ CHECK YOUR LEARNING

11-3 In 1999, Forsyth and Kerr presented a poster at the annual meeting of the American Psychological Association (also reported in Forsyth, Lawrence, Burnette, and Baumeister, 2006). They studied the effect of e-mail messages on students' final exam grades. Participants included students whose first exam grade was either (1) a C or (2) a D or F. Participants were randomly assigned to receive several e-mails in one of three conditions: e-mails intended to bolster their self-esteem, e-mails intended to enhance their sense of control over their grades, and e-mails with review questions. The accompanying table shows the cell means for the final exam grades (note that some of these are approximate, but all represent actual findings). For simplicity, assume there were 84 participants in the study and that they were evenly divided among cells.

	SELF-ESTEEM	SENSE OF CONTROL	REVIEW
C	67.31	69.83	71.12
D/F	47.83	60.98	62.13

a. From step 1 of hypothesis testing, list the populations for this study.

b. Conduct step 2 of hypothesis testing, listing all three sets of hypotheses.

c. Conduct step 3 of hypothesis testing, listing the comparison distributions for this study, including all degrees of freedom.

d. Conduct step 4 of hypothesis testing, listing all three critical F statistics.

e. The F statistics are 20.84 for the main effect of the independent variable of initial grade, 1.69 for the main effect of the independent variable of type of e-mail, and 3.02 for the interaction. Conduct step 6 of hypothesis testing.

> INTERACTIONS: A MORE PRECISE INTERPRETATION

Julie wanted to give herself a chance to catch whatever might be making that huge sound. And she wanted to do it before the noisy fishermen splashed their way farther downstream. Julie watched her line carefully as her wooly bugger drifted deeper into the pool.

The next "ka-boom" was the loudest, and this time Julie saw what was making the sound. In fact, it was swimming directly at her. The beaver's whiskers were high in the air, and its tail was raised to deliver one more warning to stay away from its territory. The following "ka-boom" seemed loudest of all, probably because it was so close. The sound had Julie backing up against the flow of the stream as quickly as she could. She scrambled backwards over the slippery rocks and against the current. It was the animal's directness that frightened Julie the most. The beaver was swimming directly at her, determined to repel the intruder. Its tail was raised yet again. But this time, instead of slapping the water, the beaver dove beneath the surface.

Julie's arms swung upward as she stepped backwards. Her fly rod waved wildly in the air, and she could feel her feet slipping uncontrollably underneath the water. She landed hard on her backside against the small rocks and started crab-walking backwards into the shallow water. She was safe, but embarrassed, and hoped the noisy fishermen hadn't seen her clumsy fall. She tried to scramble to her feet to get another look at the beaver, but her boots started slipping again.

"Whoa, there!" Arms on either side grabbed Julie and carried her to a dry rock, where she could put her feet up, safe and out of the water.

"Are you all right?" said one of them. "Wasn't that a beaver or something?"

"You almost got yourself wet," said the other. "Don't lose your fly." He pointed to Julie's waders and Grandpa's birthday fly, perched prominently near the toe of her boot. He plucked it off her waders and gave it to her. "That one's a work of art," he said as he handed it to her.

The value of noisy fishermen on the Willowemoc? It depends. Most of the time, these noisy fishermen ruined the water, put down the trout, spoiled Julie's privacy, and distracted her from the beauty of her favorite Catskill Mountain stream. But when they helped her find a treasured birthday present from her grandpa, Julie had to admit that she was glad that they were there.

To a nonfisherman, a trout stream looks both lovely and dangerous, a chaos of slippery rocks and unpredictable backwaters. But an experienced trout fisherman can enjoy the beauty, extract clarity from the chaos, and fish from the stream. Statistical reasoning about interactions also helps you extract clarity from the chaos of a data set. Students don't always like to hear this, but if you want to be an applied behavioral scientist, then you will have to become even *better* at statistics and experimental design than many other kinds of scientists because you are working in a less controlled environment. Applied statisticians don't have to be geniuses, but they do need to develop particular skills; specifically, they have to know:

1. When to use a between-groups design versus a within-groups design
2. How to analyze the data in keeping with the research design
3. How to interpret a statistically significant interaction

It is worth learning about interactions because understanding the clarity hiding behind the chaos of human behavior is the distinctive contribution that the behavioral sciences offer to the larger society. Every human behavior, from adolescent cigarette smoking to adult parenting styles, is the product of multiple, interacting variables. So this next section guides you to a more precise understanding of the meaning of a statistical interaction.

Interpreting Interactions: Toward a More Precise Statistical Understanding

Behavioral science statistics, as in other sciences, is always pushing at the boundaries of knowledge, and a more precise way of calculating interactions has emerged over the last several decades (e.g., Zuckerman, Hodgins, Zuckerman, & Rosenthal, 1993). Earlier, we presented what we will now refer to as the "traditional" way to interpret interactions. Here, we'll present the updated approach to interpreting interactions; we'll learn to calculate corrected means as we demonstrate how to isolate the effects of interactions. We'll call this the "more precise" way to interpret interactions.

The traditional way of interpreting an interaction involves an examination of the cell means, which includes both the influences of the main effects and the interaction. Because all effects are included in the cell means, traditionally main effects are not discussed if there is a statistically significant interaction. This is a tacit acknowledgment that the cell means included all effects. The statistical advance recommended by Rosnow and Rosenthal (e.g., 1989b) calculates an interaction effect independently of the main effects. If there were actual data indicating two statistically significant main effects and a statistically significant interaction, then Rosnow and Rosenthal would recommend interpreting the data as summarized by the cell means as having an interaction *plus* two main effects. The statistical significance of each of the three effects (two main effects and an interaction) would be examined separately, but they would all be part of the larger story that we examined at once by using cell means.

Most researchers report interactions the traditional way, as we did previously. It is, of course, often useful to look at the pattern of the cell means; moreover, this method is simpler, as it does not require calculating corrected means (which most statistical software still won't calculate for you). Because of this, most researchers continue to use this traditional method (Rosnow & Rosenthal, 1989a); in fact, the pattern of cell means, with both main effects and interactions included, is frequently the story that we do want to tell. In line with this, Rosnow and Rosenthal (1996) have no problem with an examination of the overall pattern of cell means instead of separate examinations of the three effects—"we do not even care if the interaction is computed" (p. 253). What they do insist on is accurate reporting of interactions when they are calculated.

Rosnow and Rosenthal call for accurate reporting because when we report the cell means, as we do with the traditional interpretation of an interaction, we are not strictly reporting an interaction. The more precise way to interpret interactions is to mathematically remove the contributions of the two main effects from the cell means before interpreting the interaction pattern. This method is like asking someone to explain the taste of chocolate milk if they have never before tasted either chocolate syrup or milk: it's uncontaminated by the effects of the individual variables. Rosnow and Rosenthal (1996) have been among the most vocal activists in the fight for more precise reporting of interactions, and they suggest calling the patterns of cell means "interaction-plus-something-more effects" (Rosnow & Rosenthal, 1991, p. 574). They urge researchers to use the term *interaction* only if they mathematically isolate the interaction effect. Let's learn how we would examine an interaction in this more precise manner.

■ With respect to interactions, a **residual** is the effect left over after the main effects of the two independent variables have been removed.

Residuals: Separating the Interaction from the Main Effect

In statistics, the word *residuals* means just about the same thing as it does in everyday usage: leftovers. The vegetables you leave on your plate are the residuals of your meal. The unpleasant thoughts and feelings after an argument has ended are your residual thoughts and emotions. In statistics, anytime we have explained some of the variance, the variance that's left over is called the residual variance. Residual variance is an exciting advance in the interpretation of statistical interactions because it contributes to a more precise way of understanding the story that the data tell.

As we mentioned in our discussion of the between-groups sum of squares for the interaction, the interaction is the variance left over—the residual—after all other sources of variance are accounted for. *With respect to interactions, a **residual** is the effect left over after the main effects of the two independent variables have been removed.* Mathematically, we must remove the effects of the two independent variables—the main effects—to determine the residuals. The concept of residuals is familiar to you and easy to understand by comparing it to leftovers that remain at the end of some process. It could be a psychological process, a mechanical process, or any other kind of process that leaves something behind after it is completed. Rosnow and Rosenthal (1996) present an overview of their explanation of residuals by quoting a scene from the Jack Nicholson movie *Five Easy Pieces*. Nicholson's

Residuals
Residuals are the leftovers. In the movie *Five Easy Pieces*, Jack Nicholson's character was told that the restaurant did not serve toast. He then explained to the waitress that she could serve a sandwich with all the ingredients removed until just toast, the residual, was left.

Getty Images/Foodcollection

TABLE 11-20. EXAMINING THE "TRUE" INTERACTION

We use our table of cells to examine the "true" interaction. We include our marginal means for the rows and columns, as well as the grand mean, seen in the lower right.

	ONE REPETITION (1)	THREE REPETITIONS (3)	
YOUNGER (Y)	0.20	0.12	0.16
OLDER (O)	0.22	0.30	0.26
	0.21	0.21	0.21

character responds to a waitress who says that the restaurant does not serve toast. "You make sandwiches, don't you?" he said, and had her remove all ingredients until just toast was left. Rosnow and Rosenthal then note the analogy to ANOVA, explaining that we want to look at the "leftover effects" (p. 253), the residuals that remain when the other components are removed.

The more precise way of understanding statistical interactions is to calculate and graph the residual means that are uncontaminated by main effects. As we demonstrate below, this can be accomplished mathematically. For those of you who go on to report interactions in your own research, especially graduate students, we recommend reading one of Rosnow and Rosenthal's (1989a, 1989b, 1991, 1995, 1996) excellent articles describing the correct process for interpreting interactions. Here, we offer the basics of their technique for interpretation of interactions for 2×2 between-groups ANOVAs.

To examine the interaction accurately, we must calculate the residuals. Let's consider what we would do for a 2×2 between-groups ANOVA. First, we conduct what Rosenthal and Rosnow call the "mean polish" (1991) or "demeaning" (1996). They use these words because the process involves removing overall means from the cell means to uncover what's left over.

1. We subtract the grand mean from each of the marginal means for the rows and then for each of the marginal means for the columns. What remains are called row effects and column effects.

2. We subtract the row effects and column effects from the cell means. This removes the main effects of the two independent variables.

3. Finally, we subtract the grand mean from each of the cell means.

TABLE 11-21. ISOLATING THE ROW EFFECTS AND COLUMN EFFECTS

The first step in the mean polish is to calculate the row effects and column effects by subtracting the grand mean from the marginal means.

	ONE REPETITION (1)	THREE REPETITIONS (3)	MARGINAL MEANS	ROW EFFECTS
YOUNGER (Y)	0.20	0.12	0.16	−0.05
OLDER (O)	0.22	0.30	0.26	0.05
MARGINAL MEANS	0.21	0.21	0.21	
COLUMN EFFECTS	0.00	0.00		

TABLE 11-22. SUBTRACTING THE ROW EFFECTS FROM THE CELL MEANS

We next subtract the row effects from each of the cell means. Remember to subtract each row effect only from the cell means in its row.

	ONE REPETITION (1)	THREE REPETITIONS (3)	MARGINAL MEANS	ROW EFFECTS
YOUNGER (Y)	0.25	0.17	0.16	−0.05
OLDER (O)	0.17	0.25	0.26	0.05
MARGINAL MEANS	0.21	0.21	0.21	
COLUMN EFFECTS	0.00	0.00		

When we interpret an interaction in this manner, we focus on the pattern of the numbers that are left rather than on the actual numbers. Let's look at the calculations for the mean polish for the data on myth-busting. Here, again, are the data, including the marginal means (Table 11-20). You'll notice that this table also includes the grand mean, 0.21, in the lower right.

Our first step is to subtract the grand mean from each of the marginal means, first for the rows and then for the columns. What remains, as seen in Table 11-21, are the row effects and the column effects.

We then subtract the row effects from the cell means, as seen in Table 11-22. We subtract the row effect for the first row from the cell means in that row. We subtract the row effect for the second row from the cell means in that row. For example, we subtract -0.05 from the two cell means in the top row, 0.20 and 0.12.

We next subtract the column effects from the cell means. Remember to subtract each column effect only from the cell means in its column. In this case, we are subtracting 0 from each cell mean, so the new cell means will be exactly the same as those in Table 11-22 from which we already subtracted the row effects.

Finally, we subtract the grand mean from each cell mean (which have already had row effects and column effects subtracted from them). Table 11-23 shows the cell means after this step.

If we want to create a bar graph of the interaction, we would go back one step in our calculations. We would use the numbers from before we subtracted the grand mean from the cell means (Table 11-22), as these numbers will make

TABLE 11-23. SUBTRACTING THE GRAND MEAN FROM THE CELL MEANS

Finally, we subtract the grand mean from the cell means that have already had the row effects and column effects removed.

	ONE REPETITION (1)	THREE REPETITIONS (3)	MARGINAL MEANS	ROW EFFECTS
YOUNGER (Y)	0.04	−0.04	0.16	−0.05
OLDER (O)	−0.04	0.04	0.26	0.05
MARGINAL MEANS	0.21	0.21	0.21	
COLUMN EFFECTS	0.00	0.00		

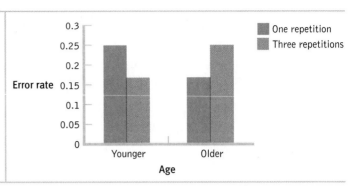

FIGURE 11-15
A "True" Interaction

If we want to see our interaction after performing a mean polish, we graph the cell means after subtracting the row effects and column effects, but before subtracting the grand mean from them.

more sense; these are the numbers in Table 11-22, which have had the row effects and column effects, but not the grand mean, subtracted from them. Figure 11-15 shows the bar graph of the interaction based on these means. Note that if we removed the row effects, column effects, and grand mean from the cell means, the remaining interaction—if indeed there is an interaction—will show intersecting lines when the bars are connected. We are now looking at the true interaction, without the main effects. The calculations to observe the pattern and to graph the interaction are not difficult. If you learn them, you will be among the few researchers who correctly interpret and report interactions!

On the other hand, remember that we do not always wish to separate main effects and interactions. We are often interested in the overall pattern of cell means, as explored in the traditional interpretation of ANOVA. "The 2×2 ANOVA is not some 'Mt. Everest' that must be scaled just because 'it is there'" (Rosnow & Rosenthal, 1996; p. 254). *Before* conducting analyses, ask yourself exactly what question you want your data to answer.

In summary, there are two ways to interpret an interaction. The traditional way, presented earlier, involves explaining the overall pattern of the cell means and discounting any significant main effects. The more precise way involves mathematically removing the contributions of the main effects from the cell means before interpreting the overall pattern. Although the latter way is the "correct" way to interpret interactions, many times we want to tell the story only through the cell means. Regardless of the method we use, we should aim to report it accurately.

⊙ CHECK YOUR LEARNING

11-4 Let's say that you conducted a two-way between-groups ANOVA with the independent variables of beverage (grapefruit juice or water) and medication (Lipitor or placebo) and the dependent variable of absorption rates. If you had a statistically significant interaction for the data shown in the accompanying table, how would you interpret the interaction in the more precise way? Show all your calculations using a series of tables.

	LIPITOR (L)	PLACEBO (P)	
GRAPEFRUIT JUICE (G)	60	4	32
WATER (W)	30	4	17
	45	4	24.5

■ DIGGING DEEPER INTO THE DATA: VARIATIONS ON ANOVA

We've already experienced the flexibility that ANOVA offers in terms of both independent variables and research design. Yet ANOVA is even more flexible than we've seen so far in this chapter and the last. Earlier, we described within-groups ANOVAs in which the participants experience all of the research conditions. Researchers have also developed a term for slightly more complicated designs. *A **mixed-design ANOVA** is used to analyze the data from a study with at least two nominal independent variables and an interval dependent variable; at least one independent variable must be within-groups and at least one independent variable must be between-groups.* In other words, a mixed design includes both a between-groups variable and a within-groups variable.

There are even more variations on ANOVA. There is a type of ANOVA that can handle multiple *dependent* variables, as well as one that can statistically subtract the effect of a possible third variable, much like we saw with partial correlation in Chapter 5. And yet another type of ANOVA can do both at the same time: handle multiple dependent variables *and* subtract the effect of a possible third variable. And all these can have a between-groups or within-groups design, or even a mixed design. In this section, we'll explore the variations on ANOVA using examples from the research literature. You'll see that your understanding of between-groups factorial ANOVAs easily maps on to more complicated ANOVAs. When you read journal articles in other courses in your social science major, you'll frequently see more complicated ANOVAs. From what you've already learned, you can approach almost any write-up of an ANOVA and come away with an understanding of the story the researchers want to tell.

Within-Groups and Mixed Designs: When the Same Participants Experience More Than One Condition

In this chapter, we considered two-way between-groups ANOVAs, but in the real world of research, there is an array of research designs. Fortunately, the principles that you learned in the context of between-groups ANOVAs apply to within-groups designs and mixed designs as well; the interpretations of main effects and interactions are essentially the same. In Check Your Learning 11-3, we discussed a study by Forsyth, Lawrence, Burnette, and Baumeister (2006). These researchers explored the effects of different types of e-mails on final exam grades for two groups of students, those with a grade of C on the first exam and those with a grade of D or F on the first exam.

When Forsyth and colleagues first presented these data, they conducted a three-way ANOVA; they used three independent variables. The first two were the same as those described in Check Your Learning 11-3: initial grade (C and D/F) and type of e-mail (self-esteem, sense of control, and no message). Both of these independent variables are between-groups. However, these researchers also included a third independent variable in their analyses. They included not only final exam grades but also grades on a second exam, a midterm exam. So they had another independent variable, exam, with two levels: midterm and final. Because every student took both exams, this independent variable is within-groups. This means that the research design had two between-groups independent variables and one within-groups independent variable. This is an example of a mixed-design ANOVA. Specifically,

■ A **mixed-design ANOVA** is used to analyze the data from a study with at least two nominal independent variables and an interval dependent variable; at least one independent variable must be within-groups and at least one independent variable must be between-groups.

this ANOVA would be referred to as a 2 (grade: C, D/F) × 3 (type of e-mail: self-esteem, sense of control, no message) × 2 (exam: midterm, final) mixed design ANOVA.

The authors reported two interesting findings based on the independent variable of exam. They found a main effect of exam, such that final exam grades tended to be lower than midterm exam grades. They also found an interaction of initial grade, type of e-mail, and exam. There was a particular drop, on average, from the midterm exam to the final exam among students who received an initial grade of D or F and who received e-mail messages aimed at increasing self-esteem. The e-mails aimed at enhancing self-esteem led to a *decrease* in average, grades among these students! This average drop did not occur to this degree among C students or among D and F students in the other two e-mail conditions. Based on this finding, the authors subtitled their paper "An Intervention That Backfired." Boosting self-esteem in the classroom might not have the effect that many claim it will.

MANOVA, ANCOVA, and MANCOVA: Multiple Dependent Variables and Covariates

Within-groups designs and mixed designs offer many more alternatives to researchers, but there are also ways we can expand our ANOVAs. We can have more than one dependent variable, one or more covariates, or both.

MANOVA: Multiple Dependent Variables

Frequently, there are several dependent variables in a study that all measure similar constructs. In such cases, we can use a ***multivariate analysis of variance (MANOVA),*** *a form of ANOVA in which there is more than one dependent variable.* The word *multivariate* refers to the number of dependent variables, not the number of independent variables. (Remember, a plain old ANOVA can already handle multiple independent variables.) The dependent variables can be different measures of the same construct or measures of slightly different constructs that are correlated. Regardless, the dependent variables "should 'make sense' as a group of variables" (Mertler & Vannata, 2005, p. 119). For example, if we want to study aggression among first graders, we might want to use two multiple dependent variables such as teacher observations and the number of times the child hits someone else. However, we would not want to include a variable unlikely to be related to aggression, such as eye color. The use of a carefully selected group of dependent variables can make a study stronger, much like the use of multiple manifest variables for each latent variable in structural equation modeling (SEM), discussed in the Digging Deeper into the Data section of Chapter 6.

Aside from the use of multiple dependent variables, a MANOVA is not all that different from an ANOVA. Essentially, the calculations treat the group of dependent variables as one dependent variable. Although one can follow up a MANOVA by considering the different univariate (single dependent variable) ANOVAs embedded in the MANOVA, we are often most interested in the effect of the independent variables on the composite of dependent variables.

ANCOVA: Correcting for a Third Variable

There are often situations in which we suspect that a third variable might be affecting our dependent variable. We might, for example, have levels of education as one of our independent variables and worry that age, which is likely

▪ A **multivariate analysis of variance (MANOVA)** is a form of ANOVA in which there is more than one dependent variable.

related to level of education, is actually what is influencing the dependent variable, not education. In this case, we could include age as *a covariate*, an interval variable that we suspect associates, or covaries, with our independent variable of interest. So, **analysis of covariance (ANCOVA)** *is a type of ANOVA in which a covariate is included so that statistical findings reflect effects after an interval variable has been statistically removed.* The inclusion of a covariate is much like the calculation of a partial correlation, in which a correlation between two variables is calculated after statistically removing the effect of a third variable.

When a covariate is included, statisticians use a variety of words that all convey the same idea; we often refer to analysis of covariance as *partialing out a variable, controlling for a variable,* or *holding a variable constant.* The third of these phrases nicely captures the essential logic of ANCOVA. At its most basic, conducting an ANCOVA is almost like conducting an ANOVA at each level of the covariate. If age were our covariate with level of education as the independent variable and income as the dependent variable, then we'd essentially be looking at a regular ANOVA for each age. We want to answer the question: Given a certain age, does education predict income? Of course, this is a simplified explanation, but that's the logic behind the procedure. If the calculations find that education has an effect on income among 33-year-olds, 58-year-olds, and individuals of every other age, then we know that there is a main effect of education on income over and above the effect of age. Including covariates helps us isolate the effects of variables so that we can move toward unambiguous conclusions.

MANCOVA: Multiple Dependent Variables and a Covariate

We bet you can guess what MANCOVA is. Yes, *a **multivariate analysis of covariance (MANCOVA)** is an ANOVA with multiple dependent variables and the inclusion of a covariate.* There are no new concepts to learn for MANCOVA; we're just combining concepts we've already learned.

To illustrate the expansion of an ANOVA to include multiple dependent variables and at least one covariate, we'll discuss a study by McLeland and Sutton (2005) that examined military service and marital status within the context of men's satisfaction within their romantic relationships. The independent variables were military service (military, nonmilitary) and marital status (married, unmarried), and there were two measures of relationship satisfaction, the Kansas Marital Satisfaction Scale (KMSS) and the ENRICH Marital Satisfaction Scale (EMS). The use of two relationship satisfaction measures suggests that the overall dependent variable is more valid than either measure would be on its own (given, of course, that each is reasonably reliable and valid). The researchers also included the covariate of age. Initial analyses also found that age was significantly associated with relationship satisfaction; older men tended to be more satisfied than younger men. The researchers wanted to be certain that it was military status and marital status, not age, that affected relationship status, so they controlled for age as a covariate.

Because they had more than one dependent variable and at least one covariate, the researchers conducted a MANCOVA. The MANCOVA led to only one statistically significant finding: military men were less satisfied than nonmilitary men with respect to their relationships when controlling for the age of the men. That is, given a certain age, military men of that age were likely to be less satisfied with their relationships than were nonmilitary men of that age.

> ■ A **covariate** is an interval variable that we suspect associates, or covaries, with our independent variable of interest.
>
> ■ **Analysis of covariance (ANCOVA)** is a type of ANOVA in which a covariate is included so that statistical findings reflect effects after an interval variable has been statistically removed.
>
> ■ A **multivariate analysis of covariance (MANCOVA)** is an ANOVA with multiple dependent variables and the inclusion of a covariate.

TABLE 11-24. VARIATIONS ON ANOVA

There are many variations on ANOVA that allow us to analyze a variety of research designs. A MANOVA allows us to include more than one dependent variable. An ANCOVA allows us to include covariates to correct for third variables that might influence our study. A MANCOVA allows us to include both more than one dependent variable and a covariate.

	INDEPENDENT VARIABLES	DEPENDENT VARIABLES	COVARIATE
ANOVA	Any number	Only one	None
MANOVA	Any number	More than one	None
ANCOVA	Any number	Only one	At least one
MANCOVA	Any number	More than one	At least one

Table 11-24 summarizes the variations on ANOVA.

Statistics based on analysis of variance allow us to implement a wide range of research designs. But it's important to remember that just because we are able to conduct a certain analysis doesn't mean that it's the wisest course. As Cohen (1990) proclaims in his classic article, "Things I Have Learned (So Far)," "less is more"; a study with fewer well-chosen independent variables and dependent variables tends to be superior to a study with more variables. Design the simplest study that answers your research questions, knowing that there are sophisticated analyses that you can use if necessary but also knowing that simpler analyses are often the best ones.

In summary, factorial ANOVAs can have a within-groups design or a mixed design in addition to a between-groups design. In a mixed design, at least one of the independent variables is between-groups and at least one of the independent variables is within-groups. We can also include multiple dependent variables, not just multiple independent variables, in a single study, analyzed with a MANOVA. Alternately, we can add a covariate to our ANOVA and conduct an ANCOVA that allows us to partial out the effect of a variable that we believe might be related to our independent variable. Finally, we can include multiple dependent variables *and* a covariate in an analysis called a MANCOVA. And we can throw all of these words around in conversation with our friends and sound really smart!

⊙ CHECK YOUR LEARNING

11-5 Cox, Thomas, Hinton, and Donahue (2006) studied the effects of exercise on perceived fatigue. There were three independent variables: age (18–20 years old, 35–45 years old), intensity of exercise (low, moderate, high), and time point (15, 20, 25, and 30 minutes). The dependent variable was positive well-being. Every participant was assessed at all intensity levels and all time points. (Generally, moderate-intensity and high-intensity exercise led to higher levels of positive well-being than low-intensity exercise.)

a. What type of ANOVA would they conduct?

b. The researchers included two covariates related to the physical effects of exercise, measures of hemoglobin and serum ferritin. What statistical test would they use? Explain.

c. The researchers conducted separate analyses for three dependent variables: perceived fatigue, psychological distress, and positive well-being. If they wanted to include all three dependent variables in the analysis described in part (a), what statistical test would they use? Explain.

d. If they wanted to use all three dependent variables in the analysis described in part (b), what statistical test would they use? Explain.

> ## Two-Way ANOVA: When the Outcome Depends on More Than One Variable

Factorial ANOVAs (also called *multifactorial ANOVAs*), those with more than one independent variable, are both practical and elegant. They permit us to test more than one hypothesis in a single study—a savings of time and resources. They also allow us to examine *interactions* between independent variables. Factorial ANOVAs are often named by referring to the levels of their independent variables, or *factors* (e.g., 2 × 2) rather than the number of independent variables (e.g., two-way). With a two-way ANOVA, we can examine two *main effects*, one for each independent variable and one for their interaction, the way in which the two variables might work together to influence the dependent variable. Because we are examining three hypotheses (two main effects and one interaction), we calculate three sets of statistics for a two-way ANOVA.

> ## The Layers of ANOVA: Understanding Interactions

The traditional way to interpret interactions is to examine the overall pattern of cell means. A *cell* is one condition in a study. We typically write the mean of a group in its cell. We write the means for each row to the right of the cells, and the means for each column below the cells; these are called *marginal means*. If the main effect of one independent variable is stronger under certain conditions of the second independent variable, there is a *quantitative interaction*. If the direction of the main effect actually reverses under certain conditions of the second independent variable, there is a *qualitative interaction*.

> ## The Expanded Source Table: Conducting a Two-Way Between-Groups ANOVA

A two-way between-groups ANOVA uses the same six steps of hypothesis testing that we have used previously, with only minor changes. First, because we have to test for two main effects and one interaction, each step is broken down into three parts, one for each possible effect. Specifically, we have three sets of hypotheses, three comparison distributions, three critical *F* values, three *F* statistics, and three conclusions. We use an expanded source table to aid in our calculations of the three *F* statistics.

> Interactions: A More Precise Interpretation

The more precise, although less frequently used, way to interpret an interaction is to mathematically remove the main effects from the cell means so that we are interpreting *only* the interaction. Once we mathematically remove the main effects of the two independent variables, we are left with just the *residual* effect of the interaction, and we can see the interaction without the input of the main effects.

▪ DIGGING DEEPER INTO THE DATA: VARIATIONS ON ANOVA

We demonstrated the steps for a between-groups ANOVA, but factorial ANOVAs can also have a within-groups design or a *mixed design ANOVA*. As with a one-way ANOVA, a within-groups design indicates that every participant is in every group. Each participant is represented in each cell. In a *mixed design*, at least one of the independent variables is between-groups and at least one of the independent variables is within-groups.

There are even more complex versions of ANOVA that we can use for more complex hypotheses. A *multivariate analysis of variance*, or *MANOVA*, is an ANOVA with more than one dependent variable; usually, the dependent variables assess the same or related constructs. *Analysis of covariance*, or *ANCOVA*, is an ANOVA that includes a *covariate*, a third variable hypothesized to be associated with both the independent and dependent variables. ANCOVA allows us to examine the effect of an independent variable on a dependent variable over and above a third variable. *Multivariate analysis of covariance*, or *MANCOVA*, is a type of ANOVA that includes both multiple dependent variables and at least one covariate.

SPSS GUIDELINES FOR CHAPTER 11: TWO-WAY ANOVA

The two-way ANOVA is used when we want to make comparisons between the groups belonging to two nominal independent variables. For example, we might want to compare three different breeds of dogs (the first independent variable) and the gender of each breed of dog (the second independent variable) in how easy they are to train (the interval dependent variable). This would be called a 3×2 between-groups ANOVA.

We can instruct SPSS to analyze our ANOVA by selecting:

Analyze → General Linear Model → Univariate and selecting the variables. A two-way ANOVA requires two fixed factors (independent variables) and a dependent variable. We can include specific descriptive statistics by selecting "Options."

We can request post-hoc comparisons of the means by selecting:

Analyze → General Linear Model → Univariate → Post Hoc and selecting the appropriate post-hoc test, and the independent variable of interest.

EXERCISES

11.1 The many varieties of ANOVA—myth-busting: Consider the study we used as an example for a two-way between-groups ANOVA. Older and younger people were randomly assigned to hear either one repetition or three repetitions of a health-related myth, accompanied by the accurate information that "busted" the myth.

a. Explain why this study is a between-groups ANOVA.

b. How could this study be redesigned so that we would use a within-groups ANOVA? (*Hint:* Think long term.)

11.2 The many varieties of ANOVA—memory for names: In a fictional study introduced in the end-of-chapter exercises for Chapter 10, a cognitive psychologist studied memory for names after a group activity that lasted 20 minutes. The researcher randomly assigned 120 participants to one of three conditions: (1) group members introduced themselves once (one introduction only), (2) group members were introduced by the experimenter and by themselves (two introductions), and (3) group members were introduced by the experimenter and themselves, and wore nametags throughout the group activity (two introductions and nametags).

a. What could the researcher do to redesign this study so it would be analyzed with a two-way between-groups ANOVA? Be specific. (*Note:* There are several possible ways that the researcher could do this.)

b. What could the researcher do to redesign this study so it would be analyzed with a two-way within-groups ANOVA? Be specific. (*Note:* There are several possible ways the researcher could do this.)

11.3 Naming ANOVAs—personal ads: A researcher wondered about the degree to which age was a factor for those posting personal ads on Match.com. He randomly selected 200 ads and examined data about the posters (the people who posted the ads). Specifically, for each ad, he calculated the difference between the poster's age and the oldest age he or she would be open to in a romantic prospect. So, if someone were 23 years old and would date someone as old as 30, his or her score would be 7; if someone were 25 and would date someone as old as 23, his or her score would be −2. He calculated these scores for all 200 posters and categorized them into male versus female and homosexual versus heterosexual.

a. List any independent variables, along with the levels.

b. What is the dependent variable?

c. What kind of ANOVA is this?

d. Now name the ANOVA using the more specific language that enumerates the numbers of levels.

e. Use your answer to part (d) to calculate the number of cells. Explain how you made this calculation.

f. Draw a table that depicts the cells of this ANOVA

11.4 Naming ANOVAs—motivated skepticism: A study on motivated skepticism examined whether participants were more likely to be skeptical when it served their self-interest (Ditto & Lopez, 1992). Ninety-three participants completed a fictitious medical test that told them they had high levels of a certain enzyme, TAA. Participants were randomly assigned to be told either that high levels of TAA had potentially unhealthy consequences or that high levels of TAA had potentially healthy consequences. They were also randomly assigned to complete a dependent measure before or after the TAA test. The dependent measure assessed their perception of the accuracy of the TAA test on a scale of 1 (very inaccurate) to 9 (very accurate).

a. State the independent variables and their levels.

b. State the dependent variable.

c. What kind of ANOVA would be used to analyze these data? State the name using the original language as well as the more specific language.

d. Use the more specific language of ANOVA to calculate the number of cells in this research design.

e. Draw a table that depicts the cells of this ANOVA.

11.5 Interpreting an ANOVA's results—motivated skepticism: In the study described in Exercise 11.4, Ditto and Lopez (1992) found the following means for those who completed the dependent measure prior to taking the TAA test: unhealthy result, 6.9; healthy result, 6.6. They found the following means for those who completed the dependent measure after taking the TAA test: unhealthy result, 5.6; healthy result, 7.3. From their ANOVA, they reported statistics for two findings. For the main effect of test outcome, they reported the following statistic: $F(1,73) = 7.74$, $p < 0.01$. For the interaction of test outcome and timing of the dependent measure, they reported the following statistic: $F(1,73) = 4.01$, $p < 0.05$.

a. Draw a table of cell means that includes the actual means for this study. Include the marginal means and the grand mean. To calculate the marginal means and grand mean, assume that there were equal numbers of participants in each cell (even though this was not the case in the actual study).

b. Describe the significant main effect in your own words.

c. Draw a bar graph that depicts the main effect.

d. Why is the main effect misleading on its own?

e. Is the main effect qualified by a statistically significant interaction? Explain. Describe the interaction in your own words.

f. Draw a bar graph that depicts the interaction. Include lines that connect the tops of the bars and show the pattern of the interaction.

g. Is this a quantitative or qualitative interaction? Explain.

11.6 Interactions and motivated skepticism: Consider again the study in Exercise 11.5.

a. Change the cell mean for the participants who had a healthy test outcome and who completed the dependent measure prior to the TAA test so that this is now a quantitative interaction.

b. Draw a bar graph depicting the pattern that includes the new cell mean.

c. Change the cell mean for the participants who had a healthy test outcome and who completed the dependent measure prior to the TAA test so that there is now no interaction.

d. Draw a bar graph that depicts the pattern that includes the new cell mean.

11.7 Interpreting an ANOVA's results—political orientation and racism: In a study of racism, Nail, Harton, and Decker (2003) had participants read a scenario in which a police officer assaulted a motorist. Half the participants read about an African American officer who assaulted a European American motorist, and half read about a European American officer who assaulted an African American motorist. Participants were categorized into three categories based on political orientation: liberal, moderate, or conservative. Participants were told that the officer was acquitted of assault charges in state court but was found guilty of violating the motorist's rights in federal court. Double jeopardy occurs when an individual is tried twice for the same crime. Participants were asked to rate, on a scale of 1–7, the degree to which the officer had been placed in double jeopardy by the second trial. The researchers reported the interaction as $F(2, 58) = 10.93$, $p < 0.0001$. The means for the *liberal* participants were 3.18 for those who read about the African American officer and 1.91 for those who read about the European American officer. The means for the *moderate* participants were 3.50 for those who read about the African American officer and 3.33 for those who read about the European American officer. The means for the *conservative* participants were 1.25 for those who read about the African American officer and 4.62 for those who read about the European American officer.

a. Draw a table of cell means that includes the actual means for this study.

b. Do the reported statistics indicate that there is a significant interaction? If yes, describe the interaction in your own words.

c. Draw a bar graph that depicts the interaction. Include lines that connect the tops of the bars and show the pattern of the interaction.

d. Is this a quantitative or qualitative interaction? Explain.

11.8 Interactions, political orientation, and racism: Consider again the study in the Exercise 11.7.

a. Change the cell means for the moderate and conservative participants who read about an African American officer so that this is now a quantitative interaction.

b. Draw a bar graph that depicts the pattern that includes the new cell means.

c. Change the cell means for the moderate and conservative participants who read about an African American officer so that there is now no interaction.

d. Draw a bar graph that depicts the pattern that includes the new cell means.

11.9 Self-interest and interactions: Ratner and Miller (2001) wondered whether people are uncomfortable when they act in a way that's not obviously in their own self-interest. They randomly assigned 33 women and 32 men to read a fictional passage saying that federal funding would soon be cut for research into a gastrointestinal illness that mostly affected either (1) women or (2) men. They were then asked how comfortable, on a 1–7 scale, they would be "attending a meeting of concerned citizens who share your position" on this cause (p. 11). The journal article reported the statistics for the interaction as $F(1, 58) = 9.83$, $p < 0.01$. Women who read about women had a mean of 4.88, whereas those who read about men had a mean of 3.56. Men who read about women had a mean of 3.29, whereas those who read about men had a mean of 4.67.

a. What are the independent variables and their levels? What is the dependent variable?

b. What kind of ANOVA did the researchers conduct?

c. Do the reported statistics indicate that there is a significant interaction? Explain your answer.

d. Draw a table that includes the cells of the study, and the cell means.

e. Draw a bar graph that depicts these findings.

f. Describe the pattern of the interaction in words. Is this a qualitative or a quantitative interaction? Explain your answer.

11.10 Self-interest and different patterns of interaction: Consider the interaction described in Exercise 11.9.

a. Draw a new table of cells, but change the means for male participants so that there is now a quantitative rather than a qualitative, interaction.

b. Draw a bar graph that represents the means in part (a).

c. Draw a new table of cells, but change the means for male participants so that there is no interaction.

d. Draw a bar graph that represents the means in part (b).

11.11 Interactions and the cross-race effect: Hugenberg, Miller, and Claypool (2007) conducted a study to better understand the cross-race effect, in which individuals have a difficult time recognizing members of different racial groups—colloquially known as the "they-all-look-the-same-to-me" effect. In a variation on Hugenberg and colleagues' study, white participants viewed either 20 black faces or 20 white faces for three seconds each. Half the participants were told to pay particular attention to distinguishing features of the faces. Later, participants were shown 40 black faces or 40 white faces (the same race as in the prior stage of the experiment), 20 of which were new. Each participant received a score that measured their recognition accuracy. The researchers reported two effects, one for the race of the pictures, $F(1, 136) = 23.06$, $p < 0.001$, and one for the interaction of the race of the pictures and the instructions, $F(1, 136) 5 5.27$, $p < 0.05$. When given no instructions, the mean recognition scores were 1.46 for white faces and 1.04 for black faces. When given instructions to pay attention to distinguishing features, the mean recognition scores were 1.38 for white faces and 1.23 for black faces.

a. What are the independent variables and their levels? What is the dependent variable?

b. What kind of ANOVA did the researchers conduct?

c. Do the reported statistics indicate that there is a significant main effect? If yes, describe it.

d. Why is the main effect not sufficient in this situation to understand the findings? Be specific about why the main effect is misleading on its own.

e. Do the reported statistics indicate that there is a significant interaction? Explain your answer.

f. Draw a table that includes the cells of the study and the cell means.

g. Draw a bar graph that depicts these findings.

h. Describe the pattern of the interaction in words. Is this a qualitative or a quantitative interaction? Explain your answer.

11.12 Calculating an ANOVA and the Greek system: A sample of students from our statistics classes reported their GPAs, indicated their genders, and stated whether they were in the university's Greek system (i.e., in a fraternity or sorority). Following are the GPAs for the different groups of students:

Men in a fraternity: 2.6, 2.4, 2.9, 3.0

Men not in a fraternity: 3.0, 2.9, 3.4, 3.7, 3.0

Women in a sorority: 3.1, 3.0, 3.2, 2.9

Women not in a sorority: 3.4, 3.0, 3.1, 3.1

a. What are the independent variables and their levels? What is the dependent variable?

b. Draw a table that lists the cells of the study design. Include the cell means.

c. Conduct all six steps of hypothesis testing.

d. Draw a bar graph for all significant effects.

e. Is there a significant interaction? If yes, describe it in words, indicate whether it is a qualitative or a quantitative interaction. Explain.

11.13 Match.com and conducting a two-way ANOVA, Part I: The online dating Web site Match.com allows people to post personal ads to meet other people. People are asked to specify a range from the youngest age that would be acceptable in a dating partner to the oldest age that would be acceptable. The following data were randomly selected from the ads of 25-year-old people living in the New York area. The scores represent the youngest acceptable ages listed by those in the sample.

25-year-old women seeking men: 26, 24, 25, 24, 25

25-year-old men seeking women: 18, 21, 22, 22, 18

25-year-old women seeking women: 22, 25, 22, 25, 25

25-year-old men seeking men: 23, 25, 24, 22, 20

a. What are the independent variables and their levels? What is the dependent variable?

b. Draw a table that lists the cells of the study design. Include the cell means.

c. Conduct all six steps of hypothesis testing.

d. Is there a significant interaction? If yes, describe it in words, indicate whether it is a quantitative or a qualitative interaction, and draw a bar graph.

11.14 Match.com and conducting a two-way ANOVA, Part II: These data were from the same 25-year-old participants described in Exercise 11.13, but now the scores represent the oldest age that would be acceptable in a dating partner.

25-year-old women seeking men: 40, 35, 29, 35, 35

25-year-old men seeking women: 26, 26, 28, 28, 28

25-year-old women seeking women: 35, 35, 30, 35, 45

25-year-old men seeking men: 33, 35, 35, 36, 38

a. What are the independent variables and their levels? What is the dependent variable?

b. Draw a table that lists the cells of the study design. Include the cell means.

c. Conduct all six steps of hypothesis testing.

d. Is there a significant interaction? If yes, describe it in words, indicate whether it is a quantitative or a qualitative interaction, and draw a bar graph.

11.15 Motivated skepticism and the more precise interpretation of ANOVA: The study by Ditto and Lopez (1992), described in Exercises 11.4–11.6, reported the following means for those who completed the dependent measure prior to taking the TAA test: unhealthy result, 6.9; healthy result, 6.6. They found the following means for those who completed the dependent measure after taking the TAA test: unhealthy result, 5.6; healthy result, 7.3. Reinterpret the interaction of test result and timing of the dependent measure using the more precise method to interpret interactions. Show your calculations of corrected cell means and a bar graph.

11.16 Match.com and the more precise interpretation of ANOVA, Part I: Conduct a mean polish on the interaction of gender of seeker and gender of person being sought from Exercise 11.13 with the data for the youngest acceptable age. Show your calculations of corrected cell means and a bar graph.

11.17 Match.com and the more precise interpretation of ANOVA, Part II: Conduct a mean polish on the interaction of gender of seeker and gender of person being sought from Exercise 11.14 with the data for the oldest acceptable age. Show your calculations of corrected cell means and a bar graph.

11.18 The language of statistics—*interaction:* In your own words, define the word *interaction*, first as you would use it in everyday conversation and then as a statistician would use it.

11.19 The language of statistics—*cell:* In your own words, define the word *cell*, first as you would use it in everyday conversation and then as a statistician would use it.

11.20 The language of statistics—*residual:* In your own words, define the word *residual*, first as you would use it in everyday conversation and then as a statistician would use it.

■ **DIGGING DEEPER INTO THE DATA**

11.21 Health-related myths and variations on ANOVA: Consider the study we used as an example for a two-way between-groups ANOVA. Older and younger people were randomly assigned to hear either one repetition or three repetitions of a health-related myth, accompanied by the accurate information that "busted" the myth.

a. How could this study be redesigned so that we would use a within-groups ANOVA? (*Hint:* Think long term).

b. How could this study be redesigned so that we would use a mixed-design ANOVA?

11.22 Study design and football players' black grease: In the end-of-chapter exercises in Chapter 10, we described a study conducted at Yale University in which researchers randomly assigned 46 participants to place one of three substances below their eyes: black grease, black antiglare stickers, or petroleum jelly (DeBroff & Pahk, 2003). They assessed eye glare using a contrast chart that gives a value for each participant on an interval scale. Black grease led to a reduction in glare compared with the two other conditions, antiglare stickers or petroleum jelly.

a. List any independent variables, along with their levels.

b. What is the dependent variable?

c. What kind of ANOVA is this?

d. Let's say that every participant was tested twice, once during broad daylight and again under the artificial lights used at night. What are the independent variables and their levels now? What kind of ANOVA is this?

11.23 Covariates, weight, and career success: A nutritional and diet software program called DietPower offers encouragement to its users when they sign on each day; in one instance, for example, the program states that people at their ideal body weight tend to have higher salaries than do people who are overweight—and then explicitly states that losing weight might lead to an increase in pay!

a. Why is this a problematic statement? List at least two confounding variables that might affect this finding.

b. Imagine that you were going to conduct a study that compared two groups, people who were overweight and people who were at their ideal body weight, with respect to salary. Why would it be useful to include one or more covariates? What interval variables might you include as covariates?

11.24 Multiple dependent variables, weight, and career success: Imagine that you were going to conduct a study based on the scenario in Exercise 11.23.

a. What is the dependent variable? How is it operationalized?

b. Under what circumstances might you want to use more than one dependent variable?

c. What other dependent variables might you use here?

d. How could you design this study as a MANCOVA? (Hint: Think about your answer to the previous exercise.)

TERMS

two-way ANOVA (p. 480)

factorial analysis of variance (p. 480)

factor (p. 480)

cell (p. 482)

main effect (p. 483)

interaction (p. 484)

quantitative interaction (p. 488)

qualitative interaction (p. 488)

marginal means (p. 488)

residual (p. 511)

mixed-design ANOVA (p. 515)

multivariate analysis of variance (MANOVA) (p. 516)

covariate (p. 517)

analysis of covariance (ANCOVA) (p. 517)

multivariate analysis of covariance (MANCOVA) (p. 517)

FORMULAS

$df_{Rows} = N_{Rows} - 1$
$df_{Columns} = N_{Columns} - 1$
$df_{Interaction} = (df_{Rows})(df_{Columns})$
$SS_{Total} = \Sigma(X - GM)^2$ for each score

$SS_{Between/rows} = \Sigma(M_{Row} - GM)^2$ for each score

$SS_{Between/columns} = \Sigma(M_{Column} - GM)^2$ for each score

$SS_{Within} = \Sigma(X - M_{Cell})^2$ for each score

$SS_{Interaction} = SS_{Total} - (SS_{Rows} + SS_{Columns} + SS_{Within})$

CHAPTER TWELVE

BEYOND HYPOTHESIS TESTING
CONFIDENCE INTERVALS, EFFECT SIZE, AND POWER

"STOP!! FREEZE!!" Professor and fight master J. Allen Suddeth leapt from his seat in the theater and ran on stage. The two student actors froze—except for the one pointing the gun, who slowly lowered her tired arm. The director, stage manager, and backstage crew also stopped. All eyes were on the actors and the fight master. Suddeth gently took the gun out of her hand, breached it, and then handed it to a props person. "Sheila, tell me whom you were trying to shoot?" he asked her.

"My husband," she said. "I'm about to kill him."

"But you could have killed Jason, your fellow actor," Professor Suddeth told her. "Sheila, you just demonstrated why we don't rehearse with blanks," he replied. "Hold out your finger and shoot Jason."

She raised her arm and said, "Bang." The tip of her finger was within a foot of his head.

"Firing a gun with blanks sets off an explosion," he said. "It doesn't send any bullets out of the barrel, but it does send out a dangerous burst of air called a gas column. Sheila, go out into the audience and watch this. Tell us if it looks convincing." While Sheila left the stage, Professor Suddeth moved into Sheila's spot and whispered instructions to Jason.

Professor Suddeth raised his arm and shot Jason, who fell dramatically.

"You killed him, all right," called out Sheila.

"People interpret what happened by the effects," said Professor Suddeth. "That gunshot looked convincing because of the consequences—the way Jason fell. But I was pointing my finger far away from Jason. Whenever we see a dramatic effect, we naturally look for what caused it."

A Margin of Error
From free falls (injuries when landing) to food fights (a slippery stage), live theater requires staging dangerous activities several times per week with an extremely small margin for error.

Sheila came back on stage. "He really wasn't aiming at you?" she asked Jason.

"Not even close," Jason replied.

Professor Suddeth added, "Sheila, we'll establish a point off-stage for you to aim at, called the firing lane, and it will be 15 degrees away from Jason. That way, even if you trip or mishandle the gun, we have a pointing margin of error of 15 degrees, plus distance enough for the gas column to dissipate. Anything more than 15 degrees and the audience won't believe you; anything less than 15 degrees and we're not being safe."

Sheila looked annoyed. "Is all this really necessary?" she finally asked. "Aren't we making too much out of a something that's very unlikely to happen anyway?"

"Think about it statistically," said Professor Suddeth. "This show is scheduled for 16 performances plus two full-dress rehearsals. It has three scenes that either threaten or portray extreme violence. Three scenes performed at 16 shows plus two dress rehearsals are 54 opportunities to seriously injure at least one member of the cast. With so many opportunities for an accident, it's quite likely that something will happen at least once, just by chance. So it's my job to train you to portray the kind of violence the playwright intended while keeping you and the audience completely safe."

Statistical reasoning figured into Professor Suddeth's decision making in several different ways. Creating a firing lane decreased the chances of an on-stage accident, a statistical probability that increased with every additional performance. But Professor Suddeth didn't instruct Sheila to shoot at the floor or in some direction 180 degrees away from Jason. Instead, his firing lane was designed to strike a balance between avoiding two types of possible errors (personal danger versus an unconvincing performance), the same way a statistician tries to strike a balance between the chances of a Type I error (rejecting the null hypothesis even though it is true) and the chances of a Type II error (not rejecting the null hypothesis even though it is false). Professor (aka fight master) Suddeth also established a set of procedures for handling the gun both on and off stage and instituted a fight call, a mandatory mini-rehearsal of the fight before every performance. In this chapter, we'll demonstrate that the statistical concepts of confidence intervals and effect sizes as well as guidelines for statistical power are all represented by Professor Suddeth's creation of a firing lane, the constraints needed to produce a dramatic theatrical effect, and his establishment of sensible preperformance procedures.

> BEYOND HYPOTHESIS TESTING: REDUCING MISINTERPRETATIONS

There are two reasons for going beyond hypothesis testing when we analyze data. First, we want to learn everything that we can from the data. Second, hypothesis testing by itself can be misleading. For example, listen to the story the data tell about a controversial research area: gender differences in mathematical reasoning ability. We'll start with a study that examined all the other studies conducted on this topic.

Men, Women, and Math: An Accurate Understanding of Differences

"Want to go shopping? OK, meet me at the mall."

"Math class is tough."

With these two phrases, and 268 others, the Mattel toy company introduced the Teen Talk Barbie doll. The technologically advanced Barbie was programmed to say four randomly chosen statements from a pool of 270 statements, including those about math and shopping. She went on sale in July 1992 and by September was criticized by the media and women's organizations for her adherence to gender stereotypes, particularly her negative message about math. At first, Mattel refused to pull the doll from the shelves, citing other more positive phrases in Barbie's repertoire, like "I'm studying to be a doctor." But the bad press escalated, and Mattel removed the phrase from the new dolls' microchips that October. The controversy took a while to subside, however, even showing up as a parody on a 1994 *Simpsons* episode when Lisa Simpson boycotted the fictional Malibu Stacy doll who says: "Thinking too much gives you wrinkles."

The controversy over gender differences in mathematical reasoning ability began shortly after publication of a study in the prestigious journal *Science*. Benbow and Stanley (1980) reported results from a sample of about 10,000 male and female students in grades 7–10. Their study included only students who were in the top 2–3% on standardized tests of mathematics and who took the SATs as part of a talent search. Our knowledge of the assumptions associated with hypothesis testing should make us particularly sensitive to that last detail about the sample. It was a select group of high-achieving students, not a representative sample. So we know that we want to be cautious about suggesting that what was true for this group would be true for the general population. In other words, we're hearing only one side of a larger story. But there's more to this particular story than a concern about its external validity.

Benbow and Stanley (1980) reported that the boys' average scores on the mathematics portion of the SAT test were, on average, 32 points higher than the girls' scores. That is why they were able to reject the null hypothesis that there was no difference between boys and girls with respect to SAT math scores. This study gained an enormous amount of media attention, so much that a pair of researchers decided to investigate the effects of the media's portrayal of the data from Benbow and Stanley's study. The abstract from Jacob and Eccles's (1982) study of the media's effects describes two conclusions:

> Results indicated that exposure to the media reports of the Benbow and Stanley study did affect parents' attitudes. As predicted, exposure had its largest impact on mothers of daughters and fathers of sons. Both became more stereotyped in their beliefs. Unexpectedly, media exposure also had a positive effect on fathers of daughters . . . fathers exposed to the campaign thought their daughters had slightly more ability than they had previously believed (p. 1).

The way the media translated Benbow and Stanley's study into the popular culture appeared to (1) mainly reinforce gender stereotypes and (2) slightly adjust gender stereotypes. But it is difficult to fault the media for getting so excited. After all, gender differences make good press, and the results from

"Math Class is Tough" Teen Talk Barbie, with her negative proclamation about math class, was a lightning rod for discussions about gender stereotypes and the evidence for actual gender differences. Some of Barbie's negative press related not to the fact that girls *can* do math well, but rather that Barbie's message might doom them to even poorer performance. The media tend to play up gender differences instead of the less interesting (and more frequent) realities of gender similarities.

Michael Newman/Photoedit

FIGURE 12-1
A Gender Difference in Mathematics Performance

This graph represents the amount of overlap that would be expected if the distributions for males and females differed, on average, by the amount that Hyde and colleagues (1990) reported in their meta-analysis of gender differences in mathematics performance. The vast amount of overlap emphasizes the futility of predicting an individual's mathematics performance solely based on gender.

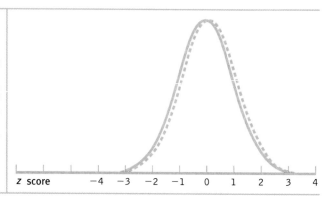

10,000 participants published in a prestigious journal are convincing. But statistical significance in a large study (using many participants) is not the same as a large effect (a big differences between groups). So in this case we want to ask whether a large gender difference is really what the data tell us. Let's go beyond hypothesis testing.

There is a specific, but profound, danger when reporting a statistically significant difference between two groups: Reporting a statistically significant difference can falsely imply that all or most of the members of one group are different from all or most of the members of the other group. As we can see in Figure 12-1, such an assertion about gender differences in mathematical reasoning ability would be far from the truth. Part of this misunderstanding is caused by the language of statistics: "statistically significant" does *not* mean "very important."

The distinction between "significant" and "important" is at the root of a central flaw of hypothesis testing. We decide that a finding is statistically significant if our test statistic is beyond our critical value or cutoff. But what if it just barely falls short of the cutoff? Two similar findings could lead to opposing conclusions. In one case, a test statistic is just beyond the cutoff, and we reject the null hypothesis. In a second case, a test statistic barely fails to beat the cutoff, and we fail to reject the null hypothesis. Yet the apparent difference between these two findings could disappear if just one or two participants scored a bit higher or lower on the dependent variable.

If we rely solely on hypothesis testing, then we would not see that these two findings are almost identical in practical importance. Travel writer Bill Bryson (1989) indirectly addressed this issue when he commented that national parks in the United States are regulated by "a belief that no commercial activities must be allowed inside the park, but permitting unrestrained development outside, even though the landscape there may be just as outstanding" (p. 119). Like the borders of a national park, the cutoff based on a *p* level of 0.05 is not a natural boundary, and good researchers, journalists, and everyday consumers of statistical information always keep this in mind.

The word *significant* ignores the more specific statistical reality:

1. Each distribution has variability.

2. The two distributions are overlapping.

The word *significant* also ignores the fact that the cutoff to which we compare the test statistic is somewhat arbitrary. We need more information.

It is so easy to read past those two important words, *on average*, to focus on the word *significant* and conclude that there's something about mathematics that girls just can't understand. Benbow and Stanley (1980) did not report the individual means for each gender, nor did they report the standard deviations that described the spread that surrounded each of those means. They did not emphasize the overlapping ranges for girls and boys, and the journalists followed their lead. So a study that used a large number of people was now perceived, inaccurately, as a study that had produced a large effect.

It took a meta-analysis, a study of all the studies about a particular topic, to hear the other sides of the story about gender differences in mathematical reasoning ability. Hyde, Fennema, and Lamon (1990) compiled results from all the studies they could identify about gender differences in mathematical reasoning ability, finding reports of 259 pairs of means for samples of male and female participants. These 259 mean differences represent data from 1,968,846 male participants and 2,016,836 female participants. Here's what they discovered:

1. Gender differences in overall mathematical reasoning ability were very small.

2. When samples of individuals at the extreme tails of the distribution, those in remedial programs or those identified as gifted (the population studied by Benbow and Stanley), were eliminated, the size of the gender difference was even tinier *and* reversed direction, now favoring women and girls rather than men and boys.

3. The superiority of one gender over another depended on the mathematical task. For example, women and girls tended to perform better than men and boys on mathematical computation, whereas men and boys tended to perform better than women and girls on mathematical problem solving.

The authors of this meta-analysis included a graph of two normal distributions that represent the small difference in favor of male participants that they found in their overall examination of studies (see Figure 12-1). Are you surprised that a small (but statistically significant) gender difference is almost completely overlapping? This is a case in which hypothesis testing alone inadvertently encouraged a profound misunderstanding (Jacob & Eccles, 1986).

The misunderstanding that derived from Benbow and Stanley's study spread from the researchers to the media and then from the media to the general public. Based only on this negative publicity, Teen Talk Barbie might have been surprised when she met one of the GI Joe dolls doctored by the guerrilla art group, the Barbie Liberation Organization. Members of the group switched the computer chips in many talking Barbies and talking GI Joes in 1993 and then put them back on the shelves of stores. Suddenly, it was GI Joe telling us, in a voice uncannily like Barbie's, that "math class is tough."

Beyond Hypothesis Testing: The "Telling" Details in Our Samples' Stories

As a social science major, you understand better than most people that misinterpretations don't necessarily lie around in our consciousness as harmless little mental events. Misinterpretations contribute to the kinds of stereotypes that undermine academic performance, even among high-achieving students (e.g., Aronson et al., 1999). An incompletely expressed statistical finding becomes a label ("Girls are less competent than boys at mathematics"). The label becomes a self-fulfilling prophecy ("I probably find math difficult because I'm a girl"). The self-fulfilling prophecy gets passed along from one generation to the next ("I wasn't any good at math, either.") Gradually, entire groups of people become trapped in talent-wasting stereotypes that have taken on a life of their own.

Fortunately, we don't have to live with such superficial misunderstandings. Here are three additional ways to listen more thoroughly to the story that the data tell. First, we'll compute confidence intervals. Rather than presenting just the mean difference between our samples, we'll present a range of plausible mean differences for the population. Second, we'll learn to compute effect sizes, so we can report that differences are small, medium, or large (just as Hyde and colleagues did in their meta-analysis). Third, we'll learn to compute statistical power so that we can be sure we have a sufficient sample size to detect any real difference that exists in the population; this helps us avoid Type II errors.

In summary, reports of the outcome of hypothesis testing can be misleading. A difference between means described as "significant" can be misinterpreted as "important." A statistically significant difference need not be of practical importance. In addition, knowing a difference between means is only useful if we also know the spread of each of the distributions. Two distributions that have a great deal of overlap might not provide much information about differences, despite a statistically significant mean difference, and that can lead to gross misinterpretations. These problems can be addressed through the calculation of confidence intervals and effect sizes as well as a consideration of statistical power.

⊙ CHECK YOUR LEARNING

12-1 A friend reads in her *Introduction to Psychology* text about a minority group in Japan, the Burakumin, who are racially the same as other Japanese people but are viewed as outcasts because their ancestors were employed in positions that involved the handling of dead animals (e.g., butchers). In Japan, the text reported, mean IQ scores of Burakumin were 10–15 points below mean IQ scores of other Japanese. In the United States, where Burakumin experienced no discrimination, there was no mean difference (from Ogbu, 1986, as reported in Hockenbury & Hockenbury, 2003). Your friend says to you: "Wow—when I taught English in Japan last summer, I had a Burakumin student. He seemed smart; perhaps I was fooled." What is your friend missing in her appraisal? Specifically, what should she consider about the two distributions, the one for Burakumin people and the one for other Japanese people?

> CONFIDENCE INTERVALS: AN ALTERNATIVE TO HYPOTHESIS TESTING

Sheila complained to the chair of the department that Professor Suddeth had embarrassed her.

"What does he have you aiming at?" asked Professor Weary.

"A red light on the catwalk off-stage left," Sheila said. "It's easy to spot and it's always on."

"Professor Suddeth gave you a point to aim at for several reasons," Professor Weary told her. "First, you need something to orient you during the chaos of a performance, when your attention should be focused on the scene rather than aiming a gun safely. But we all know that even with a real gun, you probably couldn't hit the red bulb."

"I've never shot a real gun," Sheila agreed.

"So what we're really doing is creating a zone of probability around your point, the red light on the catwalk. I'm willing to consider it a success if you miss the light but still come close. What we don't want is for you to be so far off the mark to one side that you don't convince the audience that the shooting is real, just as we don't want you so far off the mark to the other side that you endanger Jason. I'm glad that Professor Suddeth is being so firm with you," Professor Weary concluded. "The last thing I want is another injury."

"*Another* injury?" Sheila asked.

Professor Weary sighed and then said, "Three years ago, when you were still in high school, two of our students were playing around with the prop gun. It had blanks in it, so they thought they were safe. One of the students, Douglas, playfully aimed the gun at his own head and pulled the trigger. Doug suffered a traumatic brain injury when the gas column hit him on the side of his head. If he'd held the gun any closer or aimed any better, he probably would have died. As it is, he probably has some permanent brain damage."

"Where did they get the gun?"

"Douglas and his friend had gotten the gun out of a locked cabinet and without permission, but the university was sued anyway. As part of the settlement, we now have Professor Suddeth as staff consultant; the insurance company had a statistician investigate our program and calculate the probability of another injury, both with him and without him. I just wish we'd had Professor Suddeth working here before the accident. He brings much more to our department than an added measure of safety. By the time you graduate, you'll know how to fight with swords and staffs, fall down stairs, shoot blanks, wrestle, and have fistfights, and do all those and many other things convincingly and safely—and those are skills that make you much more employable as an actor. But in the bigger picture, training our students in stage combat reduces our margin for error. That's why Professor Suddeth established the red light as your target point; he estimated a range that was safe for you to point at and then used the red light as the midpoint of that estimation."

How Wide a Margin of Error?
Fight director J. Allen Suddeth used established principles of perception to stage this publicity photo using blanks and noted that, "Despite appearances, we were aiming far off target, for safety!"

Interval Estimation: A Range of Plausible Means

Hypothesis testing, by itself, is like hearing only one side of a complicated story. Just as Professor Suddeth was teaching his students how to use multiple techniques to increase the probability of a safe performance, social scientists teach their students to use multiple techniques to increase the probability of hearing the entire story that the data tell. Professor Suddeth instructed Shelia to aim her gun at the red light even though he knew she was unlikely to hit her target because the space just to the left and to the right of the light represented an acceptably safe interval. Similarly, when a sample produces a mean value, we know we probably haven't hit the target (the population mean) precisely, but the values just to the left and to the right of the mean represent an acceptably safe interval of estimation. So let's use this distinction between point estimation

∎ A **point estimate** is a summary statistic from a sample that is just one number as an estimate of the population parameter.

∎ An **interval estimate** is based on our sample statistic; it conveys the range of sample statistics we could expect if we conducted repeated hypothesis tests using samples from the same population.

Popularity Contest
Joanne Woodward and Paul Newman beat out the second-place couple, Angelina Jolie and Brad Pitt, as the celebrity couple that Americans most want to meet. The globe-trotting darlings of the tabloids, Angelina and Brad, were chosen by 18% of the 800 respondents, 11 percentage points behind Woodward and Newman. This 18% is a point estimate. There was a margin of error of ±3.5%, giving an interval estimate of 14.5–21.5%.

AP Photo/Matt Sayles

and interval estimation to better understand the controversy surrounding Benbow and Stanley's (1980) study of gender differences in mathematical reasoning ability.

Benbow and Stanley's study found that the average SAT mathematics score for boys was 32 points higher than the average SAT mathematics score for girls. That certainly sounds like convincing evidence. But let's dig a little deeper into the data. Benbow and Stanley calculated a mean difference by subtracting the mean score for girls from the mean score for boys. All three summary statistics—the mean for boys, the mean for girls, and the difference between them—are point estimates. *A **point estimate** is a summary statistic from a sample that is just one number as an estimate of the population parameter.* Point estimates are the red light that Sheila was aiming at, specific points rather than more realistic margins for safety. Point estimates are useful for gauging the central tendency but by themselves can be misleading. Even a point estimate based on a large, randomly selected sample is unlikely to represent the population exactly, just as Sheila was unlikely to hit the red light with her prop gun.

Sampling implies uncertainty, and that is why we are wiser to use interval estimates rather than point estimates. *An **interval estimate** is based on our sample statistic; it conveys the range of sample statistics we could expect if we conducted repeated hypothesis tests using samples from the same population.* An interval estimate is the range of probability around Sheila's red light, her margin of error that keeps everyone both safe and performing effectively. It is the pattern of hits around the red light that would probably result if Sheila were shooting a gun many times. Interval estimates are frequently used in media reports, particularly when reporting political polls. The important details, however, are often buried in the fine print in newspapers, at the bottom of television screens, or spoken at high speed by radio announcers.

For example, one survey (the polling company, inc., 2006) asked 800 adult respondents to select one out of six celebrity couples that they'd most like to meet. Film legends Paul Newman and Joanne Woodward came out on top, chosen by 29% of respondents, ahead of more in-the-news couples like Madonna and Guy Ritchie or Katie Holmes and Tom Cruise. The margin of error was reported to be ± 3.5%, giving an interval estimate of 25.5–32.5% for Newman and Woodward. Interval estimates remind us that the point estimate is not necessarily equal to the population percentage; they also provide us with a range of plausible values. The researcher was quantifying the uncertainty in the point estimation by reporting the margin of error.

What's particularly useful about margins of error is that we can figure out more than one interval for the same poll to see if they overlap. Angelina Jolie and Brad Pitt came in second with 18%, giving an interval estimate of 14.5–21.5%. There's no overlap with the first-place couple, a strong indication that Newman/Woodward really are the most popular couple among those in the entire population as well as those in this sample. However, what if Jolie/Pitt had 23% of the vote instead of 18% of the vote, but with the same margin of error? That would place them only 5% behind Newman/Woodward, and they'd have an interval estimate of 19.5–26.5%. This range would have overlapped with that for Newman/Woodward, an indication that it was plausible that both couples had the same percentage popularity in the general population.

In social science research, the idea of a margin of error is expressed as an interval estimate, usually a confidence interval. *A **confidence interval** is a calculated interval estimate that surrounds the point estimate.* More specifically, a confidence interval around a sample statistic includes the true population parameter a certain percentage of the time, were we to sample from the same population repeatedly. Note, though, that the use of the word *confidence* in this manner has been criticized (e.g., Frick, 1995). We are not saying that we are confident that the population mean falls in the interval; we are merely saying that we expect to find the population mean in this interval 95% of the time that we conduct this same study. The confidence interval, like the hypothesis test, is based on the sampling distribution, but it is centered around the mean of the sample rather than the mean according to the null hypothesis. In hypothesis testing, the most common cutoff level is 0.05, indicating the most extreme 5%. For a confidence interval, the counterpart to the cutoff *p* level of 0.05 is the 95% confidence level. This indicates the 95% that falls *between* the two tails (i.e., 100 − 5 = 95). Note the terms used here: the confidence *level* is 95%, but the confidence *interval* will be the range of values bounded by the actual means at each end of the interval that surrounds the sample mean.

> ■ A **confidence interval** is an interval estimate, based on the sample statistic, that includes the population mean a certain percentage of the time, were we to sample from the same population repeatedly.

Professor Suddeth established a point estimate for gun safety by having the actor aim the gun 15 degrees away from the person she was pretending to shoot. Notice how his decision strikes a balance between different risks the same way that scientists strike a balance between the risk of committing Type I and Type II errors. A point estimate less then 15 degrees away from the on-stage target increases the risk of harming a fellow actor. A point estimate more than 15 degrees from the on-stage target increases the risk of the shooting not looking real to the audience. In the following sections, we will learn how to aim the tools of science so that we establish a 95% confidence interval, first with the *z* distribution and then with *t* distributions.

z Distributions: Calculating Confidence Intervals

The symmetry of the *z* distribution, when based on a normal distribution makes it easy to calculate confidence intervals, so let's briefly refresh our knowledge from Chapter 6:

1. We use a *z* distribution when we know the population mean and population standard deviation.

2. We conduct a *z* test by collecting data from a sample and then comparing its mean to that of the population.

Let's use an example from Chapter 6 that some behavioral science majors might find interesting as they start competing in the job market and for spots in graduate school: scores on the Major Field Test in Psychology (MFTP). We already conducted hypothesis testing for this example in Chapter 6; now we will calculate a confidence interval. Frazier and Edmonds (2002) presented data comparing the average score of students at Ursuline College to the population mean for all students who took the MFTP nationwide. The population mean was 156.5, and the population standard deviation was assumed to be 14.6. The 97 students in the Ursuline College sample had a mean MFTP score of 156.11. When we conducted hypothesis testing, we centered our curve around the mean according to the null hypothesis, 156.5. We determined critical values based on this mean and compared our sample mean to these cutoffs. These two means

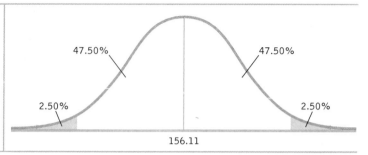

FIGURE 12-2
A 95% Confidence Interval, Part I

To begin calculating a confidence interval for a *z* distribution, we draw a normal curve, place the sample mean at its center, and indicate the percentages within and beyond the confidence interval.

are very close together, so it is not surprising that we were not able to reject the null hypothesis that there was no mean difference between the two groups. The test statistic was not beyond the cutoff *z* statistic.

To calculate a confidence interval, we will first draw a normal curve (see Figure 12-2) that has the *sample* mean, 156.11, at its center instead of the *population* mean, 156.5. We will draw a vertical line from the mean to the top of the curve. For a 95% confidence interval, we also will draw two much smaller vertical lines indicating the middle 95% (2.5% in each tail for a total of 5%) of the normal curve. (Note that we can use different confidence levels; a 99% confidence interval would coincide with a *p* level of 0.01, or 1%; a 90% confidence interval would coincide with a *p* level of 0.10, or 10%.) We will then write the appropriate percentages under the segments of the curve. The curve is symmetric, so half of the 95% would fall above and half would fall below the mean. Half of 95 is 47.5, so we would write 47.5% in the segments on either side of the mean. In the tails beyond the two lines that indicate the end of the middle 95%, we also will write the appropriate percentages. Because 50% falls on each side of the mean and 47.5% falls between the mean and each end of the confidence interval, we know that 50 − 47.5 = 2.5% falls beyond each end of the confidence interval.

We now can turn back to our versatile *z* table in Appendix B. Remember that the *z* table provides *z* statistics based on the percentage between the mean and the score of interest. It provides only positive *z* statistics because the curve is symmetric and the negative *z* statistics will be of the same magnitude. The percentage between the mean and each of our *z* scores is 47.5%. When we look up this percentage in the *z* table, we find a *z* statistic of 1.96. Note that this is identical to the cutoffs for the *z* test; this will always be the case because the *p* level of 0.05 corresponds to a confidence level of 95%. We can now add the *z* statistics of −1.96 and 1.96 to our curve, as seen in Figure 12-3.

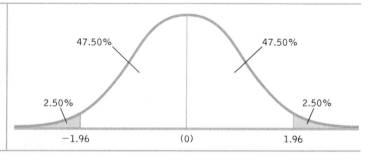

FIGURE 12-3
A 95% Confidence Interval, Part II

The next step in calculating a confidence interval is identifying the *z* statistics that indicate each end of the interval. Because the curve is symmetric, the *z* statistics will have the same magnitude—one will be negative and one will be positive (−1.96 and 1.96).

We now turn the z statistics back into raw means. We use the formula for this conversion, but first we must identify the appropriate mean and standard deviation. There are two important points to remember. First, we center our interval around the *sample* mean, not the *population* mean. So we use the sample mean of 156.11 in our calculations. Second, because we have a sample *mean*, rather than an individual *score*, we use a distribution of means. So we will have to calculate standard error as our measure of spread: $\sigma_M = \dfrac{\sigma}{\sqrt{N}} = \dfrac{14.6}{\sqrt{97}} = 1.482$.

Notice that this is the same standard error that we calculated previously when we conducted a hypothesis test.

Now we can calculate the raw mean at each end of the confidence interval, the lower end and the upper end, and add them to our curve as in Figure 12-4:

$$M_{Lower} = -z(\sigma_M) + M_{Sample} = -1.96(1.482) + 156.11 = 153.21$$

$$M_{Upper} = z(\sigma_M) + M_{Sample} = 1.96(1.482) + 156.11 = 159.01$$

Our 95% confidence interval, reported in parentheses as is typical, is (153.21, 159.01). We can check that this makes sense. The sample mean should fall exactly in the middle of the two ends of the interval. $153.21 - 156.11 = -2.9$ and $159.01 - 156.11 = 2.9$. We have a match. The confidence interval ranges from -2.9 below the sample mean to 2.9 above the sample mean. Many people refer to this number, 2.9, as the margin of error. The confidence interval, then, can be thought of as the range comprised by the sample mean plus and minus the margin of error.

To recap the steps for creation of a confidence interval:

1. *Draw* a normal curve with the sample mean in the center.

2. *Indicate* the bounds of the confidence interval on either end, and write the percentages under each segment of the curve.

3. *Look up* the z statistics for the lower and upper ends of the confidence interval in the z table.

4. *Convert* the z statistics to raw means for the lower and upper ends of the confidence interval.

5. *Check* your answer; each end of the confidence interval should be exactly the same distance from the sample mean.

If we were to sample 97 Ursuline College psychology majors from the same population over and over, the interval would include the population mean 95% of the time. Note that the population mean for all students taking the MFTP,

Formula: $M_{Lower} = -z(\sigma_M) + M_{Sample}$

Formula: $M_{Upper} = z(\sigma_M) + M_{Sample}$

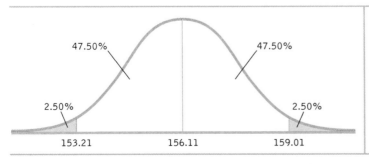

FIGURE 12-4
A 95% Confidence Interval, Part III

The final step in calculating a confidence interval is converting the *z* statistics that indicate each end of the interval into raw means.

156.5, falls within this interval. Because the population mean is within the confidence interval, it is plausible that the sample of Ursuline College psychology students who took the MFTP comes from the population according to the null hypothesis—all psychology students who took the MFTP. We cannot conclude that the sample comes from a different population; that is, we cannot conclude that Ursuline College students performed any better or worse than the national population on the MFTP. The conclusions from both statistical techniques are the same, but the confidence interval gives us more information. We not only have made the same determination that we made with a hypothesis test but we have a more realistic interval estimate—not just a point estimate. The story the data tell using confidence intervals has exactly the same ending as the story the data tell using hypothesis testing. But now we have an estimate of how strongly we can believe that story.

t Distributions: Calculating Confidence Intervals

Confidence intervals for the different kinds of *t* tests are calculated using the same logic we used for the *z* test. Here, we'll focus on the independent-samples *t* test, for which we'll create a confidence interval for the *difference between means* rather than for the means themselves. So we will use the difference between means for our samples and the standard error for the difference between means, $s_{Difference}$, that we calculate in an identical manner to that used in hypothesis testing. But we're still creating an interval around a number (now a difference between means) based on some measure of variability (now the standard error for the difference between means). We must also use the formula for the appropriate *t* statistic when calculating our raw differences between means. To do this, we will use algebra on our original formula for an independent-samples *t* test to isolate the upper and lower mean differences, just as we used algebra in Chapter 5 to change our *z* score formula to a raw-score formula.

Here is the original *t* statistic formula:

$$t = \frac{(M_X - M_Y) - (\mu_X - \mu_Y)}{s_{Difference}}$$

We now replace the population mean difference, $(\mu_X - \mu_Y)$, with the sample mean difference, $(M_X - M_Y)_{Sample}$, because that is what the confidence interval is centered around. We also indicate that the first mean difference in the numerator refers to the bounds of the confidence intervals, the upper bound in this case:

$$t_{Upper} = \frac{(M_X - M_Y)_{Upper} - (M_X - M_Y)_{Sample}}{s_{Difference}}$$

With algebra, we can isolate the upper bound of the confidence interval to create the following formula for the upper bound of the confidence interval:

$$(M_X - M_Y)_{Upper} = t(s_{Difference}) + (M_X - M_Y)_{Sample}$$

> Formula: $(M_X - M_Y)_{Upper} = t(s_{Difference}) + (M_X - M_Y)_{Sample}$
>
> Formula: $(M_X - M_Y)_{Lower} = {}^-t(s_{Difference}) + (M_X - M_Y)_{Sample}$

We create the formula for the lower bound of the confidence interval in exactly the same way:

$$(M_X - M_Y)_{Lower} = {}^-t(s_{Difference}) + (M_X - M_Y)_{Sample}$$

And now the steps are the same as the confidence interval for a *z* statistic. Let's consider another example that we also used in Chapter 6. Researchers at Stanford University used functional magnetic resonance imaging (fMRI) to compare the brain activity of women and men in the presence of humorous

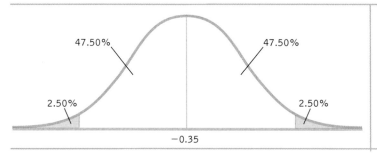

FIGURE 12-5
A 95% Confidence Interval for Differences Between Means, Part I

As with a confidence interval for a single-sample mean, we start the confidence interval for a difference between means by drawing a curve with the sample difference between means in the center.

cartoons (Azim, Mobbs, Jo, Menon, & Reiss, 2005). As part of the study, Azim and colleagues examined whether men or women were more likely to find humorous cartoons funny to begin with. Here are the fictional data that we used in Chapter 6.

Percentage of cartoons labeled as "funny."

Women: 84, 97, 58, 90

Men: 88, 90, 52, 97, 86

Previously, we calculated the difference between the means of these samples to be $82.25 - 82.6 = -0.35$; the standard error for the differences between means, $s_{Difference}$, to be 11.847; and the degrees of freedom to be 7. (Note that the order of subtraction in calculating the difference between means is irrelevant; we could just as easily have subtracted 82.25 from 82.6 and gotten a positive result, 0.35.) If we had not already calculated them for the hypothesis test, we would, of course, have to calculate them for the confidence interval. Here are the steps for determining a confidence interval for a difference between means.

1. *Draw* a normal curve with the sample difference between means in the center (see Figure 12-5).

2. *Indicate* the bounds of the confidence interval on either end, and write the percentages under each segment of the curve (see Figure 12-5).

3. *Look up* the *t* statistics for the lower and upper ends of the confidence interval in the *t* table. We will look up the *t* statistic for a two-tailed test and a *p* level of 0.05 (which corresponds to a 95% confidence interval). We will use the degrees of freedom—7—that we calculated in Chapter 6. The table indicates a *t* statistic of 2.365. Because the normal curve is symmetric, the bounds of our confidence interval fall at *t* statistics of −2.365 and 2.365. (Note that these are identical to the cutoffs used for the independent-samples *t* test. This will always be the case for a given sample size because the *p* level of 0.05 corresponds to a confidence level of 95%.) We will now add those *t* statistics to our normal curve, as in Figure 12-6.

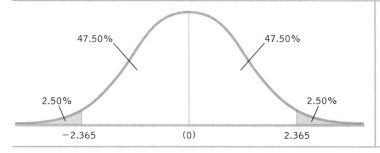

FIGURE 12-6
A 95% Confidence Interval for Differences Between Means, Part II

The next step in calculating a confidence interval is identifying the *t* statistics that indicate each end of the interval. Because the curve is symmetric, the *t* statistics will have the same magnitude—one will be negative and one will be positive.

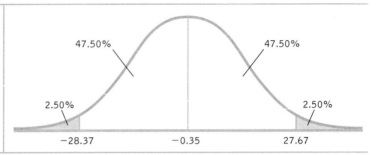

FIGURE 12-7
A 95% Confidence Interval for Differences Between Means, Part III

The final step in calculating a confidence interval is converting the *t* statistics that indicate each end of the interval into raw differences between means.

47.50%   47.50%

2.50%   2.50%

−28.37   −0.35   27.67

4. *Convert* the *t* statistics to raw differences between means for the lower and upper ends of the confidence interval. Be sure to pay attention to the negative signs in your calculations. For the lower end: $(M_X - M_Y)_{Lower} = {}^-t(s_{Difference}) + (M_X - M_Y)_{Sample} = -2.365(11.847) + (-0.35) = -28.37$. For the upper end: $(M_X - M_Y)_{Upper} = t(s_{Difference}) + (M_X - M_Y)_{Sample} = 2.365(11.847) + (-0.35) = 27.67$. The confidence interval is $(-28.37, 27.67)$, as shown in Figure 12-7.

5. *Check* your answer; each end of the confidence interval should be exactly the same distance from the sample mean.

$$-28.37 - (-0.35) = -28.02$$
$$27.67 - (-0.35) = 28.02$$

Our interval checks out, and we know that our margin of error is 28.02; the bounds of the confidence interval are calculated as the difference between sample means plus or minus 28.02.

The confidence interval is quite wide, indicating many plausible values for the difference between means. If we were to conduct this study many times, 95% of the time the population mean would be in our confidence interval. In this case, we have not pinpointed our estimate very closely. In addition, 0 falls within the interval, an indication that the two distributions could actually be identical. (Whenever 0 falls within the interval, it is plausible that there is no difference.) We cannot reject the null hypothesis and can only conclude that these data do not provide evidence of a difference between sample means.

As in the previous example, we can compare the conclusion drawn from our confidence interval to that drawn from our hypothesis test. When we conducted the independent-samples *t* test in Chapter 6, we also failed to reject the null hypothesis. Both statistical techniques led to the same outcome, but the confidence interval provided more information by using an interval estimate rather than a point estimate. In fact, we can see from our confidence interval that we have a range of possible differences between means that is quite wide. The fact that confidence intervals give us the same information as a hypothesis test, along with even more information, is the major reason that their proponents lobby for using them routinely (Cohen, 1994) and that some call for an outright boycott of hypothesis tests altogether (Schmidt, 1996). Confidence intervals allow us to hear the data speak more clearly. But there's still more to the story that the data want to tell. In the next section, we will learn how to listen to that story by calculating effect sizes.

In summary, a point estimate is just a single number, such as a mean, whereas an interval estimate is a range of numbers indicating several possibilities for a summary statistic such as a mean. A confidence interval is one kind of interval estimate. A confidence interval can be created with a z distribution around a sample mean or with a t distribution around a sample mean or around a difference between means. The confidence interval is created by adding and subtracting a margin of error from the mean or difference between means around which the interval is centered. The confidence interval matches the results of the hypothesis test. If the null hypothesis is rejected, the confidence interval will not include 0; similarly, if we fail to reject the null hypothesis, the confidence interval will include 0.

⊙ CHECK YOUR LEARNING

12-2 Check Your Learning 6-3 asked you to calculate a z test based on the following information, adapted from a study by Petrocelli (2003) that used the Consideration of Future Consequences (CFC) scale as the dependent variable. The population mean CFC score was 3.51, with a standard deviation of 0.61. The sample of interest was composed of 45 students who joined a career discussion group, and the study examined whether this might have changed CFC scores. The mean for this group is 3.7.

a. Calculate a 95% confidence interval for this study.

b. Explain what this confidence interval tells us.

c. Why is this confidence interval superior to the hypothesis test that we conducted in Chapter 6?

➤ EFFECT SIZE: JUST HOW BIG IS THE DIFFERENCE?

An evil-looking bullwhip was lying in the middle of the gymnasium floor. All the students noticed it as they wandered in for their fight choreography class. Professor Weary was seated in an office chair far away from the bleachers. Professor Suddeth stood near the bullwhip. "You can stage almost everything with a high degree of safety," Professor Suddeth told the class as they were getting settled. "Theater speaks by creating an illusion of reality, not the reality itself. So we only need to create the illusion of violence, not the violence itself."

Professor Suddeth picked up the bullwhip and began prowling back and forth before the class, coiling and uncoiling the long whip. He recounted the history and uses of a bullwhip and showed them its frayed, lethal-looking tip.

Professor Suddeth then looked across to his department chairperson. "Are you ready?" he asked Professor Weary.

"Ready!"

Professor Suddeth drew the whip back and forth across the floor like a snake until he reached a particular spot on the floor. Then he spoke directly to Professor Weary. "I've never liked you very much, Weary." Professor Suddeth started twirling the whip over his head.

A Bull Whip
The size of your margin of error depends on the situation. In theater, the research on perception can help you create the illusion of a big (dramatic) effect. In statistics, a larger distance between means and a smaller standard deviation can help you discover a big (statistical) effect.

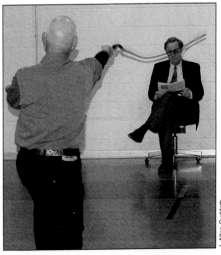
J. Allen Suddeth

Misinterpreting Statistical Significance
Statistical significance that is achieved by merely collecting a very large sample can make a research finding appear to be far more important than it really is, just as a curved mirror can exaggerate a person's size.

"You don't pay me enough," he told Weary. "You don't respect what I do. You don't . . . oh, what the . . . ?" And with that, Professor Suddeth reached back and whistled the bullwhip forward and then snapped it back with the sound of a frightening crack. Professor Weary screamed, clutched his left eye, and fell off the chair. The class was horrified and confused until Professor Weary calmly got up, looked at them all, and smiled.

Professor Suddeth took the butt end of the bullwhip and placed it on the floor at the spot where he had been standing. "Here's my mark," he told the class, pointing to a small piece of masking tape on the floor. He then straightened the whip toward the chair where Professor Weary had been sitting. It wasn't even close, perhaps twice as far as the whip could possibly reach! Professor Weary had been perfectly safe the entire time! But the combination of whistle, crack, scream, Suddeth's acted-out intention to harm Professor Weary, and his audience's reduced depth perception had convinced each of them that Suddeth had flicked the tip of the whip directly into the department chairperson's left eye. "I'm only interested in the size of the effect we can produce on the audience," Professor Suddeth told the class, "not how close I can come to Professor Weary. We're not interested in close calls; we're interested in big effects."

Researchers also tend to be interested in big effects, but we need them to be genuine discoveries rather than theatrical illusions. Unfortunately, hypothesis testing used alone can create an illusion of exaggerated importance—the same way a curved mirror can exaggerate a person's size. In research, the easiest way to inflate the impression of an important finding is by increasing sample size. Note that we are not asserting that it is sometimes wrong to increase sample size. On the contrary, increasing sample size is almost always a good thing. Indeed, the only thing that's wrong with increasing our sample size is that it tends to increase the costs of a study in terms of time and money. A large sample size, however, can mislead the reader into believing that a statistically significant study is far more important than it really is. *Statistically significant* does *not* mean that the findings from a study are consequential or important; it only means that those findings are unlikely to occur if in fact the null hypothesis is true.

To demonstrate the difference between statistical significance and practical importance, Cohen (1990) offered the example of a "definite" correlation between height and IQ observed in a sample of 14,000 children and reported by the popular media to be a statistically significant but small effect. Cohen did some calculations based on the correlation coefficient of 0.11; if there were a causal connection, to increase IQ by 30 points (2 standard deviations), one would have to grow by 3.5 feet, and to reverse causality and increase height by 4 inches, one would have to increase one's IQ by 233 points! Height may have been significantly related to IQ, but there was only a very small effect with no practical real-world applications. Statistical significance, by itself, can distort the story the data tell. Here's why a large sample can make a small difference between means appear to be a large effect.

Misunderstandings from Hypothesis Testing: When "Significant" Isn't Very Significant

In earlier chapters, we demonstrated how increasing the sample size can lead to an increased test statistic during hypothesis testing. As you may have noticed when scanning the z, t, and F tables, as the number of observations increases (usually the number of people in behavioral science research), the number needed to declare statistical significance decreases. In other words, it becomes progressively easier to declare statistical significance as we increase our sample size, the N. In many ways, this makes sense. When we have more participants in a sample, our confidence should be higher that any patterns you find in the sample genuinely describe the population. After all, if we heard a rumor about a friend of ours from one person with a reputation for being a gossip, then we might be reluctant to believe it. But if we heard the same story from seven other people, then we would be much more inclined to believe it.

But many people believing and repeating the same rumor doesn't make it true or important. A larger sample size should influence our level of confidence that the story is true, but it shouldn't increase our confidence that the story is important. The importance of one piece of gossip (hearing that a friend has suffered a serious accident and needs our help) is more important than another piece of gossip (a friend wore mismatched clothing). Both might be true, but they are not equally important. Furthermore, hearing about the terrible accident from one person is more consequential for us than hearing about the mismatched clothing from seven people.

Many people repeating the same rumor doesn't make it important. And achieving statistical significance merely by adding participants to a study doesn't make the findings important, either. In Chapter 6 we used data from the GRE psychology test to specifically demonstrate that an ever-increasing sample size leads to an ever-increasing z statistic. A small difference between a sample mean and a population mean *might not* be statistically significant with a small sample *but could* be statistically significant with a somewhat larger sample and *would almost certainly* be statistically significant with an extremely large sample size. The confusion reveals itself when students (and researchers) mistakenly refer to the latter type of finding as "very statistically significant" or, even more misleadingly, "very significant." This gives the potentially false impression that one test statistic that is far beyond the cutoff is more important than a second one that is just barely beyond the cutoff. Or that one test statistic that is just beyond the cutoff is important, whereas a second test statistic that does not quite reach the cutoff, but is almost the same as the first, is not important. *Statistical significance does not indicate practical importance.*

What Effect Size Is: Standardization Across Studies

A statistically significant finding, particularly one from a study using a large sample, may indicate a genuine but trivial difference between groups. That's where effect size comes in. *Effect size is a standardized value that indicates the size of a difference with respect to a measure of spread, but is not affected by sample size.* Effect size tells us how much two populations (the ones from which the participants come) *do not* overlap; that is, how different the two distributions are from each other. Simply put, the less overlap, the bigger the effect size. The amount of overlap between two distributions can be decreased in two ways (that we hope are familiar to you by now). Two populations can overlap *less* if either of the following is true:

1. Their means are farther apart.

2. The variation within each population is smaller.

■ **Effect size** is a standardized value that indicates the size of a difference with respect to a measure of spread, but is not affected by sample size.

Figure 12-8 shows that overlap decreases and effect size increases when means are farther apart. Figure 12-9 shows that overlap decreases and the effect size increases when the variability within each distribution becomes smaller. Because effect size takes into account both the mean difference and the variability of the population distributions based on individual scores (not the sampling distribution of means), it captures both ways in which the overlap of two distributions is affected.

When we investigated the story of gender differences in mathematical reasoning ability, you may have noticed that we described Hyde's (e.g., 2005) reporting of the size of findings as small, medium, or large. These adjectives were not arbitrarily assigned; rather, they were based on effect sizes that Hyde and

FIGURE 12-8
Effect Size and Mean Differences

When two population means are farther apart, as in the bottom of these two sets of curves, the overlap of the distributions is less and the effect size is bigger.

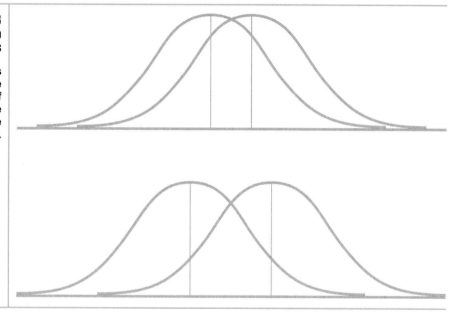

FIGURE 12-9
Effect Size and Standard Deviation

When two population distributions decrease their spread, as in the bottom of these two sets of curves, the overlap of the distributions is less and the effect size is bigger.

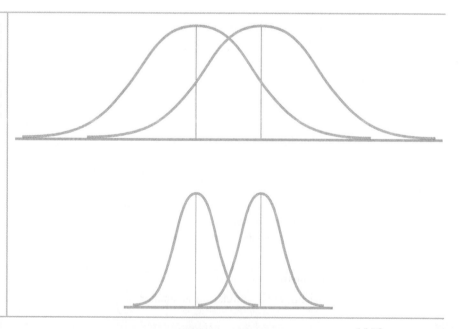

colleagues (1990) calculated for the various studies. Because effect size is a standardized measure that is based on scores rather than means, we can compare different studies with one another—an incredibly useful tool when examining many studies, as researchers do in meta-analysis. A study based on large sample sizes that shows statistical significance might have a smaller effect size than a study based on small sample sizes that is not statistically significant. Only the effect sizes allow for comparisons across studies with different sample sizes. Figure 12-10 provides a visual demonstration of why we use the distribution of scores instead of the distribution of means.

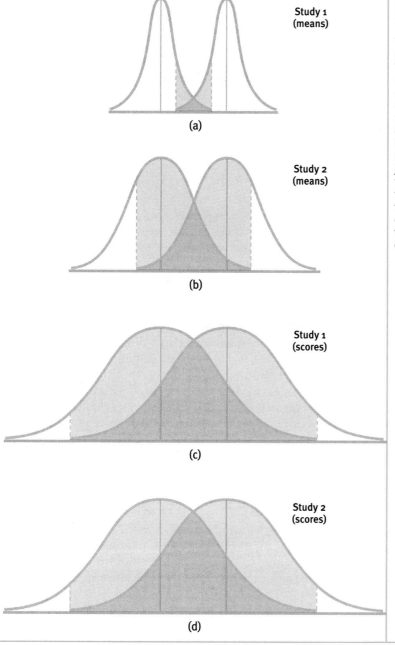

Study 1
(means)

(a)

Study 2
(means)

(b)

Study 1
(scores)

(c)

Study 2
(scores)

(d)

FIGURE 12-10
Making Fair Comparisons

The top two pairs of curves (a and b) depict two studies, study 1 and study 2. The first study (a) compared two samples with very large sample sizes, so each curve was very narrow. The second study (b) compared two samples with much smaller sample sizes, so each curve was wider. The first study has less overlap, but that doesn't mean it has a bigger effect than study 2; we just can't compare the effects. The bottom two pairs (c & d) depict the same two studies, but using standard deviation for individual scores. Now they are comparable and we see that they have the same amount of overlap—the same effect sizes.

▪ **Cohen's *d*** is a measure of effect size that assesses the difference between two means in terms of standard deviation, not standard error.

First of all, assume that each of these distributions is based on the same underlying population. Second, notice that all means represented by the vertical lines are identical. The only differences are those due to the spread of the distributions. Because sample size influences the spread of a distribution, we can't make an honest estimate of overlap (effect size) unless we avoid sampling distributions of means and compare distributions of scores. A difference in the amount of overlap caused simply by how many observations were made is an artificial difference.

Let's examine these distributions. The small degree of overlap in the tall, skinny distributions in Figure 12-10a is the result of a very large sample size. The greater degree of overlap in the somewhat wider distributions in Figure 12-10b is the result of a smaller sample size. By contrast, the distributions represented in Figures 12-10c and 12-10d are the result of actual scores rather than sample means for these two studies. Because these flatter, wider distributions include actual scores, sample size is irrelevant.

In this case, the amounts of real overlap in Figures 12-10c and 12-10d are identical. We can directly compare the amount of overlap and see that they have the same effect size. As we have learned, hypothesis testing alone can provide a distorted perception of statistical significance and the ambiguous meanings of the word "significance" encourage this misperception. Fortunately, the various effect-size statistics focus only on the amount of overlap between distributions of scores, which is what we are really interested in most of the time.

Cohen's *d*: The Effect Size for a *z* Test or a *t* Test

Symbols: Cohen's *d* (or just *d*)

There are many different effect-size statistics, but they are all created by finding ways to ignore the influence of sample size. Our particular choice of effect-size statistic depends on what hypothesis test we have conducted. When we have conducted *z* or *t* tests, the effect-size statistic of choice is Cohen's *d*, developed by Jacob Cohen (Cohen, 1988). ***Cohen's d is a measure of effect size that assesses the difference between two means in terms of standard deviation, not standard error.*** In other words, Cohen's *d* allows us to measure the difference between means using the number of standard deviations much like we did when calculating a *z* or *t* statistic. We accomplish that by using a form of standard deviation in the denominator, rather than a form of standard error. Why? Remember that standard error makes an adjustment for sample size, and effect size aims to disregard the influence of sample size.

Let's calculate Cohen's *d* for the two situations for which we constructed confidence intervals. We simply substitute standard deviation for standard error. When we calculated the test statistic for the 97 Ursuline College students on the MFTP, we first calculated the standard error: $\sigma_M = \dfrac{\sigma}{\sqrt{N}} = \dfrac{14.6}{\sqrt{97}} = 1.482$. We were told that the population mean was 156.5 and the sample mean was 156.11. We calculated the *z* statistic as $z = \dfrac{(M - \mu_M)}{\sigma_M} = \dfrac{(156.11 - 156.5)}{1.482} = -0.26$.

To calculate our Cohen's *d*, we simply use the formula for the *z* statistic, substituting σ for σ_M (and μ for μ_M, even though these means are always the same). We use 14.6, therefore, instead of 1.482 in the denominator. The Cohen's *d* is now based on the spread of the distribution of individual scores, rather than the distribution of means.

Formula: Cohen's $d = \dfrac{(M - \mu)}{\sigma}$

for a *z* distribution

$$\text{Cohen's } d = \frac{(M - \mu)}{\sigma} = \frac{(156.11 - 156.5)}{14.6} = -0.03$$

TABLE 12-1. COHEN'S CONVENTIONS FOR EFFECT SIZES: *d*

Jacob Cohen has published guidelines (or conventions), based on the overlap between two distributions, to help researchers determine whether an effect is small, medium, or large. These numbers are not cutoffs, merely rough guidelines to aid researchers in their interpretation of results.

EFFECT SIZE	CONVENTION	OVERLAP
Small	0.2	85%
Medium	0.5	67%
Large	0.8	53%

Now that we have our effect size, often written in shorthand as $d = -0.03$, what does it mean? First, we know that it indicates that the two sample means are 0.03 standard deviation apart. When you recall that 1 standard deviation corresponds to 34% of the normal distribution, 0.03 standard deviation doesn't sound like a very big difference, and it isn't. But we can go even further than that as we attempt to listen to the data. Jacob Cohen, the guru of effect sizes, developed guidelines—often called conventions by statisticians—for what constitutes a small, medium, or large effect. Table 12-1 displays these guidelines, along with the amount of overlap between two curves that is indicated by an effect of that size. No sign is provided because it is the magnitude of an effect size that matters; an effect size of -0.5 is the same size as one of 0.5. It is important to note that these guidelines are *not* cutoffs; rather, they are rough indicators. In fact, effects are often referred to as "small to medium" or as "medium to large" if they fall in between the conventions. Moreover, an effect that is close to medium, even if it is not quite as large as the convention, is simply called "medium." These conventions are the same whether Cohen's *d* is used for data analyzed with a *z* distribution, a *t* distribution used with a single sample, or a *t* distribution used with two samples.

Based on these numbers, the effect size for our study of Ursuline College students, -0.03, is not even at the level of a small effect. It's practically 0. And this makes sense because the average score of the Ursuline College students on the psychology test was almost identical to that of the general population of psychology students who had also taken that test.

So now let's listen again to some data analyzed with an independent-samples *t* test. As noted earlier, Azim and colleagues (2005) wondered whether women or men were more likely to label cartoons as "funny." Our fictional data provided means of 82.25 for women and 82.6 for men. Previously, we calculated a standard error for the difference between means, $s_{Difference}$, of 11.847.

Here are the calculations we performed:

Stage 1 (variance for each sample):
$$s_X^2 = \frac{\Sigma(X - M)^2}{N - 1} = 289.584; \ s_Y^2 = \frac{\Sigma(Y - M)^2}{N - 1} = 328.6$$

Stage 2 (combining variances):
$$s_{Pooled}^2 = \left(\frac{df_X}{df_{Total}}\right)s_X^2 + \left(\frac{df_Y}{df_{Total}}\right)s_Y^2 = 311.878$$

Stage 3 (variance form of standard error for each sample):
$$s_{M_X}^2 = \frac{s_{Pooled}^2}{N} = 77.970; \ s_{M_X}^2 = \frac{s_{Pooled}^2}{N} = 62.376$$

Stage 4 (combining variance forms of standard error):
$$s^2_{Difference} = s^2_{M_X} + s^2_{M_Y} = 140.346$$

Stage 5 (converting variance to standard error):
$$s_{Difference} = \sqrt{s^2_{Difference}} = 11.847$$

Because our goal is to disregard the influence of sample size in order to calculate Cohen's d, we want to use the standard deviation in the denominator, not the standard error. So we can ignore the last three stages, all of which contribute to the calculation of standard error. That leaves stages 1 and 2. It makes more sense to use the one that includes information from both samples, so we'll focus our attention on stage 2. Here is where many students make a mistake. What we have calculated in stage 2 is pooled *variance*, not pooled *standard deviation*. We must take the square root of the pooled variance to get the pooled standard deviation, the appropriate value for the denominator of our Cohen's d.

$$s_{Pooled} = \sqrt{s^2_{Pooled}} = \sqrt{311.878} = 17.660$$

The test statistic that we calculated for this study was:

$$t = \frac{(M_X - M_Y) - (\mu_X - \mu_Y)}{s_{Difference}} = \frac{(82.25 - 82.6) - (0)}{11.847} = -0.03$$

For Cohen's d, we'll simply replace the denominator with standard deviation, s_{Pooled}, instead of standard error, $s_{Difference}$.

Formula: Cohen's
$$d = \frac{(M_X - M_Y) - (\mu_X - \mu_Y)}{s_{Pooled}}$$
for a *t* distribution for a difference between means.

$$\text{Cohen's } d = \frac{(M_X - M_Y) - (\mu_X - \mu_Y)}{s_{Pooled}} = \frac{(82.25 - 82.6) - (0)}{17.660} = -0.02$$

For this study, the effect size can be reported as: $d = -0.02$. The two sample means are only 0.02 standard deviation apart. According to Cohen's conventions, this is not even near the level of a small effect. Cohen's d, however, doesn't apply to every situation because it only works when we compare two groups. Here's how we calculate effect sizes for ANOVA when we consider the differences among three or more groups.

R^2: The Effect Size for ANOVA

Because Cohen's d is calculated based on a difference between means, we can only use it in situations in which we have two means—the same situations in which we use a z test or a t test. Any experimental design involving three or more groups requires the use of an ANOVA. With ANOVA, we calculate a statistic called R^2. *R^2 is the proportion of variance in the dependent variable that is accounted for by the independent variable.* It is pronounced "r squared." Sometimes researchers will use the very similar measure of effect size, "eta squared," which is symbolized by the Greek symbol: η^2. We interpret η^2 exactly as we interpret R^2.

Because R^2 is the proportion of variance accounted for by the independent variable, out of all possible variance, we calculate it by constructing a ratio. We use sums of squares as indicators of variability. The numerator is a measure of the variability that takes into account just the differences among means; we use the between-groups sum of squares, $SS_{Between}$, for this because it assesses only the variability among the means, without regard to the variability within each sample. The denominator is a measure of the total

Symbols: R^2 (or sometimes η^2)

■ R^2 is the proportion of variance in the dependent variable that is accounted for by the independent variable.

TABLE 12-2. CALCULATING R^2 FROM A SOURCE TABLE

We can calculate R^2 directly from a completed source table. We simply divide the between-groups sum of squares by the total sum of squares to figure out the proportion of variance in the dependent variable accounted for by the independent variable.

SOURCE	SS	df	MS	F
Between	3.866	3	1.289	3.94
Within	4.256	13	0.327	
Total	8.122	16		

variability. For this, we use the total sum of squares, SS_{Total}, because it takes both between-groups and within-groups variance into account. The formula, therefore, is

$$R^2 = \frac{SS_{Between}}{SS_{Total}}$$

Formula: $R^2 = \dfrac{SS_{Between}}{SS_{Total}}$

Let's apply this to the example we considered in Chapter 10 for a one-way between-groups ANOVA. Ruby (2007) studied the reasons that foreign graduate students chose their current graduate institutions in the United States. She compared the students in different types of graduate programs with respect to their ratings of different criteria, including financial factors (e.g., scholarships, research assistantships). We used the following abbreviated set of data to conduct a one-way between-groups ANOVA:

Arts and sciences: 4, 5, 4, 3, 4

Education: 4, 3, 4, 4

Law: 3, 3, 2, 3

Business: 4, 4, 4, 3

From these data, we calculated the statistics in the source table shown in Table 12-2. We can use the numbers in the source table to calculate our R^2: $R^2 = \dfrac{SS_{Between}}{SS_{Total}} = \dfrac{3.866}{8.122} = 0.48.$

As you might guess, there are also conventions for R^2 that let us know whether our effect size is approximately small, medium, or large. Table 12-3 displays the conventions for R^2. From this table, we can see that our R^2 of 0.48 is very large. This is not surprising. With such small sample sizes, an effect would have to be quite large for the test statistic to be large enough that we could reject the null hypothesis. We can also turn our proportion into the more familiar language of percentages by multiplying by 100. We can then say that a specific percentage of the variance in the dependent variable was accounted for by the independent variable. In this case, we could say that 48% of the variability in ratings of the importance of financial factors is due to the type of program in which graduate students are enrolled.

TABLE 12-3. COHEN'S CONVENTIONS FOR EFFECT SIZES: R^2

The following guidelines, called conventions by statisticians, are meant to help researchers decide how important an effect is. These numbers are not cutoffs, merely rough guidelines to aid researchers in their interpretation of results.

EFFECT SIZE	CONVENTION
Small	0.01
Medium	0.06
Large	0.14

In the next section, we'll learn a way to turn up the volume on the data so that we can hear more clearly the story that the data tell. We'll do that by understanding how to calculate an important idea called statistical power.

In summary, a statistically significant result is not necessarily one with practical importance. The calculation of effect sizes takes statistical reasoning beyond hypothesis testing by giving us a sense of the amount of overlap of two distributions. Effect sizes are calculated with respect to scores, rather than means, and so are not contingent on sample size. Two common measures of effect size are Cohen's d, which is calculated much like a z or t statistic, and R^2, which is a measure of the proportion of variability in a dependent variable accounted for by a given independent variable. Cohen has published conventions for both these measures so that a statistician can get a sense of whether an effect is small, medium, or large.

⊙ CHECK YOUR LEARNING

12-3 In Check Your Learning 12-2, we calculated a confidence interval based on CFC data. The population mean CFC score was 3.51, with a standard deviation of 0.61. The sample was composed of 45 students who joined a career discussion group, and the study examined whether this might have changed CFC scores. The mean for this group is 3.7.

  a. Calculate the appropriate effect size for this study.

  b. Citing Cohen's conventions, explain what this effect size tells us.

  c. Now consider the effect of the effect size. Does this finding have any consequences or implications for anyone's life?

What is Power?
Professor Suddeth demonstrates his definition of power—sensitivity—by balancing a fragile balloon on a very sharp sword blade.

> STATISTICAL POWER AND SENSITIVITY: CORRECTLY REJECTING THE NULL HYPOTHESIS

Professor Suddeth displayed a range of weapons used in theater and opened his presentation with, "Oh, the many ways we have invented to kill one another." It was so gruesome a statement that some of the class began giggling, which apparently did not bother fight master J. Allen Suddeth in the slightest. Everything was fine with him as long as it was done safely.

Drawing on his extensive private collection, Professor Suddeth showed the class various broadswords, a mace, a halberd (ax-headed, with points and a hook for tripping men and horses), a war hammer (with a point and "can opener" for piercing armor), a gauntlet, and various firearms (guns and rifles from different periods). "Weapons are a means to obtain power," Professor Suddeth told the class. "Theater is also about power. In fact, there's no point in putting on a play if it doesn't have enough power to achieve the effect it intends. So now I will show you what I think may be the greatest power ever displayed in theater." Professor Suddeth took out one of his swords and sliced through some leather he had placed on a table. "So it's sharp," he told them convincingly. Then he took out a large yellow balloon, blew it up, tied it off, and tossed it into the air. As it floated in the quiet air, Professor Suddeth took the sword and toyed with the balloon using the flat side of the sword and then the tip.

"Sensitivity," said Professor Suddeth, "is another way to think of power. A powerful microscope detects tiny structures that our normal vision cannot perceive." He flipped the yellow balloon higher in the air and watched it drift. "Power is being sensitive to and aware of small details," he told them. He paused and prepared to thrust his sword into the slowly descending balloon, but then caught it at the last moment with the flat of his blade and gently lowered it the floor. "Power," he said, "is being sensitive to the details that really matter."

A powerful microscope is sensitive because it can detect observations that we would not otherwise know about. A powerful government can influence its citizens by being sensitive to the details of what is going on in each region and neighborhood. And a statistical test is powerful when it is able to detect real patterns that exist in a data set. As with a play that doesn't have the power to have an effect on its audience, there's no point in conducting a study if there isn't sufficient power to detect genuine patterns in the data.

Power is yet another word that statisticians use in a very specific way. ***Statistical power*** *is a measure of our ability to reject the null hypothesis given that the null hypothesis is false.* In other words, statistical power is the probability that we will reject the null hypothesis when we *should* reject the null hypothesis—the probability that we will not make a Type II error. We don't want to believe there is a pattern in the data when there really isn't one (a Type I error), but we also don't want to miss a genuine pattern in the data when there really is one (a Type II error). A powerful test, therefore, is one that has the capacity to do the job that we ask it to: to reject the null hypothesis when it should.

We don't normally equate power with sensitivity, but it is an idea that makes more sense as we keep thinking about it. For example, what if all prospective romantic partners were required to wear a badge revealing their personal sensitivity/power rating; that is, their ability to detect and respond appropriately to our every mood? "Hello, my name is Andrea and my sensitivity/power rating is 72." It sounds like a crazy idea, of course, but it would be powerful information to know *before* beginning a relationship. However, the American Psychological Association (APA) actually recommends that each study we conduct wear such a badge revealing its calculated sensitivity/power rating *before* we begin collecting any data. It gives us an idea of how seriously we can take this particular study.

Our calculation of statistical power ranges from a probability of 0.00 to a probability of 1.00 (or from 0 to 100%). It indicates the probability that we will be able to reject the null hypothesis given a specific sample size and a specific effect size. Statisticians have historically used a probability of 0.80 as the

▪ **Statistical power** is a measure of our ability to reject the null hypothesis given that the null hypothesis is false.

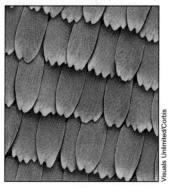

Statistical Power
Statistical power, like the progressive powers of a microscope to show the fine details of a butterfly's wing, refers to our ability to detect differences that really exist.

minimum for conducting a study. If we have an 80% chance of correctly rejecting the null hypothesis, then it is deemed appropriate to proceed.

The calculation of statistical power by hand is a bit time consuming and in some circumstances can be complicated, so we will simplify the process in two ways. First, we will calculate statistical power for the most basic hypothesis test, the z test. Second, we will calculate statistical power for a one-tailed test, so we will have to consider only one of the tails; this cuts our work in half. The logic is the same for more sophisticated hypothesis tests, so this simpler calculation allows us to understand where the numbers come from when we use a computer to calculate power for our own research.

Calculation of Statistical Power: How Sensitive Is a z Test?

There are three general steps in the calculation of statistical power, none of which introduces any new techniques. Our knowledge of the normal curve, the z statistic, and the z table is all we need for each of the steps in the calculation of statistical power for a z test. First, we'll summarize the steps to calculate statistical power; then we'll demonstrate the process with an example.

Step 1. The Numbers.

We determine the characteristics of the two populations of interest: the population to which we're comparing our sample (population 1) and the population that we believe our sample represents (population 2). We represent these two populations visually as two overlapping curves. Drawing the anticipated distributions helps clarify your thinking, so get out your pencil and start sketching!

Step 2. The Cutoff.

Using the curve for population 1, we calculate the *raw mean* that determines the critical value beyond which we reject our null hypothesis. Because we're using a one-tailed test, there will be just one critical value.

Step 3. Power.

Now, switching to the curve for population 2, we determine the percentage that falls above the raw mean that is at the critical value. In this step, it's important to remember to use the curve for population 2. The percentage (or proportion) above the raw mean that falls at the critical value on the curve for population 2 is statistical power.

Now let's work an example.

Step 1. The Numbers.

This step takes the most time of the three, but it involves concepts we already know. Let's consider a variation on a study we used as an example in Chapters 2 and 6, a study aimed at determining whether an intervention changes the mean number of sessions attended at university counseling centers. We'll assume that the population mean number of sessions attended is 4.6, with a population standard deviation of 6.3. Let's say that we plan to have students sign contracts to attend a certain number of sessions, in the hope that this will improve attendance. More specifically, we hypothesize that a sample of 9 counseling center clients will have a mean number of sessions of 7.75, an increase in the mean of just over 3. Because we have a sample of 9, we'll need to convert our standard deviation to standard error; to do this, we divide the standard deviation by the square root of the sample size and find that the standard error is 2.1. These numbers are summarized in Table 12-4.

TABLE 12-4. THE INGREDIENTS FOR THE CALCULATION OF STATISTICAL POWER

To calculate statistical power for a z test, we must know the original population means and population standard deviation. We must calculate the standard error using the planned sample size. We must also have an estimate of the mean of population 2, our expectation of what the sample mean will be. It is useful to determine all these numbers before beginning.

INGREDIENTS FOR CALCULATING POWER	COUNSELING CENTER STUDY
Mean of population 1	$\mu_{M_1} = \mu = 4.6$
Standard deviation of the population	$\sigma = 6.3$
Standard error (using the planned sample size)	$\sigma_M = \dfrac{\sigma}{\sqrt{N}} = \dfrac{6.3}{\sqrt{9}} = 2.1$
Planned sample size	$N = 9$
Mean of population 2 (expected sample mean)	$M = 7.75;\ \mu_{M_2} = 7.75$

We can never know, particularly prior to a study, what the actual effect size is. Population 2, therefore, is hypothetical; that is, we can't actually see it or know its summary parameters, so, ultimately, we're making an educated guess. Researchers typically estimate the mean of population 2 in one of three ways (Murphy & Myors, 2004). (1) They examine the existing research literature to see what effect sizes other researchers have found in studies that used the same variables. (2) They use theories developed from studies in related areas to make an educated estimate about what effect size they might find. (3) They decide what effect size would make the study worthwhile. For example, a researcher investigating a drug for treating Alzheimer's disease might decide that a study is likely to find only a small effect but that even a small effect (a Cohen's d of around 0.2) would be of practical importance. She wants a far more powerful—a more sensitive—test than most other researchers.

Whether our estimate comes from the research literature or from a desire to detect a certain effect size, we usually start with an effect size. But what we want to know is not effect size itself, but an estimate of the mean of population 2. Here, we simply use algebra to find the mean of population 2 from Cohen's d. We know that the formula for Cohen's d is: $d = \dfrac{(M - \mu)}{\sigma}$. We put all the numbers that we do know into the formula and then solve for the one number that we don't know, the expected sample mean (M). In this example, let's say we wanted to be able to detect a medium effect, a Cohen's d of 0.5. Using the formula, we have $d = \dfrac{(M - \mu)}{\sigma}$, for which we substitute numbers where possible: $0.5 = \dfrac{(M - 4.6)}{6.3}$. Solving for M, we have $M = 0.5(6.3) + 4.6 = 7.75$. The M that we have calculated is our estimate for the mean of population 2, symbolized as μ_2. (You'll notice that this is the number we used in our estimate in Table 12-4. We calculated that number in the way that we just showed you.)

[For those of you who prefer to avoid algebra, here's a simpler formula you can use: $M = d(\sigma) + \mu$].

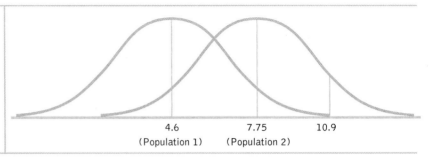

FIGURE 12-11
Calculating Statistical Power, Step 1

The first step in calculating statistical power is using the numbers that characterize the two populations of interest to draw two curves. These curves represent the hypothetical distributions of means for the two populations.

Now that we have all our numbers, we can draw a picture. This picture will have two overlapping curves, as seen in Figure 12-11. The first curve is centered around the mean of population 1, which is 4.6. The second curve is centered around the mean of the estimate for population 2, which is 7.75. We decide roughly where to place the second mean by considering our standard error. We know from Chapter 5 that all, or nearly all, scores fall within 3 standard errors of the mean. The standard error here is 2.1, and $3 \times 2.1 = 6.3$. The tail of the curve for population 1 will end 6.3 above the mean of 4.6, or at around 10.9 (calculated by addition: $6.3 + 4.6 = 10.9$). Knowing that the upper half of the curve goes from 4.6 to around 10.9 enables us to place the mean of our second curve at roughly the correct location.

Step 2. The Cutoff.

The next step is adding a cutoff to the curve for population 1. (Note that in this step, we're concerned with the curve for *population 1*. We ignore the curve for population 2 for now.) We'll use a critical p level of 0.05, and because we decided to conduct a one-tailed test, the entire 0.05 (or 5%) will be placed in one tail of the curve. We'll place it in the upper tail because we anticipate that our intervention will increase the mean number of student visits to the counseling center. To determine accurate placement for this cutoff, or critical value, we'll need to know the critical value in terms of a raw mean (we are determining a raw mean, rather than a raw score, because we are working with distributions of means).

First, we'll use a z table to find the z statistic that falls at the cutoff for the upper 5% of the curve. We know that 50% of the curve falls between the mean and the z statistic of interest. Because 5% falls beyond the cutoff, we know that $50 - 5 = 45\%$ falls between the mean of population 1 and the z statistic. The z table tells us that the z statistic associated with 45% is 1.64. To convert a z statistic into a raw mean, we use our formula from Chapter 5: $X = z(\sigma) + \mu$. However, because we are using a distribution of means rather than a distribution of scores, we'll use slightly different symbolic notation, replacing the X with M and the σ and μ with σ_M and μ_M, respectively. The formula for converting a z statistic into a raw mean, therefore, is $M = z(\sigma_M) + \mu_M$. Using the z score that we just looked up as well as the mean and standard error of population 1, we calculate: $M = 1.64(2.1) + 4.6 = 8.04$. We can now add that cutoff mean to our drawing, knowing roughly where to place it. The critical value of 8.04 will be placed just above the mean of population 2, 7.75, as seen in Figure 12-12.

This critical value has the same meaning as it did in hypothesis testing. If the test statistic for a sample falls above this cutoff, then we can reject the null hypothesis. Notice that the mean that we estimated for population 2 does *not* fall above the cutoff. If the actual difference between the two populations—

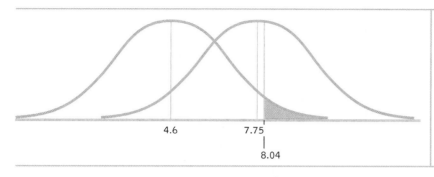

FIGURE 12-12
Calculating Statistical Power, Step 2

The second step in calculating statistical power is determining the cutoff for a one-tailed test with a *p* level of 0.05. This cutoff is determined for the curve for population 1.

counseling center clients who do not sign a contract and counseling center clients who do sign a contract—is what we expect, then we can already see that there is a good chance that we will not reject the null hypothesis. This indicates that we might not have enough statistical power. Let's move on to step 3 and calculate the actual statistical power for this study.

Step 3. Power.

In step 3, we forget about population 1. Yes, that's right; we pretend it never existed. Create a new drawing—one that includes just the curve for population 2. On this curve, include both the estimated mean of population 2, 7.75, and the cutoff mean based on population 1, 8.04. Shade the portion of the curve that falls above the critical value of 8.04. Even though the cutoff mean was determined in reference to the mean of population 1, we still forget about population 1 for the time being. Now, we'll consider the cutoff mean of 8.04 in reference to the mean of population 2. The new drawing should look like that in Figure 12-13.

The proportion of the curve above the critical value is statistical power. Remember, statistical power is the chance of rejecting the null hypothesis if we *should* reject the null hypothesis. If in fact population 2 exists, then the intervention really helps; it raises the mean number of sessions from 4.6 to 7.75, and as we know from our earlier calculations, this is a medium effect. We want to reject the null hypothesis in this case. The distribution of means for population 2 can help us determine how likely it is that we'll happen to select a sample with a given mean. Here, we know that we will *not* reject the null hypothesis unless the mean of the sample is at least 8.04. So what we want to know is how likely it is that we'll select a sample from population 2 that has a mean of at least 8.04. And that's why we shaded the portion above 8.04 in Figure 12-13.

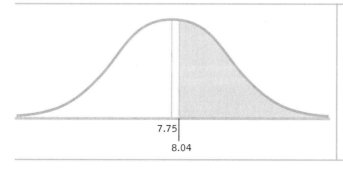

FIGURE 12-13
Ignoring Population 1, for Now

To avoid making mistakes when calculating statistical power, at this point it's best to pretend population 1 never existed. We can restore the curve for population 1 after we have calculated statistical power. Here we see just the curve for population 2.

▪ **Alpha** is another name for the p level and is the chance of making a Type I error; sometimes written α.

Now, we use the magic of the z statistic and the z table to calculate the percentage of population 2 that falls above the cutoff. We first convert the raw mean of 8.04 into a z statistic using the formula from Chapter 5: $z = \dfrac{(M - \mu_M)}{\sigma_M}$. We use the mean and standard error of population 2, not population 1, in this formula. Our drawing that includes only population 2 helps us remember to use the appropriate numbers. The mean of population 2 is 7.75; we use the same standard error, 2.1, that we used for population 1, under the assumption that the two populations have roughly equal spread. The z statistic associated with 8.04, in reference to population 2, is $z = \dfrac{(M - \mu_M)}{\sigma_M} = \dfrac{(8.04 - 7.75)}{2.1} = 0.14$. We add the z statistic to our drawing as in Figure 12-14.

We can use the z table to determine the percentage that falls between the mean of 7.75 and the z statistic of 0.14. According to the table, that percentage is 5.57%. But what we want to know is the percentage *above* 0.29, not the percentage between the mean and 0.29. We know that 50% of the curve falls above the mean, so we can subtract 11.41 from 50 to find the percentage above the z statistic of 0.14: $50 - 5.57 = 44.43\%$. We can see the portion of the curve to which this 44.43% applies in Figure 12-14.

Figure 12-15 shows this same statistical power calculation in the context of the two curves. At this point, we have conducted our calculations and can no longer be confused by the inclusion of the curve for population 1. We can restore population 1 to our drawing to see the whole picture.

From Figure 12-15, we can see the cutoff, or critical value, as determined in reference to population 1. We can see that the percentage of the distribution of means for population 1 that falls above the cutoff is 0.05, or 5%. We decided to use this cutoff level, as we have throughout hypothesis testing in this text, because it is standard in social science research. If we use a cutoff level of 0.05, the percentage of the distribution of means for population 1 that is above the cutoff is, by definition, 5%. This percentage is often called alpha. ***Alpha is another name for the*** p ***level and is the chance of making a Type I error.*** (Sometimes alpha is written as a symbol, α.) When we turn to the distribution of means for population 2, the percentage above that same cutoff is statistical power. Given that population 2 exists, 44.43% of the time that we select a sample of size 9 from this population, we will be able to reject the null hypothesis. This is far below the 80% considered accurate when conducting a study.

Symbol: α

FIGURE 12-14
Calculating Statistical Power, Step 3

Using the distribution of means for population 2, we can calculate the z statistic of 0.14 from the raw mean of 8.04 and then use the z table to determine the percentage above 0.14. That percentage, 44.43, is our statistical power for a study with this sample size and this expected effect size.

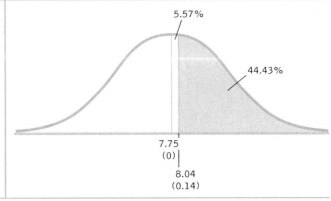

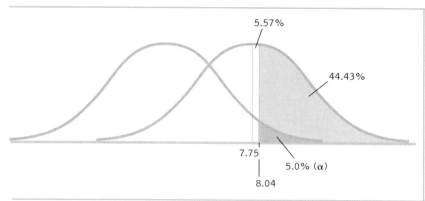

5.57%

44.43%

7.75

5.0% (α)

8.04

FIGURE 12-15
Statistical Power: The Whole Picture

Now we can visualize statistical power in the context of two populations. Statistical power is the percentage of the distribution of means for population 2 that is above the cutoff. Alpha is the percentage of the distribution of means for population 1 that is above the cutoff; alpha is set by the researcher and is usually 0.05, or 5%.

At a practical level for most behavioral science studies, statistical power calculations tell us how many participants we're probably going to need to conduct a study whose finding we can trust. Like a bargain hunter, statistical power helps us calculate whether a particular study is worth the investment of recruiting and working with a certain number of participants. If we have easy access to hundreds of undergraduate students who are eager to participate in our study for extra credit, it's not a great concern. But if we need to pay each participant $300 to come back several times and submit to a variety of intrusive tests, then statistical power calculations can provide meaningful guidance. Remember, however, that statistical power is based, to some degree, on hypothetical information. It is helpful guidance, but it is an estimate, not an exact number.

In addition to pre-study calculations, statistical power calculations should be re-examined in the context of the study's eventual results, particularly the measure of the actual, rather than hypothetical, effect size. This involves using power analysis as a "diagnostic tool" (Murphy & Myors, 2004). It enables us to ask: Given that the sample mean accurately represented its underlying population, how much power did we have? We'll turn next to several factors that affect statistical power.

Beyond Sample Size: Other Factors That Affect Statistical Power

We've already discussed the effect of increasing sample size on the likelihood of rejecting the null hypothesis, but there are other ways to influence statistical power. All told, there are five ways to increase the power of a statistical test so that it can detect genuine patterns within the data. Here they are, listed in order from what is usually the easiest to the most difficult to include when you first design your study:

1. Increase alpha. (Change the rules for "success.")
2. Turn a two-tailed hypothesis into a one-tailed hypothesis. (Form a more specific, directional hypothesis.)
3. Increase N. (Add more participants to our study.)
4. Exaggerate the levels of your independent variable. (Design our experiment to test for more obvious differences.)
5. Decrease the standard deviation by doing the following:
   a. Measure the dependent variable more reliably. (Improve the scale.)
   b. Select participants with homogeneity. (Only allow people into the study who are similar to one another on the dependent variable.)

FIGURE 12-16
Increasing Alpha

As we increase our alpha from the standard of 0.05 to a larger level such as 0.10, our statistical power increases. Because this also increases the probability of a Type I error, this is not usually a good method for increasing statistical power.

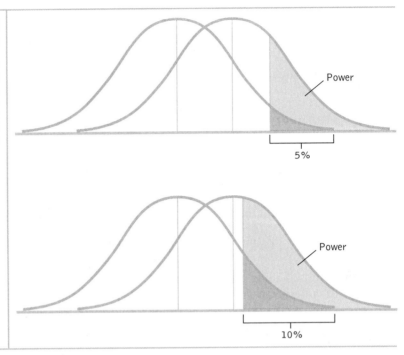

Increase Alpha

In Figure 12-16, we see how statistical power increases when we take a *p* level of 0.05 and increase it to 0.10. This has the side effect of increasing the probability of a Type I error from 5% to 10%, however, so researchers choose to increase their statistical power in this manner only under particular circumstances. For example, a medical researcher testing a drug that maintains the heart rate during open-heart surgery probably wants a very small alpha because rejecting the null hypothesis when it shouldn't be rejected means that the patient dies. But a medical researcher trying to slow the effects of Alzheimer's disease may be willing to tolerate a large alpha because the patient is already suffering from a terrible progressive disease.

Turn a Two-Tailed Hypothesis into a One-Tailed Hypothesis

We have been using a simpler one-tailed test; however, researchers often begin with the more conservative two-tailed test. In Figure 12-17, we see the difference in power between a two-tailed test (top pair of curves) and a one-tailed test (bottom pair of curves). The top pair of curves, with a two-tailed test, shows statistical power of less than 50%; the bottom pair of curves, with a one-tailed test, shows statistical power of just over 50%. If we are interested *only* in an outcome in one direction, we may consider a one-tailed test; however, it is usually best to be conservative and use a two-tailed test.

Increase *N*

Increasing sample size leads to an increase in the test statistic, making it is easier to reject the null hypothesis because a larger test statistic is more likely to fall beyond our cutoff. The influence of sample size on statistical power is demonstrated in Figure 12-18. The upper pair of curves represents a small

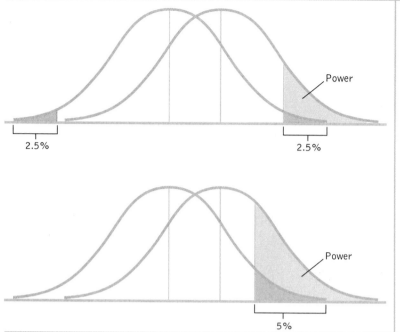

FIGURE 12-17
Two-Tailed Versus One-Tailed Tests

A two-tailed test divides alpha into two tails. When we use a one-tailed test, putting our entire alpha into just one tail, we increase our chances of rejecting the null hypothesis, which translates into an increase in statistical power.

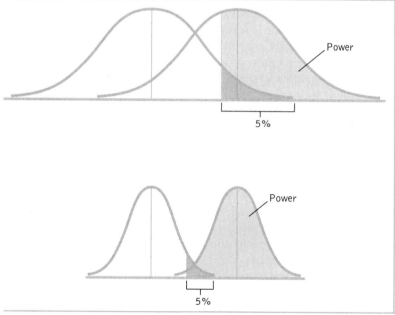

FIGURE 12-18
Increasing Sample Size or Decreasing Standard Deviation

As sample size increases (from the top to the bottom sets of curves), the distributions of means become more narrow and there is less overlap. Less overlap means more statistical power. The same effect occurs when we decrease standard deviation. As standard deviation decreases (also reflected from the top to the bottom sets of curves), the curves are narrower and there is less overlap—and more statistical power.

sample size, and the lower pair represents a larger sample size. In the upper pair, the curves are fairly wide because of a small sample size. In the lower pair, the curves are narrower because a larger sample size means a smaller standard error. A larger sample size means a larger denominator and a smaller standard error. We have direct control over the size of our samples, so simply increasing N is often an easy way to increase statistical power.

FIGURE 12-19
Increasing the Difference Between the Means

As the difference between means becomes larger, there is less overlap between curves. Here, the lower pair of curves has less overlap than the upper pair. Less overlap means more statistical power.

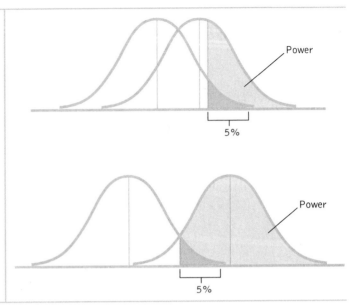

Exaggerate the Levels of Your Independent Variable

We also can affect statistical power by changing the difference between our means. As seen in Figure 12-19, the mean of population 2 is farther from the mean of population 1 in the lower set of curves than in the upper set of curves. The difference between means is not something easily changed, but it can be done. For instance, if we were studying the effectiveness of group therapy for social phobia, we could implement group therapy for 6 months rather than just 12 weeks. It is possible that a longer program might lead to a bigger change in means, as compared to a group that received no treatment, than the shorter program would. This might result in a larger effect size when the study used the longer group therapy program.

Decrease the Standard Deviation

We will see the same effect on statistical power if we find a way to decrease the standard deviation. Look again at Figure 12-18 for increasing the sample size. The curves can become narrower not only because the denominator is larger but also because the numerator is smaller. When the standard deviation is smaller to begin with, standard error will be smaller, and the curves will be narrower. Narrower curves have less overlap, and there is more statistical power. We can reduce measurement error and therefore the standard deviation in two ways: (1) use reliable measures from the beginning of the study so that there will be less error and (2) sample from a more homogeneous group in which participants' responses are more likely to be similar to begin with.

Because power is affected by so many variables, it is important to consider it when reading journal articles of others' research, particularly when they fail to reject the null hypothesis. Always ask yourself whether there was likely sufficient statistical power to detect a real finding. Most important, were there enough participants in the sample? Often the journal article provides enough information for you to run a statistical power analysis yourself using software or an online power calculator.

CALCULATING STATISTICAL POWER

Statistical power is most frequently determined by using published statistical power tables or a computerized statistical power calculator. One of the best published tables is by Jacob Cohen in his 1992 article, "A Power Primer." Cohen provides a table of sample sizes necessary to achieve 0.80 statistical power (the amount considered adequate by most researchers) with various effect sizes for eight different hypothesis tests. Also, many statistical power calculators can be found by conducting an online search for "power calculator." Or you can download the free software, G*Power, available for Mac or PC (Erdfelder, Faul, & Buchner, 1996; search online, go to http://www.psycho.uni-duesseldorf.de/app/projects/gpower/, or connect through the Web site for this text).

For most online power calculators, we simply put in the information that we gathered earlier to calculate power by hand, summarized in the accompanying table. For example, with G*Power, in the upper-right side, we select "post hoc" to let the computer know that we want to determine power for a completed study. Then, if we select "Tests" and then "t-Test (means)," we can calculate the power for an independent-samples t test. Imagine that we conducted a study that yielded a Cohen's d of 0.5 with a p level of 0.05, a two-tailed test, and 20 participants in each sample. On G*Power, we would input 0.5 as our effect size, 0.05 as our alpha (or p level), and 20 as each of our sample sizes; we would then click "two tailed" on the right-hand side. Finally, we would click "Calculate."

EXPERIENCE IT FOR YOURSELF

THE INGREDIENTS FOR ONLINE STATISTICAL POWER CALCULATION

To calculate statistical power for a z test online, we typically need to know the same numbers that we need for the calculation of statistical power by hand.

INGREDIENTS FOR CALCULATING STATISTICAL POWER	VALUES
Effect size (Cohen's d)	0.5
p level (alpha)	0.05
Type of hypothesis test	two-tailed
Samples sizes	20 and 20

What did you calculate for statistical power?

You'll notice that the statistical power is 0.3379, or 33.8%, lower than the 0.80 we would like. Let's test the different ways to increase statistical power. After each question, leave the changes made in the earlier questions. (For example, for question 2, leave the sample sizes at 30, and then change the effect size to 0.6.)

1. What is the statistical power if you increase the sample sizes from 20 to 30?

2. What is the statistical power if you increase the effect size to 0.6?

3. What is the statistical power if you choose a one-tailed test?

4. What is the statistical power if you increase the significance level from 0.05 to 0.10?

Check to be sure your answers match these. Notice that each adjustment led to an increase in statistical power.

1. 0.598
2. 0.755
3. 0.845
4. 0.917

Now change back from a one-tailed to a two-tailed test. What is the statistical power now? _____

Did you get 0.845? If we use a two-tailed test with a p level of 0.10, that puts 0.05 into each tail. That is the same, therefore, as a one-tailed test with a p level of 0.05, because a one-tailed test puts the whole 0.05 in one tail. That is why the statistical power for a one-tailed test with a p level of 0.05 is the same as for a two-tailed test with a p level of 0.10.

You should always conduct a statistical power analysis prior to beginning a study. In fact, you'll often find that you are required to submit statistical power analyses by agencies to which you might apply to fund your research through grants as well as by your university or organization's Institutional Review Board. *An **Institutional Review Board (IRB)** is a committee that institutions are legally mandated to have to vet research that uses human or animal participants prior to beginning the study.* IRBs exist to be sure that research is ethical and that the scientific merit of the study justifies the time and resources required to conduct it. In practice, we know that sample size is often the most logical factor to manipulate if we want to increase the statistical power of our study. Knowing this, we can reverse the logic we learned earlier by deciding what level of statistical power we want and then calculating the sample size necessary to achieve that statistical power.

On G*Power, we can select "a priori" to tell the program that we want to determine an appropriate sample size before conducting a study. We can then input an effect size of 0.5, an alpha (p level) of 0.05, power of 0.80, and a two-tailed test. When we click "Calculate," we'll get the sample size necessary for this configuration. Try it. What did you get?

The power calculator should have told you that to achieve 0.80 (or 80%) statistical power, you needed a total sample size of 128, half of which would go in each sample of a study designed to use an independent-samples t test.

In summary, statistical power is our ability to reject the null hypothesis if indeed we should reject it. We can calculate statistical power for a z test by examining the portion of the distribution of means from which a sample comes that is beyond the cutoff z statistic of the distribution of means based on the population. Anything beyond the cutoff z statistic would lead us to reject the null hypothesis. This proportion (or percentage) is our statistical power. Ideally, a study is not conducted unless the researcher has 80% statistical power, but because statistical power calculations are based on hypothetical effect sizes, they are not always exact measures of statistical power. Statistical power is affected by several factors, but most directly by sample size. Because of this, many researchers use statistical power calculations, often conducted with online statistical power calculators or by using published tables, to determine the number of participants necessary to achieve 80% statistical power with a certain effect size.

⊙ CHECK YOUR LEARNING

12-4 Check Your Learning 12-2 and 12-3 discussed a study aimed at changing CFC scores through a career discussion group. Imagine that you now had two groups: a career discussion group of 45 students with a mean CFC score of 3.7, and a control group of 45 students with a mean CFC score of 3.51. The appropriate measure of standard deviation is 0.61.

a. Use a computerized statistical power calculator to determine statistical power for this test.

b. Explain what this number (i.e., statistical power) means.

c. Using the online calculator, determine the minimum number of participants we would need to have at least 0.80 (or 80%) statistical power.

d. Describe five ways in which the researchers might increase statistical power.

■ DIGGING DEEPER INTO THE DATA: META-ANALYSIS

"Meta-analysis is probably the most radical departure from significance testing [hypothesis testing] seen in the social sciences in the past 50 years" (Newton & Rudestam, 1999, p. 281). *A **meta-analysis** is a study that involves the calculation of a mean effect size from the individual effect sizes of many studies.* Meta-analysis has four main benefits. It can do all of the following:

1. Provide added confidence in our conclusions by considering many studies at once

2. Decrease the bias inherent in drawing subjective conclusions from a broad literature

3. Help to resolve debates fueled by contradictory research findings (Lam & Kennedy, 2005)

4. Articulate the next logical step in the overall research process

As Schmidt (1992) observed, "No single primary study can resolve an issue or answer a question" (p. 1179). Meta-analysis allows us to think of each individual study as just one data point in a larger study to come, the meta-analysis.

Meta-Analysis: A Study of Studies

Gene Glass (1976) is credited with coining the word *meta-analysis*. The logic of meta-analysis, as well as much of the process, is surprisingly simple.

1. Choose the topic, and make a list of criteria for which studies will be included.

2. Gather every study that can be found on a given topic.

3. Calculate an effect size for every study that was found.

4. Determine the mean effect size (and related statistics) across all studies.

It really is as simple as that. Each of these steps involves much effort and innumerable decisions to arrive at an accurate overall picture; a good meta-analysis can take a great deal of time to complete. Yet this time and effort must not be confused with complexity; as Rosenthal (1995) avows, "In 20 years of reviewing meta-analytic literature syntheses, I have never seen a meta-analysis that was

■ A **meta-analysis** is a study that involves the calculation of a mean effect size from the individual effect sizes of many studies.

'too simple,' but I have often seen meta-analyses that were very fancy and very much in error" (p. 183). As with any type of research, a careful plan is key to achieving a simple but illuminating meta-analysis.

The Steps for Conducting a Meta-Analysis

Step 1: The first step in conducting a meta-analysis is to select the topic of interest and decide exactly how we will proceed. It is important to make all decisions about gathering journal articles and other study findings before beginning to track down articles. It is easy to let our subjective biases direct our decisions to include or exclude a given article. Here are some of the considerations to keep in mind before we start our meta-analysis.

1. The necessary statistical information—either effect sizes themselves or the summary statistics necessary to calculate effect sizes—must be available in the article or from the author of the article.

2. Some meta-analyses select only studies in which participants meet certain criteria, such as age, gender, or geographic location.

3. Some meta-analyses select only studies in which participants' scores on the dependent variable fall within a certain range. In their meta-analysis on gender differences in math performance, Hyde and colleagues (1990) calculated a mean effect size that used all studies, including those like Benbow and Stanley's (1980) that had a restricted range, and a separate mean effect size for those that sampled from a general population.

4. Some meta-analyses eliminate studies based on the research design, for example, because they were not experimental in nature or did not use measures that met certain reliability and validity criteria.

Eagly, Chen, Chaiken, and Shaw-Barnes (1999) conducted a meta-analysis to examine whether people tend to better remember facts that conform to their existing attitudes and beliefs, known as the "congeniality effect on memory" (p. 64). *Before* they began their meta-analysis, they developed criteria for the studies they would include; for example, they decided to include only studies that were true experiments.

Step 2: The second step in conducting a meta-analysis is to locate every study that has been conducted and meets our criteria. An obvious place to start is PsycINFO and other electronic databases, but there are many studies that have been conducted but have not been published, despite their sound "methodological rigor" (Conn, Valentine, Cooper, & Rantz, 2003). Much of this "fugitive literature" (Rosenthal, 1995, p. 184) or "gray literature" (Lam & Kennedy, 2005) is unpublished simply because the null hypothesis was not rejected, and this creates a bias in the overall literature.

Fortunately, there are several ways we can respond to these problems, but they all require effort. We can do all of the following:

1. Read the tables of contents of the most relevant journals to find articles that may not have surfaced in our searches of electronic databases

Is Memory Affected by Our Preexisting Attitudes? Eagly and colleagues (1999) conducted a meta-analysis on the congeniality effect, the hypothesis that people tend to remember information that fits with their beliefs and attitudes better than information that does not. If you are against nuclear power, for example, do you more readily remember facts that support your stance? These meta-analysts found only a small congeniality effect.

Joseph Sohm; Visions of America/Corbis

2. Examine the proceedings of relevant conferences to locate research that might have been presented but not published

3. Contact the primary researchers in the field to obtain any relevant unpublished findings

4. Read the references lists of each article we locate to track down additional articles, sometimes called the "ancestors" of an article

5. Use electronic citation indices to locate articles that cited the papers we already found, sometimes called the "descendents" of an article (e.g., Newton & Rudestam, 1999).

For example, in their meta-analysis on the congeniality effect, Eagly and colleagues (1999) started with searches of electronic databases (e.g., PsycLIT, Dissertation Abstracts International), using search words such as "opinion," "belief," "congruent," "consistent," "memory," and "recall." They used the Social Sciences Citation Index to find articles that cited some of the major experiments in this area, and they sought appropriate experiments in the reference lists of the articles they found.

Step 3: The third step in conducting a meta-analysis is to calculate an effect size, often Cohen's *d*, for every study. When the effect size has not been reported, the researcher must calculate the effect size from summary statistics that were reported. Eagly and colleagues (1999) were able to calculate 271 effect sizes from the 70 studies they examined (some studies reported more than one effect).

Step 4: The last step in conducting a meta-analysis is to calculate statistics—ideally summary statistics, a hypothesis test, a confidence interval, and a visual display of the effect sizes (Rosenthal, 1995). Most important, researchers calculate a mean effect size for all studies and often a median effect size as well, particularly if there are outlier effect sizes. Now that we have a statistical study of the studies, we can apply all the statistical insights we learned to apply to individual studies: means, medians, standard deviations, confidence intervals and hypothesis testing, and visual displays such as box plots or stem-and-leaf plots.

In their meta-analysis on the congeniality effect, Eagly and colleagues (1999) calculated a mean and median based on the weighted effect sizes of the individual studies. Their mean *d* was 0.23; they were able to reject the null hypothesis. Moreover, the confidence interval did not include zero. The median, however, was 0.10, and only 60% of studies had a positive effect size (we'd expect 50% just by chance). These findings suggest that an outlier or outliers contributed to the mean effect. The researchers found that when they omitted both positive and negative outliers, the mean effect dropped from 0.23 to 0.08, a smaller effect, but still statistically significant. The researchers included a stem-and-leaf plot of the effect sizes (Figure 12-20). Although this seems to be evidence for the congeniality effect, the effect decreased over the years, perhaps because of the more sound research designs implemented more recently (e.g., blind designs).

Eagly and colleagues (1999) concluded that the congeniality effect was extremely small or nonexistent when "methodologically suspect data sets were removed" (p. 84), when only the best measures of memory were used, and when more recent data were considered. However, they found numerous circumstances in which the congeniality effect was stronger; for example, when memory was measured after a delay or when the attitude was closely related

FIGURE 12-20
A Visual Display of the Individual Effect Sizes in a Meta-Analysis

Researchers often use a box plot or a stem-and-leaf plot as a visual display of the effect sizes used in a meta-analysis. Here, Eagly and colleagues (1999) depict the effect sizes for their meta-analysis on the congeniality effect in a stem-and-leaf plot. From this graph, we can easily see the outlier of 8.7.

Stem	Leaf
8.7	4
·	
·	
·	
2.2	0
2.1	
1.9	
1.8	
1.7	2
1.6	
1.5	
1.4	
1.3	7
1.2	
1.1	
1.0	4
0.9	
0.8	0.24
0.7	9
0.6	379
0.5	0337
0.4	5566
0.3	25
0.2	2458
0.1	0024566
0.0	013389
−0.0	9998876333221
−0.1	87210
−0.2	92
−0.3	5
−0.4	61
−0.5	5
−0.6	
−0.7	
−0.8	2
−0.9	
−1.0	
−1.1	
−1.2	4

■ A **file drawer statistic** is a statistical calculation, following a meta-analysis, of the number of studies with null results that would have to exist so that a mean effect size is no longer statistically significant.

to participants' personal values. Only a meta-analysis could tell this more general story—providing a mean effect and, at the same time, examining what variables moderated the effect. Clearly, meta-analysis is a valuable, albeit time-consuming, tool to supplement the primary research of individual studies.

The File Drawer Statistic: Where Are All the Null Results?

Much of the fugitive literature of unpublished studies exists because studies with null results are less likely to appear in press (e.g., Begg, 1994). Twenty-nine percent of the studies included in the meta-analysis conducted by Eagly and colleagues (1999) were unpublished, and the inclusion of these studies led to a lower mean effect size than that calculated from just the published studies. This has been called "the file drawer problem," because such studies are often filed away, and Rosenthal (1991) has proposed a solution to it, aptly known as the *file drawer statistic, a calculation, following a meta-analysis, of the number of studies with null results that would have to exist so that a mean effect size is no longer statistically significant.* If just a few studies could render a mean effect size nonsignificant—that is, no longer statistically significantly different from zero—then the effect size should be viewed as likely to be an inflated estimate. If it would take several hundred studies in researchers' "file drawers" to render the effect nonsignificant, then it is safe to conclude that there really is a significant effect. For most well-designed research topics, it is not likely that there are hundreds of unpublished studies.

A good meta-analysis, carefully constructed and interpreted, can have a profound impact. Hunter and Schmidt (1996) report complaints from policymakers that behavioral research—whether pertaining to reduction of crime, best educational practices, the efficacy of psychotherapy, ways to increase production, or treatments for substance use—is fraught with contradictions, making it difficult to develop policies with confidence. Meta-analysis, Hunter and Schmidt state, can resolve this problem, and many a meta-analysis has shown that across an entire field of studies, the evidence is really not contradictory. Choosing a few studies in a subjective manner can highlight contradictions, but a clear picture can emerge from an objectively implemented meta-analysis, which can make cumulative knowledge possible in the social sciences.

In summary, a meta-analysis is a study of studies that provides a more objective measure of an effect size than does an individual study. A meta-analyst chooses a topic, decides on guidelines for a study's inclusion, tracks down every study on a given topic, and calculates an effect size for each. A mean effect size is calculated and is often reported along with a standard deviation, median, significance testing, confidence interval, and appropriate graphs. A file drawer statistic can be calculated to determine how many unpublished studies that failed to reject the null hypothesis must exist for the effect size to be rendered nonsignificantly different from zero.

⊙ CHECK YOUR LEARNING

12-5 Imagine that you wanted to find out everything that was known about the career path of undergraduate behavioral science majors within the first 10 years after they graduated. Keep in mind the benefits, logic, and steps required to conduct a meta-analysis as you answer each of these questions.

a. What database(s) might be most productive as you use your computer savvy to find out what happens to behavioral science majors?

b. What search words could you use to track down all the articles that would tell you about what happens to behavioral science majors? Where could you look to get ideas for alternative search words?

c. Explain why some articles may not appear in the database to begin with.

> ## Beyond Hypothesis Testing: Reducing Misinterpretations

Hypothesis testing can be misleading because it can suggest that a difference between two mean scores represents a difference between everyone in one group and everyone in another group. The overlap between two distributions can be ignored, and a statistically significant finding can be misconstrued as important, even when the difference is quite small. Specifically, a large sample size can lead even a small difference to be detected as statistically significant. These problems can be addressed through several statistical techniques, including the calculation of confidence intervals, the calculation of effect sizes, and the consideration of statistical power.

> ## Confidence Intervals: An Alternative to Hypothesis Testing

A summary statistic, such as a mean, is a *point estimate* of the population mean. A more useful estimate is an *interval estimate*, a range of plausible numbers for the population mean. The most commonly used interval estimate in the social sciences is the *confidence interval*, which can be created around a mean or around a difference between means using a z distribution or a t distribution. The confidence interval is created by subtracting and adding a *margin of error* from a mean or difference between means. The confidence interval provides the same information as a hypothesis test but also gives us a range of values; thus, it is more useful than a hypothesis test.

> ## Effect Size: Just How Big Is the Difference?

Knowing that a difference is statistically significant does not provide information about the size of the effect. A study with a large sample size might find a small effect to be statistically significant, whereas a study with a small sample might fail to detect a large effect. To understand the importance of a finding, we must calculate an *effect size*. Effect sizes are independent of sample size because they are based on distributions of scores rather than distributions of means. Common effect-size measures are *Cohen's d*, used when a z test or a t test has been conducted, and R^2, often used when an ANOVA has been conducted. We can compare our effect sizes with guidelines developed by Cohen to get a sense of how large they are.

> Statistical Power and Sensitivity: Correctly Rejecting the Null Hypothesis

Statistical power is a measure of our ability to correctly reject the null hypothesis; that is, the chance that we will not commit a Type II error when the research hypothesis is true. For a *z* test, we can calculate the proportion (or percentage) of a distribution of means for our hypothesized second population that is beyond the cutoff for the population based on the null hypothesis. This proportion is our statistical power. Statistical power is affected most directly by sample size, but it is also affected by the choice of *alpha* (cutoff *p* level), the decision to use a one-tailed or two-tailed test, the magnitude of the difference between means, and the size of the standard deviation of the population. Researchers often use a computerized statistical power calculator to determine the appropriate sample size to achieve 0.80, or 80%, statistical power, given certain considerations (e.g., expected effect size, alpha). Pre-study statistical power analyses are frequently required by an *Institutional Review Board* before a researcher can proceed with a study.

> Digging Deeper into the Data: Meta-Analysis

A *meta-analysis* is a study of many studies on a given topic. Because it averages the effect sizes of many studies, meta-analyses allow a more objective exploration of differences between means. After choosing a topic, a meta-analyst develops specific guidelines for the inclusion of studies. Studies are tracked down through many different sources, including electronic databases, citation indices, and conference proceedings. Effect sizes are calculated for every study, and the effect sizes are averaged. In addition to the mean, meta-analysts usually report a standard deviation, a median, the results of significance testing, a confidence interval, and any appropriate graphs. The researcher might also report a *file drawer statistic* that reports how many null results must exist before the effect size is no longer statistically significant.

SPSS GUIDELINES FOR CHAPTER 12

Conceptually, these three statistical ideas are like three sides of a triangle because changes in one side provoke changes in the other two. For all of its procedures, SPSS allows us to override the default confidence level of 95%. The numbers representing the confidence interval appear in the output screen as "Lower" and "Upper." SPSS also allows us to select effect sizes as one of its output options, but the name of the particular effect-size statistic varies with the type of hypothesis test.

When conducting a single-sample *t* test, we can adjust the confidence interval by selecting:

Analyze → Compare Means → One-Sample t test → Options. We can now select a confidence level of 95% or another confidence level, such as 99%.

We can calculate effect sizes using a couple of different approaches. For example, we can calculate the effect size (eta squared or R^2) of an ANOVA by selecting:

Analyze → Compare Means → Means → Options → ANOVA table and eta squared. The effect size of R^2 (listed under eta squared), is reported at the bottom of the source table in your output screen. It is under the heading "Measures of Association."

Another option for calculating the effect size (R squared) of an ANOVA is by selecting:

Analyze → General Linear Model → Univariate → Options → Estimates of Effect Size. The effect size (R^2) is reported at the very bottom of the source table as "R squared."

EXERCISES

12.1 Law school acceptance and overlapping distributions: A midwestern university reported that its social science majors tended to outperform its humanities majors on the LSATs (which gives them an edge at getting into law school). Sadie, an English major, and Kofi, a sociology major, both just took the LSAT.

a. Can we tell which student will do better on the LSAT? Explain your answer.

b. Draw a picture that represents what the two distributions, that for social science majors and that for humanities majors at this institution, might look like with respect to one another.

12.2 Fantasy baseball and overlapping data: Your roommate is reading *Fantasyland: A Season on Baseball's Lunatic Fringe* (Walker, 2006) and is intrigued by the statistical methods used by competitors in fantasy baseball leagues (in which competitors select their own team of baseball players from across all major league teams, and win the fantasy league if their eclectic roster of players outperforms the chosen mixes of other fantasy competitors). Among the many statistics reported in the book is a finding that major league baseball players who have a third child show more of a decline in performance than players who have a first child or a second child. Your friend remembers that Johnny Damon had a third child within the last couple of years and drops him from consideration for his fantasy team.

a. Explain to your friend why a difference between means doesn't provide information about any specific individual. Include a drawing of overlapping curves as part of your answer. On the drawing, mark places on the x-axis that might represent an individual from the distribution of those who recently had a third child (mark with an X) scoring *above* an individual from the distribution of those who recently had a first or second child (mark with a Y).

b. Explain to your friend that a statistically significant difference doesn't necessarily indicate a large effect size. How might a measure of effect size, such as Cohen's d, help us understand the importance of these findings and compare them to other predictors of performance that might have larger effects?

c. Given that the reported association is true, can we conclude that having a third child *causes* a decline in performance? Explain your answer. What confounds might lead to the difference observed in this study?

d. Given the relatively limited numbers of major league baseball players (and the relatively limited numbers of those who recently had a child—whether first, second, or third), what general guess would you make about the likely statistical power of this analysis?

12.3 Division I college football and confidence intervals: Exercise 8.7 asked whether college football teams tend to be more likely or less likely to be mismatched in the upper National Collegiate Athletic Association (NCAA) divisions. During week 11 of the fall 2006 college football season, the population of 53 Division I games had a mean spread (winning score minus losing score) of 16.189, with a standard deviation of 12.128. We took a sample of four games that were played that week in the next-highest league, Division I-AA, to see if the spread were different; one of the many leagues within Division I-AA, the Patriot League, played four games that weekend. Their mean was 8.75.

a. Calculate the 95% confidence interval for this sample.

b. State in your own words what we learn from this confidence interval.

c. What information does the confidence interval give us that we also get from the hypothesis test we conducted in Chapter 8?

d. What additional information does the confidence interval give us that we do not get from the hypothesis test we conducted in Chapter 8?

12.4 The Graded Naming Test and confidence intervals: Exercise 8.11 examined the Graded Naming Test (GNT), which asks respondents to name objects in a set of 30 black-and-white drawings in order to detect brain damage. The GNT population norm for adults in England is 20.4. Roberts (2003) wondered whether a sample of Canadian adults had different scores from adults in England. If they were different, the English norms would not be valid for use in Canada. The mean for 30 Canadian adults was 17.5. For the purposes of the exercise in Chapter 8, we assumed that the standard deviation of the adults in England is 3.2.

a. Calculate the 95% confidence interval for these data.

b. Calculate the 90% confidence interval for these data.

c. How are the confidence intervals different from each other? Explain why they are different.

12.5 Hypnosis, the Stroop effect, and confidence intervals: In Exercise 9.10 we considered a study by Raz, Fan, and Posner (2005) that used brain-imaging techniques [i.e., functional magnetic resonance imaging (fMRI)] to explore whether posthypnotic suggestion led highly hypnotizable individuals to see Stroop words as nonsense words. One of the exercises asked you to conduct an independent-samples t test on two samples—one consisting of those who received no posthypnotic suggestion (X) and one consisting of people who received a posthypnotic suggestion (Y). Here are some of the calculations we made while conducting the independent-samples t test:

$$M_X = 12.55; \; s_X^2 = \frac{\Sigma(X - M)^2}{N - 1} = 0.600; \; M_Y = 9.5; \; s_Y^2 = \frac{\Sigma(Y - M)^2}{N - 1} = 0.680$$

$$df_X = N - 1 = 6 - 1 = 5; \; df_Y = N - 1 = 6 - 1 = 5; \; df_{total} = df_X + df_Y = 5 + 5 = 10$$

$$s_{Pooled}^2 = \left(\frac{df_X}{df_{Total}}\right) s_X^2 + \left(\frac{df_Y}{df_{Total}}\right) s_Y^2 = 0.300 + 0.340 = 0.640$$

a. Calculate the 95% confidence interval for these data.

b. State in your own words what we learn from this confidence interval.

c. What information does the confidence interval give us that we also get from the hypothesis test we conducted in Chapter 9?

d. What additional information does the confidence interval give us that we do not get from the hypothesis test we conducted in Chapter 9?

12.6 Getting ready for a date and confidence intervals: In an example we used on Chapter 9, we reported data from our statistics classes in which male and female students were asked how long, in minutes, they typically spend getting ready for a date. Here are the data:

Men: 28, 35, 52, 14

Women: 30, 82, 53, 61

And here are some of the calculations needed to conduct an independent-samples t test:

$$M_X = 32.25; s_X^2 = \frac{\Sigma(X - M)^2}{N - 1} = 249.584; M_Y = 56.5; s_Y^2 = \frac{\Sigma(Y - M)^2}{N - 1} = 461.667$$

$$df_X = N - 1 = 4 - 1 = 3; df_Y = N - 1 = 4 - 1 = 3; df_{total} = df_X + df_Y = 3 + 3 = 6$$

$$s_{Pooled}^2 = \left(\frac{df_X}{df_{Total}}\right)s_X^2 + \left(\frac{df_Y}{df_{Total}}\right)s_Y^2 = 124.792 + 230.834 = 355.626$$

$$s_{M_X}^2 = \frac{s_{Pooled}^2}{N} = \frac{355.626}{4} = 88.907; s_{M_Y}^2 = \frac{s_{Pooled}^2}{N} = \frac{355.626}{4} = 88.907$$

$$s_{Difference}^2 = s_M^2 + s_{M_Y}^2 = 88.907 + 88.907 = 177.814$$

$$s_{Difference} = \sqrt{s_{Difference}^2} = \sqrt{177.814} = 13.335$$

a. Calculate the 95% confidence interval for these data.

b. Calculate the 90% confidence interval for these data.

c. How are the confidence intervals different from each other? Explain why they are different.

12.7 Division I college football, z test, and effect size: In Exercise 8.7 and again in Exercise 12.3, we considered the study of week 11 of the fall 2006 college football season, during which the population of 53 Division I games had a mean spread (winning score minus losing score) of 16.189, with a standard deviation of 12.128. The sample of four games that were played that week in the next highest league, Division I-AA, had a mean of 8.75.

a. Calculate the appropriate measure of effect size for this sample.

b. Based on Cohen's conventions, is this a small, medium, or large effect size?

c. Why is it useful to have this information in addition to the results of a hypothesis test?

12.8 The Graded Naming Test, z test, and effect size: In Exercise 8.11 and again in Exercise 12.4, we examined a study of the Graded Naming Test (GNT), which has a population norm for adults in England of 20.4. Roberts (2003) found a mean for 30 Canadian adults of 17.5, and we assumed a standard deviation of adults in England of 3.2.

a. Calculate the appropriate measure of effect size for this sample.

b. Based on Cohen's conventions, is this a small, medium, or large effect size?

c. Why is it useful to have this information in addition to the results of a hypothesis test?

12.9 Hypnosis, independent-samples t test, and effect size: In Exercise 9.11 and again in Exercise 12.5, we considered a study by Raz and colleagues (2005) for which we conducted an independent-samples t test. En route to calculating our test statistic, we made the following calculations:

$$M_X = 12.55; s_X^2 = \frac{\Sigma(X - M)^2}{N = 1} = 0.600; M_Y = 9.5; s_Y^2 = \frac{\Sigma(Y - M)^2}{N - 1} = 0.680$$

$$df_X = N - 1 = 6 - 1 = 5; df_Y = N - 1 = 6 - 1 = 5;$$
$$df_{total} = df_X + df_Y = 5 + 5 = 10$$

$$s_{Pooled}^2 = \left(\frac{df_X}{df_{Total}}\right)s_X^2 + \left(\frac{df_Y}{df_{Total}}\right)s_Y^2 = 0.300 + 0.340 = 0.640$$

a. Calculate the appropriate measure of effect size for this sample.

b. Based on Cohen's conventions, is this a small, medium, or large effect size?

c. Why is it useful to have this information in addition to the results of a hypothesis test?

12.10 Getting ready for a date, independent-samples t test, and effect size: In an example we used in Exercise 9.10 and again in Exercise 12.6, we reported data from our statistics classes in which male and female students were asked how long, in minutes, they typically spend getting ready for a date. Here are some of the calculations needed to conduct an independent samples t test:

$$M_X = 32.25;\ s_X^2 = \frac{\Sigma(X-M)^2}{N-1} = 249.584;\ M_Y = 56.5;\ s_Y^2 = \frac{\Sigma(Y-M)}{N-1} = 461.667$$

$$df_X = N - 1 = 4 - 1 = 3;\ df_Y = N - 1 = 4 - 1 = 3;\ df_{total} = df_X + df_Y = 3 + 3 = 6$$

$$s_{Pooled}^2 = \left(\frac{df_X}{df_{Total}}\right)s_X^2 + \left(\frac{df_Y}{df_{Total}}\right)s_Y^2 = 124.792 + 230.834 = 355.626$$

$$s_{M_X}^2 = \frac{s_{Pooled}^2}{N} = \frac{355.626}{4} = 88.907;\ s_{M_Y}^2 = \frac{s_{Pooled}^2}{N} = \frac{355.626}{4} = 88.907$$

$$s_{Difference}^2 = s_M^2 + s_{M_Y}^2 = 88.907 + 88.907 = 177.814$$

$$s_{Difference} = \sqrt{s_{Difference}^2} = \sqrt{177.814} = 13.335$$

a. Calculate the appropriate measure of effect size for this sample.

b. Based on Cohen's conventions, is this a small, medium, or large effect size?

c. Why is it useful to have this information in addition to the results of a hypothesis test?

12.11 eBay, one-way ANOVA, and effect size: In Exercise 10.13 we used a one-way ANOVA to explore whether some genres of music tended to sell for more money than other genres on eBay. CDs were randomly selected from the eBay lists for four genres: classical, rap/hip-hop, pop, and jazz. The prices were:

Classical: $2.99, $1.91, $1.45

Rap/hip-hop: $0.99, $0.01, $0.99, $0.77

Pop: $0.99, $1.00, $0.01

Jazz: $5.79, $14.99, $8.99, $0.99

And here's the source table for this ANOVA:

SOURCE	SS	df	MS	F
Between	127.999	3	42.663	4.02
Within	106.023	10	10.602	
Total	234.022	13		

a. Calculate the appropriate measure of effect size for this sample.

b. Based on Cohen's conventions, is this a small, medium, or large effect size?

c. Why is it useful to have this information in addition to the results of a hypothesis test?

d. Why is it not possible to calculate Cohen's d as the measure of effect size for these data?

12.12 Orthodontics, one-way ANOVA, and effect size: In Exercise 10.14, we discussed Iranian researchers who studied factors affecting patients' likelihood of wearing orthodontic appliances, including stage of schooling: primary school, junior high school, or high school. The scores below are daily hours of wearing one's orthodontic appliance:

Primary school: 16, 13, 18

Junior high school: 8, 13, 14, 12

High school: 20, 15, 16, 18

And here's the source table for this ANOVA:

SOURCE	SS	df	MS	F
Between	63.475	2	31.738	5.27
Within	48.167	8	6.021	
Total	111.64	10		

a. Calculate the appropriate measure of effect size for this sample.

b. Based on Cohen's conventions, is this a small, medium, or large effect size?

c. Why is it useful to have this information in addition to the results of a hypothesis test?

12.13 Medical myths, two-way ANOVA, and effect size: In Chapter 11, we discussed a study that examined the effectiveness of myth-busting (Skurnik, Yoon, Park, & Schwarz, 2005). The researchers compared two groups of adults: one group of 6 younger adults, ages 18–25, and a second group of 6 older adults, ages 71–86, who were presented with a series of claims and were told that each claim was either true or false. In some cases, the claim was shown once; in other cases, the claim was repeated three times. So there were two independent variables: age with two levels (younger and older) and number of repetitions with two levels (once and three times). The dependent variable was error rate after a three-day delay. A two-way between-groups ANOVA was used to analyze the data, and the following source table was calculated.

SOURCE	SS	df	MS	F
Age (A)	0.0300	1	0.0300	13.04
Repetitions (R)	0.0000	1	0.0000	0.00
A × R	0.0192	1	0.0190	8.26
Within	0.0180	8	0.0023	
Total	0.0672	11		

a. Calculate effect size for the independent variable of age. (*Hint:* Effect size is calculated using the between sum of squares for that independent variable.)

b. Based on Cohen's conventions, is this a small, medium, or large effect size?

c. Calculate effect size for the independent variable of number of repetitions. (*Hint:* Effect size is calculated using the between sum of squares for that independent variable.)

d. Based on Cohen's conventions, is this a small, medium, or large effect size?

e. Calculate effect size for the interaction of age and number of repetitions. (*Hint:* Effect size is calculated using the between sum of squares for the interaction.)

f. Based on Cohen's conventions, is this a small, medium, or large effect size?

g. Which effect—the main effect of age, the main effect of number of repetitions, or their interaction—accounts for the most variance? Explain your answer.

12.14 Division I college football and statistical power: In Exercise 8.7 and again in Exercises 12.3 and 12.7, we considered the study of week 11 of the fall 2006 college football season, during which the population of 53 Division I games had a mean spread (winning score minus losing score) of 16.189, with a standard deviation of 12.128. The sample of four games that were played that week in the next-highest league, Division I-AA, had a mean of 8.75.

a. Calculate statistical power for this study. (To make your life easier, remember to use a one-tailed test to calculate statistical power.)

b. What does the statistical power suggest about how we should view the findings of this study?

12.15 The Graded Naming Test and statistical power: In Exercise 8.11 and again in Exercises 12.4 and 12.8, we examined a study of the Graded Naming Test (GNT), which has a population norm for adults in England of 20.4. Roberts (2003) found a mean for 30 Canadian adults of 17.5, and we assumed a standard deviation of adults in England of 3.2.

a. Calculate statistical power for this study.

b. What does the statistical power suggest about how we should view the findings of this study?

12.16 Hypnosis, the Stroop effect, and statistical power: In Exercise 9.11 and again in Exercises 12.5 and 12.9, we considered a study by Raz and colleagues (2005) for which we conducted an independent-samples t test. En route to calculating our test statistic, we made the following calculations:

$$M_X = 12.55; \; s_X^2 = \frac{\Sigma(X - M)^2}{N - 1} = 0.600; \; M_Y = 9.5; \; s_Y^2 = \frac{\Sigma(Y - M)^2}{N - 1} = 0.680$$

$$df_X = N - 1 = 6 - 1 = 5; \; df_Y = N - 1 = 6 - 1 = 5; \; df_{total} = df_X + df_Y = 5 + 5 = 10$$

$$s_{Pooled}^2 = \left(\frac{df_X}{df_{Total}}\right) s_X^2 + \left(\frac{df_Y}{df_{Total}}\right) s_Y^2 = 0.300 + 0.340 = 0.640$$

a. Use a computerized statistical power calculator such as G*Power to calculate statistical power for this study. Use a p level, or alpha, of 0.05 and a two-tailed test. (*Hint:* Use the above information to calculate the effect size. *Another hint:* You can figure out sample size from the calculations for degrees of freedom.)

b. Using a computerized statistical power calculator, determine exactly how many participants are needed, in total, to attain statistical power of 0.80.

12.17 Getting ready for a date and statistical power: In an example we used in Exercise 9.10 and again in Exercises 12.6 and 12.10, we reported data from our statistics classes in which male and female students were asked how long, in minutes, they typically spend getting ready for a date. Here are some of the calculations needed to conduct an independent-samples t test:

$$M_X = 32.25; \; s_X^2 = \frac{\Sigma(X - M)^2}{N - 1} = 249.584; \; M_Y = 56.5; \; s_Y^2 = \frac{\Sigma(Y - M)^2}{N - 1} = 461.667$$

$$df_X = N - 1 = 4 - 1 = 3; \; df_Y = N - 1 = 4 - 1 = 3; \; df_{total} = df_X + df_Y = 3 + 3 = 6$$

$$s_{Pooled}^2 = \left(\frac{df_X}{df_{Total}}\right) s_X^2 + \left(\frac{df_Y}{df_{Total}}\right) s_Y^2 = 124.792 + 230.834 = 355.626$$

$$s_{M_X}^2 = \frac{s_{Pooled}^2}{N} = \frac{355.626}{4} = 88.907; \; s_{M_Y}^2 = \frac{s_{Pooled}^2}{N} = \frac{355.626}{4} = 88.907$$

$$s_{Difference}^2 = s_M^2 + s_{M_Y}^2 = 88.907 + 88.907 = 177.814$$

$$s_{Difference} = \sqrt{s_{Difference}^2} = \sqrt{177.814} = 13.335$$

a. Use a computerized statistical power calculator such as G*Power to calculate statistical power for this study. Use a p level, or alpha, of 0.05 and a two-tailed test. (*Hint:* Use the above information to calculate the effect size. *Another hint:* You can figure out sample size from the calculations for degrees of freedom.)

b. Exactly how many participants are needed in total, to attain statistical power of 0.80?

12.18 Medical myths and statistical power: In Chapter 11 and Exercise 12.13, we discussed a study that examined the effectiveness of myth-busting (Skurnik, Yoon, Park, & Schwartz, 2005). The researchers compared two groups of adults: one group of 6 younger adults, ages 18–25, and a second group of 6 older adults, ages 71–86, who were presented with a series of claims and were told that each claim was either true or false. In some cases, the claim was shown once; in other cases, the claim was repeated three times. So there were two independent variables: age with two levels (younger and older) and number of repetitions with two levels (once and three times). The dependent variable was error rate after a three-day delay. List five specific ways the researchers could increase statistical power for the independent variable of number of repetitions.

12.19 The language of statistics—*confidence*: In your own words, define the word *confidence*—first as you would use it in everyday conversation and then as a statistician would use it in the context of a confidence interval.

12.20 The language of statistics—*effect*: In your own words, define the word *effect*—first as you would use it in everyday conversation and then as a statistician would use it.

12.21 The language of statistics—*power*: In your own words, define the word *power*—first as you would use it in everyday conversation and then as a statistician would use it.

12.22 The symbols of statistics: For each of the following, (i) identify the incorrect symbol, (ii) state what the correct symbol should be, and (iii) explain why the initial symbol was incorrect.

a. $M_{Lower} = -z(\sigma) + M_{Sample}$

b. $d = \dfrac{(M_X - M_Y) - (\mu_X - \mu_Y)}{s^2_{Pooled}}$

c. $R^2 = \dfrac{SS_{Within}}{SS_{Total}}$

d. $(M_X - M_Y)_{Upper} = z_{Upper}(s_{Difference}) + (M_X - M_Y)_{Sample}$

e. $d = \dfrac{(M - \mu)}{\sigma_M}$

■ DIGGING DEEPER INTO THE DATA

12.23 Meta-analysis and culturally adapted therapy: A meta-analysis examined studies that compared two types of mental health treatments for ethnic and racial minorities—the standard available treatments and treatments that were adapted to clients' cultures (Griner & Smith, 2006). An excerpt from the abstract follows:

> Many previous authors have advocated that traditional mental health treatments be modified to better match clients' cultural contexts. Numerous studies evaluating culturally adapted interventions have appeared, and the present study used meta-analytic methodology to summarize these data. Across 76 studies the resulting random effects weighted average effect size was $d = .45$, indicating a . . . benefit of culturally adapted interventions. (p. 531)

a.   What is the topic chosen by these meta-analysts?

b.   Suggest at least one criterion that the researchers might have used to select the studies for the meta-analysis.

c.   What effect size did the researchers calculate for each study in the meta-analysis?

d.   What was the mean effect size that they found? According to Cohen's conventions, how large is this effect?

e.   If a study chosen for the meta-analysis does not include an effect size, what summary statistics would the researchers use to calculate an effect size?

12.24 Meta-analysis, culturally adapted therapy, and confidence intervals: The paper on culturally targeted therapy described in Exercise 12.23 reported:

> Across all 76 studies, the random effects weighted average effect size was $d = .45$ ($SE = .04$, $p < .0001$), with a 95% confidence interval of $d = .36$ to $d = .53$. The data consisted of 72 nonzero effect sizes, of which 68 (94%) were positive and 4 (6%) were negative. Effect sizes ranged from $d = -.48$ to $d = 2.7$ (pg. 535).

a. What is the confidence interval? What does the confidence interval suggest about the overall story that the studies on this topic are telling?

b. Based on the confidence interval, would a hypothesis test (with the null hypothesis that the effect size is 0) lead us to reject the null hypothesis? Explain.

c. Why would a graph, such as a stem-and-leaf plot, be useful when conducting a meta-analysis like this one? (*Hint:* Consider the problems when using a mean as a measure of central tendency.)

12.25 Meta-analysis and electronic databases: Let's say that you read about a study suggesting that single mothers are more likely to be depressed than single fathers. You decide to do a meta-analysis to see whether this finding holds up across studies. Conduct a search on an electronic social science database such as Sociological Abstracts or PsycINFO.

a. First, conduct a literature search using the search words "gender" and "depression." How many articles did you find? Does this seem like it's too many or too few?

b. Now, conduct a literature search using the search words "gender," "depression," and "single-parent." How many articles did you find? Does this seem like it's too many or too few?

c. Look through the abstracts of the articles you located in the second search. Roughly, what percentage of these articles seems relevant to the meta-analysis you want to do?

d. What other search words might help to better target your search?

e. What do these searches suggest about the difficulties in choosing search words when conducting a meta-analysis?

12.26 File drawer statistic: Why is it necessary to calculate a file drawer statistic when conducting a meta-analysis? That is, what are the limitations of the traditional sources (e.g., electronic databases, conference proceedings) of studies used in meta-analysis?

TERMS

---

point estimate (p. 534)	Cohen's d (p. 546)	Institutional Review Board
interval estimate (p. 534)	R^2 (p. 548)	(IRB) (p. 562)
confidence interval (p. 535)	statistical power (p. 551)	meta-analysis (p. 563)
effect size (p. 543)	alpha (p. 556)	file drawer statistic (p. 566)

SYMBOLS

Cohen's d (or just d)

R^2 (or sometimes η^2)

α

FORMULAS

$M_{Lower} = -z(\sigma_M) + M_{Sample}$

$M_{Upper} = z(\sigma_M) + M_{Sample}$

$(M_X - M_Y)_{Lower} = {}^-t(s_{Difference}) + (M_X - M_Y)_{Sample}$

$(M_X - M_Y)_{Upper} = t(s_{Difference}) + (M_X - M_Y)_{Sample}$

Cohen's $d = \dfrac{(M - \mu)}{\sigma}$ for a z distribution

Cohen's $d = \dfrac{(M_X - M_Y) - (\mu_X - \mu_Y)}{s_{Pooled}}$ for a t distribution for a difference between means

$R^2 = \dfrac{SS_{Between}}{SS_{Total}}$

CHI SQUARE
EXPECTATIONS VERSUS OBSERVATIONS

Karl Pearson fought with people. Why? Perhaps it was because of the many gaps between what he expected from life and what he actually experienced. There was a gap between the love he expected from his parents and the discord he experienced with them, another gap between the ideals of Christianity and the everyday life of Christians he observed, and the troubling gap between the intellectually coherent life he longed for and the compartmentalized life he actually lived. These private conflicts evolved into a gap between the passionate Karl Pearson and the scientifically detached Karl Pearson who looked to statistics as a way to attain an unbiased perspective. Karl Pearson's private conflicts about how best to live could be summed up this way: passion versus probability.

The historical record is clear: Karl Pearson was publicly brilliant and privately vicious (to those who disagreed with him). He was acerbic, judgmental, sure that he was making history, yet disappointed that he was accomplishing so little. When he was 16, he informed his mother that he could never be happy, and he seemed to spend his entire life trying to keep that promise. As a young man in Victorian England, Pearson considered himself an "intellectual buccaneer," and his independence, brilliance, and torment showed in many ways. He scored dramatically higher than any of his peers at King's College on tests, yet disdained testing as a distraction from true intellectual issues. He demanded (and won) an end to compulsory attendance at chapel because "freedom is the essence of Religion" yet attended chapel after winning his case; his objection was to *coerced* attendance at religious services, not to religion itself. There are many other ways to express the intellectual and emotional conflicts within Karl Pearson: appearance versus reality, superstition versus science, subjective experience versus objective experimentation, and intuition versus information. These forces and many more were all at war within Pearson, and he spent a lifetime trying to broker a peace. He didn't succeed. When he thought he was dying, he told his wife that "a curve or a symbol will be called 'Pearson's' & nothing more remembered of the toil of the years."

Porter (p. 314) suggests that modern science still struggles for acceptance due to the gap between the passionate, poetic Pearson and the aloof, impartial Pearson. Pearson left us this legacy because he was inventing statistics (still used across the sciences) at the same time Darwin's ideas were invigorating the sciences. That legacy includes the chi-square distribution that enables us to test the difference between what we observe and what we can expect by chance. And it does so in the simplest way possible: by counting. More specifically, the chi-square statistic requires only that the researcher count the frequency of an observation (the observed) and compare it to what would be expected by chance (the expected). That's all there is to the chi-square statistic, but that is also why it can be a liberating statistic for students in the behavioral sciences: the entire universe of variables is now available for statistical analysis, even variables that don't even come close to meeting the assumptions associated with more conventional statistical tests.

The chi-square statistic adds an important tool to the statistician's toolbox because it allows us to test the relations between variables when they are nominal. As long as we can count the frequency of any event and assign those frequencies to discrete (nonoverlapping) categories, the chi-square statistic empowers us to test for the independence of those categories, estimate effect sizes, transform those observations into percentages, and portray those findings in a graph. Perhaps that is why people like Karl Pearson were so attracted to statistics: If something varies, statisticians have invented a way to explore that variability.

Karl Pearson
Karl Pearson worried that "a curve or a symbol will be called 'Pearson's' & nothing more remembered of the toil of the years."

> NONPARAMETRIC STATISTICS: WHEN WE'RE NOT EVEN CLOSE TO MEETING THE ASSUMPTIONS

A team of Israeli physician-researchers found that live entertainment by clowns—yes, clowns!—was associated with higher rates of conception (Rockwell, 2006). Out of 93 women receiving in vitro fertilization (IVF) treatment, 33 who were entertained by a clown (35%) conceived compared to 19% in a group that did not enjoy the entertaining clown. The idea of clown therapy was popularized when Robin Williams portrayed a healing clown-doctor in the 1998 movie *Patch Adams*, but the lead researcher for this study was Dr. Shevach Friedler, a trained mime as well as a physician (Ryan, 2006). Women, especially those participating in IVF treatment, probably don't think of pregnancy as a laughing matter, especially during the 15 minutes immediately following embryo transfer, so that is when Friedler had a professional clown entertain the women by playing the role of a comedy chef—something that would *not* remind the women of children (Brinn, 2006). "We had to devise a different concept . . . some magic and a few bits of slapstick," the clown, Algosi, said (Brinn, 2006). The question inspired by statistical reasoning has probably already occurred to you: Is this a one-time, chance finding? How seriously can we take clown therapy?

The media were amused by this study, and "Send in the Clowns" headlines proliferated in the days following this study's presentation at the annual meeting of the European Society of Human Reproduction and Embryology (Reuters, 2006).

Humor as a Medical Treatment
Does humor lead to improved physical functioning? An Israeli study showed that entertainment by clowns led to higher pregnancy rates in women who had received in vitro fertilization. When the independent variable and dependent variable are nominal, we analyze data using the chi-square statistic. A hypothesis test based on chi square could explore the preventive effect of one variable: *Triumph, the Insult Comic Dog* (*Triumph* DVDs versus no *Triumph* DVDs) on a second variable, the common cold (cold versus no cold).

One reporter even opened her article by stating: "You're going to think we're making this up" (Rockwell, 2006). You have no doubt noticed that the studies that show up in the media tend to be those that make for the most entertaining reading. Would a study of a new medication that boosted fertility rates among those undergoing IVF receive this level of press? The clown study is fun to read about, but we should withhold our final judgment on this treatment's efficacy. Of course, it's not entirely surprising that aspects of one's psychological well-being would affect physical well-being, but this study will require many replications before insurance companies consider paying for clown therapy. But if replicated in numerous contexts, it might become an empirically validated treatment. Imagine getting a prescription for the *Triumph, the Insult Comic Dog* DVD collection!

Nonparametric Tests: Using the Right Statistical Tool for the Right Statistical Job

Nonparametric tests are hypothesis tests, just as parametric tests are; both use precisely the same logic, but nonparametric tests are statistical tools that should be reserved for particular statistical circumstances. For example, what if we were to conduct a replication of the clown study? What new statistical tools would we need? Let's consider the variables of interest. The independent variable is type of post-IVF treatment with two levels (clown therapy versus no clown therapy). The dependent variable is outcome with two levels (becomes pregnant versus does not become pregnant). The hypothesis is that whether a woman becomes pregnant depends on whether she receives clown therapy. Each participant, however, does *not* receive a score on some interval variable; rather, we simply record what level (pregnancy, no pregnancy) of a category she falls in. We have encountered a new situation: both the independent variable and the dependent variable are nominal.

This new situation calls for a new statistic. Until now, we have considered several types of research designs (Table 13-1), some in which both the independent and dependent variables are interval (correlation, regression) and others in which the independent variable is nominal and the dependent variable is interval (z tests, all kinds of t tests, and all kinds of ANOVAs). But we have not yet considered situations in which both the independent and dependent variables are nominal. This new situation requires a test that uses the chi-square distribution; the chi-square statistic is symbolized as χ^2 (pronounced "kai

Symbol: χ^2

TABLE 13-1. A SUMMARY OF RESEARCH DESIGNS

We have encountered several research designs so far, most of which fall in one of two categories. Some designs—those listed in category I—include an interval independent variable and an interval dependent variable. Other designs—those listed in category II—include a nominal independent variable and an interval dependent variable. Until now, we have not encountered a research design with a nominal independent variable and a nominal dependent variable.

I. INTERVAL INDEPENDENT VARIABLE AND INTERVAL DEPENDENT VARIABLE	II. NOMINAL INDEPENDENT VARIABLE AND INTERVAL DEPENDENT VARIABLE
Correlation	z test
Regression	All kinds of t tests
	All kinds of ANOVAs

square"—rhymes with *sky*). The chi-square statistic belongs to the class of statistics identified as nonparametric.

You may recall our discussion of parametric statistics and nonparametric statistics from Chapter 8. To refresh your memory, we defined parametric tests as statistical analyses that assume that the population is normally distributed. By contrast, we defined nonparametric tests as statistical analyses that *do not* assume that the population is normally distributed. Nonparametric tests are sometimes referred to as distribution-free tests because the data do not need to conform to any particular distribution, normal or otherwise. In situations that we have not yet encountered, such as the clown study above, we would have to use a nonparametric test.

Nonparametric Tests: When to Use Them

Although nonparametric statistical tests make us more versatile, they should be reserved for those circumstances when we have to choose between using nonparametric statistics and not doing the study at all. There are three circumstances when we commonly use a nonparametric test: (1) when the dependent variable is nominal (for example, in the clown study, our dependent variable—whether a woman becomes pregnant—is nominal), (2) when either the independent variable or the dependent variable is ordinal, or (3) when the sample size is small and we suspect that the underlying population of interest is skewed. The saving grace of conducting a possibly flawed study is our ability to do it again: replication. However, scarce resources (usually money) and the peculiar demands of individual studies don't always give us that luxury. So knowing when it is appropriate to use a nonparametric test is as important a skill as knowing how to analyze the data using software such as SPSS.

The first circumstance, when a dependent variable is nominal, is fairly common. Because you can't be just a little bit pregnant, the dependent variable in the clown study is nominal: whether a woman becomes pregnant. Each woman in the study is placed in a category on the dependent variable, rather than receiving a score. It doesn't make sense to try to compute a mean value for the 33 women who became pregnant and the 60 who did not—we can only count how many people fit into each discrete category. Similarly, what would we do when the dependent variable is gender? What would be the mean, for example, of 15 individuals who are men and 12 who are women? It wouldn't make sense to calculate such a mean; we can only count people as being in one of the two categories: male or female. As we have emphasized from the very first chapter, we need to transform observations into numbers with statistical integrity; that is, the numbers must genuinely represent their observations.

The second circumstance in which we use a nonparametric test occurs when either our independent variable or dependent variable is ordinal. Recall that an ordinal variable is one in which the participants are ranked, such as class rank in high school or the finishing rankings in a marathon. As with a nominal variable, it really wouldn't make sense to calculate the mean for an ordinal variable. We could not use the Pearson correlation coefficient because it requires two interval variables. And we could not use a t test or ANOVA because both require a nominal independent variable in addition to an interval dependent variable. Once again, researchers tend to take a conservative approach to statistical analysis, so we use a nonparametric test whenever one of the variables is ordinal.

The third circumstance that calls for a nonparametric statistic is when we have a small sample size and we suspect that the population of interest is from a skewed distribution. For example, what if we were studying the adjustment capabilities or mental health of people known as prodigious savants, dramatized by the Dustin Hoffman film *Rainman*? Prodigious savants are exceedingly rare individuals who are cognitively disabled in many ways but display spectacular isolated abilities. Or what if we were studying brain patterns on functional magnetic resonance imaging (fMRI) tests among individuals who have won the Nobel Prize in literature? No matter how hard we tried or how much we paid people to participate, we would be unlikely to recruit a sample of at least 30 individuals, the number of people needed for the central limit theorem to work its peculiar magic at transforming a skewed distribution into a normal distribution.

The problem of a small sample and the possibility of skewed data are often two sides of the same problem. If the data from a small sample appeared normally distributed, it would likely be safe to proceed with a parametric analysis (although, of course, we can never guarantee that this particular sample represents the underlying population). But we really don't know if the data are skewed unless we take the extra time to examine our data visually. For example, Micceri (1989) reported that many achievement tests do not lead to normal distributions of data; moreover, he noted that when conducting his study, 75% of the researchers whom he contacted were unable to easily provide frequency distributions for published data on achievement tests, an indication that many researchers may not be exploring the shape of their data prior to statistical analysis. Whenever possible, and especially when our data might be skewed, we should aim for a large sample size even if it involves more effort. When a large sample size is not possible and the sample data indicate that the population distribution might be skewed, we can still proceed using a nonparametric statistic.

To recap, there are three main situations in which we use nonparametric statistics:

1. The dependent variable is nominal.
2. Either the independent variable or the dependent variable is ordinal.
3. The sample size is small, and the data suggest that the underlying population might be skewed.

In this chapter, we will learn techniques for dealing with the first situation, when the dependent variable is nominal. In the next chapter, we will learn techniques to deal with the latter two situations.

Nonparametric Tests: Why to Avoid Them Whenever Possible

When we use a nonparametric technique, it is typically because we have no other choice. The good news is that nonparametric hypothesis tests allow us to analyze data that we could not analyze with a parametric hypothesis test. Although this greatly expands the range of variables available for statistical analysis, the bad news is that nonparametric tests have some severe limitations.

First, confidence intervals and effect-size measures don't make as much sense when we have nominal or ordinal data. Because nominal data provide only categories and ordinal data provide only information about the rankings of observations (rather than the magnitude of differences between observations), our estimates of differences are less precise and therefore less trustworthy. So nonparametric tests are like looking at a photograph that is out of focus—we just can't see the details very clearly.

Second, nonparametric tests tend to have less statistical power than parametric tests. This increases the risk of a Type II error, especially in cases in which a researcher has access to interval data from a normally distributed population. There is one particularly common way in which researchers decide to change an interval variable to a nominal variable: by using a median split. That is, researchers take the median of an interval variable and assign every score below the median to one category and every score above the median to a second category. Using a median split reduces statistical power (Cohen, 1983), so we are less likely to reject the null hypothesis when we should reject the null hypothesis—that is, when there is a real difference between groups. We wouldn't want to miss out on a potential cure for a disease because we were overly conservative.

Third, if the initial observation can reasonably be construed as interval, then interval data are almost always better at explaining the data. There is no need to resort to nonparametric tests simply for the sake of being conservative. If we do so, then we might miss some important relation between variables that actually exists; that is, we might commit a Type II error. Table 13-2 (page 584) provides an example of the importance of matching the right statistical test to the right kind of observation.

Let's consider all three of our choices (nominal, ordinal, and interval) by looking at Boston and New York and their predicted temperatures. Let's say you're going away for the weekend and want to decide where in the Northeast to go based on weather. You can get Saturday's forecast as a nominal, ordinal, or interval variable. As a nominal observation, Boston is predicted to be hot; New York is predicted to be very hot. How different are their temperatures when we treat them as a nominal variable? It's hard to say with just two categories, mainly because we don't know how far Boston is from being considered "very hot." (Note that some might argue that this is, to some degree, an ordinal variable because we know that New York is hotter than Boston. Regardless, researchers often used ranked variables as nominal when there are just a few categories.)

What if we look at the data as an ordinal observation? Boston is ranked fourth among northeastern cities in temperature; New York is ranked first. Ordinal observations are more meaningful, but we still don't know precisely how far Boston's temperature is from New York's without knowing the range of

TABLE 13-2. WHICH VARIABLE PROVIDES THE MOST INFORMATION?

The same construct could be operationalized with different types of variables. As the variables go from nominal to ordinal to interval, we get increasingly more useful information.

CITY	NOMINAL VARIABLE (type of weather)	ORDINAL VARIABLE (rank during month)	INTERVAL VARIABLE (temperature)
Boston	Hot	Fourth hottest in the Northeast	85°F
New York	Very hot	Hottest in the Northeast	98°F

temperatures in this region. We cannot really know how different they are based on this ordinal variable, even though it's much more informative than the nominal variable. In fact, we cannot know much about either city's temperature; in both cases, you would find yourself asking "how hot?"

The most useful information is provided by the interval variable. New York is predicted to be 98° and Boston is predicted to be 85°. Finally, we can see the magnitude of the difference in predicted temperatures. Using the interval variable gives us the most statistical power to detect differences between groups when there really are differences to detect. So we're least likely to make a Type II error, failing to detect a real difference, when we have an interval dependent variable and can use a parametric test. Always strive for the highest level of information. When possible, choose an ordinal scale over a nominal scale and choose an interval scale over either a nominal or an ordinal scale.

Fortunately, ongoing research is clarifying the middle ground when it comes to the choice between using parametric and nonparametric tests. There are some indications that for data meeting the assumptions for a parametric test, the outcomes are very similar with the nonparametric equivalent of that test (Agresti & Franklin, 2006). For example, we could take interval data and conduct the appropriate parametric hypothesis test, and then convert it to ranks (ordinal data) and conduct the equivalent nonparametric test for that research design; we will often have the same statistical conclusions as with the parametric test. In addition, we must remember that in cases where the assumptions are clearly violated, nonparametric tests often have more statistical power (Sawilowsky & Blair, 1992). Still, all things considered, it's best to use the parametric test when we can.

In summary, there are several research situations in which we cannot meet the assumptions of a parametric test, primarily the assumptions of having an interval dependent variable and a normally distributed population. In these cases, we can use a nonparametric test, one that is distribution free. The most common situations in which we use a nonparametric test are when we have a nominal dependent variable, an ordinal independent variable or an ordinal dependent variable, or a small sample in which the data for the dependent variable suggest that the underlying population distribution might be skewed. Nonparametric tests are valuable because they give us a tool when we cannot use a parametric test, but when possible we should use a parametric test. Parametric tests have more statistical power, and they use an interval dependent variable, which gives us more information than does a nominal dependent variable or an ordinal dependent variable. To maximize your statistical power, match the particular type of observation to the appropriate statistical test.

⊙ CHECK YOUR LEARNING

13-1 For each of the following situations state (i) the independent variable and what type of variable it is (nominal, ordinal, or interval), (ii) the dependent variable and what type of variable it is (nominal, ordinal, or interval), and (iii) the category (I or II) from Table 13-1 from which you would choose the appropriate hypothesis test. If you would not choose a test from either category I or II, simply list category III—other. Explain why you chose I, II, or III.

a. Bernstein (1996) reported that Francis Galton created a "beauty map" by recording the numbers of women he encountered in different cities in England who were either pretty or not so pretty. London women, he found, were the most likely to be pretty and Aberdeen women the least likely.

b. Imagine that Galton instead gave every woman a beauty score on a scale of 1–10 and then compared means for the women in each of five cities. Let's say he found, again, that London women were the prettiest, on average, and Aberdeen the least pretty, on average.

c. Galton was famous for discounting the intelligence of most women (Bernstein, 1996). Imagine that he assessed the intelligence of 50 women and then applied the beauty scale of part (b). Let's say he found that women with higher intelligence were more likely to be pretty, whereas women with lower intelligence were less likely to be pretty.

d. Imagine that Galton took 50 women and ranked them from 1 to 50 on their beauty and on their intelligence. Let's say he again found that women with higher intelligence tended to be more beautiful, whereas women with lower intelligence tended to be less beautiful.

> CHI-SQUARE TEST FOR GOODNESS-OF-FIT: WHEN WE HAVE ONE NOMINAL VARIABLE

Seven years before he decided that statistics would be his life's primary endeavor, Karl Pearson established the Men and Women's Club, earnestly hoping to build a bridge of respect and understanding between men and women through the ideal of pure intellectual love. For women who had been oppressed by strict Victorian codes of conduct, this was a liberating opportunity to exercise their intellect in public. The Men and Women's Club was probably comparable to a singles event sponsored by your local public radio station or like an Internet-organized "meet-up" targeted at the intellectually curious, except it was a far more radical endeavor against the backdrop of Victorian England. The clubs, organized around social causes and intellectual ideas, were a great success in many respects—depending on how you defined success. For better or worse, members of the Men and Women's Club kept falling in love with each other as psychological intimacy and sexual attraction kept overwhelming Pearson's ideal of pure intellectual love (Porter, 2004).

Olive Schreiner
Olive Schreiner was one of several women eager to explore relationships between men and women by developing a nonsexual friendship with Karl Pearson. Although the members of the Men and Women's Club expected ideal, asexual friendships, they often experienced intense attachments and sexual attraction.

From S.C. Cronwright-Schreiner, *The Life of Olive Schreiner*, 1924

■ The **chi-square test for goodness-of-fit** is a nonparametric hypothesis test used with one nominal variable.

■ The **chi-square test for independence** is a nonparametric test used with two nominal variables.

Pearson exchanged letters with several of the women in the club, and they all strove to discuss sexuality candidly, as mature adults; they failed (Porter, 2004). For Pearson, what he expected in the Men and Women's Club was the ideal of intellectual love, but what he observed was sexual attraction. He even developed strong feelings for the club secretary, Maria Sharpe, whom he later married, and for Olive Schreiner, who also fell in love with him. We don't know whether Pearson ever made the connection between his experience in the Men and Women's Club and the logic of chi-square analysis that he would develop later in his career. Nevertheless, the discrepancy between the observed and the expected described his own life. Pearson brought these internal conflicts into his marriage, where his passionate nature wrestled with his insistence on scientific aloofness for the remainder of his life.

So why did Karl Pearson, already a successful novelist, poet, physicist, historian, and philosopher, decide to become a statistician? First of all, statistical probability was a way for Pearson to achieve scientific detachment. He recognized that both subjective passion and scientific probability were ways of explaining human behavior, but he couldn't integrate them successfully within his own life. Whenever passion wrestled with probability, probability won. Like so many of our students, Pearson was also looking for the career that fit his personality, and statistics was a good fit for his inquisitive personality. The notion of a "good fit" between personality and career is also a way of expressing the relation between variables in one of the most commonly used forms of chi-square analysis.

There are two related chi-square hypothesis tests. *The **chi-square test for goodness-of-fit** is a nonparametric hypothesis test used with one nominal variable. The **chi-square test for independence** is a nonparametric test used with two nominal variables.* These two tests are the most commonly used of all the nonparametric tests. Moreover, both answer the question that Pearson asked at so many different levels: How do the data that we observe fit with the data we would expect according to our null hypothesis? If our observed data do not deviate much from what we would expect just by chance, then we cannot reject the null hypothesis. If the observed data are different enough from what we expect just by chance, then we can reject the null hypothesis. The logic of the chi-square test should sound familiar; it's just another application of hypothesis testing and involves the same familiar six steps we have used with previous statistics.

Chi-Square Test for Goodness-of-Fit: The Six Steps of Hypothesis Testing

Both chi-square tests require a new statistic. Instead of a t or an F or an r as our statistic, we calculate a chi-square statistic: χ^2. Both chi-square statistics are based on the chi-square distribution. As is true for t distributions and F distributions, there are also several chi-square distributions, depending on the degrees of freedom. For both types of chi-square tests, we use the appropriate chi-square distribution based on the degrees of freedom for that particular research design.

In one small but sometimes useful way, the chi-square test for goodness-of-fit is slightly different from other hypothesis tests we have learned (and from the chi-square test for independence). It calculates a statistic based on just one variable. There's really no independent variable or dependent variable, just one categorical variable with two or more categories into which participants are placed.

In fact, the chi-square test for goodness-of-fit received its name because of what it tells us; it gives us a measure of how good the fit is between the observed data in the various categories of a single nominal variable and the data that we would expect according to the null hypothesis. If there's a really good fit with the null hypothesis, then we cannot reject the null hypothesis. If we're hoping that our research hypothesis will receive empirical support, then we're actually hoping for a *bad fit* between our observed data and what we expect according to the null hypothesis. Let's look at an example.

Gary Steinman (2006), an obstetrician and gynecologist, studied whether a woman's diet could affect the likelihood that she would have twins. Insulin-like growth factor (IGF), often found in diets that include animal products, is hypothesized to lead to higher rates of twin births. Rates of twin births have increased, along with rates of IGF in animal products, which are a direct result of growth hormones aimed at increasing the production of products like milk and beef. Steinman wondered whether women who were vegans (those who eat neither meat nor dairy products) would have lower rates of twin births than would women who were vegetarians but consumed dairy products or women who ate both meat and dairy products. Steinman reported that in the general population, 1.9% of births result in twins (without the aid of reproductive technologies). In Steinman's study of 1042 vegans who gave birth (without reproductive technologies), there were four sets of twins. We can use Steinman's data to conduct a chi-square test for goodness-of-fit.

We'll conduct our test within the framework of the six steps of hypothesis testing. You'll notice many similarities between this framework and its language and those we used in earlier hypothesis tests. For example, we use the term *cells* for chi square in the same way we used it for ANOVA, only now we'll have counts in the cells rather than means. In addition, statisticians usually call the numbers in cells *frequencies*. This is the same word that we used in Chapter 2 when we introduced frequency tables. In both cases, *frequency* refers to the fact that there are counts in the tables.

Rick Gomez/Masterfile

Diet and Twins
Does a diet high in meat lead to an increased rate of twin births? When we have a single nominal variable such as births (twins, singleton), we use a chi-square test for goodness-of-fit. Using data from Steinman (2006), a chi-square test for goodness-of-fit showed that rates of twin births were lower among women who were vegans than among women in the general population.

Step 1: Identify the populations, distribution, and assumptions.

There are always two populations when conducting a chi-square test, one population that matches the frequencies of participants in cells like those we observed and another population that matches the frequencies of participants in cells like what we would expect according to the null hypothesis. In the current case, we'd have a population of vegan recent mothers like those we observed and a population of vegan recent mothers like those in the general population. The comparison distribution is the chi-square distribution. When there's just one nominal variable, we'll conduct a chi-square test for goodness-of-fit.

The first assumption is that the variable of interest is nominal. The second assumption is that each observation must be independent of all of the other observations. This means that no single participant can be in more than one category. The third assumption is that participants should be randomly selected. If not, we will be limited in our ability to generalize beyond our sample. Finally, the fourth assumption is that there should be a minimum number of expected participants in every cell. A common guideline is that the minimum expected frequency in each cell should be no lower than 5 (or, preferably, 10). However, an alternative guideline (Delucchi, 1983) suggests that there should be at least five times as many participants as cells. The chi-square tests seem robust to violations of this third assumption. For many students, the practical consequence of both these guidelines is to be sure to have as many randomly selected observations (usually people in social science experiments) as you can. Every study requires a great deal of work at many different levels, and we don't want to undermine our own efforts by not having enough participants.

Summary: Population 1 is vegans who recently gave birth like those whom we observed. Population 2 is vegans who recently gave birth who are like the general population of mostly nonvegans.

The comparison distribution is a chi-square distribution. The hypothesis test will be a chi-square test for goodness-of-fit because we have one nominal variable only. This study meets three of the four assumptions. The one variable is nominal. Every participant is in only one cell [a vegan woman is not counted as having twins *and* as having a singleton (one child)]. There are far more than five times as many participants as cells (there are 1042 participants and only 2 cells). The participants were not, however, randomly selected. We learn from the published research paper that participants were recruited with the assistance of "various vegan societies." This limits our ability to generalize beyond women like those in our sample.

Step 2: State the null and research hypotheses.

For chi-square tests, it's easiest to simply state the hypotheses in words, rather than in both words and symbols.

Summary: Null hypothesis: Vegan women give birth to twins at the same rate as the general population.

Research hypothesis: Vegan women give birth to twins at a different rate from the general population.

Step 3: Determine the characteristics of the comparison distribution.

Our only task at this step is to determine the degrees of freedom. In most previous hypothesis tests, the degrees of freedom have been based on sample size. For the chi-square hypothesis tests, however, the degrees of freedom are based on the numbers of categories, or cells, in which participants can be counted. The degrees of freedom for chi square is the number of categories minus 1: $df_{\chi^2} = k - 1$. Here, k is the symbol for the number of categories. In the situation with the vegan mothers, there are only two categories. Each mother either had one child (a singleton) or twins: $df_{\chi^2} = 2 - 1 = 1$.

Symbol: k

Formula: $df_{\chi^2} = k - 1$

TABLE 13-3. EXCERPT FROM THE χ^2 TABLE

We use the χ^2 table to determine critical values for a given p level, based on the degrees of freedom.

df	PROPORTION IN CRITICAL REGION		
	.10	0.05	0.01
1	2.71	3.84	6.64
2	4.61	5.99	9.21
3	6.25	7.82	11.35
.			
.			
.			

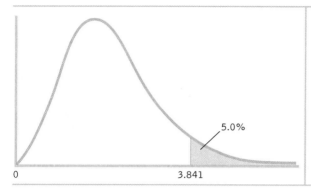

FIGURE 13-1
Determining the Cutoff for a Chi-Square Statistic

We look up the critical value for a chi-square statistic, based on a certain p level and degrees of freedom, in the chi-square table. Because the chi-square statistic is squared, it is never negative, so there is only one critical value.

Summary: The comparison distribution is the chi-square distribution, which has 1 degree of freedom: $df_{\chi^2} = 2 - 1 = 1$.

Step 4: Determine critical values, or cutoffs.

To determine the cutoff, or critical value, for the chi-square statistic, we use— you guessed it—the chi-square table. Like the cutoff for F used in ANOVA, there is only one critical value for chi square. Both F and χ^2 are based on squares and can never be negative, so there is just one critical value even for a two-tailed test. The chi-square table is perhaps the simplest of all of the tables in which we look up cutoffs and we provided you with an excerpt from Appendix B in Table 13-3 that applies to this particular finding. We look under the p level that we're using, usually 0.05, and across from our degrees of freedom, in this case, 1. For this situation, our cutoff chi-square statistic is 3.841.

Summary: Our cutoff χ^2, based on a p level of 0.05 and 1 degree of freedom, is 3.841, as seen in the curve in Figure 13-1. (*Note:* It is helpful to include a drawing of the chi-square distribution in your answers to exercises; indicate the cutoff χ^2 on the drawing.)

Step 5: Calculate the test statistic.

To calculate a chi-square statistic, we first determine our observed frequencies and our expected frequencies, as seen in Table 13-4. The expected frequencies are determined from the information we have about the general population. We know that in the general population, 1.9% of births are twins, a proportion of 0.019. Of the 1042 vegan mothers in the study, therefore, we would expect to find that they gave birth to $(0.019)(1042) = 19.798$ sets of twins if these mothers are no different from the general population of mothers. We also know that in the general population, $100 - 1.9 = 98.1\%$, or 0.981, of births are singletons. So we would expect to find that the vegan mothers gave birth to $(0.981)(1042) = 1022.202$ singletons if they are no different from the general population of mothers.

We want to point out two things about the expected frequencies. First, of course, we cannot actually have 19.798 or 1022.202 births; but this is fine for our purposes. The expected frequencies will often include decimals, even though it doesn't make sense to have a fraction of a person. Second, the two (or more) expected frequencies will always add up to the total number of participants in the study. Try it:

TABLE 13-4. OBSERVED FREQUENCIES AND EXPECTED FREQUENCIES

The first step in calculating the chi-square statistic is creating two tables, one with cells that display the observed frequencies of births among vegan mothers and one with cells that display the expected frequencies.

OBSERVED (among vegan mothers)	
SINGLETON	TWINS
1038	4

EXPECTED (based on the general population)	
SINGLETON	TWINS
1022.202	19.798

TABLE 13-5. THE CHI-SQUARE CALCULATIONS

As with many other statistics, we calculate the chi-square statistic using columns to keep track of our work. We calculate the difference between the observed frequency and the expected frequency, square the difference, then divide each square by its appropriate expected frequency. Finally, we add up the numbers in the sixth column, and that's our chi-square statistic.

CATEGORY	OBSERVED (O)	EXPECTED (E)	$O - E$	$(O - E)^2$	$\dfrac{(O - E)^2}{E}$
Singleton	1038	1022.202	15.798	249.577	0.244
Twins	4	19.798	−15.798	249.577	12.606

$19.798 + 1022.202 = 1042$. This is a good check on our calculations, as is merely considering whether the numbers make sense.

If we can eyeball the difference between the observed frequencies and the expected frequencies, then we can see that the vegan mothers had fewer sets of twins than did the mothers in the general population. But are the observed frequencies different enough from the expected frequencies that we're willing to conclude that this did *not* happen by chance? As usual, that's why we conduct hypothesis testing, and that's why we calculate a test statistic to compare with our critical value.

The next step in calculating our chi-square statistic is to determine the differences between each observed frequency and its matching expected frequency. This is usually done in columns, and we'll use this format even though we have only two categories. The first three columns of Table 13-5 show us the categories, observed frequencies, and expected frequencies, respectively. The fourth column displays the differences. As in the past, if we add up the differences, they'll cancel out because some are positive and some are negative. So we use our usual trick of squaring them. The fifth column shows the squared differences. Finally, we divide each squared difference by the expected value for its cell, as seen in the sixth column.

As an example, here are the calculations for the category "twins":

$$O - E = (4 - 19.798) = -15.798$$

$$(O - E)^2 = (-15.798)^2 = 249.577$$

$$\frac{(O = E)^2}{E} = \frac{249.577}{19.798} = 12.606$$

Once we have our table completed, the last step is easy. We just add up the numbers in the sixth column. In this case, our chi-square statistic is $0.244 + 12.606 = 12.85$. We can finish our formula by adding a summation sign to the formula in the sixth column. The formula for chi square is

Formula: $\chi^2 = \Sigma \left[\dfrac{(O - E)^2}{E} \right]$

$$\chi^2 = \Sigma \left[\frac{(O - E)^2}{E} \right]$$

Summary: $\chi^2 = \Sigma \left[\dfrac{(O - E)^2}{E} \right] = (0.244 + 12.606) = 12.85$ (*Note:* It is helpful to include all calculations in your summary.)

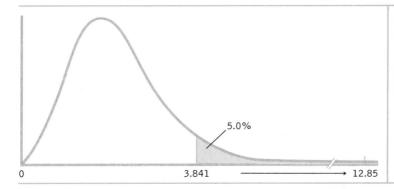

FIGURE 13-2
Making a Decision

As with other hypothesis tests, we make a decision with a chi-square test by comparing our test statistic to the cutoff, or critical value. 12.85 would be *far* to the right of 3.841.

Step 6: Make a decision.

This step is identical to that for every other hypothesis test we've encountered. We reject the null hypothesis if our test statistic is beyond the critical value, and we fail to reject the null hypothesis if our test statistic is not beyond the critical value. In this case, our test statistic, 12.85, is beyond the cutoff, 3.841, as seen in Figure 13-2. So we reject the null hypothesis. There are only two categories, so it's clear where the difference lies. It appears that vegan mothers are less likely to have twins than are mothers in the general population. (If we had failed to reject the null hypothesis, we could only have concluded that these data did not provide sufficient evidence to conclude that vegan mothers have a different likelihood of having twins from mothers in the general population.)

Summary: Reject the null hypothesis; it appears that vegan mothers are less likely to have twins than are mothers in the general population.

The statistics, as reported in a journal article, follow almost the same format that we've seen previously. We report the degrees of freedom, the value of the test statistic, and whether the p value associated with the test statistic was less than or greater than the cutoff based on the p level of 0.05. In addition, we report the sample size within the parentheses with degrees of freedom. In the current example, the statistics would read: $\chi^2(1, N = 1042) = 12.85, p < 0.05$.

A More Typical Chi-Square Test for Goodness-of-Fit: Evenly Divided Expected Frequencies

In the vegan mother example, the expected data were 1.9% in one category and 98.1% in another. We chose this example for a reason. We wanted to demonstrate that we cannot simply divide the number of participants by 2 (or 3 if there are three categories, or 4 if there are four categories, etc.) and use that as our expected frequency for each cell. In the above situation, it would not have made sense to expect 50% of vegans to have had twins! This would be so far above the rate in the general population as to be ridiculous. In the everyday reality of research, there are many circumstances in which our expected data are not divided evenly among categories. It's always important to carefully examine each specific situation to determine what the correct expected data are. Let's look at another situation that exemplifies the more typical case for chi-square goodness-of-fit, in which the expected data simply reflect a division among all possible categories.

Gero Breloer/dpa/Corbis

Are Elite Soccer Players Born in the Early Months of the Year?
Dubner and Levitt (2006) reported that elite soccer players are far more likely to be born in the first three months of the year than in the last three months of the year. Based on data on elite German youth soccer players, a chi-square test goodness-of-fit test showed a significant effect: players were significantly more likely to be born in the first three months than in the last three months of the year.

Dubner and Levitt (2006) reported that the best soccer players in the world were more likely to have been born early in the year than later. As one example, they reported that 52 elite youth players in Germany (those on the national youth teams and from which the World Cup players are frequently drawn) were born in January, February, or March, whereas only 4 players were born in October, November, or December. These are the observed data: 52 of these players were born in the first quarter of the year and 4 were born in the last quarter of the year.

What would you expect just by chance? That is, what would you expect according to the null hypothesis? Here, the null hypothesis would be that the time of year in which one was born did *not* affect one's likelihood of becoming an elite soccer player. (The research hypothesis would be that the time of year in which one was born *would* affect one's likelihood of becoming an elite soccer player.) Given an assumption that births are evenly distributed across the months of the year, the null hypothesis would posit equal numbers, or frequencies, of elite soccer players born in the first three months and the last three months. There are 56 participants in this study (52 born in the first three months and 4 in the last three months), so equal frequencies would mean that we would expect 28 in the first three months and 28 in the last three months just by chance. We won't conduct the chi-square test, but you could probably guess the outcome. In fact, this has a whopping chi-square statistic of 41.14—well higher than the relevant critical value.

As always, however, we must remember that when we do not randomly assign participants to conditions, we cannot assume causality. And, of course, these players' parents were not assigned to conceive their children at particular times of the year. Dubner and Levitt (2006) ask why this association might occur and offer four ideas: "a) certain astrological signs confer superior soccer skills; b) winter-born babies tend to have higher oxygen capacity, which increases soccer stamina; c) soccer-mad parents are more likely to conceive children in springtime, at the annual peak of soccer mania; d) none of the above." What's your guess?

Dubner and Levitt (2006) pick (d) and offer one possible answer. They cite work by psychologist Anders Ericsson, who has shown in numerous studies that "expert performers" are likely "made, not born." There is, Ericsson would say, some degree of innate talent requisite for elite status. But without outside influences and internal motivation, that talent is unlikely to translate into superiority. How does this fit with soccer and birth dates? Dubner and Levitt report that the various levels of soccer leagues have age limits and the cutoff date for each of these leagues is December 31. Those born in January, almost a year before the cutoff, are likely to be physically larger and psychologically more mature than their counterparts born 11 months later in December, just before the cutoff. The January players are more likely to be chosen for the best soccer leagues and therefore are more likely to receive the kind of practice and feedback that leads to superiority. All this from a simple chi-square test!

In summary, the chi-square tests are used when the variable or variables are nominal. The chi-square test for goodness-of-fit is used with one nominal variable; technically, therefore, there is neither an independent variable nor a dependent variable. We simply see whether participants fit into levels of one categorical variable as we would expect them to just by chance. The chi-square test for independence is used with two nominal variables; usually one can be designated as the independent variable and one as the dependent variable. Both chi-square hypothesis tests use the same six steps of hypothesis testing with which we are familiar. As with all research, if participants are not randomly assigned to conditions, we cannot assume causality from an association.

⊙ CHECK YOUR LEARNING

13-2 In the example above, we saw that 52 elite German youth soccer players were born in the first three months of the year and only 4 were born in the last three months of the year. We presented a chi-square statistic, 41.14, but did not conduct the steps of hypothesis testing or show the calculations. Conduct all six steps of a chi-square test for goodness-of-fit for this example.

> CHI-SQUARE TEST FOR INDEPENDENCE: WHEN WE HAVE TWO NOMINAL VARIABLES

Pearson developed the chi-square statistic to extend the insights of statistics to non-normal distributions, but he was never able to apply its logic of a good fit to his own life. He could be enormously helpful to colleagues who supported him, but if he suspected disloyalty, he could be vindictive and petty. His most bitter fight was with the equally combative statistician Ronald Aylmer Fisher. Fisher turned down a prestigious university appointment because it required that he subordinate himself to Pearson. Instead, Fisher created a scientific laboratory in a distant agricultural station, where he developed most of the enduring experimental designs that continue to guide researchers across all the sciences. These two brilliant men defined the meaning of statistics and experimental design during a critical period in the history of science, yet they couldn't stand the sight of each other.

Their differences are partly revealed by how they treated their colleagues. Although Pearson inspired appreciation from his many female assistants (who had few other opportunities for scientific research), he also "recognized that he could hire the same level of competence for a lower salary, and get greater loyalty or at least continuity into the bargain, by recruiting women" (Porter, 2004, p. 274). When Beatrice Cave asked Pearson to release her from her contract so she could accept a better position, he accused her of disloyalty. When she agreed to stay on a little longer, he went to the provost and terminated her contract. Fisher, by contrast, treated his colleagues more graciously. He was unemployed and almost unemployable when he finally received the offer to work under Pearson. But Pearson insisted on approving everything that Fisher would teach and publish, so Fisher turned down the financial security, prestige, and opportunities associated with a university position, opting for a six-month position at the Rothamsted agricultural station.

Fortunately, Fisher's genius was quickly recognized, and as the laboratory slowly grew, he treated his colleagues with a respect he had not received from Pearson. When the first female scientist, Miss W. Benchley, was hired at his laboratory in 1906, the five male scientists already on staff were uncertain how to behave and, in typical English fashion, immediately instituted afternoon tea. Afternoon tea soon became a pleasant ritual, now made famous in Salsburg's (2001) *The Lady Tasting Tea*, in honor of Fisher's experiment to test Dr. Muriel Bristol's claim that she could taste whether tea or cream had first been poured into a tea cup. Fisher was the quintessential warm-hearted, absent-minded professor, spilling his scientific opinions on his listeners as freely as he spilled pipe tobacco on his clothes. He reserved most of his anger and bitterness for Karl Pearson.

Fisher's biographer and daughter, statistician Joan Box (1978), asserts that Fisher saw Pearson as an out-of-touch, self-promoting, often careless academic. She also suggests that Pearson perceived Fisher as misguided and disloyal to the grander mission of discovering and articulating the rules of science. Pearson was journal editor and head of the laboratory established by his mentor, Francis Galton (Darwin's cousin). At various times, Pearson refused to publish Fisher's papers, modified them substantially, or took credit for them almost entirely. When Fisher replaced Pearson at the Galton laboratories, he physically removed reminders of Pearson, including Pearson's collection of skulls. So Pearson's dismal prophecy about his own life came true: most students today only know of "Pearson's" correlation coefficient; they are unaware of the conflicted personality behind the symbol.

Pearson's legacy is not what he hoped for. His image of cold rationality does not fit with the "hot rationality" of John Snow walking through cholera-stricken neighborhoods to discover a correlation, the "impassioned statistician" Florence Nightingale creating life-saving graphs, or the thousands of social science professors who year after year conduct research despite minimal financial support while fulfilling extensive teaching responsibilities. Pearson's legacy urges students to ask themselves about the goodness-of-fit between their own ambitions and how well the modern social sciences can satisfy those ambitions.

The idea of goodness-of-fit is also at the heart of statistical tests, such as the chi square, which evaluate the goodness-of-fit between theory and observation. Specifically, the chi-square test for independence allows researchers to study more than one nominal variable at a time, and Cramer's *V* statistic is way to estimate effect sizes for chi square. Finally, graphing percentages adds visual clarity to the logic of chi square, especially as we use the chi-square statistic to estimate the probability of any particular outcome. But all of these statistical tools are only useful when they can accommodate the complexity of the personalities and circumstances we are hoping to analyze.

Chi-Square Test for Independence: The Six Steps of Hypothesis Testing

Chi-square tests for goodness-of-fit are limited by their ability to analyze just one nominal variable. Their slightly more complicated counterpart, the chi-square test for independence, enables us to analyze two nominal variables. When we have two nominal variables, we can often identify one as the independent and one as the dependent variable. For example, in the study on IVF pregnancy rates with and without clown therapy (Rockwell, 2006), we would identify clown therapy (clown versus no clown) as the independent variable and IVF outcome (becoming pregnant versus not becoming pregnant) as the dependent variable. It makes sense that an eventual pregnancy might depend on whether or not a clown is present but does not make sense that the presence of a clown might depend on an eventual pregnancy.

With the chi-square test for independence, however, we do not have to identify a specific independent and dependent variable. Like the correlation coefficient, the chi-square statistic will be identical even if we switch the independent variable and dependent variable. The main reason we identify a specific independent variable and dependent variable is to help us understand the hypothesis that inspired this particular research design in the first place. The chi-square test for independence is so named because we are trying to determine whether the two variables—no matter which one we consider to be the independent variable—are independent of one another. Here, we'll ask whether pregnancy rates are independent of (that is, depend) on whether one is entertained by a clown post-IVF treatment.

In the clown study reported by the mass media (Ryan, 2006), 186 women were randomly assigned to receive IVF treatment only or to receive IVF treatment followed by 15 minutes of clown entertainment. Eighteen out of 93 who received IVF treatment only became pregnant, whereas 33 of the 93 who received both IVF treatment and clown entertainment became pregnant. The cells for these observed frequencies are in Table 13-6. The table of cells for a chi-square test for independence is called a contingency table because we are trying to see if the outcome of one variable (e.g., becoming pregnant versus not becoming pregnant) is contingent upon the other variable (clown versus no clown). Let's implement the six steps of hypothesis testing for a chi-square test for independence.

Clown Therapy
Israeli researchers tested whether entertainment by a clown led to higher pregnancy rates after in vitro fertilization treatment. Their study had two nominal variables—entertainment (clown, no clown) and pregnancy (pregnant, not pregnant)—and could have been analyzed with a chi-square test for independence.

Step 1: Identify the populations, distribution, and assumptions.

Population 1 is women receiving IVF treatment like those whom we observed. Population 2 is women receiving IVF treatment for whom the presence of a clown is not associated with eventual pregnancy.

The comparison distribution is a chi-square distribution. The hypothesis test will be a chi-square test for independence because we have two nominal variables. This study meets three of the four assumptions. The two variables are nominal; every participant is in only one cell; and there are more than five times as many participants as cells (186 participants and 4 cells). The participants were not, however, randomly selected from the population of all women undergoing IVF treatment. We must be cautious in generalizing beyond the sample of Israeli women at this particular hospital.

Step 2: State the null and research hypotheses.

Null hypothesis: Pregnancy rates are independent of whether one is entertained by a clown after IVF treatment.

Research hypothesis: Pregnancy rates depend on whether one is entertained by a clown after IVF treatment.

Step 3: Determine the characteristics of the comparison distribution.

For a chi-square test for independence, we calculate degrees of freedom for each variable and then multiply the two to get the overall degrees of freedom. The degrees of freedom for the variable in the rows of the contingency table is

TABLE 13-6. OBSERVED PREGNANCY RATES

This table depicts the cells and their frequencies for the study on whether entertainment by a clown is associated with pregnancy rates among women undergoing in vitro fertilization.

	OBSERVED	
	PREGNANT	NOT PREGNANT
Clown	33	60
No Clown	18	75

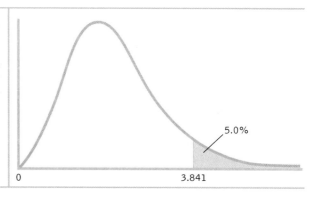

FIGURE 13-3
The Cutoff for a Chi-Square Test for Independence

The shaded region is beyond the critical value for a chi-square test for independence with a *p* level of 0.05 and 1 degree of freedom. If the test statistic falls within this shaded area, we will reject the null hypothesis.

5.0%

0   3.841

Formula:

$$df_{\chi^2} = (k_{Row} - 1)(k_{Column} - 1)$$

$df_{Row} = k_{Row} - 1$. The degrees of freedom for the variable in the columns of the contingency table is $df_{Column} = k_{Column} - 1$. And then the overall degrees of freedom is $df_{\chi^2} = (df_{Row})(df_{Column})$. To expand this last formula, we write $df_{\chi^2} = (k_{Row} - 1)(k_{Column} - 1)$.

The comparison distribution is the chi-square distribution, which has 1 degree of freedom: $df_{\chi^2} = (k_{Row} - 1)(k_{Column} - 1) = (2 - 1)(2 - 1) = 1$.

Step 4: Determine critical values, or cutoffs.

Our critical value, or cutoff χ^2, based on a *p* level of 0.05 and 1 degree of freedom, is 3.841. (*Note:* It is helpful to include a drawing of the chi-square distribution with the cutoff, as seen in Figure 13-3.)

Step 5: Calculate the test statistic.

The next step, the determination of the appropriate expected frequencies, is the most important in the calculation of the chi-square test for independence. Errors commonly occur in this step, and if the wrong expected frequencies are used, the chi-square statistic derived from them will also be wrong. Many students want to divide the total number of participants (here, 186) by 4 and place equivalent frequencies in all cells for the expected data. Here, that would mean that the expected frequencies would be 46.5. But this would not make sense. Of the 186 women, only 51 became pregnant; 51/186 = 0.274, or 27.4%, of these women became pregnant. If pregnancy rates do not depend on clown entertainment, then we would expect the same percentage of successful pregnancies, 27.4%, regardless of exposure to clowns. If we have expected frequencies of 46.5 in all four cells, then we have a 50%, not a 27.4%, pregnancy rate. We must always consider the specifics of our situation.

In the current study, we have already calculated that 27.4% of women who received IVF treatment became pregnant. If pregnancy rates are independent of whether a woman is entertained by a clown, then we would expect 27.4% of the women who were entertained by a clown to become pregnant and 27.4% of women who were not entertained by a clown to become pregnant. Based on this percentage, 100 − 27.4 = 72.6% of women did not become pregnant. We would expect, therefore, that 72.6% of women who were entertained by a clown to fail to become pregnant and 72.6% of women who were not entertained by a clown to fail to become pregnant. Again, we're expecting the same pregnancy and nonpregnancy rates in both groups—those who were and were not entertained by clowns.

Table 13-7 shows our observed data once again, now with totals for each row, each column, and the whole table.

From Table 13-7, we see that 93 women were entertained by a clown after IVF treatment. As we calculated above, we would expect 27.4% of them to become pregnant: (0.274)(93) = 25.482. There were 93 women who were not

TABLE 13-7. OBSERVED FREQUENCIES WITH TOTALS

This table includes the observed frequencies for each of the four cells, along with row totals (93, 93), column totals (51, 135), and the grand total for the whole table (186).

	OBSERVED		
	PREGNANT	NOT PREGNANT	
Clown	33	60	93
No Clown	18	75	93
	51	135	186

TABLE 13-8. EXPECTED FREQUENCIES WITH TOTALS

This table includes the expected frequencies for each of the four cells. The expected frequencies should still add up to the row totals (93, 93), column totals (51, 135), and the grand total for the whole table (186).

	EXPECTED		
	PREGNANT	NOT PREGNANT	
Clown	25.482	67.518	93
No Clown	25.482	67.518	93
	51	135	186

entertained by a clown, and we would expect 27.4% of them to become pregnant if clowning is independent of pregnancy rates: $(0.274)(93) = 25.482$. We now repeat the same procedure for not becoming pregnant. We would expect that 72.6% of women in both groups to fail to become pregnant. For the women who were entertained by a clown, we would expect $(0.726)(93) = 67.518$ nonpregnancies. For the women who were not entertained by a clown, we would expect $(0.726)(93) = 67.518$ nonpregnancies. (Note that the two expected frequencies for the first row are the same as the two expected frequencies for the second row; this occurred only because there were the same number of people in each clown condition, 93. Were these numbers different, we would not see the same frequencies in the two rows.)

The way of calculating the expected frequencies that we described above is ideal because it is directly based on our own thinking about the frequencies in the rows and in the columns. Sometimes, however, our thinking can get muddled, particularly when the two (or more) row totals do not match and the two (or more) column totals do not match. For these situations, there is a simple rubric that will lead to accurate expected frequencies. For each cell, we divide its column total ($Total_{Column}$) by the grand total (N) and multiply that by the row total ($Total_{Row}$):

$$\frac{Total_{Column}}{N}(Total_{Row}).$$

As an example, the observed frequency of those who became pregnant and were entertained by a clown is 33. The row total for this cell is 93. The column total is 51. The grand total, N, is 186. The expected frequency, therefore, is:

$\frac{Total_{Column}}{N}(Total_{Row}) = \frac{51}{186}(93) = (0.274)(93) = 25.482$. Notice that this is identical to what we calculate without a formula. The middle step above shows that, even with the formula, we actually did calculate the pregnancy rate overall, by dividing the column total (51) by the grand total (186). We then calculated how many in that row of 93 participants we would expect to get pregnant using this overall rate: $(0.274)(93) = 25.482$. The formula follows our logic, but it also keeps us on track when there are multiple calculations.

As a final check on our calculations, shown in Table 13-8, we can add up the frequencies to be sure that they still match the row, column, and grand totals. For example, if we add the two numbers in the first column, 25.482 and 25.482, we get 50.964 (different from 51 only because of rounding decisions). If we had

Formula: Expected frequency for each cell $= \dfrac{Total_{Column}}{N}(Total_{Row})$, where we use the overall number of participants, N, along with the totals for the rows and columns for each particular cell.

TABLE 13-9. THE CHI-SQUARE CALCULATIONS

For the calculations for the chi-square test for independence, we use the same format as we did for the chi-square test for goodness-of-fit. We calculate the difference between the observed frequency and the expected frequency, square the difference, then divide each square by its appropriate expected frequency. Finally, we add up the numbers in the last column, and that's our chi-square statistic.

CATEGORY	OBSERVED (O)	EXPECTED (E)	$O - E$	$(O - E)^2$	$\dfrac{(O - E)^2}{E}$
Clown; pregnant	33	25.482	7.518	56.520	2.218
Clown; not pregnant	60	67.518	−7.518	56.520	0.837
No clown; pregnant	18	25.482	−7.482	55.980	2.197
No clown; not pregnant	75	67.518	7.482	55.980	0.829

made the mistake of dividing the 186 participants into cells by dividing by 4, we would have had 46.5 in each cell; then the total for the first column would have been 46.5 + 46.5 = 93, not a match with 51. This final check will ensure that we have the appropriate expected frequencies in the cells.

The remainder of the fifth step is identical to that for a chi-square test for goodness-of-fit, as seen in Table 13-9. As before, we calculate the difference between each observed frequency and its matching expected frequency, square these differences, and divide each squared difference by the appropriate expected frequency. We add up the numbers in the final column of our table to calculate our chi-square statistic: $\chi^2 = \Sigma \left[\dfrac{(O - E)^2}{E} \right] = (2.218 + 0.837 + 2.197 + 0.829) = 6.081$.

Step 6: Make a decision.

Reject the null hypothesis. It appears that pregnancy rates depend on whether a woman receives clown entertainment following IVF treatment. (*Note*: It is helpful to add the test statistic to the drawing that included the cutoff, as seen in Figure 13-4).

The statistics, as reported in a journal article, would follow the format we learned for a chi-square test for goodness-of-fit as well as for other hypothesis tests in earlier chapters. We report the degrees of freedom and sample size, the value of the test statistic, and whether the *p* value associated with the test statistic was less than or greater than the critical value based on the *p* level of 0.05. In the current example, the statistics would read: $\chi^2(1, N = 186) = 6.08$, $p < 0.05$.

FIGURE 13-4
The Decision

Because the chi-square statistic, 6.081, is beyond the critical value, 3.841, we can reject the null hypothesis. It is unlikely that the pregnancy rates for those who received clown therapy versus those who did not were this different from each other just by chance.

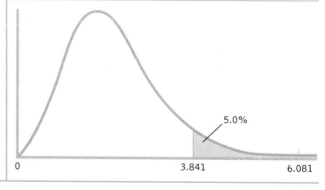

Cramer's *V*: The Effect Size for Chi Square

Like all hypothesis tests, the chi-square hypothesis tests have limitations. A hypothesis test tells us only that there is a likely effect—that the observed effect was unlikely to have occurred merely by chance if the null hypothesis were true. But a hypothesis test, including those based on the chi-square statistic, does not tell us how large an effect there is. We have to calculate an additional statistic, an effect size, before we can make claims about the importance of a study's finding.

Cramer's **V**, *also called* ***Cramer's phi***, *symbolized as ϕ (pronounce "fie"—rhymes with fly), is the standard effect size used with the chi-square test for independence.* Once we have calculated our test statistic, it is easy to calculate Cramer's V by hand. The formula is

Symbol: Cramer's *V*
Symbol: Cramer's ϕ

$$\text{Cramer's } V = \sqrt{\frac{\chi^2}{(N)(df_{Row/Column})}}$$

where χ^2 is the test statistic we just calculated, N is the total number of participants in the study (the lower-right number in the contingency table), and $df_{Row/Column}$ is to the degrees of freedom for either the category in the rows or the category in the columns, whichever is smaller. For the clown example, we calculated a chi-square statistic of 6.081, there were 186 participants, and the degrees of freedom for both categories were 1. When neither degrees of freedom is smaller than the other, of course, it doesn't matter which one we choose. Our effect size for the clown study, therefore, is

Formula:

$$\text{Cramer's } V = \sqrt{\frac{\chi^2}{(N)(df_{Row/Column})}}$$

$$\text{Cramer's } V = \sqrt{\frac{\chi^2}{(N)(df_{Row/Column})}} = \sqrt{\frac{6.081}{(186)(1)}} = \sqrt{0.033} = 0.181.$$

Now that we have our effect size, what does it mean? As with other effect sizes, Jacob Cohen (1992) has developed guidelines, shown in Table 13-10, for determining whether a particular effect is small, medium, or large. The guidelines vary based on the size of the contingency table. When the smaller of the two degrees of freedom for the row and column is 1, we use the guidelines in the second column. When the smaller of the two degrees of freedom is 2, we use the guidelines in the third column. And when it is 3, we use the guidelines in the fourth column. As with the other guidelines for judging effect sizes, such as those for Cohen's d, the guidelines are not cutoffs. Rather, they are rough indicators to help researchers gauge a finding's importance.

Our effect size for the clowning and pregnancy study was 0.18. The smaller of the two degrees of freedom, that for the row and that for the column, was 1 (in fact, both were 1). So we use the second column in Table 13-10. Our Cramer's V falls about halfway between the effect-size guidelines for a small effect (0.10)

TABLE 13-10. CONVENTIONS FOR DETERMINING EFFECT SIZE BASED ON CRAMER'S *V*

Jacob Cohen (1992) developed guidelines to determine whether particular effect sizes should be considered small, medium, or large. The effect-size guidelines vary depending on the size of the contingency table. There are different guidelines based on whether the smaller of the two degrees of freedom (row or column) is 1, 2, or 3.

EFFECT SIZE	WHEN $df_{ROW/COLUMN} = 1$	WHEN $df_{ROW/COLUMN} = 2$	WHEN $df_{ROW/COLUMN} = 3$
Small	0.10	0.07	0.06
Medium	0.30	0.21	0.17
Large	0.50	0.35	0.29

and a medium effect (0.30). We would call this a small-to-medium effect. We can build on our report of the statistics by adding the Cramer's V to the end: $\chi^2(1) = 6.08$, $p < 0.05$, Cramer's $V = 0.18$.

Graphing Chi-Square Percentages: Depicting the Relation Visually

In addition to calculating a Cramer's V, we also can graph our data. A visual depiction of the pattern of results is an effective way to understand the size of the relation between two variables assessed using the chi-square statistic. We cannot just graph the frequencies, however, for the same reason that we cannot just divide the total number of participants evenly into the cells for expected frequencies. If one group (say, individuals who were entertained by a clown) were much larger than the other group (individuals not entertained by a clown), it would not be surprising that the first group had more pregnancies; there would be more women who could possibly get pregnant in the first place.

Instead, we graph proportions or percentages. For the women entertained by a clown, we calculate the proportion who became pregnant and the proportion who did not. For the women not entertained by a clown, we again calculate the proportion who became pregnant and the proportion who did not. In each case, we're dividing the number of women with a given outcome by the total number of women in that group. The proportions are called conditional proportions because we're not calculating the proportions out of all women in the study; we're calculating proportions of women in a certain condition. We calculate the proportion of women who became pregnant, for example, conditional on their having been entertained by a clown:

Entertained by a clown

Became pregnant: 33/93 = 0.355

Did not become pregnant: 60/93 = 0.645

Not entertained by a clown

Became pregnant: 18/93 = 0.194

Did not become pregnant: 75/93 = 0.806

We can put those proportions into a table, as shown in Table 13-11. For each category of entertainment (clown, no clown), the proportions should add up to 1.00; if we used percentages, they should add up to 100%.

TABLE 13-11. CONDITIONAL PROPORTIONS

To construct a graph depicting the results of a chi-square test for independence, we first calculate conditional proportions. For example, we calculate the proportions of women who got pregnant, conditional on having been entertained by a clown post-IVF: 33/93 = 0.355.

	CONDITIONAL PROPORTIONS		
	PREGNANT	NOT PREGNANT	
Clown	0.355	0.645	1.00
No Clown	0.194	0.806	1.00

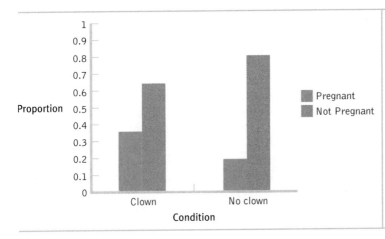

FIGURE 13-5
Graphing and Chi Square

When we graph the data for a chi-square test for independence, we graph conditional proportions rather than frequencies. The proportions allow us to compare the rates at which women became pregnant in the two conditions.

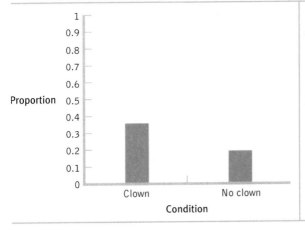

FIGURE 13-6
A Simpler Graph of Conditional Probabilities

Because the rates at which women did not become pregnant are based on the rates at which they did become pregnant, we can simply graph one set of rates. Here we see the rates at which women became pregnant in each of the two clown conditions.

We can now graph our conditional proportions, as in Figure 13-5. Alternately, as in Figure 13-6, we could simply graph the two rates at which women got pregnant—0.355 and 0.194—given that the rates at which they did not become pregnant are based on these rates. In both cases, we include the scale of proportions on the y-axis from 0 to 1.0 so that our graph will not mislead the viewer into thinking the rates are higher than they are.

Relative Risk: How Much Higher Are the Chances of an Outcome?

Another way to think about the size of an effect with chi square is through *relative risk*, *a measure created by making a ratio of two conditional proportions.* (Relative risk is also called *relative likelihood* or *relative chance*.) As when we created Figure 13-5, we calculate the chance of getting pregnant with post-IVF clown entertainment by dividing the number of pregnancies in this group by the total number of women entertained by clowns: 33/93 = 0.355. We then calculate the chance of getting pregnant with no post-IVF clown entertainment by dividing the number of pregnancies in this group by the total number of women not entertained by clowns: 18/93 = 0.194. If we divide the chance of getting pregnant having been entertained by clowns by the chance of getting pregnant not having been entertained by clowns,

▪ **Relative risk** is a measure created by making a ratio of two conditional proportions; also called *relative likelihood* or *relative chance*.

we get a relative likelihood of 0.355/0.194 = 1.804. The chance of getting pregnant when IVF is followed by clown entertainment is 1.80 times the chance of getting pregnant when IVF is not followed by clown entertainment. This matches the impression that we get from Figure 13-5. The bar for the pregnancy rate of women who were entertained by clowns looks to be almost twice as tall as the bar for the pregnancy rate of women who were not entertained by clowns.

Alternately, you can reverse the ratio, dividing the chance of becoming pregnant without clown entertainment, 0.194, by the chance of becoming pregnant following clown entertainment, 0.355. This gives us a relative likelihood of 0.194/0.355 = .55. This number gives us the same information in a different way. The chance of getting pregnant when IVF is followed by no entertainment is 0.55 (or about half) the chance of getting pregnant when IVF is followed by clown entertainment. Again, this matches Figure 13-5; one bar is about half that of the other.

When this simple calculation is made with respect to diseases, rather than a happy outcome like a much-hoped-for pregnancy, it's referred to as relative risk, rather than relative likelihood. You'll often see relative risks reported in the news. For example, *Health and Medicine Week* reported on a study of a lifestyle and dietary education program to prevent diabetes in individuals who were determined to be at high risk for the disease ("Lifestyle Education Reduced," 2006). Compared to those who received no lifestyle education, those in the program had a relative risk of developing diabetes of 0.50. The chance of developing diabetes, therefore, was 50% lower among those in the lifestyle education program.

We should be careful when relative risks are reported, however. We must always be aware of base rates. If, for example, a certain disease occurs in just 0.01% of the population (that is, 1 in 10,000) and is twice as likely to occur among people who eat ice cream, that means that among those who eat ice cream, the rate is just 0.02% (2 in 10,000). Relative risks can be used to scare the general public unnecessarily. Be sure to be clear when you report your own statistics; be careful not to mislead your readers—whether intentionally or unintentionally.

In summary, the six steps of hypothesis testing for the chi-square test for independence are almost identical to those for the chi-square test for goodness-of-fit. The main difference is that more care has to be taken when determining the expected frequencies. After completing the hypothesis test, it is wise to calculate an effect size as well. The appropriate effect-size measure for the chi-square test for independence is Cramer's *V*. Jacob Cohen developed guidelines for interpreting Cramer's *V* that depend on the size of the contingency table. We can depict the effect size visually by calculating and graphing conditional proportions so that we can compare the rates of a certain outcome in each of two or more groups. Another way to consider the size of an effect is through relative risk, a ratio of conditional proportions for each of two groups.

⊙ CHECK YOUR LEARNING

13-3 The Chicago Police Department conducted a study comparing two types of lineups for suspect identification: simultaneous lineups and sequential lineups (Mecklenburg, Malpass, & Ebbesen, 2006). In simultaneous lineups, witnesses saw the suspects all at once, either live or in photographs, and then made their selection. In sequential lineups, witnesses saw the people in the lineup one at a time, either live or in photographs, and said yes or no to suspects one at a time. After numerous high-profile cases in which DNA evidence exonerated people who had been convicted, including many on death row, many police departments shifted to sequential lineups in the hope of reducing incorrect identifications. Several previous studies had indicated the superiority of sequential lineups with respect to accuracy. Over one year, three jurisdictions in Illinois compared the two types of lineups. Of 319 simultaneous lineups, 191 led to identification of the suspect, 8 led to identification of another person in the lineup, and 120 led to no identification. Of 229 sequential lineups, 102 led to identification of the suspect, 20 led to identification of another person in the lineup, and 107 led to no identification.

a. Who or what would the participants in this study be? Identify the independent variable and its levels as well as the dependent variable and its levels.

b. Conduct all six steps of hypothesis testing.

c. Calculate the appropriate measure of effect size for this study.

d. Report the statistics as you would in a journal article.

e. Why is this study an example of the importance of using two-tailed rather than one-tailed hypothesis tests?

■ DIGGING DEEPER INTO THE DATA: A DEEPER UNDERSTANDING OF CHI SQUARE

Hypothesis tests based on the chi-square statistic are among the simplest to compute by hand. Despite their simplicity, however, there are several more sophisticated ways to think about chi square. First, we'll consider a method to determine which observed cell frequencies are likely to be different from their corresponding expected cell frequencies. Second, we'll explore the debate about the minimum expected frequencies necessary to conduct a chi-square hypothesis test. We introduced the controversy earlier, but we will explore it more in depth here.

Standardized Residuals: A Post-Hoc Test for Chi Square

When we discussed ANOVAs, we observed that a significant hypothesis test does not tell us everything we need to know. With ANOVA, when our F statistic is beyond the critical value, we know only that there is a difference somewhere, but not exactly where the difference is. For example, for a one-way ANOVA for which the independent variable has three levels (A, B, C), a significant result might indicate that all three groups are different, that A is different from both B and C (but that B and C are not significantly different), and several other possible patterns. We conduct a post-hoc test to determine exactly which pairs are significantly different.

Chi-square tests, when there are more than two cells, offer a similar problem. A significant chi-square hypothesis test means only that at least some of the cells' observed frequencies are statistically significantly different from their corresponding expected frequencies. We cannot know how many cells or exactly which ones without an additional step, the calculation of an additional set of statistics for each cell based on residuals. A cell's residual is the difference between the expected frequency and the observed frequency for that cell, but we take it a step further. We calculate an ***adjusted standardized residual***, *the difference between the observed frequency and the expected frequency for a cell in a chi-square research design, divided by the standard error*. In other words, an adjusted standardized residual (often called just "adjusted residual" by software and "standardized residual" by

■ An **adjusted standardized residual** is the difference between the observed frequency and the expected frequency for a cell in a chi-square research design, divided by the standard error.

statisticians) is a measure of the number of standard errors that an observed frequency falls from its associated expected frequency.

Does this sound familiar? The adjusted standardized residual is kind of like a z score for each cell (Agresti & Franklin, 2006). A larger adjusted standardized residual indicates that an observed frequency is farther from its expected frequency than is a smaller standardized residual. And like a z score, we're not concerned with the sign. A large positive adjusted standardized residual and a large negative adjusted standardized residual tell us the same thing. If it's large enough, then we're willing to conclude that the observed frequency really is different from what we would expect if the null hypothesis were true—that is, if the two variables were independent of each other.

Also like a z score, anytime a cell has an adjusted standardized residual that is at least 2 (whether the sign is positive or negative), we are willing to conclude that the cell's observed frequency is different from its expected frequency. Some statisticians prefer a more stringent criterion, drawing this conclusion only if an adjusted standardized residual is larger than 3 (again, whether the sign is positive or negative). You may recall that in Chapter 7 we talked about percentages that fell under different parts of the normal distribution. We told you that 96% of all scores fell within 2 standard deviations of the mean on either side and that all (or practically all) scores fell within 3 standard deviations of the mean on either side. Regardless of the criterion used, the method and logic for determining the probabilities of z scores and of adjusted standardized residuals are the same.

Adjusted standardized residuals are too complicated to calculate without the aid of a computer, but we'll show you a software printout of the adjusted standardized residuals for the study of whether entertainment by clowns led to increased pregnancy rates among women post-IVF treatment. Figure 13-7 shows the printout from the SPSS software package. The row labeled "count" includes the observed frequencies. The row labeled "expected count" includes the expected frequencies. The row labeled "adjusted residual" includes the adjusted standardized residuals. So, for example, the upper-left cell is for women who became pregnant following post-IVF entertainment by a clown; the observed frequency for this cell was 33; the expected frequency was 25.5; and the adjusted standardized residual was 2.5. Any adjusted standardized residual greater than 2 or less than −2 indicates that the observed frequency is farther from the expected frequency than we would expect if the two variables were independent of each other. In this case, all four adjusted standardized residuals are either 2.5 or −2.5, so we can conclude that all four observed frequencies are farther from their corresponding expected frequencies than would likely occur if the null hypothesis were true.

FIGURE 13-7
Adjusted Standardized Residuals

Software calculates an adjusted standardized residual, called "adjusted residual" by most software packages, for each cell. It is calculated by taking the residual for each cell, the difference between the observed frequency and expected frequency, and dividing by standard error. When an adjusted standardized residual is greater than 2, we typically conclude that the observed frequency is greater than the expected frequency.

Type of Entertainment* Result of IVF Crosstabulation

			Result of IVF		Total
			pregnant	not pregnant	
Type of Entertainment	Clown	Count	33	60	93
		Expected Count	25.5	67.5	93.0
		Adjusted Residual	2.5	−2.5	
	no clown	Count	18	75	93
		Expected Count	25.5	67.5	93.0
		Adjusted Residual	−2.5	2.5	
Total		Count	51	135	186

Chi-Square Controversies: Expectations About Expected Frequencies

Nonparametric tests, often viewed merely as backups for situations in which we cannot use parametric tests, have been controversial over the last several decades. Some controversies are specific to individual nonparametric hypothesis tests, whereas others pertain to all nonparametric testing. We will introduce the main controversy related to chi-square hypothesis tests here, and then we will discuss other specific controversies in the Digging Deeper into the Data section of the next chapter.

We alluded to the major controversy in chi-square hypothesis tests in the main part of this chapter. When we introduced the assumptions of chi-square hypothesis tests, we provided information on the lowest expected frequencies for each cell that would be permissible with this procedure. There has been a great deal of debate since the days of Pearson, Galton, and Fisher. In fact, Fisher himself suggested that each cell have a minimum expected frequency of 10 (Delucchi, 1983). Over the years, statisticians have suggested anywhere from 1 to 20 as the lowest expected frequency possible to conduct a valid chi-square hypothesis test. The most common suggested minimum expected frequency, however, is 5 per cell (e.g., Lewis & Burke, 1949). (Remember, these recommendations are for the *expected* frequencies, not the *observed* frequencies. There are no suggested minimum observed frequencies.)

Delucchi (1983) conducted a major review of the literature on chi square in an attempt to resolve the controversy. Noting the robustness of chi-square tests in the face of this assumption, Delucchi stated that smaller expected frequencies are not necessarily problematic. For example, he noted several other criteria that can outweigh a small expected value. Both chi-square tests for goodness of fit and chi-square tests of independence are robust, Delucchi said, even if they have small expected values, as long as several criteria are met; for example, the total number of participants should be at least five times the total number of cells and the *average* expected value should be at least 5. Delucchi also cited the even more lenient Cochran's rule, which allows an expected value as low as 1, as long as no more than 20% of the expected values are less than 5.

However, Delucchi (1983) also noted that very small expected frequencies are associated with low statistical power. It becomes harder to reject the null hypothesis (when we should reject it) if expected frequencies are low. This suggests that if we manage to reject the null hypothesis in the face of low expected frequencies, we are likely detecting a fairly large effect, but it raises the risk of a Type II error, failing to reject the null hypothesis when we should.

When conducting your own chi-square hypothesis tests, it is important to consider the sizes of your expected values. If any expected value is below 5, see if you at least meet Cochran's rule. Are no more than 20% of your expected values below 5? Better yet, is the total number of participants more than five times the number of cells? If you can answer yes to both these questions, it is probably safe to proceed with a chi-square test.

In summary, a statistically significant chi-square hypothesis test tells us only that the observed frequencies in at least some cells are farther from their expected frequencies than would occur if the two variables were independent. It does not tell us exactly which cells these are. We must calculate adjusted standardized residuals, the amounts that the observed frequencies are from their corresponding expected frequencies in terms of standard errors. If the absolute value of an adjusted standardized residual is large (greater than 2 or 3, depending on the chosen criterion), then we can conclude that there is a difference. We also encountered a controversy concerning chi square. Some argue that there must be a minimum expected frequency, such as 5, in each cell in order to proceed; others argue that smaller expected frequencies are not problematic if certain criteria are met (e.g., no more than 20% of cells have an expected frequency less than 5).

⊙ CHECK YOUR LEARNING

13-4 In Check Your Learning 13-3, we introduced the example of the Chicago Police Department's study of lineups (Mecklenburg et al., 2006). The accompanying printout from SPSS software shows the data for the six cells.

a. For simultaneous lineups, what is the observed frequency for the identification of suspects?

b. For sequential lineups, what is the expected frequency for the identification of a person other than the suspect?

c. For simultaneous lineups, what is the adjusted standardized residual for cases in which there was no identification? What does this number indicate?

d. If you were to use an adjusted standardized residual criterion of 2 (regardless of the sign), for which cells would you conclude that the difference between observed frequency and expected frequency is greater than you would expect if the two variables were independent?

e. Repeat part (d) for an adjusted standardized residual criterion of 3 (regardless of the sign).

			Type of Lineup		Total
			Simultaneous	sequential	
Identification	Suspect	Count	191	102	293
		Expected Count	170.6	122.4	293.0
		Adjusted Residual	3.5	-3.5	
	another person	Count	8	20	28
		Expected Count	16.3	11.7	28.0
		Adjusted Residual	-3.3	3.3	
	no identification	Count	120	107	227
		Expected Count	132.1	94.9	227.0
		Adjusted Residual	-2.1	2.1	
Total		Count	319	229	548

> Nonparametric Statistics: When We're Not Even Close to Meeting the Assumptions

Nonparametric hypothesis tests are used when we do not meet the assumptions of a parametric test. This often occurs when we have a nominal dependent variable, an ordinal independent or dependent variable, or a small sample in which the data suggest a skewed population distribution. Given the choice, we should use a parametric test because these tests tend to have more statistical power. Moreover, interval variables tend to provide more information than do nominal variables and ordinal variables.

R E V I E W   O F   C O N C E P T S

> Chi-Square Test for Goodness-of-Fit: When We Have One Nominal Variable

When we have a nominal dependent variable, we analyze our data using a chi-square test. We use the *chi-square test for goodness-of-fit* when we have only one variable and it is nominal. We use the *chi-square test for independence* when we have two nominal variables, one of which can usually be thought of as an independent variable and one of which can usually be thought of as a dependent variable. In both cases, we analyze whether the data that we observe match what we would expect according to the null hypothesis. Both tests use the same basic six steps of hypothesis testing that we learned previously.

> Chi-Square Test for Independence: When We Have Two Nominal Variables

We conduct a chi-square test for independence using almost exactly the same six steps that we use for the chi-square test for goodness-of-fit. We usually calculate an effect size as well; the most commonly calculated effect size with chi square is *Cramer's V* also called *Cramer's phi*. We can also create a graph that depicts the conditional proportions of an outcome for each group. Alternately, we can calculate a *relative risk* to more easily compare the rates of certain outcomes in each of two groups.

> Digging Deeper into the Data: A Deeper Understanding of Chi Square

As with ANOVA, when we reject the null hypothesis with a chi-square hypothesis test, we know only that the observed frequencies in at least some cells are farther from their expected frequencies than would occur if the two variables were independent. We do not know, however, exactly which cells these are. We can determine this by calculating *adjusted standardized residuals*, the distances of the observed frequencies from their corresponding expected frequencies in terms of standard errors. If an adjusted standardized residual is large (farther from 0 than 2 or −2, or 3 or −3, depending on the chosen criterion), we can conclude that there is a difference between a cell's observed frequency and its expected frequency. We also presented a controversy related to chi-square hypothesis tests. Some researchers claim that we cannot proceed with this test unless we have a minimum expected frequency, such as 5, in each cell; however, further data suggest that it is fine to proceed with smaller expected frequencies if other criteria are met.

SPSS GUIDELINES FOR CHAPTER 13: CHI SQUARE

Chi-square tests are used when comparing expectations against actual observations. The chi-square test for independence evaluates whether there is a statistically significant relation between two nominal variables. For example, we might want to examine the relation between our participants' ethnicities and whether or not they have experienced discrimination.

In SPSS, we would conduct a chi-square test for independence by selecting:

Analyze → Descriptive Statistics → Crosstabs (select a nominal variable for the row and a nominal variable for the column) → Statistics → Chi-Square and Phi & Cramer's V (for effect sizes). Click continue, and then click "OK" to run the analysis.

We can include more descriptive information, such as percentages, by selecting:

Cells → Any of the options under "Percentages."

We can also compare the observed frequencies to the expected frequencies by selecting:

Cells → Select "Expected" option under "Counts." (Notice that "Observed" is automatically selected.)

EXERCISES

13.1 Type of research design and student evaluations: Weinberg, Fleisher, and Hashimoto (2007) studied almost 50,000 students' evaluations of their professors in almost 400 economics courses at The Ohio State University over a 10-year period. For each of their findings, outlined below, state (i) the independent variable or variables, and their levels where appropriate, (ii) the dependent variable(s), and (iii) what category of research design is being used:

I—interval independent variable(s) and interval dependent variable

II—nominal independent variable(s) and interval dependent variable

III—only nominal variables

Explain your answer to part (iii).

a. The researchers found that students' ratings of their professors were predictive of grades in the class for which the professor was evaluated.

b. The researchers also found that students' ratings of their professors were not predictive of grades for other, related future classes. (The researchers stated that these first two findings suggest that student ratings of professors are tied to their current grades but not to learning—which would affect future grades.)

c. The researchers found that male professors received statistically significantly higher student ratings, on average, than did female professors.

d. The researchers reported, however, that average levels of students learning (as assessed by grades in related future classes) were not statistically significantly different for those who had male and those who had female professors.

e. The researchers might have been interested in whether there were proportionally more female professors teaching upper-level than lower-level courses and proportionally more male professors teaching lower-level than upper-level courses (perhaps a reason for the lower average ratings of female professors).

f. The researchers found no statistically significant differences in average student evaluations among non–tenure-track lecturers, graduate student teaching associates, and tenure-track faculty members.

13.2 Type of research design and grade inflation: A *New York Times* article on grade inflation reported several findings related to a tendency for average grades to rise over the years and a tendency for the top-ranked institutions to give the highest average grades (Archibold, 1998). For each of the findings outlined below, state (i) the independent variable or variables, and their levels where appropriate, (ii) the dependent variable(s), and (iii) what category of research design is being used:

I—interval independent variable(s) and interval dependent variable

II—nominal independent variable(s) and interval dependent variable

III—only nominal variables

Explain your answer to part (iii).

a. In 1969, 7% of all grades were As; in 1994, 25% of all grades were As.

b. The average GPA for the graduating students of elite schools is 3.2; the average GPA for graduating students at selective schools (the level below elite schools) is 3.04; and the average GPA for graduating students at state colleges is 2.95.

c. At Dartmouth College, an elite university, SAT scores of incoming students have risen along with their subsequent college GPAs (perhaps an explanation for grade inflation).

13.3 Type of research design and obituaries: The public editor of the *Chicago Tribune*, Timothy McNulty (2006), reported that men were the subjects of 73% of the *Tribune*'s obituaries. McNulty sarcastically asked, "Could it be that more men die than women? Unlikely, you say." McNulty examined data as far back as 1998 both when there was a male lead obituary writer and when there was a female lead obituary writer. Moreover, the difference was similar or even more pronounced at other U.S. newspapers. McNulty questioned what society values in its members, noting that newspapers tended to define achievement as "great wealth or social achievement" and put a particular emphasis on accomplishments in the business world, which tends to be dominated by men. He cites others who point out that women live longer than men and thus may die well after they have left the world of work; perhaps their accomplishments have faded in memory by then. (*Hint:* For the following questions, draw the cells of the study to help determine the research design.)

a. If McNulty statistically analyzed his data to determine whether the proportion of obituaries for men is higher than that for women, would he use a parametric or a nonparametric hypothesis test? Explain your answer, citing any variables he would examine. What specific hypothesis test would he use? Explain your answer.

b. If McNulty wanted to explore whether women die longer after they've stopped working, on average, than men, would he use a parametric or a nonparametric hypothesis test? Explain your answer, citing any variables he would examine. What specific hypothesis test would he use? Explain your answer.

c. Let's say that McNulty decided to examine men's and women's obituaries to determine if there were a gender difference in whether the primary accomplishment were related to wealth, social achievement, or another type of achievement. Would he use a parametric or a nonparametric hypothesis test? Explain your answer, citing any variables he would examine. What specific hypothesis test would he use? Explain your answer.

13.4 Types of variables and performance in high school: Here are three ways to assess one's performance in high school: (1) GPA at graduation, (2) whether one graduated with honors (as indicated by graduating with a GPA of at least 3.5), and (3) class rank at graduation. For example, Abdul had a 3.98 GPA, graduated with honors, and was ranked 10th in his class.

a. Which of these variables could be considered to be a nominal variable? Explain.

b. Which of these variables is most clearly an ordinal variable? Explain.

c. Which of these variables is an interval variable? Explain.

d. Which of these variables gives us the most information about Abdul's performance?

e. If we were to use one of these variables in an analysis, which variable (as the dependent variable) would lead to the lowest chance of a Type II error? Explain why.

13.5 Types of variables and Super Bowl television advertisements: Imagine that you plan to conduct a study of the success of the latest crop of advertisements that aired during the Super Bowl.

a. State one way in which you could operationalize that construct using a nominal variable. List the levels of the nominal variable that you chose. (Note that there are several possible answers for each part of these question.)

b. State one way in which you could operationalize that construct using an ordinal variable.

c. State one way in which you could operationalize that construct using an interval variable.

13.6 The cells of research design and studies of immigrants: "Do Immigrants Make Us Safer?" asked the title of a *New York Times Magazine* article (Press, 2006). The article reported findings from several studies, including several conducted by Harvard sociologist Robert Sampson in Chicago. For each of the following findings, draw the table of cells that would comprise the research design.

a. Mexicans were more likely to be married (versus single) than either blacks or whites.

b. People living in immigrant neighborhoods were 15% less likely than were people living in nonimmigrant neighborhoods to commit crimes. This finding was true among both those living in households headed by a married couple and those living in households not headed by a married couple.

c. There was a higher crime rate among second-generation than among first-generation immigrants; moreover, there was a higher crime rate among third-generation than among second-generation immigrants.

13.7 Chi square and sex selection: Across all of India, there are only 933 girls for every 1000 boys (Lloyd, 2006), evidence of a bias that leads many parents to illegally select for boys or to kill their infant girls. (Note that this translates into a proportion of girls of 0.483.) In Punjab, a region of India in which residents tend to be more educated than in other regions, there are only 798 girls for every 1000 boys. Assume that you are a researcher interested in whether sex selection is more or less prevalent in educated regions of India and that 1798 children from Punjab constitute the entire sample. (*Hint:* You will use the proportions from the national database for comparison.)

a. How many variables are there in this study? What are the levels of any variable you identified?

b. What hypothesis test would be used to analyze these data? Justify your answer.

c. Conduct the six steps of hypothesis testing for this example. (*Note:* Be sure to use the correct proportions for the expected values, not the actual numbers for the population.)

d. Report the statistics as you would in a journal article.

13.8 Chi square and journalist genders: Richards (2006) reported data from a study by the *American Prospect* on the genders of op-ed writers who covered the topic of abortion in the *New York Times*. Over a two-year period, the *American Prospect* counted 124 articles that discussed abortion (from a wide range of political and ideological perspectives). Of these, just 21 were written by women.

a. How many variables are there in this study? What are the levels of any variable you identified?

b. What hypothesis test would be used to analyze these data? Justify your answer.

c. Conduct the six steps of hypothesis testing for this example.

d. Report the statistics as you would in a journal article.

13.9 Chi square and the prisoner's dilemma: In a classic prisoner's dilemma game with money for prizes, players who cooperate with each other both earn good prizes. If, however, your opposing player cooperates but you do not (the term used is *defect*), you receive an even bigger payout and your opponent receives nothing. If you cooperate but your opposing player defects, he or she receives that bigger payout and you receive nothing. If both defect, they each get a small prize. Because of this, most players of such games choose to defect, knowing that if they cooperate but their partners don't, they won't win anything. The strategies of U.S. and Chinese students were compared. The researchers hypothesized that those from the market economy (United States) would cooperate less (i.e., would defect more often) than would those from the nonmarket economy (China).

	DEFECT	COOPERATE
China	31	36
United States	41	14

a. How many variables are there in this study? What are the levels of any variables you identified?

b. What hypothesis test would be used to analyze these data? Justify your answer.

c. Conduct the six steps of hypothesis testing for this example, using the above data.

d. Calculate the appropriate measure of effect size. According to Cohen's conventions, what size effect is this?

e. Report the statistics as you would in a journal article.

13.10 Chi square and poor growth in children: Grimberg, Kutikov, and Cucchiara (2005) wondered whether there were a gender bias in referrals of children for poor growth. They believed that boys were more likely to be referred even when there was no problem—bad for boys because families of short boys might falsely view their height as a medical problem. They also believed that girls were less likely to be referred even when there was a problem—bad for girls because real problems might not be diagnosed and treated. They studied all new patients at The Children's Hospital of Philadelphia Diagnostic and Research Growth Center who were referred for potential problems related to short stature. Of the 182 boys who were referred, 27 had an underlying medical problem, 86 did not but were below norms for their age, and 69 were of normal height according to growth charts. Of the 96 girls who were referred, 39 had an underlying medical problem, 38 did not but were below norms for their age, and 19 were of normal height according to growth charts.

a. How many variables are there in this study? What are the levels of any variable you identified?

b. What hypothesis test would be used to analyze these data? Justify your answer.

c. Conduct the six steps of hypothesis testing for this example.

d. Calculate the appropriate measure of effect size. According to Cohen's conventions, what size effect is this?

e. Report the statistics as you would in a journal article.

13.11 Graphing, chi square, and the prisoner's dilemma: Refer to the prisoner's dilemma example in Exercise 13.9.

a. Draw a table that includes the conditional proportions for participants from China and from the United States.

b. Create a graph with bars showing the proportions for all four conditions.

c. Create a graph showing the proportions for just two bars (just for defections for each country).

13.12 Graphing, chi square, and poor growth in children: Refer to the study of poor growth in children in Exercise 13.10.

a. Draw a table that includes the conditional proportions for boys and for girls.

b. Create a graph with bars showing the proportions for all six conditions.

13.13 Relative risk and the prisoner's dilemma: Refer to the prisoner's dilemma example in Exercise 13.9.

a. Calculate the relative risk of defecting given that one is from China as opposed to the United States. Show your calculations.

b. Explain what we learn from this relative risk.

c. Now calculate the relative risk of defecting given that one is from the United States as opposed to China. Show your calculations.

d. Explain what we learn from this relative risk.

e. Explain how the calculations in parts (a) and (c) provide us with the same information in two different ways.

13.14 Relative risk and poor growth in children: Refer to the study of poor growth in children in Exercise 13.10. Consider only those boys and girls who were below norms for their age groups. That is, ignore those who turned out to have normal heights according to growth charts.

a. Among only children who are below height norms, calculate the relative risk of having an underlying medical condition if one is a boy. Show your calculations.

b. Explain what we learn from this relative risk.

c. Now calculate the relative risk of having an underlying medical condition if one is a girl. Show your calculations.

d. Explain what we learn from this relative risk.

e. Explain how the calculations in parts (a) and (c) provide us with the same information in two different ways.

13.15 The drawbacks of relative risk: Friedman (2007) reported findings from a study, conducted in the Netherlands, that found that pessimistic people were 45% more likely to die over a 10-year period than were optimistic people. The writer, a physician, reacted to the findings by worrying about his pessimistic friends: "After all, if the findings are valid, how much can anyone really do about a gloomy disposition?"

a. Based on the information above, what is the relative risk of dying given that one is pessimistic as compared to optimistic?

b. Should pessimists be worried that they're about to die? Why or why not? What additional information would a pessimist need to determine how worried to be?

c. What if you were to find out that the proportion of deaths in the population of optimists is 0.01 over 10 years? Should pessimists be overly worried about the increased risk of dying?

d. What if you were to find out that the proportion of deaths in the population of optimists is 0.40 over 10 years? Should pessimists be more or less worried than you indicated in part (b)? Explain.

e. Should we conclude that pessimism causes fatal illnesses? Explain how the causal direction might be the reverse. Explain how a third variable might be involved.

f. The article also reports that those with depression have double the relative risk of dying of heart disease or having an initial heart attack compared to those without depression. How might this finding connect to the finding about pessimism and death?

13.16 Tying it all together—chi square, the General Social Survey (GSS), and an exciting life: Go to the GSS Web site at www.icpsr.umich.edu/GSS/. During several years of the GSS, participants were asked "In general, do you find life exciting, pretty routine, or dull?" (a variable called LIFE) and were also asked "When you were 16 years old, were you living in the same (city/town/country)?" (a variable called MOBILE16). Near the top of the GSS Web site, click "Analyze" (if you don't see boxes next to the words "Row" and "Column," also click the circle for "Frequencies or crosstabluation" and click "Start"). Enter MOBILE16 in the space next to "Column" and

LIFE in the space next to "Row." Next to "Selection Filter(s)," type "MOBILE16(1-3), LIFE(1-3); Year (1972–2004)" to limit the responses you will examine. Click the button that says "Run the Table."

a. What are the variables being examined in this analysis? List the levels of each variable. (*Note:* "Same st, dif city" means that the respondent lives in the same state but in a different city from when they were 16.)

b. Using the observed frequencies provided by the GSS, conduct all six steps of hypothesis testing for a chi-square test for independence. (The frequencies are the bottom numbers in each cell of the frequency distribution table. For example, the observed frequency for those who live in the same city and find life exciting is 4890.)

c. Calculate Cramer's *V* for these data. According to Cohen's conventions, what size effect is this?

d. Report the statistics as you would in a journal article.

e. Construct a table that shows only the appropriate conditional proportions for this example. Note that the frequency distribution table includes the conditional percentages already. For example, the percentage of people who find life exciting, given that they live in the same city, is 42.4. The proportion, therefore, is 0.424.

f. Construct a graph that displays these conditional proportions.

g. Calculate the relative risk (or relative likelihood) of finding life exciting if one lives in a different state compared to the same city.

13.17 Tying it all together—chi square, the General Social Survey (GSS), and the law: Are people who believe in an afterlife more or less likely to endorse breaking the law in exceptional circumstances than are those who do not believe in an afterlife? Again, go to the GSS Web site at www.icpsr.umich.edu/GSS/. During several years of the GSS, participants were asked "In general, would you say that people should obey the law without exception, or are there exceptional circumstances in which people should follow their consciences even if it means breaking the law?" (a variable called OBEYLAW) and "Do you believe there is a life after death?" (a variable called POSTLIFE). Near the top of the GSS Web site, click "Analyze." Enter OBEYLAW in the space next to "Row" and POSTLIFE in the space next to "Column." Next to "Selection Filter(s)," type "YEAR (1972–2004)." In the "Table Options" section, click "Statistics." Finally, click the button that says "Run the Table."

a. What are the variables being examined in this analysis? List the levels of each variable.

b. Scroll down to the section titled "Summary Statistics." The chi-square statistic is listed next to "Chisq(P)." What is the chi-square statistic?

c. What is the degrees of freedom for this analysis? Based on this degrees of freedom, what is the critical chi-square value? Can we reject the null hypothesis?

d. What is the *p* value next to the chi-square statistic? Is it lower or higher than the designated *p* level of 0.05? Does this concur with the conclusion in part (c)?

e. Calculate Cramer's phi for these data. According to Cohen's conventions, what size effect is this?

f. Report the statistics as you would in a journal article.

g. Construct a table that shows only the appropriate conditional proportions for this example. Note that the frequency distribution table includes the conditional percentages already. For example, the percentage of people who say we should always obey the law given that they believe in an afterlife, is 44.7. The proportion, therefore, is 0.447.

h. Construct a graph that displays these conditional proportions.

13.18 The language of statistics—*independence* again: List two ways in which statisticians use the word *independence* or *independent* with respect to concepts introduced earlier in this text. Then describe how *independence* is used by statisticians with respect to chi square.

13.19 The symbols of statistics: For each of the following, (i) identify the incorrect symbol, (ii) state what the correct symbol should be, and (iii) explain why the initial symbol was incorrect.

a. For the chi-square test for goodness-of-fit: $df_{\chi^2} = N - 1$

b. For the chi-square test for independence: $df_{\chi^2} = (k_{Row} - 1) + (k_{Column} - 1)$

c. $\chi^2 = \Sigma \left[\dfrac{(M - E)^2}{E} \right]$

d. Cramer's $V = \sqrt{\dfrac{\chi^2}{(N)(k_{Row/Column})}}$

e. Expected frequency for each cell $= \dfrac{k_{Column}}{N\,(k_{Row})}$

▪ DIGGING DEEPER INTO THE DATA

13.20 Adjusted standardized residuals and poor growth in children: Refer to the study of poor growth in children in Exercise 13.10. The accompanying printout from SPSS software depicts the data for the six cells. For each cell, there is an observed frequency (count), expected frequency (expected count), and adjusted standardized residual (adjusted residual).

Gender * Problem Crosstabulation

			Problem			
			Underlying medical condition	Below norms	Normal height	Total
Gender	Boy	Count	27	86	69	182
		Expected Count	43.2	81.2	57.6	182.0
		Adjusted Residual	-4.8	1.2	3.1	
	Girl	Count	39	38	19	96
		Expected Count	22.8	42.8	30.4	96.0
		Adjusted Residual	4.8	-1.2	-3.1	
Total		Count	66	124	88	278
		Expected Count	66.0	124.0	88.0	278.0

a. For boys, what is the observed frequency for having an underlying medical condition?

b. For boys, what is the expected frequency for having an underlying medical condition?

c. For boys, what is the adjusted standardized residual for those with an underlying medical condition? What does this number indicate?

d. If you were to use an adjusted standardized residual criterion of 2 (regardless of the sign), for which cells would you conclude that the difference between observed frequency and expected frequency is greater than you would expect if the two variables were independent?

e. Repeat part (d) for an adjusted standardized residual criterion of 3 (regardless of the sign). Are the results different from those in part (d)? If yes, explain how they're different.

13.21 Adjusted standardized residuals, GSS, and an exciting life: Refer to the GSS example in Exercise 13.16 that explored whether one's perception of the excitement of life depended on whether one had moved since age 16. Follow the steps outlined in Exercise 13.16, but now also click "Show Z-statistic" under "Table Options" before clicking "Run the Table." The adjusted standardized residuals are the middle numbers in the cells. For example, the adjusted standardized residual for the cell for those who live in the same city and say that they lead an exciting life is −10.43.

a. If you were to use an adjusted standardized residual criterion of 2 (regardless of the sign), for which cells would you conclude that the difference between observed frequency and expected frequency is greater than you would expect if the two variables were independent?

b. Repeat part (b) for an adjusted standardized residual criterion of 3 (regardless of the sign). Are the results different from those in part (b)? If yes, explain how they're different.

13.22 Expected frequencies and poor growth: Refer to the study on poor growth in Exercise 13.10. Imagine that the study was conducted by a much smaller clinic that had fewer patients. The accompanying printout from SPSS software shows the observed frequency, expected frequency, and adjusted standardized residual for each cell. The proportions in each cell are roughly similar to those in the entire study, and the chi-square statistic is still statistically significant.

Gender * Problem Crosstabulation

			Problem			
			Underlying medical condition	Below norms	Normal height	Total
Gender	Boy	Count	6	21	18	45
		Expected Count	8.9	21.4	14.8	45.0
		Adjusted Residual	-2.1	-.2	2.0	
	Girl	Count	6	8	2	16
		Expected Count	3.1	7.6	5.2	16.0
		Adjusted Residual	2.1	.2	-2.0	
Total		Count	12	29	20	61
		Expected Count	12.0	29.0	20.0	61.0

a. What is the lowest expected frequency for this study?

b. Why is it potentially problematic to have one or more very low expected frequencies?

c. Is it appropriate to conduct a chi-square hypothesis test according to Cochran's rule? Explain.

d. Cite at least one other criterion that can help us to determine whether any of our expected values is too low. Do we meet this criterion for this study? Explain.

e. If you were to use an adjusted standardized residual criterion of 2 (regardless of the sign), for which cells would you conclude that the difference between observed frequency and expected frequency is greater than you would expect if the two variables were independent?

f. Repeat part (e) for an adjusted standardized residual criterion of 3 (regardless of the sign). Are the results different from those in part (e)? If yes, explain how they're different.

TERMS

---

chi-square test for goodness-of-fit (p. 586)

the chi-square test for independence (p. 586)

Cramer's *V* (p. 599)

relative risk (p. 601)

adjusted standardized residual (p. 603)

SYMBOLS

χ^2

k

Cramer's V

Cramer's ϕ

FORMULAS

$df_{\chi^2} = k - 1$

$\chi^2 = \Sigma \left[\dfrac{(O - E)^2}{E} \right]$

$df_{\chi^2} = (k_{Row} - 1)(k_{Column} - 1)$

Expected frequency for each cell $= \dfrac{Total_{Column}}{N}(Total_{Row})$, where we use the overall number of participants, N, along with the totals for the rows and columns for each particular cell

Cramer's $V = \sqrt{\dfrac{\chi^2}{(N)(df_{Row/Column})}}$

CHAPTER FOURTEEN

BEYOND CHI SQUARE
NONPARAMETRIC TESTS WITH ORDINAL DATA

Wilson Grainer sat in the corner and watched his wife, Alice, slowly disappear. He tried to explain to Albert, the daytime nurse, what it felt like to be married to someone who was physically but not mentally there. "It's like a parallel world," he said. "It's her body, but it's not her. One world is normal and the other one, well, isn't. I don't even know how to communicate with her."

"I think," said Albert, "that when people say, 'for better or worse,' they're usually only thinking of the 'better' part." He prepared Alice's medications by crushing them in a small paper cup and then mixing them with applesauce, trying to find a way she might accept her medicine. "She sounds normal," he said, "but she might not remember to eat, recognize your voice, or even know her own name." He dipped a tiny plastic spoon into the sweetened medicine as he approached Alice. "We have to modify the rules that apply in the normal world if we want to get anything done in her abnormal world."

"Like what?"

"One, approach her slowly. Every time she sees you, you're someone new and possibly threatening. Two, speak quietly, but often. Let her associate your voice with calmness and safety. Three, crouch as low as you can so you don't hover over her. She needs lots of reassurance. Emphasizing the simplest rules is our only chance of getting done what needs to be done. Today, we want to find out what kind of ice cream she prefers. If she keeps forgetting to eat, she can forget how to swallow."

"How can a person forget how to swallow?" Wilson asked.

"The dietician and the speech therapist suggested we use ice cream as recreational swallowing. They hope to mix a little nutrition in with her favorite flavor."

"Vanilla," said Wilson. "Sixty years of vanilla ice cream, and now she can't even remember what flavor she likes. I wonder if she even has a preference anymore."

Alice woke up, suddenly. "Hello, Will," she said.

"It's you," Wilson replied.

"Who else would I be?"

"Good morning, Mrs. Grainer," said Albert. "Are you hungry?"

"Famished. Any ice cream?"

Albert held up three labels of ice cream: strawberry, chocolate, and vanilla. "Which do you prefer?" he asked.

She looked from the labels to her nurse and back again. "Oh, just any old flavor will do," she said.

"Well, which one would you like me to get for you?"

She looked confused and then smiled at her nurse. "You decide for me," she said.

"Is it this one?" Albert asked, holding out the label with the picture of strawberry ice cream.

"I don't know. You're confusing me."

"Sorry." Albert turned away. "I'll get any ice cream I can find," he said and hurried out the door. Wilson went to the bed and kissed his wife.

"Hi. Can I get you anything?"

"You know, I think I'd like some ice cream," she replied. "I'm a little hungry."

"What kind would you like?"

"I don't care. Anything. You decide."

"Well, give me a hint." He held up the three pictures.

"Just give me the red one!"

"That's what I'll do," he promised. "I'll tell Albert."

His wife stared at him and then said, "Marrying you was the worst decision I ever made." She threw back the covers from her bed and moved with surprising agility toward the open door and then stopped. "Where am I?" she said.

Wilson never moved from his chair. "It's like a hospital," he said.

"Why? I'm not sick. I don't feel sick. What's going on, Will?"

Wilson went to his wife and put his arm around her shoulders. "The doctor thinks you have Alzheimer's disease," he said.

Measuring Environmental Characteristics
Measuring the type of environment preferred by people with disorders such as Alzheimer's disease often presents unique challenges that can be met by using nonparametric statistical tests.

Behavioral scientists need to learn the special skills needed to work with populations that don't fit the definition of "normal" behavior. Social workers, health psychologists, clinical psychologists, and psychiatrists recognize that the rules are different for people with Alzheimer's disease. Yet for some of the research on difficult-to-study topics, including some aspects of Alzheimer's disease, we don't come close to meeting the assumptions for parametric statistics. Fortunately, for every parametric statistic that assumes a normal distribution, there is a parallel nonparametric statistic that allows us to conduct valid statistical tests even under nonnormal circumstances.

All the statistics you have learned prior to Chapter 13 were based on assumptions, particularly that the distribution either approached or could be transformed (through the central limit theorem) into a normal, bell-shaped curve. It is not surprising that these are called parametric statistics because they are based on samples that estimate the population parameter. But this parallel world of nonparametric statistics is available to us whenever the situation doesn't allow us to meet assumptions about the distribution. We still do correlations, *t* tests, ANOVAs, and other parametric tests in some situations, but when it's clear we are far from meeting the assumptions, then we conduct nonparametric hypothesis tests. And nonparametric tests are based on a slightly different set of rules.

As we learned in Chapter 13, we use nonparametric statistics in one of several situations: when all variables are nominal, when either the independent variable or the dependent variable is ordinal, or when the sample size is small and the sample indicates that the underlying population distribution is not likely to be normally distributed. The previous chapter focused on situations in which all variables are nominal and in which we use a hypothesis test based on the chi-square distribution. This chapter will focus on the latter two situations: (1) those in which the data are ordinal and (2) those in which it makes sense to convert the sample data from interval to ordinal because of a small sample size and a likely skewed population distribution.

There are numerous settings in which researchers use nonparametric data. For example, an architect might hire a health psychologist to learn about the experiential world of people suffering from dementia. That researcher would likely resort to rank-ordering his or her data. Researchers use rank-ordering in such situations because the people they are trying to help can often indicate a preference even though they are not able to articulate how much more they prefer one thing over another. It might be a preference for the color of the walls, the type of ice cream, or even the intensity of lighting. The skillful use of nonparametric statistics allows people like Alice Grainer to benefit from research, even though there may be profound limitations to their ability to provide important information.

The set of statistical tests you will learn about in this chapter allows you to increase the validity of the conclusions you draw from observations that do not meet the assumptions for a parametric test, such as when we have rank-ordered observations. That is why nonparametric statistics significantly expand the range of human behaviors that psychologists can study. So let's experience that versatility by shifting our statistical microscope from interpersonal, clinical insights into Alzheimer's disease to international, comparative observations about national pride.

> NONPARAMETRIC STATISTICS: WHEN THE DATA ARE ORDINAL

The University of Chicago News Office published a press release on March 1, 2006. "Americans and Venezuelans Lead the World in National Pride," announced the headline. Researchers Smith and Kim (2006) of the University of Chicago's National Opinion Research Center (NORC) surveyed individuals in 33 countries. Then they developed two different kinds of national pride scores: pride in specific accomplishments of their nations (which they called domain-specific national pride) and a more general national pride. The accomplishment-related national pride scale asked respondents to rate their level of pride in their countries' accomplishments in specific areas such as international political

National Pride

University of Chicago researchers ranked 33 countries in terms of national pride. Venezuela, along with the United States, came out on top. Ordinal data such as these are analyzed using nonparametric statistics.

influence, social security, equality across societal groups, science and technology, and sports. The general national pride scale included questions related to a country's general superiority over other countries. Individuals were asked to rate their degree of agreement or disagreement with items such as "People should support their country even if the country is in the wrong."

Based on citizens' responses to these items, Smith and Kim developed two sets of national pride scores—accomplishment-related and general—for each country. They then converted the scores to ranks and reported the rankings of the 33 countries in the study. When results on the two scales were merged, Venezuela and the United States were tied for first place. These findings suggest many hypotheses about what creates and inflates national pride. The authors examined several of their own hypotheses. They noted that countries that were settled as colonies tend to rank higher than their "mother country," that ex-socialist countries tend to rank lower than other countries, and that countries in Asia tend to rank lower than those from other continents. They also reported that increases in national pride occurred among countries that had experienced recent terrorist attacks against their citizens.

We wondered about other possible precursors of high levels of national pride. What traits, such as competitiveness, might be associated with national pride? What categories of nations, such as those for which English is a primary language, might have higher levels of national pride than other categories of nations? Because Smith and Kim provided ordinal data, the only way we can explore these interesting questions is by using nonparametric statistics.

Hypothesis Tests with Ordinal Data: A Nonparametric Equivalent for Every Parametric Test

Rank-ordered variables should be analyzed with one of the statistical tests specifically designed to assess the relations among rank-ordered variables. For example, the ordinal rankings of countries in Smith and Kim's study should be analyzed using one of the nonparametric statistics. Parametric statistics are appropriate for interval data but not for ordinal data. The very nature of an ordinal variable means that it will not meet the assumptions of an interval dependent variable and a normally distributed population. As we can see in Figure 14-1, the shape of a distribution of ordinal variables is rectangular because every individual has a different rank. It is not even possible to have a

FIGURE 14-1
A Histogram of Ordinal Data

When ordinal data are graphed in a histogram, the resulting distribution is rectangular. These are data for ranks 1–10; for each rank, there is one individual. Ordinal data are never normally distributed.

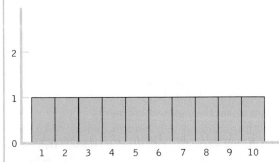

bell-shaped distribution with observations that are rank-ordered because there can only be one individual at every possible value.

Fortunately, the logic of many nonparametric statistics will be familiar to you. That is because many of the nonparametric statistical tests serve as specific alternatives to parametric statistical tests. These alternative, nonparametric tests may be used whenever assumptions for a parametric test are not met. In this chapter, we'll consider four such tests; the parametric tests and their alternative nonparametric tests are listed as pairs in Table 14-1. First, we'll learn the nonparametric equivalent for the Pearson correlation coefficient, the Spearman rank-order correlation coefficient: a nonparametric statistic that quantifies the association between two ordinal variables. Second, we'll learn a nonparametric equivalent for the paired-samples *t* test, the Wilcoxon signed-rank test: a nonparametric hypothesis test used when there are two groups, a within-groups design, and an ordinal dependent variable. Third, we'll learn a nonparametric equivalent for the independent-samples *t* test, the Mann–Whitney *U* test: a nonparametric hypothesis test used when there are two groups, a between-groups design, and an ordinal dependent variable. Fourth, we'll learn a nonparametric equivalent for the one-way between-groups ANOVA, the Kruskal–Wallis *H* test: a nonparametric hypothesis test used when there are more than two groups, a between-groups design, and an ordinal dependent variable. There is almost always an established nonparametric alterative to a parametric test. When we are far from meeting the assumptions of the parametric test that we'd like to conduct, we can choose the nonparametric test that is appropriate for our particular data.

These four statistical tests let us conduct a hypothesis test when it is clear that we should not conduct a parametric test—that is, when our assumptions, particularly that for a normal population distribution, appear to be severely violated. One drawback of nonparametric methods, however, is the lack of effect-size estimates for many of these tests. Confidence intervals pose a similar problem, although they can be developed around the median instead of the mean in many situations in which we want to use a nonparametric test. So we are less able to comply with the American Psychological Association's (APA) recommendations to include confidence intervals and effect sizes with many nonparametric

TABLE 14-1. PARAMETRIC AND NONPARAMETRIC PARTNERS

Most parametric hypothesis tests have at least one equivalent nonparametric alternative. Here, all the parametric tests call for interval dependent variables, and their nonparametric counterparts all call for ordinal dependent variables.

DESIGN	PARAMETRIC TEST	NONPARAMETRIC TEST
Association between two variables	Pearson correlation coefficient	Spearman rank-order correlation coefficient
Two groups; within-groups design	Paired-samples *t* test	Wilcoxon signed-rank test
Two groups; between-groups design	Independent-samples *t* test	Mann–Whitney *U* test
More than two groups; between-groups design	One-way between-groups ANOVA	Kruskal–Wallis *H* test

tests. As a result, many researchers believe we should use parametric procedures whenever possible, going to the backup procedures only when the emerging data indicate that we cannot justify using a parametric hypothesis test.

Examining the Data: Deciding to Use a Nonparametric Test for Ordinal Data

Nonparametric tests for ordinal data are typically used in one of two situations. First and most obviously, we use them when our sample data are ordinal. Second, we use them when our dependent variable suggests that the underlying population distribution is greatly skewed, a situation that often develops when we have a small sample size. It is likely for this second reason that Smith and Kim (2006) converted their data to ranks. Figure 14-2 shows a histogram of their full set of data for the variable accomplishment-related national pride, which we will use for many examples in this chapter. The data appear to be positively skewed, probably because Venezuela and the United States seem to be outliers. When we want to use a nonparametric test despite having interval data, we have to transform our data from interval to ordinal.

Transforming interval data to ordinal data is not uncommon. For example, when we are calculating a Spearman correlation coefficient, both of the variables would have to be ordinal; if one or both of the variables were interval, then we'd have to convert the interval scores to ranks. This conversion can help in situations like that described above: when the data from a small sample are skewed. Look what happens to the following five data points for income when we change the data from interval to ordinal. In the first row, the interval data,

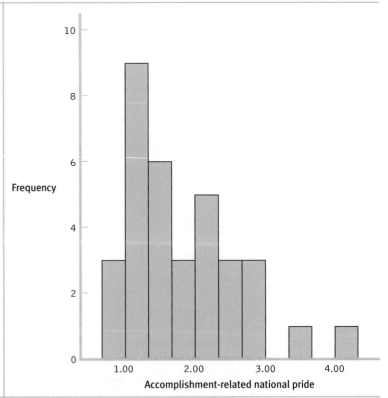

FIGURE 14-2
Skewed Data

The sample data for the variable, accomplishment-related national pride, are skewed. This indicates the possibility that the underlying population distribution is skewed. It is likely for this reason that Smith and Kim (2006) chose to report their data as ranks.

there is a severe outlier ($550,000), suggesting a skewed distribution. In the second row, the ordinal data, the severe outlier merely becomes the first ranking. The ranked data do not have an outlier.

Interval:	$24,000	$27,000	$35,000	$46,000	$550,000
Ordinal:	5	4	3	2	1

In summary, nonparametric statistics are used when all variables are nominal (as covered in Chapter 13), when one or more variables are ordinal, and when the sample suggests that the underlying population distribution is skewed and the sample size is small. Nonparametric tests for ordinal data are used when the data are already ordinal or when it is clear that the assumptions are severely violated. In the latter case, the interval data must be converted to ordinal data.

⊙ CHECK YOUR LEARNING

14-1 Here are IQ scores for 10 individuals:

$$88, 90, 91, 99, 103, 102, 104, 112, 114, 139$$

a. Why might it be better to use a nonparametric test than a parametric test in this case?

b. Convert the scores for IQ (an interval variable) to ranks (an ordinal variable).

c. What happens to the outlier when the scores are converted from an interval scale to an ordinal scale?

► SPEARMAN RANK-ORDER CORRELATION COEFFICIENT: QUANTIFYING THE ASSOCIATION BETWEEN TWO ORDINAL VARIABLES

Six months after his wife's diagnosis, Wilson Grainer read the newspaper out loud to her as she slowly disappeared. There was a time, at the beginning of her disease, when Alice was keenly aware that she was disappearing and it frightened her so deeply that she had been very careful not to tell anyone. Now she was in and out of self-awareness. She appeared to be sleeping as he read to her, but Wilson hoped that the sound of his voice was somehow soothing to his wife.

"I'm sorry she started being so mean to you," Albert told Wilson as he maneuvered his cart into the room. "It's the disease. I'm sure she doesn't want to be that way."

Alice woke up and startled them both with a question. "What's that noise outside?" she asked.

Wilson put down his paper, bent back a window blind, and peered outside. He looked at a brick wall and a smokestack, but he didn't tell Alice that. He said, "There's a track meet across the street at the high school."

"Oh, I love track meets!" exclaimed Alice. "The wonderful thing about track-and-field is that there's an event that's right for every type of person," Alice said. "That's the key to success in track, finding the event that's right for you. Big, husky people can throw the shot put. Tall, lanky people can run hurdles or high-jump. All kinds of people can run long distances. I ran cross-country in college. Did you know that?"

Dennis MacDonald/Photo Edit

Rank Order and Races
The outcomes of races are often presented as ordinal data. If you finish first, it does not matter what your interval score—your time—is; you've won.

"Yes," said Wilson. "They're running one of the long races right now. Two women have been running in the lead. One is wearing orange, the other black. They're ringing the bell. There is just one more lap to go. A third woman is starting to kick!" he said. "She's gaining on both of them. Oh, this is going to be quite a finish!"

"Tell me!" Alice insisted.

"The woman in third is wearing red and she's really moving! I don't think the other two even know she's catching them. Now all three are starting to kick! Orange is pulling away from black. The woman in black is fading!"

"What about the woman in red?"

"She just passed the orange runner and is still gaining on black. It's going to be close, so close!" He was quiet, staring out the window. "It's over," he said.

"Who won?"

"Orange held on for the win; red came in second. Black faded and came in third, just a little behind her" said Wilson.

"But she still came in third," said Alice. "Third is third, no matter how far away you are from second. You still get a medal for finishing third."

Wilson looked at his wife and her bright, shining eyes. "How do you know so much about track?" he asked.

She returned his smile, but with confusion. "How do I know what?" she asked.

Wilson desperately tried to salvage a few more sentences with his wife. "About running. How do you know so much about running?"

Her bright eyes suddenly narrowed with suspicion. "Get away from me!" she ordered him. "Stay away from me! I'll scream," she threatened.

"Thank you, Mrs. Grainer," Albert said to her.

"For what?" she said, surprised by his comment.

"I got you exactly what you wanted," Albert continued. "Applesauce. It's just what you wanted."

Alice Grainer revealed a rich understanding of statistical ideas during her brief period of lucidity. For instance, she knew that everything works better when you match the answer to the question, whether it is matching a particular body type to a particular event in track-and-field or matching the appropriate statistical test to the appropriate kind of observation. And her observation that "third is third, no matter how far away you are from second" expresses the distinction between Spearman's rank-ordered (nonparametric) correlation statistic and Pearson's interval (parametric) correlation statistic. Rank-ordered data are how we think about many everyday statistical observations and decisions, such as who comes in first in a race, whom to vote for as president, our preferred flavor of ice cream, or which romantic partner we select. When we have to bet, vote, prefer, or select, it doesn't matter how close second place was. We made a rank-ordered decision, so we need rank-ordered statistics that match our rank-ordered behavior. When we collect rank-ordered observations from many people, we analyze the data using nonparametric statistics.

Calculating Spearman's Correlation: Converting Interval Observations to Rank-Ordered Observations

■ The **Spearman rank-order correlation coefficient** is a nonparametric statistic that quantifies the association between two ordinal variables.

You, too, are already familiar with the ideas behind the nonparametric statistics you will learn about in this chapter; they parallel the world of parametric statistics presented in previous chapters. The logic of hypothesis testing, effect sizes, and Type I and Type II errors is the same even though the assumptions underlying the tests are different. But, like Alice Grainer, you will understand the value of these ideas even more as you find a way to apply statistical reasoning to your own life. But how does that reasoning actually lead to calculating a correlation when one variable is ordinal and the other variable is interval? The answer is the ***Spearman rank-order correlation coefficient***, *a nonparametric statistic that quantifies the association between two ordinal variables.*

Earlier, when we introduced Smith and Kim's study of national pride (2006), we noted that they described two types of national pride: Accomplishment-related pride based on specific achievements and general pride. We learned that Venezuela and the United States tied for first in overall national pride. Yet, when Smith and Kim examined rankings by type of national pride (accomplishment-related versus general pride), there were some differences in rankings. For example, the United States was number one in accomplishment-related national pride, but it was number two, behind Venezuela, in general pride. Other countries showed a similar discrepancy; the United Kingdom was 12th in accomplishment-related and 24th in general pride. New Zealand was 6th in accomplishment-related and 11th in general pride.

As so often happens with descriptive data such as national rankings, we started wondering how the descriptive data might be related to other variables. The stimulus for that curiosity was a very ordinary observation: One of the authors has a tennis-playing friend from one of the countries on the list, a person who is both very proud of his heritage and extremely competitive. But just because this friend is very competitive doesn't mean that everyone else from his nation is also competitive. It is easy to be tricked by the "someone who" error when we know "someone who" fits one pattern and leads us to believe that it must be true for everyone else in that particular group. In order to play fair with our own curiosity, we thought that a statistical test would be a way to help us overcome our own biases and create a fair test of whether accomplishment-related national pride is related to the underlying trait of competitiveness.

So we randomly selected 10 countries from this list and compiled their scores for accomplishment-related national pride. We also located rankings of competitiveness compiled by an international business school (IMD, 2001). If there were a correlation between these variables, this would be some evidence that countries' levels of accomplishment-related national pride is tied to the level of competitiveness in these countries. This research question involves two variables. The competitiveness variable we borrowed from the business school rankings is already ordinal. However, the accomplishment-related national pride variable was initially an interval variable. Because just one of the variables is ordinal, we cannot use the Pearson correlation coefficient. So we substitute the Spearman rank-order correlation coefficient, often called just the Spearman correlation coefficient, or Spearman's rho; its symbol is almost like that for the Pearson correlation coefficient, but it now has the subscript S to indicate that it is Spearman's correlation coefficient: r_S.

The current case exemplifies the use of Spearman's correlation when one of the variables is already ordinal. As with the Pearson correlation coefficient, we do not have to have a specific independent variable and a specific dependent variable, but it often helps to think of the variables in this way. In this example, the

Adam Pretty/Getty Images

Competitiveness and National Pride: French Tennis Star Amélie Mauresmo
The correlation between competitiveness and accomplishment-related national pride can be tested using Spearman's rho, a rank-ordered, nonparametric version of Pearson's parametric correlation coefficient. Using statistics helps us avoid deceiving ourselves with the false consensus bias, also known as the "someone who" error. Just because we happen to know "someone who" fits one pattern doesn't mean that it applies to others.

Symbol: r_s

variable that might be thought of as the independent variable is competitiveness. The variable that might be thought of as the dependent variable is accomplishment-related national pride; these scores were initially on an interval scale, and so they have to be converted to an ordinal scale. The hypothesis is that accomplishment-related national pride depends on a country's level of competitiveness.

When we conduct nonparametric analyses based on ordinal data, sometimes our data are already ordinal, such as the competitiveness data. Other times our data are interval and need to be converted to ordinal, as with the national pride data. As noted earlier, the data must be converted from interval to ordinal in two cases. The first is in a situation like the one we're encountering here. One variable is already ordinal, so we convert the other variable to match the first. We cannot calculate a Spearman correlation coefficient if only one variable is ordinal. In the second situation, the data are interval but it is clear that we do not meet the assumptions for a parametric test. As discussed earlier, a nonparametric test is recommended when the data for either variable suggest that the underlying population is skewed.

To convert interval data, we simply organize our data from highest to lowest and then rank them. (We also could organize our data from lowest to highest if that makes more sense, as it does when reporting the finishing times in a race; in a race, the lowest number is the fastest and is best indicated by a rank of 1.) Table 14-2 shows the conversion from interval data to ordinal data for accomplishment-related national pride. Sometimes, as seen for Austria and Canada, we have a tie. Both of these countries had an accomplishment-related national pride score of 2.4. When we rank the data, these countries take the third and fourth positions, but they must have the same rank because their scores are the same. So we take the average of the two ranks they would hold if the scores were different: $(3 + 4)/2 = 3.5$. Both of these countries receive the rank of 3.5. We handle tied ranks in this way no matter what nonparametric test for ordinal data we're using—not just for the Spearman correlation.

TABLE 14-2. CONVERTING PRIDE SCORES TO RANKS

When we convert interval data to ordinal data, we simply arrange the data from highest to lowest (or lowest to highest if that makes more sense) and then rank them. These are the data for accomplishment-related national pride. In cases of ties, we average the two ranks that these participants—countries, in this case—would hold.

COUNTRY	PRIDE SCORE	PRIDE RANK
United States	4.00	1
South Africa	2.70	2
Austria	2.40	3.5
Canada	2.40	3.5
Chile	2.30	5
Japan	1.80	6
Hungary	1.60	7
France	1.50	8
Norway	1.30	9
Slovenia	1.10	10

Sometimes professional golfers also experience the conversion between interval data and ordinal data when it comes to distributing prize money. Imagine that the first-place winner of a golf tournament is awarded $100,000; the second-place finisher, $75,000; and the third-place finisher, $25,000. In golf, if two players are tied at the end of regulation play, they participate in a play-off to determine first and second places, and the prize money is distributed accordingly. However, if the second- and third-place golfers finish in a tie, they split the rank and the prize money; each golfer will receive $50,000 [($75,000 + $25,000)/2].

Now that we have our ranks, we can compute our Spearman correlation coefficient. We learned the Pearson correlation coefficient as a descriptive statistic, but it can be used as an inferential statistic as well. As an inferential statistic, we would test the null hypothesis that the correlation coefficient is 0, and we would use Table B.6 in the appendix. If we reject the null hypothesis, then we conclude that the correlation is significantly different from 0. Similarly, we will learn the Spearman correlation coefficient as a descriptive statistic rather than an inferential statistic, even though we can conduct a hypothesis test with the null hypothesis that the correlation coefficient is 0. For the hypothesis test associated with the Spearman correlation coefficient, we would use Table B.6 in the appendix. This means that we will not use the six steps of hypothesis testing. However, it is possible to conduct a hypothesis test with the null hypothesis that the correlation between the two variables is 0.

Whether we treat the Spearman correlation as a descriptive statistic or an inferential statistic, we first need to include both sets of ranks in the same table, as in the second and third columns in Table 14-3. We then calculate the difference between each pair of ranks, as in the fourth column. The differences will always add up to 0, so we must square the differences, as in the last column. As we have frequently done with squared differences in the past, we'll sum them—another

---

TABLE 14-3. CALCULATING A SPEARMAN CORRELATION COEFFICIENT

The first step in calculating a Spearman correlation coefficient is creating a table that includes the ranks for all participants—countries, in this case—on both variables of interest (accomplishment-related national pride and competitiveness). We then calculate differences for each participant (i.e., country) and square each difference.

COUNTRY	PRIDE RANK	COMPETITIVENESS RANK	DIFFERENCE (D)	SQUARED DIFFERENCE (D^2)
United States	1	1	0	0
South Africa	2	10	−8	64
Austria	3.5	2	1.5	2.25
Canada	3.5	3	0.5	0.25
Chile	5	5	0	0
Japan	6	7	−1	1
Hungary	7	8	−1	1
France	8	6	2	4
Norway	9	4	5	25
Slovenia	10	9	1	1

variation on the concept of a sum of squares. The sum of these squared differences is: $\Sigma D^2 = (0 + 64 + 2.25 + 0.25 + 0 + 1 + 1 + 4 + 25 + 1) = 98.5$.

The formula for calculating the Spearman correlation coefficient includes the sum of the squared differences that we just calculated, 98.5. The formula is

Formula: $r_s = 1 - \dfrac{6(\Sigma D^2)}{N(N^2 - 1)}$

$$r_s = 1 - \frac{6(\Sigma D^2)}{N(N^2 - 1)}$$

In addition to the sum of squared differences, the only other information we need is the sample size, N, which is 10 in this example. (The number 6 is a constant; it is always included in the calculation of the Spearman correlation coefficient.) Our Spearman correlation coefficient, therefore, is

$$r_s = 1 - \frac{6(\Sigma D^2)}{N(N^2 - 1)} = 1 - \frac{6(98.5)}{10(10^2 - 1)} = \frac{591}{10(100 - 1)} =$$

$$1 - \frac{591}{10(99)} = 1 - \frac{591}{990} = 1 - 0.597 = 0.403$$

The Spearman correlation coefficient is 0.40.

The interpretation of the Spearman correlation coefficient is identical to that for the Pearson correlation coefficient. The coefficient can range from -1, a perfect negative correlation, to 1, a perfect positive correlation. A correlation coefficient of 0 indicates no relation between the two variables. As with the Pearson correlation coefficient, it is not the sign of the Spearman correlation coefficient that indicates the strength of a relation. So, for example, a coefficient of -0.66 indicates a stronger association than does a coefficient of 0.23.

Let's consider how the formula works. If there were a perfect positive correlation, all the difference scores would be 0. The first-ranked participant (or, in this case, country) on one scale would also be ranked first on the other scale, and the difference would be 0; the participant ranked second on one scale would be ranked second on the other, and the difference would be 0; this would be true for all participants. When we sum the squares of a column of 0s, we get 0, so our formula would simplify to $1 - 0$ and the correlation coefficient would be 1. As the differences become larger than 0, the correlation coefficient gets smaller and closer to 0 because we're subtracting a number larger than 0 from 1. However, at a certain point, the differences become so large that when we subtract them from 1, the coefficient is negative, an indication of a negative relation between the two variables. Eventually, the differences become so large that we reach a perfect negative correlation of -1. In the case of a perfect negative correlation coefficient, the first-ranked country on one scale would be the last-ranked country on the other scale. The second-ranked country on one scale would be the second-to-last-ranked country on the other scale, and so on across the entire data set. Summing the squared differences and inputting that sum into the formula would produce a coefficient of -1.

Eyeballing the Data: Using Your Scientific Common Sense

The easiest way to get a sense of how the Spearman correlation coefficient works may surprise you: eyeball the data. For instance, a positive correlation means that the two variables move up and down together, the same way we hope that the two ends of a window washer's scaffold move up and down together. And a negative correlation means that as one variable increases, the other variable tends to decrease, the same way the two ends of a teeter-totter move up and down in opposition to each other. So let's take a close look at the individual data points in Table 14-3.

The country ranked number one in competitiveness (the United States) is also ranked number one in accomplishment-related national pride. That sounds like the start of a positive correlation because the nation highest on one variable is also highest on the other variable. Now look at the lowest-ranked (10th) nation in national pride, Slovenia. This country is ranked next to lowest (9th) in competitiveness. That looks like more evidence for a positive correlation because the nation low on one variable is also low on the other variable. After these two initial observations, the two variables of competitiveness and accomplishment-related national pride seem to be moving up and down together: a positive correlation.

But wait! The country ranked 10th in competitiveness (South Africa) is ranked 2nd in accomplishment-related national pride. This sounds like evidence for a negative correlation because the nation low on one variable ranks high on the other variable. As we continue to eyeball the data, we notice that the pattern is not quite as clear as we might hope. That is precisely why we need a mathematical formula: to clarify the relation between the two variables. In this case (as we already know), the Spearman rank-order correlation is positive (0.40), in spite of the individual exceptions to that rule (South Africa and Norway). Eyeballing the data is easier to do with rank-ordered data because we can identify the extremes (highest and lowest) right away. But we can't always trust our eyeballs! Sometimes our judgment is clouded by something as simple as the pair of data points that we happen to look at first. Trust the formula more than your private impressions when estimating the relation between the two variables in an unbiased way so that you can reach a sensible conclusion without being tricked by a first-impression bias.

Rankings of National Pride
Does a country's ranking on accomplishment-related national pride correlate with its ranking on competitiveness? When we have ordinal data, we must calculate a Spearman correlation coefficient rather than a Pearson correlation coefficient.

PREDICTING FROM A CORRELATION COEFFICIENT

EXPERIENCE IT FOR YOURSELF

What about the competitive tennis-playing friend of one of the authors? Well, the friend is from Spain, but Spain was not selected to be part of our smaller study, purely because of random selection. Smith and Kim's (2006) data indicate that Spain, with a score of 1.60, would have been ranked toward the bottom of our set of 10 countries with respect to accomplishment-related national pride. Can we use the findings from this study to make any statements about Spain? Because this question goes to the heart of random sampling, you can experience the answer to this question for yourself. Given the positive correlation of 0.40 between accomplishment-related national pride and competitiveness in this random sample of 10 countries, answer True or False to each of the following statements:

1. T F   We cannot make any prediction about Spain's competitiveness because it wasn't part of the sample.

2. T F   We can make a firm statement that Spain would be low in competitiveness because we used a random sample.

3. T F   Our best guess is that Spain would be low in competitiveness, but we wouldn't be surprised if it were not.

4. T F   Gathering data from fans at a Spanish tennis tournament would be the best way to answer the question.

5. T F   This positive correlation indicates that competitiveness causes national pride.

6. T F   This positive but imperfect (less than 1.00) correlation indicates that competitiveness might cause national pride.

Here is a final word of caution to help you think through some of your answers to the questions in Experience It for Yourself: Predicting From a Correlation Coefficient. The Spearman correlation coefficient, like the Pearson correlation coefficient, provides information about the relation, or association, between two variables. So item 3 is true; we can make an educated guess about Spain based on the relation between two variables.

It does not, however, tell us about causation. As with the Pearson correlation coefficient, it is possible that there is a causal relation in one of two directions. The relation between competitiveness (variable A) and accomplishment-related national pride (variable B) is 0.40, a fairly strong positive correlation. It is possible that competitiveness (variable A) causes a country to feel prouder (variable B) of its accomplishments; if one nation is competitive, perhaps its accomplishments mean more and are a greater source of pride. On the other hand, it is also possible that accomplishment-related national pride (variable B) causes competitiveness (variable A); perhaps a country that feels very proud of its accomplishments feels an enhanced sense of competition in order to maintain that pride. Finally, it is also possible that a third variable, C, causes both of the other two variables (A and B). For example, a high gross domestic product (variable C) might cause both a sense of competitiveness with other economic powerhouses (variable A) and a feeling of national pride at this economic accomplishment (variable B). So item 6 is true; competitiveness *might* cause national pride. It's one of several possible explanations for the relation between the two variables. (Note that no items other than 3 and 6 are true.) A strong correlation indicates only a strong association; we can draw no conclusions about causation.

In summary, when we want to determine a correlation between two ordinal variables, we calculate a Spearman correlation coefficient, which is interpreted in the same way as the Pearson correlation coefficient: 1 is a perfect positive correlation, −1 is a perfect negative correlation, and 0 means no correlation. As with the Pearson correlation coefficient, the Spearman correlation coefficient does not tell us about causation. It simply quantifies the magnitude and direction of association between two ordinal variables.

⊙ CHECK YOUR LEARNING

14-2 The accompanying table includes ranks for accomplishment-related national pride, along with numbers of medals won at the 2000 Sydney Olympics

COUNTRY	PRIDE RANK	OLYMPIC MEDALS
United States	1	97
South Africa	2	5
Austria	3	3
Canada	4	14
Chile	5	1
Japan	6	18
Hungary	7	17
France	8	38
Norway	9	10
Slovenia	10	2

by the same countries in our random sample. (Of course, this might not be the best way to operationalize the variable of Olympic performance; perhaps we should be ranking Olympic medals per capita.)

a. Calculate the Spearman correlation coefficient for these two variables. Remember to convert numbers of Olympic medals to ranks.

b. What does the coefficient tell us about the relation between these two variables?

c. We had interval data for accomplishment-related national pride, and number of Olympic medals is an interval variable. Why might it not have been a good idea to calculate a Pearson correlation coefficient for these data?

> NONPARAMETRIC HYPOTHESIS TESTS: COMPARING GROUPS USING RANKS

Two years after Alice Grainer was diagnosed with Alzheimer's disease, her cruelty was all that remained for her husband. Wilson came to see his wife for two hours on Mondays, Wednesdays, and Sundays and always in the mornings. He had settled into a routine he could live with.

Albert entered her room with a cart full of medications.

Wilson folded his newspaper. "The Cubs are in first place," he said.

"It won't last," said Albert. "They've been in first place at the mid-season All-Star break lots of times, but they haven't won the World Series since 1908."

"That's interesting," said Wilson. "You would think that their rank in the standings after the first half of the season would predict their rank at the end of the season." He looked across the room at his wife. "It's just like my marriage," he said. "The first part was great, but these last few years have been very difficult."

"You're lucky, Mr. Grainer," Albert said. "I have a Red Sox marriage—usually very frustrating, but occasionally wonderful."

"Men," said Alice Grainer, shaking her head. She surprised them both, but then returned to staring at her hands. She had disappeared as quickly as she had arrived.

Wilson stared at his wife for a long time and then said, "The newspaper says that the prevalence rates for Alzheimer's disease get worse the older you get. It's a positive correlation. The older you get, the higher your chances are of developing Alzheimer's disease."

"Planning any track meets today?" Albert asked.

"It makes her happy," Wilson replied. "She remembers."

Albert had been waiting for the right moment to ask a question. "Mr. Grainer," he said. "Why do you come? If it were my wife, I'm not sure I could keep coming, to be honest."

"She doesn't have anyone else," said Wilson. "My life wasn't normal after Alice got sick. I had to impose some normality on the chaos, and I found a way to do it. For me, it was working out the three-days-per-week schedule. But I couldn't pretend life was normal when it wasn't. I had to find a way to make it as normal as I possibly could."

Predicting from Rankings
A baseball team's rank in the standings at the All-Star break does not perfectly predict how they will finish the season. To quantify a correlation of ordinal variables, we'd use a nonparametric statistic.

Scott Olson/Getty Images

"Can you really make something normal if it's really not normal?" Albert asked.

"People do it all the time," said Wilson.

Alice got up from her chair and started wandering about the room. She picked up a framed picture of their wedding and stared at it for a long time. The two men watched her carefully. Then Alice dropped it on the floor, cracking the glass. She pointed at her husband, said "Traitor," then climbed back into bed.

Wilson stared at his own hands as Albert cleaned up the glass. "What would you like me to do with the photo?" Albert asked. There was no answer, so Albert quietly put it into a drawer. "I'd like to let some light in," he said. Wilson still said nothing in reply, so Albert pulled up the blinds. "A brick wall and a smoke-stack," he said. "Not much of a view. Nobody would judge you, Mr. Grainer, if you just left. No one would say you're a bad person for not letting yourself be treated like that anymore."

"I made a promise," Wilson said.

People who suffer from Alzheimer's disease have families who also suffer in different ways. As you may recall from a social science class, there are several competing definitions for what is "abnormal." One of those is a statistical defi-nition in which *abnormal* simply means "statistically unusual." Alice Grainer's be-havior was abnormal, but only when compared to her behavior in her previous life. However, it was not abnormal compared to the behavior of others suffering from Alzheimer's disease. When we try to help people who behave in an "ab-normal" and harmful way, we impose one or more of those definitions of abnor-mal and then compare that person's behavior to the standard we call normal.

Fortunately, there are several nonparametric hypothesis tests that can be used to answer the kinds of urgent research questions—often based on nonnormal data—raised by disorders such as Alzheimer's disease. In this section, we'll learn how to conduct three of these tests: the Wilcoxon signed-rank test, the non-parametric equivalent of the paired-samples t test; the Mann–Whitney U test, the nonparametric equivalent of the independent-samples t test; and the Kruskal–Wallis H test, the nonparametric equivalent for the one-way between-groups ANOVA. We will use these new statistics to test more hypotheses about the ranked data on national pride.

The Wilcoxon Signed-Rank Test for Matched Pairs: A Nonparametric Test for Within-Groups Designs

Smith and Kim (2006) provided data on national pride for two periods, 1995–1996 and 2003–2004. We examined the data from the six countries for which English is the primary language: the United States, Australia, Ireland, Canada, Great Britain, and New Zealand. We wondered whether the score on accomplishment-related national pride were different between these two peri-ods. The scores for each period are listed in Table 14-4, with the differences between the two periods for each country. The differences are calculated by subtracting the first score from the second. So, for example, for the United States, there was an increase of $4.00 - 3.11 = 0.89$; for Ireland, there was a de-crease of $2.90 - 3.36 = -0.46$.

The independent variable for this analysis is period, with two levels: 1995–1996 and 2003–2004. The dependent variable is accomplishment-related national pride. This is a within-groups design because every participant, or coun-try, had a score for each level of the independent variable. Were we to use the

---

TABLE 14-4. ACCOMPLISHMENT-RELATED NATIONAL PRIDE SCORES
....
Smith and Kim (2006) provided scores on accomplishment-related national pride for two periods, 1995–1996 and 2003–2004. Here are the data for the countries for which English is a primary language. For each country, there are scores for each time period, as well as a difference score, calculated by subtracting the first score from the second.

COUNTRY	1995–1996	2003–2004	DIFFERENCE
United States	3.11	4.00	0.89
Australia	2.10	2.90	0.80
Ireland	3.36	2.90	−0.46
New Zealand	2.62	2.60	−0.02
Canada	2.56	2.40	−0.16
Great Britain	2.09	2.20	0.11

---

interval scores on accomplishment-related national pride, we would use a dependent-samples *t* test. But because these data are better analyzed as ordinal data than as interval data, we will use a nonparametric equivalent for the dependent-samples *t* test, the ***Wilcoxon signed-rank test*** *for matched pairs, a nonparametric hypothesis test used when there are two groups, a within–groups design, and an ordinal dependent variable.* The test statistic for this test is symbolized with a *T*; be sure to capitalize the *T* so that it is not mistaken for the test statistic in *t* tests.

Symbol: *T*

For nonparametric tests, the six steps of hypothesis testing are very similar to those for parametric tests. The good news is that these six steps for nonparametric hypothesis tests are usually easier to compute, and some of the steps, such as the one for assumptions, are shorter. We will outline the six steps for hypothesis testing with the Wilcoxon signed-rank test for matched pairs in the context of this example about possible changes in accomplishment-related national pride rankings.

Step 1. Determine the assumptions.

There are three assumptions: (1) The differences between pairs must be able to be ranked. (2) We should use random selection; otherwise, our ability to generalize will be limited. (3) The difference scores should come from a symmetric population distribution. This third assumption, combined with the fact that the paired-samples *t* test is robust with respect to violations of the assumption that the population distribution is normal, means that the *t* test is often the preferred choice. Only when the assumption of a normal population distribution is seriously questioned should researchers use the Wilcox signed-rank test for matched pairs.

Summary: We will convert our data from interval to ordinal. The researchers did not indicate whether they used random selection to choose the countries in the sample, so we must be cautious when generalizing from these results. It is difficult to know from a small sample whether the difference scores come from a symmetric population distribution.

Step 2. State the null and research hypotheses.

We will state the null and research hypotheses only in words, not in symbols.

■ The **Wilcoxon signed-rank test** is a nonparametric hypothesis test used when there are two groups, a within-groups design, and an ordinal dependent variable.

Summary: Null hypothesis: English-speaking countries in 1995–1996 did not differ in accomplishment-related national pride from English-speaking countries in 2003–2004.

Research hypothesis: English-speaking countries in 1995–1996 differed in accomplishment-related national pride from English-speaking countries in 2003–2004.

Step 3. Determine the characteristics of the comparison distribution.

The Wilcoxon signed-rank test for matched pairs compares the T statistic to the T distribution. The main reason we have to determine the characteristics of the comparison distribution is so that we can move on to later steps; in step 4, we determine a cutoff, or critical value. To do so, we need to (1) decide on the cutoff level (usually 0.05), (2) clarify whether we're using a one-tailed test or a two-tailed test (usually two-tailed), and (3) determine the sample size. The sample size for this test is a bit different from that for other tests; it is the number of difference scores that are *not* 0. For this example, all difference scores are *not* 0, so our sample size will be 6. (Note that for samples larger than 50, the T distribution looks like the z distribution, and we can use a z test instead.)

Summary: We will use a p level of 0.05 and a two-tailed test. Our sample size is 6.

Step 4. Determine critical values, or cutoffs.

We'll use Table B.9 from the appendix to determine the cutoff, or critical value, for the Wilcoxon signed-rank test for matched pairs. In the table, we'll find the sample size down the left-hand column and the appropriate number of tails and p level across the top row. There is an important difference between this critical value and those we considered with parametric tests. We can reject the null hypothesis only if our test statistic is equal to or *smaller than* the critical value.

Summary: The cutoff for a Wilcoxon signed-rank test for matched pairs with $N = 6$ for a p level of 0.05 and a two-tailed test is 0. This critical value suggests that our sample size is too small to have sufficient statistical power. We must be wary of the validity of our decision in this case. (*Note:* For the hypothesis test, we calculate two statistics. We want the *smaller* of the test statistics to be equal to or *smaller than* this critical value; that is, we compare only the smaller test statistic to the cutoff.)

Step 5. Calculate the test statistic.

We start our calculations by organizing our difference scores from highest to lowest in terms of absolute value, as seen in Table 14-5. Because we are organizing by absolute value, -0.46 is higher than 0.11, for example. We then rank the absolute values of the differences, as seen in the third column. We then separate the ranks into two columns, the fourth and fifth columns. The fourth column includes only the ranks associated with positive differences, and the fifth column includes only the ranks associated with negative differences.

Table 14-5, incidentally, also serves as a graph. We can tell by the pattern of the ranks in the last two columns whether there seems to be a difference. The pattern for these data suggests that there has been more of an increase than a decrease in accomplishment-related national pride among English-speaking countries. We can draw no conclusions, however, until we have compared our test statistic to our critical value.

The final step in calculating the test statistic is to sum the ranks for the positive scores and the ranks for the negative scores:

$$\Sigma R_+ = (1 + 2 + 5) = 8$$
$$\Sigma R_- = (3 + 4 + 6) = 13$$

TABLE 14-5. **ORGANIZING DATA FOR A WILCOXON SIGNED-RANK TEST FOR MATCHED PAIRS**

To conduct a Wilcoxon signed-rank test for matched pairs, we first organize our data from highest to lowest in terms of absolute value. We rank the absolute values and then create two separate columns—one for ranks associated with positive scores and one for ranks associated with negative scores.

COUNTRY	DIFFERENCE	RANKS	RANKS FOR POSITIVE DIFFERENCES	RANKS FOR NEGATIVE DIFFERENCES
United States	0.89	1	1	
Australia	0.80	2	2	
Ireland	−0.46	3		3
Canada	−0.16	4		4
Great Britain	0.11	5	5	
New Zealand	−0.02	6		6

The work is done. The smaller of these is the test statistic, T. The formula for T, therefore, is

$$T = \Sigma R_{Smaller}$$

In this case, $T = \Sigma R_+ = 8$.

> **Summary:** $T = \Sigma R_{Smaller} = 8$. (*Note:* It is helpful to show all calculations in your summary.)

Formula: $T = \Sigma R_{Smaller}$

Step 6. Make a decision.

The test statistic, 8, is not smaller than the critical value, 0, and so we fail to reject the null hypothesis. We expected this from the very small critical value; we likely did not have sufficient statistical power to detect any real differences that might exist. We cannot conclude that the two groups are different with respect to accomplishment-related national pride rankings.

After completing our hypothesis test, we want to present the primary statistical information in a report, just as we did with the outcomes of parametric tests. We'll use a format similar to that used for parametric tests. In our write-up, we'll list the totals for positive ranks, 8, and negative ranks, 13. There are no degrees of freedom, so the test statistic is reported only as $T = 8$, $p > 0.05$.

The Mann–Whitney *U* Test: Comparing Two Independent Groups Using Ordinal Data

Smith and Kim (2006) observed that countries with recent communist pasts tended to have lower ranks on national pride. We'll choose 10 European countries, 5 of which were communist during part of the previous century. Our independent variable is type of country, with two levels: former communist and not former communist. The dependent variable is rank on accomplishment-related national pride. This exemplifies a common research situation in the social sciences, one in which we want to compare two independent samples. When our data suggest that we meet the assumptions for a parametric test, we use the independent-samples *t* test; however, when we are far from meeting the assumptions and must use a nonparametric test, we often use the Mann–Whitney *U* test, one of the nonparametric

TABLE 14-6. COMPARING TWO GROUPS

Here are the data for two samples: European countries that were recently communist and European countries that were not recently communist. The data in this table are interval; because we do not meet the assumptions for a parametric test, we will have to convert our data from interval to ordinal as one step of our calculations.

COUNTRY	PRIDE SCORE
Not Communist	
Ireland	2.90
Austria	2.40
Spain	1.60
Portugal	1.60
Sweden	1.20
Communist	
Hungary	1.60
Czech Republic	1.30
Slovenia	1.10
Slovakia	1.10
Poland	0.90

Symbol: *U*

equivalents of the independent-samples *t* test. The **Mann–Whitney U test** *is a nonparmaetric hypothesis test used when there are two groups, a between-groups design, and an ordinal dependent variable.* It is symbolized as *U*.

As in previous situations, we may have started with ordinal data, or we may have converted interval data to ordinal data because we were far from meeting the assumptions of a parametric test. Table 14-6 shows the accomplishment-related national pride scores for the 10 countries.

As noted earlier, nonparametric tests use the same six steps of hypothesis testing as parametric tests but are usually easier to calculate.

Step 1. Determine the assumptions.

There are three assumptions: (1) The data must be ordinal. (2) We should use random selection; otherwise, our ability to generalize will be limited. (3) Ideally, no ranks are tied. The Mann–Whitney *U* test is robust with respect to violations of the third assumption; if there are only a few ties, then it is usually safe to proceed.

Summary: We will convert our data from interval to ordinal. The researchers did not indicate whether they used random selection to choose the European countries in the sample, so we must be cautious when generalizing from these results. There are some ties, but we will assume that there are not so many as to render the results of the test invalid.

Step 2: State the null and research hypotheses.

We will state the null and research hypotheses only in words, not in symbols.

Summary: Null hypothesis: European countries with recent communist histories and those without recent communist histories do not differ in accomplishment-related national pride.

Research hypothesis: European countries with recent communist histories and those without recent communist histories differ in accomplishment-related national pride.

■ The **Mann–Whitney *U* test** is a nonparametric hypothesis test used when there are two groups, a between-groups design, and an ordinal dependent variable.

one-way between-groups ANOVA. The same six steps of hypothesis testing are used for both parametric and nonparametric tests, but the steps and the calculations for the nonparametric tests tend to be simpler.

■ DIGGING DEEPER INTO THE DATA: TRANSFORMING SKEWED DATA, THE MEANING OF INTERVAL DATA, AND BOOTSTRAPPING

In addition to nonparametric tests, one method for handling skewed data is a data transformation. Specifically, interval data can be mathematically transformed (e.g., *square root transformation, log transformations*) so that the distribution is more normal. Since the development of nonparametric tests, there has been a great deal of debate about their use. Some advocate that they be used more, arguing that most psychological measures are not interval. Others argue that parametric tests are robust and are usually the best—and typically more statistically powerful—choice. Others have developed new techniques, adding to the array of statistical choices. An increasingly used technique is *bootstrapping*, in which the researcher continually samples with replacement from the original sample. The enormous number of calculations necessary to do this can only be carried out with today's fast computers. This technique allows us to develop a 95% confidence interval from the middle 95% of the means of the many samples.

SPSS GUIDELINES FOR CHAPTER 14: OTHER PARAMETRIC TESTS

SPSS offers multiple ways to analyze ordinal data. For example, we can examine the correlation between two ordinal variables by conducting a Spearman's correlation.

We can do this by selecting:

Analyze → Correlate → Bivariate → Select "Spearman" under "Correlation Coeffecient." Choose two ordinal variables under "Variables."

We may also need to compare the ordinal data of two independent groups by conducting a Mann–Whitney *U* test.

We can do this by selecting:

Analyze → Nonparametric Tests → Two Independent-Samples Tests → Select Mann Whitney *U* as the test type → Select "Descriptive" under "Options" if you want the descriptive data as well. The dependent variable goes under "Test Variable List" and the independent goes under "Grouping Variable." Be sure to define your groups by clicking "Define Groups" and telling SPSS what you have called each of your conditions (e.g., 1 and 2).

EXERCISES

14.1 Parametric versus nonparametric—choosing the type of test: For each of the following research questions, state whether a parametric or nonparametric hypothesis test is more appropriate. Explain your answers.

a. Are women more or less likely than men to be economics majors?

b. At a small company with 15 staff and 1 big boss, do those with college educations tend to make a different amount of money from those without them?

c. At your high school, did athletes or nonathletes tend to have higher grade point averages?

d. At your high school, did athletes or nonathletes tend to have higher class ranks?

e. Compare car accidents in which the occupants were wearing seat belts with accidents in which the occupants were not wearing seat belts. Do seat belts seem to make a difference in the numbers of accidents that lead to no injuries, nonfatal injuries, and fatal injuries?

f. Compare car accidents in which the occupants were wearing seat belts with accidents in which the occupants were not wearing seat belts. Were those wearing seat belts driving at slower speeds, on average, than those not wearing seat belts?

14.2 The shape of a distribution and cell phone bills: In Chapter 3, we displayed data that depicted the relation between students' monthly cell phone bills and the number of hours they report that they study per week.

a. What does the accompanying scatterplot suggest about the shape of the distribution for hours studied per week? What does it suggest about the shape of the distribution for monthly cell phone bill?

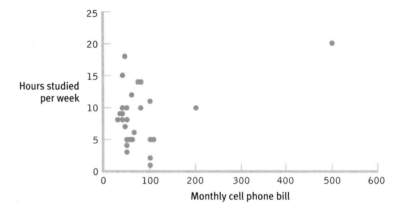

b. What does the accompanying grouped frequency histogram suggest about the shape of the distribution for monthly cell phone bill?

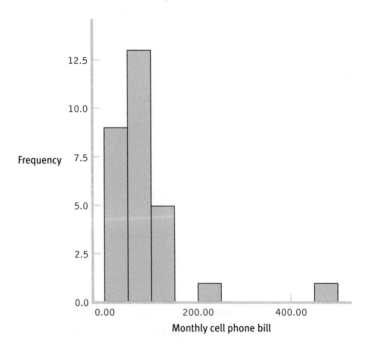

c. Is it a good idea to use a parametric hypothesis test for these data? Explain.

14.3 Interval versus ordinal data and cell phone bills: Here are the monthly cell phone bills displayed in the graphs in Exercise 14.2:

100	60	35	50	50	50	60	65
0	75	100	55	50	40	80	
200	30	50	108	500	100	45	
40	45	50	40	40	100	80	

a. Convert these data from interval to ordinal. (Don't forget to put them in order first.) What happens to the outlier when you convert these data to ordinal?

b. Roughly, what shape would the distribution of these data be? Would they likely be normally distributed? Explain why the distribution of ordinal data is never normal.

c. Why does it not matter if the ordinal variable is normally distributed? (*Hint:* Think about what kind of hypothesis test you'll conduct.)

14.4 Ordinal data—choosing from among hypothesis tests for ranked data, Part I: You're applying to graduate school and have found a list of the top 50 PhD programs for your area of study. For each of the following scenarios, state which nonparametric hypothesis test is most appropriate: Spearman rank-order correlation coefficient, Wilcoxon signed-rank test, Mann–Whitney U test, or Kruskal–Wallis H test. Explain your answers.

a. You want to determine which institutions tend to be higher ranked: those that fund students primarily by offering fellowships, those that fund students primarily by offering teaching assistantships, or those that don't have full funding for most students.

b. You wonder whether rankings are related to the typical GRE scores of incoming students.

c. You decide to compare the rankings of institutions within a three-hour drive of your current home and those beyond a three-hour drive.

14.5 Ordinal data—choosing from among hypothesis tests for ranked data, Part II: CNN.com reported on a 2005 study that ranked the world's cities in terms of how livable they are (http://www.cnn.com/2005/WORLD/europe/10/04/eui.survey/) using a range of criteria related to stability, health care, culture and environment, education, and infrastructure. Vancouver came out on top. For each of the following research questions, state which nonparametric hypothesis test is most appropriate: Spearman rank-order correlation coefficient, Wilcoxon signed-rank test, Mann–Whitney U test, or Kruskal–Wallis H test. Explain your answers.

a. Which cities tend to receive higher rankings—those north or south of the equator?

b. Did the top-10 cities tend to change their rankings since the previous study?

c. Are the livability rankings related to a city's economic status?

14.6 Spearman correlation coefficient and fantasy baseball: In fantasy baseball, groups of 12 league participants conduct a draft in which they can "buy" any baseball players from any teams across one of the leagues (i.e., the American League or National League). These makeshift teams are compared on the basis of the combined statistics of the individual baseball players. Statistics such as home runs are awarded points, and each fantasy team receives a total score of all combined points for its baseball players, regardless of their real-life team. Many in the fantasy and real-life baseball worlds have wondered how success in fantasy leagues maps onto the real-life success of winning baseball games. Walker (2006) compared the fantasy league performances of the players for each American League team with their actual American League finishes for the 2004 season, the year the Red Sox broke the curse and won the World Series. The data, sorted from highest to lowest fantasy league score, are shown in the accompanying table.

TEAM	FANTASY LEAGUE POINTS	ACTUAL AMERICAN LEAGUE FINISH
Boston	117.5	2
New York	109.5	1
Anaheim	108	3.5
Minnesota	97	3.5
Texas	85	6
Chicago	80	7
Cleveland	79	8
Oakland	77	5
Baltimore	74.5	9
Detroit	68.5	10
Seattle	51	13
Tampa Bay	47.5	11
Toronto	35.5	12
Kansas City	20	14

a. What are the two variables of interest? For each variable, state whether it's interval or ordinal.

b. Calculate the Spearman correlation coefficient for these two variables. Remember to convert any interval variables to ranks.

c. What does the coefficient tell us about the relation between these two variables?

d. Why could we not have calculated a Pearson correlation coefficient?

14.7 Spearman correlation coefficient and test-taking speed: Does speed in completing a test correlate with one's grade? Here are test scores for eight students in one of our statistics classes. They are arranged in order from the student who turned in the test first to the student who turned in the test last.

$$98 \quad 74 \quad 87 \quad 92 \quad 88 \quad 93 \quad 62 \quad 67$$

a. What are the two variables of interest? For each variable, state whether it's interval or ordinal.

b. Calculate the Spearman correlation coefficient for these two variables. Remember to convert any interval variables to ranks.

c. What does the coefficient tell us about the relation between these two variables?

d. Why could we not have calculated a Pearson correlation coefficient?

14.8 Interpreting Spearman correlation and test-taking speed: Consider again the two variables described in Exercise 14.7, test grade and speed in taking the test. Imagine that each of the following numbers represents the Spearman correlation coefficient that quantifies the relation between these two variables—test grade converted to ranks such that the top grade of 98 is ranked 1, and speed in taking the test with the fastest person ranked 1. What does each coefficient suggest about the relation between the variables? Using the guidelines for the Pearson correlation coefficient, indicate whether each coefficient is roughly small (0.10), medium (0.30), or large (0.50). Specify which of these coefficients suggests the strongest relation between the two variables as well as which coefficient suggests the weakest relation between the two variables. [You calculated the actual correlation between these variables in Exercise 14.7(b).]

a. 1.00

b. −0.001

c. 0.52

d. −0.27

e. −0.98

f. 0.09

14.9 Spearman correlation, causation, and test-taking speed: Exercise 14.7 presented data to enable you to calculate the Spearman correlation coefficient that quantifies the relation between the speed of taking the test and the test grade.

a. Does this correlation coefficient suggest that students should take their tests as quickly as possible? That is, does it indicate that taking the test quickly *causes* a good grade? Explain your answer.

b. What third variables might be responsible for this correlation? That is, what third variables might cause both speedy test-taking and a good test grade?

14.10 Wilcoxon signed-rank test for matched pairs and the NHL: Are Canadian professional hockey teams consistent over time? Here are the wins per season (out of 82 games) for the six Canadian teams in the National Hockey League (NHL). For comparison, in 1995–1996, the top team in the Eastern Conference was the Pittsburgh Penguins with 49 wins, and the top team in the Western Conference was the Detroit Red Wings with 62 wins. In 2005–2006, the top team in the Eastern Conference was the Ottawa Senators with 52 wins, and the top team in the Western Conference was, again, Detroit with 58 wins. (The Winnipeg Jets moved and became the Phoenix Coyotes in 1996, so we didn't include them here.)

TEAM	1995–1996 SEASON	2005–2006 SEASON
Calgary Flames	34	46
Edmonton Oilers	30	41
Montreal Canadiens	40	42
Ottawa Senators	18	52
Toronto Maple Leafs	34	41
Vancouver Canucks	32	42

a. What is the independent variable, and what are its levels? What is the dependent variable?

b. Is this a between-groups or within-groups design? Explain.

c. Why might it be preferable to use a nonparametric hypothesis test for these data?

d. Conduct all six steps of hypothesis testing for a Wilcoxon signed-rank test for matched pairs.

e. How would you present these statistics in a journal article?

14.11 Wilcoxon signed-rank test for matched pairs and airline fares: Which Web site offers better fares—CheapTickets.com or Expedia.com? We conducted searches in February 2007 for the cheapest fares for round-trip international flights during peak summer travel season: leaving on July 7, 2007, and returning on July 28, 2007. We conducted a search for each itinerary using both search engines.

ITINERARY	CHEAPTICKETS.COM	EXPEDIA.COM
Athens, GA, to Johannesburg, South Africa	$2403	$2580
Chicago to Chennai, India	1884	2044
Columbus, OH to Belgrade, Serbia	1259	1436
Denver to Geneva, Switzerland	1392	1412
Montreal to Dublin, Ireland	1097	1152
New York City to Reykjavik, Iceland	935	931
San Antonio to Hong Kong	1407	1400
Toronto to Istanbul, Turkey	1261	1429
Tulsa to Guadalajara, Mexico	565	507
Vancouver to Melbourne, Australia	1621	1613

a. What is the independent variable, and what are its levels? What is the dependent variable?

b. Is this a between-groups or within-groups design? Explain.

c. Conduct all six steps of hypothesis testing for a Wilcoxon signed-rank test for matched pairs.

d. How would you present these statistics in a journal article?

14.12 Mann–Whitney U test and graduate school in sociology: Do public or private universities tend to have better sociology graduate programs? *U.S. News & World Report* publishes online rankings of graduate schools across a range of disciplines. Here is their 2005 list of the top 21 sociology PhD programs, along with an indication of whether they're public or private institutions. Schools listed at the same rank are tied.

1	University of Wisconsin, Madison (public)
2	University of California, Berkeley (public)
3	University of Michigan, Ann Arbor (public)
4.5	University of Chicago (private)
4.5	University of North Carolina (public)
6.5	Princeton University (private)
6.5	Stanford University (private)
8.5	Harvard University (private)
8.5	University of California, Los Angeles (public)
10	University of Pennsylvania (private)
12	Columbia University (private)
12	Indiana University, Bloomington (public)
12	Northwestern University (private)
15	Cornell University (private)
15	Duke University (private)
15	University of Texas, Austin (public)
18	Pennsylvania State University–University Park (public)
18	University of Arizona (public)
18	University of Washington (public)
20.5	The Ohio State University (public)
20.5	Yale University (private)

a. What is the independent variable, and what are its levels? What is the dependent variable?

b. Is this a between-groups or within-groups design? Explain.

c. Why do we have to use a nonparametric hypothesis test for these data?

d. Conduct all six steps of hypothesis testing for a Mann–Whitney U test.

e. How would you present these statistics in a journal article?

14.13 Mann-Whitney U test and voter turnout: Do red states (U.S. states whose residents tend to vote Republican) have different voter turnouts from blue states (U.S. states whose residents tend to vote Democratic)? The accompanying table shows voter turnouts (in percentages) for the 2004 presidential election for eight randomly selected red states and eight randomly selected blue states (from http://elections.gmu.edu/Voter_Turnout_2004.htm).

RED STATES	%	BLUE STATES	%
Georgia	57.38	California	60.01
Idaho	64.89	Illinois	60.73
Indiana	55.69	Maine	73.40
Louisiana	60.78	New Jersey	64.54
Missouri	66.89	Oregon	70.50
Montana	64.36	Vermont	66.19
Texas	53.35	Washington	67.42
Virginia	61.50	Wisconsin	76.73

a. What is the independent variable, and what are its levels? What is the dependent variable?

b. Is this a between-groups or within-groups design? Explain.

c. Conduct all six steps of hypothesis testing for a Mann–Whitney U test.

d. How would you present these statistics in a journal article?

14.14 Kruskal–Wallis H test and political science graduate programs: In what region do political science graduate programs tend to have the best rankings—East Coast (E), West Coast (W), or Midwest (M)? Here are data from *U.S. News & World Report*'s 2005 online rankings of graduate schools. These are the top 17 PhD programs in political science. Schools listed at the same rank are tied.

1	Harvard University (E)
2	Stanford University (W)
3	University of Michigan, Ann Arbor (M)
4	Princeton University (E)
5.5	University of California, Berkeley (W)
5.5	Yale University (E)
7	University of California, Davis (W)
8.5	Duke University (E)
8.5	University of Chicago (M)
11	Columbia University (E)
11	Massachusetts Institute of Technology (E)
11	University of California, Los Angeles (W)
14	The Ohio State University (M)
14	University of North Carolina, Chapel Hill (E)
14	University of Rochester (E)
16.5	University of Wisconsin, Madison (M)
16.5	Washington University in St. Louis (M)

a. What is the independent variable, and what are its levels? What is the dependent variable?

b. Is this a between-groups or within-groups design? Explain.

c. Why do we have to use a nonparametric hypothesis test for these data?

d. Conduct all six steps of hypothesis testing for a Kruskal–Wallis *H* test.

e. How would you present these statistics in a journal article?

f. Explain why a statistically significant Kruskal–Wallis *H* statistic does not tell us exactly where the specific differences lie.

14.15 Kruskal–Wallis *H* test and smart states: The Morgan Quitno Press regularly ranks U.S. states on how "smart" they are based on 21 criteria, including per-student school expenditures, percent of population with high school degrees, high school dropout rate, average class size, and "percent of 4th graders whose parents have strict rules about getting homework done." Here are the rankings for all 50 states for 2004. Do the Northeast (NE), Midwest (MW), and South (S) tend to have different rankings from one another?

1. Massachusetts (NE)	26. Missouri (MW)
2. Connecticut (NE)	27. Delaware
3. Vermont (NE)	28. Utah
4. New Jersey (NE)	29. Idaho
5. Wisconsin (MW)	30. Washington
6. New York (NE)	31. Michigan (MW)
7. Minnesota (MW)	32. South Carolina (S)
8. Iowa (MW)	33. Texas
9. Pennsylvania (NE)	34. West Virginia
10. Montana	35. Oregon
11. Maine (NE)	36. Arkansas (S)
12. Virginia (S)	37. Kentucky (S)
13. Nebraska (MW)	38. Georgia (S)
14. New Hampshire (NE)	39. Florida (S)
15. Kansas (MW)	40. Oklahoma
16. Wyoming	41. Tennessee (S)
17. Indiana (MW)	42. Hawaii
18. Maryland	43. California
19. North Dakota	44. Alabama (S)
20. Ohio (MW)	45. Alaska
21. Colorado	46. Louisiana (S)
22. South Dakota	47. Mississippi (S)
23. Rhode Island (NE)	48. Arizona
24. Illinois (MW)	49. Nevada
25. North Carolina (S)	50. New Mexico

a. What is the independent variable, and what are its levels? What is the dependent variable?

b. Is this a between-groups or within-groups design? Explain.

c. Why do we have to use a nonparametric hypothesis test for these data?

d. Conduct all six steps of hypothesis testing for a Kruskal–Wallis *H* test. Note that you'll have to rank just the states included in this study, separate from the original ranking list.

e. How would you present these statistics in a journal article?

f.   Explain why a statistically significant Kruskal–Wallis H statistic does not tell us exactly where the specific differences lie. If there is a statistically significant finding for this example, determine where the difference lies by calculating Kruskal–Wallis H statistics for each pair.

14.16 Tying it all together—reading the results of a nonparametric test and dreams: Spanish researchers reported the following: "Using the Mann-Whitney nonparametrical statistical test on the gender differences, we found a significant difference between boys and girls in Group 1 for overall [aggression] $(U = 44.00, p = 0.004)$ and received aggression $(U = 48.00, p = 0.005)$. So, in their dreams, younger boys not only had a higher level of general aggression but also received more *severe* aggressive acts than girls of the same age" (emphasis in original) (Oberst, Charles, & Chamarro, 2005 p. 175).

a.   What is the independent variable, and what are its levels? What is the dependent variable?

b.   Is this a between-groups or within-groups design?

c.   What hypothesis test did the researchers conduct? Why might they have chosen a nonparametric test? Why do you think they chose this particular nonparametric test?

d.   Describe what they found in your own words.

e.   Can we conclude that gender caused a difference in levels of aggression in dreams? Explain. Provide at least two reasons why gender might not cause certain levels of aggression in dreams even though these variables are associated.

14.17 The symbols of statistics: For each of the following, (i) identify the incorrect symbol, (ii) state what the correct symbol should be, and (iii) explain why the initial symbol was incorrect.

a. $r = 1 - \dfrac{6(\Sigma D^2)}{N(N^2 - 1)}$

b. $H = \left[\dfrac{12}{N(N + 1)}\right][\Sigma n(\mu - GM)^2]$

c. $U_1 = (n_1)(n_2) + \dfrac{n_1(n_1 + 1)}{2} - \Sigma R_1^2$

d. $t = \Sigma R_{Smaller}$

▪ DIGGING DEEPER INTO THE DATA

14.18 Data transformations and cell phone bills: The following data from monthly cell phone bills were presented in Exercise 14.3.

100	60	35	50	50	50	60	65
0	75	100	55	50	40	80	
200	30	50	108	500	100	45	
40	45	50	40	40	100	80	

a.   Apply a square root transformation to every observation.

b.   Sketch a histogram of the data after the transformation.

c.   Compare the histogram you drew for part (b) to the one shown in Exercise 14.2(b). Describe the shape of both distributions with respect to skew. How did the distribution change following the transformation?

14.19 When are the same differences not really the same?: For the following situations, state which difference seems like more (even if, as in one case below, it's actually less), and explain why it seems like more. Note that part (d) is not a fourth scenario; rather it's a different, but related, question.

a. You are deciding between two boxes of cereal, and one costs $5 more than the other. You are deciding between two flat-screen TVs, and one costs $5 more than the other.

b. Some background information: In major league baseball, few players have ever broken a batting average of 0.400 in a single season. On the other hand, hitting below 0.250 is considered poor performance. The all-time league average is approximately 0.270. Roberto Clemente, a Puerto Rican native, played baseball for the Pittsburgh Pirates from 1955 to 1972, the year he died when the cargo plane on which he was a passenger crashed while traveling to Nicaragua with relief supplies for earthquake victims. He was elected to the Baseball Hall of Fame in 1973, the first year in which he was eligible. For the year 1955, Clemente hit 0.255; the next year, he hit 0.311. The increase in batting average was 0.056. In 1966, Clemente hit 0.317; the next year, he hit 0.357. The increase was 0.040, a smaller increase than the one Clemente achieved from 1955 to 1956.

c. Imagine that you received a 60 on your first statistics quiz and a 70 on your second. Your friend received an 88 on his first statistics quiz and a 98 on his second. Another friend received a 5 on her first statistics quiz and a 15 on her second. Assume that all scores are out of a possible 100.

d. We have defined an interval variable as one in which the differences between scores have some standard meaning. In light of this, explain why the phenomenon you observed in parts (a) through (c) might lead us to question whether the variables that we study in the behavioral sciences are truly interval variables. Cite an example from the behavioral sciences in your answer.

14.20 Bootstrapping and Angelman syndrome: Angelman syndrome is a rare genetic disease in which children are delayed developmentally and exhibit unusual symptoms, such as inappropriate and prolonged laughter, difficulty with speaking or inability to speak, and seizures. Imagine that a researcher was able to obtain vocabulary data for six children with Angelman syndrome and wants to develop an estimate of the mean vocabulary score of the population of children with this disorder. (Although those with Angelman syndrome often cannot speak, they are usually able to understand at least some simple language and they may learn to communicate with sign language.) The General Social Survey asks children the meaning of 10 words using a multiple-choice format; the GSS data have a mean of 6.1 with a standard deviation of 2.1. The fictional data for the six children with Angelman syndrome are: 0, 1, 1, 2, 3, and 4. Write each of these six numbers on a separate, small piece of paper.

a. Put the six pieces of paper in a bowl or hat, and then pull six out, one at a time, replacing each one and mixing them up before pulling the next. List the numbers and take the mean. Repeat this two more times so that you have three lists and three means.

b. We did this 20 times and got the following 20 means:

1.833   1.167   2.000   2.333   1.333   1.333   2.000   1.667   1.667   1.667

1.500   1.000   1.500   1.667   1.833   1.500   1.667   2.333   2.167   2.000

Determine the 90% confidence interval for these means. (*Hint:* Arrange them in order, and then choose the middle 90% of scores.) Remember, were we really to bootstrap our data, we would have a computer do it because 20 means is far too few.

c. Why is bootstrapping a helpful technique in this particular situation?

14.21 The language of statistics—*transformation*: In your own words, define the word *transformation*—first as you would use it in everyday conversation and then as a statistician would use it.

14.22 The language of statistics—*bootstrap:* In your own words, define the verb *to bootstrap*—first as you would use it in everyday conversation and then as a statistician would use it.

TERMS

Spearman rank-order correlation coefficient (p. 624)

Wilcoxon signed-rank test (p. 633)

Mann–Whitney U test (p. 636)

Kruskal–Wallis H test (p. 639)

square root transformation (p. 644)

log transformation (p. 644)

logarithm (p. 644)

bootstrapping (p. 646)

SYMBOLS

r_S

T

U

H

FORMULAS

$$r_S = 1 - \frac{6(\sum D^2)}{N(N^2 - 1)}$$

$$T = \sum R_{Smaller}$$

$$U_1 = (n_1)(n_2) + \frac{n_1(n_1 + 1)}{2} = \sum R_1$$

$$U_2 = (n_1)(n_2) + \frac{n_2(n_2 + 1)}{2} = \sum R_2$$

$$H = \left[\frac{12}{N(N + 1)} \right][\sum n(M - GM)^2]$$

CHOOSING A STATISTICAL TEST AND REPORTING THE RESULTS
THE PROCESS OF STATISTICS

On August 9, 1945, chance spared the city of Kokura. Cloud cover diverted a B-29 bomber to its secondary target, a port city in southern Japan. But chance was not kind to the city of Nagasaki. A brief opening in the cloud cover allowed the crew to confirm their location, then release and explode their plutonium-based atomic bomb about 550 meters (1800 feet) above a tennis court. Like Hiroshima three days earlier, most of the city of Nagasaki simply disappeared. Chance variability matters.

An estimated 70,000 to 74,000 people died immediately in Nagasaki. Six days later, Japan surrendered unconditionally and World War II at last came to its bloody end. But the war didn't come to an end for the additional 70,000 people from Nagasaki who later died from bomb-related illnesses such as radioactive poisoning. And the war didn't end psychologically for the surviving families and returning soldiers from every country who had witnessed the worst that humanity had yet inflicted on itself. So how is it possible that only sixty years later, the city of Nagasaki is a thriving port city with almost half a million people? Today, it is an export center for Mitsubishi and other Japanese manufacturers, and the local citizens are especially proud of their new symbol of prosperity, the magnificent Megami Ohashi (Goddess) Bridge.

How did geographically tiny Japan re-create itself from such thorough devastation? The country did not have the natural resources that other nations could use to bootstrap their way back to economic independence. The emperor was forbidden to exercise any political authority. And General Douglas MacArthur was a virtual dictator, charged with directing the ruined nation back to some safer form of democratic prosperity. To do this, MacArthur needed to

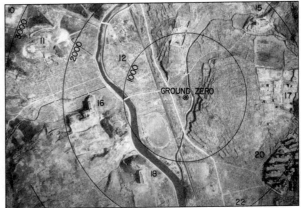

Nagasaki, Two Days Before the Atomic Bomb

Nagasaki, Three Days After the Atomic Bomb

communicate across all of Japan's many islands and remote regions, so he directed the Japanese industrial sector to manufacture transistor radios (Bowles, 1994). "Made in Japan" transistor radios were among the first postwar Japanese products to cross the ocean into the United States.

More important, Japanese business leaders looked to manufacturing as their path to economic self-revitalization. To help, MacArthur called in a relatively obscure, but innovative, statistician from the U. S. Census Bureau, W. Edwards Deming, to consult with Japanese leaders about how to manufacture better products for less money. General MacArthur might not have appointed Deming if he had realized that he was an independent-thinking contrarian. If everyone turned left, Deming's impulse was to look to the right to see what was happening. For example, nearly everyone believed that the postwar United States was the world's foremost industrial power and would remain that way for the foreseeable future. Deming didn't see it that way, however, and it required a lot of conviction to be an economic contrarian in the 1950s.

After the war, the tag "Made in the USA" was so potent a symbol of industrial might that the struggling Japanese created the village of Usa so they, too, could label products with "Made in USA" (Magnier, 1999). The entire world looked to the United States to supply its many material needs, and the United States was glad to sell products to former allies and enemies alike. But Deming had a different way of thinking, and he remained unimpressed with the quality of American products and the process by which they were created.

Why was Deming so independent a thinker? Perhaps it was the struggle for economic survival in the tar-paper shack that he grew up in, the long annual fight against the elements of Wyoming winters, his parents' deep belief in education, or his academic training in mathematics and physics. Whatever the cause, Deming thought that American manufacturers were headed for trouble, even though they were living through a period of unparalleled prosperity.

Deming didn't just believe that U.S. manufacturers were headed for trouble; he believed that their methods were counterproductive, and his convictions were the product of statistical reasoning. Japan's leading postwar engineers and businessmen gathered in 1950 for a seminar to be taught by Deming and immediately began applying his ideas. The Japanese industrial miracle was about to be triggered by W. Edwards Deming's ability to translate the insights from one statistical idea—variability—into thousands of different solutions.

This chapter provides the very small details that allow us to select and then report the sources of variability as they are customarily presented in professional journals. Deming would have suggested that getting these small details right matters because the same statistics that test the reliability of small questions (such as the reliability of a measurement of room temperature) also test the larger questions (such as whether Earth is warming, cooling, or experiencing normal fluctuations). Deming believed that when we ask the right questions, the little reporting details can provide critical insights into the reliability and validity of those larger issues. At a more practical level, learning how to report statistics convinces reviewers, editors, professors, and our eventual audience that we really know what we're doing. So, if we want our research to be heard by a larger audience, then we need to to report statistics accurately.

> BEFORE WE EVEN BEGIN: CHOOSING THE RIGHT STATISTICAL TEST

The authors of this text have worked as statistical consultants in several different contexts. A recurring issue in this work is the tendency for individuals with no research training to believe that they can design and implement research and then just hire a statistician to swoop in and analyze the results. We have seen this practice lead to a range of problems: the lack of random selection when it might have been possible, an absence of random assignment when it was warranted, inclusion of obvious confounds, and misleading operational definitions. We'll present three real-life cases (with identifying details disguised) to show how a poorly designed study can lead to results that are difficult to interpret. Then we'll demonstrate how statistical reasoning and accurate reporting can help to avoid post-data collection regret that is common within organizations.

Planning Your Statistics First: How to Avoid Post–Data Collection Regret

Case 1: A project assessing the effectiveness of different Web site characteristics for a major North American company implemented a research design that confounded color with shape. The company had identified the variables it was interested in and included variations of them on the homepage of its Web site. The first independent variable of interest was the color of the Web site, with three levels: blue, red, and yellow. The second was the shape of the image on the Web site, also with three levels: let's say square, circle, and triangle. In one sense, of course, these are artistic decisions, but that doesn't mean that we can't use statistical reasoning to determine which artistic choices best serve the company's interests. Here's where the company went wrong.

In their flawed attempt to conduct a controlled study, the project managers randomly varied the homepage that each Internet surfer saw, and they tracked the number of seconds that each individual spent on the site (their dependent variable)—so far, so good. But their research design had just three cells (Table 15-1) instead of the nine cells they really needed (Table 15-2). In their research design, the variable, color of Web site, was confounded with the variable, shape of image. If the blue square led to the longest amount of time spent on the Web site, we can't know whether it was because of the blue color or the square shape. There is no way to separate these confounded variables; there is no way

TABLE 15-1. POOR RESEARCH DESIGN

A study comparing the time spent on a company's Web site contingent on variations in the characteristics of the Web site included three levels of two independent variables; the first independent variable was color of Web site, represented here by the levels of blue, red, and yellow; the second independent variable was shape of Web site, represented here by the levels square, circle, and triangle. The company wanted to know which color and which shape worked best, but the two variables were confounded with each other.

Blue square	Red circle	Yellow triangle

to assess the effect of the blue color without the square shape or of the square shape without the blue color. This same problem also existed in each of the other two cells.

What the researchers really needed was a crossed design, in this case a 3×3 ANOVA research design. Participants would be assigned to one particular level of each independent variable, separate from the other independent variable. Each participant would be randomly assigned to one of nine variations of the Web site homepage. (Remember, we calculate the number of cells by multiplying the levels of each independent variable: $3 \times 3 = 9$.) One participant might be assigned to view a homepage with a blue square, another to view a homepage with a red square, another to view a homepage with a blue triangle, and so on, as illustrated in Table 15-2.

This research design would allow the project managers to separate the effects of each of the two independent variables. If more time was spent on the Web site with the blue color than on the Web sites with the other two colors, *regardless of the accompanying design*, then we would know that it was color, not shape, that was having the effect. Statistically, we would refer to that outcome as a main effect of color of Web site on the dependent variable of time spent on the Web site. We would also have the opportunity to discover whether there was an interaction between these two variables. For example, perhaps the blue color led to a particularly long time spent on the Web site when combined with the triangle, but not with the square or circle. That would show up as a statistical interaction. Why? The effect of the independent variable color of Web site on the dependent variable time spent on Web site *depended* on a particular level of shape of image—in this case, the triangle. But without a crossed, 3×3

TABLE 15-2. BETTER RESEARCH DESIGN

What the company really needed was a crossed design in which each Internet surfer was randomly assigned to a homepage based first on color and then separately on shape. Each individual would be randomly assigned one of nine variations: a blue square, a blue circle, a blue triangle, a red square, a red circle, and so on.

	BLUE	RED	YELLOW
SQUARE	Blue square	Red square	Yellow square
CIRCLE	Blue circle	Red circle	Yellow circle
TRIANGLE	Blue triangle	Red triangle	Yellow triangle

research design, the curious insight that a Web site using a blue triangle was most effective would be lost. In reality, research time and money were wasted and potential customers became frustrated as they tried to work their way through an unappealing Web site. The only satisfying piece of that particular puzzle was the consulting fee.

Case 2. A survey designed to assess public opinion with respect to women's issues in a small town included the question: Do you agree that women should have equal rights to men? But this study had a sampling problem. Specifically, the study was administered by leaving a stack of surveys at the entrance to the town's municipal building with a box in which to place completed surveys. Every respondent except for two elderly men responded "yes." This question had a socially acceptable answer: yes. Even if someone thought that women should not have equal rights, there is enormous societal pressure to keep such a view to oneself. So there wasn't likely to be much variability.

An additional problem, also related to sampling, was that the sample included only people who were entering the municipal building *and* were interested enough in women's issues to respond. Moreover, it is debatable whether the administration of the survey provided any sense of anonymity. Even if the sample were representative of the population and provided anonymity, it was too vague. What was meant by "equal rights"? With practically no variability in the answer, no hypothesis tests could be conducted using this as either an independent or dependent variable. (Remember, variables vary; most statistics involve calculations of variability.) This survey was merely a waste of time for the respondents, the researchers, and the trees that contributed the paper on which it was distributed. Even worse, one can easily imagine a misleading newspaper headline reporting "Study Proves Town Is Not Biased."

Case 3. A doctoral student in one of the social sciences created two scales to assess his construct of interest. One scale included a number of items, but when it was analyzed after the study, it showed poor internal consistency—a low coefficient alpha. Specifically, the individual items on that scale did not appear to measure the same thing, an indication that the measure was not reliable and therefore unlikely to be valid. A pilot study before the real study or the use of an existing measure might have allowed this student to proceed with a reliable and valid scale. A second scale included only one item. There is no way to calculate a coefficient alpha on a scale with just one item. (Remember, a coefficient alpha is essentially the average of all possible split-half reliabilities.) If the scale cannot be split in half (because there's just one item), then we cannot calculate any split-half reliabilities. Neither scale is likely to allow the researcher to gather reliable and valid data. This student was taking an unnecessary and costly detour on the way to earning a PhD.

In all of the cases above, individuals with no research training or limited research skills began a project without consulting someone with research and statistical experience. A consultation could have led to a redesign of the methodology of all these studies, which would have led to data that could be statistically analyzed more readily. Such planning would have saved a great deal of time and money. Confounding variables (case 1), poor sampling (case 2), and using inappropriate scales (case 3) are common mistakes, even among those well versed in research methods and statistics. Such mistakes are almost always due to lack of forethought, and they can be expensive, embarrassing, and frustrating. But now you don't have to make them.

There are four main questions we can ask ourselves to make sure we gather data that can be statistically analyzed in an appropriate way:

1. What is the goal of this research?
2. What are the specific hypotheses?
3. What are the variables, and what are the levels of those variables?
4. What statistical analyses do we plan to use?

In case 1, the goal is fairly obvious. What attributes of a Web site lead to increased time spent there and more purchases of the product for sale? (In fact, the company did include a separate dependent variable related to sales.) No thought was given, however, to the hypotheses or the planned statistical analyses. The researchers assumed that a statistician could work with whatever data were handed over and just "find the pattern in the data." Had the hypotheses been outlined and the statistics planned in advance, then the confound would have been clear. The two nominal independent variables and the interval dependent variable would have been identified, and the appropriate statistical test could have been chosen in advance. The research design would have enabled the statistician to conduct a 3 × 3 between-groups ANOVA using color of Web site (blue, red, yellow) and shape of image (square, circle, triangle) as the two independent variables. And that research design could have produced a great deal of useful information.

In case 2, the goal of the research was to document the opinions of community residents. Had that goal been explicitly stated, the researchers might have devised a method to reach residents who did not visit the municipal building and who would not go out of their way to complete a survey on women's rights. Further, their goal was to identify actions that would help women in their community and ways in which these actions might succeed, despite some anticipated opposition. Rather than asking a single vague question, the researchers could have asked a series of questions aimed at gauging public response to the possible interventions that might be implemented in the community. These questions together might have formed a single scale, an interval variable.

If the researchers had carefully considered the specific goals of their research, then they would have been better equipped to outline specific hypotheses and to use the appropriate statistical analyses. This process probably would have led the researchers to list the variables that they wished to examine in the same analyses with the locals' views on women's rights. Were they interested in demographic variables such as gender, marital status, age, and ethnicity? Were they interested in program variables such as cost, availability, and time to implement? Probably. Only a clear outline of hypotheses and statistical analyses can ensure that a survey is generating the needed data.

In case 3, one of the goals of the study was to assess individuals on a new scale. A researcher who creates a new scale must demonstrate that the scale is both reliable and valid. In fact, an entire doctoral thesis could be devoted to the development of a new scale. Had this researcher thought about the statistical analyses necessary to demonstrate reliability and validity, he would have realized that they were impossible with just one item. Moreover, he would have realized that it was probably a waste of time

Planning Survey Research
Survey research is conducted every day, but researchers often approach such research without a specific plan. Carefully outlined hypotheses, thoughtfully designed measures, and clever survey methodology will lead to far better data.

Richard Lord/Photo Edit

and money to conduct his final study using a scale before he had examined its psychometric properties. Researchers often conduct a pilot study to assess a scale's reliability and validity. Feedback from the pilot study often leads researchers to reshape their research plan. Or, they may decide to use an existing scale that has the necessary psychometric characteristics of reliability and validity. After all, we want to be able to believe our own research findings when we're done.

Beyond the Statistical Plan: Tips for a Successful Study

Jacob Cohen, the pioneer and activist who advanced the concept of effect size, has been a major proponent of the improved reporting of statistics in general. The title of his classic treatise, "Things I Have Learned (So Far)" (Cohen, 1990), captures the humility of a great thinker and lifelong learner. Among the things he has learned are several lessons that should be applied to the development of our own research designs. As Cohen says, "In planning research, I think it wise to *plan* the research" (p. 1310; italics in original).

"Less is more, except of course for sample size" (Cohen, 1990, p. 1304). Cohen advocates limiting the number of independent variables and dependent variables to avoid the Type I errors that occur when there are too many comparisons in a single study. It is important, he argues, to focus on the most important variables before we start collecting data on every concept imaginable. Cohen (1990) says that his emphasis on having many participants and few variables has been mocked by his students, who "have spread the rumor that my idea of the perfect study is one with 10,000 cases and no variables. They go too far" (p. 1305). When planning a study, read the literature, develop a theory and specific hypotheses, and zero in on the most central variables.

"Simple is better" (Cohen, 1990, p. 1305). In a similar admonition, Cohen argues for simplicity in both the analysis and the reporting of data. He laments the reporting of statistics to many decimal places, both suggesting a level of precision that does not exist and cluttering the text and tables. (A sign in Montenegro directs motorists to a hotel that is "41 meters" off the main road, a level of precision that is simply funny. Avoid this in your reporting of statistics.) Cohen also encourages a minimalist approach to showing the pattern of data; a simple graph such as a frequency polygon provides more information, he suggests, than does a litany of descriptive statistics: the numerical representations of mean, standard deviation, skew, and kurtosis. The graph can show gaps in the data, outliers, and other aspects of the distribution that the numbers cannot. When planning a study, know in advance how you want to explore and display the data graphically. Even though software provides us with complex analyses that have fancy-sounding names and elaborate graphing techniques, we should aim for the simplest procedures necessary to illuminate our findings. Design your studies with this in mind.

When he discovered the benefits of power analysis, Cohen (1990) felt as if he "had died and gone to heaven" (p. 1308). Finally, he could have a sense of what sample size to aim for in his research. Cohen conducted a meta-analysis and found that the median power in published studies (to reject the null hypothesis with a medium effect size) was 0.46 (46%), well below the hoped for 0.80 (80%). In the past, the absence of pre–data collection power analyses led to absurdly low statistical power and perhaps much wasted time and money. Yet even now, when statistical power is easily calculated using tables or computers, a striking number of researchers fail to use it to guide their decisions on the appropriate sample size.

Always conduct a power analysis as part of the development of a study; the process of doing so forces us to think about our sample, the population, and the size of the effect we hope to find, all considerations that will help us to plan a valid—and useful—study. In fact, the process of calculating statistical power often uncovers flaws in the study; perhaps the expected effect size is detectable with statistical power of 0.80 only with an impossibly large sample size. So, be kind to yourself: Assess your power.

Finally, and perhaps most important, Cohen calls for the researcher's own judgment to play a central role in the process of research design and data analysis. Blind acceptance of a computer's output—say, the results of a statistical power analysis—is almost as bad as reliance only on our judgment without objective data. Always think about the numbers, ask yourself whether they make sense, and use your judgment in all phases of research, from the planning to the reporting of results.

We have argued in this section that the most important part of the pre–data collection process is the plan for the statistics. Only a very specific statistical strategy can show us what we've missed in our research design. Integral to the development of a simple, straightforward, and workable plan is the skill of identifying which statistical test is used for which situations. In the next part of this chapter, we'll introduce a rubric that will help do just that.

In summary, it is easy to miss important aspects of research design when the elements of a study are not carefully outlined prior to collecting data. Before beginning data collection, it is important to consider the goal of the research, hypotheses, and statistical analyses that will be conducted. As Cohen (1990) tells us, in research design, less is more, simple is better, and power analyses can help keep us on track. A plan that includes all this information can pinpoint areas of the research design that need to be tweaked or changed entirely, saving both time and money.

⊙ CHECK YOUR LEARNING

15-1 The dean of a college asked a member of the university's evaluation department to analyze survey data he had collected from students about their perceived effectiveness of the general education programs offered by the college. When the evaluator asked who had responded to the survey, the dean looked confused by the question and then replied, "Students who took the general education courses, of course." The evaluator then asked whether every student taking a general education course had filled out the survey, and the dean replied, "No, initially only two faculty volunteered to hand out the surveys to their class, so I asked a few of the professors I know well to hand it out for me."

a. What did the dean do incorrectly when conducting this study?

b. Can the evaluator fix the problem?

c. What should the evaluator tell the dean?

❯ GUIDELINES FOR REPORTING STATISTICS: THE COMMON LANGUAGE OF RESEARCH

Deming's ideas helped Japan to rebuild, but they were not well received in the United States. There seem to be at least three reasons for this. First, it was difficult to argue against an American system that was producing such magnificent prosperity. Second, Deming's personal style was blunt. Third, he pinned responsibility for industrial failures on the people most likely to hire him as a consultant: upper management. Deming contrasted management's habit of using statistics to identify which workers to blame with the more sensible approach of using statistics to identify the causes of product variability. Deming also resisted management fads such as TQM (total quality management): as Deming (quoted in Salsburg, 2001, p. 251) asserted

> You have a slogan, posted everywhere, urging everyone to do perfect work, nothing else. I wonder how anyone could live up to it. . . . How can he, when he is handicapped with defective materials, change of supply, machines out of order? Another roadblock is management's supposition that the production workers are responsible for all the trouble: that there would be no problems in production if only the production workers would do their jobs in the way that they know to be right.

Although American business managers rejected Deming, the Japanese industrial leadership embraced him, especially his belief that management was responsible for establishing and improving the systems that generated product variability. In fact, Deming boldly told the Japanese leaders that they could transform their manufacturing in approximately five years and later declared that they had accomplished it in only three.

Deming's core statistical insight was that high-quality products have low variability. That's it. Deming himself acknowledged that if there was one word that captured his entire philosophy of business management, it was the word *variability*. The idea that variability predicts quality is not a surprising insight at all, once we stop to think about it. For example, part of what makes Roger Federer and Rafael Nadal such a thrilling tennis rivalry is their high quality of play. During their tense, four-set championship battle at Wimbledon in 2006, both players had a statistical edge in different categories. Federer served more aces (Federer, 13; Nadal, 8), but Nadal had fewer unforced errors (Federer, 32; Nadal, 26). And between the two players, they double-faulted (missed two serves in a row) only four times (Federer, once, out of 119 total service points; Nadal, three times, out of 127 total service points). The mark of high-quality championship tennis is high reliability. So Deming's core insight is hardly an insight at all; it simply reframes a familiar idea (variability) as way to describe the quality of outcomes, whether we're talking about automobiles, electronic games, or tennis.

Once we accept the idea that high quality corresponds with low variability (around a high mean), we clarify that our management task is to reduce anything that contributes to product variability (an unreliable product). So our more specific task as a manager is to separate random (i.e., uncontrollable) variability from manageable variability, the variability that we can control. The goal is to increase the reliability of our product by reducing the manageable variability. In tennis, manageable variability might be due to using different racquets, spending less time practicing, or not warming up properly. In manufacturing, manageable variability might be due to using different parts suppliers selected by the lowest bid, using worn-out machinery to save money in the short term, or making working conditions

Wimbledon, 2006
Deming's statistical idea that high quality is characterized by low variability applies to everything from factory productivity to tennis championships. In a tense, four-set championship match at Wimbledon in 2006, Roger Federer defeated Rafael Nadal. According to the U.S. Tennis Association Web site, Federer double-faulted only once in 119 service points and Nadal double-faulted only three times in 127 service points.

AP Photo/Alastair Grant

unpleasant for employees. Deming insisted that it was management's job to plan organizational systems so that they produced low variability. He was especially insistent that management take responsibility for the systems rather than blame workers for variability that was beyond the workers' control.

Deming asserted that managing variability meant that cars and ships lasted longer, cameras worked better, quality steel was produced within specific parameters, electronic devices maintained their appeal, and consumers were eager to buy those products. Indeed, many of the products that are now familiar consumer items are the result of the way Japanese industries responded to Deming's ideas about managing variability in the 1950s. To this day, the Japanese are very specific about why they were able to transform their nation so swiftly from an economic disaster after World War II to an enduring industrial leader: The honor belongs to W. Edwards Deming. The Japanese leadership was so impressed with Deming, especially after he returned his consulting fees, that they created an annual Deming Prize. The education ministry even established "an annual Statistics Day, when students competed for prizes by creating presentations in statistics" (Salsburg, 2001, p. 249). The statistician W. Edwards Deming made the analysis of variability the central focus of his wildly successful management philosophy, and it worked—in Japan.

The Statistical Path to Improved Products
Many Japanese companies followed Deming's advice closely and reduced the variability in their products, leading to more reliable products and increased sales.

We want to transform your understanding of statistical ideas into statistical skills you can use to first ask a good question and then devise a way to discover a trustworthy answer. (As a practical matter, you should be aware that the guidelines we offer here correspond with the way that SPSS, and most other computer statistics programs, ask you to provide information about each variable.) The skills you need to select the statistical test appropriate for your particular situation are based on the following three familiar ideas:

1. How to transform observations into numbers (Chapter 1)
2. How to distinguish between independent and dependent variables (Chapter 1)
3. How to identify your research design (Chapters 5–14)

Three Skills Needed to Select the Appropriate Statistical Test: Transforming Observations into Numbers, Identifying Variables, and Selecting a Research Design

Skill 1: We provided a mnemonic device in Chapter 1 for remembering how to transform observations into numbers: N-O-I-R. Those letters represent nominal, ordinal, interval, and ratio numbers. Nominal numbers are used only for naming an observation, such as when we assign the number 1 to represent men and the number 2 to represent women as levels of the nominal variable gender. Similarly, the nominal variable religious tradition could have levels indicated by numbers such as 1 (for Muslim), 2 (for Christian), 3 (Jewish), 4 (other), and 5 (no religious tradition). Nominal numbers are only naming devices. Ordinal numbers are used when the data can be rank-ordered. So bettors at the racetrack are most interested in where their horses finish rather than how fast they finish: 1 (first place), 2 (second place), 3 (third place), and so on. Ordinal numbers inform us about who won, but not by how much. The more specific question "How much?" is an interval observation, just as the precise time needed to finish a race is a more precise observation than the order of finish in a race. Interval and ratio observations are often lumped together and called scale observations (as they are in SPSS) because they use the same type of statistical tests based on the assumption of equal intervals between observations. (And as we've done throughout the text, we'll continue to refer to both as "interval.") That's all we need to know in order to match the right type of observation to the right category of statistical tests: N-O-I-R. And it is even simpler because the I (interval) and R (ratio) are represented in SPSS as S (scale) observations: N-O-S.

Skill 2: Also in Chapter 1, we clarified that there are only three classes of variables: independent, dependent, and confounding variables. The first two are necessary for research, but confounding variables are its enemy. We try to control confounding variables through our research design because they tend to disrupt the logic of causality between the independent and the dependent variable. The behavioral sciences substitute many words for *independent variables* and *dependent variables*, such as *cause* and *effect*, *stimulus* and *response*, and *predictor* and *predicted*. They all imply some kind of predictable association between variables.

Skill 3: If we have become skillful at these first two tasks, then recognizing the research design is fairly simple, especially because there are only two general types of research designs. The first type of research design is a between-groups design in which different participants are randomly assigned to or naturally belong to (e.g., gender) different levels of the independent variable. The second type is a within-groups design in which the same participants all experience all levels of every independent variable. But there's one more question to answer in order to select the statistical test that is appropriate for our data. If our independent variable is nominal, then we need to count how many levels it has. Remember, variables vary, but only nominal variables vary in terms of qualitatively different levels. For example, gender is a between-groups variable with two levels: male and female. Religious tradition is (usually) a between-groups variable that may have several levels, depending on what we are interested in comparing, such as Muslim, Christian, or Jewish religious traditions.

These three skills are all you need to select the statistical test that is appropriate for your data: transforming observations into numbers, identifying the kinds of variables, and identifying the research design.

Let's look at an example (which has been simplified somewhat for teaching purposes). Stacy Dale and Alan Krueger (1999) conducted a study comparing two groups of students, those who attended a highly selective college and those who attended a moderately selective college. Both groups of students had been accepted at both types of institutions. In this way, students who were accepted at Harvard but chose not to go there, for example, could be compared with students who actually went to Harvard.

Krueger and Dale (1999) wanted to examine the hypothesis that those who attended highly selective colleges had higher levels of postgraduation earnings than did those who attended moderately selective colleges, as assessed by the income of graduates who were working full-time during their first year out of school. Their research was driven by the growing tendency of top high school

The Value of a Brand Name
Does a prestigious, brand-name institution like Northwestern University, pictured here, lead to a better outcome for its graduates? Among students who were accepted by both highly selective and moderately selective colleges, researchers found few differences in outcome between students who then chose to attend the top institutions versus students who chose to attend somewhat lower-ranked institutions.

Sarah Hadley/Alamy

students to view an Ivy League education as the only road to the highest levels of success. The researchers did not find a statistically significant difference between the postgraduation earnings of the two groups of students. They concluded that an individual student's characteristics, such as internal motivation, were better predictors of success than was the type of college attended.

First, we'll identify any independent variables in this study. If we can't figure out which is which, we should ask which of the variables might depend on one or more of the other variables. Would the type of college that one attends depend on one's earnings during the first year after graduation? Or would one's earnings during the first year after graduation depend on the type of college one attends? It makes more sense that postgraduation earnings might depend on type of college rather than the other way around. This means that the independent variable is type of college and the dependent variable is income the first year out of college. There is only the one independent variable: type of college. One's score on type of college is one of two categories, so it is a nominal scale. The levels of this independent variable are the two categories: highly selective and moderately selective. We already identified the dependent variable as income the first year out of school. Income in dollars is an interval variable.

Using this information, we'll create two tables to help us decide which statistical test to use. Table 15-3 shows the research design. There are just two cells in this study, one for students who attended selective schools and one for students who attended moderately selective schools. Table 15-4 summarizes the information about the independent variable and the dependent variable. With these two tables, we are ready to apply the rubric that we'll learn in the next section.

Let's look at a second example (again simplified a bit for teaching purposes). Researchers at Duke University (Cooper, Robinson, & Patall, 2006) studied the effects of homework on the success of students in grades 7–12. They assessed the time spent on homework per night as well as students' academic achievement, assessed by scores on standardized tests. The study hypothesized that the amount of time spent on homework would be associated with academic achievement among students in grades 7–12. The researchers expected that achievement would depend on time spent on homework. So we can consider achievement to be the dependent variable; achievement is assessed by a score on a standardized test, so it is an interval variable. The independent variable, therefore, is time spent on homework; time, measured in minutes, is also an interval variable. With two interval variables, we will not create a table of cells because a

TABLE 15-3.	**THE RESEARCH DESIGN**
It is useful to create a table of the research design—just two cells in this case—to help us determine the appropriate statistical test to use.	
Selective	Moderately selective

TABLE 15-4. SUMMARIZING THE VARIABLES

To determine the appropriate statistical test, it is useful to summarize the characteristics of the independent variable(s) and dependent variable in a table.

	NAME OF VARIABLE	TYPE	NUMBER OF LEVELS (FOR NOMINAL VARIABLES ONLY)	NAMES OF LEVELS (FOR NOMINAL VARIABLES ONLY)
Independent variable (or variables)	Type of college	Nominal	Two	1. Selective 2. Moderately selective
Dependent variable	Income	Interval		

TABLE 15-5. SUMMARIZING THE VARIABLES

To determine the appropriate statistical test, it is useful to summarize the characteristics of the independent variable(s) and dependent variable in a table. Here there are two interval variables. The last two columns are left blank because there are no nominal variables.

	NAME OF VARIABLE	TYPE	NUMBER OF LEVELS (FOR NOMINAL VARIABLES ONLY)	NAMES OF LEVELS (FOR NOMINAL VARIABLES ONLY)
Independent variable	Time spent on homework	Interval		
Dependent variable	Achievement	Interval		

continuous, interval variable can't be divided into discrete cells. However, we will create a table summarizing the variables (Table 15-5).

Choosing the Right Statistical Test: A Guideline

Once we have developed the two tables for each hypothesis, the bulk of the work in identifying the appropriate statistical analysis is done. There are four categories of statistical tests that we have learned:

1. Statistical tests in which all variables are interval
2. Statistical tests in which the independent variable (or variables) is nominal, but the dependent variable is interval
3. Statistical tests in which all variables are nominal
4. Statistical tests in which any variable is ordinal

Use the accompanying tables to decide which category, then use the guidelines below to decide which test to use within that category.

Category 1: Two Interval Variables

If we have a research design with only interval variables, we have two choices about how to analyze the data: the Pearson correlation coefficient or a regression analysis. The only question we have to ask ourselves is whether the research question pertains to an association, or relation, between two variables or to the degree to which one variable predicts the other. If the research question is about association, then we choose the Pearson correlation coefficient. If it is about prediction, then we choose regression. The decisions for category 1 are represented in Table 15-6.

TABLE 15-6. CATEGORY 1 STATISTICS

When both the independent variable and the dependent variable are interval, we calculate either a Pearson correlation coefficient or a regression equation.

RESEARCH QUESTION: ASSOCIATION (RELATION)	RESEARCH QUESTION: PREDICTION
Pearson correlation coefficient	Regression equation

Category 2: Nominal Independent Variable(s) and Interval Dependent Variable

If our research design includes one or more nominal independent variables and an interval dependent variable, then we have several choices. The next question pertains to the number of independent variables.

1. If there is *just one independent variable*, then we ask ourselves how many levels it has.
    a. If there are *two levels, but just one sample*—that is, one level is represented by the sample and one level by the population—then we will use either a *z* test or a single-sample *t* test. It is unusual to know enough about a population that we need to collect data only from a single sample. If this is the case, however, and we know the

population mean and standard deviation, then we can use a z test. If this is the case but we know only the population mean, not the population standard deviation, then we use the single-sample t test.

b. If there are *two levels, each represented by a sample* (either a single sample in which everyone participates in both levels or two different samples, one for each level), then we will use either a paired-samples t test (if all participants are in both levels of the independent variable) or an independent-samples t test (if participants are in only one level of the independent variable).

c. If there are *three or more levels*, then we will use a form of a one-way ANOVA. We can use Table 11-1 for naming ANOVAs to decide whether it's a between-groups ANOVA (participants in just one level of the independent variable) or a within-groups ANOVA (participants in all levels of the independent variable).

The decisions for data that fall into parts a, b, or c in Part 1 of category 2 are summarized in Table 15-7.

2. If there are *at least two independent variables*, we must use a form of ANOVA. We can return to Table 11-1 for naming ANOVAs at this point. Remember, we name ANOVAs by the number of independent variables (one-way, two-way, three-way) and the research design (between-groups, within-groups).

TABLE 15-7. CATEGORY 2 STATISTICS

When there are one or more nominal independent variables and an interval dependent variable, we have several choices. Start by selecting the appropriate number of independent variables. For *one independent variable*, use the accompanying chart. To use this chart, look at the first two columns, those that identify the number of levels of the independent variable and the number of samples. For two levels but one sample, it's a choice between the z test and single-sample t test; for two levels and two samples, it's a choice between the paired-samples t test and the independent-samples t test. For three or more levels (and the matching number of samples), we use either a one-way within-groups ANOVA or a one-way between-groups ANOVA. For *two independent variables* or *three independent variables*, we'll use a form of ANOVA and refer to Table 11-1 on naming ANOVAs. One independent variable:

NUMBER OF LEVELS OF INDEPENDENT VARIABLE	NUMBER OF SAMPLES	INFORMATION ABOUT POPULATION	HYPOTHESIS TEST
Two	One (compared to the population)	Mean and standard deviation	z test
Two	One (compared to the population)	Mean only	Single-sample t test

NUMBER OF LEVELS OF INDEPENDENT VARIABLE	NUMBER OF SAMPLES	RESEARCH DESIGN	HYPOTHESIS TEST
Two	Two	Within-groups	Paired-samples t test
Two	Two	Between-groups	Independent-samples t test
Three (or more)	Three (or more)	Between-groups	One-way between-groups ANOVA
Three (or more)	Three (or more)	Within-groups	One-way within-groups ANOVA

TABLE 15-8. CATEGORY 3 STATISTICS

When we have only nominal variables, then we choose one of the two chi-square tests.

ONE NOMINAL VARIABLE	TWO NOMINAL VARIABLES
Chi-square test for goodness-of-fit	Chi-square test for independence

Category 3: One or Two Nominal Variables

If we have a design with only nominal variables—that is, counts, not means, in the cells—then we have two choices, both nonparametric tests: the chi-square test for goodness-of-fit and the chi-square test for independence. The only question we have to ask ourselves is whether there are one or two nominal variables. If there is one nominal variable, then we choose the chi-square test for goodness of fit. If there are two nominal variables, then we choose the chi-square test for independence. The decision for category 3 is represented in Table 15-8.

Category 4: At Least One Ordinal Variable

If we have a design with even one ordinal variable or a design in which it makes sense to convert our data from interval to ordinal, then we have several choices, as seen in Table 15-9. All these choices have parallel parametric hypothesis tests, as seen in Table 15-10. For situations in which we want to investigate the relation between two ordinal variables, we use the Spearman rank-order correlation coefficient. For situations in which we have a within-groups research design and two groups, we use the Wilcoxon signed-rank test. When we have a between-groups design with two groups, we use a Mann–Whitney U test. And when we have a between-groups design with more than two groups, we use a Kruskal–Wallis H test.

The decisions we've outlined above are summarized in Figure 15-1. Let's apply the four-category rubric to the two research situations mentioned earlier.

TABLE 15-9. CATEGORY 4 STATISTICS

When at least one variable is ordinal, we have several choices. If both variables are ordinal, or can be converted to ordinal, and we are interested in quantifying the relation between them, we use the Spearman rank-order correlation coefficient. If the independent variable is nominal and the dependent variable is ordinal, we choose the correct nonparametric test based on the research design and the number of levels of the independent variable.

TYPE OF INDEPENDENT VARIABLE (AND NUMBER OF LEVELS IF APPLICABLE)	RESEARCH DESIGN	QUESTION TO BE ANSWERED	HYPOTHESIS TEST
Ordinal	Not applicable	Are two variables related?	Spearman rank-order correlation coefficient
Nominal (two levels)	Within-groups	Are two groups different?	Wilcoxon signed-rank test
Nominal (two levels)	Between-groups	Are two groups different?	Mann–Whitney U test
Nominal (three or more levels)	Between-groups	Are three or more groups different?	Kruskal–Wallis H test

TABLE 15-10. NONPARAMETRIC STATISTICS AND THEIR PARAMETRIC COUNTERPARTS

Every parametric hypothesis test has at least one nonparametric counterpart. If our data are far from meeting the assumptions for a parametric test or at least one variable is ordinal, we should use the appropriate nonparametric test instead of a parametric test.

DESIGN	PARAMETRIC TEST	NONPARAMETRIC TEST
Association between two variables	Pearson correlation coefficient	Spearman rank-order correlation coefficient
Two groups; within-groups design	Paired-samples t test	Wilcoxon signed-rank test
Two groups; between-groups design	Independent-samples t test	Mann–Whitney U test
More than two groups; between-groups design	One-way between-groups ANOVA	Kruskal–Wallis H test

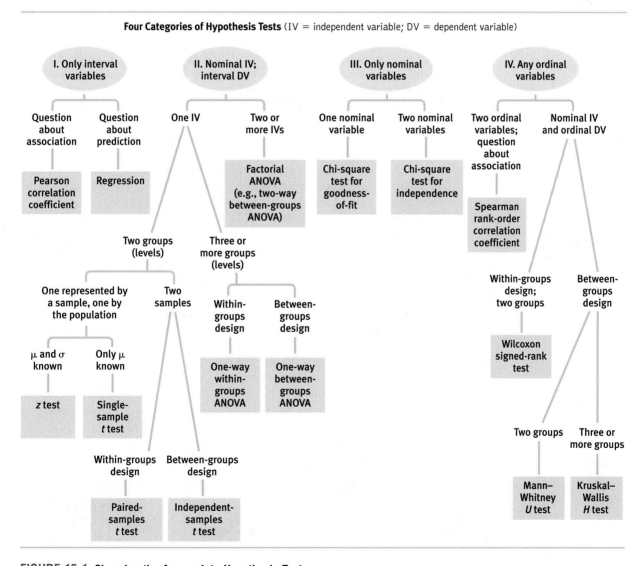

Four Categories of Hypothesis Tests (IV = independent variable; DV = dependent variable)

FIGURE 15-1 Choosing the Appropriate Hypothesis Test

By asking the right questions about our variables and research design, we can choose the appropriate hypothesis test for our research.

TABLE 15-11. SUMMARIZING THE VARIABLES

We use our summary table to determine the appropriate statistical test.

	NAME OF VARIABLE	TYPE	NUMBER OF LEVELS (FOR NOMINAL VARIABLES ONLY)	NAMES OF LEVELS (FOR NOMINAL VARIABLES ONLY)
Independent variable	Type of college	Nominal	Two	1. Selective 2. Moderately selective
Dependent variable	Income	Interval		

First, we'll examine the study of whether attending a selective college leads to a higher income than does attending a moderately selective college (given that you were accepted at both). Table 15-11 shows the summary of variables that was presented earlier.

The independent variable is nominal, and the dependent variable is interval, which puts this research design in category 2. Next, we ask ourselves how many independent variables there are. In this case, there is just one, type of college. The next question addresses the number of levels of the independent variable; here, there are two levels, selective and moderately selective. We then ask whether each level is represented by a separate sample or whether there are sample data for just one level and information about the population for the other level. Here, we have separate sample data for each level. The final question asks about the research design—whether it is within-groups or between-groups. In this study, we could not have within-groups data; a student could not attend both a highly selective and a moderately selective college. The design, therefore, is between-groups. We must use an independent-samples t test.

The second study discussed earlier attempted to uncover an association between time spent on homework and academic achievement among students in grades 7-12. Table 15-12 shows the summary of variables.

Here, we have two interval variables, which narrows our choice of statistics to the Pearson correlation coefficient and the regression equation. Now we ask ourselves whether the research question concerns (1) an association, or relation, between two variables or (2) the prediction of one variable from the other variable. Because the researchers stated an interest in determining an association between the two variables, the appropriate statistic is the Pearson correlation coefficient. In this text, the Pearson correlation coefficient was used as a

TABLE 15-12. SUMMARIZING THE VARIABLES

We can use our summary table to determine the appropriate statistical test.

	NAME OF VARIABLE	TYPE	NUMBER OF LEVELS (FOR NOMINAL VARIABLES ONLY)	NAMES OF LEVELS (FOR NOMINAL VARIABLES ONLY)
Independent variable	Time spent on homework	Interval		
Dependent variable	Achievement	Interval		

descriptive statistic. However, as we noted previously, it also can be used as an inferential statistic. The hypothesis-testing procedure tests whether the coefficient is statistically significantly different from a correlation of 0, and uses Table B.6 in the appendix.

The researchers calculated correlation coefficients. For homework times up to two hours, they found a linear relation between the two variables. There was a positive correlation between time spent on homework and academic achievement; those who spent more time on homework tended to perform better than those who spent less time. However, after that two-hour period, time spent on homework was not correlated with academic achievement. Also, in previous research by Cooper, Valentine, Nye, and Lindsay (1999), time spent on extracurricular activities was also positively correlated with achievement, suggesting that after those two hours of homework, students should get out there and do something. (But time spent watching television was negatively correlated with achievement, so that "something" should not be TV!) And we also have to remember, as we've discussed throughout this text, that a correlational finding does not indicate whether there is a causal relation. We need random assignment to draw causal conclusions.

Regardless of the test we choose, it's important to check our assumptions—which we've outlined for each hypothesis test throughout this text—before conducting the test. We must make sure that we meet them or that the test is robust to violations of any assumptions we fail to meet. And we must report any instance in which we do not meet an assumption so that our readers can be cautious in interpreting them and applying them beyond our study.

In summary, there are three skills we need to select the statistical test that is appropriate for our particular situation. They are each based on concepts that should, by now, be familiar ones: (1) how to transform observations into numbers, (2) how to distinguish between independent and dependent variables, and (3) how to identify the research design. For nominal variables, we also need to count how many levels the variable has. This information can help us to determine the appropriate statistical test. In this text, we learned about four types of statistical tests: those with an interval independent variable and an interval dependent variable (Pearson correlation, regression), those with one or more nominal independent variables and an interval dependent variable (z test, t tests, and ANOVAs), those with only nominal variables (chi-square nonparametric tests), and those with at least one ordinal variable (the nonparametric tests discussed in Chapter 14).

⊙ CHECK YOUR LEARNING

15-2 The British magazine *The Economist* wanted to increase sales in North America (Elliott, 2006). It chose two cities, Baltimore and Pittsburgh, both deemed prototypical of the United States. In Baltimore, it implemented a six-week, $500,000 advertising campaign that included newspaper ads, posters, radio spots, sponsored events, and even café umbrellas that included the slogan "Talk about more than just the weather." In Pittsburgh, there was no ad campaign. The magazine planned to compare the cities with respect to the mean level of awareness of *The Economist*, as assessed by a survey, in the two cities before versus after the campaign. From the description of the study, it appears that the researchers surveyed different people at each time point. If the ad campaign appeared to increase the average level of awareness (and boost subscriptions, another variable in their study), then the magazine would commence similar campaigns in other North American cities.

a. What is the dependent variable in this study, and what type of variable is it?

b. List any independent variables and the type of variables they are. For any nominal variables, list their levels.

c. How many cells are there in this study? Draw a table that shows the cells. Would the cells include counts (or numbers) of participants or means of participants' scores?

d. What are the hypotheses of this study?

e. Create a table summarizing the variables in the study.

f. What statistical test would be used to analyze these data? Outline the steps by which you made your decision.

> REPORTING THE STATISTICS: THE RESULTS SECTION OF AN APA-STYLE PAPER

When asked why they buy Japanese cars, most Americans simply shrug and say, "They work better." The heart of such consumer decisions, Deming tried to tell America's upper management, is about trusting the product; the statistical name for trust is reliability. Buyers don't expect perfection—random variability is simply a fact of life. But consumers will pay for reliability. So, according to Deming, the purpose of quality control in auto manufacturing, health care, or any other endeavor is to identify and then manage the sources of variability that lead to an unreliable, low-quality product. Does identifying the sources of variability sound familiar? That's all a statistical report conveys: the sources of variability. And that is precisely what we do when creating a source table.

Unfortunately, American management still ignored Deming's statistical insights even as the American steel industry melted away and American consumers turned to less variable (more trustworthy) Japanese automobiles. But a turning point arrived in 1980 when an NBC television documentary asked a point-blank question: "If Japan can, why can't we?" The focus was on Deming's statistical work on analyzing and managing the causes of product variability—the statistical reasoning that is represented in every statistical report. W. Edwards Deming became an overnight media star, sought after by every struggling industry.

Several formerly well-established American industries had been flailing about for answers for decades. Textiles, automobiles, electronics, and steel were rapidly moving overseas because America could no longer compete—not only on the costs of labor but also on the quality of the product. Fortunately, Deming the statistician had never just had a job; he had a mission. He may have been 80 years old by the time American management recognized him, but he still believed he could improve people's lives through the statistical analysis of variability.

In 1989, at the age of 82, Deming published what is perhaps his most famous book, *Out of the Crisis*. He gave seminars at corporations all over the country, insisting that their presidents be in attendance. He championed statistical reasoning by demonstrating how it could be applied to problems involving the intersection among economics, industrial productivity, and psychology. The focus of statistical reports, he emphasized, should be on determining the causes of variability, not on "catching" employees who are statistically identified as unproductive (quite possibly because of management decisions or chance influences beyond their control). He continued his work from his wheelchair until he died at the age of 93, revered as the management guru who helped save Japan in the 1950s; revitalized the Ford Motor Company in the 1980s; and developed a comprehensive, statistically inspired business philosophy that made management responsible for continuous improvement of its own systems.

W. Edwards Deming provided specific, practical guidelines so that businesses could find ways to analyze and then manage product variability. Statisticians also need guidelines to report statistics in a way that everyone can understand. Fortunately, all these reporting guidelines follow a similar format, modified just slightly to accommodate the particular features of particular statistics. But the core purpose of statistical reports remains the same as the core purpose identified by Deming: quantify and report the sources of variability.

The causes of variability represent the content of statistical reports, but students should recognize that report writing is also a part of being a behavioral scientist. Reporting variability is what you do whether you work as a psychological therapist (reporting progress notes), as a geographic epidemiologist specializing in geographic information systems (reporting on clusters of diseases), as a criminologist (reporting on age trends relative to types of crimes), as an industrial/organizational psychologist (reporting on changing employment patterns), as a sociologist (documenting socioeconomic trends), as a school psychologist (interpreting test data for students, families, and administrators), as a political scientist (following trends through polling and other research methods), as a forensic specialist (reporting to lawyers, judges, and law enforcement), or as a statistician in the attorney general's office prosecuting abusive nursing homes (reporting on the frequency of falls, and hip fractures, and their impact on life expectancy). If you're serious about a career in the behavioral sciences, then you're joining a community of professionals who have developed their own standards so that they can speak to one another about the particulars of their research and practice. And the particulars always convey statistical ideas related to variability.

But what if you don't become a public health professional, forensic specialist, sociologist, or psychological therapist? Well, if you're not the psychologist writing the report, at some point you will probably be the person the psychologist (or some other professional) is writing about. And if you're not the sociologist examining immigrant trends in urban centers, you may live in the urban center being studied—and the findings may affect your life. At various points in your life you may play the role of a client in therapy, an employee being assessed, a teacher making recommendations about a young student, a judge ruling on the admissibility of evidence, or an academic conducting research on career satisfaction. Or you may just be among the population to whom research results are intended to generalize.

Variability is the answer to each of these questions: How much has a person changed in therapy, if at all? How different is this student from his peers? How likely is this person to commit another crime if we parole her? It's all about variability. So now you will be able to read reports across many different disciplines, understand the reports that others are writing about you, and even create new knowledge that can be shared with the larger community.

Catherine Karnow/Corbis

W. Edwards Deming's Mission
W. Edwards Deming was a multitalented individual who used his statistical talents to forward his goal of intelligent research design across industries.

Telling Our Story: What to Include in a Results Section

Think of a career in statistics as that of a storyteller, someone uniquely trained to communicate both overall trends and underlying details hidden inside a data set. For example, in Chapter 9, we introduced a story about gender differences in humor in a study by researchers at Stanford University (Azim, Mobbs, Jo, Menon, & Reiss, 2005). The researchers compared women's and men's responses to humor using functional magnetic resonance imaging (fMRI). They found many similarities between the genders but noted that, on average, women were more likely than men to use language and executive functioning when processing humor. Women also had more activity than men in their brains' reward centers when they found something funny. The researchers wondered whether one gender were more likely to find humorous stimuli funny, and so they had men and women rate a series of cartoons.

Let's recap the results of the analyses conducted in Chapters 9 and 12 and then use this information to craft the report (the story) of these findings in a Results section of an APA-style paper. In the analyses in this text, we used fictional data that had the same means as the actual study. We used the following raw data for the percentage of cartoons the participants labeled as "funny."

> Women: 84, 97, 58, 90
>
> Men: 88, 90, 52, 97, 86

In Chapter 9, we conducted an independent-samples t test and found a test statistic, t, of -0.03. This test statistic was not beyond the cutoff, so we failed to reject the null hypothesis. We can *not* conclude that men or women find different percentages of the cartoons to be funny; we can only conclude that this study did not provide evidence that women and men are different on this variable. In Chapter 9, we noted that the statistics, as reported in a journal article, would include the symbol for the statistic, the degrees of freedom, the value of the test statistic, and whether the p value associated with the test statistic was less than or greater than the cutoff p level of 0.05. In the humor example, the statistics would read: $t(7) = -0.03$, $p > 0.05$. We also noted that we would report the means and standard deviations for the two samples: Women: $M = 82.25$, $SD = 17.02$; Men: $M = 82.60$, $SD = 18.13$.

In Chapter 12, we calculated a confidence interval for these data. The confidence interval, centered around the difference between means of $82.25 - 82.60 = -0.35$, is $(-28.37, 27.67)$. We also calculated the effect size for this study, a Cohen's d of -0.02. We now have sufficient information to write up these findings for a Results section. There are four topics to consider when writing a Results section (*Note:* Some statistical findings actually go in the Methods section. We'll alert you in those cases.), all covered in various sections of the *Publication Manual of the American Psychological Association* [American Psychological Association (APA), 2001]. First, we want to defend our study by including information about the statistical power, reliability, and validity of any measures we used. Second, we will report the "traditional" statistics, which include any relevant descriptive statistics and often the results of hypothesis testing. Third, we will include the newer statistics that are now highly encouraged by the APA and often required by journal editors. Finally, there are several things that should *not* be included in the Results section, such as the individual raw scores and references for commonly used statistical tests.

Defending Our Study: Convincing the Reader That the Results Are Worth Reading

The first step in persuading critical readers that we have done good research is to report the statistical information relative to how trustworthy our study is. That is why we should first report the results of statistical power analyses that were conducted prior to data collection and then report any information related to the reliability and validity of the ways in which we measured your variables. Readers should be convinced that we had enough statistical power to reject the null hypothesis when the null hypothesis was false. And readers should be convinced that we measured our variables in a sensible way likely to yield helpful information. Because this information is what readers need to be convinced by the rest of the study, this information usually goes in the Methods rather than the Results section.

If a study does not have sufficient statistical power, any cases in which we failed to reject the null hypothesis have a higher chance of being a Type II error. For the same reason, we should also include information about the reliability and validity of our measures. Reliability is usually reported as a coefficient alpha. Validity is usually reported as correlation coefficients of the scale with other scales with which it is believed to correlate. That is, based on the existing research literature, researchers predict a correlation between the new scale and existing scales; those coefficients tell us about the validity of a scale. The psychometric statistics are usually reported in the Methods section, along with descriptions of the scales and any psychometric data reported in previous research.

To summarize this aspect of the findings (which is included in the Methods, not the Results, section), we include:

1. Statistical power analyses

2. Psychometric data for each scale used (reliability and validity information)

In the study on humor, we have not yet calculated statistical power based on our small sample. We can do that now, using G*Power, the software described in Chapter 12. We can calculate the effect size, Cohen's d, from the two sample means, 82.25 for women and 82.60 for men, and the pooled standard deviation, 17.66. In fact, when we calculated the effect size in Chapter 12, we found that it was very small, -0.02. In G*Power, on the upper-right side, we click "post hoc" to indicate that we are calculating power after the fact and "Two tailed" to let the computer know that we conducted a two-tailed test. We enter the effect size of 0.02 (the sign doesn't affect the magnitude of an effect size), the alpha of 0.05, and the sample sizes of 4 and 5. We then click "Calculate," and the computer tells us that our statistical power is an abysmally low 0.050 (or 5%).

Remember, we want power to be at least 0.80 (or 80%). In other words, we probably don't have the statistical power necessary to detect this very small difference between means if in fact it represents a real difference in the population. It's always best to conduct the power analysis before the study based on the effect size that would actually be useful to detect. We really would be much better off with more than just 9 participants! Ideally, in the Methods section, we'd include the results of a statistical power analysis that was conducted before data

Reporting Findings on Gender and Humor
If you understand the basics of what constitutes an excellent Results section, you will be able to create your own Results sections as well as understand those created by others. The findings of the study on gender and humor are clearer when they're presented in a standard format.

VStock/Alamy

were collected. We might, for example, conduct a power analysis to determine the sample size necessary to achieve 0.80 power in the study on humor. As we demonstrated in Chapter 12, using G*Power, we can select "a priori" to tell the program that we want to determine power before conducting a study. We can then input the effect size we anticipate (let's say 0.5 for this example), an alpha (p level) of 0.05, power of 0.80, and a two-tailed test. When we click "Calculate," we'll get the sample size necessary for this configuration, 128, half of which would go in each sample of a study designed to use an independent-samples t test.

In addition, we would ideally include information on the reliability and validity of all measures. However, for this study, we cannot report psychometric data because we do not have the individual data points, nor do we have data on additional scales that might be theoretically related to this scale. We would need to have individuals' ratings of each cartoon in order to calculate coefficient alpha, and we would need to have other scales that assessed constructs such as "sense of humor" to assess validity.

So, here's what we would include in our Methods section if we did in fact recruit a sample of the size indicated by our power analysis: "An a priori statistical power analysis indicated that we needed 128 participants to achieve 0.80 power to detect an effect with a Cohen's d of 0.50 with a two-tailed test and an alpha of 0.05. Based on this analysis, we recruited 128 participants for this study, 64 of whom were randomly assigned to each sample."

If we had data on reliability and validity, then we would write something like this: "Psychometric analyses indicate that this scale is likely to be both reliable and valid. Coefficient alpha is 0.86. Moreover, this scale was significantly correlated with two scales that are theoretically related to it: the Sense of Humor scale ($r = 0.67$) and the Witticism scale ($r = 0.43$)."

Alternately, if psychometric data were available from previous studies, then we could write something like this, usually in the Methods section: "Previous research has documented the psychometric properties of this scale (Smith, 2000). It has been shown to have good reliability, with coefficient alphas ranging from 0.81 to 0.94. It also appears to be valid; it showed strong positive correlations with the Sense of Humor scale ($r = 0.67$) and the Witticism scale ($r = 0.43$). Coefficient alpha in the current study was 0.86." This information gives the readers a better sense of how strongly they can believe in the results of this particular study.

"Traditional" Statistics: The Long-Standing Way of Reporting Results

Results sections should include any relevant descriptive statistics. For analyses with an interval dependent variable, include means, standard deviations, and sample sizes for each cell in the research design. For analyses with a nominal dependent variable (chi-square analyses), include the frequencies (counts) for each cell; there won't be means or standard deviations because there are no scores on an interval scale. Descriptive statistics are sometimes presented first in a Results section but are more typically presented after a summary of each hypothesis test. If there are only two or three cells, then the descriptive statistics are typically presented in the text; if there are more cells, then a table or figure that displays these numbers makes it easier for readers to see the pattern in the data.

When reporting descriptive statistics, it is particularly important to be sure that they are clear. Hoffrage, Lindsey, Hertwig, and Gigerenzer (2000) reported that most people have difficulty making sense of statistical information even if it relates to a field in which they are expert. Citing examples from medicine, they demonstrate that it is easier to comprehend frequencies than probabilities. The following question about a cancer screening test was answered correctly by only 1 of 24 medical doctors:

> The probability of colorectal cancer can be given as 0.3% [base rate]. If a person has colorectal cancer, the probability that the . . . test is positive is 50% [sensitivity]. If a person does not have colorectal cancer, the probability that he still tests positive is 3% [false-positive rate]. What is the probability that a person who tests positive actually has colorectal cancer? (p. 1261)

The correct answer is 5%. Did you get it? Don't worry if you didn't; you're in good company. To solve this problem, we would start with the disease's base rate of 0.3%. Let's take 10,000 people; 0.3% of 10,000 is 30 people, so 30 of 10,000 people have colorectal cancer. Of these 30, 50%, or 15, will correctly test positive. The remaining 9970 people have a 3% chance of testing positive, even though they do not have cancer. So approximately 300 of them will test positive—a false positive. That means that about 315 people will test positive, but only 15 will have cancer: 15 is approximately 5% of 315. That's a lot of mental math for the reader to do!

The researchers then asked the same question of 24 different medical doctors, but phrased it in terms of frequencies rather than probabilities.

> A restatement of the same problem in terms of natural frequencies would be that out of every 10,000 people, 30 have colorectal cancer. Of these, 15 will have a positive . . . test. Out of the remaining 9970 people without colorectal cancer, [about] 300 will still test positive. How many of those who test positive actually have colorectal cancer? (p. 1261)

Using the numbers provided, this question is much easier to answer: 15 people with cancer had a positive test, and 300 people who did not have cancer had a positive test. So 315 people had a positive test, but only 15 out of those 315 (or about 5%) actually had cancer. That's it.

Similarly, Cohen (1990) advocated for easily understandable numbers in the Results section. For example, he suggested that when the meaning of scores is intuitive, as with measures like IQ and income, it makes sense to report not only effect sizes but also mean differences. Knowing that a difference in income between two groups was $10,000, for example, is far more readily understood than knowing that the effect size was a Cohen's d of 0.23. Follow the lead of Hoffman and colleagues and of Cohen; be sure that the presentation of your statistics, particularly of your descriptive statistics, tells the story of the data clearly and intuitively.

Reports of hypothesis tests typically begin by reiterating the hypothesis to be tested and then describing the test that was conducted, including the independent and dependent variables. The results of the hypothesis test are then presented, usually including the symbol for the statistic, the degrees of freedom, the actual value of the statistic, and whether the statistic is less than or greater than the cutoff test statistic. The format for reporting this information has been presented after each hypothesis test in this text and is presented again

TABLE 15-13. THE FORMAT FOR THE RESULTS OF A HYPOTHESIS TEST

There is a general format for reporting the results of hypothesis tests. The symbol for the statistic is followed by the degrees of freedom in parentheses, then the value of the test statistic, and finally information on whether the test statistic fell beyond the cutoff. This table presents the way that format would be implemented for several of the test statistics discussed in this text. Note that the information about the cutoff will vary depending the specific case; p could be listed as <0.001, <0.01, <0.05, or <0.10, or it could be listed as >0.05 or >0.10. Pay attention to your particular situation.

SYMBOL	DEGREES OF FREEDOM	VALUE OF TEST STATISTIC	INFORMATION ABOUT THE CUTOFF	EFFECT SIZE	EXAMPLE
z	(df)	$= XX,$	$p < 0.XX$ (or $p > 0.XX$),	$d = XX$	$z(54) = 0.60$, $p > 0.10$, $d = 0.08$
t	(df)	$= XX,$	$p < 0.XX$, (or $p > 0.XX$),	$d = XX$	$t(143) = 2.05$, $p < 0.05$, $d = 0.17$
F	$(df_{Between}, df_{Within})$	$= XX,$	$p < 0.XX$ (or $p > 0.XX$),	$R^2 = XX$	$F(2, 31) = 3.49$, $p < 0.05$, $R^2 = 0.18$
χ^2	$(df, N = XX)$	$= XX,$	$p < 0.XX$ (or $p > 0.XX$),	$V = XX$	$\chi^2(1, N = 733) = 8.89$, $p < 0.01$, $V = 0.11$
T	None	$= XX,$	$p < 0.XX$ (or $p > 0.XX$),	None	$T = 7$, $p > 0.05$
U	None	$= XX,$	$p < 0.XX$ (or $p > 0.XX$),	None	$U = 3$, $p > 0.05$

in Table 15-13 for each statistic. After the statistics are presented, a brief statement summarizes the results, indicating the direction of any effects but not drawing conclusions beyond the actual finding. That is, in the Results section, we do not discuss the finding in terms of the general theories in the field or in terms of its potential implications or applications. Such discussions go in the section titled, appropriately enough, the Discussion. We should present the results of all hypothesis tests that we conducted, even those in which we failed to reject the null hypothesis.

To summarize this aspect of Results sections, we include the following:

1. Descriptive statistics (often included after each hypothesis test): means, standard deviations, and sample sizes for each cell when the dependent variable is interval; frequencies (counts) for each cell when the dependent variable is nominal

2. For each hypothesis test conducted:
   - Brief summary of hypotheses and hypothesis test
   - Results of hypothesis testing: the symbol for the statistic used, degrees of freedom, the actual value of the statistic, and whether the test statistic is less than or greater than the cutoff test statistic
   - A statement that summarizes the results of hypothesis testing
   - Tables or figures when they make the pattern of data clearer

3. All results, even for nonsignificant findings (especially important for future meta-analyses)

The statistics for the study that compared the mean percentages of cartoons that women and men found funny might be reported as follows: "To examine the hypothesis that women and men, on average, find different percentages of cartoons funny, we conducted an independent-samples t test. The independent variable was gender, with two levels: female and male. The dependent variable was the percentage of cartoons deemed funny. There was not a statistically significant effect of gender [$t(7) = -0.03$, $p > 0.05$]; this study does not provide evidence that women ($M = 82.25$, $SD = 17.02$) and men ($M = 82.60$, $SD = 18.13$), on average, deem different percentages of cartoons to be funny. The difference between the mean percentages for women and men is just 0.35%."

Statistics Strongly Encouraged by the APA: Essential Additions to the "Traditional" Statistics

It is no longer enough simply to present the descriptive statistics and the results of the hypothesis test. The APA (2001) strongly encourages the inclusion of effect sizes: "It is almost always necessary to include some index of effect size or strength of relationship in your Results section" (p. 25). The effect-size estimate is often included as part of the report of the statistics, just after the indication of whether the p value was less than or greater than the cutoff p level. There is also usually a statement that indicates the size of the effect in words, not just in numbers.

Although many different statistical symbols are used to indicate effect size, they all refer to the same idea: how much of the total variance has been accounted for by the independent variables. When possible, a confidence interval should also be presented, either in addition to or in place of a hypothesis test. The APA (2001) states that confidence intervals "are, in general, the best reporting strategy" and strongly encourages their inclusion in reports (p. 22). Note that nonparametric tests often do not have associated measures of effect size or confidence intervals. In these cases, be sure to provide enough descriptive information so that readers can interpret your findings for themselves.

To summarize this aspect of the Results sections, we include the following:

1. Effect sizes, along with a statement about the size of the effect
2. Confidence intervals, when possible, along with a statement interpreting the confidence interval in the context of the study (confidence intervals sometimes replace the results of hypothesis testing)

For the study on humor, we might report the effect size as part of the traditional statistics that we described above: "There was not a statistically significant effect of gender [$t(7) = -0.03$, $p > 0.05$, $d = -0.02$]; this was a small, almost nonexistent, effect. In fact, there is only a 0.35% difference between the mean percentages for women and men." Alternately, we could include this information after reporting the traditional statistics. For example, we could write: "There is a small, almost nonexistent, effect size ($d = -0.02$), reflected by a difference between means of only 0.35%."

The confidence interval is typically reported in place of or after the results of the hypothesis test: "The 95% confidence interval for the difference between means is (-28.37, 27.67); because 0 falls within this rather large confidence interval, it is plausible that there is no difference between these means. This study does not provide evidence that men and women, on average, rate different percentages of cartoons as funny."

What Not to Include in a Results Section: Keeping the Story Focused

The primary role of statistics in research is to tell the data's story, *not* to interpret that story. We can do that in the Discussion section. The descriptive statistics summarize that story, and the inferential statistics help us to draw conclusions beyond our data, to test the probability that this story describes the population. The whole reason for calculating statistics is so that we don't have to look at scads of individual data points that wouldn't allow us to perceive a genuine pattern. This is why we do not present the individual scores in a Results section. In most cases, individual data points would not be useful to readers, and would probably make the Results section seem more confusing than it actually is. Moreover, there are often ethical considerations with respect to the disclosure of individual data points. In many cases, participants are told that their individual data will be kept confidential and that results will be presented only in the aggregate—that is, only summaries, not individual scores, will be published. Imagine that IQ data were collected in a primary school classroom; if there are only 20 students and only 1 is a seven-year-old Hispanic male, a presentation of individual data points would make it clear who that individual is, and his IQ score would be public knowledge.

We also do not include references for individual hypothesis tests or statistics. The statistics presented in this text will be familiar to most researchers, and we do not have to cite sources for them. We should cite a reference only when we use an unusual statistical procedure. Moreover, for common statistical procedures, it is not necessary to describe the procedure, show calculations, or explain our reason for choosing them. It is only necessary to describe or show calculations for unusual statistical procedures. And it is only necessary to explain our choice of procedure if our choice was *not* the obvious one. For example, we might explain why we used a parametric test even though several assumptions appear to have been violated.

Finally, the Results section is meant to be a matter-of-fact statement of findings. Conclusions that go beyond the findings, as well as discussions of the implications of the findings for the particular research area and their potential applications within the field generally, are not appropriate for a Results section. What often happens in our undergraduate (and graduate) classes is that as students start writing about their results, they become overexcited about what their research might mean and can't refrain from discussing the implications of their results right away. But be patient; these extensions beyond the statistics will be part of the Discussion section. In the Results section, just present the unadorned findings.

To summarize, we should *not* report the following:

1. Individual participants' scores
2. References for our hypothesis tests, unless they are likely to be unfamiliar to most readers
3. Formulas and calculations for common statistical tests
4. Discussion of what the results mean for the research area or for the field

For the humor study, we can now pull all the parts of the results together. The first part goes in the Methods section; if we actually collected data for 128 participants, we would write: "An a priori statistical power analysis indicated that we needed 128 participants to achieve 0.80 power to detect an effect with a Cohen's *d* of 0.50 with a two-tailed test and an alpha of 0.05. Based on this analysis, we recruited 128 participants for this study, 64 of whom were randomly assigned to each sample."

If we had data on reliability and validity, we would then write: "Previous research has documented the psychometric properties of this scale (Smith, 2000). It has been shown to have good reliability, with coefficient alphas ranging from

0.81 to 0.94. It also appears to be valid; it showed strong positive correlations with the Sense of Humor scale ($r = 0.67$) and the Witticism scale ($r = 0.43$). Coefficient alpha in the current study was 0.86."

The rest goes in the Results section: "To examine the hypothesis that women and men, on average, find different percentages of cartoons funny, we conducted an independent-samples t test. The independent variable was gender, with two levels: female and male. The dependent variable was the percentage of cartoons deemed funny. There was not a statistically significant effect of gender [$t(7) = -0.03$, $p > 0.05$, $d = -0.02$]; this was a small, almost nonexistent, effect. Moreover, the 95% confidence interval for the difference between means is $(-28.37, 27.67)$; because 0 falls within this rather large confidence interval, it is plausible that there is no difference between these means. Based on the hypothesis test and the confidence interval, this study does not provide evidence that women ($M = 82.25$, $SD = 17.02$) and men ($M = 82.60$, $SD = 18.13$), on average, deem different percentages of cartoons to be funny. In fact, there is only a very small difference between the mean percentages for women and men, just 0.35%."

Two Excerpts from Results Sections: Understanding the Statistical Story

Every research article is a story with a beginning (the Literature Review), a middle (the Methods section), and a data-driven end (the Results section). The Discussion section is like the denouement that tries to tie up loose ends, resolve any remaining concerns, and set you up for the next story. Now that you know the basics of the Results section, you will be able to understand the ending of the many research stories published in scientific journal articles.

For example, let's examine Safran's (2006) study of the effectiveness of positive behavior supports in three rural Ohio schools. If you hope to use your training in behavioral sciences to help disadvantaged students, you will want to pay particular attention because this study was trying to address a variety of disruptive behavioral problems among students. So, first, the researcher wanted to take a statistical picture of four different types of social support already available to students. He noted that this particular research story was embedded within a larger economic story that probably contributed to these behavioral problems: the students in this study were disadvantaged in a variety of ways. For example, there was no major employer in their geographical area; because the school system depended on property taxes in a depressed region of Appalachia in southeastern Ohio, these children received far less financial support per child than most other students in the state. It was, therefore, important to understand the situation that existed before implementing a program of positive behavioral supports.

The formal program being tested was called Positive Behavior Support (PBS); by the end of the study, the researcher wanted to understand not only whether PBS consistently improved life for these children but also how big an effect the PBS program had on them. So he first needed to assess the situation by comparing the different types of social support already available to students. In other words, Safran wanted to measure whether there were any reliable differences in the type of social support (as measured by the hypothesis test and indicated by a p value) and how small or large these differences were (as measured by the effect-size statistic, the partial eta squared statistic, η^2. This statistic is analogous to partial R^2 and is interpreted the same way. Note that the word *partial* indicates that this is the effect size for one independent variable, above and beyond the effects of other independent variables.)

As taxpayers, we all want "the most bang for our buck," and that is precisely the information that the effect-size statistic can provide. Safran conducted and reported a variety of analyses that compared the amount of support (the dependent variable) among four different types of support (the independent variable). The levels of the independent variable, type of support, were:

> Level 1: Schoolwide support (such as workshops involving all students, teachers, and staff)
>
> Level 2: Nonclassroom support (such as interactions between teachers and students in hallways or cafeterias)
>
> Level 3: Classroom support (such as the customary classroom setting)
>
> Level 4: Individual support (usually for students whose problematic behavior required personal interventions by staff, such as fighting)

After the analysis, Safran (2006) concluded that there was a large effect of type of support on amount of support, and he summarized that general finding as part of the results section of his article:

> A one-way ANOVA contrasted the mean scores . . . with effect size measured by partial eta squared (η^2). Results indicate significant differences across the four subscales, $F(3, 316) = 78.336$, $p < .001$, $\eta^2 = .43$, reflecting what Cohen (1987) would consider a large effect size (p. 6).

So, something seemed to be going on in this particular study. We know there is a statistically significant effect not only because the author tells us there are "significant differences" but also because the p value is very small—less than 0.001. But remember, a p value does not indicate anything about effect size. The small p value could be due to the very large sample.

We know there is a large effect because the η^2 is 0.43, well above Cohen's convention for a large effect size, 0.14. But just knowing that something statistically significant is going on somewhere in this study isn't a very satisfying story—we want to know the details. To understand the story these data tell, we need to dig deeper into the data by reading a table or looking at a graph that describes or portrays those statistically significant differences, and understanding the meaning of effect size statistics.

Let's look at the second example. The story that interested Jaswal and Neely (2006) was about how very young children manage to absorb language so fluently. They investigated children's particular perceptions of others' credibility by examining whether children would use a word presented by actors in a videotape. There were four conditions; in the pretest phase, the 58 three- and four-year-old children were presented with one of four videotapes. In one condition, called "both-reliable," both a child actor and an adult actor were "reliable"; that is, they both labeled an unfamiliar object correctly, albeit differently. For example, one called an athletic shoe a "shoe" and the other called it a "sneaker." In a second condition, "reliable-adult," only the adult called the object by its correct name; the child called it by an incorrect name, such as calling a shoe a "glass." In a third condition, "reliable-child," only the child called the object by its correct name. And in the fourth condition, "both-unreliable," the child and the adult called the object by different incorrect names—for example, calling the shoe a "glass" and a "telephone," respectively. In other words, Jaswal and Neely had designed a study that allowed the story of how children absorb new words to have at least four different possible endings—and then allowed the statistical analysis to tell them which story-ending they should believe.

During the subsequent test phase of the study, a different videotape was shown to all participants; that is, the children all viewed the same videotape. On this videotape, all the objects were unfamiliar (e.g., a paint roller) and all the names were invented (e.g., the child might say "blicket" and the adult might say "wug"). One of the dependent variables was the number of times that the participants chose the word that the adult said.

An analysis of variance on the number of times children selected the adult actor's novel label revealed a significant effect of condition, $F(3, 54) = 13.31, p_{rep} = .99, \eta^2 = .43$. Children in the both-reliable and reliable-adult conditions selected the adult actor's label more often than those in the reliable-child condition, and children in the reliable-adult condition selected the adult actor's label more often than those in the both-unreliable condition (Tukey's *HSD*, $p < .05$) (Jaswal & Neely, 2006, p. 758).

Symbol: p_{rep}

[*Note:* As in the previous example, the authors used the effect-size measure η^2, which can be interpreted as we interpret R^2. They also used p_{rep} instead of p. p_{rep} is the probability of replicating an effect given this population and sample size. The Association for Psychological Science prefers p_{rep} to p and strongly recommends its use in the journals that it publishes. One can interpret p_{rep} as: "This effect will replicate $100(p_{rep})\%$ of the time" (Killeen, 2005, p. 349). In this case, the effect would replicate, given the same population and sample size, 99% of the time.]

This excerpt tells us which hypothesis test was conducted (analysis of variance) as well as the variables of interest—the independent variable of condition and the dependent variable of number of times children selected the adult actor's novel label. It also provides a great deal of information about the findings. Specifically, it indicates that there was a statistically significant effect of videotape condition on the number of words invented by adults (versus children) that participants repeat. This excerpt tells us that the effect is "significant," that it would replicate 99% of the time under these conditions, and that, by Cohen's conventions, it is a large effect (η^2 well above 0.14). See Figure 15-2 for the mean numbers of times the participants chose the word used by the adult, the child, or neither.

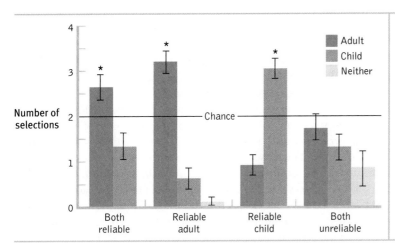

FIGURE 15-2
Reliable Adults

All things being equal, children will believe what an adult says over what a child says. But if an adult proves to be unreliable, then children will believe a child's word over an adult's. The asterisk (*) indicates a statistically significant difference. The differences are statistically significant when the black error bars (around the top of each bar) do not overlap with one another.

In addition, a post-hoc Tukey *HSD* test suggested that participants were more likely to repeat adults' words if they had viewed the "both-reliable" or "reliable-adult" videotapes than if they had viewed the "reliable-child" videotape, and were more likely to repeat adults' words if they had viewed the "reliable-adult" videotape than if they had viewed the "both-unreliable" videotape. In this Results section, means and standard errors were presented in a bar graph. A well-written Results section, accompanied by well-designed visuals, can provide a great deal of clear information in a small amount of space. To understand the story these data tell about how children absorb language, we need to understand the differences revealed by the Tukey *HSD* statistic.

Unfamiliar Statistics: How to Approach Any Results Section with Confidence

Knowing the framework of a Results section can help us read any journal article with confidence; we examined two studies above that used statistical methods we covered in this text. But even if we have never heard of a statistical technique, we can still understand a Results section by looking for clues. First, look for a *p* value. If the author reports a *p* value or lets you know that the *p* is less than or greater than a given cutoff, then we know that a hypothesis test has been conducted. If the *p* value is less than 0.05, then you know that the results were statistically significant and that the researcher was able to reject the null hypothesis. (And now you know what p_{rep} means as well. Contrary to *p*, a reliable effect would have a p_{rep} very close to 1.00 as opposed to very close to 0.00.)

Second, look for descriptive statistics. Almost always, the researcher will report means and standard deviations, or frequencies. Even if the hypothesis test is unfamiliar to us, the descriptive statistics always have the same meaning.

Third, look for explanations of the results. The author will typically include a statement that describes each finding. The researcher should explicitly state whether there were a difference between means, a difference between proportions, or a relation between two or more variables.

Fourth, look for a measure of effect size. We have introduced three common measures of effect size in this text—Cohen's d,, R^2, and Cramer's *V*. Cohen's *d* is typically used when a researcher compares two groups and uses the *t* statistic. ANOVA and regression are among the most commonly used statistical techniques, and R^2 is the usual effect-size measure with these analyses. And researchers who conduct chi-square analyses often include Cramer's *V* as the measure of effect size. (Remember, $df_{Row/Column}$ refers to the degrees of freedom for either the rows or the columns, whichever is smaller.) We can easily look up the conventions for these basic effect size measures, summarized in Table 15-14, and then we will be able to understand the size of an effect even if we do not know which hypothesis test was conducted.

Finally, read the Discussion section, the last major section of an APA-style paper. The Discussion section usually begins with a summary of the results, along with an interpretation of the findings and an examination of their implications and applications. The Discussion section omits reference to statistics and is usually more readily comprehensible than the Results section. Once we've read the Discussion and know what to expect, it's much easier to read, or reread, the Results section.

Results sections that include unfamiliar statistics can seem overwhelming, but we have the skills to get a basic understanding of almost any story that statistics

TABLE 15-14. CONVENTIONS FOR COMMON MEASURES OF EFFECT SIZE

A general sense of the meaning of the common measures of effect size will help us interpret findings when we read about studies in journal articles.

MEASURES OF EFFECT SIZE	SMALL	MEDIUM	LARGE
Cohen's d	0.20	0.50	0.80
R^2	0.01	0.06	0.14
Cramer's V ($df_{Row/Column} = 1$)	0.10	0.30	0.50
Cramer's V ($df_{Row/Column} = 2$)	0.07	0.21	0.35
Cramer's V ($df_{Row/Column} = 3$)	0.06	0.17	0.29

try to tell. The key is to slow down and to focus on the components of the Results with which we are familiar. It's easier than we think to decipher findings from a novel statistical method, and we'll also find that, with time, we get better and better at reading the Results sections.

In summary, we present the findings of our study in the Results section of an APA-style paper. In the Methods section, include background information on statistical power and on the reliability and validity of any measures used. Then in the Results section, traditionally, we reiterate our hypotheses, state the independent and dependent variables, name the statistical test that we are conducting, and present its results in both numbers and words. We also present descriptive statistics. It has become increasingly important to include measures of effect size as well as confidence intervals when it is possible to calculate them. We do not include individual data points, references, or explanations for commonly used statistics, statistical calculations, or discussions of the implications or applications of our findings.

⊙ CHECK YOUR LEARNING

15-3 In Chapter 10, we conducted a one-way between-groups ANOVA on data collected by Ruby (2006), with the independent variable of type of academic program, with four levels (arts and sciences, education, law, and business), and the dependent variable of importance of financial aspects. We used an F distribution with 3 between degrees of freedom and 13 within degrees of freedom. The cutoff p value was 3.41, and the test statistic was 3.94. We conducted a Tukey HSD post-hoc test, which indicated that foreign graduate students in U.S. arts and sciences programs rate the importance of financial factors higher, on average, than do foreign graduate students in U.S. law programs. In Chapter 12, we calculated a measure of effect size: $R^2 = 0.48$.

a. Report the traditional statistics for a Results section for this study. Also include a measure of effect size. Be sure to include a summary of the analysis, a recap of the hypothesis, and statements that summarize the results in addition to the statistics.

b. What other information would be reported? Be specific.

■ DIGGING DEEPER INTO THE DATA: REPORTING MORE SOPHISTICATED STATISTICAL ANALYSES

In several of the Digging Deeper into the Data sections of this text, we've introduced more sophisticated statistical analyses. Often, they are more complex and flexible versions of the hypothesis tests that we learned in the chapter. The reporting of these statistics is very similar to the reporting of their more basic counterparts. First, we defend our study by citing power analyses and psychometric data, usually in the Methods section. Those aspects are identical to what we learned earlier. Similarly, we omit the same information from the Results section that we omit from all the other hypothesis tests; for example, we do not include individual data points or definitions of the statistics we used (unless they're obscure statistics). In this section, we'll outline what we'll report for the traditional statistics and the analyses, such as effect size, that are now strongly encouraged by the APA. We'll focus on one of the more complex statistical analyses introduced in this text, MANCOVA. We'll see how reporting of the more complex statistics is merely an elaboration on the reporting of the more basic statistics, and we'll be able to extrapolate this reporting to other types of statistics.

For example, in Chapter 11, we discussed a study by McLeland and Sutton (2005) that examined the effects of military service and marital status on men's satisfaction within their romantic relationships. The researchers conducted a multivariate analysis of covariance (MANCOVA). There were two independent variables, military service (military, nonmilitary) and marital status (married, unmarried). There were two measures of the dependent variable (relationship satisfaction): the Kansas Marital Satisfaction Scale (KMSS) and the ENRICH Marital Satisfaction Scale (EMSS). They also included the covariate of age.

This is an excerpt from their Results section. You'll notice that they refer to their independent variables as quasi-independent; researchers sometimes use this language to indicate that participants were not randomly assigned to these variables. (Remember that η^2 is interpreted the same as R^2.)

> Because age was associated with the dependent variable, we used age as a covariate in a two-way MANCOVA to examine differences among the groups formed by the two quasi-independent variables of military

From ANOVA to MANOVA to MANCOVA
A 2 × 2 ANOVA examining relationship satisfaction in military and non-military couples becomes a MANOVA by using more than one dependent variable (*M* stands for "multiple") and then becomes a MANCOVA by controlling for the variable of age (*C* stands for "covariate").

service and marital relationship. MANCOVA results for military status were significant, Wilkes $\Lambda = .79$, $F(2,40) = 5.28$, $p = .009$, $\eta^2 = .21$. The results for marital status and the interaction were not significant ($ps > .05$) (p. 180).

With our knowledge of statistics, we can learn a great deal from this excerpt. First, because the researchers stated that they included age as a covariate, we know that the researchers controlled for age (see Digging Deeper into the Data section of Chapter 11). That is, any effect of an independent variable is beyond the effect of age. The possible third variable of age has been accounted for. Second, we know that there was one significant main effect—that of military service (military, nonmilitary). The two most important pieces of information here are the p value of 0.009, well below the usual cutoff of 0.05, and the η^2 (or R^2) of 0.21, a large effect. This tells us that there was a large main effect of military service (military, nonmilitary) on marital satisfaction, over and above the effect of age on marital satisfaction. Third, we know that there was neither a significant main effect of marital relationship (married, unmarried) nor a significant interaction; the authors do not tell us the specific p values for these two effects, but they do tell us that both p values were greater than the cutoff of 0.05. Ideally, the authors would have provided measures of effect size for these two effects as well.

The authors provided information on the psychometrics of the two relationship scales in the Methods section. They included coefficient alphas for both scales from both previous research and their own study; their study produced coefficient alphas of 0.84 and 0.92, both adequate for research. The authors did not report power analyses.

In addition to the statistics reported in the excerpt above, the researchers presented the Pearson correlation coefficient, $r = 0.48$, to demonstrate that the two dependent variables were correlated. Moreover, they presented descriptive statistics for the overall sample and, to demonstrate the pattern of the significant main effect, the difference between the two military status groups.

In summary, the more sophisticated statistics that we introduced in this text are reported very similarly to the more basic statistics. We still include background information (psychometrics, statistical power analyses), results of hypothesis tests, and descriptive statistics, as well as effect sizes and confidence intervals when possible. Your knowledge of statistics is more than adequate to tackle most Results sections that you will encounter in your academic career. Most reports of statistical analyses, even ones that are unfamiliar to you, will include at least some information that will be familiar to you—from p values to means to correlation coefficients. By looking for familiar language, symbols, and numbers, you will usually be able to understand enough of the Results section to understand the story that the data tell.

⊙ CHECK YOUR LEARNING

15-4 Emdad, Sondergaard, and Theorell (2005) studied short-term memory in individuals suffering from post-traumatic stress disorder (PTSD). The independent variable, therefore, was diagnosis, with two levels: PTSD and none. The dependent variable was a measure of memory, Thurstone's Picture Memory Test. They included several covariates that might both associate with PTSD and affect memory: age, years of education, and the score on an intelligence test

[Raven Standard Progressive Matrices (RSPM)]. Here is an excerpt from their Results section:

> Using ANCOVA, there was a significant difference between the PTSD group and the control group with regard to the TPMT . . . adjusted for age, years of education, and RSPM ($M = 15.69$, $SD = 7.63$ for those with PTSD versus $M = 20.90$, $SD = 4.99$ for the controls, $F = 4.14$, $p = 0.05$) (p. 37).

a. Why did the researchers use an ANCOVA?

b. What can we learn from this excerpt? Be specific.

c. Do the researchers need to conduct a post-hoc test for this finding? Explain.

d. In what way do the researchers deviate from the typical reporting of a hypothesis test?

e. What other aspects of a Results section are not in this excerpt and should be included? Be specific about what should be included. (Note that the researchers did include some other important aspects in the rest of their Results section.)

R E V I E W   O F   C O N C E P T S

> Before We Even Begin: Choosing the Right Statistical Test

For a study to attain valid results, it is essential that a research design be carefully planned with consideration of the anticipated statistical analyses. Prior to data collection, researchers must be specific about the goals and hypotheses of the study as well as the statistical analyses that will be conducted. When designing a study, it is wise to adhere to Cohen's admonitions that less is more, simple is better, and power analyses can prevent a study that is a waste of time. A careful research plan will lead to the best use of valuable resources and help us avoid the potential consequences that might result from flawed conclusions.

> Guidelines for Reporting Statistics: The Common Language of Research

To choose the appropriate statistical test, we first identify the independent and dependent variables and ascertain whether they are nominal, ordinal, or interval. For nominal variables, we specify the number of levels, or categories. When the independent variable and dependent variable are interval, we typically use either Pearson correlation or regression. When there is one or more nominal independent variable and an interval dependent variable, we typically use a z test, t test, or ANOVA. When there are only nominal variables, we typically use one of the chi-square tests. And when there is at least one ordinal variable, we use another nonparametric test, such as one of those introduced in Chapter 14.

> Reporting the Statistics: The Results Section of an APA-Style Paper

The summary of statistical analyses is reported in the Results section of an APA-style paper. But first in the Methods section, we include the results of a statistical power analysis, as well as any psychometric analyses that were conducted. These analyses alert the reader that the study was carefully designed. In the Results section, if we conducted hypothesis tests, we report the hypotheses, specify the independent and dependent variables, identify the hypothesis test that we are conducting, and present the results in both numbers and words. Descriptive statistics are included to quantify the pattern of results. The APA strongly encourages the inclusion of measures of effect size and confidence intervals whenever possible. Results sections do not include individual participants' scores; references or explanations for statistical procedures that are likely to be familiar to readers; statistical calculations; or interpretations, implications, or applications of the findings.

> Digging Deeper into the Data: Reporting More Sophisticated Statistical Analyses

Statistical analyses that may initially seem unfamiliar, such as MANOVA, are complicated only by the addition of another dependent variable. That is why the reporting of a MANOVA is merely an elaboration on the reporting of the more basic statistics. Similarly, the reporting of other more sophisticated statistics, such as ANCOVA and MANCOVA, are usually based on the principles you learned when reporting more basic statistics. Recognizing the ideas behind the APA recommendations will help us figure out how to read and report other types of statistics.

SPSS GUIDANCE FOR CHAPTER 15: A STEP-BY-STEP SUMMARY OF HOW TO ANALYZE YOUR DATA

We recommend a two-step approach to analyzing any data set:

1. understand the individual variables in the study in three ways: conceptually, visually, and then numerically;

2. understand the relations between those variables in the same three ways: conceptually, visually, and numerically.

The first step in a conceptual understanding of individual variables begins by going to the *Variable View* screen in SPSS and identifying the

Name, Label, Values, and Measure for each variable. We now have a variable labeled with a meaningful name, numbers assigned to the various levels of the variable, and a description of whether each variable is parametric (scale) or nonparametric (ordinal or nominal). If the dependent variable is parametric, then we must use a parametric test; if the dependent variable is nonparametric, then we must use a nonparametric test.

Our variables will appear in the SPSS *Data View* screen, so we can now enter our data. Now we can describe each individual variable visually using a table or a graph.

We can reorder the variables in a table from lowest to highest and then impose a normal distribution over the graph of the resulting histogram by selecting:

Analyze → Descriptive Statistics → Frequencies → Charts → Histograms with normal curve. Click Continue, and the OK, to run the table.

We can look at the standardized (z) versions of these same variables by selecting:

Analyze → Descriptive Statistics → Descriptives and checking the box labeled "Save as standardized variables."

Now that we have a conceptual and a visual understanding of individual variables, we can move on to a numerical description. Numerical descriptions of individual variables may be obtained by selecting:

Analyze → Descriptive Statistics → Frequencies → Statistics and selecting from a variety of descriptive statistics such as the mean, standard deviation, median, mode, skewness, kurtosis, and so forth.

The second step in analyzing our data is to understand how these individual variables relate to one another. Our conceptual understanding shapes our decision about which statistic to use. First, ask if the dependent variable is parametric (scale) or nonparametric (ordinal and nominal). Second, determine if the research design is between-groups (different individuals in different comparison groups) or within-groups (the same individuals being compared under different conditions).

Based on this understanding of the data, we can choose the appropriate statistical analysis and conduct it using the SPSS steps outlined in earlier chapters. We can generate the appropriate graphs to accompany the analysis, also using instructions outlined through the SPSS sections in this book.

In conclusion, we recommend a simple two-step approach to any data analysis:

1. Understand each individual variable in three ways: conceptually, visually, and numerically;

2. Understand the relations between the variables of interest in the same three ways: conceptually, visually, and numerically.

Not so long ago, people like Abraham DeMoivre, Florence Nightingale, and W.S. Gossett spent many hours carefully calculating numbers so that they could test vital ideas related to statistical reasoning. Today, we conduct those same analyses in fractions of a second. SPSS (and other statistical programs) make the calculations relatively easy. By combining a conceptual, visual, and numerical understanding of each variable, and how variables relate to one another, we are able to listen more powerfully to the underlying story the data tell.

EXERCISES

15.1 Before collecting data and improving statistics performance: Do real-life examples help teach statistics? Imagine that you plan to conduct research to test whether the use of real-life examples (versus fictional data) better helps students learn statistical concepts. There are four main questions you can ask yourself to gather data that can be statistically analyzed in an appropriate way. Answer each of these questions with respect to a possible study on this topic. [*Note:* The answers to these questions will be different for each student, particularly for parts (c) and (d).]

a. What is the goal of this research?

b. What are the specific hypotheses?

c. What are the independent variable and dependent variable that will be measured, and, if appropriate, what are the levels of those variables?

d. What statistical analyses will be conducted?

15.2 Cohen's guidelines and improving statistics performance: Cohen offers advice to social science researchers. Explain in your own words how you would apply each of the following pieces of advice to the study you described in Exercise 15.1 and why following each of these admonitions is important.

a. "Less is more, except of course for sample size."

b. "Simple is better."

c. Conduct a statistical power analysis before collecting data.

15.3 Choice of statistical test and revenge: The media reported a study by Dr. Tania Singer on revenge among men and women (Rosenthal, 2006). Using magnetic resonance imaging (MRI), she and her colleagues observed neurological patterns in women and men. All participants had interacted with a person who behaved in a selfish manner toward them, then later watched that person receive a mild electric shock. Singer observed whether the brain areas associated with pleasure lit up or didn't light up; these areas lit up when participants enjoyed watching selfish people get their due. She found that these brain areas typically lit up in men but not in women.

a. What is the dependent variable in this study, and what type of variable is it?

b. List any independent variables and the type of variables they are. For any nominal variables, list their levels.

c. Will this research design have cells? Explain. If yes, how many cells are there in this study? Draw a table that shows the cells. Would the cells include counts (or numbers) of participants or means of participants' scores?

d. Create a table summarizing the variables in the study.

e. What statistical test would be used to analyze these data? Outline the steps by which you made your decision as to which statistical test to use.

15.4 Choice of statistical test, GPA, and graduate school admission: Social science researchers studying men's and women's perceptions of criteria for graduate school admission found that women, more than men, thought a high GPA was important (Rajecki, Lauer, & Metzner, 1998). On a scale of 1–7, women rated the importance of GPA as 6.06, on average, and men rated its importance as 5.57, on average.

a. What is the dependent variable in this study, and what type of variable is it?

b. List any independent variables and the type of variables they are. For any nominal variables, list their levels.

c. Will this research design have cells? Explain. If yes, how many cells are there in this study? Draw a table that shows the cells. Would the cells include counts (or numbers) of participants or means of participants' scores?

d. Create a table summarizing the variables in the study.

e. What statistical test would be used to analyze these data? Outline the steps by which you made your decision as to which statistical test to use.

15.5 Choice of statistical test, course requirements, and graduate school admission: The same study described in Exercise 15.4 found that psychology students' ratings of their likelihood of attending graduate school tended to become *lower* as students completed *more* of the course requirements in their major.

a. What is the dependent variable in this study, and what type of variable is it?

b. List any independent variables and the type of variables they are. For any nominal variables, list their levels.

c. Will this research design have cells? Explain. If yes, how many cells are there in this study? Draw a table that shows the cells. Would the cells include counts (or numbers) of participants or means of participants' scores?

d. Create a table summarizing the variables in the study.

e. What statistical test would be used to analyze these data? Outline the steps by which you made your decision as to which statistical test to use.

f. Why can't we conclude that taking psychology courses causes one's interest in graduate school in psychology to decrease? Name at least one third variable that might play a role in this relation. Explain.

15.6 Choice of statistical test and filmmaking: Makers of comedy films run test screenings to determine which jokes are likely to garner the largest audience response (Snyder, 2006), and there is debate about the best method of assessing an audience's perception of what is funny. Some film companies rely on the audience's self-report of what is funny, whereas others believe that the audience's actual behavioral reaction is a more valid indicator. For example, the producer of the film *Dumb and Dumber* stated a preference for observing audience reactions versus crunching survey numbers, describing a scene in which a female character "playfully" tosses a snowball at a male character who then responds by pummeling her with a snowball. This scene was greeted with silence when there was blood beneath the female character's nose and with loud laughter when the blood was removed. Let's say that a social scientist wondered whether survey ratings were related to the volume of laughter and gathered data on both for 100 movie-goers.

a. What is the dependent variable in this study, and what type of variable is it?

b. List any independent variables and the type of variables they are. For any nominal variables, list their levels.

c. Will this research design have cells? Explain. If yes, how many cells are there in this study? Draw a table that shows the cells. Would the cells include counts (or numbers) of participants or means of participants' scores?

d. Create a table summarizing the variables in the study.

e. What statistical test would be used to analyze these data? Outline the steps by which you made your decision as to which statistical test to use.

f. Explain how volume of laughter and survey ratings are two different ways of operationalizing an audience's enjoyment of a film. Why might the volume of laughter be a better measure of audience response than survey ratings?

15.7 Choice of statistical test and consumer surveys: The magazine *Consumer Reports* (consumerreports.org) conducted a telephone survey of a representative sample of 1016 people from what it called telephone households (that is, people who have a landline). Men reported that they would spend $1734, on average, on a flat-screen TV. Women reported that they would spend $1495, on average, on a flat-screen TV.

a. What is the dependent variable in this study, and what type of variable is it?

b. List any independent variables and the type of variables they are. For any nominal variables, list their levels.

c. Will this research design have cells? Explain. If yes, how many cells are there in this study? Draw a table that shows the cells. Would the cells include counts (or numbers) of participants or means of participants' scores?

d. Create a table summarizing the variables in the study.

e. What statistical test would be used to analyze these data? Outline the steps by which you made your decision as to which statistical test to use.

f. What aspects of this sample might limit external validity?

15.8 Choice of statistical test, race, and teachers: Tough (2006), a journalist, documented racial inequities in the school system. From the article: "The best teachers tend to go where they are needed the least. A study that the Education Trust issued in June used data from Illinois to demonstrate the point. Illinois measures the quality of its teachers and divides their scores into four quartiles, and those numbers show glaring racial inequities. In majority-white schools, bad teachers are rare; just 11 percent of the teachers are in the lowest quartile. But in schools with practically no white students, 88 percent of the teachers are in the worst quartile" (p. 77).

a. What is the dependent variable in this study, and what type of variable is it?

b. List any independent variables and the type of variables they are. For any nominal variables, list their levels.

c. Will this research design have cells? Explain. If yes, how many cells are there in this study? Draw a table that shows the cells. Would the cells include counts (or numbers) of participants or means of participants' scores?

d. Create a table summarizing the variables in the study.

e. What statistical test would be used to analyze these data? Outline the steps by which you made your decision.

f. What is the relative risk of a bad teacher given that one is in a school with almost no white students (versus a majority-white school)?

g. Construct a graph that depicts the proportions reported here.

h. What third variables might be at play in this finding?

15.9 Statistical tests—a snapshot of studies reported in the *New York Times*, Part I: You'll notice statistical findings everywhere now that you're aware of them. The following quotes are from articles that appeared during just a few days (between March 4, 2007, and March 8, 2007), many in the science or health sections. (A background in statistics is incredibly helpful for many journalists as they translate scientific findings into language the general public can understand.) For each finding, state what hypothesis test the researchers might have used. Explain your answer, citing the independent and dependent variables.

a. A total of 3246 smokers were screened with CT scans for lung cancer: "The scans detected lung cancer in 144 people. That, the researchers calculated, is 300 percent more than would be expected without screening. ... But, they note, the number who died from lung cancer—38—was about the same as it would have been without screening" (Kolata, 2007).

b. A study of medical errors found that "poor penmanship, careless listening, or bad arithmetic caused patients to get doses [of medication] 10 or even 50 times as high as they should" (McNeil, 2007).

c. Studies examined the effects of antioxidants (e.g., vitamin E) on the speed of muscle recovery in people who exercise: "Researchers have recently speculated that those who exercise less vigorously could possibly benefit more from antioxidant supplements than could elite athletes, whose bodies, the thinking now goes, might be better equipped to combat oxidative stress" (Reynolds, 2007).

d. Knowing that a quick emergency room response can mean the difference between life and death for a heart attack patient, the University of California, San Francisco, Medical Center changed procedures to improve its response time. The best cardiologists carried a special pager for heart attack patients, electrocardiograms were required to be read immediately, and a bright red toolbox containing the basics for heart attack treatment was placed in a prominent position in the ER. From 2002 to 2003, "the hospital had cut its response time to about 90 minutes," on average, per patient (Leonhardt, 2007).

e. A study of airline pilot performance assessed pilots in a flight simulator. In tests of ability to avoid traffic, "the older pilots improved more than the younger ones" (Nagourney, 2007c).

15.10 Statistical tests—a snapshot of studies reported in the *New York Times*, Part II: These quotes appeared in articles during the same few days as those in Exercise 15.9. As in Exercise 15.9, for each finding, state what hypothesis test the researchers might have used. Explain your answer, citing the independent and dependent variables.

a. "A survey by Morgan Stanley found that only 10 percent of consumers interviewed in 2006 considered diet colas a healthy choice, compared with 14 percent in 2003" (Martin, 2007).

b. Although research has suggested that minorities tend to get poorer health care treatment than whites, one "study found that blacks and Hispanics were about twice as likely as whites to report having been counseled by a doctor about alcohol," despite the fact that "there is no evidence that blacks and Hispanics drink more than whites" (Nagourney, 2007a).

c. A study that assessed children's body mass index at several time points over a year found that children's "biggest gain in body mass index ... came during the summer" (Nagourney, 2007b).

d. Despite beliefs that restrooms have the most bacteria of any public place, a study found that "public restrooms [fall] behind playgrounds and just ahead of handrails in terms of contamination levels" (O'Connor, 2007).

e. Can smells help our memory? "Scientists studying how sleep affects memory have found that the whiff of a familiar scent can help a slumbering brain better remember things that it learned the evening before. A rose bouquet—delivered to people's nostrils as they studied and, later, as they slept—improved their performance on a memory test by almost 15 percent" (Carey, 2007b).

15.11 Statistics in the news and an interaction: One of the studies described in Exercises 15.9 and 15.10 reported an interaction.

a. Which study reported an interaction? Explain why this is an interaction.

b. Draw a graph that depicts what this interaction might look like. (*Note:* If the interaction involves time, remember that increased time is slower and decreased time is faster.)

c. What is the only type of parametric hypothesis test that we've learned that can uncover an interaction? Explain.

15.12 Designing a study and red lipstick, Part I: Another way to practice choosing the correct statistical test is to work the other way around—to try to design a study so that you will be able to use a particular statistical test. In real life, you wouldn't design a study this way, but it's good practice! So here's a claim with no data to back it up. Near the beginning of *Lipstick: A Celebration of the World's Favorite Cosmetic*, Jessica Pallingston (1998) wrote a single sentence on an otherwise blank page: "Studies show that women who wear red lipstick smile more." That's it—no citation, no data, nothing.

a. Let's say you decided to test this assertion and wanted to analyze your data using a chi-square test for independence. State your independent variable. What type of variable is it? If it's nominal, what are its levels? State your dependent variable. What type of variable is it? If it's nominal, what are its levels?

b. Now let's say you want to use an independent-samples *t* test. State your independent variable. What type of variable is it? If it's nominal, what are its levels? State your dependent variable. What type of variable is it? If it's nominal, what are its levels?

c. What if you wanted to use a paired-samples *t* test? State your independent variable. What type of variable is it? If it's nominal, what are its levels? State your dependent variable. What type of variable is it? If it's nominal, what are its levels?

15.13 Designing a study and red lipstick, Part II: Consider the assertion about lipstick from Exercise 15.12. Let's consider how we might examine it using ANOVA.

a. Let's say you decided to test this assertion and wanted to analyze your data using a one-way between-groups ANOVA. State your independent variable. What type of variable is it? If it's nominal, what are its levels? State your dependent variable. What type of variable is it? If it's nominal, what are its levels?

b. What if you wanted to use a two-way between-groups ANOVA? State your independent variables. What type of variables are they? If they're nominal, what are their levels? State your dependent variable. What type of variable is it? If it's nominal, what are its levels?

15.14 Defending your data and red lipstick: If you conducted a study on the effects of lipstick on smiling, it would be important to defend your data when you write your Methods and Results sections.

a. In the context of this example, explain why it would be wise to conduct a statistical power analysis prior to data collection.

b. Why is it important to include information on your preliminary statistical power analysis in the Methods and Results section?

c. Why is it important to be certain that your outcome measures are reliable and valid? Explain one way in which you might check the reliability of your measure of smiling. Explain one way in which you might check the validity of your measure of smiling as an assessment of happiness.

15.15 Writing a Results section and mismatched teams: Do college football teams tend to be more likely or less likely to be mismatched in the upper National Collegiate Athletic Association (NCAA) divisions? During one week in 2006, the 53 Division I games had a mean spread (winning score minus losing score) of 16.189, with a standard deviation of 12.128. We compared a sample of four Division I-AA games, with a mean of 6.25, to the population of Division I games. In Exercises 8.7–8.9, we conducted a z test to examine this question. In Exercise 12.3, we calculated a confidence interval for the mean score of the sample of Division I-AA teams, and in Exercise 12.7, we calculated the effect size. Using the findings from the earlier chapters (or calculating these findings now), write a brief Results section for these data. (For the purposes of this exercise, you may omit information on statistical power and psychometric analyses.)

15.16 Writing a Results section and medical myths: In Chapter 11, we introduced the six steps of hypothesis testing for a two-way between-subjects ANOVA by using the example of medical myth-busting. In Exercise 12.13, we asked you to calculate the effect sizes for this ANOVA. Using the findings from Chapter 11 and the effect sizes from Exercise 12.13 (calculate them now if you did not previously), write a brief Results section for these data. (For the purposes of this exercise, you may omit information on statistical power and psychometric analyses.)

15.17 Writing a Results section and clown therapy: In Chapter 13, we introduced the six steps of hypothesis testing for a chi-square test for independence through the example of clown therapy and fertility. Using the findings from Chapter 13, write a brief Results section for these data. (For the purposes of this exercise, you may omit information on statistical power and psychometric analyses.)

15.18 Excerpt from a Results section and sexist language: Hyde (1984) conducted a now-classic study on sexist language. Elementary school students read a passage that included one of three pronouns; "he," "they," or "he or she" was included in the blank space in this excerpt from the passage: "When a kid goes to school, ___ often feels excited on the first day." In the Results section, Hyde reported: "The main effect of pronoun was also significant, $\chi^2(2, N = 310) = 28.81$, $p < .001$. When the pronoun was 'he' or 'his,' overall 12% of the stories were about females; when it was 'they' or 'their,' 18% were female, and when the pronoun was 'his or her' ('he or she'), 42% of the stories were about females" (p. 701).

a. What is the independent variable in this study? What are its levels?

b. What is the dependent variable in this story? What are its levels?

c. What statistical test did Hyde conduct? Why did she choose this test?

d. Is this finding statistically significant? State two ways in which this excerpt tells you this.

e. How many degrees of freedom were there? Where does it state this in the excerpt? How could you calculate the degrees of freedom without seeing the number in the Results section?

f. How many elementary school children participated in the study? How do you know this from the excerpt?

g. What is Hyde's overall finding?

h. What nontraditional statistic might Hyde have included to provide more information about this finding? Calculate this statistic from the information provided here.

15.19 Excerpt from a Results section: A study by Barch, Csernansky, Conturo, and Snyder (2002) examined memory deficits among people with schizophrenia. They compared two groups (individuals with schizophrenia with individuals who did not have schizophrenia) and two types of material [verbal memory tasks (memory for words) and nonverbal memory tasks (memory for faces)]. Here is an excerpt from the Results section: "The ANOVA for accuracy in the WM [working memory] tasks indicated significant main effects of group, $F(1,82) = 14.13$, $p < .002$, and material, $F(1,82) = 7.38$, $p < .01$, but no Group X Material interaction, $F(1,82) = 0.0001$, $p > .90$. As expected, participants with schizophrenia performed significantly worse than controls (see Table 2), but were equally impaired with verbal and nonverbal materials. All participants performed better with words than faces" (p. 482). Note that the authors refer to a table that includes means and standard deviations.

a. What are the independent variables in this study? What are their levels?

b. What is the dependent variable in this study?

c. What statistical test did the researchers conduct? Why did they choose this test?

d. Are any main effects statistically significant? Explain how you know this.

e. Is the interaction significant? Explain how you know this.

f. What nontraditional statistic might the authors have included to provide more information about these findings?

▪ DIGGING DEEPER INTO THE DATA

15.20 Choice of statistical test and dependent personalities: In yet another study reported in the *New York Times* during just a few days (see Exercises 15.9 and 15.10); "Psychologists rated 48 men and women attending Gettysburg College in Pennsylvania on measures of dependency, and calculated their grade-point averages. After controlling for the students' SAT scores and the difficulty of their course schedules, among other factors, the researchers found, to their surprise, that those students who scored highly on measures of dependency were doing significantly better, on average, than those who were more self-sufficient" (Carey, 2007a).

a. What is the dependent variable in this study, and what type of variable is it?

b. List any independent variables and the types of variables they are. For any nominal variables, list their levels.

c. What statistical test would be used to analyze these data? Outline the steps by which you made your decision.

d. The researchers refer to factors for which they controlled. List these variables. Why might the researchers have chosen to control for these variables?

e. Can you think of other third variables that might play a role in this finding?

15.21 Excerpt from a Results section—MANOVA: Cheng, Chan, and Tong (2006) conducted a study of online friendships (such as on MySpace or Facebook). Cheng and colleagues included three independent variables in their study: gender of participant (male, female), gender of online friend (same-sex, opposite-sex), and the length of the online friendship (less than one year, one to two years, more than two years). So far, this is a 2 × 2 × 3 between-subjects ANOVA. But they included four dependent variables: intimacy, trust, self-disclosure, and relationship satisfaction. One of their findings is described in this excerpt from their Results section: "The interaction effect between gender of online friends and duration was found on intimacy, $F(2, 158) = 13.44$, $p < .001$, trust, $F(2, 158) = 6.22$, $p < .01$, self-disclosure, $F(2, 158) = 6.99$, $p < .01$, and relational satisfaction, $F(2, 158) = 13.23$, $p < .001$. Specifically, qualities of cross-sex friendships were higher than those of same-sex online friendships at the later stage of friendship development. Again, differences were relatively small at the early stage" (pp. 17–18).

a. Why did the researchers use a MANOVA?

b. What can we learn from this excerpt? Be specific, and state how the statistics helped you understand the finding.

c. What other aspects of a Results section are not in this excerpt and should be included? Be specific.

15.22 Excerpt from a Results section—unusual statistical technique: Rholes, Simpson, Tran, Martin, and Friedman (2007) studied attachment and information-seeking in romantic relationships; one of the questions they explored was whether people (whom they called "actors" in this study) who were avoidant in relationships were less interested in knowing aspects of their romantic partners' feelings and thoughts. The authors used the Actor-Partner Interdependence Model (APIM) to conduct statistical analyses. Here is an excerpt from the Results section: "The results revealed significant main effects for actor avoidance predicting all three information-seeking categories, with more avoidant individuals seeking less information about their romantic partners across all three categories. Specifically, greater avoidance was associated with less seeking of intimate information, $b = -.28$, $t(147) = -3.32$, $p < .003$, less seeking of future-oriented information, $b = 2.42$, $t(147) = -3.93$, $p < .001$, and surprisingly less seeking of nonrelationship material interests, $b = -.41$, $t(147) = -3.19$, $p < .01$" (pp. 426–427). If you do not know what APIM is or what b means in this context, it is still possible to understand these findings.

a. How do the authors convey their findings in words in this excerpt? State in your own words what they found.

b. What statistics are familiar to you? How do these statistics help us to understand the findings without knowing what b is?

c. What nontraditional statistic might the authors have included to provide more information about this finding?

SYMBOLS

---

p_{rep}

REFERENCE FOR BASIC MATHEMATICS

This appendix serves as a reference for the basic mathematical operations that take place in the book. We provide quick reference tables to help you with symbols and notation; instruction on the order of operations for equations with multiple operations; guidelines for converting fractions, decimals, and percentages; and examples of how to solve basic algebraic equations. Some of you will need a more extensive review than is presented in these pages. That review, which involves greater detail and instruction, can be found on the book's companion Web site. Most of you will be familiar with much of this material. However, the inclusion of this reference can help you to solve problems throughout this text, particularly when you come across material that appears unfamiliar.

We include a diagnostic quiz for you to assess your current comfort level with this material. Following the diagnostic test, we provide instruction and reference tables for each section so that you can review the concepts, apply the concepts through worked problems, and review your skills with a brief self-quiz.

Section A.1 Diagnostic Test

Section A.2 Symbols and Notation: Arithmetic Operations

Section A.3 Order of Operations

Section A.4 Proportions: Fractions, Decimals, and Percentages

Section A.5 Solving Equations with a Single Unknown Variable

Section A.6 Answers to Diagnostic Test and Self Quizzes

A.1 DIAGNOSTIC TEST: SKILLS EVALUATION

This diagnostic test is divided into four parts that correspond with sections to the basic mathematics review that follows. The purpose of the diagnostic test is to help you understand which areas you need to review prior to completing work in this text. (Answers to each of the questions can be found at the end of the review on page A-7.)

SECTION 1 (Symbols and Notation: Arithmetic Operations)

1. $8 + 2 + 14 + 4 =$ _____
2. $4 \times (-6) =$ _____
3. $22 - (-4) + 3 =$ _____
4. $8 \times 6 =$ _____
5. $36 \div (-9) =$ _____
6. $13 + (-2) + 8 =$ _____
7. $44 \div 11 =$ _____
8. $-6 \, (-3) =$ _____
9. $-6 - 8 =$ _____
10. $-14 \, / -2 =$ _____

SECTION 2 (Order of Operations)

1. $3 \times (6 + 4) - 30 =$ _____
2. $4 + 6(2 + 1) + 6 =$ _____
3. $(3 - 6) \times 2 + 5 =$ _____
4. $4 + 6 \times 2 =$ _____
5. $16/2 + 6(3 - 1) =$ _____
6. $2^2 \, (12 - 8) =$ _____
7. $5 - 3(4 - 1) =$ _____
8. $7 \times 2 - (9 - 3) \times 2 =$ _____
9. $15 \div 5 + (6 + 2)/2 =$ _____
10. $15 - 3^2 + 5(2) =$ _____

SECTION 3 (Proportions: Fractions, Decimals, and Percentages)

1. Convert .42 into a fraction _____
2. Convert $^6/_{10}$ into a decimal _____
3. Convert $^4/_5$ into a percentage _____
4. $^6/_{13} + ^4/_{13} =$ _____
5. $.8 \times .42 =$ _____
6. 40% of 120 = _____
7. $^2/_7 + ^2/_5 =$ _____
8. $^2/_5 \times 80 =$ _____
9. $^1/_4 \div ^1/_3 =$ _____
10. $^4/_7 \times ^5/_9 =$ _____

SECTION 4 (Solving Equations with a Single Unknown Variable)

1. $5X - 13 = 7$ _____
2. $3(X - 2) = 9$ _____
3. $X/3 + 2 = 10$ _____
4. $X(-3) + 2 = -16$ _____
5. $X(6 - 4) + 3 = 15$ _____
6. $X/4 + 3 = 6$ _____
7. $3X + (-9)/(-3) = 24$ _____
8. $9 + X/4 = 12$ _____
9. $4X - 5 = 19$ _____
10. $5 + (-2) + 3X = 9$ _____

A.2 SYMBOLS AND NOTATION: ARITHMETIC OPERATIONS

SYMBOLS AND NOTATION

The basic mathematical symbols used throughout this textbook are located in Table A.1. These are the most common arithmetic operations, and most of you will find that you are familiar with them. However, it is worth your time to review the reference table and material that outline the operations using positive and negative numbers. For those of you who have spent little time solving math equations recently, familiarizing yourselves with this material can be quite helpful in avoiding common mistakes.

TABLE A.1 SYMBOLS AND NOTATION

+	Addition	$8 + 3 = 11$
−	Subtraction	$14 - 6 = 8$
×, ( )	Multiplication	$4 \times 3 = 12$, $4(3) = 12$
÷, /	Division	$12 \div 6 = 2$, $^{12}/_6 = 2$
>	Greater than	$7 > 5$
<	Less than	$4 < 9$
≥	Greater than or equal to	$7 \geq 5$, $4 \geq 4$
≤	Less than or equal to	$5 \leq 9$, $6 \leq 6$
≠	Not equal to	$5 \neq 3$

ARITHMETIC OPERATIONS: Worked Examples

Adding, Subtracting, Multiplying, and Dividing with Positive and Negative Numbers

1. Adding with positive numbers: Add the two (or series of) numbers to produce a sum.
   a. $4 + 7 = 11$
   b. $7 + 4 + 9 = 20$
   c. $4 + 6 + 7 + 2 = 19$

2. Adding with negative numbers: Sum the absolute values of each number and place a negative sign in front of the sum. (*Hint:* When a positive sign directly precedes a negative sign, change both signs to a single negative sign.)
   a. $-6 + (-4) = -10$
      $-6 - 4 = -10$
   b. $-3 + (-2) = -5$
      $-3 - 2 = -5$

3. Adding two numbers with opposite signs: Find the difference between the two numbers and assign the sign (positive or negative) of the larger number.
   a. $17 + (-9) = 8$
   b. $-16 + 10 = -6$

4. Subtracting one number from another number. (*Hint:* When subtracting a negative number from another number, two negative signs come in sequence, as in part (a). To solve the equations, change the two sequential negative signs into a single positive sign.)
   a. $5 - (-4) = 9$
      $5 + 4 = 9$
   b. $5 - 8 = -3$
   c. $-6 - 3 = -9$

5. Multiplying two positive numbers produces a positive result.
   a. $6 \times 9 = 54$
   b. $6(9) = 54$
   c. $4 \times 3 = 12$
   d. $4(3) = 12$

6. Multiplying two negative numbers produces a positive result.
   a. $-3 \times -9 = 27$
   b. $-3(-9) = 27$
   c. $-4 \times -3 = 12$
   d. $-4(-3) = 12$

7. Multiplying one positive and one negative number produces a negative result.
   a. $-3 \times 9 = -27$
   b. $-3(9) = -27$
   c. $4 \times -3 = -12$
   d. $4(-3) = -12$

8. Dividing two positive numbers produces a positive result.
   a. $12 \div 4 = 3$
   b. $12 / 4 = 3$
   c. $16 \div 8 = 2$
   d. $16 / 8 = 2$

9. Dividing two negative numbers produces a positive result.
   a. $-12 \div -4 = 3$
   b. $-12 / -4 = 3$
   c. $-16 \div -8 = 2$
   d. $^-16 / -8 = 2$

10. Dividing a positive number by a negative number (or dividing a negative number by a positive number) produces a negative result.
    a. $-12 \div 4 = -3$
    b. $-12 / 4 = -3$
    c. $16 \div -8 = -2$
    d. $16 / -8 = -2$

SELF-QUIZ #1: Symbols and Notation: Arithmetic Operations

(Answers to this quiz can be found on page A-7.)

1. $4 \times 7 =$

2. $6 + 3 + 9 =$

3. $-6 - 3 =$

4. $-27 / 3 =$

5. $4(9) =$

6. $12 + (-5) =$

7. $16(-3) =$

8. $-24 / -3 =$

9. $75 \div 5 =$

10. $-7(-4) =$

A.3 ORDER OF OPERATIONS

Equations and formulas often include a number of mathematical operations combining addition, subtraction, multiplication, and division. Some will also include exponents and square roots. In complex equations with more than one operation, it is important to perform the operations in a specific sequence. Deviating from this sequence can produce a wrong answer. Table A.2 lists the order of operations for quick reference.

ORDER OF OPERATIONS: Worked Examples

1.
$-3 + 6(4) - 7 =$	Multiplication
$-3 + 24 - 7 =$	Addition
$21 - 7 =$	Subtraction
$14 = 14$	Answer

2.
$2(8) + 6 / 3 \times 8 =$	Multiplication. Remember to move left to right
$16 + 6 / 3 \times 8 =$	Division
$16 + 2 \times 8 =$	Multiplication
$16 + 16 =$	Addition
$32 = 32$	Answer

3.
$3^2 + 6 / 3 - 12(2) =$	Square (raise exponent)
$9 + 6 / 3 - 12(2) =$	Division
$9 + 2 - 12(2) =$	Multiplication
$9 + 2 - 24 =$	Addition
$11 - 24 =$	Subtraction
$-13 = -13$	Answer

4.
$(10 + 6) - 6^2 / 4 + 3(10) =$	Within parentheses
$16 - 6^2 / 4 + 3(10) =$	Square (raise exponent)
$16 - 36 / 4 + 3(10) =$	Division
$16 - 9 + 3(10) =$	Multiplication
$16 - 9 + 30 =$	Subtraction
$7 + 30 =$	Addition
$37 = 37$	Answer

5.
$8 + (-4) + 3(12 - 8) =$	Within parentheses
$8 + (-4) + 3(4) =$	Multiplication
$8 + (-4) + 12 =$	Addition
$4 + 12 =$	Addition
$16 = 16$	Answer

TABLE A.2 ORDER OF OPERATIONS

Rule of Operation	Example
1. Calculations within parentheses are completed first.	1a. $(6 + 2) - 4 \times 3 / 2^2 + 6 =$ 1b. $8 - 4 \times 3 / 2^2 + 6 =$
2. Squaring (or raising to another exponent) is completed second.	2a. $8 - 4 \times 3 / 2^2 + 6 =$ 2b. $8 - 4 \times 3 / 4 + 6 =$
3. From **left** to **right**, complete all multiplication and division operations. This may require multiple steps.	3a. $8 - 4 \times 3 / 4 + 6 =$ 3b. $8 - 12 / 4 + 6 =$ 3c. $8 - 12 / 4 + 6 =$ 3d. $8 - 3 + 6 =$
4. Last, complete all the addition and subtraction operations.	4a. $8 - 3 + 6 =$ 4b. $5 + 6 =$ 4c. $11 = 11$

SELF-QUIZ #2: Order of Operations

(Answers to this quiz can be found on paeg A-7.)

1. $3(7) - 12/3 + 2 =$
2. $4/2 + 6 - 2(3) =$
3. $-5(4) + 16 =$
4. $8 + (-16)/4 =$
5. $6 - 3 + 5 - 3(5) + 10 =$
6. $4^2/8 - 4(3) + (8 - 3) =$
7. $(14 - 6) + 72/9 + 4 =$
8. $(54 - 18)/4 + 7 \times 3 =$
9. $32 - 4(3 + 4) + 8 =$
10. $100 \times 3 - 87 =$

A.4 PROPORTIONS: FRACTIONS, DECIMALS, AND PERCENTAGES

A proportion is a part in relation to a whole. When we look at fractions, we understand the denominator (the bottom number) to be the number of equal parts in the whole. The numerator represents the proportion of parts of that whole that are present. Fractions can be converted into decimals by dividing the numerator by the denominator. Decimals can then be converted into percentages by multiplying by 100 (Table A.3). It is important to use the percentage symbol (%) when differentiating decimals from percentages. Additionally, decimals are often rounded to the nearest hundredth before they are converted into a percentage.

TABLE A.3 PROPORTIONS: CONVERTING FRACTIONS TO DECIMALS TO PERCENTAGES

 $= 2/8 = .25 = 25\%$

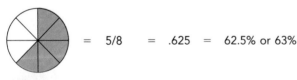 $= 5/8 = .625 = 62.5\%$ or 63%

 $= 10/20 = .50 = 50\%$

FRACTIONS

Equivalent Fractions

The same proportion can be expressed in a number of equivalent fractions. Equivalent fractions are found by multiplying both the numerator and the denominator by the same number.

$$\tfrac{1}{2} = \tfrac{2}{4} = \tfrac{6}{12} = \tfrac{30}{60}$$

In this case, we multiply each side of $\tfrac{1}{2}$ by 2 to reach the equivalent $\tfrac{2}{4}$, then by 3 to reach the equivalent $\tfrac{6}{12}$, then by 5 to reach the equivalent $\tfrac{30}{60}$. Or we could have multiplied the numerator and denominator of the original $\tfrac{1}{2}$ by 30 to reach our concluding $\tfrac{30}{60}$.

Now fractions can also be reduced to a simpler form by dividing the numerator and denominator by the same number. Be sure to divide each by a number that will result in a whole number for both the numerator and the denominator.

$$\tfrac{25}{75} = \tfrac{5}{15} = \tfrac{1}{3}$$

By dividing each side by 5, the fraction was reduced from $\tfrac{25}{75}$ to $\tfrac{5}{15}$. By further dividing by 5, we reduce the fraction to its simplest form, $\tfrac{1}{3}$. Or, we could have divided the numerator and denominator of the original $\tfrac{25}{75}$ by 25 resulting in the simplest expression of this fraction, $\tfrac{1}{3}$.

Adding and Subtracting Fractions (with the same denominator)

Finding equivalent fractions is essential to adding and subtracting two or more fractions. In order to add or subtract, each fraction must have the same denominator (bottom number). If the two fractions already have the same denominator, add or subtract the numbers in the numerators only.

$$\tfrac{2}{7} + \tfrac{1}{7} = \tfrac{3}{7} \qquad \tfrac{4}{5} - \tfrac{3}{5} = \tfrac{1}{5}$$

In each of these instances, we are adding or subtracting from the same whole (or same pie, as in line one of Table A.3). In the first equation, we are increasing our proportion of 2 by 1 to equal 3 pieces of the whole. In the second equation, we are reducing the number of proportions from 4 by 3 to equal just 1 piece of the whole.

Adding and Subtracting Fractions (with different denominators)

When adding or subtracting two proportions with different denominators, it is necessary to find a common denominator before performing the operation. It is often easiest to multiply each side by the number equal to the denominator of the other fraction. This provides an easy route to finding a common denominator.

$$\tfrac{2}{5} + \tfrac{1}{6} =$$

Multiply the numerator and denominator of $\tfrac{2}{5}$ by 6, equaling $\tfrac{12}{30}$

Multiply the numerator and denominator of $\tfrac{1}{6}$ by 5, equaling $\tfrac{5}{30}$

$$\tfrac{12}{30} + \tfrac{5}{30} = \tfrac{17}{30}$$

Multiplying Fractions

When multiplying fractions, it is not necessary to find common denominators. Just multiply the two numerators in each fraction and the two denominators in each fraction.

$$\tfrac{4}{7} \times \tfrac{5}{8} = (4 \times 5)/(7 \times 8) = \tfrac{20}{56}$$

(*Note:* This fraction can be reduced to a simpler equivalent by dividing both the numerator and denominator by 4. The result is $5/14$.)

Dividing Fractions

When dividing a fraction by another fraction, invert the second fraction and multiply as above.

$$1/3 \div 2/3 = 1/3 \times 3/2 = (1 \times 3) / (3 \times 2) = 3/6$$

(*Note:* This can be reduced to a simpler equivalent by dividing both the numerator and denominator by 3. The result is one-half, $1/2$.)

SELF-QUIZ #3: Fractions

(Answers to this quiz can be found on page A-7.)

1. $2/5 + 1/5 =$
2. $2/7 \times 4/5 =$
3. $11/15 - 2/5 =$
4. $3/5 \div 6/8 =$
5. $3/8 + 1/4 =$
6. $1/8 \div 4/5 =$
7. $8/9 - 5/9 + 2/9 =$
8. $2/7 + 1/3 =$
9. $4/15 \times 3/5 =$
10. $6/7 - 3/4 =$

DECIMALS

Converting Decimals to Fractions

Decimals represent a proportion of a whole similar to fractions. Each decimal place represents a factor of 10. So the first decimal place represents a number over 10, the second decimal place represents a number over 100, the third decimal place represents a number of 1000, the fourth decimal place represents a number of 10,000, and so on.

To convert a decimal to a fraction, take the number as the numerator and place it over 10, 100, 1000, and so on based on how many numbers are to the right of the decimal point. For example,

$$0.6 = 6/10 \qquad 0.58 = 58/100$$
$$0.926 = 926/1000 \qquad 0.7841 = 7841/10,000$$

Adding and Subtracting Decimals

When adding or subtracting decimal points, it is necessary to keep the decimal points in a vertical line. Then add or subtract each vertical row as you normally would.

$$\begin{array}{r} 3.83 \\ +1.358 \\ \hline 5.188 \end{array} \qquad \begin{array}{r} 4.4992 \\ -1.738 \\ \hline 2.7612 \end{array}$$

Multiplying Decimals

Multiplying decimals requires two basic steps. First, multiply the two decimals just as you would any numbers, paying

no concern to where the decimal point is located. Once you have completed that operation, add the number of places to the right of the decimal in each number and count off that many decimal points in the solution line. That is your answer.

$$\begin{array}{r} 4.26 \text{ (two decimal places)} \\ \times.398 \text{ (three decimal places)} \\ \hline 3408 \\ 3834 \\ 1278 \\ \hline 1.69548 \text{ (five decimal places)} \end{array}$$

$$\begin{array}{r} 0.532 \text{ (three decimal places)} \\ \times 0.8 \text{ (one decimal place)} \\ \hline .4256 \text{ (four decimal places)} \end{array}$$

Dividing Decimals

When dividing decimals, it is easiest to multiply each decimal by the factor of 10 associated with the number of places to the right of the decimal point. So, if one of the numbers has two numbers to the right of the decimal point and the other number has three, each number should be multiplied by 1000. For example,

$$0.7 \div 1.32 = {}^{.7}/_{1.32}$$

Then multiply each side by the factor of 10 associated with the most spaces to the right of the decimal point in either number. In this case, that is 2, so we multiply each side by 100.

$$0.7 \times 100 = 70$$
$$1.32 \times 100 = 132$$

So, our new fraction is $70/132$.

SELF-QUIZ #4: Decimals

(Answers to this quiz can be found on page A-7.)

1. $1.83 \times 0.68 =$
2. $2.637 + 4.2 =$
3. $1.894 - 0.62 =$
4. $0.35 \div 0.7 =$
5. $3.419 \times 0.12 =$
6. ${}^{0.82}/_{1.74} =$
7. $0.125 \div 0.625 =$
8. $0.44 \times 0.163 =$
9. $0.8 + 1.239 =$
10. $13.288 - 4.46 =$

PERCENTAGES

Converting Percentages to Fractions or Decimals

Convert a percentage into a fraction by removing the percentage symbol and placing the number over a denominator of 100.

$$82\% = 82/100 \quad \text{or} \quad 41/50 \quad \text{or} \quad .82$$
$$20\% = 20/100 \quad \text{or} \quad 1/5 \quad \text{or} \quad 0.2$$

Multiplying with Percentages

In statistics, it is often necessary to determine the percentage of a whole number when analyzing data. To multiply with a percentage, convert the percentage to a decimal (Table A.3) and solve the equation. To convert a percentage to a decimal, remove the percentage symbol and move the decimal point two places to the left.

$$80\% \text{ of } 45 = 80\% \times 45 = .80 \times 45 = 36$$
$$25\% \text{ of } 94 = 25\% \times 94 = .25 \times 94 = 23.5$$

SELF-QUIZ #5: Percentages

(Answers to this quiz can be found on page A-7.)

1. $45\% \times 100 =$

2. 22% of $80 =$

3. 35% of $90 =$

4. $80\% \times 23 =$

5. $58\% \times 60 =$

6. $32 \times 16\% =$

7. $125 \times 73\% =$

8. $24 \times 75\% =$

9. 69% of $224 =$

10. $51\% \times 37 =$

A.5 SOLVING EQUATIONS WITH A SINGLE UNKNOWN VARIABLE

When solving equations with an unknown variable, isolate the unknown variable on one side of the equation. By isolating the variable, you free up the other side of the equation so you can solve it to a single number, thus providing you with the value of the variable.

To isolate the variable, add, subtract, multiply or divide each side of the equation to solve operations on the side of the equation that contains the variable (Table A.4).

TABLE A.4 SOLVING EQUATIONS WITH A SINGLE VARIABLE

Addition

$X + 7 = 18$	Subtracting 7 from each
$X + 7 - 7 = 18 - 7$	side zeros the addition
$X = 11$	operation.

Subtraction

$X - 13 = 27$	Adding 13 to each side
$X - 13 + 13 = 27 + 13$	zeros the subtraction
$X = 40$	operation.

TABLE A.4 (continued)

Multiplication

$X \times 5 = 20$	Dividing each side by 5
$X \times 5/5 = 20/5$	zeros the multiplication
$X = 4$	operation.

Division

$X/5 = 40$	Multiplying each side by
$X/5 \times 5 = 40 \times 5$	5 zeros the division
$X = 200$	operation.

Multiple Operations

$4X + 6 = 18$	When isolating a variable,
$4X + 6 - 6 = 18 - 6$	work *backward* through
$4X = 12$	the order of operations
$4X/4 = 12/4$	(see Table A.2). Isolate
$X = 3$	addition and subtraction
	operations first. Then isolate operations for multiplication and division.

SOLVING EQUATIONS WITH A SINGLE UNKNOWN VARIABLE: Worked Examples

1.
$$X + 12 = 42$$
$$X + 12 - 12 = 42 - 12$$
$$X = 30$$

2.
$$X - 13 = -5$$
$$X - 13 + 13 = -5 + 13$$
$$X = 8$$

3.
$$(X - 3)/6 = 2$$
$$(X - 3)/6 \times 6 = 2 \times 6$$
$$X - 3 = 12$$
$$X - 3 + 3 = 12 + 3$$
$$X = 15$$

4.
$$(3X + 4)/2 = 8$$
$$(3X + 4)/2 \times 2 = 8 \times 2$$
$$3X + 4 = 16$$
$$3X + 4 - 4 = 16 - 4$$
$$3X = 12$$
$$3X/3 = 12/3$$
$$X = 4$$

5.
$$(X - 2)/3 = 7$$
$$(X - 2)/3 \times 3 = 7 \times 3$$
$$X - 2 = 21$$
$$X - 2 + 2 = 21 + 2$$
$$X = 23$$

SELF-QUIZ #6: Solving Equations with a Single Unknown Variable

(Answers to this quiz can be found on page A.7.)

1. $7X = 42$
   $X =$

2. $87 - X + 16 = 57$
   $X =$

3. $X - 17 = -6$
   $X =$

4. $5X - 4 = 21$
   $X =$

5. $X - 10 = -4$
   $X =$

6. $X / 8 = 20$
   $X =$

7. $(X + 17)/3 = 10$
   $X =$

8. $2(X + 4) = 24$
   $X =$

9. $X(3 + 12) - 20 = 40$
   $X =$

10. $34 - X/6 = 27$
    $X =$

A.6 ANSWERS TO DIAGNOSTIC TEST AND SELF QUIZZES

Answers to Diagnostic Test

Section 1

1. 28; 2. −24; 3. 29; 4. 48; 5. −4; 6. 19; 7. 4; 8. 18; 9. −14; 10. 7

Section 2

1. 0; 2. 28; 3. −1; 4. 16; 5. 20; 6. 16; 7. −4; 8. 2; 9. 7; 10. 16

Section 3

1. $^{42}/_{100}$ or $^{21}/_{50}$; 2. 0.6; 3. 80%; 4. $^{10}/_{13}$; 5. 0.336; 6. 48; 7. $^{24}/_{35}$; 8. 32; 9. $^{3}/_{4}$; 10. $^{20}/_{63}$

Section 4

1. 4; 2. 5; 3. 24; 4. 6; 5. 6; 6. 12; 7. 7; 8. 12; 9. 6; 10. 2

Answers for Self-Quiz #1: Symbols and Notation

1. 28; 2. 18; 3. −9; 4. −9; 5. 36; 6. 7; 7. −48; 8. 8; 9. 15; 10. 28

Answers for Self-Quiz #2: Order of Operations

1. 19; 2. 2; 3. −4; 4. 4; 5. 3; 6. −5; 7. 20; 8. 30; 9. 12; 10. 213

Answers for Self-Quiz #3: Fractions

1. $^{3}/_{5}$; 2. $^{8}/_{35}$; 3. $^{1}/_{3}$ or $^{5}/_{15}$ or $^{25}/_{75}$; 4. $^{24}/_{30}$ or $^{4}/_{5}$; 5. $^{5}/_{8}$; 6. $^{5}/_{32}$; 7. $^{5}/_{9}$; 8. $^{13}/_{21}$; 9. $^{12}/_{75}$ or $^{4}/_{25}$; 10. $^{3}/_{28}$

Answers for Self-Quiz #4: Decimals

1. 1.244; 2. 6.837; 3. 1.274; 4. $^{35}/_{70}$ or $^{1}/_{2}$ or 0.5; 5. 0.41028; 6. $^{82}/_{174}$ or $^{41}/_{87}$ or 0.47; 7. $^{125}/_{625}$ or $^{1}/_{5}$ or 0.2; 8. 0.07172; 9. 2.039; 10. 8.828

Answers for Self-Quiz #5: Percentages

1. 45; 2. 17.6; 3. 31.5; 4. 18.4; 5. 34.8; 6. 5.12; 7. 91.25; 8. 18; 9. 154.56; 10. 18.87

Answers for Self-Quiz #6: Solving Equations

1. 6; 2. 46; 3. 11; 4. 5; 5. 6; 6. 160; 7. 13; 8. 8; 9. 4; 10. 42

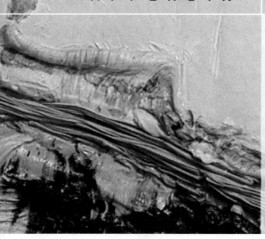

STATISTICAL TABLES

TABLE B.1 THE z DISTRIBUTION

Normal curve columns represent percentage between the mean and the z score and percentage beyond the z score in the tail.

z	% MEAN TO z	% IN TAIL	z	% MEAN TO z	% IN TAIL
.00	0.00	50.00	.23	9.10	40.90
.01	0.40	49.60	.24	9.48	40.52
.02	0.80	49.20	.25	9.87	40.13
.03	1.20	48.80	.26	10.26	39.74
.04	1.60	48.40	.27	10.64	39.36
.05	1.99	48.01	.28	11.03	38.97
.06	2.39	47.61	.29	11.41	38.59
.07	2.79	47.21	.30	11.79	38.21
.08	3.19	46.81	.31	12.17	37.83
.09	3.59	46.41	.32	12.55	37.45
.10	3.98	46.02	.33	12.93	37.07
.11	4.38	45.62	.34	13.31	36.69
.12	4.78	45.22	.35	13.68	36.32
.13	5.17	44.83	.36	14.06	35.94
.14	5.57	44.43	.37	14.43	35.57
.15	5.96	44.04	.38	14.80	35.20
.16	6.36	43.64	.39	15.17	34.83
.17	6.75	43.25	.40	15.54	34.46
.18	7.14	42.86	.41	15.91	34.09
.19	7.53	42.47	.42	16.28	33.72
.20	7.93	42.07	.43	16.64	33.36
.21	8.32	41.68	.44	17.00	33.00
.22	8.71	41.29	.45	17.36	32.64

z	% MEAN TO z	% IN TAIL	z	% MEAN TO z	% IN TAIL
.46	17.72	32.28	.89	31.33	18.67
.47	18.08	31.92	.90	31.59	18.41
.48	18.44	31.56	.91	31.86	18.14
.49	18.79	31.21	.92	32.12	17.88
.50	19.15	30.85	.93	32.38	17.62
.51	19.50	30.50	.94	32.64	17.36
.52	19.85	30.15	.95	32.89	17.11
.53	20.19	29.81	.96	33.15	16.85
.54	20.54	29.46	.97	33.40	16.60
.55	20.88	29.12	.98	33.65	16.35
.56	21.23	28.77	.99	33.89	16.11
.57	21.57	28.43	1.00	34.13	15.87
.58	21.90	28.10	1.01	34.38	15.62
.59	22.24	27.76	1.02	34.61	15.39
.60	22.57	27.43	1.03	34.85	15.15
.61	22.91	27.09	1.04	35.08	14.92
.62	23.24	26.76	1.05	35.31	14.69
.63	23.57	26.43	1.06	35.54	14.46
.64	23.89	26.11	1.07	35.77	14.23
.65	24.22	25.78	1.08	35.99	14.01
.66	24.54	25.46	1.09	36.21	13.79
.67	24.86	25.14	1.10	36.43	13.57
.68	25.17	24.83	1.11	36.65	13.35
.69	25.49	24.51	1.12	36.86	13.14
.70	25.80	24.20	1.13	37.08	12.92
.71	26.11	23.89	1.14	37.29	12.71
.72	26.42	23.58	1.15	37.49	12.51
.73	26.73	23.27	1.16	37.70	12.30
.74	27.04	22.96	1.17	37.90	12.10
.75	27.34	22.66	1.18	38.10	11.90
.76	27.64	22.36	1.19	38.30	11.70
.77	27.94	22.06	1.20	38.49	11.51
.78	28.23	21.77	1.21	38.69	11.31
.79	28.52	21.48	1.22	38.88	11.12
.80	28.81	21.19	1.23	39.07	10.93
.81	29.10	20.90	1.24	39.25	10.75
.82	29.39	20.61	1.25	39.44	10.56
.83	29.67	20.33	1.26	39.62	10.38
.84	29.95	20.05	1.27	39.80	10.20
.85	30.23	19.77	1.28	39.97	10.03
.86	30.51	19.49	1.29	40.15	9.85
.87	30.78	19.22	1.30	40.32	9.68
.88	31.06	18.94	1.31	40.49	9.51

TABLE B.1 continued

z	% MEAN TO z	% IN TAIL	z	% MEAN TO z	% IN TAIL
1.32	40.66	9.34	1.75	45.99	4.01
1.33	40.82	9.18	1.76	46.08	3.92
1.34	40.99	9.01	1.77	46.16	3.84
1.35	41.15	8.85	1.78	46.25	3.75
1.36	41.31	8.69	1.79	46.33	3.67
1.37	41.47	8.53	1.80	46.41	3.59
1.38	41.62	8.38	1.81	46.49	3.51
1.39	41.77	8.23	1.82	46.56	3.44
1.40	41.92	8.08	1.83	46.64	3.36
1.41	42.07	7.93	1.84	46.71	3.29
1.42	42.22	7.78	1.85	46.78	3.22
1.43	42.36	7.64	1.86	46.86	3.14
1.44	42.51	7.49	1.87	46.93	3.07
1.45	42.65	7.35	1.88	46.99	3.01
1.46	42.79	7.21	1.89	47.06	2.94
1.47	42.92	7.08	1.90	47.13	2.87
1.48	43.06	6.94	1.91	47.19	2.81
1.49	43.19	6.81	1.92	47.26	2.74
1.50	43.32	6.68	1.93	47.32	2.68
1.51	43.45	6.55	1.94	47.38	2.62
1.52	43.57	6.43	1.95	47.44	2.56
1.53	43.70	6.30	1.96	47.50	2.50
1.54	43.82	6.18	1.97	47.56	2.44
1.55	43.94	6.06	1.98	47.61	2.39
1.56	44.06	5.94	1.99	47.67	2.33
1.57	44.18	5.82	2.00	47.72	2.28
1.58	44.29	5.71	2.01	47.78	2.22
1.59	44.41	5.59	2.02	47.83	2.17
1.60	44.52	5.48	2.03	47.88	2.12
1.61	44.63	5.37	2.04	47.93	2.07
1.62	44.74	5.26	2.05	47.98	2.02
1.63	44.84	5.16	2.06	48.03	1.97
1.64	44.95	5.05	2.07	48.08	1.92
1.65	45.05	4.95	2.08	48.12	1.88
1.66	45.15	4.85	2.09	48.17	1.83
1.67	45.25	4.75	2.10	48.21	1.79
1.68	45.35	4.65	2.11	48.26	1.74
1.69	45.45	4.55	2.12	48.30	1.70
1.70	45.54	4.46	2.13	48.34	1.66
1.71	45.64	4.36	2.14	48.38	1.62
1.72	45.73	4.27	2.15	48.42	1.58
1.73	45.82	4.18	2.16	48.46	1.54
1.74	45.91	4.09	2.17	48.50	1.50

z	% MEAN TO z	% IN TAIL	z	% MEAN TO z	% IN TAIL
2.18	48.54	1.46	2.61	49.55	.45
2.19	48.57	1.43	2.62	49.56	.44
2.20	48.61	1.39	2.63	49.57	.43
2.21	48.64	1.36	2.64	49.59	.41
2.22	48.68	1.32	2.65	49.60	.40
2.23	48.71	1.29	2.66	49.61	.39
2.24	48.75	1.25	2.67	49.62	.38
2.25	48.78	1.22	2.68	49.63	.37
2.26	48.81	1.19	2.69	49.64	.36
2.27	48.84	1.16	2.70	49.65	.35
2.28	48.87	1.13	2.71	49.66	.34
2.29	48.90	1.10	2.72	49.67	.33
2.30	48.93	1.07	2.73	49.68	.32
2.31	48.96	1.04	2.74	49.69	.31
2.32	48.98	1.02	2.75	49.70	.30
2.33	49.01	.99	2.76	49.71	.29
2.34	49.04	.96	2.77	49.72	.28
2.35	49.06	.94	2.78	49.73	.27
2.36	49.09	.91	2.79	49.74	.26
2.37	49.11	.89	2.80	49.74	.26
2.38	49.13	.87	2.81	49.75	.25
2.39	49.16	.84	2.82	49.76	.24
2.40	49.18	.82	2.83	49.77	.23
2.41	49.20	.80	2.84	49.77	.23
2.42	49.22	.78	2.85	49.78	.22
2.43	49.25	.75	2.86	49.79	.21
2.44	49.27	.73	2.87	49.79	.21
2.45	49.29	.71	2.88	49.80	.20
2.46	49.31	.69	2.89	49.81	.19
2.47	49.32	.68	2.90	49.81	.19
2.48	49.34	.66	2.91	49.82	.18
2.49	49.36	.64	2.92	49.82	.18
2.50	49.38	.62	2.93	49.83	.17
2.51	49.40	.60	2.94	49.84	.16
2.52	49.41	.59	2.95	49.84	.16
2.53	49.43	.57	2.96	49.85	.15
2.54	49.45	.55	2.97	49.85	.15
2.55	49.46	.54	2.98	49.86	.14
2.56	49.48	.52	2.99	49.86	.14
2.57	49.49	.51	3.00	49.87	.13
2.58	49.51	.49	3.50	49.98	.02
2.59	49.52	.48	4.00	50.00	.00
2.60	49.53	.47	4.50	50.00	.00

TABLE B.2 THE *t* DISTRIBUTION

	One-Tailed Tests			Two-Tailed Tests		
df	.10	.05	.01	.10	.05	.01
1	3.078	6.314	31.821	6.314	12.706	63.657
2	1.886	2.920	6.965	2.920	4.303	9.925
3	1.638	2.353	4.541	2.353	3.182	5.841
4	1.533	2.132	3.747	2.132	2.776	4.604
5	1.476	2.015	3.365	2.015	2.571	4.032
6	1.440	1.943	3.143	1.943	2.447	3.708
7	1.415	1.895	2.998	1.895	2.365	3.500
8	1.397	1.860	2.897	1.860	2.306	3.356
9	1.383	1.833	2.822	1.833	2.262	3.250
10	1.372	1.813	2.764	1.813	2.228	3.170
11	1.364	1.796	2.718	1.796	2.201	3.106
12	1.356	1.783	2.681	1.783	2.179	3.055
13	1.350	1.771	2.651	1.771	2.161	3.013
14	1.345	1.762	2.625	1.762	2.145	2.977
15	1.341	1.753	2.603	1.753	2.132	2.947
16	1.337	1.746	2.584	1.746	2.120	2.921
17	1.334	1.740	2.567	1.740	2.110	2.898
18	1.331	1.734	2.553	1.734	2.101	2.879
19	1.328	1.729	2.540	1.729	2.093	2.861
20	1.326	1.725	2.528	1.725	2.086	2.846
21	1.323	1.721	2.518	1.721	2.080	2.832
22	1.321	1.717	2.509	1.717	2.074	2.819
23	1.320	1.714	2.500	1.714	2.069	2.808
24	1.318	1.711	2.492	1.711	2.064	2.797
25	1.317	1.708	2.485	1.708	2.060	2.788
26	1.315	1.706	2.479	1.706	2.056	2.779
27	1.314	1.704	2.473	1.704	2.052	2.771
28	1.313	1.701	2.467	1.701	2.049	2.764
29	1.312	1.699	2.462	1.699	2.045	2.757
30	1.311	1.698	2.458	1.698	2.043	2.750
35	1.306	1.690	2.438	1.690	2.030	2.724
40	1.303	1.684	2.424	1.684	2.021	2.705
60	1.296	1.671	2.390	1.671	2.001	2.661
80	1.292	1.664	2.374	1.664	1.990	2.639
100	1.290	1.660	2.364	1.660	1.984	2.626
120	1.289	1.658	2.358	1.658	1.980	2.617
∞	1.282	1.645	2.327	1.645	1.960	2.576

TABLE B.3 THE *F* DISTRIBUTIONS

WITHIN-GROUPS *df*	SIGNIF-ICANCE (*p*) LEVEL	BETWEEN-GROUPS DEGREES OF FREEDOM					
		1	2	3	4	5	6
1	.01	**4,052**	**5,000**	**5,404**	**5,625**	**5,764**	**5,859**
	.05	162	200	216	225	230	234
	.10	*39.9*	*49.5*	*53.6*	*55.8*	*57.2*	*58.2*
2	.01	**98.50**	**99.00**	**99.17**	**99.25**	**99.30**	**99.33**
	.05	18.51	19.00	19.17	19.25	19.30	19.33
	.10	*8.53*	*9.00*	*9.16*	*9.24*	*9.29*	*9.33*
3	.01	**34.12**	**30.82**	**29.46**	**28.71**	**28.24**	**27.91**
	.05	10.13	9.55	9.28	9.12	9.01	8.94
	.10	*5.54*	*5.46*	*5.39*	*5.34*	*5.31*	*5.28*
4	.01	**21.20**	**18.00**	**16.70**	**15.98**	**15.52**	**15.21**
	.05	7.71	6.95	6.59	6.39	6.26	6.16
	.10	*4.55*	*4.33*	*4.19*	*4.11*	*4.05*	*4.01*
5	.01	**16.26**	**13.27**	**12.06**	**11.39**	**10.97**	**10.67**
	.05	6.61	5.79	5.41	5.19	5.05	4.95
	.10	*4.06*	*3.78*	*3.62*	*3.52*	*3.45*	*3.41*
6	.01	**13.75**	**10.93**	**9.78**	**9.15**	**8.75**	**8.47**
	.05	5.99	5.14	4.76	4.53	4.39	4.28
	.10	*3.78*	*3.46*	*3.29*	*3.18*	*3.11*	*3.06*
7	.01	**12.25**	**9.55**	**8.45**	**7.85**	**7.46**	**7.19**
	.05	5.59	4.74	4.35	4.12	3.97	3.87
	.10	*3.59*	*3.26*	*3.08*	*2.96*	*2.88*	*2.83*
8	.01	**11.26**	**8.65**	**7.59**	**7.01**	**6.63**	**6.37**
	.05	5.32	4.46	4.07	3.84	3.69	3.58
	.10	*3.46*	*3.11*	*2.92*	*2.81*	*2.73*	*2.67*
9	.01	**10.56**	**8.02**	**6.99**	**6.42**	**6.06**	**5.80**
	.05	5.12	4.26	3.86	3.63	3.48	3.37
	.10	*3.36*	*3.01*	*2.81*	*2.69*	*2.61*	*2.55*
10	.01	**10.05**	**7.56**	**6.55**	**6.00**	**5.64**	**5.39**
	.05	4.97	4.10	3.71	3.48	3.33	3.22
	.10	*3.29*	*2.93*	*2.73*	*2.61*	*2.52*	*2.46*
11	.01	**9.65**	**7.21**	**6.22**	**5.67**	**5.32**	**5.07**
	.05	4.85	3.98	3.59	3.36	3.20	3.10
	.10	*3.23*	*2.86*	*2.66*	*2.54*	*2.45*	*2.39*

WITHIN-GROUPS df	SIGNIF-ICANCE (p) LEVEL	BETWEEN-GROUPS DEGREES OF FREEDOM					
		1	2	3	4	5	6
12	.01	9.33	6.93	5.95	5.41	5.07	4.82
	.05	4.75	3.89	3.49	3.26	3.11	3.00
	.10	3.18	2.81	2.61	2.48	2.40	2.33
13	.01	9.07	6.70	5.74	5.21	4.86	4.62
	.05	4.67	3.81	3.41	3.18	3.03	2.92
	.10	3.14	2.76	2.56	2.43	2.35	2.28
14	.01	8.86	6.52	5.56	5.04	4.70	4.46
	.05	4.60	3.74	3.34	3.11	2.96	2.85
	.10	3.10	2.73	2.52	2.40	2.31	2.24
15	.01	8.68	6.36	5.42	4.89	4.56	4.32
	.05	4.54	3.68	3.29	3.06	2.90	2.79
	.10	3.07	2.70	2.49	2.36	2.27	2.21
16	.01	8.53	6.23	5.29	4.77	4.44	4.20
	.05	4.49	3.63	3.24	3.01	2.85	2.74
	.10	3.05	2.67	2.46	2.33	2.24	2.18
17	.01	8.40	6.11	5.19	4.67	4.34	4.10
	.05	4.45	3.59	3.20	2.97	2.81	2.70
	.10	3.03	2.65	2.44	2.31	2.22	2.15
18	.01	8.29	6.01	5.09	4.58	4.25	4.02
	.05	4.41	3.56	3.16	2.93	2.77	2.66
	.10	3.01	2.62	2.42	2.29	2.20	2.13
19	.01	8.19	5.93	5.01	4.50	4.17	3.94
	.05	4.38	3.52	3.13	2.90	2.74	2.63
	.10	2.99	2.61	2.40	2.27	2.18	2.11
20	.01	8.10	5.85	4.94	4.43	4.10	3.87
	.05	4.35	3.49	3.10	2.87	2.71	2.60
	.10	2.98	2.59	2.38	2.25	2.16	2.09
21	.01	8.02	5.78	4.88	4.37	4.04	3.81
	.05	4.33	3.47	3.07	2.84	2.69	2.57
	.10	2.96	2.58	2.37	2.23	2.14	2.08
22	.01	7.95	5.72	4.82	4.31	3.99	3.76
	.05	4.30	3.44	3.05	2.82	2.66	2.55
	.10	2.95	2.56	2.35	2.22	2.13	2.06
23	.01	7.88	5.66	4.77	4.26	3.94	3.71
	.05	4.28	3.42	3.03	2.80	2.64	2.53
	.10	2.94	2.55	2.34	2.21	2.12	2.05

WITHIN-GROUPS df	SIGNIF-ICANCE (p) LEVEL	BETWEEN-GROUPS DEGREES OF FREEDOM					
		1	2	3	4	5	6
24	.01	7.82	5.61	4.72	4.22	3.90	3.67
	.05	4.26	3.40	3.01	2.78	2.62	2.51
	.10	2.93	2.54	2.33	2.20	2.10	2.04
25	.01	7.77	5.57	4.68	4.18	3.86	3.63
	.05	4.24	3.39	2.99	2.76	2.60	2.49
	.10	2.92	2.53	2.32	2.19	2.09	2.03
26	.01	7.72	5.53	4.64	4.14	3.82	3.59
	.05	4.23	3.37	2.98	2.74	2.59	2.48
	.10	2.91	2.52	2.31	2.18	2.08	2.01
27	.01	7.68	5.49	4.60	4.11	3.79	3.56
	.05	4.21	3.36	2.96	2.73	2.57	2.46
	.10	2.90	2.51	2.30	2.17	2.07	2.01
28	.01	7.64	5.45	4.57	4.08	3.75	3.53
	.05	4.20	3.34	2.95	2.72	2.56	2.45
	.10	2.89	2.50	2.29	2.16	2.07	2.00
29	.01	7.60	5.42	4.54	4.05	3.73	3.50
	.05	4.18	3.33	2.94	2.70	2.55	2.43
	.10	2.89	2.50	2.28	2.15	2.06	1.99
30	.01	7.56	5.39	4.51	4.02	3.70	3.47
	.05	4.17	3.32	2.92	2.69	2.53	2.42
	.10	2.88	2.49	2.28	2.14	2.05	1.98
35	.01	7.42	5.27	4.40	3.91	3.59	3.37
	.05	4.12	3.27	2.88	2.64	2.49	2.37
	.10	2.86	2.46	2.25	2.11	2.02	1.95
40	.01	7.32	5.18	4.31	3.83	3.51	3.29
	.05	4.09	3.23	2.84	2.61	2.45	2.34
	.10	2.84	2.44	2.23	2.09	2.00	1.93
45	.01	7.23	5.11	4.25	3.77	3.46	3.23
	.05	4.06	3.21	2.81	2.58	2.42	2.31
	.10	2.82	2.43	2.21	2.08	1.98	1.91
50	.01	7.17	5.06	4.20	3.72	3.41	3.19
	.05	4.04	3.18	2.79	2.56	2.40	2.29
	.10	2.81	2.41	2.20	2.06	1.97	1.90
55	.01	7.12	5.01	4.16	3.68	3.37	3.15
	.05	4.02	3.17	2.77	2.54	2.38	2.27
	.10	2.80	2.40	2.19	2.05	1.96	1.89

TABLE B.3 continued

WITHIN-GROUPS df	SIGNIF-ICANCE (p) LEVEL	BETWEEN-GROUPS DEGREES OF FREEDOM					
		1	2	3	4	5	6
60	.01	**7.08**	**4.98**	**4.13**	**3.65**	**3.34**	**3.12**
	.05	4.00	3.15	2.76	2.53	2.37	2.26
	.10	2.79	2.39	2.18	2.04	1.95	1.88
65	.01	**7.04**	**4.95**	**4.10**	**3.62**	**3.31**	**3.09**
	.05	3.99	3.14	2.75	2.51	2.36	2.24
	.10	2.79	2.39	2.17	2.03	1.94	1.87
70	.01	**7.01**	**4.92**	**4.08**	**3.60**	**3.29**	**3.07**
	.05	3.98	3.13	2.74	2.50	2.35	2.23
	.10	2.78	2.38	2.16	2.03	1.93	1.86
75	.01	**6.99**	**4.90**	**4.06**	**3.58**	**3.27**	**3.05**
	.05	3.97	3.12	2.73	2.49	2.34	2.22
	.10	2.77	2.38	2.16	2.02	1.93	1.86
80	.01	**6.96**	**4.88**	**4.04**	**3.56**	**3.26**	**3.04**
	.05	3.96	3.11	2.72	2.49	2.33	2.22
	.10	2.77	2.37	2.15	2.02	1.92	1.85
85	.01	**6.94**	**4.86**	**4.02**	**3.55**	**3.24**	**3.02**
	.05	3.95	3.10	2.71	2.48	2.32	2.21
	.10	2.77	2.37	2.15	2.01	1.92	1.85
90	.01	**6.93**	**4.85**	**4.01**	**3.54**	**3.23**	**3.01**
	.05	3.95	3.10	2.71	2.47	2.32	2.20
	.10	2.76	2.36	2.15	2.01	1.91	1.84
95	.01	**6.91**	**4.84**	**4.00**	**3.52**	**3.22**	**3.00**
	.05	3.94	3.09	2.70	2.47	2.31	2.20
	.10	2.76	2.36	2.14	2.01	1.91	1.84
100	.01	**6.90**	**4.82**	**3.98**	**3.51**	**3.21**	**2.99**
	.05	3.94	3.09	2.70	2.46	2.31	2.19
	.10	2.76	2.36	2.14	2.00	1.91	1.83
200	.01	**6.76**	**4.71**	**3.88**	**3.41**	**3.11**	**2.89**
	.05	3.89	3.04	2.65	2.42	2.26	2.14
	.10	273	2.33	2.11	1.97	1.88	1.80
1000	.01	**6.66**	**4.63**	**3.80**	**3.34**	**3.04**	**2.82**
	.05	3.85	3.00	2.61	2.38	2.22	2.11
	.10	2.71	2.31	2.09	1.95	1.85	1.78
∞	.01	**6.64**	**4.61**	**3.78**	**3.32**	**3.02**	**2.80**
	.05	3.84	3.00	2.61	2.37	2.22	2.10
	.10	2.71	2.30	2.08	1.95	1.85	1.78

TABLE B.4 THE CHI-SQUARE DISTRIBUTION

df	.10	SIGNIFICANCE (p) LEVEL .05	.01
1	2.706	3.841	6.635
2	4.605	5.992	9.211
3	6.252	7.815	11.345
4	7.780	9.488	13.277
5	9.237	11.071	15.087
6	10.645	12.592	16.812
7	12.017	14.067	18.475
8	13.362	15.507	20.090
9	14.684	16.919	21.666
10	15.987	18.307	23.209

TABLE B.5 THE q STATISTIC (TUKEY HSD TEST)

WITHIN-GROUPS df	SIGNIF-ICANCE (p) LEVEL	\(k\) = NUMBER OF TREATMENTS (LEVELS) 2	3	4	5	6	7	8	9	10	11	12
5	.05	3.64	4.60	5.22	5.67	6.03	6.33	6.58	6.80	6.99	7.17	7.32
	.01	5.70	6.98	7.80	8.42	8.91	9.32	9.67	9.97	10.24	10.48	10.70
6	.05	3.46	4.34	4.90	5.30	5.63	5.90	6.12	6.32	6.49	6.65	6.79
	.01	5.24	6.33	7.03	7.56	7.97	8.32	8.61	8.87	9.10	9.30	9.48
7	.05	3.34	4.16	4.68	5.06	5.36	5.61	5.82	6.00	6.16	6.30	6.43
	.01	4.95	5.92	6.54	7.01	7.37	7.68	7.94	8.17	8.37	8.55	8.71
8	.05	3.26	4.04	4.53	4.89	5.17	5.40	5.60	5.77	5.92	6.05	6.18
	.01	4.75	5.64	6.20	6.62	6.96	7.24	7.47	7.68	7.86	8.03	8.18
9	.05	3.20	3.95	4.41	4.76	5.02	5.24	5.43	5.59	5.74	5.87	5.98
	.01	4.60	5.43	5.96	6.35	6.66	6.91	7.13	7.33	7.49	7.65	7.78
10	.05	3.15	3.88	4.33	4.65	4.91	5.12	5.30	5.46	5.60	5.72	5.83
	.01	4.48	5.27	5.77	6.14	6.43	6.67	6.87	7.05	7.21	7.36	7.49
11	.05	3.11	3.82	4.26	4.57	4.82	5.03	5.20	5.35	5.49	5.61	5.71
	.01	4.39	5.15	5.62	5.97	6.25	6.48	6.67	6.84	6.99	7.13	7.25

TABLE B.5 continued

WITHIN-GROUPS df	SIGNIF-ICANCE (p) LEVEL	k = NUMBER OF TREATMENTS (LEVELS)										
		2	3	4	5	6	7	8	9	10	11	12
12	.05	3.08	3.77	4.20	4.51	4.75	4.95	5.12	5.27	5.39	5.51	5.61
	.01	4.32	5.05	5.50	5.84	6.10	6.32	6.51	6.67	6.81	6.94	7.06
13	.05	3.06	3.73	4.15	4.45	4.69	4.88	5.05	5.19	5.32	5.43	5.53
	.01	4.26	4.96	5.40	5.73	5.98	6.19	6.37	6.53	6.67	6.79	6.90
14	.05	3.03	3.70	4.11	4.41	4.64	4.83	4.99	5.13	5.25	5.36	5.46
	.01	4.21	4.89	5.32	5.63	5.88	6.08	6.26	6.41	6.54	6.66	6.77
15	.05	3.01	3.67	4.08	4.37	4.59	4.78	4.94	5.08	5.20	5.31	5.40
	.01	4.17	4.84	5.25	5.56	5.80	5.99	6.16	6.31	6.44	6.55	6.66
16	.05	3.00	3.65	4.05	4.33	4.56	4.74	4.90	5.03	5.15	5.26	5.35
	.01	4.13	4.79	5.19	5.49	5.72	5.92	6.08	6.22	6.35	6.46	6.56
17	.05	2.98	3.63	4.02	4.30	4.52	4.70	4.86	4.99	5.11	5.21	5.31
	.01	4.10	4.74	5.14	5.43	5.66	5.85	6.01	6.15	6.27	6.38	6.48
18	.05	2.97	3.61	4.00	4.28	4.49	4.67	4.82	4.96	5.07	5.17	5.27
	.01	4.07	4.70	5.09	5.38	5.60	5.79	5.94	6.08	6.20	6.31	6.41
19	.05	2.96	3.59	3.98	4.25	4.47	4.65	4.79	4.92	5.04	5.14	5.23
	.01	4.05	4.67	5.05	5.33	5.55	5.73	5.89	6.02	6.14	6.25	634
20	.05	2.95	3.58	3.96	4.23	4.45	4.62	4.77	4.90	5.01	5.11	5.20
	.01	4.02	4.64	5.02	5.29	5.51	5.69	5.84	5.97	6.09	6.19	6.28
24	.05	2.92	3.53	3.90	4.17	4.37	4.54	4.68	4.81	4.92	5.01	5.10
	.01	3.96	4.55	4.91	5.17	5.37	5.54	5.69	5.81	5.92	6.02	6.11
30	.05	2.89	3.49	3.85	4.10	4.30	4.46	4.60	4.72	4.82	4.92	5.00
	.01	3.89	4.45	4.80	5.05	5.24	5.40	5.54	5.65	5.76	5.85	5.93
40	.05	2.86	3.44	3.79	4.04	4.23	4.39	4.52	4.63	4.73	4.82	4.90
	.01	3.82	4.37	4.70	4.93	5.11	5.26	5.39	5.50	5.60	5.69	5.76
60	.05	2.83	3.40	3.74	3.98	4.16	4.31	4.44	4.55	4.65	4.73	4.81
	.01	3.76	4.28	4.59	4.82	4.99	5.13	5.25	5.36	5.45	5.53	5.60
120	.05	2.80	3.36	3.68	3.92	4.10	4.24	4.36	4.47	4.56	4.64	4.71
	.01	3.70	4.20	4.50	4.71	4.87	5.01	5.12	5.21	5.30	5.37	5.44
∞	.05	2.77	3.31	3.63	3.86	4.03	4.17	4.28	4.39	4.47	4.55	4.62
	.01	3.64	4.12	4.40	4.60	4.76	4.88	4.99	5.08	5.16	5.23	5.29

TABLE B.6 THE PEARSON CORRELATION

To be significant, the sample correlation, r, must be greater than or equal to the critical value in the table.

	LEVEL OF SIGNIFICANCE FOR ONE-TAILED TEST			LEVEL OF SIGNIFICANCE FOR TWO-TAILED TEST	
$df = N - 2$	.05	.01	$df = N - 2$	.05	.01
1	.988	.9995	1	.997	.9999
2	.900	.980	2	.950	.990
3	.805	.934	3	.878	.959
4	.729	.882	4	.811	.917
5	.669	.833	5	.754	.874
6	.622	.789	6	.707	.834
7	.582	.750	7	.666	.798
8	.549	.716	8	.632	.765
9	.521	.685	9	.602	.735
10	.497	.658	10	.576	.708
11	.476	.634	11	.553	.684
12	.458	.612	12	.532	.661
13	.441	.592	13	.514	.641
14	.426	.574	14	.497	.623
15	.412	.558	15	.482	.606
16	.400	.542	16	.468	.590
17	.389	.528	17	.456	.575
18	.378	.516	18	.444	.561
19	.369	.503	19	.433	.549
20	.360	.492	20	.423	.537
21	.352	.482	21	.413	.526
22	.344	.472	22	.404	.515
23	.337	.462	23	.396	.505
24	.330	.453	24	.388	.496
25	.323	.445	25	.381	.487
26	.317	.437	26	.374	.479
27	.311	.430	27	.367	.471
28	.306	.423	28	.361	.463
29	.301	.416	29	.355	.456
30	.296	.409	30	.349	.449
35	.275	.381	35	.325	.418
40	.257	.358	40	.304	.393
45	.243	.338	45	.288	.372
50	.231	.322	50	.273	.354
60	.211	.295	60	.250	.325
70	.195	.274	70	.232	.302
80	.183	.256	80	.217	.283
90	.173	.242	90	.205	.267
100	.164	.230	100	.195	.254

TABLE B.7 THE SPEARMAN CORRELATION

To be significant, the sample correlation, r_s, must be greater than or equal to the critical value in the table.

LEVEL OF SIGNIFICANCE FOR ONE-TAILED TEST			LEVEL OF SIGNIFICANCE FOR TWO-TAILED TEST		
N	.05	.01	N	.05	.01
4	1.000	—	4	—	—
5	0.900	1.000	5	1.000	—
6	0.829	0.943	6	0.886	1.000
7	0.714	0.893	7	0.786	0.929
8	0.643	0.833	8	0.738	0.881
9	0.600	0.783	9	0.700	0.833
10	0.564	0.745	10	0.648	0.794
11	0.536	0.709	11	0.618	0.755
12	0.503	0.671	12	0.587	0.727
13	0.484	0.648	13	0.560	0.703
14	0.464	0.622	14	0.538	0.675
15	0.443	0.604	15	0.521	0.654
16	0.429	0.582	16	0.503	0.635
17	0.414	0.566	17	0.485	0.615
18	0.401	0.550	18	0.472	0.600
19	0.391	0.535	19	0.460	0.584
20	0.380	0.520	20	0.447	0.570
21	0.370	0.508	21	0.435	0.556
22	0.361	0.496	22	0.425	0.544
23	0.353	0.486	23	0.415	0.532
24	0.344	0.476	24	0.406	0.521
25	0.337	0.466	25	0.398	0.511
26	0.331	0.457	26	0.390	0.501
27	0.324	0.448	27	0.382	0.491
28	0.317	0.440	28	0.375	0.483
29	0.312	0.433	29	0.368	0.475
30	0.306	0.425	30	0.362	0.467
35	0.283	0.394	35	0.335	0.433
40	0.264	0.368	40	0.313	0.405
45	0.248	0.347	45	0.294	0.382
50	0.235	0.329	50	0.279	0.363
60	0.214	0.300	60	0.255	0.331
70	0.190	0.278	70	0.235	0.307
80	0.185	0.260	80	0.220	0.287
90	0.174	0.245	90	0.207	0.271
100	0.165	0.233	100	0.197	0.257

TABLE B.8A MANN-WHITNEY U FOR a α = .05 FOR A ONE-TAILED TEST

To be significant, the U must be equal to or less than the value in the table.

N_A/N_B	1	2	3	4	5	6	7	8	9	10	11	12	13	14	15	16	17	18	19	20
1	—	—	—	—	—	—	—	—	—	—	—	—	—	—	—	—	—	—	0	0
2	—	—	—	—	0	0	0	1	1	1	1	2	2	2	3	3	3	4	4	4
3	—	—	0	0	1	2	2	3	3	4	5	5	6	7	7	8	9	9	10	11
4	—	—	0	1	2	3	4	5	6	7	8	9	10	11	12	14	15	16	17	18
5	—	0	1	2	4	5	6	8	9	11	12	13	15	16	18	19	20	22	23	25
6	—	0	2	3	5	7	8	10	12	14	16	17	19	21	23	25	26	28	30	32
7	—	0	2	4	6	8	11	13	15	17	19	21	24	26	28	30	33	35	37	39
8	—	1	3	5	8	10	13	15	18	20	23	26	28	31	33	36	39	41	44	47
9	—	1	3	6	9	12	15	18	21	24	27	30	33	36	39	42	45	48	51	54
10	—	1	4	7	11	14	17	20	24	27	31	34	37	41	44	48	51	55	58	62
11	—	1	5	8	12	16	19	23	27	31	34	38	42	46	50	54	57	61	65	69
12	—	2	5	9	13	17	21	26	30	34	38	42	47	51	55	60	64	68	72	77
13	—	2	6	10	15	19	24	28	33	37	42	47	51	56	61	65	70	75	80	84
14	—	2	7	11	16	21	26	31	36	41	46	51	56	61	66	71	77	82	87	92
15	—	3	7	12	18	23	28	33	39	44	50	55	61	66	72	77	83	88	94	100
16	—	3	8	14	19	25	30	36	42	48	54	60	65	71	77	83	89	95	101	107
17	—	3	9	15	20	26	33	39	45	51	57	64	70	77	83	89	96	102	109	115
18	—	4	9	16	22	28	35	41	48	55	61	68	75	82	88	95	102	109	116	123
19	0	4	10	17	23	30	37	44	51	58	65	72	80	87	94	101	109	116	123	130
20	0	4	11	18	25	32	39	47	54	62	69	77	84	92	100	107	115	123	130	138

TABLE B.8B MANN-WHITNEY U FOR a α = .05 FOR A TWO-TAILED TEST

To be significant, the U must be equal to or less than the value in the table.

N_A/N_B	1	2	3	4	5	6	7	8	9	10	11	12	13	14	15	16	17	18	19	20
1	—	—	—	—	—	—	—	—	—	—	—	—	—	—	—	—	—	—	—	—
2	—	—	—	—	—	—	—	0	0	0	0	1	1	1	1	1	2	2	2	2
3	—	—	—	—	0	1	1	2	2	3	3	4	4	5	5	6	6	7	7	8
4	—	—	—	0	1	2	3	4	4	5	6	7	8	9	10	11	11	12	13	13
5	—	—	0	1	2	3	5	6	7	8	9	11	12	13	14	15	17	18	19	20
6	—	—	1	2	3	5	6	8	10	11	13	14	16	17	19	21	22	24	25	27
7	—	—	1	3	5	6	8	10	12	14	16	18	20	22	24	26	28	30	32	34
8	—	0	2	4	6	8	10	13	15	17	19	22	24	26	29	31	34	36	38	41
9	—	0	2	4	7	10	12	15	17	20	23	26	28	31	34	37	39	42	45	48
10	—	0	3	5	8	11	14	17	20	23	26	29	33	36	39	42	45	48	52	55
11	—	0	3	6	9	13	16	19	23	26	30	33	37	40	44	47	51	55	58	62
12	—	1	4	7	11	14	18	22	26	29	33	37	41	45	49	53	57	61	65	69
13	—	1	4	8	12	16	20	24	28	33	37	41	45	50	54	59	63	67	72	76
14	—	1	5	9	13	17	22	26	31	36	40	45	50	55	59	64	67	74	78	83
15	—	1	5	10	14	19	24	29	34	39	44	49	54	59	64	70	75	80	85	90
16	—	1	6	11	15	21	26	31	37	42	47	53	59	64	70	75	81	86	92	98
17	—	2	6	11	17	22	28	34	39	45	51	57	63	67	75	81	87	93	99	105
18	—	2	7	12	18	24	30	36	42	48	55	61	67	74	80	86	93	99	106	112
19	—	2	7	13	19	25	32	38	45	52	58	65	72	78	85	92	99	106	113	119
20	—	2	8	13	20	27	34	41	48	55	62	69	76	83	90	98	105	112	119	127

TABLE B.9 WILCOXON SIGNED-RANKS TEST FOR MATCHED PAIRS (T)

LEVEL OF SIGNIFICANCE (p LEVEL) FOR ONE-TAILED TEST			LEVEL OF SIGNIFICANCE (p LEVEL) FOR TWO-TAILED TEST		
N	.05	.01	N	.05	.01
5	0	—	5	—	—
6	2	—	6	0	—
7	3	0	7	2	—
8	5	1	8	3	0
9	8	3	9	5	1
10	10	5	10	8	3
11	13	7	11	10	5
12	17	9	12	13	7
13	21	12	13	17	9
14	25	15	14	21	12
15	30	19	15	25	15
16	35	23	16	29	19
17	41	27	17	34	23
18	47	32	18	40	27
19	53	37	19	46	32
20	60	43	20	52	37
21	67	49	21	58	42
22	75	55	22	65	48
23	83	62	23	73	54
24	91	69	24	81	61
25	100	76	25	89	68
26	110	84	26	98	75
27	119	92	27	107	83
28	130	101	28	116	91
29	140	110	29	126	100
30	151	120	30	137	109
31	163	130	31	147	118
32	175	140	32	159	128
33	187	151	33	170	138
34	200	162	34	182	148
35	213	173	35	195	159
36	227	185	36	208	171
37	241	198	37	221	182
38	256	211	38	235	194
39	271	224	39	249	207
40	286	238	40	264	220
41	302	252	41	279	233
42	319	266	42	294	247

LEVEL OF SIGNIFICANCE (*p* LEVEL) FOR ONE-TAILED TEST			LEVEL OF SIGNIFICANCE (*p* LEVEL) FOR TWO-TAILED TEST		
N	.05	.01	N	.05	.01
43	336	281	43	310	261
44	353	296	44	327	276
45	371	312	45	343	291
46	389	328	46	361	307
47	407	345	47	378	322
48	426	362	48	396	339
49	446	379	49	415	355
50	466	397	50	434	373

TABLE B.10 RANDOM DIGITS

101	19223	95034	05756	28713	96409	12531	42544	82853
102	73676	47150	99400	01927	27754	42648	82425	36290
103	45467	71709	77558	00095	32863	29485	82226	90056
104	52711	38889	93074	60227	40011	85848	48767	52573
105	95592	94007	69971	91481	60779	53791	17297	59335
106	68417	35013	15529	72765	85089	57067	50211	47487
107	82739	57890	20807	47511	81676	55300	94383	14893
108	60940	72024	17868	24943	61790	90656	87964	18883
109	36009	19365	15412	39638	85453	46816	83485	41979
110	38448	48789	18338	24697	39364	42006	76688	08708
111	81486	69487	60513	09297	00412	71238	27649	39950
112	59636	88804	04634	71197	19352	73089	84898	45785
113	62568	70206	40325	03699	71080	22553	11486	11776
114	45149	32992	75730	66280	03819	56202	02938	70915
115	61041	77684	94322	24709	73698	14526	31893	32592
116	14459	26056	31424	80371	65103	62253	50490	61181
117	38167	98532	62183	70632	23417	26185	41448	75532
118	73190	32533	04470	29669	84407	90785	65956	86382
119	95857	07118	87664	92099	58806	66979	98624	84826
120	35476	55972	39421	65850	04266	35435	43742	11937
121	71487	09984	29077	14863	61683	47052	62224	51025
122	13873	81598	95052	90908	73592	75186	87136	95761
123	54580	81507	27102	56027	55892	33063	41842	81868

TABLE B.10 RANDOM DIGITS

124	71035	09001	43367	49497	72719	96758	27611	91596
125	96746	12149	37823	71868	18442	35119	62103	39244
126	96927	19931	36809	74192	77567	88741	48409	41903
127	43909	99477	25330	64359	40085	16925	85117	36071
128	15689	14227	06565	14374	13352	49367	81982	87209
129	36759	58984	68288	22913	18638	54303	00795	08727
130	69051	64817	87174	09517	84534	06489	87201	97245
131	05007	16632	81194	14873	04197	85576	45195	96565
132	68732	55259	84292	08796	43165	93739	31685	97150
133	45740	41807	65561	33302	07051	93623	18132	09547
134	27816	78416	18329	21337	35213	37741	04312	68508
135	66925	55658	39100	78458	11206	19876	87151	31260
136	08421	44753	77377	28744	75592	08563	79140	92454
137	53645	66812	61421	47836	12609	15373	98481	14592
138	66831	68908	40772	21558	47781	33586	79177	06928
139	55588	99404	70708	41098	43563	56934	48394	51719
140	12975	13258	13048	45144	72321	81940	00360	02428
141	96767	35964	23822	96012	94591	65194	50842	53372
142	72829	50232	97892	63408	77919	44575	24870	04178
143	88565	42628	17797	49376	61762	16953	88604	12724
144	62964	88145	83083	69453	46109	59505	69680	00900
145	19687	12633	57857	95806	09931	02150	43163	58636
146	37609	59057	66967	83401	60705	02384	90597	93600
147	54973	86278	88737	74351	47500	84552	19909	67181
148	00694	05977	19664	65441	20903	62371	22725	53340
149	71546	05233	53946	68743	72460	27601	45403	88692
150	07511	88915	41267	16853	84569	79367	32337	03316

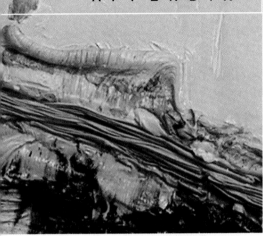

ANSWERS TO ODD-NUMBERED END-OF-CHAPTER PROBLEMS

CHAPTER 1

1.1 AVERAGE WEIGHTS OF GIRLS IN THE UNITED STATES

a. The average weight for a 10-year-old girl was 77.4 pounds in 1963 and nearly 88 pounds in 2002.

b. No; the CDC would not be able to weigh every single girl in the United States. It would be too expensive and too time-consuming.

c. It is a descriptive statistic because it is a numerical summary of a sample. It is an inferential statistic because the researchers drew conclusions about the population's average weight based on this information from a sample.

1.3 THE KENTUCKY DERBY AND TYPES OF VARIABLES

a. Ordinal

b. Interval/ratio

c. Interval/ratio

d. Nominal

e. Nominal

d. Discrete

e. Continuous

1.5 RELIABILITY AND VALIDITY OF THE RORSCHACH INKBLOT TEST

a. They relate more to validity because they suggest that the Rorschach is not really measuring what it intends to measure.

b. A Rorschach test might be consistent; for example, five clinicians might interpret the responses in one Rorschach in the same way. Yet the interpretation might not be accurate—it might not be a valid measure of a person's personality.

1.7 RELIABILITY AND VALIDITY AND PERSONALITY TESTING

a. A reliable test is one that provides consistent results. If you took the test twice, you should get the same results, an indication of reliability.

b. A valid test is one that measures that which it intends to measure. This test has the stated intention of measuring personality. If in fact it is measuring personality accurately, then it is a valid test.

1.9 OPERATIONALIZING DEPENDENT VARIABLES

Answers will be different for each student. The following are possible answers.

a. Final score on a video game; average reaction time on a video game task

b. Parental measure of child aggression; number of aggressive acts observed in an hour of play

c. Weight loss measured in pounds or kilograms; weight loss measured by change in waist size

d. Average test score for the semester; overall grade for the semester

e. Minutes to fall asleep from when participant goes to bed; actual time at which the participant falls asleep

1.11 CONSIDERATION OF FUTURE CONSEQUENCES AND VARIABLES

a. Independent: CFC level; dependent: credit card debt and tendency to buy on impulse

b. There are many possible answers to this question. As one example, the scale might have asked: "When you go grocery shopping, how often do you buy an item that is not on your list?"

1.13 CHOLERA AND HIV

a. Researchers could have randomly assigned some individuals who are HIV-positive to take the oral vaccine and other such individuals not to take the oral vaccine. The second group would likely take a placebo.

b. This would have been a between-groups experiment because the individuals who are HIV-positive would have been in only one group: either vaccine or no vaccine (i.e., placebo).

c. The researchers might observe individuals who are HIV-positive and were given the oral vaccine and other individuals who are HIV-positive and were not given the vaccine. The two groups would be those who did or did not take the vaccine anyway; they would not have been randomly assigned to these conditions. The researchers would then compare the rates of cholera in the two groups.

d. This limits their ability to draw causal conclusions because those who received the vaccine may have been different in some way from those who did not receive the vaccine. There may have been a confounding variable that led to these findings. For example, those who received the vaccine might have had better access to health care and better sanitary conditions to begin with, making them less likely to contract cholera regardless of the vaccine's effectiveness.

1.15 IMPLEMENTING RANDOM ASSIGNMENT

We could recruit a sample of people who are HIV-positive. Half would be randomly assigned to take the oral vaccine; half would be randomly assigned to take a placebo. A double-blind procedure would be used to ensure that participants did not know which they received. They would be followed to determine whether they developed cholera.

1.17 THE LANGUAGE OF STATISTICS—*SCALE*

Statisticians use *scale* as another term for an interval measure. They also use *scale* as a word for many measurement tools, particularly those that involve a series of items that test-takers must complete.

1.19 THE LANGUAGE OF STATISTICS— *EXPERIMENT*

In everyday language, people often use the word *experiment* to refer to something they are trying out to see what will happen. Researchers use the term to refer to a type of study in which participants are randomly assigned to levels of the independent variable.

1.21 OUTLIER ANALYSIS

a. The individual would be considered an outlier because his or her score was far from the scores of all the others in the study.

b. Outlier analysis might be useful to find out why this person gained so much despite the exercise program. For example, was the person eating much more because he or she incorrectly assumed the exercise would burn all the extra calories?

c. We are looking for any reason that might explain why this outlier exists. Is there something about this individual that provides evidence for our hypothesis, when, on the face of it, the outlier seems to discredit our hypothesis?

CHAPTER 2

2.1 FREQUENCIES AND THE NATIONAL SURVEY OF STUDENT ENGAGEMENT (NSSE)

a. Frequency table:

PERCENT-AGES	FREQUENCY	PERCENT	CUMULATIVE PERCENT
10	1	5.26	100.00
9	0	0.0	94.74
8	0	0.0	94.74
7	0	0.0	94.74
6	0	0.0	94.74
5	2	10.53	94.74
4	2	10.53	84.21
3	4	21.05	73.68
2	4	21.05	52.63
1	5	26.32	31.58
0	1	5.26	5.26

b. 10.53% of these schools had exactly 4% of their students report that they wrote between five and 10 20-page papers that year.

c. 84.21% of these schools had 4% or fewer of their students report that they wrote between five and 10 20-page papers that year.

d. This is not a random sample. It includes schools that chose to participate in this survey and opted to have their results made public.

2.3 GROUPED HISTOGRAM AND FREQUENCY POLYGON

a. Grouped histogram:

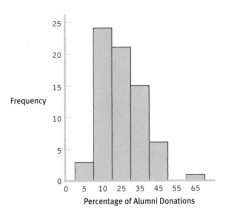

b. Frequency polygon:

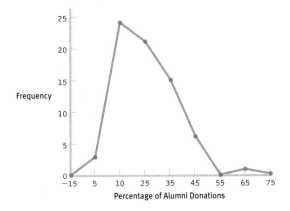

c. There is one potential outlier—the score of 61. The distribution appears to be positively skewed. The center of the distribution seems to be in the 10–29 range. The distribution is unimodal.

2.5 CENTRAL TENDENCY AND ALUMNI DONATIONS

a. $M = \dfrac{\Sigma X}{N} = (48 + 61 + 45 + 39 + 46 \ldots$
$+ 16 + 13) / 70 = 1759/70 = 25.13$

b. The scores would be arranged in order. There are 70 scores; if we divide 70 by 2, and add $^1/_2$, we get 35.5. The mean of the 35th score (24) and the 36th score (25) is 24.5. Thus, the median is 24.5.

2.7 CENTRAL TENDENCY AND THE BUSINESS OF WEIGHT LOSS

a. The answers will be different for each student, but most ads will promote a product that offers purportedly fast, easy, substantial weight loss.

b. The answers will be different for each student, but such ads typically offer little or no data. Testimonials abound.

c. It would be most useful to see a median; the mean could be skewed higher by the occasional person who loses a great deal of weight (and maybe not even from this diet product specifically). The mean would not be representative of the typical person's weight loss.

d. We would tell a friend to look at the data for the *typical* person—the median, or middle score. The company clearly chooses the biggest "losers" for its ad testimonials.

2.9 VARIANCE, STANDARD DEVIATION, AND NSSE

a. $M = \dfrac{\Sigma X}{N} = (0 + 5 + 3 + 3 + 1 \ldots +$
$3 + 5)/19 = 53/19 = 2.789$

b. The formula for variance is $SD^2 = \dfrac{\Sigma(X - M)^2}{N}$.

We will start by creating three columns: one for the scores, one for the deviations of the scores from the mean, and one for the squares of the deviations.

X	X − M	(X − M)²
0	−2.789	7.779
5	2.211	4.889
3	0.211	0.045
3	0.211	0.045
1	−1.789	3.201
10	7.211	51.999
2	−0.789	0.623
2	−0.789	0.623
3	0.211	0.045
1	−1.789	3.201
2	−0.789	0.623
4	1.211	1.467
2	−0.789	0.623
1	−1.789	3.201
1	−1.789	3.201
1	−1.789	3.201
4	1.211	1.467
3	0.211	0.045
5	2.211	4.889

We can now calculate variance: $SD^2 = \frac{\Sigma(X - M)^2}{N} = (7.779 + 4.889 + 0.045 + 0.045 \ldots + 0.045 + 4.889)/19 = 91.167/19 = 4.798$

c. Standard deviation is calculated just like we calculated variance, but we then take the square root: $SD = \sqrt{\frac{\Sigma(X - M)^2}{N}} = 2.19$

d. The typical score is around 2.79, and the typical deviation from 2.79 is around 2.19.

2.11 MEAN, MEDIAN, AND THE SHAPE OF DISTRIBUTIONS

There are many possible answers to these questions. The following are only examples.

a. 70, 70. There is no skew; the mean is not pulled away from the median.

b. 80, 70. There is positive skew; the mean is pulled up, but the median is unaffected.

c. 60, 70. There is negative skew; the mean is pulled down, but the median is unaffected.

2.13 NUMBER OF MODES

a. Bimodal. There would be newborn infants and mothers of childbearing age.

b. Unimodal. Most people would fall in the middle, with some exhibiting no depression and others reporting to be very depressed.

c. Unimodal. Most people would score around 500, with some scoring down toward 200 and others up toward 800.

d. Bimodal. The first world countries would charge much more for the drug than the third world countries.

2.15 UNDERSTANDING YOUR DISTRIBUTION—WINS IN THE NBA

a. Grouped frequency table:

INTERVALS	FREQUENCIES
60–69	1
50–59	7
40–49	10
30–39	7
20–29	2
10–19	3

b. Histogram:

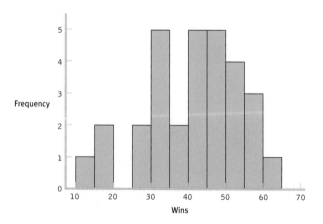

c. $M = \frac{\Sigma X}{N} = (45 + 43 + 42 + 33 + 33 \ldots + 45 + 18)/30 = 1230/30 = 41.00$

With 30 scores, the median would be between the 15th and 16th scores [(30/2) + 0.5 = 15.5]. The 15th and 16th scores are 43 and 44, respectively, and so the median would be 43.5

The mode is 45; there are three scores of 45.

d. Software reports that the range is 49 and the standard deviation is 12.69.

e. The summary will differ for each student but will include the following information: The data appear to be roughly symmetric and unimodal, maybe a bit negatively skewed. There are no glaring outliers.

f. There are many possible answers to this question. For example, one might ask whether teams with older players do better or worse than those with younger players. Another study might examine whether team budget relates to wins; there's a salary cap, but some teams might choose to pay the "luxury tax" in order to spend more. Does spending make a difference?

2.17 THE LANGUAGE OF STATISTICS— INTERVAL

Statisticians might use *interval* to describe a type of variable. Interval variables have numbers as their values, and the distance (or interval) between numbers is assumed to be equal. Statisticians might also use *interval* to refer to the range of values that will be used in a grouped frequency table, histogram, or polygon.

2.19 KURTOSIS, PLATYKURTIC, LEPTOKURTIC, AND MESOKURTIC

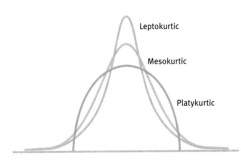

The answers will be different for each student depending on the distribution of GPAs at her or his school.

2.21 INTERQUARTILE RANGE AND DETERMINATION OF OUTLIERS

$IQR \times 1.5 = 17(1.5) = 25.5$

$Q1 - 25.5 = 16 - 25.5 = -9.5$

$Q3 + 25.5 = 33 + 25.5 = 58.5$

There is one potential outlier: 61.

2.23 INFERENTIAL STATISTICS AND VARIANCE

The answers will be different for each student. For example, a swimming instructor might want to compare variabilities of students in her swimming classes. In one class, all the students might be beginners; thus, there would be little variability among abilities. In a more advanced class, there might be some students who are still struggling with basics and others who are chafing to learn more advanced techniques. If there is lower variability in some classes than in others, she can be more targeted in her instruction.

CHAPTER 3

3.1 CROSS-COUNTRY CYCLING AND SCATTERPLOTS

a. Scatterplot of mileage and climb:

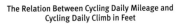

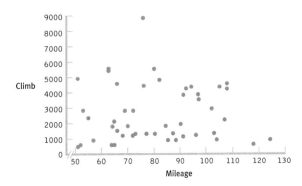

b. For the most part, the points on the scatterplot do not seem to indicate any particular relation, whether linear or curvilinear. Low-mileage days (50s, 60s) have some low-climb and some high-climb days, and mid-mileage days (90s, 100s) have some low-climb and some high-climb days. Only the two very long mileage days (around 120) have low climbs, perhaps indicating a tiny relation.

c. The cyclists experience the mileage and climbs as difficult and tend to notice days on which both are high. The organizers want to convince cyclists to sign up and pay the trip costs so they can make money; a promise that long mileage days won't have big climbs helps them recruit cyclists. The staff have no vested interest either way.

3.3 ORGAN DONATION AND TIME SERIES

a. Time series plot of organ donation rates, 1994–2004:

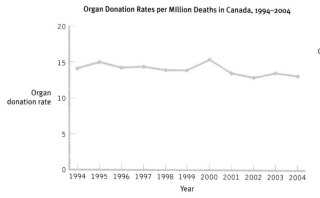

Organ Donation Rates per Million Deaths in Canada, 1994–2004

b. These data suggest that, although there are some fluctuations, there seems to have been a slight decrease in organ donation between 1994 and 2004.

c. We might predict a continued decline, but it would be dangerous to do so. Predicting beyond our data is an example of the extrapolation lie. Because we cannot know what events might occur to affect organ donation, we cannot safely predict beyond our data.

d. There are many possible answers to this question. As one example, you might be interested in how characteristics of families or types of deaths distinguish between agreeing to and declining to donate.

3.5 G8 AND PARETO CHART

a. A Pareto chart is organized from the highest bar to the lowest bar, whereas a bar graph might be organized in a number of different ways (e.g., alphabetical).

b. Bar graph using alphabetical order:

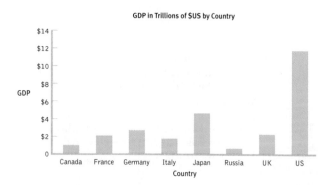

GDP in Trillions of $US by Country

c. Pareto chart:

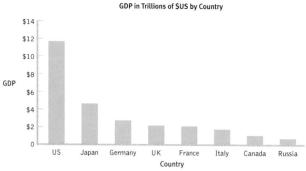

GDP in Trillions of $US by Country

d. The Pareto chart allows us to make comparisons more easily than does the bar graph. Moreover, we can very easily identify the countries with the highest and lowest GDPs.

3.7 PICTORIAL GRAPH AND ALUMNI DONATIONS

a. Pictures could be used instead of bars. For example, dollar signs might be used to represent the three quantities.

b. If the dollar signs become wider as they get taller, as often happens with pictorial graphs, the overall size will be proportionally larger than the increase in donation rate it is meant to represent. A bar graph is not subject to this problem, because graphmakers are not likely to make bars wider as they get taller.

3.9 SATISFACTION WITH GRADUATE ADVISORS AND DEFAULTS

a. Example of bar graph after changes:

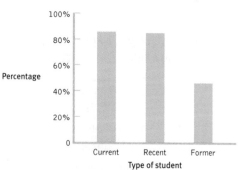

Percentage Satisfied with Graduate Advisors Among Current Students, Recent Graduates, and Former Students Who Did Not Complete a PhD

b. The default options that students choose to override will differ. For the bar graph here, we (1) added a title, (2) labeled the x-axis, (3) labeled the y-axis, (4) rotated the y-axis label so that it read from left to right, (5) eliminated the box around the whole graph, (6) eliminated the right and top borders around the part of the graph that contains the bars, (7) muted the color of the grid lines, (8) muted the color of the axes, (9) eliminated background color, and (10) eliminated the black lines around the bars themselves.

3.11 INVENT A SCENARIO

The examples will differ for each student. Correct answers will include the following numbers and types of variables.

a. Frequency polygon: one interval variable, such as times for rats to complete a maze on the x-axis and frequencies for each time on the y-axis

b. Line graph (line of best fit): two interval variables, such as hours of maze-training for rats on the x-axis and predicted times for rats to complete a maze on the y-axis

c. Bar graph (one independent variable): one nominal independent variable and one interval dependent variable, such as gender of rat on the x-axis and time to complete a maze on the y-axis

d. Scatterplot: two interval variables, such as hours of maze-training for rats on the x-axis and times for rats to complete a maze on the y-axis

e. Time series plot: one time independent variable (e.g., minute, week, year, decade) on the x-axis, such as years since the founding of a university, and one interval dependent variable on the y-axis, such as mean GPA of incoming students

f. Pie chart: Trick question! Don't use one; use a bar graph instead.

g. Bar graph (two independent variables): two nominal independent variables, such as gender of rat and reinforcement schedule for rat, on the x-axis, and an interval dependent variable, such as time to complete a maze, on the y-axis.

3.13 RATE MY PROFESSOR AND THE SNEAKY SAMPLE LIE

a. The examples will be different for each student.

b. The examples will be different for each student.

c. In general, only the students who feel most strongly about a professor (i.e., they either adore or detest the professor) take the time to post their views.

d. Only students who feel very strongly about a professor—whether in a positive or negative direction—tend to take the time to post on Web sites like this.

e. There many examples of chartjunk on this Web site. Here are several that were present in 2006: Emoticons are ducks, and they are redundant (there are numerical scores). The checkmarks that say "rate" are ducks. The color scheme, particularly the white writing, makes it difficult to read comments and scores; it has some of the effect of a moiré pattern. There is a distracting grid pattern that uses alternating shades of blue and white lines.

3.15 PULLING IT ALL TOGETHER—THE POPULAR MEDIA

The articles and subsequent responses will be different for each student.

3.17 PULLING IT ALL TOGETHER AND PSYCHOLOGY DEGREES

a. This is a time plot. The researchers chose this type of graph because they wanted to show changes in the number of psychology degrees over time.

b. This graph suggests a fairly large increase in bachelor's degrees over time, with smaller increases in master's degrees and doctoral degrees.

c. The independent variable is year; it is an interval/ratio variable. The dependent variable is number of psychology degrees. It is also an interval/ratio variable.

d. There are several possible answers to this question. For example, the y-axis starts at 0, there is a clear title, and all labels read from left to right.

e. There are several possible answers to this question. For example, the graph creators should have labeled the y-axis and they could have toned down the grid behind the data points. The y-axis is too "busy"; intervals of 10,000 would be better.

f. It is dangerous to extrapolate—that is, to predict beyond our available data—because we do not know what factors may change that will affect current trends.

g. There are several possible answers to this question. For example, we could track percentage out of all such degrees (e.g., percentage of psychology bachelor's degrees conferred out of *all* bachelor's degrees conferred).

h. There are several possible answers to this question. For example, we might examine what types of careers psychology undergraduates pursue that do not require a master's or doctorate in psychology.

3.19 THE LANGUAGE OF STATISTICS— *DEFAULT*

In everyday language, we use the term *default* to indicate a failure to fulfill an obligation, such as "to default on a loan." We also use the term to indicate a predetermined option or outcome, such as "his default Monday night activity is to watch football." With respect to computer software, the meaning of *default* is closer to the second of the everyday definitions. Defaults are the predetermined options built into the software. Unless we actively select an alternative, the decisions made by a programmer will be implemented.

■ DIGGING DEEPER INTO THE DATA

3.21 BOX PLOTS AND OUTLIERS

a. $IQR = 33 - 16 = 17$

b. $IQR \times 1.5 = 17(1.5) = 25.5$

$Q1 - 25.5 = 9 - 25.5 = -16.5$; $Q3 + 25.5 = 33 + 25.5 = 58.5$. Based on this criterion, any score below -16.5 (note that it is not possible to have a negative score in this case, so we already know there will be no potential outliers below the median) and any score above 58.5 will be considered potential outliers.

c. According to this criterion, there is one outlier in this data set: 61.

CHAPTER 4

4.1 RANDOM SELECTION AND U.S. SCHOOL PSYCHOLOGISTS

a. The targeted population is the 5000 school psychologists with doctoral degrees.

b. The researcher would like to recruit 100 of these doctoral-level school psychologists.

c. The researcher would number the members of the population from 0001 to 5000, then select the first 100 four-digit numbers from a random numbers table that were between 0001 and 5000, ignoring doubles (e.g., two 2549's).

d. The first 10 participants would be 449, 3524, 2463, 3824, 4586, 2510, 2561, 549, 4640, and 1599.

4.3 RANDOM ASSIGNMENT AND U.S. SCHOOL PSYCHOLOGISTS

a. The independent variable is type of news information with two levels: information about an improving job market and information about a declining job market.

b. The dependent variable is attitudes toward careers.

c. Because participants are randomly assigned to levels of the independent variable, this study qualifies as an experiment.

d. There are two levels of the independent variable; these levels would be given numbers, such as 0 and 1 for "improving" and "declining," respectively. A random numbers table or computerized random numbers generator would be used to generate a list of 0's and 1's. Each participant would be assigned to the condition that matched the next number on the random numbers list. If a random numbers table were used, any numbers except 0 and 1 would be ignored. Thus, if the first three relevant numbers were 001, then the first participant would read the article about the improving job market, as would the second. The third would read the article about the declining job market. As soon as 50 participants are assigned to one of the levels of the independent variable, the remaining individuals are assigned to the other condition.

e. With 0 representing "improving" and 1 representing "declining," the first 10 participants would be assigned to condition as follows: 0010000100.

f. These numbers don't appear to be random because there are so many more 0s than 1s. In the short run, lists of randomly generated numbers may not appear to be random. It is only in the long run that proportions tend to reflect the actual underlying probabilities.

4.5 RANDOM SELECTION AND AUSTRALIAN SCHOOL PSYCHOLOGISTS

a. The population is composed of the 2000 school psychologists in Australia.

b. The desired sample is the 30 school psychologists who will be recruited to participate in the study.

c. We could tell the randomizer to generate one set of 30 numbers between 0001 and 2000. We would specify that we want unique numbers because no individual will be in the study more than once. We can ask the randomizer to sort the numbers, if we wish, to more easily identify the participants who will comprise our sample.

d. The list will be different for each student.

e. The second list will also be different for each student. It is likely that the two lists will include strings of numbers and will not always appear to be random.

4.7 RANDOM NUMBERS AND THE HELPFUL ROOMMATE

Although humans believe we can think randomly if we want to, we do not, in fact, generate numbers independently of the ones that came before. We tend to glance at the preceding numbers in order to make the next ones "random." Yet once we do this, the numbers are not independent and therefore are not random. Moreover, even if we can keep ourselves from looking at the previous numbers, the numbers that we generate are not likely to be random. If we were born on the 6th of the month, then we may be more likely, for example, to choose 6s than other digits. Humans just don't think randomly.

4.9 VOLUNTEER SAMPLES AND U.S. COLLEGE FOOTBALL

a. The typical study volunteer is likely someone who cares deeply about U.S. college football. Moreover, it is particularly the fans of the top ACC teams, who themselves are likely extremely biased, who are most likely to vote.

b. External validity refers to our ability to generalize beyond our current sample. In this case, it is likely that fans of the top ACC teams are voting and that results do not reflect opinions of U.S. college football fans at large.

c. There are several possible answers to this question. As one example, only eight options were provided. Even though one of these options was "other," this limited the possible range of answers that respondents would be likely to provide.

4.11 VOLUNTEER SAMPLES AND U.S. POLITICAL LEANINGS

a. These numbers are not likely representative. This is a volunteer sample.

b. Those most likely to volunteer are those who have stumbled across, or searched for, this Web

site: a site that advocates for self-government. Those who respond are more likely to tend toward supporting self-government than are those who do not respond (or even find this Web site).

c. This description of libertarians suggests they would advocate for self-government, the title of the Web site, a likely explanation for the predominance of libertarians who responded to this survey. Also, the chart has "Liberation" at top, and the word "Liberation" appears in the icon beside the question, "How can you support this Web site?"

d. It doesn't matter how big our sample is if it's not representative. With respect to external validity, it would be far preferable to have a smaller but representative sample than a very large but nonrepresentative sample.

4.13 BIASES AND HOROSCOPES

a. An illusory correlation is the phenomenon of perceiving a correlation between variables when no such correlation exists. In this case, the friend has perceived an illusory correlation between horoscopes and his own life experiences.

b. A confirmation bias is the tendency to look for evidence that confirms our existing beliefs and to ignore evidence that contradicts them. In this case, the friend notices instances in which his horoscope seemed to match the events in his life and ignores instances in which it does not.

c. There are several possible answers to this question. As one example, we might give our friend two horoscopes each day—one for his actual sign and one for another sign. At the end of each day, he must choose the horoscope that seems to be more accurate. If, over the course of a number of days, he performs better than chance, then he would have some evidence for his hypothesis. If, on the other hand, he performs at chance, getting only around 50% correct, then he would not have evidence for his hypothesis.

4.15 CONFIRMATION BIAS, PROFESSORS, AND DEAD GRANDMOTHERS

You might point out to your professor that she might have an existing belief—an expectation that students will lie to get out of exams, particularly if they're doing poorly in a given course. In this case, her confirmation bias might lead her to recall the cases in which students did lie, ignoring the many more instances in which they did not. Moreover, she might not always check her inferences; for example, she might assume a student had lied about a grandmother's death prior to an exam without checking it. This would confirm her existing belief, but might not be true!

4.17 SHORT-RUN PROPORTIONS VERSUS LONG-RUN PROBABILITIES

a. In the short run, there are often strings of one outcome or another. In the short run, there might be proportions far below or above the actual probability of observing a success. In the long run, these balance out and the proportion approaches the actual probability.

b. The expected long-run probability would be 0.50. Over time, you'd expect half heads and half tails, although there may be many strings of one or the other along the way.

c. Answers will be different for each student.

d. In many cases, the individual proportions likely do not match the expected long-run probability of 0.50. Any number of combinations of heads and tails could occur in a short series of 10 flips. Over a very large number of trials, however, the short-run fluctuations would balance out and the proportion would approach the true probability of 0.50.

e. We would explain that in the short run, we're very likely to see strings of heads or tails. In the long run, however, the proportion would approach 0.50. We could suggest that our friend flip the coin 100 times or, even better, 1000 times to confirm that the proportion does in fact approach 0.50.

4.19 GAMBLER'S FALLACY AND INDEPENDENT TRIALS

a. (i) The trials are independent. (ii) The dice have no memory of the previous rolls. (iii) The quote is definitely fallacious; the Monopoly player is not more likely to get double sixes on her next turn than any other possible combination of two numbers.

b. (i) It is possible that the trials are dependent. (ii) The Buckeyes may have lost because of factors (e.g., injuries, decreased morale) related to their previous games. (iii) It is possible that this quote is accurate because the next game might actually depend to some degree on the previous games.

c. (i) These trials are likely to be pretty much independent (although probably not entirely independent). (ii) The car does not remember that is has been starting every day and that it owes you a bad day. (iii) This quote is likely

fallacious. The previous successful starts do not likely mean an unsuccessful attempt today. (If anything, the week of successes and the recent tune-up might be positive indicators.)

d. (i) The trials are independent. (ii) Each pair of stockings has no connection to any other pair, particularly because they were purchased at different stores. (iii) The quote is likely fallacious. The probability that the third pair will fail is the same as the probability that the first or the second would fail. (On the other hand, the stockings are worn by the same person. Her behavior is likely contributing to the outcomes with the stockings, so the trials might not be independent.)

4.21 NULL HYPOTHESIS AND RESEARCH HYPOTHESIS

a. The null hypothesis is that the tendency to develop false memories is either unchanged or is lowered by the repetition of false information. The research hypothesis is that false memories are higher—when false information is repeated than when it is not.

b. The null hypothesis is that outcome is the same or worse when whether or not structured assessments are used. The research hypothesis is that outcome is better when structured assessments are used than when they are not used.

c. The null hypothesis is that mean employee morale is the same whether employees work in enclosed offices or cubicles. The research hypothesis is that mean employee morale is different when employees work in enclosed offices versus cubicles.

d. The null hypothesis is that ability to speak one's native language is the same, on average, whether or not a second language was taught to children from birth. The research hypothesis is that ability to speak one's native language is different, on average, when a second language is taught from birth than when no second language is taught.

4.23 TYPE I AND TYPE II ERRORS

a. If this conclusion is incorrect, we have made a Type I error. We have rejected the null hypothesis when the null hypothesis is really true. (Of course, we never know whether we have made an error! We just have to acknowledge the possibility.)

b. If this conclusion is incorrect, we have made a Type I error. We have rejected the null hypothesis when the null hypothesis is really true.

c. If this conclusion is incorrect, we have made a Type II error. We have failed to reject the null hypothesis when the null hypothesis is not true.

d. If this conclusion is incorrect, we have made a Type II error. We have failed to reject the null hypothesis when the null hypothesis is not true.

4.25 TYING IT ALL TOGETHER: TREATMENT FOR ALCOHOL PROBLEMS IN COLLEGE STUDENTS

a. The population of interest is male students with alcohol problems. The sample is the 64 students who were ordered to meet with a school counselor.

b. Random selection was not used. The sample was comprised of 64 male students who had been ordered to meet with a school counselor; they were not chosen out of all male students with alcohol problems.

c. Random assignment was used. Each participant had an equal chance of being assigned to each of the two conditions.

d. The independent variable is type of counseling. It has two levels: BMI and AE. The dependent variable is number of alcohol-related problems at follow-up.

e. The null hypothesis is that the mean number of alcohol-related problems is the same regardless of type of counseling (BMI or AE). The research hypothesis is that students who undergo BMI have different mean numbers of alcohol-related problems at follow-up than do students who participate in AE.

f. The researchers rejected the null hypothesis.

g. If the researchers were incorrect in their decision, they made a Type I error. If this is the case, they rejected the null hypothesis when the null hypothesis was true. The consequences of this type of error are that a new treatment that is no better, on average, than the standard treatment will be implemented. This might lead to unnecessary costs to train counselors to implement the new treatment.

4.27 THE LANGUAGE OF STATISTICS— *PROBABILITY*

We use the word *probability* to refer to our estimate of the likelihood that something will occur. Known as subjective (or personal) probability, this is just an estimate or guess. We might say there's a 50% chance that we'll have dessert tonight at dinner. Statisticians use the word *probability* to mean the underlying actual frequency with which a given outcome occurs out of a given number of trials. *Probability* refers to what we expect in the long run and is often phrased as the expected relative-frequency probability. The probability of heads when we flip a coin is 0.50.

4.29 THE LANGUAGE OF STATISTICS—*PROVE*

The logic of science involves debunking null hypotheses, rather than proving a hypothesis. Our goal is to find evidence against a hypothesis. If we continue to fail to find evidence against a hypothesis, we start to have confidence in that hypothesis. Because most of science is based on probability, we can conclude only that a given outcome is very unlikely; we cannot conclude that it is impossible or that it is absolutely true. We can never have proof, just lots of evidence.

■ **DIGGING INTO THE DATA**

4.31 MEDICAL RESEARCH, THE MEDIA, AND TYPE I ERRORS: REDUCING BONE FRACTURES

a. Studies with exciting findings typically receive the most press. Given a certain number of studies, some will have an exciting outcome just by chance and will get more press than all the boring outcomes. In fact, Sterne and Smith (2001) estimated that almost half of published medical results were actually Type I errors.

b. There are a number of possible answers. Here are four examples. (1) We would like evidence that this sample is representative of the population to which the researchers are generalizing. (2) Ideally, random assignment to statins versus no statins would have been used. (3) The control group (no statins) would have received a placebo that resembled statins. (4) The design would have been double-blind. Neither the participants nor the researchers would know to which conditions the participants were assigned.

c. It is possible that the men who already used statins were different in some important way from the men who did not use statins to begin with. First, we know that the men who took statins had high cholesterol. Does high cholesterol protect against bone fractures? It also is possible that these men were prescribed statins because they visit their physicians frequently and are more health-conscious. Perhaps many men in the other group would have received statins had they visited their doctors. It is possible that it is health-consciousness—and the good nutrition and exercise that accompany it— that leads to a reduced risk of bone fractures.

CHAPTER 5

5.1 SLEEP AND THE MEAN AND STANDARD DEVIATION OF THE z DISTRIBUTION

a. The mean of the z distribution is always 0.

b. $z = \dfrac{(X - \mu)}{\sigma} = \dfrac{(6.65 - 6.65)}{1.24} = 0$

c. The standard deviation of the z distribution is always 1.

d. A student 1 standard deviation above the mean would have a score of $6.65 + 1.24 = 7.89$. This person's z score would be:

$z = \dfrac{(X - \mu)}{\sigma} = \dfrac{(7.89 - 6.65)}{1.24} = 1$

e. The answer will differ for each student but will involve substituting one's own score for X in this equation: $z = \dfrac{(X - 6.65)}{1.24}$.

5.3 BREAKFAST AND z SCORES

a. $z = \dfrac{(X - \mu)}{\sigma} = \dfrac{(6 - 4.1)}{2.4} = 0.792$

b. $z - \dfrac{(X - \mu)}{\sigma} = \dfrac{(2 - 4.1)}{2.4} = -0.875$

c. The answer will differ for each student but will involve substituting one's own score for X in this equation: $= \dfrac{(X - 4.1)}{2.4}$.

5.5 CORRELATION, BODY FAT INDEX, AND AGE AT DEATH

a. Obesity, as measured by body fat index, and age at death are likely to be negatively correlated. Those with high body fat indices are likely to be younger, on average, when they die, and those with low body fat indices are likely to be older, on average, when they die.

b. There are many possible scatterplots, but the accompanying one depicts a negative correlation between body fat index and age at death.

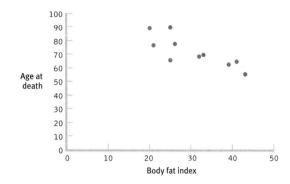

5.7 EXTERNALIZING, ANXIETY, AND SCATTERPLOTS OF RAW SCORES

a. The accompanying scatterplot depicts the relation between anxiety and externalizing behaviors. Note that we could have chosen to represent anxiety along the x-axis and externalizing along the y-axis.

b. The scatterplot suggests that there is a positive linear relation between externalizing and anxiety; as externalizing scores increase, anxiety scores also increase.

c. Yes, it would be appropriate to calculate a Pearson correlation coefficient for this set of data because there appears to be a linear relation between the two variables, and the Pearson correlation coefficient assesses the direction and magnitude of that linear relation.

d. The scatterplot appears here. We would expect a positive correlation, but one that is smaller in magnitude than that depicted in the previous scatterplot.

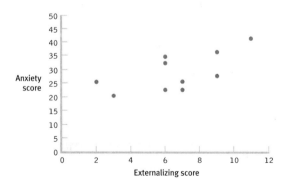

e. The one participant who was added had an extremely high anxiety score (outside the range of the other scores) and an extremely low externalizing score. This participant is an outlier on both of the measured variables. Because each of the variables has an extreme outlier, the mean of each of the variables is affected, which in turn affects the calculation of the z scores for each of the variables on which the calculation of the correlation is based. Furthermore, the relation between anxiety and externalizing is very different for this participant than for other participants in the sample. So the positive correlation is reduced in magnitude when we include this participant.

5.9 EXPECTED CORRELATIONS IN YOUR EVERYDAY LIFE

a. You might expect there to be a positive correlation between how hard the rain is falling and your commuting time, because as it rains harder, people tend to drive more slowly, which means your commuting time would increase with the increasing rain.

b. You would expect there to be a negative correlation between how often you say no to dessert and your body fat. People who say no to dessert more often should tend to have lower body fat than people who say yes more often.

c. You would expect there to be a negative correlation between the amount of wine you consume with dinner and your alertness after dinner. As the number of glasses of wine consumed increases, alertness should decrease, on average.

5.11 DRAWING SCATTERPLOTS OF CAT OWNERSHIP AND MENTAL HEALTH

There are many possible scatterplots one could draw for each of the following.

a. The accompanying scatterplot depicts a weak positive correlation between cat ownership and mental health:

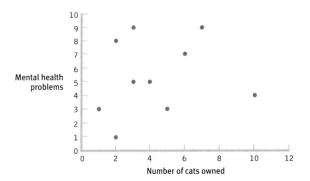

b. The accompanying scatterplot depicts a strong positive correlation.

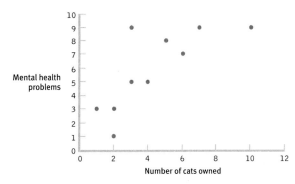

c. The accompanying scatterplot depicts a perfect positive correlation.

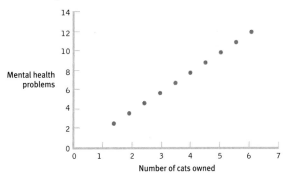

d. The accompanying scatterplot depicts a weak negative correlation.

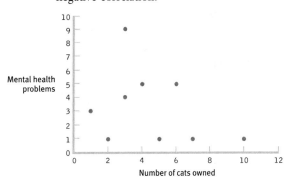

e. The accompanying scatterplot depicts a strong negative correlation.

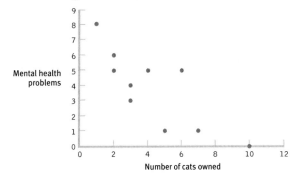

f. The accompanying scatterplot depicts a perfect negative correlation.

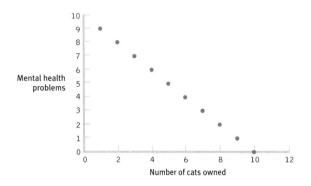

g. The accompanying scatterplot depicts almost no correlation between these variables:

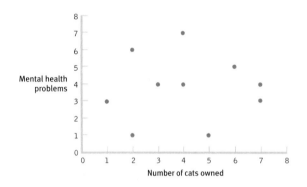

5.13 CORRELATION COEFFICIENTS AND GRADUATE SCHOOL

a. A 1.00 correlation coefficient reflects a perfect positive relation between students' ratings of the likelihood of attending graduate school and the number of completed psychology credits. This is the strongest correlation of the options.

b. A −0.001 correlation coefficient reflects a lack of relation between students' ratings and the number of completed psychology credits. This is the weakest correlation of the options.

c. A 0.56 correlation coefficient reflects a large positive relation between students' ratings and the number of completed psychology credits.

d. A −0.27 correlation coefficient reflects a medium negative relation between students' ratings and the number of completed psychology credits.

e. A −0.98 correlation coefficient reflects a large (close to perfect) negative relation between students' ratings and the number of completed psychology credits.

f. A 0.09 correlation coefficient reflects a small positive relation between students' ratings and the number of completed psychology credits.

5.15 CALCULATING A CORRELATION COEFFICIENT FOR TRAUMA AND MASCULINITY

a. The accompanying scatterplot depicts a positive linear relation between perceived trauma and perceived masculinity. The data appear to be linearly related; therefore, it is appropriate to calculate a Pearson correlation coefficient.

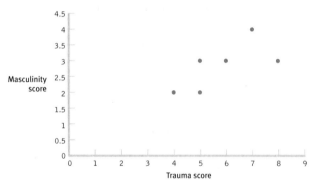

b. Intermediate steps for calculating the correlation coefficient are depicted in the accompanying table. To obtain the Pearson correlation coefficient, we calculate $r = \dfrac{\sum[(z_X)(z_Y)]}{N}$. The first step is to turn the traumatic and masculinity variables into z scores. These scores appear in the third and fourth columns of the table. The second step is to obtain the cross-product of the z scores for the two variables (column 5). Finally, we calculate r as the average of the cross-products. The cross-products sum to 4.165. Dividing this sum by 6, the number of participants for whom we have scores, gives us the correlation coefficient of 0.69.

TRAUMATIC	MASCULINITY	z TRAUMATIC	z MASCULINITY	(z TRAUMATIC) (z MASCULINITY)
5	3	−0.622	0.243	−0.151
6	3	0.125	0.243	0.030
4	2	−1.368	−1.213	1.659
5	2	−0.622	−1.213	0.754
7	4	0.871	1.699	1.480
8	3	1.617	0.243	0.393

c. The correlation indicates that there is a large positive relation between perceived trauma and perceived masculinity.

d. For most of the participants, the sign of the z score for the traumatic variable is the same as that for the masculinity variable, which indicates that those participants scoring above the mean on one variable also tended to score above the mean on the second variable (and vice versa). Because the scores are changing in the same direction, this is a positive relation.

e. When the person was a woman, the perception of the situation as traumatic was strongly negatively correlated with the perception of the woman as feminine. This relation is opposite that observed when the person was a man. When the person was a man, the perception of the situation as traumatic was strongly positively correlated with the perception of the man as feminine. Regardless of whether the person was a man or a woman, there was a positive correlation between the perception of the situation as traumatic and perception of masculinity, but the observed correlation was stronger for the perceptions of women than for the perceptions of men.

5.17 ILLUSORY CORRELATIONS, INTELLIGENCE, AND AN AMAZING SWISS WATERFALL

The Thurlemanns relied on friends' anecdotes rather than precisely measuring whether thinking ability improved after drinking the water. Because the Thurlemanns relied on the subjective reports of a limited number of people, they were susceptible to errors. So the Thurlemanns perceived a correlation between the amount of water consumed and intelligence. If they had, however, randomly selected a large sample of participants and randomly assigned some to drink the water from the Swiss waterfall and others to drink plain tap water, they would likely have found no causal effect of the Swiss water on intelligence.

5.19 CORRELATION, CAUSATION, AND TYPE OF SCHOOL

a. The researchers are suggesting that attending a private school causes a student to have better test scores.

b. It could be that those students who perform better on standardized tests tend to choose to go to private schools over public schools.

c. There are many possible answers. For example, the socioeconomic status of the student's family

may account for both better test scores and private school attendance, with higher socioeconomic status causing both improved test scores and private school attendance.

5.21 CORRELATION, CAUSATION, AND GOLFING AS DIPLOMACY

One possibility is that a lack of war causes golfing. Prolonged periods of peace may allow a country's citizens to develop leisure activities and, as such, golfing is more likely to emerge as an activity in peaceful nations than in nations waging wars. A second possibility is that golfing causes peace. Golfing may act as a release from the stress and tensions that would otherwise lead a people to wage war. Finally, a third variable, such as economic prosperity, may cause both peace and golfing. More prosperous countries may be both satisfied with their place in the world and therefore less likely to wage war and may afford more time and money for their citizens to engage in leisure activities such as golfing.

5.23 VALIDITY AND ROMANCE

a. The construct this measure is trying to assess is passionate love.

b. If the PLS were valid, then it would mean that the scale provides an accurate measure of how much passionate love an individual feels for another.

c. To assess postdictive validity, we would correlate individuals' scores on the PLS with a measure of a past behavior that would also be indicative of passionate love. For example, we could correlate the PLS scores with a count of the number of times participants called a significant other over the past week (as assessed via cell phone records). We would expect higher numbers of phone calls to one's romantic partner to be associated with greater passionate love scores.

d. To assess concurrent validity, we would correlate individuals' scores on the PLS with another concurrently measured indicator of passionate love. For example, while they are taking the PLS, we might ask participants to look at a picture of their significant other and measure galvanic skin response (GSR), which is an indicator of autonomic nervous system activity. We could then correlate the GSR scores with the scores on the PLS. We would expect increased GSR to be associated with greater passionate love scores.

e. To assess the predictive validity of the PLS, we could ask participants who have taken the PLS to report how many days they continued to date their significant other. We would expect higher passionate love scores to be related to a longer dating relationship.

5.25 VALIDITY AND BROWNIE THE COW

a. If students were marked down for talking about the rooster, not the cow, the reading test item would not meet the established criteria. The question asked on the test is ambiguous because the information regarding what caused the cow's behavior to change is not explicitly stated in the story. Furthermore, the correct answer to the question provided on the Web site is not actually an answer to the question itself. The question asks, "What caused Brownie's behavior to change?" The answer that the cow started out kind and ended up mean is a description of *how* her behavior changed, not what caused her behavior to change. This does not appear to be a valid question because it does not appear to provide an accurate assessment of students' *writing* ability.

b. The postdictive validity of this test could be assessed by determining the correlation between students' scores on this test and their grades on previous writing assignments.

c. The concurrent validity of this test could be assessed by determining whether students' performance correlates with their performance on another test already believed to be a valid test of writing ability.

d. The predictive validity of this test could be assessed by determining how well students' scores on the test correlate with grades on future writing assignments.

e. One possible third variable that could lead to better performance in some schools over others is the average socioeconomic status of the families whose students attend the schools. Schools in wealthier areas or counties would tend to have students of higher socioeconomic status who might be expected to perform better on a test of writing skill and would tend to attract better teachers and administrators.

5.27 THE LANGUAGE OF STATISTICS—*VALID*

In everyday language the word *valid* is used to refer to something that is accurate and recognized as such. A valid passport is one that is accurate and is authenticated by the government, indicating the government's recognition of the passport.

A valid claim is one that is honest and accurate. Similarly, in statistics, *validity* refers to the accuracy of a measure. A valid measure is one that accurately assesses the construct that it claims to measure as supported by evidence from other measures of the same construct.

■ DIGGING DEEPER INTO THE DATA

5.29 PARTIAL CORRELATION

a. The correlation between depression and anxiety is 0.368, which is a moderate positive correlation. The correlation indicates that when depression is higher, anxiety also tends to be higher.

b. The correlation between anxiety and externalizing is 0.356, which is a moderate positive correlation. The correlation indicates that adolescents who have higher levels of anxiety tend to exhibit a higher frequency of externalizing behaviors.

c. The partial correlation between anxiety and externalizing (0.17) controlling for depression is lower than that correlation calculated when not controlling for depression (0.356).

d. The partial correlation differs from the original Pearson correlation coefficient because the partial correlation has removed the common variability in anxiety and externalizing that could be accounted for by the variable of depression. By calculating the partial correlation, we learned that although depression is related to both anxiety levels and externalizing behaviors, there is still part of the relation between anxiety and externalizing behaviors that cannot be explained away by depression.

CHAPTER 6

6.1 CORRELATION VERSUS SIMPLE LINEAR REGRESSION VERSUS MULTIPLE REGRESSION

a. A correlation means that the two variables are related to each other. In general, people's scores on one variable are related to their scores on the other variable.

b. You could ask whether weight predicts blood pressure.

c. In simple linear regression, there is one independent variable that is being examined as a possible predictor of the dependent variable. In multiple regression, several independent variables are examined.

d. There are several possible answers to this question. You could, for example, include a measure of body fat, cholesterol levels, or age.

6.3 AGE, STUDYING, AND PREDICTING ONE z SCORE FROM ANOTHER z SCORE

a. $z_{X\hat{Y}} = (r_{XY})(z_X)$, so her predicted z score for hours studied per week would be $(0.49)(-0.82)$, or -0.402.

b. $z_{\hat{Y}} = (r_{XY})(z_X)$, so his predicted z score for hours studied per week would be $(0.49)(1.2)$, or 0.588.

c. We would predict that his z score for the number of hours studied per week would be 0 because $(0.49)(0) = 0$.

d. In part (c), regression to the mean is not relevant because Eugene's score on the independent variable is exactly at the mean (which is why he has a z score of 0). We then predict that his score on the dependent variable is at the mean of that variable. The idea of regression to the mean is not relevant and we do not need to *calculate* the regression because Eugene is already right at the mean.

6.5 THE GRE, z SCORES, AND RAW SCORES

a.   i. 650 (1.5 standard deviations above the mean)

ii. 450 (0.05 standard deviation below the mean)

iii. 300 (2 standard deviations below the mean)

b.   i. $X = Z(\sigma) + \mu = 1.5\ (100) + 500 = 650$

ii. $X = Z(\sigma) + \mu = -0.5\ (100) + 500 = 450$

iii. $X = Z(\sigma) + \mu = -2.0\ (100) + 500 = 300$

6.7 STUDYING, GPA, AND PREDICTING FROM A REGRESSION EQUATION

a. 3.12

b. 3.16

c. 3.18

d. The accompanying graph depicts the scatterplot of the GPA and hours studied scores with the regression line.

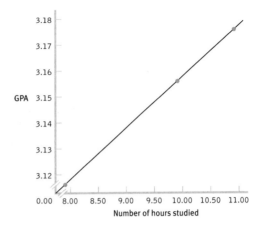

e. We can calculate the number of hours one would need to study in order to earn a 4.0 by substituting 4.0 for $\hat{Y}$ in our regression equation and solving for X: $4.0 = 2.96 + 0.02(X)$. To isolate the X, we subtract 2.96 from the left side of the equation and divide by 0.02: $X = (4.0 - 2.96)/0.02 = 52$. This regression equation predicts that we would have to study 52 hours a week in order to earn a 4.0. It is misleading to make predictions about what will happen when a person studies this many hours because the regression equation for prediction is based on a sample that studied far fewer hours. Even though the relation between hours studied and GPA was linear within the range of studied scores, outside of that range it may have a different slope or no longer be linear, or the relation may not even exist.

6.9 REGRESSION FROM SCRATCH

a. The accompanying scatterplot depicts the relation between number of candidates supported by a company and that company's profits.

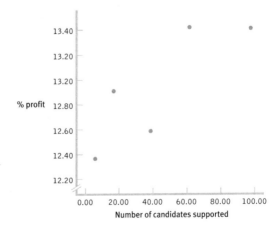

b. The mean number of candidates supported was 44.40 with a standard deviation of 36.869.

c. The mean profit was 12.94 with a standard deviation of 0.479.

d. The correlation between the number of candidates supported and profit is 0.834.

e. To calculate the regression equation, we need to find the intercept and the slope. We determine the intercept by calculating what we predict for Y when X equals zero. Given the means, standard deviations, and the correlation calculated above, we first find z_X, which is -1.204. We then calculate the predicted z score for profit, which is -2.038. Finally, we transform the predicted profit z score into the predicted raw score, which gives us the intercept of 12.45. To determine the slope, we calculate what we would predict for Y when X equals 1 and determine how much that differs from what we would predict when X equals 0. The z score for X corresponding to our raw score of 1 is -1.177. Our predicted z score for Y would be -0.982, and the raw score for Y is 12.47. The difference between our predicted Y when X equals 1 (12.47) and that when X equals 0 (12.46) yields our slope, which is 0.01. So the regression equation is $\hat{Y} = 12.45 + 0.01(X)$.

f. The accompanying graph shows the regression for predicting profit from the number of candidates.

g. These data suggest that companies profit by supporting political candidates, reflecting a possible quid pro quo in the political process.

h. There are many possible answers to this question. One possibility is that profitable companies overall have more money and are therefore able to spend money to back more political candidates.

6.11 ERROR MATHEMATICALLY

a. To calculate the proportionate reduction in error the long way, we first calculate the predicted Y scores (3rd column) for each of the observed X scores in our data set and determine how much those predicted Y scores differ from the observed Y scores (4th column) and then we square them (5th column).

AGE	OBSERVED HOURS STUDIED	PREDICTED HOURS STUDIED	OBSERVED − PREDICTED	SQUARE OF OBSERVED − PREDICTED	OBSERVED − MEAN	SQUARE OF OBSERVED − MEAN
19	5	11.16	−6.16	37.946	−9.2	84.64
20	20	12.69	7.31	53.436	5.8	33.64
20	8	12.69	−4.69	21.996	−6.2	38.44
21	12	14.22	−2.22	4.928	−2.2	4.84
21	18	14.22	3.78	14.288	3.8	14.44
23	25	17.28	7.72	59.598	10.8	116.64
22	15	15.75	−0.75	0.563	0.8	0.64
20	10	12.69	−2.69	7.236	−4.2	17.64
19	14	11.16	2.84	8.066	−0.2	0.04
25	15	20.34	−5.34	28.516	0.8	0.64

We then calculate SS_{Error}, which is the sum of the squared error when using the regression equation as the basis of prediction. This sum, calculated by adding the numbers in column 5, is 236.573. We then subtract the mean from each score (column 6), and square these differences (column 7). Next, we calculate SS_{Total}, which is the sum of the squared error when using the mean as the basis of prediction. This sum is 311.6. Finally, we calculate the proportionate reduction in error as

$$r^2 = \frac{(SS_{Total} - SS_{Error})}{SS_{Total}} = 0.24.$$

b. The r^2 calculated in part (a) indicates that 24% of the variability in hours studied is accounted for by a student's age. By using the regression equation, we have reduced the error of our prediction by 24%.

c. To calculate the proportionate reduction in error the short way, we would square the correlation coefficient. The correlation between age and hours studied, given in Exercise 6.8, is 0.49. Squaring 0.49 yields 0.24. It makes sense that the correlation coefficient could be used to determine how useful the regression equation will be because the correlation coefficient is a measure of the strength of association between two variables. If two variables are strongly related, we are better able to use one of the variables to predict the values of the other.

6.13 RAIN, VIOLENCE, REGRESSION, AND CAUSATION

a. The independent variable in this study is the amount of rainfall.

b. The dependent variable is the incidence of civil war in African countries.

c. The economic prosperity of African countries relies on agriculture, which is heavily dependent upon rain. As rainfall decreases, crop yields are likely to decrease, as will economic prosperity. A decrease in economic prosperity could lead to unrest and war.

6.15 TUTORING AND THE LIMITS OF REGRESSION

First, the increase in mathematics ability might be due to regression to the mean. It was the poorest students who were offered this program, and there's nowhere for them to go but up in terms of mathematics ability. Second, we do not know if it is the weeks spent with a tutor that makes a difference; it might not be a causal relation. The direction of the effect could be the reverse. It could be that students who were progressing were more likely to continue with tutoring because parents attributed the improvement to the tutoring. Or there could be a third variable. It might be that the students from families with the most financial resources were the ones to send their children to tutors for more weeks, and it might have something to do with money, rather than the tutoring per se. Third, it is always dangerous to extrapolate. The longest number of weeks in this study was 20; we do not know what will happen if parents send their children for two years—104 weeks.

6.17 DEPRESSION, ANXIETY, AND THE OUTPUT OF SIMPLE LINEAR REGRESSION

a. $\hat{Y} = 24.698 + 0.161\ (X)$, or predicted year-3 anxiety $= 24.698 + 0.161$ (year-1 depression)

b. As depression at year 1 increases by 1 point, predicted anxiety at year 3 increases, on average, by the slope of the regression equation, which is 0.161.

c. We would predict that her year-3 anxiety score would be 26.31.

d. We would predict that his year-3 anxiety score would be 25.02.

6.19 SYMBOLS OF STATISTICS

The equations that were incorrect are shown, along with their corrected versions.

INCORRECT	CORRECT
$X = z(\sigma) + M$	$X = Z(\sigma) + \mu$
$z_Y = (r_{XY})(z_X)$	$z_{\hat{Y}} = (r_{XY})(z_X)$

■ DIGGING DEEPER INTO THE DATA

6.21 THE LANGUAGE OF STATISTICS—*LATENT VARIABLES* AND *MANIFEST VARIABLES*

A latent variable is one that cannot be observed or directly measured. It is a construct believed to exist and influence behavior. A manifest variable is an indicator of the latent variable that can be observed and directly measured. For example, a latent variable could be a person's concern about the environment. This latent variable could be measured by different manifest behaviors, such as how much a person recycles and whether the person donates to environmental organizations such as the Natural Resources Defense Council.

6.23 STRUCTURAL EQUATION MODELING (SEM) AND NEIGHBORHOOD SOCIAL DISORDER

a. The four latent variables are social disorder, distress, injection frequency, and sharing behavior.

b. There are seven manifest variables: beat up, sell drugs, burglary, loitering, litter, vacant houses, and vandalism. By "social disorder," it appears that the authors are referring to physical or crime-related factors that lead a neighborhood to be chaotic.

c. Among the latent variables, injection frequency and sharing behavior seem to be most strongly related to each other. The number on this path, 0.26, is positive, an indication that as the frequency of injection increases, the frequency of sharing behaviors also tends to increase.

d. The overall story seems to be that social disorder increases the level of distress in a community. Distress in turn increases both the frequency of injection and sharing behavior. The frequency of injection also leads to an increase in sharing behavior. Ultimately, social disorder leads to dangerous drug use behaviors.

CHAPTER 7

7.1 THE NORMAL CURVE IN REAL LIFE

a. Yes, the distribution of the number of movies a college student rents in a year would likely approximate a normal curve. You can imagine that a small number of students rent an enormous number of movies and that a small number rent very few but that most rent a moderate number of movies between these two extremes.

b. Yes, the number of full-page advertisements in a magazine is likely to approximate a normal curve. We could find magazines that have no or just one or two full-page advertisements and some that are chock full of them, but most magazines will have some intermediate number of full-page advertisements.

c. Yes, human birth weights in Canada could be expected to approximate a normal curve. There will be few infants weighing in at the extremes of very light or very heavy, and the weight of most infants will cluster around some intermediate value.

7.3 GETTING READY FOR A DATE AND THE NORMAL CURVE

a. Histogram for the 10 scores:

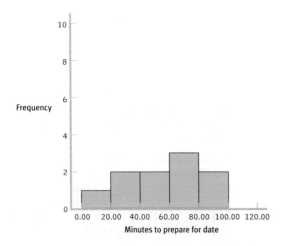

b. Histogram for all 40 scores:

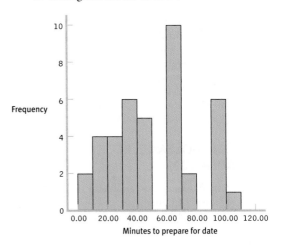

c. The shape of the distribution became more normal as the number of scores increased. If we added more scores, the distribution would become more and more normal. This occurs because many physical, psychological, and behavioral variables are normally distributed. With smaller samples, this might not be clear. But as the sample size approaches the size of the population, the shape of the sample distribution approaches that of the population.

d. This is a distribution of scores because each individual score is represented in the histogram on its own, not as part of a mean.

e. There are several possible answers to this question. For example, instead of retrospective self-report, we could have had students call a number or send an e-mail as they began to get ready; they would then have called the same number or sent another e-mail when they were ready. This would have led to scores that would be closer to the actual time it took students to get ready.

f. There are several possible answers to this question. For example, we could examine whether there was a gender difference in time spent getting ready for a date.

7.5 BREAKFAST, z SCORES, AND PERCENTILES

a. A student who eats breakfast four times per week is approximately at the mean and would be at roughly the 50th percentile.

b. The student who eats breakfast six times per week is a little over 1 standard deviation above the mean. We can determine the student's percentile by adding the 50% of students who are below the mean to the 34% who are within 1 standard above the mean (50 + 34). The student would be at approximately the 98th percentile.

c. The student who eats breakfast twice a week is about 1 standard deviation below the mean. Fifty percent of the students are below the mean and 34% fall between the mean and 1 standard deviation below the mean. This student would be at the 50 − 34 = 16th percentile.

7.7 STANDARDIZING MARIA SHARAPOVA AND TIGER WOODS

a. $z = \dfrac{(X - \mu)}{\sigma} = \dfrac{(18.2 - 11.58)}{6.58} = 1.01$

b. Fifty percent of scores fall below the mean and about 34% fall between the mean and a z score of 1.0: 50 + 34 = 84. Sharapova is at approximately the 84th percentile among the top-10 tennis players.

c. $z = \dfrac{(X - \mu)}{\sigma} = \dfrac{(89.4 - 30.01)}{28.86} = 2.06$

d. Fifty percent of scores fall below the mean; about 34% fall between the mean and 1 standard deviation above the mean; and about 14% fall between 1 and 2 standard deviations above the mean: 50 + 34 + 14 = 98. Woods is at approximately the 98th percentile among the top-10 golfers.

e. In comparison to the top-10 earners in their respective sports, Woods outearned Sharapova.

f. These data appear to be positively skewed; there are two potential outliers, one of whom is Woods. Alternately, we could consider these data to be bimodal, with one hump between 10 million and 25 million and another around 80 million. The normal curve percentages associated with the z distribution should be used with scores only when the data are approximately normally distributed. It might not be appropriate to use the z distribution in this situation.

7.9 SPORTS TEAMS AND RAW SCORES

a. $X = z(\sigma) + \mu = -0.18(10.83) + 81.00 = 79$ games (rounded to a whole number)

b. $X = z(\sigma) + \mu = -1.475(3.39) + 8.0 = 3$ games (rounded to a whole number)

c. Fifty percent of scores fall below the mean, so 34% (84 − 50 = 34) fall between the mean and the Steelers' score. We know that 34% of scores fall between the mean and a z score of 1.0, so the Steelers have a z score of 1.0. $X = z(\sigma) + \mu = 1(3.39) + 8.0 = 11$ games (rounded to a whole number)

d. We can examine our answers to be sure that negative z scores match up with answers that are below the mean and positive z scores match up with answers that are above the mean.

7.11 DIFFERENT TYPES OF DISTRIBUTIONS AND LANGUAGE ACQUISITION

a. The sample is the 50 eight-year-old children in the study, and the population is all eight-year-old Canadian children.

b. We could take the vocabulary scores of every eight-year-old child in Canada and put them in a giant container. Then, one by one, we could randomly pull out scores and plot them on a histogram, returning scores to the container in between pulls. If we did this long enough, we'd start to have the distribution of scores for the population.

c. We could take the vocabulary scores of every eight-year-old child in Canada and put them in a giant container. Then we would pull 50 random scores at a time and take their mean, returning the scores to the container in between pulls. We would plot these means on a histogram. If we did this long enough, we'd start to have the distribution of means for samples of size 50 for this population.

d. The mean would be the same.

e. The standard deviation would be smaller. We would divide the standard deviation by the square root of the sample size; the standard deviation would now be called standard error.

f. The specialist would use the distribution of means if he wanted to compare the mean of his sample with established norms. When comparing a single score, we use the distribution of scores; when comparing a mean of a sample, we use the distribution of means.

g. Based on the central limit theorem, we can typically use the z distribution if the population is skewed, as long as we have at least 30 individuals in our sample. Distributions of means for samples of at least 30 individuals are usually approximately normal.

7.13 THE z STATISTIC, DISTRIBUTIONS OF MEANS, AND APARTMENT RENTALS

a. $\mu_M = \mu = 1225.15; \sigma_M = \dfrac{\sigma}{\sqrt{N}} = \dfrac{777.50}{100}$
$= 77.75$

b. $z = \dfrac{(M - \mu_M)}{\sigma_M} = \dfrac{(868.86 - 1225.15)}{77.75}$
$= -4.58.$

c. The z statistic is so large probably because the distribution is not normal. With housing costs, the mean is likely to be influenced by outliers—the few homes or apartments with high prices. The median is typically a better measure of central tendency for housing costs.

d. With sample sizes of at least 30, the distribution of means is likely to be approximately normally distributed. (*Note:* An additional problem here, however, is that the apartment prices probably have a very different spread—probably much smaller—than do the overall prices.)

7.15 THE GSS AND z SCORES

a. You would compare his score to a distribution of scores. When we compare an individual score, we need to use the distribution of individual scores because it is this distribution that indicates the variability we should expect to see in individual scores.

b. $z - \dfrac{(X - \mu)}{\sigma} = \dfrac{(18 - 7.44)}{10.98} = 0.96$. His z score of 0.96 is approximately 1 standard deviation above the mean. Because 50% of people are below the mean and 34% are between the mean and 1 standard deviation above it, he would be at approximately the 84th percentile.

c. It may not make sense to calculate the percentile for this person because the distribution is positively skewed and is wide and flat (i.e., it is not normal). As such, we cannot be as sure of the percentage of people who fall along different parts of the distribution as we can be with the normal distribution.

d. You would compare this sample mean to a distribution of means. When we are making a comparison involving a sample mean, we need to use the distribution of means because it is this distribution that indicates the variability we are likely to see in sample means.

e. $z = \dfrac{(M = \mu_M)}{\sigma_M} = \dfrac{(8.7 - 7.44)}{1.23} = 1.02$. This z score of 1.02 is approximately 1 standard deviation above the mean. Because 50% of the people are below the mean and 34% are between the mean and 1 standard deviation above it, this person would be at approximately the 84th percentile.

f. It does make sense to calculate a percentile for this sample. Given the central limit theorem and the size of the sample used to calculate the

mean (80), we would expect the distribution of the sample means to be approximately normal.

7.17 THE LANGUAGE OF STATISTICS— *STANDARDIZE*

People sometimes use the word *standardize* to refer to making everything the same. Statisticians use the word to refer to situations in which they take various raw scores and put them all on the same scale, often on the z distribution.

7.19 THE SYMBOLS OF STATISTICS

a. (i.) μ is incorrect. (ii.) The symbol should be σ, and the formula should be $\sigma_M = \dfrac{\sigma}{\sqrt{N}}$.

(iii.) To obtain the standard error (or the standard deviation of the distribution of sample means), you need to divide the population standard deviation by the square root of N.

b. (i.) μ is incorrect. (ii.) The symbol should be μ, and the formula should be $z = \dfrac{(M - \mu_M)}{\sigma_M}$.

(iii.) This is the formula for the z statistic for comparing a sample mean (M) to the distribution of sample means.

c. (i.) σ is incorrect. (ii.) The symbol should be σ_M and the formula should be $z = \dfrac{(M + \mu_M)}{\sigma_M}$.

(iii.) To calculate the z statistic for comparing a sample mean to the distribution of sample means, we must divide by the standard error.

d. (i.) σ_M is incorrect. (ii.) The symbol should be σ, and the formula should be $z = \dfrac{(X - \mu)}{\sigma}$.

(iii.) This is the formula to calculate a z score from a raw score and is used when comparing an individual score to the distribution of scores in the population. As such, we need to use the population standard deviation as represented by σ.

■ DIGGING DEEPER INTO THE DATA

7.21 DETECTION OF CREDIT CARD THEFT AND THE z DISTRIBUTION

Because you will get a call from your credit card company any time that your purchases for the month exceed the 98th percentile, this means that any month in which you spend more than 2 standard deviations more than your mean spending you will receive a call. One standard deviation is $75, and multiplying that by 2 yields $150. We then add \$150 to the mean of \$280 to arrive at \$430. If you spend more than \$430 in a given month on your credit card, you will get a call from your credit card company.

CHAPTER 8

8.1 THE z TABLE—WEATHER PATTERNS

a.

X	$(X - \mu)$	$(X - \mu)^2$
4.41	0.257	0.066
8.24	4.087	16.704
4.69	0.537	0.288
3.31	−0.843	0.711
4.07	−0.083	0.007
2.52	−1.633	2.667
10.65	6.497	42.211
3.77	−0.383	0.147
4.07	−0.083	0.007
0.04	−4.113	16.917
0.75	−3.403	11.580
3.32	−0.833	0.694

$\mu = 4.153$; $SS = \Sigma(X - \mu)^2 = 91.999$;

$\sigma^2 = \dfrac{\Sigma(X - \mu)^2}{N} = (91.999)/12 = 7.667$;

$\sigma = \sqrt{\sigma^2} = \sqrt{7.667} = 2.769$

August: $X = 3.77$

$z = \dfrac{(X - \mu)}{\sigma} = \dfrac{(3.77 - 4.153)}{2.769} = -0.138$

b. The table tells us that 5.57% of scores fall between the mean and a z score of −0.138. Thus, (50 − 5.57) = 44.43% of scores fall below that z score. The percentile for August is 44.43%. This is surprising because it is below the mean, and it was the month in which a devastating hurricane hit New Orleans. (*Note:* It is helpful to draw a picture of the curve when calculating this answer.)

c. Paragraphs will be different for each student but will include the fact that a monthly total based on missing data is inaccurate. The mean and the standard deviation based on this population, therefore, are inaccurate. Moreover, even if we had these data points, they would likely be large and would increase the total precipitation for August; August would likely be an outlier, skewing the overall mean. The median would be a more accurate measure of

central tendency than the mean under these circumstances.

d. With 10% in each tail, we would look up (50 − 10) = 40% between the mean and the score of interest. The z scores that mark the points 40% below and above the mean are −1.28 and 1.28. (*Note:* It is helpful to draw a picture of the curve that includes these z scores.) We can then convert these z scores to raw scores. $X = z(\sigma) + \mu = -1.28(2.769) + 4.153 = 0.609$; $X = z(\sigma) + \mu = 1.28(2.769) + 4.153 = 7.697$. Only October (0.04) is below 0.609. Only February (8.24) and July (10.65) are above 7.697. These data are likely inaccurate, however, because the mean and the standard deviation of the population are based on an inaccurate mean from August. Moreover, it is quite likely that August would have been in the most extreme upper 10% if there were complete data for this month.

8.3 WHICH SIBLING IS TALLER?

a. Kari's and Jacob's scores are on different scales. Kari needs to be compared to girls of her age, and Jacob needs to be compared to boys of his age. It's like comparing pounds and kilograms; we need to convert to the same scale so that we can compare directly. With statistics, we can convert both heights to the same scale; we can turn both into z scores that gives us a sense of how far Kari and Jacob are from the average for their age and gender. We can compare these two z scores to each other directly, or we can use the z scores to look up their percentiles and compare those directly.

b. Kari: $z = \dfrac{(X - \mu)}{\sigma} = \dfrac{(60 - 63)}{2.7} = -1.111$

Jacob: $z = \dfrac{(X - \mu)}{\sigma} = \dfrac{(59 - 61.8)}{3.2} = -0.875$

Jacob's z score is less negative, and so he is taller with respect to his peers than Kari is with respect to hers.

c. For each z score, we draw a curve on which we can include all percentages and z scores. The percentage between the mean and a z score of −1.111 is 36.65. Kari's percentile rank is (50 − 36.65) = 13.35%. The percentage between the mean and a z score of −0.875 is 31.06. Jacob's percentile rank is (50 − 31.06) = 18.94%.

8.5 STEP 1—TESTING OF PSYCHIATRIC INPATIENTS

a. Population 1 is adult psychiatric inpatients. Population 2 is normal adults.

b. The comparison distribution would be a distribution of means. Boone would compare his sample of 150 psychiatric inpatients to a distribution of all possible samples of 150 individuals.

c. We would use a z test because we have one sample and we're comparing it to a population for which we know the mean and the standard deviation.

d. (1) The dependent variable, intrasubtest scatter, seems to be an interval variable from the description. (2) The sample includes 150 adult psychiatric inpatients. It is unlikely that they were randomly selected from all adult psychiatric inpatients; thus, we must be cautious about generalizing from this sample. (3) We do not know if the population distributions are normal, but we have more than 30 participants (i.e., 150), so the sampling distribution is likely to be normal.

e. Boone uses the word *significantly* as an indication that he rejected the null hypothesis.

8.7 DIVISION I COLLEGE FOOTBALL AND THE ASSUMPTIONS FOR HYPOTHESIS TESTING

a. The independent variable is the division. Teams were drawn from either Division I or Division I-AA. The dependent variable is the spread.

b. Random selection was not used. Random selection would entail having some process for randomly selecting Division I games and Division I-AA games for inclusion in the sample. The researchers do not describe such a process and, in fact, took all their Division I-AA teams from the same league within that division.

c. The populations of interest are football games between teams in the upper divisions of the NCAA (Division I-A and Division I-AA).

d. The comparison distribution would be the distribution of sample means.

e. The first assumption—that the dependent variable is on an interval scale—is met in this example. The dependent variable is point spread, which is an interval measure. The second assumption—that participants are randomly selected—is not met. As described in part (b), the teams for inclusion in the sample were not randomly selected. The third assumption—that the distribution of scores in the population of interest must be normal—is likely to be met. We can imagine that there is some average point spread around which most point spreads fall and that on occasion you see extremely high or extremely low point spreads.

8.9 DIVISION I COLLEGE FOOTBALL AND A z TEST

a. *Step 3:* $\mu_M = \mu = 16.189$; $\sigma_M = \dfrac{\sigma}{\sqrt{N}} = \dfrac{12.128}{\sqrt{4}} = 6.064$

Step 4: When we adopt 0.05 as the p level for significance and have a two-tailed hypothesis, we need to divide the 0.05 by 2 to obtain the z score cutoff for each end of the distribution (high and low). Dividing 0.05 by 2 yields 0.025. The z score corresponding to a probability of 0.025 is 1.96. Therefore, our cutoffs are +1.96 and −1.96.

Step 5: We first must obtain the mean spread in our sample. The games with their spreads are listed below:

GAME	SPREAD
Holy Cross, 27/Bucknell, 10	7
Lehigh, 23/Colgate, 15	8
Lafayette, 31/Fordham, 24	7
Georgetown, 24/Marist, 21	3

Mean spread = 8.75

$$z = \frac{(M - \mu_M)}{\sigma_M} = \frac{(8.75 - 16.189)}{6.064} = -1.23$$

Step 6: Given that the z statistic of −1.23 does not exceed our cutoff value of −1.96, we would fail to reject the null hypothesis. We can conclude only that we do not have sufficient evidence that the point spread of Division I-AA teams is different, on average, from that of Division I-A teams.

b. It would be unwise to generalize these findings beyond the sample. The sample of games was not randomly selected from all Division I-AA team games that week. It is possible that this particular league differs from other leagues and therefore is not representative of Division I-AA as a whole.

8.11 z TEST—THE GRADED NAMING TEST AND CROSS-CULTURAL DIFFERENCES

a. *Step 1:* Population 1 is Canadian adults. Population 2 is English adults. The comparison distribution will be a distribution of means. The hypothesis test will be a z test because we have only one sample and we know the population mean and the standard deviation. This study meets two of the three assumptions and may meet the third. The dependent variable appears to be interval. In addition, there are 30 participants in the sample, indicating that the comparison distribution will be normal. The data were not likely randomly selected, however, so we must be cautious when generalizing.

Step 2: Null hypothesis: Canadian adults have the same average GNT scores as do English adults. $H_0: \mu_1 = \mu_2$

Research hypothesis: Canadian adults have different average GNT scores from English adults. $H_0: \mu_1 \neq \mu_2$

Step 3:

$$\mu_M = \mu = 20.4; \ \sigma_M = \frac{\sigma}{\sqrt{N}} = \frac{3.2}{\sqrt{30}} = 0.584$$

Step 4: Our cutoff z statistics, based on a p level of 0.05 and a two-tailed test, are −1.96 and 1.96. (*Note:* It is helpful to draw a picture of the normal curve and include these z statistics on it.)

$$\text{*Step 5:* } z = \frac{(M - \mu_M)}{\sigma_M} = \frac{(17.5 - 20.4)}{0.583}$$

= −4.97. (*Note:* It is helpful to add this z statistic to your drawing of the normal curve that includes the cutoff z statistics.)

Step 6: Reject the null hypothesis. It appears that Canadian adults have lower average GNT scores than English adults.

b. Sometimes the people on whom the test was normed have characteristics in common that other people might not have. Often, when a test that was normed with one cultural group is used with another cultural group, the average scores are different, not because the groups are actually different on the variable of interest but because some items are biased toward one group.

8.13 *p* LEVELS—THE GRADED NAMING TEST

a. *Step 4:* Our cutoff z statistics, based on a p level of 0.01 and a two-tailed test, are −2.58 and 2.58. (*Note:* It is helpful to draw a picture of the normal curve and include these z statistics on it.)

b. *Step 6:* Reject the null hypothesis; it appears that Canadian adults have lower average GNT scores than English adults.

c. A p level of 0.01 leads to more extreme cutoff statistics than a p level of 0.05, making it more difficult to reject the null hypothesis. When the tails are limited to 1% versus 5%, the tails beyond the cutoffs are smaller and the cutoffs are more extreme.

d. The difference between the mean of the population and the mean of the sample is identical

in both cases, as is the test statistic. The only aspect that is affected is the critical value.

8.15 CHEATING WITH HYPOTHESIS TESTING

a. (1) We could use a one-tailed, rather than a two-tailed test. (2) We could use a less stringent p level (0.05 versus 0.01). (3) We could use a much larger sample size.

b. None of these tactics would change the actual difference between samples. This is a potential problem with hypothesis testing because an identical difference between means could be statistically significant under some circumstances but not others. Statistical significance, therefore, does not necessarily translate into importance of a finding.

8.17 TYING IT ALL TOGETHER—FACILITATED COMMUNICATION

a. The independent variable was experimental series with three levels: A, B, and C. In series A (but not B and C), the facilitator saw the same picture cards as the patients. The population of patients whose facilitators viewed the same picture cards (A) were being compared with two populations of patients whose facilitators did not view the same picture cards (B and C).

b. The dependent variable was whether the patient's answer matched the picture card the patient saw.

c. Null hypothesis: Patients have the same mean number of answers that match the picture card they saw when their facilitators are also viewing the card as when the facilitators are not viewing the card. $H_0: \mu_1 = \mu_2$

Research hypothesis: Patients have different mean numbers of answers that match the picture card they saw when their facilitators are also viewing the card versus when the facilitators are not viewing the card. $H_1: \mu_1 \neq \mu_2$

d. Null hypothesis: Patients do not have more answers, on average, that match the picture card they saw when their facilitators are also viewing the card as when the facilitators are not viewing the card. $H_0: \mu_1 \leq \mu_2$

Research hypothesis: Patients have more answers, on average, that match the picture card they saw when their facilitators are also viewing the card versus when the facilitators are not viewing the card. $H_1: \mu_1 > \mu_2$

e. *Step 6:* Reject the null hypothesis. It appears that patients are more likely, on average, to have their answers match the picture card they viewed when the facilitators are viewing that same card than when the facilitators are not viewing that card.

f. If the decision were in error, this would be a Type I error. The researchers would be rejecting the null hypothesis of no difference when in fact there really was no difference.

8.19 THE LANGUAGE OF STATISTICS— *CRITICAL REGIONS* AND *CUTOFFS*

a. *Critical region* may have been chosen because values of a test statistic that are significant will appear in a particular area, or region, on the normal distribution.

b. *Cutoff* may have been chosen because any values more extreme than the cutoff are considered significant. Therefore, these values indicate which test statistics make the cutoff and which do not. Just like we may have cutoffs for qualifying for sports teams, here we have cutoffs for qualifying for significance.

8.21 THE LANGUAGE AND SYMBOLS OF STATISTICS

a. (i) $\sigma_1 = \sigma_2$ is used incorrectly. (ii) Research hypotheses would not include an "=" sign; only null hypotheses would. (iii) $\mu_1 = \mu_2$.

b. (i) "p level" is used incorrectly. (ii) First, statistics should always be italicized. Second, the cutoff listed here is a z statistic, not a p level. A p level would be something like 0.05. (iii) z statistic.

c. (i) The reference to calculating standard error from the scores in the sample is incorrect. (ii) The scientist must know the population standard deviation and must calculate standard error from that. (iii) The scientist must use the standard deviation from the population to calculate the standard error.

d. (i) X is used incorrectly. (ii) When calculating a z statistic for a sample, we subtract the population mean from the sample mean, not from a score. (iii) M.

■ DIGGING DEEPER INTO THE DATA

8.23 MOVIE EARNINGS AND USING THE z DISTRIBUTION TO IDENTIFY OUTLIERS

a. It appears that there may be three scores that are outliers: *Star Wars: Episode III*, *Wedding Crashers*, and *Walk the Line*.

b.

X	$(X - \mu)$	$(X - \mu)^2$
120.000	33.800	1142.440
75.000	−11.200	125.440
26.000	−60.200	3624.040
380.000	293.800	86,318.440
42.000	−44.200	1953.640
34.000	−52.200	2724.840
30.000	−56.200	3158.440
64.000	−22.200	492.840
53.000	−33.200	1102.240
209.000	122.800	15,079.840
53.000	−33.200	1102.240
48.000	−38.200	1459.240
29.000	−57.200	3271.840
47.000	−39.200	1536.640
83.000	−3.200	10.240

$\mu = 86.2$; $SS = \Sigma(X - \mu)^2 = 221301.44$;
$\sigma^2 = \dfrac{\Sigma(X - \mu)^2}{N} = (221{,}301.44)/15 = 14{,}753.429$;
$\sigma = \sqrt{\sigma^2} = \sqrt{14753.429} = 121.464$

The standard deviation is 90.592. To determine if a movie gross is more than 2 standard deviations above the mean we need to calculate $2 \times 90.592 + 86.2 = 267.38$ and to calculate $86.2 - (2 \times 90.592) = -94.98$. We then compare these values to the box office grosses. Only one movie is more than 2 standard deviations from the mean: *Star Wars: Episode III*.

c. To be more than 3 standard deviations above the mean a movie would have to have grossed more than $357.97 million or to have grossed less than −$185.57 million. No movies are more than 3 standard deviations from the mean.

d. Outliers may distort what is otherwise a very clear pattern in the data, particularly if all but one or two of your scores tell the same story.

e. The decision about how to identify and deal with outliers should be made prior to the collection of the data because it is dishonest for a researcher to tweak his or her data set until the expected results are achieved. The safest route to take is to identify how you will deal with outliers ahead of time in an effort to avoid even unintentional dishonesty.

CHAPTER 9

9.1 THE t STATISTIC AND THE *PRINCETON REVIEW*

a. The appropriate mean: $\mu_M = \mu = 210$

The calculations for the appropriate standard deviation (in this case, the standard error, s_M): $M = \frac{\Sigma X}{N} = \frac{(160 + 240 + 340 + 70 + 250)}{5} = 212$

X	X − M	(X − M)²
20	−2.8	7.84
19	−3.8	14.44
27	4.2	17.64
24	1.1	1.44
25	2.2	4.84

Numerator: $\Sigma(X - M)^2 = \Sigma(2{,}704 + 784 + 16{,}384 + 20{,}164 + 1444) = 41{,}480$

$s = \sqrt{\frac{\Sigma(X - M)^2}{(N - 1)}} = \sqrt{\frac{41{,}480}{(5 - 1)}} = \sqrt{10{,}370}$
$= 101.833$

$s_M = \frac{s}{\sqrt{N}} = \frac{101.833}{\sqrt{5}} = 45.541$

b. $t = \frac{(M - \mu_M)}{s_M} = \frac{(212 - 210)}{45.541} = 0.04$

c. There are several possible answers to this question. Here are some examples. (1) Is the improvement of 210 points based on practice tests or actual GRE scores? (2) Does your sample include all students who took the course or a subset (e.g., students who attended every class or another group that is not likely to be representative)? (3) What is the mean improvement for a student who takes the GRE twice without a course in between administrations? That is, how much better is an improvement of 210 points than simply taking the test twice?

9.3 A DISTRIBUTION OF DIFFERENCES BETWEEN MEANS AND DEPRESSION IN CHINA

a. The populations of interest are all Chinese boys and all Chinese girls. The samples are the 134 boys and 127 girls who participated in this study.

b. To construct a distribution of differences between means, we would randomly select 134 boys from the population and calculate their mean CDI score; we would randomly select 127 girls from the population and calculate their mean CDI score; and then we would subtract the second mean from the first to get a difference between means. (After selecting each individual score, we would return it to the population before selecting the next.) We would then repeat the process to get a second difference between means. We would do this many, many, many times, plotting the differences between means.

c. The mean would be 0. If there is no difference between the actual population means (and that is the distribution to which we will compare the difference between means of our sample), then some of the time the boys' mean will be higher just by chance, some of the time the girls' mean will be higher just by chance, and some of the time they will be the same. These differences will cancel each other out, and the mean of the differences between means will be 0.

9.5 STEP 1—SHOULD WE SEPARATE TWINS IN THE CLASSROOM?

a. Population 1 is twins who are separated from their twins throughout their school years. Population 2 is twins who are not separated from their twins throughout their school years.

b. The comparison distribution is a distribution of differences between means. There are two samples, and no child is in both samples. Each child is either separated from or placed together with his or her twin. So we will calculate a mean for each sample and take the difference between the means. This difference between means will be compared to a distribution of all possible differences between means for samples of these sizes.

c. We would use an independent-samples t test because there are two samples and the participants in each sample are different individuals.

d. (1) The dependent variable, academic performance, is likely interval; for example, high school grade point average could be used. (2) The sample is randomly selected. (3) Without data, we cannot tell if the samples indicate that the populations are likely normally distributed, but because the sample size is 200 (well over 30), the comparison distribution is likely to be normal.

9.7 STEP 2—TWINS AND BIG BOX SCORES

a. Null hypothesis: Twins who were separated from their twins have the same outcomes, on average, as twins who were kept together with their twins—$H_0: \mu_1 = \mu_2$.

Research hypothesis: Twins who were separated from their twins had different outcomes, on average, from twins who were kept together with their twins—H_1: $\mu_1 \neq \mu_2$.

b. Null hypothesis: Local retailers have the same earnings, on average, in the presence of big box stores as in the absence of big box stores—H_0: $\mu_1 = \mu_2$.
Research hypothesis: Local retailers have different earnings, on average, in the presence of big box stores than in the absence of big box stores—H_1: $\mu_1 \neq \mu_2$.

9.9 PAIRED-SAMPLES t TEST—MINIMUM GPAS

a. There are two samples of universities; the same universities are in each sample.

b. *Step 1:* Population 1 is university psychology programs. Population 2 is university history programs. The comparison distribution will be a distribution of mean differences. The hypothesis test will be a paired-samples t test because we have two samples and all participants are in both samples. This study meets two of the three assumptions and may meet the third. The dependent variable, GPA, is interval/ratio. The data were randomly selected. We do not know whether the population is normally distributed, there are not at least 30 participants, and there is not much variability in the data in our samples, so we should proceed with caution.

Step 2: Null hypothesis: University psychology programs require the same minimum GPA, on average, as university history programs—H_0: $\mu_1 = \mu_2$.
Research hypothesis: University psychology programs require different minimum GPAs, on average, from university history programs—H_1: $\mu_1 \neq \mu_2$.

Step 3: $\mu_M = \mu = 0$; $s_M = 0.062$

(*Note:* Remember to cross out the original scores once you have created the difference scores so you won't be tempted to use them in your calculations.)

X	Y	DIFFERENCE	$(X - M)$	$(X - M)^2$
3.0	2.75	0.25	0.15	0.023
3.0	3.0	0	−0.1	0.01
3.0	2.75	0.25	0.15	0.023
3.0	3.0	0	−0.1	0.01
3.0	3.0	0	−0.1	0.01

$M_{Difference} = 0.1$

$SS = \Sigma(X - M)^2 = \Sigma(0.023 + 0.01 + 0.023 + 0.01 + 0.01) = 0.076$

$s = \sqrt{\dfrac{\Sigma(X - M)^2}{(N - 1)}} = \sqrt{\dfrac{SS}{(N - 1)}} = \sqrt{\dfrac{0.076}{(5 - 1)}}$
$= \sqrt{0.019} = 0.138$

$s_M = \dfrac{s}{\sqrt{N}} = \dfrac{0.138}{\sqrt{5}} = 0.062$

Step 4: $df = N - 1 = 5 - 1 = 4$; our critical values, based on 4 degrees of freedom, a p level of 0.05, and a two-tailed test, are -2.776 and 2.776. (*Note:* It is helpful to draw a curve that includes these cutoffs.)

Step 5: $t = \dfrac{(M_{Difference} = \mu_{Difference})}{s_M} =$

$\dfrac{(0.1 - 0)}{0.062} = 1.61$ (*Note:* It is helpful to add this t statistic to the curve that you drew in step 4.)

Step 6: Fail to reject the null hypothesis; we conclude that there is no evidence from this study to support the research hypothesis.

c. $t(4) = 1.61$, $p > 0.05$

9.11 INDEPENDENT-SAMPLES t TEST—HYPNOSIS AND THE STROOP EFFECT

a. *Step 1:* Population 1 is highly hypnotizable individuals who receive a posthypnotic suggestion. Population 2 is highly hypnotizable individuals who do not receive a posthypnotic suggestion. The comparison distribution will be a distribution of differences between means. The hypothesis test will be an independent-samples t test because we have two samples and every participant is in only one sample. This study meets one of the three assumptions and may meet another. The dependent variable, reaction time in seconds, is interval/scale. The data were not likely randomly selected, so we should be cautious when generalizing beyond our sample. We do not know whether the population is normally distributed and there are not at least 30 participants, but our sample data do not suggest skew.

Step 2: Null hypothesis: Highly hypnotizable individuals who receive a posthypnotic suggestion will have the same average Stroop reaction times as will highly hypnotizable individuals who receive no posthypnotic suggestion—H_0: $\mu_1 = \mu_2$.

Research hypothesis: Highly hypnotizable individuals who receive a posthypnotic suggestion will have different average Stroop reaction times from highly hypnotizable individuals who receive no posthypnotic suggestion—H_1: $\mu_1 \neq \mu_2$.

Step 3: $(\mu_1 = \mu_2) = 0$; $s_{Difference} = 0.463$

Calculations:

$M_X = 12.55$

X	X − M	(X − M)²
12.6	0.05	0.003
13.8	1.25	1.563
11.6	−0.95	0.903
12.2	−0.35	0.123
12.1	−0.45	0.203
13.0	0.45	0.203

$$s_X^2 = \frac{\Sigma(X - M)^2}{N - 1}$$
$$= \frac{(0.003 + 1.563 + 0.903 + 0.123 + 0.203 + 0.203)}{6 - 1}$$
$$= 0.600$$

$M_Y = 9.5$

Y	Y − M	(Y − M)²
8.5	−1.0	1.000
9.6	0.1	0.010
10.0	0.5	0.250
9.2	−0.3	0.090
8.9	−0.6	0.360
10.8	1.3	1.690

$$s_Y^2 = \frac{\Sigma(Y - M)^2}{N - 1}$$
$$= \frac{(1.0 + 0.01 + 0.25 + 0.09 + 0.36 + 2.56)}{6 - 1}$$
$$= 0.680$$

$df_X = N - 1 = 6 - 1 = 5$

$df_Y = N - 1 = 6 - 1 = 5$

$df_{total} = df_X + df_Y = 5 + 5 = 10$

$$s_{Pooled}^2 = \left(\frac{df_X}{df_{Total}}\right)s_X^2 + \left(\frac{df_Y}{df_{Total}}\right)s_Y^2$$
$$= \left(\frac{5}{10}\right)0.600 + \left(\frac{5}{10}\right)0.680$$
$$= 0.300 + 0.340 = 0.640$$

$$s_{M_X}^2 = \frac{s_{Pooled}^2}{N} = \frac{0.640}{6} = 0.107$$

$$s_{M_Y}^2 = \frac{s_{Pooled}^2}{N} = \frac{0.640}{6} = 0.107$$

$$s_{Difference}^2 = s_{M_Y}^2 + s_{M_X}^2 = 0.107 + 0.107 = 0.214$$
$$s_{Difference} = \sqrt{s_{Difference}^2} = \sqrt{0.214} = 0.463$$

Step 4: Our critical values, based on a two-tailed test, a p level of 0.05, and df_{Total} of 10, are −2.228 and 2.228. (*Note:* It is helpful to draw a curve that includes these cutoffs.)

Step 5: $t = \dfrac{(12.55 - 9.50) - (0)}{0.463} = \dfrac{3.05}{0.463} = 6.59$. (*Note:* It is helpful to add this t statistic to the curve that you drew in step 4.)

Step 6: Reject the null hypothesis; it appears that highly hypnotizable people have faster Stroop reaction times when they receive a posthypnotic suggestion than when they do not.

b. $t(10) = 6.59$, $p < 0.05$

c. The test statistic becomes smaller when you move to two separate samples. It would be easier to reject the null hypothesis with a within-groups design. The larger test statistic of the paired-samples t test more than makes up for the slightly more extreme cutoff t values.

d. A large source of variance—individual differences—is eliminated in a within-groups design because the participants serve as their own controls. This reduces the standard error of the mean difference and thereby increases the magnitude of the t statistic.

9.13 ONE-TAILED VERSUS TWO-TAILED TESTS—STROOP AND HYPNOSIS

a. *Step 2:* Null hypothesis: The average Stroop reaction time of highly hypnotizable individuals who receive a posthypnotic suggestion is greater than or equal to that of highly hypnotizable individuals who receive no posthypnotic suggestion—H_0: $\mu_1 \geq \mu_2$.
Research hypothesis: Highly hypnotizable individuals who receive a posthypnotic suggestion will have faster (i.e., lower number) average Stroop reaction times than highly hypnotizable individuals who receive no posthypnotic suggestion—H_1: $\mu_1 < \mu_2$.

b. *Step 4:* $df = N - 1 = 6 - 1 = 5$; our critical value, based on 5 degrees of freedom, a p level of 0.05, and a one-tailed test, is −2.015. (*Note:* It is helpful to draw a curve that includes this cutoff.)

c. *Step 6:* Reject the null hypothesis; it appears that highly hypnotizable people have faster Stroop reaction times when they receive a post-hypnotic suggestion than when they do not.

d. It is easier to reject the null hypothesis with a one-tailed test. Although we rejected the null hypothesis under both conditions, the cutoff *t* value is less extreme with a one-tailed test because the entire 0.05 (5%) critical region is in one tail instead of divided between two.

e. The difference between the means of the samples is identical, as is the test statistic. The only aspect that is affected is the critical value.

9.15 EFFECT OF SAMPLE SIZE—STROOP AND HYPNOSIS

a. *Step 3:* $\mu_M = \mu = 0$; $S_M = 0.850$

(*Note:* Remember to cross out the original scores once you have created the difference scores so you won't be tempted to use them in your calculations.)

X	Y	DIFFERENCE	$(X - M)$	$(X - M)^2$
~~12.6~~	~~8.5~~	−4.1	−0.8	0.64
~~13.8~~	~~9.6~~	−4.2	−0.9	0.81
~~11.6~~	~~10.0~~	−1.6	1.7	2.89

$s = M_{Difference} = -3.3$

$SS = \Sigma(X - M)^2 = \Sigma(0.64 + 0.81 + 2.89) = 4.34$

$s = \sqrt{\dfrac{\Sigma(X - M)^2}{(N - 1)}} = \sqrt{\dfrac{SS}{(N - 1)}} = \sqrt{\dfrac{4.34}{(3 - 1)}}$
$= \sqrt{2.17} = 1.473$

$s_M = \dfrac{s}{\sqrt{N}} = \dfrac{1.473}{\sqrt{3}} = 0.850$

Step 4: $df = N - 1 = 3 - 1 = 2$; our critical values, based on 2 degrees of freedom, a *p* level of 0.05, and a two-tailed test, are −4.303 and 4.303. (*Note:* It is helpful to draw a curve that includes these cutoffs.)

Step 5: $t = \dfrac{(M_{Difference} - \mu_{Difference})}{s_M}$

$\dfrac{(-3.3 - 0)}{0.850} = -3.88$. (*Note:* It is helpful to add this *t* statistic to the curve that you drew in step 4.)

b. This test statistic is no longer beyond the critical value. Reducing the sample size makes it more difficult to reject the null hypothesis

because it results in a larger standard error and therefore a smaller test statistic. It also results in more extreme critical values.

9.17 CHOOSE THE CORRECT TEST, PART II

a. We would use a single-sample *t* test because we have one sample of figure skaters and are comparing that sample to a population (women with eating disorders) for which we know the mean.

b. We would use an independent-samples *t* test because we have two samples, and no participant can be in both samples. One cannot have both a high level and a low level of knowledge about a topic.

c. We would use a paired-samples *t* test because we have two samples, but every student is assigned to both samples—one night of sleep loss and one night of no sleep loss.

9.19 MANY DIFFERENT HYPOTHESIS TESTS, ONE RESEARCH QUESTION

a. We could compare one sample to known norms. We would need the mean and the standard deviation for weight for the population of children in the United States (or North America). One flaw is that the students in our sample might be different from the population on some important variable to begin with.

b. We would conduct the study as described in part (a), but we would need only the population mean, not the standard deviation.

c. We would need two samples, with all participants in both samples. Students could be weighed before and after participation in the Edible Schoolyard program. We would, of course, have to adjust for children's expected weight gain over a year.

d. In all cases, we are comparing two means, whether both from samples or one from a sample and one from a population, in terms of a measure of spread. We divide the difference between means by a type of standard error.

9.21 THE LANGUAGE OF STATISTICS—CONSERVATIVE

In everyday conversation, conservative is typically used to refer to someone's political leanings. People who ally themselves with the Republican Party, for example, might be considered conservative or we might use the word *conservative* to refer to someone, perhaps an investor, who does not like to take risks. Scientists use the word conservative to refer to a judgment that is unlikely to be an over-estimate and errs on the side of caution. A scientist might use the word conservative to refer to a particularly stringent test of a hypothesis or to particularly stringent criteria for a hypothesis test. A conservative test is one that errs on the side of caution and stacks the cards against finding significant test statistics.

■ DIGGING DEEPER INTO THE DATA

9.23 GRAPHING AND STROOP REACTION TIMES

a. Stem-and-leaf plot:

17	2
16	
15	0189
14	1458
13	011368999
12	0112335555799
11	023467789
10	122467
9	119
8	1

b. Dot plot:

Dot Plot of Seconds

Seconds

c. The data appear to be fairly normally distributed, although there are potential outliers in both tails of the distribution.

CHAPTER 10

10.1 THE *DAILY SHOW* AS REAL NEWS AND *t* TESTS VERSUS ANOVAS

a. The independent variable is type of program. The levels are *The Daily Show* and network news. The dependent variable is amount of substantive video and audio reporting per second.

b. The hypothesis test that Fox would use is an independent-samples *t* test.

c. The independent variable is still type of program, but now the levels are *The Daily Show*, network news, and cable news. Because there are three levels of the independent variable, Fox would need to use a one-way ANOVA.

10.3 WHICH DISTRIBUTION? PART II

a. *t* distribution; we are comparing the mean IQ of a sample of 10 to the population mean of 100; this student knows only the population mean—not the population standard deviation.

b. *F* distribution; we are comparing the mean ratings of four samples—families with no books visible, with only children's books visible, with only adult books visible, and with both types of books visible.

c. *t* distribution; we are comparing the average vocabulary of two groups.

10.5 ESCALATING TYPE I ERROR—TOO MANY *t* TESTS

a. For three groups there would be three comparisons (group 1 versus group 2, group 1 versus group 3, and group 2 versus group 3). The probability of a Type I error for a single comparison (given our *p* level of 0.01) is 0.01, and the probability of not having a Type I error is 0.99. The probability of not having a Type I error in three comparisons is $(0.99)(0.99)(0.99) = (0.99)^3 = 0.97$. So the probability of making a Type I error in one of our three comparisons is $1 - 0.97$, or 0.03.

b. With six groups there would be 15 possible comparisons. The probability of not having a Type I error in any of those comparisons would be $(0.99)^{15} = 0.86$. So the probability of making a Type I error in one of the 15 comparisons is $1 - 0.86$, or 0.14.

c. When we make many comparisons, having the more conservative *p* level of 0.01 does not help much; our chances of making a Type I error still go up exponentially.

10.7 THE MANY VARIETIES OF ANOVA— MEMORY FOR NAMES

a. A one-way between-groups ANOVA should be used.

b. The researcher could have some members of the same group introduced only once, others introduced twice, and others introduced twice and also wearing nametags. The researcher could then ask the participants to remember all the names of those working in their group. This way, all participants would be in all three experimental conditions.

10.9 STUDY DESIGN AND FOOTBALL PLAYERS' EYE BLACK GREASE

a. The independent variable is the type of substance placed beneath the eyes and its levels are black grease, black antiglare stickers, and petroleum jelly.

b. The dependent variable is eye glare.

c. This is a one-way between-groups ANOVA.

10.11 BETWEEN AND WITHIN ALGEBRA CLASSROOMS

a. Between variance is the variability in performance on the mathematics exam that we would expect to see between the three different treatment groups. That is, we might expect the mean of the remedial class to be the lowest, the mean of the normal class to be in the middle, and the mean of the advanced class to be the highest. It is this difference among the means of the treatment groups that is between variance.

b. Within variance is the variability we would expect to see within each of the classrooms. For example, even though all students in the remedial class receive the same instruction, all these students will not perform exactly the same on their mathematics test. The difference among the students within the treatment groups is within variance.

c. There are different ways in which these distributions could be drawn, but you would expect that the distribution for the remedial class would be farthest to the left (poorer performance), the distribution for the normal class in the middle, and the distribution for the advanced class farthest to the right. You would expect to see some overlap in these distributions, but not a lot. The width of each distribution would represent the within variance, and the distance between the peak of each distribution would represent the between variance.

10.13 ONE-WAY ANOVA AND EBAY

a. The independent variable is genre of music, and its levels are classical, rap/hip-hop, pop, and jazz.

b. The dependent variable is lowest starting bid.

c. *Step 1:* Population 1 is all classical CDs offered on eBay. Population 2 is all rap/hip-hop CDs offered on eBay. Population 3 is all pop CDs offered on eBay. Population 4 is all jazz CDs offered on eBay. The comparison distribution will be an F distribution. The hypothesis test will be a one-way between-groups ANOVA. The study description indicates that these CDs were randomly selected from those within their genre, which means that we meet the first assumption of ANOVA: random selection. We do not know if the underlying population distributions are normal; because our sample sizes are relatively small, the distribution of sample means based on these samples may not be normal. Finally, to see if we meet the homoscedasticity assumption, we check to see if the largest variance is no greater than twice the smallest variance. The variance calculations appear in the table below. From this table we can see that we have violated the homoscedasticity assumption. The largest variance, 34.49, is more than twice the smallest variance, 0.216.

SAMPLE	CLASSICAL	RAP	POP	JAZZ
Squared deviations	0.762	0.090	0.104	3.610
	0.043	0.462	0.111	53.290
	0.444	0.090	0.432	1.690
	0.006	44.890		
Sum of squares:	1.249	0.648	0.647	103.48
$N - 1$	2	3	2	3
Variance	0.6245	0.216	0.3235	34.49

Step 2: Null hypothesis: The average starting bid price of CDs offered on eBay does not differ depending on the genre of music—H_0: $\mu_1 = \mu_2 = \mu_3$.
Research hypothesis: The average starting bid price of CDs offered on eBay depends on the genre of music.

Step 3: $df_{Between} = N_{Groups} - 1 = 4 - 1 = 3$

$df_1 = 3 - 1 = 2$; $df_2 = 4 - 1 = 3$;
$df_3 = 3 - 1 = 2$; $df_4 = 4 - 1 = 3$

$df_{Within} = 2 + 3 + 2 + 3 = 10$

The comparison distribution will be the F distribution with 3 and 10 degrees of freedom.

Step 4: The cutoff for the F statistic based on a p level of 0.05 is 3.71.

1 line short

Step 5: $df_{Total} = N - 1 = 14 - 1 = 13$

$GM = 2.991$

$SS_{Total} = \Sigma(X - GM)^2 = 234.027$

SAMPLE	X	(X − GM)	(X − GM)²
Classical	2.99	−0.001	0.000
	1.91	−1.081	1.169
	1.45	−1.541	2.375
Rap/hip-hop	0.99	−2.001	4.004
	0.01	−2.981	8.886
	0.99	−2.001	4.004
	0.77	−2.221	4.933
Pop	0.99	−2.001	4.004
	1.00	−1.991	3.964
	0.01	−2.981	8.886
Jazz	5.79	2.799	7.834
	14.99	11.999	143.976
	8.99	5.999	35.988
	0.99	−2.001	4.004

$SS_{Within} = \Sigma(X - M)^2 = 106.023$

SAMPLE	X	(X − M)	(X − M)²
Classical	2.99	0.873	0.762
$M_{Classical} = 2.117$	1.91	−0.207	0.043
	1.45	−0.667	0.444
Rap/hip-hop	0.99	0.300	0.090
$M_{Rap} = 0.69$	0.01	−0.680	0.462
	0.99	0.300	0.090
	0.77	0.080	0.006
Pop	0.99	0.323	0.104
$M_{Pop} = 0.667$	1.00	0.333	0.111
	0.01	−0.657	0.432
Jazz	5.79	−1.900	3.610
$M_{Jazz} = 7.69$	14.99	7.300	53.290
	8.99	1.300	1.690
	0.99	−6.700	44.890

$SS_{Between} = \Sigma(X - GM)^2 = 127.99 \quad GM = 2.991$

SAMPLE	X	(M − GM)	(M − GM)²
Classical	2.99	−0.874	0.764
$M_{Classical} = 2.117$	1.91	−0.874	0.764
	1.45	−0.874	0.764
Rap, Hip-Hop	0.99	−2.301	5.295
$M_{Rap} = 0.69$	0.01	−2.301	5.295
	0.99	−2.301	5.295
	0.77	−2.301	5.295
Pop	0.99	−2.324	5.401
$M_{Pop} = 0.667$	1.00	−2.324	5.401
	0.01	−2.324	5.401
Jazz	5.79	4.699	22.081
$M_{Jazz} = 7.69$	14.99	4.699	22.081
	8.99	4.699	22.081
	0.99	4.699	22.081

$SS_{Total} = SS_{Within} + SS_{Between} = 106.023 + 127.999 = 234.022$

$$MS_{Between} = \frac{SS_{Between}}{df_{Between}} = \frac{127.999}{3} = 42.662$$

$$MS_{Within} = \frac{SS_{Within}}{df_{Within}} = \frac{106.023}{10} = 10.602$$

$$F = \frac{MS_{Between}}{MS_{Within}} = \frac{42.662}{10.602} = 4.024$$

SOURCE	SS	df	MS	F
Between	127.999	3	42.663	4.02
Within	106.023	10	10.602	
Total	234.022	13		

Step 6: Our *F* statistic, 4.02, is beyond the cutoff of 3.71. We can reject the null hypothesis. It seems that CDs from different genres of music have different average starting bid prices on eBay.

d. $F(3, 10) = 4.02$, $p < 0.05$

10.15 THE LANGUAGE OF STATISTICS— *SOURCE*

One way that we use the word *source* in everyday conversation is to refer to the place from which people got their information. For example, a reporter would have a source for information that she prints. Another way in which we use the word *source* in everyday conversation is to refer to where a product originally comes from. For example, a distributor of bottled water might claim that the water was "bottled at its source." Similarly, one might talk about the source of a problem, referring to where the problem originated. Statisticians use the word *source* in a similar way. For example, when referring to the source of variance, statisticians are referring to where the variance comes from or what the variance can be attributed to.

10.17 THE SYMBOLS OF STATISTICS

a. (i) The symbol for sample variance, s, is used incorrectly. (ii) This is the symbol for standard deviation. (iii) The between variance in an ANOVA is symbolized by $MS_{Between}$.

b. (i) The X symbol for a raw score is used incorrectly, and the formula is missing the summation symbol, Σ. (ii) When calculating the $SS_{Between}$, you sum the squared differences between the treatment condition mean and the grand mean. (iii) The formula should read $SS_{Between} = \Sigma(M - GM)^2$.

c. (i) The formula is missing the summation symbol, Σ, and it is missing the squared term. (ii) When calculating SS_{Within}, you must square the deviation of each score from its own group mean and then sum those deviation scores. (iii) The formula should read $SS_{Within} = \Sigma(X - M)^2$.

d. (i) The square root symbol is on the wrong side of the equation. (ii) F is a term based on variance, which means it is a squared term. t is the square root of F. (iii) The formula should read $t = \sqrt{F}$.

10.19 A COMPARISON OF GPAS—STATISTICAL SOFTWARE OUTPUT AND THE RELATION BETWEEN t AND F DISTRIBUTIONS

a. $F = \dfrac{MS_{Between}}{MS_{Within}} = \dfrac{4.623}{0.522} = 8.856$

b. $t = \sqrt{F} = \sqrt{8.856} = 2.98$

c. The "Sig." for t is the same as that for the ANOVA, 0.005, because the F distribution reduces to the t distribution when we are dealing with two groups.

■ **DIGGING DEEPER INTO THE DATA**

10.21 POST-HOC TESTS AND CHANGING CRITICAL VALUES

a. For three means, we will make three comparisons, and so our p level for each comparison will be $(0.05/3) = 0.017$.

b. For a desired p level of 0.01 overall, our p level for each comparison will be $(0.01/3) = 0.003$.

CHAPTER 11

11.1 THE MANY VARIETIES OF ANOVA—MYTH-BUSTING

a. This study would be analyzed with a between-groups ANOVA because different groups of participants were assigned to the different treatment conditions.

b. This study could be redesigned to use a within-groups ANOVA by testing the same group of participants on some myths repeated once and some repeated three times both when they are young and then again when they are old.

11.3 NAMING ANOVAS—PERSONAL ADS

a. There are two independent variables. The first is gender, and its levels are male and female. The second is sexual orientation, and its levels are homosexual and heterosexual.

b. The dependent variable is the preferred maximum age difference.

c. This would be analyzed with a two-way between-groups ANOVA.

d. This is a 2×2 between-groups ANOVA.

e. The ANOVA would have four cells. This number is obtained by multiplying the number of levels of each independent variable (2×2).

f.

	MALE	FEMALE
Homosexual	homosexual; male	homosexual; female
Heterosexual	heterosexual; male	heterosexual; female

11.5 INTERPRETING ANOVA'S RESULTS—MOTIVATED SKEPTICISM

a.

	PERCEPTION BEFORE	PERCEPTION AFTER	
Told Unhealthy	6.6	5.6	6.1
Told Healthy	6.9	7.3	7.1
	6.75	6.45	6.6

b. There appears to be a main effect of whether participants were told a high TAA level was associated with healthy or unhealthy consequences. Overall, those told that it was associated with healthy consequences perceived the TAA test to be more accurate, on average, than did those told it was associated with unhealthy consequences.

c. Bar graph depicting the main effect of test outcome:

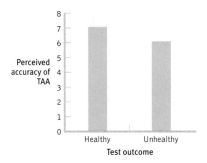

d. The main effect is misleading on its own because, based on the cell means, the effect of test outcome appears to depend on whether perception were assessed before or after the TAA test.

e. Based on the cell means, there does appear to be an interaction. When perceptions of the TAA test were taken after the test, those told that high levels were associated with healthy consequences perceived the test to be more accurate, on average, than did those told high levels were associated with unhealthy consequences. Having been told the outcome of the test, these participants were motivated to believe in the test's accuracy to different degrees. But for those whose perceptions were assessed prior to the TAA test, there does not appear to be an effect of the outcome of the test on perceptions of the test. Not knowing the outcome, they had no motivation toward a certain perception of accuracy.

f. Here is the bar graph of the interaction with lines to show the pattern of the interaction:

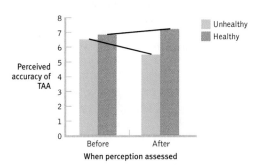

g. The interaction is qualitative because the direction of the effect of when the perception is assessed switches depending on whether participants were told that high TAA levels were associated with healthy or unhealthy consequences.

11.7 INTERPRETING AN ANOVA'S RESULTS— POLITICAL ORIENTATION AND RACISM

a. Table of means:

	LIBERAL	MODERATE	CONSERVATIVE
African American	3.18	3.50	1.25
European American	1.91	3.33	4.62

b. The reported statistics indicate a significant interaction. Conservative participants gave higher mean double jeopardy ratings to the European American officer than to the African American officer, whereas the liberal participants gave higher mean double jeopardy ratings to the African American officer than to the European American officer.

c. Bar graph depicting interaction:

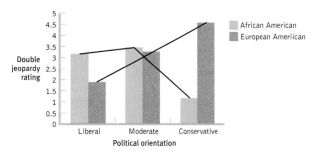

d. This is a qualitative interaction; the pattern of double jeopardy ratings switches direction between the liberal participants and the conservative participants.

11.9 SELF-INTEREST AND INTERACTIONS

a. The first independent variable is the gender said to be most affected by the illness, and its levels are men and women. The second independent variable is the gender of the participant, and its levels are male and female.

b. The researchers conducted a two-way between-groups ANOVA.

c. The reported statistics do indicate that there is a significant interaction because the probability associated with the F statistic for the interaction is less than 0.05.

d.

	FEMALE PARTICIPANTS	MALE PARTICIPANTS
Illness Affects Women	4.88	3.29
Illness Affects Men	3.56	4.67

e. Bar graph for the interaction:

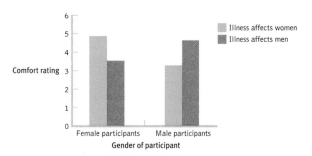

f. This is a qualitative interaction. Female participants indicated greater average comfort for attending a meeting regarding an illness that affects women than for attending a meeting regarding an illness that affects men. Male participants had the opposite pattern of results; male participants indicated greater average comfort for attending a meeting regarding an illness that affects men as opposed to one that affects women.

11.11 INTERACTIONS AND THE CROSS-RACE EFFECT

a. The first independent variable is the race of the face, and its levels are white and black. The second independent variable is the type of instruction given to the participants, and its levels are no instruction and instruction to attend to distinguishing features. The dependent variable is the measure of recognition accuracy.

b. The researchers conducted a two-way between-groups ANOVA.

c. The reported statistics indicate that there is a significant main effect of race. On average, the white participants who saw white faces had higher recognition scores than did white participants who saw black faces.

d. The main effect is misleading because those who received instructions to attend to distinguishing features actually had lower mean recognition scores for the white faces than did those who received no instruction, whereas those who received instructions to attend to distinguishing features had higher mean recognition scores for the black faces than did those who received no instruction.

e. The reported statistics do indicate that there is a significant interaction because the probability associated with the F statistics for the interaction is less than 0.05.

f.

	BLACK FACE	WHITE FACE
No Instruction	1.04	1.46
Distinguishing Features Instruction	1.23	1.38

g. Bar graph of findings:

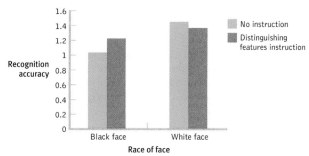

h. When given instructions to pay attention to distinguishing features of the faces, participants' average recognition of the black faces was higher than when given no instructions, whereas their average recognition of the white faces was worse than when given no instruction. This is a qualitative interaction because the direction of the effect changes between black and white.

11.13 MATCH.COM AND CONDUCTING A TWO-WAY ANOVA, PART I

a. The first independent variable is gender of the seeker, and its levels are men and women. The second independent variable is gender of the person being sought, and its levels are men and women. The dependent variable is the youngest acceptable age of the person being sought.

b.

	WOMEN SEEKERS	MEN SEEKERS
Men Sought	24.8	22.8
Women Sought	23.8	20.2

c. *Step 1:* Population 1 (women, men) is women seeking men. Population 2 (men, women) is men seeking women. Population 3 (women, women) is women seeking women. Population 4 (men, men) is men seeking men. The comparison distribution will be an F distribution. The hypothesis test will be a two-way between-groups ANOVA. Assumptions: The data are not from random samples, so we must generalize with caution. The homogeneity of variance assumption is violated because the largest variance (4.20) is more than five times as large as the smallest variance (0.70).

Step 2: Main effect of first independent variable—gender of seeker:

Null hypothesis: On average, men and women report the same youngest acceptable ages for their partners—$\mu_M = \mu_W$.
Research hypothesis: On average, men and women report different youngest acceptable ages for their partners—$\mu_M \neq \mu_W$.

Main effect of second independent variable—gender of person sought:

Null hypothesis: On average, those seeking men and those seeking women report the same youngest acceptable ages for their partners—$\mu_M - \mu_W$.
Research hypothesis: On average, those seeking men and those seeking women report different youngest acceptable ages for their partners—$\mu_M \neq \mu_W$.

Interaction: Seeker × sought:

Null hypothesis: The effect of the gender of the seeker does not depend on the gender of the person sought.
Research hypothesis: The effect of gender of the seeker does depend on gender of the person sought.

Step 3: $df_{Columns(seeker)} = 2 - 1 = 1$

$df_{Rows(sought)} = 2 - 1 = 1$

$df_{Interaction} = (1)(1) = 1$

$df_{Within} = df_{W,M} + df_{M,W} + df_{W,W} + df_{M,M} = 4 + 4 + 4 + 4 = 16$

Main effect of gender of seeker: F distribution with 1 and 16 df

Main effect of gender of sought: F distribution with 1 and 16 df

Interaction of seeker and sought: F distribution with 1 and 16 df

Step 4: Cutoff F for main effect of seeker: 4.49

Cutoff F for main effect of sought: 4.49

Cutoff F for interaction of seeker and sought: 4.49

Step 5: Total sum of squares = $\Sigma(X - GM)^2 = 103.800$

Sum of squares for column/seeker = $\Sigma(M_{Column(seeker)} - GM)^2 = 39.200$

Sum of squares for row/sought = $\Sigma(M_{Row(sought)} - GM)^2 = 16.200$

Sum of squares within = $\Sigma(X - M_{Cell})^2 = 45.200$

Sum of squares for interaction = $SS_{Total} - (SS_{Row} + SS_{Column} + SS_{Within}) = 3.200$

SOURCE	SS	df	MS	F
Seeker gender	39.200	1	39.200	13.876
Sought gender	16.200	1	16.200	5.736
Seeker × sought	3.200	1	3.200	1.133
Within	45.200	16	2.825	
Total	103.800	19		

Step 6: There is a significant main effect of gender of the seeker and a significant main effect of gender of the person being sought. We can reject the null hypotheses for both of these main effects. Male seekers are more willing to accept younger partners, on average, than are female seekers. Those seeking women are willing to accept younger partners, on average, than are those seeking men. We cannot reject the null hypothesis for the interaction; we can only conclude that there is not sufficient evidence that the effect of the gender of the seeker depends on the gender of the person sought.

d. There is not a significant interaction.

11.15 MOTIVATED SKEPTICISM AND THE MORE PRECISE INTERPRETATION OF ANOVA

Step 1: Subtract the grand mean from each of the marginal means.

	PERCEPTION BEFORE	PERCEPTION AFTER	
Told Healthy	6.6	7.3	6.95 − 6.6 = 0.35
Told Unhealthy	6.9	5.6	6.25 − 6.6 = −0.35
	6.75 − 6.6 = 0.15	6.45 − 6.6 = −.15	6.6

Step 2: Subtract row effects and column effects from each cell.

	PERCEPTION BEFORE	PERCEPTION AFTER	
Told Healthy	6.6 − 0.35 − 0.15 = 6.1	7.3 − 0.35 − (−0.15) = 7.1	−0.50
Told Unhealthy	6.9 − (−0.35) − 0.15 = 7.1	5.6 − (−0.35) − (−0.15) = 6.1	0.50
	0.15	−0.15	6.6

Step 3: Subtract grand mean from each cell mean.

	PERCEPTION BEFORE	PERCEPTION AFTER	
Told Healthy	6.1 − 6.6 = −0.5	7.1 − 6.6 = 0.5	0.35
Told Unhealthy	7.1 − 6.6 = 0.5	6.1 − 6.6 = −0.5	−0.35
	0.15	−0.15	6.6

The accompanying bar graph depicts the cell means of the interaction corrected for the main effects. We went back a step in the calculations to create this graph, however, so that the means would be positive and easier to interpret. Here we can clearly see the interaction of the two independent variables.

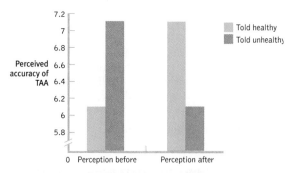

11.17 MATCH.COM AND THE MORE PRECISE INTERPRETATION OF ANOVA, PART II

Step 1: Subtract grand mean from row and column means.

	WOMEN SEEKERS	MEN SEEKERS	
Men Sought	34.80	35.40	35.1 − 33.35 = 1.75
Women Sought	36.00	37.20	31.6 − 22.9 = 8.7
	35.4 − 33.35 = 2.05	31.3 − 33.35 = 2.05	33.35

Step 2: Subtract row and column effects from cell means.

	WOMEN SEEKERS	MEN SEEKERS	
Men Sought	34.8 − 1.75 − 2.05 = 31	35.4 − 1.75 − (−2.05) = 35.7	1.75
Women Sought	36.0 − (−1.75) − 2.05 = 35.7	27.2 − (−1.75) − (−2.05) = 31	−1.75
	2.05	−2.05	33.35

Step 3: Subtract grand mean from the cell means (that already have had row and column effects removed):

	WOMEN SEEKERS	MEN SEEKERS	
Men Sought	31 − 33.35 = −2.35	35.7 − 33.35 = 2.35	1.75
Women Sought	35.7 − 33.35 = 2.35	31 − 33.35 = −2.35	−1.75
	2.05	−2.05	33.35

The accompanying bar graph depicts the new cell means for the interaction corrected for the main effects. We went back one step in our calculations so that all the bars would be positive and easier to interpret. We can now see that there is no interaction. Were we to draw lines between the two green columns for "men sought" and the two orange columns for "women sought," they would be parallel.

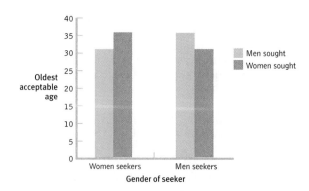

11.19 THE LANGUAGE OF STATISTICS—CELL

In everyday conversation the word *cell* conjures up images of a prison or a small room in which someone is forced to stay, or of one of the building blocks of a plant or animal. In statistics, the word *cell* refers to a single condition in a factorial ANOVA that is characterized by its values on each of the independent variables.

■ **DIGGING DEEPER IN THE DATA**

11.21 HEALTH-RELATED MYTHS AND VARIATIONS ON ANOVA

a. In a within-groups design, every participant is in every cell. We could follow the same people, exposing them to the experimental stimuli when they were young and then again when they are old. (This would be impractical, of course, because it would take too long to conduct the study. In addition, there might be a practice effect: Those who participated in the study when they were young might have become attuned to health-related myths through that participation.)

b. We could keep age (younger, older) as a between-groups independent variable but make repetitions (one, three) within-groups. All participants would have some myths debunked one time and other myths debunked three times to see which way led to the most accurate reports of the true health fact. In fact, this is exactly the way this study was conducted in real life.

11.23 COVARIATES, WEIGHT, AND CAREER SUCCESS

a. This is problematic because it suggests a causal connection for correlational data. There are many possible confounds. It could be that people with high energy are more likely both to exercise (and lose weight) and to work long hours (and make more money). It could be that education level is associated with both weight and income. The act of losing weight might not cause one's income to change at all.

b. If you can include covariates, you can eliminate alternative explanations. There are several possible interval variables that could be included as a covariate. For example, if you include education level as a covariate, and there still is a link between weight and income, you can eliminate education level as a possible confound.

CHAPTER 12

12.1 LAW SCHOOL ACCEPTANCE AND OVERLAPPING DISTRIBUTIONS

a. No, we cannot tell which student will do better on the LSAT. It is likely that the distributions of LSAT scores for the two groups (humanities majors and social science majors) have a great deal of overlap. Just because one group, on average, does better than another group does not mean that every student in one group does better than every student in another group.

b. Answers to this will vary, but the two distributions should overlap and the mean of the distribution for the social sciences majors should be farther to the right (i.e., higher) than the mean of the distribution for the humanities majors.

12.3 DIVISION I COLLEGE FOOTBALL AND CONFIDENCE INTERVALS

a. Given $\mu = 16.189$ and $\sigma = 12.128$, we calculate $\sigma_M = \dfrac{\sigma}{\sqrt{N}} = \dfrac{12.128}{\sqrt{4}} = 6.064$. To calculate the 95% confidence interval, we find the z values that mark off the most extreme 0.025 in each tail, which are -1.96 and 1.96. We calculate the lower end of the interval as $M_{Lower} = -z(\sigma_M) + M_{Sample} = -1.96(6.064) + 8.75 = -3.14$ and the upper end of the interval as $M_{Upper} = z(\sigma_M) + M_{Sample} = 1.96(6.064) + 8.75 = 20.64$. The confidence interval around the mean of 8.75 is $(-3.14, 20.64)$.

b. Because 16.189, the null-hypothesized value of the population mean, falls within this confidence interval, it is plausible that the point spreads of Division I-AA schools are the same, on average, as the point spreads of Division I schools. It is plausible that they come from the same population of point spreads.

c. Because the confidence interval includes 16.189, we know that we would fail to reject the null hypothesis if we conducted a hypothesis test. In fact, when we conducted a z test in Chapter 8, we failed to reject the null hypothesis. It is plausible that the sample came from a population with $\mu = 16.189$ by chance. We did not have sufficient evidence to conclude that the point spreads of Division I-AA schools are from a different population from the point spreads of Division I schools.

d. In addition to letting us know that it is plausible that the Division I-AA point spreads are from the same population as those for the Division I schools, the confidence interval tells us a range of plausible values for the mean point spread.

12.5 HYPNOSIS, THE STROOP EFFECT, AND CONFIDENCE INTERVALS

a. To calculate the 95% confidence interval, first calculate $s_{Difference} = \sqrt{s^2_{Difference}} = \sqrt{s^2_{M_X} + s^2_{M_Y}} =$

$$\sqrt{\frac{s^2_{Pooled}}{N_X} + \frac{s^2_{Pooled}}{N_Y}} = \sqrt{\frac{0.640}{6} + \frac{0.640}{6}}$$

$= \sqrt{0.214} = 0.463$. The t statics for a distribution with $df = 10$ that correspond to a p level of 0.05—that is, the values that mark off the most extreme 0.025 in each tail—are -2.228 and 2.228. Then calculate:

$(M_X - M_Y)_{Lower} = t_{Lower}(s_{Difference}) +$
$(M_X - M_Y)_{Sample} = -2.228(0.463) +$
$(12.55 - 9.5) = -1.032 + 3.05 = 2.02$

$(M_X - M_Y)_{Upper} = t_{Upper}(s_{Difference}) +$
$(M_X - M_Y)_{Sample} = -2.228(0.463) +$
$(12.55 - 9.5) = 1.032 + 3.05 = 4.08.$

The 95% confidence interval around the difference between means of 3.05 is (2.02, 4.08).

b. Were we to draw repeated samples (of the same sizes) from these two populations, 95% of the time the confidence interval will contain the true population parameter.

c. Because the confidence interval does not include 0, it is not plausible that there is no difference between means. Were we to conduct a hypothesis test, we would be able to reject the null hypothesis and could conclude that the means of the two samples are different. In fact, the hypothesis test that we conducted in Chapter 9 led us to reject the null hypothesis.

d. In addition to determining statistical significance, the confidence interval allows us to determine a range of plausible differences between means. An interval estimate gives us a better sense than does a point estimate of how precisely we can estimate from this study.

12.7 DIVISION I COLLEGE FOOTBALL, z TEST, AND EFFECT SIZE

a. The appropriate measure of effect size for a z statistic is Cohen's d, which is calculated as
$$d = \frac{M - \mu}{\sigma} = \frac{8.75 - 16.189}{12.128} = {}^-0.613.$$

b. Based on Cohen's conventions, this is a medium to large effect size.

c. The hypothesis test tells us only whether a sample mean is likely to have been obtained by chance, whereas the effect size gives us the additional information of how much overlap there is

between the distributions. Cohen's d, in particular, tells us how far apart two means are in terms of standard deviation. Because it's based on standard deviation, not standard error, Cohen's d is independent of sample size and therefore has the added benefit of allowing us to compare across studies. In summary, effect size tells us the magnitude of the effect, giving us a sense of how important or practical this finding is, and allows us to standardize the results of the study. Here, we know that there's a medium to large effect.

12.9 HYPNOSIS, INDEPENDENT-SAMPLES t TEST, AND EFFECT SIZE

a. The appropriate measure of effect size for a t statistic is Cohen's d, which is calculated as
$$d = \frac{(M_X - M_Y) - (\mu_X - \mu_Y)}{s_{Pooled}} =$$
$$\frac{(12.55 - 9.5) - (0)}{\sqrt{0.640}} = 3.81.$$

b. Based on Cohen's conventions, this is a large effect size.

c. It is useful to have effect-size information because the hypothesis test tells us only whether we were likely to have obtained our sample mean by chance. The effect size tells us the magnitude of the effect, giving us a sense of how important or practical this finding is, and allows us to standardize the results of the study so that we can compare across studies. Here, we know that there's a large effect.

12.11 EBAY, ONE-WAY ANOVA, AND EFFECT SIZE

a. One appropriate measure of effect size for ANOVA is R^2.
$$R^2 = \frac{SS_{Between}}{SS_{Total}} = \frac{127.999}{234.022} = 0.55.$$

b. Based on Cohen's conventions, this is a large effect size.

c. Although the hypothesis test tells us whether the variability among our groups is likely due to chance or to our effect, it does not tell us the size of our effect. R^2 tells us how much variability in the dependent measure is attributable to an independent variable (or to the interaction of two independent variables). So it is a measure of the magnitude of an effect, telling us how important or practical a finding is. In this case, we know that there's a large effect. In addition, because it's not dependent on sample size, R^2 can standardize findings so that we can compare across studies.

d. It is not possible to calculate Cohen's d when you have more than two groups because the numerator of Cohen's d requires taking the difference between two means. Here, we have four group means.

12.13 MEDICAL MYTHS, TWO-WAY ANOVA, AND EFFECT SIZE

a. The effect size for the independent variable of age is $R^2 = \dfrac{SS_{Between}}{SS_{Total}} = \dfrac{0.0300}{0.0672} = 0.45$.

b. Based on Cohen's conventions, this is a large effect size.

c. The effect size for the independent variable of repetitions is $R^2 = \dfrac{SS_{Between}}{SS_{Total}} = \dfrac{0.0000}{0.0672} = 0.00$.

d. Based on Cohen's conventions, this is not even a small effect size.

e. The effect size for the interaction between age and repetitions is $R^2 = \dfrac{SS_{Between}}{SS_{Total}} = \dfrac{0.0192}{0.0672} = 0.29$.

f. Based on Cohen's conventions, this is a large effect.

g. The main effect of age accounts for the most variance; 45% of the variability in memory errors is explained by age. Only 29% of the variability in errors is explained by the interaction between age and repetitions, and none of the variability is explained by the main effect of repetitions.

12.15 THE GRADED NAMING TEST AND STATISTICAL POWER

a. *Step 1:* To calculate statistical power, we need to know the mean of population 1, which is $\mu_1 = 20.4$, and the population standard deviation, which is $\sigma = 3.2$. We need to calculate standard error based on our expected sample size of $N = 30$. In this case, our standard error is $\sigma_M = \dfrac{\sigma}{\sqrt{N}} = \dfrac{3.2}{\sqrt{30}} = 0.584$. Finally, the mean of population 2 (which, for the sake of calculating statistical power, we're assuming is represented by the mean of our sample) is 17.5.

Step 2: Looking only at population 1, we find the raw mean (of this distribution of means) that marks off the bottom 5% of the distribution; we

choose the bottom 5% because the sample mean is lower than the mean of population 1. To find the raw mean, we find the critical z value for that point, -1.645, and convert it to a raw mean: $M = z(\sigma_M) + \mu_M = -1.645(0.584) + 20.4 = 19.439$. See the accompanying figure, which shows where this z statistic falls on the distribution with respect to the mean of population 1.

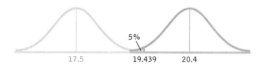

Step 3: At this step, we're focusing just on the second distribution, the one centered around 17.5. The accompanying figure shows where the raw mean of 19.439 falls relative to the mean of population 2 (the sample mean), 17.5. We will now compare the raw mean we just calculated, 19.439, with the mean of population 2, 17.5, by calculating the z statistic for 19.439 with respect to 17.5: $z = \dfrac{19.439 - 17.5}{0.584} = 3.320$. We now look up now look up the z value of 3.32 in the z table (the closest z is 3.50), and we find that approximately 49.98% of the distribution falls between the z value and the mean; if we add this to 50%, the percentage that falls on the other side of the mean, we find that 99.98% of scores fall beyond the point at which we would reject the null hypothesis. In this case, our statistical power to detect an effect is about 99.98%. If the population represented by the second distribution really does exist, we have a 99.98% chance of randomly selecting a sample with a mean different enough from that in population 1 that we will reject the null hypothesis.

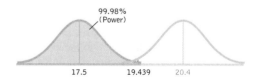

b. Statistical power of 80% is typically considered acceptable. In this study, we had very good statistical power to detect our effects. So, if we were to fail to obtain a significant difference between the means, we would know that it was not due to a lack of statistical power to detect the effect.

12.17 GETTING READY FOR A DATE AND STATISTICAL POWER

a. From a computerized statistical power calcu-lator: For an alpha of 0.05, a two-tailed test, a sample size of 4, and the calculated effect size

of $d = 32.25 - \dfrac{56.5}{\sqrt{355.625}} = 1.29$, our

statistical power is 0.339.

b. From a computerized statistical power calculator: Given this effect size, you would need a total sample size of 22 to obtain statistical power of 0.80.

12.19 THE LANGUAGE OF STATISTICS— *CONFIDENCE*

In everyday language, we use the word *confidence* to refer to how sure we are of something or someone. In statistics, however, when we use the word *confidence* in the phrase *confidence interval*, we are referring to a range of means (or differences between means) that are plausible for a given population (or populations).

12.21 THE LANGUAGE OF STATISTICS—*POWER*

In everyday language, we use the word *power* to mean either an ability to get something done or an ability to make others do things. Statisticians use the word *power* to refer to the ability to detect an effect, given that one exists.

■ **DIGGING DEEPER INTO THE DATA**

12.23 META-ANALYSIS AND CULTURALLY ADAPTED THERAPY

a. The topic is whether culturally adapted therapies are effective.

b. They might decide to include only studies that had included a control-group comparison.

c. The researchers used Cohen's *d* as a measure of effect size for each study in the analysis.

d. The mean effect size they found was 0.45. According to Cohen's conventions, this is a medium effect.

e. The researchers could use the group means and standard deviations to calculate a measure of effect size.

12.25 META-ANALYSIS AND ELECTRONIC DATABASES

Answers to items *a* through *d* will vary.

a. For a search using the search words "gender" and "depression," most of you will get many, many abstracts.

b. When the search also includes the search word "single-parent," the number of abstracts will be far reduced.

c. For most of you, you'll discover that a far smaller percentage of abstracts than you might imagine are actually useful to you.

d. As you read abstracts, you'll learn which words show up in the most useful abstracts, and you'll add them to your search. You'll also learn which words show up only in the least useful abstracts, and you can search for abstracts that *don't* have those terms.

e. When conducting a meta-analysis, it's easy to overlook studies that use synonyms for the constructs of interest that we haven't considered. It's important to methodically track down all possible words that might be used to describe the constructs that we're studying in our meta-analysis.

CHAPTER 13

13.1 TYPE OF RESEARCH DESIGN AND STUDENT EVALUATIONS

a. (i) Students' ratings of the professors. (ii) Students' grades. (iii) This is a category I research design because it is likely that students filled out an interval rating scale, and students' grades can be assumed to be measured on an interval scale—that is, the difference between each "step" should be the same (e.g., going from a B− to a B is the same distance as going from an A− to an A; or in terms of GPA, going from a 2.6 to a 2.7 is the same distance as going from a 3.3 to a 3.4).

b. (i) Students' ratings of the professors. (ii) Students' grades in future classes. (iii) This is a category I research design because it is likely that students filled out an interval rating scale, and students' grades in future classes would also be based on an interval measure.

c. (i) Gender of the professor, male or female. (ii) Students' ratings of the professor. (iii) This is a category II research design because the independent variable is categorical (i.e., nominal) and the dependent variable is a rating on an interval scale.

d. (i) Gender of the professor, male or female. (ii) Students' grades in related future classes. (iii) This is a category II research design because the independent variable of gender is categorical (i.e., nominal) and the dependent variable of students' grades is interval.

e. (i) Gender of the professor, male or female. (ii) Level of the course, upper or lower. (iii) This is a category III research design because both the independent variable and the dependent variable are categorical.

f. (i) Position of instructor: non-tenure-track, graduate student, tenure-track. (ii) Students' ratings of instructor. (iii) This is a category II research design because the independent variable is categorical (i.e., nominal) and the dependent variable is interval.

13.3 TYPE OF RESEARCH DESIGN AND OBITUARIES

a. To determine whether the proportion of obituaries for men is higher than that for women, McNulty would use a nonparametric test, the chi-square test for goodness-of-fit, because he is assessing a single nominal variable. He could compare whether the proportion of obituaries for men and women differs from a 50/50 split—what we would expect if the proportions for the two genders were equal.

b. To determine whether women die longer after they've stopped working than do men, McNulty could use a parametric test. Gender of the deceased, man or woman, would be the independent variable, and years postretirement at time of death would be the dependent variable. Because the independent variable is nominal and the dependent variable is interval, McNulty could use a parametric test, the independent samples t test.

c. To determine if the type of accomplishment documented in the obituary differed by gender, McNulty would use a nonparametric test, the chi-square test for independence, because he would need to use a nominal independent variable and a nominal dependent variable. The independent variable would be gender, male or female, and the dependent variable would be type of accomplishment—wealth, social, or other.

13.5 TYPES OF VARIABLES AND SUPER BOWL TELEVISION ADVERTISEMENTS

a. One way we could operationalize the success of the Super Bowl advertisements using a nominal variable would be to categorize whether each product's sales in the one-week period following the Super Bowl were different from its sales in the week prior to the Super Bowl.

b. One way we could operationalize the success of the Super Bowl advertisements using a ordinal variable would be to rank each product's sales in the one-week period following the Super Bowl as either higher or lower than its sales in the week prior to the Super Bowl.

c. One way we could operationalize the success of the Super Bowl advertisements using an interval variable would be to measure the difference in a product's net profit in the week prior to and the week following the Super Bowl.

13.7 CHI SQUARE AND SEX SELECTION

a. There is one variable, gender of the children. Its levels are girls and boys.

b. A chi-square test for goodness-of-fit would be used because we have one sample, the children from Punjab, and we are comparing proportions of children that fall within each level of gender (a nominal variable) to expectations based on national proportions.

c. *Step 1:* Population 1 is children with gender proportions like those that we observed in Punjab. Population 2 is children with gender proportions similar to those in India as a whole. The comparison distribution is a chi-square distribution. The hypothesis test will be a chi-square test for goodness-of-fit because we have only one nominal variable. This study meets three of the four assumptions. The variable under study is nominal. Each observation is independent of the others. There are more than five times as many participants as there are cells (there are 1798 children in the sample and only 2 cells). We do not know, however, whether this is a randomly selected sample of the more educated people, so we must generalize with caution.

Step 2: Null hypothesis: The proportions of boys and girls in Punjab are the same as those of India as a whole.

Research hypothesis: The proportions of boys and girls in the Punjab area are different from those in India as a whole.

Step 3: The comparison distribution is a chi-square distribution that has 1 degree of freedom: $df_{\chi^2} = 2 - 1 = 1$.

Step 4: Our critical χ^2, based on a p level of 0.05 and 1 degree of freedom, is 3.841.

Step 5:

OBSERVED (PROPORTIONS OF BOYS AND GIRLS)	
BOYS	GIRLS
1000	798

EXPECTED (FROM THE GENERAL POPULATION)	
BOYS	GIRLS
929.566	868.434

CATEGORY	OBSERVED (O)	EXPECTED (E)	O − E	$(O - E)^2$	$\dfrac{(O - E)^2}{E}$
Boys	1000	929.566	70.434	4960.948	5.337
Girls	798	868.434	−70.434	4960.948	5.713

$$\chi^2 = \Sigma \left[\frac{(O - E)^2}{E} \right] = 5.337 + 5.713 = 11.05$$

Step 6: Reject the null hypothesis. Our calculated chi-square value exceeds our critical value. It appears that the proportion of girls in Punjab is less than that in the general population of India.

d. $\chi^2(1) = 19.53$, $p < 0.05$

13.9 CHI SQUARE AND THE PRISONER'S DILEMMA

a. There are two variables in this study. The independent variable is the country the student is from (United States, China). The dependent variable is the choice the student made (defect, cooperate).

b. A chi-square test for independence would be used because we have data on two nominal variables.

c. *Step 1:* Population 1 contains students like those in this sample. Population 2 contains students from a population in which country of origin and choice to defect or cooperate are independent. The comparison distribution is a chi-square distribution. The hypothesis test will be a chi-square test for independence because we have two nominal variables. This study meets three of the four assumptions. The two variables are nominal; every participant is in only one cell; and there are more than five times as many participants as there are cells (there are 122 participants and

4 cells). The students were not randomly selected, however, so we should use caution when generalizing beyond this sample.

Step 2: Null hypothesis: The proportion of Chinese students who choose to defect as opposed to cooperate is similar to the proportion for U.S. students.
Research hypothesis: The proportion of Chinese students who choose to defect as opposed to cooperate is different from the proportion for U.S. students.

Step 3: The comparison distribution is a chi-square distribution that has 1 degree of freedom:. $df_{\chi^2} = (k_{Row} - 1)$ $(k_{Column} - 1) =$ $(2 - 1)(2 - 1) = 1$.

Step 4: Our cutoff χ^2, based on a p level of 0.05 and 1 degree of freedom, is 3.841.

Step 5:

	OBSERVED		
	DEFECT	COOPERATE	
China	31	36	67
United States	41	14	55
	72	50	122

$$\frac{Total_{Column}}{N}(Total_{Row}) = \frac{72}{122}(67) = 39.541$$

$$\frac{Total_{Column}}{N}(Total_{Row}) = \frac{72}{122}(55) = 32.459$$

$$\frac{Total_{Column}}{N}(Total_{Row}) = \frac{50}{122}(67) = 27.459$$

$$\frac{Total_{Column}}{N}(Total_{Row}) = \frac{50}{122}(55) = 22.541$$

	EXPECTED		
	DEFECT	COOPERATE	
China	39.541	27.459	67
United States	32.459	22.541	55
	72	50	122

See table at the top of the next page and use this equation:

$$\chi^2 = \Sigma \left[\frac{(O - E)^2}{E} \right]$$
$$= 1.849 + 2.657 + 2.247 + 3.236 = 9.989$$

CATEGORY	OBSERVED (O)	EXPECTED (E)	O − E	(O − E)²	$\dfrac{(O-E)^2}{E}$
China; defect	31	39.451	−8.541	72.949	1.849
China; cooperate	36	27.459	8.541	72.949	2.657
U.S.; defect	41	32.459	8.541	72.949	2.247
U.S.; cooperate	14	22.541	−8.541	72.949	3.236

Step 6: Reject the null hypothesis. Our calculated chi-square value exceeds our critical value. It appears that the proportion of participants who choose to defect is higher among U.S. students than among Chinese students.

d. Cramer's $V = \sqrt{\dfrac{\chi^2}{(N)(df_{Row/Column})}} =$

$\sqrt{\dfrac{9.989}{(122)(1)}} = 0.286$. According to Cohen's conventions, this is a medium effect.

e. $\chi^2(1, N = 122) = 9.99$, $p < 0.05$, Cramer's $V = 0.29$

13.11 GRAPHING, CHI SQUARE, AND THE PRISONER'S DILEMMA

a. The accompanying table shows the conditional proportions.

	DEFECT	COOPERATE	
China	0.463	0.537	1.00
United States	0.745	0.255	1.00

b. The accompanying graph shows the conditional proportions for all four conditions.

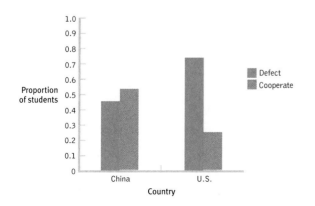

c. The accompanying graph shows only the bars for defects.

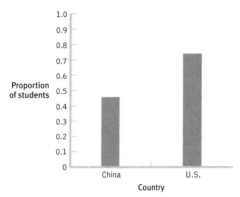

13.13 RELATIVE RISK AND THE PRISONER'S DILEMMA

a. The chance of defecting given that one is from China as opposed to the United States is equal to the conditional probability of defecting among those from China divided by the conditional probability of defecting among those from the United States, or $\dfrac{0.463}{0.745} = 0.621$.

b. This indicates that a student from China is only about 62% as likely to defect as a student from the United States.

c. The chance of defecting given that one is from the United States as opposed to China is equal to the conditional probability of defecting among those from the United States divided by the conditional probability of defecting among those from China, or $\dfrac{0.745}{0.463} = 1.609$.

d. This indicates that a student from the United States is approximately 1.6 times more likely to defect than a student from China.

e. The two likelihood ratios give us complementary information. If students from the United States defect 1.6 as many times as do students from China, that implies that students from

China defect about 40% less of the time than do students from the United States.

13.15 THE DRAWBACKS OF RELATIVE RISK

a. The relative risk of dying given that one is pessimistic (versus optimistic) is 1.45.

b. Based on just this information, pessimists should not be worried that they are about to die. It would be very important to know the base rate, or the rate of deaths during the 10-year period.

c. No, pessimists should not be worried about the increase risk of dying. If the base rate for optimists is a proportion of 0.01 and pessimists are 45% more likely to die, then the death rate for pessimists would be 0.0145. (To obtain this value, we multiply 0.01 by the relative risk, 1.45.)

d. If the base rate were 0.40, pessimists should be more worried. A base rate of 0.40 multiplied by 1.45 is 0.58. With a larger base rate, the increased risk for pessimists results in many more deaths.

e. It may be that those people with fatal illnesses are more pessimistic—that having a fatal illness causes one to be a pessimist.

f. It could be that having depression causes both pessimism and the fatal condition, leading to the observed association between death and pessimism.

13.17 TYING IT ALL TOGETHER—CHI SQUARE, THE GENERAL SOCIAL SURVEY (GSS), AND THE LAW

a. One variable is whether a person believes it is OK to break the law in exceptional circumstances (always obey law, obey conscience). The second variable is whether a person believes in an afterlife (yes, no).

b. $\chi^2 = 0.93$

c. The degrees of freedom is 1. Based on this *df*, our chi-square critical value at a *p* level of 0.05 is 3.84. We cannot reject the null hypothesis.

d. The *p* value next to the chi-square statistic is 0.34. This number is higher than our designated *p* level and so leads us to the same conclusion that we came to in part (c).

e Cramer's $V = \sqrt{\dfrac{\chi^2}{(N)(df_{Row/Column})}}$

$= \sqrt{\dfrac{0.93}{(1,431)(1)}} = 0.025.$

This [$V = 0.025$] is much lower than even a small effect size.

f. $\chi^2(1, N = 1,431) = 0.93$, Cramer's $V = 0.03$

g. The accompanying table shows the conditional proportions.

	POSTLIFE YES	POSTLIFE NO
Obey Law	0.447	0.415
Follow Conscience	0.553	0.584

h. The accompanying graph shows these conditional proportions.

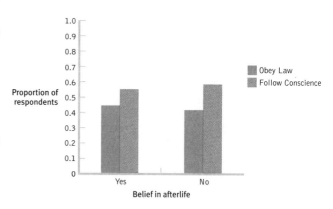

13.19 THE SYMBOLS OF STATISTICS

a. (i) N is incorrect. (ii) k is the correct symbol. (iii) Degrees of freedom for the chi-square test of goodness-of-fit is based on the number of groups, symbolized by k.

b. (i) + is incorrect. (ii) The multiplication symbol is the correct symbol. (iii) When obtaining the degrees of freedom for the chi-square test for independence, we multiply the degrees of freedom associated with each variable.

c. (i) M is incorrect. (ii) O is the correct symbol. (iii) Calculation of chi square involves calculating the difference between observed (O) and expected frequencies.

d. (i) k is incorrect. (ii) *df* is the correct symbol. (iii) Calculation of Cramer's ϕ involves dividing by the *df*, not the number of groups.

e. (i) both ks are incorrect. (ii) *Total* is the correct symbol. (iii) Calculation of the expected values is based on the total counts for the rows and the columns, not the numbers of categories.

■ **DIGGING DEEPER IN THE DATA**

13.21 ADJUSTED STANDARDIZED RESIDUALS, GSS, AND AN EXCITING LIFE

a. Using a criterion of 2, all the cells (exciting, routine, and dull) for those people who live in the same city differ significantly from expected values, as do the cells for exciting and routine for those people living in a different state.

b. Changing the criterion to 3 does not change the results obtained in part (b).

CHAPTER 14

14.1 PARAMETRIC VERSUS NONPARAMETRIC—CHOOSING THE TYPE OF TEST

a. A nonparametric test would be appropriate because both of the variables are nominal.

b. A nonparametric test is more appropriate for this question because the sample size is small and the data are unlikely to be normal; the "big boss" is likely to have a much higher income than the other employees. This outlier would lead to a nonnormal distribution.

c. A parametric test would be appropriate because the independent variable (type of student: athlete versus nonathlete) is nominal and the dependent variable (grade point average) is interval.

d. A nonparametric test would be appropriate because the independent variable (athlete versus nonathlete) is nominal and the dependent variable (class rank) is ordinal.

e. A nonparametric test would be appropriate because the research question is about the relation between two nominal variables: seat-belt wearing and fatal injuries.

f. A parametric test would be appropriate because the independent variable (seat-belt use: no seat belt versus seatbelt) is nominal and the dependent variable (speed) is interval.

14.3 INTERVAL VERSUS ORDINAL DATA AND CELL PHONE BILLS

a. The accompanying table shows the ordered data and corresponding ranks. When converted to ordinal data, the outlier is still at the top of the distribution but is no longer very different from the rest of the scores in the distribution. Prior to converting to ordinal data, the outlier, 500, was well above the next-highest observation, 200. Now the scores of 500 and 200 are ranked 29 and 28, respectively.

PHONE BILL	PHONE RANK	PHONE BILL (CONT.)	PHONE RANK (CONT.)
0	1	55	16
30	2	60	17.5
35	3	60	17.5
40	5.5	65	19
40	5.5	75	20
40	5.5	80	21.5
40	5.5	80	21.5
45	8.5	100	24.5
45	8.5	100	24.5
50	12.5	100	24.5
50	12.5	100	24.5
50	12.5	108	27
50	12.5	200	28
50	12.5	500	29
50	12.5		

b. The distribution is likely to be somewhat rectangular and not normal. However, the distribution of ordinal data is never normal because each score is assigned a rank, which means that each individual raw score usually has a different rank from the others. In most cases (unless there are ties), all frequencies would be 1.

c. It does not matter that the ordinal transformation is not normally distributed because we will be using nonparametric statistics to analyze the data. Nonparametric statistics do not require the assumption that the underlying distribution is normal.

14.5 ORDINAL DATA—CHOOSING FROM AMONG HYPOTHESIS TESTS FOR RANKED DATA, PART II

a. The Mann–Whitney U test would be most appropriate because it is a nonparametric equivalent to the independent-samples t test. It is used when we have a nominal independent variable with two levels (here, they are north and south of the equator), a between-groups research design, and an ordinal dependent variable (here, it is the ranking of the city).

b. The Wilcoxon signed-rank test would be most appropriate because we have a nominal independent variable with two levels (the time of the previous study versus 2005), a within-groups research design, and an ordinal dependent variable (ranking).

c. The Spearman rank-order correlation would be most appropriate because we are asking a question about the relation between two ordinal variables.

14.7 SPEARMAN CORRELATION COEFFICIENT AND TEST-TAKING SPEED

a. The first variable of interest is test grade, which is an interval variable. The second variable of interest is the order in which students completed the test, which is an ordinal variable.

b. The accompanying table shows test grade converted to ranks, difference scores, and squared differences.

GRADE PERCENTAGE	SPEED	GRADE RANK	D	D^2
98	1	1	0	0
93	6	2	4	16
92	4	3	1	1
88	5	4	1	1
87	3	5	−2	4
74	2	6	−4	16
67	8	7	1	1
62	7	8	−1	1

We calculate the Spearman correlation coefficient as:

$$r_S = 1 - \frac{6(\Sigma D^2)}{N(N^2 - 1)} = 1 - \frac{6(40)}{8(64 - 1)}$$
$$= 1 - \frac{240}{504} = 0.524$$

c. The coefficient tells us that there is a rather large positive relation between the two variables. Students who completed the test more quickly also tended to score higher.

d. We would not have calculated a Pearson correlation coefficient because one of our variables, order in which students turned in the test, is ordinal.

14.9 SPEARMAN CORRELATION, CAUSATION, AND TEST-TAKING SPEED

a. This correlation does not indicate that students should attempt to take their tests as quickly as possible. Correlation does not provide evidence for a particular causal relation. A number of underlying causal relations could produce this observed correlation.

b. A third variable that might cause both speedy test-taking and a good test grade is knowledge of the material. Students with better knowledge of and more practice with the material would be able to get through the test more quickly and get a better grade.

14.11 WILCOXON SIGNED-RANK TEST FOR MATCHED PAIRS AND AIRLINE FARES

a. The independent variable is Web site, and its levels are cheaptickets.com and expedia.com. The dependent variable is the cost of the fare.

b. This is a within-groups design because the fares to each destination are represented twice, once for each Web site. In this case, the itineraries are our participants.

c. *Step 1:* We will convert the interval data into ordinal data. These 10 trips were unlikely to have been randomly selected from all possible trips, so we must generalize with caution. It is difficult to know from this small sample whether the difference scores come from a symmetric population distribution.

Step 2: Null hypothesis: There is no difference between the rankings of the fares posted on cheaptickets.com and expedia.com. Research hypothesis: There is a difference between the rankings of the fares posted on cheaptickets.com and expedia.com.

Step 3: Our comparison distribution will be a *T* distribution. We will use a *p* level of 0.05 and a two-tailed test. Our sample size is 10.

Step 4: The critical *T* value is 8. Our calculated *T* value must be less than or equal to 8 to be statistically significant.

Step 5:

TRIP	CHEAP-TICKETS	EXPEDIA	D	D RANK	POSITIVE DIFFERENCE	NEGATIVE DIFFERENCE
Athens, GA, to Johannesburg, South Africa	2403	2580	177	1.5	1.5	
Chicago to Chennai, India	1884	2044	160	4	4	
Columbus, OH, to Belgrade, Serbia	1259	1436	177	1.5	1.5	
Denver to Geneva, Switzerland	1392	1412	20	7	7	
Montreal to Dublin, Ireland	1097	1152	55	6	6	
New York City to Reykjavik, Iceland	935	931	−4	10		10
San Antonio to Hong Kong	1407	1400	−7	9		9
Toronto to Istanbul, Turkey	1261	1429	168	3	3	
Tulsa to Guadalajara, Mexico	565	507	−58	5		5
Vancouver to Melbourne, Australia	1621	1613	−8	8		8

$$\Sigma\, R_+ = (1.5 + 4 + 1.5 + 7 + 6 + 3) = 32$$
$$\Sigma\, R_- = (10 + 9 + 5 + 8) = 32$$
$$T = \Sigma\, R_{Smaller} = 23$$

Step 6: The test statistic, 23, is greater than our critical value, so we fail to reject the null hypothesis. We conclude that there is not sufficient evidence that there tends to be a difference between the fares posted on cheaptickets.com and expedia.com.

d. $T = 23$, $p > 0.05$

14.13 MANN–WHITNEY *U* TEST AND VOTER TURNOUT

a. The independent variable is type of state, and its levels are red and blue. The dependent variable is the percentage of registered voters who voted.

b. This is a between-groups design because each state is either a red state or a blue state but cannot be both.

c. *Step 1:* We will convert our data to an ordinal measure. The states were randomly selected, so we can assume that they are representative of their populations. Finally, there are no tied ranks.

Step 2: Null hypothesis: There will be no difference between the voter turnout in red and blue states. Research hypothesis: There will be a difference between the voter turnout in red and blue states.

Step 3: There are eight red and eight blue states.

Step 4: The critical value for a Mann–Whitney *U* test with two groups of eight, a *p* level of 0.05 and a two-tailed test is 15. The smaller calculated statistic will need to be less than or equal to this critical value to be considered statistically significant.

Step 5:

STATE	TURNOUT	TURNOUT RANK	STATE TYPE	RED RANK	BLUE RANK
Wisconsin	76.73	1	Blue		1
Maine	73.4	2	Blue		2
Oregon	70.5	3	Blue		3
Washington	67.42	4	Blue		4
Missouri	66.89	5	Red	5	
Vermont	66.19	6	Blue		6
Idaho	64.89	7	Red	7	
New Jersey	64.54	8	Blue		8
Montana	64.36	9	Red	9	
Virginia	61.5	10	Red	10	
Louisiana	60.78	11	Red	11	
Illinois	60.73	12	Blue		12
California	60.01	13	Blue		13
Georgia	57.38	14	Red	14	
Indiana	55.69	15	Red		
Texas	53.35	16	Red		

$$\Sigma R_{Red} = 5 + 7 + 9 + 10 + 11 + 14 + 15 + 16 = 87$$

$$\Sigma R_{Blue} = 1 + 2 + 3 + 4 + 6 + 8 + 12 + 13 = 49$$

$$U_{Red} = (8)(8) + \frac{8(8+1)}{2} - 87 = 13$$

$$U_{Blue} = (8)(8) + \frac{8(8+1)}{2} - 49 = 51$$

Step 6: The smaller calculated *U*, 13, is less than the critical value of 15, so we reject the null hypothesis. There is a statistically significant difference between voter turnout in red and blue states. Voter turnout tends to be higher in blue states than in red states.

d. $U = 13$, $p < 0.05$

14.15 KRUSKAL–WALLIS *H* TEST AND SMART STATES

a. The independent variable is region of the country, and its levels are Northeast, Midwest, and South. The dependent variable is "smart" ranking.

b. This is a between-groups design because a state is in only one region of the country.

c. We need to use a nonparametric test because our dependent measure is ordinal.

d. *Step 1:* Our data are ordinal. (This list includes all states in the regions of interest, so the assumption of random selection is not relevant.)

Step 2: Null hypothesis: The "smart" ranking of a state does not tend to vary with its geographical region.
Research hypothesis: The "smart" ranking of a state does tend to vary with its geographical region.

Step 3: We will use the chi-square distribution as our comparison distribution with degrees of freedom of $3 - 1 = 2$.

Step 4: The critical value with a *df* of 2 and *p* level of 0.05 is 5.991. Our calculated statistic will need to be larger than this critical value to be considered statistically significant.

Step 5:

STATE	RANK	NE RANK	MW RANK	S RANK
Massachusetts	1	1		
Connecticut	2	2		
Vermont	3	3		
New Jersey	4	4		
Wisconsin	5		5	
New York	6	6		
Minnesota	7		7	
Iowa	8		8	
Pennsylvania	9	9		
Maine	10	10		
Virginia	11			11
Nebraska	12		12	
New Hampshire	13	13		
Kansas	14		14	
Indiana	15		15	
Ohio	16		16	
Rhode Island	17	17		
Illinois	18		18	
North Carolina	19			19
Missouri	20		20	
Michigan	21		21	
South Carolina	22			22
Arkansas	23			23
Kentucky	24			24
Georgia	25			25
Florida	26			26
Tennessee	27			27
Alabama	28			28
Louisiana	29			29
Mississippi	30			30

$$M_{NE} = \frac{\Sigma R_{NE}}{n} = \frac{65}{9} = 7.222$$

$$M_{MW} = \frac{\Sigma R_{MW}}{n} = \frac{136}{10} = 13.60$$

$$M_S = \frac{\Sigma R_S}{n} = \frac{264}{11} = 24.00$$

$$GM = \frac{\Sigma R}{N} = \frac{465}{30} = 15.50$$

$$H = \left[\frac{12}{N(N+1)}\right][\Sigma n(M = GM)^2]$$

$$= \left[\frac{12}{30(30+1)}\right][(9(7.222 - 15.5)^2)$$

$$+ (10(13.6 - 15.5)^2 + (11(24 - 15.5)^2)]$$
$$= (0.013)(1447.578) = 18.819$$

Step 6: Our calculated statistic, 18.819, exceeds the critical value of 5.992, so we reject the null hypothesis. The "smart" ranking for a state does tend to vary with the geographical location of that state.

e. $H = 18.82$, $p < 0.05$

f. Like an omnibus ANOVA, the Kruskal–Wallis H statistic when used with more than two groups just indicates that there is a difference among the groups, but it does not indicate where that difference is. Separate Kruskal–Wallis H tests for each group comparison in the current example appear below. For each test the degrees of freedom is 1 and the critical value, given a p level of 0.05, is 3.84.

Northeast versus South: $H = 13.02$, $p < 0.05$

Northeast versus Midwest: $H = 4.86$, $p < 0.05$

Midwest versus South: $H = 10.49$, $p < 0.05$

All regions are statistically significantly different from each another. The states in the Northeast tend to have the highest rankings, followed by those in the Midwest, and then by those in the South.

14.17 THE SYMBOLS OF STATISTICS

a. (i) The r is incorrect. (ii) r_S is the correct symbol. (iii) This is the formula for the Spearman rank-order correlation, which requires the subscript S.

b. (i) μ is incorrect. (ii) M is the correct symbol. (iii) In the formula for the Kruskal–Wallis H test, we do not use population parameters (μ); we use the mean of the ranks for the group (M).

c. (i) ΣR_1^2 is incorrect. (ii) ΣR_1 is the correct symbol. (iii) In the Mann–Whitney U test, we do not square the ranks before we sum them; we just sum the ranks.

d. (i) t is incorrect. (ii) T is the correct symbol. (iii) The Wilcoxon signed-ranks tests is symbolized with a T.

■ DIGGING DEEPER INTO THE DATA

14.19 WHEN ARE THE SAME DIFFERENCES NOT REALLY THE SAME?

a. The first $5 difference seems like more. When shopping for a box of cereal, a $5 increase in the price is enormous. Most of us would switch brands rather than pay $5 more for our favorite brand. When shopping for a flat-screen television, a $5 increase is trivial. Most of us would not even notice if we arrived at the store and the price were $5 more than advertised. A difference of $5 does not always mean the same thing.

b. Most baseball fans would agree that an increase from 0.317 to an impressive 0.357 is far more deserving of applause than one from a relatively abysmal 0.255 to an above-average 0.311. It's just not as impressive when a good player improves from a mediocre performance to a solid one as when he improves from a solid performance to a stellar one. It's more difficult to make the leap to the highest echelons of performance.

c. An increase from a 5 to a 15 on a quiz is not that impressive. An increase from a 60 to a 70 is more impressive. But if someone improved from an already strong 88 to a practically perfect 98, that 10 points is far more meaningful because it is more difficult to improve when already at high levels.

d. The problem of the meaning of difference scores is particularly pronounced in behavioral science fields in which many measures are composites of ratings on a number of items. A measure of eating behaviors, for example, might ask individuals to provide ratings of their own behaviors and attitudes on a number of items. Some items might represent far more damaging behaviors or attitudes than other items but might lead to the same net increase in overall score. An increase of 3 on a measure of eating behaviors might be more meaningful when we know that the client achieved this increase because she endorsed an item indicating she frequently binged and purged. Another client's increase of 3 may have resulted from an endorsement of an item indicating that he frequently thought about his next meal. But the two 3-point increases don't have the same meaning.

14.21 THE LANGUAGE OF STATISTICS— *TRANSFORMATION*

In everyday conversation we use the word *transformation* to refer to a radical change. Similarly, statisticians use the word *transformation* to refer to a systematic change applied to the data.

CHAPTER 15

15.1 BEFORE COLLECTING DATA AND IMPROVING STATISTICS PERFORMANCE

a. The goal of this research is to determine whether real-life examples as opposed to fictional data are better at helping students learn statistics.

b. One specific hypothesis might be that students who learn with real-life examples will perform better, on average, on a statistics exam than students who learn with fictional data.

c. The independent variable might be type of data used to illustrate a statistical example, and its levels would be real and fictional. The dependent variable could be students' performance on a quiz assessing their knowledge of that statistical concept.

d. This is a study that would most appropriately be run between groups so that you could use the same quiz for two separate groups of students who learned with the different kinds of examples. Therefore, we would use an independent-samples t test.

15.3 CHOICE OF STATISTICAL TEST AND REVENGE

a. The nominal dependent variable is whether the areas associated with pleasure lit up, and its levels are lit up or did not light up.

b. The nominal independent variable is gender, and its levels are men and women.

c. This research design will have cells because there are discrete categories into which our observations will fall. There would be four cells in this study that would contain counts. The accompanying table shows the cells.

	PLEASURE AREA LIT UP	PLEASURE AREA DID NOT LIGHT UP
Men		
Women		

d. The accompanying table summarizes the variables.

	NAME OF VARIABLE	TYPE	NUMBER OF LEVELS	NAMES OF LEVELS
Independent variable	Gender	Nominal	Two	1. Women 2. Men
Dependent variable	Activity in pleasure area	Nominal	Two	1. Lit up 2. Did not light up

e. A chi-square test for independence would be used to analyze these data because we have two nominal variables (category 3 research).

15.5 CHOICE OF STATISTICAL TEST, COURSE REQUIREMENTS, AND GRADUATE SCHOOL ADMISSION

a. The dependent variable is students' ratings of their likelihood of attending graduate school. This is an interval variable.

b. The independent variable is the amount of coursework completed within the major. If this is measured as number of credit hours, this would be an interval/ratio variable.

c. This research design will not have cells because there are no discrete levels of either of our variables.

d. The accompanying table summarizes the variables.

	NAME OF VARIABLE	TYPE	NUMBER OF LEVELS	NAMES OF LEVELS
Independent variable	Amount of coursework completed	Interval		
Dependent variable	Likelihood of attending graduate school	Interval		

e. We would calculate a Pearson correlation coefficient because we have two variables that are measured on interval scales (category 1 research) and our research question has to do with association rather than prediction.

f. Causal interpretations are warranted only when participants have been randomly assigned to conditions. We cannot randomly assign students to have completed different levels of coursework, so we cannot infer that taking more coursework causes one's interest in graduate school to decrease. As a student is taking more coursework, that student is maturing in a number of ways. It may be that as time passes—a variable correlated with both completing more coursework and maturation in adolescent students—students learn about other career options that are open to them with a bachelor's degree.

15.7 CHOICE OF STATISTICAL TEST AND CONSUMER SURVEYS

a. The dependent variable is how much people indicate they would spend on a flat-screen TV. This is an interval variable.

b. The independent variable is gender, and its levels are men and women.

c. This research design will have cells because our independent variable is a nominal variable that has discrete levels. The study will have two cells, and these cells would include the means of participants' scores. The accompanying table shows the cells.

Men	Women

d. The accompanying table summarizes the variables.

	NAME OF VARIABLE	TYPE	NUMBER OF LEVELS	NAMES OF LEVELS
Independent variable	Gender	Nominal	Two	1. Women 2. Men
Dependent variable	Amount willing to spend	Interval		

e. The statistical test used to analyze these data would be an independent-samples t test. Because we have a nominal independent variable and an interval dependent variable (category 1 research) and because we have two independent samples (given that the men and women are not from the same households), we would use the independent-samples t test.

f. The sample is not a random sample of all adults because it is limited to those who have landlines and those who were willing to take the time to respond to the phone survey. This group might not be representative of other adults (e.g., people who do not have landlines or people who do but are unwilling to participate in the survey).

15.9 STATISTICAL TESTS—A SNAPSHOT OF STUDIES REPORTED IN THE *NEW YORK TIMES*, PART I

a. It is likely that the researchers conducted a chi-square test for independence, for their two research questions. First, did the number of people diagnosed with lung cancer (144) with the CT screening differ from the number of people diagnosed who did not have the CT screening? In this case there are two nominal independent variables, whether a smoker had the screening (levels: screened, not screened) and whether a smoker were diagnosed with lung cancer (levels: diagnosis, no diagnosis). The cells contain counts of people, not mean scores. Second, was the number who died from lung cancer different in the group that was screened than in the group that was not screened? This again would require a chi-square test for independence because there are two nominal variables, whether one had the screening and whether one died or lived. The cells again would contain counts of people.

b. It is possible that the researcher conducted a one-way between-groups ANOVA. The independent variable, type of medical error (levels: no error, poor penmanship, careless listening, bad arithmetic), is nominal and the dependent variable, dosage, is interval/ratio.

c. The researchers may have used a two-way between-groups ANOVA. There are two independent variables manipulated between groups: (1) presence of antioxidants (present, not present) and (2) athletic ability (elite, nonelite). The dependent variable is an interval/ratio variable.

d. The researchers may have used an independent-samples t test. The independent variable is the year during which response time was measured (2002 or 2003). The dependent variable is response time, which is an interval/ratio variable. The patients would be different in each of these years—two independent groups.

e. The researchers likely used an independent-samples t test. The independent variable is age of the pilot (young or old) and the dependent variable is an assessment of the level of improvement in a pilot's ability to avoid traffic, which may have been measured on an interval scale.

15.11 STATISTICS IN THE NEWS AND AN INTERACTION

a. The study described in Exercise 15.9(c) reports an interaction. An interaction occurs whenever the effect of one independent variable depends on the level of the other independent variable. In this case, the effect of taking vitamin E depends on whether a person is an elite athlete or not. For elite athletes, it has no effect. For nonelite athletes, it improves muscle recovery.

b. The accompanying graph is one possibility.

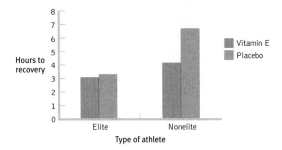

c. A two-way ANOVA uncovers an interaction because it allows us to look at two independent variables simultaneously. More specifically, it takes into account any variability among the group means after the main effects have been taken into account.

15.13 DESIGNING A STUDY AND RED LIPSTICK, PART II

a. Using a one-way ANOVA, we could have a nominal independent variable of lipstick color with several levels (e.g., red, mauve, pink, or even a control group of no lipstick). We would then need to choose an interval/ratio dependent variable such as the number of seconds the woman smiled during a three-minute period.

b. Using a two-way between-groups ANOVA, we would need to introduce a second independent variable. Our first independent variable could be that described in part (a), the color of lipstick worn. We could introduce a second nominal independent variable such as environment: social setting (e.g., party) versus academic setting (e.g., classroom). Our dependent variable, an interval variable, could be the same as that introduced in part (a): the number of seconds the woman smiled during a three-minute period.

15.15 WRITING A RESULTS SECTION AND MISMATCHED TEAMS

Answers may vary. Here is one possible Results section: "A z test comparing the point spread of Division I-AA teams to that of the population of Division I games ($\mu = 16.189$) revealed that the point spread of Division I-AA teams was not significantly different from that of Division I-A teams,

$z = -1.23$, $p > 0.05$, $d = 0.61$, a large effect. The 95% confidence interval around the mean spread ($M = 8.75$) for the Division I-AA teams is (-3.14, 20.64). (*Note:* The fact that a large effect is not statistically significant is an indication that our statistical power is very low. It would be wise to replicate this study with a larger sample.)"

15.17 WRITING A RESULTS SECTION AND CLOWN THERAPY

Answers may vary. Here is one possible Results section: "A chi-square test for independence was used to determine whether pregnancy after in vitro fertilization (got pregnant, did not get pregnant) varied with whether a woman received clown entertainment (clown, no clown). The chi-square test for independence revealed that pregnancy did vary with clown entertainment, $\chi^2(1) = 6.08$, $p < 0.05$, Cramer's $V = 0.18$. Of the women who were entertained by the clown, 35.5% got pregnant. Of the women who were not entertained by the clown, only 19.4% got pregnant. Women entertained by the clown were 1.8 more times as likely to get pregnant than women not entertained by the clown."

15.19 EXCERPT FROM A RESULTS SECTION

a. The independent variables are whether a person has schizophrenia (present, absent) and the type of material to be remembered (verbal, nonverbal).

b. The dependent variable is accuracy on the working memory tasks.

c. The researchers conducted a mixed two-way ANOVA, with the factor of schizophrenia manipulated between groups and the factor of type of material manipulated within groups.

d. The two main effects are significant. We know this because the authors both explicitly state that they were significant and provide the p levels associated with the F statistic for both of the main effects. Because both p levels are less than 0.05, we know both effects are significant.

e. The interaction is not significant. We know this because the authors both explicitly state that the interaction was not significant and provide the p level associated with the F statistic for the interaction. Because this p level is greater than 0.05, we know the interaction is not significant.

f. The authors might also include a measure of effect size (R^2) for each of the main effects in the ANOVA.

■ **DIGGING DEEPER INTO THE DATA**

15.21 EXCERPT FROM A RESULTS SECTION— MANOVA

a. The researchers used a MANOVA because they had multiple dependent variables.

b. For cross-sex friendships the measures of intimacy, trust, and relational satisfaction were greater for older friendships than for younger friendships. There was not a pronounced difference in the quality of same-sex and cross-sex friendships for the younger friendships versus the older friendships. The statistics listed behind each significant measure make it apparent on which of the dependent variables in the MANOVA the researchers found significant effects.

c. The authors should have included effect sizes (R^2) for each of the significant effects and the Pearson correlation coefficients for the correlations between the dependent variables.

ANSWERS TO CHECK YOUR LEARNING PROBLEMS

CHAPTER 1

1-1 **a.** 100 selected students

b. 12,500 students at the university

c. 100 students have an average score of 18, a moderately high stress level.

d. The whole population of students at this university have a moderately high stress level, on average. The sample mean, 18 is an estimate of the unknown population mean.

1-2 **a.** The levels of gender, male and female, have no numerical meaning even if they are arbitrarily labeled 1 and 2

b. The three levels of hair length (short, mid-length, and long) are arranged in order, but we do not know the magnitude of the differences in length.

c. The distances between probability scores are assumed to be equal.

1-3 **a.** Whether or not a student declared a major

b. Declared a major; did not declare a major

c. Anxiety score

d. The scores would be consistent over time unless a student's anxiety level changed.

e. The anxiety scale was actually measuring anxiety.

1-4 For (ii), there are several possible answers other than the ones given here.

a. **i.** Deaths as ascertained in household from an interview

ii. Hospital or morgue death rates

b. **i.** Distance from well

ii. Cups of well water consumed

1-5 **a.** Researchers could randomly assign a certain number of women to be told that there was a gender difference on this test and randomly assign a certain number of other women to be told that there was no gender difference on this test.

b. If researchers did not use random assignment, any gender differences might be due to confounding variables. The women in the two groups might be different in some way (e.g., in math ability, or belief in stereotypes) to begin with.

c. There are many possible confounds. Women who already believed the stereotype might do so because they had always performed poorly in mathematics, whereas those who did not believe the stereotype might be those who always did particularly well in math. Women who believed the stereotype might be those who were discouraged from studying math because "girls can't do math," whereas those who did not believe the stereotype might be those who were encouraged to study math because "girls are just as good as boys in math."

d. Researchers would not want participants to be aware of the two conditions in the study, because they might guess the hypothesis and respond accordingly. In addition, it is best if the researchers themselves do not know to which group the women have been assigned because they might inadvertently discourage those in the "stereotype" group and encourage those in the "no-stereotype" group.

e. Researchers could have two math tests that are similar in difficulty. All women would take the first test after being told that women tend not to do as well as men on this test. After taking that test, they would be given the second test after being told that women tend to do as well as men on this test.

f. The participants might do better on the second test merely because they've practiced by taking the first or they might do worse due to fatigue.

g. Counterbalancing would reduce order effects. Half the women would take test 1 first, and half would take test 2 first. (Even better, the two sets of instructions as well as the tests themselves would be counterbalanced.)

1-6 a. Archival research; because the professor used existing data (class records)

b. Archival research; because the pharmacist is using existing data (the pharmacy's call logs)

c. Outlier research; because the researcher is examining the few cases that differ from the majority (those who did not conform to intense peer pressure)

d. Outlier research; because the researcher is examining the few cases that differ from the majority (those whose seizures worsened following surgery)

CHAPTER 2

2-1 a. Grouped frequency table:

INTERVALS	FREQUENCIES
50–59	2
40–49	1
30–39	1
20–29	2
10–19	4
0–9	7

b. Histogram:

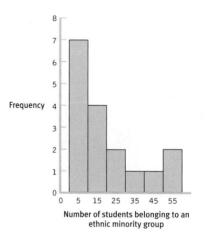

c. Frequency polygon:

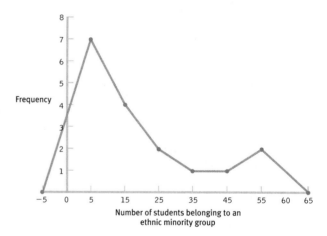

d. We can now get a sense of the overall pattern of the data.

e. Percentages might be more useful because they allow us to compare programs. Two programs might have the same numbers of minority students, but if one program has far more students overall, it is less diverse than the one with fewer students overall.

f. It is possible that schools did not provide data if they had no or few minority students. Thus, this data set might be composed of the schools with more diverse student bodies. This is a volunteer sample; schools are not obligated to report these data to petersons.com.

2-2 a. $M = \dfrac{\sum X}{N}$ $= (1 + 0 + 1 + 2 + 5 \ldots +$
$4 + 6)/20 = 50/20 = 2.50$

b. In this case, the scores would comprise a sample taken from the whole population, and this mean would be a statistic. The symbol, therefore, would be either M or $\overline{X}$.

c. In this case, the scores would constitute the entire population of interest, and the mean would be a parameter. Thus, the symbol would be μ.

d. We would arrange the scores in order: 0, 0, 1, 1, 1, 1, 2, 2, 2, 2, 2, 2, 3, 3, 3, 3, 4, 5, 6, 7. We would then divide the total number of scores, 20, by 2, and add $1/2$. This would give us 10.5. The median, therefore, is the mean of the 10th and 11th scores. Both of these scores are 2; therefore, the median is 2.

e. The mode is the most common score—in this case, there are six 2's, so the mode is 2.

f. The mean is a little higher than the median. This indicates that there are potential outliers pulling the mean higher; outliers would not affect the median.

2-3 a. range $= X_{highest} - X_{lowest} = 1460 - 450 = 1010$

b. We do not know whether scores cluster at some point in the distribution—for example, near one end of the distribution—or whether the scores are more evenly spread out.

c. The formula for variance is $SD^2 = \dfrac{\Sigma(X - M)^2}{N}$. The first step is to calculate the mean, which is 927.50. We then create three columns: one for the scores, one for the deviations of the scores from the mean, and one for the squares of the deviations.

X	$X - M$	$(X - M)^2$
450	-477.5	228,006.25
670	-257.5	66,306.25
1130	202.5	41,006.25
1460	532.5	283,556.25

We can now calculate variance: $SD^2 = \dfrac{\Sigma(X - M)^2}{N} = (228,006.25 + 66,306.25 + 41,006.25 + 283,556.25)/4 = 618,875/4 = 154,718.75$.

d. Standard deviation is calculated just like we calculated variance, but we then take the square root. $SD = \sqrt{\dfrac{\Sigma(X - M)^2}{N}} = \sqrt{154,718.75} = 393.34$.

e. If the researcher were interested only in these four students, these scores would represent the entire population of interest, and the variance and standard deviation would be parameters. Therefore, the symbols would be σ^2 and σ, respectively.

f. If the researcher hoped to generalize from these four students to all students at the university, these scores would represent a sample, and the variance and standard deviation would be statistics. Therefore, the symbols would be SD^2, s^2, or MS for variance and SD or s for standard deviation.

2-4 a. There is more than one possible answer. If we imagine a very popular restaurant where most people have reservations but a few walk in and choose to wait a long time, the distribution would be positively skewed. But if we imagine a very popular restaurant that does not take reservations, most people have to wait a long time, but a few who have perfect timing get seated very quickly; in this case, the distribution would be negatively skewed.

b. There is more than one possible answer. If some people rarely take public transportation—say, just to go out at night or on the weekend—there would likely a "hump" around those people. But if others take it frequently—say, to commute to work—there would be a second "hump" around those people. In this case, the distribution would be bimodal.

c. The income of high school teachers is probably not very variable, so the distribution would likely be leptokurtic.

2-5 a. First, we arrange the data in order: 1, 1, 1, 2, 2, 2, 2, 3, 3, 3, 3, 3, 3, 4, 4, 5, 6, 7, 7, 8, and 12. Then we'll calculate the median. There are 21 scores; 21 divided by 2 plus $1/2$ equals 11. The median is the 11th score, which is 3.

Next, we take the 10 scores below the median—1, 1, 1, 2, 2, 2, 2, 3, 3, and 3—and calculate their median: 2. This is $Q1$. Then we take the 10 scores above the median and calculate their median: 5.5. This is $Q3$. $IQR = Q3 - Q1 = 5.5 - 2 = 3.5$, and $IQR \times 1.5 = 5.25$.

We now subtract 5.25 from $Q1$ and add it to $Q3$ to get the bounds of what might be potential outliers: $Q1 - 5.25 = 2 - 5.25 = -3.25$. There cannot be data below 0, so the lower bound is technically 0. $Q3 + 5.25 = 5.5 + 5.25 = 10.75$. The bounds, therefore, are 0 and 10.75. Anything beyond these scores is a potential outlier. Only one score, 12, is a potential outlier.

b. i. In either group, blue-collar or white-collar, there might be families who are outliers—families who have a very large number of books in their homes. However, this might be particularly true of the white-collar families. The mean of the white-collar families would be inflated by these extreme outliers. Because medians would not be affected by outliers, they would be better measures of central tendency in these circumstances.

ii. It would be interesting to study whether one group were more variable than the other. We might expect the white-collar families to have more variability, with some using their higher levels of income to buy many books. Alternatively, we might expect the blue-collar families to be more variable: perhaps white-collar families have many more books than blue-collar families but all have roughly the same number of books, whereas blue-collar families are more spread out, with a few spending a great deal of discretionary income on books.

CHAPTER 3

3-1 The graph on the left is misleading. It shows a sharp decline in Connecticut annual traffic deaths from 1955 to 1956, but we cannot draw valid conclusions from just two data points. The graph on the right is a more accurate and complete depiction of the data. It includes nine, rather than two, data points and suggests that the sharp one-year decline is the beginning of a clear downward trend in traffic fatalities that extends through 1959. It also shows that there had been previous one-year declines of similar magnitude—from 1951–1952 and from 1953–1954. The graph on the right is a more accurate depiction of the data.

3-2 **a.** A scatterplot is the best graph choice to depict the relation between two interval variables such as depression and stress.

b. A time plot, or time series plot, is the best graph choice to depict the change in an interval variable, such as number of fatalities, over time.

c. For one interval/ratio variable, such as number of siblings, the best graph choice would be either a frequency histogram or frequency polygon.

d. In this case, there is a nominal variable, region of the United States, and an interval/ratio variable, years of education. The best choice would be a bar graph, with one bar depicting the mean years of education for each region. A Pareto

chart would arrange the bars from highest to lowest, allowing for easier comparisons.

e. Calories and hours are both interval/ratio variables, and the question is about prediction rather than relation. In this case, we'd calculate and graph a line of best fit.

3-3 The accompanying graph improves on the chartjunk graph in several ways. First, it has a clear, specific caption. Second, all axes are labeled left to right. Third, there are no abbreviations. The units of measurement, IQ and hours of sunlight per day, are included. The *y*-axis has 0 as its minimum, the colors are simple and muted, and all chartjunk has been eliminated. This graph wasn't as much fun to create, but it offers a far clearer presentation of the data! (*Note:* we are treating ours as a nominal variable.)

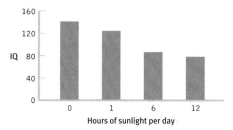

The Effect of Sunlight on IQ Scores

3-4 **a.** The interpolation lie. We see only three data points in this time plot. It is possible that there was a decrease (after adjusting for inflation) between 1950 and 1975 or between 1975 and 2000.

b. The false face validity lie. Statistics grades may correlate somewhat with intelligence scores, but statistics tests do not measure intelligence.

c. The extrapolation lie. There may have been a decrease in job openings over the past 10 years, but that doesn't guarantee the decrease will continue.

d. The biased scale lie. Students are offered only three choices: never, rarely, and always. What about something in between rarely and always, like often? (This also could fall under the limited range lie, although the range is not limited by its minimum and maximum—just the options in between.)

e. The sneaky sample lie. The students who choose to complete the online survey might not be representative of the overall student body. For one thing, they are choosing to shop at the bookstore and so might provide more favorable responses.

f. There are several possible lies here! The false face validity lie: Does receiving a punishment, perhaps for verbal aggression, indicate a girl is violent? The extrapolation lie: We don't know any data points beyond these two years. The false impression lie: Just because the school is now cracking down on offenses doesn't mean that the offenses were not there in the past.

3-5 a. The mean for the "computer" group is 19.20, and the mean for the "by-hand" group is 17.47. The "by-hand" group seems to be faster than the "computer" group (i.e., shorter time to completion).

b. The five-number summaries:

	MIN	Q1	MDN	Q3	MAX
Computer	11	12	15	17	84
By hand	14	15	17	19	24

c. The box plot shows us that the median for the "computer" group is lower than the median for the "by-hand" group. There is an extreme outlier (the 10 above the outlier indicates the sample size) that influences the mean but not the median.

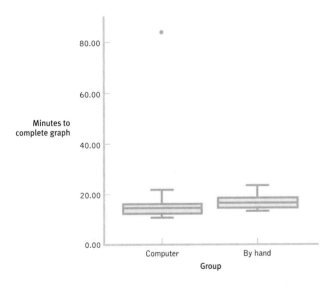

d. *Computer*: $IQR = 17 - 12 = 5$; $IQR \times 1.5 = 5(1.5) = 7.5$; $Q1 - 7.5 = 12 - 7.5 = 4.5$; $Q3 + 7.5 = 17 + 7.5 = 24.5$; based on this criterion, there is one potential outlier, 84, in the computer group.

By hand: $IQR = 19 - 15 = 4$; $IQR \times 1.5 = 4(1.5) = 6$; $Q1 - 6 = 15 - 6 = 9$; $Q3 + 6 = 19 + 6 = 25$; based on this criterion, there are no potential outliers.

e. The "computer" group, overall, now appears to construct their graphs more quickly than does the "by-hand" group.

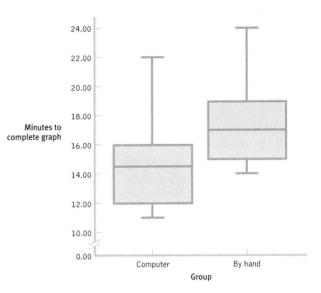

CHAPTER 4

4-1 a. The likely population is all patients who will undergo surgery; the researcher would not be able to access this population, and therefore random selection could not be used. Random assignment, however, could be used. The psychologist could randomly assign half of the patients to counseling and half to a control group.

b. The population is all children in this school system; the psychologist could identify all of these children and thus could use random selection. The psychologist also could use random assignment. She could randomly assign half the children to one kind of textbook and half to the other.

c. The population is 2006 Olympic athletes. Because all of these athletes could be identified, random selection could be used. Random assignment, however, could not be used. It would not be possible to assign athletes to be from a Western or Eastern country.

d. The population is people diagnosed as HIV-positive; because the researcher could not identify all people who are HIV-positive, he could not use random selection. He could, however, use random assignment. Patients in the sample could be assigned either to receive a beeper or not to receive a beeper.

e. The population is patients in therapy; because the whole population could not be identified, random selection could not be used. Moreover, random assignment could not be used. It is not possible to assign people to either have or not have a diagnosed personality disorder.

4-2 a. Given that the population is high school students in Marseille and in Lyons, it is possible that the researcher can compile a list of all members of the population, allowing her to use random selection. She could not, however, use random assignment because she could not assign the students to have lived in Marseille or Lyons.

b. The population in this study is much larger than that in the previous study comparing Marseille and Lyons. It is not likely that the researcher can identify all members of the population so as to be able to use random selection. He can, however, use random assignment. Members of the affected communities who are recruited to participate can be assigned to either a job skills program or a control group without such a program.

4-3 a. Spectacular plane crashes are far more likely to be front-page news than are typically less spectacular car crashes. An illusory correlation between flying and crashes is perceived, and someone might then pay more attention to plane crashes than to car crashes, thus confirming this belief.

b. Someone might have observed an illusory correlation of caring female nurses and less caring male nurses (or, more likely, had a preconceived gender bias) and then looked for evidence to confirm this belief. Given that there are currently more female than male nurses (a demographic that is rapidly changing), it might be easier to find examples of caring female nurses than caring male nurses.

c. Although dog attacks are more common, they don't get the attention that shark attacks do. The media help us to confirm this belief by providing us with more evidence, albeit neither statistical nor objective, of shark attacks.

d. Someone might have known of cases in which a depressed person was abused as a child, thus perceiving an illusory correlation. An ensuing confirmation bias might lead to ongoing attention to other such cases and a lack of attention to depression cases without such a history.

e. Someone who is prejudiced against gay men might readily notice gay men who present themselves in a sexualized manner, while failing to notice gay men who do not present in

this way. Moreover, it is possible that such a person might perceive any man who presents in a sexualized manner as gay, regardless of his actual sexual orientation—confirmation bias at work. Or this person might be overly aware of the behavior of someone he knows to be gay—perceiving a number of behaviors as sexualized in a gay man that he would not perceive as sexualized in a straight man.

4-4 a. In the short run, we might see a wide range of numbers of successes. It would not be surprising to have several in a row or none in a row. In the short run, our observations seem almost like chaos.

b. Given the assumptions listed for this problem, in the long run, we'd expect 0.50, or 50%, to be women, although there will likely be strings of men and of women along the way.

c. This is an example of the gambler's fallacy. If each trial is independent, each trial has no memory of the outcome of the last. The next ATM user is as likely to be a man as a woman.

4-5 a. The null hypothesis is that a decrease in temperature does not affect academic performance (or does not decrease academic performance).

b. The research hypothesis is that a decrease in temperature does affect academic performance (or decreases academic performance).

c. The researchers would reject the null hypothesis.

d. The researchers would fail to reject the null hypothesis.

4-6 a. This may be a Type I error. A Type I error occurs when the null hypothesis is rejected but is really true. If the virtual-reality glasses really don't have any effect.

b. This may be a Type II error. A Type II error occurs when the researchers fail to reject the null hypothesis, but the null hypothesis is not true. If the research hypothesis is true, the virtual-reality glasses really do have an effect.

4-7 a. Testimonials are often more persuasive than empirical evidence and objective data. The pedigree, the publishers hope, establishes the testimonial writer's expertise in the field, rendering him more believable.

b. Ideally, the publishing company would offer empirical evidence that this book is more entertaining, or more educational, than other books on statistics. The best circumstance would involve a true experiment in which readers were assigned to read this text or another. To the knowledge of these authors, no publishing company has ever conducted such a true experiment.

c. Even if you tend to agree with the authors on many counts, their report constitutes merely another testimonial from statistics geeks. Why should you rely on them for suggestions of what books might entertain you? (However, it really is good!)

d. We could randomly assign students to read and study a chapter with or without anecdotes. Then, we could test both groups immediately and two weeks later on the content of the chapters.

4-8 a. Because findings are typically published only when the null hypothesis is rejected, a certain number of reported findings are bound to be Type I errors. In fact, some researchers estimate that almost 50% of reported findings are Type I errors. Given that a rigorously designed experiment did not support the efficacy of echinacea, it is likely that earlier, less well-designed studies reported Type I errors.

b. It is likely that the researchers used random assignment; that is, participants were equally likely to receive Echinacea or an alternative. That alternative was likely to have been a placebo, a drug that looked just liked echinacea, but without the active ingredients. Finally, it is likely that this study used a double-blind design; that is, neither the participants nor the experimenters knew to what condition the participants had been assigned.

c. Confirmation bias would lead strong believers in the powers of echinacea to attend to studies that supported its efficacy and ignore those that did not. Echinacea proponents might find a way to discredit this study despite its careful design.

CHAPTER 5

5-1 a. $z = \dfrac{(X - \mu)}{\sigma} = \dfrac{(4.2 - 3.51)}{0.61} = 1.13$;

this answer makes sense because the score is above the mean of 3.51 and the z score is positive.

b. $z = \dfrac{(X - \mu)}{\sigma} = \dfrac{(3.0 - 3.51)}{0.61} = -0.84$; this answer makes sense because the score is below the mean of 3.51 and the z score is negative.

c. The mean always has a z score of 0. The mean for this distribution is 3.51, so if you had a z score of 0, your CFC score would be 3.51.

5-2 The scatterplot:

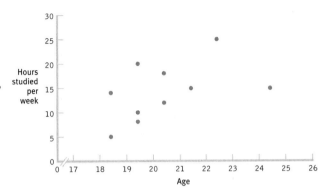

The correlation coefficient, based on the calculations in the accompanying table, is: $r = \dfrac{\sum[(z_X)(z_Y)]}{N} = \dfrac{4.907}{10} = 0.49$. The absence of a sign indicates that this is a positive correlation. Higher ages tend to be associated with longer hours spent studying, and lower ages tend to be associated with fewer hours spent studying. This is what we would expect given that pairs of scores for each student tend to be either both above the mean or both below the mean.

STUDENT	AGE (X)	HOURS (Y)	z_X	z_Y	$(z_X)(z_Y)$
1	19	5	−1.118	−1.648	1.843
2	20	20	−0.559	1.039	−0.581
3	20	8	−0.559	−1.111	0.621
4	21	12	0.000	−0.394	0.000
5	21	18	0.000	0.681	0.000
6	23	25	1.118	1.935	2.163
7	22	15	0.559	0.143	0.080
8	20	10	−0.559	−0.752	0.421
9	19	14	−1.118	−0.036	0.401
10	25	15	2.236	0.143	0.320

5-3 a. It is possible that training while listening to music (A) causes an increase in a country's average finishing time (B), perhaps because music decreases one's focus on running. It also is possible that high average finishing times (B) cause an increase in the percentage of marathon runners in a country who train while listening to music (A), perhaps because slow runners tend to get bored and need music to get through their runs. It also is possible that a third variable, such as a country's level of wealth (C), causes a higher percentage of runners who train while listening to music (because of the higher presence of technology in wealthy countries) (A) and also causes higher (slower) finishing times (perhaps because long-distance running is a less popular sport in wealthy countries with access to so many sport and entertainment options) (B). Without a true experiment, we cannot know the direction of causality.

b. We are looking only at marathoners. The correlation coefficient might be different from the one we would calculate if we included all runners, no matter their usual distance.

c. If there were one country with an extremely high percentage of training while listening to music, but also really low (fast) finishing times, this country's data point might decrease the positive correlation or even reverse it.

5-4 a. The psychometrician could assess test–retest reliability by administering the quiz to 100 heterosexual female readers and then one week later readministering the test to the same 100 female readers. If their scores at the two times are highly correlated, the test would have high test–retest reliability. She also could calculate a coefficient alpha using computer software. The computer would essentially calculate correlations for every possible two groups of five items and then would calculate the average of all of these split-half correlations.

b. The psychometrician could assess criterion-related validity by choosing criteria that she believed assessed the underlying construct of interest, a boyfriend's devotion to his girlfriend. There are many possible criteria. Postdictive validity could be examined by correlating the measure with the amount of money each participant's boyfriend spent on her last birthday. Concurrent validity could be examined by correlating the measure with the number of minutes the participant spent on the phone with her boyfriend today. Predictive validity could be examined by correlating the measure with the number of months the relationship ends up lasting.

c. Of course, we assume that these other measures actually assess the underlying construct of a boyfriend's devotion, which may or may not be true! For example, the amount of money that the boyfriend spent on the participant's last birthday might be a measure of his income, not his devotion.

5-5 a. The correlation coefficient is 0.372. Percentage of homework completed and extra credit earned are positively correlated. Those who complete a higher percentage of homework tend to earn more extra credit, whereas those who complete a lower percentage of homework tend to earn less extra credit.

b. The correlation coefficient is 0.621. Mean exam grade and extra credit earned are positively correlated. Those who achieve higher mean exam grades tend to earn more extra credit, whereas those who achieve lower mean exam grades tend to earn less extra credit.

c. Even when controlling for the third variable of percentage of homework completed, extra credit earned and mean exam grade are strongly positively associated, with a partial correlation coefficient of 0.539. Earning extra credit is associated with mean exam grade, independent of completion of homework.

CHAPTER 6

6-1 First, we'll calculate what we would predict for Y when X equals 0; that number, -17.908, is our intercept.

$$z_X = \frac{(X - M_X)}{SD_X} = \frac{(0 - 21)}{1.789} = -11.738$$

$$z_{\hat{Y}} = (r_{XY})(z_X) = (0.49)(-11.738) = -5.752$$

$$\hat{Y} = z_{\hat{Y}}(SD_Y) + M_Y = -5.752(5.582) + 14.2 = -17.908$$

Note that the reason this prediction is negative (it doesn't make sense to have a negative number of hours) is that the number for age, 0, is not a number that would actually be used in this situation—it's another example of the dangers of extrapolation, but it still is necessary to determine our regression equation.

Then we'll calculate what we would predict for Y when X equals 1: the amount that that number, -16.378, differs from the prediction when X equals 0 is the slope.

$$z_X = \frac{(X - M_X)}{SD_X} = \frac{(1 - 21)}{1.789} = -11.739$$

$$z_{\hat{Y}} = (r_{XY})(z_X) = (0.49)(-11.179) = -5.478$$

$$\hat{Y} = z_{\hat{Y}}(SD_Y) + M_Y = -5.478(5.582) + 14.2 = -16.378$$

When X equals 0, -17.908 is the prediction for Y. When X equals 1, -16.378 is the prediction for Y. The latter number is 1.530 higher $[-16.378 - (-17.908) = 1.530]$—that is, more positive—than the former. Remember when you're calculating the difference to consider whether the prediction for Y was more positive or more negative when X increased from 0 to 1.

Thus, the regression equation is:
$\hat{Y} = -17.91 + 1.53(X)$

6-2 Tell Coach Parcells that prediction suffers from the same limitations as correlation. First, just because two variables are associated doesn't mean one causes the other. This is not a true experiment, and if we didn't randomly assign athletes to appear on a *Sports Illustrated* cover or not, then we cannot determine if a cover appearance causes sporting failure. Moreover, we have a limited range; by definition, those lauded on the cover are the best in sports. Would the association be different among those with a wider range of athletic ability? Finally, and most important, there is the very strong possibility of regression to the mean. Those chosen for a cover appearance are at the very top of their game. There is nowhere to go but down, so it is not surprising that those who merit a cover appearance would soon thereafter experience a decline. There's likely no need to avoid that cover, Coach.

6-3 a. $\hat{Y} = 2.695 + 0.069(X_1) + 0.015(X_2) - 0.072(X_3)$

b. $\hat{Y} = 2.695 + 0.069(6) + 0.015(20) - 0.072(4) = 3.121$

c. The negative sign in the slope (-0.072) tells us that those with higher levels of admiration for Pamela Anderson tend to have lower GPAs, and those with lower levels of admiration for Pamela Anderson tend to have higher GPAs.

6-4 a. Student success might be predicted by the latent, or invisible, variables of intelligence, motivation, and effort.

b. The latent variable of intelligence might be represented by the manifest variables of SAT score, GPA, and IQ score. The latent variable of motivation might be represented by the manifest variables of one's score on the Consideration of Future Consequences (CFC) scale, a measure of parental pressure to do well, and a measure of desire to pursue higher education. The latent variable of effort might be represented by the manifest variables of class attendance, hours spent studying, and percentage of homework problems completed.

c. Student success might be represented by the manifest variable of GPA at graduation or, later in life, by income, hours spent contributing to society (e.g., community service), or, in the school's self-interest, alumni donations.

d.

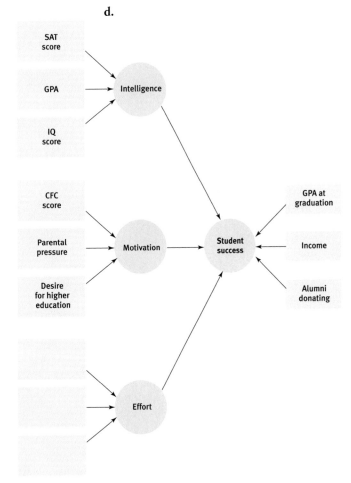

CHAPTER 7

7-1 a. Histogram for five students:

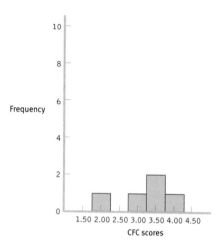

b. Histogram for 30 students:

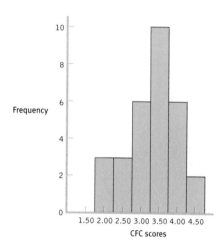

c. The shape of the distribution becomes more normal as the size of the sample increases (although the larger sample appears to be somewhat negatively skewed).

7-2 a. $z = \dfrac{(X - \mu)}{\sigma} = \dfrac{(2.3 - 3.51)}{0.61} = -1.98$; this score is in the bottom 50%. We see that 34% fall between the mean and one z score below the mean, and 14% fall between one z score and two z scores from the mean. So $34 + 14 = 48\%$ of scores fall between the mean and two z scores below the mean. So $50 - 48 = 2\%$ of scores fall below this z score.

b. $z = \dfrac{(X - \mu)}{\sigma} = \dfrac{(4.7 - 3.51)}{0.61} = 1.95$; this score is in the upper 50%. We see that 34% fall between the mean and one z score above the mean, and 14% fall between one z score and two z scores from the mean. So $34 + 14 = 48\%$ of scores fall between the mean and two z scores above the mean. And another 50% fall below the mean. So $50 + 48 = 98\%$ of scores fall below this z score.

c. A percentile rank of 84% (50% below the mean + 34% between the mean and a z score of 1) corresponds to z score of about 1.0.

d. $X = z(\sigma) + \mu = 1(0.61) + 3.51 = 4.12$; this answer makes sense because the z score is positive and the raw score is above the mean. More specifically, the raw score is 1 standard deviation above the mean.

7-3 a. The scores range from 2.0 to 4.5.

b. The means are 3.4 for the first row, 3.4 for the second row, and 3.15 for the third row [e.g., for the first row, $M = (3.5 + 3.5 + 3.0 + 4.0 + 2.0 + 4.0 + 2.0 + 4.0 + 3.5 + 4.5)/10 = 3.4$]. These three means range from 3.15 to 3.40.

c. The range is smaller for the means of samples of 10 scores than for the individual scores because the more extreme scores will be balanced by lower scores when samples of 10 are taken. Individual scores are not attenuated in that way.

d. The mean of the distribution of means will be the same as the mean of the individual scores: $\mu_M = \mu = 3.32$. The standard error will be smaller than the standard deviation; we must divide by the square root of the sample size of 10: $\sigma_M = \dfrac{\sigma}{\sqrt{N}} = \dfrac{0.69}{\sqrt{10}} = 0.22$.

7-4 a. It would not make sense because we would be comparing a mean to a distribution of scores. Because the distribution of scores would include some extreme scores, it would have a larger spread. The distribution of means includes sample means; within a given sample, the occasional extreme score is balanced by less extreme scores, and so the overall distribution has a smaller spread. Means are less likely to be extreme than are scores. A sample mean, therefore, is unlikely to appear extreme when compared to the wider range of scores.

b. The null hypothesis would predict that the videos do not change CFC scores; the research hypothesis would predict that the videos do change CFC scores.

c. $\mu_M = \mu = 3.51$

$$\sigma_M = \frac{\sigma}{\sqrt{N}} = \frac{0.61}{\sqrt{40}} = 0.096$$

d. $z = \frac{(M - \mu_M)}{\sigma_M} = \frac{(3.62 - 3.51)}{0.096} = 1.15$

e. This sample mean is about 1 standard deviation above the mean, and we know that about 34% of a distribution falls between the mean and 1 standard deviation above the mean (i.e., a z statistic of 1). We also know that 50% fall below the mean, because the z distribution is symmetric. The percentile would be about $50 + 34 = 84\%$.

7-5 a. The median is 67.

b. The distribution is not bell-shaped. If the score of 99 did not exist, the curve would be negatively skewed. Most scores are in the 60s, with a few trailing out toward the 40s and 30s.

c. We might suspect the student with the score of 99. She or he is well above the median. There is a large gap between that student's score and the next highest score, 72.

d. No; it is possible that this student really did perform much better than her or his classmates.

e. The student may be particularly intelligent. She or he may have studied much more than all of the other students. She or he may be a graduate student in a class of undergraduates. There are many more possible explanations, as well.

f. Given that the student who earned a 99 is an outlier, it may not be fair for the professor to give that student an A, and then the next-highest student a C, and then all others a D or below. Without that outlier, a number of students did well relative to their classmates.

CHAPTER 8

8-1 a. $\mu_M = \mu = 156.8$

$$\sigma_M = \frac{\sigma}{\sqrt{N}} = \frac{14.6}{\sqrt{36}} = 2.433$$

$$z = \frac{(M - \mu_M)}{\sigma_M} = \frac{(164.6 - 156.8)}{2.433} = 3.21$$

50% below the mean; 49.9% above the mean; $50 + 49.9 = 99.9$th percentile

b. $100 - 99.9 = 0.1\%$ of samples of this size scored higher than the students at Baylor.

c. We would want to know how Baylor selected the students in its sample. For instance, do all Baylor psychology majors take the test? If not, how are those who take the test different from those who do not?

8-2 a. (1) The dependent variable, diagnosis (correct vs. incorrect) is nominal, not interval, so this assumption is not met. Based only on this, we should not proceed with a hypothesis test based on a z distribution. (2) The samples include only outpatients seen over two specific months and only those at one community mental health center. The sample is not randomly selected, so we must be cautious about generalizing from it. (3) The populations are not normally distributed because the dependent variable is nominal.

b. (1) The dependent variable, health score, is likely interval. (2) The data were randomly selected; all wild cats in zoos in North American had an equal chance of being selected for this study. (3) The data are not normally distributed; we are told that a few animals had very high scores, so the data are likely positively skewed. Moreover, there are fewer than 30 participants in this study. It probably is not a good idea to proceed with a hypothesis test based on a z distribution.

8-3 *Step 1:* Population 1 is all students in career discussion groups. Population 2 is all students who do participate in career discussion groups. The comparison distribution will be a distribution of means. The hypothesis test will be a z test because we have only one sample and we know the population mean and the standard deviation. This study meets two of the three assumptions and may meet the third. The dependent variable is interval. In addition, there are more than 30 participants in the sample, indicating that the comparison distribution will be normal. The data were not randomly selected, however, so we must be cautious when generalizing.

Step 2: The null hypothesis is that students who participate in career discussion groups have the same CFC scores, on average, as students who do not participate ($H_0: \mu_1 = \mu_2$). The research hypothesis is that students who participate in career discussion groups have different CFC scores, on average, from students who do not participate ($H_1: \mu_1 \neq \mu_2$).

Step 3:

$$\mu_M = \mu = 3.51; \sigma_M = \frac{\sigma}{\sqrt{N}} = \frac{0.61}{\sqrt{45}} = 0.091$$

Step 4: Our cutoff z statistics are -1.96 and 1.96.

Step 5: $z = \dfrac{(M - \mu_M)}{\sigma_M} = \dfrac{(3.7 - 3.51)}{0.091} = 2.09$

Step 6: Reject the null hypothesis. It appears that students who participate in career discussions have higher CFC scores, on average, than do students who do not participate.

8-4 (Numbered steps indicate steps in the z test.)

a. *Step 3:*

$\mu_M = \mu = 3.51$; $\sigma_M = \dfrac{\sigma}{\sqrt{N}} = \dfrac{0.61}{\sqrt{5}} = 0.273$

Step 5:

$z = \dfrac{(M - \mu_M)}{\sigma_M} = \dfrac{(3.7 - 3.51)}{0.273} = 0.696$

b. *Step 3:*

$\mu_M = \mu = 3.51$; $\sigma_M = \dfrac{\sigma}{\sqrt{N}} = \dfrac{0.61}{\sqrt{1000}} = 0.019$

Step 5:

$z = \dfrac{(M - \mu_M)}{\sigma_M} = \dfrac{(3.7 - 3.51)}{0.019} = 10.0$

c. *Step 3:*

$\mu_M = \mu = 3.51$; $\sigma_M = \dfrac{\sigma}{\sqrt{N}} = \dfrac{0.61}{\sqrt{1,000,000}}$

$= 0.0006$

Step 5:

$z = \dfrac{(M - \mu_M)}{\sigma_M} = \dfrac{(3.7 - 3.51)}{0.0006} = 316.667$

d. As sample size increases, the standard error decreases. This makes sense because means derived from larger samples would be less extreme—would have less spread. As standard error decreases, the test statistic becomes larger. A larger test statistic is more likely to fall in the tails of the distribution, beyond the cutoff values.

e. An identical difference between means might lead to different conclusions based on sample size. If the sample size is large enough, even a small difference can lead to a large test statistic. The larger the sample size, the larger the test statistic, and the easier it is to reject the null hypothesis. So a significant finding might be small and not practically important.

8-5 **a.** We cannot include data from these 3 participants in our analyses because we do not have their scores on the dependent variable. We would report this in the Methods section.

b. For the 2 participants who left one item blank, we have several choices, although we should make the choice *before* we collect our data. We could assign the participants the modal (or mean) score of all participants on that variable; we could assign the participants their own modal (or mean) score for all other items on the physical activity scale; or we could assign them a random number within the range of possible responses. Regardless of the technique that we used, we should report it in the Methods section.

c. For the 4 participants who left out all information about eating habits, we would not be able to conduct analyses with eating habits as a variable. When too many data points on a scale are missing, we would not want to fill them in with a mode, mean, or random number. We would conduct only analyses predicting blood sugar levels from physical activity. We would report this in the Methods section, and we would attempt to find a better measure of eating habits for future research.

d. Without 7 of the participants, we have only 10 participants in our study. We do not have a sufficient sample size to assume that our sampling distribution would be approximately normally distributed. It would not be wise to rely on findings from this study. It would make sense to replicate this research with a larger sample size.

CHAPTER 9

9-1. **a.** We will use a distribution of means, specifically a t distribution. It is a distribution of means because we have a sample consisting of more than one individual. It is a t distribution because we are comparing one sample to a population, but we know only the population mean, not its standard deviation.

b. The appropriate mean: $\mu_M = \mu = 25$

The calculations for the appropriate standard deviation (in this case, standard error, s_M):

$M = \dfrac{\Sigma X}{N} = \dfrac{(20 + 19 + 27 + 24 + 18)}{5} = 21.6$

X	X − M	(X − M)²
20	−1.6	2.56
19	−2.6	6.76
27	5.4	29.16
24	2.4	5.76
18	−3.6	12.96

Numerator: $\Sigma(X - M)^2 = (2.56 + 6.76 + 29.16 + 5.76 + 12.96) = 57.2$

$$s = \sqrt{\frac{\Sigma(X - M)^2}{(N - 1)}} = \sqrt{\frac{57.2}{5 - 1}}$$

$$= \sqrt{14.3} = 3.782$$

$$s_M = \frac{s}{\sqrt{N}} = \frac{3.782}{\sqrt{5}} = 1.691$$

c. $\quad t = \dfrac{(M - \mu_M)}{s_M} = \dfrac{(22.8 - 25)}{2.033} = -1.08 =$

$$= \frac{(21.6 - 25)}{1.691} = -2.01$$

9-2 *Step 1:* Population 1 is all students in career discussion groups. Population 2 is all students who did not participate in career discussion groups. The comparison distribution will be a distribution of means. The hypothesis test will be a single-sample *t* test because we have only one sample and we know the population mean but not the population standard deviation. This study meets two of the three assumptions and may meet the third. The dependent variable is interval. In addition, there are more than 30 participants in the sample, indicating that the comparison distribution will be normal. The students were not randomly selected, however, so we must be cautious when generalizing.

Step 2: Null hypothesis: Students who participate in career discussion groups have the same CFC scores, on average, as students who do not participate—$H_0: \mu_1 = \mu_2$.
 Research hypothesis: Students who participated in career discussion groups had different CFC scores, on average, from students who did not participate—$H_1: \mu_1 \neq \mu_2$.

Step 3:
$$\mu_M = \mu = 3.51; s_M = \frac{s}{\sqrt{N}} = \frac{0.52}{\sqrt{45}} = 0.078$$
Step 4: $df = N - 1 = 45 - 1 = 44$; Our critical values based on a two-tailed test, a *p* level of 0.05, and *df* of 44 are −2.012 and 2.021. (*Note:* It is helpful to draw a curve that includes the cutoffs.)
Step 5: $t = \dfrac{(M - \mu_M)}{s_M} = \dfrac{(3.7 - 3.51)}{0.078} = 2.44$
(*Note:* It is helpful to add this *t* statistic to the curve you drew in step 4.)

Step 6: Reject the null hypothesis. It appears that students who participate in career discussions have higher CFC scores, on average, than do students who do not participate.

9-3 *Step 1:* Population 1 is people with a monthly cell phone plan. Population 2 is people with a prepaid cell phone plan. The comparison distribution will be a distribution of differences between means based on the null hypothesis. The hypothesis test will be an independent-samples *t* test because we have two samples comprised of different groups of participants. This study meets two of the three assumptions and may meet the third; the dependent variable is minutes, which is interval (ratio, actually). We do not know whether the population is normally distributed, and there are not at least 30 participants, but the sample data do not indicate skew. Finally, the participants were randomly selected.

Step 2: Null hypothesis: On average, people with a monthly cell phone plan use the same number of minutes as the people with a prepaid plan—$H_0: \mu_1 = \mu_2$.
 Research hypothesis: On average, people with a monthly cell phone plan use a different number of minutes from the people with a prepaid plan—$H_1: \mu_1 \neq \mu_2$.

Step 3: $(\mu_1 - \mu_2) = 0$; $s_{Difference} = 98.698$.

Calculations:

$M_X = 1100.25$

X	X − M	(X − M)²
955	−145.25	21,097.563
1067	−33.25	1,105.563
1121	20.75	430.625
1258	157.75	24,885.063

$$s_X^2 = \frac{\Sigma(X - M)^2}{N - 1}$$

$$= \frac{(21,097.563 + 1105.563 + 430.625 + 24,885.063)}{4 - 1}$$

$$= 15,839.605$$

$M_Y = 862.667$

Y	Y − M	(Y − M)²
856	−6.667	44.449
1000	137.333	18,860.353
732	−130.667	17,073.865

$$s_Y^2 = \frac{\Sigma(Y - M)^2}{N - 1}$$

$$= \frac{(44.449 + 18,860.353 + 17,073.865)}{3} - 1$$

$$= 17,989.334$$

$df_X = N - 1 = 4 - 1 = 3$

$df_Y = N - 1 = 3 - 1 = 2$

$df_{Total} = df_X + df_Y = 3 + 2 = 5$

$$s^2_{Pooled} = \left(\frac{df_X}{df_{Total}}\right) s^2_X + \left(\frac{df_Y}{df_{Total}}\right) s^2_Y :$$

$$= \left(\frac{3}{5}\right) 15,839.605 + \left(\frac{2}{5}\right) 17,989.334$$

$$= 9,503.763 + 7195.734 = 16,699.497$$

$$s^2_{M_X} = \frac{s^2_{Pooled}}{N} = \frac{16,699.497}{4} = 4174.874$$

$$s^2_{M_Y} = \frac{s^2_{Pooled}}{N} = \frac{16,699.497}{3} = 5566.499$$

$$s^2_{Difference} = s^2_{M_X} + s^2_{M_Y} = 4174.874 + 5566.499$$

$$= 9741.373$$

$$s_{Difference} = \sqrt{s^2_{Difference}} = \sqrt{9741.373} = 98.698$$

Step 4: Our critical values, based on a two-tailed test, a *p* level of 0.05, and df_{Total} of 5, are -2.571 and 2.571. (*Note:* It is helpful to draw a curve that includes the cutoffs.)

Step 5: $t = \dfrac{(1100.25 - 862.667) - (0)}{98.698} = 2.407$

(*Note:* It is helpful to add this *t* statistic to the curve you drew in step 4.)

Step 6: Fail to reject the null hypothesis; we conclude that there is no evidence from this study to support the research hypothesis.

9-4 a. Stem-and-leaf plot:

4	00055
3	00005555555
2	0055

b. Dot plot:

Dot Plot of CFC Score

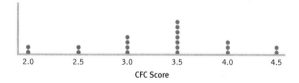

CFC Score

c. The distribution shows a central tendency around 3.5, and the scores range from 2.0 to 4.5. There might be some negative skew. No outliers appear.

CHAPTER 10

10-1 a. We will use an *F* distribution because there are more than two samples.

b. We would determine the variance among the three sample means—the means for those in the control group, for those in the two-hour communication ban, and for those in the four-hour communication ban.

c. We would determine the variance within each of the three samples, and we would take a weighted average of the three variances.

d. $F = \dfrac{MS_{Between}}{MS_{Within}} = \dfrac{8.6}{3.7} = 2.32$

10-2 a. This is a one-way ANOVA because there is only one independent variable, year in school, and it has more than two levels. The four levels are freshman, sophomore, junior, and senior.

b. This is a between-groups ANOVA because participants are in only one level of the independent variable. They cannot be both a freshman and a junior, for example.

c. This study would be analyzed with a one-way within-groups ANOVA if all participants were in *every* level of the independent variable. He could take the same set of participants and assess their CFC scores every year for four years.

10-3 a. The independent variable was attendance, with three levels: <5 sessions, 5–8 sessions, and 9–12 sessions. The dependent variable was number of minutes of exercise per week. This is a scale variable because we can assume that the distance between minutes has the same meaning for every level of minutes.

b. *Step 1:* Population 1 is postmenopausal women who attended fewer than 5 sessions of a group exercise education program. Population 2 is postmenopausal women who attended 5–8 sessions of a group exercise education program. Population 3 is postmenopausal women who attended 9–12 sessions of a group exercise education program. The comparison distribution will be an *F* distribution. The hypothesis test will be a one-way between-groups ANOVA. The data are not selected randomly, so we must generalize only with caution. We do not know if the underlying population distributions are normal, but the sample data do not indicate severe skew. To see if we meet the homoscedasticity assumption, we will check to see if the largest variance is no greater than twice the smallest variance. From the accompanying table, we see that the largest variance, 387, is not more than twice the smallest, 208.67, and so we have met the homoscedasticity assumption. (The information in the table comes from the calculation of SS_{Within}.)

SAMPLE	<5	5–8	9–12
Squared deviations	400	324	324
	225	441	4
	25	9	289
			9
Sum of squares	650	774	626
N − 1	2	2	3
Variance	**325**	**387**	**208.67**

Step 2: Null hypothesis: Postmenopausal women in different categories of attendance at a group exercise education program exercise the same average number of minutes per week—H_0: $\mu_1 = \mu_2 = \mu_3$.
Research hypothesis: Postmenopausal women in different categories of attendance at a group exercise education program exercise different average numbers of minutes per week.

Step 3: $df_{Between} = N_{Groups} - 1 = 3 - 1 = 2$

$df_1 = 3 - 1 = 2$; $df_2 = 3 - 1 = 2$; $df_3 = 4 - 1 = 3$

$df_{Within} = 2 + 2 + 3 = 7$

The comparison distribution will be the F distribution with 2 and 7 degrees of freedom.

Step 4: The cutoff for the F statistic based on a p level of 0.05 is 4.74.

Step 5: $df_{Total} = 2 + 7 = 9$ or $df_{Total} = 10 - 1 = 9$

$SS_{Total} = \Sigma(X - GM)^2 = 12,222.40$

SAMPLE	X	(X − GM)	(X − GM)²
<5	155	−24.6	605.16
$M_{<5} = 135$	120	−59.6	3552.16
	130	−49.6	2460.16
5–8	199	19.4	376.36
$M_{5–8} = 181$	160	−19.6	384.16
	184	4.4	19.36
9–12	230	50.4	2540.16
$M_{9–12} = 212$	214	34.4	1183.36
	195	15.4	237.16
	209	29.4	864.36
GM = 179.6			SS_{Total} = **12,222.40**

$$SS_{Within} = \Sigma(X - M)^2 = 2050.00$$

SAMPLE	X	(X − M)	(X − M)²
<5	155	20	400
$M_{<5} = 135$	120	−15	225
	130	−5	25
5–8	199	18	324
$M_{5–8} = 181$	160	−21	441
	184	3	9
9–12	230	18	324
$M_{9–12} = 212$	214	2	4
	195	−17	289
	209	−3	9
GM = 179.6			SS_{Within} = **2,050.00**

$$SS_{Between} = \Sigma(X - GM)^2 = 10,172.40$$

SAMPLE	X	(M − GM)	(M − GM)²
<5	155	−44.6	1989.16
$M_{<5} = 135$	120	−44.6	1989.16
	130	−44.6	1989.16
5–8	199	1.4	1.96
$M_{5–8} = 181$	160	1.4	1.96
	184	1.4	1.96
9–12	230	32.4	1049.76
$M_{9–12} = 212$	214	32.4	1049.76
	195	32.4	1049.76
	209	32.4	1049.76
GM = 179.6			SS_{Total} = **10,172.40**

$SS_{Total} = SS_{Within} + SS_{Between}$: $12,222.40 = 2,050.00 + 10,172.40$

$$MS_{Between} = \frac{SS_{Between}}{df_{Between}} = \frac{10,172.40}{2} = 5086.20$$

$$MS_{Within} = \frac{SS_{Within}}{df_{Within}} = \frac{2050.00}{7} = 292.857$$

SOURCE	SS	df	MS	F
Between	10,172.40	2	5,086.200	**17.37**
Within	2,050.00	7	292.857	
Total	12,222.40	9		

Step 6: Our F statistic, 17.37, is beyond the cutoff of 4.74. We can reject the null hypothesis. It appears that postmenopausal women in different categories of attendance at a group exercise education program exercise different average numbers of minutes per week.

c. We do not know where specific differences lie. The ANOVA only tells us that there is at least one difference between means. We must calculate a follow-up statistic called a post-hoc test to determine exactly what pairs of means are different.

d. The researchers did not use random assignment. The participants placed themselves in categories by their attendance at program sessions. It is possible that those who were more motivated to attend sessions were also more motivated to exercise. It might be motivation, not attendance at sessions, that affected the number of minutes exercised per week. Motivation might be the confounding variable.

10-4 a. We rejected the null hypothesis and concluded that postmenopausal women in different categories of attendance at a group exercise education program exercise different average numbers of minutes per week. We could not be more specific because ANOVA only tells us that there is at least one difference between pairs of means; it does not tell us exactly which pairs of means are statistically significantly different. We must conduct an additional test, called a post-hoc test, to identify the pairs of means that show a statistically significant difference.

b. $N' = \dfrac{N_{Groups}}{\Sigma(1/N)} = \dfrac{3}{\dfrac{1}{3} + \dfrac{1}{3} + \dfrac{1}{4}} = 3.273$

$s_M = \sqrt{\dfrac{MS_{Within}}{N'}} = \sqrt{\dfrac{292.857}{3.273}} = 9.460$

$HSD = \dfrac{(M_1 - M_2)}{s_M}$ for each pair of means

<5 vs. 5–8: $HSD = \dfrac{(135 - 181)}{9.460} = -4.86$

<5 vs. 9–12: $HSD = \dfrac{(135 - 212)}{9.460} = -8.14$

5–8 vs. 9–12: $HSD = \dfrac{(181 - 212)}{9.460} = -3.28$

For a p level of 0.05, the cutoff q is 4.16. (Remember, the signs do not matter because the order in which we subtract means is arbitrary.) It appears that those who attend fewer than 5 sessions have a lower average number of minutes exercised per week than do those who attend 5–8 sessions and also than do those who attend 9–12 sessions. We can draw no conclusion about the average difference between

those who attend 5–8 sessions and those who attend 9–12 sessions.

c. We did not reject the null hypothesis for the difference between the means of those who attend 5–8 sessions and those who attend 9–12 sessions. We cannot conclude that the means are the same because we can never accept the null hypothesis. It is possible that there is a difference between means that we did not detect in this study.

CHAPTER 11

11-1 a. The participants are the stocks themselves.

b. One independent variable is the type of ticker-code name, with two levels: pronounceable and unpronounceable. The second indepen-dent variable is time lapsed since the stock was initially offered, with four levels: one day, one week, six months, and one year.

c. The dependent variable is the stocks' selling price.

d. This would be a two-way between-groups ANOVA.

e. This would be a 2 (ticker code name: pronounceable, unpronounceable) × 4 (time lapsed: one day, one week, six months, one year) between-groups ANOVA, or just a 2 × 4 between-groups ANOVA.

f. This study would have eight cells: 2 × 4 = 8

11-2 a. i. Independent variables: student (Caroline, Mira); class (philosophy, psychology)

ii. Dependent variable: performance in class

iii.

	CAROLINE	MIRA
Philosophy Class		
Psychology Class		

iv. This describes a qualitative interaction because the direction of the effect reverses. Caroline does worse in philosophy class than in psychology class, whereas Mira does better.

b. i. Independent variables; game location (home, away); team (own conference, other conference)

ii. Dependent variable; number of runs

iii.

	HOME	AWAY
Own Conference		
Other Conference		

iv. This describes a qualitative interaction because the direction of the effect reverses. The team does worse at home against teams in the other conference but does well against those teams while away; the team does better at home against teams in their own conference, but performs poorly against teams in their own conference when away.

c. i. Independent variables: amount of caffeine (caffeine, none); exercise (worked out, did not work out)

ii. Dependent variable: amount of sleep

iii.

	CAFFEINE	NO CAFFEINE
Working Out		
Not Working Out		

iv. This describes a quantitative interaction because the effect of working out is particularly strong in the presence of caffeine versus no caffeine (and the presence of caffeine is particularly strong in the presence of working out versus not). The direction of the effect of either independent variable, however, does change depending on the level of the other independent variable.

11-3 **a.** Population 1 is students who received an initial grade of C who received e-mail messages aimed at bolstering self-esteem. Population 2 is students who received an initial grade of C who received e-mail messages aimed at bolstering their sense of control over their grades. Population 3 is students who received an initial grade of C who received e-mail messages with just review questions. Population 4 is students who received an initial grade of D or F who received e-mail messages aimed at bolstering self-esteem. Population 5 is students who received an initial grade of D or F who received e-mail messages aimed at bolstering their sense of control over their grades. Population 6 is students who received an initial grade of D or F who received e-mail messages with just review questions.

b. Main effect of first independent variable— initial grade:

Null hypothesis: The mean final exam grade of students with an initial grade of C is the same as that of students with an initial grade of D or F. H_0: $\mu_C = \mu_{D/F}$.
Research hypothesis: The mean final exam grade of students with an initial grade of C is not the same as that of students with an initial grade of D or F. H_0: $\mu_C \neq \mu_{D/F}$.

Main effect of second independent variable— type of e-mail:

Null hypothesis: On average, the mean exam grades among those re-ceiving different types of e-mails are the same—H_0: $\mu_{SE} = \mu_C = \mu_{NM}$.
Research hypothesis: On average, the mean exam grades among those receiving different types of e-mails are not the same.

Interaction: Initial grade $\times$ type of e-mail:

Null hypothesis: The effect of type of e-mail is not dependent on the levels of initial grade.
Research hypothesis: The effect of type of e-mail depends on the levels of initial grade.

c. $df_{Between/grade} = N_{Groups} - 1 = 2 - 1 = 1$

$df_{Between/e\text{-}mail} = N_{Groups} - 1 = 3 - 1 = 2$

$df_{Interaction} = (df_{Between/grade})(df_{Between/e\text{-}mail}) = (1)(2) = 2$

$df_{C,SE} = N - 1 = 14 - 1 = 13$

$df_{C,C} = N - 1 = 14 - 1 = 13$

$df_{C,NM} = N - 1 = 14 - 1 = 13$

$df_{D/F,SE} = N - 1 = 14 - 1 = 13$

$df_{D/F,C} = N - 1 = 14 - 1 = 13$

$df_{D/F,NM} = N - 1 = 14 - 1 = 13$

$df_{Within} = df_{C,SE} + df_{C,C} + df_{C,NM} + df_{D/F,SE} + df_{D/F,C} + df_{D/F,NM} = 13 + 13 + 13 + 13 + 13 + 13 = 78$

Main effect of initial grade: F distribution with 1 and 78 degrees of freedom

Main effect of type of e-mail: F distribution with 2 and 78 degrees of freedom

Main effect of interaction of initial grade and type of e-mail: F distribution with 2 and 78 degrees of freedom

d. There are three cutoffs (Note that when your specific df is not in the table, you should choose the more conservative—that is, larger— cutoff. In this case, we'll go with the cutoffs for a within df of 75 rather than 80.):

Main effect of initial grade: 3.97

Main effect of type of e-mail: 3.12

Interaction of initial grade and type of e-mail: 3.12

e. There is a significant main effect of initial grade because the F statistic, 20.84, is larger than the critical value of 3.97. The marginal means, seen in the accompanying table, tell us that students who earned a C on the initial exam have higher scores on the final exam than do students who earned a D or an F on the initial exam. There is no statistically significant main effect of type of e-mail, however. The F statistic of 1.69 is not larger than the critical value of 3.12. Had this main effect been significant, we would have conducted a post-hoc test to determine where the differences were. There also is not a significant interaction. The F statistic of 3.02 is not larger than the critical value of 3.12. (Had we used a cutoff based on a p level of 0.10, we would have rejected the null hypothesis for the interaction. The cutoff for a p level of 0.10 is 2.77.) If we had rejected the null hypothesis for the interaction, we would have constructed a bar graph to interpret the main effect, and, ideally, also would have examined the corrected cell means in tabular and graph form.

	SELF-ESTEEM	SENSE OF CONTROL	NO MESSAGE	
C	67.31	69.83	71.12	69.42
D/F	47.83	60.98	62.13	56.98
	57.57	65.41	66.63	

11-4 Step 1: Subtract the grand mean from each of the column and row means.

	LIPITOR	PLACEBO	
Grapefruit Juice	60	4	$32 - 24.5 = 7.5$
Water	30	4	$17 - 24.5 = -7.5$
	$45 - 24.5 = 20.5$	$4 - 24.5 = -20.5$	24.5

Step 2: Subtract the row and column effects from each cell mean.

	LIPITOR	PLACEBO	
Grapefruit Juice	$60 - 20.5 - 7.5 = 32$	$4 - (-20.5) - 7.5 = 17$	7.5
Water	$30 - 20.5 - (-7.5) = 17$	$4 - (-20.5) - (-7.5) = 32$	-7.5
	20.5	-20.5	24.5

Step 3: Subtract the grand mean from each cell mean.

	LIPITOR	PLACEBO	
Grapefruit Juice	$32 - 24.5 = 7.5$	$17 - 24.5 = -7.5$	7.5
Water	$17 - 24.5 = -7.5$	$32 - 24.5 = 7.5$	-7.5
	20.5	-20.5	24.5

The corrected cell means demonstrate that there is an interaction between type of beverage and type of drug. The corrected cell means show the interaction separate from either main effect.

11-5 **a.** They would conduct a 2 (age: 18–20, 35–45) $\times$ 3 (intensity: low, moderate, high) $\times$ 4 (time point: 15, 20, 25, and 30 minutes) mixed-design ANOVA. (It's mixed because age is between-groups but the other two independent variables are within-groups).

b. Now they would use ANCOVA because they are including covariates.

c. Now they would use MANOVA because they do not have a covariate but they do have more than one dependent variable.

d. Now they would use MANCOVA because they have two covariates and three dependent variables.

CHAPTER 12

12-1 Your friend is not considering the fact that the two distributions, that of IQ scores of Burakumin and that of IQ scores of other Japanese, will have a great deal of overlap. The fact that one mean is higher than another does not imply that all members of one group have higher IQ scores than all members of another group. Any individual member of either group, such as your friend's former student, might fall well above the mean for his group (and the other group) or well below the mean for his group (and the other group). Research reports that do not give an indication of the overlap between two distributions risk misleading their audience.

12-2 **a.** First, we draw a normal curve with the sample mean, 3.7, in the center. Then we put the bounds of the 95% confidence interval on either end, writing the appropriate percentages under the segnebts of the curve: 2.5% beyond the cutoffs on either end and 47.5% between the mean and each cutoff (see figure). Now we look up the z statistics for these cutoffs; the z statistic associated with 47.5%, the percentage between the mean and the z statistic, is 1.96. Thus, the cutoffs are -1.96 and 1.96. Next, we'll calculate standard error so that we can convert these z statistics to raw means:

$$\sigma_M = \frac{\sigma}{\sqrt{N}} = \frac{0.61}{\sqrt{45}} = 0.091$$

$$M_{Lower} = -z(\sigma_M) + M_{Sample} = -1.96(0.091) + 3.7 = 3.52$$

$$M_{Upper} = z(\sigma_M) + M_{Sample} = 1.96(0.091) + 3.7 = 3.88$$

Finally, we check to be sure our answer makes sense by demonstrating that each end of the confidence interval is the same distance from the mean. $3.52 - 3.7 = -0.18$ and $3.88 - 3.7 = 0.18$. The confidence interval is (3.52, 3.88).

    b. If we were to conduct this study over and over, determining the limits of a 95% confidence interval for each new sample, we would expect the population mean to fall in that interval 95% of the time. Thus, it provides a range of plausible values for the population mean. Because the null-hypothesized poulation mean, 3.51 is not a plausible value, we can conclude that those who attended the discussion group have higher CFC scores than those who did not. This conclusion matches that of the hypothesis test, in which we rejected the null hypothesis.

    c. The confidence interval is superior to the hypothesis test because not only does it lead to the same conclusion but it also gives us an interval estimate, rather than a point estimate, of the population mean.

12-3 a. We would calculate Cohen's d, the effect size appropriate for data analyzed with a z test. We use standard deviation in the denominator, rather than standard error, because effect sizes are for distributions of scores rather than distributions of means.

$$\text{Cohen's } d = \frac{(M - \mu)}{\sigma} = \frac{(3.7 - 3.51)}{0.61} = 0.31$$

    b. Cohen's conventions indicate that 0.2 is a small effect and 0.5 is a medium effect. This effect size, therefore, would be considered a small-to-medium effect.

    c. If the career discussion group is easily implemented in terms of time and money, the small-to-medium effect might be worth the effort. For university students, a higher level of Consideration of Future Consequences might translate into a higher level of readiness for life after graduation, a premise that we could study.

12-4 a. The inputs for G*Power are as follows. This is a two-tailed test with an effect size of

$$d = \frac{(3.7 - 3.51)}{0.61} = 0.311.$$ (Note that G*Power

will calculate the effect size for you if you input the means and standard deviation.) The alpha level is 0.05, and the sample size is 45 for each group. G*Power tells us that power is 30.93%.

    b. This indicates that we have a 30.93% chance of rejecting the null hypothesis if there is an effect of this size and with samples of this size.

    c. G*Power returned a total sample size of 326 (163 per group) required to achieve 80% power.

    d. (1) The researchers could use a cutoff p level of 0.10 instead of 0.05. There would then be 5% instead of 2.5% in each tail. (2) The researchers could use a one-tailed instead of a two-tailed test, thus placing the entire cutoff region in one tail. There would then be 5% instead of 2.5% in the upper tail. (3) The researchers could use more than 45 participants. (4) The researchers could have a longer career discussion group with the aim of increasing the difference between means even more. Ostensibly, after a longer series of discussions, the mean CFC score would increase to an even higher level than 3.7. (5) The researchers could decrease the standard deviation by measuring CFC scores with a more reliable scale if one existed, or they could decrease the standard deviation by using only top students (but this would have to be true both of the sample and the population for an appropriate comparison).

12-5 a. PsycINFO, the database of psychology-related publications, would be useful, as would other behavioral science databases. One could also use a database that accesses newspaper articles, such as Lexis Nexis.

    b. There are many possible search words, including "behavioral science major," "career," "graduate school," "employment," and "salary." Alternative search words are sometimes suggested by the databases themselves, and we could look for other search words in the articles that we find.

    c. Studies conducted on the employment outcomes of behavioral science majors might not have been published if they did not find "useful" or "exciting" information.

CHAPTER 13

13-1 a. i. The independent variable is city, a nominal variable.

   ii. The dependent variable is whether a woman is pretty or not so pretty, a nominal variable.

   iii. We'd choose a hypothesis test from category III. We'd use a nonparametric test because the dependent variable is nominal and would not meet the primary assumption of a normally distributed dependent variable, even with a large sample.

b. i. The independent variable is city, a nominal variable.

   ii. The dependent variable is beauty, assessed on an interval scale of 1–10. This is an interval variable.

   iii. We'd choose a test from category II because the independent variable is nominal and the dependent variable is interval. (In fact, we'd use a one-way between-groups ANOVA because there is only one independent variable and it has more than two levels.)

c. i. The independent variable is intelligence, an interval variable.

   ii. The dependent variable is beauty, assessed on an interval scale of 1–10. This is an interval variable.

   iii. We'd choose a hypothesis test from category I because we have an interval independent variable and an interval dependent variable. (If we were assessing the *relation* between these variables, we'd use correlation. If we wondered whether intelligence *predicted* beauty, we'd use regression.)

d. i. The independent variable is ranking on intelligence, an ordinal variable.

   ii. The dependent variable is ranking on beauty, also an ordinal variable.

   iii. We'd choose a hypothesis from category III because both the independent and dependent variables are ordinal. We would not meet the assumption of having a normal distribution of the dependent variable, even if we had a large sample.

13-2 *Step 1:* Population 1 is elite German youth soccer players like those we observed. Population 2 is elite German youth soccer players with birth patterns like those in the general population. The comparison distribution is a chi-square distribution. The hypothesis test will be a chi-square test for goodness-of-fit because we have one nominal variable only. This study meets three of the four assumptions. The one variable is nominal. Every participant is in only one cell (an individual can be born in only one month). There are more than five times as many participants as cells (56 participants and only 2 cells). This is not a randomly selected sample of all elite soccer players, however. The sample includes only German youth soccer players in the elite leagues. We must be cautious in generalizing beyond young German elite players.

Step 2: Null hypothesis: Elite German youth soccer players have the same pattern of birth months as do those in the general population. Research hypothesis: Elite German youth soccer players have a different pattern of birth months from those in the general population.

Step 3: The comparison distribution is the chi-square distribution that has 1 degree of freedom: $df_{\chi^2} = 2 - 1 = 1$.

Step 4: Our cutoff χ^2, based on a p level of 0.05 and 1 degree of freedom, is 3.841. (*Note:* Include a drawing of the chi-square distribution with the cutoff.)

Step 5:

OBSERVED (WHEN ELITE PLAYERS WERE BORN)	
FIRST THREE MONTHS OF THE YEAR	LAST THREE MONTHS OF THE YEAR
52	4

EXPECTED (FROM THE GENERAL POPULATION):	
FIRST THREE MONTHS OF THE YEAR	LAST THREE MONTHS OF THE YEAR
28	28

CATEGORY	OBSERVED (O)	EXPECTED (E)	O − E	(O − E)²	$\frac{(O - E)^2}{E}$
First three months	52	28	24	576	20.571
Last three months	4	28	−24	576	20.571

$$\chi^2 = \Sigma\left[\frac{(O - E)^2}{E}\right] = (20.571 + 20.571) = 41.14$$

Step 6: Reject the null hypothesis. It appears that elite German youth soccer players are more likely to have been born in the first three months of the year, and less likely to have been born in the last three months of the year, than are those in the general population. (*Note:* Add the test statistic to the drawing that included the cutoff.)

13-3 a. The participants are the lineups. The independent variable is type of lineup (simultaneous, sequential), and the dependent variable is outcome of the lineup (suspect identification, other identification, no identification).

b. *Step 1:* Population 1 is police lineups like those we observed. Popula-tion 2 is police lineups for which type of lineup and outcome are independent. The comparison distribution is a chi-square distribution. The hypothesis test is a chi-square test for independence because we have two nominal variables. This study meets three of the four assumptions. The two variables are nominal; every participant (lineup) is in only one cell; and there are more than five times as many participants as cells (8 participants and 6 cells).

Step 2: Null hypothesis: Lineup outcome is independent of type of lineup.
Research hypothesis: Lineup outcome depends on type of lineup.

Step 3: The comparison distribution is a chi-square distribution with 2 degrees of freedom: $df_{\chi^2} = (k_{Row} - 1)(k_{Column} - 1) = (2 - 1)(3 - 1) = (1)(2) = 2$.

Step 4: Our cutoff χ^2, based on a p level of 0.05 and 2 degrees of freedom is 5.992. (*Note:* Include drawing of the chi-square distribution with the cutoff.)

Step 5:

We can calculate the expected frequencies in one of two ways. First, we can think about it. Out of the total of 548 lineups, 293 led to identification of the suspect, an identification rate of 293/548 = 0.535, or 53.5%. If identification were independent of type of lineup, we would expect the same rate for each type of lineup. For the 319 simultaneous lineups, we would expect this rate: (0.535)(319) = 170.665. For the 299 sequential lineups, we would expect this rate: (0.535)(229) = 122.515. Or we can use our formula. For these same two cells (the column labeled "suspect ID"), we calculate:

$$\frac{Total_{Column}}{N}(Total_{Row}) = \frac{293}{548}(319)$$
$$= (0.535)(319) = 170.665$$

$$\frac{Total_{Column}}{N}(Total_{Row}) = \frac{293}{548}(229)$$
$$= (0.535)(229) = 122.515$$

For the column labeled "other ID":

$$\frac{Total_{Column}}{N}(Total_{Row}) = \frac{28}{548}(319)$$
$$= (0.051)(319) = 16.269$$

$$\frac{Total_{Column}}{N}(Total_{Row}) = \frac{28}{548}(229)$$
$$= (0.051)(229) = 11.679$$

For the column labeled "no ID":

$$\frac{Total_{Column}}{N}(Total_{Row}) = \frac{227}{548}(319)$$
$$= (0.414)(319) = 132.066$$

$$\frac{Total_{Column}}{N}(Total_{Row}) = \frac{227}{548}(229)$$
$$= (0.414)(229) = 94.806$$

	OBSERVED			
	SUSPECT ID	OTHER ID	NO ID	
Simultaneous	191	8	120	319
Sequential	102	20	107	229
	293	28	227	548

	EXPECTED			
	SUSPECT ID	OTHER ID	NO ID	
Simultaneous	170.665	16.269	132.066	319
Sequential	122.515	11.679	94.806	229
	293	28	227	548

CATEGORY	OBSERVED (O)	EXPECTED (E)	O − E	(O − E)²	$\frac{(O - E)^2}{E}$
Sim; suspect	191	170.665	20.335	413.512	2.423
Sim; other	8	16.269	−8.269	68.376	4.203
Sim; no	120	132.066	−12.066	145.588	1.102
Seq; suspect	102	122.515	−20.515	420.865	3.435
Seq; other	20	11.679	8.321	69.239	5.929
Seq; no	107	94.806	12.194	148.694	1.568

$$\chi^2 = \Sigma\left(\frac{(O-E)^2}{E}\right) = (2.423 + 4.203 + 1.102$$
$$+ 3.435 + 5.929 + 1.568) = 18.660$$

Step 6: Reject the null hypothesis. It appears that the outcome of a lineup depends on the type of lineup. In general, simultaneous lineups tend to lead to a higher rate than expected of suspect identification, lower rates than expected of identification of other members of the lineup, and lower rates than expected of no identification at all. (*Note:* Add the test statistic to the drawing that included the cutoff).

c. Cramer's $V = \sqrt{\dfrac{\chi^2}{(N)(df_{Row/Column})}} =$

$$\sqrt{\frac{18.660}{(548)(1)}} = \sqrt{0.034} = 0.184. \text{ This is a}$$

small-to-medium effect.

d. $\chi^2(1, N = 548) = 18.66, p < 0.05$, Cramer's $V = 0.18$.

e. The findings of this study were opposite to what had been expected by the investigators; the report of results noted that, prior to this study, police departments believed that the sequential lineup led to more accurate identification of suspects. This situation occurs frequently in behavioral research, a reminder of the importance of conducting two-tailed hypothesis tests. (Of course, the fact that this study produced different results doesn't end the debate. Future researchers should explore why there are different findings in different contexts in an effort to target the best lineup procedures based on specific situations.)

13-4 a. For simultaneous lineups, the observed frequency for the identification of suspects is 191.

b. For sequential lineups, the expected frequency for the identification of a person other than the suspect is 11.7.

c. For simultaneous lineups, the adjusted standardized residual for cases in which there was no identification is −2.1. This number indicates that the observed frequency for this cell, 120, is 2.1 standard errors below the expected frequency for this cell, 132.1.

d. If we were to use an adjusted standardized residual criterion of 2 (regardless of the sign), we would conclude that the observed frequencies in all cells are farther from their expected frequencies than would occur if the two variables (type of lineup and type of identification) were independent.

e. If we were to use an adjusted standardized residual criterion of 3 (regardless of the sign), we would conclude that the observed frequencies for four cells (the identification of the suspect or of another person in simultaneous lineups, and the identification of the suspect or of another person in sequential lineups) are farther from their expected frequencies than would occur if the two variables (type of lineup and type of identification) were independent.

CHAPTER 14

14-1 a. There is an extreme outlier, 139, suggesting that the underlying population distribution might be skewed. Moreover, the sample size is small.

b. 1, 2, 3, 4, 5, 6, 7, 8, 9, 10 (we chose to rank this way, but you could do the reverse, from 10 to 1).

c. The outlier was 25 IQ points $(139 - 114 = 25)$ behind the next-highest score of 114. It now is ranked 10, compared to the next-highest score's rank of 9.

14-2 a.

COUNTRY	PRIDE RANK	OLYMPIC MEDALS	MEDALS RANK	DIFFERENCE (D)	SQUARED DIFFERENCE (D^2)
United States	1	97	1	0	0
South Africa	2	5	7	−5	25
Austria	3	3	8	−5	25
Canada	4	14	5	−1	1
Chile	5	1	10	−5	25
Japan	6	18	3	3	9
Hungary	7	17	4	3	9
France	8	38	2	6	36
Norway	9	10	6	3	9
Slovenia	10	2	9	1	1

$\Sigma R = (0 + 25 + 25 + 1 + 25 + 9 + 9 + 36 + 9 + 1) = 140$

$r_S = 1 - \dfrac{6(\Sigma D^2)}{N(N^2 - 1)} = 1 - \dfrac{6(140)}{10(10^2 - 1)}$

$\quad = 1 - \dfrac{840}{10(100 - 1)} = 1 - \dfrac{840}{990}$

$\quad = 1 - 0.848 = 0.152$

b. The Spearman correlation coefficient of 0.152 indicates a small positive association.

c. We might not want to use the interval data because the United States, with a score of 97, appears to be an outlier. Its score is likely to inflate the strength of the correlation.

14-3 **a.** *Step 1:* We convert our data from interval to ordinal. The researchers did not indicate whether they used random selection to choose the countries in the sample, so we must be cautious when generalizing from these results. There are some ties, but we will assume that there are not so many as to render the results of the test invalid.

COUNTRY	PRIDE SCORE	PRIDE RANK	ENGLISH LANGUAGE	OTHER RANKS	RANKS
United States	4.0	1	E	1	
Australia	2.9	2.5	E	2.5	
Ireland	2.9	2.5	E	2.5	
South Africa	2.7	4	E	4	
New Zealand	2.6	5	E	5	
Canada	2.4	6	E	6	
Chile	2.3	7	NE		7
Great Britain	2.2	8	E	8	
Japan	1.8	9	NE		9
France	1.5	10	NE		10
Czech Republic	1.3	11.5	NE		11.5
Norway	1.3	11.5	NE		11.5
Slovenia	1.1	13	NE		13
South Korea	1.0	14	NE		14

Step 2: Null hypothesis: Countries in which English is a primary language and countries in which English is not a primary language do not tend to differ in accomplishment-related national pride.
Research hypothesis: Countries in which English is a primary language and countries in which English is not a primary language differ in accomplishment-related national pride.

Step 3: There are seven countries in the English-speaking group and seven countries in the non-English-speaking group.

Step 4: The cutoff, or critical value, for a Mann–Whitney U test with two groups of seven participants (countries), a p level of 0.05, and a two-tailed test is 8.

Step 5: (*Note:* E stands for English-speaking, and NE stands for non-English-speaking.)

$\Sigma R_E = 1 + 2.5 + 2.5 + 4 + 5 + 6 + 8 = 29$

$\Sigma R_{NE} = 7 + 9 + 10 + 11.5 + 11.5 + 13 + 14 = 76$

$U_E = (n_E)(n_{NE}) + \dfrac{n_E(n_E + 1)}{2} - \Sigma R_E$

$\quad = (7)(7) + \dfrac{7(7 + 1)}{2} - 29$

$\quad = 49 + 28 - 29 = 48$

$U_{NE} = (n_E)(n_{NE}) + \dfrac{n_{NE}(n_E + 1)}{2} - \Sigma R_{NE}$

$\quad = (7)(7) + \dfrac{7(7 + 1)}{2} - 76$

$\quad = 49 + 28 - 76 = 1$

$U_E = 48; N_{NE} = 1$

Step 6: The smaller test statistic, 1, is smaller than the critical value, 8. We can reject the null hypothesis; it appears that English-speaking countries have higher accomplishment-related national pride than non-English-speaking countries.

14-4

INCOME	SQUARE ROOT
20,238	142.26
21,763	147.52
22,876	151.25
23,776	154.19
26,871	163.92
28,774	169.63
29,452	171.62
31,743	178.17
32,638	180.66
34,658	186.17
34,779	186.49
45,876	214.19
56,452	237.60
75,884	275.47
126,993	356.36

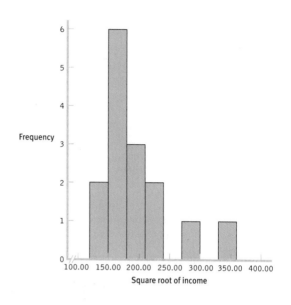

Histogram of incomes: Before being transformed, these data are positively skewed.

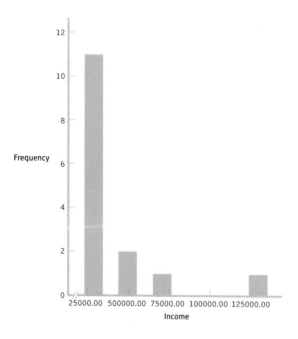

Histogram of square roots of incomes: After being transformed, the distribution is only somewhat positively skewed. Overall, it is much closer to a normal distribution than prior to the transformation. [Note that the x-axis of the previous histogram goes up to 125,000, whereas the x-axis of this histogram only goes up to 400.]

Although both the histogram of incomes and the histogram of square roots of incomes show some positive skew, the skewness is far less in the histogram of the square roots. After the square root transformation, the distribution of income was closer to a normal curve.

CHAPTER 15

15-1 a. The dean used a biased sample that included mostly students of professors he knew well. This sample is unlikely to be representative of the population.

b. The evaluator cannot solve the problem; it is impossible to change the sample at this point.

c. The evaluator should tell the dean that he should use extreme caution when generalizing beyond this sample.

15-2 a. The dependent variable is level of awareness of *The Economist*, as assessed by a survey; we know that this is an interval variable because it is referred to as the *mean* level of awareness.

b. There are two independent variables, both nominal. The first independent variable is presence of the ad campaign, with two levels: ad campaign (Baltimore) and no ad campaign (Pittsburgh). The second is time point, with two levels: before ad campaign and after ad campaign.

c. We can calculate the number of cells by multiplying the numbers of levels of the independent variables: $2 \times 2 = 4$. So there are four cells in this study, as shown in the accompanying table. The cells would contain means of survey scores for the participants in that cell.

	BALTIMORE; ADS	PITTSBURGH; NO ADS
Before		
After		

d. The study hypothesized that after the advertising campaign, the mean level of awareness of *The Economist* would be different—they hoped higher—in the city with the ad campaign, Baltimore, than in the city with no ad campaign, Pittsburgh. They did not expect such a difference before the campaign. They are hypothesizing an interaction. The effect of one variable, city, depends on the level of the other variable, before or after the advertising campaign.

e. The accompanying table summarizes the variables in the study.

	NAME OF VARIABLE	TYPE	NUMBER OF LEVELS (FOR NOMINAL VARIABLES ONLY)	NAMES OF LEVELS (FOR NOMINAL VARIABLES ONLY)
Independent variable 1	Presence of ad campaign	Nominal	Two	1. Baltimore (ad campaign) 2. Pittsburgh (no ad campaign)
Independent variable 2	Time point	Nominal	Two	1. Before 2. After
Dependent variable	Level of awareness	Interval		

f. The independent variables are nominal, and the dependent variable is interval, so this is a category 2 situation. We then ask how many independent variables there are. Because there are two, we know we will use some kind of two-way ANOVA. Using the guideline for naming ANOVAs from Chapter 11, we ask ourselves whether each variable is within-groups or between-groups. City must be between-groups; someone cannot live in both cities at once. Time point also is between groups; we presume from the media report of this study that different participants were surveyed at each time point. The analysis, therefore, will be a two-way between-groups ANOVA.

15-3 a. A one-way between-groups ANOVA was conducted on these data with the independent variable of type of academic program (arts and sciences, education, law, and business) and the dependent variable of importance of financial aspects. The researcher had hypothesized that foreign graduate students in different programs would give different ratings, on average, to the importance of financial factors. There was a significant effect of type of academic program, $F(3, 13) = 3.94$, $p < 0.05$, $R^2 = 0.48$. A Tukey HSD post-hoc test indicated a significantly higher rating among students in arts and sciences programs than among students in law programs. This is a large effect.

b. We also would report (likely in a Methods section) information on statistical power analyses to justify the number of participants in the study, as well as psychometric statistics to demonstrate the reliability and validity of the financial factors scale.

15-4 a. The researchers used an ANCOVA because they had a nominal independent variable, an interval dependent variable, and several interval covariates.

b. This excerpt tells us that memory scores were higher, on average, among those in the control group than among those in the PTSD group. This is a statistically significant difference, not accounted for by differences in age, years of education, or intelligence scores.

c. The researchers do not need to conduct a post-hoc test because there are only two groups, so we know where the difference lies.

d. The researchers do not include the degrees of freedom in their reporting of the statistics.

e. In this excerpt, the researchers did not include a measure of effect size. Moreover, because there are only two groups, the researchers could have reported a confidence interval around the mean difference. The researchers also should have included the results of a statistical power analysis and psychometric statistics on their interval variables, although these would likely be in the Methods section.

GLOSSARY

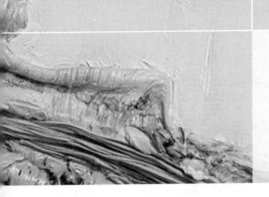

A

adjusted standardized residual The difference between the observed frequency and the expected frequency for a cell in a chi-square research design, divided by the standard error.

alpha The chance of making a Type I error and another name for the p level; symbolized as α.

analysis of covariance (ANCOVA) A type of ANOVA in which a covariate is included so that statistical findings reflect effects after an interval variable has been statistically removed.

analysis of variance (ANOVA) A hypothesis test typically used with one or more nominal independent variables (with at least three groups overall) and an interval dependent variable.

archival study The analysis of existing records or documents rather than newly collected data.

assumptions A requirement that the population from which we are sampling has a specific characteristic that will allow us to make accurate inferences.

B

bar graph A visual depiction of data when the independent variable is nominal and the dependent variable is interval. Each bar typically represents the mean value of the dependent variable for each category.

between-groups ANOVA A hypothesis test in which there are more than two samples, and each sample is composed of different participants.

between-groups variance An estimate of the population variance based on the differences among the means.

between-groups research design An experimental design in which participants experience one, and only one, level of the independent variable.

bimodal A distribution that has two modes, or most common scores.

Bonferroni test A post-hoc test that provides a more stringent critical value for every comparison of means; sometimes called the *Dunn Multiple Comparison test.*

bootstrapping A statistical process by which the original sample data are used to represent the entire population, and we repeatedly take samples from the original sample data to form a confidence interval.

box plot A graph that depicts the overall distribution of a data set. The lower end of the box marks the first

quartile, and the upper end marks the third quartile. A line through the middle indicates the median. Whiskers extend to the minimum and maximum scores.

C

ceiling effect A situation in which a constraint prevents a variable from taking on values above a given number.

cell A box that depicts one unique combination of levels of the independent variables in a factorial design.

central limit theorem The idea that a distribution of sample means is a more normal distribution than a distribution of scores even when the population distribution is not normal.

central tendency A descriptive statistic that best represents the center of a data set, the particular value that all the other data seem to be gathering around.

chartjunk Any unnecessary information or feature in a graph that distracts from a viewer's ability to understand the data.

chi-square test for goodness-of-fit A nonparametric hypothesis test used with one nominal variable.

chi-square test for independence A nonparametric test used with two nominal variables.

cluster sampling A selection method in which all of the clusters in a population are identified and a certain number of those clusters selected randomly. Everyone in the selected clusters would then be recruited to participate in the study.

coefficient alpha A commonly used estimate of a test's or measure's reliability that is calculated by taking the average of all possible split-half correlations and symbolized as α; sometimes called *Cronbach's alpha.*

Cohen's *d* A measure of effect size that assesses the difference between two means in terms of standard deviation, not standard error.

concurrent validity A type of criterion-related validity in which we correlate the scale or measure of interest with a criterion measured at the same time.

confidence interval An interval estimate, based on the sample statistic, that includes the population mean a certain percentage of the time, were we to sample from the same population repeatedly.

confirmation bias Our usually unintentional tendency to pay attention to evidence that confirms what we already believe and to ignore evidence that would disconfirm our beliefs.

confounding variable A variable that systematically co-varies with the independent variable so that we cannot logically determine which variable is at work; also called a *confound*.

control group A level of the independent variable that is designed to match the experimental group in all ways but the experimental manipulation itself.

construct A hypothetical idea that is developed (or constructed) to describe and explain human behavior.

continuous observation Observed data point that can take on a full range of values (e.g., numbers out to many decimal points); there is an infinite number of potential values.

convenience sample A subset of a population whose members are chosen strictly because they are readily available, as opposed to randomly selecting participants from the entire population of interest.

correlation An association between two or more variables.

correlation coefficient A statistic that quantifies a relation between two variables.

counterbalancing The minimization of order effects by varying the order of presentation of different levels of the independent variable from one participant to the next.

covariate An interval variable that we suspect associates, or covaries, with our independent variable of interest.

Cramer's *V* The standard effect size used with the chi-square test for independence; also called Cramer's phi, symbolized as ϕ.

criterion-related validity A type of validity whereby the scale or measure of interest is correlated with a criterion, which is some external standard.

critical region The area in the tails of the distribution within which we will reject the null hypothesis if our test statistic falls there.

critical value Test statistic value beyond which we will reject the null hypothesis; often called *cutoff*.

cumulative percentage The percentage of individuals who have scores at a given value or lower.

D

default An option that the software designer has preselected. This is a built-in decision that the software will implement if we do not instruct it otherwise.

degrees of freedom The number of scores that are free to vary when estimating a population parameter from a sample.

demand characteristic When experimenters inadvertently cue participants to offer certain responses.

dependent variable The outcome variable that we hypothesize to be related to, or caused by, changes in the independent variable.

descriptive statistic Statistical technique used to organize, summarize, and communicate a group of numerical observations.

deviation from the mean The amount that a score in a sample differs from the mean of the sample; also called *deviation*.

discrete observation Observed data point that can take on only specific values (e.g., whole numbers); no other values can exist between these numbers.

distribution The pattern of a set of numbers.

distribution of means A distribution composed of many means that are calculated from all possible samples of a given size, all taken from the same population.

dot plot A graph that displays all the data points in a sample, with the range of scores along the *x*-axis and a dot for each data point above the appropriate value.

double-blind experiment An experiment in which neither the experimenters conducting the study nor the participants in the study know the conditions to which participants have been assigned.

duck A form of chartjunk where features of the data have been dressed up in a graph to be something other than merely data.

E

effect size A standardized value that indicates the size of a difference with respect to a measure of spread, but is not affected by sample size.

expected relative-frequency probability The outcome expected if a trial were repeated many, many times.

experiment A study in which participants are randomly assigned to a condition or level of one or more independent variables.

experimental group A level of the independent variable that receives the treatment or intervention of interest in an experiment.

extraneous variable A randomly distributed influence that detracts from the experimenter's efforts to measure what was intended to be measured.

F

F statistic A ratio of two measures of variance: (1) between-groups variance, which indicates differences among sample means, and (2) within-groups variance, which is essentially an average of the sample variances.

factor A term used to describe an independent variable in a study with more than one independent variable.

factorial analysis of variance A statistical analysis used with one interval dependent variable and at least two nominal independent variables (also called factors); also called a *multifactorial analysis of variance*.

figure Any visual presentation of data other than a table, such as a photograph, drawing, or graph.

file drawer statistic A statistical calculation, following a meta-analysis, of the number of studies with null results that would have to exist so that a mean effect size is no longer statistically significant.

first quartile The 25th percentile of a data set.

floor effect A situation in which a constraint prevents a variable from taking values below a certain point.

frequency polygon A line graph with the x-axis representing values (or midpoints of intervals) and the y-axis representing frequencies. A point is placed at the frequency for each value (or midpoint), and the points are connected.

frequency table A visual depiction of data that shows how often each value occurred; that is, how many scores were at each value. Values are listed in one column, and the numbers of individuals with scores at that value are listed in the second column.

G

gambler's fallacy A type of biased thinking in which an individual believes that a previous occurrence has an effect on an ensuing occurrence, when in fact the two events are unrelated.

generalizability The ability to apply findings from one sample or in one context to other samples or contexts; also called *external validity*.

grand mean The mean of every score in a study, regardless of which sample the score came from.

grid A form of chartjunk that takes the form of a background pattern, almost like graph paper, on which the data representations, such as bars, are superimposed on a graph.

grouped frequency table A visual depiction of data that reports the frequencies within a given interval rather than the frequencies for a specific value.

groupthink The overconfident, biased decision making that occurs when a group of people confirm one anothers' beliefs rather than relying on objective evidence.

H

heteroscedastic A term given to populations that have different variances.

hierarchical multiple regression A type of multiple regression in which the researcher adds independent variables into the equation in an order determined by theory.

histogram A graph similar to a bar graph typically used to depict interval data with the values of the variable on the x-axis and the frequencies on the y-axis.

homoscedastic A term given to populations that have the same variance; also called *homogeneity of variance*.

hypothesis testing The process of drawing conclusions about whether a particular relation between variables is supported by the evidence.

I

illusory correlation The phenomenon of believing that one sees an association between variables when no such association exists.

independent-samples t test A hypothesis test used to compare two means for a between-groups design, a situation in which each participant is assigned to only one condition.

independent variable A variable that we either manipulate or observe to determine its effects on the dependent variable.

inferential statistic Statistical technique that uses sample data to make general estimates about the larger population.

Institutional Review Board (IRB) A committee that institutions are legally mandated to have to vet research that uses human or animal participants prior to beginning the study.

interaction The statistical result achieved in a factorial design when the two independent variables have an effect in combination that we do not see when we examine each independent variable on its own.

intercept The predicted value for Y when X is equal to 0, or the point at which the line crosses, or intercepts, the y-axis.

interquartile range The difference between the first and third quartiles of a data set.

interval estimate Based on our sample statistic, the range of sample statistics we could expect if we conducted repeated hypothesis tests using samples from the same population.

interval variable A variable that has numbers as its values; the distance (or interval) between pairs of consecutive numbers is assumed to be equal.

K

Kruskal–Wallis H test A nonparametric hypothesis test used when there are more than two groups, a between-groups design, and an ordinal dependent variable.

kurtosis The degree to which a curve's width and the thickness of its tails deviate from a normal curve—from very tall and skinny with thicker tails to very flat and wide with thinner tails.

L

latent variable A construct that we want to research but cannot directly measure.

leptokurtic The description for distributions that are taller and thinner with thicker tails.

level A discrete value or condition that a variable can take on.

line graph A graph used to illustrate the relation between different interval variables; sometimes the line represents the predicted y scores for each x value, and sometimes the line represents change in a variable over time.

linear relation A relation between two variables best described by a straight line.

log transformation A transformation that compresses the positive side of a skewed distribution and extends the smaller values on the negative side of the distribution.

logarithm The power (exponent) a base number must be raised to in order to get the original number.

longitudinal study An investigation that looks at ideas (constructs) by following a sample over time.

M

main effect A result occuring in a factorial design when one of the independent variables has an influence on the dependent variable.

manifest variable A variable in a study that we can observe and measure.

Mann–Whitney *U* test A nonparametric hypothesis test used when there are two groups, a between-groups design, and an ordinal dependent variable.

marginal mean The mean of a row or a column in a table that shows the cells of a study with a two-way ANOVA design.

mean The arithmetic average of a group of scores. It is calculated by summing all the scores and dividing by the total number of scores.

median The middle score of all the scores in a sample when the scores are arranged in ascending order. If there is no single middle score, the median is the mean of the two middle scores.

mesokurtic The description given to a normal distribution.

meta-analysis A type of statistical analysis that simultaneously examines as many studies as possible for a given research topic, and involves the calculation of a mean effect size from the individual effect sizes of these studies.

mixed-design ANOVA A hypothesis test used to analyze the data from a study with at least two nominal independent variables and an interval dependent variable; at least one independent variable must be within-groups and at least one independent variable must be between-groups.

mode The most common score of all the scores in a sample.

moiré vibration A form of chartjunk that take the form of any of the patterns that computers provide as options to fill in bars on a graph.

multimodal A distribution that has more than two modes, or most common scores.

multiple regression A statistical technique that includes two or more predictor variables in a prediction equation.

multivariate analysis of covariance (MANCOVA) An ANOVA with multiple dependent variables and the inclusion of a covariate.

multivariate analysis of variance (MANOVA) A form of ANOVA in which there is more than one dependent variable.

N

negative correlation An association between two variables in which participants with high scores on one variable tend to have low scores on the other variable.

negatively skewed data An asymmetric distribution whose tail extends to the left, in a negative direction.

noise Any factors that influence an experiment by making the relations between variables less clear than they really are.

nominal variable A variable used for observations that have categories, or names, as their values.

nonexperiment or quasi-experiment A study in which participants are not randomly assigned to conditions.

nonlinear relation A relation between variables best described by a line that breaks or curves in some way.

nonparametric test Inferential statistical analysis that is not based on a set of assumptions about the population.

normal curve A specific bell-shaped curve that is unimodal, symmetric, and defined mathematically.

normal distribution A specific frequency distribution in the shape of a bell-shaped, symmetric, unimodal curve.

null hypothesis A statement that postulates that there is no difference between populations or that the difference is in a direction opposite from that anticipated by the researcher.

O

one-tailed test A hypothesis test in which the research hypothesis is directional, positing either a mean decrease or a mean increase, but not both, as a result of the independent variable.

one-way ANOVA A hypothesis test that includes one nominal independent variable with more than two levels, and an interval dependent variable.

operational definition The operations or procedures used to measure or manipulate a variable.

order effect The effect produced when a participant's behavior changes when the dependent variable is assessed a second time; also called *practice effect*.

ordinal variable A variable used for observations that have rankings (i.e., 1st, 2nd, 3rd, . . .) as their values.

orthogonal variable An independent variable that makes a separate and distinct contribution to the prediction of a dependent variable, as compared with another variable.

outcome In reference to probability, the result of a trial.

outlier An extreme score that is either very high or very low in comparison with the rest of the scores in a sample.

outlier analysis A study that examines the extreme scores in an effort to understand the factors that influence the dependent variable.

P

***p* level** The probability used to determine the critical values, or cutoffs, in hypothesis testing.

paired-samples *t* test A test used to compare two means for a within-groups design, a situation in which every participant is in both samples; also called a *dependent-samples t test*.

parameter A number based on the whole population; it is usually symbolized by a Greek letter.

parametric test Inferential statistical analysis that is based on a set of assumptions about the population.

Pareto chart A type of bar graph in which the categories along the x-axis are ordered from highest bar on the left to lowest bar on the right.

partial correlation A technique that quantifies the degree of association between two variables, after statistically removing the association of a third variable with both of those two variables.

path The term statisticians use to describe the connection between two variables in a statistical model.

path analysis A statistical method that examines a hypothesized model, usually by conducting a series of regression analyses that quantify the paths at each succeeding step in the model.

Pearson correlation coefficient A statistic that quantifies a linear relation between two interval variables.

pictorial graph A visual depiction of data typically used for an independent variable with very few levels (categories) and an interval dependent variable. Each category uses a picture or symbol to represent its value on the interval dependent variable.

pie chart A graph in the shape of a circle with a slice for every category. The size of each slice represents the proportion (or percentage) of each category.

placebo effect The result achieved when an expectation of an outcome either causes or appears to cause that outcome to take place.

planned comparison A test conducted when there are multiple groups of scores but specific comparisons have been specified prior to data collection; also called an *a priori* comparison.

platykurtic The description for distributions that are shorter and fatter with thinner tails.

point estimate A summary statistic from a sample that is just one number as an estimate of the population parameter.

pooled variance A weighted average of the two estimates of variance—one from each sample—that are calculated when conducting an independent-samples t test.

population All of the possible observations about which we'd like to know something.

positive correlation An association between two variables such that participants with high scores on one variable tend to have high scores on the other variable as well, and those with low scores on one variable tend to have low scores on the other variable as well.

positively skewed data An asymmetric distribution whose tail extends to the right, in a positive direction.

postdictive validity A type of criterion-related validity in which we correlate the scale or measure of interest with a criterion measured in the past.

post-hoc test A statistical procedure frequently carried out after we reject the null hypothesis in an analysis of variance; it allows us to make multiple comparisons among several means.

predictive validity How well a measuring instrument (such as a personality scale) predicts future behavior.

proportionate reduction in error A statistic that quantifies how much more accurate our predictions are when we use the regression line instead of the mean as a prediction tool; also called *coefficient of determination*, symbolized as R^2.

psychometrician A statistician and psychologist who develops tests and measures.

psychometrics The branch of statistics used in the development of tests and measures.

Q

qualitative interaction A particular type of quantitative interaction of two (or more) independent variables in which one independent variable reverses its effect depending on the level of the other independent variable.

quantitative interaction An interaction in which one independent variable exhibits a strengthening or weakening of its effect at one or more levels of the other independent variable, but the direction of the initial effect does not change.

R

R^2 The proportion of variance in the dependent variable that is accounted for by the independent variable.

random assignment The protocol established for an experiment whereby every participant in a study has an equal chance of being assigned to any of the groups, or experimental conditions, in the study.

random sample A subset of a population selected using a method that ensures that every member of the population has an equal chance of being selected into the study.

randomized block design A method of developing a study that creates equivalent groups by matching the participants with regard to important characteristics and then uses randomization only within blocks, or groups, of participants who are similar on one or more of these characteristics.

range A measure of variability calculated by subtracting the lowest score (the minimum) from the highest score (the maximum).

range-frame A scatterplot or related graph that indicates only the range of the data on each axis; the lines extend only from the minimum to the maximum scores.

ratio variable A variable that meets the criteria for interval variables but also has meaningful zero points.

raw score Data point that has not yet been transformed or analyzed.

regression to the mean The tendency of scores that are particularly high or low to drift toward the mean over time.

relative risk A measure created by making a ratio of two conditional proportions; also called *relative likelihood* or *relative chance*.

reliability The consistency of a measure.

replication The duplication of scientific results, ideally in a different context or with a sample that has different characteristics.

research hypothesis A statement that postulates that there is a difference between populations, or sometimes, more specifically, that there is a difference in a certain direction, positive or negative; also called the *alternate hypothesis*.

residual The effect, with respect to interactions, left over after the effects of the two independent variables have been removed.

robust A term given to a hypothesis test that produces fairly accurate results even when the data suggest that the population might not meet some of the assumptions.

S

sample A set of observations drawn from the population of interest that, it is hoped, share the same characteristics as the population of interest.

scatterplot A graph that depicts the relation between two interval variables. The values of each variable are marked along the two axes, and a mark is made to indicate the intersection of the two scores for each participant. The mark will be above the individual's score on the *x*-axis and across from the score on the *y*-axis.

simple linear regression A statistical tool that enables us to predict an individual's score on a dependent variable from his or her score on one independent variable.

single-blind experiment An experiment in which participants do not know the condition to which they have been assigned. This reduces the possibility that participants will respond as they believe they are expected to respond to a given situation.

single-sample *t* test A hypothesis test in which we compare data from one sample to a population for which we know the mean but not the standard deviation.

skewness A measure of how much one of the tails of the distribution is pulled away from the center.

slope The amount that *Y* is predicted to increase for an increase of 1 in *X*.

source table A table that presents the important calculations and final results of an ANOVA in a consistent and easy-to-read format.

sparkline Dataword that is a data-intense, design-simple, word-sized graphics that may be inserted into a sentence.

Spearman rank-order correlation coefficient A non-parametric statistic that quantifies the association between two ordinal variables.

split-half reliability A measure of the internal consistency of a test or measure that is calculated by correlating the odd-numbered items with the even-numbered items.

square root transformation A transformation that reduces skewness by compressing both the negative and positive sides of a skewed distribution.

standard deviation The typical amount that the scores in a sample vary, or deviate, from the mean.

standard error The name for the standard deviation of a distribution of means.

standard error of the estimate A statistic indicating the typical distance between a regression line and the actual data points.

standard normal distribution A normal distribution of the *z* score.

standardization A process that converts individual scores from different normal distributions to a shared normal distribution with a known mean, standard deviation, and percentiles.

statistically significant A name given to a finding for which we have rejected the null hypothesis because the pattern in the data differs from what we would expect by chance.

statistical (or theoretical) model A hypothesized network of relations, often portrayed graphically, among multiple variables.

statistical power A measure of our ability to reject the null hypothesis given that the null hypothesis is false.

statistic A number based on a sample taken from a population; it is usually symbolized by a Latin letter.

stem-and-leaf plot A graph that displays all the data points of a single variable both numerically and visually.

stepwise multiple regression A type of multiple regression in which computer software determines the order in which independent variables are included in the equation.

stratified sampling A selection method in which strata, usually levels of a nominal variable, are identified, and then a random sample of the same size is taken from each stratum.

structural equation modeling (SEM) A statistical technique that quantifies how well sample data "fit" a theoretical model that hypothesizes a set of relations among multiple variables.

subjective probability An individual's opinion or judgment about the likelihood that an event will occur; also called *personal probability*.

success In reference to probability, the outcome for which we're trying to determine the probability.

sum of squares The sum of the squared deviations from the mean for each score. Symbolized as *SS*.

T

***t* statistic** A statistic that indicates the distance of a sample mean from a population mean in terms of standard error.

table A presentation of data, typically quantitative, that is typed as text in rows and columns (e.g., frequency table).

test–retest reliability A method that determines whether the scale being used provides consistent information every time the test is taken.

third quartile The 75th percentile of a data set.

time plot or **time series plot** A graph that plots an interval variable on the y-axis as it changes over an increment of time (e.g., second, day, century) labeled on the x-axis.

trial In reference to probability, each occasion that a given procedure is carried out.

two-tailed test A hypothesis test in which the research hypothesis does not indicate a direction of mean difference or change in the dependent variable but merely indicates that there will be a mean difference.

two-way ANOVA A hypothesis test that includes two nominal independent variables, regardless of their numbers of levels, and an interval dependent variable.

Tukey _HSD_ test A widely used post-hoc test that determines the differences between means in terms of standard error; the _HSD_ is compared to a critical value; sometimes called the _q test_.

Type I error The result when we reject the null hypothesis, but the null hypothesis is correct.

Type II error The result when we fail to reject the null hypothesis, but the null hypothesis is false.

U

ubiquity of the normal curve The concept that posits that the bell-shaped curve describes the approximate shape of the distributions of a surprising number of characteristics that vary.

unimodal A distribution that has one mode, or most common score.

V

validity The extent to which a test actually measures what it was intended to measure.

variable Any observation of a physical, attitudinal, or behavioral characteristic that can take on different values.

variance The average of the squared deviations from the mean.

volunteer sample A special kind of convenience sample in which participants actively choose to participate in a study; also called a _self-selected sample_.

W

whiskers The lines that extend from either end of the box in a box plot. The ends of the whiskers indicate the minimum and maximum scores in a sample.

Wilcoxon signed-rank test A nonparametric hypothesis test used when there are two groups, a within-groups design, and an ordinal dependent variable.

within-groups ANOVA A hypothesis test in which there are more than two samples, and each sample is composed of the same participants; also called a _repeated measures ANOVA_.

within-groups research design An experimental design in which the different levels of the independent variable are experienced by all participants in the study; also called a _repeated-measures design_.

within-groups variance An estimate of the population variance based on the differences within each of the three (or more) sample distributions.

Z

z score The number of standard deviations a particular score is from the mean.

z distribution A normal distribution of standardized scores.

Abelson, R. (2006, August 18). Heart procedure is off the charts in an Ohio city. *New York Times.* Retrieved on November 12, 2006, from http://www.nytimes.com

Adams, M. (1990). The dead grandmother/exam syndrome and the potential downfall of American society. *The Connecticut Review, 12,* 70–74.

Adema, A. (2005). Investigating space shuttle *Columbia's* accident: A four-phase systemic model of structure, technology, environment, and transformation. *Dissertation Abstracts International Section A: Humanities and Social Sciences, 66*(2-A), 411.

Agresti, A. & Franklin, C. (2006). *Statistics: The art and science of learning from data.* Upper Saddle River, NJ: Prentice Hall.

Alter, A., & Oppenheimer, D. (2006). Predicting short-term stock fluctuations by using processing fluency. *Proceedings of the National Academy of Sciences of the United States of America, 103,* 9369–9372.

Alterman, E. (2005). Think again: Conservative media, liberal nation, *Media & Culture.* July 7, retrieved February 6, 2007, from http://www.americanprogress.org/issues/2005/07

Amabile, T. M. (1983). The social psychology of creativity: A componential conceptualization. *Journal of Personality and Social Psychology, 45,* 357–376.

American Academy of Physician Assistants. (2005). Income reported by PAs who graduated in 2004. *American Academy of Physician Assistants.* Retrieved November 20, 2006, from http://www.aapa.org/research/05newgrad-income.pdf

American Psychological Association. (1994). *Resolution on Facilitated Communication,* Washington, DC: Author.

American Psychological Association (APA). (2001). *Publication manual of the American Psychological Association.* Washington, DC: Author.

American Psychological Association. (2005). *Graduate study in psychology 2005* (rev. ed.). Washington, DC: Author.

Archibold, R. C. (1998, February 18). Just because the grades are up, are Princeton students smarter? *New York Times.* Retrieved November 14, 2006, from http://www.nytimes.com

Aron, A., & Aron, E. N. (2002). *Statistics for psychology* (3rd ed.). Upper Saddle River, NJ: Pearson Education.

Aron, A., Fisher, H., Mashek, D. J., Strong, G., Li, H., & Brown, L. L. (2005). Reward, motivation, and emotion systems associated with early-stage intense romantic love. *Journal of Neurophysiology, 94,* 327–337.

Aronson, J., Justina, M. J., Good, C., Keough, K., Stelle, C. M., & Brown, J. (1999). When white men can't do math: Necessary and sufficient factors in stereotype threat. *Journal of Experimental Social Psychology, 35,* 29–46.

Azim, E., Mobbs, D., Jo, B., Menon, V., & Reiss, A. L. (2005). Sex differences in brain activation elicited by humor. *Proceedings of the National Academy of Sciences, 102,* 16496–16501. Retrieved February 10, 2006, from http://www.pnas.org/cgi/doi/10.1073/pnas.0408456102

Bailey, D. G., & Dresser, G. K. (2004). Natural products and adverse drug interactions. *Canadian Medical Association Journal, 170,* 1531–1532.

Bakalar, N. (2005, October 4). Prevention: Statin drugs appear to reduce risks to bones. *New York Times.* Retrieved October 8, 2005, from http://www.nytimes.com

Baker, F., Wigram, T. & Gold, C. (2005). The effects of a song-singing programme on the affective speaking intonation of people with traumatic brain injury. *Brain Injury, 19,* 519–528.

Banks, J., Marmot, M., Oldfield, Z., & Smith, J. P. (2006). Disease and disadvantage in the United States and England. *Journal of the American Medical Association, 295,* 2037–2045.

Barch, D. M., Csernansky, J. G., Conturo, T., & Snyder, A. Z. (2002). Working and long-term memory deficits in schizophrenia: Is there a common prefrontal mechanism? *Journal of Abnormal Psychology, 111,* 478–494.

Bardwell, W. A., Ensign, W. Y., & Mills, P. J. (2005). Negative mood endures after completion of high-altitude military training. *Annals of Behavioral Medicine, 29,* 64–69.

Bartsh, R. A. (2006). Improving attitudes towards statistics in the first class. *Teaching Psychology, 33,* 197–198.

Basoglu, M., Mineka, S., Parker, M., Aker, T., Livanou, M., & Gök, S. (1997). Psychological preparedness for trauma as a protective factor in survivors of torture. *Psychological Medicine, 27,* 1421–1433.

Bauerline, M. (2004, November 12). Liberal groupthink is anti-intellectual. *Chronicle of Higher Education.*

Begg, C. B. (1994). Publication bias. In H. Cooper & L. V. Hedges (Eds.), *The handbook of research synthesis* (pp. 399–409). New York: Russell Sage Foundation.

Behenam, M., & Pooya, O. (2006). Factors affecting patients cooperation during orthodontic treatment. *The Orthodontic CYBERjournal.* Retrieved on November 21, 2006, from http://www.oc-j.com/nov06/cooperation.htm

Belkin, L. (2002, August 11). The odds of that. *New York Times.* Retrieved August 11, 2002, from http://www.nytimes.com

Bellafante, G. (2006, February 24). To keep twins in the same class, parents seek legislators' help. *New York Times.* Retrieved February 24, 2006, from http://www.nytimes.com

Bellosta, S., Paoletti, R., & Corsini, A. (2004). Safety of statins: Focus on clinical pharmacokinetics and drug interactions. *Circulation, 109*, III-50–III-57.

Belluck, P. (2005). What it means to be human. *Princeton Alumni Weekly Online*. Retrieved October 13, 2005, from http://www.princeton.edu/~paw/archive_new/PAW04-05/15-0608/features1.html

Benbow, C. P., & Stanley, J. C. (1980). Sex differences in math ability: Fact or artifact? *Science, 210*, 1262–1264.

Ben-Peretz, M. (2002). Retired teachers reflect on learning from experience. *Teachers and Teaching: Theory and Practice, 8*, pp. 313–323.

Bernstein, P. L. (1996). *Against the gods: The remarkable story of risk*. New York: Wiley.

Beubow, C. P., & Stanley, J. C. (1980). Sex differences in mathematical ability: Fact or artifact? *Science, 210*, 1262–1264.

Birney, R. C., Burdick, H., & Teevan, R. C. (1969). *Fear of failure*. New York: Van Nostrand Reinhold.

Boone, D. E. (1992). WAIS-R scatter with psychiatric inpatients: I. Intrasubtest scatter. *Psychological Reports, 71*, 483–487.

Borsari, B., & Carey, K. B. (2005). Two brief alcohol interventions for mandated college students. *Psychology of Addictive Behaviors, 19*, 296–302.

Bowen, W. G., & Bok, D. (2000). *The shape of the river: Long-term consequences of considering race in college and university admissions*. Princeton, NJ: Princeton University Press.

Bowles, J. (1994). W.E. Deming obituary. *Q-Tips Newsletter*, January 1994. Retrieved July 22, 2006, from http://deming.eng.clemson.edu/pub/den/files/wedobit.txt

Box, J. (1978). *R. A. Fisher: The life of a scientist*. New York: Wiley.

Brinn, D. (2006, June 25). Israeli "clown therapy" boosts fertility treatment birthrate. *Health*. Retrieved April 6, 2007, from http://www.Israel21c.org

Bryson, B. (1989). *The lost continent: Travels in small-town America*. London: Black Swan.

Buekens, P., Xiong, X., & Harville, E. (2006). Hurricanes and pregnancy. *Birth, 33*, 91–93.

Burns, D. S., Sledge, R. B., & Fuller, L. A. (2005). Cancer patients' interest and preferences for music therapy. *Journal of Music Therapy, 42*, 185–199.

Bushweller, K. (1999). Generation of cheaters. *American School Board Journal*. Retrieved October 24, 2006, from http://www.asbj.com/199904/0499inprint.html

Canadian Institute for Health Information (CIHI). (2005). More patients receiving transplants than 10 years ago, despite stagnant organ donation rate. Retrieved July 15, 2005, from http://secure.cihi.ca/cihiweb/dispPage.jsp?cw_page=media_13apr2005_e

Cancer Research UK. (2003). *Cancer deaths in the UK*. Retrieved June 15, 2005, from http://info.cancerresearchuk.org/cancerstats/mortality/cancerdeaths/

Carey, B. (2006, February 21). The unconscious mind: A great decision maker. *New York Times*. Retrieved February 21, 2006, from http://www.nytimes.com

Carey, B. (2007a, March 6). Insufferable clinginess, or healthy dependence? *New York Times*. Retrieved March 8, 2007, from http://www.nytimes.com

Carey, B. (2007b, March 8). Scent activates memory during sleep, study says. *New York Times*. Retrieved March 8, 2007, from http://www.nytimes.com

Centers for Disease Control (CDC). (2004). *Americans slightly taller, much heavier than four decades ago*. Retrieved May 26, 2005, from http://www.cdc.gov/nchs/pressroom/04news/americans.htm

Cheng, G. H. L., Chan, D. K. S., & Tong, P. Y. (2006). Qualities of online friendships with different gender compositions and durations. *CyberPsychology and Behavior, 9*, 14–21.

Chen, X., Rubin, K. H., & Li, B.-S. (1995). Depressed mood in Chinese children: Relations with school performance and family environment. *Journal of Consulting and Clinical Psychology, 63*, 938–947.

Christianson, S. (1992). Emotional stress and eyewitness testimony: A critical review. *Psychological Bulletin, 112*, 284–309.

Christopher, A. N., & Walter, M. I. (2006). An assignment to help students learn to navigate primary sources of information. *Teaching Psychology, 33*, 42–45.

Cohen, J. (1983). The cost of dichotomization. *Applied Psychological Measurement, 7*, 249–253.

Cohen, J. (1988). *Statistical power analysis for the behavioral sciences* (2nd ed.). Hillsdale, NJ: Erlbaum.

Cohen, J. (1990). Things I have learned (so far). *American Psychologist, 45*, 1304–1312.

Cohen, J. (1992). A power primer. *Psychological Bulletin, 112*, 155–159.

Cohen, J. (1994). The earth is round ($p < .05$). *American Psychologist, 49*, 997–1003.

Conn, V. S., Valentine, J. C., Cooper, H. M., & Rantz, M. J. (2003). Grey literature in meta-analyses. *Nursing Research, 52*, 256–261.

Cooper, H., Robinson, J. C., & Patall, E. A. (2006). Does homework improve academic achievement? A synthesis of research, 1987–2003. *Review of Educational Research, 76*, 1–62.

Cooper, H., Valentine, J. C., Nye, B., & Lindsay, J. J. (1999). Relationships between five after-school activities and academic achievement. *Journal of Educational Psychology, 91*, 369–378.

Cooper, M. J., Gulen, H., & Ovtchinnikov, A. V. (2007). *Corporate political contributions and stock returns*. Available at SSRN: http://ssrn.com/abstract-940790.

Corsi, A., & Ashenfelter, O. (2001, April). *Wine quality: Experts' ratings and weather determinants* [Electronic version]. Poster session presented at the annual meeting of the European Association of Agricultural Economists, Zaragoza, Spain.

Cortina, J. M. (1993). What is coefficient alpha? An examination of theory and applications. *Journal of Applied Psychology, 78*, 98–104.

Cox, R. H., Thomas. T. R., Hinton, P. S., Donahue, W. M. (2006). Effects of acute bouts of aerobic exercise of varied intensity on subjective mood experiences in women of different age groups across time. *Journal of Sport Behavior, 29,* 40–59.

Coyne, J. C. (1976). Toward an interactional description of depression. *Psychiatry: Journal for the Study of Interpersonal Processes, 39,* 28–40.

Creighton, C. (1965). *History of epidemics in Britain* (Vol. 2). London: Cassell.

Cunliffe, S. (1976). Interaction. *Journal of the Royal Statistical Society, A, 139,* 1–19.

Czerwinski, M., Smith, G., Regan, T., Meyers, B., Robertson, G., & Starkweather, G. (2003). Toward characterizing the productivity benefits of very large displays. In M. Rauterberg et al. (Eds.), *Human-computer interaction-INTERACT '03 (pp. 9–16).* IOS Press.

Dale, S. B., & Krueger, A. B. (1999). Estimating the payoff to attending a more selective college: An application of selection on observables and unobservables (Working Paper No. 7322). National Bureau of Economic Research. Retrieved July 30, 2006, from http://www.nber.org/papers/w7322

Darlin, D. (2006, July 1). Air fare made easy (or easier). *New York Times.* Retrieved July 1, 2006, from http://www.nytimes.com

Darwin, C. (1839). *The Voyage of the Beagle.* London: Smith, Eldo, & Co.

Darwin, C. (1859). *On the Origin of Species by Means of Natural Selection.* London: W. Clowes and Sons. Retrieved from http://darwin-online.org.uk, March 26, 2007

Darwin, C. (1862, 1877). *On the various contrivances by which British and foreign orchids are fertilized by insects, and on the good effects of intercrossing.* John Murray: London. (Original work published 1862).

Dean, G., & Kelly, I. W. (2003). Is astrology relevant to consciousness and PSI? *Journal of Consciousness Studies, 10,* 175–198.

Dean, G., Mather, A., & Kelly, I. W. (1996). Astrology. In G. Stein (Ed.), *The encyclopedia of the paranormal* (pp. 47–99) Amherst, NY: Prometheus.

DeBroff, B. M., & Pahk, P. J. (2003). The ability of periorbitally applied antiglare products to improve contrast sensitivity in conditions of sunlight exposure. *Archives of Ophthalmology, 121,* 997–1001.

DeCarlo, L. T. (1997). On the meaning and use of kurtosis. *Psychological Methods, 2,* 292–307.

Delucchi, K. L. (1983). The use and misuse of chi square: Lewis and Burke revisited. *Psychological Bulletin, 94,* 166–176.

Deming, W. E. (1989). *Out of the crisis.* Cambridge, MA: Massachusetts Institute of Technology, Center for Advanced Engineering Study.

DeVellis, R. F. (1991). *Scale development: Theory and applications.* Newbury Park, CA: Sage.

Diekman, A. B., & Murnan, S. K. (2004). Learning to be little women and little men: The inequitable gender equality of nonsexist children's literature. *Sex Roles, 50,* 373–385.

Dijksterhuis, A., Bos, M. W., Nordgren, L. F., & van Baaren, R. B. (2006). On making the right choice: The deliberation-without-attention effect. *Science, 311,* 1005–1007.

Ditto, P. H., & Lopez, D. L. (1992). Motivated skepticism: Use of differential decision criteria for preferred and nonpreferred conclusions. *Journal of Personality and Social Psychology, 63,* 568–584.

Doctors Without Borders. (2006). Trying to halt cholera in Angola: Access to safe and free water not guaranteed. Retrieved August 2, 2006, from http://www.doctorswithoutborders.org/pr/2006/05-17-2006.cfm

Dubner, S. J., & Levitt, S. D. (2006, November 5). The Way We Live Now: Freakonomics; The price of climate change. *New York Times,* Retrieved on March 7, 2007 from http://www.nytimes.com.

Dubner, S. J., & Levitt, S. D. (2006, May 7). A star is made: The birth-month soccer anomaly. *New York Times.* Retrieved May 7, 2006, from http://www.nytimes.com

Duggan, M., & Levitt, S. D. (2002). Winning isn't everything: Corruption in sumo wrestling. *American Economic Review, 92,* 1594–1605.

Eagly, A. H., Chen, S., Chaiken, S., & Shaw-Barnes, K. (1999). The impact of attitudes on memory: An affair to remember. *Psychological Bulletin, 125,* 64–89.

Eckles, E., Joireman, J., Sprott, D., & Spangenberg, E. (2003, May). *Individual differences in the consideration of future consequences predict fiscal responsibility* [Electronic version]. Poster session presented at the annual meeting of the American Psychological Society, Atlanta.

Eid, J., & Morgan, C. A. (2006). Dissociation, hardiness, and performance in military cadets participating in survival training. *Military Medicine, 171,* 436–442.

Elliott, S. (2006, March 20). A magazine's blitz of Baltimore. *The New York Times.* Retrieved March 20, 2006 from http://www.nytimes.com

Emdad, R., Sondergaard, H. P., & Theorell, T. (2005). Short communication: Impairments in short-term memory, and figure logic, in PTSD patients compared to healthy controls with the same ethnic background. *Stress and Health: Journal of the International Society for the Investigation of Stress, 21,* 33–44.

Engle-Friedman, M., Riela, S., Golan, R., Ventuneac, A. M., Davis, C. M., Jefferson, A. D., & Major, D. (2003). The effect of sleep loss on next day effort. *Journal of Sleep Research, 12,* 113–124.

Erdfelder, E., Faul, F., & Buchner, A. (1996). GPOWER: A general power analysis program. *Behavior Research Methods, Instruments, and Computers, 28,* 1–11.

Feingold, A. (1992). The greater male variability controversy. *Review of Educational Research, 62,* 89–90.

Feynman, R. P. (1986). Personal observations on the reliability of the shuttle. In *Report of the Presidential Commission on the Space Shuttle* Challenger *Accident: Feynman's appendix to the Rogers Commission Report.* Committee on Science and Technology, House of Representatives. Washington, DC.

Forsyth, D. R., & Kerr, N. A. (1999, August). *Are adaptive illusions adaptive?* Poster presented at the annual meeting of the American Psychological Association, Boston, MA.

Forsyth, D. R., Lawrence, N. K., Burnette, J. L., & Baumeister, R. F. (2006). *Attempting to improve the academic performance of struggling college students by bolstering their self-esteem: An intervention that backfired.* Unpublished manuscript.

Frantz, C. M., & Bennigson, C. (2005). Better late than early: The influence of timing on apology effectiveness. *Journal of Experimental Social Psychology, 41*, 201–207.

Frazier, T. W., & Edmonds, C. L. (2002). Curriculum predictors of performance on the Major Field Test in Psychology II. *Journal of Instructional Psychology, 29*, 29–32.

Freedman, O., Pisani, R., & Purves, R. (1998). *Statistics.* New York: W. W. Norton.

Frick, R. W. (1995). A problem with confidence intervals. *American Psychologist, 50*, 1102–1003.

Friedman, R. A. (2007, January 9). Yet another worry for those who believe the glass is half-empty. *New York Times.* Retrieved February 19, 2007, from http://www.nytimes.com

Friendly, M. (2002). Visions and re-visions of Charles Joseph Minard. *Journal of Educational and Behavioral Statistics, 27*, pp. 31–52.

Friendly, M. (2005). Gallery of data visualization. Retrieved July 21, 2005, from http://www.math.yorku.ca/SCS/Gallery/

Galton, F. (1889). *Natural Inheritance.* London: MacMillan.

Georgiou, C. C., Betts, N. M., Hoerr, S. L., Keim, K., Peters, P. K., Stewart, B., & Voichick, J. (1997). Among young adults, college students and graduates practiced more healthful habits and made more healthful food choices than did nonstudents. *Journal of the American Dietetic Association, 97*, 754–759.

Gerber, A., & Malhotra, N. (2006). Can political science literatures be believed? A study of publication bias in the *APSR* and the *AJPS.* Retrieved from http://www.jspure.org/news2.htm on March 23, 2007.

Gill, G. (2005). *Nightingales: The extraordinary upbringing and curious life of Miss Florence Nightingale.* Random House Trade Paperbacks: New York.

Gilovich, T., & Medvec, V. H. (1995). The experience of regret: What, when, and why. *Psychological Review, 102*, 379–395.

Gimbarzevsky, B. (1995). Canadian homicide trends 1961–1994. Retrieved July 6, 2005, from http://teapot.usask.ca/cdn-firearms/Gimbarzevsky/homicide.html

Glass, G. V. (1976). Primary, secondary, and meta-analysis of research. *Educational Researcher, 5*, 3–8.

Goodwin, L. D., & Leech, N. L. (2006). Understanding correlation: Factors that affect the size of *r*. *The Journal of Experimental Education, 74*, 251–266.

Gossett, W. S. (1908). The probable error of a mean. *Biometrics, 6*, 1–24.

Gossett, W. S. (1942). *"Student's" collected papers* (E. S. Pearson, J. Wishart, Eds). Cambridge University Press, Cambridge: U.K.

Grimberg, A., Kutikov, J. K., & Cucchiara, A. J. (2005). Sex differences in patients referred for evaluation of poor growth. *Journal of Pediatrics, 146*, 212–216.

Grimes, W. (2005, November 18). Winnowing the field of America to one representative. *New York Times.* Retrieved on November 18, 2005, from http://www.nytimes.com

Griner, D., & Smith, T. B. (2006). Culturally adapted mental health intervention: A meta-analytic review. *Psychotherapy: Research, Practice, Training, 43*, 531–548.

Grove, W. M., Zald, D. H., Lebow, B. S., Snits, B. E., & Nelson, C. E. (1996). Clinical vs. mechanical prediction: A meta-analysis. *Psychological Assessment, 12*, 19–30.

Guttmannova, K., Shields, A. L. & Caruso, J. C. (2005). Promoting conceptual understanding of statistics: Definitional versus computational formulas, *Teaching of Psychology, 32*, 251–253.

Hancock, P. A., & Warm, J. S. (1989). A dynamic model of stress and sustained attention. *Human Factors, 31*, 519–537.

Hartmann, P., Reuter, M., & Nyborg, H. (2006). The relationship between date of birth and individual differences in personality and general intelligence: A large-scale study. *Personality and Individual Differences, 40*, 1349–1362.

Harwood, W., & Navias, R. (1986). The *Challenger* timeline. United Press International. Washington, DC.

Hatchett, G. T. (2003). Does psychopathology predict counseling duration? *Psychological Reports, 93*, 175–185.

Hatfield, E., & Sprecher, S. (1986). Measuring passionate love in intimate relationships. *Journal of Adolescence, 9*, 383–410.

Hays, W. L. (1994). *Statistics* (5th ed.). Fort Worth, TX: Harcourt Brace College Publishers.

Heading for the hills. (2005, March 12). *New Zealand Herald* [Electronic version].

Headquarters Counseling Center. (2005). Myths and facts about suicide. Retrieved February 12, 2007, from http://www.hqcc.lawrence.ks.us/suicide_prevention/myths_facts.html

Healey, J. R. (2006, October 13). Driving the hard (top, that is) way. *USA Today*, Page 1B.

Herszenhorn, D. M. (2006, May 5). As test-taking grows, test-makers grow rarer. *New York Times.* Retrieved May 5, 2006 from http://www.nytimes.com

Hidden persuaders (2006). *Skeptics Dictionary*, http://skeptic.com/hiddenpersuaders.html. Retrieved on February 12, 2007.

Hockenbury, D. H., & Hockenbury, S. E. (2003). *Psychology* (3rd ed.). New York: Worth.

Hoffrage, U., Lindsey, S., Hertwig, R., & Gigerenzer, G. (2000). Communicating statistical information. *Science, 290*, 2261–2262. [Electronic version]

Holiday, A., & Nolan, S. (2007). Perceptions of depression based on etiology and gender. Unpublished manuscript.

Houlder, V. (2004, October 18). Confusing formulae that muddy the waters of the fiscal debate. *Financial Times* (London), p. 3.

Howard, K. I., Moras, K., Brill, P. L., Martinovich, Z., & Lutz, W. (1996). Efficacy, effectiveness, and patient progress. *American Psychologist, 51*, 1059–1064.

Hugenberg, K., Miller, J., & Claypool, H. (2007). Categorization and individuation in the cross-race recognition deficit: Toward a solution to an insidious problem. *Journal of Experimental Social Psychology, 43*, 334–340.

Hunter, J. E., & Schmidt, F. L. (1996). Cumulative research knowledge and social policy formulation: The critical role of meta-analysis. *Psychology, Public Policy, and Law, 2*, 324–347.

Hyde, J. S. (1984). Children's understanding of sexist language. *Developmental Psychology, 20*, 697–706.

Hyde, J. S., Fennema, E., & Lamon, S. J. (1990). Gender differences in mathematics performance: A meta-analysis. *Psychological Bulletin, 107*, 139–155.

Hyde, J. S. (2005). The gender similarities hypothesis. *American Psychologist, 60*, 581–592.

IMD International (2001). Competitiveness rankings as of April 2001. Retrieved on June 29, 2006 from http://www.photius.com/wfb1999/rankings/competitiveness.html

Indiana University Media Relations. (2006). It's no joke: IU study finds *The Daily Show* with Jon Stewart to be as substantive as network news. Retrieved December 10, 2006, from http://newsinfo.iu.edu/news/page/normal/4159.html

Irwin, M. L., Tworoger, S. S., Yasui, Y., Rajan, B., McVarish, L., LaCroix, K., et al. (2004). Influence of demographic, physiologic, and psychosocial variables on adherence to a year-long moderate-intensity exercise trial in postmenopausal women. *Preventive Medicine, 39*, 1080–1086.

Jacob, J. E., & Eccles, J. (1982). Science and the media: Benbow and Stanley revisited. Report funded by the National Institute of Education, Washington, D.C. ERIC # ED235925.

Jacob, J. E., & Eccles, J. (1986). Social forces shape math attitudes and performance. *Signs, 11*, 367–380.

Jacobsen, J. W., Malick, J. A., & Schwartz, A. A. (1995). A history of facilitated communication: Science, pseudoscience, and anti-science. *American Psychologist, 50*, 750–765.

Janis, L. (1972). *Victims of groupthink: A psychological study of foreign-policy decisions and fiascoes.* Oxford, UK: Houghton Mifflin.

Jaswal, V. K., & Neely, L. A. (2006). Adults don't always know best: Preschoolers use past reliability over age when learning new words. *Psychological Science, 17*, 757–758.

Johnson, S. (2006). *The ghost map: The story of London's deadliest epidemic—and how it changed the way we think about disease, cities, science, and the modern world.* New York: Riverhead.

Johnson, W. B., Koch, C., Fallow, G. O., & Huwe, J. M. (2000). Prevalence of mentoring in clinical versus experimental doctoral programs: Survey findings, implications, and recommendations. *Psychotherapy: Theory, Research, Practice, Training, 37*, 325–334.

Kaufman, J. C., & Bristol, A. S. (2001). When Allport met Freud: Using anecdotes in the teaching of psychology. *Teaching of Psychology, 28*, pp. 44–46.

Kennedy, R., & Scott, A. (2005). A pilot study: The effects of music therapy interventions on middle school students' ESL skills. *Journal of Therapy Music, 42*, 244–261.

Kilian, R., Matschinger, H., Loeffler, W., Roick, C., & Angermeyer, M. C. (2002). A comparison of methods to handle skew distributed cost variables in the analysis of the resource consumption in schizophrenia treatment. *Journal of Mental Health Policy Economics, 5*, 21–31.

Killeen, P. B. (2005). An alternative to null-hypothesis significance tests. *Psychological Science, 16*, 345–353.

Klewe, L. (1993). An empirical evaluation of spelling boards as a means of communication for the multihandicapped. *Journal of Autism and Developmental Disorders, 23*, 559–566.

Kocich, J. (2005, April 20). How to calculate life expectancy [Letter to the editor]. *Financial Times* (London), p. 12.

Kolata, G. (2001, June 5). On research frontier, basic questions. *New York Times*, pp. F1, F9.

Kolata, G. (2005, July 28). Study says echinacea has no effect on colds. *New York Times.* Retrieved July 28, 2005, from http://www.nytimes.com

Kolata, G. (2007, March 7). Researchers dispute benefits of CT scans for lung cancer. *New York Times.* Retrieved March 8, 2007, from http://www.nytimes.com

Kramer, R. M. (1998). Revisiting the Bay of Pigs and Vietnam decisions 25 years later: How well has the groupthink hypothesis stood the test of time? *Organizational Behavior and Human Decision Processes, 73*, 236–271.

Kressel, N. J., & Kressel, D. F. (2002). *Stack and sway: The new science of jury consulting.* Boulder, CO: Westview.

Krugman, P. (2006, May 5). Our sick society. *New York Times.* Retrieved May 5, 2006, from http://www.nytimes.com

Kuck, V. J., Buckner, J. P., Marzabadi, C. H., & Nolan, S. A. (2007). A review and study on graduate training and academic hiring of chemists. *Journal of Chemical Education, 84*, 277–284.

Kunicki, M., & Heinzen, T. E. (1996). *Who wrote it—he or she?: Thirty-five years of gender inequity in the New York Times.* Paper presented at the third annual undergraduate psychology conference at William Paterson University of New Jersey, Wayne, New Jersey.

Lam, R. W., & Kennedy, S. H. (2005). Using meta-analysis to evaluate evidence: Practical tips and traps. *Canadian Journal of Psychiatry, 50*, 167–174.

Landrum, E. (2005). Core terms in undergraduate statistics. *Teaching of Psychology, 32*, 249–251.

Lansing, A. (1960). *Shackleton's valiant voyage.* New York: Scholastic Book Services.

Latkin, C. A., Williams, C. T., Wang, J., & Curry, A. D. (2005). Neighborhood social disorder as a determinant of drug injection behaviors: A structural equation modeling approach. *Health Psychology, 24*, 96–100.

Leippe, M. R., Eisenstadt, D., Rauch, S. M., & Seib, H. M. (2004). Timing of eyewitness expert testimony, jurors' need for cognition, and case strength as determinants of trial verdicts. *Journal of Applied Psychology, 89*, 524–541.

Leonhardt, D. (2007, March 7). The data tell a different story on heart patients. *New York Times.* Retrieved March 8, 2007 from http://www.nytimes.com

Levitt, S. D., & Dubner, S. J. (2005). *Freakonomics: A rogue economist explores the hidden side of everything.* New York: Morrow.

Lewis, D., & Burke, C. J. (1949). The use and misuse of the chi-square test. *Psychological Bulletin, 46,* 433–489.

Lewis, M. (2003). *Money ball.* New York: Norton.

Lexis, W. (1903). *Abhandlungen zur theorie der bevolkerungs-und moralstatistik.* Jena: Gustav Fisher. Treatises to the theory of population statistics and morality statistics. Kostock, Germany.

Lieberman, J. K., & Rhodes, N. S. (1976). *The complete CB handbook: Everything you have to know to own and operate a citizens band two-way radio.* New York: Avon Books.

Lifestyle education reduced both 2-h plasma glucose and relative risk. (2006, March 6). *Health and Medicine Week.* Retrieved July 9, 2006, from http://www.newsrx.com

Lloyd, C. (2006, December 14). Saved, or sacrificed? *Salon.com.* Retrieved February 26, 2007, from http://www.salon.com/mwt/broadsheet/2006/12/14/selection/index.html

Lucas, M. E. S., Deen, J. L., von Seidlein, L., Wang, X., Ampuero, J., Puri, M., et al. (2005). Effectiveness of mass oral cholera vaccination in Beira, Mozambique. *New England Journal of Medicine, 352,* 757–767.

Luttke, H. B. (2004). Experiments within the Milgram paradigm. *Gruppendynamik und Organisationsasberatung, 35,* 431–464.

Lynn, M. (1988). The effects of alcohol consumption on restaurant tipping. *Personality and Social Psychology Bulletin, 14,* 87–91.

Maddi, S. R. (2006). Hardiness: The courage to grow from stress. *Journal of Positive Psychology, 1,* 160–168.

Magnier, M. (1999, October 25). The 50: People who most influenced business this century. *Los Angeles Times,* p. U-8.

Manning, W. G., & Mullahy, J. (2001). Estimating log models: To transform or not to transform? *Journal Health Economics, 20,* 461–494.

Mark, G., Gonzalez, V. M., & Harris, J. (2005, April). No task left behind? Examining the nature of fragmented work. *Proceedings of the Association for Computing Machinery Conference on Human Factors in Computing Systems* (ACM CHI 2005), Portland, OR, 321–330. New York: ACM Press.

Markoff, J. (2005, July 18). Marrying maps to data for a new web service. *New York Times.* Retrieved July 18, 2005, from http://www.nytimes.com

Martin, A. (2007, March 7). Makers of sodas try a new pitch: They're healthy. *New York Times.* Retrieved March 8, 2007, from www.nytimes.com

Massey, C., & Thaler, R. H. (2005). *Overconfidence vs. market efficiency in the National Football League.* Retrieved June 6, 2005, from http://www.nber.org/papers/w11270

Matlin, M. W., & Kalat, J. W. (2001). Demystifying the GRE psychology test: A brief guide for students. *Eye on Psi Chi, 5,* 22–25. Retrieved January 7, 2006, from http://www.psichi.org/pubs/articles/article_66.asp

McCabe, D. L., Trevino, L. K., & Butterfield, K. D. (2001). Cheating in academic institutions: A decade of research. *Ethics & Behavior, 11,* 219–232.

McKinney, B. C. (1986). Decision making in the president's commission on the assassination of President Kennedy: A descriptive analysis employing Irving Janis' groupthink hypothesis. *Dissertation Abstracts International, 46*(9-A), 2483.

McLeland, K. C., & Sutton, G. W. (2005). Military service, marital status, and men's relationship satisfaction. *Individual Difference Research, 3,* 177–182.

McNeil, D. G., Jr. (2007, March 7). Medication errors are studied. *New York Times.* Retrieved March 8, 2007, from http://www.nytimes.com

McNulty, T. (2006, November 13). Gender gap, even in death. *Chicago Tribune.* Retrieved November 13, 2006, from http://www.chicagotribune.com

Mecklenburg, S. H., Malpass, R. S., & Ebbesen, E. (2006, March 17). Report to the legislature of the State of Illinois: The Illinois Pilot Program on Sequential Double-Blind Identification Procedures. Retrieved April 19, 2006, from http://eyewitness.utep.edu

Mertler, C. A., & Vannata, R. A. (2005). *Advanced and multivariate statistical methods: Practical application and interpretation* (3rd ed.). Los Angeles: Pyrczak.

Micceri, T. (1989). The unicorn, the normal curve, and other improbable creatures. *Psychological Bulletin, 105,* 156–166.

Mitchell, P. (1999). Grapefruit juice found to cause havoc with drug uptake. *Lancet, 353,* 1355.

Miyamura, M., & Kano, Y. (2006). Robust Gaussian graphical modeling. *Journal of Multivariate Analysis, 97,* 1525–1550.

Morris, R. J. (1975). Religion and medicine: The cholera pamphlets of Oxford, 1832, 1849, and 1854 [Electronic version]. *Medical History, 19.* Retrieved June 10, 2005, from http://www.pubmedcentral.nih.gov/picrender.fcgi?artid=1081641&blobtype=pdf.

Murphy, K. R., & Myors, B. (2004). *Statistical power analysis: A simple and general model for traditional and modern hypothesis tests.* Mahwah, NJ: Erlbaum.

Nagourney, E. (2007a, March 6). Disparities: Singling out minorities for alcohol counseling. *New York Times.* Retrieved March 8, 2007, from http://www.nytimes.com

Nagourney, E. (2007b, March 6). On the scales: Pounds add up on summer break, study says. *New York Times.* Retrieved March 8, 2007, from http://www.nytimes.com

Nagourney, E. (2007c, March 6). Performance: Tests of pilots show age may be advantageous. *New York Times.* Retrieved March 8, 2007, from http://www.nytimes.com

Nail, P. R., Harton, H. C., & Decker, B. P. (2003). Political orientation and modern versus aversive racism: Tests of Dovidio and Gaertner's (1998) integrated model. *Journal of Personality and Social Psychology, 84,* 754–770.

National Center for Health Statistics. (2000). *National Health and Nutrition Examination Survey, CDC growth charts: United States.* Retrieved January 6, 2006, from http://www.cdc.gov/nchs/about/major/nhanes/growthcharts/charts.htm.

Neck, C. P., & Moorhead, G. (1992). Jury deliberation in the trial of *U.S. v. John DeLorean:* A case analysis of groupthink avoidance and an enhanced framework. *Human Relations, 45,* 1077–1091.

Neuman, W. (2005, June 7). In Manhattan, apartments still selling at record highs. *New York Times*, p. 6.

Newell, C. E., Rosenfeld, P., & Culbertson, A. L. (1995). Sexual harassment experiences and equal opportunity perceptions of Navy women. *Sex Roles, 32,* 159–168.

Newman, A. (2006, November 11). Missed the train? Lost a wallet? Maybe it was all Mercury's fault. *New York Times,* p. B3.

Newton, R. R., & Rudestam, K. E. (1999). *Your statistical consultant: Answers to your data analysis questions.* Thousand Oaks, CA: Sage.

Nickerson, R. S. (2000). Null hypothesis significance testing: A review of an old and continuing controversy. *Psychological Methods, 5,* 241–301.

Nolan, S. A., Flynn, C., & Garber, J. (2003). Prospective relations between rejection and depression in young adolescents. *Journal of Personality and Social Psychology, 85,* 745–755.

Nolan, S. A., Flynn, C., & Garber, J. (2003). The relation of rejection to depression in adolescents. *Journal of Personality and Social Psychology, 85,* 745–755.

Nunnally, J. C., & Bernstein, I. H. (1994). *Psychometric theory* (3rd ed.). New York: McGraw-Hill.

Oberst, U., Charles, C., & Chamarro, A. (2005). Influence of gender and age in aggressive dream content of Spanish children and adolescents. *Dreaming, 15,* 170–177.

O'Connor, A. (2007, March 6). The claim: Restrooms are the dirtiest public areas. *New York Times.* Retrieved March 8, 2007, from http://www.nytimes.com

Ogbu, J. U. (1986). The consequences of the American caste system. In U. Neisser (Ed.), *The school achievement of minority children: New perspectives.* Hillsdale, NJ: Erlbaum. 19–56.

O'Keefe, K. (2005). *The average American: the extraordinary search for the nation's most ordinary citizen.* New York: Public Affairs.

Omilusik, K. (2007). From dyes to peptides; The evaluation of antibiotic drugs. *The Science Creative Quarterly, 2,* retrieved February 28, 2007 from http://www.scq.abc.ca/?=407.

Optimal graphs and statistics win child custody. (2005). Retrieved July 21, 2005, from http://www.parentingtime.net/info_statistics.htm

Osborne, J. (2002). Notes on the use of data transformations. *Practical Assessment, Research & Evaluation, 8.* Retrieved September 22, 2006, from http://PAREonline.net/getvn.asp?v=8&n=6

Pallingston, J. (1998). *Lipstick: A celebration of the world's favorite cosmetic.* New York: St. Martin's Press.

Parker-Pope, T. (2005, December 13). A weight guessing game: Holiday gains fall short of estimates, but pounds hang on. *Wall Street Journal,* p. 31.

Pearson, K. (1978). *The history of statistics in the 17ᵗʰ and 18ᵗʰ centuries, against the Changing Background of Intellectual, Scientific, and Religious Thought (Lectures from 1921–1933).* London: Charles Griffin. Edited by E. S. Pearson.

Peterson's Guides. (2004). *Graduate programs in psychology 2004.* Lawrenceville, NJ: Author.

Peters, W. S. (1986). *Counting for something: Statistical principles and personalities.* New York: Springer-Verlag.

Petrocelli, J. V. (2003). Factor validation of the Consideration of Future Consequences Scale: Evidence for a shorter version. *Journal of Social Psychology, 143,* 405–413.

Plotz, D. (2000, June 4). Greens peace: A controversial new theory about the true causes of war and peace—in 18 holes or less. *New York Times Magazine,* pp. 32, 37.

Popkin, S. J. & Woodley, W. (2002). *Hope VI Panel Study.* Urban Institute: Washington, D.C.

Porter, T. M. (1986). *The rise of statistical thinking: 1820–1900.* Princeton, NJ: Princeton University Press.

Porter, T. M. (2004). *Karl Pearson: The scientific life in a statistical age.* Princeton, NJ: Princeton University Press

Press, E. (2006, December 3). Do immigrants make us safer? *New York Times Magazine,* pp. 20–24.

Public vs. private schools [Editorial]. (2006, July 19). *New York Times.* Retrieved July 19, 2006, from http://www.nytimes.com

Rajecki, D. W., Lauer, J. B., & Metzner, B. S. (1998). Early graduate school plans: Uninformed expectations. *Journal of College Student Development, 39,* 629–632.

Ratner, R. K., & Miller, D. T. (2001). The norm of self-interest and its effects on social action. *Journal of Personality and Social Psychology, 81,* 5–16.

Raven, B. H. (1998). Groupthink, Bay of Pigs, and Watergate reconsidered. *Organizational Behavior and Human Decision Processes, 73,* 352–361.

Raz, A. (2005). Attention and hypnosis: Neural substrates and genetic associations of two converging processes. *International Journal of Clinical and Experimental Hypnosis, 53,* 237–258.

Raz, A., Fan, J., & Posner, M. I. (2005). Hypnotic suggestion reduces conflict in the human brain. *Proceedings of the National Academy of Sciences.*

Regal, R., Rooney, J. R., & Wandas, T. (1994). Facilitated communication: An experimental evaluation. *Journal of Autism and Developmental Disorders, 24,* 344–355.

Report of the Presidential Commission on the Space Shuttle Challenger Accident (PCSSA). Presented to President Ronald Regan June 9, 1986, by William P. Rogers, Neil Armstrong, Sally Ride, David C. Acheson, Eugene Covert, Robert Hotz, et al. Washington, DC: Author.

Reuters. (2006, June 21). Send in the clowns to boost IVF success. Retrieved June 25, 2006, from http://msnbc.msn.com

Reynolds, G. (2007, March 4). Give us this day our daily supplements. *New York Times.* Retrieved March 8, 2007, from http://www.nytimes.com

Rholes, W. S., Simpson, J. A., Tran, S., Martin, A. M., & Friedman, M. (2007). Attachment and information seeking in romantic relationships. *Personality and Social Psychology Bulletin, 33,* 422–438.

Richards, S. E. (2006, March 22). Women silent on abortion on NYT op-ed page. *Salon.com*. Retrieved March 22, 2006, from http://www.salon.com.

Rockwell, P. (2006, June 23). Send in the clowns: No joke: "Medical clowning" seems to help women conceive. *Salon.com*. Retrieved June 25, 2006, from http://www.salon.com

Roberts, P. M. (2003). Performance of Canadian adults on the Graded Naming Test. *Aphasiology, 17*, 933–946.

Robison, W., Boisjoly, R., Hoeker, D., & Young S. (2003). Representation and misrepresentation: Tufte and the Morton Thiokol engineers on the *Challenger*. *Science and Engineering Ethics, 8*, 59–81.

Rosenthal, E. (2006, January 19). When bad people are punished, men smile (but women don't). *New York Times*. Retrieved January 19, 2006, from http://www.nytimes.com

Rosenthal, R. (1991). *Meta-analytic procedures for social research*. Newbury Park, CA: Sage.

Rosenthal, R. (1995). Writing meta-analytic reviews. *Psychological Bulletin, 118*, 183–192.

Rosnow, R. L., & Rosenthal, R. (1989a). Definition and interpretation of interaction effects. *Psychological Bulletin, 105*, 143–146.

Rosnow, R. L., & Rosenthal, R. (1989b). Statistical procedures and the justification of knowledge in psychological science. *American Psychologist, 44*, 1276–1284.

Rosnow, R. L., & Rosenthal, R. (1991). If you're looking at the cell means, you're not looking at *only* the interaction (unless all main effects are zero). *Psychological Bulletin, 10*, 574–576.

Rosnow, R. L., & Rosenthal, R. (1995). "Some things you learn aren't so": Cohen's paradox, Asch's paradigm, and the interpretation of interaction. *Psychological Science, 6*, 3–9.

Rosnow, R. L., & Rosenthal, R. (1996). Contrasts and interactions redux: Five easy pieces. *Psychological Science, 7*, 253–257.

Roster of the dead. (2005, October 26). *New York Times*. Retrieved November 1, 2005, from http://www.nytimes.com

Rubarth-Lay, J. (1997). Napoleon's Invasion of Russia. Retrieved November 5, 2006, from http://uts.cc.utexas.edu/~jrubarth/gslis/lis385t.16/Napoleon/

Ruby, C. (2006). *Coming to America: An examination of the factors that influence international students' graduate school choices*. Draft of dissertation.

Ruhm, C. J. (2000). Are recessions good for your health? *Quarterly Journal of Economics, 115*, 617–650.

Ruhm, C. J. (2006). *Healthy living in hard times* (NBEB Working Paper No. 9468). Cambridge, MA: National Bureau of Economic Research. Retrieved May 30, 2006, from http://www.nber.org/papers/w9468

Rummel, R. J. (1994). *Death by government: Genocide and mass murder since 1900*. New Brunswick: NJ: Transaction.

Runco, M. A. (2006). The development of children's creativity. In B. Spodek & O. N. Saracho (Eds.), *Handbook of research on the education of young children* (2nd ed., pp. 121–131). Mahwah, NJ: Erlbaum.

Ryan, C. (2006, June 21). "Therapeutic clowning" boosts IVF. *BBC News*. Retrieved June 25, 2006, from http://news.bbc.co.uk

Safran, S. P. (2006). Using the effective behavior supports survey to guide development of schoolwide positive behavior support. *Journal of Positive Behavior Interventions, 8*, 3–9.

Salsburg, D. (2001). *The lady tasting tea: How statistics revolutionized science in the twentieth century*. New York: W. H. Freeman.

Sanchez, A. (2002). The effect of alcohol consumption and patronage frequency on restaurant tipping. *Journal of Foodservice Business Research, 5*, 19–36.

Sandberg, D. E., Bukowski, W. M., Fung, C. M., & Noll, R. B. (2004). Height and social adjustment: Are extremes a cause for concern and action? *Pediatrics, 114*, 744–750.

Sawilowsky, S. S., & Blair, R. C. (1992). A more realistic look at the robustness and Type II error properties of the *t* test to departures from population normality. *Psychological Bulletin, 111*, 352–360.

Scarr, S. (1997). Rules of evidence: A large context for the statistical debate. *Psychological Science, 8*, 16–17.

Schackman, B. R., Gebo, K. A., Walensky, R. P., Losina, E., Muccio, T., Sax, P. E., et al. (2006). The lifetime cost of current human immunodeficiency virus care in the United States. *Medical Care, 44*, 990–997.

Schmidt, F. L. (1992). What do data really mean? Research findings, meta-analysis, and cumulative knowledge in psychology. *American Psychologist, 47*, 1173–1181.

Schmidt, F. L. (1996). Statistical significance testing and cumulative knowledge in psychology: Implications for training of researchers. *Psychological Methods, 1*, 115–129.

Seymour, C. (2006). Listen while you run. *Runner's World*. Retrieved May 24, 2006, from http://msn.runnersworld.com

Shah, P., & Hoeffner, J. (2002). Review of graph comprehension research: Implications for instruction. *Educational Psychology Review, 14*, 47–69.

Sherman, J. D., Honegger, S. D., & McGivern, J. L. (2003). *Comparative indicators of education in the United States and other G-8 countries: 2002*, NCES 2003-026. Washington, D.C.: U.S. Department of Education, National Center for Health Statistics, http://scsvt.org/resource/global_ed_compare2002.pdf

Simonton, D. K. (1988). Age and outstanding achievement: What do we know after a century of research? *Psychological Bulletin, 104*, 252–267.

Simonton, D. K. (1999). Historical trends in art and art criticism: A historiometric perspective. *Psychoanalysis and Contemporary Thought, 22*, 687–703.

Simonton, D. K. (2004). *Creativity in science: Chance, logic, genius, and zeitgeist*. Cambridge, UK: Cambridge University Press.

Simonton, D. K. (2005). Cinematic creativity and production budgets: Does money make the movie? *Journal of Creative Behavior, 39*, 1–15.

Skurnik, I., Yoon, C., Park, D. C., & Swarz, N. (2005). How warnings about false claims become recommendations. *Journal of Consumer Research, 31*, 713–724.

Smith, T. W., & Kim, S. (2006). National pride in cross-national and temporal perspective. *International Journal of Public Opinion Research, 18*, 127–136.

Snow, J. (1855). On the mode of communication of cholera. John Churchill: London.

Snyder, G. (2006, November 12). The humor index. *New York Times Magazine*, p. 33.

Spencer, S. J., Steele, C. M., & Quinn, D. M. (1999). Stereotype threat and women's math performance. *Journal of Experimental Social Psychology, 35*, 1–28.

Stampone, E. (1993). Effects of gender of rater and a woman's hair length on the perceived likelihood of being sexually harassed. The 46th Annual Undergraduate Psychology Conference, Mount Holyoke College, MA.

Steinman, G. (2006). Mechanisms of twinning: VII. Effect of diet and heredity on human twinning rate. *Journal of Reproductive Medicine, 51*, 405–410.

Sterling, T. D., Rosenbaum, W. L., & Weinkam, J. J. (1995). Publication decisions revisited: The effect of the outcome of statistical tests on the decision to publish and vice versa. *The American Statistician, 49*, 108–112.

Sterne, J. A. C., & Smith, G. D. (2001). Sifting the evidence—what's wrong with significance tests? *British Medical Journal, 322*, 226–231.

Stigler, S. M. (1986). *The history of statistics: The measurement of uncertainty before 1900*. Cambridge, MA: Belknap Press of Harvard University Press.

Stigler, S. M. (1999). *Statistics on the table: The history of statistical concepts and methods*. Harvard University Press: Cambridge, MA.

Strathman, A., Gleicher, F., Boninger, D. S., & Edwards, C. S. (1994). The consideration of future consequences: Weighing immediate and distant outcomes of behavior. *Journal of Personality and Social Psychology, 66*, 742–752.

Strayer, D. L., Drews, F. A., & Johnston, W. A. (2003). Cell phone induced failures of visual attention during simulated driving. *Journal of Experimental Psychology: Applied, 9*, 23–32.

Suddeth, J. A. (1996). *Fight directing for the theatre*. Portsmouth, NH: Heineman.

Suicide Prevention Action Network. (2004). National Strategy for Suicide Prevention Benchmark Survey. Retrieved July 7, 2005, from http://www.spanusa.org.pdf/NSSP_Benchmark_Survey_Results.pdf

Suls, J., Martin, R., & Wheeler, L. (2002). Social comparisons: Why, with whom, and with what effect? *Current Directions in Psychological Science, 11*, 159–163.

Szempruch, J., & Jacobsen, J. W. (1993). Evaluating the facilitated communications of people with developmental disabilities. *Research in Developmental Disabilities, 14*, 253–264.

Talarico, J. M., & Rubin, D. C. (2003). Confidence, not consistency, characterizes flashbulb memories. *Psychological Science, 14*, 455–461.

Taylor, G. M. & Ste. Marie, D. M. (2001). Eating disorders symptoms in Canadian female pair and dance figure skaters. *International Journal of Sports Psychology, 32*, 21–28.

Taubenberger, J. K., & Morens, D. M. (2006). 1918 influenza: The mother of all pandemics. *Emerg Infect Dis, 12*. Retrieved October 8, 2006, from http://www.cdc.gov/ncidod/EID/vol12no01/05-0979.htm

the polling company, inc. (2006). Oprah named top choice for meetings we'd love to have, says Citrix GoToMeeting poll. Retrieved April, 10, 2006, http://www.pollingcompany.com/viewPage.asp?pid=134

The top 25 jobs for 2005–2009. (2005). *Fast Company*. Retrieved October 8, 2006, from http://www.fastcompany.com/articles/2005/01/top-jobs-main.html

Tiger files and 2000 U.S. Census. (2005). Retrieved July 21, 2005 from http://www.esri.com/data/download/census2000_tigerline/

Toppo, G. (2005, July 14). Younger students excel in reading. *USA Today*. Retrieved July 15, 2005, from http://www.usatoday.com

Tough, P. (2006, November 26). Can teaching poor children to act more like middle-class children help close the education gap? *New York Times Magazine*, pp. 44–51, 69–72, 77.

Tucker, K. L., Morita, K., Qiao, N., Hannan, M. T., Cupples, A., & Kiel, D. P. (2006). Colas, but not other carbonated beverages, are associated with low bone mineral density in older women: The Framingham Osteoporosis Study. *American Journal of Clinical Nutrition, 84*, 936–942.

Tufte, E. R. (1990). *Envisioning information*. Cheshire, CT: Graphics Press.

Tufte, E. R. (1997). *Visual explanations*. Cheshire, CT: Graphics Press.

Tufte, E. R. (2005). *Visual explanations* (2nd ed.) (original work published 1997) Cheshire, CT: Graphics Press.

Tufte, E. R. (2006). *Beautiful evidence*. Cheshire, CT: Graphics Press.

Tufte, E. R. (2006). *The visual display of quantitative information* (2nd ed.) (original work published 2001) Cheshire, CT: Graphics Press.

Turner, R. B., Bauer, R., Woelkart, K., Hulsey, T. C., & Gangemi, J. D. (2005). An evaluation of *Echinacea angustifolia* in experimental rhinovirus infections. *New England Journal of Medicine, 353*, 341–348.

Upton, P, & Eiser, C. (2006). School experiences after treatment for a brain tumour. *Child: Care, Health and Development, 32*, 9–17.

Urbaniak, G. C., & Plous, S. (2005). Research randomizer. Retrieved August 3, 2005, from http://www.randomizer.org

Van den Broek, P., Lynch, J. S., & Naslund, J. (2003). The development of comprehension of main ideas in narratives: Evidence from the selection of titles. *Journal of Educational Psychology, 95*, 707–718.

Vinten-Johansen P., Brody H., Paneth N., Rachman, S., & Rip, M. (2003). *Cholera, chloroform, and the science of medicine: A life of John Snow*. Oxford University Press New York.

Wallace, A. (1867). Creation by law. *Quarterly Journal of Science, 4*, 470–488.

Walker, S. (2006). *Fantasyland: A season on baseball's lunatic fringe*. New York: Penguin.

Wansink, B., & van Ittersum, K. (2003). Bottoms up! The influence of elongation and pouring on consumption volume. *Journal of Consumer Research, 30*, 455–463.

Waters, A. (2006, February 24). Eating for credit. *New York Times*. Retrieved February 24, 2006 from http://www.nytimes.com

Weinberg, B. A., Fleisher, B. M., & Hashimoto, M. (2007). *Evaluating methods for evaluating instruction: The case of higher education* (National Bureau of Economic Research Working Paper No. 12844). Cambridge, MA: National Bureau of Economic Research.

Weis, R. (2004). Using an undergraduate human service practicum to promote unified psychology. *Teaching of psychology, 31*, 43–46.

Wiley, J. (2005). A fair and balanced look at the news: What affects memory for controversial arguments. *Journal of Memory and Language, 53*, 95–109.

Wisniewski, S. R., Leon, A. C., Otton, M. W., & Trevedi, M. H. (2006). Prevention of missing data in clinical research studies. *Biological Psychiatry, 59*, 997–1000.

Wolff, A. (2007). Is the SI jinx for real? *Sports Illustrated*, January 26.

Wood, J. M., Nezworski, M. T., Lilienfeld, S. O., & Garb, H. N. (Eds.). (2003). *What's wrong with the Rorschach? Science confronts the controversial inkblot test*. San Francisco: Jossey-Bass.

World Health Organization. (2007). Myths and realities in disaster situations. Retrieved February 12, 2007, from http://www.who.int/hac/techguidance/ems/myths/en/index.html

Youden, W. J. (1972). Enduring Values. *Technometrics, 14*, 1–11.

Yule, G. U., & Kendall, M. G. (1950). *An introduction to the theory of statistics*. New York: Hafner.

Zuckerman, M., Hodgins, H. S., Zuckerman, A., & Rosenthal, R. (1993). Contemporary issues in the analysis of data: A survey of 551 psychologists. *Psychological Science, 4*, 49–53.

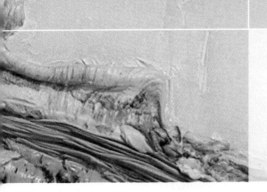

INDEX

FORMULAS

CHAPTER 10

One-Way ANOVA (pp. 445–458)

$df_{between} = N_{Groups} - 1$

$df_{Within} = df_1 + df_2 + \ldots + df_{Last}$

(in which df_1 etc. are the degrees of freedom, $N - 1$, for each sample)

$df_{Total} = df_{Between} + df_{Within}$
or $df_{Total} = N_{Total} - 1$

$GM = \dfrac{\Sigma(X)}{N_{Total}}$

$SS_{Total} = \Sigma(X - GM)^2$

$SS_{Within} = \Sigma(X - M)^2$

$SS_{Between} = \Sigma(M - GM)^2$

$SS_{Total} = SS_{Within} + SS_{Between}$

$MS_{Between} = \dfrac{SS_{Between}}{df_{Between}}$

$MS_{Within} = \dfrac{SS_{Within}}{df_{Within}}$

$F = \dfrac{MS_{Between}}{MS_{Within}}$

Tukey *HSD* post-hoc test (p. 463)

$HSD = \dfrac{(M_1 - M_2)}{s_M}$, for any two sample means

$s_M = \sqrt{\dfrac{MS_{Within}}{N}}$, if equal sample sizes

$N' = \dfrac{N_{Groups}}{\Sigma(1/N)}$

$s_M = \sqrt{\dfrac{MS_{Within}}{N'}}$, if unequal sample sizes

CHAPTER 11

Two-Way ANOVA (pp. 502–507)

$df_{Rows} = N_{Rows} - 1$

$df_{Columns} = N_{Columns} - 1$

$df_{Interaction} = (df_{Rows})(df_{Columns})$

$SS_{Total} = \Sigma(X - GM)^2$ for each score

$SS_{Between\ (rows)} = \Sigma(M_{Row} - GM)^2$ for each score

$SS_{Between\ (columns)} = \Sigma(M_{Column} - GM)^2$ for each score

$SS_{Within} = \Sigma(X - M_{Cell})^2$ for each score

$SS_{Interaction} = SS_{Total} - (SS_{Rows} + SS_{Columns} + SS_{Within})$